FLORIDA RULES OF JUDICIAL ADMINISTRATION

2013 EDITION

Rules reflect all changes through 37 FLW S643. Subsequent amendments, if any, can be found at www.floridasupremecourt.org/decisions/rules.shtml. The Florida Bar also updates the rules on its website at www.FloridaBar.org (on the home page, click "Rules Updates").

THE FLORIDA BAR

CONTINUING LEGAL EDUCATION

Distributed by LexisNexis®
1275 Broadway, Albany, NY 12204-2694
800/833-9844 • Fax: 800/643-1280
www.lexisnexis.com

D1456431

THE FLORIDA BAR

LexisNexis®

The Florida Bar and LexisNexis

working together for Florida's Lawyers

Through a joint publishing relationship, The Florida Bar and LexisNexis have combined their expertise to best serve the information needs of those practicing law in Florida. The Florida Bar Continuing Legal Education staff writes and edits the publications; LexisNexis provides printing, CD duplication, distribution, and customer service support.

If you have any questions:

Contact The Florida Bar
For questions regarding content, authors, CLE schedules, member benefits, and other Bar matters.

> The Florida Bar
> 651 East Jefferson Street
> Tallahassee, FL 32399-2300
> Phone: 850/561-5600
> Fax: 850/561-5826
> www.floridabar.org

Contact LexisNexis
For questions regarding billing, subscriptions, purchases, or other Florida Bar products.

> LexisNexis
> 1275 Broadway
> Albany, NY 12204-2694
> Phone: 800/833-9844
> Fax: 800/643-1280
> www.lexisnexis.com/flabar
> customer.support@lexisnexis.com

International Standard Book Number: 978-0-7698-6030-5
Library of Congress Control Number: 2008907430

22736-23

(Pub No. 22736)

CITATIONS TO OPINIONS ADOPTING OR AMENDING RULES

ORIGINAL ADOPTION, effective 7-1-78: 360 So.2d 1076.

OTHER OPINIONS:

Effective 1-1-79:	364 So.2d 466.	Amended 2.070(f).
Effective 7-1-79:	372 So.2d 449.	Amended 2.010–2.130.
Effective 2-21-80:	380 So.2d 1027.	Amended 2.060(b).
Effective 1-1-81:	389 So.2d 202.	Four-year-cycle revision. Amended 2.050(e), 2.130.
Effective 1-1-81:	391 So.2d 214.	Amended 2.040(b)(3), 2.050(c).
Effective 1-1-82:	403 So.2d 926.	Added 2.075.
Effective 12-1-83:	442 So.2d 198.	Added 2.035.
Effective 2-23-84:	446 So.2d 87.	Amended 2.035.
Effective 1-1-85:	458 So.2d 1110.	Four-year-cycle revision. Amended 2.140(b)(2); added 2.130(b)(5); renumbered 2.130(b)(6).
Effective 1-1-85:	462 So.2d 444.	Added 2.071.
Effective 3-1-85:	465 So.2d 1217.	Added 2.125.
Effective 7-1-86:	493 So.2d 423.	Added 2.085.
Effective 2-1-87:	500 So.2d 524.	Amended 2.040(a)(2), 2.050(c).
Effective 7-1-87:	507 So.2d 1390.	Amended 2.050(d), 2.070(e).
Effective 7-1-87:	509 So.2d 276.	Amended 2.130(f).
Effective 1-1-88:	518 So.2d 258.	Added 2.150.
Effective 1-1-89:	532 So.2d 667.	See revised opinion at 536 So.2d 195.
Effective 1-1-89:	536 So.2d 195.	Four-year-cycle revision. Amended 2.050(c), 2.060(d), (h)–(j), 2.070(h), 2.085(a), (c).
Effective 6-1-89:	543 So.2d 1244.	Added 2.125(b)(1)(I), (b)(1)(J).
Effective 11-9-89:	552 So.2d 194.	Added 2.125(b)(1)(K).
Effective 1-11-90:	555 So.2d 848.	Added 2.125(b)(1)(L).
Effective 1-18-90:	550 So.2d 457.	Added 2.055.
Effective 6-15-90:	560 So.2d 786.	Added 2.030(a)(3)(D).
Effective 10-22-92:	607 So.2d 39.	Amended 2.130(b)(3).
Effective 10-29-92:	608 So.2d 472.	Added 2.051.
Effective 1-1-93:	609 So.2d 465.	Four-year-cycle revision. Substantively amended 2.040(b)(5), 2.055, 2.060, 2.071, 2.085, 2.130; added 2.160, 2.170.
Effective 12-23-93:	634 So.2d 604.	Amended 2.110(b).
Effective 2-9-95:	650 So.2d 30.	Amended 2.170.
Effective 2-23-95:	650 So.2d 38.	Amended 2.070.
Effective 3-23-95:	651 So.2d 1185.	Amended 2.051.
Effective 3-30-95:	652 So.2d 811.	Amended 2.125.
Effective 5-9-95:	654 So.2d 917.	Amended 2.070(d)(2).
Effective 6-15-95:	656 So.2d 926.	Amended 2.125.
Effective 1-1-96:	661 So.2d 806.	Amended 2.070(b).
Effective 1-1-96:	665 So.2d 218.	Amended 2.035.
Effective 4-11-96:	672 So.2d 523.	Amended 2.050(b)(4), 2.050(b)(7); added 2.050(h).
Effective 6-27-96:	675 So.2d 1376.	Added 2.072.
Effective 8-29-96:	678 So.2d 1285.	Added court commentary to 2.050.
Effective 1-1-97:	681 So.2d 698.	Added 2.060(f), renumbered 2.060(f)–(l); amended 2.075, 2.090.
Effective 1-1-97:	682 So.2d 89.	Four-year-cycle revision. Added 2.030(a)(2)(B)(iv), 2.052, 2.065, 2.135, 2.180; amended 2.050(c), (e)(1)(F), (e)(3), (h), 2.055(c), 2.125 (for style); deleted 2.055(e).
Effective 2-7-97:	688 So.2d 320.	Added 2.050(b)(10).

Effective 7-17-97:	697 So.2d 144.	Partially suspended application of 2.055(c) until January 1, 1999.
Effective 1-1-98:	701 So.2d 1164.	Amended 2.060(f), 2.090(c).
Effective 11-20-97:	701 So.2d 864.	Amended 2.050(b)(10).
Effective 1-1-99:	711 So.2d 29.	Amended 2.055(c), added a new (d), and redesignated former (d) as (e).
Effective 2-1-99:	746 So.2d 1073.	Amended 2.051(c)(7).
Effective 5-25-00:	766 So.2d 999.	Added 2.071(f).
Effective 7-14-00:	772 So.2d 532.	Added 2.070(i).
Effective 12-1-00:	774 So.2d 625.	Added 2.053.
Effective 1-1-01:	780 So.2d 819.	Four-year-cycle revision. Amended 2.020, 2.053(b)(1)(A), 2.060, 2.070, 2.071(d), 2.130(a), (c), (e)–(g); added 2.061, 2.140(c).
Effective 7-1-01:	796 So.2d 477.	Added 2.054.
Effective 10-1-01:	797 So.2d 1213.	Amended 2.050(b).
Effective 1-1-02:	812 So.2d 401.	Amended 2.054(e).
Effective 3-7-02:	825 So.2d 889.	Amended 2.030, 2.040, 2.051, 2.075; added 2.076 and Judicial Branch Retention Schedule for Administrative Records.
Effective 10-1-02:	826 So.2d 233.	Amended 2.050, 2.052, 2.085.
Effective 9-19-02:	828 So.2d 994.	Amended 2.130.
Effective 7-10-03:	851 So.2d 698.	Amended 2.050, 2.053, 2.130.
Effective 1-1-04:	851 So.2d 698.	Two-year-cycle revision. Amended 2.060, 2.070, 2.085, 2.160, 2.170.
Effective 1-1-04:	860 So.2d 394.	Amended 2.060.
Effective 10-14-04:	888 So.2d 614.	Amended 2.035.
Effective 1-1-05:	885 So.2d 870.	Amended 2.160.
Effective 1-1-05:	889 So.2d 68.	Amended 2.085.
Effective 5-12-05:	907 So.2d 1138.	Amended 2.061.
Effective 11-3-05:	915 So.2d 157.	Two-year-cycle revision. Amended 2.130.
Effective 1-1-06:	915 So.2d 157.	Two-year-cycle revision. Amended 2.050, 2.051, 2.060, 2.071, 2.085.
Effective 1-1-06:	915 So.2d 145.	Amended 2.030.
Effective 2-16-06:	921 So.2d 615.	Adopted 2.036.
Effective 3-2-06:	923 So.2d 1160.	Amended 2.050.
Effective 7-1-06:	933 So.2d 504.	Adopted 2.073(a)–(d), (f).
Effective 7-6-06:	933 So.2d 1136.	Amended 2.035.
Effective 9-21-06:	939 So.2d 966.	Reorganization of rules. Adopted 2.140(g).
Effective 9-28-06:	939 So.2d 1051.	Amended 2.235.
Effective 4-5-07:	954 So.2d 16.	Amended 2.420.
Effective 5-17-07:	957 So.2d 1168.	Adopted 2.244.
Effective 11-3-07:	915 So.2d 145.	Amended 2.150(b)(3) [2.320(b)(3)].
Effective 1-1-08:	967 So.2d 178.	Adopted 2.256, 2.430(l)
Effective 1-17-08:	973 So.2d 437.	Amended 2.430.
Effective 1-31-08:	974 So.2d 1066.	Amended 2.240.
Effective 4-1-08:	978 So.2d 805.	Amended 2.215.
Effective 7-1-08:	933 So.2d 504.	Adopted 2.073(e) [2.560(e)].
Effective 10-1-08:	992 So.2d 237.	Amended 2.215.
Effective 1-1-09:	986 So.2d 560.	Three-year-cycle revision. Amended 2.130, 2.140, 2.215, 2.330.
Effective 1-1-09:	991 So.2d 842.	Amended 2.510.
Effective 7-16-09:	13 So.3d 1044.	Amended 2.535.
Effective 3-18-10:	31 So.3d 756.	Amended 2.420.
Effective 5-20-10:	41 So.3d 881.	Amended 2.540.

Effective 7-1-10:	41 So.3d 128.	Adopted 2.236.
Effective 10-1-10:	31 So.3d 756.	Amended 2.420(d).
Effective 12-9-10:	51 So.3d 1151.	Amended 2.320(a)(2).
Effective 2-24-11:	36 FLW S87.	Amended 2.215(b)(10)(C).
Effective 7-7-11:	68 So.3d 228.	Amended 2.420(d)(1)(B)(xx).
Effective 10-1-11:	36 FLW S331.	Adopted 2.425.
Effective 10-6-11:	75 So.3d 203.	Amended 2.545(d)(2).
Effective 1-1-12:	73 So.3d 210.	Three-year-cycle revision. Amended 2.505(f)(1), 2.510(a), (b)(2), 2.530(d)(1); adopted 2.525(g), 2.526.
Effective 2-9-12:	37 FLW S82.	Amended 2.205, 2.210, 2.215, 2.220, 2.225, 2.230, 2.235, 2.244.
Effective 7-12-12:	95 So.3d 115.	Amended 2.425.
Effective 9-1-12	37 FLW S643.	Amended 2.515, Adopted 2.516.
Effective 10-01-12:	95 So.3d 96.	Adopted 2.514.
Effective 6-21-12:	37 FLW S638.	Amended 2.430, 2.510, 2.516, 2.520, 2.525, 2.535.

NOTE TO USERS: Rules reflect all changes through 37 FLW S643. Subsequent amendments, if any, can be found at www.floridasupremecourt.org/decisions/rules.shtml. The Florida Bar also updates the rules on its website at www.FloridaBar.org (on the homepage click "Rules Updates").

TRACING TABLE

Former Florida Rules of Judicial Administration — Current Florida Rules of Judicial Administration

Former	Current	Former	Current	Current	Former	Current	Former
2.010	2.110	2.130(a)	2.140(d)	2.110	2.010	2.520	2.055
2.020	2.120		2.140(a)	2.120	2.020	2.525	2.090
2.030	2.205		2.140(b)	2.130	2.135	2.530	2.071
2.035	2.240		2.140(c)	2.140(a)	2.130(b)	2.535	2.070
2.036	2.241		2.140(e)	(b)	2.130(c)	2.540	2.065
2.040	2.210		2.140(f)	(c)	2.130(d)	2.545(a)	2.085(a)
2.050	2.215		2.140(g)	(d)	2.130(a)		2.085(b)
2.051	2.420		2.140(h)	(e)	2.130(e)		2.085(c)
2.052	2.550	2.135	2.130	(f)	2.130(f)		2.085(d)
2.053	2.230	2.140	2.310	(g)	---		2.085(e)
2.054	2.235	2.150	2.320	(h)	2.130(g)	2.550	2.052
2.055	2.520	2.160	2.330	2.205	2.030	2.555(a)	2.080(c)
2.060(a)	2.505(a)	2.170	2.450	2.210	2.040	(b)	2.080(d)
(b)	2.505(b)	2.180	2.260	2.215	2.050	(c)	2.080(e)
(c)	2.515(a)			2.220(c)	2.120	2.560	2.073
(d)	2.515(b)			2.225	2.125		
(e)	2.515(c)			2.230	2.053		
(f)	2.505(c)			2.235	2.054		
(g)	2.505(d)			2.240	2.035		
(h)	2.505(e)			2.241	2.036		
(i)	2.505(f)			2.244	---		
(j)	2.505(g)			2.245(a)	2.080(a)		
(k)	2.505(h)			(b)	2.080(b)		
2.061	2.510			2.250(a)	2.085(f)		
2.065	2.540			(b)	2.085(g)		
2.070	2.535			2.255	2.100		
2.071	2.530			2.256	---		
2.072	2.410			2.260	2.180		
2.073	2.560			2.265	2.110		
2.075	2.430			2.310	2.140		
2.076	2.440			2.320	2.150		
2.080(a)	2.245(a)			2.330	2.160		
(b)	2.245(b)			2.410	2.072		
(c)	2.555(a)			2.420	2.051		
(d)	2.555(b)			2.430	2.075		
(e)	2.555(c)			2.440	2.076		
2.085(a)	2.545(a)			2.450	2.170		
(b)	2.545(b)			2.505(a)	2.060(a)		
(c)	2.545(c)			(b)	2.060(b)		
(d)	2.545(d)			(c)	2.060(f)		
(e)	2.545(e)			(d)	2.060(g)		
(f)	2.250(a)			(e)	2.060(h)		
(g)	2.250(b)			(f)	2.060(i)		
2.090	2.525			(g)	2.060(j)		
2.100	2.255			(h)	2.060(k)		
2.110	2.265			2.510	2.061		
2.120	2.220			2.515(a)	2.060(c)		
2.125	2.225			(b)	2.060(d)		
				(c)	2.060(e)		

[NOTE: The Florida Rules of Judicial Administration were reorganized and renumbered in *In Re: Amendments to the Florida Rules of Judicial Administration — Reorganization of the Rules*, 939 So.2d 966 (Fla. 2006).]

TABLE OF CONTENTS

PART I. GENERAL PROVISIONS

PART II. STATE COURT ADMINISTRATION

PART III. JUDICIAL OFFICERS

PART IV. JUDICIAL PROCEEDINGS AND RECORDS

PART V. PRACTICE OF LAW

A. ATTORNEYS

FLORIDA RULES OF JUDICIAL ADMINISTRATION

PART I. GENERAL PROVISIONS

RULE 2.110. SCOPE AND PURPOSE

These rules, cited as "Florida Rules of Judicial Administration" and abbreviated as "Fla. R. Jud. Admin.," shall take effect at 12:01 a.m. on July 1, 1979. They shall apply to administrative matters in all courts to which the rules are applicable by their terms. The rules shall be construed to secure the speedy and inexpensive determination of every proceeding to which they are applicable. These rules shall supersede all conflicting rules and statutes.

RULE 2.120. DEFINITIONS

The following terms have the meanings shown as used in these rules:

(a) Court Rule: A rule of practice or procedure adopted to facilitate the uniform conduct of litigation applicable to all proceedings, all parties, and all attorneys.

(b) Local Court Rule:

(1) A rule of practice or procedure for circuit or county application only that, because of local conditions, supplies an omission in or facilitates application of a rule of statewide application and does not conflict therewith.

(2) A rule that addresses other matters that are required by the Florida Constitution, general law, rules of court, or a supreme court opinion to be adopted by or in a local rule.

(c) Administrative Order: A directive necessary to administer properly the court's affairs but not inconsistent with the constitution or with court rules and administrative orders entered by the supreme court.

RULE 2.130. PRIORITY OF FLORIDA RULES OF APPELLATE PROCEDURE

The Florida Rules of Appellate Procedure shall control all proceedings in the supreme court and the district courts, and all proceedings in which the circuit courts exercise their appellate jurisdiction, notwithstanding any conflicting rules of procedure.

RULE 2.140. AMENDING RULES OF COURT

(a) Amendments Generally. The following procedure shall be followed for consideration of rule amendments generally other than those adopted under subdivisions (d), (e), (f), and (g):

(1) Proposals for court rules, amendments to them, or abrogation of them may be made by any person.

(2) Proposals shall be submitted to the clerk of the supreme court in writing and shall include a general description of the proposed rule change or a specified proposed change in content. The clerk of the supreme court shall refer proposals to the appropriate committee under subdivision (a)(3).

(3) The Florida Bar shall appoint the following committees to consider rule proposals: Civil Procedure Rules Committee, Criminal Procedure Rules Committee, Small Claims Rules Committee, Traffic Court Rules Committee, Appellate Court Rules Committee, Juvenile Court Rules Committee, Code and Rules of Evidence Committee, Rules of Judicial Administration Committee, Probate Rules Committee, and Family Law Rules Committee.

(4) Each committee shall be composed of attorneys and judges with extensive experience and training in the area of practice of the committee calling for regular, frequent use of the rules. The members of the committee shall serve for 3-year staggered terms. The president of The Florida Bar shall appoint the chair and vice chair of each committee.

(5) The Rules of Judicial Administration Committee shall also serve as a rules coordinating committee. Each rules committee shall have at least 1 of its members appointed to the Rules of Judicial Administration Committee to serve as liaison. All committees shall provide a copy of any proposed rules changes to the Rules of Judicial Administration Committee within 30 days of a committee's affirmative vote to recommend the proposed change to the supreme court. The Rules of Judicial Administration Commit-

tee shall then refer all proposed rules changes to those rules committees that might be affected by the proposed change.

(6) The committees shall consider and vote on each proposal. The committees may originate proposals and are charged with the duty of regular review and reevaluation of the rules to advance orderly and inexpensive procedures in the administration of justice. The committees may accept or reject proposed amendments or may amend proposals. The committees shall keep minutes of their activities, which minutes shall reflect the action taken on each proposal. Copies of the minutes shall be furnished to the clerk of the supreme court, to the board of governors of The Florida Bar, and to the proponent of any proposal considered at the meeting.

(b) Schedule for Rules Proposals.

(1) Each committee shall report all proposed rule changes on a staggered basis (with the first cycle starting in 2006). Reports shall be made by the Criminal Procedure Rules Committee, the Traffic Court Rules Committee, and the Juvenile Court Rules Committee in 2006; by the Civil Procedure Rules Committee, the Probate Rules Committee, the Small Claims Rules Committee, and the Code and Rules of Evidence Committee in 2007; and by the Family Law Rules Committee, the Appellate Court Rules Committee, and the Rules of Judicial Administration Committee in 2008. Thereafter, the cycle shall repeat.

(2) No later than June 15 of the year prior to each reporting year or such other date as the board of governors of The Florida Bar may set, each reporting committee shall submit all proposed rule changes to the board of governors with the committee's final numerical voting record on each proposal. Contemporaneously with reporting proposed rule changes to the board of governors, each committee report shall be furnished to the Speaker of the Florida House of Representatives, the President of the Florida Senate, and the chairs of the House and Senate committees as designated by the Speaker and the President, and published on the Internet website of The Florida Bar, and in the Florida Bar Journal or Florida Bar News. Any person desiring to comment upon proposed rule

changes shall submit written comments to the appropriate committee chair no later than August 1 of the year prior to each reporting year. Each committee shall consider any comments submitted and thereafter report to the board of governors, no later than October 15 of the year prior to each reporting year, any revisions to the proposed rule changes. Contemporaneously with reporting any revisions to the board of governors, each committee's revised proposed rule changes shall be furnished to the Speaker of the Florida House of Representatives, the President of the Florida Senate, and the chairs of the House and Senate committees as designated by the Speaker and the President, and published on the Internet website of The Florida Bar, and in the Florida Bar Journal or Florida Bar News. Any person desiring to comment thereafter shall submit written comments to the supreme court in accordance with subdivision (b)(6).

(3) No later than December 15 of the year prior to each reporting year, the board of governors shall consider the proposals and shall vote on each proposal to recommend acceptance, rejection, or amendment.

(4) No later than February 1 of each reporting year, each committee shall file a report of its proposed rule changes with the supreme court. Each committee may amend its recommendations to coincide with the recommendations of the board of governors or may decline to do so or may amend its recommendations in another manner. Any such amendments shall also be reported to the supreme court. The report shall include:

(A) a list of the proposed changes, together with a detailed explanation of each proposal and the name and address of the proponent of each change if other than the rules committee;

(B) the final numerical voting record of the proposals in the committee;

(C) a report of the action taken by the committee on comments submitted in accordance with subdivision (b)(2);

(D) a report of the action and voting record of the board of governors;

(E) any dissenting views of the committee and, if available, of the board; and

(F) an appendix containing all comments submitted to the committee and a two-column chart setting forth the proposed changes in legislative format in the first column and a brief explanation of each change in the second column.

The report and the proposed rule changes shall be filed with the supreme court, in legislative format, both on paper and in an electronic format approved by the supreme court.

(5) If oral argument is deemed necessary, the supreme court shall establish a date during the month of May or June of each reporting year for oral argument on the proposals. Notice of the hearing on the proposals and a copy of the proposals shall be furnished to the affected committee chair and vice chair, the executive director of The Florida Bar, all members of the Judicial Management Council, the clerk and chief judge of each district court of appeal, the clerk and chief judge of each judicial circuit, the Speaker of the Florida House of Representatives, the President of the Florida Senate, the chairs of the House and Senate committees as designated by the Speaker and the President, and any person who has asked in writing filed with the clerk of the supreme court for a copy of the notice. The clerk may provide the notice electronically. If the committee modifies its recommendations after considering comments submitted in accordance with subdivision (b)(2), the recommendations or a resume of them shall be published on the internet websites of the supreme court and the Florida Bar and in the Florida Bar Journal or Florida Bar News before the hearing. Notice of the hearing shall also be published on the internet websites of the supreme court and the Florida Bar and in the Florida Bar Journal or Florida Bar News.

(6) Before the date of oral argument, any person may file comments concerning the proposals. All comments and other submissions by interested persons shall be filed with the clerk of the supreme court and served on the chair of the appropriate rules committee, and on the proponent of the rule change if other than the rules committee. The chair of the rules committee shall file a response to all comments within the time period set by the court. All comments and other submissions regarding the rule change proposals, in addition to being filed with the supreme court in paper format, shall also be filed in an electronic format approved by the supreme court. Prior to the date of oral argument and as soon as practicable after the date of filing, the clerk of the supreme court shall publish on the Internet websites of the supreme court and The Florida Bar, all comments and the responses of the chair of the rules committee that have been filed concerning the rule change proposals. All requests or submissions by a rules committee made in connection with a pending rule change proposal shall be filed with the clerk of the supreme court and thereafter published by the clerk of the supreme court on the Internet websites of the supreme court and The Florida Bar.

(7) Orders of the supreme court on said proposals should be adopted in sufficient time to take effect on January 1 of the year following the reporting year. The supreme court may permit motions for rehearing to be filed on behalf of any person, The Florida Bar, any bar association, and the affected committee.

(c) Rejected Proposals. If a committee rejects a proposal, the proponent may submit the proposed rule to the board of governors and shall notify the chair and vice chair of the affected committee of the submission of the proposed rule to the board of governors. Minority reports of committees are allowed and may be submitted to both the board of governors and the supreme court.

(d) Emergency Amendments by Court. The supreme court, with or without notice, may change court rules at any time if an emergency exists that does not permit reference to the appropriate committee of The Florida Bar for recommendations. If a change is made without reference to the committee, the change may become effective immediately or at a future time. In either event, the court shall fix a date for further consideration of the change. Any person may file comments concerning the change, seeking its abrogation or a delay in the effective date, in accordance with the procedures set forth in subdivision (b)(6) of this rule. The court may allow oral argument in support of such comments by The Florida Bar, by its sections and committees, and by other bar associations. Notice of the hearing on the change and a copy of the change shall be furnished to the affected committee chair and vice chair, the executive director of the Florida Bar, all members of the Judicial Management Council, the clerk and chief judge of each district court of appeal, the clerk and chief judge of each judicial circuit, the Speaker of the Florida House of Representatives, the President of the Florida Senate, the chairs of the House and Senate committees as designated by the speaker and the President, and any person who has asked in writing filed with the clerk of the supreme court for a copy of the notice. The clerk may provide the notice electronically. The change shall be published on the internet websites of the supreme court and the Florida Bar, and in the Florida Bar Journal or Florida Bar News before the hearing. Notice of the hearing shall also be published on the internet websites of the supreme court and the Florida Bar, and in the Florida Bar Journal or Florida Bar News.

(e) Emergency Recommendations by Committee. If, in the opinion of a committee, a proposal is of an emergency nature, and the board of governors concurs, proposals may be made at any time to the supreme court. If the court agrees that an emergency exists, the court may set a time for oral argument and consideration of the proposal. Notice of the hearing on the proposals and a copy of the proposals shall be furnished to the affected committee chair and vice chair, the executive director of the Florida Bar, all members of the Judicial Management Council, the clerk and chief judge of each district court of appeal, the clerk and chief judge of each judicial circuit, the Speaker of the Florida House of Representatives, the President of the Florida Senate, the chairs of the House and Senate committees as designated by the Speaker and the President, and any person who has asked in writing filed with the clerk of the supreme court for a copy of the notice. The clerk may provide the notice electronically. The recommendations or a resume of them shall be published on the internet websites of the supreme court and the Florida Bar, and in the Florida Bar Journal or Florida Bar News before the hearing. Notice of the hearing shall also be

published on the internet websites of the supreme court and the Florida Bar, and in the Florida Bar Journal or Florida Bar News.

(f) Request by Court. The supreme court may direct special consideration of a proposal at times other than those specified in this rule and may require a committee to report its recommendation with the recommendations of the board of governors. All requests or submissions by a rules committee made in connection with a request under this subdivision shall be filed with the clerk of the supreme court. The supreme court may set oral argument on the report at any time. Notice of the hearing on the proposals and a copy of the proposals shall be furnished to the affected committee chair and vice chair, the executive director of the Florida Bar, all members of the Judicial Management Council, the clerk and chief judge of each district court of appeal, the clerk and chief judge of each judicial circuit, the Speaker of the Florida House of Representatives, the President of the Florida Senate, the chairs of the House and Senate committees as designated by the Speaker and the President, and any person who has asked in writing filed with the clerk of the supreme court for a copy of the notice. The clerk may provide the notice electronically. The recommendations or a resume of them shall be published on the internet websites of the supreme court and the Florida Bar, and in the Florida Bar Journal or Florida Bar News before the hearing. Notice of the hearing shall also be published on the internet websites of the supreme court and the Florida Bar, and in the Florida Bar Journal or Florida Bar News.

(g) Amendments to the Rules of Judicial Administration.

(1) Amendments Without Referral to Rules Committee. Changes to the Rules of Judicial Administration contained in Part II, State Court Administration, of these rules, and rules 2.310, and 2.320, contained in Part III, Judicial Officers, generally will be considered and adopted by the supreme court without reference to or proposal from the Rules of Judicial Administration Committee. The supreme court may amend rules under this subdivision at any time, with or without notice. If a change is made without notice, the court shall fix a date for future consideration of the change and the change shall be published on the Internet websites of the supreme court and The Florida Bar and in the Florida Bar Journal or Florida Bar News. Any person may file comments concerning the change, in accordance with the procedures set forth in subdivision (b)(6) of this rule. The court may hear oral argument on the change. Notice of the hearing on the change and a copy of the change shall be provided in accordance with subdivision (d) of this rule.

(2) Other Amendments. Amendments to all other Rules of Judicial Administration shall be referred to or proposed by the Rules of Judicial Administration Committee and adopted by the supreme court as provided in subdivisions (a), (b), (c), (d), (e), and (f) of this rule.

(h) Local Rules Proposed by Trial Courts. The foregoing procedure shall not apply to local rules proposed by a majority of circuit and county judges in the circuit. The chief justice of the supreme court may appoint a Local Rule Advisory Committee to consider and make recommendations to the court concerning local rules and administrative orders submitted pursuant to rule 2.215(e).

Committee Notes

1980 Amendment. Rule 2.130 [renumbered as 2.140 in 2006] is entirely rewritten to codify the procedures for changes to all Florida rules of procedure as set forth by this court in *In re Rules of Court: Procedure for Consideration of Proposals Concerning Practice and Procedure,* 276 So.2d 467 (Fla.1972), and to update those procedures based on current practice. The Supreme Court Rules Advisory Committee has been abolished, and the Local Rules Advisory Committee has been established.

PART II. STATE COURT ADMINISTRATION

RULE 2.205. THE SUPREME COURT

(a) Internal Government.

(1) Exercise of Powers and Jurisdiction.

(A) The supreme court shall exercise its powers, including establishing policy for the judicial branch, and jurisdiction en banc. Five justices shall constitute a quorum and the concurrence of 4 shall be necessary to a decision. In cases requiring only a panel of 5, if 4 of the 5 justices who consider the case do not concur, it shall be submitted to the other 2 justices.

(B) Consistent with the authority of the supreme court to establish policy, including recommending state budget and compensation priorities for the judicial branch, no judge, supreme court created committee, commission, task force, or similar group, and no conference (Conference of District Court of Appeal Judges, Conference of Circuit Court Judges, Conference of County Court Judges) is permitted to recommend state budget priorities, including compensation and benefits, to the legislative or executive branch that have not been approved by the supreme court. This subdivision is not intended to apply to judges expressing their personal views who affirmatively make it explicitly clear that they are not speaking on behalf of the judicial branch.

(C) Newly created judicial branch commissions, committees, task forces, work groups, and similar study or advisory groups must be established by the supreme court, not solely by the chief justice. Such study or advisory groups may be created and charged by rule adopted by the court, or by administrative order issued by the chief justice in accordance with court action. Members of such groups shall be appointed by administrative order of the chief justice, after consultation with the court. When practicable, ad hoc committees and other ad hoc study or advisory groups, which should be used to address specific problems, shall be established under the umbrella of an existing committee or commission, which should be used to address long-term problems.

(2) Chief Justice.

(A) The chief justice shall be chosen by majority vote of the justices for a term of 2 years commencing on July 1, 2012. The selection of the chief justice should be based on managerial, administrative, and leadership abilities, without regard to seniority only. A chief justice may serve successive terms limited to a total of 8 years. The chief justice may be removed by a vote of 4 justices. If a vacancy occurs, a successor shall be chosen promptly to serve the balance of the unexpired term.

(B) The chief justice shall be the administrative officer of the judicial branch and of the supreme court and shall be responsible for the dispatch of the business of the branch and of the court and direct the implementation of policies and priorities as determined by the supreme court for the operation of the branch and of the court. The administrative powers and duties of the chief justice shall include, but not be limited to:

(i) the responsibility to serve as the primary spokesperson for the judicial branch regarding policies and practices that have statewide impact including, but not limited to, the judicial branch's management, operation, strategic plan, legislative agenda and budget priorities;

(ii) the power to act on requests for stays during the pendency of proceedings, to order the consolidation of cases, to determine all procedural motions and petitions relating to the time for filing and size of briefs and other papers provided for under the rules of this court, to advance or continue cases, and to rule on other procedural matters relating to any proceeding or process in the court;

(iii) the power to assign active or retired county, circuit, or appellate judges or justices to judicial service in this state, in accordance with subdivisions (a)(3) and (a)(4) of this rule;

(iv) the power, upon request of the chief judge of any circuit or district, or sua sponte, in the event of natural disaster, civil disobedience, or other emergency situation requiring the closure of courts or other circumstances inhibiting the ability of litigants to comply with deadlines imposed by rules of procedure applicable in the courts of this state, to enter such order or orders as may be appropriate to suspend, toll, or otherwise grant relief from time deadlines imposed by otherwise applicable statutes and rules of procedure for such period as may be appropriate, including, without limitation, those affecting speedy trial procedures in criminal and juvenile proceedings, all civil process and proceedings, and all appellate time limitations;

(v) the authority to directly inform all judges on a regular basis by any means, including, but not limited

to, email on the state of the judiciary, the state of the budget, issues of importance, priorities and other matters of statewide interest; furthermore, the chief justice shall routinely communicate with the chief judges and leaders of the district courts, circuit and county court conferences by the appropriate means;

(vi) the responsibility to exercise reasonable efforts to promote and encourage diversity in the administration of justice; and

(vii) the power to perform such other administrative duties as may be required and which are not otherwise provided for by law or rule.

(C) The chief justice shall be notified by all justices of any contemplated absences from the court and the reasons therefor. When the chief justice is to be temporarily absent, the chief justice shall select the justice longest in continuous service as acting chief justice.

(D) If the chief justice dies, retires, or is unable to perform the duties of the office, the justice longest in continuous service shall perform the duties during the period of incapacity or until a successor chief justice is elected.

(E) The chief justice shall meet on a regular basis with the chief judges of the district courts and the chief judges of the circuit courts to discuss and provide feedback for implementation of policies and practices that have statewide impact including, but not limited to, the judicial branch's management, operation, strategic plan, legislative agenda and budget priorities. Such meetings shall, if practicable, occur at least quarterly and be conducted in-person. At the discretion of the chief justice, any of these meetings may be combined with other judicial branch and leadership meetings and, where practicable include the justices of the supreme court.

(3) **Administration.**

(A) The chief justice may, either upon request or when otherwise necessary for the prompt dispatch of business in the courts of this state, temporarily assign justices of the supreme court, judges of district courts of appeal, circuit judges, and judges of county courts to any court for which they are qualified to serve. Any consenting retired justice or judge may be assigned to judicial service and receive compensation as provided by law.

(B) For the purpose of judicial administration, a "retired judge" is defined as a judge not engaged in the practice of law who has been a judicial officer of this state. A retired judge shall comply with all requirements that the supreme court deems necessary relating to the recall of retired judges.

(C) When a judge who is eligible to draw retirement compensation has entered the private practice of law, the judge may be eligible for recall to judicial service upon cessation of the private practice of law and approval of the judge's application to the court. The application shall state the period of time the judge has not engaged in the practice of law, and must be approved by the court before the judge shall be eligible for recall to judicial service.

(D) A "senior judge" is a retired judge who is eligible to serve on assignment to temporary judicial duty.

(4) Assignments of Justices and Judges.

(A) When a justice of the supreme court is unable to perform the duties of office, or when necessary for the prompt dispatch of the business of the court, the chief justice may assign to the court any judge who is qualified to serve, for such time as the chief justice may direct.

(B) When a judge of any district court of appeal is unable to perform the duties of office, or when necessary for the prompt dispatch of the business of the court, the chief judge shall advise the chief justice and the chief justice may assign to the court any judge who is qualified to serve, for such time or such proceedings as the chief justice may direct.

(C) When any circuit or county judge is unable to perform the duties of office, or when necessary for the prompt dispatch of the business of the court, the chief judge of the circuit may assign any judge in the circuit

to temporary service for which the judge is qualified, in accordance with rule 2.215. If the chief judge deems it necessary, the chief judge may request the chief justice to assign a judge to the court for such time or such proceedings as the chief justice may direct.

(b) Clerk.

(1) Appointment. The supreme court shall appoint a clerk who shall hold office at the pleasure of the court and perform such duties as the court directs. The clerk's compensation shall be fixed by law. The clerk's office shall be in the supreme court building. The clerk shall devote full time to the duties of the office and shall not engage in the practice of law while in office.

(2) Custody of Records, Files, and Seal. All court records and the seal of the court shall be kept in the office and the custody of the clerk. The clerk shall not allow any court record to be taken from the clerk's office or the courtroom, except by a justice of the court or upon the order of the court.

(3) Records of Proceedings. The clerk shall keep such records as the court may from time to time order or direct. The clerk shall keep a docket or equivalent electronic record of all cases that are brought for review to, or that originate in, the court. Each case shall be numbered in the order in which the notice, petition, or other initial pleading originating the cause is filed in the court.

(4) Filing Fee. In all cases filed in the court, the clerk shall require the payment of a fee as provided by law when the notice, petition, or other initial pleading is filed. The payment shall not be exacted in advance in appeals in which a party has been adjudicated insolvent for the purpose of an appeal or in appeals in which the state is the real party in interest as the moving party. The payment of the fee shall not be required in habeas corpus proceedings, or appeals therefrom, arising out of or in connection with criminal actions.

(5) Issuance of Mandate; Recordation and Notification. The clerk shall issue such mandate or process as may be directed by the court. Upon the issuance of any mandate, the clerk shall record the issuance in a book or equivalent electronic record kept for that purpose, in which the date of issuance and the manner of transmittal of the process shall be noted. In proceedings in which no mandate is issued, upon final adjudication of the pending cause the clerk shall transmit to the party affected thereby a copy of the court's order or judgment. The clerk shall notify the attorneys of record of the issuance of any mandate or the rendition of any final judgment. The clerk shall furnish without charge to all attorneys of record in any cause a copy of any order or written opinion rendered in such action.

(6) Return of Original Papers. Upon the conclusion of any proceeding in the supreme court, the clerk shall return to the clerk of the lower court the original papers or files transmitted to the court for use in the cause.

(c) Librarian.

(1) Appointment. The supreme court shall appoint a librarian of the supreme court and such assistants as may be necessary. The supreme court library shall be in the custody of the librarian, but under the exclusive control of the court. The library shall be open to members of the bar of the supreme court, to members of the legislature, to law officers of the executive or other departments of the state, and to such other persons as may be allowed to use the library by special permission of the court.

(2) Library Hours. The library shall be open during such times as the reasonable needs of the bar require and shall be governed by regulations made by the librarian with the approval of the court.

(3) Books. Books shall not be removed from the library except for use by, or upon order of, any justice.

(d) Marshal.

(1) Appointment. The supreme court shall appoint a marshal who shall hold office at the pleasure of the court and perform such duties as the court directs. The marshal's compensation shall be fixed by law.

(2) Duties. The marshal shall have power to execute process of the court throughout the state and such other powers as may be conferred by law. The marshal may deputize the sheriff or a deputy sheriff in any county to execute process of the court and shall perform such clerical or ministerial duties as the court may direct or as required by law. Subject to the direction of the court, the marshal shall be custodian of the supreme court building and grounds.

(e) State Courts Administrator.

(1) Appointment. The supreme court shall appoint a state courts administrator who shall serve at the pleasure of the court and perform such duties as the court directs. The state courts administrator's compensation shall be fixed by law.

(2) Duties. The state courts administrator shall supervise the administrative office of the Florida courts, which shall be maintained at such place as directed by the supreme court; shall employ such other personnel as the court deems necessary to aid in the administration of the state courts system; shall represent the state courts system before the legislature and other bodies with respect to matters affecting the state courts system and functions related to and serving the system; shall supervise the preparation and submission to the supreme court, for review and approval, of a tentative budget request for the state courts system and shall appear before the legislature in accordance with the court's directions in support of the final budget request on behalf of the system; shall inform the judiciary of the state courts system's final budget request and any proposed substantive law changes approved by the supreme court; shall assist in the preparation of educational and training materials for the state courts system and related personnel, and shall coordinate or assist in the conduct of educational and training sessions for such personnel; shall assist all courts in the development of improvements in the system, and submit to the chief justice and the court appropriate recommendations to improve the state courts system; and shall collect and compile uniform financial and other statistical data or information reflective of the cost, workloads, business, and other functions related to the state courts system. The state courts administrator is the custodian of all records in the administrator's office.

(f) Open Sessions. All sessions of the court shall be open to the public, except proceedings designated as confidential by the court and conference sessions held for the discussion and consideration of pending cases, for the formulation of opinions by the court, and for the discussion or resolution of other matters related to the administration of the state courts system.

(g) Designation of Assigned Judges. When any judge of another court is assigned for temporary service on the supreme court, that judge shall be designated, as author or participant, by name and initials followed by the words "Associate Justice."

RULE 2.210. DISTRICT COURTS OF APPEAL

(a) Internal Government.

(1) Exercise of Powers and Jurisdiction. Three judges shall constitute a panel for and shall consider each case, and the concurrence of a majority of the panel shall be necessary to a decision.

(2) Chief Judge.

(A) The selection of a chief judge should be based on managerial, administrative, and leadership abilities, without regard to seniority only.

(B) The chief judge shall be the administrative officer of the court, and shall, consistent with branch-wide policies, direct the formation and implementation of policies and priorities for the operation of the court. The chief judge shall exercise administrative supervision over all judges and court personnel. The chief judge shall be responsible to the chief justice of the supreme court. The chief judge may enter and sign administrative orders. The administrative powers and duties of the chief judge include, but are not limited to, the power to order consolidation of cases, and to assign cases to the judges for the preparation of opinions, orders, or judgments. The chief judge shall have the authority to require all judges of the court, court officers and court personnel, to comply with all court and judicial branch policies, administrative orders, procedures, and administrative plans.

(C) The chief judge shall maintain liaison in all judicial administrative matters with the chief justice of the supreme court, and shall, considering available resources, ensure the efficient and proper administration of the court. The chief judge shall develop an administrative plan that shall include an administrative organization capable of effecting the prompt disposition of cases, the assignment of judges, other court officers, and court personnel, and the control of dockets. The administrative plan shall include a consideration of the statistical data developed by the case reporting system.

(D) All judges shall inform the chief judge of any contemplated absences that will affect the progress of the court's business. If a judge is temporarily absent, is disqualified in an action, or is unable to perform the duties of the office, the chief judge or the chief judge's designee may assign a matter pending before the judge to any other judge or any additional assigned judge of the same court. If it appears to the chief judge that the speedy, efficient, and proper administration of justice so requires, the chief judge shall request the chief justice of the supreme court to assign temporarily an additional judge or judges from outside the court to duty in the court requiring assistance, and shall advise the chief justice whether or not the approval of the chief judge of the court from which the assignment is to be made has been obtained. The assigned judges shall be subject to administrative supervision of the chief judge for all purposes of this rule. Nothing in this rule shall restrict the constitutional powers of the chief justice of the supreme court to make such assignments as the chief justice shall deem appropriate.

(E) The chief judge shall regulate the use of all court facilities, regularly examine the dockets of the courts under the chief judge's administrative supervision, and require a report on the status of the matters on the docket. The chief judge may take such action as may be necessary to cause the docket to be made current.

(F) The chief judge shall be chosen by a majority of the active judges of the court for a term commencing on July 1 of each odd-numbered year, and shall serve for a term of 2 years. A chief judge may serve for successive terms but in no event shall the total term as chief judge exceed 8 years. In the event of a vacancy, a successor shall be chosen promptly to serve the balance of the unexpired term. If the chief judge is unable to discharge these duties, the judge longest in continuous service or, as between judges with equal continuous service, the one having the longest unexpired term and able to do so, shall perform the duties of chief judge pending the chief judge's return to duty. Judges shall notify the chief judge of any contemplated absence from the court and the reasons therefor. A chief judge may be removed as chief judge by the supreme court, acting as the administrative supervisory body of all courts, or by a two-thirds vote of the active judges.

(G) The failure of any judge to comply with an order or directive of the chief judge shall be considered neglect of duty and may be reported by the chief judge to the chief justice of the supreme court who shall have the authority to take such corrective action as may be appropriate. The chief judge may report the neglect of duty by a judge to the Judicial Qualifications Commission or other appropriate person or body, or take such other corrective action as may be appropriate.

(H) At the call of the chief justice, the chief judges of the circuit court and district courts of appeal shall meet on a regular basis and with each other and with the chief justice to discuss and provide feedback for implementation of policies and practices that have statewide impact including, but not limited to, the judicial branch's management, operation, strategic plan, legislative agenda and budget priorities. Such meetings shall, if practicable, occur at least quarterly and be conducted in person. At the discretion of the chief justice, any of these meetings may be combined with other judicial branch and leadership meetings.

(I) The chief judge shall have the responsibility to exercise reasonable efforts to promote and encourage diversity in the administration of justice.

(b) Clerk.

(1) Appointment. The court shall appoint a clerk who shall hold office at the pleasure of the court and perform such duties as the court directs. The clerk's compensation shall be fixed by law. The clerk's office

shall be in the headquarters of the court. The clerk's time shall be devoted to the duties of the office and the clerk shall not engage in the private practice of law while serving as clerk. All court records and the seal of the court shall be kept in the office and the custody of the clerk. The clerk shall not allow any court record to be taken from the clerk's office or the courtroom, except by a judge of the court or upon order of the court.

(2) Records of Proceedings. The clerk shall keep such records as the court may from time to time order or direct. The clerk shall keep a docket or equivalent electronic record of all cases that are brought for review to, or that originate in, the court. Each case shall be numbered in the order that the notice, petition, other initial pleading originating the proceeding is filed in the court.

(3) Filing Fee. In all cases filed in the court, the clerk shall require the payment of a fee as provided by law at the time the notice, petition, or other initial pleading is filed. The payment shall not be exacted in advance in appeals in which a party has been adjudicated insolvent for the purpose of an appeal or in appeals in which the state is the real party in interest as the moving party. The payment of the fee shall not be required in habeas corpus proceedings or appeals therefrom.

(4) Issuance of Mandate; Recordation and Notification. The clerk shall issue such mandates or process as may be directed by the court. If the court directs that a mandate record shall be maintained, then upon the issuance of any mandate the clerk shall record the issuance in a book or equivalent electronic record kept for that purpose, in which shall be noted the date of issuance and the manner of transmittal of the process. In proceedings in which no mandate is issued, upon final adjudication of the pending cause the clerk shall transmit to the party affected thereby a copy of the court's order or judgment. The clerk shall notify the attorneys of record of the issuance of any mandate or the rendition of any final judgment. The clerk shall furnish without charge to all attorneys of record in any cause a copy of any order or written opinion rendered in such action.

(5) Return of Original Papers. The clerk shall retain all original papers, files, and exhibits transmitted to the court for a period of not less than 30 days after rendition of the opinion or order denying any motion pursuant to Florida Rule of Appellate Procedure 9.330, whichever is later. If no discretionary review proceeding or appeal has been timely commenced in the supreme court to review the court's decision within 30 days, the clerk shall transmit to the clerk of the trial court the original papers, files, and exhibits. If a discretionary review proceeding or appeal has been timely commenced in the supreme court to review the court's decision, the original papers, files, and exhibits shall be retained by the clerk until transmitted to the supreme court or, if not so transmitted, until final disposition by the supreme court and final disposition by the court pursuant to the mandate issued by the supreme court.

(c) Marshal.

(1) Appointment. The court shall appoint a marshal who shall hold office at the pleasure of the court and perform such duties as the court directs. The marshal's compensation shall be fixed by law.

(2) Duties. The marshal shall have power to execute process of the court throughout the district, and in any county therein may deputize the sheriff or a deputy sheriff for such purpose. The marshal shall perform such clerical or ministerial duties as the court may direct or as are required by law. The marshal shall be custodian of the headquarters occupied by the court, whether the headquarters is an entire building or a part of a building.

(d) Open Sessions. All sessions of the court shall be open to the public, except conference sessions held for the discussion and consideration of pending cases, for the formulation of opinions by the court, and for the discussion or resolution of other matters related to the administration of the court.

(e) Designation of Assigned Judges. When any justice or judge of another court is assigned for temporary service on a district court of appeal, that justice or judge shall be designated, as author or

participant, by name and initials followed by the words "Associate Judge."

RULE 2.215. TRIAL COURT ADMINISTRATION

(a) Purpose. The purpose of this rule is to fix administrative responsibility in the chief judges of the circuit courts and the other judges that the chief judges may designate. When these rules refer to the court, they shall be construed to apply to a judge of the court when the context requires or permits.

(b) Chief Judge.

(1) The chief judge shall be a circuit judge who possesses managerial, administrative, and leadership abilities, and shall be selected without regard to seniority only.

(2) The chief judge shall be the administrative officer of the courts within the circuit and shall, consistent with branch-wide policies, direct the formation and implementation of policies and priorities for the operation of all courts and officers within the circuit. The chief judge shall exercise administrative supervision over all judges and court personnel within the judicial circuit. The chief judge shall be responsible to the chief justice of the supreme court. The chief judge may enter and sign administrative orders, except as otherwise provided by this rule. The chief judge shall have the authority to require that all judges of the court, other court officers, and court personnel comply with all court and judicial branch policies, administrative orders, procedures and administrative plans.

(3) The chief judge shall maintain liaison in all judicial administrative matters with the chief justice of the supreme court, and shall, considering available resources, ensure the efficient and proper administration of all courts within that circuit. The chief judge shall develop an administrative plan that shall be filed with the supreme court and shall include an administrative organization capable of effecting the prompt

disposition of cases; assignment of judges, other court officers, and all other court personnel; control of dockets; regulation and use of courtrooms; and mandatory periodic review of the status of the inmates of the county jail. The plan shall be compatible with the development of the capabilities of the judges in such a manner that each judge will be qualified to serve in any division, thereby creating a judicial pool from which judges may be assigned to various courts throughout the state. The administrative plan shall include a consideration of the statistical data developed by the case reporting system. Questions concerning the administration or management of the courts of the circuit shall be directed to the chief justice of the supreme court through the state courts administrator.

(4) The chief judge shall assign judges to the courts and divisions, and shall determine the length of each assignment. The chief judge is authorized to order consolidation of cases, and to assign cases to a judge or judges for the preparation of opinions, orders, or judgments. All judges shall inform the chief judge of any contemplated absences that will affect the progress of the court's business. If a judge is temporarily absent, is disqualified in an action, or is unable to perform the duties of the office, the chief judge or the chief judge's designee may assign a proceeding pending before the judge to any other judge or any additional assigned judge of the same court. The chief judge may assign any judge to temporary service for which the judge is qualified in any court in the same circuit. If it appears to the chief judge that the speedy, efficient, and proper administration of justice so requires, the chief judge shall request the chief justice of the supreme court to assign temporarily an additional judge or judges from outside the circuit to duty in the court requiring assistance, and shall advise the chief justice whether or not the approval of the chief judge of the circuit from which the assignment is to be made has been obtained. The assigned judges shall be subject to administrative supervision of the chief judge for all purposes of this rule. When assigning a judge to hear any type of postconviction or collateral relief proceeding brought by a defendant who has been sentenced to death, the chief judge shall assign to such cases a judge qualified to conduct such proceedings under

subdivision (b)(10) of this rule. Nothing in this rule shall restrict the constitutional powers of the chief justice of the supreme court to make such assignments as the chief justice shall deem appropriate.

(5) The chief judge may designate a judge in any court or court division of circuit or county courts as "administrative judge" of any court or division to assist with the administrative supervision of the court or division. To the extent practical, the chief judge shall assign only one administrative judge to supervise the family court. The designee shall be responsible to the chief judge, shall have the power and duty to carry out the responsibilities assigned by the chief judge, and shall serve at the pleasure of the chief judge.

(6) The chief judge may require the attendance of prosecutors, public defenders, clerks, bailiffs, and other officers of the courts, and may require from the clerks of the courts, sheriffs, or other officers of the courts periodic reports that the chief judge deems necessary.

(7) The chief judge shall regulate the use of all court facilities, regularly examine the dockets of the courts under the chief judge's administrative supervision, and require a report on the status of the matters on the dockets. The chief judge may take such action as may be necessary to cause the dockets to be made current. The chief judge shall monitor the status of all pending postconviction or collateral relief proceedings brought by defendants who have been sentenced to death and shall take the necessary actions to assure that such cases proceed without undue delay. On the first day of every January, April, July, and October, the chief judge shall inform the chief justice of the supreme court the status of all such pending cases.

(8) The chief judge or the chief judge's designee shall regularly examine the status of every inmate of the county jail.

(9) The chief judge may authorize the clerks of the courts to maintain branch county court facilities. When so authorized, clerks of court shall be permitted to retain in such branch court facilities all county court permanent records of pending cases, and may

retain and destroy these records in the manner provided by law.

(10)(A) The chief judge shall not assign a judge to preside over a capital case in which the state is seeking the death penalty, or collateral proceedings brought by a death row inmate, until that judge has become qualified to do so by:

(i) presiding a minimum of 6 months in a felony criminal division or in a division that includes felony criminal cases, and

(ii) successfully attending the "Handling Capital Cases" course offered through the Florida Court Education Council. A judge whose caseload includes felony criminal cases must attend the "Handling Capital Cases" course as soon as practicable, or upon the direction of the chief judge.

(B) The chief justice may waive these requirements in exceptional circumstances at the request of the chief judge.

(C) Following attendance at the "Handling Capital Cases" course, a judge shall remain qualified to preside over a capital case by attending a "Capital Case Refresher" course once during each of the subsequent continuing judicial education (CJE) reporting periods. A judge who has attended the "Handling Capital Cases" course and who has not taken the "Capital Case Refresher" course within any subsequent continuing judicial education reporting period must requalify to preside over a capital case by attending the refresher course.

(D) The refresher course shall be at least a 6-hour course and must be approved by the Florida Court Education Council. The course must contain instruction on the following topics: penalty phase, jury selection, and proceedings brought pursuant to Florida Rule of Criminal Procedure 3.851.

(11) The failure of any judge to comply with an order or directive of the chief judge shall be considered neglect of duty and may be reported by the chief judge to the chief justice of the supreme court who shall have the authority to take any corrective action as may be appropriate. The chief judge may report the neglect of duty by a judge to the Judicial Qualifications Commission or other appropriate person or body, or take such other corrective action as may be appropriate.

(12) At the call of the chief justice, the chief judges of the circuit court and district courts of appeal shall meet on a regular basis and with each other and with the chief justice to discuss and provide feedback for implementation of policies and practices that have statewide impact including, but not limited to, the judicial branch's management, operation, strategic plan, legislative agenda and budget priorities. Such meetings shall, if practicable, occur at least quarterly and be conducted in person. At the discretion of the chief justice, any of these meetings may be combined with other judicial branch and leadership meetings.

(13) The chief judge shall have the responsibility to exercise reasonable efforts to promote and encourage diversity in the administration of justice.

(c) **Selection.** The chief judge shall be chosen by a majority of the active circuit and county court judges within the circuit for a term of 2 years commencing on July 1 of each odd-numbered year, or if there is no majority, by the chief justice, for a term of 2 years. The election for chief judge shall be held no sooner than February 1 of the year during which the chief judge's term commences beginning July 1. All elections for chief judge shall be conducted as follows:

(1) All ballots shall be secret.

(2) Any circuit or county judge may nominate a candidate for chief judge.

(3) Proxy voting shall not be permitted.

(4) Any judge who will be absent from the election may vote by secret absentee ballot obtained from and returned to the Trial Court Administrator.

A chief judge may be removed as chief judge by the supreme court, acting as the administrative supervisory body of all courts, or may be removed by a two-thirds vote of the active judges. The purpose of this rule is to fix a 2-year cycle for the selection of the chief judge in each circuit. A chief judge may serve for successive terms but in no event shall the total term as chief judge exceed 8 years. A chief judge who is to be temporarily absent shall select an acting chief judge from among the circuit judges. If a chief judge dies, retires, fails to appoint an acting chief judge during an absence, or is unable to perform the duties of the office, the chief justice of the supreme court shall appoint a circuit judge to act as chief judge during the absence or disability, or until a successor chief judge is elected to serve the unexpired term. When the office of chief judge is temporarily vacant pending action within the scope of this paragraph, the duties of court administration shall be performed by the circuit judge having the longest continuous service as a judge or by another circuit judge designated by that judge.

(d) Circuit Court Administrator. Each circuit court administrator shall be selected or terminated by the chief judge subject to concurrence by a majority vote of the circuit and county judges of the respective circuits.

(e) Local Rules and Administrative Orders.

(1) Local court rules as defined in rule 2.120 may be proposed by a majority of the circuit and county judges in the circuit. The judges shall notify the local bar within the circuit of the proposal, after which they shall permit a representative of the local bar, and may permit any other interested person, to be heard orally or in writing on the proposal before submitting it to the supreme court for approval. When a proposed local rule is submitted to the supreme court for approval, the following procedure shall apply:

(A) Local court rule proposals shall be submitted to the supreme court in January of each year. The supreme court may accept emergency proposals submitted at other times.

(B) Not later than February 15 of each year, the clerk of the supreme court shall submit all local court rule proposals to the Supreme Court Local Rules Advisory Committee created by rule 2.140. At the same time, the clerk of the supreme court shall send copies of the proposed rules to the appropriate committees of The Florida Bar. The Florida Bar committees, any interested local bar associations, and any other interested person shall submit any comments or responses that they wish to make to the Supreme Court Local Rules Advisory Committee on or before March 15 of the year.

(C) The Supreme Court Local Rules Advisory Committee shall meet on or before April 15 to consider the proposals and any comments submitted by interested parties. The committee shall transmit its recommendations to the supreme court concerning each proposal, with the reasons for its recommendations, within 15 days after its meeting.

(D) The supreme court shall consider the recommendations of the committee and may resubmit the proposals with modifications to the committee for editorial comment only. The supreme court may set a hearing on any proposals, or consider them on the recommendations and comments as submitted. If a hearing is set, notice shall be given to the chief judge of the circuit from which the proposals originated, the executive director of The Florida Bar, the chair of the Rules of Judicial Administration Committee of The Florida Bar, any local bar associations, and any interested persons who made comments on the specific proposals to be considered. The supreme court shall act on the proposals promptly after the recommendations are received or heard.

(E) If a local court rule is approved by the supreme court, it shall become effective on the date set by that court.

(F) A copy of all local court rules approved by the supreme court shall be indexed and recorded by the clerk of the circuit court in each county of the circuit where the rules are effective. A set of the recorded copies shall be readily available for inspection as a public record, and copies shall be provided to any requesting party for the cost of duplication. The chief judge of the circuit may provide for the publication of the rules. The clerk of the supreme court shall furnish copies of each approved local court rule to the executive director of The Florida Bar.

(2) Any judge or member of The Florida Bar who believes that an administrative order promulgated

under subdivision (b)(2) of this rule is a court rule or a local rule as defined in rule 2.120, rather than an administrative order, may apply to the Supreme Court Local Rules Advisory Committee for a decision on the question. The decisions of the committee concerning the determination of the question shall be reported to the supreme court, and the court shall follow the procedure set forth in subdivision (D) above in considering the recommendation of the committee.

(3) All administrative orders of a general and continuing nature, and all others designated by the chief judge, shall be indexed and recorded by the clerk of the circuit court in each county where the orders are effective. A set of the recorded copies shall be readily available for inspection as a public record, and copies shall be provided to any requesting party for the cost of duplication. The chief judge shall, on an annual basis, direct a review of all local administrative orders to ensure that the set of copies maintained by the clerk remains current and does not conflict with supreme court or local rules.

(4) All local court rules entered pursuant to this section shall be numbered sequentially for each respective judicial circuit.

(f) Duty to Rule within a Reasonable Time. Every judge has a duty to rule upon and announce an order or judgment on every matter submitted to that judge within a reasonable time. Each judge shall maintain a log of cases under advisement and inform the chief judge of the circuit at the end of each calendar month of each case that has been held under advisement for more than 60 days.

(g) Duty to Expedite Priority Cases. Every judge has a duty to expedite priority cases to the extent reasonably possible. Priority cases are those cases that have been assigned a priority status or assigned an expedited disposition schedule by statute, rule of procedure, case law, or otherwise. Particular attention shall be given to all juvenile dependency and termination of parental rights cases, cases involving families and children in need of services, and challenges involving elections and proposed constitutional amendments.

(h) Neglect of Duty. The failure of any judge, clerk, prosecutor, public defender, attorney, court reporter, or other officer of the court to comply with an order or directive of the chief judge shall be considered neglect of duty and shall be reported by the chief judge to the chief justice of the supreme court. The chief justice may report the neglect of duty by a judge to the Judicial Qualifications Commission, and neglect of duty by other officials to the governor of Florida or other appropriate person or body.

(i) Status Conference After Compilation of Record in Death Case. In any proceeding in which a defendant has been sentenced to death, the circuit judge assigned to the case shall take such action as may be necessary to ensure that a complete record on appeal has been properly prepared. To that end, the judge shall convene a status conference with all counsel of record as soon as possible after the record has been prepared pursuant to rule of appellate procedure 9.200(d) but before the record has been transmitted. The purpose of the status conference shall be to ensure that the record is complete.

Committee Notes

2008 Amendment. The provisions in subdivision (g) of this rule should be read in conjunction with the provisions of rule 2.545(c) governing priority cases.

Court Commentary

1996 Court Commentary. Rule 2.050(h) [renumbered as 2.215(h) in 2006] should be read in conjunction with Florida Rule of Appellate Procedure 9.140(b)(4)(A).

1997 Court Commentary. [Rule 2.050(b)(10), renumbered as 2.215(b)(10) in 2006]. The refresher course may be a six-hour block during any Florida Court Education Council approved course offering sponsored by any approved Florida judicial education provider, including the Florida College of Advanced Judicial Studies or the Florida Conference of Circuit Judges. The block must contain instruction on the following topics: penalty phase, jury selection, and rule 3.850 proceedings.

Failure to complete the refresher course during the three-year judicial education reporting period will necessitate completion of the original "Handling Capital Cases" course.

2002 Court Commentary. Recognizing the inherent differences in trial and appellate court dockets, the last sentence of subdivision (g) is intended to conform to the extent practicable with appellate rule 9.146(g), which requires appellate courts to give priority to appeals in juvenile dependency and termination of parental rights cases, and in cases involving families and children in need of services.

RULE 2.220. CONFERENCES OF JUDGES

(a) Conference of County Court Judges.

(1) **Creation.** There shall be a "Conference of County Court Judges of Florida," consisting of the active and senior county court judges of the State of Florida.

(2) **Purpose.** The purpose of the conference shall be:

(A) the betterment of the judicial system of the state;

(B) the improvement of procedure and practice in the several courts;

(C) to conduct conferences and institutes for continuing judicial education and to provide forums in which the county court judges of Florida may meet and discuss mutual problems and solutions; and

(D) to provide input to the Unified Committee on Judicial Compensation on judicial compensation and benefit issues, and to assist the judicial branch in soliciting support and resources on these issues.

(3) **Officers.** Management of the conference shall be vested in the officers of the conference, an executive committee, and a board of directors.

(A) The officers of the conference shall be:

(i) the president, president-elect, immediate past president, secretary, and treasurer, who shall be elected at large; and

(ii) one vice-president elected from each appellate court district.

(B) The executive committee shall consist of the officers of the conference and an executive secretary.

(C) The board of directors shall consist of the executive committee and a member elected from each judicial circuit.

(D) There shall be an annual meeting of the conference.

(E) Between annual meetings of the conference, the affairs of the conference shall be managed by the executive committee.

(4) **Authority.** The conference may adopt governance documents, the provisions of which shall not be inconsistent with this rule.

Editor's Note: Subdivision (b) shall become effective upon the repeal of section 26.55, Florida Statutes (2011). See the Editor's Notes at the end of the rule.

(b) Conference of Circuit Court Judges.

(1) **Creation.** There shall be a "Conference of Circuit Court Judges of Florida", consisting of the active and senior circuit judges of the several judicial circuits of the state.

(2) **Purpose.** The purpose of the conference shall be:

(A) the betterment of the judicial system of the state;

(B) the improvement of procedure and practice in the several courts;

(C) to conduct conferences and institutes for continuing judicial education and to provide forums in which the circuit court judges of Florida may meet and discuss mutual problems and solutions; and

(D) to provide input to the Unified Committee on Judicial Compensation on judicial compensation and benefit issues, and to assist the judicial branch in soliciting support and resources on these issues.

(3) **Officers.** Management of the conference shall be vested in the officers of the conference, an executive committee, and a board of directors.

(A) The officers of the conference shall be:

(i) the president, president-elect, immediate past president, secretary, and treasurer, who shall be elected at large; and

(ii) one vice-president elected from each appellate court district.

(B) The executive committee shall consist of the officers of the conference and an executive secretary.

(C) The board of directors shall consist of the executive committee and a member elected from each judicial circuit.

(D) There shall be an annual meeting of the conference.

(E) Between annual meetings of the conference, the affairs of the conference shall be managed by the executive committee.

(4) Authority. The conference may adopt governance documents, the provisions of which shall not be inconsistent with this rule.

(c) Conference of District Court of Appeal Judges.

(1) Creation. There shall be a "Florida Conference of District Court of Appeal Judges," consisting of the active and senior district court of appeal judges of the State of Florida.

(2) Purpose. The purpose of the conference shall be:

(A) the betterment of the judicial system of the state;

(B) the improvement of procedure and practice in the several courts;

(C) to conduct conferences and institutes for continuing judicial education and to provide forums in which the district court of appeal judges of Florida may meet and discuss mutual problems and solutions; and

(D) to provide input to the Unified Committee on Judicial Compensation on judicial compensation and benefit issues, and to assist the judicial branch in soliciting support and resources on these issues.

(3) Officers. Management of the conference shall be vested in the officers of the conference and an executive committee.

(A) The officers of the conference shall be the president, president-elect, and secretary-treasurer.

(B) The executive committee shall consist of the president and president-elect of the conference and the chief judge of each district court of appeal.

(C) There shall be an annual meeting of the conference.

(D) Between annual meetings of the conference, the affairs of the conference shall be managed by the executive committee.

(4) Authority. The conference may adopt governance documents, the provisions of which shall not be inconsistent with this rule.

Editor's Notes: — The amendments to Subdivision (a) and the enactment of new Subdivision (c) were effective immediately, while the enactment of new Subdivision (b) is effective contingent on the repeal by the legislature of section 26.55 of the Florida Statutes. See *In re Implementation of Judicial Branch Study Group Recommendations - Amendments to the Florida Rules of Judicial Administration*, 37 FLW S82 (Fla. 2012), which provides in relevant part:

"Based on a Study Group recommendation, we amend rule 2.220 (Conference of County Court Judges) to create a conference of active and senior judges for each level of court. Much of the current rule creating the Conference of County Court Judges is retained in new subdivision (a). New subdivision (b) is added to recreate by rule the Conference of Circuit Court Judges, which is currently created by section 26.55, Florida Statutes (2011). New subdivision (b) will become effective upon the repeal of the statute. New subdivision (c) is added to the rule to formally create the Conference of District Court of Appeal Judges. Among the other purposes for the conferences stated in the rule, each conference will provide input to the newly created Unified Committee on Judicial Compensation, discussed below, on judicial compensation and benefit issues and will assist the judicial branch in soliciting support and resources on those issues." Id. at 3.

"New rule 2.220(b) (Conference of Circuit Court Judges) shall become effective upon the repeal of section 26.55, Florida Statutes (2011). The remainder of the amendments shall become effective immediately upon release of this opinion." Id. at 5.

As adopted, subdivision (c)(3) includes subdivisions (D) and (E), which the editors have redesignated as current (C) and (D), respectively.

RULE 2.225. JUDICIAL MANAGEMENT COUNCIL

(a) Creation and Responsibilities. There is hereby created the Judicial Management Council of

Florida, which shall meet at least quarterly, and be charged with the following responsibilities:

(1) identifying potential crisis situations affecting the judicial branch and developing strategy to timely and effectively address them;

(2) identifying and evaluating information that would assist in improving the performance and effectiveness of the judicial branch (for example, information including, but not limited to, internal operations for cash flow and budget performance, and statistical information by court and type of cases for (i) number of cases filed, (ii) aged inventory of cases – the number and age of cases pending, (iii) time to disposition – the percentage of cases disposed or otherwise resolved within established time frames, and (iv) clearance rates – the number of outgoing cases as a percentage of the number of incoming cases);

(3) developing and monitoring progress relating to long-range planning for the judicial branch;

(4) reviewing the charges of the various court and Florida Bar commissions and committees, recommending consolidation or revision of the commissions and committees, and recommending a method for the coordination of the work of those bodies based on the proposed revisions; and

(5) addressing issues brought to the council by the supreme court.

(b) Referrals. The chief justice and the supreme court shall consider referring significant new issues or problems with implications for judicial branch policy to the Judicial Management Council prior to the creation of any new committees.

(c) Supreme Court Action on Recommendations by the Judicial Management Council. The supreme court may take any or all of the following actions on recommendations made by the Judicial Management Council:

(1) adopt the recommendation of the council in whole or in part, with or without conditions, including but not limited to:

(A) directing that action be taken to influence or change administrative policy, management practices, rules, or programs that are the subject of the recommendations;

(B) including the recommendation in the judicial branch's legislative agenda or budget requests;

(2) refer specific issues or questions back to the council for further study or alternative recommendations;

(3) reject the recommendation or decision in whole or in part;

(4) refer the recommendation to other entities, such as the Florida Legislature, the governor, the cabinet, executive branch agencies, or The Florida Bar, as the supreme court deems appropriate; or

(5) take alternative action.

(d) Membership.

(1) The council shall consist of 15 voting members, including the chief justice, who shall chair the council, an additional justice of the supreme court, representatives from each level of court, and public members.

(2) All voting members shall be appointed by the supreme court. Each member, other than the chief justice, will initially be appointed for a 2- or 4- year term, with the terms staggered to ensure continuity and experience on the council and for 4-year terms thereafter.

(3) The state courts administrator shall be a non-voting member. The council may request other non-voting persons to participate on an as-needed temporary basis to gain expertise and experience in certain issues on review.

(e) Staff Support and Funding. The Office of the State Courts Administrator shall provide primary staff support to the Judicial Management Council. Adequate staffing and other resources shall be made available to the Office of the State Courts Administrator to ensure the effective and efficient completion of tasks assigned to the Judicial Management Council. Sufficient resources shall also be provided for meetings of the Judicial Management Council and its committees or subcommittees, and other expenses necessary to the satisfactory completion of its work.

RULE 2.230. TRIAL COURT BUDGET COMMISSION

(a) Purpose. The purpose of this rule is to establish a Trial Court Budget Commission that will have the responsibility for developing and overseeing the administration of trial court budgets in a manner which ensures equity and fairness in state funding among the 20 judicial circuits.

(b) Responsibilities. The Trial Court Budget Commission is charged with specific responsibility to:

(1) establish budgeting and funding policies and procedures consistent with judicial branch plans and policies, directions from the supreme court, and in consideration of input from the Commission on Trial Court Performance and Accountability and other supreme court committees and from the Florida Conference of Circuit Court Judges and the Florida Conference of County Court Judges;

(2) make recommendations to the supreme court on the trial court component of the annual judicial branch budget request;

(3) advocate for the trial court component of the annual judicial branch budget request and associated statutory changes;

(4) make recommendations to the supreme court on funding allocation formulas and budget implementation and criteria as well as associated accountability mechanisms based on actual legislative appropriations;

(5) monitor trial court expenditure trends and revenue collections to identify unanticipated budget problems and to ensure the efficient use of resources;

(6) recommend statutory and rule changes related to trial court budgets;

(7) develop recommended responses to findings on financial audits and reports from the Supreme Court Inspector General, Auditor General, Office of Program Policy Analysis and Government Accountability, and other governmental entities charged with auditing responsibilities regarding trial court budgeting when appropriate;

(8) recommend to the supreme court trial court budget reductions required by the legislature;

(9) identify potential additional sources of revenue for the trial courts;

(10) recommend to the supreme court legislative pay plan issues for trial court personnel, except the commission shall not make recommendations as to pay or benefits for judges; and

(11) request input from the Commission on Trial Court Performance and Accountability on recommendations from that commission that may impact the trial court budget or require funding.

(c) Operational Procedures. The Trial Court Budget Commission will establish operating procedures necessary to carry out its responsibilities as outlined in subdivision (b), subject to final approval by the supreme court. These procedures shall include:

(1) a method for ensuring input from interested constituencies, including the chief judges and trial court administrators of the trial courts, other members of the trial court judiciary, the Judicial Management Council, the Commission on Trial Court Performance and Accountability, and other judicial branch committees and commissions; and

(2) a method for appeal of the decisions of the Trial Court Budget Commission. Appeals may be made only by a chief judge on behalf of a circuit. Appeals may be heard only by the Trial Court Budget Commission unless the appeal is based on the failure of the commission to adhere to its operating procedures, in which case the appeal may be made to the supreme court.

(d) Action by Supreme Court or Chief Justice on Recommendations of Trial Court Budget Com-

mission. The supreme court or chief justice, as appropriate, may take any or all of the following actions on recommendations made by the Trial Court Budget Commission:

(1) The adoption of the recommendations of the commission made in accordance with the discharge of its responsibilities listed in subdivision (b) in whole.

(2) The adoption of the recommendations in part and referral of specific issues or questions back to the commission for further study or alternative recommendations.

(e) Membership and Organization. The Trial Court Budget Commission will be composed of 21 voting members appointed by the chief justice who will represent the interests of the trial courts generally rather than the individual interests of a particular circuit or division. The respective presidents of the Conference of Circuit Court Judges, and the Conference of County Court Judges, and the chair of the Commission on Trial Court Performance and Accountability shall serve as ex officio nonvoting members of the Commission. The chief justice will make appointments to ensure that the broad interests of the trial courts are represented by including members who have experience in different divisions, who have expertise in court operations or administrative matters, and who offer geographic, racial, ethnic, and gender diversity.

(1) The membership must include 14 trial court judges and 7 trial court administrators.

(2) The chief justice will appoint 1 member to serve as chair and 1 member to serve as vice chair, each for a 2-year term.

(3) A supreme court justice will be appointed by the chief justice to serve as supreme court liaison.

(4) No circuit will have more than 2 members on the commission.

(5) The original members of the commission will be appointed as follows:

(A) 7 members shall be appointed for a 2-year term;

(B) 7 members shall be appointed for a 4-year term; and

(C) 7 members shall be appointed for one 6-year term.

All subsequent members will each be appointed for one 6-year term. In the event of a vacancy, the chief justice will appoint a new member to serve for the remainder of the departing member's term.

(6) The commission may establish subcommittees as necessary to satisfactorily carry out its responsibilities. Subcommittees may make recommendations only to the commission as a whole. The chair of the commission may appoint a non-commission member to serve on a subcommittee.

(f) Staff Support and Funding. The Office of the State Courts Administrator will provide primary staff support to the commission. Adequate staffing and resources will be made available to the Office of the State Courts Administrator to ensure the commission is able to fulfill its responsibilities as outlined in the rule. Sufficient resources will also be provided for the commission and its subcommittees to meet and otherwise complete its work.

RULE 2.235. DISTRICT COURT OF APPEAL BUDGET COMMISSION

(a) Purpose. The purpose of this rule is to establish a District Court of Appeal Budget Commission with responsibility for developing and overseeing the administration of district court budgets in a manner which ensures equity and fairness in state funding among the 5 districts.

(b) Responsibilities. The District Court of Appeal Budget Commission is charged with specific responsibility to:

(1) establish budgeting and funding policies and procedures consistent with judicial branch plans and policies, directions from the supreme court, and in consideration of input from the Commission on District Court of Appeal Performance and Accountability, and other supreme court committees;

(2) make recommendations to the supreme court on a unitary district court component of the annual judicial branch budget request;

(3) advocate for the district court component of the annual judicial branch budget request;

(4) make recommendations to the supreme court on funding allocation formulas and/or criteria as well as associated accountability mechanisms based on actual legislative appropriations;

(5) monitor district court expenditure trends and revenue collections to identify unanticipated budget problems and to ensure the efficient use of resources;

(6) recommend statutory and rule changes related to district court budgets;

(7) develop recommended responses to findings on financial audits and reports from the Supreme Court Inspector General, Auditor General, Office of Program Policy Analysis and Government Accountability, and other governmental entities charged with auditing responsibilities regarding district court budgeting when appropriate;

(8) recommend to the supreme court district court budget reductions required by the legislature;

(9) identify potential additional sources of revenue for the district courts;

(10) recommend to the supreme court legislative pay plan issues for district court personnel, except the commission shall not make recommendations as to pay or benefits for judges; and

(11) request input from the Commission on District Court of Appeal Performance and Accountability on recommendations from that commission that may impact the district court budget or require funding.

(c) Operational Procedures. The District Court of Appeal Budget Commission will establish operating procedures necessary to carry out its responsibilities as outlined in subdivision (b), subject to final approval by the supreme court. These procedures shall include:

(1) a method for ensuring input from interested constituencies, including the chief judges, marshals, and clerks of the district courts, other members of the district court judiciary, the Judicial Management Council, the Commission on District Court of Appeal Performance and Accountability, and other judicial branch committees and commissions; and

(2) a method for appeal of the decisions of the District Court of Appeal Budget Commission. Appeals may be made only by a chief judge on behalf of the district. Appeals may be heard only by the District Court of Appeal Budget Commission unless the appeal is based on the failure of the commission to adhere to its operating procedures, in which case the appeal may be made to the supreme court.

(d) Action by Supreme Court or Chief Justice on Recommendations of the District Court of Appeal Budget Commission. The supreme court or chief justice, as appropriate, may take any or all of the following actions on recommendations made by the District Court of Appeal Budget Commission:

(1) The adoption of the recommendations of the commission made in accordance with the discharge of its responsibilities listed in subdivision (b) in whole.

(2) The adoption of the recommendations in part and referral of specific issues or questions back to the commission for further study or alternative recommendations.

(e) Membership and Organization. The District Court of Appeal Budget Commission will be composed of 10 voting members appointed by the chief justice who will represent the interests of the district courts generally rather than the individual interests of a particular district.

(1) The membership shall include the chief judge of each district court of appeal, who shall serve for his or her term as chief judge. The membership shall also include one additional judge from each district court of appeal, appointed by the chief justice, with advice from each chief judge. The marshal of each district court of appeal shall serve as a nonvoting member. Ex officio nonvoting members shall also include the chairs of the District Court of Appeal Performance and Accountability Commission and the Appellate Court Technology Committee, and the president of the District Court of Appeal Judges Conference.

(2) The chief justice will appoint 1 member to serve as chair and 1 member to serve as vice chair, each for a four-year term, or until the member's term on the commission expires.

(3) The commission may establish subcommittees as necessary to satisfactorily carry out its responsibilities. Subcommittees may make recommendations only to the commission as a whole. The chair of the commission may appoint a non-commission member to serve on a subcommittee.

(4) Effective July 1, 2013, the commission shall be reconstituted with staggered terms for voting members, as follows: (A) The chief judge of each district will be appointed for his or her term as chief judge. (B) The additional judge from each odd-numbered district will be appointed for a four-year term. (C) The additional judge from each even-numbered district will be appointed for a two-year term, and thereafter to four-year terms. (D) Each nonvoting member will serve so long as he or she continues to hold the office which entitles him or her to membership on the commission.

(f) Staff Support and Funding. The Office of the State Courts Administrator will provide primary staff support to the commission. Adequate staffing and resources will be made available to the Office of the State Courts Administrator to ensure the commission is able to fulfill its responsibilities as outlined in this rule. Sufficient resources will also be provided for the commission and its subcommittees to meet and otherwise complete its work.

RULE 2.236. FLORIDA COURTS TECHNOLOGY COMMISSION

(a) Purpose. The purpose of this rule is to establish a Florida Courts Technology Commission with responsibility for overseeing, managing, and directing the development and use of technology within the judicial branch under the direction of the supreme court as specified in this rule. For the purpose of this rule, the term "judicial branch" does not include The Florida Bar, the Florida Board of Bar Examiners, or the Judicial Qualifications Commission.

(b) Responsibilities. The Florida Courts Technology Commission is charged with specific responsibility to:

(1) make recommendations to the supreme court on all matters of technology policy impacting the judicial branch to allow the supreme court to establish technology policy in the branch;

(2) make recommendations to the supreme court regarding policies for public access to electronic court records;

(3) make recommendations to the supreme court about the relative priorities of various technology projects within the judicial branch so that the supreme court can establish priorities. The commission should coordinate with the Trial Court Budget Commission and District Court of Appeal Budget Commission to secure funds for allocation of those priorities;

(4) direct and establish priorities for the work of all technology committees in the judicial branch, including the Appellate Court Technology Committee, and review and approve recommendations made by any court committee concerning technology matters or otherwise implicating court technology policy;

(5) establish, periodically review, and update technical standards for technology used and to be used in the judicial branch to receive, manage, maintain, use, secure, and distribute court records by electronic means, consistent with the technology policies established by the supreme court. These standards shall be coordinated with the strategic plans of the judicial branch, rules of procedure, applicable law, and directions from the supreme court, and shall incorporate input from the public, clerks of court, supreme court committees and commissions, and other groups involved in the application of current technology to the judicial branch;

(6) create procedures whereby courts and clerks and other applicable entities can apply for approval of new systems, or modifications to existing systems, that involve the application of technology to the receipt, management, maintenance, use, securing, and distribution of court records within the judicial branch, and between the public and the judicial branch;

(7) evaluate all such applications to determine whether they comply with the technology policies

established by the supreme court and the procedures and standards created pursuant to this rule, and approve those applications deemed to be effective and found to be in compliance;

(8) develop and maintain security policies that must be utilized to ensure the integrity and availability of court technology systems and related data;

(9) ensure principles of accessibility are met for all court technology projects, with consideration and application of the requirements of the Americans with Disabilities Act of 1990 and any other applicable state or federal disability laws;

(10) ensure that the technology utilized in the judicial branch is capable of required integration;

(11) periodically review and evaluate all approved technology in the judicial branch to determine its adherence to current supreme court technology policies and standards;

(12) review annual and periodic reports on the status of court technology systems and proposals for technology improvements and innovation throughout the judicial branch;

(13) recommend statutory and rule changes or additions relating to court technology and the receipt, maintenance, management, use, securing, and distribution of court records by electronic means;

(14) identify technology issues that require attention in the judicial branch upon:

(A) referral from the chief justice;

(B) referral from the supreme court; or

(C) identification by the Florida Courts Technology Commission on its own initiative based on recommendations of the public, commission members, judges, justice system partners, The Florida Bar, clerks of court, the Florida Legislature (either informally or through the passage of legislation), the Governor, the cabinet, or executive branch agencies; and

(15) coordinate proposed amendments to rules of court procedure and judicial administration necessary to effectuate the commission's charge with appropriate Florida Bar rules committees.

If a program, system, or application is found not to comply with the policies established by the supreme court or the standards and procedures established by the commission, the commission may require that it be terminated or modified or subject to such conditions as the commission deems appropriate.

(c) Operational Procedures. The Florida Courts Technology Commission shall establish operating procedures necessary to carry out its responsibilities as outlined in subdivision (b), subject to final approval by the supreme court. These procedures shall include:

(1) a method for ensuring input from all interested constituencies in the state of Florida;

(2) a method for monitoring the development of new court technology projects, reviewing reports on new technology projects, and reviewing the annual reports;

(3) a method whereby courts and clerks and other applicable entities can apply for approval of new technology systems or applications, or modifications to existing systems or applications, that affect the receipt, management, maintenance, use, securing, and distribution of court records;

(4) a system to evaluate all applications for new or modified technology systems to determine whether they comply with the policies and technical standards established by the supreme court and the procedures created pursuant to this rule, and are otherwise appropriate to implement in the judicial branch;

(5) a process for making decisions on all applications for new or modified technology systems and communicating those decisions to interested parties. If an application is found to comply with technology policies and standards, the commission may approve the application and its written approval shall authorize the applicant to proceed. For all applications that are not approved, the commission shall assist the appli-

cant in remedying any deficiencies that the commission identifies;

(6) a method to monitor all technology programs, systems, and applications used in the judicial branch to ensure that such programs, systems, and applications are operating in accordance with the technology policies established by the supreme court and technical standards established by the commission. The commission may ask any operator of a program, system, or application to appear before it for examination into whether the program, system, or application complies with technology policies and standards;

(7) a process to conduct the limited, short-term work of the commission through work groups that it may constitute from time to time. Work groups may make recommendations to the commission as a whole. The chair of the commission may appoint non-commission members to serve on any work group; and

(8) a process to conduct substantial work of the commission requiring long-term commitment through subcommittees. Subcommittees may make recommendations to the commission as a whole. The chair of the commission may appoint non-commission members to serve on any subcommittee.

(d) Action by Supreme Court or Chief Justice on Recommendations of or Decisions by Florida Courts Technology Commission. The supreme court or chief justice, as appropriate, may take any of the following actions on recommendations or decisions made by the Florida Courts Technology Commission:

(1) Adopt the recommendation or decision of the commission in whole or in part, with or without conditions.

(2) Refer specific issues or questions back to the commission for further study or alternative recommendations.

(3) Reject the recommendation or decision in whole or in part.

(4) Take alternative action.

(e) Membership and Organization.

(1) The Florida Courts Technology Commission shall be composed of 25 voting members appointed by the chief justice after consultation with the court. All members shall represent the interests of the public and of Florida courts generally rather than the separate interests of any particular district, circuit, county, division, or other organization. The membership shall include members who have experience in different divisions of courts, in court operations, and in using technology in court for case processing, management, and administrative purposes, and shall provide geographic, racial, ethnic, gender, and other diversity.

(2) The membership shall include 2 district court judges, 5 circuit court judges (1 of whom must be a chief judge), 2 county court judges, 3 court administrators, 3 court technology officers, 4 clerks of court (1 of whom must be a clerk of an appellate court), 4 members of The Florida Bar (1 of whom must be a member of the Board of Governors of The Florida Bar), and 2 members of the public at large.

(3) The members of the commission who are judicial officers, court technology officers, and court administrators must constitute a majority of the commission and must constitute a majority of any quorum at all meetings of the commission.

(4) A supreme court justice shall be appointed by the chief justice to serve as supreme court liaison to the commission.

(5) Each member will be initially appointed for a 1-, 2-, or 3-year term, with the terms staggered to ensure continuity and experience on the commission and for three year terms thereafter. Retention and reappointment of each member will be at the discretion of the chief justice.

(6) The chief justice shall appoint 1 member to serve as chair for a two-year term.

(f) Schedule of Reports. The Florida Courts Technology Commission shall prepare an annual report of its activities, which shall include its recommendations for changes or additions to the technology policies or standards of Florida courts, its recommendations for setting or changing priorities among the programs within the responsibility of the commission to assist with budget resources available, its recommendations for changes to rules, statutes, or regulations that affect technology in Florida courts and the work of the commission. The report also shall include recommendations of the Appellate Court Technology Committee that implicate court technology policy and the action taken on those recommendations by the commission. This report shall be submitted to the supreme court on April 1 of each year.

(g) Appellate Court Technology Committee.

(1) Purpose. The purpose of this subdivision is to establish the Appellate Court Technology Committee as a standing committee of the Florida Courts Technology Commission responsible for providing technical guidance and consultation to the commission regarding information systems development and operational policies and procedures relating to automation in the district courts of appeal.

(2) Responsibilities. The Appellate Court Technology Committee is charged with specific responsibility to:

(A) coordinate with and provide advice to the Florida Courts Technology Commission regarding the development of standards and policies for implementing new technologies, system security, public access to district court information, and system support;

(B) develop, recommend, and implement policy and procedures consistent with the overall policy of the supreme court relating to technology issues affecting the district courts of appeal;

(C) recommend and coordinate the purchase and upgrade of hardware and software in relation to the district courts' office automation systems and networks;

(D) oversee and direct expenditures of designated state court system trust funds for technology needs in the district courts;

(E) promote orientation and education programs on technology and its effective utilization in the district court environment;

(F) ensure principles of accessibility are met for all court technology projects, with consideration and application of the requirements of the Americans with Disabilities Act of 1990 and any other applicable state or federal disability laws;

(G) propose amendments to rules of court procedure and judicial administration necessary to effectuate the committee's charge, after coordination with appropriate Florida Bar rules committees; and

(H) identify budget issues and funding sources and coordinate with the District Court of Appeal Budget Commission on recommendations requiring additional funding or resources for implementation in the district courts of appeal.

(3) Membership and Terms.

(A) The chief justice will select the chair of the committee from among the judges of the district courts, with input from the chief judges.

(B) The chief judges of the remaining district courts will designate a representative from each of their courts to serve as member of the committee.

(C) The chair and members will serve 3-year terms. Retention and reappointment of the chair will be at the discretion of the chief justice. Retention and reappointment of the representative from each district court will be at the discretion of the district court chief judge.

(4) Commission Approval and Reporting of Policy Recommendations. Committee recommendations that implicate court technology policy must be reviewed and approved by the commission. The commission will report the committee's policy recommendations and the action taken on them by the commission to the supreme court. The committee may submit to the court a companion report on its recommendations, supporting or opposing the action taken by the commission.

(h) Staff Support and Funding. The Office of the State Courts Administrator shall provide primary staff support to the Florida Courts Technology Commission and the Appellate Court Technology Committee. Adequate staffing and resources shall be made available by the Office of the State Courts Administrator to ensure that the commission and committee are able to fulfill their responsibilities under this rule.

RULE 2.240. DETERMINATION OF NEED FOR ADDITIONAL JUDGES

(a) Purpose. The purpose of this rule is to set forth uniform criteria used by the supreme court in determining the need for additional judges, except supreme court justices, and the necessity for decreasing the number of judges, pursuant to article V, section 9, Florida Constitution. These criteria form the primary basis for the supreme court's determination of need for additional judges. Unforeseen developments, however, may have an impact upon the judiciary resulting in needs which cannot be foreseen or predicted by statistical projections. The supreme court, therefore, may also consider any additional information found by it to be relevant to the process. In establishing criteria for the need for additional appellate court judges, substantial reliance has been placed on the findings and recommendations of the Commission on District Court of Appeal Performance and Accountability. *See In re Report of the Comm'n on Dist. Court of Appeal Performance and Accountability—Rule of Judicial Admin. 2.035, 933 So.2d 1136 (Fla. 2006).*

(b) Criteria.

(1) Trial Courts.

(A) Assessment of judicial need at the trial court level is based primarily upon the application of case weights to circuit and county court caseload statistics supplied to the Office of the State Courts Administrator by the clerks of the circuit courts, pursuant to rule 2.245, Florida Rules of Judicial Administration. Such case weights provide a quantified measure of judicial time spent on case-related activity, translating judicial caseloads into judicial workload by factoring in the relative complexity by case type in the following manner:

(i) The circuit court case weights are applied to forecasted case filings, which include circuit criminal (includes felony, drug court, and worthless check

cases), circuit civil (includes matters involving claims of $15,000.01 and above), family (includes domestic relations, juvenile dependency, and juvenile delinquency cases), and probate (includes guardianship, mental health, and trust cases).

(ii) The county court case weights are applied to forecasted filings, which include county criminal (includes misdemeanor, violations of county and municipal ordinance, worthless check, driving under the influence, and other criminal traffic cases), and county civil (includes small claims, matters involving claims ranging from $5,000.01 to $15,000, landlord-tenant, and civil traffic infraction cases).

(B) Other factors may be utilized in the determination of the need for one or more additional judges. These factors include, but are not limited to, the following:

(i) The availability and use of county court judges in circuit court.

(ii) The availability and use of senior judges to serve on a particular court.

(iii) The availability and use of magistrates and hearing officers.

(iv) The extent of use of alternative dispute resolution.

(v) The number of jury trials.

(vi) Foreign language interpretations.

(vii) The geographic size of a circuit, including travel times between courthouses in a particular jurisdiction.

(viii) Law enforcement activities in the court's jurisdiction, including any substantial commitment of additional resources for state attorneys, public defenders, and local law enforcement.

(ix) The availability and use of case-related support staff and case management policies and practices.

(x) Caseload trends.

(C) The Commission on Trial Court Performance and Accountability shall review the trial court workload trends and case weights and consider adjustments no less than every five years.

(2) District Courts of Appeal.

(A) The criteria for determining the need to certify the need for increasing or decreasing the number of judges on a district court of appeal shall include the following factors:

(i) workload factors to be considered include: trends in case filings; trends in changes in case mix; trends in the backlog of cases ready for assignment and disposition; trends in the relative weight of cases disposed on the merits per judge; and changes in statutes, rules of court, and case law that directly or indirectly impact judicial workload.

(ii) efficiency factors to be considered include: a court's ability to stay current with its caseload, as indicated by measurements such as trend in clearance rate; trends in a court's percentage of cases disposed within the time standards set forth in the Rules of Judicial Administration and explanation/justification for cases not resolved within the time standards; and a court's utilization of resources, case management techniques and technologies to maximize the efficient adjudication of cases, research of legal issues, and preparation and distribution of decisions.

(iii) effectiveness factors to be considered include the extent to which each judge has adequate time to: thoroughly research legal issues, review briefs and memoranda of law, participate in court conferences on pending cases, hear and dispose of motions, and prepare correspondence, orders, judgments and opinions; expedite appropriate cases; prepare written opinions when warranted; develop, clarify, and maintain consistency in the law within that district; review all decisions rendered by the court; perform administrative duties relating to the court; and participate in the administration of the justice system through work in statewide committees.

(iv) professionalism factors to be considered include: the extent to which judges report that they have time to participate, including teaching, in education programs designed to increase the competency and efficiency of the judiciary and justice system as well as the competency of lawyers; provide guidance and instruction for the professional development of court support staff; and participate in appropriate activities of the legal profession at both the state and local levels to improve the relationship between the bench and bar, to enhance lawyer professionalism, and to improve the administration of justice.

(B) The court will presume that there is a need for an additional appellate court judgeship in any district for which a request is made and where the relative weight of cases disposed on the merits per judge would have exceeded 280 after application of the proposed additional judge(s).

(i) The relative weight of cases disposed on the merits shall be determined based upon case disposition statistics supplied to the state courts administrator by the clerks of the district courts of appeal, multiplied by the relative case weights established pursuant to subdivision (b)(2)(B)(ii), and divided by 100.

(ii) The Commission on District Court of Appeal Performance and Accountability shall review the workload trends of the district courts of appeal and consider adjustments in the relative case weights every four years.

(c) Additional Trial Court Workload Factors. Because summary statistics reflective of the above criteria do not fully measure judicial workload, the supreme court will receive and consider, among other things, information about the time to perform and volume of the following activities, which also comprise the judicial workload of a particular jurisdiction:

(1) review appellate court decisions;

(2) research legal issues;

(3) review briefs and memoranda of law;

(4) participate in court conferences on pending cases;

(5) hear and dispose of motions;

(6) prepare correspondence, orders, judgments, and decisional opinions;

(7) review presentence investigative reports and predispositional reports in delinquency and dependency cases;

(8) review petitions and motions for post-conviction relief;

(9) perform administrative duties relating to the court;

(10) participate in meetings with those involved in the justice system; and

(11) participate in educational programs designed to increase the competency and efficiency of the judiciary.

(d) Certification Process. The process by which certification of the need to increase or decrease the number of judges shall include:

(1) The state courts administrator will distribute a compilation of summary statistics and projections to each chief judge at a time designated by the chief justice.

(2) Each chief judge shall submit to the chief justice a request for any increase or decrease in the number of judges:

(A) Trial Courts. Each chief judge will then consider these criteria, additional workload factors, and summary statistics, and submit to the chief justice a request for any increases or decreases under article V, section 9, of the Florida Constitution that the chief judge feels are required.

(B) District Courts. Each chief judge will then consider the criteria of this rule and the summary statistics; if a new judge is requested, the chief judge shall prepare a report showing the need for a new judge based upon the application of the criteria in this rule.

(i) Any request for a new district court judge shall be submitted to the District Court of Appeal Budget Commission for review and approval.

(ii) The chief judge of a district court of appeal shall submit the report showing the need together with the approval of the District Court of Appeal Budget Commission to the chief justice.

(3) The chief justice and the state courts administrator may then visit the chief judge and other representatives of the court submitting the request as well as representatives of The Florida Bar and the public to gather additional information and clarification about the need in the particular jurisdiction.

(4) The chief justice will submit recommendations to the supreme court, which will thereafter certify to the legislature its findings and recommendations concerning such need.

Court Commentary

1983 Adoption. Article V, section 9, of the Florida Constitution authorizes the establishment, by rule, of uniform criteria for the determination of the need for additional judges, except supreme court justices, the necessity for decreasing the number of judges and for increasing, decreasing, or redefining appellate districts and judicial circuits. Each year since the adoption of article V in 1972, this court, pursuant to section 9, has certified its determination of need to the legislature based upon factors and criteria set forth in our certification decisions. This rule is intended to set forth criteria and workload factors previously developed, adopted, and used in this certification process, as summarized and specifically set forth in *In re Certificate of Judicial Manpower,* 428 So. 2d 229 (Fla. 1983); *In re Certificate of Judicial Manpower,* 396 So. 2d 172 (Fla. 1981); and *In re Certification,* 370 So. 2d 365 (Fla. 1979).

2004 Amendment. Subdivision (b)(2) was amended to provide more specific criteria and workload factors to be used in determining the need for increasing or decreasing the number of judges on the District Courts of Appeal. In addition, the caseload level at which the court will presume that there is a need for an additional appellate judge has been increased from 250 to 350 filings per judge.

2006 Amendment. Subdivision (a) is amended to be consistent with the 2006 adoption of rule 2.036 relating to the criteria for determining the necessity and for increasing, decreasing, or redefining appellate districts and judicial circuits, pursuant to article V, section 9, Florida Constitution. The Court adopts the Commission on District Court of Appeal Performance and Accountability's conclusion that a single case filing threshold is insufficient to capture the intricacies that make up judicial workload in the district courts. The Commission's alternative to the 350-filings-per-judge threshold is a weighted case dispositions per judge, which the Commission determined to be a meaningful measure of judicial workload.

The relative weighted caseload is determined by surveying a representative sample of judges on the relative degree of judicial effort put into each category of cases based upon an agreed typical case having a value of 100. Each category was assigned a relative weight number based upon the statewide average of the weight calculated through the survey. These weights were then applied to each court's dispositions on the merits to determine the weighted caseload value and divided by 100.

This approach accommodates the important distinction between the number of cases filed and the judicial effort required to dispose of those cases. While the number of cases continues to increase, trends in the types of cases filed have dramatically changed the nature of the work that the district court judges handle. The weighted caseload approach not only accommodates the differences in types of cases by measuring their relative workload demands for judges, but it also accommodates the work performed by legal support staff.

Subdivision (b)(2)(B) establishes a presumption that the relative weight of cases disposed on the merits should fall below 280 per judge. Chief judges must consider the impact that the addition of a judge would have on this measure when applied to their courts' dispositions on the merits for the previous year.

Every four years the Commission will measure the relative judicial effort associated with the cases disposed on the merits for the year immediately preceding. This will be accomplished by asking a representative sample of judges to approximate the relative weight of cases in relation to a mid-ranked case. The resulting weights will then be applied to each court's dispositions on the merits to determine the weighted caseload value per judge.

RULE 2.241. DETERMINATION OF THE NECESSITY TO INCREASE, DECREASE, OR REDEFINE APPELLATE DISTRICTS

(a) Purpose. The purpose of this rule is to establish uniform criteria for the supreme court's determination of necessity for increasing, decreasing, or redefining appellate districts as required by Article V, section 9, of the Florida constitution. This rule also provides for an assessment committee and a certification process to assist the court both in certifying to the legislature its findings and recommendations concerning such need and in making its own rules affecting appellate court structure and jurisdiction.

(b) Assessment Committee. At least once during every eight-year period, beginning after review year 2006, the chief justice shall appoint a committee that shall assess the capacity of the district courts to effectively fulfill their constitutional and statutory duties. The committee shall make a recommendation to the supreme court concerning the decisions that it should make during the process described in subdivision (c).

(1) The assessment committee shall consist of three members from each district: one attorney, one district judge, and one circuit judge.

(2) The committee should be appointed no later than August 31 of the year prior to the review year. It must report its recommendations to the chief justice in writing no later than July 1 of the review year.

(3) The chief justice shall select the chair of the committee.

(4) Prior to the preparation of its report, the committee shall solicit written input from the public and shall hold at least one public hearing.

(5) The Office of the State Courts Administrator, in consultation with the clerks and marshals of the district courts of appeal, shall provide staff support to the committee.

(6) The chief justice shall submit the committee's recommendations to the supreme court. On or before November 15 of the review year, the supreme court shall certify to the legislature its findings and recommendations.

(c) Certification Process. The certification process balances the potential impact and disruption caused by changes in appellate districts against the need to address circumstances that limit the quality and efficiency of, and public confidence in, the appellate review process. Given the impact and disruption that can arise from any alteration in judicial structure, prior to recommending a change in districts, the assessment committee and the supreme court shall consider less disruptive adjustments including, but not limited to, the addition of judges, the creation of branch locations, geographic or subject-matter divisions within districts, deployment of new technologies, and increased ratios of support staff per judge.

(1) The supreme court shall certify a necessity to increase, decrease, or redefine appellate districts when it determines that the appellate review process is adversely affected by circumstances that present a compelling need for the certified change.

(2) The supreme court may certify a necessity to increase, decrease, or redefine appellate districts when

it determines that the appellate review process would be improved significantly by the certified change.

(d) Criteria. The following criteria shall be considered by the supreme court and the assessment committee:

(1) Effectiveness. The factors to be considered for this criterion are the extent to which:

(A) each court expedites appropriate cases;

(B) each court's workload permits its judges to prepare written opinions when warranted;

(C) each court functions in a collegial manner;

(D) each court's workload permits its judges to develop, clarify, and maintain consistency in the law within that district, including consistency between written opinions and per curiam affirmances without written opinions;

(E) each court's workload permits its judges to harmonize decisions of their court with those of other district courts or to certify conflict when appropriate;

(F) each court's workload permits its judges to have adequate time to review all decisions rendered by the court;

(G) each court is capable of accommodating changes in statutes or case law impacting workload or court operations; and

(H) each court's workload permits its judges to serve on management committees for that court and the judicial system.

(2) Efficiency. The factors to be considered for this criterion are the extent to which:

(A) each court stays current with its caseload, as indicated by measurements such as the clearance rate;

(B) each court adjudicates a high percentage of its cases within the time standards set forth in the Rules of Judicial Administration and has adequate procedures to ensure efficient, timely disposition of its cases; and

(C) each court utilizes its resources, case management techniques, and other technologies to improve the efficient adjudication of cases, research of legal issues, and preparation and distribution of decisions.

(3) Access to Appellate Review. The factors to be considered for this criterion are the extent to which:

(A) litigants, including self-represented litigants, have meaningful access to a district court for mandatory and discretionary review of cases, consistent with due process;

(B) litigants are afforded efficient access to the court for the filing of pleadings and for oral argument when appropriate; and

(C) orders and opinions of a court are available in a timely and efficient manner.

(4) Professionalism. The factors to be considered for this criterion are the extent to which:

(A) each court's workload permits its judges to have adequate time and resources to participate in continuing judicial education opportunities and to stay abreast of the law in order to maintain a qualified judiciary;

(B) each court is capable of recruiting and retaining qualified staff attorneys, clerk's office staff, and other support staff; and

(C) each court's staff has adequate time to participate in continuing education and specialized training opportunities.

(5) Public Trust and Confidence. The factors to be considered for this criterion are the extent to which:

(A) each court's workload permits its judges to have adequate time to conduct outreach to attorneys and the general public within the district;

(B) each court provides adequate access to oral arguments and other public proceedings for the general public within its district;

(C) each court's geographic territory fosters public trust and confidence;

(D) each court's demographic composition fosters public trust and confidence; and

(E) each court attracts an adequate, diverse group of well-qualified applicants for judicial vacancies within its district, including applicants from all circuits within the district.

Committee Notes

District Court of Appeal Workload and Jurisdiction Committee Notes 2006 Adoption. Article V, section 9 of the Florida constitution states that:

"The supreme court shall establish by rule uniform criteria for the determination of the need for additional judges except supreme court justices, the *necessity* for decreasing the number of judges and for increasing, decreasing or redefining appellate districts. If the supreme court finds that a *need* exists for . . . increasing, decreasing or redefining appellate districts . . . , it shall, prior to the next regular session of the legislature, certify to the legislature its findings and recommen dations concerning such need."

(Emphasis added.) Thus, the constitution uses only "need" when describing the uniform criteria for certifying additional judges, but uses both "necessity" and "need" when describing the uniform criteria for increasing, decreasing, or redefining appellate districts. The supreme court has never determined whether this language compels differing tests for the two certifications. Subdivision (c) of this rule uses the phrase "certify a necessity." The Committee on District Court of Appeal Workload and Jurisdiction determined that the two standards set forth in that subdivision recognize the supreme court's obligation to recommend a change to the structure of the district courts when circumstances reach the level of necessity that compels a change, but also recognize the court's discretion to recommend a change to the structure of the district courts when improvements are needed.

The criteria set forth in this rule are based on studies of the workload, jurisdiction, and performance of the appellate courts, and the work of the Committee on District Court of Appeal Workload and Jurisdiction in 2005. In establishing these criteria, substantial reliance was placed on empirical research conducted by judicial branch committees and on other statistical data concerning cases, caseloads, timeliness of case processing, and manner for disposition of cases, collected by the Office of the State Courts Administrator Office as required by section 25.075, Florida Statutes (2004), and Florida Rule of Judicial Administration 2.030(e)(2).

The workload and jurisdiction committee considered the impact of computer technology on appellate districts. It is clear that, at this time or in the future, technology can be deployed to allow litigants efficient access to a court for filing of pleadings and for participation in oral argument, and that it can expand the general public's access to the courts. It is possible that technology will substantially alter the appellate review process in the future and that appellate courts may find that technology permits or even requires different districting techniques. This rule was designed to allow these issues to be addressed by the assessment committee and the supreme court without mandating any specific approach.

The five basic criteria in subdivision (d) are not listed in any order of priority. Thus, for example, the workload and jurisdiction committee did not intend efficiency to be a more important criterion than engendering public trust and confidence.

Subdivision (d)(2)(A) recognizes that the court currently provides the legislature with an annual measurement of the appellate courts' "clearance rate," which is the ratio between the number of cases that are resolved during a fiscal year and the new cases that are filed during the same period. Thus, a clearance rate of one hundred percent reflects a court that is disposing of pending cases at approximately the same rate that new cases arrive. Given that other measurements may be selected in the future, the rule does not mandate sole reliance on this measurement.

Subdivision (d)(5)(E) recognizes that a district court's geographic territory may be so large that it limits or discourages applicants for judicial vacancies from throughout the district and creates the perception that a court's judges do not reflect the makeup of the territory.

RULE 2.244. JUDICIAL COMPENSATION

(a) Statement of Purpose. The purpose of this rule is to set forth the official policy of the judicial branch of state government concerning the appropriate salary relationships between justices and judges at the various levels of the state courts system and the mechanism for advancing judicial compensation and benefits issues. Although ultimate discretion in establishing judicial compensation is vested in the Florida Legislature, the salary relationships referenced in this rule reflect the policy of the judicial branch when requesting adjustments to judicial salaries.

(b) Annual Salaries. The annual salary of a district court of appeal judge should be equal to 95 percent of the annual salary of a supreme court justice. The annual salary of a circuit court judge should be equal to 90 percent of the annual salary of a supreme court justice. The annual salary of a county court judge should be equal to 85 percent of the annual salary of a supreme court justice.

(c) Unified Committee on Judicial Compensation.

(1) Creation. There shall be created a Unified Committee on Judicial Compensation to address judicial pay and benefits issues.

(2) Purpose. The purpose of the Unified Committee on Judicial Compensation shall be to:

(A) develop and recommend to the supreme court judicial pay and benefits priorities; and

(B) advocate for judicial pay and benefits issues approved by the supreme court for inclusion in the annual judicial branch budget request.

(3) Membership. The membership shall include the chief justice of the supreme court, the presidents and presidents-elect of the Conference of District Court of Appeal Judges, the Conference of Circuit Court Judges, and the Conference of County Court Judges, and the chairs and vice-chairs of the District Court Budget Commission and the Trial Court Budget Commission.

(4) Staffing. The Office of the State Courts Administrator will provide primary staff support to the committee.

RULE 2.245. CASE REPORTING SYSTEM FOR TRIAL COURTS

(a) Reporting. The clerk of the circuit court shall report the activity of all cases before all courts within the clerk's jurisdiction to the supreme court in the manner and on the forms established by the office of the state courts administrator and approved by order of the court. In those jurisdictions where separate offices of the clerk of the circuit court and clerk of the county court have been established by law, the clerk of the circuit court shall report the activity of all cases before the circuit court, and the clerk of the county court shall report the activity of all cases before the county court.

(b) Uniform Case Numbering System.

(1) The clerk of the circuit court and the clerk of the county court, where that separate office exists, shall use the Uniform Case Numbering System. The uniform case number shall appear upon the case file, the docket and minute books (or their electronic equivalent), and the complaint.

(2) The office of the state courts administrator shall distribute to the respective clerks of the circuit and county courts appropriate instructions regarding the nature and use of the Uniform Case Numbering System.

RULE 2.250. TIME STANDARDS FOR TRIAL AND APPELLATE COURTS AND REPORTING REQUIREMENTS

(a) Time Standards. The following time standards are hereby established as a presumptively reasonable time period for the completion of cases in the trial and appellate courts of this state. It is recognized that there are cases that, because of their complexity, present problems that cause reasonable delays. However, most cases should be completed within the following time periods:

(1) Trial Court Time Standards.

(A) Criminal.

Felony—180 days (arrest to final disposition)

Misdemeanor—90 days (arrest to final disposition)

(B) Civil.

Jury cases—18 months (filing to final disposition)

Non-jury cases—12 months (filing to final disposition)

Small Claims—95 days (filing to final disposition)

(C) Domestic Relations.

Uncontested—90 days (filing to final disposition)

Contested—180 days filing to final disposition)

(D) Probate.

Uncontested, no federal estate tax return—12 months (from issuance of letters of administration to final discharge)

Uncontested, with federal estate tax return—12 months (from the return's due date to final discharge)

Contested—24 months (from filing to final discharge)

(E) Juvenile Delinquency.

Disposition hearing—120 days (filing of petition or child being taken into custody to hearing)

Disposition hearing (child detained)—36 days (date of detention to hearing)

(F) Juvenile Dependency.

Disposition hearing (child sheltered)—88 days (shelter hearing to disposition)

Disposition hearing (child not sheltered)—120 days (filing of petition for dependency to hearing)

(G) Permanency Proceedings.

Permanency hearing—12 months (date child is sheltered to hearing)

(2) Supreme Court and District Courts of Appeal Time Standards. Rendering a decision — within 180 days of either oral argument or the submission of the case to the court panel for a decision without oral argument, except in juvenile dependency or termination of parental rights cases, in which a decision should be rendered within 60 days of either oral argument or submission of the case to the court panel for a decision without oral argument.

(3) Florida Bar Referee Time Standards: Report of referee—within 180 days of being assigned to hear the case

(4) Circuit Court Acting as Appellate Court:

Ninety days from submission of the case to the judge for review

(b) Reporting of Cases. The time standards require that the following monitoring procedures be implemented:

All pending cases in circuit and district courts of appeal exceeding the time standards shall be listed separately on a report submitted quarterly to the chief justice. The report shall include for each case listed the case number, type of case, case status (active or inactive for civil cases and contested or uncontested for domestic relations and probate cases), the date of arrest in criminal cases, and the original filing date in civil cases. The Office of the State Courts Administrator will provide the necessary forms for submission of this data. The report will be due on the 15th day of the month following the last day of the quarter.

RULE 2.255. STATEWIDE GRAND JURY

(a) Procedure. The chief judge of each judicial circuit shall cause a list of those persons whose names have been drawn and certified for jury duty in each of the counties within that circuit to be compiled. The lists shall be taken from the male and female population over the age of 18 years and having the other constitutional and statutory qualifications for jury duty in this state not later than the last day of the first week of December of each year. From the lists so compiled, the chief judge shall cause to be selected, by lot and at random, and by any authorized method including mechanical, electronic, or electrical device, a list of prospective grand jurors from each county whose number shall be determined on the basis of 3 jurors for each 3,000 residents or a fraction thereof in each county. The lists from which the names are drawn may be, but are not required to be, the same lists from which petit and grand juries are drawn in each county and circuit. After compilation, the statewide grand jury lists shall be submitted to the state courts administrator not later than February 15 of each year.

(b) Population. For the purposes of this rule, the population of each county shall be in accordance with the latest United States Decennial Census as set forth in the Florida Statutes.

(c) Excuses.

(1) The judge appointed to preside over the statewide grand jury may issue an order appointing the chief judge of the judicial circuit where a prospective grand juror resides to determine whether service on the statewide grand jury will result in an unreasonable personal or financial hardship because of the location or projected length of the grand jury investigation.

(2) The chief judge of the circuit shall determine whether a prospective grand juror fails to meet the

qualifications of a juror in the county where the person resides. The determination shall be made only for those prospective grand jurors who contact the chief judge and request disqualification.

(3) The chief judge of the circuit shall excuse any prospective grand juror who requests and is qualified for exemption from grand jury service pursuant to general law, or from service as a juror in the county where the person resides. The chief judge shall inform the judge appointed to preside over the statewide grand jury without delay of any determination.

RULE 2.256. JUROR TIME MANAGEMENT

(a) **Optimum Use.** The services of prospective jurors should be employed so as to achieve optimum use with a minimum of inconvenience to jurors.

(b) **Minimum Number.** A minimally sufficient number of jurors needed to accommodate trial activity should be determined. This information and appropriate management techniques should be used to adjust both the number of individuals summoned for jury duty and the number assigned to jury panels, consistent with any administrative orders issued by the Chief Justice.

(c) **Courtroom Assignment.** Each prospective juror who has reported to the courthouse should be assigned a courtroom for voir dire before any prospective juror is assigned a second time.

(d) **Calendar Coordination.** Jury management and calendar management should be coordinated to make effective use of jurors.

RULE 2.260. CHANGE OF VENUE

(a) **Preliminary Procedures.** Prior to entering an order to change venue to a particular circuit in a criminal case or in any other case in which change of venue will likely create an unusual burden for the transferee circuit, the chief judge in the circuit in which the case originated shall contact the chief judge in the circuit to which the case is intended to be moved to determine the receiving county's ability to accommodate the change of venue. It is the intent of this rule that the county identified to receive the case

shall do so unless the physical facilities or other resources in that county are such that moving the case to that county would either create an unsafe situation or adversely affect the operations of that court. Any conflict between the circuits regarding a potential change of venue shall be referred to the chief justice of the Florida Supreme Court for resolution.

(b) **Presiding Judge.** The presiding judge from the originating court shall accompany the change of venue case, unless the originating and receiving courts agree otherwise.

(c) **Reimbursement of Costs.** As a general policy the county in which an action originated shall reimburse the county receiving the change of venue case for any ordinary expenditure and any extraordinary but reasonable and necessary expenditure that would not otherwise have been incurred by the receiving county. For purposes of this section, ordinary expenditure, extraordinary expenditure, and nonreimbursable expenditure are defined as follows:

(1) Ordinary expenditures include:

(A) juror expenses not reimbursed by the State of Florida;

(B) court reporter expenses, including appearances by either official or freelance reporters, transcripts, and other expenses associated with the creation of a court record;

(C) court interpreters;

(D) maintenance of evidence, including the cost of handling, storing, or maintaining the evidence beyond the expenses normally incurred by the receiving county;

(E) services and supplies purchased as a result of the change of venue;

(F) overtime expenditures for regular court and clerk staff attributable to the change of venue; and

(G) trial-related expenses, including conflict attorney fees; all expert, law enforcement, or ordinary witness costs and expenses; and investigator expenses.

(2) Extraordinary but reasonable and necessary expenses include:

(A) security-related expenditures, including overtime for security personnel;

(B) facility remodeling or renovation; and

(C) leasing or renting of space or equipment.

Except in emergencies or unless it is impracticable to do so, a receiving county should give notice to the chief judge and clerk of the county in which the action originated before incurring any extraordinary expenditures.

(3) Nonreimbursable expenses include:

(A) normal operating expenses, including the overhead of the receiving county; and

(B) equipment that is purchased and kept by the receiving county that can be used for other purposes or cases.

(d) Documentation of Costs. No expenses shall be submitted for reimbursement without supporting documentation, such as a claim, invoice, bill, statement, or time sheet. Any required court order or approval of costs shall also be sent to the originating court.

(e) Timing of Reimbursement. Unless both counties agree to other terms, reimbursement of all expenses by the originating county shall be paid or disputed in writing on or before the sixtieth day after the receipt of the claim for reimbursement. Payment of a disputed amount shall be made on or before the sixtieth day after the resolution of this dispute. Any amount subject to dispute shall be expeditiously resolved by authorized representatives of the court administrator's office of the originating and receiving counties.

(f) Media Relations. Procedures to accommodate the media shall be developed by the receiving county immediately upon notice of the change of venue when the change of venue is reasonably expected to generate an unusual amount of publicity. These procedures must be approved by the chief judge of the receiving circuit and implemented pursuant to administrative order by the presiding judge. The presiding judge shall obtain the concurrence of the chief judge before entering any orders that vary from or conflict with existing administrative orders of the receiving circuit.

(g) Case File. The clerk of the circuit court in the originating county shall forward the original case file to the clerk in the receiving county. The receiving clerk shall maintain the file and keep it secure until the trial has been concluded. During the trial, any documents or exhibits that have been added shall be properly marked and added to the file in a manner consistent with the policy and procedures of the receiving county. After the conclusion of the trial, the file shall be returned to the clerk in the county of origin.

RULE 2.265. MUNICIPAL ORDINANCE VIOLATIONS

(a) References to Abolished Municipal Courts. All references to a municipal court or municipal judge in rules promulgated by the supreme court, in the Florida Statutes, and in any municipal ordinance shall be deemed to refer, respectively, to the county court or county court judge.

(b) Costs in County Courts. The chief judge of a circuit shall by administrative order establish a schedule of costs, in conformity with any provisions of law, to be assessed against a defendant in the county court and paid to the county for violations of municipal ordinances which are prosecuted in county court. The costs shall be assessed as a set dollar amount per conviction, not to exceed $50 excluding any other statutory costs.

(c) Collection of Outstanding Fines. All cases for which outstanding fines, civil penalties, and costs are being collected by a municipality shall be retained by the municipality until collected or until the offender defaults on payment. If a default occurs, the municipality may institute summary claims proceedings to collect the outstanding fines.

(d) Judicial Notice of Municipal Ordinances. The judges of the county courts may take judicial notice of any municipal ordinance if a certified copy of the ordinance has been filed in the office of the clerk of circuit court or, in those counties having a clerk of the county court, filed in that office, and if a certified copy of the ordinance is presented to the court.

(e) Style of Municipal Ordinance Cases. All prosecutions for violations of municipal ordinances in county court shall have the following style: City of .... v. ....

PART III. JUDICIAL OFFICERS

RULE 2.310. JUDICIAL DISCIPLINE, REMOVAL, RETIREMENT, AND SUSPENSION

(a) Filing. Any recommendations to the supreme court from the Judicial Qualifications Commission pursuant to article V, section 12, of the Florida Constitution shall be in writing. The original and 7 copies shall be filed with the clerk of the court, and a copy shall be served expeditiously on the justice or judge against whom action is sought.

(b) Procedure.

(1) Promptly upon the filing of a recommendation from the commission, the court shall determine whether the commission's recommendation complies with all requirements of the constitution and the commission's rules. Upon determining that the recommendation so complies, and unless the court otherwise directs, an order shall issue directing the justice or judge to show cause in writing why the recommended action should not be taken.

(2) The justice or judge may file a response in writing within the time set by the court in its order to show cause, and the commission may serve a reply within 20 days from service of the response.

(3) If requested by the commission, or by a justice or judge at the time of filing a response, the court may allow oral argument on the commission's recommendation.

(c) Costs. The supreme court may award reasonable and necessary costs, including costs of investigation and prosecution, to the prevailing party. Neither attorneys' fees nor travel expenses of commission personnel shall be included in an award of costs. Taxable costs may include:

(1) court reporters' fees, including per diem fees, deposition costs, and costs associated with the preparation of the transcript and record; and

(2) witness expenses, including travel and out-of-pocket expenses.

RULE 2.320. CONTINUING JUDICIAL EDUCATION

(a) Purpose. This rule sets forth the continuing education requirement for all judges in the state judicial system.

(b) Education Requirements.

(1) Applicability. All Florida county, circuit, and appellate judges and Florida supreme court justices shall comply with these judicial education requirements. Retired judges who have been approved by the supreme court to be assigned to temporary active duty as authorized by section 25.073, Florida Statutes (1991), shall also comply with the judicial education requirements.

(2) Minimum Requirements. Each judge and justice shall complete a minimum of 30 credit hours of approved judicial education programs every 3 years. Beginning January 1, 2012, 4 hours must be in the area of judicial ethics; prior to that date, 2 hours in the area of judicial ethics are required. Approved courses in fairness and diversity also can be used to fulfill the judicial ethics requirement. In addition to the 30-hour requirement, every judge new to a level of trial court must complete the Florida Judicial College program in that judge's first year of judicial service following selection to that level of court; every new appellate court judge or justice must, within 2 years following selection to that level of court, complete an approved appellate-judge program. Every new appellate judge who has never been a trial judge or who has never attended Phase I of the Florida Judicial College as a magistrate must also attend Phase I of the Florida Judicial College in that judge's first year of judicial service following the judge's appointment. Credit for teaching a course for which mandatory judicial education credit is available will be allowed on the basis of 2 1/2 hours' credit for each instructional hour taught, up to a maximum of 5 hours per year.

(3) Mediation Training. Prior to conducting any mediation, a senior judge shall have completed a minimum of one judicial education course offered by the Florida Court Education Council. The course shall specifically focus on the areas where the Code of Judicial Conduct or the Florida Rules for Certified and Court-Appointed Mediators could be violated.

(c) Course Approval. The Florida Court Education Council, in consultation with the judicial conferences, shall develop approved courses for each state court jurisdiction. Courses offered by other judicial and legal education entities must be approved by the council before they may be submitted for credit.

(d) Waiver. The Florida Court Education Council is responsible for establishing a procedure for considering and acting upon waiver and extension requests on an individual basis.

(e) Reporting Requirements and Sanctions. The Florida Court Education Council shall establish a procedure for reporting annually to the chief justice on compliance with this rule. Each judge shall submit to the Court Education Division of the Office of the State Courts Administrator an annual report showing the judge's attendance at approved courses. Failure to comply with the requirements of this rule will be reported to the chief justice of the Florida supreme court for such administrative action as deemed necessary. The chief justice may consider a judge's or justice's failure to comply as neglect of duty and report the matter to the Judicial Qualifications Commission.

RULE 2.330. DISQUALIFICATION OF TRIAL JUDGES

(a) Application. This rule applies only to county and circuit judges in all matters in all divisions of court.

(b) Parties. Any party, including the state, may move to disqualify the trial judge assigned to the case on grounds provided by rule, by statute, or by the Code of Judicial Conduct.

(c) Motion. A motion to disqualify shall:

(1) be in writing;

(2) allege specifically the facts and reasons upon which the movant relies as the grounds for disqualification;

(3) be sworn to by the party by signing the motion under oath or by a separate affidavit; and

(4) include the dates of all previously granted motions to disqualify filed under this rule in the case and the dates of the orders granting those motions.

The attorney for the party shall also separately certify that the motion and the client's statements are made in good faith. In addition to filing with the clerk, the movant shall immediately serve a copy of the motion on the subject judge as set forth in Florida Rule of Civil Procedure 1.080.

(d) Grounds. A motion to disqualify shall show:

(1) that the party fears that he or she will not receive a fair trial or hearing because of specifically described prejudice or bias of the judge; or

(2) that the judge before whom the case is pending, or some person related to said judge by consanguinity or affinity within the third degree, is a party thereto or is interested in the result thereof, or that said judge is related to an attorney or counselor of record in the cause by consanguinity or affinity within the third degree, or that said judge is a material witness for or against one of the parties to the cause.

(e) Time. A motion to disqualify shall be filed within a reasonable time not to exceed 10 days after discovery of the facts constituting the grounds for the motion and shall be promptly presented to the court for an immediate ruling. Any motion for disqualification made during a hearing or trial must be based on facts discovered during the hearing or trial and may be stated on the record, provided that it is also promptly reduced to writing in compliance with subdivision (c) and promptly filed. A motion made during hearing or trial shall be ruled on immediately.

(f) Determination—Initial Motion. The judge against whom an initial motion to disqualify under subdivision (d)(1) is directed shall determine only the legal sufficiency of the motion and shall not pass on the truth of the facts alleged. If the motion is legally sufficient, the judge shall immediately enter an order granting disqualification and proceed no further in the action. If any motion is legally insufficient, an order denying the motion shall immediately be entered. No other reason for denial shall be stated, and an order of denial shall not take issue with the motion.

(g) Determination—Successive Motions. If a judge has been previously disqualified on motion for alleged prejudice or partiality under subdivision (d)(1), a successor judge shall not be disqualified based on a successive motion by the same party unless the successor judge rules that he or she is in fact not fair or impartial in the case. Such a successor judge may rule on the truth of the facts alleged in support of the motion.

(h) Prior Rulings. Prior factual or legal rulings by a disqualified judge may be reconsidered and vacated or amended by a successor judge based upon a motion for reconsideration, which must be filed within 20 days of the order of disqualification, unless good cause is shown for a delay in moving for reconsideration or other grounds for reconsideration exist.

(i) Judge's Initiative. Nothing in this rule limits the judge's authority to enter an order of disqualification on the judge's own initiative.

(j) Time for Determination. The judge shall rule on a motion to disqualify immediately, but no later than 30 days after the service of the motion as set forth in subdivision (c). If not ruled on within 30 days of service, the motion shall be deemed granted and the moving party may seek an order from the court directing the clerk to reassign the case.

PART IV. JUDICIAL PROCEEDINGS AND RECORDS

RULE 2.410. POSSESSION OF COURT RECORDS

No person other than judges and authorized court employees shall remove court records as defined in rule 2.430 from the clerk's office except by order of the chief judge or chief justice upon a showing of good cause.

Court Commentary

1996 Adoption. This rule was written as a result of the problems being encountered in the removal of files from clerks' offices. While the purpose of the rule is to discourage the removal of court files, it is not intended to prohibit chief judges or the chief justice from issuing for good cause a general order providing that attorneys or authorized individuals may be allowed to check out files on a routine basis to assist in the administrative efficiency of a court. We note that section 28.13, Florida Statutes (1995), similarly prohibits the removal of files from clerks' offices.

RULE 2.420. PUBLIC ACCESS TO JUDICIAL BRANCH RECORDS

(a) Scope and Purpose. Subject to the rulemaking power of the Florida Supreme Court provided by article V, section 2, Florida Constitution, the following rule shall govern public access to the records of the judicial branch of government. The public shall have access to all records of the judicial branch of government, except as provided below.

(b) Definitions.

(1) "Records of the judicial branch" are all records, regardless of physical form, characteristics, or means of transmission, made or received in connection with the transaction of official business by any judicial branch entity and consist of:

(A) "court records," which are the contents of the court file, including the progress docket and other similar records generated to document activity in a case, transcripts filed with the clerk, documentary exhibits in the custody of the clerk, and electronic records, videotapes, or stenographic tapes of depositions or other proceedings filed with the clerk, and electronic records, videotapes, or stenographic tapes of court proceedings; and

(B) "administrative records," which are all other records made or received pursuant to court rule, law, or ordinance, or in connection with the transaction of official business by any judicial branch entity.

(2) "Judicial branch" means the judicial branch of government, which includes the state courts system, the clerk of court when acting as an arm of the court, The Florida Bar, the Florida Board of Bar Examiners, the Judicial Qualifications Commission, and all other entities established by or operating under the authority of the supreme court or the chief justice.

(3) "Custodian." The custodian of all administrative records of any court is the chief justice or chief judge of that court, except that each judge is the custodian of all records that are solely within the possession and control of that judge. As to all other records, the custodian is the official charged with the responsibility of maintaining the office having the care, keeping, and supervision of such records. All references to "custodian" mean the custodian or the custodian's designee.

(4) "Confidential," as applied to information contained within a record of the judicial branch, means that such information is exempt from the public right of access under article I, section 24(a) of the Florida Constitution and may be released only to the persons or organizations designated by law, statute, or court order. As applied to information contained within a court record, the term "exempt" means that such information is confidential. Confidential information includes information that is confidential under this rule or under a court order entered pursuant to this rule. To the extent reasonably practicable, restriction of access to confidential information shall be implemented in a manner that does not restrict access to any portion of the record that is not confidential.

(5) "Affected non-party" means any non-party identified by name in a court record that contains confidential information pertaining to that non-party.

(c) **Confidential and Exempt Records.** The following records of the judicial branch shall be confidential:

(1) Trial and appellate court memoranda, drafts of opinions and orders, court conference records, notes, and other written materials of a similar nature prepared by judges or court staff acting on behalf of or at the direction of the court as part of the court's judicial decision-making process utilized in disposing of cases and controversies before Florida courts unless filed as a part of the court record;

(2) Memoranda or advisory opinions that relate to the administration of the court and that require confidentiality to protect a compelling governmental interest, including, but not limited to, maintaining court security, facilitating a criminal investigation, or protecting public safety, which cannot be adequately protected by less restrictive measures. The degree, duration, and manner of confidentiality imposed shall be no broader than necessary to protect the compelling governmental interest involved, and a finding shall be made that no less restrictive measures are available to protect this interest. The decision that confidentiality is required with respect to such administrative memorandum or written advisory opinion shall be made by the chief judge;

(3)(A) Complaints alleging misconduct against judges until probable cause is established;

(B) Complaints alleging misconduct against other entities or individuals licensed or regulated by the courts, until a finding of probable cause or no probable cause is established, unless otherwise provided. Such finding should be made within the time limit set by law or rule. If no time limit is set, the finding should be made within a reasonable period of time;

(4) Periodic evaluations implemented solely to assist judges in improving their performance, all information gathered to form the bases for the evaluations, and the results generated therefrom;

(5) Only the names and qualifications of persons applying to serve or serving as unpaid volunteers to assist the court, at the court's request and direction, shall be accessible to the public. All other information contained in the applications by and evaluations of persons applying to serve or serving as unpaid volunteers shall be confidential unless made public by court order based upon a showing of materiality in a pending court proceeding or upon a showing of good cause;

(6) Copies of arrest and search warrants and supporting affidavits retained by judges, clerks, or other court personnel until execution of said warrants or until a determination is made by law enforcement authorities that execution cannot be made;

(7) All records made confidential under the Florida and United States Constitutions and Florida and federal law;

(8) All records presently deemed to be confidential by court rule, including the Rules for Admission to the Bar, by Florida Statutes, by prior case law of the State of Florida, and by the rules of the Judicial Qualifications Commission;

(9) Any court record determined to be confidential in case decision or court rule on the grounds that

(A) confidentiality is required to

(i) prevent a serious and imminent threat to the fair, impartial, and orderly administration of justice;

(ii) protect trade secrets;

(iii) protect a compelling governmental interest;

(iv) obtain evidence to determine legal issues in a case;

(v) avoid substantial injury to innocent third parties;

(vi) avoid substantial injury to a party by disclosure of matters protected by a common law or privacy right not generally inherent in the specific type of proceeding sought to be closed;

(vii) comply with established public policy set forth in the Florida or United States Constitution or statutes or Florida rules or case law;

(B) the degree, duration, and manner of confidentiality ordered by the court shall be no broader than necessary to protect the interests set forth in subdivision (A); and

(C) no less restrictive measures are available to protect the interests set forth in subdivision (A).

(10) The names and any identifying information of judges mentioned in an advisory opinion of the Judicial Ethics Advisory Committee.

(d) Procedures for Determining Confidentiality of Court Records.

(1) The clerk of the court shall designate and maintain the confidentiality of any information contained within a court record that is described in subdivision (d)(1)(A) or (d)(1)(B) of this rule. The following information shall be maintained as confidential:

(A) information described by any of subdivisions (c)(1) through (c)(6) of this rule; and

(B) except as provided by court order, information subject to subdivision (c)(7) or (c)(8) of this rule that is currently confidential or exempt from section 119.07, Florida Statutes, and article I, section 24(a) of the Florida Constitution under any of the following statutes or court rules as they may be amended or renumbered:

(i) Chapter 39 records relating to dependency matters, termination of parental rights, guardians ad litem, child abuse, neglect, and abandonment. § 39.0132(3), Fla. Stat.

(ii) Adoption records. § 63.162, Fla. Stat.

(iii) Social Security, bank account, charge, debit, and credit card numbers in court records. § 119.0714(1)(i)-(j), (2)(a)-(e), Fla. Stat. (Unless redaction is requested pursuant to 119.0714(2), this information is exempt only as of January 1, 2011.)

(iv) HIV test results and patient identity within those test results. § 381.004(3)(e), Fla. Stat.

(v) Sexually transmitted diseases - test results and identity within the test results when provided by the Department of Health or the department's authorized representative. § 384.29, Fla. Stat.

(vi) Birth and death certificates, including court-issued delayed birth certificates and fetal death certificates. §§ 382.008(6), 382.025(1)(a), Fla. Stat.

(vii) Identifying information in a petition by a minor for waiver of parental notice when seeking to terminate pregnancy. § 390.01116, Fla. Stat.

(viii) Identifying information in clinical mental health records under the Baker Act. § 394.4615(7), Fla. Stat.

(ix) Records of substance abuse service providers which pertain to the identity, diagnosis, and prognosis of and service provision to individuals who have received services from substance abuse service providers. § 397.501(7), Fla. Stat.

(x) Identifying information in clinical records of detained criminal defendants found incompetent to proceed or acquitted by reason of insanity. § 916.107(8), Fla. Stat.

(xi) Estate inventories and accountings. § 733.604(1), Fla. Stat.

(xii) The victim's address in a domestic violence action on petitioner's request. § 741.30(3)(b), Fla. Stat.

(xiii) Information identifying victims of sexual offenses, including child sexual abuse. §§ 119.071(2)(h), 119.0714(1)(h), Fla. Stat.

(xiv) Gestational surrogacy records. § 742.16(9), Fla. Stat.

(xv) Guardianship reports and orders appointing court monitors in guardianship cases. §§ 744.1076, 744.3701, Fla. Stat.

(xvi) Grand jury records. Ch. 905, Fla. Stat.

(xvii) Information acquired by courts and law enforcement regarding family services for children. § 984.06(3)-(4), Fla. Stat.

(xviii) Juvenile delinquency records. §§ 985.04(1), 985.045(2), Fla. Stat.

(xix) Information disclosing the identity of persons subject to tuberculosis proceedings and records of the Department of Health in suspected tuberculosis cases. §§ 392.545, 392.65, Fla. Stat.

(xx) Presentence investigation reports and attached psychological or psychiatric evaluations. Fla. R. Crim. P. 3.712; §§ 921.231(1)(i), 948.015(9), Fla. Stat.

(2) Any person filing any document containing confidential information shall, at the time of filing, file with the clerk a "Notice of Confidential Information within Court Filing" in order to: (A) indicate that confidential information described in subdivision (d)(1)(B) of this rule is included within the document being filed; (B) identify the provision of subdivision (d)(1)(B) of this rule that applies to the identified information; and (C) identify the precise location of the confidential information within the document being filed. A form Notice of Confidential Information within Court Filing accompanies this rule. The clerk of court shall review filings identified by filers as containing confidential information to determine whether the purported confidential information is facially subject to confidentiality under the identified provision in subdivision (d)(1)(B). If the clerk determines that filed information is not subject to confidentiality under the identified provision, the clerk shall notify the person who filed the document in writing within 5 days of the filing and thereafter shall maintain the information as confidential for 10 days from the day such notice is served. The information shall not be held as confidential for more than 10 days, unless the filer has filed a motion pursuant to subdivision (d)(3).

(3) Any person filing a document with the court shall ascertain whether any information contained within the document may be confidential under subdivision (c) of this rule notwithstanding that such information is not itemized at subdivision (d)(1) of this rule. A person filing information that he or she believes in good faith to be confidential but that is not described in subdivision (d)(1) of this rule shall request that the information be maintained as confidential by filing a "Motion to Determine Confidentiality of Court Records" under the procedures set forth in subdivision (e), (f), or (g), unless (A) the person filing the information is the only individual whose

confidential information is included in the document to be filed or is the attorney representing all such individuals; and (B) a knowing waiver of the confidential status of that information is intended by the person filing the information. Any interested person may request that information within a court file be maintained as confidential by filing a motion as provided in subdivision (e), (f), or (g).

(4) If a notice of confidential information is filed pursuant to subdivision (d)(2), or a motion is filed pursuant to subdivision (e)(1) seeking to determine that information contained in court records is confidential, or pursuant to subdivision (e)(5) seeking to vacate an order that has determined that information in a court record is confidential or seeking to unseal information designated as confidential by the clerk of court, then the person filing the notice or motion shall give notice of such filing to any affected non-party. Notice pursuant to this provision must:

(A) be filed with the court;

(B) identify the case by docket number;

(C) describe the confidential information with as much specificity as possible without revealing the confidential information, including specifying the precise location of the information within the court record; and

(D) include:

(i) in the case of a request to deem materials confidential, a statement that if the motion is denied then the subject material will not be treated as confidential by the clerk; and

(ii) in the case of a motion to unseal confidential records or a motion to vacate an order deeming records confidential, a statement that if the motion is granted, the subject material will no longer be treated as confidential by the clerk.

Any notice described herein must be served together with the motion that gave rise to the notice in accordance with subdivision (e)(5) or (g)(5). When serving the notice and motion described in this subdivision on a non-party, the server shall use reasonable efforts to locate the non-party and may serve such non-party by any method set forth in Florida Rule of Civil Procedure 1.080(b).

(e) Request to Determine Confidentiality of Trial Court Records in Noncriminal Cases.

(1) A request to determine the confidentiality of trial court records in noncriminal cases under subdivision (c)(9) must be made in the form of a written motion captioned "Motion to Determine Confidentiality of Court Records." A motion made under this subdivision must:

(A) identify the particular court records or a portion of a record that the movant seeks to have determined as confidential with as much specificity as possible without revealing the information subject to the confidentiality determination;

(B) specify the bases for determining that such court records are confidential; and

(C) set forth the specific legal authority and any applicable legal standards for determining such court records to be confidential.

Any motion made under this subdivision must include a signed certification by the party or the attorney for the party making the request that the motion is made in good faith and is supported by a sound factual and legal basis. Information that is subject to such a motion must be treated as confidential by the clerk pending the court's ruling on the motion. Notwithstanding any of the foregoing, the court may not determine that the case number, docket number, or other number used by the clerk's office to identify the case file is confidential.

(2) Except when a motion filed under subdivision (e)(1) represents that all parties agree to all of the relief requested, the court must, as soon as practicable but no later than 30 days after the filing of a motion under this subdivision, hold a hearing before ruling on the motion. Whether or not any motion filed under subdivision (e)(1) is agreed to by the parties, the court may in its discretion hold a hearing on such motion.

Any hearing held under this subdivision must be an open proceeding, except that any person may request that the court conduct all or part of the hearing in camera to protect the interests set forth in subdivision (c). Any person may request expedited consideration of and ruling on the motion. The moving party shall be responsible for ensuring that a complete record of any hearing held pursuant to this subdivision be created, either by use of a court reporter or by any recording device that is provided as a matter of right by the court. The court may in its discretion require prior public notice of the hearing on such a motion in accordance with the procedure for providing public notice of court orders set forth in subdivision (e)(4) or by providing such other public notice as the court deems appropriate. The court must issue a ruling on the motion within 30 days of the hearing.

(3) Any order granting in whole or in part a motion filed under subdivision (e) must state the following with as much specificity as possible without revealing the information subject to the confidentiality determination:

(A) The type of case in which the order is being entered;

(B) The particular grounds under subdivision (c) for determining the information confidential;

(C) Whether any party's name is determined to be confidential and, if so, the particular pseudonym or other term to be substituted for the party's name;

(D) Whether the progress docket or similar records generated to document activity in the case are determined to be confidential;

(E) The particular information that is determined to be confidential;

(F) Identification of persons who are permitted to view the confidential information;

(G) That the court finds that: (i) the degree, duration, and manner of confidentiality ordered by the court are no broader than necessary to protect the interests set forth in subdivision (c) and (ii) no less restrictive measures are available to protect the interests set forth in subdivision (c) and

(H) That the clerk of the court is directed to publish the order in accordance with subdivision (e)(4).

(4) Except as provided by law or court rule, notice must be given of any order granting in whole or in part a motion made under subdivision (e)(1) as follows. Within 10 days following the entry of the order, the clerk of court must post a copy of the order on the clerk's website and in a prominent, public location in the courthouse. The order must remain posted in both locations for no less than 30 days. This subdivision shall not apply to orders determining that court records are confidential under subdivision (c)(7) or (c)(8).

(5) If a nonparty requests that the court vacate all or part of an order issued under subdivision (e), or requests that the court order the unsealing of records designated as confidential under subdivision (d), the request must be made by a written motion, filed in that court, that states with as much specificity as possible the bases for the request. The motion must set forth the specific legal authority and any applicable legal standards supporting the request. The movant must serve all parties and all affected non-parties with a copy of the motion. If the subject order determines that the names or addresses of one or more parties confidential, the movant must state prominently in the caption of the motion "Confidential Party—Court Service Requested." When a motion so designated is filed, the court shall be responsible for providing a copy of the motion to all parties and all affected non-parties in such a way as not to reveal the confidential information to the movant. Except when a motion filed under this subdivision represents that all parties agree to all of the relief requested, the court must, as soon as practicable but no later than 30 days after the filing of a motion under this subdivision, hold a hearing on the motion. Regardless of whether any motion filed under this subdivision is agreed to by the parties, the court may in its discretion hold a hearing on such motion. Any person may request expedited consideration of and ruling on the motion. Any hearing held under this subdivision must be an

open proceeding, except that any party may request that the court conduct all or part of the hearing in camera to protect the interests set forth in subdivision (c). The court must issue a ruling on the motion within 30 days of the hearing. The movant shall be responsible for ensuring that a complete record of any hearing held under this subdivision be created, either by use of a court reporter or by any recording device that is provided as a matter of right by the court. This subdivision shall not apply to orders determining that court records are confidential under subdivision (c)(7) or (c)(8).

(6) After notice and an opportunity to respond, the court may impose sanctions against any party or non-party and/or their attorney, if:

(A) the court determines that a designation made under subdivision (d) or a motion made under subdivision (d)(3) or (e) was not made in good faith and was not supported by a sound legal or factual basis, or

(B) a document is filed in violation of subdivision (d)(2) or (d)(3).

(f) Request to Determine Confidentiality of Court Records in Criminal Cases.

(1) Subdivision (e) shall apply to any motion by the state or a defendant to determine the confidentiality of trial court records under subdivision (c), except as provided in subdivision (f)(3). As to any motion filed in the trial court under subdivision (f)(3), the following procedure shall apply:

(A) Unless the motion represents that both the movant and any other party subject to the motion agree to all of the relief requested, as evidenced by all such parties signing the motion, the court shall hold a hearing on a motion filed under this subdivision within 15 days of the filing of the motion. Any hearing held under this subdivision must be an open proceeding, except that any person may request that the court conduct all or part of the hearing in camera to protect the interests set forth in subdivision (c)(9)(A).

(B) The court shall issue a written ruling on a motion filed under this subdivision within 10 days of the hearing on a contested motion or within 10 days of the filing of an agreed motion.

(2) Subdivision (g) shall apply to any motion to determine the confidentiality of appellate court records under subdivision (c), except as provided in subdivision (f)(3). As to any motion filed in the appellate court under subdivision (f)(3), the following procedure shall apply:

(A) The motion may be made with respect to a record that was presented or presentable to a lower tribunal, but no determination concerning confidentiality was made by the lower tribunal, or a record presented to an appellate court in an original proceeding.

(B) A response to a motion filed under this subdivision may be served within 10 days of service of the motion.

(C) The court shall issue a written ruling on a motion filed under this subdivision within 10 days of the filing of a response on a contested motion or within 10 days of the filing of an uncontested motion.

(3) Any motion to determine whether a court record that pertains to a plea agreement, substantial assistance agreement, or other court record that reveals the identity of a confidential informant or active criminal investigative information is confidential under subdivision (c)(9)(A)(i), (c)(9)(A)(iii), (c)(9)(A)(v), or (c)(9)(A)(vii) of this rule may be made in the form of a written motion captioned "Motion to Determine Confidentiality of Court Records." Any motion made pursuant to this subdivision must be treated as confidential and indicated on the docket by generic title only, pending a ruling on the motion or further order of the court. As to any motion made under this subdivision, the following procedure shall apply:

(A) Information that is the subject of such motion must be treated as confidential by the clerk pending the court's ruling on the motion. Filings containing the information must be indicated on the docket in a manner that does not reveal the confidential nature of the information.

(B) The provisions of subdivisions (e)(3)(A)-(G), (e)(6), and (g)(7) shall apply to motions made under this subdivision. The provisions of subdivisions (e)(1), (e)(2), (e)(3)(H), (e)(4), and (e)(5) shall not apply to motions made under this subdivision.

(C) No order entered under this subdivision may authorize or approve the sealing of court records for any period longer than is necessary to achieve the objective of the motion, and in no event longer than 120 days. Extensions of an order issued hereunder may be granted for 60-day periods, but each such extension may be ordered only upon the filing of another motion in accordance with the procedures set forth under this subdivision. In the event of an appeal or review of a matter in which an order is entered under this subdivision, the lower tribunal shall retain jurisdiction to consider motions to extend orders issued hereunder during the course of the appeal or review proceeding.

(D) The clerk of the court shall not publish any order of the court issued hereunder in accordance with subdivision (e)(4) or (g)(4) unless directed by the court. The docket shall indicate only the entry of the order.

(4) This subdivision does not authorize the falsification of court records or progress dockets.

(g) Request to Determine Confidentiality of Appellate Court Records in Noncriminal Cases.

(1) A motion to determine the confidentiality of appellate court records in noncriminal cases under subdivision (c) must be filed in the appellate court an d must be in compliance with the guidelines set forth in subdivision (e)(1). Such a motion may be made with respect to a record that was presented or presentable to a lower tribunal, but no determination concerning confidentiality was made by the lower tribunal, or a record presented to an appellate court in an original proceeding.

(2) A response to a motion filed under subdivision (g)(1) may be served within 10 days of service of the motion.

(3) Any order granting in whole or in part a motion filed under subdivision (g)(1) must be in compliance with the guidelines set forth in subdivisions (e)(3)(A)-(H). Any order requiring the sealing of an appellate court record operates to also make those same records confidential in the lower tribunal during the pendency of the appellate proceeding.

(4) Except as provided by law, within 10 days following the entry of an order granting a motion under subdivision (g)(1), the clerk of the appellate court must post a copy of the order on the clerk's website and must provide a copy of the order to the clerk of the lower tribunal, with directions that the clerk is to seal the records identified in the order. The order must remain posted for no less than 30 days.

(5) If a nonparty requests that the court vacate all or part of an order issued under subdivision (g)(3), or requests that the court order the unsealing of records designated as confidential under subdivision (d), the request must be made by a written motion, filed in that court, that states with as much specificity as possible the bases for the request. The motion must set forth the specific legal authority and any applicable legal standards supporting the request. The movant must serve all parties and all affected non-parties with a copy of the motion. If the subject order determines that the names or addresses of one or more parties are confidential, the movant must state prominently in the caption of the motion "Confidential Party—Court Service Requested." When a motion so designated is filed, the court shall be responsible for providing a copy of the motion to all parties and all affected non-parties in such a way as not to reveal the confidential information to the movant. A response to a motion may be served within 10 days of service of the motion.

(6) The party seeking to have an appellate record sealed under this subdivision has the responsibility to ensure that the clerk of the lower tribunal is alerted to the issuance of the order sealing the records and to ensure that the clerk takes appropriate steps to seal the records in the lower tribunal.

(7) Upon conclusion of the appellate proceeding, the lower tribunal may, upon appropriate motion showing changed circumstances, revisit the appellate court's order directing that the records be sealed.

(8) If the court determines that a designation made under subdivision (d) or a motion made under subdivision (g)(1) was not made in good faith and was not supported by a sound legal or factual basis, the court may impose sanctions on the movant after notice and an opportunity to respond.

(9) Records of a lower tribunal determined to be confidential by that tribunal must be treated as confidential during any review proceedings. In any case where information has been determined to be confidential under this rule, the clerk of the lower tribunal shall so indicate in the index transmitted to the appellate court. If the information was determined to be confidential in an order, the clerk's index must identify such order by date or docket number. This subdivision does not preclude review by an appellate court, under Florida Rule of Appellate Procedure 9.100(d), or affect the standard of review by an appellate court, of an order by a lower tribunal determining a record to be confidential.

(h) Denial of Access Request for Administrative Records. Expedited review of denials of access to administrative records of the judicial branch shall be provided through an action for mandamus or other appropriate relief in the following manner:

(1) Where a judge who has denied a request for access to records is the custodian, the action shall be filed in the court having appellate jurisdiction to review the decisions of the judge denying access. Upon order issued by the appellate court, the judge denying access to records shall file a sealed copy of the requested records with the appellate court.

(2) All other actions under this rule shall be filed in the circuit court of the circuit in which such denial of access occurs.

(i) Procedure. Requests and responses to requests for access to records under this rule shall be made in a reasonable manner.

(1) Requests for access to records shall be in writing and shall be directed to the custodian. The request shall provide sufficient specificity to enable the custodian to identify the requested records. The reason for the request is not required to be disclosed.

(2) The custodian shall be solely responsible for providing access to records of the custodian's entity. The custodian shall determine whether the requested record is subject to this rule and, if so, whether the record or portions of the record are exempt from disclosure. The custodian shall determine the form in which the record is provided. If the request is denied, the custodian shall state in writing the basis for the denial.

(3) Fees for copies of records in all entities in the judicial branch of government, except for copies of court records, shall be the same as those provided in section 119.07, Florida Statutes (2001).

Committee Notes

1995 Amendment. This rule was adopted to conform to the 1992 addition of article I, section 24, to the Florida Constitution. Amendments to this rule were adopted in response to the 1994 recommendations of the Study Committee on Confidentiality of Records of the Judicial Branch.

Subdivision (b) has been added by amendment and provides a definition of "judicial records" that is consistent with the definition of "court records" contained in rule 2.075(a)(1) [renumbered as 2.430(a)(1) in 2006] and the definition of "public records" contained in chapter 119, Florida Statutes. The word "exhibits" used in this definition of judicial records is intended to refer only to documentary evidence and does not refer to tangible items of evidence such as firearms, narcotics, etc. Judicial records within this definition include all judicial records and data regardless of the form in which they are kept. Reformatting of information may be necessary to protect copyrighted material. *Seigle v. Barry,* 422 So. 2d 63 (Fla. 4th DCA 1982), *review denied,* 431 So. 2d 988 (Fla. 1983).

The definition of "judicial records" also includes official business information transmitted via an electronic mail (e-mail) system. The judicial branch is presently experimenting with this new technology. For example, e-mail is currently being used by the judicial branch to transmit between judges and staff multiple matters in the courts including direct communications between judges and staff and other judges, proposed drafts of opinions and orders, memoranda concerning pending cases, proposed jury instructions, and even votes on proposed opinions. All of this type of information is exempt from public disclosure under rules 2.051(c)(1) and (c)(2) [renumbered as 2.420(c)(1) and (c)(2) in 2006]. With few exceptions, these examples of e-mail transmissions are sent and received between judicial officials and employees within a particular court's jurisdiction. This type of e-mail is by its very nature almost always exempt from public record disclosure pursuant to rule 2.051(c). In addition, official business e-mail transmissions sent to or received by judicial officials or employees using dial-in equipment, as well as the use of on-line outside research facilities such as Westlaw, would also be exempt email under rule 2.051(c). On the other hand, we recognize that not all e-mail sent and received within a particular court's jurisdiction will fall into an exception under rule 2.051(c). The fact that a non-exempt e-mail message made or received in connection with official court business is transmitted intra-court does not relieve judicial officials or employees from the obligation of properly having a record made of such messages so they will be available to the public similar to any other written communications. It appears that official business e-mail that is sent or received by persons outside a particular court's jurisdiction is largely non-exempt and is subject to recording in some form as a public record. Each court should develop a means to properly make a record of non-exempt official business e-mail by either electronically storing the mail or by making a hard copy. It is important to note that, although official business communicated by e-mail transmissions is a matter of public record under the rule, the exemptions provided in rule 2.051(c) exempt many of these judge/staff transmissions from the public record. E-mail may also include transmissions that are clearly not official business and are, consequently, not required to be recorded as a public record. Each court should also publish an e-mail address for public access. The individual e-mail addresses of judicial officials and staff are exempt under rule 2.051(c)(2) to protect the compelling interests of maintaining the uninterrupted use of the computer for research, word-processing, preparation of opinions, and communication during trials, and to ensure computer security.

Subdivision (c)(3) was amended by creating subparts (a) and (b) to distinguish between the provisions governing the confidentiality of complaints against judges and complaints against other individuals or entities licensed or regulated by the Supreme Court.

Subdivision (c)(5) was amended to make public the qualifications of persons applying to serve or serving the court as unpaid volunteers such as guardians ad litem, mediators, and arbitrators and to make public the applications and evaluations of such persons upon a showing of materiality in a pending court proceeding or upon a showing of good cause.

Subdivision (c)(9) has also been amended. Subdivision (c)(9) was adopted to incorporate the holdings of judicial decisions establishing that confidentiality may be required to protect the rights of defendants, litigants, or third parties; to further the administration of justice; or to otherwise promote a compelling governmental interest. *Barron v. Florida Freedom Newspapers, Inc.*, 531 So.2d 113 (Fla.1988); *Miami Herald Publishing Co. v. Lewis*, 426 So.2d 1 (Fla.1982). Such confidentiality may be implemented by court rule, as well as by judicial decision, where necessary for the effective administration of justice. *See, e.g.*, Fla.R.Crim.P. 3.470, (Sealed Verdict); Fla.R.Crim.P. 3.712, (Presentence Investigation Reports); Fla.R.Civ.P. 1.280(c), (Protective Orders).

Subdivision (c)(9)(D) requires that, except where otherwise provided by law or rule of court, reasonable notice shall be given to the public of any order closing a court record. This subdivision is not applicable to court proceedings. Unlike the closure of court proceedings, which has been held to require notice and hearing prior to closure, *see Miami Herald Publishing Co. v. Lewis*, 426 So. 2d 1 (Fla.1982), the closure of court records has not required prior notice. Requiring prior notice of closure of a court record may be impractical and burdensome in emergency circumstances or when closure of a court record requiring confidentiality is requested during a judicial proceeding. Providing reasonable notice to the public of the entry of a closure order and an opportunity to be heard on the closure issue adequately protects the competing interests of confidentiality and public access to judicial records. *See Florida Freedom Newspapers, Inc. v. Sirmons*, 508 So.2d 462 (Fla. 1st DCA 1987), *approved, Barron v. Florida Freedom Newspapers, Inc.*, 531 So.2d 113 (Fla.1988); *State ex rel.Tallahassee Democrat v. Cooksey, 371 So.2d 207 (Fla. 1st DCA 1979). Subdivision (c)(9)(D), however, does not preclude the giving of prior notice of closure of a court record, and the court may elect to give prior notice in appropriate cases.*

Court Commentary

2002 Court Commentary. The custodian is required to provide access to or copies of records but is not required either to provide information from records or to create new records in response to a request. Op. Atty. Gen. Fla. 80- 57 (1980); Wootton v. Cook, 590 So.2d 1039 (Fla. 1st DCA 1991); Seigle v. Barry, 422 So.2d 63 (Fla. 4th DCA 1982).

The writing requirement is not intended to disadvantage any person who may have difficulty writing a request; if any difficulty exists, the custodian should aid the requestor in reducing the request to writing.

It is anticipated that each judicial branch entity will have policies and procedures for responding to public records requests.

The 1995 commentary notes that the definition of "judicial records" added at that time is consistent with the definition of "court records" contained in rule 2.075(a)(1) [renumbered as 2.430(a)(1) in 2006] and the definition of "public records" contained in chapter 119, Florida Statutes. Despite the commentary, these definitions are not the same. The definitions added in 2002 are intended to clarify that records of the judicial branch include court records as defined in rule 2.075(a)(1) and administrative records. The definition of records of the judicial branch is consistent with the definition of "public records" in chapter 119, Florida Statutes.

2005 Court Commentary. Under courts' inherent authority, appellate courts may appoint a special magistrate to serve as commissioner for the court to make findings of fact and oversee discovery in review proceedings under subdivision (d) of this rule. Cf. State ex rel. Davis v. City of Avon Park, 158 So. 159 (Fla. 1934) (recognizing appellate courts' inherent authority to do all things reasonably necessary for administration of justice within the scope of courts' jurisdiction, including the appointment of a commissioner to make findings of fact); Wessells v. State, 737 So. 2d 1103 (Fla. 1st DCA 1998) (relinquishing jurisdiction to circuit court for appointment of a special master to serve as commissioner for court to make findings of fact).

2007 Court Commentary. New subdivision (d) applies only to motions that seek to make court records in noncriminal cases confidential in accordance with subdivision (c)(9).

2007 Committee Commentary. Subdivision (d)(2) is intended to permit a party to make use of any court-provided recording device or system that is available generally for litigants' use, but is not intended to require the court system to make such devices available where they are not already in use and is not intended to eliminate any cost for use of such system that is generally borne by a party requesting use of such system.

IN THE _____ COURT, _____
JUDICIAL CIRCUIT, IN AND
FOR _____ COUNTY, FLORIDA

CASE NO.: _____

_____
Plaintiff/Petitioner,

v.

_____
Defendant/Respondent.
_____/

NOTICE OF CONFIDENTIAL INFORMATION WITHIN COURT FILING

Pursuant to Florida Rule of Judicial Administration 2.420(d)(2), the filer of a court record at the time of filing shall indicate whether any confidential information is included within the document being filed; identify the confidentiality provision that applies to the identified information; and identify the precise location of the confidential information within the document being filed.

Title/Type of Document(s): _____

Indicate the applicable confidentiality provision(s) below from Rule 2.420(d)(1)(B), by specifying the location within the document on the space provided:

_____ Chapter 39 records relating to dependency matters, termination of parental rights, guardians ad litem, child abuse, neglect, and abandonment. § 39.0132(3), Fla. Stat. (If the document is filed within a Chapter 39 case, this form is not required.)

_____ Adoption records. § 63.162, Fla. Stat. (If the document is filed within a Chapter 63 adoption case, this form is not required.)

_____ Social Security, bank account, charge, debit, and credit card numbers in court records. § 119.0714(1)(i)-(j), (2)(a)-(e), Fla. Stat. (Unless redaction is requested pursuant to § 119.0714(2), this information is exempt only as of January 1, 2011.)

_____ HIV test results and patient identity within the HIV test results. § 381.004(3)(e), Fla. Stat.

_____ Sexually transmitted diseases — test results and identity within the test results when provided by the Department of Health or the department's authorized representative. § 384.29, Fla. Stat.

_____ Birth and death certificates, including court-issued delayed birth certificates and fetal death certificates. §§ 382.008(6), 382.025(1)(a), Fla. Stat.

_____ Identifying information in petition by minor for waiver of parental notice when seeking to terminate pregnancy. § 390.01116, Fla. Stat. (If the document is filed within a Ch. 390 waiver of parental notice case, this form is not required.)

_____ Identifying information in clinical mental health records under the Baker Act. § 394.4615(7), Fla. Stat.

_____ Records of substance abuse service providers which pertain to the identity, diagnosis, and prognosis of and service provision to individuals who have received services from substance abuse service providers. § 397.501(7), Fla. Stat.

_____ Identifying information in clinical records of detained criminal defendants found incompetent to proceed or acquitted by reason of insanity. § 916.107(8), Fla. Stat.

_____ Estate inventories and accountings. § 733.604(1), Fla. Stat.

_____ Victim's address in domestic violence action on petitioner's request. § 741.30(3)(b), Fla. Stat.

_____ Information identifying victims of sexual offenses, including child sexual abuse. §§ 119.071(2)(h), 119.0714(1)(h), Fla. Stat.

_____ Gestational surrogacy records. § 742.16(9), Fla. Stat.

_____ Guardianship reports and orders appointing court monitors in guardianship cases. §§ 744.1076, 744.3701, Fla. Stat.

_____ Grand jury records. Ch. 905, Fla. Stat. (If the document is filed in a Ch. 905 grand jury proceeding, this form is not required.)

_____ Information acquired by courts and law enforcement regarding family services for children. § 984.06(3)-(4), Fla. Stat. (If the document is filed in a Ch. 984 family services for children case, this form is not required.)

_____ Juvenile delinquency records. §§ 985.04(1), 985.045(2), Fla. Stat. (If the document is filed in a Ch. 985 juvenile delinquency case, this form is not required.)

_____ Information disclosing the identity of persons subject to tuberculosis proceedings and records of the Department of Health in suspected tuberculosis cases. §§ 392.545, 392.65, Fla. Stat.

_____ Presentence investigation reports and attached psychological or psychiatric evaluations. Fla. R. Crim. P. 3.712; §§ 921.231(1)(i), 948.015(9), Fla. Stat.

CERTIFICATE OF SERVICE

I HEREBY CERTIFY that a copy of the foregoing was furnished by U.S. mail/personal service to: _____, on _____, 20 _____.

Attorney Name ....
Address ....
Phone ....
Florida Bar No. ....

NOTE: The clerk of court shall review filings identified as containing confidential information to determine whether the information is facially subject to confidentiality under the identified provision. The clerk shall notify the filer in writing within 5 days if the clerk determines that the information is NOT subject to confidentiality, and the records shall not be held as confidential for more than 10 days, unless a motion is filed pursuant to subdivision (d)(3) of the Rule. Fla. R. Jud. Admin. 2.420(d)(2).

RULE 2.425. MINIMIZATION OF THE FILING OF SENSITIVE INFORMATION

(a) Limitations for Court Filings. Unless authorized by subdivision (b), statute, another rule of court, or the court orders otherwise, designated sensitive information filed with the court must be limited to the following format:

(1) The initials of a person known to be a minor;

(2) The year of birth of a person's birth date;

(3) No portion of any

(A) social security number,

(B) bank account number,

(C) credit card account number,

(D) charge account number, or

(E) debit account number,

(4) The last four digits of any

(A) taxpayer identification number (TIN),

(B) employee identification number,

(C) driver's license number,

(D) passport number,

(E) telephone number,

(F) financial account number, except as set forth in subdivision (a)(3),

(G) brokerage account number,

(H) insurance policy account number,

(I) loan account number,

(J) customer account number, or

(K) patient or health care number;

(5) A truncated version of any

(A) email address,

(B) computer user name,

(C) password, or

(D) personal identification number (PIN); and

(6) A truncated version of any other sensitive information as provided by court order.

(b) Exceptions. Subdivision (a) does not apply to the following:

(1) An account number which identifies the property alleged to be the subject of a proceeding;

(2) The record of an administrative or agency proceeding;

(3) The record in appellate or review proceedings;

(4) The birth date of a minor whenever the birth date is necessary for the court to establish or maintain subject matter jurisdiction;

(5) The name of a minor in any order relating to parental responsibility, time-sharing, or child support;

(6) The name of a minor in any document or order affecting the minor's ownership of real property;

(7) The birth date of a party in a writ of attachment or notice to payor;

(8) In traffic and criminal proceedings;

(A) a pro se filing;

(B) a court filing that is related to a criminal matter or investigation and that is prepared before the filing of a criminal charge or is not filed as part of any docketed criminal case;

(C) an arrest or search warrant or any information in support thereof;

(D) a charging document and an affidavit or other documents filed in support of any charging document, including any driving records;

(E) a statement of particulars;

(F) discovery material introduced into evidence or otherwise filed with the court; and

(G) all information necessary for the proper issuance and execution of a subpoena duces tecum;

(9) Information used by the clerk for case maintenance purposes or the courts for case management purposes; and

(10) Information which is relevant and material to an issue before the court.

(c) Remedies. Upon motion by a party or interested person or sua sponte by the court, the court may order remedies, sanctions or both for a violation of subdivision (a). Following notice and an opportunity to respond, the court may impose sanctions if such filing was not made in good faith.

(d) Motions Not Restricted. This rule does not restrict a party's right to move for protective order, to move to file documents under seal, or to request a determination of the confidentiality of records.

(e) Application. This rule does not affect the application of constitutional provisions, statutes, or rules of court regarding confidential information or access to public information.

RULE 2.430. RETENTION OF COURT RECORDS

This rule is subject to an implementation schedule. See the Editor's Notes at the end of the rule.

(a) Definitions. The following definitions apply to this rule:

(1) "Court records" mean the contents of the court file, including the progress docket and other similar records generated to document activity in a case, transcripts filed with the clerk, documentary exhibits in the custody of the clerk, and electronic records, video tapes, or stenographic tapes of depositions or other proceedings filed with the clerk, and electronic records, videotapes or stenographic tapes of court proceedings.

(2) "After a judgment has become final" means:

(A) when a final order, final judgment, final docket entry, final dismissal, or nolle prosequi has been entered as to all parties, no appeal has been taken, and the time for appeal has expired; or

(B) when a final order, final judgment, or final docket entry has been entered, an appeal has been taken, the appeal has been disposed of, and the time for any further appellate proceedings has expired.

(3) "Permanently recorded" means that a document has been microfilmed, optically imaged, or recorded onto an electronic record keeping system in accordance with standards adopted by the Supreme Court of Florida.

(b) Permanently Recorded Records.

Text of rule effective prior to amendment by Florida Supreme Court in case number SC11-399. See also text of rule as amended by Florida Supreme Court in case number SC11-399 below.

Court records, except exhibits, that have been permanently recorded may be destroyed or otherwise disposed of by the clerk at any time after a judgment has become final.

(b) Permanently Recorded Records.

Text of rule as amended by Florida Supreme Court in case number SC11-399. See also text of rule prior to amendment by Florida Supreme Court in case number SC11-399 above.

(1) Court records, except exhibits, that have been permanently recorded may be destroyed or otherwise disposed of by the clerk at any time after a judgment has become final.

(2) Any physical media submitted to the clerk for the purpose of filing information contained in the

media may be destroyed, retained, or otherwise disposed of by the clerk once the contents of the media have been made a part of the court record.

(c) Records Not Permanently Recorded. No court records under this subdivision shall be destroyed or disposed of until the final order, final docket entry, or final judgment is permanently recorded for, or recorded in, the public records. The time periods shall not apply to any action in which the court orders the court records to be kept until the court orders otherwise. When an order is entered to that effect, the progress docket and the court file shall be marked by the clerk with a legend showing that the court records are not to be destroyed or disposed of without a further order of court. Any person may apply for an order suspending or prohibiting destruction or disposition of court records in any proceeding. Court records, except exhibits, that are not permanently recorded may be destroyed or disposed of by the clerk after a judgment has become final in accordance with the following schedule:

(1) For trial courts

(A) 60 days — Parking tickets and noncriminal traffic infractions after required audits have been completed.

(B) 2 years — Proceedings under the Small Claims Rules, Medical Mediation Proceedings.

(C) 5 years — Misdemeanor actions, criminal traffic violations, ordinance violations, civil litigation proceedings in county court other than those under the Small Claims Rules, and civil proceedings in circuit court except marriage dissolutions and adoptions.

(D) 10 years — Probate, guardianship, and mental health proceedings.

(E) 10 years — Felony cases in which no information or indictment was filed or in which all charges were dismissed, or in which the state announced a nolle prosequi, or in which the defendant was adjudicated not guilty.

(F) 75 years — Juvenile proceedings containing an order permanently depriving a parent of custody of a child, and adoptions, and all felony cases not previously destroyed.

(G) Juvenile proceedings not otherwise provided for in this subdivision shall be kept for 5 years after the last entry or until the child reaches the age of majority, whichever is later.

(H) Marriage dissolutions — 10 years from the last record activity. The court may authorize destruction of court records not involving alimony, support, or custody of children 5 years from the last record activity.

(2) For district courts of appeal

(A) 2 years — noncriminal court records.

(B) 5 years — Criminal court records.

(3) For the Supreme Court

(A) 5 years — All cases disposed of by order not otherwise provided for in this rule.

(B) 10 years — Cases disposed of by order involving individuals licensed or regulated by the court and noncriminal court records involving the unauthorized practice of law.

(d) Records to Be Retained Permanently. The following court records shall be permanently recorded or permanently retained:

(1) progress dockets, and other similar records generated to document activity in a case, and

(2) court records of the supreme court in which the case was disposed of by opinion.

(e) Court Reporters' Notes. Court reporters or persons acting as court reporters for judicial or discovery proceedings shall retain the original notes or electronic records of the proceedings or depositions until the times specified below:

(1) 2 years from the date of preparing the transcript — Judicial proceedings, arbitration hearings, and

discovery proceedings when an original transcript has been prepared.

(2) 10 years — Judicial proceedings in felony cases when a transcript has not been prepared.

(3) 5 years — All other judicial proceedings, arbitration hearings, and discovery proceedings when a transcript has not been prepared.

When an agreement has been made between the reporter and any other person and the person has paid the reasonable charges for storage and retention of the notes, the notes or records shall be kept for any longer time agreed on. All reporters' notes shall be retained in a secure place in Florida.

(f) Exhibits.

(1) Exhibits in criminal proceedings shall be disposed of as provided by law.

(2) All other exhibits shall be retained by the clerk until 90 days after a judgment has become final. If an exhibit is not withdrawn pursuant to subdivision (i) within 90 days, the clerk may destroy or dispose of the exhibits after giving the parties or their attorneys of record 30 days' notice of the clerk's intention to do so. Exhibits shall be delivered to any party or attorney of record calling for them during the 30-day time period.

(g) Disposition Other Than Destruction. Before destruction or disposition of court records under this rule, any person may apply to the court for an order requiring the clerk to deliver to the applicant the court records that are to be destroyed or disposed of. All parties shall be given notice of the application. The court shall dispose of that court record as appropriate.

(h) Release of Court Records. This rule does not limit the power of the court to release exhibits or other parts of court records that are the property of the person or party initially placing the items in the court records. The court may require copies to be substituted as a condition to releasing the court records under this subdivision.

(i) Right to Expunge Records. Nothing in this rule shall affect the power of the court to order records expunged.

(j) Sealed Records. No record which has been sealed from public examination by order of court shall be destroyed without hearing after such notice as the court shall require.

(k) Destruction of Jury Notes. At the conclusion of the trial and promptly following discharge of the jury, the court shall collect all juror notes and immediately destroy the juror notes.

Editor's Notes: — On October 18, 2012, the Supreme Court of Florida issued a revised opinion in case number SC11-399, which was originally issued on June 21, 2012. See *In re Amendments to the Florida Rules of Judicial Administration*, 37 FLW S643 (Fla. 2012). The opinion provides in relevant part:

"First, the new electronic filing requirements the Court adopts will become effective in the civil, probate, small claims, and family law divisions of the trial courts, as well as for appeals to the circuit courts in these categories of cases, on April 1, 2013, at 12:01 a.m., except as may be otherwise provided by administrative order. Electronic filing will be mandatory in these divisions pursuant to rule 2.525 on that date. However, until the new rules take effect in these divisions, any clerk who is already accepting documents filed by electronic transmission under the current rules should continue to do so; attorneys in these counties are encouraged to file documents electronically under the current rules.

"Next, the new electronic filing requirements the Court adopts will become effective in the criminal, traffic, and juvenile divisions of the trial courts, as well as for appeals to the circuit court in these categories of cases, on October 1, 2013, at 12:01 a.m., except as may be otherwise provided by administrative order. Electronic filing will be mandatory in these divisions under rule 2.525 on that date. The new e-filing requirements, as they apply in proceedings brought pursuant to the Florida Mental Health Act (Baker Act), Chapter 394, Part I, Florida Statutes, and the Involuntary Commitment of Sexually Violent Predators Act (Jimmy Ryce), Chapter 394, Part V, Florida Statutes, will also not be mandatory in these cases until October 1, 2013. As stated above, until the new rules take effect in these divisions and proceedings, any clerk who is already accepting electronically filed documents under the current rules should continue to do so; attorneys are again encouraged to utilize existing electronic filing procedures under the current rules.

"However, until the new rules and procedures take effect in the district courts, any clerk who is already accepting documents filed by electronic transmission may continue to do so; attorneys in these districts are encouraged to file documents electronically. Clerks will not be required to electronically transmit the record on appeal until July 1, 2013, at 12:01 a.m. Until July 1, we encourage clerks, whenever possible, to electronically transmit the record under the new rules and requirements.

"(W)e note that, in all types of cases, pursuant to amended rule 2.525(d) self-represented parties and self-represented nonparties, including nonparty governmental or public agencies, and attorneys excused from e-mail service under Florida Rule of Judicial Administration 2.516 will be permitted, but not required, to file documents electronically.

By order of November 28, 2012, in case number SC11-399, the Court released a revised implementation schedule, which provides, in pertinent part: "The e-filing rules adopted in the October 2012 opinion will be mandatory in this (Supreme) Court on February 27, 2013, at 12:01 a.m.; and effective earlier on a voluntary basis as will be indicated by further administrative order of the chief justice.

"Thereafter, the e-filing rules will be mandatory in the Second District Court of Appeal on July 22, 2013, at 12:01 a.m.; in the Third District Court of Appeal on September 27, 2013, at 12:01 a.m.; in the Fourth District Court of Appeal on October 31, 2013, at 12:01 a.m.; in the Fifth District Court of Appeal on November 27, 2013 at 12:01 a.m.; and in the First District Court of Appeal on December 27, 2013, at 12:01 a.m., unless made mandatory earlier by the chief judge of the applicable district court of appeal. The e-filing rules will be effective earlier on a voluntary trial basis in the district courts of appeal as will be indicated by further administrative order by the chief judge of the applicable district court."

RULE 2.440. RETENTION OF JUDICIAL BRANCH ADMINISTRATIVE RECORDS

(a) Definitions.

(1) "Judicial branch" means the judicial branch of government, which includes the state courts system, the clerk of court when acting as an arm of the court, The Florida Bar, the Florida Board of Bar Examiners, the Judicial Qualifications Commission, and all other entities established by or operating under the authority of the supreme court or the chief justice.

(2) "Records of the judicial branch" means all records, regardless of physical form, characteristics, or means of transmission, made or received in connection with the transaction of official business by any judicial branch entity and consists of:

(A) "court records," which means the contents of the court file, including the progress docket and other similar records generated to document activity in a case, transcripts filed with the clerk, documentary exhibits in the custody of the clerk, and electronic records, videotapes, or stenographic tapes of depositions or other proceedings filed with the clerk, and electronic records, videotapes, or stenographic tapes of court proceedings; and

(B) "administrative records," which means all other records made or received pursuant to court rule, law, or ordinance, or in connection with the transaction of official business by any judicial branch entity.

(b) Retention requirements. Administrative records in the judicial branch shall be retained in accordance with the Judicial Branch Records Retention Schedule approved by the supreme court.

Court Commentary

2002 Court Commentary. This rule does not apply to court records and files that are governed by rule 2.075 [renumbered as 2.430 in 2006]. This rule applies to administrative records.

To provide a consistent schedule for retention of administrative records in the judicial branch, the Supreme Court Workgroup on Public Records recommended that the Court adopt the Judicial Branch Records Retention Schedule. This schedule uses the legislatively authorized Department of State retention schedules, as appropriate, and includes a schedule for other records that are unique to the judicial branch. *[This schedule is set forth at the end of these rules.]*

RULE 2.450. TECHNOLOGICAL COVERAGE OF JUDICIAL PROCEEDINGS

(a) Electronic and Still Photography Allowed. Subject at all times to the authority of the presiding judge to: (i) control the conduct of proceedings before the court; (ii) ensure decorum and prevent distractions; and (iii) ensure the fair administration of justice in the pending cause, electronic media and still photography coverage of public judicial proceedings in the appellate and trial courts of this state shall be allowed in accordance with the following standards of conduct and technology promulgated by the Supreme Court of Florida.

(b) Equipment and Personnel.

(1) At least 1 portable television camera, operated by not more than 1 camera person, shall be permitted in any trial or appellate court proceeding. The number of permitted cameras shall be within the sound discretion and authority of the presiding judge.

(2) Not more than 1 still photographer, using not more than 2 still cameras, shall be permitted in any proceeding in a trial or appellate court.

(3) Not more than 1 audio system for radio broadcast purposes shall be permitted in any proceeding in a trial or appellate court. Audio pickup for all media purposes shall be accomplished from existing audio systems present in the court facility. If no technically

suitable audio system exists in the court facility, microphones and related wiring essential for media purposes shall be unobtrusive and shall be located in places designated in advance of any proceeding by the chief judge of the judicial circuit or district in which the court facility is located.

(4) Any "pooling" arrangements among the media required by these limitations on equipment and personnel shall be the sole responsibility of the media without calling upon the presiding judge to mediate any dispute as to the appropriate media representative or equipment authorized to cover a particular proceeding. In the absence of advance media agreement on disputed equipment or personnel issues, the presiding judge shall exclude all contesting media personnel from a proceeding.

(c) Sound and Light Criteria.

(1) Only television photographic and audio equipment that does not produce distracting sound or light shall be used to cover judicial proceedings. No artificial lighting device of any kind shall be used in connection with the television camera.

(2) Only still camera equipment that does not produce distracting sound or light shall be used to cover judicial proceedings. No artificial lighting device of any kind shall be used in connection with a still camera.

(3) It shall be the affirmative duty of media personnel to demonstrate to the presiding judge adequately in advance of any proceeding that the equipment sought to be used meets the sound and light criteria enunciated in this rule. A failure to obtain advance judicial approval for equipment shall preclude its use in any proceeding.

(d) Location of Equipment Personnel.

(1) Television camera equipment shall be positioned in such location in the court facility as shall be designated by the chief judge of the judicial circuit or district in which such facility is situated. The area designated shall provide reasonable access to coverage. If and when areas remote from the court facility that permit reasonable access to coverage are provided, all television camera and audio equipment shall be positioned only in such area. Videotape recording equipment that is not a component part of a television camera shall be located in an area remove from the court facility.

(2) A still camera photographer shall position himself or herself in such location in the court facility as shall be designated by the chief judge of the judicial circuit or district in which such facility is situated. The area designated shall provide reasonable access to coverage. Still camera photographers shall assume a fixed position within the designated area and, once established in a shooting position, shall act so as not to call attention to themselves through further movement. Still camera photographers shall not be permitted to move about in order to obtain photographs of court proceedings.

(3) Broadcast media representatives shall not move about the court facility while proceedings are in session, and microphones or taping equipment once positioned as required by subdivision (b)(3) shall not be moved during the pendency of the proceeding.

(e) Movement During Proceedings. News media photographic or audio equipment shall not be placed in or removed from the court facility except before commencement or after adjournment of proceedings each day, or during a recess. Neither television film magazines nor still camera film or lenses shall be changed within a court facility except during a recess in the proceeding.

(f) Courtroom Light Sources. With the concurrence of the chief judge of a judicial circuit or district in which a court facility is situated, modifications and additions may be made in light sources existing in the facility, provided such modifications or additions are installed and maintained without public expense.

(g) Conferences of Counsel. To protect the attorney-client privilege and the effective right to counsel, there shall be no audio pickup or broadcast of conferences that occur in a court facility between attorneys and their clients, between co-counsel of a client, or between counsel and the presiding judge held at the bench.

(h) Impermissible Use of Media Material. None of the film, videotape, still photographs, or audio reproductions developed during or by virtue of coverage of a judicial proceeding shall be admissible as evidence in the proceeding out of which it arose, in any proceeding subsequent or collateral thereto, or upon retrial or appeal of such proceedings.

(i) Appellate Review. Review of an order excluding the electronic media from access to any proceeding, excluding coverage of a particular participant, or upon any other matters arising under these standards shall be pursuant to Florida Rule of Appellate Procedure 9.100(d).

Court Commentary

1994 Amendment. This rule was copied from Canon 3A(7) of the Code of Judicial Conduct. Canon 3A(7) represented a departure from former Canon 3A(7) [ABA Canon 35]. The former canon generally proscribed electronic media and still photography coverage of judicial proceedings from within and in areas immediately adjacent to the courtroom, with three categories of exceptions - (a) use for judicial administration, (b) coverage of investitive, ceremonial, and naturalization proceedings, and (c) use for instructional purposes in educational institutions. Subject to the limitations and promulgation of standards as mentioned therein, the revised canon constituted a general authorization for electronic media and still photography coverage for all purposes, including the purposes expressed as exceptions in the former canon. Limited only by the authority of the presiding judge in the exercise of sound discretion to prohibit filming or photographing of particular participants, consent of participants to coverage is not required. The text of the rule refers to public judicial proceedings. This is in recognition of the authority reposing in the presiding judge, upon the exercise of sound discretion, to hold certain judicial proceedings or portions thereof in camera, and in recognition of the fact that certain proceedings or portions thereof are made confidential by statute. The term "presiding judge" includes the chief judge of an appellate tribunal.

PART V. PRACTICE OF LAW

A. Attorneys

RULE 2.505. ATTORNEYS

(a) Scope and Purpose. All persons in good standing as members of The Florida Bar shall be permitted to practice in Florida. Attorneys of other states who are not members of the Florida Bar in good standing shall not engage in the practice of law in Florida except to the extent permitted by rule 2.510.

(b) Persons Employed by the Court. Except as provided in this subdivision, no full-time employee of the court shall practice as an attorney in any court or before any agency of government while continuing in that position. Any attorney designated by the chief justice or chief judge may represent the court, any court employee in the employee's official capacity, or any judge in the judge's official capacity, in any proceeding in which the court, employee, or judge is an interested party. An attorney formerly employed by a court shall not represent anyone in connection with a matter in which the attorney participated personally and substantially while employed by the court, unless all parties to the proceeding consent after disclosure.

(c) Attorney Not to Be Surety. No attorneys or other officers of court shall enter themselves or be taken as bail or surety in any proceeding in court.

(d) Stipulations. No private agreement or consent between parties or their attorneys concerning the practice or procedure in an action shall be of any force unless the evidence of it is in writing, subscribed by the party or the party's attorney against whom it is alleged. Parol agreements may be made before the court if promptly made a part of the record or incorporated in the stenographic notes of the proceedings, and agreements made at depositions that are incorporated in the transcript need not be signed when signing of the deposition is waived. This rule shall not apply to settlements or other substantive agreements.

(e) Appearance of Attorney. An attorney may appear in a proceeding in any of the following ways:

(1) By serving and filing, on behalf of a party, the party's first pleading or paper in the proceeding.

(2) By substitution of counsel, but only by order of court and with written consent of the client, filed with the court. The court may condition substitution upon payment of, or security for, the substituted attorney's fees and expenses, or upon such other terms as may be just.

(3) By filing with the court and serving upon all parties a notice of appearance as counsel for a party that has already appeared in a proceeding pro se or as co-counsel for a party that has already appeared in a proceeding by non-withdrawing counsel.

(f) Termination of Appearance of Attorney. The appearance of an attorney for a party in a proceeding shall terminate only in one of the following ways:

(1) Withdrawal of Attorney. By order of court, where the proceeding is continuing, upon motion and hearing, on notice to all parties and the client, such motion setting forth the reasons for withdrawal and the client's last known address, telephone number, including area code, and email address.

(2) Substitution of Attorney. By order of court, under the procedure set forth in subdivision (e)(2) of this rule.

(3) Termination of Proceeding. Automatically, without order of court, upon the termination of a proceeding, whether by final order of dismissal, by final adjudication, or otherwise, and following the expiration of any applicable time for appeal, where no appeal is taken.

(4) Filing of Notice of Completion. For limited representation proceedings under Florida Family Law Rule of Procedure 12.040, automatically, by the filing of a notice of completion titled "Termination of Limited Appearance" pursuant to rule 12.040(c).

(g) Law Student Participation. Eligible law students shall be permitted to participate as provided under the conditions of chapter 11 of the Rules Regulating The Florida Bar as amended from time to time.

(h) Attorney as Agent of Client. In all matters concerning the prosecution or defense of any proceeding in the court, the attorney of record shall be the agent of the client, and any notice by or to the attorney or act by the attorney in the proceeding shall be accepted as the act of or notice to the client.

Court Commentary

1997 Amendment. Originally, the rule provided that the followup filing had to occur within ten days. In the 1997 amendment to the rule, that requirement was modified to provide that the follow-up filing must occur "immediately" after a document is electronically filed. The "immediately thereafter" language is consistent with language used in the rules of procedure where, in a somewhat analogous situation, the filing of a document may occur after service. See, e.g., Florida Rule of Civil Procedure 1.080(d) ("All original papers shall be filed with the court either before service or *immediately thereafter.*") (emphasis added). "Immediately thereafter" has been interpreted to mean "filed with reasonable promptness." *Miami Transit Co. v. Ford,* 155 So. 2d 360 (Fla. 1963).

The use of the words "other person" in this rule is not meant to allow a nonlawyer to sign and file pleadings or other papers on behalf of another. Such conduct would constitute the unauthorized practice of law.

2003 Amendment. Rule Regulating the Florida Bar 4-1.12(c), which addresses the imputed disqualification of a law firm, should be looked to in conjunction with the rule 2.060(b) [renumbered as 2.505(b) in 2006] restriction on representation by a former judicial staff attorney or law clerk.

RULE 2.510. FOREIGN ATTORNEYS

This rule is subject to an implementation schedule. See the Editor's Notes at the end of the rule.

(a) Eligibility. Upon filing a verified motion with the court, an attorney who is an active member in good standing of the bar of another state and currently eligible to practice law in a state other than Florida may be permitted to appear in particular cases in a Florida court upon such conditions as the court may deem appropriate, provided that a member of The Florida Bar in good standing is associated as an attorney of record. The foreign attorney must make application in each court in which a case is filed even if a lower tribunal granted a motion to appear in the same case. In determining whether to permit a foreign attorney to appear pursuant to this rule, the court may consider, among other things, information provided under subdivision (b)(3) concerning discipline in other jurisdictions. No attorney is authorized to appear pursuant to this rule if the attorney (1) is a Florida resident, unless the attorney has an application pending for admission to The Florida Bar and has not previously been denied admission to The Florida Bar; (2) is a member of The Florida Bar but is ineligible to practice law; (3) has previously been disciplined or held in contempt by reason of misconduct committed while engaged in representation permitted pursuant to this rule provided, however, the contempt is final and has not been reversed or abated; (4) has failed to provide notice to The Florida Bar or pay the filing fee as required by subdivision (b)(7); or (5) is engaged in a "general practice" before Florida courts. For purposes of this rule, more than 3 appearances within a

365-day period in separate cases shall be presumed to be a "general practice." Appearances at different levels of the court system in the same case shall be deemed 1 appearance for the purposes of determining whether a foreign attorney has more than 3 appearances within a 365-day period. In cases involving indigent clients, the court may waive the filing fee for good cause shown.

(b) Contents of Verified Motion. A form verified motion accompanies this rule and shall be utilized by the foreign attorney. The verified motion required by subdivision (a) shall include:

(1) a statement identifying all jurisdictions in which the attorney is an active member in good standing and currently eligible to practice law including all assigned bar numbers and attorney numbers;

(2) a statement identifying by date, case name, and case number all other matters in Florida state courts in which pro hac vice admission has been sought in the preceding 5 years, including any lower tribunals for the case in which the motion is filed, and whether such admission was granted or denied;

(3) a statement identifying all jurisdictions in which the attorney has been disciplined in any manner in the preceding 5 years and the sanction imposed, or in which the attorney has pending any disciplinary proceeding, including the date of the disciplinary action and the nature of the violation;

(4) a statement identifying the date on which the legal representation at issue commenced, and the party or parties represented;

(5) a statement that all applicable provisions of these rules and the rules regulating the Florida bar have been read, and that the verified motion complies with those rules;

(6) the name, record bar address, and membership status of the Florida bar member or members associated for purposes of the representation;

(7) a certificate indicating service of the verified motion upon all counsel of record in the matter in which leave to appear pro hac vice is sought and upon The Florida Bar at its Tallahassee office accompanied by a nonrefundable $250.00 filing fee made payable to The Florida Bar or notice of the waiver of the fee; and

(8) a verification by the attorney seeking to appear pursuant to this rule and the signature of the Florida bar member or members associated for purposes of the representation.

IN THE _____ COURT OF THE _____ JUDICIAL CIRCUIT,
_____ IN AND FOR _____, COUNTY, FLORIDA

Case No. _____

_____
    Plaintiff

Division _____

vs.

_____
    Defendant

VERIFIED MOTION FOR ADMISSION TO APPEAR *PRO HAC VICE* PURSUANT TO FLORIDA RULE OF JUDICIAL ADMINISTRATION 2.510

Comes now _____, Movant herein, and respectfully represents the following:

1. [ ] Movant resides in _____, _____. Movant
                       (City)   (State)
is not a resident of the State of Florida.
    [ ] Movant is a resident of the State of Florida and has an application pending for admission to The Florida Bar and has not previously been denied admission to The Florida Bar.

2. Movant is an attorney and a member of the law firm of (or practices law under the name of) _____ with offices at _____(Street Address)_____, _____(City)_____, _____(County)_____ _____(State)_____ _____(Zip Code)_____ _____(Telephone)_____ .

3. Movant has been retained personally or as a member of the above-named law firm on __(Date Representation Commenced)__ by _____Name of Party or Parties_____ to provide legal representation in connection with the above-styled matter now pending before the above-named court of the State of Florida.

4. Movant is an active member in good standing and currently eligible to practice law in the following jurisdiction(s): Include attorney or bar number(s). (Attach an additional sheet if necessary.)

JURISDICTION   ATTORNEY/BAR NUMBER

_____
_____
_____
_____
_____

5. There are no disciplinary proceedings pending against Movant, except as provided below (give jurisdiction of disciplinary action, date of disciplinary action, nature of the violation and the sanction, if any, imposed): (Attach an additional sheet if necessary.)

_____

_____

_____

_____

_____

6. Within the past five (5) years, Movant has not been subject to any disciplinary proceedings, except as provided below (give jurisdiction of disciplinary action, date of disciplinary action, nature of the violation and the sanction, if any, imposed):
(Attach an additional sheet if necessary.)

_____

_____

_____

_____

_____

7. Movant has never been subject to any suspension proceedings, except as provided below (give jurisdiction of disciplinary action, date of disciplinary action, nature of the violation and the sanction, if any, imposed):
(Attach an additional sheet if necessary.)

_____

_____

_____

_____

_____

8. Movant has never been subject to any disbarment proceedings, except as provided below (give jurisdiction of disciplinary action, date of disciplinary action, nature of the violation and the sanction, if any, imposed):
(Attach an additional sheet if necessary.)

_____

_____

_____

_____

9. Movant, either by resignation, withdrawal, or otherwise, never has terminated or attempted to terminate Movant's office as an attorney in order to avoid administrative, disciplinary, disbarment, or suspension proceedings.

10. Movant is not an inactive member of The Florida Bar.

11. Movant is not now a member of The Florida Bar.

12. Movant is not a suspended member of The Florida Bar.

13. Movant is not a disbarred member of The Florida Bar nor has Movant received a disciplinary resignation from The Florida Bar.

Text of rule effective prior to amendment by Florida Supreme Court in case number SC11-399. See also text of rule as amended by Florida Supreme Court in case number SC11-399 below.

14. Movant has not previously been disciplined or held in contempt by reason of misconduct committed while engaged in representation pursuant to Florida Rule of Judicial Administration 2.510, except as provided below (give date of disciplinary action or contempt, reasons there for, and court imposing contempt):
(Attach an additional sheet if necessary.)

_____
_____
_____
_____
_____

Text of rule as amended by Florida Supreme Court in case number SC11-399. See also text of rule prior to amendment by Florida Supreme Court in case number SC11-399 above.

14. Movant has not previously been disciplined or held in contempt by reason of misconduct committed while engaged in representation pursuant to Florida Rule of Judicial Administration 2.510, except as provided below (give date of disciplinary action or contempt, reasons therefor, and court imposing contempt):
(Attach an additional sheet if necessary.)

_____
_____
_____
_____
_____

Text of rule effective prior to amendment by Florida Supreme Court in case number SC11-399. See also text of rule as amended by Florida Supreme Court in case number SC11-399 below.

15. Movant has filed motion(s) to appear as counsel in Florida state courts during the past five (5) years in the following matters: (attach additional sheet if necessary)

Date of Motion	Case Name	Case Number	Court	Date Motion	Granted/Denied

Text of rule as amended by Florida Supreme Court in case number SC11-399. See also text of rule prior to amendment by Florida Supreme Court in case number SC11-399 above.

15. Movant has filed motion(s) to appear as counsel in Florida state courts during the past five (5) years in the following matters: (Attach an additional sheet if necessary)

Date of Motion	Case Name	Case Number	Court	Date Motion	Granted/Denied

16. Local counsel of record associated with Movant in this matter is (Name and Florida Bar Number)   who is an active member in good standing of The Florida Bar and has offices at _____(Street Address)_____, _____(City)_____, _____(County)_____, Florida, _(Zip Code)_   (Telephone with area code)   .

(If local counsel is not an active member of The Florida Bar in good standing, please provide information as to local counsel's membership status _____)

17. Movant has read the applicable provisions of Florida Rule of Judicial Administration 2.510 and Rule 1-3.10 of the Rules Regulating The Florida Bar and certifies that this verified motion complies with those rules.

18. Movant agrees to comply with the provisions of the Florida Rules of Professional Conduct and consents to the jurisdiction of the courts and the Bar of the State of Florida.

WHEREFORE, Movant respectfully requests permission to appear in this court for this cause only.

Dated this _____ day of _____, 20_____.

Text of rule effective prior to amendment by Florida Supreme Court in case number SC11-399. See also text of rule as amended by Florida Supreme Court in case number SC11-399 below.

_____
Movant

_____
Address

_____
Address

_____
City, State, Zip Code

_____
Telephone Number

STATE OF _____

COUNTY OF _____

I, _____, do hereby swear or affirm under penalty of perjury that I am the Movant in the above-styled matter; that I have read the foregoing Motion and know the contents thereof, and the contents are true of my own knowledge and belief.

_____
Movant

I hereby consent to be associated as local counsel of record in this cause pursuant to Florida Rule of Judicial Administration 2.510.

Dated this _____ day of _____, 20____.

_____
Local Counsel of Record

_____
Address

_____
Address

_____
City, State, Zip Code

_____
Telephone Number

_____
Florida Bar Number

CERTIFICATE OF SERVICE

I HEREBY CERTIFY that a true and correct copy of the foregoing motion was furnished by U.S. mail to PHV Admissions, The Florida Bar, 651 East Jefferson Street, Tallahassee, Florida 32399-2333 accompanied by payment of the $250.00 filing fee made payable to The Florida Bar and to _____
_____
_____

Name and Address of All Counsel of Record and of Parties Not Represented by Counsel this _____ day of _____, 20____.

_____
Movant

Text of rule as amended by Florida Supreme Court in case number SC11-399. See also text of rule prior to amendment by Florida Supreme Court in case number SC11-399 above.

_____
Movant

_____
Address

_____
Address

_____
City, State, Zip Code

_____

Telephone Number

_____

E-mail Address

STATE OF _____

COUNTY OF _____

I, _____, do hereby swear or affirm under penalty of perjury that I am the Movant in the above-styled matter; that I have read the foregoing Motion and know the contents thereof, and the contents are true of my own knowledge and belief.

_____

Movant

I hereby consent to be associated as local counsel of record in this cause pursuant to Florida Rule of Judicial Administration 2.510.

Dated this _____ day of _____, 20_____.

_____

Local Counsel of Record

_____

Address

_____

Address

_____

City, State, Zip Code

_____

Telephone Number

_____

Florida Bar Number

_____

E-mail Address

CERTIFICATE OF SERVICE

I HEREBY CERTIFY that a true and correct copy of the foregoing motion was served on (insert the name or names and addresses used for service) by (e-mail) (delivery) (mail) (fax) to PHV Admissions, The Florida Bar, 651 East Jefferson Street, Tallahassee, Florida 32399-2333 accompanied by payment of the $250.00 filing fee made payable to The Florida Bar and to _____

_____

_____

Name and Address of All Counsel of Record and of Parties Not Represented by Counsel this _____ day of _____, 20____.

_____

Movant

Editor's Notes: — On October 18, 2012, the Supreme Court of Florida issued a revised opinion in case number SC11-399, which was originally issued on June 21, 2012. See *In re Amendments to the Florida Rules of Judicial Administration*, 37 FLW S643 (Fla. 2012). The opinion provides in relevant part:

"First, the new electronic filing requirements the Court adopts will become effective in the civil, probate, small claims, and family law divisions of the trial courts, as well as for appeals to the circuit courts in these categories of cases, on April 1, 2013, at 12:01 a.m., except as may be otherwise provided by administrative order. Electronic filing will be mandatory in these divisions pursuant to rule 2.525 on that date. However, until the new rules take effect in these divisions, any clerk who is already accepting documents filed by electronic transmission under the current rules should continue to do so; attorneys in these counties are encouraged to file documents electronically under the current rules.

"Next, the new electronic filing requirements the Court adopts will become effective in the criminal, traffic, and juvenile divisions of the trial courts, as well as for appeals to the circuit court in these categories of cases, on October 1, 2013, at 12:01 a.m., except as may be otherwise provided by administrative order. Electronic filing will be mandatory in these divisions under rule 2.525 on that date. The new e-filing requirements, as they apply in proceedings brought pursuant to the Florida Mental Health Act (Baker Act), Chapter 394, Part I, Florida Statutes, and the Involuntary Commitment of Sexually Violent Predators Act (Jimmy Ryce), Chapter 394, Part V, Florida Statutes, will also not be mandatory in these cases until October 1, 2013. As stated above, until the new rules take effect in these divisions and proceedings, any clerk who is already accepting electronically filed documents under the current rules should continue to do so; attorneys are again encouraged to utilize existing electronic filing procedures under the current rules.

"However, until the new rules and procedures take effect in the district courts, any clerk who is already accepting documents filed by electronic transmission may continue to do so; attorneys in these districts are encouraged to file documents electronically. Clerks will not be required to electronically transmit the record on appeal until July 1, 2013, at 12:01 a.m. Until July 1, we encourage clerks, whenever possible, to electronically transmit the record under the new rules and requirements.

"(W)e note that, in all types of cases, pursuant to amended rule 2.525(d) self-represented parties and self-represented nonparties, including nonparty governmental or public agencies, and attorneys excused from e-mail service under Florida Rule of Judicial Administration 2.516 will be permitted, but not required, to file documents electronically.

By order of November 28, 2012, in case number SC11-399, the Court released a revised implementation schedule, which provides, in pertinent part: "The e-filing rules adopted in the October 2012 opinion will be mandatory in this (Supreme) Court on February 27, 2013, at 12:01 a.m.; and effective earlier on a voluntary basis as will be indicated by further administrative order of the chief justice.

"Thereafter, the e-filing rules will be mandatory in the Second District Court of Appeal on July 22, 2013, at 12:01 a.m.; in the Third District Court of Appeal on September 27, 2013, at 12:01 a.m.; in the Fourth District Court of Appeal on October 31, 2013, at 12:01 a.m.; in the Fifth District Court of Appeal on November 27, 2013 at 12:01 a.m.; and in the First District Court of Appeal on December 27, 2013, at 12:01 a.m., unless made mandatory earlier by the chief judge of the applicable district court of appeal. The e-filing rules will be effective earlier on a voluntary trial basis in the district courts of appeal as will be indicated by further administrative order by the chief judge of the applicable district court."

RULE 2.514. COMPUTING AND EXTENDING TIME

(a) Computing Time. The following rules apply in computing time periods specified in any rule of procedure, local rule, court order, or statute that does not specify a method of computing time.

(1) Period Stated in Days or a Longer Unit. When the period is stated in days or a longer unit of time

(A) exclude the day of the event that triggers the period;

(B) count every day, including intermediate Saturdays, Sundays, and legal holidays; and

(C) include the last day of the period, but if the last day is a Saturday, Sunday, or legal holiday, or falls within any period of time extended through an order of the chief justice under Florida Rule of Judicial Administration 2.205(a)(2)(B)(iv), the period continues to run until the end of the next day that is not a Saturday, Sunday, or legal holiday and does not fall within any period of time extended through an order of the chief justice.

(2) Period Stated in Hours. When the period is stated in hours

(A) begin counting immediately on the occurrence of the event that triggers the period;

(B) count every hour, including hours during intermediate Saturdays, Sundays, and legal holidays; and

(C) if the period would end on a Saturday, Sunday, or legal holiday, or during any period of time extended through an order of the chief justice under Florida Rule of Judicial Administration 2.205(a)(2)(B)(iv), the period continues to run until the same time on the next day that is not a Saturday, Sunday, or legal holiday and does not fall within any period of time extended through an order of the chief justice.

(3) Period Stated in Days Less Than Seven Days. When the period stated in days is less than 7 days, intermediate Saturdays, Sundays, and legal holidays shall be excluded in the computation.

(4) "Last Day" Defined. Unless a different time is set by a statute, local rule, or court order, the last day ends

(A) for electronic filing or for service by any means, at midnight; and

(B) for filing by other means, when the clerk's office is scheduled to close.

(5) "Next Day" Defined. The "next day" is determined by continuing to count forward when the period is measured after an event and backward when measured before an event.

(6) "Legal Holiday" Defined. "Legal holiday" means

(A) the day set aside by section 110.117, Florida Statutes, for observing New Year's Day, Martin Luther King, Jr.'s Birthday, Memorial Day, Independence Day, Labor Day, Veterans' Day, Thanksgiving Day, the Friday after Thanksgiving Day, or Christmas Day, and

(B) any day observed as a holiday by the clerk's office or as designated by the chief judge.

(b) Additional Time after Service by Mail or E-mail. When a party may or must act within a specified time after service and service is made by mail or e-mail, 5 days are added after the period that would otherwise expire under subdivision (a).

B. Practice and Litigation Procedures

RULE 2.515. SIGNATURE OF ATTORNEYS AND PARTIES

This rule is subject to an implementation schedule. See the Editor's Notes at the end of the rule.

(a) Attorney Signature. Every pleading and other document of a party represented by an attorney shall be signed by at least 1 attorney of record in that attorney's individual name whose current record Florida Bar address, telephone number, including area code, primary e-mail address and secondary e-mail addresses, if any, and Florida Bar number shall be stated, and who shall be duly licensed to practice law in Florida or who shall have received permission to appear in the particular case as provided in rule 2.510. The attorney may be required by the court to give the address of, and to vouch for the attorney's authority to represent, the party. Except when otherwise specifically provided by an applicable rule or statute, pleadings need not be verified or accompanied by affidavit. The signature of an attorney shall constitute a certificate by the attorney that the attorney has read the pleading or other document; that to the best of the attorney's knowledge, information, and belief there is good ground to support it; and that it is not interposed for delay. If a pleading is not signed or is signed with intent to defeat the purpose of this rule, it may be stricken and the action may proceed as though the pleading or other document had not been served.

(b) Pro Se Litigant Signature. A party who is not represented by an attorney shall sign any pleading or other paper and state the party's address and telephone number, including area code.

(c) Form of Signature.

(1) The signatures required on pleadings and documents by subdivisions (a) and (b) of this rule may be:

(A) original signatures;

(B) original signatures that have been reproduced by electronic means, such as on electronically transmitted documents or photocopied documents;

(C) electronic signatures using the "/s/," "s/," or "/s" formats by or at the direction of the person signing; or

(D) any other signature format authorized by general law, so long as the clerk where the proceeding is pending has the capability of receiving and has obtained approval from the Supreme Court of Florida to accept pleadings and documents with that signature format.

(2) An attorney, party, or other person who files a pleading or paper by electronic transmission that does not contain the original signature of that attorney, party, or other person shall file that identical pleading or paper in paper form containing an original signature of that attorney, party, or other person (hereinafter called the follow-up filing) immediately thereafter. The follow-up filing is not required if the Supreme Court of Florida has entered an order directing the clerk of court to discontinue accepting the follow-up filing.

Editor's Notes: — On October 18, 2012 the Supreme Court of Florida issued a revision to its opinion in SC10-2101, originally issued on June 21, 2012. It provides in relevant part: "We accept the [Criminal Procedure Rules Committee and Florida Public Defender Association] workgroup's recommendation to delay mandatory e-mail service in the criminal, traffic, and juvenile divisions of the trial court until electronic filing is also mandatory in these divisions. Accordingly, the rule amendments that we adopt in this case are effective, nunc pro tunc, September 1, 2012, at 12:01 a.m.; however, they will be implemented as set forth in this opinion.

First, e-mail service will be mandatory for attorneys practicing in the civil, probate, small claims, and family law divisions of the trial courts, as well as in all appellate cases, when the rule amendments take effect on September 1, 2012.

Second, when the rules take effect on September 1, attorneys practicing in the criminal, traffic, and juvenile divisions of the trial court may voluntarily choose to serve documents by e-mail under the new procedures, or they may continue to operate under the existing rules. E-mail service will be mandatory for attorneys practicing in these divisions on October 1, 2013, at 12:01 a.m. (the date on which electronic filing will be mandatory in these divisions). See In re Electronic Filing, No. SC11-399, slip op. at 22 (Fla. June 21, 2012). Additionally, the new e-mail service requirements, as they apply in proceedings brought pursuant to the Florida Mental Health Act (Baker Act), Chapter 394, Part I, Florida Statutes, and the Involuntary Commitment of Sexually Violent Predators Act (Jimmy Ryce), Chapter 394, Part V, Florida Statutes, will also not be mandatory in these cases until October 1, 2013, at 12:01 a.m.

Finally, we note that, pursuant to rule 2.516(b)(1), self-repre-

sented parties involved in any type of case in any Florida court, may, but are not required to, serve documents by e-mail. Attorneys excused from e-mail service are also not obligated to comply with the new e-mail service requirements."

RULE 2.516. SERVICE OF PLEADINGS AND DOCUMENTS

This rule is subject to an implementation schedule. See the Editor's Notes at the end of the rule.

(a) Service; When Required. Unless the court otherwise orders, or a statute or supreme court administrative order specifies a different means of service, every pleading subsequent to the initial pleading and every other document filed in any court proceeding, except applications for witness subpoenas and documents served by formal notice or required to be served in the manner provided for service of formal notice, must be served in accordance with this rule on each party. No service need be made on parties against whom a default has been entered, except that pleadings asserting new or additional claims against them must be served in the manner provided for service of summons.

(b) Service; How Made. When service is required or permitted to be made upon a party represented by an attorney, service must be made upon the attorney unless service upon the party is ordered by the court.

(1) Service by Electronic Mail ("e-mail"). All documents required or permitted to be served on another party must be served by e-mail, unless this rule otherwise provides. When, in addition to service by e-mail, the sender also utilizes another means of service provided for in subdivision (b)(2), any differing time limits and other provisions applicable to that other means of service control.

(A) Service on Attorneys. Upon appearing in a proceeding, an attorney must serve a designation of a primary e-mail address and may designate no more than two secondary e-mail addresses. Thereafter, service must be directed to all designated e-mail addresses in that proceeding. Every document filed by an attorney thereafter must include the primary e-mail address of that attorney and any secondary e-mail addresses. If an attorney does not designate any e-mail address for service, documents may be served on that attorney at the e-mail address on record with The Florida Bar.

(B) Exception to E-mail Service on Attorneys. Service by an attorney on another attorney must be made by e-mail unless excused by the court. Upon motion by an attorney demonstrating that the attorney has no e-mail account and lacks access to the Internet at the attorney's office, the court may excuse the attorney from the requirements of e-mail service. Service on and by an attorney excused by the court from e-mail service must be by the means provided in subdivision (b)(2) of this rule.

(C) Service on and by Parties Not Represented by an Attorney. Any party not represented by an attorney may serve a designation of a primary e-mail address and also may designate no more than two secondary e-mail addresses to which service must be directed in that proceeding by the means provided in subdivision (b)(1) of this rule. If a party not represented by an attorney does not designate an e-mail address for service in a proceeding, service on and by that party must be by the means provided in subdivision (b)(2) of this rule.

(D) Time of Service. Service by e-mail is complete when it is sent.

(i) An e-mail is deemed served on the date it is sent.

(ii) If the sender learns that the e-mail did not reach the address of the person to be served, the sender must immediately send another copy by e-mail, or by a means authorized by subdivision (b)(2) of this rule.

(iii) E-mail service is treated as service by mail for the computation of time.

(E) Format of E-mail for Service. Service of a document by e-mail is made by an e-mail sent to all addresses designated by the attorney or party with either (a) a copy of the document in PDF format attached or (b) a link to the document on a website maintained by a clerk.

(i) All documents served by e-mail must be sent by an e-mail message containing a subject line beginning with the words "SERVICE OF COURT DOCU-MENT" in all capital letters, followed by the case number of the proceeding in which the documents are being served.

(ii) The body of the e-mail must identify the court in which the proceeding is pending, the case number, the name of the initial party on each side, the title of each document served with that e-mail, and the sender's name and telephone number.

(iii) Any document served by e-mail may be signed by any of the "/s/," "/s," or "s/" formats, as long as the filed original is signed in accordance with the applicable rule of procedure.

(iv) Any e-mail which, together with its attached documents, exceeds five megabytes (5MB) in size, must be divided and sent as separate e-mails, no one of which may exceed 5MB in size and each of which must be sequentially numbered in the subject line.

(2) Service by Other Means. In addition to, and not in lieu of, service by e-mail, service may also be made upon attorneys by any of the means specified in this subdivision (b)(2). Service on and by all parties who are not represented by an attorney and who do not designate an e-mail address, and on and by all attorneys excused from e-mail service, must be made by delivering a copy of the document or by mailing it to the party or attorney at their last known address or, if no address is known, by leaving it with the clerk of the court. Service by mail is complete upon mailing. Delivery of a copy within this rule is complete upon:

(A) handing it to the attorney or to the party,

(B) leaving it at the attorney's or party's office with a clerk or other person in charge thereof,

(C) if there is no one in charge, leaving it in a conspicuous place therein,

(D) if the office is closed or the person to be served has no office, leaving it at the person's usual place of abode with some person of his or her family above 15 years of age and informing such person of the contents, or

(E) transmitting it by facsimile to the attorney's or party's office with a cover sheet containing the sender's name, firm, address, telephone number, and facsimile number, and the number of pages transmitted. When service is made by facsimile, a copy must also be served by any other method permitted by this rule. Facsimile service occurs when transmission is complete.

(F) Service by delivery shall be deemed complete on the date of the delivery.

(c) Service; Numerous Defendants. In actions when the parties are unusually numerous, the court may regulate the service contemplated by these rules on motion or on its own initiative in such manner as may be found to be just and reasonable.

(d) Filing. All original documents must be filed with the court either before service or immediately thereafter, unless otherwise provided for by general law or other rules. If the original of any bond or other document is not placed in the court file, a certified copy must be so placed by the clerk.

(e) Filing Defined.

Text of rule effective prior to amendment by Florida Supreme Court in case number SC11-399. See also text of rule as amended by Florida Supreme Court in case number SC11-399 below.

The filing of documents with the court as required by these rules must be made by filing them with the clerk, except that the judge may permit documents to be filed with the judge, in which event the judge must note the filing date before him or her on the documents and transmit them to the clerk. The date of filing is that shown on the face of the document by the judge's notation or the clerk's time stamp, whichever is earlier.

(e) Filing Defined.

Text of rule as amended by Florida Supreme Court in case number SC11-399. See also text of rule prior to amendment by Florida Supreme Court in case number SC11-399 above.

The filing of documents with the court as required by these rules must be made by filing them with the clerk in accordance with rule 2.525, except that the judge may permit documents to be filed with the judge, in which event the judge must note the filing date before him or her on the documents and transmit them to the clerk. The date of filing is that shown on the face of the document by the judge's notation or the clerk's time stamp, whichever is earlier.

(f) Certificate of Service. When any attorney certifies in substance:

"I certify that a copy hereof has been furnished to (here insert name or names and addresses used for service) by (e-mail) (delivery) (mail) (fax) on .....(date).....

———————————————————

Attorney"

the certificate is taken as prima facie proof of such service in compliance with this rule.

(g) Service by Clerk. When the clerk is required to serve notices and other documents, the clerk may do so by e-mail as provided in subdivision (b)(1) or by any other method permitted under subdivision (b)(2). Service by a clerk is not required to be by e-mail.

(h) Service of Orders.

(1) A copy of all orders or judgments must be transmitted by the court or under its direction to all parties at the time of entry of the order or judgment. No service need be made on parties against whom a default has been entered except orders setting an action for trial and final judgments that must be prepared and served as provided in subdivision (h)(2). The court may require that orders or judgments be prepared by a party, may require the party to furnish the court with stamped, addressed envelopes for service of the order or judgment, and may require that proposed orders and judgments be furnished to all parties before entry by the court of the order or judgment. The court may serve any order or judgment by e-mail to all attorneys who have not been excused from e-mail service and to all parties not represented by an attorney who have designated an e-mail address for service.

(2) When a final judgment is entered against a party in default, the court must mail a conformed copy

of it to the party. The party in whose favor the judgment is entered must furnish the court with a copy of the judgment, unless it is prepared by the court, with the address of the party to be served. If the address is unknown, the copy need not be furnished.

(3) This subdivision is directory and a failure to comply with it does not affect the order or judgment, its finality, or any proceedings arising in the action.

Editor's Notes: — On October 18, 2012 the Supreme Court of Florida issued a revision to its opinion in SC10-2101, originally issued on June 21, 2012. It provides in relevant part: "We accept the [Criminal Procedure Rules Committee and Florida Public Defender Association] workgroup's recommendation to delay mandatory e-mail service in the criminal, traffic, and juvenile divisions of the trial court until electronic filing is also mandatory in these divisions. Accordingly, the rule amendments that we adopt in this case are effective, nunc pro tunc, September 1, 2012, at 12:01 a.m.; however, they will be implemented as set forth in this opinion.

First, e-mail service will be mandatory for attorneys practicing in the civil, probate, small claims, and family law divisions of the trial courts, as well as in all appellate cases, when the rule amendments take effect on September 1, 2012.

Second, when the rules take effect on September 1, attorneys practicing in the criminal, traffic, and juvenile divisions of the trial court may voluntarily choose to serve documents by e-mail under the new procedures, or they may continue to operate under the existing rules. E-mail service will be mandatory for attorneys practicing in these divisions on October 1, 2013, at 12:01 a.m. (the date on which electronic filing will be mandatory in these divisions). See In re Electronic Filing, No. SC11-399, slip op. at 22 (Fla. June 21, 2012). Additionally, the new e-mail service requirements, as they apply in proceedings brought pursuant to the Florida Mental Health Act (Baker Act), Chapter 394, Part I, Florida Statutes, and the Involuntary Commitment of Sexually Violent Predators Act (Jimmy Ryce), Chapter 394, Part V, Florida Statutes, will also not be mandatory in these cases until October 1, 2013, at 12:01 a.m.

Finally, we note that, pursuant to rule 2.516(b)(1), self-represented parties involved in any type of case in any Florida court, may, but are not required to, serve documents by e-mail. Attorneys excused from e-mail service are also not obligated to comply with the new e-mail service requirements."

On October 18, 2012, the Supreme Court of Florida issued a revised opinion in case number SC11-399, which was originally issued on June 21, 2012. See *In re Amendments to the Florida Rules of Judicial Administration*, 37 FLW S643 (Fla. 2012). The opinion provides in relevant part:

"First, the new electronic filing requirements the Court adopts will become effective in the civil, probate, small claims, and family law divisions of the trial courts, as well as for appeals to the circuit courts in these categories of cases, on April 1, 2013, at 12:01 a.m., except as may be otherwise provided by administrative order. Electronic filing will be mandatory in these divisions pursuant to

rule 2.525 on that date. However, until the new rules take effect in these divisions, any clerk who is already accepting documents filed by electronic transmission under the current rules should continue to do so; attorneys in these counties are encouraged to file documents electronically under the current rules.

"Next, the new electronic filing requirements the Court adopts will become effective in the criminal, traffic, and juvenile divisions of the trial courts, as well as for appeals to the circuit court in these categories of cases, on October 1, 2013, at 12:01 a.m., except as may be otherwise provided by administrative order. Electronic filing will be mandatory in these divisions under rule 2.525 on that date. The new e-filing requirements, as they apply in proceedings brought pursuant to the Florida Mental Health Act (Baker Act), Chapter 394, Part I, Florida Statutes, and the Involuntary Commitment of Sexually Violent Predators Act (Jimmy Ryce), Chapter 394, Part V, Florida Statutes, will also not be mandatory in these cases until October 1, 2013. As stated above, until the new rules take effect in these divisions and proceedings, any clerk who is already accepting electronically filed documents under the current rules should continue to do so; attorneys are again encouraged to utilize existing electronic filing procedures under the current rules.

"However, until the new rules and procedures take effect in the district courts, any clerk who is already accepting documents filed by electronic transmission may continue to do so; attorneys in these districts are encouraged to file documents electronically. Clerks will not be required to electronically transmit the record on appeal until July 1, 2013, at 12:01 a.m. Until July 1, we encourage clerks, whenever possible, to electronically transmit the record under the new rules and requirements.

"(W)e note that, in all types of cases, pursuant to amended rule 2.525(d) self-represented parties and self-represented nonparties, including nonparty governmental or public agencies, and attorneys excused from e-mail service under Florida Rule of Judicial Administration 2.516 will be permitted, but not required, to file documents electronically.

By order of November 28, 2012, in case number SC11-399, the Court released a revised implementation schedule, which provides, in pertinent part: "The e-filing rules adopted in the October 2012 opinion will be mandatory in this (Supreme) Court on February 27, 2013, at 12:01 a.m.; and effective earlier on a voluntary basis as will be indicated by further administrative order of the chief justice.

"Thereafter, the e-filing rules will be mandatory in the Second District Court of Appeal on July 22, 2013, at 12:01 a.m.; in the Third District Court of Appeal on September 27, 2013, at 12:01 a.m.; in the Fourth District Court of Appeal on October 31, 2013, at 12:01 a.m.; in the Fifth District Court of Appeal on November 27, 2013 at 12:01 a.m.; and in the First District Court of Appeal on December 27, 2013, at 12:01 a.m., unless made mandatory earlier by the chief judge of the applicable district court of appeal. The e-filing rules will be effective earlier on a voluntary trial basis in the district courts of appeal as will be indicated by further administrative order by the chief judge of the applicable district court."

RULE 2.520. DOCUMENTS

Text of rule effective prior to amendment by Florida Supreme Court in case number SC11-399. See also text of rule as amended by Florida Supreme Court in case number SC11-399 below.

(a) Type and Size. All pleadings, motions, petitions, briefs, notices, orders, judgments, decrees, opinions, and other papers and official documents filed in any court shall be filed on recycled paper measuring 8 1/2 by 11 inches. For purposes of this rule, paper is recycled if it contains a minimum content of 50 percent waste paper. Xerographic reduction of legal-size (8 1/2 by 14 inches) documents to letter size (8 1/2 by 11 inches) is prohibited.

(b) Exhibits. Any exhibit or attachment filed with pleadings or papers may be filed in its original size.

(c) Recording Space. On all papers and documents prepared and filed by the court or by any party to a proceeding which are to be recorded in the public records of any county, including but not limited to final money judgments and notices of lis pendens, a 3-inch by 3-inch space at the top right-hand corner on the first page and a 1-inch by 3-inch space at the top right-hand corner on each subsequent page shall be left blank and reserved for use by the clerk of court.

(d) Exceptions to Recording Space. Any papers or documents created by persons or entities over which the filing party has no control, including but not limited to wills, codicils, trusts, or other testamentary documents; documents prepared or executed by any public officer; documents prepared, executed, acknowledged, or proved outside of the State of Florida; or documents created by State or Federal government agencies, may be filed without the space required by this rule.

(e) Noncompliance. No clerk of court shall refuse for filing any document or paper because of noncompliance with this rule. However, upon request of the clerk of court, noncomplying documents shall be resubmitted in accordance with this rule.

Court Commentary

1989 Adoption. Rule 2.055 [renumbered as 2.520 in 2006] is new. This rule aligns Florida's court system with the federal court system and the court systems of the majority of our sister states by requiring in subdivision (a) that all pleadings, motions, petitions, briefs, notices, orders, judgments, decrees, opinions, or other papers filed with any Florida court be submitted on paper measuring 8 1/2

by 11 inches. Subdivision (e) provides a 1-year transition period from the effective date of January 1, 1990, to January 1, 1991, during which time filings that traditionally have been accepted on legal-size paper will be accepted on either legal- or letter-size paper. The 1-year transition period was provided to allow for the depletion of inventories of legal-size paper and forms. The 1-year transition period was not intended to affect compliance with Florida Rule of Appellate Procedure 9.210(a)(1), which requires that typewritten appellate briefs be filed on paper measuring 8 1/2 by 11 inches. Nor was it intended that the requirement of Florida Rule of Appellate Procedure 9.210(a)(1) that printed briefs measure 6 by 9 inches be affected by the requirements of subdivision (a).

Subdivision (b), which recognizes an exception for exhibits or attachments, is intended to apply to documents such as wills and traffic citations which traditionally have not been generated on lettersize paper.

Subdivision (c) was adopted to ensure that a 1 1/2 inch square at the top right-hand corner of all filings is reserved for use by the clerk of court. Subdivision (d) was adopted to ensure that all papers and documents submitted for filing will be considered filed on the date of submission regardless of paper size. Subdivision (d) also ensures that after the 1-year transition period of subdivision (e), filings that are not in compliance with the rule are resubmitted on paper measuring 8 1/2 by 11 inches.

This rule is not intended to apply to those instruments and documents presented to the clerk of the circuit court for recording in the Official Records under section 28.222, Florida Statutes (1987). It is also not intended to apply to matters submitted to the clerk of the circuit court in the capacity as ex officio clerk of the board of county commissioners pursuant to article VIII, section (1)(d), Florida Constitution.

1996 Amendment. Subdivision (c) was amended to make the blank space requirements for use by the clerk of the court consistent with section 695.26, Florida Statutes (1995). Subdivision (e) was eliminated because the transition period for letter-size and recycled paper was no longer necessary.

RULE 2.520. DOCUMENTS

Text of rule as amended by Florida Supreme Court in case number SC11-399. See also text of rule prior to amendment by Florida Supreme Court in case number SC11-399 above. This rule is subject to an implementation schedule. See the Editor's Notes at the end of the rule.

(a) Electronic Filing Mandatory. All documents filed in any court shall be filed by electronic transmission in accordance with rule 2.525. "Documents" means pleadings, motions, petitions, memoranda, briefs, notices, exhibits, declarations, affidavits, orders, judgments, decrees, writs, opinions, and any other paper or writing submitted to a court.

(b) Type and Size. Documents subject to the exceptions set forth in rule 2.525(d) shall be filed on recycled paper measuring 8 1/2 by 11 inches. For purposes of this rule, paper is recycled if it contains a minimum content of 50 percent waste paper. Xerographic reduction of legal-size (8 1/2 by 14 inches) documents to letter size (8 1/2 by 11 inches) is prohibited. All other documents filed by electronic transmission shall be filed in a format capable of being printed in a format consistent with the provisions of this rule.

(c) Exhibits. Any exhibit or attachment filed with pleadings or papers may be filed in its original size.

(d) Recording Space. On all papers and documents prepared and filed by the court or by any party to a proceeding which are to be recorded in the public records of any county, including but not limited to final money judgments and notices of lis pendens, a 3-inch by 3-inch space at the top right-hand corner on the first page and a 1-inch by 3-inch space at the top right-hand corner on each subsequent page shall be left blank and reserved for use by the clerk of court.

(e) Exceptions to Recording Space. Any papers or documents created by persons or entities over which the filing party has no control, including but not limited to wills, codicils, trusts, or other testamentary documents; documents prepared or executed by any public officer; documents prepared, executed, acknowledged, or proved outside of the State of Florida; or documents created by State or Federal government agencies, may be filed without the space required by this rule.

(f) Noncompliance. No clerk of court shall refuse for filing any document or paper because of noncompliance with this rule. However, upon request of the clerk of court, noncomplying documents shall be resubmitted in accordance with this rule.

Editor's Notes: — On October 18, 2012, the Supreme Court of Florida issued a revised opinion in case number SC11-399, which was originally issued on June 21, 2012. See *In re Amendments to the Florida Rules of Judicial Administration*, 37 FLW S643 (Fla. 2012). The opinion provides in relevant part:

"First, the new electronic filing requirements the Court adopts will become effective in the civil, probate, small claims, and family law divisions of the trial courts, as well as for appeals to the circuit courts in these categories of cases, on April 1, 2013, at 12:01 a.m., except as may be otherwise provided by administrative order.

Electronic filing will be mandatory in these divisions pursuant to rule 2.525 on that date. However, until the new rules take effect in these divisions, any clerk who is already accepting documents filed by electronic transmission under the current rules should continue to do so; attorneys in these counties are encouraged to file documents electronically under the current rules.

"Next, the new electronic filing requirements the Court adopts will become effective in the criminal, traffic, and juvenile divisions of the trial courts, as well as for appeals to the circuit court in these categories of cases, on October 1, 2013, at 12:01 a.m., except as may be otherwise provided by administrative order. Electronic filing will be mandatory in these divisions under rule 2.525 on that date. The new e-filing requirements, as they apply in proceedings brought pursuant to the Florida Mental Health Act (Baker Act), Chapter 394, Part I, Florida Statutes, and the Involuntary Commitment of Sexually Violent Predators Act (Jimmy Ryce), Chapter 394, Part V, Florida Statutes, will also not be mandatory in these cases until October 1, 2013. As stated above, until the new rules take effect in these divisions and proceedings, any clerk who is already accepting electronically filed documents under the current rules should continue to do so; attorneys are again encouraged to utilize existing electronic filing procedures under the current rules.

"However, until the new rules and procedures take effect in the district courts, any clerk who is already accepting documents filed by electronic transmission may continue to do so; attorneys in these districts are encouraged to file documents electronically. Clerks will not be required to electronically transmit the record on appeal until July 1, 2013, at 12:01 a.m. Until July 1, we encourage clerks, whenever possible, to electronically transmit the record under the new rules and requirements.

"(W)e note that, in all types of cases, pursuant to amended rule 2.525(d) self-represented parties and self-represented nonparties, including nonparty governmental or public agencies, and attorneys excused from e-mail service under Florida Rule of Judicial Administration 2.516 will be permitted, but not required, to file documents electronically.

By order of November 28, 2012, in case number SC11-399, the Court released a revised implementation schedule, which provides, in pertinent part: "The e-filing rules adopted in the October 2012 opinion will be mandatory in this (Supreme) Court on February 27, 2013, at 12:01 a.m.; and effective earlier on a voluntary basis as will be indicated by further administrative order of the chief justice.

"Thereafter, the e-filing rules will be mandatory in the Second District Court of Appeal on July 22, 2013, at 12:01 a.m.; in the Third District Court of Appeal on September 27, 2013, at 12:01 a.m.; in the Fourth District Court of Appeal on October 31, 2013, at 12:01 a.m.; in the Fifth District Court of Appeal on November 27, 2013 at 12:01 a.m.; and in the First District Court of Appeal on December 27, 2013, at 12:01 a.m., unless made mandatory earlier by the chief judge of the applicable district court of appeal. The e-filing rules will be effective earlier on a voluntary trial basis in the district courts of appeal as will be indicated by further administrative order by the chief judge of the applicable district court."

Court Commentary

1989 Adoption. Rule 2.055 [renumbered as 2.520 in 2006] is new. This rule aligns Florida's court system with the federal court system and the court systems of the majority of our sister states by requiring in subdivision (a) that all pleadings, motions, petitions, briefs, notices, orders, judgments, decrees, opinions, or other papers filed with any Florida court be submitted on paper measuring 8 1/2 by 11 inches. Subdivision (e) provides a 1-year transition period from the effective date of January 1, 1990, to January 1, 1991, during which time filings that traditionally have been accepted on legal-size paper will be accepted on either legal- or letter-size paper. The 1-year transition period was provided to allow for the depletion of inventories of legal-size paper and forms. The 1-year transition period was not intended to affect compliance with Florida Rule of Appellate Procedure 9.210(a)(1), which requires that typewritten appellate briefs be filed on paper measuring 8 1/2 by 11 inches. Nor was it intended that the requirement of Florida Rule of Appellate Procedure 9.210(a)(1) that printed briefs measure 6 by 9 inches be affected by the requirements of subdivision (a).

Subdivision (b), which recognizes an exception for exhibits or attachments, is intended to apply to documents such as wills and traffic citations which traditionally have not been generated on lettersize paper.

Subdivision (c) was adopted to ensure that a 1 1/2 inch square at the top right-hand corner of all filings is reserved for use by the clerk of court. Subdivision (d) was adopted to ensure that all papers and documents submitted for filing will be considered filed on the date of submission regardless of paper size. Subdivision (d) also ensures that after the 1-year transition period of subdivision (e), filings that are not in compliance with the rule are resubmitted on paper measuring 8 1/2 by 11 inches.

This rule is not intended to apply to those instruments and documents presented to the clerk of the circuit court for recording in the Official Records under section 28.222, Florida Statutes (1987). It is also not intended to apply to matters submitted to the clerk of the circuit court in the capacity as ex officio clerk of the board of county commissioners pursuant to article VIII, section (1)(d), Florida Constitution.

1996 Amendment. Subdivision (c) was amended to make the blank space requirements for use by the clerk of the court consistent with section 695.26, Florida Statutes (1995). Subdivision (e) was eliminated because the transition period for letter-size and recycled paper was no longer necessary.

RULE 2.525. ELECTRONIC FILING

Text of rule effective prior to amendment by Florida Supreme Court in case number SC11-399. See also text of rule as amended by Florida Supreme Court in case number SC11-399 below.

(a) Definition. "Electronic transmission of documents" means the transmission by electronic signals, to or from a court or clerk of the court, of information which when received can be transformed and stored or reproduced on paper, microfilm, magnetic storage device, optical imaging system, or other electronic record keeping system authorized by the Supreme Court of Florida in a format sufficient to communicate the information on the original document in a readable format.

(b) Application. Any court or clerk of the court may accept the electronic transmission of documents for filing after the clerk, together with input from the chief judge of the circuit, has obtained approval of the procedures and program for doing so from the Supreme Court of Florida.

(c) Documents Affected.

(1) All documents that are court records, as defined in rule 2.430(a)(1), may be filed by electronic transmission provided that:

(A) the clerk of court has the ability to accept and retain such documents;

(B) the clerk of court or the chief judge of the circuit has requested permission to accept documents filed by electronic transmission; and

(C) the Supreme Court of Florida has entered an order granting permission to the clerk of court to accept documents filed by electronic transmission.

Any attorney, party, or other person who files a document by electronic transmission shall, immediately thereafter, file the identical document, in paper form, with an original signature of the attorney, party, or other person if a signature is otherwise required by these rules (hereinafter called the follow-up filing).

(2) The follow-up filing of any document that has previously been filed by electronic transmission may be discontinued if:

(A) after a 90-day period of accepting electronically filed documents, the clerk of court or the chief judge of the circuit certifies to the Supreme Court of Florida that the electronic filing system is efficient, reliable, and meets the demands of all parties;

(B) the clerk of court or the chief judge of the circuit requests permission to discontinue that portion of the rule requiring a follow-up filing of documents in paper form, except as otherwise required by general law, statute, or court rule; and

(C) the Supreme Court of Florida enters an order directing the clerk of court to discontinue accepting the follow-up filing.

(d) Service. Paper documents and other submissions may be manually submitted to the clerk or court:

(1) Electronic transmission may be used by a court for the service of all orders of whatever nature provided the clerk, together with input from the chief judge of the circuit, has obtained approval from the Supreme Court of Florida of the specific procedures and program to be used in transmitting the orders. All other requirements for the service of such an order shall be met.

(2) Any document electronically transmitted to a court or clerk of the court shall also be served on all parties and interested persons in accordance with the applicable rules of court.

(e) Transmission Difficulties. Any attorney, party, or other person who elects to file any document by electronic transmission shall be responsible for any delay, disruption, interruption of the electronic signals, and readability of the document, and accepts the full risk that the document may not be properly filed with the clerk as a result.

(f) Administration.

(1) Any clerk of the court who, after obtaining Supreme Court of Florida approval, accepts for filing documents that have been electronically transmitted shall:

(A) provide electronic or telephonic access to its equipment during regular business hours; and

(B) accept electronic transmission of documents up to 10 pages in length.

(2) All attorneys, parties, or other persons using this rule to file documents are required to make arrangements with the court or clerk of the court for

the payment of any charges authorized by general law or the Supreme Court of Florida before filing any document by electronic transmission.

(3) The filing date for an electronically transmitted document shall be the date the last page thereof is received by the court or clerk of the court.

(4) Any court or clerk of the court may extend the hours of access or increase the page limitations set forth in this subdivision.

(g) Accessibility. All documents transmitted in any electronic form under this rule must comply with the accessibility requirements of Florida Rule of Judicial Administration 2.526.

Court Commentary

1997 Amendment. Originally, the rule provided that the follow-up filing had to occur within ten days. In the 1997 amendment to the rule, that requirement was modified to provide that the follow-up filing must occur "immediately" after a document is electronically filed. The "immediately thereafter" language is consistent with language used in the rules of procedure where, in a somewhat analogous situation, the filing of a document may occur after service. *See, e.g.,* Florida Rule of Civil Procedure 1.080(d) ("All original papers shall be filed with the court either before service or *immediately thereafter.*") (emphasis added). "Immediately thereafter" has been interpreted to mean "filed with reasonable promptness." *Miami Transit Co. v. Ford,* 155 So.2d 360 (Fla.1963).

The use of the words "other person" in this rule is not meant to allow a nonlawyer to sign and file pleadings or other papers on behalf of another. Such conduct would constitute the unauthorized practice of law.

RULE 2.525. ELECTRONIC FILING

Text of rule as amended by Florida Supreme Court in case number SC11-399. See also text of rule prior to amendment by Florida Supreme Court in case number SC11-399 above. This rule is subject to an implementation schedule. See the Editor's Notes at the end of the rule.

(a) Definition. "Electronic transmission of documents" means the sending of information by electronic signals to, by or from a court or clerk which when received can be transformed and stored or transmitted on paper, microfilm, magnetic storage device, optical imaging system, CD-ROM, flash drive, other electronic data storage system, server, case maintenance system ("CM"), electronic court filing ("ECF") system, statewide or local electronic portal ("e-portal"), or other electronic record keeping system authorized by the supreme court in a format sufficient to communicate the information on the original document in a readable format. Electronic transmission of documents includes electronic mail ("e-mail") and any internet-based transmission procedure, and may include procedures allowing for documents to be signed or verified by electronic means.

(b) Application. Any court or clerk may accept the electronic transmission of documents for filing and may send documents by electronic transmission after the clerk, together with input from the chief judge of the circuit, has obtained approval of the procedures, programs, and standards for electronic filing from the supreme court ("ECF Procedures"). All ECF Procedures must comply with the then-current e-filing standards, as promulgated by the supreme court in Administrative Order No. AOSC09-30, or subsequent administrative order.

(c) Documents Affected.

(1) All documents that are court records, as defined in rule 2.430(a)(1), must be filed by electronic transmission provided that:

(A) the clerk has the ability to accept and retain such documents;

(B) the clerk or the chief judge of the circuit has requested permission to accept documents filed by electronic transmission; and

(C) the supreme court has entered an order granting permission to the clerk to accept documents filed by electronic transmission.

(2) The official court file is a set of electronic documents stored in a computer system maintained by the clerk, together with any supplemental non-electronic documents and materials authorized by this rule. It consists of:

(A) documents filed by electronic transmission under this rule;

(B) documents filed in paper form under subdivision (d) that have been converted to electronic form by the clerk;

(C) documents filed in paper form before the effective date of this rule that have been converted to electronic form by the clerk;

(D) documents filed in paper form before the effective date of this rule or under subdivision (d), unless such documents are converted into electronic form by the clerk;

(E) electronic documents filed pursuant to subdivision (d)(5); and

(F) materials and documents filed pursuant to any rule, statute or court order that either cannot be converted into electronic form or are required to be maintained in paper form.

(3) The documents in the official court file are deemed originals for all purposes except as otherwise provided by statute or rule.

(4) Any document in paper form submitted under subdivision (d) is filed when it is received by the clerk or court and the clerk shall immediately thereafter convert any filed paper document to an electronic document. "Convert to an electronic document" means optically capturing an image of a paper document and using character recognition software to recover as much of the document's text as practicable and then indexing and storing the document in the official court file.

(5) Any storage medium submitted under subdivision (d)(5) is filed when received by the clerk or court and the clerk shall immediately thereafter transfer the electronic documents from the storage device to the official court file.

(6) If the filer of any paper document authorized under subdivision (d) provides a self-addressed, postage-paid envelope for return of the paper document after it is converted to electronic form by the clerk, the clerk shall place the paper document in the envelope and deposit it in the mail. Except when a paper

document is required to be maintained, the clerk may recycle any filed paper document that is not to be returned to the filer.

(7) The clerk may convert any paper document filed before the effective date of this rule to an electronic document. Unless the clerk is required to maintain the paper document, if the paper document has been converted to an electronic document by the clerk, the paper document is no longer part of the official court file and may be removed and recycled.

(d) Exceptions. Paper documents and other submissions may be manually submitted to the clerk or court:

(1) when the clerk does not have the ability to accept and retain documents by electronic filing or has not had ECF Procedures approved by the supreme court;

(2) for filing by any self-represented party or any self-represented nonparty unless specific ECF Procedures provide a means to file documents electronically. However, any self-represented nonparty that is a governmental or public agency and any other agency, partnership, corporation, or business entity acting on behalf of any governmental or public agency may file documents by electronic transmission if such entity has the capability of filing documents electronically;

(3) for filing by attorneys excused from e-mail service in accordance with rule 2.516(b);

(4) when submitting evidentiary exhibits or filing non-documentary materials;

(5) when the filing involves documents in excess of 25 megabytes (25MB) in size. For such filings, documents may be transmitted using an electronic storage medium that the clerk has the ability to accept, which may include a CD-ROM, flash drive, or similar storage medium;

(6) when filed in open court, as permitted by the court;

(7) when paper filing is permitted by any approved statewide or local ECF procedures; and

(8) if any court determines that justice so requires.

(e) Service.

(1) Electronic transmission may be used by a court or clerk for the service of all orders of whatever nature, pursuant to rule 2.516(h), and for the service of any documents pursuant to any ECF Procedures, provided the clerk, together with input from the chief judge of the circuit, has obtained approval from the supreme court of ECF Procedures containing the specific procedures and program to be used in transmitting the orders and documents. All other requirements for the service of such orders must be met.

(2) Any document electronically transmitted to a court or clerk must also be served on all parties and interested persons in accordance with the applicable rules of court.

(f) Administration.

(1) Any clerk who, after obtaining supreme court approval, accepts for filing documents that have been electronically transmitted must:

(A) provide electronic or telephonic access to its equipment, whether through an e-portal or otherwise, during regular business hours, and all other times as practically feasible;

(B) accept electronic transmission of documents up to 25 megabytes (25MB) in size, or until e-filing has been fully implemented, accept facsimile transmissions of documents up to 10 pages in length; and

(C) accept filings in excess of 25 megabytes (25MB) in size by electronic storage device or system, which may include a CD-ROM, flash drive, or similar storage system.

(2) All attorneys, parties, or other persons using this rule to file documents are required to make arrangements with the court or clerk for the payment of any charges authorized by general law or the supreme court before filing any document by electronic transmission.

(3) The filing date for an electronically transmitted document is the date and time that such filing is

acknowledged by an electronic stamp or otherwise, pursuant to any procedure set forth in any ECF Procedures approved by the supreme court, or the date the last page of such filing is received by the court or clerk.

(4) Any court or clerk may extend the hours of access or increase the page or size limitations set forth in this subdivision.

(g) Accessibility. All documents transmitted in any electronic form under this rule must comply with the accessibility requirements of Florida Rule of Judicial Administration 2.526.

Editor's Notes: — On October 18, 2012, the Supreme Court of Florida issued a revised opinion in case number SC11-399, which was originally issued on June 21, 2012. See *In re Amendments to the Florida Rules of Judicial Administration*, 37 FLW S643 (Fla. 2012). The opinion provides in relevant part:

"First, the new electronic filing requirements the Court adopts will become effective in the civil, probate, small claims, and family law divisions of the trial courts, as well as for appeals to the circuit courts in these categories of cases, on April 1, 2013, at 12:01 a.m., except as may be otherwise provided by administrative order. Electronic filing will be mandatory in these divisions pursuant to rule 2.525 on that date. However, until the new rules take effect in these divisions, any clerk who is already accepting documents filed by electronic transmission under the current rules should continue to do so; attorneys in these counties are encouraged to file documents electronically under the current rules.

"Next, the new electronic filing requirements the Court adopts will become effective in the criminal, traffic, and juvenile divisions of the trial courts, as well as for appeals to the circuit court in these categories of cases, on October 1, 2013, at 12:01 a.m., except as may be otherwise provided by administrative order. Electronic filing will be mandatory in these divisions under rule 2.525 on that date. The new e-filing requirements, as they apply in proceedings brought pursuant to the Florida Mental Health Act (Baker Act), Chapter 394, Part I, Florida Statutes, and the Involuntary Commitment of Sexually Violent Predators Act (Jimmy Ryce), Chapter 394, Part V, Florida Statutes, will also not be mandatory in these cases until October 1, 2013. As stated above, until the new rules take effect in these divisions and proceedings, any clerk who is already accepting electronically filed documents under the current rules should continue to do so; attorneys are again encouraged to utilize existing electronic filing procedures under the current rules.

"However, until the new rules and procedures take effect in the district courts, any clerk who is already accepting documents filed by electronic transmission may continue to do so; attorneys in these districts are encouraged to file documents electronically. Clerks will not be required to electronically transmit the record on appeal until July 1, 2013, at 12:01 a.m. Until July 1, we encourage clerks, whenever possible, to electronically transmit the record under the new rules and requirements.

"(W)e note that, in all types of cases, pursuant to amended rule 2.525(d) self-represented parties and self-represented nonparties, including nonparty governmental or public agencies, and attorneys excused from e-mail service under Florida Rule of Judicial Administration 2.516 will be permitted, but not required, to file documents electronically.

By order of November 28, 2012, in case number SC11-399, the Court released a revised implementation schedule, which provides, in pertinent part: "The e-filing rules adopted in the October 2012 opinion will be mandatory in this (Supreme) Court on February 27, 2013, at 12:01 a.m.; and effective earlier on a voluntary basis as will be indicated by further administrative order of the chief justice.

"Thereafter, the e-filing rules will be mandatory in the Second District Court of Appeal on July 22, 2013, at 12:01 a.m.; in the Third District Court of Appeal on September 27, 2013, at 12:01 a.m.; in the Fourth District Court of Appeal on October 31, 2013, at 12:01 a.m.; in the Fifth District Court of Appeal on November 27, 2013 at 12:01 a.m.; and in the First District Court of Appeal on December 27, 2013, at 12:01 a.m., unless made mandatory earlier by the chief judge of the applicable district court of appeal. The e-filing rules will be effective earlier on a voluntary trial basis in the district courts of appeal as will be indicated by further administrative order by the chief judge of the applicable district court."

Court Commentary

1997 Amendment. Originally, the rule provided that the follow-up filing had to occur within ten days. In the 1997 amendment to the rule, that requirement was modified to provide that the follow-up filing must occur "immediately" after a document is electronically filed. The "immediately thereafter" language is consistent with language used in the rules of procedure where, in a somewhat analogous situation, the filing of a document may occur after service. See, e.g., Florida Rule of Civil Procedure 1.080(d) ("All original papers shall be filed with the court either before service or *immediately thereafter.*") (emphasis added). "Immediately thereafter" has been interpreted to mean "filed with reasonable promptness." *Miami Transit Co. v. Ford,* 155 So.2d 360 (Fla.1963).

The use of the words "other person" in this rule is not meant to allow a nonlawyer to sign and file pleadings or other papers on behalf of another. Such conduct would constitute the unauthorized practice of law.

RULE 2.526. ACCESSIBILITY OF INFORMATION AND TECHNOLOGY

Any document that is or will become a judicial branch record, as defined in rule 2.420(b)(1), and that is transmitted in an electronic form, as defined in rule 2.525, must be formatted in a manner that complies with all state and federal laws requiring that electronic judicial records be accessible to persons with disabilities, including without limitation the Americans with Disabilities Act and Section 508 of the federal Rehabilitation Act of 1973 as incorporated into Florida law by section 282.603(1), Florida Statutes (2010), and any related federal or state regulations or administrative rules.

RULE 2.530. COMMUNICATION EQUIPMENT

(a) **Definition.** Communication equipment means a conference telephone or other electronic device that permits all those appearing or participating to hear and speak to each other, provided that all conversation of all parties is audible to all persons present.

(b) **Use by all Parties.** A county or circuit court judge may, upon the court's own motion or upon the written request of a party, direct that communication equipment be used for a motion hearing, pretrial conference, or a status conference. A judge must give notice to the parties and consider any objections they may have to the use of communication equipment before directing that communication equipment be used. The decision to use communication equipment over the objection of parties will be in the sound discretion of the trial court, except as noted below.

(c) **Use Only by Requesting Party.** A county or circuit court judge may, upon the written request of a party upon reasonable notice to all other parties, permit a requesting party to participate through communication equipment in a scheduled motion hearing; however, any such request (except in criminal, juvenile, and appellate proceedings) must be granted, absent a showing of good cause to deny the same, where the hearing is set for not longer than 15 minutes.

(d) **Testimony.**

(1) **Generally.** A county or circuit court judge, general magistrate, special magistrate, or hearing officer may allow testimony to be taken through communication equipment if all parties consent or if permitted by another applicable rule of procedure.

(2) **Procedure.** Any party desiring to present testimony through communication equipment shall, prior to the hearing or trial at which the testimony is to be presented, contact all parties to determine whether each party consents to this form of testimony. The party seeking to present the testimony shall move for permission to present testimony through communication equipment, which motion shall set forth good cause as to why the testimony should be allowed in this form.

(3) **Oath.** Testimony may be taken through communication equipment only if a notary public or other person authorized to administer oaths in the witness's jurisdiction is present with the witness and administers the oath consistent with the laws of the jurisdiction.

(4) **Confrontation Rights.** In juvenile and criminal proceedings the defendant must make an informed waiver of any confrontation rights that may be abridged by the use of communication equipment.

(5) **Video Testimony.** If the testimony to be presented utilizes video conferencing or comparable two-way visual capabilities, the court in its discretion may modify the procedures set forth in this rule to accommodate the technology utilized.

(e) **Burden of Expense.** The cost for the use of the communication equipment is the responsibility of the requesting party unless otherwise directed by the court.

(f) **Override of Family Violence Indicator.** Communications equipment may be used for a hearing on a petition to override a family violence indicator under Florida Family Law Rule of Procedure 12.650.

RULE 2.535. COURT REPORTING

This rule is subject to an implementation schedule. See the Editor's Notes at the end of the rule.

(a) **Definitions.**

(1) "Approved court reporter" means a court employee or contractor who performs court reporting services, including transcription, at public expense and who meets the court's certification, training, and other qualifications for court reporting.

(2) "Approved transcriptionist" means a court employee, contractor, or other individual who performs

transcription services at public expense and who meets the court's certification, training, and other qualifications for transcribing proceedings.

(3) "Civil court reporter" means a court reporter who performs court reporting services in civil proceedings not required to be reported at public expense, and who meets the court's certification, training, and other qualifications for court reporting.

(4) "Court reporting" means the act of making a verbatim record of the spoken word, whether by the use of written symbols, stenomask equipment, stenographic equipment, or electronic devices, in any proceedings pending in any of the courts of this state, including all discovery proceedings conducted in connection therewith, any proceedings reported for the court's own use, and all proceedings required by statute to be reported by a certified or officialan approved court reporter or civil court reporter. It does not mean the act of taking witness statements not intended for use in court as substantive evidence.

(5) "Electronic record" means the audio, analog, digital, or video record of a court proceeding.

Text of rule effective prior to amendment by Florida Supreme Court in case number SC11-399. See also text of rule as amended by Florida Supreme Court in case number SC11-399 below.

(6) "Official record" means the transcript, which is the written record of court proceedings and depositions prepared in accordance with the requirements of subdivision (f).

Text of rule as amended by Florida Supreme Court in case number SC11-399. See also text of rule prior to amendment by Florida Supreme Court in case number SC11-399 above.

(6) "Official record" means the transcript, which is the written or electronically stored record of court proceedings and depositions prepared in accordance with the requirements of subdivision (f).

(b) When Court Reporting Required. Any proceeding shall be reported on the request of any party. The party so requesting shall pay the reporting fees, but this requirement shall not preclude the taxation of costs as authorized by law.

(c) Record. When trial proceedings are being reported, no part of the proceedings shall be omitted unless all of the parties agree to do so and the court approves the agreement. When a deposition is being reported, no part of the proceedings shall be omitted unless all of the parties and the witness so agree. When a party or a witness seeks to terminate or suspend the taking of a deposition for the time necessary to seek a court order, the court reporter shall discontinue reporting the testimony of the witness.

(d) Ownership of Records. The chief judge of the circuit in which a proceeding is pending, in his or her official capacity, is the owner of all records and electronic records made by an official court reporter or quasi-judicial officer in proceedings required to be reported at public expense and proceedings reported for the court's own use.

(e) Fees. The chief judge shall have the discretion to adopt an administrative order establishing maximum fees for court reporting services. Any such order must make a specific factual finding that the setting of such maximum fees is necessary to ensure access to the courts. Such finding shall include consideration of the number of court reporters in the county or circuit, any past history of fee schedules, and any other relevant factors.

Text of rule effective prior to amendment by Florida Supreme Court in case number SC11-399. See also text of rule as amended by Florida Supreme Court in case number SC11-399 below.

(f) Transcripts. Transcripts of all judicial proceedings, including depositions, shall be uniform in and for all courts throughout the state. The form, size, spacing, and method of printing transcripts are as follows:

Text of rule as amended by Florida Supreme Court in case number SC11-399. See also text of rule prior to amendment by Florida Supreme Court in case number SC11-399 above.

(f) Transcripts. Transcripts of all judicial proceedings, including depositions, shall be uniform in and for all courts throughout the state and shall be stored in an electronic format sufficient to communicate the information contained in proceedings in a readable format, and capable of being transmitted electronically as set forth in rule 2.525. Any transcripts stored in electronic form must be capable of being printed in accordance with this rule. The form, size, spacing, and method of printing transcripts are as follows:

(1) All proceedings shall be printed on paper 8 1/2 inches by 11 inches in size and bound on the left.

(2) There shall be no fewer than 25 printed lines per page with all lines numbered 1 through 25, respectively, and with no more than a double space between lines.

(3) Font size or print shall be 9 or 10 pica, 12-point courier, or 12-point Times New Roman print with no less than 56 characters per line on questions and answers unless the text of the speaker ends short of marginal requirements.

(4) Colloquy material shall begin on the same line following the identification of the speaker, with no more than 2 spaces between the identification of the speaker and the commencement of the colloquy. The identification of the speaker in colloquy shall begin no more than 10 spaces from the left margin, and carry-over colloquy shall be indented no more than 5 spaces from the left margin.

(5) Each question and answer shall begin on a separate line no more than 5 spaces from the left margin with no more than 5 spaces from the "Q" or "A" to the text. Carry-over question and answer lines shall be brought to the left margin.

(6) Quoted material shall begin no more than 10 spaces from the left margin with carry-over lines beginning no more than 10 spaces from the left margin.

(7) Indentations of no more than 10 spaces may be used for paragraphs, and all spaces on a line as herein provided shall be used unless the text of the speaker ends short of marginal requirements.

(8) One-line parentheticals may begin at any indentation. Parentheticals exceeding 1 line shall begin no more than 10 spaces from the left margin, with carry-over lines being returned to the left margin.

(9) Individual volumes of a transcript, including depositions, shall be no more than 200 pages in length, inclusive of the index.

(10) Deviation from these standards shall not constitute grounds for limiting use of transcripts in the trial or appellate courts.

(g) Officers of the Court. Approved court reporters, civil court reporters, and approved transcriptionists are officers of the court for all purposes while acting as court reporters in judicial proceedings or discovery proceedings or as transcriptionists. Approved court reporters, civil court reporters, and approved transcriptionists shall comply with all rules and statutes governing the proceeding that are applicable to court reporters and approved transcriptionists.

(h) Court Reporting Services at Public Expense.

(1) When Reporting Is Required. All proceedings required by law, court rule, or administrative order to be reported shall be reported at public expense.

(2) When Reporting May Be Required. Proceedings reported for the court's own use may be reported at public expense.

(3) Circuit Plan. The chief judge, after consultation with the circuit court and county court judges in the circuit, shall enter an administrative order developing and implementing a circuit-wide plan for the court reporting of all proceedings required to be reported at public expense using either full or part time court employees or independent contractors. The plan shall ensure that all court reporting services are provided by approved court reporters or approved transcriptionists. This plan may provide for multiple service delivery strategies if they are necessary to ensure the efficient provision of court reporting services. Each circuit's plan for court reporting services shall be developed after consideration of guidelines issued by the Office of the State Courts Administrator.

(4) Electronic Recording and Transcription of Proceedings Without Court Reporters. A chief judge may enter a circuit-wide administrative order, which shall be recorded, authorizing the electronic recording and subsequent transcription by approved court reporters or approved transcriptionists, of any judicial proceedings, including depositions, that are otherwise required to be reported by a court reporter. Appropriate procedures shall be prescribed in the order which shall:

(A) set forth responsibilities for the court's support personnel to ensure a reliable record of the proceedings;

(B) provide a means to have the recording transcribed by approved court reporters or approved transcriptionists, either in whole or in part, when necessary for an appeal or for further use in the trial court; and

(C) provide for the safekeeping of such recordings.

(5) Safeguarding Confidential Communications When Electronic Recording Equipment Is Used in the Courtroom.

(A) Court personnel shall provide notice to participants in a courtroom proceeding that electronic recording equipment is in use and that they should safeguard information they do not want recorded.

(B) Attorneys shall take all reasonable and available precautions to protect disclosure of confidential communications in the courtroom. Such precautions may include muting microphones or going to a designated location that is inaccessible to the recording equipment.

(C) Participants have a duty to protect confidential information.

(6) Grand Jury Proceedings. Testimony in grand jury proceedings shall be reported by an approved court reporter, but shall not be transcribed unless required by order of court. Other parts of grand jury proceedings, including deliberations and voting, shall not be reported. The approved court reporter's work product, including stenographic notes, electronic recordings, and transcripts, shall be filed with the clerk of the court under seal.

(i) Court Reporting Services in Capital Cases. The chief judge, after consultation with the circuit court judges in the circuit, shall enter an administrative order developing and implementing a circuit-wide plan for court reporting in all trials in which the state seeks the death penalty and in capital postconviction proceedings. The plan shall require the use of all measures necessary to expedite the preparation of the transcript, including but not limited to:

(1) where available, the use of an approved court reporter who has the capacity to provide real-time transcription of the proceedings;

(2) if real-time transcription services are not available, the use of a computer-aided transcription qualified court reporter;

(3) the use of scopists, text editors, alternating court reporters, or other means to expedite the finalization of the certified transcript; and

(4) the imposition of reasonable restrictions on work assignments by employee or contract approved court reporters to ensure that transcript production in capital cases is given a priority.

(j) Juvenile Dependency and Termination of Parental Rights Cases. Transcription of hearings for appeals of orders in juvenile dependency and termination of parental rights cases shall be given priority, consistent with rule 2.215(g), over transcription of all other proceedings, unless otherwise ordered by the court based upon a demonstrated exigency.

Editor's Notes: — On October 18, 2012, the Supreme Court of Florida issued a revised opinion in case number SC11-399, which was originally issued on June 21, 2012. See *In re Amendments to the Florida Rules of Judicial Administration*, 37 FLW S643 (Fla. 2012). The opinion provides in relevant part:

"First, the new electronic filing requirements the Court adopts will become effective in the civil, probate, small claims, and family law divisions of the trial courts, as well as for appeals to the circuit courts in these categories of cases, on April 1, 2013, at 12:01 a.m., except as may be otherwise provided by administrative order. Electronic filing will be mandatory in these divisions pursuant to rule 2.525 on that date. However, until the new rules take effect in these divisions, any clerk who is already accepting documents filed by electronic transmission under the current rules should continue to do so; attorneys in these counties are encouraged to file documents electronically under the current rules.

"Next, the new electronic filing requirements the Court adopts will become effective in the criminal, traffic, and juvenile divisions of the trial courts, as well as for appeals to the circuit court in these categories of cases, on October 1, 2013, at 12:01 a.m., except as may be otherwise provided by administrative order. Electronic filing will be mandatory in these divisions under rule 2.525 on that date. The new e-filing requirements, as they apply in proceedings brought pursuant to the Florida Mental Health Act (Baker Act), Chapter 394, Part I, Florida Statutes, and the Involuntary Commitment of Sexually Violent Predators Act (Jimmy Ryce), Chapter 394, Part V, Florida Statutes, will also not be mandatory in these cases until October 1, 2013. As stated above, until the new rules take effect in these divisions and proceedings, any clerk who is already accepting electronically filed documents under the current rules should continue to do so; attorneys are again encouraged to utilize existing electronic filing procedures under the current rules.

"However, until the new rules and procedures take effect in the district courts, any clerk who is already accepting documents filed by electronic transmission may continue to do so; attorneys in these districts are encouraged to file documents electronically. Clerks will not be required to electronically transmit the record on appeal until July 1, 2013, at 12:01 a.m. Until July 1, we encourage clerks, whenever possible, to electronically transmit the record under the new rules and requirements.

"(W)e note that, in all types of cases, pursuant to amended rule 2.525(d) self-represented parties and self-represented nonparties, including nonparty governmental or public agencies, and attorneys excused from e-mail service under Florida Rule of Judicial Administration 2.516 will be permitted, but not required, to file documents electronically.

By order of November 28, 2012, in case number SC11-399, the Court released a revised implementation schedule, which provides, in pertinent part: "The e-filing rules adopted in the October 2012 opinion will be mandatory in this (Supreme) Court on February 27, 2013, at 12:01 a.m.; and effective earlier on a voluntary basis as will be indicated by further administrative order of the chief justice.

"Thereafter, the e-filing rules will be mandatory in the Second District Court of Appeal on July 22, 2013, at 12:01 a.m.; in the Third District Court of Appeal on September 27, 2013, at 12:01 a.m.; in the Fourth District Court of Appeal on October 31, 2013, at 12:01 a.m.; in the Fifth District Court of Appeal on November 27, 2013 at 12:01 a.m.; and in the First District Court of Appeal on December 27, 2013, at 12:01 a.m., unless made mandatory earlier by the chief judge of the applicable district court of appeal. The e-filing rules will be effective earlier on a voluntary trial basis in the district courts of appeal as will be indicated by further administrative order by the chief judge of the applicable district court."

Committee Notes

The definitions of "electronic record" in subdivision (a)(5) and of "official record" in subdivision (a)(6) are intended to clarify that when a court proceeding is electronically recorded by means of audio, analog, digital, or video equipment, and is also recorded via a written transcript prepared by a court reporter, the written transcript shall be the "official record" of the proceeding to the exclusion of all electronic records. While the term "record" is used within Rule 2.535 and within Fla. R. App. P. 9.200, it has a different meaning within the unique context of each rule. Accordingly, the meaning of the term "record" as defined for purposes of this rule does not in any way alter, amend, change, or conflict with the meaning of the term "record" as defined for appellate purposes in Fla. R. App. P. 9.200(a).

RULE 2.540. REQUESTS FOR ACCOMMODATIONS BY PERSONS WITH DISABILITIES

(a) Duties of Court. Qualified individuals with a disability will be provided, at the court's expense, with accommodations, reasonable modifications to rules, policies, or practices, or the provision of auxiliary aids and services, in order to participate in programs or activities provided by the courts of this state. The court may deny a request only in accordance with subdivision (e).

(b) Definitions. The definitions encompassed in the Americans with Disabilities Act of 1990, 42 U.S.C. § 12101, et seq., are incorporated into this rule.

(c) Notice Requirement.

(1) All notices of court proceedings to be held in a public facility, and all process compelling appearance at such proceedings, shall include the following statement in bold face, 14-point Times New Roman or Courier font:

"If you are a person with a disability who needs any accommodation in order to participate in this proceeding, you are entitled, at no cost to you, to the provision of certain assistance. Please contact [identify applicable court personnel by name, address, and telephone number] at least 7 days before your scheduled court appearance, or immediately upon receiving this notification if the time before the scheduled appearance is less than 7 days; if you are hearing or voice impaired, call 711."

(2) Each trial and appellate court shall post on its respective website and in each court facility the procedures for obtaining an accommodation as well as the grievance procedure adopted by that court.

(d) Process for Requesting Accommodations. The process for requesting accommodations is as follows:

(1) Requests for accommodations under this rule may be presented on a form approved or substantially similar to one approved by the Office of the State Courts Administrator, in another written format, or orally. Requests must be forwarded to the ADA coordinator, or designee, within the time frame provided in subdivision (d)(3).

(2) Requests for accommodations must include a description of the accommodation sought, along with a statement of the impairment that necessitates the accommodation and the duration that the accommodation is to be provided. The court, in its discretion, may require the individual with a disability to provide additional information about the impairment. Requests for accommodation shall not include any information regarding the merits of the case.

(3) Requests for accommodations must be made at least 7 days before the scheduled court appearance, or immediately upon receiving notification if the time before the scheduled court appearance is less than 7 days. The court may, in its discretion, waive this requirement.

(e) Response to Accommodation Request. The court must respond to a request for accommodation as follows:

(1) The court must consider, but is not limited by, the provisions of the Americans with Disabilities Act of 1990 in determining whether to provide an accommodation or an appropriate alternative accommodation.

(2) The court must inform the individual with a disability of the following:

(A) That the request for accommodation is granted or denied, in whole or in part, and if the request for accommodation is denied, the reason therefor; or that an alternative accommodation is granted;

(B) The nature of the accommodation to be provided, if any; and

(C) The duration of the accommodation to be provided.

If the request for accommodation is granted in its entirety, the court shall respond to the individual with a disability by any appropriate method. If the request is denied or granted only in part, or if an alternative accommodation is granted, the court must respond to the individual with a disability in writing, as may be appropriate, and if applicable, in an alternative format.

(3) If the court determines that a person is a qualified person with a disability and an accommodation is needed, a request for accommodation may be denied only when the court determines that the requested accommodation would create an undue financial or administrative burden on the court or would fundamentally alter the nature of the service, program, or activity.

(f) Grievance Procedure.

(1) Each judicial circuit and appellate court shall establish and publish grievance procedures that allow for the resolution of complaints. Those procedures may be used by anyone who wishes to file a complaint alleging discrimination on the basis of disability in the provision of services, activities, programs, or benefits by the Florida State Courts System.

(2) If such grievance involves a matter that may affect the orderly administration of justice, it is within the discretion of the presiding judge to stay the proceeding and seek expedited resolution of the grievance.

RULE 2.545. CASE MANAGEMENT

(a) Purpose. Judges and lawyers have a professional obligation to conclude litigation as soon as it is reasonably and justly possible to do so. However parties and counsel shall be afforded a reasonable time to prepare and present their case.

(b) Case Control. The trial judge shall take charge of all cases at an early stage in the litigation and shall control the progress of the case thereafter until the case is determined. The trial judge shall take specific steps to monitor and control the pace of litigation, including the following:

(1) assuming early and continuous control of the court calendar;

(2) identifying priority cases as assigned by statute, rule of procedure, case law, or otherwise;

(3) implementing such docket control policies as may be necessary to advance priority cases to ensure prompt resolution;

(4) identifying cases subject to alternative dispute resolution processes;

(5) developing rational and effective trial setting policies; and

(6) advancing the trial setting of priority cases, older cases, and cases of greater urgency.

(c) Priority Cases.

(1) In all noncriminal cases assigned a priority status by statute, rule of procedure, case law, or otherwise, any party may file a notice of priority status explaining the nature of the case, the source of the priority status, any deadlines imposed by law on any aspect of the case, and any unusual factors that may bear on meeting the imposed deadlines.

(2) If, in any noncriminal case assigned a priority status by statute, rule of procedure, case law, or otherwise, a party is of the good faith opinion that the case has not been appropriately advanced on the docket or has not received priority in scheduling consistent with its priority case status, that party may seek review of such action by motion for review to the chief judge or to the chief judge's designee. The filing of such a motion for review will not toll the time for seeking such other relief as may be afforded by the Florida Rules of Appellate Procedure.

(d) Related Cases.

(1) The petitioner in a family case shall file with the court a notice of related cases, if related cases are known or reasonably ascertainable. A case is related when:

(A) it involves any of the same parties, children, or issues and it is pending at the time the party files a family case; or

(B) it affects the court's jurisdiction to proceed; or

(C) an order in the related case may conflict with an order on the same issues in the new case; or

(D) an order in the new case may conflict with an order in the earlier litigation.

(2) "Family cases" include dissolution of marriage, annulment, support unconnected with dissolution of marriage, paternity, child support, UIFSA, custodial care of and access to children, proceedings for temporary or concurrent custody of minor children by extended family, adoption, name change, declaratory judgment actions related to premarital, marital, or postmarital agreements, civil domestic, repeat violence, dating violence, and sexual violence injunctions, juvenile dependency, termination of parental rights, juvenile delinquency, emancipation of a minor, CINS/FINS, truancy, and modification and enforcement of orders entered in these cases.

(3) The notice of related cases shall identify the caption and case number of the related case, contain a brief statement of the relationship of the actions, and contain a statement addressing whether assignment to one judge or another method of coordination will conserve judicial resources and promote an efficient determination of the actions.

(4) The notice of related cases shall be filed with the initial pleading by the filing attorney or self-represented petitioner.

(5) Each party has a continuing duty to inform the court of any proceedings in this or any other state that could affect the current proceeding.

(6) Whenever it appears to a party that two or more pending cases present common issues of fact and that assignment to one judge or another method of coordination will significantly promote the efficient administration of justice, conserve judicial resources, avoid inconsistent results, or prevent multiple court appearances by the same parties on the same issues, the party may file a notice of related cases requesting coordination of the litigation.

(7) The notice of related cases shall be served on all parties in the related cases, the presiding judges,

and the chief judge or family law administrative judge.

(e) Continuances. All judges shall apply a firm continuance policy. Continuances should be few, good cause should be required, and all requests should be heard and resolved by a judge. All motions for continuance shall be in writing unless made at a trial and, except for good cause shown, shall be signed by the party requesting the continuance. All motions for continuance in priority cases shall clearly identify such priority status and explain what effect the motion will have on the progress of the case.

Committee Notes

The provisions in subdivision (c) of this rule governing priority cases should be read in conjunction with the provisions of rule 2.215(g), governing the duty to expedite priority cases.

RULE 2.550. CALENDAR CONFLICTS

(a) Guidelines. In resolving calendar conflicts between the state courts of Florida or between a state court and a federal court in Florida, the following guidelines must be considered:

(1) Any case priority status established by statute, rule of procedure, case law, or otherwise shall be evaluated to determine the effect that resolving a calendar conflict might have on the priority case or cases.

(2) Juvenile dependency and termination of parental rights cases are generally to be given preference over other cases, except for speedy trial and capital cases.

(3) Criminal cases are generally to be given preference over civil cases.

(4) Jury trials are generally to be given preference over non-jury trials.

(5) Appellate arguments, hearings, and conferences are generally to be given preference over trial court proceedings.

(6) The case in which the trial date has been first set should generally take precedence.

(b) Additional Circumstances. Factors such as cost, numbers of witnesses and attorneys involved, travel, length of trial, age of case, and other relevant matters may warrant deviation from these case guidelines.

(c) Notice and Agreement; Resolution by Judges. When an attorney is scheduled to appear in 2 courts at the same time and cannot arrange for other counsel to represent the clients' interests, the attorney shall give prompt written notice of the conflict to opposing counsel, the clerk of each court, and the presiding judge of each case, if known. If the presiding judge of the case cannot be identified, written notice of the conflict shall be given to the chief judge of the court having jurisdiction over the case, or to the chief judge's designee. The judges or their designees shall confer and undertake to avoid the conflict by agreement among themselves. Absent agreement, conflicts should be promptly resolved by the judges or their designees in accordance with the above case guidelines.

Committee Notes

1996 Adoption. The adoption of this rule was prompted by the Resolution of the Florida State-Federal Judicial Council Regarding Calendar Conflicts Between State and Federal Courts, which states as follows:

WHEREAS, the great volume of cases filed in the state and federal courts of Florida creates calendar conflicts between the state and federal courts of Florida which should be resolved in a fair, efficient and orderly manner to allow for judicial efficiency and economy; and

WHEREAS, the Florida State-Federal Judicial Council which represents the Bench and Bar of the State of Florida believes that it would be beneficial to formally agree upon and publish recommended procedures and priorities for resolving calendar conflicts between the state and federal courts of Florida;

NOW, THEREFORE, BE IT RESOLVED

In resolving calendar conflicts between the state and federal courts of Florida, the following case priorities should be considered:

1. Criminal cases should prevail over civil cases.

2. Jury trials should prevail over non-jury trials.

3. Appellate arguments, hearings, and conferences should prevail over trials.

4. The case in which the trial date has been first set should take precedence.

5. Circumstances such as cost, numbers of witnesses and attorneys involved, travel, length of trial, age of case and other

relevant matters may warrant deviation from this policy. Such matters are encouraged to be resolved through communication between the courts involved.

Where an attorney is scheduled to appear in two courts - trial or appellate, state or federal - at the same time and cannot arrange for other counsel in his or her firm or in the case to represent his or her client's interest, the attorney shall give prompt written notice to opposing counsel, the clerk of each court, and the presiding judge of each case, if known, of the conflict. If the presiding judge of a case cannot be identified, written notice of the conflict shall be given to the chief judge of the court having jurisdiction over the case, or to his or her designee. The judges or their designees shall confer and undertake to avoid the conflict by agreement among themselves. Absent agreement, conflicts should be promptly resolved by the judges or their designees in accordance with the above case priorities.

In jurisdictions where calendar conflicts arise with frequency, it is recommended that each court involved consider appointing a calendar conflict coordinator to assist the judges in resolving calendar conflicts by obtaining information regarding the conflicts and performing such other ministerial duties as directed by the judges.

REVISED AND READOPTED at Miami, Florida, this 13th day of January, 1995.

Court Commentary

2002 Court Commentary. As provided in subdivision (c), when a scheduling conflict involves different courts, the presiding judges should confer and undertake to agree on a resolution, using the guidelines provided in this rule.

RULE 2.555. INITIATION OF CRIMINAL PROCEEDINGS

(a) Major Statutory Offense. Law enforcement officers, at the time of the filing of a complaint with the clerk of court, shall designate whether the most serious charge on the complaint is a felony or a misdemeanor. The state attorney or the state attorney's designee, at the time of the filing of an original information or an original indictment with the clerk of court, shall designate whether the most serious offense on the information or the indictment is a felony or misdemeanor. Complaints, original informations, and original indictments on which the most serious charge is a felony shall be filed with the clerk of the circuit court.

(b) Ordinance Violations. In cases when the state attorney has the responsibility for the prosecution of county or municipal ordinance violations, where such ordinances have state statutory equivalents, the state

attorney or the state attorney's designee shall set forth at the top of the face of the accusatory instrument the exact statute number of the single most serious offense charged.

(c) Information or Indictment after County Court Proceedings Begun. When action in a criminal case has been initiated in county court, and subsequently the state attorney files a direct information or the grand jury indicts the defendant, the state attorney or the state attorney's designee shall notify the clerk without delay.

RULE 2.560. APPOINTMENT OF INTERPRETERS FOR NON-ENGLISH-SPEAKING PERSONS

(a) Criminal or Juvenile Delinquency Proceedings. In any criminal or juvenile delinquency proceeding in which a non-English-speaking person is the accused, an interpreter for the non-English-speaking person shall be appointed. In any criminal or juvenile delinquency proceeding in which a non-English-speaking person is a victim, an interpreter shall be appointed unless the court finds that the victim does not require the services of a court-appointed interpreter.

(b) Other Proceedings. In all other proceedings in which a non-English-speaking person is a litigant, an interpreter for the non-English-speaking litigant shall be appointed if the court determines that the litigant's inability to comprehend English deprives the litigant of an understanding of the court proceedings, that a fundamental interest is at stake (such as in a civil commitment, termination of parental rights, paternity, or dependency proceeding), and that no alternative to the appointment of an interpreter exists.

(c) Witnesses. In any proceeding in which a non-English-speaking person is a witness, the appointment of an interpreter shall be governed by the applicable provisions of the Florida Evidence Code.

(d) Compliance with Title VI of the Civil Rights Act of 1964. In making determinations regarding the appointment of an interpreter, the court should ensure compliance with the requirements of Title VI of the Civil Rights Act of 1964.

(e) Qualifications of Interpreter.

(1) Appointment of Interpreters when Certified or Duly Qualified Interpreters Are Available. Whenever possible, a certified or duly qualified interpreter, as defined in the Rules for Certification and Regulation of Court Interpreters, shall be appointed.

(2) Appointment of Interpreters when Certified or Duly Qualified Interpreters Are Unavailable. If, after diligent search, a certified or duly qualified interpreter is not available, an interpreter who is neither certified nor duly qualified may be appointed if the judge or hearing officer presiding over the proceeding finds that:

(A) good cause exists for the appointment of an interpreter who is neither certified nor duly qualified, such as the prevention of burdensome delay, the request or consent of the non-English-speaking person, or other unusual circumstance; and

(B) the proposed interpreter is competent to interpret in the proceedings.

(3) On-the-Record Objections or Waivers in Criminal and Juvenile Delinquency Proceedings. In any criminal or juvenile delinquency proceeding in which the interpreter is neither certified nor duly qualified, the court shall advise the accused, on the record, that the proposed interpreter is not certified or duly qualified pursuant to the Rules for Certification and Regulation of Court Interpreters. The accused's objection to the appointment of a proposed interpreter, or the accused's waiver of the appointment of a certified or duly qualified interpreter, shall also be on the record.

(4) Additional on-the-Record Findings, Objections, and Waivers Required at Subsequent Proceedings. The appointment of an interpreter who is neither certified nor duly qualified shall be limited to a specific proceeding and shall not be extended to subsequent proceedings in a case without additional findings of good cause and qualification as required by subdivision (e)(2) of this rule, and additional compliance with the procedures for on-the-record objections or waivers provided for in subdivision (e)(3) of this rule.

(f) Privileged Communications. Whenever a person communicates through an interpreter to any person under circumstances that would render the communication privileged and such person could not be compelled to testify as to the communication, the privilege shall also apply to the interpreter.

Appendix
State of Florida
Judicial Branch
Records Retention Schedule
for Administrative Records.

GENERAL APPLICATION.

This record retention schedule does not impose a duty to create records contained in the schedule. The purpose of the schedule is to authorize destruction of records after the retention period has elapsed. The records custodian may retain records longer than required by the schedule. This schedule authorizes destruction of records unless otherwise provided by court rule.

The retention period should be calculated from the time that the record is completed. For purposes of calculating the retention period, fiscal records should be considered completed at the end of a fiscal year. All retention periods are subject to the caveat "provided that applicable audits have been released."

The records custodian of the judicial branch entity that creates a record creates the "record copy" and is responsible for its retention in accordance with this schedule. The records custodian of the judicial branch entity that properly receives a record from outside the judicial branch has the "record copy" and is responsible for its retention in accordance with this schedule. Duplicates are only required to be retained until obsolete, superseded or administrative value is lost.

"Record Series" means a group of related documents arranged under a single filing arrangement or kept together as a unit because they consist of the same form, relate to the same subject, result from the same activity, or have certain common characteristics.

ACQUISITION RECORDS: LIBRARY. This record series consists of information on the acquisition of library materials including: books, periodicals, filmstrips, software, compact discs, video/audio tapes, and other non-print media. This information may include the accession date and method, the publisher and cost, the date entered into the collection, dates removed from collection, and method of final disposal.
RETENTION: Retain for life of material.

ADMINISTRATIVE CONVENIENCE RECORDS. This record series consists of a subject file, generally filed alphabetically, which is located away from the official files, such as in the Director's and other supervisory offices. The file contains DUPLICATES of correspondence, reports, publications, memoranda, etc., and is used as a working file or reference file on subjects which are currently significant or which may become significant in the near future. The material filed in this series is NOT the official file or record copy but is maintained for the convenience of the officials in carrying out their elected or appointed duties.
RETENTION: Retain until obsolete, superseded or administrative value is lost.

ADMINISTRATIVE RECORDS: PUBLIC OFFICIALS/COURT ADMINISTRATORS. This record series consists of office files documenting the substantive actions of elected or appointed officials and the court administrator. These records constitute the official record of a judicial branch entity's performance of its functions and formulation of policy and program initiative. This series will include various types of records such as correspondence; memoranda; statements prepared for delivery at meetings, conventions or other public functions that are designed to advertise and promote programs, activities and policies of the judicial branch entity; interviews; and reports concerning development and implementation of activities of the judicial branch entity. **"These records may have archival value."**
RETENTION: 10 years.

ADMINISTRATIVE SUPPORT RECORDS. This record series consists of records accumulated relative to internal administrative activities rather than the functions for which the office exists. Normally, these records

document procedures; the expenditure of funds, including budget material; day-to-day management of office personnel including training and travel; supplies, office services and equipment requests and receipts and other recorded experiences that do not serve as official documentation of the programs of the office. However, because the content of these records vary so greatly in content and value (containing some duplicates and record copies), a relatively large proportion of them are of continuing value and may be subject to the audit process. Note: Reference a more applicable records series first if one exists. **"These records may have archival value."**
RETENTION: 2 years.

ADVERTISEMENTS: LEGAL. This record series consists of advertisements which have appeared in newspapers or in the "Administrative Weekly" on matters pertaining to the judicial branch entity and other legal ads which may or may not indirectly affect the judicial branch entity; i.e., bid invitations for construction jobs, public hearings or notices, public sales. See also "BID RECORDS: CAPITAL IMPROVEMENT SUCCESS-FUL BID", "BID RECORDS: CAPITAL IMPROVEMENT UNSUCCESSFUL BIDS" and "BID RECORDS: NON-CAPITAL IMPROVEMENT."
RETENTION: 5 years.

AFFIRMATIVE ACTION RECORDS. This record series consists of copies of reports submitted to the Equal Employment Opportunity Commission (EEOC) per their requirements for the judicial branch entity's affirmative action plan. It may also include discrimination complaints, correspondence and investigative papers pertaining to the judicial branch entity's affirmative action plan. See also "EQUAL EMPLOYMENT OPPORTUNITY COMPLIANCE RECORDS."
RETENTION: 2 years.

APPLICATIONS: GUARDIAN AD LITEM, MEDIATION, OTHERS. This record series consists of applications, supporting documents, correspondence and reports relating to the application of a person to be certified as a mediator, a program to be approved to offer training for mediators, a volunteer to be approved by the Guardian ad Litem Program, or other persons or programs regulated in the judicial branch.
RETENTION: 5 years after the person or program is no longer regulated by the judicial branch.

APPLICATIONS: LIBRARY CARDS. This record series consists of library card applications which must be renewed on an annual, bi-annual, or other basis. The application may include the patron's name, address, telephone number, date of birth, as well as a statement of liability for the care and timely return of all materials checked out or utilized by the patron.
RETENTION: Retain for 30 days after expiration.

APPRAISALS: LAND PURCHASES (NOT PURCHASED). This record series consists of documents pertaining to land not purchased by a judicial branch entity and all supporting documents. See also "APPRAISALS: LAND PURCHASES (PURCHASED)."
RETENTION: 3 years.

APPRAISALS: LAND PURCHASES (PURCHASED). This record series consists of documents pertaining to land purchased by a judicial branch entity and all supporting documents. See also "APPRAISALS: LAND PURCHASES (NOT PURCHASED)."
RETENTION: Retain as long as judicial branch entity retains property.

ARCHITECTURAL PLANS/SPECIFICATIONS: PRELIMINARY DRAWINGS. This record series consists of those graphic and engineering preliminary drawing records that depict conceptual as well as precise measured information essential for the planning and construction of facilities.
RETENTION: Retain until completion and acceptance.

ATTENDANCE AND LEAVE RECORDS. This record series consists of requests or applications for vacation, sick, family medical leave (FMLA) and other types of leave including leave of absences, timesheets or timecards

along with any required documentation (medical statements or excuses from a physician, jury duty summons, or military orders, etc.) submitted by an employee to document authorized absences.
RETENTION: 3 years.

AUDITS: INDEPENDENT. This record series consists of a report issued by an independent auditor to establish the position of the judicial branch entity being audited against its standard of performance. See also, "AUDITS: INTERNAL," "AUDITS: STATE/FEDERAL" and "AUDITS: SUPPORTING DOCUMENTS."
RETENTION: 10 years.

AUDITS: INTERNAL. This record series consists of a report issued by an internal auditor to establish the position of a judicial branch entity being audited against its standard of performance. See also, "AUDITS: INDEPENDENT," "AUDITS: STATE/FEDERAL" and "AUDITS: SUPPORTING DOCUMENTS."
RETENTION: 3 years.

AUDITS: STATE/FEDERAL. This record series consists of a report issued by a federal or state auditor to establish the position of a judicial branch entity being audited against its standard of performance. See also, "AUDITS: INDEPENDENT," "AUDITS: INTERNAL" and "AUDITS: SUPPORTING DOCUMENTS." **"These records may have archival value."**
RETENTION: 10 years.

AUDITS: SUPPORTING DOCUMENTS. This record series consists of the documentation and supporting documents used to develop the audit report with all bills, accounts, records and transactions. See also "AUDITS: INDEPENDENT," "AUDITS: INTERNAL" and "AUDITS: STATE/FEDERAL."
RETENTION: 3 years.

BACKGROUND/Security Checks. This record series consists of background/security checks for potential new hires and promotions. These checks may include a background and driver's license screening, reference check, and verification of academic standing. The files might include notices of not being hired based on the outcome of a security check and a opportunity for rebuttal. Supporting documentation consists of fingerprint cards, copy of the driver's license, copy of the transcript release form, returned form reference letters, and other necessary information.
RETENTION: 4 anniversary years.

BANK ACCOUNT AUTHORIZATION RECORDS. This record series consists of an authorization to maintain a bank account and who is authorized to sign off on the account.
RETENTION: 1 year after superseded by new authorization.

BAR APPLICANTS: ADMITTED. This record series consists of bar applications, supporting documents, all investigative materials, of administrative value, correspondence, reports, and similar materials accumulated during the bar admissions process regarding bar applicants who were subsequently admitted to The Florida Bar.
RETENTION: Bar application and fingerprint card, 5 years; all other materials, 1 year.

BAR APPLICANTS: NOT ADMITTED (WITH NO RECOMMENDATION). This record series consists of bar applications, supporting documents, all investigative materials of administrative value, correspondence, reports, and similar materials accumulated during the bar admissions process regarding bar applicants who have not been admitted to The Florida Bar and who have not received an unfavorable recommendation by the Florida Board of Bar Examiners.
RETENTION: 20 years or the death of the applicant, whichever is earlier.

BAR APPLICANTS: NOT ADMITTED (WITH UNFAVORABLE RECOMMENDATION). This record series consists of bar applications, supporting documents, all investigative materials of administrative value, correspondence, reports, and similar materials accumulated during the bar admissions process regarding bar applicants who have not been admitted to The Florida Bar and who have received an unfavorable

recommendation by the Florida Board of Bar Examiners by either a negotiated consent judgment or the issuance of findings of fact and conclusions of law.
RETENTION: 40 years or the death of the applicant, whichever is earlier.

BAR EXAMINATION/ANSWERS. This record series consists of answers to essay questions and answer sheets to machine-scored questions submitted by bar applicants during the bar examination administered by the Florida Board of Bar Examiners.
RETENTION: Until the conclusion of the administration of the next successive general bar examination.

BAR EXAMINATION/FLORIDA PREPARED PORTION. This record series consists of the portion of the bar examination prepared by the Florida Board of Bar Examiners.
RETENTION: 10 years from the date of the administration of the examination.

BID RECORDS: CAPITAL IMPROVEMENT SUCCESSFUL BIDS. This record series consists of information relative to the processing and letting of capital improvement successful bids including legal advertisements, "Requests for Proposal," technical specifications, correspondence, "Invitations to Bid," bid tabulations and bid responses. "Capital Improvements" shall mean enhancement to buildings, fixtures and all other improvements to land. See also "BID RECORDS: CAPITAL IMPROVEMENT UNSUCCESSFUL BIDS" and "BID RECORDS: NON-CAPITAL IMPROVEMENT."
RETENTION: 10 years.

BID RECORDS: CAPITAL IMPROVEMENT UNSUCCESSFUL BIDS. This record series consists of information relative to the processing and letting of capital improvement unsuccessful bids including legal advertisements, "Requests for Proposal," technical specifications, correspondence, "Invitations to Bid," bid tabulations and bid responses. "Capital Improvements" shall mean enhancement to buildings, fixtures and all other improvements to land. See also "BID RECORDS: CAPITAL IMPROVEMENT SUCCESSFUL BIDS" and "BID RECORDS: NON-CAPITAL IMPROVEMENT."
RETENTION: 5 years.

BID RECORDS: NON-CAPITAL IMPROVEMENT. This record series consists of information relative to the processing and letting of successful and unsuccessful noncapital improvement bids including legal advertisements, "Requests for Proposal," technical specifications, correspondence, "Invitations to Bid," bid tabulations and bid responses. See also "BID RECORDS: CAPITAL IMPROVEMENT SUCCESSFUL BIDS" and "BID RECORDS: CAPITAL IMPROVEMENT UNSUCCESSFUL BIDS."
RETENTION: 5 years.

BIOGRAPHICAL FILES. This record series consists of vitas, biographies, photographs and newspaper clippings of employees.
RETENTION: Retain until obsolete, superseded or administrative value is lost.

BUDGET RECORDS: APPROVED ANNUAL BUDGET. This record series consists of the approved annual budget and its amendments. See also "BUDGET RECORDS: SUPPORTING DOCUMENTS" **"These records may have archival value."**
RETENTION: Permanent.

BUDGET RECORDS: SUPPORTING DOCUMENTS. This record series consists of any supporting documentation supporting budget matters and is filed chronologically. See also "BUDGET RECORDS: APPROVED ANNUAL BUDGET."
RETENTION: 3 years.

BUILDING PLANS. This record series consists of graphic and engineering records that depict conceptual as well as precise measured information essential for the planning and construction of buildings. See also "ARCHITECTURAL PLANS/SPECIFICATIONS: PRELIMINARY DRAWINGS."
RETENTION: Retain for life of structure.

CALENDARS. This record series consists of a calendar showing official daily appointments and meetings.
RETENTION: 1 year.

CASE RELATED RECORDS NOT IN THE CUSTODY OF THE CLERK AND /OR NOT IN CASE FILE. This record series includes records that are related to a trial court records as defined in Rule 2.420, Florida Rules of Judicial Administration, because they are not filed with the clerk of court and are not included in the court file. These records include, but are not limited to, drug court evaluation and progress reports, mediation reports, deferred prosecution and diversion records, and arbitration reports. Case-related trial court documents may be destroyed or disposed of after a judgment has become final in record accordance with the following schedule:
RETENTION:

(A) 60 days- Parking tickets and noncriminal traffic infractions after required audits have been completed.

(B) 2 years- Proceedings under the Small Claims Rules, Medical Mediation Proceedings.

(C) 5 years- Misdemeanor actions, criminal traffic violations, ordinance violations, civil litigation proceedings in county court other than those under the Small Claims Rules, and civil proceedings in circuit court except marriage dissolutions and adoptions.

(D) 10 years- Probate, guardianship, and mental health proceedings.

(E) 10 years- Felony cases in which no information or indictment was filed or in which all charges were dismissed, or in which the state announced a nolle prosequi, or in which the defendant was adjudicated not guilty.

(F) 75 years- juvenile proceedings containing an order permanently depriving a parent of custody of a child, and adoptions and all felony cases not previously destroyed.

(G) Juvenile proceedings not otherwise provided for in this subdivision shall be kept for 5 years after the last entry or until the child reaches the age of majority, whichever is later.

(H) Marriage dissolutions- 10 years from the last record activity. The court may authorize destruction of court records not involving alimony, support, or custody of children 5 years from the last record activity.

CERTIFICATION FORWARD DOCUMENTS. This record series consists of lists of encumbrances to be applied against certified forward money which is money brought forward from the previous fiscal year for goods and services which were not received until the current fiscal year. See also "ENCUMBRANCE RECORDS."
RETENTION: 3 years.

CHILD SUPPORT/ALIMONY DISBURSEMENT RECORDS: DETAIL. This series consists of records documenting disbursement of child support or alimony. The series includes, but is not limited to, check registers, check stubs, cancelled checks, cancelled warrants, disbursement ledgers, transaction journals, vendor invoice, refund records and other accounts payable related documentation.
RETENTION: 5 fiscal years.

CHILD SUPPORT/ALIMONY DISBURSEMENT RECORDS: SUMMARY. This series consists of records providing summary or aggregate documentation of expenditures or transfers moneys for child support or alimony. The series may include, but is not limited to, trail balance reports, check logs and registers, summary reports, summary journal transactions and other accounts payable summary related documentation.
RETENTION: 10 fiscal years.

CHILD SUPPORT/ALIMONY RECEIPT/REVENUE RECORDS: DETAIL. This series consists of records documenting specific receipts/revenues collected for child support or alimony. The series may include, but is not limited to, cash receipts, receipt books, deposit receipts, bank validated deposit slips, depository ledger reports filed with Clerk of Court, transaction journals, refund records, bad check records and other accounts receivable related documentation.
RETENTION: 5 fiscal years.

CHILD SUPPORT/ALIMONY RECEIPT/REVENUE RECORDS: SUMMARY. This series consists of records providing summary or aggregate documentation of receipts/revenues collected for child support or alimony. The series may include, but is not limited to, monthly statements of bank accounts, trial balance reports, bank statements, credit and debit card reports, collection balance sheets and other receivable summary related documentation.
RETENTION: 10 fiscal years.

COMPLAINTS: CITIZENS/CONSUMERS/EMPLOYEES. This record series consists of individual complaints received from citizens, consumers or employees. This file may include the name, address, date of complaint, telephone number, the complaint to whom referred and date, action taken and signature of person taking the action.
RETENTION: 1 year.

CONTINUING EDUCATION RECORDS. This record series consists of continuing education records, including records of judicial education.
RETENTION: 2 years.

CONTRACTS/LEASES/AGREEMENTS: CAPITAL IMPROVEMENT/REAL PROPERTY. This record series consists of legal documents, correspondence, reports, etc., relating to the negotiation, fulfillment and termination of capital improvement or real property contracts, leases or agreements to which the agency is a party, including contracts, leases or agreements with architects, engineers, builders, and construction companies. "Capital Improvements" shall mean improvements to real property (land, buildings, including appurtenances, fixtures and fixed equipment, structures, etc.), that add to the value and extend the useful life of the property, including construction of new structures, replacement or rehabilitation of existing structures (e.g., major repairs such as roof replacement), or removal of closed structures. 'Real Property' means land, buildings, and fixtures. The terms "land," "real estate," "realty" and "real property" may be used interchangeably. See also "CONTRACTS/LEASES/AGREEMENTS: NON-CAPITAL IMPROVEMENT."
RETENTION: 10 fiscal years after completion or termination of contract/lease/agreement.

CONTRACTS/LEASES/AGREEMENTS: NON-CAPITAL IMPROVEMENT. This record series consists of legal documents, correspondence, reports, etc., relating to the negotiation, fulfillment and termination of non-capital improvement contracts, leases or agreements to which the agency is a party. In addition, it includes the various contracts, leases or agreements entered into for the purchase of goods and services such as the purchase of gas, fuel oil and annual purchases of inventory-maintained items. See also "CONTRACTS/LEASES/AGREEMENTS: CAPITAL IMPROVEMENT/REAL PROPERTY."
RETENTION: 5 fiscal years after completion or termination of contract/lease/agreement.

CORRESPONDENCE & MEMORANDA: ADMINISTRATIVE. This record series consists of routine correspondence and memoranda of a general nature that is associated with administrative practices but that does not create policy or procedure, document the business of a particular program, or act as a receipt. See also "INFORMATION REQUEST RECORDS." **"These records may have archival value."**
RETENTION: 3 years.

CORRESPONDENCE & MEMORANDA: PROGRAM AND POLICY DEVELOPMENT. This record series consists of correspondence and memoranda of any nature that is associated with a specific program or the

development of policy and procedure. **"These records may have archival value."**
RETENTION: 5 years.

COURT REGISTRY. This record series consists of records, ledgers and journals showing amounts paid into the Court Registry, held by the Court, and paid out by the Court.
RETENTION: Permanent.

COURT REPORTS. This record series consists of court reports, including SRS, jury management, witness management, uniform case reporting system records, and other statistical court reports.
RETENTION: 3 years.

DEEDS: PROPERTY. This record series consists of property deeds. Series may include appraisals, surveys, and other supporting documents.
RETENTION: Retain as long as property is retained.

DELAYED BIRTH (APPLICATION/CERTIFICATE/AFFIDAVITS, ETC.) This record series consists of an application signed by a judge for a birth (other than in a hospital usually). This record is filed with the County Court pursuant to Section 382.0195(4)(a), Florida Statutes. Once signed, the application becomes an order. The record copy is sent to Vital Statistics.
RETENTION: Permanent.

DIRECTIVES/POLICIES/PROCEDURES. This record series consists of the official management statements of policy for the organization, supporting documents, and the operating procedures which outline the methods for accomplishing the functions and activities assigned to the judicial branch entity. It includes all memoranda and correspondence generated relating to the policies and procedures which are to be followed by employees. See also "CORRESPONDENCE & MEMORANDA: PROGRAM AND POLICY DEVELOPMENT." **"These records may have archival value."**
RETENTION: 2 years.

DISASTER PREPAREDNESS DRILLS. This record series consists of the results of disaster preparedness exercises and the supporting documents including scenarios, location of safety related drills, time tables, response times, probable outcomes, areas of difficulties, descriptions of how difficulties were resolved, and areas for improvement. Types of drills include: fire, tornado, safety, hurricane and SARA chemical spills. See also "DIRECTIVES/POLICIES/PROCEDURES" and "DISASTER PREPAREDNESS PLANS."
RETENTION: 3 years.

DISASTER PREPAREDNESS PLANS. This record series consists of disaster preparedness and recovery plans adopted by a judicial branch entity. See also "DIRECTIVE/POLICIES/PROCEDURES."
RETENTION: Retain until obsolete, superseded or administrative value is lost.

DISBURSEMENT RECORDS: DETAIL. This series consists of records documenting specific expenditures or transfers of agency moneys for the procurement of commodities and services and other purposes. The series may include, but is not limited to, procurement records such as requisitions, requisition logs, purchase orders, contracts, purchasing card (p-card) receipts, vendor invoices, receiving reports, acceptances of contract deliverables, approvals, and related documentation; and expenditure records for disbursements made through checks, warrants, electronic fund transfers (EFT), purchasing cards, or other methods, such as payment vouchers, approvals, check registers, cancelled checks, check stubs, cancelled warrants, disbursement ledgers, journal transactions, expenditure detail reports, refund records and other accounts payable and related documentation. Retention is based on s. 95.11(2), F.S., Statute of Limitations on contracts, obligations, or liabilities. See also "DISBURSEMENT RECORDS: SUMMARY," "PURCHASING RECORDS," and "TRAVEL RECORDS."
RETENTION: 5 fiscal years.

DISBURSEMENT RECORDS: SUMMARY. This series consists of records providing summary or aggregate documentation of expenditures or transfers of agency moneys for the procurement of commodities and services

and other purposes. The series may include, but is not limited to, summary records such as trial balance reports, check logs and registers, summary expenditure reports, federal grant final closeout reports, summary journal transactions, and other accounts payable summary and related documentation. See also "DISBURSEMENT RECORDS: DETAIL."
RETENTION: 10 fiscal years.

DISCIPLINARY CASE FILES. This record series consists of both sustained formal or informal disciplinary cases investigated that allege employee misconduct or violations of department regulations and orders, and state/federal statutes. It includes statements by the employee, witnesses, and the person filing the complaint. "Formal discipline" is defined as disciplinary action involving demotion, removal from office, suspension, or other similar action. "Informal discipline" is defined as any disciplinary action involving written and verbal reprimands, memoranda, or other similar action. This record series also can consist of formal and informal disciplinary cases that were determined as not sustained, unfounded, or exonerated charges. See also "PERSONNEL RECORDS".
RETENTION: 5 years.

DRAFTS AND WORKING PAPERS. This record series consists of documents, correspondence, reports, memos, and other materials in preliminary or developmental form before their iteration as a final product. Drafts may include copies of materials circulated for review for grammar, spelling, and content. Working papers may include notes and miscellaneous documents and materials used in compiling and assembling the final product. Note that some draft documents and working papers may have long-term value; such documents may even have archival or historical value. Such records might be better placed under the record series "Administrator Records: Public Officials/Court Administrators."
RETENTION: Retain until obsolete, superseded or administrative value is lost.

DRUG TEST RECORDS. This record series consists of the positive or negative results of a drug test under the Drug Free Workplace Act or as required for CDL or other drivers under US DOT regulations as well as records related to canceled tests. This series might include documents generated in decisions to administer reasonable suspicion or post-accident testing, or in verifying the existence of a medical explanation of the inability of the driver to provide adequate breath or to provide a urine specimen for testing. In addition, the case file could include: the employer's copy of an alcohol test form, including the results of the test; a copy of the controlled substances test chain of custody control form; documents sent by the Medical Review Officer (MRO) to the employer; notice to report for testing; affidavit signed by the employee stating any prescription drugs or over the counter medication currently taken; and final clearance to resume working. This record series can also consist of documentation, including memorandum and correspondence, related to an employee's refusal to take or submit samples for an alcohol and/or controlled substances test(s).
RETENTION: 5 years.

ELECTRONIC FUNDS TRANSFER RECORDS. This record series consists of documentation necessary to establish and maintain the electronic transfer of funds from one financial institution to another. The documentation may include, but is not limited to: an agreement between the two parties; a form which lists both institutions' names, their routing numbers, the name of the account holder, and the account's authorizing signature; a canceled deposit slip or check; and the paperwork for the termination of service or transfer of service to a new institution. This series does not include the paperwork on a specific individual deposit or payment.
RETENTION: 5 fiscal years.

ELECTRONIC RECORDS SOFTWARE. This record series consists of proprietary and non-proprietary software as well as related documentation that provides information about the content, structure and technical specifications of computer systems necessary for retrieving information retained in machine-readable format. These records may be necessary to an audit process.
RETENTION: Retain as long as there are software dependent records.

EMPLOYEE PRE-COUNSELING RECORDS. This record series consists of material and supporting documentation which provide documentation of initial contact with an employee regarding incidents which may or may not lead to disciplinary action. This series is not considered in and of itself a part of the employee discipline record.
RETENTION: 1 year.

EMPLOYMENT EXAMINATION RECORDS. This record series consists of test plans, announcements, grades, grading scales, keyed exams, test monitor's list of candidates, any research toward the development of the tests, and any other selection or screening criteria. See "PERSONNEL RECORDS" and "RECRUITMENT & SELECTION PACKAGES."
RETENTION: 4 anniversary years.

ENCUMBRANCE RECORDS. This record series consists of documents and reports which document funds that have been encumbered. See also "CERTIFICATION FORWARD DOCUMENTS."
RETENTION: 3 years.

ENDOWMENTS, BEQUESTS AND TRUST FUND RECORDS. This record series consists of creating, establishing or contributing to endowments, bequests and trust fund records. **"These records may have archival value."**
RETENTION: Permanent.

ENVIRONMENTAL REGULATION RECORDS. This record series consists of permits, reviews, supporting documents and correspondence resulting from environmental regulation requirements.
RETENTION: 5 years.

EQUAL EMPLOYMENT OPPORTUNITY COMPLIANCE RECORDS. This record series consists of EEO-5 and supporting documents, reviews, background papers and correspondence relating to employment papers and correspondence relating to employment statistics (race, sex, age, etc.). See also "AFFIRMATIVE ACTION RECORDS."
RETENTION: 4 anniversary years after final action.

EQUIPMENT/VEHICLE MAINTENANCE RECORDS. This record series documents service, maintenance, and repairs to agency equipment and vehicles, including program changes to electronic equipment. The series may include, but is not limited to, work orders and documentation of dates/history of repairs, locations, cost of parts, hours worked, etc. Records for all agency vehicles, including ground, air, and water vehicles, are covered by this series. See also "VEHICLE RECORDS."
RETENTION: 1 fiscal year after disposition of equipment.

EQUIPMENT/VEHICLE USAGE RECORDS. This record series documents use of agency equipment and vehicles, including, but not limited to, vehicle logs indicating driver, destination, fuel/service stops, and odometer readings and/or total trip mileage; equipment usage logs and/or reports; and other usage documentation. See also "VEHICLE RECORDS."
RETENTION:

a) Record copy. 1 calendar year.

b) Duplicates. Retain until obsolete, superseded, or administrative value is lost.

EXPENDITURE PLANS: CAPITAL. This record series consists of capital improvement expenditure plans.
RETENTION: Permanent.

FACILITY RESERVATION/Rental records. This record series consists of forms generated in the process of renting or scheduling a public meeting hall or room, conference site, to a citizen or family, private organization,

or other public agency. These forms include, but are not limited to, name of renter, renter's address and telephone number, method of payment, acknowledgment of rules, liability, damage waivers, and the date and time of the rental as well as what facility or portion of a facility is to be reserved. These forms may contain a check number, corresponding receipt number, an amount as well as deposit information. There may also be a floor plan denoting the desired arrangement of tables or chairs as requested by the renter.
RETENTION: 5 fiscal years.

FEASIBILITY STUDY RECORDS. This record series consists of working papers, correspondence, consulting firm reports and management committee reports investigating various projects of the judicial branch entity.
RETENTION: 3 years.

FEDERAL AND STATE TAX FORMS/REPORTS. This record series consists of W-2 Forms, W-4 Forms, W-9 Forms, 940 Forms, 941-E Forms, 1099 Forms, 1099 Reports and UTC-6 Forms. The retention period mentioned below for the record (master) copy was established pursuant to Section 26 CFR 31.6001-1(2).
RETENTION: 4 calendar years.

GENERAL LEDGERS: ANNUAL SUMMARY. This record series consists of ledgers containing accounts to which debits and credits are posted from supporting documents of original entry. It includes all permanent ledger entries.
RETENTION: Permanent.

GRAND JURY NOTES. This record series consists of stenographic records, notes, and transcriptions made by the court reporter or stenographer during the grand jury session. These records are normally kept in a sealed container and are not subject to public inspection pursuant to Section 905.17(1), Florida Statutes. A Court order must be obtained for disposition.
RETENTION: 10 years from closing of session.

GRAND JURY RECORDS. This record series consists of jury summons, requests for recusal, juror payments, information to jurors' employers, lists of jurors, juror questionnaires, and other records related to a grand jury. This record series includes records related to a grand jury and the statewide grand jury.
RETENTION: 2 years.

GRANT FILES. This record series consists of financial, management and any other related material which is generated subsequent to application for or expenditure of grant funds. These files include all applications, supporting documentation, contracts, agreements, and routine reports. Check with applicable grant agency for any additional requirements. Project completion has not occurred until all reporting requirements are satisfied and final payments have been received. See also "PROJECT FILES: FEDERAL", and "PROJECT FILES: NONCAPITAL IMPROVEMENT". **"These records may have archival value."**
RETENTION: 5 fiscal years after completion of project.

GRIEVANCE FILES (EMPLOYMENT). This record series consists of records of all proceedings in the settlement of disputes between employer and employee. See also "PERSONNEL RECORDS."
RETENTION: 3 years.

HEALTH RECORDS: BLOOD BORNE PATHOGEN/ASBESTOS/EXPOSURE. This record series consists of medical records of employees who may have or did come into contact with blood or other potentially hazardous materials. These confidential records include the employee's name, social security number, hepatitis B vaccination status including the dates of testing, results of examinations, medical testing, and follow up procedures, a copy of the healthcare professional's written opinion, a list of complaints which may be related to the exposure, and a copy of information provided to the healthcare professional. This record series can also consist of documents which record the exposure or possible exposure of an employee to a blood borne pathogen, contagion, radiation and chemicals above the acceptable limits or dosage. These documents may include

statistical analyses, incident reports, material safety data sheets, copies of medical records or reports, risk management assessments, and other necessary data to support the possibility of exposure. *Please refer to 20 CFR 1910.1030.*
RETENTION: 30 years after termination, retirement, or separation from employment.

INCIDENT REPORTS. This record series consists of reports of incidents which occur at a public facility or on publicly owned property. It may include alarm malfunctions, suspicious persons, maintenance problems, or any other circumstance that should be noted for future reference or follow up.
RETENTION: 4 years.

INFORMATION REQUEST RECORDS. This record series consists of correspondence accumulated in answering inquiries from the public. See also "CORRESPONDENCE & MEMORANDA: ADMINISTRA-TIVE."
RETENTION: 1 year.

INSPECTION RECORDS: FIRE/SECURITY/SAFETY. This record series consists of inspection reports for fire, security, and safety.
RETENTION: 4 years.

INSPECTION REPORTS: FIRE EXTINGUISHER (ANNUAL). This records series consists of annual fire extinguisher inspection reports.
RETENTION: 1 anniversary year or life of equipment, whichever is sooner.

INSURANCE RECORDS. This record series consists of all policies, claim filing information, correspondence and claims applications made by an agency, premium payment records which includes fire, theft, liability, medical, life, etc. on agency's property or employees. The record series also consists of a list of any insurance carriers and the premium payment amounts paid to them.
RETENTION: 5 years after final disposition of claim or expiration of policy.

INVENTORY RECORDS: PHYSICAL. This record series consists of all information regarding the physical inventory of all Operating Capital Outlay (O.C.O.) items which require an identification number and tag. Included in these reports are items sold through the auctions process as well as the Fixed Inventory Report showing all property owned by the judicial branch entity. See also "SUPPLY RECORDS."
RETENTION: 3 years.

JQC — JUDICIAL FINANCIAL DISCLOSURE FORMS. This record consists of all financial disclosure forms filed by the judiciary with the Judicial Qualifications Commission.
RETENTION: 10 years.

JQC — JUDICIAL COMPLAINTS. This record consists of individual complaints received from citizens, judges, or lawyers against members of the judiciary.
RETENTION: 3 years if complaint summarily dismissed. For the lifetime of the judge against whom the complaint has been filed in all other cases.

JUROR NOTES. Juror notes shall consist of any written notes taken by jurors during civil or criminal trials.
RETENTION: Immediate destruction upon issuance of a verdict or if the trial ends prematurely as a result of a mistrial, plea, or settlement.

JURY RECORDS. This record series consists of jury summons, requests for recusal, juror payments, information to jurors' employers, lists of jurors, juror questionnaires, and other records related to the jury pool. This record series includes records related to petit juries.
RETENTION: 2 years.

KEY AND BADGE ISSUANCE RECORDS. This record series consists of the key control system which includes receipts for keys and security or identification badges issued by employees. See also "VISITOR

LOGS".
RETENTION: Retain as long as employee is employed.

LAW OFFICE MANAGEMENT ASSISTANCE SERVICE RECORDS. This record series consists of all materials in connection with consultations or advice given in the course of office management assistance services provided to an attorney, legal office, or law firm.
RETENTION: Retain until obsolete, superseded or administrative value is lost.

LEAVE TRANSACTION REPORTS. This record series consists of the printed record generated through COPES of the total hours used and the accrual earned during a pay period. It also consists of the leave balances of vacation, sick and compensatory leave for all employees in the agency.
RETENTION: 3 years.

LEGISLATION RECORDS. This record series consists of proposed legislation for the Florida Legislature and all supporting documentation, analysis or tracking information. **"These records may have archival value."**
RETENTION: Retain until obsolete, superseded or administrative value is lost.

LIBRARY CIRCULATION RECORDS. This record series consists of the transactions devised to make library materials and equipment available to the entire library clientele. Also, includes delinquent records and charges, copies of incoming and outgoing interlibrary loan requests for books, magazine articles, microfilms, renewals and subject searches.
RETENTION: 3 years.

LITIGATION CASE FILES. This record series consists of legal documents, notes, reports, background material, etc. created in the preparation of handling legal disputes involving a judicial branch entity. See also, "OPINIONS: LEGAL (ATTORNEY)," and "OPINIONS: LEGAL (SUPPORTING DOCUMENTS)."
RETENTION: 5 years after case closed or appeal process expired.

MAIL: UNDELIVERABLE FIRST CLASS. This record series consists of mail from any judicial branch entity, returned due to an incorrect address or postage. See also "MAILING LISTS" and "POSTAGE RECORDS."
RETENTION: 1 year.

MAILING LISTS. This record series consists of mailing lists. See also "MAIL: UNDELIVERABLE FIRST CLASS" and "POSTAGE RECORDS."
RETENTION: Retain until obsolete, superseded or administrative value is lost.

MANAGEMENT SURVEYS/STUDIES: INTERNAL. This record series consists of the raw data and work papers for any survey conducted to study management issues such as client/patron/employee satisfaction and service improvement. This data may include survey response cards, the results of telephone polls, tally sheets, opinion cards for suggestion boxes, and other records related to the study of internal operations. This does not include a consultant report. The final computation of the data is produced as a survey report and may be scheduled either as part of a feasibility study, project case file, or an operational/statistical report - depending on the nature and depth of the survey/study.
RETENTION: 1 year after final data or report released.

MATERIALS SAFETY RECORDS. This record series consists of a list of toxic substances to which an employee is, has been or may be exposed to during the course of their employment with an employer who manufacturers, produces, uses, applies or stores toxic substances in the work place.
RETENTION: 30 years.

MEMORANDA - LEGAL: Court's decision-making. This record series consists of memoranda, drafts or other documents involved in a court's judicial decision-making process.
RETENTION: Retain until obsolete, superseded or administrative value is lost.

MINUTES: OFFICIAL MEETINGS. This record series consists of the minutes of meetings convened to establish policy or precedent and includes meetings of the Board of Governors of The Florida Bar and The Florida Board of Bar Examiners, and court administrative conferences. See also "MINUTES: OTHER MEETINGS" and "MINUTES: OFFICIAL MEETINGS (AUDIO/VISUAL RECORDINGS)." **"These records may have archival value."**
RETENTION: Permanent.

MINUTES: OFFICIAL MEETINGS (AUDIO/VISUAL RECORDINGS). This record series consists of official audio and video recordings of meetings. See also, "MINUTES: OTHER MEETINGS."
RETENTION: Until minutes are prepared.

MINUTES: OFFICIAL MEETINGS (SUPPORTING DOCUMENTS). This record series consists of the agenda and supporting documents for official meetings. See also "MINUTES: OTHER MEETINGS" and "MINUTES: OFFICIAL MEETINGS (AUDIO/VISUAL RECORDINGS)."
RETENTION: 3 years.

MINUTES: OTHER MEETINGS. This record series consists of minutes from all meetings which are not included in "MINUTES: OFFICIAL MEETINGS."
RETENTION: 1 year.

MONTHLY DISTRIBUTION OF FINES. This record series consists of monthly reports, prepared by the clerk, of all fines imposed under the penal laws of the state and the proceeds of all forfeited bail bonds or recognizance which are paid into the fine and forfeiture fund. The report contains the amount of fines imposed by the court and of bonds forfeited and judgments rendered on said forfeited bonds, and into whose hands they had been paid or placed for collection, the date of conviction in each case, the term of imprisonment, and the name of the officer to whom commitment was delivered.
RETENTION: 3 fiscal years.

NEWS RELEASES. This record series consists of news releases distributed by the judicial branch entity and news releases received from other offices for informational purposes. See also "PUBLIC INFORMATION CASE FILES," and "PRE-PUBLICATIONS AND MEDIA ITEM RECORDS." **"These records may have archival value."**
RETENTION: 90 days.

OPERATIONAL AND STATISTICAL REPORT RECORDS: OFFICE. This record series consists of daily, weekly, monthly, biannual, and annual narrative and statistical reports of office operations made within and between judicial branch entities. Also included in this series are activity reports demonstrating the productivity of an employee or the work tasks completed for a period of time (hourly/daily/weekly).
RETENTION: Retain until obsolete, superseded or administrative value is lost.

OPINIONS: ETHICS. This record series consists of advisory ethical opinions issued by the appropriate committee in response to an inquiry from a regulated person or entity. **"These records may have archival value."**
RETENTION: Permanent.

OPINIONS: ETHICS (SUPPORTING DOCUMENTS). This record series consists of supporting documents relating to advisory ethical opinions.
RETENTION: 3 years.

OPINIONS: LEGAL (ATTORNEY). This record series consists of written opinions of lasting significance establishing policy or precedent answering legal questions involving questions of interpretation of Florida or federal law. This does not include memoranda, drafts or other documents involved in a court's judicial decision-making process. See also "CORRESPONDENCE & MEMORANDA: PROGRAM AND POLICY

DEVELOPMENT", "LITIGATION CASE FILES," "MEMORANDA — LEGAL" and "OPINIONS: LEGAL (SUPPORTING DOCUMENTS)." **"These records may have archival value."**
RETENTION: Permanent.

OPINIONS: LEGAL (SUPPORTING DOCUMENTS). This record series consists of the supporting documentation to the opinions that answer legal questions involving questions of interpretation of Florida or Federal law. See also "LITIGATION CASE FILES" and "OPINIONS: LEGAL (ATTORNEY)."
RETENTION: 3 years.

ORDERS: ADMINISTRATIVE. This record series consists of administrative orders as defined in Rule of Judicial Administration 2.020(c).
RETENTION: Permanent.

ORGANIZATION CHARTS. This record series consists of organizational charts that show lines of authority and responsibility within and between judicial branch entities. See also "DIRECTIVES/POLICIES/PROCE-DURES."
RETENTION: Retain until obsolete, superseded or administrative value is lost.

OTHERWISE UNCATEGORIZED RECORDS. This record series consists of all records which are not otherwise specified in this schedule.
RETENTION: Retain until obsolete, superseded or administrative value is lost.

PARKING DECAL/PERMIT RECORDS. This record series consists of parking applications for automobile and motor bike decals for employees. See also "VEHICLE RECORDS."
RETENTION: 2 years.

PAYROLL RECORDS. This record series consists of the following: a form used by staff to rectify errors in payroll processing including: wrong name, incorrect deductions or salary, inaccurate tax information, or other problems; forms authorizing direct deductions for insurance, union dues, credit unions, savings bonds, charitable contributions, deferred compensation, day care, etc.; any payroll record posted to the employee's applicable retirement plan, in any format (plus indices, if applicable), which are used to document payment for retirement or other purposes during an employee's duration of employment and also lists each rate(s) of pay changes.
RETENTION: 4 years.

PAYROLL RECORDS: REGISTERS (POSTED). This record series consists of records posted to the employee's retirement plan, in any format (plus indexes, if applicable), which are used to document payment for retirement or other purposes during an employee's duration of employment and also lists each rate of pay. Please note that the information in this record series should be posted to an applicable retirement plan. See also other "PAYROLL RECORDS" and "SOCIAL SECURITY CONTROLLED SUMMARY RECORDS."
RETENTION: 4 years.

PERSONNEL RECORDS. This record series consists of an application for employment, resume, personnel action reports, directly related correspondence, oath of loyalty, fingerprints, medical examination reports, performance evaluation reports, worker's compensation reports, and other related materials. See also "EM-PLOYMENT EXAMINATION RECORDS," "DISCIPLINARY CASE FILES," and other "PERSONNEL RECORDS."
RETENTION: 25 years after separation or termination of employment.

PERSONNEL RECORDS: LOCATOR. This record series consists of a log or card of where to locate personnel including name of individual, location to be found, date, address, emergency contact and other general information.
RETENTION: Retain until obsolete, superseded or administrative value is lost.

PERSONNEL RECORDS: OPS/TEMPORARY EMPLOYMENT. This record series consists of all information relating to each O.P.S. or temporary employee within each judicial branch entity. Also, records may

include an employment application, resume, personnel action forms and any correspondence relating to that individual. Temporary employment may include personnel from a local employment agency. See also "EMPLOYMENT EXAMINATION RECORDS," "DISCIPLINARY CASE FILES," and other "PERSONNEL RECORDS."
RETENTION: 3 years.

PETTY CASH DOCUMENTATION RECORDS. This record series consists of receipts, bills and monthly balances indicating amount needed for replenishing this revolving account.
RETENTION: 3 years.

POSITION DESCRIPTION RECORDS. This record series consists of specifically assigned duties and responsibilities for a particular position, including percentage breakdown of duties.
RETENTION: 2 years after superseded.

POSTAGE RECORDS. This record series consists of a detailed listing showing the amount of postage used, date, unused balance and purpose. See also "MAILING LISTS" and "MAIL: UNDELIVERABLE FIRST CLASS."
RETENTION: 3 years.

PRE-PUBLICATIONS AND MEDIA ITEM RECORDS. This record series consists of records used to generate publications such as catalogs, pamphlets and leaflets and other media items including rough, blue lined, and final copies. See also "NEWS RELEASES" and "PUBLIC INFORMATION CASE FILES".
RETENTION: Retain until receipt of final copy.

PROCLAMATIONS/RESOLUTIONS. This record series consists of an expression of a governing body or public official concerning administrative matters, an expression of a temporary character or a provision for the disposition of a particular item of the administrative business of a governing body or judicial branch entity. See also, "DIRECTIVES/POLICIES/PROCEDURES." **These records may have archival value.**
RETENTION: Permanent.

PROCLAMATIONS/RESOLUTIONS: SUPPORTING DOCUMENTS. This record series consists of documents that were used to prepare a proclamation or resolution. See also "PROCLAMATIONS/RESOLU-TIONS" and "DIRECTIVES/POLICIES/PROCEDURES."
RETENTION: 3 years.

PROGRAM/SUBJECT/REFERENCE FILES. This record series may contain correspondence, reports, memoranda, studies, articles, etc. regarding topics of interest to or addressed by a judicial branch entity. See also, "ADMINISTRATIVE RECORDS: PUBLIC OFFICIALS/COURT ADMINISTRATORS".
RETENTION: Retain until obsolete, superseded, or administrative value is lost.

PROJECT FILES: CAPITAL IMPROVEMENT. This record series consists of correspondence or memo-randa, drawings, resolutions, narratives, budget revisions, survey information, change orders, computer runs and reports all pertaining to capital improvement projects, construction and contract specifications for various proposed projects sent out for bid. See also "PROJECT FILES: FEDERAL," and "PROJECT FILES: NON-CAPITAL IMPROVEMENT."
RETENTION: 10 years.

PROJECT FILES: FEDERAL. This record series consists of original approved project contracts, agreements, awards, and line-item budgets, budget amendments, cash requests, correspondence and audit reports. See also "GRANT FILES" and "PROJECT FILES: CAPITAL IMPROVEMENT."
RETENTION: 5 years.

PROJECT FILES: NON-CAPITAL IMPROVEMENT. This record series consists of correspondence or memoranda, drawings, resolutions, narratives, budget revisions, survey information, change orders, computer

runs and reports all pertaining to projects in progress, construction and contract specifications for various proposed projects sent out for bid. See also "GRANT FILES," "PROJECT FILES: CAPITAL IMPROVE-MENT," and "PROJECT FILES: FEDERAL."
RETENTION: 5 years.

PROPERTY TRANSFER FORMS. This record series consists of all capital and non-capital property transfer forms to declare surplus or transfer to another unit of local or state government. This series does not include real property transfers.
RETENTION: 1 year.

PUBLIC INFORMATION CASE FILES. This record series consists of speeches and drafts, contact prints, negatives, enlargements from negatives and transparencies created as illustrations in publications or as visual displays of activities of the judicial branch entity. See also "NEWS RELEASES," and "PRE-PUBLICATIONS AND MEDIA ITEM RECORDS." **"These records may have archival value."**
RETENTION: 90 days.

PUBLIC PROGRAM/EVENT RECORDS: CONTRACTED. This record series consists of case files of events or programs which are available to the public or segments of the public. Files may include copies of contracts or agreements, participant or performer information, program details and arrangements, photo or video tapes. See also "PUBLIC PROGRAM/EVENT RECORDS: NON-CONTRACTED."
RETENTION: 5 years.

PUBLIC PROGRAM/EVENT RECORDS: NON-CONTRACTED. This record series consists of case files of events or programs which are available to the public or segments of the public. Files may include, copies of contracts or agreements, participant or performer information, program details and arrangements, photo or video tapes. See also "PUBLIC PROGRAM/EVENT RECORDS: CONTRACTED."
RETENTION: 3 years.

PURCHASING RECORDS. This record series consists of a copy of the purchase order which is retained by the originating office while another is sent by the purchasing office to the appropriate vendor for action. The series may include, but is not limited to, copies of requisitions sent by the originating office to supply, purchasing, graphics, duplicating, or other sections for action; copies of receiving reports; and a log of outstanding and paid requisitions and purchase orders used for cross-referencing purposes. See also "DIS-BURSEMENT RECORDS: DETAIL."
RETENTION: 5 fiscal years.

RECEIPT/REVENUE RECORDS: DETAIL. This series consists of records documenting specific receipts/revenues collected by an agency through cash, checks, electronic fund transfers (EFT), credit and debit cards, or other methods. The series may include, but is not limited to, records such as cash collection records and reports, cash receipt books, cash register tapes, deposit/transfer slips, EFT notices, credit and debit card records, receipt ledgers, receipt journal transactions and vouchers, refund records, bad check records, and other accounts receivable and related documentation. Retention is based on s. 95.11(2), F.S., Statute of Limitations on contracts, obligations, or liabilities. See also "RECEIPT/REVENUE RECORDS: SUMMARY."
RETENTION: 5 fiscal years provided applicable audits have been released.

RECEIPT/REVENUE RECORDS: SUMMARY. This series consists of records providing summary or aggregate documentation of receipts/revenues collected by an agency. The series may include, but is not limited to, records such as trial balance reports, bank statements, credit and debit card reports, revenue reconciliations, collection balance sheets, and other accounts receivable summary and related documentation. See also "RECEIPT/REVENUE RECORDS: DETAIL."
RETENTION: 10 fiscal years provided applicable audits have been released.

RECEIPTS: REGISTERED AND CERTIFIED MAIL. This record series consists of receipts for registered and certified mail sent out or received by a particular judicial branch entity. See also "MAIL: UNDELIVER-

ABLE FIRST CLASS," and "POSTAGE RECORDS."
RETENTION: 1 year.

RECRUITMENT & SELECTION PACKAGES. This record series consists of all records which document the selection process and justify the selection process and justify the selection decision including: details of the job analysis and identification of the knowledge, skills and abilities necessary to perform the job; application forms and/or resumes for employment including demographic data of applicants including but not limited to race, sex, age and veteran status; list of all applicants' name and ratings or rankings (if applicable) for each selection technique; description of the selection process; selection techniques used, including samples, supplemental applications, etc.; the current position description; the names and titles of all persons administering the selection process or participating in making selection decisions; the job opportunity announcement and any other recruitment efforts; and other information that affects the selection decisions. See also "EMPLOYMENT EXAMINATION RECORDS".
RETENTION: 4 anniversary years after personnel action and any litigation is resolved.

SALARY COMPARISON REPORTS. This record series consists of a report which is distributed and provided for reference purposes only. This data is compiled from records located in the Personnel Office.
RETENTION: 1 year.

SALARY SCHEDULES. This record series consists of a pay grade comparison chart or log indicating the salary classification for each position.
RETENTION: 10 years.

SEARCH COMMITTEE RECORDS. This record series consists of minutes, reports, vitas, resumes, interview score sheets, interview results, list of priority hires, a personnel requisition, references of applicants and the affirmative action compliance report.
RETENTION: 180 days.

SEARCH WARRANTS SERVED: NO ARREST/NO CASE FILED. This record series consists of the original affidavit for search warrant, search warrant and return of the search warrant. Series may also include property inventory and receipt, if any property was obtained. After execution of the warrant it is filed with the Clerk of Court as served with no arrest having been made. Since no court case is generated, these are kept as a separate record series.
RETENTION: 1 year after date of return.

SOCIAL SECURITY CONTROLLED SUMMARY RECORDS. This record series consists of a judicial branch entity's copy of the State's FICA report mailed to the Division of Retirement. Report lists the total taxable wages plus the amount withheld from employee wages plus employer's contribution. See also "PAYROLL RECORDS."
RETENTION: 4 calendar years after due date of tax.

STATE AUTOMATED MANAGEMENT ACCOUNTING SYSTEM (SAMAS) REPORTS. This record series consists of reports of all updated transactions entered into the system and a financial statement for each month for all divisions of judicial branch entities.
RETENTION: 3 years.

STATE AWARDS AND RECOGNITION FILES. This record series consists of data relating to the State Meritorious Service Awards Program. File contains employee suggestion forms (Form DMS/EPE.AWP01), evaluations, adoption forms and payment records. It also contains Superior Accomplishment nomination forms and payment records. Summary information submitted to the Department of Management Services for Annual Workforce Report (Form DMS/EPE.AWP02) is also contained in this record series.
RETENTION: 3 years.

SUPPLY RECORDS. This record series consists of documentation of a perpetual inventory of expendable supplies located in a central supply office for use by judicial branch entity employees. Included in this series is a listing of all available supplies which is distributed periodically or upon request. See also "INVENTORY RECORDS: PHYSICAL."
RETENTION: 3 years.

SURVEILLANCE VIDEO TAPES. This record series consists of surveillance video tapes created to monitor activities occurring both within and outside of public buildings. This tape may play an integral part in prosecution or disciplinary actions.
RETENTION: 30 days, then erase and reuse provided any necessary images are saved.

TELEPHONE CALL RECORDS: LONG DISTANCE. This record series consists of documentation and logs of separately billed long distance telephone service.
RETENTION: 1 year.

TRAINING MATERIAL RECORDS. This record series consists of materials used in training, such as films, slides, commentaries, manuals, workbooks and other related items. This records series does not include individual training records.
RETENTION: Retain until obsolete, superseded or administrative value is lost.

TRAINING RECORDS: EMPLOYEE. This record series consists of a record for each employee which may include all educational and training records of the employee. See also "PERSONNEL RECORDS."
RETENTION: 3 years.

TRANSITORY MESSAGES. This record series consists of those records that are created primarily for the communication of information, as opposed to communications designed for the perpetuation of knowledge. Transitory messages do not set policy, establish guidelines or procedures, certify a transaction, or become a receipt. The informal tone of transitory messages might be compared to the communication that might take place during a telephone conversation or a conversation in an office hallway. Transitory messages would include, but would not be limited to: E-mail messages with short-lived, or no administrative value, voice mail, self-sticking notes, and telephone messages.
RETENTION: Retain until obsolete, superseded or administrative value is lost.

TRAVEL RECORDS. This record series consists of records required to support reimbursement of expenses incurred during official travel.
RETENTION: 5 fiscal years.

UNCLAIMED PROPERTY RECORDS. This record series consists of forms required by the State Comptroller's Office for the registration of abandoned tangible or intangible property. These forms are required under Chapter 717 of the Florida Statutes. The judicial branch entity holding the unclaimed property is to maintain a list of the specific type of property, amount, name, and last known address of the owner.
RETENTION: 5 years after the property becomes reportable.

UNEMPLOYMENT COMPENSATION RECORDS. This record series consists of reports submitted to the State on a quarterly basis stating the name of each employee, employee number, amount of wages paid during quarter subject to unemployment benefits, social security number, number of weeks covered and other pertinent information which is retained by the State for determination of unemployment benefits due to applicants for same. Also includes, receipts and statements of charges.
RETENTION: 5 fiscal years.

VEHICLE ACCIDENT REPORTS. This record series consists of reports of employees that are involved in accidents in a judicial branch entity vehicle or in their own vehicle during the course of official business. See also "VEHICLE RECORDS."
RETENTION: 4 anniversary years.

VEHICLE RECORDS. This record series consists of all pertinent records pertaining to each vehicle owned by the judicial branch entity. The records usually consist of the vehicle registration papers, copy of the title, inspection information, maintenance agreements, credit card information, confidential tag issuance information and any other information relating to the vehicle. See also "VEHICLE ACCIDENT REPORTS."
RETENTION: 1 year after disposition of vehicle.

VENDOR FILES. This record series consists of vendor invoices for items purchased or leased, received and paid for.
RETENTION: 3 years.

VISITOR LOGS. This record series consists of records documenting employees' and visitors' entrance into a judicial branch entity's building during and after office hours. See also "KEY AND BADGE ISSUANCE RECORDS."
RETENTION: 30 days.

WIRE AND ORAL COMMUNICATIONS: APPLICATIONS, ORDERS AND AUDIO RECORDINGS. This record series consists of applications for an order authorizing the interception of a wire or oral communications and orders granted pursuant to Chapter 934, Florida Statutes. Also included are original recordings of the contents of any wire or oral communication made pursuant to Section 934.09, Florida Statutes. They shall not be destroyed except upon an order of the issuing or denying judge, or that judge's successor in office, and in any event shall be kept for ten (10) years.
RETENTION: 10 years (upon permission of the Court).

WITNESS SUBPOENAS/LISTS. This record series consists of subpoena lists that may be used to establish witness payments.
RETENTION: 3 years.

WORK ORDERS. This record series consists of information reflecting the individual history of major or minor maintenance or services requiring a work order request. Work order includes dates, locations, cost of labor, hours worked, equipment cost per hour, material used and cost, and other pertinent details. This item does not include equipment maintenance records. See also "EQUIPMENT/VEHICLE MAINTENANCE RECORDS."
RETENTION: 3 years.

WORK SCHEDULES. This record series consists of any scheduling documentation for shift or part time employees. These records may include hours scheduled to work, the switching of hours with another employee, the location or route of work assignment, and anticipated starting and ending times.
RETENTION: 1 year.

WORKERS' COMPENSATION RECORDS. This record series consists of the first report of injury and the employer's supplemental reports including, if used, OSHA Form No. 200 as well as its predecessor forms No. 100 and 102 and OSHA Form No. 101. These records are created pursuant to Florida Statutes Section 440.09 and OSHA standards 1904.2, 1904.4, and 1904.5.
RETENTION: 5 years.

INDEX TO FLORIDA RULES OF JUDICIAL ADMINISTRATION

FLORIDA PROBATE RULES

2013 EDITION

*(Includes probate and guardianship rules, Florida Probate Code,
Florida Guardianship Law, and related rules, statutes,
and constitutional provisions)*

Rules reflect all changes through 37 FLW S643. Subsequent amendments, if any, can be found at www.floridasupremecourt.org/decisions/rules.shtml. The Florida Bar also updates the rules on its website at www.FloridaBar.org (on the home page, click "Rules Updates"). Statutes are current through the 2012 Legislative Session.

THE FLORIDA BAR

CONTINUING LEGAL EDUCATION PUBLICATIONS

CITATIONS TO OPINIONS ADOPTING OR AMENDING RULES

ORIGINAL ADOPTION, effective 1-1-68: 201 So.2d 409.

OTHER OPINIONS:

Effective 1-1-76:	324 So.2d 38	Complete revision (temporary rules).
Effective 7-1-77:	344 So.2d 828	Complete revision.
Effective 1-1-81:	387 So.2d 949	Four-year-cycle revision. Amended 5.020, 5.040, 5.340, 5.345, 5.400, 5.440, 5.520, 5.540, 5.550, 5.560, 5.570, 5.630, 5.660, 5.690; added 5.205.
Effective 1-1-85:	458 So.2d 1079	Four-year-cycle revision. Amended 5.020–5.040, 5.080, 5.110, 5.150, 5.170, 5.180, 5.210, 5.230, 5.240–5.270, 5.340–5.420, 5.440, 5.460–5.490, 5.510–5.560, 5.600, 5.620, 5.660, 5.670; deleted 5.280, 5.290, 5.410, 5.450, 5.500, 5.570; added 5.041, 5.042, 5.065, 5.395, 5.401, 5.405, 5.406.
Effective 1-1-85:	460 So.2d 906	Amended 5.340.
Effective 12-23-87:	517 So.2d 675	Amended 5.540, 5.560; added 5.710.
Effective 1-1-89:	531 So.2d 1261	Four-year-cycle revision. Amended 5.015, 5.025, 5.042, 5.050, 5.080, 5.110, 5.160, 5.180, 5.205–5.240, 5.270, 5.340, 5.360, 5.400, 5.405–5.420, 5.440, 5.490, 5.510, 5.620, 5.630, 5.650–5.670, 5.690; deleted 5.190, 5.390, 5.540, 5.590; added 5.122, 5.171, 5.201, 5.235, 5.275, 5.346, 5.355, 5.385, 5.386, 5.475, 5.495.
Effective 10-1-89:	551 So.2d 452	Amended 5.015, 5.550, 5.560, 5.610–5.660, 5.680–5.700; added 5.590, 5.800.
Effective 10-1-91:	584 So.2d 964	Amended 5.010, 5.040, 5.050, 5.240, 5.550, 5.560, 5.590–5.630, 5.650–5.680, 5.700–5.800; amended and re-numbered 5.690 to 5.695; deleted 5.495; added 5.540, 5.541, 5.555, 5.635, 5.690, 5.696, 5.697, 5.705, 5.900.
Effective 1-1-93:	607 So.2d 1306	Four-year-cycle revision. Amended 5.025, 5.120, 5.200, 5.240, 5.260, 5.310, 5.346, 5.400, 5.470, 5.690, 5.695, 5.900; added 5.496, 5.636.
Effective 1-1-97:	683 So.2d 78	Four-year-cycle revision. Amended 5.040, 5.041, 5.080, 5.100, 5.180, 5.210, 5.235, 5.240, 5.346, 5.370, 5.400, 5.401, 5.405, 5.406, 5.470, 5.560, 5.590, 5.680.
Effective 1-1-01:	778 So.2d 272	Four-year-cycle revision. Amended 5.015, 5.040, 5.041, 5.065, 5.100, 5.110, 5.555, 5.560, 5.705.
Effective 10-11-01:	807 So.2d 622, 816 So.2d 1095	Amended 5.025, 5.340, 5.360; added 5.365.
Effective 5-2-02, applicable to decedents dying after December 31, 2001:	824 So.2d 849	Amended 5.080, 5.200, 5.205, 5.210, 5.240, 5.310, 5.340, 5.345, 5.346, 5.385, 5.405, 5.440, 5.510, 5.530; deleted 5.070, 5.520; added 5.215, 5.216, 5.241, 5.341, 5.404.
Effective 6-19-03, applicable to decedents dying after December 31, 2001:	848 So.2d 1069	Two-year-cycle revision. Amended 5.122, 5.205, 5.240, 5.385, 5.430, 5.496; added 5.342.
Effective 1-1-04:	848 So.2d 1069	Two-year-cycle revision. Amended 5.555, 5.680; added 5.407, 5.552.
Effective 10-1-04:	887 So.2d 1090	Amended 5.697.

Effective 1-1-06:	912 So.2d 1178	Two-year-cycle revision. Amended 5.040, 5.041, 5.042, 5.240, 5.241, 5.270, 5.345, 5.346, 5.360, 5.400, 5.404, 5.475, 5.496, 5.530, 5.620; added 5.402, 5.403, 5.498, 5.499, 5.625.
Effective 2-1-07:	948 So.2d 735	Amended 5.180, 5.550, 5.552, 5.555, 5.560, 5.625, 5.630, 5.636, 5.660, 5.680, 5.695; added 5.646, 5.647, 5.685, 5.720, 5.725.
Effective 7-12-07:	964 So.2d 140	Amended 5.015, 5.240, 5.241; added 5.648.
Effective 1-1-08:	959 So.2d 1170	Three-year-cycle revision. Amended 5.040, 5.041, 5.200, 5.210, 5.241, 5.490, 5.496, 5.498, 5.499, 5.530, 5.650, 5.670, 5.697, 5.710; added 5.095, 5.645.
Effective 7-10-08:	986 So.2d 576	Amended 5.015, 5.030, 5.040, 5.050, 5.120, 5.540, 5.541, 5.620, 5.625, 5.640, 5.650, 5.660, 5.680, 5.720; added 5.649, 5.681.
Effective 1-11-11:	50 So.3d 578	Three-year cycle review. Amended 5.020, 5.030, 5.040, 5.041, 5.060, 5.110, 5.200, 5.205, 5.210, 5.235, 5.260, 5.330, 5.340, 5.346, 5.360, 5.405, 5.406, 5.440, 5.470, 5.496, 5.696, 5.710, and 5.725.
Effective 1-1-11:	51 So.3d 1146	Amended 5.201, 5.260, 5.360 and created 5.3425.
Effective 7-7-11:	67 So.3d 1035	Amended 5.260.
Effective 9-28-11:	73 So.3d 205	Amended 5.025, 5.240.
Effective 10-1-11:	78 So.3d 1045	Amended 5.200, 5.210, 5.530.
Effective 9-1-12:	37 FLW S643	Amended 5.030, 5.040, 5.041, 5.060, 5.120. 5.200, 5.340, 5.342, 5.350, 5.355, 5.360, 5.370, 5.380, 5.385, 5.386, 5.400, 5.401, 5.402, 5.403, 5.405, 5.406, 5.407, 5.430, 5.440, 5.460, 5.470, 5.475, 5.496, 5.498, 5.499, 5.510, 5.530, 5.620, 5.630, 5.650, 5.660, 5.670, 5.680, 5.690. 5.695, 5.696, 5.700
Effective 10-1-12:	95 So.3d 96	Amended 5.042.
Effective 4-1-13:	37 FLW S638	Adopted 5.043.

NOTE TO USERS: Rules in this pamphlet are current through 37 FLW S643. Subsequent amendments, if any, can be found at www.floridasupremecourt.org/decisions/rules.shtml. The Florida Bar also updates the rules on its website at www.FloridaBar.org (on the homepage click "Rules Updates").

TABLE OF CONTENTS

FLORIDA PROBATE RULES

PART I. GENERAL

PART II. PROBATE

PART III. GUARDIANSHIP

PART IV. EXPEDITED JUDICIAL INTERVENTION CONCERNING MEDICAL TREATMENT PROCEDURES

PART I. GENERAL

RULE 5.010. SCOPE

These rules govern the procedure in all probate and guardianship proceedings and shall be known as the Florida Probate Rules and may be cited as Fla. Prob. R. Part I applies to all proceedings. Part II applies to probate alone, Part III applies to guardianship alone, and Part IV applies to expedited judicial intervention concerning medical treatment procedures. The Florida Rules of Civil Procedure apply only as provided herein.

Committee Notes

Rule History

1975 Revision: These rules shall govern the procedures to be followed in all matters pending on or commenced after January 1, 1976, including procedures for the enforcement of substantive rights that have vested before that date. See section 731.011, Florida Statutes.

1977 Revision: The changes in these rules shall take effect on July 1, 1977.

1988 Revision: In the opinion reported at 460 So. 2d 906, the Florida Supreme Court directed the Probate and Guardianship Rules Committee to study the statutes and attempt to identify those portions of the Florida Probate Code, the Florida Guardianship Law, and other statutes that contained procedural provisions. When those procedural provisions were identified, the committee was charged to promulgate rules incorporating those procedures.

The committee has reviewed the statutes and has found a substantial measure of procedure that was contained only in the statutes for which there were no corresponding rules. The committee also determined that much of the procedure in the statutes already had a rule counterpart.

New rules added, or prior rules amended, in 1988 to add procedural matters previously found only in the statutes are rules 5.050, 5.122, 5.171, 5.180, 5.201, 5.235, 5.270, 5.275, 5.355, 5.360, 5.385, 5.386, 5.400, 5.440, 5.475, 5.490, and 5.510. With only one exception (see rule 5.050), the only portion of the statutes that has been reviewed in detail, and for which rules have been created, is the Florida Probate Code. Other portions of the statutes mentioned in the opinion cited above remain for the next cycle of this committee to review.

As the committee wrote rules to transfer the statutory procedure into these rules, an attempt was made to write the rule without changing the meaning of the statute. It was not possible or advisable to use the exact wording of the statute in some instances, and in those instances the committee rewrote the statutory language in the format used in the rules generally. Even under those circumstances, the committee attempted to transfer the entire procedural portion of the statute without changing its meaning. Where it was specifically intended in a few instances to add to existing statutory procedure, that fact is noted in the relevant committee note. The committee felt strongly that it would be detrimental to the orderly process of estate probate and related procedures if a rule specified a different procedure than was specified in the related statute, even though the statute must, under the Florida Constitution, yield to the rule when there is a conflict.

The committee, through the proper channels in the Florida Bar (initially, the Probate Law Committee of the Real Property, Probate and Trust Law Section), intends to ask the legislature to repeal those portions of the statutes that are procedural when there are similar rules already in place, or when similar new rules are added by this opinion. It is the opinion of the committee that continuing to maintain procedure in the statutes when there is a rule specifying that procedure is detrimental to the orderly process of the court and the public that it serves, especially when, over time, the statute and the rule may diverge.

Although the supreme court has adopted these recommended rules, it has not specifically determined that all of the provisions of the statutes that were procedural have now been adopted as a rule. This is a continuing project for the committee and although these new rules and changes represent a substantial transition of procedure into the rules, the committee does not suggest that the transition is complete. The court is not precluded from examining any particular statute or rule in the context of a particular actual dispute.

1991 Revision: Rule revised to reflect addition of new Part IV dealing with expedited judicial intervention concerning medical treatment procedures.

1992 Revision: In 1989, the Florida Legislature enacted a comprehensive revision to Florida's guardianship law. In response, the Florida Supreme Court appointed an ad hoc committee to recommend temporary rules of procedure for the new law. In an opinion at 551 So. 2d 452 (Fla. 1989), the court adopted the temporary rules recommended by the ad hoc committee, to replace Part III of the then-existing Florida Probate Rules, effective October 1, 1989. In its opinion, the court also directed the Florida Probate Rules Committee to review the new laws and, on a priority basis, to recommend permanent rules of procedure.

The committee reviewed the Florida Guardianship Law enacted in 1989, as well as revisions to the law enacted in 1990, and presented its rule recommendations to the court in 1991. The court, in an opinion at 584 So. 2d 964, adopted the recommendations with minor exceptions, to be effective October 1, 1991.

In 1990, the court also rendered its opinion in In re Guardianship of Browning, 568 So. 2d 4 (Fla. 1990), regarding a person's right to refuse lifeprolonging medical procedures. In that decision, the court directed the committee to recommend a response, the committee created a new Part IV of these rules and recommended rule 5.900, which was adopted by the court, with minor changes, in its opinion at 584 So. 2d 964, effective October 1, 1991.

The committee continued its efforts to review the Florida Probate Code and to promulgate or amend rules regarding any procedural portions of those statutes. As a result of those efforts, as well as the efforts described above, the committee recommended amendments to rules 5.010, 5.025, 5.040, 5.050, 5.200, 5.240, 5.310, 5.346, 5.400, 5.470, 5.550, 5.560, 5.590, 5.600, 5.610, 5.620, 5.630, 5.640, 5.650, 5.660, 5.670, 5.680, 5.695, 5.700, 5.710, and 5.800; creation of new rules 5.496, 5.540, 5.541, 5.555, 5.635, 5.636, 5.690, 5.696, 5.697, 5.705, and 5.900; and deletion of rule 5.495. In addition, the committee recommended editorial changes in virtually all the rules so that they would conform stylistically to one another and to all other rules promulgated by the supreme court.

2003 Revision: The committee has promulgated numerous changes in the rules and in the committee notes to many of the rules, in response to legislative amendments that deleted procedural aspects of a number of statutes in the Florida Probate Code, including deletion and re-titling of some statutes. See Ch. 2001-226, Laws of Fla.

Rule References

Fla. Prob. R. 5.025 Adversary proceedings.

Fla. Prob. R. 5.040(a)(3)(B) Notice.

Fla. Prob. R. 5.050 Transfer of proceedings.

Fla. Prob. R. 5.080 Discovery and subpoena.

Fla. Prob. R. 5.230(e) Commission to prove will.

Fla. R. App. P. 9.800 Uniform citation system.

RULE 5.015. GENERAL DEFINITIONS

(a) General. The definitions and rules of construction stated or referred to in sections 1.01 and 393.12, Florida Statutes, and chapters 731, 732, 733, 734, 735, 736, 738, 739, and 744, Florida Statutes, as amended from time to time, shall apply to these rules, unless otherwise defined in these rules.

(b) Specific Definitions. When used in these rules

(1) "certified copy" means a copy of a document signed and verified as a true copy by the officer to whose custody the original is entrusted;

(2) "formal notice" means notice under rule 5.040(a);

(3) "informal notice" means notice under rule 5.040(b);

(4) "judge" means a judge of the circuit court, including any judge elected, appointed, substituted, or assigned to serve as judge of the court;

(5) "guardian advocate" means a person appointed for a person with a developmental disability pursuant to section 393.12, Florida Statutes;

(6) "guardian" means a person appointed pursuant to chapter 744, Florida Statutes, or a guardian advocate unless a rule indicates otherwise;

(7) "ward" means an individual for whom a guardian is appointed.

Committee Notes

Rule History

1977 Revision: No change in rule. Correction of typographical error in committee note.

This is intended to simplify drafting of these rules and should be liberally construed. See Fla. Prob. R. 5.190 and 5.540 and also §§ 731.201 and 744.102, Fla. Stat.

1988 Revision: Rule was expanded due to deletion of rule 5.190. Committee notes expanded. Citation form changes in rule and committee notes.

1992 Revision: Citation form changes in rule and committee notes.

2000 Revision: Subdivision (b)(2) amended to delete outdated reference to rule 5.550(c).

2007 Revision: Subdivision (a) amended to add reference to chapter 736, Florida Statutes, which was added to the statutes effective July 1, 2007, and which replaces deleted chapter 737, and to add reference to chapter 739, Florida Statutes, which was added effective July 1, 2005. Committee notes revised.

2008 Revision: Subdivision (a) amended to add reference to section 393.12, Florida Statutes, which governs guardian advocates for persons with developmental disabilities, As provided by section 744.102(11), the term "guardian advocate" as used in the Florida Guardianship Law and these rules does not include a guardian advocate appointed for a person determined to lack capacity to consent to treatment under section 394,4598, Florida Statutes. Subdivisions (b)(5) through (b)(7) added to reflect 2008 amendments to section 393.12, Florida Statutes. Committee notes revised.

Statutory References

§ 1.01, Fla. Stat. Definitions.

§ 393.063, Fla. Stat. Definitions.

§ 393.12, Fla. Stat. Capacity; appointment of guardian advocate.

§ 731.201, Fla. Stat. General definitions.

§ 736.0103, Fla. Stat. Definitions.

§ 738.102, Fla. Stat. Definitions.

§ 739.102, Fla. Stat. Defintions.

§ 744.102, Fla. Stat. Definitions.

RULE 5.020. PLEADINGS; VERIFICATION; MOTIONS

(a) Forms of Pleading. Pleadings shall be signed by the attorney of record, and by the pleader when required by these rules. All technical forms of pleadings are abolished. No defect of form impairs substantial rights, and no defect in the statement of jurisdictional facts actually existing renders any proceeding void.

(b) Petition. A petition shall contain a short and plain statement of the relief sought, the grounds therefor, and the jurisdiction of the court where the jurisdiction has not already been shown.

(c) Motions. Any other application to the court for an order shall be by written motion, unless made orally during a hearing or trial. The motion shall state with particularity the grounds therefor and shall set forth the relief or order sought.

(d) Rehearing. A motion for rehearing of any order or judgment shall be served not later than 10 days after the date of filing the order or judgment with the clerk as shown on the face of the order or judgment.

(e) Verification. When verification of a document is required, the document filed shall include an oath, affirmation, or the following statement:

"Under penalties of perjury, I declare that I have read the foregoing, and the facts alleged are true, to the best of my knowledge and belief."

Committee Notes

The time for determining when a motion for rehearing must be served has been clarified in view of Casto v. Casto, 404 So. 2d 1046 (Fla. 1981).

Rule History

1977 Revision: Editorial change (rule) and expansion of committee note. Subdivisions (a), (b), and (d) substantially the same as subdivisions (a), (b), and (f) of prior rule 5.030. Subdivision (c) taken from section 731.104, Florida Statutes. For adversary proceedings see new rule 5.025. Notice of administration is not a pleading within the meaning of this rule.

1980 Revision: Subdivisions (c) and (d) have been redesignated as (e) and (f). New subdivisions (c) and (d) are added to provide for the use of motions in probate proceedings other then adversary proceedings and to specifically authorize a procedure for rehearing.

1984 Revision: Minor editorial changes. Subdivision (f) of prior rule has been deleted as it is now covered under the adversary rules.

1988 Revision: Editorial change in caption of (a). Committee notes revised. Citation form change in committee notes.

1992 Revision: Editorial changes. Committee notes revised. Citation form changes in rule and committee notes.

2003 Revision: Committee notes revised.

2008 Revision: Committee notes revised.

2010 Revision: Committee notes revised.

Statutory References

§ 393.12, Fla. Stat. Capacity; appointment of guardian advocate.

§ 731.104, Fla. Stat. Verification of documents.

§ 731.201, Fla. Stat. General definitions.

§ 733.202, Fla. Stat. Petition.

§ 733.604(1), Fla. Stat. Inventories and accountings; public records exemptions.

§ 733.901, Fla. Stat. Final discharge.

§ 735.203, Fla. Stat. Petition for summary administration.

§ 744.104, Fla. Stat. Verification of documents.

§ 744.3085, Fla. Stat. Guardian advocates.

§ 744.3201, Fla. Stat. Petition to determine incapacity.

§ 744.331, Fla. Stat. Procedures to determine incapacity.

§ 744.334, Fla. Stat. Petition for appointment of guardian or professional guardian; contents.

Rule References

Fla. Prob. R. 5.025 Adversary proceedings.

Fla. Prob. R. 5.200 Petition for administration.

Fla. Prob. R. 5.205(b) Filing evidence of death.

Fla. Prob. R. 5.320 Oath of personal representative.

Fla. Prob. R. 5.330 Execution by personal representative.

Fla. Prob. R. 5.350 Continuance of unincorporated business or venture.

Fla. Prob. R. 5.370(a) Sales of real property where no power conferred.

Fla. Prob. R. 5.405(b) Proceedings to determine homestead real property.

Fla. Prob. R. 5.530 Summary administration.

Fla. Prob. R. 5.550 Petition to determine incapacity.

Fla. Prob. R. 5.560 Petition for appointment of guardian of an incapacitated person.

Fla. Prob. R. 5.600 Oath.

Fla. Prob. R. 5.649 Guardian advocate.

RULE 5.025. ADVERSARY PROCEEDINGS

(a) Specific Adversary Proceedings. The following are adversary proceedings unless otherwise ordered by the court: proceedings to remove a personal representative, surcharge a personal representative, remove a guardian, surcharge a guardian, probate a lost or destroyed will or later-discovered will, determine beneficiaries, construe a will, reform a will, modify a will, cancel a devise, partition property for the purposes of distribution, determine pretermitted status, determine pretermitted share, determine amount of elective share and contribution, and for revocation of probate of a will.

(b) Declared Adversary Proceedings. Other proceedings may be declared adversary by service on interested persons of a separate declaration that the proceeding is adversary.

(1) If served by the petitioner, the declaration must be served with the petition to which it relates.

(2) If served by the respondent, the declaration and a written response to the petition must be served at the earlier of:

(A) within 20 days after service of the petition, or

(B) prior to the hearing date on the petition.

(3) When the declaration is served by a respondent, the petitioner must promptly serve formal notice on all other interested persons.

(c) Adversary Status by Order. The court may determine any proceeding to be an adversary proceeding at any time.

(d) Notice and Procedure in Adversary Proceedings.

(1) Petitioner must serve formal notice.

(2) After service of formal notice, the proceedings, as nearly as practicable, must be conducted similar to suits of a civil nature, including entry of defaults. The Florida Rules of Civil Procedure govern, except for rule 1.525.

(3) The court on its motion or on motion of any interested person may enter orders to avoid undue delay in the main administration.

(4) If a proceeding is already commenced when an order is entered determining the proceeding to be adversary, it must thereafter be conducted as an adversary proceeding. The order must require interested persons to serve written defenses, if any, within 20 days from the date of the order. It is not necessary to re-serve the petition except as ordered by the court.

(5) When the proceedings are adversary, the caption of subsequent pleadings, as an extension of the probate caption, must include the name of the first petitioner and the name of the first respondent.

Editor's Notes: — Florida Supreme Court Order No. SC11-1575, effective July 12, 2012, provides in part, "[W]e clarify that the amendments to Florida Probate Rule 5.025(d)(2) [by Order No. SC11-1575, effective September 28, 2011, reported as In re Amendments to the Florida Probate Rules, 73 So. 3d 205 (Fla. 2011)] apply to all proceedings commenced on or after the September 28, 2011, effective date. The amendments also apply to all proceedings that were pending on the effective date, but only as to all judgments, orders, or notices that were filed on or after that date."

Committee Notes

The court on its initiative or on motion of any party may order any proceeding to be adversary or nonadversary or enter any order that will avoid undue delay. The personal representative would be an interested person in all adversary proceedings. A prescribed form for the caption is provided that will facilitate the clerk's and the court's ability to segregate such adversary proceeding from other adversary proceedings and from the main probate file:

Court

Case #

In Re Estate of John B. Jones   )

)

·   Julia Jones,   )

Petitioner,   )

v.   )

Harold Jones, as Personal   )

Representative, et al.,   )

)

Respondents.   )

Rule History

1975 Revision: New rule. 324 So. 2d 38.

1977 Revision: Editorial changes to (a)(1).

1984 Revision: Extensive changes, committee notes revised and expanded.

1988 Revision: Changes in (a) add proceedings to remove a guardian and to surcharge a guardian to the list of specific adversary proceedings and delete proceedings to determine and award the elective share from the list. Change in (b)(4) clarifies on whom the petitioner must serve formal notice. Editorial change in (d)(2) and (d)(5). Committee notes revised. Citation form changes in committee notes.

1992 Revision: Deletion of (b)(3) as unnecessary. Former (b)(4) renumbered as new (b)(3). Committee notes revised. Citation form changes in committee notes.

2001 Revision: Change in (a) to add determination of amount of elective share and contribution as specific adversary proceedings. Committee notes revised.

2003 Revision: Committee notes revised.

2008 Revision: Committee notes revised.

2011 Revision: Subdivision (a) revised to add "reform a will, modify a will" and "determine pretermitted status." Subdivision (d)(2) modified to insure that an award of attorneys' fees in a probate or guardianship proceeding follows the law and procedures established for such proceedings, rather than the law and procedures for civil proceedings. *See Amendments to the Florida Family Law Rules of Procedure (Rule 12.525), 897 So. 2d 467 (Fla. 2005).* Editorial changes to conform to the court's guidelines for rules submissions as set forth in Administrative Order AOSC06-14. Committee notes revised.

Statutory References

§ 393.12, Fla. Stat. Capacity; appointment of guardian advocate.

§§ 732.201-732.2155, Fla. Stat. Elective share of surviving spouse.

§ 732.301, Fla. Stat. Pretermitted spouse.

§ 732.302, Fla. Stat. Pretermitted children.

§ 732.507, Fla. Stat. Effect of subsequent marriage, birth, or dissolution of marriage.

§§ 732.6005-732.611, Fla. Stat. Rules of construction.

§ 732.615, Fla. Stat. Reformation to correct mistakes.

§ 732.616, Fla. Stat. Modification to achieve testator's tax objectives.

§ 733.105, Fla. Stat. Determination of beneficiaries.

§ 733.107, Fla. Stat. Burden of proof in contests; presumption of undue influence.

§ 733.109, Fla. Stat. Revocation of probate.

§ 733.207, Fla. Stat. Establishment and probate of lost or destroyed will.

§ 733.208, Fla. Stat. Discovery of later will.

§ 733.504, Fla. Stat. Removal of personal representative; causes for removal.

§ 733.505, Fla. Stat. Jurisdiction in removal proceedings.

§ 733.506, Fla. Stat. Proceedings for removal.

§ 733.5061, Fla. Stat. Appointment of successor upon removal.

§ 733.603, Fla. Stat. Personal representative to proceed without court order.

§ 733.609, Fla. Stat. Improper exercise of power; breach of fiduciary duty.

§ 733.619(2), (4), Fla. Stat. Individual liability of personal representative.

§ 733.814, Fla. Stat. Partition for purpose of distribution.

§ 744.3085, Fla. Stat. Guardian advocates.

§ 744.474, Fla. Stat. Reasons for removal of guardian.

§ 744.477, Fla. Stat. Proceedings for removal of a guardian.

Rule References

Fla. Prob. R. 5.040 Notice.

Fla. Prob. R. 5.270 Revocation of probate.

Fla. Prob. R. 5.360 Elective share.

Fla. Prob. R. 5.365 Petition for dower.

Fla. Prob. R. 5.440 Proceedings for removal.

Fla. Prob. R. 5.649 Guardian advocate.

Fla. Prob. R. 5.660 Proceedings for removal of guardian.

Fla. Prob. R. 5.681 Restoration of rights of person with developmental disability.

Fla. R. Civ. P. 1.140 Defenses.

Fla. R. Civ. P. 1.160 Motions.

Fla. R. Civ. P. 1.200 Pretrial procedure.

Fla. R. Civ. P. 1.280 General provisions governing discovery.

Fla. R. Civ. P. 1.290 Depositions before action or pending appeal.

Fla. R. Civ. P. 1.310 Depositions upon oral examination.

Fla. R. Civ. P. 1.340 Interrogatories to parties.

Fla. R. Civ. P. 1.380 Failure to make discovery; sanctions.

RULE 5.030. ATTORNEYS

(a) Required; Exception. Every guardian and every personal representative, unless the personal representative remains the sole interested person, shall be represented by an attorney admitted to practice in Florida. A guardian or personal representative who is an attorney admitted to practice in Florida may represent himself or herself as guardian or personal representative. A guardian advocate is not required to be represented by an attorney unless otherwise required by law or the court.

(b) Limited Appearance without Court Order. An attorney of record for an interested person in a proceeding governed by these rules shall be the attorney of record in all other proceedings in the administration of the same estate or guardianship, except service of process in an independent action on a claim, unless at the time of appearance the attorney files a notice specifically limiting the attorney's appearance only to the particular proceeding or matter in which the attorney appears. At the conclusion of that proceeding or matter, the attorney's role terminates upon the attorney filing notice of completion of limited appearance and serving a copy on the client and other interested persons.

(c) Withdrawal or Limited Appearance with Court Order. An attorney of record may withdraw or limit the attorney's appearance with approval of the court after filing a motion setting forth the reasons and serving a copy on the client and other interested persons.

Committee Notes

The appearance of an attorney in an estate is a general appearance unless (i) specifically limited at the time of such appearance or (ii) the court orders otherwise. This rule does not affect the right of a party to employ additional attorneys who, if members of the Florida Bar, may appear at any time.

Rule History

1975 Revision: Subdivision (a) is same as prior rule 5.040 with added provision for withdrawal of attorney similar to Florida Rule of Appellate Procedure 2.3(d)(2). Subdivision (b) reflects ruling in case of State ex rel. Falkner v. Blanton, 297 So. 2d 825 (Fla. 1974).

1977 Revision: Editorial change requiring filing of petition for withdrawal and service of copy upon interested persons. Editorial change in citation forms in rule and committee note.

1984 Revision: Minor editorial changes and addition of subdivision (c). Committee notes expanded.

1988 Revision: Editorial changes and order of subdivisions rearranged. Committee notes expanded. Citation form changes in committee notes.

1992 Revision: Editorial changes. Committee notes revised. Citation form changes in committee notes.

2003 Revision: Committee notes revised.

2005 Revision: Committee notes revised.

2006 Revision: Committee notes revised.

2008 Revision: Subdivision (a) amended to reflect that a guardian advocate may not be required to be represented by an attorney in some instances. Committee notes revised.

2010 Revision: Subdivisions (b) and (c) amended to clarify the procedure for termination of an attorney's representation of an interested person either with or without court order.

2012 Revision: Committee notes revised.

Statutory References

§ 393.12, Fla. Stat. Capacity; appointment of guardian advocate.

§ 731.301, Fla. Stat. Notice.

§ 733.106, Fla. Stat. Costs and attorney fees.

§ 733.212, Fla. Stat. Notice of administration; filing of objections.

§ 733.6175, Fla. Stat. Proceedings for review of employment of agents and compensation of personal representatives and employees of estate.

§ 744.108, Fla. Stat. Guardian's and attorney's fees and expenses.

§ 744.3085, Fla. Stat. Guardian advocates.

Rule References

Fla. Prob. R. 5.041 Service of pleadings and documents.

Fla. Prob. R. 5.110(b), (c) Resident agent.

Fla. R. Jud. Admin. 2.505 Attorneys.

Fla. R. Jud. Admin. 2.516 Service of pleadings and documents.

Fla. R. App. P. 9.440 Attorneys.

RULE 5.040. NOTICE

(a) Formal Notice.

(1) When formal notice is given, a copy of the pleading or motion shall be served on interested persons, together with a notice requiring the person served to serve written defenses on the person giving notice within 20 days after service of the notice, exclusive of the day of service, and to file the original of the written defenses with the clerk of the court either before service or immediately thereafter, and notifying the person served that failure to serve written defenses as required may result in a judgment or order for the relief demanded in the pleading or motion, without further notice.

(2) After service of formal notice, informal notice of any hearing on the pleading or motion shall be served on interested persons, provided that if no written defense is served within 20 days after service of formal notice on an interested person, the pleading or motion may be considered ex parte as to that person, unless the court orders otherwise.

(3) Formal notice shall be served:

(A) by sending a copy by any commercial delivery service requiring a signed receipt or by any form of mail requiring a signed receipt as follows:

(i) to the attorney representing an interested person; or

(ii) to an interested person who has filed a request for notice at the address given in the request for notice; or

(iii) to an incapacitated person or a person with a developmental disability to the person's usual place of abode and to the person's legal guardian, if any, at the guardian's usual place of abode or regular place of business; or, if there is no legal guardian, to the incapacitated person or person with a developmental disability at the person's usual place of abode and on the person, if any, having care or custody of the incapacitated person or person with a developmental disability at the usual place of abode or regular place of business of such custodian; or

(iv) to a minor whose disabilities of nonage are not removed, by serving the persons designated to accept service of process on a minor under chapter 48, Florida Statutes; or

(v) on any other individual to the individual's usual place of abode or to the place where the individual regularly conducts business; or

(vi) on a corporation or other business entity to its registered office in Florida or its principal business office in Florida or, if neither is known after reasonable inquiry, to its last known address; or

(B) as provided in the Florida Rules of Civil Procedure for service of process; or

(C) as otherwise provided by Florida law for service of process.

(4) Service of formal notice pursuant to subdivision (3)(A) shall be complete on receipt of the notice. Proof of service shall be by verified statement of the person giving the notice; and there shall be attached to the verified statement the signed receipt or other evidence satisfactory to the court that delivery was made to the addressee or the addressee's agent.

(5) If service of process is made pursuant to Florida law, proof of service shall be made as provided therein.

(b) Informal Notice. When informal notice of a petition or other proceeding is required or permitted, it shall be served as provided in rule 5.041.

(c) "Notice" Defined. In these rules, the Florida Probate Code, and the Florida Guardianship Law "notice" shall mean informal notice unless formal notice is specified.

(d) Formal Notice Optional. Formal notice may be given in lieu of informal notice at the option of the person giving notice unless the court orders other-

wise. When formal notice is given in lieu of informal notice, formal notice shall be given to all interested persons entitled to notice. When formal notice is given in lieu of informal notice, that notice does not modify any time period otherwise specified by statute or these rules.

Committee Notes

Formal notice is the method of service used in probate proceedings and the method of service of process for obtaining jurisdiction over the person receiving the notice. "The manner provided for service of formal notice" is as provided in rule 5.040(a)(3).

Informal notice is the method of service of notice given to interested persons entitled to notice when formal notice is not given or required.

Reference in this rule to the terms "mail" or "mailing" refers to use of the United States Postal Service.

Rule History

1975 Revision: Implements section 731.301, Florida Statutes.

1977 Revision: Reference to elisor.

1980 Revision: Editorial changes. Clarification of time for filing defenses after formal notice. Authorizes court to give relief to delinquent respondent from ex parte status; relief from service on numerous persons; allows optional use of formal notice.

1984 Revision: Editorial changes. Eliminates deadline for filing as opposed to serving defenses after formal notice; defines procedure subsequent to service of defenses after formal notice; new requirements for service of formal notice on incompetents and corporations; defines when service of formal notice is deemed complete; provisions relating to method of service of informal notice transferred to new rules 5.041 and 5.042; eliminates waiver of notice by will.

1988 Revision: Editorial changes. Committee notes revised. Citation form changes in committee notes.

1991 Revision: Subdivision (b) amended to define informal notice more clearly.

1992 Revision: Editorial changes. Committee notes revised. Citation form changes in committee notes.

1996 Revision: Subdivision (a) amended to permit service of formal notice by commercial delivery service to conform to 1993 amendment to section 731.301(1), Florida Statutes. Editorial changes.

2001 Revision: Editorial changes in subdivision (a)(3)(A) to clarify requirements for service of formal notice.

2003 Revision: Committee notes revised.

2005 Revision: Subdivision (a)(3)(A) amended to delete requirement of court approval of commercial delivery service.

2006 Revision: Committee notes revised.

2007 Revision: Committee notes revised.

2007 Revision: New subdivision (a)(3)(A)(iv) inserted in response to Cason ex rel. Saferight v. Hammock, 908 So. 2d 512 (Fla.

5th DCA 2005), and subsequent subdivisions renumbered accordingly. Committee notes revised.

2008 Revision: Subdivision (a)(3)(A)(iii) revised to include "person with a developmental disability." Committee notes revised.

2010 Revision: Subdivision (d) amended to clarify that the optional use of formal notice when only informal notice is required does not modify any time period otherwise specified by statute or rule. Committee notes revised.

2012 Revision: Subdivision (b) revised to reflect amendment to rule 5.041.

Statutory References

§ 1.01(3), Fla. Stat. Definitions.

ch. 48, Fla. Stat. Process and service of process.

ch. 49, Fla. Stat. Constructive service of process.

§ 393.12, Fla. Stat. Capacity; appointment of guardian advocate.

§ 731.105, Fla. Stat. In rem proceeding.

§ 731.201(18), (22), Fla. Stat. General definitions.

§ 731.301, Fla. Stat. Notice.

§ 731.302, Fla. Stat. Waiver and consent by interested person.

§ 733.212, Fla. Stat. Notice of administration; filing of objections.

§ 733.2123, Fla. Stat. Adjudication before issuance of letters.

§ 733.502, Fla. Stat. Resignation of personal representative.

§ 733.613, Fla. Stat. Personal representative's right to sell real property.

§ 733.6175, Fla. Stat. Proceedings for review of employment of agents and compensation of personal representatives and employees of estate.

§ 733.901, Fla. Stat. Final discharge.

ch 743, Fla. Stat. Disability of nonage of minors removed.

§ 744.106, Fla. Stat. Notice.

§ 744.301, Fla. Stat. Natural guardians.

§ 744.3085, Fla. Stat. Guardian advocates.

§ 744.3201, Fla. Stat. Petition to determine incapacity.

§ 744.331, Fla. Stat. Procedures to determine incapacity.

§ 744.3371, Fla. Stat. Notice of petition for appointment of guardian and hearing.

§ 744.441, Fla. Stat. Powers of guardian upon court approval.

§ 744.447, Fla. Stat. Petition for authorization to act.

§ 744.477, Fla. Stat. Proceedings for removal of a guardian.

Rule References

Fla. Prob. R. 5.025 Adversary proceedings.

Fla. Prob. R. 5.030 Attorneys.

Fla. Prob. R. 5.041 Service of pleadings and documents.

Fla. Prob. R. 5.042 Time.

Fla. Prob. R. 5.060 Request for notices and copies of pleadings.

Fla. Prob. R. 5.180 Waiver and consent.

Fla. Prob. R. 5.560 Petition for appointment of a guardian of an incapacitated person.

Fla. Prob. R. 5.649 Guardian advocate.

Fla. Prob. R. 5.681 Restoration of rights of person with developmental disability.

Fla. R. Jud. Admin. 2.505 Attorneys.

Fla. R. Jud. Admin. 2.516 Service of pleadings and documents.

Fla. R. Civ. P. 1.070 Process.

Fla. R. Civ. P. Form 1.902 Summons.

RULE 5.041. SERVICE OF PLEADINGS AND DOCUMENTS

Unless the court orders otherwise, every petition or motion for an order determining rights of an interested person, and every other pleading or document filed in the particular proceeding which is the subject matter of such petition or motion, except applications for witness subpoenas, shall be served on interested persons as set forth in Florida Rule of Judicial Administration 2.516 unless these rules, the Florida Probate Code, or the Florida Guardianship Law provides otherwise. No service need be made on interested persons against whom a default has been entered, or against whom the matter may otherwise proceed ex parte, unless a new or additional right or demand is asserted. For purposes of this rule an interested person shall be deemed a party under rule 2.516. If the interested person is a minor whose disabilities of nonage are not removed, and who is not represented by an attorney, then service shall be on the persons designated to accept service of process on a minor under chapter 48, Florida Statutes.

Committee Notes

Derived from Florida Rule of Civil Procedure 1.080. Regulates the service of pleadings and papers in proceedings on petitions or motions for determination of rights. It is not applicable to every pleading and paper served or filed in the administration of a guardianship or decedent's estate.

Rule History

1984 Revision: New rule. Subdivision (c) is same as former rule 5.040(d).

1988 Revision: Committee notes revised. Citation form changes in committee notes.

1992 Revision: Editorial changes. Committee notes revised. Citation form changes in committee notes.

1996 Revision: Subdivision (b) amended to allow service to be made by facsimile. Committee notes revised.

2000 Revision: Subdivision (b) amended to clarify requirements for service of pleadings and papers. Subdivision (e) amended to clarify date of filing. Editorial changes in subdivision (f).

2003 Revision: Committee notes revised.

2005 Revision: Changes in subdivisions (b) and (f) to clarify service requirements, and editorial changes in (e).

2006 Revision: Committee notes revised.

2007 Revision: Provisions regarding service on a minor added in subdivision (b) in response to *Cason ex rel. Saferight v. Hammock*, 908 So. 2d 512 (Fla. 5th DCA 2005). Committee notes revised.

2008 Revision: Committee notes revised.

2010 Revision: Committee notes revised.

2012 Revision: Portions of subdivision (b) and all of subdivisions (d), (e), (f), and (g) deleted in response to creation of Rule 2.516 of the Rules of Judicial Administration. Committee notes revised.

Statutory References

ch. 39, Fla. Stat. Proceedings relating to children.

ch. 48, Fla. Stat. Process and service of process.

ch. 61, Fla. Stat. Dissolution of marriage; support; time-sharing.

ch. 63, Fla. Stat. Adoption.

§ 393.12, Fla. Stat. Capacity; appointment of guardian advocate.

§ 731.301, Fla. Stat. Notice.

§ 733.212, Fla. Stat. Notice of administration; filing of objections.

§ 733.2123, Fla. Stat. Adjudication before issuance of letters.

§ 733.705(2), (4), Fla. Stat. Payment of and objection to claims.

ch. 743, Fla. Stat. Disability of nonage of minors removed.

§ 744.3085, Fla. Stat. Guardian advocates.

§ 744.3201, Fla. Stat. Petition to determine incapacity.

§ 744.331, Fla. Stat. Procedures to determine incapacity.

§ 744.3371, Fla. Stat. Notice of petition for appointment of guardian and hearing.

§ 744.447, Fla. Stat. Petition for authorization to act.

ch. 751, Fla. Stat. Temporary custody of minor children by extended family.

Rule References

Fla. Prob. R. 5.020 Pleadings; verification; motions.

Fla. Prob. R. 5.025 Adversary proceedings.

Fla. Prob. R. 5.030 Attorneys.

Fla. Prob. R. 5.040 Notice.

Fla. Prob. R. 5.042 Time.

Fla. Prob. R. 5.150(c) Order requiring accounting.

Fla. Prob. R. 5.180 Waiver and consent.

Fla. Prob. R. 5.240(a) Notice of administration.

Fla. Prob. R. 5.340(d) Inventory.

Fla. Prob. R. 5.550 Petition to determine incapacity.

Fla. Prob. R. 5.560 Petition for appointment of a guardian of an incapacitated person.

Fla. Prob. R. 5.649 Guardian advocate.

Fla. Prob. R. 5.681 Restoration of rights of person with developmental disability.

Fla. R. Civ. P. 1.080 Service of pleadings and papers.

Fla. R. Jud. Admin. 2.505 Attorneys.

Fla. R. Jud. Admin. 2.516 Service of pleadings and documents.

RULE 5.042. TIME

(a) Computation. Computation of time shall be governed by Florida Rule of Judicial Administration 2.514.

(b) Enlargement. When an act is required or allowed to be done at or within a specified time by these rules, by order of court, or by notice given thereunder, for cause shown the court at any time in its discretion

(1) with or without notice may order the period enlarged if request therefor is made before the expiration of the period originally prescribed or as extended by a previous order, or

(2) on motion made and notice after the expiration of the specified period may permit the act to be done when failure to act was the result of excusable neglect. The court under this rule may not extend the time for serving a motion for rehearing or to enlarge any period of time governed by the Florida Rules of Appellate Procedure.

(c) Service for Hearings. A copy of any written petition or motion which may not be heard ex parte and a copy of the notice of the hearing thereon shall be served a reasonable time before the time specified for the hearing.

(d) Additional Time After Service by Mail or E-mail. Except when serving formal notice, or when serving a motion, pleading, or other document in the manner provided for service of formal notice, Florida Rule of Judicial Administration 2.514 shall apply to the computation of time following service.

Committee Notes

This rule is derived from Florida Rule of Civil Procedure 1.090.

Rule History

1984 Revision: New rule.

1988 Revision: Editorial changes in (a) and (b). Subdivision (a) enlarged to include closing of the clerk's office as a legal holiday. In *Clara P. Diamond, Inc. v. Tam-Bay Realty, Inc.*, 462 So. 2d 1168 (Fla. 2d DCA 1984), the Second District Court of Appeal suggested that Florida Rule of Civil Procedure 1.090(b) be clarified to leave no question that the court may not extend the time for rehearing, appeal, or petition for certiorari regardless of whether a request to enlarge the time therefor was made before the expiration of the time allowed. Because the format of rule 5.042(b) was substantially the same as the format of rule 1.090(b), subdivision (b) is amended to conform for the sake of clarity. Committee notes revised.

1992 Revision: Editorial changes. Committee notes revised. Citation form changes in committee notes.

2003 Revision: Committee notes revised.

2005 Revision: Subdivision (d) amended to clarify exception to mailing rule for service of formal notice and service in the manner provided for service of formal notice. Committee notes revised.

2008 Revision: Committee notes revised.

2012 Revision: Subdivision (a) revised to refer to Rule 2.514 and delete duplicative provisions. Subdivision (d) revised to incorporate service by e-mail and the filing and service of documents, rather than papers. Committee notes revised.

Statutory References

§ 393.12, Fla. Stat. Capacity; appointment of guardian advocate.

§ 683.01, Fla. Stat. Legal holidays.

§ 731.301, Fla. Stat. Notice.

§ 732.107, Fla. Stat. Escheat.

§ 732.2135, Fla. Stat. Time of election; extensions; withdrawal.

§ 732.402, Fla. Stat. Exempt property.

§ 732.901, Fla. Stat. Production of wills.

§ 733.104, Fla. Stat. Suspension of statutes of limitation in favor of the personal representative.

§ 733.212, Fla. Stat. Notice of administration; filing of objections.

§ 733.2121, Fla. Stat. Notice to creditors; filing of claims.

§ 733.701, Fla. Stat. Notifying creditors.

§ 733.702, Fla. Stat. Limitations on presentation of claims.

§ 733.705, Fla. Stat. Payment of and objection to claims.

§ 733.710, Fla. Stat. Limitations on claims against estates.

§ 733.816, Fla. Stat. Disposition of unclaimed property held by personal representatives.

§ 744.3085, Fla. Stat. Guardian advocates.

Rule References

Fla. Prob. R. 5.040(a)(1) Notice.

Fla. Prob. R. 5.150 Order requiring accounting.

Fla. Prob. R. 5.240 Notice of administration.

Fla. Prob. R. 5.241 Notice to creditors.

Fla. Prob. R. 5.340(a)-(b) Inventory.

Fla. Prob. R. 5.345 Accountings other than personal representatives' final accountings.

Fla. Prob. R. 5.395 Notice of federal estate tax return.

Fla. Prob. R. 5.400 Distribution and discharge.

Fla. Prob. R. 5.649 Guardian advocate.

Fla. Prob. R. 5.681 Restoration of rights of person with developmental disability.

Fla. Prob. R. 5.700 Objections to guardianship reports.

Fla. R. Civ. P. 1.090 Time.

Fla. R. Jud. Admin. 2.514 Computing and extending time.

RULE 5.043. DEPOSIT OF WILLS AND CODICILS

This rule is subject to an implementation schedule. See the Editor's Notes at the end of the rule.

Notwithstanding any rule to the contrary, and unless the court orders otherwise, any original executed will or codicil deposited with the court must be retained by the clerk in its original form and must not be destroyed or disposed of by the clerk for 20 years after submission regardless of whether the will or codicil has been permanently recorded as defined by Florida Rule of Judicial Administration 2.430.

Editor's Notes: — On October 18, 2012, the Supreme Court of Florida issued a revised opinion in case number SC11-399, which was originally issued on June 21, 2012. See In re Amendments to the Florida Rules of Judicial Administration, 37 FLW S643 (Fla. 2012). The opinion provides in relevant part:

"First, the new electronic filing requirements the Court adopts will become effective in the civil, probate, small claims, and family law divisions of the trial courts, as well as for appeals to the circuit courts in these categories of cases, on April 1, 2013, at 12:01 a.m., except as may be otherwise provided by administrative order. Electronic filing will be mandatory in these divisions pursuant to rule 2.525 on that date. However, until the new rules take effect in these divisions, any clerk who is already accepting documents filed by electronic transmission under the current rules should continue to do so; attorneys in these counties are encouraged to file documents electronically under the current rules.

"Next, the new electronic filing requirements the Court adopts will become effective in the criminal, traffic, and juvenile divisions of the trial courts, as well as for appeals to the circuit court in these categories of cases, on October 1, 2013, at 12:01 a.m., except as may be otherwise provided by administrative order. Electronic filing will be mandatory in these divisions under rule 2.525 on that date. The new e-filing requirements, as they apply in proceedings brought pursuant to the Florida Mental Health Act (Baker Act), Chapter 394, Part I, Florida Statutes, and the Involuntary Commitment of Sexually Violent Predators Act (Jimmy Ryce), Chapter 394, Part V, Florida Statutes, will also not be mandatory in these cases until October 1, 2013. As stated above, until the new rules take effect in these divisions and proceedings, any clerk who is already accepting electronically filed documents under the current rules should continue to do so; attorneys are again encouraged to utilize existing electronic filing procedures under the current rules.

"However, until the new rules and procedures take effect in the district courts, any clerk who is already accepting documents filed by electronic transmission may continue to do so; attorneys in these districts are encouraged to file documents electronically. Clerks will not be required to electronically transmit the record on appeal until July 1, 2013, at 12:01 a.m. Until July 1, we encourage clerks, whenever possible, to electronically transmit the record under the new rules and requirements.

"(W)e note that, in all types of cases, pursuant to amended rule 2.525(d) self-represented parties and self-represented nonparties, including nonparty governmental or public agencies, and attorneys excused from e-mail service under Florida Rule of Judicial Administration 2.516 will be permitted, but not required, to file documents electronically.

By order of November 28, 2012, in case number SC11-399, the Court released a revised implementation schedule, which provides, in pertinent part: "The e-filing rules adopted in the October 2012 opinion will be mandatory in this (Supreme) Court on February 27, 2013, at 12:01 a.m.; and effective earlier on a voluntary basis as will be indicated by further administrative order of the chief justice.

"Thereafter, the e-filing rules will be mandatory in the Second District Court of Appeal on July 22, 2013, at 12:01 a.m.; in the Third District Court of Appeal on September 27, 2013, at 12:01 a.m.; in the Fourth District Court of Appeal on October 31, 2013, at 12:01 a.m.; in the Fifth District Court of Appeal on November 27, 2013 at 12:01 a.m.; and in the First District Court of Appeal on December 27, 2013, at 12:01 a.m., unless made mandatory earlier by the chief judge of the applicable district court of appeal. The e-filing rules will be effective earlier on a voluntary trial basis in the district courts of appeal as will be indicated by further administrative order by the chief judge of the applicable district court."

Committee Notes

2012 Adoption. Florida Rule of Judicial Administration 2.525 requires that all documents be filed with the court electronically. Although the Florida Statutes direct the deposit of a will, rather than the filing of the will, the committee believes that original wills and codicils should be retained in their original form longer than other documents filed with the court due to the unique evidentiary aspects of the actual document. These unique aspects could be lost forever if the original document were converted to electronic form and the original destroyed.

Rule History

2012 Revision: New Rule.

Statutory References

§ 731.201(16), Fla. Stat. General definitions.

§ 732.901, Fla. Stat. Production of wills.

Rule References

Fla. R. Jud. Admin. 2.430 Retention of court records.

Fla. R. Jud. Admin. 2.525 Electronic filing.

RULE 5.050. TRANSFER OF PROCEEDINGS

(a) Incorrect Venue. When any proceeding is filed laying venue in the wrong county, the court may transfer the proceeding in the same manner as provided in the Florida Rules of Civil Procedure. Any action taken by the court or the parties before the transfer is not affected because of the improper venue.

(b) Change of Residence of Ward. When the residence of a ward is changed to another county, the guardian of the person or the guardian advocate shall have the venue of the guardianship changed to the county of the acquired residence.

Committee Notes

Subdivision (b) of this rule represents a rule implementation of the procedure found in section 744.202(3), Florida Statutes.

Rule History

1975 Revision: Same as section 733.101(3), Florida Statutes.

1977 Revision: Title changed to indicate that the rule is one dealing with transfer.

1988 Revision: Prior rule renumbered as (a). New (b) is rule implementation of procedure in section 744.202(2), Florida Statutes. Editorial changes. Committee notes expanded. Citation form changes in rule and committee notes.

1991 Revision: Editorial changes.

1992 Revision: Committee notes revised. Citation form changes in committee notes.

2003 Revision: Committee notes revised.

2008 Revision: Change in (b) to add reference to guardian advocate. Committee notes revised.

Statutory References

ch. 47, Fla. Stat. Venue.

§ 393.12, Fla. Stat. Capacity; appointment of guardian advocate.

§ 733.101, Fla. Stat. Venue of probate proceedings.

§ 744.106, Fla. Stat. Notice.

§ 744.201, Fla. Stat. Domicile of ward.

§ 744.202, Fla. Stat. Venue.

§ 744.2025, Fla. Stat. Change of ward's residence.

§ 744.306, Fla. Stat. Foreign guardians.

§ 744.3085, Fla. Stat. Guardian advocates.

§ 744.3201, Fla. Stat. Petition to determine incapacity.

Rule References

Fla. Prob. R. 5.200(d) Petition for administration.

Fla. Prob. R. 5.240(b)(3), (d) Notice of administration.

Fla. Prob. R. 5.649 Guardian advocate.

Fla. R. Civ. P. 1.060 Transfers of actions.

RULE 5.060. REQUEST FOR NOTICES AND COPIES OF PLEADINGS

(a) Request. Any interested person who desires notice of proceedings in the estate of a decedent or ward may file a separate written request for the notice of further proceedings, designating therein such person's residence and post office address. When such person's residence or post office address changes, a new designation of such change shall be filed in the proceedings. A person filing such request, or address change, shall also deliver a copy thereof to the clerk, who shall forthwith mail it to the attorney for the personal representative or guardian, noting on the original the fact of mailing.

(b) Notice and Copies. A party filing a request shall be served thereafter by the moving party with notice of further proceedings and with copies of subsequent pleadings and papers as long as the party is an interested person.

Committee Notes

Rule History

1975 Revision: This rule substantially incorporates the provisions of prior rule 5.060 except that now a copy of the request shall be mailed by the clerk only to the attorney for the personal representative or guardian. Even though a request under this rule has not been made, informal notice as provided in rule 5.040(b)(3) may still be required.

1977 Revision: Editorial and citation form change in committee note.

1980 Revision: Caveat, the personal representative may want to give notice to parties even though not required, for example, where an independent action has been filed on an objected claim.

1988 Revision: Captions added to subdivisions. Committee notes expanded. Citation form changes in committee notes.

1992 Revision: Editorial changes. Committee notes revised. Citation form changes in committee notes.

2003 Revision: Committee notes revised.

2010 Revision: Committee notes revised.

2012 Revision: Committee notes revised.

Statutory References

§ 731.201, Fla. Stat. General definitions.

§ 733.604, Fla. Stat. Inventories and accountings; public records exemptions.

Rule References

Fla. Prob. R. 5.040 Notice.

Fla. Prob. R. 5.041 Service of pleadings and documents.

Fla. Prob. R. 5.340 Inventory.

Fla. Prob. R. 5.341 Estate information.

Fla. R. Jud. Admin. 2.516 Service of pleadings and documents.

RULE 5.065. NOTICE OF CIVIL ACTION OR ANCILLARY ADMINISTRATION

(a) Civil Action. A personal representative and a guardian shall file a notice when a civil action has been instituted by or against the personal representative or the guardian. The notice shall contain:

(1) the names of the parties;

(2) the style of the court and the case number;

(3) the county and state where the proceeding is pending;

(4) the date of commencement of the proceeding; and

(5) a brief statement of the nature of the proceeding.

(b) Ancillary Administration. The domiciliary personal representative shall file a notice when an ancillary administration has commenced, which notice shall contain:

(1) the name and residence address of the ancillary personal representative; and

(2) the information required in subdivisions (a)(2), (3), and (4) above.

(c) Copies Exhibited. A copy of the initial pleading may be attached to the notice. To the extent an attached initial pleading states the required information, the notice need not restate it.

Committee Notes

This rule reflects a procedural requirement not founded on a statute or rule.

Rule History

1984 Revision: New rule.

1988 Revision: Committee notes expanded.

1992 Revision: Editorial change. Citation form changes in committee notes.

2000 Revision: Subdivision (b) amended to eliminate requirement to set forth nature and value of ancillary assets.

Statutory References

§ 733.612(20), Fla. Stat. Transactions authorized for the personal representative; exceptions.

§ 744.441(11), Fla. Stat. Powers of guardian upon court approval.

RULE 5.080. DISCOVERY AND SUBPOENA

(a) Adoption of Civil Rules. The following Florida Rules of Civil Procedure shall apply in all probate and guardianship proceedings:

(1) Rule 1.280, general provisions governing discovery.

(2) Rule 1.290, depositions before action or pending appeal.

(3) Rule 1.300, persons before whom depositions may be taken.

(4) Rule 1.310, depositions upon oral examination.

(5) Rule 1.320, depositions upon written questions.

(6) Rule 1.330, use of depositions in court proceedings.

(7) Rule 1.340, interrogatories to parties.

(8) Rule 1.350, production of documents and things and entry upon land for inspection and other purposes.

(9) Rule 1.351, production of documents and things without deposition.

(10) Rule 1.360, examination of persons.

(11) Rule 1.370, requests for admission.

(12) Rule 1.380, failure to make discovery; sanctions.

(13) Rule 1.390, depositions of expert witnesses.

(14) Rule 1.410, subpoena.

(b) Limitations and Costs. In order to conserve the assets of the estate, the court has broad discretion to limit the scope and the place and manner of the discovery and to assess the costs, including attorneys' fees, of the discovery against the party making it or against 1 or more of the beneficiaries of the estate or against the ward in such proportions as the court determines, considering, among other factors, the benefit derived therefrom.

(c) Application. It is not necessary to have an adversary proceeding under rule 5.025 to utilize the rules adopted in subdivision (a) above. Any interested person may utilize the rules adopted in subdivision (a).

Committee Notes

Subdivision (b) is not intended to result in the assessment of costs, including attorney's fees, in every instance in which discovery is sought. Subdivision (c) is not intended to overrule the holdings in *In re Estate of Shaw*, 340 So. 2d 491 (Fla. 3d DCA 1976), and *In re Estate of Posner*, 492 So. 2d 1093 (Fla. 3d DCA 1986).

Rule History

1975 Revision: This rule is the same as prior rule 5.080, broadened to include guardianships and intended to clearly permit the use of discovery practices in nonadversary probate and guardianship matters.

1977 Revision: Editorial change in citation form in committee note.

1984 Revision: Florida Rules of Civil Procedure 1.290, 1.300, 1.351, and 1.410 have been added.

1988 Revision: Subdivision (a)(15) deleted as duplicative of rule 5.070 Subpoena. Editorial change in (b). Citation form change in committee notes.

1992 Revision: Editorial changes. Committee notes revised. Citation form changes in committee notes.

1996 Revision: Reference to rule 1.400 eliminated because of deletion of that rule from the Florida Rules of Civil Procedure. Editorial change.

2002 Revision: Reference to rule 1.410 transferred to subdivision (a) from former rule 5.070. Subdivision (b) amended to give court discretion to assess attorneys' fees. Subdivision (c) added. Committee notes revised.

2006 Revision: Committee notes revised.

2007 Revision: Committee notes revised.

Statutory References

§ 731.201(23), Fla. Stat. General definitions.

§ 733.106, Fla. Stat. Costs and attorney's fees.

§ 744.105, Fla. Stat. Costs.

§ 744.108, Fla. Stat. Guardian's and attorney's fees and expenses.

Rule References

Fla. Prob. R. 5.025 Adversary proceedings.

Fla. R. Jud. Admin. 2.535 Court reporting.

RULE 5.095. GENERAL AND SPECIAL MAGISTRATES

(a) **General Magistrates.** The court may appoint general magistrates as the court finds necessary. General magistrates shall be members of The Florida Bar and shall continue in office until removed by the court. The order making an appointment shall be recorded. Each general magistrate shall take the oath required of officers by the Florida Constitution. The oath shall be recorded before the magistrate begins to act.

(b) **Special Magistrates.** The court may appoint members of The Florida Bar as special magistrates for any particular service required by the court. Special magistrates shall be governed by all laws and rules relating to general magistrates, except special magistrates shall not be required to make oath unless specifically required by the court. For good cause shown, the court may appoint a person other than a member of The Florida Bar as a special magistrate.

(c) **Reference.** No referral shall be made to a magistrate without the consent of the parties. When a referral is made to a magistrate, either party may set the action for hearing before the magistrate.

(d) **General Powers and Duties.** Every magistrate shall act under the direction of the court. Process issued by a magistrate shall be directed as provided by law. All grounds for disqualification of a judge shall apply to magistrates.

(e) **Bond.** When not otherwise provided by law, the court may require magistrates who are appointed to dispose of real or personal property to give bond and surety conditioned for the proper payment of all money that may come into their hands and for the due performance of their duties. The bond shall be made payable to the State of Florida and shall be for the benefit of all persons aggrieved by any act of the magistrate.

(f) **Hearings.** Hearings before any magistrate may be held in the county where the action is pending or at any other place by order of the court for the convenience of the witnesses or the parties. The magistrate shall assign a time and place for proceedings as soon as reasonably possible after a referral is made and give notice to all parties. If any party fails to appear, the magistrate may proceed ex parte or may continue the hearing to a future day, with notice to the absent party. The magistrate shall proceed with reasonable diligence and the least practicable delay. Any party may apply to the court for an order directing the magistrate to accelerate the proceedings and to make a report promptly. Evidence shall be taken in writing or by electronic recording by the magistrate or by some other person under the magistrate's authority in the magistrate's presence and shall be filed with the magistrate's report. The magistrate may examine and take testimony from the parties and their witnesses under oath on all matters contained in the referral and may require production of all books, papers, writings, vouchers, and other documents applicable to those matters. The magistrate shall admit only evidence that would be admissible in court. The magistrate may take all actions concerning evidence that may be taken by the court. All parties accounting before a magistrate shall bring in their accounts in the form of accounts payable and receivable, and any other parties who are not satisfied with the account may examine the accounting party orally or by interrogatories or deposition as the magistrate directs. All depositions and documents that have been taken or used previously in the action may be used before the magistrate.

(g) **Magistrate's Report.** The magistrate's report shall contain a description of the matters considered and the magistrate's conclusion and any recommendations. No part of any statement of facts, account, charge, deposition, examination, or answer used before the magistrate shall be recited.

(h) **Filing Report; Notice; Exceptions.** The magistrate shall file the report and serve copies on the parties. The parties may serve exceptions to the report within 10 days from the time it is served on them. If no exceptions are filed within that period, the court shall take appropriate action on the report. All timely filed exceptions shall be heard on reasonable notice by either party.

(i) **Application of Rule.** This rule shall not apply to the appointment of magistrates for the specific purpose of reviewing guardianship inventories, accountings, and plans as otherwise governed by law and these rules.

Committee Notes

Rule History

2007 Revision: This rule, patterned after Florida Rule of Civil Procedure 1.490, is created to implement the use of magistrates in probate and guardianship proceedings other than those specifically addressed in rule 5.697.

Rule References

Fla. Prob. R. 5.697 Magistrates' review of guardianship inventories, accountings, and plans.

Fla. R. Civ. P. 1.490 Magistrates.

RULE 5.100. RIGHT OF APPEAL

Appeal of final orders and discretionary appellate review of non-final orders are governed by the Florida Rules of Appellate Procedure.

Committee Notes

For purposes of appellate review, the service of a motion for rehearing postpones rendition of final orders only. A motion for rehearing of a non-final order does not toll the running of the time to seek review of that order.

Rule History

1975 Revision: Same as prior rule 5.100 with editorial changes.

1977 Revision: Citation form change in committee note.

1988 Revision: Committee notes expanded. Citation form changes in rule and committee notes.

1992 Revision: Editorial changes. Citation form changes in committee notes.

1996 Revision: Superseded by Florida Rules of Appellate Procedure 9.110(a)(2).

2000 Revision: Rewritten because former rule was superseded. Revisions to committee notes to amend text and to include cross-references to other rules.

2003 Revision: Committee notes revised.

Rule References

Fla. Prob. R. 5.020(d) Pleadings; verifications; motions.

Fla. R. App. P. 9.020(h) Definitions.

Fla. R. App. P. 9.110(a)(2), (b) Appeal proceedings to review final orders of lower tribunals and orders granting new trial in jury and non-jury cases.

Fla. R. App. P. 9.130(b) Proceedings to review non-final orders and specified final orders.

RULE 5.110. ADDRESS DESIGNATION FOR PERSONAL REPRESENTATIVE OR GUARDIAN; DESIGNATION OF RESIDENT AGENT AND ACCEPTANCE

(a) **Address Designation of Personal Representative or Guardian.** Before letters are issued, the personal representative or guardian shall file a designation of its residence street address and mailing address. The personal representative or guardian shall notify the court of any change in its residence street address or mailing address within 20 days of the change.

(b) **Designation of Resident Agent.** Before letters are issued, a personal representative or guardian shall file a designation of resident agent for service of process or notice, and the acceptance by the resident agent. A designation of resident agent is not required if a personal representative or guardian is (1) a corporate fiduciary having an office in Florida, or (2) a Florida Bar member who is a resident of and has an office in Florida. The designation shall contain the name, residence street address, and mailing address of the resident agent. A Florida office street address and mailing address for the attorney as resident agent may be designated in lieu of a residence address.

(c) **Residency Requirement.** A resident agent, other than a member of The Florida Bar who is a resident of Florida, must be a resident of the county where the proceedings are pending.

(d) **Acceptance by Resident Agent.** The resident agent shall sign a written acceptance of its designation.

(e) **Incorporation in Other Pleadings.** The designation of the address of the personal representative or guardian, the designation of resident agent, or acceptance may be incorporated in the petition for administration, the petition for appointment of guardian, or the personal representative's or guardian's oath.

(f) Effect of Designation and Acceptance. The designation of and acceptance by the resident agent shall constitute consent to service of process or notice on the agent and shall be sufficient to bind the personal representative or guardian:

(1) in its representative capacity in any action; and

(2) in its personal capacity only in those actions in which the personal representative or guardian is sued personally for claims arising from the administration of the estate or guardianship.

(g) Successor Agent. If the resident agent dies, resigns, or is unable to act for any other reason, the personal representative or guardian shall appoint a successor agent within 10 days after receiving notice that such event has occurred.

Committee Notes

Rule History

1977 Revision: Change in committee note to conform to statutory renumbering.

Substantially the same as prior rule 5.210, except that under prior rule, designation was required to be filed within 10 days after letters issued.

1984 Revision: Captions added to subdivisions. New subdivision (b) added. Requires filing acceptance at the same time as filing designation. Committee notes revised.

1988 Revision: Change in (c) to clarify that the personal representative, if a member of The Florida Bar, may not also serve as resident agent for service of process or notice. Citation form change in committee notes.

1992 Revision: Editorial changes. Committee notes revised. Citation form changes in committee notes.

2000 Revision: Extensive editorial changes to rule. Rule reformatted for clarity and revised to permit an attorney serving as resident agent to designate a business address in lieu of a residence address.

2003 Revision: Committee notes revised.

2008 Revision: Committee notes revised.

2010 Revision: Subdivision (a) amended to require the personal representative or guardian to notify the court of any change of address to facilitate timely communication with the personal representative or guardian.

Rule References

Fla. Prob. R. 5.200 Petition for administration.

Fla. Prob. R. 5.320 Oath of personal representative.

Fla. Prob. R. 5.560 Petition for appointment of guardian of an incapacitated person.

Fla. Prob. R. 5.649 Guardian advocate.

RULE 5.120. ADMINISTRATOR AD LITEM AND GUARDIAN AD LITEM

(a) Appointment. When it is necessary that the estate of a decedent or a ward be represented in any probate or guardianship proceeding and there is no personal representative of the estate or guardian of the ward, or the personal representative or guardian is or may be interested adversely to the estate or ward, or is enforcing the personal representative's or guardian's own debt or claim against the estate or ward, or the necessity arises otherwise, the court may appoint an administrator ad litem or a guardian ad litem, as the case may be, without bond or notice for that particular proceeding. At any point in a proceeding, a court may appoint a guardian ad litem to represent the interests of an incapacitated person, an unborn or unascertained person, a minor or any other person otherwise under a legal disability, a person with a developmental disability, or a person whose identity or address is unknown, if the court determines that representation of the interest otherwise would be inadequate. If not precluded by conflict of interest, a guardian ad litem may be appointed to represent several persons or interests. The administrator ad litem or guardian ad litem shall file an oath to discharge all duties faithfully and upon the filing shall be qualified to act. No process need be served upon the administrator ad litem or guardian ad litem, but such person shall appear and defend as directed by the court.

(b) Petition. The petition for appointment of a guardian ad litem shall state to the best of petitioner's information and belief:

(1) the name and residence address of each minor, person with a developmental disability, or incapacitated person and birth date of each minor who has an interest in the proceedings;

(2) the name and address of any guardian appointed for each minor, person with a developmental disability, or incapacitated person;

(3) the name and residence address of any living natural guardians or living natural guardian having legal custody of each minor, person with a developmental disability, or incapacitated person;

(4) a description of the interest in the proceedings of each minor, person with a developmental disability, or incapacitated person; and

(5) the facts showing the necessity for the appointment of a guardian ad litem.

(c) Notice. Within 10 days after appointment, the petitioner shall serve conformed copies of the petition for appointment of a guardian ad litem and order to any guardian, or if there is no guardian, to the living natural guardians or the living natural guardian having legal custody of the minor, person with a developmental disability, or incapacitated person.

(d) Report. The guardian ad litem shall serve conformed copies of any written report or finding of the guardian ad litem's investigation and answer filed in the proceedings, petition for compensation and discharge, and the notice of hearing on the petition to any guardian, or in the event that there is no guardian, to the living natural guardians or the living natural guardian having legal custody of the minor, person with a developmental disability, or incapacitated person.

(e) Service of Petition and Order. Within 10 days after appointment, the petitioner for an administrator ad litem shall serve conformed copies of the petition for appointment and order to the attorney of record of each beneficiary and to each known beneficiary not represented by an attorney of record.

(f) Enforcement of Judgments. When an administrator ad litem or guardian ad litem recovers any judgment or other relief, it shall be enforced as other judgments. Execution shall issue in favor of the administrator ad litem or guardian ad litem for the use of the estate or ward and the money collected shall be paid to the personal representative or guardian, or as otherwise ordered by the court.

(g) Claim of Personal Representative. The fact that the personal representative is seeking reimbursement for claims against the decedent paid by the personal representative does not require appointment of an administrator ad litem.

Committee Notes

Rule History

1977 Revision: Editorial change in (a) limiting application of rule to probate and guardianship proceedings. In (b) the petition for appointment of a guardian need not be verified. Deletion of (g) as being substantive rather than procedural and changing former (h) to new (g). Change in committee note to conform to statutory renumbering.

This rule implements sections 731.303(5), 733.308, and 744.391, Florida Statutes, and includes some of the provisions of prior rule 5.230.

1988 Revision: Editorial changes; captions added to paragraphs. Citation form changes in committee notes.

1992 Revision: Addition of phrase in subdivision (a) to conform to 1992 amendment to section 731.303(5), Florida Statutes. Editorial changes. Committee notes revised. Citation form changes in committee notes.

2003 Revision: Committee notes revised.

2006 Revision: Committee notes revised.

2008 Revision: Subdivisions (a), (b), (c), and (d) amended to include persons with a developmental disability. Committee notes revised.

2012 Revision: The phrase "deliver or mail" in subdivisions (c), (d), and (e) has been replaced with the word "serve" to comply with other rules relating to service of pleadings and documents. Committee notes revised.

Statutory References

§ 393.12, Fla. Stat. Capacity; appointment of guardian advocate.

§ 731.303, Fla. Stat. Representation.

§ 733.308, Fla. Stat. Administrator ad litem.

§ 733.708, Fla. Stat. Compromise.

§ 744.3025, Fla. Stat. Claims of minors.

§ 744.3085, Fla. Stat. Guardian advocates.

§ 744.387, Fla. Stat. Settlement of claims.

§ 744.391, Fla. Stat. Actions by and against guardian or ward.

§ 744.446, Fla. Stat. Conflicts of interest; prohibited activities; court approval; breach of fiduciary duty.

Rule References

Fla. Prob. R. 5.041 Service of pleadings and documents.

Fla. R. Jud. Admin. 2.516 Service of pleadings and documents.

RULE 5.122. CURATORS

(a) Petition for Appointment. The petition for appointment of a curator shall be verified and shall contain:

(1) the petitioner's name, address, and interest, if any, in the estate;

(2) the decedent's name, address, date and place of death, and state and county of domicile;

(3) the names and addresses of the persons apparently entitled to letters of administration and any known beneficiaries;

(4) the nature and approximate value of the assets;

(5) a statement showing venue;

(6) a statement as to why a curator should be appointed; and

(7) the name and address of any proposed curator.

The court may appoint a curator sua sponte.

(b) Appointment. Before letters of curatorship are issued, the curator shall file a designation of resident agent and acceptance, and an oath, as is required for personal representatives under these rules. The court shall issue letters of curatorship that shall entitle the curator to possess or control the decedent's property, which the court may enforce through contempt proceedings.

(c) Notice. Formal notice shall be given to the person apparently entitled to letters, if any. If it is likely that the decedent's property will be wasted, destroyed, or removed beyond the jurisdiction of the court and if the appointment of a curator would be delayed by giving notice, the court may appoint a curator without notice.

(d) Powers. By order, the court may authorize the curator to perform any duty or function of a personal representative, including publication and service of notice to creditors, or if a will has been admitted, service of notice of administration.

(e) Inventory and Accounting. The curator shall file an inventory within 30 days after issuance of letters of curatorship. When the personal representative is appointed, the curator shall account for and deliver all estate assets in the curator's possession to the personal representative within 30 days after issuance of letters of administration.

(f) Petition to Reconsider. If a curator has been appointed without notice, any interested party who did not receive notice may, at any time, petition to reconsider the appointment.

(g) Subject to Other Provisions. Curators shall be subject to the provisions of these rules and other applicable law concerning personal representatives.

Committee Notes

This rule implements the procedure found in section 733.501, Florida Statutes, as amended in 1997 and 2001. The rule has been modified, in part, to reflect the addition of new rule 5.241 regarding notice to creditors. Because the fundamental concern of curatorship is protection of estate property, the procedure facilitates speed and flexibility while recognizing due process concerns. It is not intended that this rule change the effect of the statute from which it has been derived, but the rule has been reformatted to conform to the structure of these rules. Furthermore, the Committee does not intend to create a new procedure, except that subdivision (d) specifies certain acts that the court may authorize the curator to perform. This specificity of example, while not included in the statute, is not intended to limit the authorized acts to those specified in the rule. The appointment of a curator without notice is tantamount to a temporary injunction. Thus, due process considerations suggest an expedited hearing to reconsider the appointment of a curator by any interested party who did not receive notice.

Rule History

1988 Revision: New rule.

1992 Revision: Editorial changes. Citation form changes in committee notes.

2003 Revision: Extensive changes to rule to clarify procedure for appointment of curator. Committee notes revised.

Statutory References

§ 733.402, Fla. Stat. Bond of fiduciary; when required; form.

§ 733.501, Fla. Stat. Curators.

Rule Reference

Fla. Prob. R. 5.020 Pleadings; verification; motions.

RULE 5.150. ORDER REQUIRING ACCOUNTING

(a) Accountings Required by Statute. When any personal representative or guardian fails to file an accounting or return required by statute or rule, the court on its own motion or on the petition of an interested person shall order the personal representative or guardian to file the accounting or return within 15 days from the service on the personal representative or guardian of the order, or show cause why he or she should not be compelled to do so.

(b) Accountings Not Required by Statute. On the petition of an interested person, or on its own motion, the court may require the personal representative or guardian to file an accounting or return not otherwise required by statute or rule. The order requiring an accounting or return shall order the personal representative or guardian to file the accounting or return within a specified time from service on the personal representative or guardian of the order, or show cause why he or she should not be compelled to do so.

(c) Service. A copy of the order shall be served on the personal representative or guardian and the personal representative's or guardian's attorney.

Committee Notes

The court on its motion or on petition of an interested person may require a personal representative or guardian to file an accounting or return not otherwise required by statute.

Rule History

1977 Revision: Change in committee notes.

1984 Revision: Extensive editorial changes. Committee notes revised and expanded.

1992 Revision: Editorial changes. Committee notes revised. Citation form changes in committee notes.

2003 Revision: Committee notes revised.

2008 Revision: Committee notes revised.

Statutory References

§ 38.22, Fla. Stat. Power to punish contempts.

§ 38.23, Fla. Stat. Contempts defined.

§ 393.12(2)(h), Fla. Stat. Capacity; appointment of guardian advocate.

§ 733.5036, Fla. Stat. Accounting and discharge following resignation.

§ 733.508, Fla. Stat. Accounting and discharge of removed personal representatives upon removal.

§ 783.901, Fla. Stat. Final discharge.

ch. 738, Fla. Stat. Principal and income.

§ 744.3085, Fla. Stat. Guardian advocates.

§ 744.367, Fla. Stat. Duty to file annual guardianship report.

§ 744.3678, Fla. Stat. Annual accounting.

§ 744.3685, Fla. Stat. Order requiring guardianship report; contempt.

§ 744.369, Fla. Stat. Judicial review of guardianship reports.

§ 744.467, Fla. Stat. Resignation of guardian.

§ 744.511, Fla. Stat. Accounting upon removal.

§ 744.517, Fla. Stat. Proceedings for contempt.

§ 744.521, Fla. Stat. Termination of guardianship.

§ 744.524, Fla. Stat. Termination of guardianship on change of domicile of resident ward.

§ 744.527, Fla. Stat. Final reports and applications for discharge; hearing.

Rule References

Fla. Prob. R. 5.649 Guardian advocate.

Fla. Prob. R. 5.650 Resignation or disqualification of guardian; appointment of successor.

Fla. Prob. R. 5.560 Proceedings for removal of guardian.

Fla. Prob. R. 5.670 Termination of guardianship on change of domicile of resident ward.

Fla. Prob. R. 5.680 Termination of guardianship.

Fla. Prob. R. 5.681 Restoration of rights of person with developmental disability.

Fla. Prob. R. 5.695 Annual guardianship report.

Fla. Prob. R. 5.696 Annual accounting.

Fla. Prob. R. 5.697 Magistrates' review of guardianship accountings and plans.

RULE 5.160. PRODUCTION OF ASSETS

On the petition of an interested person, or on its own motion, the court may require any personal representative or guardian to produce satisfactory evidence that the assets of the estate are in the possession or under the control of the personal representative or guardian and may order production of the assets in the manner and for the purposes directed by the court.

Committee Notes

Rule History

1977 Revision: Change in committee notes.

1984 Revision: Minor editorial changes. Committee notes revised.

1988 Revision: Editorial changes.

1992 Revision: Editorial changes Committee notes revised.

Statutory Reference

§ 744.373, Fla. Stat. Production of property.

RULE 5.170. EVIDENCE

In proceedings under the Florida Probate Code and the Florida Guardianship Law the rules of evidence in civil actions are applicable unless specifically changed by the Florida Probate Code, the Florida Guardianship Law, or these rules.

Committee Notes

Rule History.

1977 Revision: New rule.

1984 Revision: To further clarify the intent of the rule to incorporate the provisions of the Florida Evidence Code (chapter 90, Florida Statutes) when not in conflict with the Florida Probate Code or Florida Guardianship Law, or rules applicable to these particular proceedings.

1992 Revision: Citation form changes in committee notes.

2003 Revision: Committee notes revised.

Statutory References.

ch. 90, Fla. Stat. Florida Evidence Code.

§ 733.107, Fla. Stat. Burden of proof in contests; presumption of undue influence.

RULE 5.171. EVIDENCE OF DEATH

In a proceeding under these rules, the following shall apply:

(a) Death certificate. An authenticated copy of a death certificate issued by an official or agency of the place where the death purportedly occurred or by an official or agency of the United States is prima facie proof of the fact, place, date, and time of death and the identity of the decedent.

(b) Other records. A copy of any record or report of a governmental agency, domestic or foreign, that a person is dead, alive, missing, detained, or, from the facts related, presumed dead is prima facie evidence of the status, dates, circumstances, and places disclosed by the record or report.

(c) Extended absence. A person who is absent from the place of that person's last known domicile for a continuous period of 5 years and whose absence is not satisfactorily explained after diligent search and inquiry is presumed dead. The person's death is presumed to have occurred at the end of the period unless there is evidence establishing that death occurred earlier.

Committee Notes

This rule represents a rule implementation of the procedure found in section 731.103, Florida Statutes. It is not intended to

change the effect of the statute from which it was derived but has been reformatted to conform with the structure of these rules. It is not intended to create a new procedure or modify an existing procedure, except that additional language has been added which was not in the statute, to permit issuance of a death certificate by an official or agency of the United States. An example would be such a certificate issued by the Department of State or the Department of Defense.

Rule History

1988 Revision: New rule.

1992 Revision: Editorial changes. Committee notes revised. Citation form changes in committee notes.

Statutory References

§ 731.103, Fla. Stat. Evidence as to death or status.

§ 744.521, Fla. Stat. Termination of guardianship.

Rule References

Fla. Prob. R. 5.205 Filing evidence of death.

Fla. Prob. R. 5.680 Termination of guardianship.

RULE 5.180. WAIVER AND CONSENT

(a) Manner of Execution. A waiver or consent as authorized by law shall be in writing and signed by the person executing the waiver or consent.

(b) Contents. The waiver or consent shall state:

(1) the person's interest in the subject of the waiver or consent;

(2) if the person is signing in a fiduciary or representative capacity, the nature of the capacity;

(3) expressly what is being waived or consented to; and

(4) if the waiver pertains to compensation, language declaring that the waiving party has actual knowledge of the amount and manner of determining the compensation and, in addition, either:

(A) that the party has agreed to the amount and manner of determining that compensation and waives any objection to payment; or

(B) that the party has the right to petition the court to determine the compensation and waives that right.

(c) Filing. The waiver or consent shall be filed.

Committee Notes

One person who serves in two fiduciary capacities may not waive or consent to the person's acts without the approval of those whom the person represents. This rule represents a rule implementation of the procedure found in section 731.302, Florida Statutes.

Rule History

1977 Revision: Extends right of waiver to natural guardian; clarifies right to waive service of notice of administration.

1984 Revision: Extends waiver to disclosure of compensation and distribution of assets. Committee notes revised.

1988 Revision: Procedure from section 731.302, Florida Statutes, inserted as new (1)(f), and a new requirement that the waiver be in writing has been added. Editorial changes. Committee notes expanded. Citation form changes in committee notes.

1992 Revision: Editorial changes. Committee notes revised. Citation form changes in committee notes.

1996 Revision: Addition of specific fee waiver disclosure requirements found in 733.6171(9), Florida Statutes, and expanded to cover all fees.

2003 Revision: Committee notes revised.

2006 Revision: Rule extensively amended to remove references to interested persons' right to waive or consent, which is governed by section 731.302, Florida Statutes, and to address manner of execution and contents of waiver. Committee notes revised.

Statutory References

§ 731.302, Fla. Stat. Waiver and consent by interested person.

§ 731.303, Fla. Stat. Representation.

§ 733.6171, Fla. Stat. Compensation of attorney for the personal representative.

PART II. PROBATE

RULE 5.200. PETITION FOR ADMINISTRATION

The petition for administration shall be verified by the petitioner and shall contain:

(a) a statement of the interest of the petitioner, the petitioner's name and address, and the name and office address of the petitioner's attorney;

(b) the name and last known address of the decedent, last 4 digits of the decedent's social security number, date and place of death of the decedent, and state and county of the decedent's domicile;

(c) so far as is known, the names and addresses of the surviving spouse, if any, and the beneficiaries and their relationship to the decedent and the date of birth of any who are minors;

(d) a statement showing venue;

(e) the priority, under the Florida Probate Code, of the person whose appointment as the personal representative is sought and a statement that the person is qualified to serve under the laws of Florida;

(f) a statement whether domiciliary or principal proceedings are pending in another state or country, if known, and the name and address of the foreign personal representative and the court issuing letters;

(g) a statement of the approximate value and nature of the assets;

(h) in an intestate estate, a statement that after the exercise of reasonable diligence the petitioner is unaware of any unrevoked wills or codicils, or if the petitioner is aware of any unrevoked wills or codicils, a statement why the wills or codicils are not being probated;

(i) in a testate estate, a statement identifying all unrevoked wills and codicils being presented for probate, and a statement that the petitioner is unaware of any other unrevoked wills or codicils or, if the petitioner is aware of any other unrevoked wills or codicils, a statement why the other wills or codicils are not being probated; and

(j) in a testate estate, a statement that the original of the decedent's last will is in the possession of the court or accompanies the petition, or that an authenticated copy of a will deposited with or probated in another jurisdiction or that an authenticated copy of a notarial will, the original of which is in the possession of a foreign notary, accompanies the petition.

Committee Notes

Rule History

1977 Revision: Addition to (b)(5) to require an affirmative statement that the person sought to be appointed as personal representative is qualified to serve. Committee note expanded to include additional statutory references.

Substantially the same as section 733.202, Florida Statutes, and implementing sections 733.301 through 733.305, Florida Statutes.

1988 Revision: Editorial changes. Committee notes revised.

1992 Revision: Addition of phrase in subdivision (b) to conform to 1992 amendment to section 733.202(2)(b), Florida Statutes.

Reference to clerk ascertaining the amount of the filing fee deleted in subdivision (g) because of repeal of sliding scale of filing fees. The remaining language was deemed unnecessary. Editorial changes. Committee notes revised. Citation form changes in committee notes.

2002 Revision: Addition of phrases in subdivision (j) to add references to wills probated in Florida where the original is in the possession of a foreign official. Editorial changes. Committee notes revised.

2003 Revision: Committee notes revised.

2007 Revision: Editorial changes in (h) and (i).

2007 Revision: Committee notes revised.

2010 Revision: Editorial change in (e) to clarify reference to Florida Probate Code.

2011 Revision: Subdivision (b) amended to limit listing of decedent's social security number to last four digits.

2012 Revision: Committee notes revised.

Statutory References

§ 731.201(23), Fla. Stat. General definitions.

§ 731.301, Fla. Stat. Notice.

§ 733.202, Fla. Stat. Petition.

§ 733.301, Fla. Stat. Preference in appointment of personal representative.

§ 733.302, Fla. Stat. Who may be appointed personal representative.

§ 733.303, Fla. Stat. Persons not qualified.

§ 733.304, Fla. Stat. Nonresidents.

§ 733.305, Fla. Stat. Trust companies and other corporations and associations.

Rule References

Fla. Prob. R. 5.020 Pleadings; verification; motions.

Fla. Prob. R. 5.040 Notice.

Fla. Prob. R. 5.041 Service of pleadings and documents.

Fla. Prob. R. 5.180 Waiver and consent.

Fla. Prob. R. 5.201 Notice of petition for administration.

Fla. R. Jud. Admin. 2.516 Service of pleadings and documents.

RULE 5.201. NOTICE OF PETITION FOR ADMINISTRATION

(a) Petitioner Entitled to Preference of Appointment. Except as may otherwise be required by these rules or the Florida Probate Code, no notice need be given of the petition for administration or the issuance of letters when it appears that the petitioner is entitled to preference of appointment as personal representative.

(b) Petitioner Not Entitled to Preference. Before letters shall be issued to any person who is not entitled to preference, formal notice must be served on all known persons qualified to act as personal representative and entitled to preference equal to or greater than the applicant, unless those entitled to preference waive it in writing.

(c) Service of Petition by Formal Notice. If the petitioner elects or is required to serve formal notice of the petition for administration prior to the issuance of letters, a copy of the will offered for probate must be attached to the notice.

Committee Notes

This rule represents a rule implementation of the procedure formerly found in section 733.203(2), Florida Statutes, which was repealed as procedural in 2001.

Rule History

1988 Revision: New rule.

1992 Revision: Committee notes revised. Citation form changes in committee notes.

2003 Revision: Committee notes revised.

2010 Revision: Subdivision (c) added to require service of a copy of the will offered for probate. This requirement was included in section 733.2123, Florida Statutes, but was removed in 2010 because it was deemed to be a procedural requirement. Committee notes revised. Editorial changes.

Statutory References

§ 731.301, Fla. Stat. Notice.

§ 733.212, Fla. Stat. Notice of administration; filing of objections.

§ 733.2123, Fla. Stat. Adjudication before issuance of letters.

Rule References

Fla. Prob. R. 5.040 Notice.

Fla. Prob. R. 5.060 Request for notices and copies of pleadings.

Fla. Prob. R. 5.200 Petition for administration.

RULE 5.205. FILING EVIDENCE OF DEATH

(a) Requirements for Filing. A copy of an official record of the death of a decedent shall be filed by the personal representative, if any, or the petitioner in each of the following proceedings and at the times specified:

(1) Administration of decedent's estate: not later than 3 months following the date of the first publication of the notice to creditors.

(2) Ancillary proceedings: not later than 3 months following the date of first publication of notice to creditors.

(3) Summary administration: at any time prior to entry of the order of summary administration.

(4) Disposition without administration: at the time of filing the application for disposition without administration.

(5) Determination of beneficiaries: at any time prior to entry of the final judgment determining beneficiaries.

(6) Determination of protected homestead: at any time prior to entry of the final judgment determining protected homestead status of real property.

(7) Probate of will without administration: at any time prior to entry of the order admitting will to probate.

(b) Waiver. On verified petition by the personal representative, if any, or the petitioner the court may enter an order dispensing with this rule, without notice or hearing.

(c) Authority to Require Filing. The court may, without notice or hearing, enter an order requiring the personal representative, if any, or the petitioner to file a copy of an official record of death at any time during the proceedings.

Committee Notes

A short form certificate of death, which does not disclose the cause of death, should be filed.

Rule History

1980 Revision: This rule is intended to provide a uniform procedure for filing an official record of death in any judicial or statutory proceeding upon the death of a decedent. The court may, upon ex parte application, waive compliance with this rule or require filing at any stage in the proceedings.

1984 Revision: Captions and minor editorial changes. Committee notes revised.

1988 Revision: Editorial and substantive changes. Adds (a)(8) to require filing when will is admitted to probate without administration of the estate or an order disposing of property. Committee notes revised.

1992 Revision: Editorial changes. Committee notes revised. Citation form changes in committee notes.

2002 Revision: Replaces "homestead" with "protected homestead" in (a)(7) to conform to addition of term in section 731.201(29), Florida Statutes. Committee notes revised.

2003 Revision: Revises subdivision (a)(1) to change notice of administration to notice to creditors. Deletes subdivision (a)(3) referring to family administration, and renumbers subsequent subdivisions. Committee notes revised.

2010 Revision: Committee notes revised.

Statutory References

§ 28.222(3)(g), Fla. Stat. Clerk to be county recorder.

§ 382.008(6), Fla. Stat. Death and fetal death registration.

§ 731.103, Fla. Stat. Evidence as to death or status.

§ 733.2121, Fla. Stat. Notice to creditors; filing of claims.

Rule References

Fla. Prob. R. 5.042(a) Time.

Fla. Prob. R. 5.171 Evidence of death.

Fla. Prob. R. 5.241 Notice to creditors.

RULE 5.210. PROBATE OF WILLS WITHOUT ADMINISTRATION

(a) Petition and Contents. A petition to admit a decedent's will to probate without administration shall be verified by the petitioner and shall contain:

(1) a statement of the interest of the petitioner, the petitioner's name and address, and the name and office address of the petitioner's attorney;

(2) the name and last known address of the decedent, last 4 digits of the decedent's social security number, date and place of death of the decedent, and state and county of the decedent's domicile;

(3) so far as is known, the names and addresses of the surviving spouse, if any, and the beneficiaries and their relationships to the decedent, and the date of birth of any who are minors;

(4) a statement showing venue;

(5) a statement whether domiciliary or principal proceedings are pending in another state or country, if known, and the name and address of the foreign personal representative and the court issuing letters;

(6) a statement that there are no assets subject to administration in Florida;

(7) a statement identifying all unrevoked wills and codicils being presented for probate and a statement that the petitioner is unaware of any other unrevoked

wills or codicils or, if the petitioner is aware of any other unrevoked wills or codicils, a statement why the other wills or codicils are not being probated; and

(8) a statement that the original of the decedent's last will is in the possession of the court or accompanies the petition, or that an authenticated copy of a will deposited with or probated in another jurisdiction or that an authenticated copy of a notarial will, the original of which is in the possession of a foreign notary, accompanies the petition.

(b) Service. The petitioner shall serve a copy of the petition on those persons who would be entitled to service under rule 5.240.

(c) Objections. Objections to the validity of the will shall follow the form and procedure set forth in these rules pertaining to revocation of probate. Objections to the venue or jurisdiction of the court shall follow the form and procedure set forth in the Florida Rules of Civil Procedure.

(d) Order. An order admitting the will to probate shall include a finding that the will has been executed as required by law.

Committee Notes

Examples illustrating when a will might be admitted to probate are when an instrument (such as a will or trust agreement) gives the decedent a power exercisable by will, such as the power to appoint a successor trustee or a testamentary power of appointment. In each instance, the will of the person holding the power has no legal significance until admitted to probate. There may be no assets, creditors' issues, or other need for a probate beyond admitting the will to establish the exercise or non-exercise of such powers.

Rule History

1975 Revision: Proof of will may be taken by any Florida circuit judge or clerk without issuance of commission.

1984 Revision: This rule has been completely revised to set forth the procedure for proving all wills except lost or destroyed wills and the title changed. The rule requires an oath attesting to the statutory requirements for execution of wills and the will must be proved before an order can be entered admitting it to probate. Former rules 5.280, 5.290, and 5.500 are included in this rule. Committee notes revised.

1988 Revision: Editorial and substantive changes. Change in (a)(3) to clarify which law determines validity of a notarial will; change in (a)(4) to clarify requirement that will of a Florida resident must comply with Florida law; adds new subdivision (b) to set forth required contents of petition for probate of will; moves former (b)

to (c). Committee notes expanded; citation form change in committee notes.

1992 Revision: Editorial changes. Committee notes revised. Citation form changes in committee notes.

1996 Revision: Subdivision (a)(4) changed to allow authenticated copies of wills to be admitted to probate if the original is filed or deposited in another jurisdiction.

2002 Revision: Substantial revision to the rule setting forth the requirements of a petition to admit a will to probate when administration is not required. Self proof of wills is governed by the Florida Statutes. Former subdivision (a)(4) amended and transferred to new rule 5.215. Former subdivision (a)(5) amended and transferred to new rule 5.216.

2003 Revision: Committee notes revised.

2007 Revision: Existing text redesignated as subdivision (a) and editorial change made in (a)(7). New subdivisions (b) and (c) added to provide for service of the petition and the procedure for objections consistent with the procedures for probate of a will with administration. Committee notes revised.

2010 Revision: Subdivision (b) amended to reflect that service of the petition to admit a decedent's will to probate without administration shall be served on the persons who would be entitled to service of the notice of administration in a formal administration as set forth in rule 5.240. New subdivision (d) added to provide that any order admitting the decedent's will to probate without administration contain a finding that the will was executed as required by law. Committee notes revised.

2011 Revision: Subdivision (a)(2) amended to limit listing of decedent's social security number to last four digits.

Statutory References

§ 731.201, Fla. Stat. General definitions.

§ 731.301, Fla. Stat. Notice.

§ 732.502, Fla. Stat. Execution of wills.

§ 732.503, Fla. Stat. Self-proof of will.

§ 733.103, Fla. Stat. Effect of probate.

§ 733.201, Fla. Stat. Proof of wills.

§ 733.202, Fla. Stat. Petition.

§ 733.204, Fla. Stat. Probate of a will written in a foreign language.

§ 733.205, Fla. Stat. Probate of notarial will.

§ 733.206, Fla. Stat. Probate of will of resident after foreign probate.

§ 733.207, Fla. Stat. Establishment and probate of lost or destroyed will.

§ 734.104, Fla. Stat. Foreign wills; admission to record; effect on title.

Rule References

Fla. Prob. R. 5.015 General definitions.

Fla. Prob. R. 5.020 Pleadings, verification; motions.

Fla. Prob. R. 5.205(a)(7) Filing evidence of death.

Fla. Prob. R. 5.215 Authenticated copy of will.

Fla. Prob. R. 5.216 Will written in foreign language.

Fla. Prob. R. 5.230 Commission to prove will.

Fla. Prob. R. 5.240 Notice of administration.

Fla. Prob. R. 5.270 Revocation of probate.

RULE 5.215. AUTHENTICATED COPY OF WILL

An authenticated copy of a will may be admitted to probate if the original could be admitted to probate in Florida.

Committee Notes

Rule History

2002 Revision: New rule, derived from former rule 5.210(a)(4).

2003 Revision: Committee notes revised.

Statutory References

§ 733.205, Fla. Stat. Probate of notarial will.

§ 733.206, Fla. Stat. Probate of will of resident after foreign probate.

§ 734.102, Fla. Stat. Ancillary administration.

§ 734.1025, Fla. Stat. Nonresident decedent's testate estate with property not exceeding $50,000 in this state; determination of claims.

§ 734.104, Fla. Stat. Foreign wills; admission to record; effect on title.

Rule References

Fla. Prob. R. 5.200 Petition for administration.

Fla. Prob. R. 5.210 Probate of wills without administration.

Fla. Prob. R. 5.470 Ancillary administration.

Fla. Prob. R. 5.475 Ancillary administration, short form.

RULE 5.216. WILL WRITTEN IN FOREIGN LANGUAGE

A will written in a foreign language being offered for probate shall be accompanied by a true and complete English translation. In the order admitting the foreign language will to probate, the court shall establish the correct English translation. At any time during administration, any interested person may have the correctness of the translation redetermined after formal notice to all other interested persons.

Committee Notes

Rule History

2002 Revision: New rule, derived from former rule 5.210(a)(5) and section 733.204(2), Florida Statutes.

Statutory Reference

§ 733.204, Fla. Stat. Probate of a will written in a foreign language.

RULE 5.230. COMMISSION TO PROVE WILL

(a) **Petition.** On petition the court may appoint a commissioner to take the oath of any person qualified to prove the will under Florida law. The petition shall set forth the date of the will and the place where it was executed, if known; the names of the witnesses and address of the witness whose oath is to be taken; and the name, title, and address of the proposed commissioner.

(b) **Commission.** The commission shall be directed to any person who is authorized to administer an oath by the laws of Florida, the United States of America, or the state or country where the witness may be found, and it shall empower the commissioner to take the oath of the witness to prove the will and shall direct the commissioner to certify the oath and file the executed commission, copy of the will, oath of the witness, and certificate of commissioner. An oath of the commissioner is not required.

(c) **Mailing or Delivery.** The petitioner or the petitioner's attorney shall cause the commission, together with a copy of the will, the oath, and the certificate of commissioner, to be mailed or delivered to the commissioner.

(d) **Filing.** The executed commission, copy of the will, oath of the witness, and certificate of commissioner shall be filed.

(e) **Objections.** Objections to the validity of the will shall follow the form and procedure set forth in these rules pertaining to revocation of probate. Objections to the qualifications of the personal representative shall follow the form and procedure set forth in these rules pertaining to removal of personal representatives. Objections to the venue or jurisdiction of the court shall follow the form and procedure set forth in the Florida Rules of Civil Procedure.

Committee Notes

Rule History

1975 Revision: Substantially the same as prior rule 5.130(a) and (b) and carries forward prior procedures as to a matter upon which Florida Probate Code is silent.

1984 Revision: This rule has been completely changed to set forth the procedure for the issuance and return of a commission. The rule has been broadened to allow anyone authorized by Florida Statutes or by the U.S. Code to be a commissioner as well as those authorized by the state or country where the witness resides.

The rule now provides that the petitioner or his attorney shall forward the commission to the commissioner. The rule also contemplates that a Florida notary may be appointed as commissioner to take the proof of a witness outside the State of Florida. Committee notes revised and expanded.

1988 Revision. Editorial and substantive changes. Change in (a) to provide that commissioner may take the oath of not only the attesting witness to the will but also the oath of any other person qualified to prove the will; change in (c) to permit copies other than photographic copies to be furnished to the commissioner, and to permit delivery of documents in a manner other than by mailing; change in (d) to require the filing of documents with the court. Committee notes revised. Citation form changes in rule and committee notes.

1992 Revision: Editorial change. Committee notes revised. Citation form changes in committee notes.

2003 Revision: Committee notes revised.

Statutory References

§ 92.50, Fla. Stat. Oaths, affidavits, and acknowledgments; who may take or administer; requirements.

§ 733.101, Fla. Stat. Venue of probate proceedings.

§ 733.109, Fla. Stat. Revocation of probate.

§ 733.201, Fla. Stat. Proof of wills.

§ 733.504, Fla. Stat. Removal of personal representative; causes for removal.

§ 733.506, Fla. Stat. Proceedings for removal.

22 U.S.C. 4215 Notarial acts, oaths, affirmations, affidavits, and depositions; fees.

Rule References

Fla. Prob. R. 5.050 Transfer of proceedings.

Fla. Prob. R. 5.270 Revocation of probate.

Fla. Prob. R. 5.440 Proceedings for removal.

Fla. R. Civ. P. 1.060 Transfers of actions.

RULE 5.235. ISSUANCE OF LETTERS, BOND

(a) Appointment of Personal Representative. After the petition for administration is filed and the will, if any, is admitted to probate:

(1) the court shall appoint the person entitled and qualified to be personal representative;

(2) the court shall determine the amount of any bond required. The clerk may approve the bond in the amount determined by the court; and

(3) any required oath or designation of, and acceptance by, a resident agent shall be filed.

(b) Issuance of Letters. Upon compliance with all of the foregoing, letters shall be issued to the personal representative.

(c) Bond. On petition by any interested person or on the court's own motion, the court may waive the requirement of filing a bond, require a personal representative or curator to give bond, increase or decrease the bond, or require additional surety.

Committee Notes

This rule represents a rule implementation of the procedure formerly found in sections 733.401 and 733.403(2), Florida Statutes, both of which were repealed in 2001. It is not intended to change the effect of the statutes from which it was derived but has been reformatted to conform with the structure of these rules. It is not intended to create a new procedure or modify an existing procedure.

Rule History

1988 Revision: New rule.

1992 Revision: Editorial changes. Committee notes revised. Citation form changes in committee notes.

1996 Revision: Mandate in subdivision (a)(2) prohibiting charge of service fee by clerk deleted. Statutory references added.

2003 Revision: Committee notes revised.

2010 Revision: Committee notes revised.

Statutory References

§ 28.24(19), Fla. Stat. Service charges by clerk of the circuit court.

§ 28.2401, Fla. Stat. Service charges in probate matters.

§ 733.402, Fla. Stat. Bond of fiduciary; when required; form.

§ 733.403, Fla. Stat. Amount of bond.

§ 733.405, Fla. Stat. Release of surety.

§ 733.501, Fla. Stat. Curators.

Rule References

Fla. Prob. R. 5.110 Address designation for personal representative or guardian; designation of resident agent and acceptance.

Fla. Prob. R. 5.122 Curators.

Fla. Prob. R. 5.320 Oath of personal representative.

RULE 5.240. NOTICE OF ADMINISTRATION

(a) Service. The personal representative shall promptly serve a copy of the notice of administration on the following persons who are known to the personal representative and who were not previously served under section 733.2123, Florida Statutes:

(1) the decedent's surviving spouse;

(2) all beneficiaries;

(3) a trustee of any trust described in section 733.707(3), Florida Statutes and each qualified beneficiary of the trust as defined in section 736.0103(14), if each trustee is also a personal representative of the estate; and

(4) persons who may be entitled to exempt property

in the manner provided for service of formal notice. The personal representative may similarly serve a copy of the notice on any devisee under another will or heirs or others who claim or may claim an interest in the estate.

(b) Contents. The notice shall state:

(1) the name of the decedent, the file number of the estate, the designation and address of the court in which the proceedings are pending, whether the estate is testate or intestate, and, if testate, the date of the will and any codicils;

(2) the name and address of the personal representative and of the personal representative's attorney, and that the fiduciary lawyer-client privilege in section 90.5021, Florida Statutes, applies with respect to the personal representative and any attorney employed by the personal representative;

(3) that any interested person on whom the notice is served who challenges the validity of the will, the qualifications of the personal representative, venue, or jurisdiction of the court must file any objections with the court in the manner provided in the Florida Probate Rules within the time required by law or those objections are forever barred;

(4) that any person entitled to exempt property must file a petition for determination of exempt property within the time provided by law or the right to exempt property is deemed waived; and

(5) that an election to take an elective share must be filed within the time provided by law.

(c) Copy of Will. Unless the court directs otherwise, the personal representative of a testate estate must, upon written request, furnish a copy of the will and all codicils admitted to probate to any person on whom the notice of administration was served.

(d) Objections. Objections to the validity of the will shall follow the form and procedure set forth in these rules pertaining to revocation of probate. Objections to the qualifications of the personal representative shall follow the form and procedure set forth in these rules pertaining to removal of a personal representative. Objections to the venue or jurisdiction of the court shall follow the form and procedure set forth in the Florida Rules of Civil Procedure.

(e) Waiver of Service. For the purpose of determining deadlines established by reference to the date of service of a copy of the notice of administration in cases in which service has been waived, service on a person who has waived notice is deemed to occur on the date the waiver is filed.

Committee Notes

Rule History

1977 Revision: Former subdivision (c) is deleted as being substantive rather than procedural.

1984 Revision: Editorial changes; new requirement to file proof of publication; new requirements as to form of objections to will and qualifications of personal representative. Committee notes revised.

1988 Revision: The obligation to mail notice of administration to all known or reasonably ascertainable creditors has been added to comply with the dictates of *Tulsa Professional Collection Services, Inc. v. Pope*, 485 U.S. 478, 108 S. Ct. 1340, 99 L. Ed. 2d 565 (1988).

This rule does not require sending notice of administration to creditors in estates where the time for filing claims has expired before the effective date of this rule. However, no opinion is offered whether such claims are barred by the provisions of section 733.702, Florida Statutes.

Committee notes revised. Citation form changes in committee notes.

1991 Revision: Subdivision (a) modified to make it consistent with recent changes to sections 733.212 and 733.702, Florida Statutes. Those statutes were amended to comply with the dictates of *Tulsa Professional Collection Services, Inc. v. Pope*, 485 U.S. 478, 108 S. Ct. 1340, 99 L. Ed. 2d 565 (1988). For the same reason, subdivision (e) was eliminated.

1992 Revision: Former subdivision (e) revised and reinstated to emphasize need for personal representative to determine all known or reasonably ascertainable creditors. Editorial changes; committee notes revised; citation form changes in committee notes.

1996 Revision: Subdivision (a) amended to require service of notice of administration on trustees of certain revocable trusts as defined by Florida statute. Editorial changes.

2002 Revision: Procedures for notifying creditors are now governed by new rule 5.241. Committee notes revised.

2003 Revision: Change in title of (a) to reflect elimination of publication of notice. Committee notes revised.

2005 Revision: Subdivision (a)(3) amended to make it consistent with 2003 change to section 733.212(1)(c), Florida Statutes, regarding when service on trust beneficiaries is required, and clarifying editorial change made in (a). New subdivision (b)(5) added regarding notice to file election to take elective share. Committee notes revised.

2007 Revision: Subdivision (a)(3) amended to replace reference to "beneficiary" with "qualified beneficiary" and to change reference from former section 737.303(4)(b) to new section 736.0103(14), which defines that term. Subdivision (b)(5) amended to delete the reference to the surviving spouse filing the election as another person can file the election on behalf of the surviving spouse. New subdivision (e) added to provide a deadline for objection by a person who waives service. Committee notes revised.

2011 Revision: Subdivision (b)(2) amended to conform to amendment to section 732.212, Florida Statutes, relating to attorney-client privilege for fiduciaries and their attorneys. Editorial changes to conform to the court's guidelines for rules submissions as set forth in Administrative Order AOSC06-14. Statutory reference to section 732.402, Florida Statutes, added. Committee notes revised.

Statutory References

§ 731.201(23), Fla. Stat. General definitions.

§ 731.301, Fla. Stat. Notice.

§ 731.302, Fla. Stat. Waiver and consent by interested person.

§ 732.2135, Fla. Stat. Time of election; extensions; withdrawal.

§ 732.402, Fla. Stat. Exempt property.

§ 732.5165, Fla. Stat. Effect of fraud, duress, mistake, and undue influence.

§ 733.101, Fla. Stat. Venue of probate proceedings.

§ 733.109, Fla. Stat. Revocation of probate.

§ 733.212, Fla. Stat. Notice of administration; filing of objections.

§ 733.2123, Fla. Stat. Adjudication before issuance of letters.

§ 733.302, Fla. Stat. Who may be appointed personal representative.

§ 733.303, Fla. Stat. Persons not qualified.

§ 733.305, Fla. Stat. Trust companies and other corporations and associations.

§ 733.504, Fla. Stat. Removal of personal representative; causes for removal.

§ 733.506, Fla. Stat. Proceedings for removal.

Rule References

Fla. Prob. R. 5.025 Adversary proceedings.

Fla. Prob. R. 5.040 Notice.

Fla. Prob. R. 5.050 Transfer of proceedings.

Fla. Prob. R. 5.180 Waiver and consent.

Fla. Prob. R. 5.270 Revocation of probate.

Fla. Prob. R. 5.440 Proceedings for removal.

Fla. R. Civ. P. 1.060 Transfers of actions.

RULE 5.241. NOTICE TO CREDITORS

(a) **Publication and Service.** Unless creditors' claims are otherwise barred by law, the personal representative shall promptly publish a notice to creditors and serve a copy of the notice on all creditors of the decedent who are reasonably ascertainable and, if required by law, on the Agency for Health Care Administration. Service of the notice shall be either by informal notice, or in the manner provided for service of formal notice at the option of the personal representative. Service on one creditor by a chosen method shall not preclude service on another creditor by another method.

(b) **Contents.** The notice to creditors shall contain the name of the decedent, the file number of the estate, the designation and address of the court, the name and address of the personal representative and of the personal representative's attorney, and the date of first publication of the notice to creditors. The notice shall require all creditors to file all claims against the estate with the court, within the time provided by law.

(c) **Method of Publication and Proof.** Publication shall be made as required by law. The personal representative shall file proof of publication with the court within 45 days after the date of first publication of the notice to creditors.

(d) **Statement Regarding Creditors.** Within 4 months after the date of the first publication of notice to creditors, the personal representative shall file a verified statement that diligent search has been made to ascertain the name and address of each person having a claim against the estate. The statement shall indicate the name and address of each person at that time known to the personal representative who has or may have a claim against the estate and whether such person was served with the notice to creditors or otherwise received actual notice of the information contained in the notice to creditors; provided that the statement need not include persons who have filed a timely claim or who were included in the personal representative's proof of claim.

(e) Service of Death Certificate. If service of the notice on the Agency for Health Care Administration is required, it shall be accompanied by a death certificate.

Committee Notes

It is the committee's opinion that the failure to timely file the proof of publication of the notice to creditors shall not affect time limitations for filing claims or objections.

On April 19, 1988, the United States Supreme Court decided *Tulsa Professional Collection Services, Inc. v. Pope*, 485 U.S. 478, 108 S. Ct. 1340, 99 L. Ed. 2d 565. This case substantially impacted the method for handling (and barring) creditors' claims. This case stands for the proposition that a creditor may not be barred by the usual publication if that creditor was actually known to or reasonably ascertainable by the personal representative, and the personal representative failed to give notice to the creditor by mail or other means as certain to ensure actual notice. Less than actual notice in these circumstances would deprive the creditor of due process rights under the 14th Amendment to the U.S. Constitution. Probably actual notice of the death (as in the case of a hospital where the decedent died as a patient) without notice of the institution of probate proceedings is not sufficient.

An elementary and fundamental requirement of due process in any proceeding which is to be accorded finality is notice reasonably calculated, under all the circumstances, to apprise interested persons of the pendency of the proceeding and afford them an opportunity to present their claims.

The steps to be taken by a personal representative in conducting a diligent search for creditors depends, in large measure, on how familiar the personal representative is with the decedent's affairs. Therefore, the committee believes it is inappropriate to list particular steps to be taken in each estate, since the circumstances will vary from case to case.

The statement required by this rule is not intended to be jurisdictional but rather to provide evidence of satisfaction (or lack thereof) of the due process requirements.

Rule History

2002 Revision: New rule to implement procedures consistent with new section 733.2121, Florida Statutes.

2003 Revision: Committee notes revised.

2005 Revision: Subdivision (a) amended to clarify approved methods of service on creditors. Committee notes revised.

2007 Revision: Editorial change in (a).

2007 Revision: New subdivision (e) added to require service of a copy of the decedent's death certificate on the Agency for Health

Care Administration, as is now required by section 733.2121(3)(d), Florida Statutes.

Statutory References

ch. 50, Fla. Stat. Legal and official advertisements.

§ 731.301, Fla. Stat. Notice.

§ 733.2121, Fla. Stat. Notice to creditors; filing of claims.

§ 733.702, Fla. Stat. Limitations on presentation of claims.

§ 733.703, Fla. Stat. Form and manner of presenting claim.

§ 733.704, Fla. Stat. Amendment of claims.

§ 733.705, Fla. Stat. Payment of and objection to claims.

§ 733.708, Fla. Stat. Compromise.

Rule Reference

Fla. Prob. R. 5.490 Form and manner of presenting claim.

RULE 5.260. CAVEAT; PROCEEDINGS

(a) Filing. Any creditor or interested person other than a creditor may file a caveat with the court. The caveat of an interested person, other than a creditor, may be filed before or after the death of the person for whom the estate will be, or is being, administered. The caveat of a creditor may be filed only after the person's death.

(b) Contents. The caveat shall contain the name of the person for whom the estate will be, or is being, administered, the last 4 digits of the person's social security number or year of birth, if known, a statement of the interest of the caveator in the estate, and the name and specific mailing address of the caveator.

(c) Resident Agent of Caveator; Service. If the caveator is not a resident of Florida, the caveator must file a designation of the name and specific mailing address and residence address of a resident in the county where the caveat is filed, as the caveator's agent for service of notice. The written acceptance by the person appointed as resident agent must be filed with the designation or included in the caveat. The designation and acceptance shall constitute the consent of the caveator that service of notice upon the designated resident agent shall bind the caveator. If the caveator is represented by an attorney admitted to practice in Florida who signs the caveat, it shall not be necessary to designate a resident agent under this rule.

(d) Filing after Commencement. If at the time of the filing of any caveat the decedent's will has been admitted to probate or letters of administration have been issued, the clerk must promptly notify the caveator in writing of the date of issuance of letters and the names and addresses of the personal representative and the personal representative's attorney.

(e) Creditor. When letters of administration issue after the filing of a caveat by a creditor, the clerk must promptly notify the caveator, in writing, advising the caveator of the date of issuance of letters and the names and addresses of the personal representative and the personal representative's attorney, unless notice has previously been served on the caveator. A copy of any notice given by the clerk, together with a certificate of the mailing of the original notice, must be filed in the estates proceedings.

(f) Other Interested Persons; Before Commencement. After the filing of a caveat by an interested person other than a creditor, the court must not admit a will of the decedent to probate or appoint a personal representative without service of formal notice on the caveator or the caveator's designated agent.

Committee Notes

Caveat proceedings permit a decedent's creditor or other interested person to be notified when letters of administration are issued. Thereafter, the caveator must take appropriate action to protect the caveator's interests.

This rule treats the creditor caveator different from other caveators.

An attorney admitted to practice in Florida who represents the caveator may sign the caveat on behalf of the client.

Rule History

1977 Revision: Carried forward prior rule 5.150.

1984 Revision: Changes in (a), (b), and (d) are editorial. Change in (c) eliminates resident agent requirement for Florida residents and for nonresidents represented by a Florida attorney. Service on the attorney binds caveator. Former (e) is now subdivisions (e) and (f) and treats creditor caveator differently from other interested persons. Change in (f) requires formal notice. Committee notes revised.

1988 Revision: Committee notes revised. Citation form changes in committee notes.

1992 Revision: Addition of language in subdivision (b) to implement 1992 amendment to section 731. 110(2), Florida Statutes. Editorial changes. Citation form changes in committee notes.

2003 Revision: Committee notes revised.

2010 Revision: Subdivision (c) amended to clarify that a state

agency filing a caveat need not designate an agent for service of process, and to provide that a caveator who is not a resident of the county where the caveat is filed must designate either a resident of that county or an attorney licensed and residing in Florida as the caveator's agent. Editorial changes in (d) and (e). Committee notes revised.

2010 Cycle Report Revision: Subdivision (c) amended to clarify that a state agency filing a caveat need not designate an agent for service of process, and to provide that a caveator who is not a resident of the county where the caveat is filed must designate either a resident of that county or an attorney licensed and residing in Florida as the caveator's agent. Editorial changes in (d) and (e). Committee notes revised.

2010 Out-of-Cycle Report Revision: Subdivisions (a) and (b) amended to conform with statutory changes. Subdivision (c) amended to read as it existed prior to SC10-171 (35 FLW S482) due to a subsequent legislative amendment (Chapter 2010-132, § 3, Laws of Fla.). Editorial changes in (d), (e), and (f). Committee notes revised.

2011 Revision: Subdivision (b) amended to replace language removed in 2010 out-of-cycle revision, to replace term "decedent" with "person for whom the estate will be, or is being, administered," and to limit listing of a social security number to the last four digits and a date of birth to the year of birth.

Statutory References

§ 731.110, Fla. Stat. Caveat; proceedings.

Rule Reference

Fla. Prob. R. 5.040(a) Notice.

RULE 5.270. REVOCATION OF PROBATE

(a) Petition and Contents. A petition for revocation of probate shall state the interest of the petitioner in the estate and the facts constituting the grounds on which revocation is demanded.

(b) Continued administration. Pending the determination of any issue for revocation of probate, the personal representative shall proceed with the administration of the estate as if no revocation proceeding had been commenced, except that no distribution may be made to beneficiaries in contravention of the rights of those who, but for the will, would be entitled to the property disposed of.

Committee Notes

This rule represents a rule implementation of the procedure found in section 733.109(2), Florida Statutes. It is not intended to change the effect of the statute from which it was derived but has been reformatted to conform with the structure of these rules. It is not intended to create a new procedure or modify an existing procedure. The committee believes that subsections (1) and (3) of the statute are substantive, and have therefore not been included.

Further, this rule revises subdivision (b) of the prior similar rule to track the language in the statute from which it was derived.

Rule History

1984 Revision: Extensive changes. Committee notes revised.

1988 Revision: Language of subdivision (b) of the rule rewritten to track the statute more closely. Committee notes expanded. Citation form change in committee notes.

1992 Revision: Committee notes revised. Citation form changes in committee notes.

2003 Revision: Committee notes revised.

2005 Revision: "Beneficiaries" substituted for "devisees" in subdivision (b) to conform language to section 733.109(2), Florida Statutes.

2007 Revision: Committee notes revised.

Statutory References

§ 731.201(23), Fla. Stat. General definitions.

§ 732.5165, Fla. Stat. Effect of fraud, duress, mistake, and undue influence.

§ 733.109, Fla. Stat. Revocation of probate.

§ 733.212, Fla. Stat. Notice of administration; filing of objections.

§ 733.2123, Fla. Stat. Adjudication before issuance of letters.

Rule References

Fla. Prob. R. 5.025 Adversary proceedings.

Fla. Prob. R. 5.040 Notice.

Fla. Prob. R. 5.240 Notice of administration.

RULE 5.275. BURDEN OF PROOF IN WILL CONTESTS

In all proceedings contesting the validity of a will, the burden shall be upon the proponent of the will to establish prima facie its formal execution and attestation. Thereafter, the contestant shall have the burden of establishing the grounds on which the probate of the will is opposed or revocation sought.

Committee Notes

This rule represents a rule implementation of the procedure found in section 733.107, Florida Statutes. The presumption of undue influence implements public policy against abuse of fiduciary or confidential relationships and is therefore a presumption shifting the burden of proof under sections 90.301-90.304, Florida Statutes.

Rule History

1988 Revision: New rule.

1992 Revision: Citation form changes in committee notes.

2003 Revision: Committee notes revised.

Statutory References

§ 90.301, Fla. Stat. Presumption defined; inferences.

§ 90.302, Fla. Stat. Classification of rebuttable presumptions.

§ 90.303, Fla. Stat. Presumption affecting the burden of producing evidence defined.

§ 90.304, Fla. Stat. Presumption affecting the burden of proof defined.

§ 733.107. Fla. Stat. Burden of proof in contests; presumption of undue influence.

RULE 5.310. DISQUALIFICATION OF PERSONAL REPRESENTATIVE; NOTIFICATION

Any personal representative who was not qualified to act at the time of appointment or who would not be qualified for appointment if application for appointment were then made shall immediately file and serve on all interested persons a notice describing:

(a) the reason the personal representative was not qualified at the time of appointment; or

(b) the reason the personal representative would not be qualified for appointment if application for appointment were then made and the date on which the disqualifying event occurred.

The personal representative's notice shall state that any interested person may petition to remove the personal representative.

Committee Notes

Notification under this rule or section 733.3101, Florida Statutes, does not automatically affect the authority of the personal representative to act. The personal representative may resign or interested persons or the court must act to remove the personal representative.

Rule History

1975 Revision: This is same as old rule 5.220 and old section 732.47(3), Florida Statutes. The rule sets forth the imperative need for timely action and the inherent responsibility of a fiduciary to effect orderly succession. It further implies the inherent jurisdiction of the court to control by judicial overview the succession.

1977 Revision: Citation form change in committee note.

1988 Revision: Committee notes revised. Citation form changes in committee notes.

1992 Revision: Editorial changes to clarify rule. Committee notes revised. Citation form changes in committee notes.

2002 Revision: Rule amended to implement procedures found in section 733.3101, Florida Statutes. Committee notes revised.

Statutory References

§ 731.301, Fla. Stat. Notice.

§ 733.302, Fla. Stat. Who may be appointed personal representative.

§ 733.303, Fla. Stat. Persons not qualified.

§ 733.3101, Fla. Stat. Personal representative not qualified.

§ 733.502, Fla. Stat. Resignation of personal representative.

§ 733.504, Fla. Stat. Removal of personal representative; causes for removal.

§ 733.505, Fla. Stat. Jurisdiction in removal proceedings.

§ 733.506, Fla. Stat. Proceedings for removal.

Rule References

Fla. Prob. R. 5.040 Notice.

Fla. Prob. R. 5.430 Resignation of personal representative.

Fla. Prob. R. 5.440 Proceedings for removal.

RULE 5.320. OATH OF PERSONAL REPRESENTATIVE

Before the granting of letters of administration, the personal representative shall file an oath to faithfully administer the estate of the decedent. If the petition is verified by the prospective personal representative individually, the oath may be incorporated in the petition or in the designation of resident agent.

Committee Notes

It is contemplated the oath may be signed concurrently with the petition for administration and will be valid even if it predates the order appointing the personal representative.

Rule History

1977 Revision: No change in rule. Change in committee note to conform to statutory renumbering.

This rule establishes the uniform requirement for an oath of faithful performance of fiduciary duties within the permissiveness of section 733.401(1)(d), Florida Statutes. Should be taken together with new rule 5.110, Resident Agent.

1988 Revision: Committee notes expanded. Citation form changes in committee notes.

1992 Revision: Editorial change. Committee notes revised. Citation form changes in committee notes.

2003 Revision: Committee notes revised.

Rule References

Fla. Prob. R. 5.110 Address designation for personal representative or guardian; designation of resident agent and acceptance.

Fla. Prob. R. 5.235 Issuance of letters, bond.

RULE 5.330. EXECUTION BY PERSONAL REPRESENTATIVE

Notwithstanding any other provisions of these rules, the personal representative shall sign the:

(a) inventory;

(b) accountings;

(c) petition for sale or confirmation of sale or encumbrance of real or personal property;

(d) petition to continue business of decedent;

(e) petition to compromise or settle claim;

(f) petition to purchase on credit;

(g) petition for distribution and discharge; and

(h) resignation of personal representative.

Committee Notes

Rule History

1975 Revision: Where the jurisdiction of the court is invoked voluntarily pursuant to section 733.603, Florida Statutes, or otherwise, the rule requires that the personal representative have actual knowledge of the more important steps and acts of administration.

1977 Revision: Citation form change in committee note.

1988 Revision: Editorial changes. Citation form changes in committee notes.

1992 Revision: Editorial changes. Committee notes revised. Citation form changes in committee notes.

2003 Revision: Committee notes revised.

2010 Revision: Committee notes revised.

Statutory References

§ 733.502, Fla. Stat. Resignation of personal representative.

§ 733.604, Fla. Stat. Inventories and accountings; public records exemptions.

§ 733.612(5), (22), (24), Fla. Stat. Transactions authorized for the personal representative; exceptions.

§ 733.613, Fla. Stat. Personal representative's right to sell real property.

§ 733.708, Fla. Stat. Compromise.

§ 733.901, Fla. Stat. Final discharge.

Rule References

Fla. Prob. R. 5.340 Inventory.

Fla. Prob. R. 5.345 Accountings other than personal representatives' final accountings.

Fla. Prob. R. 5.346 Fiduciary accounting.

Fla. Prob. R. 5.350 Continuance of unincorporated business or venture.

Fla. Prob. R. 5.370 Sales of real property where no power conferred.

Fla. Prob. R. 5.400 Distribution and discharge.

Fla. Prob. R. 5.430 Resignation of personal representative.

RULE 5.340. INVENTORY

(a) **Contents and Filing.** Unless an inventory has been previously filed, the personal representative shall file an inventory of the estate within 60 days after issuance of letters. The inventory shall contain notice of the beneficiaries' rights under subdivision (e), list the estate with reasonable detail, and include for each listed item (excluding real property appearing to be protected homestead property) its estimated fair market value at the date of the decedent's death. Real property appearing to be protected homestead property shall be listed and so designated.

(b) **Extension.** On petition the time for filing the inventory may be extended by the court for cause shown without notice, except that the personal representative shall serve copies of the petition and order on the persons described in subdivision (d).

(c) **Amendments.** A supplementary or amended inventory containing the information required by subdivision (a) as to each affected item shall be filed and served by the personal representative if:

(1) the personal representative learns of property not included in the original inventory; or

(2) the personal representative learns that the estimated value or description indicated in the original inventory for any item is erroneous or misleading; or

(3) the personal representative determines the estimated fair market value of an item whose value was described as unknown in the original inventory.

(d) **Service.** The personal representative shall serve a copy of the inventory and all supplemental and amended inventories on the surviving spouse, each heir at law in an intestate estate, each residuary beneficiary in a testate estate, and any other interested person who may request it in writing.

(e) **Information.** On request in writing, the personal representative shall provide the following:

(1) To the requesting residuary beneficiary or heir in an intestate estate, a written explanation of how the inventory value for an asset was determined or, if an appraisal was obtained, a copy of the appraisal.

(2) To any other requesting beneficiary, a written explanation of how the inventory value for each asset distributed or proposed to be distributed to that beneficiary was determined or, if an appraisal of that asset was obtained, a copy of the appraisal.

(f) **Notice to Nonresiduary Beneficiaries.** The personal representative shall provide to each nonresiduary beneficiary written notice of that beneficiary's right to receive a written explanation of how the inventory value for each asset distributed or proposed to be distributed to that beneficiary was determined or a copy of an appraisal, if any, of the asset.

(g) **Elective Share Proceedings.** Upon entry of an order determining the surviving spouse's entitlement to the elective share, the personal representative shall file an inventory of the property entering into the elective estate which shall identify the direct recipient, if any, of that property. The personal representative shall serve the inventory of the elective estate as provided in rule 5.360. On request in writing, the personal representative shall provide an interested person with a written explanation of how the inventory value for an asset was determined and shall permit an interested person to examine appraisals on which the inventory values are based.

(h) **Verification.** All inventories shall be verified by the personal representative.

Committee Notes

Inventories of the elective estate under subdivision (f) shall be afforded the same confidentiality as probate inventories. § 733.604(1) and (2), Fla. Stat.

Inventories are still required to be filed. Once filed, however, they are subject to the confidentiality provisions found in sections 733.604(1) and (2), Florida Statutes.

Constitutional protected homestead real property is not necessarily a probatable asset. Disclosure on the inventory of real property appearing to be constitutional protected homestead property informs interested persons of the homestead issue.

Interested persons are entitled to reasonable information about estate proceedings on proper request, including a copy of the inventory, an opportunity to examine appraisals, and other information pertinent to their interests in the estate. The rights of beneficiaries to information contained in estate inventories is limited by section 733.604(3), Florida Statutes. Inventories of the elective estate under subdivision (f) affects a broader class of interested persons who may obtain information regarding the assets disclosed therein subject to control by the court and the confidentiality afforded such inventories under section 733.604(1) and (2).

Rule History

1980 Revision: Eliminated the time limit in requesting a copy of the inventory by an interested person or in furnishing it by the personal representative.

1984 (First) Revision: Extensive changes. Committee notes revised.

1984 (Second) Revision: Subdivision (a) modified to clarify or re-insert continued filing requirement for inventory.

1988 Revision: Editorial changes in (b) and (d). Committee notes revised. Citation form changes in committee notes.

1992 Revision: Editorial changes. Committee notes revised. Citation form changes in committee notes.

2001 Revision: Subdivision (a) amended to conform to statutory changes. Subdivision (d) amended to add requirement of filing of proof of service. Subdivision (e) amended to clarify personal representative's duty to furnish explanation of how inventory values were determined. Subdivision (f) added to require personal representative to file inventory of property entering into elective share. Subdivision (g) added to require verification of inventories. Committee notes revised.

2002 Revision: Subdivision (e) amended to conform to section 733.604(3), Florida Statutes. Subdivision (f) amended to establish procedures for interested persons to obtain information about assets and values listed in the inventory of the elective estate. Committee notes revised.

2003 Revision: Committee notes revised.

2010 Revision: Subdivisions (d) and (g) (former (f)) amended to delete the requirement to serve a copy of the inventory on the Department of Revenue. Subdivision (e) amended, and new (f) created, to limit the kind of information available to nonresiduary beneficiaries, and subsequent subdivisions relettered. Editorial changes in (a), (e), and (g). Committee notes revised.

2012 Revision: The last sentence of subdivision (d) is deleted to remove duplicative requirement of filing a proof of service for a document which includes a certificate of service as provided in Fla. R. Jud. Admin. 2.516. If service of the inventory is by service in the manner provided for service of formal notice, then proof of service should be filed as provided in rule 5.040(a)(5). Committee notes revised.

Constitutional Reference

Art. X, § 4, Fla. Const.

Statutory References

§ 732.401, Fla. Stat. Descent of homestead.

§ 732.4015, Fla. Stat. Devise of homestead.

§ 733.604, Fla. Stat. Inventories and accountings; public records exemptions.

Rule References

Fla. Prob. R. 5.041 Service of pleadings and documents.

Fla. Prob. R. 5.060 Request for notices and copies of pleadings.

Fla. Prob. R. 5.340 Execution by personal representative.

Fla. Prob. R. 5.360 Elective share.

Fla. Prob. R. 5.405 Proceedings to determine homestead real property.

Fla. R. Jud. Admin. 2.516 Service of pleadings and documents.

RULE 5.341. ESTATE INFORMATION

On reasonable request in writing, the personal representative shall provide an interested person with information about the estate and its administration.

Committee Notes

This rule is not intended to overrule the holdings in *In re Estate of Shaw*, 340 So. 2d 491 (Fla. 3d DCA 1976), and *In re Estate of Posner*, 492 So. 2d 1093 (Fla. 3d DCA 1986).

Rule History

2002 Revision: New rule.

RULE 5.342. INVENTORY OF SAFE-DEPOSIT BOX

(a) Filing. The personal representative shall file an inventory of the contents of the decedent's safe-deposit box within 10 days of the initial opening of the box by the personal representative or the personal representative's attorney of record. The inventory shall include a copy of the financial institution's entry record for the box from a date that is six months prior to the decedent's date of death to the date of the initial opening by the personal representative or the personal representative's attorney of record.

(b) Verification. Each person who was present at the initial opening must verify the contents of the box by signing a copy of the inventory under penalties of perjury.

(c) Service. The personal representative shall serve a copy of the inventory on the surviving spouse, each heir at law in an intestate estate, each residuary beneficiary in a testate estate, and any other interested person who may request it in writing.

Committee Notes

Inventories and entry records, once filed, shall be afforded the same confidentiality as probate inventories.

If a safe-deposit box is opened pursuant to section 655.935 of the Florida Statutes, no written inventory of the box need be prepared or filed.

Rule History

2003 Revision: New rule.

2012 Revision: The last sentence of subdivision (c) is deleted to remove duplicative requirement of filing a proof of service for a document which includes a certificate of service as provided in Fla. R. Jud. Admin. 2.516. If service of the inventory is by service in the manner provided for service of formal notice, then proof of service should be filed as provided in rule 5.040(a)(5). Committee notes revised.

Statutory References

§ 655.935, Fla. Stat. Search procedure on death of lessee.

§ 655.936, Fla. Stat. Delivery of safe-deposit box contents or property held in safekeeping to personal representative.

§ 733.6065, Fla. Stat. Opening safe-deposit box.

Rule References

Fla. Prob. R. 5.041 Service of pleadings and documents.

Fla. Prob. R. 5.340 Inventory.

Fla. R. Jud. Admin. 2.516 Service of pleadings and documents.

RULE 5.3425. SEARCH OF SAFE DEPOSIT BOX

(a) Petition for Order Authorizing Search. The petition for an order authorizing the search of a safe deposit box leased or co-leased by a decedent must be verified and must contain:

(1) The petitioner's name, address, and interest, if any, in the estate;

(2) The decedent's name, address, date and place of death, and state and county of domicile;

(3) A description of the safe deposit box leased by the decedent and, if known, the name of any co-lessee;

(4) The name and address of the institution where the safe deposit box is located; and

(5) A statement that the petitioner believes that the decedent may have left in the safe deposit box one or more of the following:

(A) A will or codicil of the decedent, or a writing described in section 732.515 of the Code;

(B) A deed to a burial plot;

(C) A writing giving burial instructions; or

(D) Insurance policies on the life of the decedent.

(b) Order. If the Court determines that the petitioner is entitled to an order authorizing a search of the decedent's safe deposit box, it must enter an order

(1) authorizing the petitioner to open the safe deposit box in the presence of an officer of the lessor and, if requested by the petitioner, to remove and deliver

(A) to the court having probate jurisdiction in the county where the lessor is located any writing purporting to be a will or codicil of the decedent and any writing purporting to identify devises of tangible property;

(B) to the petitioner, any writing purporting to be a deed to a burial plot to give burial instructions; and

(C) to the beneficiary named therein, any document purporting to be an insurance policy on the life of the decedent.

(2) directing the officer of the lessor to make a complete copy of any document removed and delivered pursuant to the court order, together with a memorandum of delivery identifying the name of the officer, the person to whom the document was delivered, and the date of delivery, to be placed in the safe deposit box leased or co-leased by the decedent.

Committee Notes

The search of the safe deposit box is not considered an initial opening and is not subject to the inventory requirements of rule 5.342.

Rule History

2010 Revision: New rule.

Statutory References

§ 655.935, Fla. Stat. Search procedure on death of lessee.

RULE 5.345. ACCOUNTINGS OTHER THAN PERSONAL REPRESENTATIVES' FINAL ACCOUNTINGS

(a) Applicability and Accounting Periods. This rule applies to the interim accounting of any fiduciary of a probate estate, the accounting of a personal representative who has resigned or been removed, and the accounting of a curator upon the appointment of a successor fiduciary. The fiduciary may elect to file an interim accounting at any time, or the court may require an interim or supplemental accounting. The ending date of the accounting period for any accounting to which this rule applies shall be as follows:

(1) For an interim accounting, any date selected by the fiduciary, including a fiscal or calendar year, or as may be determined by the court.

(2) For the accounting of a personal representative who has resigned or has been removed, the date the personal representative's letters are revoked.

(3) For a curator who has been replaced by a successor fiduciary, the date of appointment of the successor fiduciary.

(b) Notice of Filing. Notice of filing and a copy of any accounting to which this rule applies shall be served on all interested persons. The notice shall state that objections to the accounting must be filed within 30 days from the date of service of notice.

(c) Objection. Any interested person may file an objection to any accounting to which this rule applies within 30 days from the date of service of notice on that person. Any objection not filed within 30 days from the date of service shall be deemed abandoned. An objection shall be in writing and shall state with particularity the item or items to which the objection is directed and the grounds upon which the objection is based.

(d) Service of Objections. The objecting party shall serve a copy of the objection on the fiduciary filing the accounting and other interested persons.

(e) Disposition of Objections and Approval of Accountings. The court shall sustain or overrule any objection filed as provided in this rule. If no objection is filed, any accounting to which this rule applies shall be deemed approved 30 days from the date of service of the accounting on interested persons.

(f) Substantiating Papers. On reasonable written request, the fiduciary shall permit an interested person to examine papers substantiating items in any accounting to which this rule applies.

(g) Supplemental Accountings. The court, on its own motion or on that of any interested person, may require a fiduciary who has been replaced by a successor fiduciary to file a supplemental accounting, the beginning date of which shall be the ending date of the accounting as specified in subdivision (a) of this rule and the ending date of which is the date of delivery of all of the estate's property to the successor fiduciary, or such other date as the court may order.

(h) Verification. All accountings shall be verified by the fiduciary filing the accounting.

Committee Notes

The personal representative is required to file a final accounting when administration is complete, unless filing is waived by interested persons. Additionally, a fiduciary of a probate estate may elect, but is not required, to file interim accountings at any time. An accounting is required for resigning or removed fiduciaries. The filing, notice, objection, and approval procedure is similar to that for final accounts.

Rule History

1977 Revision: Change in (a) to authorize selection of fiscal year.

1980 Revision: Change in (d) of prior rule to require the notice to state that the basis for an objection is necessary. Change in (e) of prior rule to require any person filing an objection to set forth the basis of such objection.

1984 Revision: Extensive changes. Committee notes revised.

1988 Revision: Citation form change in committee notes.

1992 Revision: Editorial change. Committee notes revised. Citation form changes in committee notes.

2002 Revision: Implements procedures for interim accountings and accountings by resigning or removed fiduciaries. Committee notes revised.

2003 Revision: Committee notes revised.

2005 Revision: Verification requirement added as new (h). Committee notes revised.

Statutory References

§ 733.3101, Fla. Stat. Personal representative not qualified.

§ 733.501, Fla. Stat. Curators.

§ 733.5035, Fla. Stat. Surrender of assets after resignation.

§ 733.5036, Fla. Stat. Accounting and discharge following resignation.

§ 733.508, Fla. Stat. Accounting and discharge of removed personal representatives upon removal.

§ 733.509, Fla. Stat. Surrender of assets upon removal.

Ch. 738, Fla. Stat. Principal and income.

Rule References

Fla. Prob. R. 5.020 Pleadings; verification; motions.

Fla. Prob. R. 5.122 Curators.

Fla. Prob. R. 5.150 Order requiring accounting.

Fla. Prob. R. 5.330 Execution by personal representative.

Fla. Prob. R. 5.346 Fiduciary accounting.

Fla. Prob. R. 5.430 Resignation of personal representative.

Fla. Prob. R. 5.440 Proceedings for removal.

RULE 5.346. FIDUCIARY ACCOUNTING

(a) Contents. A fiduciary accounting shall include:

(1) all cash and property transactions since the date of the last accounting or, if none, from the commencement of administration, and

(2) a schedule of assests at the end of the accounting period.

(b) Accounting Standards. The following standards are required for the accounting of all transactions occurring on or after January 1, 1994:

(1) Accountings shall be stated in a manner that is understandable to persons who are not familiar with practices and terminology peculiar to the administration of estates and trusts.

(2) The accounting shall begin with a concise summary of its purpose and content.

(3) The accounting shall contain sufficient information to put interested persons on notice as to all significant transactions affecting administration during the accounting period.

(4) The accounting shall contain 2 values in the schedule of assets at the end of the accounting period, the asset acquisition value or carrying value, and estimated current value.

(5) Gains and losses incurred during the accounting period shall be shown separately in the same schedule.

(6) The accounting shall show significant transactions that do not affect the amount for which the fiduciary is accountable.

(c) Accounting Format. A model format for an accounting is attached to these rules as Appendix A.

(d) Verification. All accountings shall be verified by the fiduciary filing the accounting.

Committee Notes

This rule substantially adopts the Uniform Fiduciary Accounting Principles and Model Formats adopted by the Committee on National Fiduciary Accounting Standards of the American Bar Association: Section of Real Property, Probate and Trust Law, the American College of Probate Counsel, the American Bankers Association: Trust Division, and other organizations.

Accountings shall also comply with the Florida principal and income law, chapter 738, Florida Statutes.

Attached as Appendix B to this rule are an explanation and commentary for each of the foregoing standards, which shall be considered as a Committee Note to this rule.

Accountings that substantially conform to the model formats are acceptable. The model accounting format included in Appendix A is only a suggested form.

Rule History

1988 Revision: New rule.

1992 Revision: Editorial changes throughout. Rule changed to require compliance with the Uniform Fiduciary Accounting Principles and Model Formats for accounting of all transactions occurring on or after January 1, 1994. Committee notes revised. Citation form changes in committee notes.

1996 Revision: Committee notes revised.

1999 Revision: Committee notes revised to correct rule reference and to reflect formatting changes in accounting formats.

2002 Revision: Subdivisions (a) and (b) amended to clarify contents of accounting. Comittee notes revised.

2003 Revision: Committee notes revised.

2005 Revision: Verification requirement added as new (d). Committee notes revised.

2007 Revision: Committee notes revised.

2010 Revision: Committee notes revised.

Statutory References

§ 733.501, Fla. Stat. Curators.

§ 733.5036, Fla. Stat. Accounting and discharge following resignation.

§ 733.508, Fla. Stat. Accounting and discharge of removed personal representatives upon removal.

§ 733.602(1), Fla. Stat. General duties.

§ 733.612(18), Fla. Stat. Transactions authorized for the personal representative; exceptions.

ch. 738, Fla. Stat. Principal and income.

Rule References

Fla. Prob. R. 5.020 Pleadings; verification; motions.

Fla. Prob. R. 5.040 Notice.

Fla. Prob. R. 5.122 Curators.

Fla. Prob. R. 5.180 Waiver and consent.

Fla. Prob. R. 5.330 Execution by personal representative.

Fla. Prob. R. 5.345 Accountings other than personal representatives' final accountings

Fla. Prob. R. 5.400 Distribution and discharge.

Fla. Prob. R. 5.430 Resignation of personal representative.

Fla. Prob. R. 5.440 Proceedings for removal.

APPENDIX A

IN THE CIRCUIT COURT FOR _____ COUNTY, FLORIDA

IN RE: ESTATE OF   PROBATE DIVISION

                                    File Number _____

    Deceased.

                                      Division _____

_____ ACCOUNTING OF PERSONAL REPRESENTATIVE(S)

From:_____, _____, Through:_____, _____

The purpose of this accounting is to acquaint all interested persons with the transactions that have occurred during the period covered by the accounting and the assets that remain on hand. It consists of a SUMMARY sheet and Schedule A showing all Receipts, Schedule B showing all Disbursements, Schedule C showing all Distributions, Schedule D showing all Capital Transactions and Adjustments (the effect of which are also reflected in other schedules, if appropriate), and Schedule E showing assets on hand at the end of the accounting period.

It is important that this accounting be carefully examined. Requests for additional information and any questions should be addressed to the personal representative(s) or the attorneys for the personal representative(s), the names and addresses of whom are set forth below.

Under penalties of perjury, the undersigned personal representative(s) declare(s) that I (we) have read and examined this accounting and that the facts and figures set forth in the Summary and the attached Schedules are true, to the best of my (our) knowledge and belief, and that it is a complete report of all cash and property transactions and of all receipts and disbursements by me (us) as personal representative(s) of the estate of _____ deceased, from _____, _____ through _____, _____.

Signed on _____, _____.

Attorney for Personal Representative: Personal Representative:

_____   _____
          Attorney

                                          _____

Name

Florida Bar No. _____

_____   _____

_____   _____

(address)   (address)

                                        [Print or Type Names Under All Signature Lines]

Telephone:_____

IN THE CIRCUIT COURT FOR _____ COUNTY, FLORIDA

IN RE: ESTATE OF   PROBATE DIVISION
                                   File Number _____

Deceased.   Division_____

_____ ACCOUNTING OF PERSONAL REPRESENTATIVE

From:_____, _____, Through:_____, _____

SUMMARY

	Income	Principal	Totals
I. Starting Balance Assets per Inventory or on Hand at Close of Last Accounting Period	$_____	$_____	$_____
II. Receipts Schedule A:	$_____	$_____	$_____
III. Disbursements Schedule B:	$_____	$_____	$_____
IV. Distributions Schedule C:	$_____	$_____	$_____
V. Capital Transactions and Adjustments Schedule D: Net Gain or (Loss)		$_____	$_____

VI. <u>Assets on Hand at Close of Accounting Period</u>
Schedule E: Cash and Other $_____ $_____ $_____
Assets

NOTE: Refer to Fla. Prob. R. 5.330(b), 5.345, 5.346, and 5.400.

Also see <u>Accountings</u>, Chapter 12 of Practice Under Florida Probate Code (Fla. Bar CLE).

Entries on Summary are to be taken from totals on Schedules A, B, C, D, and E.

The Summary and Schedules A, B, C, D and E are to constitute the full accounting. Every transaction occurring during the accounting period should be reflected on the Schedules.

All purchases and sales, all adjustments to the inventory or carrying value of any asset, and any other changes in the assets (such as stock splits) should be described on Schedule D.

The amount in the "Total" column for Item VI must agree with the total inventory or adjusted carrying value of all assets on hand at the close of the accounting period on Schedule E.

_____ ACCOUNTING OF PERSONAL REPRESENTATIVE,

ESTATE OF _____

From:_____, ___, Through:_____,

SCHEDULE A   Receipts

Date	Brief Description of Items	Income	Principal

NOTE: Schedule A should reflect only those items received during administration that are not shown on the inventory. Classification of items as income or principal is to be in accordance with the provisions of the Florida Uniform Principal and Income Act, Chapter 738, Florida Statutes.

Entries involving the sale of assets or other adjustments to the carrying values of assets are to be shown on Schedule D, and not on Schedule A.

_____ ACCOUNTING OF PERSONAL REPRESENTATIVE,

ESTATE OF _____

From:_____, ___, Through:_____,

SCHEDULE B
  Disbursements

Date	Brief Description of Items	Income	Principal

NOTE: Schedule B should reflect only those items paid out during the accounting period. Classification of disbursements as income or principal is to be in accordance with the provisions of the Florida Uniform Principal and Income Act, Chapter 738, Florida Statutes.

    Entries involving the purchase of assets or adjustments to the carrying values of assets are to be shown on Schedule D, and not on Schedule B.

_____ ACCOUNTING OF PERSONAL REPRESENTATIVE,

ESTATE OF _____

From:_____, ___, Through:_____,

SCHEDULE C
   Distributions

Date	Brief Description of Items	Income	Principal

NOTE: Schedule C should reflect only those items or amounts distributed to beneficiaries during the accounting period. Assets distributed should be shown at their inventory or adjusted carrying values. Classification of distributions as income or principal is to be in accordance with the provisions of the Florida Uniform Principal and Income Act, Chapter 738, Florida Statutes.

Entries involving adjustments to the carrying values of assets are to be shown on Schedule D, and not on Schedule C.

_____ ACCOUNTING OF PERSONAL REPRESENTATIVE,

ESTATE OF _____

From:_____, ___, Through:_____,

SCHEDULE D			Capital
Transactions and Adjustments			

(Does not include distributions. Distributions are shown on Schedule C.)

Date	Brief Description of Transactions	Net Gain	Net Loss
TOTAL NET GAINS AND (LOSSES)		$	$
NET GAIN OR (LOSS)		$	$

NOTE: Schedule D should reflect all purchases and sales of assets and any adjustments to the carrying values of any assets.

Entries reflecting sales should show the inventory or adjusted carrying values, the costs and expenses of the sale, and the net proceeds received. The net gain or loss should be extended in the appropriate column on the right side of Schedule D.

Entries reflecting purchases should reflect the purchase price, any expenses of purchase or other adjustments to the purchase price, and the total amount paid. Presumably no gain or loss would be shown for purchases.

Entries reflecting adjustments in capital assets should explain the change (such as a stock split) and the net gain or loss should be shown in the appropriate column on the right side of Schedule D.

The NET gain or loss should be entered in the Principal column of the Summary.

_____ ACCOUNTING OF PERSONAL REPRESENTATIVE,

ESTATE OF _____

From:_____, ___, Through:_____,

SCHEDULE E Period	Assets on Hand at Close of Accounting

(Indicate where held and legal description, certificate numbers or other identification.)

	Estimated Current Value	Carrying Value
ASSETS OTHER THAN CASH:		
OTHER ASSETS TOTAL	$	$
CASH:		
CASH TOTAL		$
TOTAL ASSETS (must agree with the Total for Item VI on Summary)		$

NOTE: Schedule E should be a complete list of all assets on hand reflecting inventory values for each item, adjusted in accordance with any appropriate entries on Schedule D.

Current market values for any assets that are known to be different from the inventory or carrying values as of the close of the accounting period should be shown in the column marked "Current Value." The total inventory or adjusted carrying value (not Current Value) must agree with the Total for Item VI on Summary.

APPENDIX B
UNIFORM FIDUCIARY ACCOUNTING PRINCIPLES

I. ACCOUNTS SHOULD BE STATED IN A MANNER THAT IS UNDERSTANDABLE BY PERSONS WHO ARE NOT FAMILIAR WITH PRACTICES AND TERMINOLOGY PECULIAR TO THE ADMINISTRATION OF ESTATES AND TRUSTS.

Commentary: In order for an account to fulfill its basic function of communication, it is essential that it be stated in a manner that recognizes that the interested parties are not usually familiar with fiduciary accounts. It is neither practical nor desirable to require that accounts be tailored to meet individual disabilities of particular parties but any account should be capable of being understood by a person of average intelligence, literate in English, and familiar with basic financial terms who has read it with care and attention.

Problems arising from terminology or style are usually a reflection of the fact that people who become versed in a particular form of practice tend to forget that terms which are familiar and useful to them may convey nothing to someone else or may even be affirmatively misleading. For example, the terms "debit" and "credit" are generally incomprehensible to people with no knowledge of bookkeeping and many people who are familiar with them in other contexts would assume that in the context of fiduciary accounting, the receipt of an item is a "credit" to the fund rather than a "debit" to the fiduciary.

While the need for concise presentation makes a certain amount of abbreviation both acceptable and necessary, uncommon abbreviation of matters essential to an understanding of the account should be avoided or explained.

No position is taken for or against the use of direct print-outs from machine accounting systems. The quality of the accounts produced by these systems varies widely in the extent to which they can be understood by persons who are not familiar with them. To endorse or object to a direct print-out because it is produced by machine from previously stored data would miss the essential point by focusing attention upon the manner of preparation rather than the product.

II. A FIDUCIARY ACCOUNT SHALL BEGIN WITH A CONCISE SUMMARY OF ITS PURPOSE AND CONTENT.

Commentary: Very few people can be expected to pay much attention to a document unless they have some understanding of its general purpose and its significance to them. Even with such an understanding, impressions derived from the first page or two will often determine whether the rest is read. The use that is made of these pages is therefore of particular significance.

The cover page should disclose the nature and function of the account. While a complete explanation of the significance of the account and the effect of its presentation upon the rights of the parties is obviously impractical for inclusion at this point, there should be at least a brief statement identifying the fiduciary and the subject matter, noting the importance of examining the account and giving an address where more information can be obtained.

It is assumed that the parties would also have enough information from other sources to understand the nature of their relationship to the fund (e.g., residuary legatee, life tenant, remainderman), the function of the account, and the obligation of the fiduciary to supply further relevant information upon request. It is also assumed that notice will be given of any significant procedural considerations such as limitation on the time within which objections must be presented. This would normally be provided by prior or contemporaneous memoranda, correspondence, or discussions.

A summary of the account shall also be presented at the outset. This summary, organized as a table of contents, shall indicate the order of the details presented in the account and shall show separate totals for the aggregate of the assets on hand at the beginning of the accounting period; transactions during the period; and the assets remaining on hand at the end of the period. Each entry in the summary shall be supported by a schedule in the account that provides the details on which the summary is based.

III. A FIDUCIARY ACCOUNT SHALL CONTAIN SUFFICIENT INFORMATION TO PUT THE INTERESTED PARTIES ON NOTICE AS TO ALL SIGNIFICANT TRANSACTIONS AFFECTING ADMINISTRATION DURING THE ACCOUNTING PERIOD.

Commentary: The presentation of the information account shall allow an interested party to follow the progress of the fiduciary's administration of assets during the accounting period.

An account is not complete if it does not itemize, or make reference to, assets on hand at the beginning of the accounting period.

Illustration:

3.1 The first account for a decedent's estate or a trust may detail the items received by the fiduciary and for which the fiduciary is responsible. It may refer to the total amount of an inventory filed elsewhere or assets described in a schedule attached to a trust agreement.

Instead of retyping the complete list of assets in the opening balance, the preparer may prefer to attach as an exhibit a copy of the inventory, closing balance from the last account, etc., as appropriate, or may refer to them if previously provided to the interested parties who will receive it.

Transactions shall be described in sufficient detail to give interested parties notice of their purpose and effect. It should be recognized that too much detail may be counterproductive to making the account understandable. In accounts covering long periods or dealing with extensive assets, it is usually desirable to consolidate information. For instance, where income from a number of securities is being accounted for over a long period of time, a statement of the total dividends received on each security with appropriate indication of changes in the number of shares held will be more readily understandable and easier to check for completeness than a chronological listing of all dividends received.

Although detail should generally be avoided for routine transactions, it will often be necessary to proper understanding of an event that is somewhat out of the ordinary.

Illustrations:

3.2 Extraordinary appraisal costs should be shown separately and explained.

3.3 Interest and penalties in connection with late filing of tax returns should be shown separately and explained.

3.4 An extraordinary allocation between principal and income such as apportionment of proceeds of property acquired on foreclosure should be separately stated and explained.

3.5 Computation of a formula marital deduction gift involving non-probate assets should be explained.

IV. A FIDUCIARY ACCOUNT SHALL CONTAIN TWO VALUES, THE ASSET ACQUISITION VALUE OR CARRYING VALUE, AND CURRENT VALUE.

Commentary: In order for transactions to be reported on a consistent basis, an appropriate carrying value for assets must be chosen and employed consistently.

The carrying value of an asset should reflect its value at the time it is acquired by the fiduciary (or a predecessor fiduciary). When such a value is not precisely determinable, the figure used should reflect a thoughtful decision by the fiduciary. For assets owned by a decedent, inventory values or estate tax values — generally reflective of date of death — would be appropriate. Assets received in kind by a trustee from a settlor of an intervivos trust should be carried at their value at the time of receipt. For assets purchased during the administration of the fund, cost would normally be used. Use of Federal income tax basis for carrying value is acceptable when basis is reasonably representative of real values at the time of acquisition. Use of tax basis as a carrying value under other circumstances could be affirmatively misleading to beneficiaries and therefore is not appropriate.

In the Model Account, carrying value is referred to as "fiduciary acquisition value." The Model Account establishes the initial carrying value of assets as their value at date of death for inventoried assets, date of receipt for subsequent receipts, and cost for investments.

Carrying value would not normally be adjusted for depreciation.

Except for adjustments that occur normally under the accounting system in use, carrying values should generally be continued unchanged through successive accounts and assets should not be arbitrarily "written up" or "written down." In some circumstances, however, with proper disclosure and explanation, carrying value may be adjusted.

Illustrations:

4.1 Carrying values based on date of death may be adjusted to reflect changes on audit of estate or inheritance tax returns.

4.2 Where appropriate under applicable local law, a successor fiduciary may adjust the carrying value of assets to reflect values at the start of that fiduciary's administration.

4.3 Assets received in kind in satisfaction of a pecuniary legacy should be carried at the value used for purposes of distribution.

Though essential for accounting purposes, carrying values are commonly misunderstood by laypersons as being a representation of actual values. To avoid this, the account should include both current values and carrying values.

The value of assets at the beginning and ending of each accounting period is necessary information for the evaluation of investment performance. Therefore, the account should show, or make reference to, current values at the start of the period for all assets whose carrying values were established in a prior accounting period.

Illustrations:

4.4 The opening balance of the first account of a testamentary trustee will usually contain assets re-

ceived in kind from the executor. Unless the carrying value was written up at the time of distribution (e.g., 4.2 or 4.3 supra) these assets will be carried at a value established during the executor's administration. The current value at the beginning of the accounting period should also be shown.

4.5 An executor's first account will normally carry assets at inventory (date of death) values or costs. No separate listing of current values at the beginning of the accounting period is necessary.

Current values should also be shown for all assets on hand at the close of the accounting period. The date on which current values are determined shall be stated and shall be the last day of the accounting period, or a date as close thereto as reasonably possible.

Current values should be shown in a column parallel to the column of carrying values. Both columns should be totalled.

In determining current values for assets for which there is no readily ascertainable current value, the source of the value stated in the account shall be explained. The fiduciary shall make a good faith effort to determine realistic values but should not be expected to incur expenses for appraisals or similar costs when there is no reason to expect that the resulting information will be of practical consequence to the administration of the estate or the protection of the interests of the parties.

Illustrations:

4.6 When an asset is held under circumstances that make it clear that it will not be sold (e.g., a residence held for use of a beneficiary) the fiduciary's estimate of value would be acceptable in lieu of an appraisal.

4.7 Considerations such as a pending tax audit or offer of the property for sale may indicate the advisability of not publishing the fiduciary's best estimate of value. In such circumstances, a statement that value was fixed by some method such as "per company books," "formula under buy-sell agreement," or "300% of assessed value" would be acceptable, but the fiduciary would be expected to provide further information to interested parties upon request.

V. GAINS AND LOSSES INCURRED DURING THE ACCOUNTING PERIOD SHALL BE SHOWN SEPARATELY IN THE SAME SCHEDULE.

Commentary: Each transaction involving the sale or other disposition of securities during the accounting period shall be shown as a separate item in one combined schedule of the account indicating the transaction, date, explanation, and any gain or loss.

Although gains and losses from the sale of securities can be shown separately in accounts, the preferred method of presentation is to present this information in a single schedule. Such a presentation provides the most meaningful description of investment performance and will tend to clarify relationships between gains and losses that are deliberately realized at the same time.

VI. THE ACCOUNT SHALL SHOW SIGNIFICANT TRANSACTIONS THAT DO NOT AFFECT THE AMOUNT FOR WHICH THE FIDUCIARY IS ACCOUNTABLE.

Commentary: Transactions such as the purchase of an investment, receipt of a stock split, or change of a corporate name do not alter the total fund for which a fiduciary is accountable but must be shown in order to permit analysis and an understanding of the administration of the fund. These can be best shown in information schedules.

One schedule should list all investments made during the accounting period. It should include those subsequently sold as well as those still on hand. Frequently the same money will be used for a series of investments. Therefore, the schedule should not be totalled in order to avoid giving an exaggerated idea of the size of the fund.

A second schedule (entitled "Changes in Investment Holdings" in the Model Account) should show all transactions affecting a particular security holding, such as purchase of additional shares, partial sales, stocksplits, change of corporate name, divestment distributions, etc. This schedule, similar to a ledger account for each holding, will reconcile opening and closing entries for particular holdings, explain changes in carrying value, and avoid extensive searches through the account for information scattered among other schedules.

RULE 5.350. CONTINUANCE OF UNINCORPORATED BUSINESS OR VENTURE

(a) **Separate Accounts and Reports.** In the conduct of an unincorporated business or venture, the personal representative shall keep separate, full, and accurate accounts of all receipts and expenditures and make reports as the court may require.

(b) **Petition.** If the personal representative determines it to be in the best interest of the estate to continue an unincorporated business or venture beyond the time authorized by statute or will, the personal representative shall file a verified petition which shall include:

(1) a statement of the nature of that business or venture;

(2) a schedule of specific assets and liabilities;

(3) the reasons for continuation;

(4) the proposed form and times of accounting for that business or venture;

(5) the period for which the continuation is requested; and

(6) any other information pertinent to the petition.

(c) **Order.** If the continuation is authorized, the order shall state:

(1) the period for which that business or venture is to continue;

(2) the particular powers of the personal representative in the continuation of that business or venture; and

(3) the form and frequency of accounting by that business or venture.

(d) **Petition by Interested Person.** Any interested person, at any time, may petition the court for an order regarding the operation of, accounting for, or termination of an unincorporated business or venture, and the court shall enter an order thereon.

Committee Notes

Rule History

1975 Revision: New rule. § 733.612.

1984 Revision: Extensive changes in rule and title. Clarifies procedural steps to be taken by a personal representative who determines it to be in the best interest of an estate to continue any unincorporated business beyond the time authorized by statute. Information required to be filed in a verified petition is specified, and normal information to be included in a court order is listed. Other pertinent information under (b)(6) may include provisions for insurance of business or venture, proposed professionals to be used in connection with such activities, how the business or venture shall be managed, the person or persons proposed for managerial positions, a list of all other employees, agents, or independent contractors employed by or affiliated with the business or venture, and proposed compensation for all such management personnel, agents, employees, and independent contractors. Committee notes revised and expanded.

1988 Revision: Editorial change in caption of (b). Committee notes revised. Citation form changes in committee notes,

1992 Revision: Committee notes revised. Citation form changes in committee notes.

2012 Revision: Committee notes revised.

Statutory References

F.S. 733.612(22), Fla. Stat. Transactions authorized for the personal representative; exceptions.

Rule References

Fla. Prob. R. 5.020 Pleadings; verification; motions.

Fla. Prob. R. 5.040 Notice.

Fla. Prob. R. 5.041 Service of pleadings and documents.

Fla. Prob. R. 5.380 Execution by personal representative.

Fla. R. Jud. Admin. 2.516 Service of pleadings and documents.

RULE 5.355. PROCEEDINGS FOR REVIEW OF EMPLOYMENT OF AGENTS AND COMPENSATION OF PERSONAL REPRESENTATIVES AND ESTATE EMPLOYEES

After notice to all interested persons and upon petition of an interested person bearing all or a part of the impact of the payment of compensation to the personal representative or any person employed by the personal representative, the propriety of the employment and the reasonableness of the compensation or payment may be reviewed by the court. The petition shall state the grounds on which it is based.

The burden of proving the propriety of the employment and the reasonableness of the compensation shall be upon the personal representative and the person employed by the personal representative. Any person who is determined to have received excessive compensation from an estate may be ordered to make appropriate refunds.

Committee Notes

This rule represents a rule implementation of the procedure formerly found in section 733.6175, Florida Statutes. It is not intended to change the effect of the statute from which it was derived but has been reformatted to conform with the structure of these rules. It is not intended to create a new procedure or modify an existing procedure.

Rule History

1988 Revision: New rule.

1992 Revision: Editorial changes. Committee notes revised. Citation form changes in committee notes.

1996 Revision: Committee notes revised.

2003 Revision: Committee notes revised.

2007 Revision: Committee notes revised.

2012 Revision: Committee notes revised.

Statutory References

§ 731.201(23), Fla. Stat. General definitions.

§ 731.301, Fla. Stat. Notice.

§ 733.612(19), Fla. Stat. Transactions authorized for the personal representative; exceptions.

§ 733.617, Fla. Stat. Compensation of personal representative.

§ 733.6171 Fla. Stat. Compensation of attorney for the personal representative.

§ 733.6175, Fla. Stat. Proceedings for review of employment of agents and compensation of personal representatives and employees of estate.

Rule References

Fla. Prob. R. 5.040 Notice.

Fla. Prob. R. 5.041 Service of pleadings and documents.

Fla. R. Jud. Admin. 2.516 Service of pleadings and documents.

RULE 5.360. ELECTIVE SHARE

(a) Election. An election to take the elective share may be filed by the surviving spouse, or on behalf of the surviving spouse by an attorney-in-fact or guardian of the property of the surviving spouse.

(1) Election by Surviving Spouse. An electing surviving spouse must file the election within the time required by law and promptly serve a copy of the election on the personal representative in the manner provided for service of formal notice.

(2) Election by Attorney-in-Fact or Guardian of the Property of Surviving Spouse.

(A) Petition for Approval. Before filing the election, the attorney-in-fact or guardian of the property of the surviving spouse must petition the court having jurisdiction of the probate proceeding for approval to make the election. The petition for approval must allege the authority to act on behalf of the surviving spouse and facts supporting the election.

(B) Notice of Petition. Upon receipt of the petition, the personal representative must promptly serve a copy of the petition by formal notice on all interested persons.

(C) Order Authorizing Election. If the election is approved, the order must include a finding that the election is in the best interests of the surviving spouse during the spouse's probable lifetime.

(D) Filing the Election. Upon entry of an order authorizing the filing of an election, the attorney-in-fact or guardian of the property must file the election within the later of the time provided by law or 30 days from service of the order and promptly serve a copy of the election on the personal representative in the manner provided for service of formal notice.

(b) Procedure for Election.

(1) Extension. Within the period provided by law to make the election, the surviving spouse or an attorney-in-fact or guardian of the property of the surviving spouse may petition the court for an extension of time for making an election or for approval to make the election. After notice and hearing the court for good cause shown may extend the time for election. If the court grants the petition for an extension, the election must be filed within the time allowed by the extension.

(2) Withdrawal of Election. The surviving spouse, an attorney-in-fact, a guardian of the property of the surviving spouse, or the personal representative

of the surviving spouse's estate may withdraw the election within the time provided by law.

(3) Service of Notice. Upon receipt of an election the personal representative must serve a notice of election within 20 days following service of the election, together with a copy of the election, on all interested persons in the manner provided for service of formal notice. The notice of election must indicate the names and addresses of the attorneys for the surviving spouse and the personal representative and must state that:

(A) persons receiving a notice of election may be required to contribute toward the satisfaction of the elective share;

(B) objections to the election must be served within 20 days after service of the copy of the notice of election; and

(C) if no objection to the election is timely served, an order determining the surviving spouse's entitlement to the elective share may be granted without further notice.

(4) Objection to Election. Within 20 days after service of the notice of election, an interested person may serve an objection to the election which must state with particularity the grounds on which the objection is based. The objecting party must serve copies of the objection on the surviving spouse and the personal representative. If an objection is served, the personal representative must promptly serve a copy of the objection on all other interested persons who have not previously been served with a copy of the objection.

(c) Determination of Entitlement.

(1) No Objection Served. If no objection to the election is timely served, the court must enter an order determining the spouse's entitlement to the elective share.

(2) Objection Served. If an objection to the election is timely served, the court must determine the surviving spouse's entitlement to the elective share after notice and hearing.

(d) Procedure to Determine Amount of Elective Share and Contribution.

(1) Petition by Personal Representative. After entry of the order determining the surviving spouse's entitlement to the elective share, the personal representative must file and serve a petition to determine the amount of the elective share. The petition must

(A) give the name and address of each direct recipient known to the personal representative;

(B) describe the proposed distribution of assets to satisfy the elective share, and the time and manner of distribution; and

(C) identify those direct recipients, if any, from whom a specified contribution will be required and state the amount of contribution sought from each.

(2) Service of Inventory. The inventory of the elective estate required by rule 5.340, together with the petition, must be served within 60 days after entry of the order determining entitlement to the elective share on all interested persons in the manner provided for service of formal notice.

(3) Petition by Spouse. If the personal representative does not file the petition to determine the amount of the elective share within 90 days from rendition of the order of entitlement, the electing spouse or the attorney-in-fact or the guardian of the property or personal representative of the electing spouse may file the petition specifying as particularly as is known the value of the elective share.

(4) Objection to Amount of Elective Share. Within 20 days after service of the petition to determine the amount of the elective share, an interested person may serve an objection to the amount of or distribution of assets to satisfy the elective share. The objection must state with particularity the grounds on which the objection is based. The objecting party must serve copies of the objection on the surviving spouse and the personal representative. If an objection is served, the personal representative must promptly serve a copy of the objection on all interested persons who have not previously been served.

(5) Determination of Amount of Elective Share and Contribution.

(A) No Objection Served. If no objection is timely served to the petition to determine the amount of the elective share, the court must enter an order on the petition.

(B) Objection Served. If an objection is timely served to the petition to determine the amount of the elective share, the court must determine the amount of the elective share and contribution after notice and hearing.

(6) Order Determining Amount of Elective Share and Contribution. The order must:

(A) set forth the amount of the elective share;

(B) identify the assets to be distributed to the surviving spouse in satisfaction of the elective share; and

(C) if contribution is necessary, specify the amount of contribution for which each direct recipient is liable.

(e) Relief from Duty to Enforce Contribution. A petition to relieve the personal representative from the duty to enforce contribution must state the grounds on which it is based and notice must be served on interested persons.

Committee Notes

The extensive rewrite of this rule in 2001 is intended to conform it with and provide procedures to accommodate amendments to Florida's elective share statutes, §§ 732.201 *et seq.*, Fla. Stat. Proceedings to determine entitlement to elective share are not specific adversary proceedings under rule 5.025(a), but may be declared adversary at the option of the party. Proceedings to determine the amount of elective share and contribution are specific adversary proceedings under rule 5.025(a). Requirements for service are intended to be consistent with the requirements for formal notice. Rule 5.040. Service of process may be required to obtain personal jurisdiction over direct recipients who are not otherwise interested persons and who have not voluntarily submitted themselves to the jurisdiction of the court. Rule 5.040(a)(3)(C); ch. 48, Fla. Stat. Process and Service of Process; ch. 49, Fla. Stat., Constructive Service of Process. An inventory of the elective estate should be afforded the same confidentiality as other estate inventories. § 733.604(1) and (2), Fla. Stat. In fulfilling his or her obligations under this rule, a personal representative is not required to make impractical or extended searches for property entering into the elective estate and the identities of direct recipients. Pre-existing rights to dower and curtesy formerly addressed in subdivision (e) of this rule are now governed by new rule 5.365.

Counsel's attention is directed to Fla. Ethics Opinion 76-16, dated April 4, 1977, for guidance regarding the duties of an attorney with respect to spousal rights.

Rule History

1984 Revision: Extensive changes. Clarifies information to be included in a petition for elective share filed by a personal representative and specifies information to be included in an order determining elective share. Committee notes revised and expanded.

1988 Revision: Extensive changes. A new procedure has been added providing for optional service of a notice of election together with a copy of the election and a procedure to expose objections to and determine right to entitlement, separate from the pre-existing procedure of determination of amount and setting aside. Subdivisions (c) and (d) represent rule implementation of procedure in statute. Committee notes revised and expanded. Citation form changes in committee notes.

1992 Revision: Editorial change. Committee notes revised. Citation form changes in committee notes.

2001 Revision: Entire rule rewritten. Committee notes revised.

2003 Revision: Committee notes revised.

2005 Revision: Subdivision (a) amended to require service in the manner of formal notice of the notice of election. Subdivision (b)(3) amended to provide time period for personal representative to service notice of election on interested persons, and title revised. Subdivision (d)(2) amended to provide time limit and service requirement for elective estate inventory and petition for determination of amount of elective share. Committee notes revised.

2010 Cycle Report Revision: Committee notes revised.

2010 Out-of-Cycle Report Revision: Subdivision (a)(2) amended to conform to an amendment to § 732.2125, Florida Statutes.

2012 Revision: Committee notes revised.

Statutory References

§ 732.201, Fla. Stat. Right to elective share.

§ 732.2025, Fla. Stat. Definitions.

§ 732.2035, Fla. Stat. Property entering into elective estate.

§ 732.2045, Fla. Stat. Exclusions and overlapping application.

§ 732.2055, Fla. Stat. Valuation of the elective estate.

§ 732.2065, Fla. Stat. Amount of the elective share.

§ 732.2075, Fla. Stat. Sources from which elective share payable; abatement.

§ 732.2085, Fla. Stat. Liability of direct recipients and beneficiaries.

§ 732.2095, Fla. Stat. Valuation of property used to satisfy elective share.

§ 732.2125, Fla. Stat. Right of election; by whom exercisable.

§ 732.2135, Fla. Stat. Time of election; extensions; withdrawal.

§ 732.2145, Fla. Stat. Order of contribution; personal representative's duty to collect contribution.

§ 733.604, Fla. Stat. Inventories and accountings; public records exemptions.

Rule References

Fla. Prob. R. 5.025 Adversary proceedings.

Fla. Prob. R. 5.040 Notice.

Fla. Prob. R. 5.041 Service of pleadings and documents.

Fla. Prob. R. 5.340 Inventory.

Fla. R. Jud. Admin. 2.516 Service of pleadings and documents.

Fla. R. App. P. 9.020(h) Definitions.

RULE 5.365. PETITION FOR DOWER

A widow may file an extraordinary petition for assignment of dower. The petition shall be filed in the court of each county where the widow's husband had conveyed land in which the widow had not relinquished her right of dower before October 1, 1973. Formal notice shall be served on persons adversely affected. The proceedings shall be as similar as possible to those formerly existing for the ordinary assignment of dower.

Committee Notes

Rule History

2001 Revision: Derived from former rule 5.360(e).

Statutory Reference

§ 732.111 Dower and curtesy abolished.

RULE 5.370. SALES OF REAL PROPERTY WHERE NO POWER CONFERRED

(a) Petition. When authorization or confirmation of the sale of real property is required, the personal representative shall file a verified petition setting forth the reasons for the sale, a description of the real property sold or proposed to be sold, and the price and terms of the sale.

(b) Order. If the sale is authorized or confirmed, the order shall describe the real property. An order authorizing a sale may provide for the public or private sale of the real property described therein, in parcels or as a whole. An order authorizing a private sale shall specify the price and terms of the sale. An order authorizing a public sale shall specify the type of notice of sale to be given by the personal representative.

Committee Notes

Petitions under the rule are governed by section 733.610, Florida Statutes, under which sales are voidable by interested persons if there was a conflict of interest without full disclosure and consent, unless the will or contract entered into by the decedent authorized the transaction or it was approved by the court after notice to all interested persons, and by section 733.609, Florida Statutes, involving bad faith actions by the personal representative. Note provisions for attorney's fees.

Rule History

1984 Revision: Extensive changes. Notice of hearing on any petition concerning sale of real property is required by statute unless waived. The requirement to record a certified copy of the order approving sale of real estate in each county where the real property or any part thereof is situated has been deleted. Committee notes revised and expanded.

1988 Revision: Committee notes expanded. Citation form changes in committee notes.

1992 Revision: Committee notes revised. Citation form changes in committee notes.

1996 Revision: Editorial changes.

2012 Revision: Committee notes revised.

Statutory References

§ 733.609, Fla. Stat. Improper exercise of power; breach of fiduciary duty.

§ 733.610, Fla. Stat. Sale, encumbrance or transaction involving conflict of interest.

§ 733.613(1), Fla. Stat. Personal representative's right to sell real property.

§ 733.810, Fla. Stat. Distribution in kind; valuation.

Rule References

Fla. Prob. R. 5.020 Pleadings; verification; motions.

Fla. Prob. R. 5.040 Notice.

Fla. Prob. R. 5.041 Service of pleadings and documents.

Fla. Prob. R. 5.180 Waiver and consent.

Fla. R. Jud. Admin. 2.516 Service of pleadings and documents.

RULE 5.380. COMPULSORY PAYMENT OF DEVISES OR DISTRIBUTIVE INTERESTS

(a) Petition. A beneficiary may file a petition setting forth the facts that entitle the beneficiary to compel payment of devises or distributive interests stating that the property will not be required for the payment of debts, family allowance, spouse's elective share, estate and inheritance taxes, claims, charges, and expenses of administration, or for providing funds for contribution or enforcing equalization in case of advancements.

(b) Order. If the court finds that the property will not be required for the purposes set forth in subdivision (a), it may enter an order describing the property to be surrendered or delivered and compelling the personal representative, prior to the final settlement of the personal representative's accounts, to do one or more of the following:

(1) Pay all or any part of a devise in money.

(2) Deliver specific personal property within the personal representative's custody and control.

(3) Pay all or any part of a distributive interest in the personal estate of a decedent.

(4) Surrender real property.

(c) Bond. Before the entry of an order of partial distribution, the court may require the person entitled to distribution to give a bond with sureties as prescribed by law.

Committee Notes

Rule History

1984 Revision: Extensive changes. Committee notes revised.

1988 Revision: Editorial change in caption of (a). Citation form change in committee notes.

1992 Revision: Editorial changes. Committee notes revised. Citation form changes in committee notes.

2003 Revision: Committee notes revised.

2012 Revision: Committee notes revised.

Statutory References

§ 731.301, Fla. Stat. Notice.

§ 733.802, Fla. Stat. Proceedings for compulsory payment of devises or distributive interest.

Rule References

Fla. Prob. R. 5.020 Pleadings verification: motions.

Fla. Prob. R. 5.040 Notice.

Fla. Prob. R. 5.041 Service of pleadings and documents.

Fla. R. Jud. Admin. 2.516 Service of pleadings and documents.

RULE 5.385. DETERMINATION OF BENEFICIARIES AND SHARES

(a) Beneficiaries and Shares. If a personal representative or other interested person is in doubt or is unable to determine with certainty beneficiaries entitled to an estate or the shares of any beneficiary of an estate, or a beneficiary entitled to any asset or interest in an estate, the personal representative or other interested person may petition the court to determine beneficiaries.

(b) Petition. The petition shall include:

(1) the names, residences, and post office addresses of all persons who may have an interest, except creditors of the decedent, known to the petitioner or ascertainable by diligent search and inquiry;

(2) a statement of the nature of the interest of each person;

(3) designation of any person believed to be a minor or incapacitated, and whether any person so designated is under legal guardianship in this state;

(4) a statement as to whether petitioner believes that there are, or may be, persons whose names are not known to petitioner who have claims against, or interest in, the estate as beneficiaries.

(c) Order. After formal notice and hearing, the court shall enter an order determining the beneficiaries or the shares and amounts they are entitled to receive, or both.

Committee Notes

This rule represents a rule implementation of the procedure formerly found in section 733.105, Florida Statutes. It is not intended to change the effect of the statute from which it was derived but has been reformatted to conform with the structure of these rules. It is not intended to create a new procedure or modify an existing procedure.

Rule History

1988 Revision: New rule.

1992 Revision: Editorial changes. Committee notes revised. Citation form changes in committee notes.

2002 Revision: Subdivision (c) added to implement procedure formerly found in section 733.105(2), Florida Statutes. Committee notes revised.

2003 Revision: Change in subdivision (c) to replace "heirs or devisees" with "beneficiaries" to incorporate term used in section 733.105, Florida Statutes. Committee notes revised.

2007 Revision: Committee notes revised.

2012 Revision: Committee notes revised.

Statutory References

ch. 49, Fla. Stat. Constructive service of process.

§ 731.201(2), (23), Fla. Stat. General definitions.

§ 731.301, Fla. Stat. Notice.

§ 733.105, Fla. Stat. Determination of beneficiaries.

Rule References

Fla. Prob. R. 5.025 Adversary proceedings.

Fla. Prob. R. 5.040 Notice.

Fla. Prob. R. 5.041 Service of pleadings and documents.

Fla. Prob. R. 5.120 Administrator ad litem and guardian ad litem.

Fla. Prob. R. 5.205(a)(5) Filing evidence of death.

Fla. R. Jud. Admin. 2.516 Service of pleadings and documents.

RULE 5.386. ESCHEAT

(a) Escheat proceeding. If it appears to the personal representative that an estate may escheat or there is doubt about the existence of any person entitled to the estate, the personal representative shall institute a proceeding to determine beneficiaries within 1 year after letters have been issued to the personal representative, and notice shall be served on the Department of Legal Affairs. If the personal representative fails to institute the proceeding within the time fixed, it may be instituted by the Department of Legal Affairs.

(b) Court's Report. On or before January 15 of each year, each court shall furnish to the Department of Legal Affairs a list of all estates being administered in which no person appears to be entitled to the property and the personal representative has not instituted a proceeding for the determination of beneficiaries.

(c) Administration. Except as herein provided, escheated estates shall be administered as other estates.

Committee Notes

This rule represents a rule implementation of the procedure formerly found in section 732.107, Florida Statutes. It is not intended to change the effect of the statute which it was derived but has been reformatted to conform with the structure of these rules. It is not intended to create a new procedure or modify as existing procedure.

Rule History

1988 Revision: New rule.

1992 Revision: Editorial change. Committee notes revised. Citation form changes in committee notes.

2003 Revision: Committee notes revised.

2012 Revision: Committee notes revised.

Statutory References

§ 732.107, Fla. Stat. Escheat.

§ 733.105, Fla. Stat. Determination of beneficiaries.

§ 733.816, Fla. Stat. Disposition of unclaimed property held by personal representatives.

Rule References

Fla. Prob. R. 5.020 Pleadings; verification; motions.

Fla. Prob. R. 5.040 Notice.

Fla. Prob. R. 5.041 Service of pleadings and documents.

Fla. Prob. R. 5.042 Time.

Fla. Prob. R. 5.385 Determination of beneficiaries and shares.

Fla. R. Jud. Admin. 2.516 Service of pleadings and documents.

RULE 5.395. NOTICE OF FEDERAL ESTATE TAX RETURN

When a federal estate tax return is required, the personal representative shall file a notice stating the due date of the return. The notice shall be filed within 12 months from the date letters are issued and copies of the notice shall be served on interested persons. Whenever the due date is subsequently extended, similar notice shall be filed and served.

Committee Notes

The purpose of the rule is to require notification to the court and all interested persons that the time for closing the estate is extended when a federal estate tax return is required.

Rule History

1984 Revision: New rule.

1988 Revision: Citation form change in committee notes.

1992 Revision: Committee notes revised. Citation form changes in committee notes.

2003 Revision: Committee notes revised.

Rule Reference

Fla. Prob. R. 5.400 Distribution and discharge.

RULE 5.400. DISTRIBUTION AND DISCHARGE

(a) Petition for Discharge; Final Accounting. A personal representative who has completed administration except for distribution shall file a final accounting and a petition for discharge including a plan of distribution.

(b) Contents. The petition for discharge shall contain a statement:

(1) that the personal representative has fully administered the estate;

(2) that all claims which were presented have been paid, settled, or otherwise disposed of;

(3) that the personal representative has paid or made provision for taxes and expenses of administration;

(4) showing the amount of compensation paid or to be paid to the personal representative, attorneys, accountants, appraisers, or other agents employed by the personal representative and the manner of determining that compensation;

(5) showing a plan of distribution which shall include:

(A) a schedule of all prior distributions;

(B) the property remaining in the hands of the personal representative for distribution;

(C) a schedule describing the proposed distribution of the remaining assets; and

(D) the amount of funds retained by the personal representative to pay expenses that are incurred in the distribution of the remaining assets and termination of the estate administration;

(6) that any objections to the accounting, the compensation paid or proposed to be paid, or the proposed distribution of assets must be filed within 30 days from the date of service of the last of the petition for discharge or final accounting; and also that within 90 days after filing of the objection, a notice of hearing thereon must be served or the objection is abandoned; and

(7) that objections, if any, shall be in writing and shall state with particularity the item or items to which the objection is directed and the grounds on which the objection is based.

(c) Closing Estate; Extension. The final accounting and petition for discharge shall be filed and served on interested persons within 12 months after issuance of letters for estates not required to file a federal estate tax return, otherwise within 12 months from the date the return is due, unless the time is extended by the court for cause shown after notice to interested persons. The petition to extend time shall state the status of the estate and the reason for the extension.

(d) Distribution. The personal representative shall promptly distribute the estate property in accordance with the plan of distribution, unless objections are filed as provided in these rules.

(e) Discharge. On receipt of evidence that the estate has been fully administered and properly distributed, the court shall enter an order discharging the personal representative and releasing the surety on any bond.

Committee Notes

The rule establishes a procedure for giving notice and serving the final accounting, petition for discharge, and plan of distribution to all interested persons prior to distribution and discharge. No distinction is made in plans of distribution which distribute estate property in kind among multiple residual beneficiaries proportionate to their respective interests and those which include equalizing adjustments in cash or property and which do not make prorated distribution. If disclosure of the compensation or disclosure of the manner of determining the compensation, in the petition for discharge is to be waived, the form of waiver must conform to rule 5.180(b).

Rule History

1980 Revision: Change in prior (a)(6) to require that an objection set forth the basis on which it is being made.

1984 Revision: This rule has been substantially revised. Portions of the prior rule are now incorporated in rules 5.400 and 5.401. The committee has included the procedure for filing and serving of objections to the final accounting, petition for discharge, plan of distribution, or compensation in rule 5.401.

1988 Revision: Subdivision (b)(1) is deleted to avoid duplication with rule 5.346. Subdivision (c) is amended to add the 12-month time specification of section 733.901(1), Florida Statutes. Committee notes revised. Citation form changes in committee notes.

1992 Revision: Subdivision (b)(5)(D) is added. Editorial changes. Committee notes revised. Citation form changes in committee notes.

1996 Revision: Addition in (a)(4) of specific attorney fee compensation disclosure requirements found in 733.6171(9), Florida Statutes, and expanded to cover all compensation. Committee notes revised.

2003 Revision: Committee notes revised.

2005 Revision: Subdivision (f) deleted to avoid duplication with rule 5.180.

2006 Revision: Committee notes revised.

2007 Revision: Committee notes revised.

2012 Revision: Committee notes revised.

Statutory References

§ 731.201(12), (23), Fla. Stat. General definitions.

§ 731.302, Fla. Stat. Waiver and consent by interested persons.

§ 733.809, Fla. Stat. Right of retainer.

§ 733.810, Fla. Stat. Distribution in kind; valuation,

§ 733.811, Fla. Stat. Distribution; right or title of distributee.

§ 733.812, Fla. Stat. Improper distribution or payment; liability of distributee or payee.

§ 733.901, Fla. Stat. Final discharge.

Rule References

Fla. Prob. R. 5.020 Pleadings; verification; motions.

Fla. Prob. R. 5.040 Notice.

Fla. Prob. R. 5.041 Service of pleadings and documents.

Fla. Prob. R. 5.042 Time.

Fla. Prob. R. 5.180 Waiver and consent.

Fla. Prob. R. 5.330 Execution by personal representative.

Fla. Prob. R. 5.346 Fiduciary accounting.

Fla. Prob. R. 5.401 Objections to petition for discharge or final accounting.

Fla. R. Jud. Admin. 2.250(a)(1)(D) Time standards for trial and appellate courts and reporting requirements.

Fla. R. Jud. Admin. 2.516 Service of pleadings and documents.

RULE 5.401. OBJECTIONS TO PETITION FOR DISCHARGE OR FINAL ACCOUNTING

(a) Objections. An interested person may object to the petition for discharge or final accounting within 30 days after the service of the later of the petition or final accounting on that interested person.

(b) Contents. Written objections to the petition for discharge or final accounting must state with particularity the items to which the objections are directed and must state the grounds on which the objections are based.

(c) Service. Copies of the objections shall be served by the objector on the personal representative and interested persons not later than 30 days after the last date on which the petition for discharge or final accounting was served on the objector.

(d) Hearing on Objections. Any interested person may set a hearing on the objections. Notice of the hearing shall be given to all interested persons. If a notice of hearing on the objections is not served within 90 days of filing of the objections, the objections shall be deemed abandoned and the personal representative may make distribution as set forth in the plan of distribution.

(e) Order on Objections. The court shall sustain or overrule any objections to the petition for discharge and final accounting and shall determine a plan of distribution.

(f) Discharge. On receipt of evidence that the estate has been distributed according to the plan determined by the court and the claims of creditors have been paid or otherwise disposed of, the court shall enter an order discharging the personal representative and releasing the surety on any bond.

Committee Notes

Rule History

1984 Revision: New rule. Objections to the petition for discharge or final accounting were formerly under prior rule 5.400. Clarifies procedure for objections.

1988 Revision: Editorial changes in (a). Committee notes revised. Citation form changes in committee notes.

1992 Revision: Committee notes revised. Citation form changes in committee notes.

1996 Revision: Subdivision (d) amended to clarify that 90-day period pertains to service of hearing notice, not the actual hearing date.

2003 Revision: Committee notes revised.

2007 Revision: Committee notes revised.

2012 Revision: Committee notes revised.

Statutory References

§ 731.201(12), (23), Fla. Stat. General definitions.

§ 733.6175, Fla. Stat. Proceedings for review of employment of agents and compensation of personal representatives and employees of estate.

§ 733.901, Fla. Stat. Final discharge.

Rule References

Fla. Prob. R. 5.020 Pleadings; verification; motions.

Fla. Prob. R. 5.040 Notice.

Fla. Prob. R. 5.041 Service of pleadings and documents.

Fla. Prob. R. 5.042 Time.

Fla. Prob. R. 5.180 Waiver and consent.

Fla. Prob. R. 5.400 Distribution and discharge.

Fla. R. Jud. Admin. 2.516 Service of pleadings and documents.

RULE 5.402. NOTICE OF LIEN ON PROTECTED HOMESTEAD

(a) Filing. If the personal representative has recorded a notice of lien on protected homestead, the personal representative shall file a copy of the recorded notice in the probate proceeding.

(b) Contents. The notice of lien shall contain:

(1) the name and address of the personal representative and the personal representative's attorney;

(2) the legal description of the real property;

(3) to the extent known, the name and address of each person appearing to have an interest in the property; and

(4) a statement that the personal representative has expended or is obligated to expend funds to preserve, maintain, insure, or protect the property and that the lien stands as security for recovery of those expenditures and obligations incurred, including fees and costs.

(c) Service. A copy of the recorded notice of lien shall be served on interested persons in the manner provided for service of formal notice.

Committee Notes

Rule History

2005 Revision: New rule.

2012 Revision: Committee notes revised.

Statutory References

§ 733.608, Fla. Stat. General power of the personal representative.

Rule References

Fla. Prob. R. 5.040 Notice.

Fla. Prob. R. 5.041 Service of pleadings and documents.

Fla. Prob. R. 5.403 Proceedings to determine amount of lien on protected homestead.

Fla. Prob. R. 5.404 Notice of taking possession of protected homestead.

Fla. Prob. R. 5.405 Proceedings to determine protected homestead real property.

Fla. R. Jud. Admin. 2.516 Service of pleadings and documents.

RULE 5.403. PROCEEDINGS TO DETERMINE AMOUNT OF LIEN ON PROTECTED HOMESTEAD

(a) Petition. A personal representative or interested person may file a petition to determine the amount of any lien on protected homestead.

(b) Contents. The petition shall be verified by the petitioner and shall state:

(1) the name and address of the personal representative and the personal representative's attorney;

(2) the interest of the petitioner;

(3) the legal description of the real property;

(4) to the extent known, the name and address of each person appearing to have an interest in the property; and

(5) to the extent known, the amounts paid or obligated to be paid by the personal representative to preserve, maintain, insure, or protect the protected homestead, including fees and costs.

(c) Service. The petition shall be served on interested persons by formal notice.

Committee Notes

Rule History

2005 Revision: New rule.

2012 Revision: Committee notes revised.

Statutory References

§ 733.608, Fla. Stat. General power of the personal representative.

Rule References

Fla. Prob. R. 5.040 Notice.

Fla. Prob. R. 5.041 Service of pleadings and documents.

Fla. Prob. R. 5.402 Notice of lien on protected homestead.

Fla. Prob. R. 5.404 Notice of taking possession of protected homestead.

Fla. Prob. R. 5.405 Proceedings to determine protected homestead real property.

Fla. R. Jud. Admin. 2.516 Service of pleadings and documents.

RULE 5.404. NOTICE OF TAKING POSSESSION OF PROTECTED HOMESTEAD

(a) Filing of Notice. If a personal representative takes possession of what appears reasonably to be protected homestead pending a determination of its homestead status, the personal representative shall file a notice of that act.

(b) Contents of Notice. The notice shall contain:

(1) a legal description of the property;

(2) a statement of the limited purpose for preserving, insuring, and protecting it for the heirs or devisees pending a determination of the homestead status;

(3) the name and address of the personal representative and the personal representative's attorney;

(4) if known, the location, date, and time the petition to determine homestead status will be heard, and

(5) if the personal representative is in possession when the notice is filed, the date the personal representative took possession.

(c) Service of Notice. The notice shall be served in the manner provided for service of formal notice on interested persons and on any person in actual possession of the property.

Committee Notes

Rule History

2002 Revision: New rule.

2005 Revision: Term "devisees" substituted for "beneficiaries" in subdivision (b)(2) to clarify the status of persons interested in protected homestead. Committee notes revised.

Statutory References

§ 732.401, Fla. Stat. Descent of homestead.

§ 732.4015, Fla. Stat. Devise of homestead.

§ 733.608(2), Fla. Stat. General power of the personal representative.

Rule References

Fla. Prob. R. 5.402 Notice of lien on protected homestead.

Fla. Prob. R. 5.403 Proceedings to determine amount of lien on protected homestead.

Fla. Prob. R. 5.405 Proceedings to determine protected homestead real property.

RULE 5.405. PROCEEDINGS TO DETERMINE PROTECTED HOMESTEAD REAL PROPERTY

(a) Petition. An interested person may file a petition to determine protected homestead real property owned by the decedent.

(b) Contents. The petition shall be verified by the petitioner and shall state:

(1) the date of the decedent's death;

(2) the county of the decedent's domicile at the time of death;

(3) the name of the decedent's surviving spouse and the names and dates of birth of the decedent's surviving lineal descendants;

(4) a legal description of the property owned by the decedent on which the decedent resided; and

(5) any other facts in support of the petition.

(c) Order. The court's order on the petition shall describe the real property and determine whether any of the real property constituted the protected homestead of the decedent. If the court determines that any of the property was the protected homestead of the decedent, the order shall identify the person or persons entitled to the protected homestead real property and define the interest of each.

Committee Notes

This rule establishes the procedure by which the personal representative or any interested person may petition the court for a determination that certain real property constituted the decedent's homestead property, in accordance with article X, section 4 of the Florida Constitution. The jurisdiction of the court to determine constitutional homestead property was established by *In re Noble's Estate*, 73 So. 2d 873 (Fla. 1954).

Rule History

1984 Revision: New rule.

1988 Revision: Editorial change in (a). Subdivision (b)(4) amended to conform to constitutional change. Committee notes revised. Citation form change in committee notes.

1992 Revision: Editorial change. Committee notes revised. Citation form changes in committee notes.

1996 Revision: Subdivision (c) amended to require description of real property that is the subject of the petition, description of any homestead property, and definition of specific interests of persons entitled to homestead real property.

2002 Revision: Replaces "homestead" with "protected homestead" throughout to conform to addition of term in section 731.201(29), Florida Statutes. Committee notes revised.

2003 Revision: Committee notes revised.

2007 Revision: Committee notes revised.

2010 Revision: Committee notes revised.

2012 Revision: Committee notes revised.

Constitutional Reference

Art. X, 4, Fla. Const.

Statutory References

§ 731.104, Fla. Stat. Verification of documents.

§ 731.201 (33), Fla. Stat. General definitions.

§ 731.401, Fla. Stat. Descent of homestead.

§ 732.4015, Fla. Stat. Devise of homestead.

§ 733.607, Fla. Stat. Possession of estate.

§ 733.608, Fla. Stat. General power of the personal representative.

Rule References

Fla. Prob. R. 5.020 Pleadings; verification; motions.

Fla. Prob. R. 5.040 Notice.

Fla. Prob. R. 5.041 Service of pleadings and documents.

Fla. Prob. R. 5.205(a)(6) Filing evidence of death.

Fla. Prob. R. 5.340 Inventory.

Fla. Prob. R. 5.404 Notice of taking possession of protected homestead.

Fla. R. Jud. Admin. 2.516 Service of pleadings and documents.

RULE 5.406. PROCEEDINGS TO DETERMINE EXEMPT PROPERTY

(a) Petition. An interested person may file a petition to determine exempt property within the time allowed by law.

(b) Contents. The petition shall be verified by the petitioner and shall:

(1) describe the property and the basis on which it is claimed as exempt property; and

(2) state the name and address of the decedent's surviving spouse or, if none, the names and addresses of decedent's children entitled by law to the exempt property and the dates of birth of those who are minors.

(c) Order. The court shall determine each item of exempt property and its value, if necessary to determine its exempt status, and order the surrender of that property to the persons entitled to it.

Committee Notes

This rule establishes the procedure by which the personal representative or any interested person may petition the court for determination of exempt property in accordance with article X, section 4 of the Florida Constitution and section 732.402, Florida Statutes.

Section 732.402, Florida Statutes, specifies the time within which the petition to determine exempt property must be filed within 4 months after the date of service of the notice of administration, unless extended as provided in the statute.

Rule History

1984 Revision: New rule.

1988 Revision: Subdivision (a) revised to reflect editorial changes and to require verification. Subdivision (b)(1) revised to require the basis for asserting exempt property status. Subdivision (b)(2) added the requirement of stating addresses of those entitled to exempt property. Subdivision (c) revised to reflect editorial changes and to require determination of the value of each item of exempt property. Committee notes revised.

1992 Revision: Committee notes revised. Citation form changes in committee notes.

1996 Revision: Editorial changes in rule to conform to similar language in rule 5.405. Committee notes revised.

2003 Revision: Committee notes revised.

2010 Revision: Subdivision (c) amended to limit the instances in which the value of the property claimed as exempt needs to be stated in the order.

2012 Revision: Committee notes revised.

Statutory References

§ 731.104, Fla. Stat. Verification of documents.

§ 732.402, Fla. Stat. Exempt property.

Rule References

Fla. Prob. R. 5.020 Pleadings; verification; motions.

Fla. Prob. R. 5.040 Notice.

Fla. Prob. R. 5.041 Service of pleadings and documents.

Fla. Prob. R. 5.042 Time.

Fla. Prob. R. 5.420 Disposition of personal property without administration.

Fla. R. Jud. Admin. 2.516 Service of pleadings and documents.

RULE 5.407. PROCEEDINGS TO DETERMINE FAMILY ALLOWANCE

(a) Petition. An interested person may file a petition to determine family allowance.

(b) Contents. The petition shall be verified by the petitioner and shall:

(1) state the names and addresses of the decedent's surviving spouse and the decedent's lineal heirs who were being supported by the decedent or who were entitled to be supported by the decedent at the time of the decedent's death, stating the dates of birth of those who are minors; and

(2) for each person for whom an allowance is sought, state the person's name and relationship to the decedent, the basis on which the allowance is claimed, and the amount sought.

(c) Order. The order shall identify the persons entitled to the allowance, the amount to which each is entitled, the method of payment, and to whom payment should be made.

Committee Notes

Rule History

2003 Revision: New rule.

2012 Revision: Editorial change in (b)(1) for gender neutrality. Committee notes revised.

Statutory References

§ 731.104, Fla. Stat. Verification of documents.

§ 732.403, Fla. Stat. Family allowance.

Rule References

Fla. Prob. R. 5.020 Pleadings; verification; motions.

Fla. Prob. R. 5.040 Notice.

Fla. Prob. R. 5.041 Service of pleadings and documents.

Fla. R. Jud. Admin. 2.516 Service of pleadings and documents.

RULE 5.420. DISPOSITION OF PERSONAL PROPERTY WITHOUT ADMINISTRATION

(a) Application. An interested person may request a disposition of the decedent's personal property without administration. An application signed by the applicant shall set forth:

(1) the description and value of the exempt property;

(2) the description and value of the other assets of the decedent;

(3) the amount of preferred funeral expenses and reasonable and necessary medical and hospital expenses for the last 60 days of the last illness together with accompanying statements or payment receipts; and

(4) each requested payment or distribution of personal property.

(b) Exempt Property. If the decedent's personal property includes exempt property, or property that can be determined to be exempt property, the application must also be signed by all persons entitled to the exempt property or by their representative.

(c) Preparation. On request, the clerk shall assist the applicant in the preparation of the required writing.

(d) Disposition. If the court is satisfied that disposition without administration is appropriate, the court may, without hearing, by letter or other writing authorize the payment, transfer, or disposition of the decedent's personal property to those persons entitled to it.

Committee Notes

Section 732.402, Florida Statutes, requires persons entitled to exempt property, which excludes property specifically or demonstratively devised, to file timely a petition to determine exempt property. Accordingly, disposition of personal property under this rule should not be granted if decedent's personal property includes exempt property without all persons entitled thereto agreeing to such disposition.

Rule History

1977 Revision: Permits the clerk to perform limited ministerial acts in the completion of the application.

1984 Revision: Editorial changes. Delineates the required contents of the application. Committee notes revised.

1988 Revision: Subparagraph (a)(3) changed to require applicant to attach accompanying statements or payment receipts regarding priority expenses. Subdivision (b) added to require persons entitled to exempt property to agree to the proposed disposition. Committee notes expanded.

1992 Revision: Editorial change. Committee notes revised. Citation form changes in committee notes.

2003 Revision: Committee notes revised.

Statutory References

§ 732.402, Fla. Stat. Exempt property.

§ 735.301, Fla. Stat. Disposition without administration.

Rule Reference

Fla. Prob. R. 5.205(a)(4) Filing evidence of death.

RULE 5.430. RESIGNATION OF PERSONAL REPRESENTATIVE

(a) Resignation. A personal representative may resign with court approval.

(b) Petition for Resignation. The personal representative seeking to resign shall file a petition for resignation. The petition shall be verified and shall state:

(1) the personal representative desires to resign and be relieved of all powers, duties, and obligations as personal representative;

(2) the status of the estate administration and that the interests of the estate will not be jeopardized if the resignation is accepted;

(3) whether a proceeding for accounting, surcharge, or indemnification or other proceeding against the resigning personal representative is pending; and

(4) whether the appointment of a successor fiduciary is necessary. If the petition nominates a successor fiduciary, it shall state the nominee's priority under the Florida Probate Code, if any, and that the nominee is qualified to serve under the laws of Florida.

(c) Service. The petition shall be served by formal notice on all interested persons and the personal representative's surety, if any.

(d) Appointment of Successor. Before accepting the resignation, the court shall determine the necessity for appointment of a successor fiduciary. If there is no joint personal representative serving, the court shall appoint a successor fiduciary.

(e) Acceptance of Resignation. The court may accept the resignation and revoke the letters of the resigning personal representative if the interests of the estate are not jeopardized. Acceptance of the resignation shall not exonerate the resigning personal representative or the resigning personal representative's surety from liability.

(f) Delivery of Records and Property. The resigning personal representative shall immediately upon acceptance of the resignation by the court deliver to the remaining personal representative or the successor fiduciary all of the records of the estate and all property of the estate, unless otherwise directed by the court.

(g) Petition for Discharge; Accounting. The resigning personal representative shall file an accounting and a petition for discharge within 30 days after the date that the letters of the resigning personal representative are revoked by the court. The petition for discharge shall be verified and shall state:

(1) that the letters of the resigning personal representative have been revoked;

(2) that the resigning personal representative has surrendered all undistributed estate assets, records, documents, papers, and other property of or concerning the estate to the remaining personal representative or the successor fiduciary; and

(3) the amount of compensation paid or to be paid the resigning personal representative and the attorney and other persons employed by the resigning personal representative.

(h) Notice, Filing, and Objections to Accounting. Notice of, filing of, and objections to the accounting of the resigning personal representative shall be as provided in rule 5.345.

(i) Notice of Filing and Objections to Petition for Discharge.

(1) Notice of filing and a copy of the petition for discharge shall be served on all interested persons. The notice shall state that objections to the petition for discharge must be filed within 30 days after the later of service of the petition or service of the accounting on that interested person.

(2) Any interested person may file an objection to the petition for discharge within 30 days after the later of service of the petition or service of the accounting on that interested person. Any objection not filed within such time shall be deemed abandoned. An objection shall be in writing and shall state with particularity the item or items to which the objection is directed and the grounds on which the objection is based.

(3) The objecting party shall serve a copy of the objection on the resigning personal representative and other interested persons.

(4) Any interested person may set a hearing on the objections. Notice of the hearing shall be given to the resigning personal representative and other interested persons.

(j) Failure to File Accounting or Deliver Records or Property. The resigning personal representative shall be subject to contempt proceedings if the resigning personal representative fails to file an accounting or fails to deliver all property of the estate and all estate records under the control of the resigning personal representative to the remaining personal representative or the successor fiduciary within the time prescribed by this rule or by court order.

(k) Discharge. The court shall enter an order discharging the resigning personal representative and releasing the surety on any bond after the court is satisfied that the resigning personal representative has delivered all records and property of the estate to the remaining personal representative or the successor fiduciary; that all objections, if any, to the accounting of the resigning personal representative have been withdrawn, abandoned, or judicially resolved; and that the liability of the resigning personal representative has been determined and satisfied.

Committee Notes

In the event of resignation of a personal representative, if a joint personal representative is not serving, the successor fiduciary must file an oath and designation of a successor resident agent.

This rule was revised to implement the revisions to the probate code that govern resignation of personal representative. The committee intended to separate the procedure with respect to resignation from removal because these proceedings may differ in practice.

Rule History

1975 Revision: The rule provides for the orderly succession of personal representatives in the event a personal representative resigns or is removed.

1977 Revision: Editorial change in committee note.

1988 Revision: Editorial changes; captions added to subdivisions. Committee notes revised. Citation form changes in committee notes.

1992 Revision: Editorial changes. Committee notes revised. Citation form changes in committee notes.

2003 Revision: Rule completely revised to comply with statutory changes. Committee notes revised.

2007 Revision: Committe notes revised.

2012 Revision: Committee notes revised.

Statutory References

§ 731.104, Fla. Stat. Verification of documents.

§ 731.201(23), Fla. Stat. General definitions.

§ 733.101, Fla. Stat. Venue of probate proceedings.

§ 733.502, Fla. Stat. Resignation of personal representative.

§ 733.503, Fla. Stat. Appointment of successor upon resignation.

§ 733.5035, Fla. Stat. Surrender of assets after resignation.

§ 733.5036, Fla. Stat. Accounting and discharge following resignation.

Rule References

Fla. Prob. R. 5.020 Pleadings; verification; motions.

Fla. Prob. R. 5.040 Notice.

Fla. Prob. R. 5.041 Service of pleadings and documents.

Fla.Prob.R. 5.180 Waiver and consent.

Fla.Prob.R. 5.310 Disqualification of personal representative; notification.

Fla.Prob.R. 5.330 Execution by personal representative.

Fla.Prob.R. 5.345 Accountings other than personal representatives' final accountings.

Fla.Prob.R. 5.346 Fiduciary accounting.

Fla.Prob.R. 5.401 Objections to petition for discharge or final accounting.

Fla. R. Jud. Admin. 2.516 Service of pleadings and documents.

RULE 5.440. PROCEEDINGS FOR REMOVAL OF PERSONAL REPRESENTATIVE

(a) Commencement of Proceeding. The court on its own motion may remove, or any interested person by petition may commence a proceeding to remove, a personal representative. A petition for removal shall state the facts constituting the grounds upon which removal is sought, and shall be filed in the court having jurisdiction over the administration of the estate.

(b) Accounting. A removed personal representative shall file an accounting within 30 days after removal.

(c) Delivery of Records and Property. A removed personal representative shall, immediately after removal or within such time prescribed by court order, deliver to the remaining personal representative or to the successor fiduciary all of the records of the estate and all of the property of the estate.

(d) Failure to File Accounting or Deliver Records and Property. If a removed personal representative fails to file an accounting or fails to deliver all property of the estate and all estate records under the control of the removed personal representative to the remaining personal representative or to the successor fiduciary within the time prescribed by this rule or by court order, the removed personal representative shall be subject to contempt proceedings.

Committee Notes

The revision of subdivision (a) of this rule by the addition of its final phrase represents a rule implementation of the procedure found in section 733.505, Florida Statutes. It is not intended to change the effect of the statute from which it was derived but has been reformatted to conform with the structure of these rules. It is not intended to create a new procedure or modify an existing procedure.

Rule History

1980 Revision: Subdivision (a) amended to require formal notice to interested persons and to delete requirement that court give directions as to mode of notice. Surety authorized to petition for removal.

1984 Revision: Editorial changes. Provisions in prior rule for contempt have been deleted since the court has the inherent power to punish for contempt. Committee notes revised.

1988 Revision: Last phrase of (a) added to implement the procedure found in section 733.505, Florida Statutes. Subdivision (b) amended to parallel interim accounting rules. Deletes ability to extend time to file and adds reference to court power to punish for contempt. Committee notes expanded. Editorial changes. Citation form changes in committee notes.

1992 Revision: Editorial changes. Committee notes revised. Citation form changes in committee notes.

2002 Revision: Entire rule amended. Contents of accountings by removed fiduciaries are now governed by rule 5.346. Editorial changes in (a), (c), and (d). Committee notes revised.

2003 Revision: Committee notes revised.

2007 Revision: Committee notes revised.

2010 Revision: Editorial change in title to clarify scope of rule.

2012 Revision: Committee notes revised.

Statutory References

§ 731.201(23), Fla. Stat. General definitions.

§ 733.504, Fla. Stat. Removal of personal representative; causes of removal.

§ 733.505, Fla. Stat. Jurisdiction in removal proceedings.

§ 733.506, Fla. Stat. Proceedings for removal.

§ 733.5061, Fla. Stat. Appointment of successor upon removal.

§ 733.508, Fla. Stat. Accounting and discharge of removed personal representative upon removal.

§ 733.509, Fla. Stat. Surrender of assets upon removal.

Rule References

Fla. Prob. R. 5.020 Pleadings; verification; motions.

Fla. Prob. R. 5.025 Adversary proceedings.

Fla. Prob. R. 5.040 Notice.

Fla. Prob. R. 5.041 Service of pleadings and documents.

Fla. Prob. R. 5.042 Time.

Fla. Prob. R. 5.150 Order requiring accounting.

Fla. Prob. R. 5.310 Disqualification of personal representative; notification.

Fla. Prob. R. 5.345 Accounting other than personal representatives' final accountings.

Fla. Prob. 5.346 Fiduciary accounting.

Fla. R. Jud. Admin. 2.516 Service of pleadings and documents.

RULE 5.460. SUBSEQUENT ADMINISTRATION

(a) Petition. If, after an estate is closed, additional property of the decedent is discovered or if further administration of the estate is required for any other reason, any interested person may file a petition for further administration of the estate. The petition shall be filed in the same probate file as the original administration.

(b) Contents. The petition shall state:

(1) the name, address, and interest of the petitioner in the estate;

(2) the reason for further administration of the estate;

(3) the description, approximate value, and location of any asset not included among the assets of the prior administration; and

(4) a statement of the relief sought.

(c) Order. The court shall enter such orders as appropriate. Unless required, the court need not revoke the order of discharge, reissue letters, or require bond.

Committee Notes

This rule establishes a procedure for further administration after estate is closed, which maybe summary in nature.

Rule History

1984 Revision: Extensive changes. Committee notes revised.

1992 Revision; Citation form change in committee notes.

2003 Revision: Committee notes revised.

2012 Revision: Committee notes revised.

Statutory Reference

§ 733.903, Fla. Stat. Subsequent administration.

Rule References

Fla. Prob. R. 5.020 Pleadings; verification; motions.

Fla. Prob. R. 5.040 Notice.

Fla. Prob. R. 5.041 Service of pleadings and documents.

Fla. R. Jud. Admin. 2.516 Service of pleadings and documents.

RULE 5.470. ANCILLARY ADMINISTRATION

(a) Petition. The petition for ancillary letters shall include an authenticated copy of so much of the domiciliary proceedings as will show:

(1) for a testate estate the will, petition for probate, order admitting the will to probate, and authority of the personal representative; or

(2) for an intestate estate the petition for administration and authority of the personal representative to act.

(b) Notice. Before ancillary letters shall be issued to any person, formal notice shall be given to:

(1) all known persons qualified to act as ancillary personal representative and whose entitlement to preference of appointment is equal to or greater than petitioner's and who have not waived notice or joined in the petition; and

(2) all domiciliary personal representatives who have not waived notice or joined in the petition.

(c) Probate of Will. On filing the authenticated copy of a will, the court shall determine whether the will complies with Florida law to entitle it to probate. If it does comply, the court shall admit the will to probate.

Committee Notes

Rule History

1975 Revision: The rule sets out the procedural requirements for issuance of ancillary letters.

1984 Revision: Editorial changes with addition of notice requirement in (b). Committee notes revised.

1988 Revision: Committee notes revised.

1992 Revision: Changed rule to require that notice be given to persons qualified to act as ancillary personal representative whose entitlement to preference of appointment is equal to or greater than petitioner's and to all domiciliary personal representatives prior to entry of an order admitting the will to probate. Committee notes revised. Citation form changes in committee notes.

1996 Revision: The requirement that a filing of an authenticated copy of a will be a "probated" will is removed from subdivision (c). There may be circumstances in which a will is on deposit or file in a foreign jurisdiction but is not being offered for probate. That should not preclude an ancillary administration in Florida of that estate. This change is not intended to allow an authenticated copy of any document other than an original instrument to be filed under this rule and considered for probate.

2003 Revision: Committee notes revised.

2005 Revision: Committee notes revised.

2010 Revision: Committee notes revised.

2012 Revision: Committee notes revised.

Statutory References

§ 731.201(1), Fla Stat. General definitions.

§ 733.212, Fla. Stat. Notice of administration; filing of objections.

§ 733.2121, Fla. Stat. Notice to creditors; filing of claims.

§ 734.102, Fla. Stat. Ancillary administration.

§ 734.1025, Fla. Stat. Nonresident decedent's testate estate with property not exceeding $50,000 in this state; determination of claims.

Rule References

Fla. Prob. R. 5.020 Pleadings; verification; motions.

Fla. Prob. R. 5.040 Notice.

Fla. Prob. R. 5.041 Service of pleadings and documents.

Fla. Prob. R. 5.042 Time.

Fla. Prob. R. 5.065(b) Notice of civil action or ancillary administration.

Fla. Prob. R. 5.205(a)(2) Filing evidence of death.

Fla. Prob. R. 5.215 Authenticated copy of will.

Fla. Prob. R. 5.240 Notice of administration.

Fla. Prob. R. 5.241 Notice to creditors.

Fla. Prob. R. 5.475 Ancillary administration, short form.

Fed. R. Civ. P. 44(a) Proving an official record.

Fla. R. Jud. Admin. 2.516 Service of pleadings and documents.

RULE 5.475. ANCILLARY ADMINISTRATION, SHORT FORM

(a) Filing Requirements. The foreign personal representative of a testate estate that meets the requirements of section 734.1025, Florida Statutes, may file with the clerk in the county where any property is located an authenticated copy of so much of the transcript of the foreign proceedings as will show:

(1) the probated will and all probated codicils of the decedent;

(2) the order admitting them to probate;

(3) the letters or their equivalent; and

(4) the part of the record showing the names of the beneficiaries of the estate or an affidavit of the foreign personal representative reciting that the names are not shown or not fully disclosed by the foreign record and specifying the names.

On presentation of the foregoing, the court shall admit the will and any codicils to probate if they comply with section 732.502(1) or section 732.502(2), Florida Statutes.

(b) Notice to Creditors. After complying with the foregoing requirements, the foreign personal representative may cause a notice to creditors to be published as required by these rules.

(c) Claims Procedure. The procedure for filing or barring claims and objecting to them and for suing on them shall be the same as for other estates, except as provided in this rule.

(d) Order. If no claims are filed against the estate within the time allowed, the court shall enter an order adjudging that notice to creditors has been duly published and proof thereof filed and that no claims have been filed against the estate or that all claims have been satisfied.

(e) Notification of Claims Filed. If any claim is filed against the estate within the time allowed, the clerk shall send to the foreign personal representative a copy of the claim and a notice setting a date for a hearing to appoint an ancillary personal representative. At the hearing, the court shall appoint an ancillary personal representative according to the preferences as provided by law.

(f) Objections to Claims. If an ancillary personal representative is appointed pursuant to this rule, the procedure for filing, objecting to, and suing on claims shall be the same as for other estates, except that the ancillary personal representative appointed shall have not less than 30 days from the date of appointment within which to object to any claim filed.

Committee Notes

This rule represents a rule implementation of the procedure found in section 734.1025, Florida Statutes. It is not intended to change the effect of the statute from which it was derived but has been reformatted to conform with the structure of these rules. It is not intended to create a new procedure or modify an existing procedure.

Rule History

1988 Revision: New rule.

1992 Revision: Editorial changes. Committee notes revised. Citation form changes in committee notes.

2003 Revision: Committee notes revised.

2005 Revision: Deletion of reference to intestate estates in subdivision (a) to conform to 2001 amendments to section 734.1025, Florida Statutes. Editorial changes throughout.

2012 Revision: Committee notes revised.

Statutory References

§ 733.2121, Fla. Stat. Notice to creditors; filing of claims.

§ 734.102, Fla. Stat. Ancillary administration.

§ 734.1025, Fla. Stat. Nonresident decedent's testate estate with property not exceeding $50,000 in this state; determination of claims.

Rule References

Fla. Prob. R. 5.020 Pleadings verification; motions.

Fla. Prob. R. 5.040 Notice.

Fla. Prob. R. 5.041 Service of pleadings and documents.

Fla. Prob. R. 5.042 Time.

Fla. Prob. R. 5.065(b) Notice of civil action or ancillary administration.

Fla. Prob. R. 5.205(a)(2) Filing evidence of death.

Fla. Prob. R. 5.215 Authenticated copy of will.

Fla. Prob. R. 5.240 Notice of administration.

Fla. Prob. R. 5.470 Ancillary administration.

Fla. R. Jud. Admin. 2.516 Service of pleadings and documents.

RULE 5.490. FORM AND MANNER OF PRESENTING CLAIM

(a) Form. A creditor's statement of claim shall be verified and filed with the clerk and shall state:

(1) the basis for the claim;

(2) the amount claimed;

(3) the name and address of the creditor;

(4) the security for the claim, if any; and

(5) whether the claim is currently due or involves an uncertainty and, if not due, then the due date and, if contingent or unliquidated, the nature of the uncertainty.

(b) Copy. At the time of filing the claim, the creditor shall also furnish the clerk with a copy thereof.

(c) Mailing. The clerk shall mail a copy of claims; noting the fact and date of mailing on the original, to the attorney for the personal representative, unless all personal representatives file a notice directing that copies of claims be mailed to a designated personal representative or attorney of record. Absent designation, a copy of claims shall be mailed to the attorney for the personal representative named first in the letters of administration.

(d) Validity of Claim. Failure to deliver or receive a copy of the claim shall not affect the validity of the claim.

(e) Amending Claims. If a claim as filed is sufficient to notify interested persons of its substance but is otherwise defective as to form, the court may permit the claim to be amended at any time.

(f) Service by Personal Representative. If the personal representative files a claim individually, or in any other capacity creating a conflict of interest between the personal representative and any interested person, then at the time the claim is filed, the personal representative shall serve all interested persons with a copy of the claim and notice of the right to object to the claim. The notice shall state that an interested person may object to a claim as provided by law and rule 5.496. Service shall be either by informal notice or in the manner provided for service of formal notice. Service on one interested person by a chosen method shall not preclude service on another interested person by another method.

Committee Notes

Subdivision (e) of this rule represents a rule implementation of the procedure found in section 733.704, Florida Statutes. It is not intended to change the effect of the statute from which it was derived but has been reformatted to conform with the structure of these rules. It is not intended to create a new procedure or modify an existing procedure.

Rule History

1975 Revision: Sets forth the claims procedure to be followed and clarifies the matter of delivery of copies where there are multiple personal representatives or where the attorney of record desires to accept such delivery.

1984 Revision: Extensive editorial changes and requires furnishing of copy of claim to the attorney for the personal representative. Committee notes revised.

1988 Revision: Clarifies the matter of delivery of copies and directs the clerk to mail the same to the attorney for the personal representative unless designations are filed by all personal representatives to the contrary. Subdivision (e) added to implement the procedure found in F.S. section 733.704, Florida Statutes. Editorial changes. Committee notes expanded. Citation form change in committee notes.

1992 Revision: Committee notes revised. Citation form changes in committee notes.

1999 Revision: Reference to repealed rule deleted from committee notes.

2003 Revision: Committee notes revised.

2007 Revision: Editorial change in (a). New (f) added, providing procedure for notice when personal representative files a claim individually or otherwise has a conflict of interest with any interested person regarding a claim.

Statutory References

§ 731.104, Fla. Stat. Verification of documents.

§ 733.2121, Fla. Stat. Notice to creditors; filing of claims.

§ 733.702, Fla. Stat. Limitations on presentation of claims.

§ 733.703, Fla. Stat. Form and Manner of presenting claim.

§ 733.704, Fla. Stat. Amendment of claims.

§ 733.708, Fla. Stat. Compromise.

§ 733.710, Fla. Stat. Limitations on claims against estates.

§ 733.102, Fla. Stat. Ancillary administration.

Rule References

Fla. Prob. R. 5.020 Pleadings; verification; motions.

Fla. Prob. R. 5.241 Notice to creditors.

Fla. Prob. R. 5.470 Ancillary administration.

Fla. Prob. R. 5.475 Ancillary administration, short form.

Fla. Prob. R. 5.530 Summary administration.

RULE 5.496. FORM AND MANNER OF OBJECTING TO CLAIM

(a) **Filing.** An objection to a claim, other than a personal representative's proof of claim, shall be in writing and filed on or before the expiration of 4 months from the first publication of notice to creditors or within 30 days from the timely filing or amendment of the claim, whichever occurs later.

(b) **Service.** A personal representative or other interested person who files an objection to the claim shall serve a copy of the objection on the claimant. If the objection is filed by an interested person other than the personal representative, a copy of the objection shall also be served on the personal representative. Any objection shall include a certificate of service.

(c) **Notice to Claimant.** An objection shall contain a statement that the claimant is limited to a period of 30 days from the date of service of an objection within which to bring an action as provided by law.

Committee Notes

This rule represents an implementation of the procedure found in section 733.705, Florida Statutes, and adds a requirement to furnish notice of the time limitation in which an independent action or declaratory action must be filed after objection to a claim.

Rule History

1992 Revision: New rule.

2003 Revision: Reference in (a) to notice of administration changed to notice to creditors. Committee notes revised.

2005 Revision: Removed provision for objections to personal representative's proof of claim, now addressed in rule 5.498, and subsequent subdivisions relettered. Reference to service on the claimant's attorney removed because service on the attorney is required by rule 5.041(b). Committee notes revised.

2007 Revision: Editorial change in (a). Second sentence of (b) added to specify that the objection must include a certificate of service.

2010 Revision: Subdivision (b) amended to delete the requirement to serve a copy of an objection to a claim within 10 days, and to clarify the requirement to include a certificate of service.

2012 Revision: Committee notes revised.

Statutory Reference

§ 731.201(4), Fla. Stat. General definitions.

§ 733.705, Fla. Stat. Payment of and objection to claims.

Rule References

Fla. Prob. R. 5.040 Notice.

Fla. Prob. R. 5.041 Service of pleadings and documents.

Fla. Prob. R. 5.498 Personal representative's proof of claim.

Fla. Prob. R. 5.499 Form and manner of objecting to personal representative's proof of claim.

Fla. R. Jud. Admin. 2.516 Service of pleadings and documents.

RULE 5.498. PERSONAL REPRESENTATIVE'S PROOF OF CLAIM

(a) **Contents.** A personal representative's proof of claim shall state:

(1) the basis for each claim;

(2) the amount claimed;

(3) the name and address of the claimant;

(4) the security for the claim, if any;

(5) whether the claim is matured, unmatured, contingent, or unliquidated;

(6) whether the claim has been paid or is to be paid; and

(7) that any objection to a claim listed as to be paid shall be filed no later than 4 months from first publication of the notice to creditors or 30 days from the date of the filing of the proof of claim, whichever occurs later.

(b) **Service.** The proof of claim shall be served at the time of filing or promptly thereafter on all interested persons.

Committee Notes

This rule represents an implementation of the procedure found in section 733.703(2), Florida Statutes, with respect to a proof of claim filed by the personal representative.

Rule History

2005 Revision: New rule.

2007 Revision: Subdivision (b) amended to eliminate the need to serve claimants listed as paid on the proof of claim, and clarifying editorial change.

2012 Revision: Committee notes revised.

Statutory References

§ 733.703(2), Fla. Stat. Form and manner of presenting claim.

§ 733.705, Fla. Stat. Payment of and objection to claims.

Rule References

Fla. Prob. R. 5.041 Service of pleadings and documents.

Fla. Prob. R. 5.499 Form and manner of objecting to personal representative's proof of claim.

Fla. R. Jud. Admin. 2.516 Service of pleadings and documents.

RULE 5.499. FORM AND MANNER OF OBJECTING TO PERSONAL REPRESENTATIVE'S PROOF OF CLAIM

(a) **Filing.** An objection to a personal representative's proof of claim shall be in writing and filed on or before the expiration of 4 months from the first publication of notice to creditors or within 30 days from the timely filing of the proof of claim, whichever occurs later.

(b) **Contents.** The objection shall identify the particular item or items to which objection is made. An objection to an item listed on the proof of claim as to be paid shall also contain a statement that the claimant is limited to a period of 30 days from the date of service of an objection within which to bring an independent action as provided by law.

(c) **Items Listed as Paid.** If an objection is filed to an item listed on the proof of claim as paid, it shall not be necessary for the claimant to file an independent action as to that item. Liability as between estate and the personal representative individually for claims listed on the proof of claim as paid, or for claims treated as if they were listed on the proof of claim as paid, shall be determined in the estate administration, in a proceeding for accounting or surcharge, or in another appropriate proceeding, whether or not an objection has been filed.

(d) **Items Paid Before Objection.** If an item listed as to be paid is paid by the personal representative prior to the filing of an objection as to that item, the item shall be treated as if it were listed on the proof of claim as paid.

(e) Service. The objector shall serve a copy of the objection on the personal representative and, in the case of any objection to an item listed as to be paid, shall also serve a copy on that claimant within 10 days after the filing of the objection. In the case of an objection to an item listed as to be paid, the objection shall include a certificate of service.

Committee Notes

This rule represents an implementation of the procedure found in section 733.705, Florida Statutes, with respect to a proof of claim filed by the personal representative. The rule recognizes the different treatment between items listed on a proof of claim as having been paid versus items listed as to be paid. An objection to an item listed as to be paid is treated in the same manner as a creditor's claim and there is a requirement to furnish notice of the time limitation in which an independent action or declaratory action must be filed after objection to a claim.

Rule History

2005 Revision: New rule.

2007 Revision: Editorial change in (a). Extensive revisions to rest of rule to clarify the differences in procedure between items listed as paid and items listed as to be paid. Committee notes revised.

2012 Revision: Committee notes revised.

Statutory Reference

§ 733.705, Fla. Stat. Payment of and objection to claims.

Rule References

Fla. Prob. R. 5.040 Notice.

Fla. Prob. R. 5.041 Service of pleadings and documents.

Fla. Prob. R. 5.496 Form and manner of objecting to claim.

Fla. Prob. R. 5.498 Personal representative's proof of claim.

Fla. R. Jud. Admin. 2.516 Service of pleadings and documents.

RULE 5.510. ESTABLISHMENT AND PROBATE OF LOST OR DESTROYED WILL

(a) Proceeding. The establishment and probate of a lost or destroyed will shall be in one proceeding.

(b) Petition. The petition, in addition to reciting information required under these rules for petition for administration, shall include a statement of the facts constituting grounds on which relief is sought, and a statement of the contents of the will or, if available, a copy of the will.

(c) Testimony. The testimony of each witness in the proceeding shall be reduced to writing and filed and may be used as evidence in any contest of the will if the witness has died or moved from the state.

(d) Notice. No lost or destroyed will shall be admitted to probate unless formal notice has been given to those who, but for the will, would be entitled to the property thereby devised.

(e) Order. The order admitting the will to probate shall state in full its terms and provisions.

Committee Notes

This rule represents a rule implementation of the procedure formerly found in section 733.207, Florida Statutes. It is not intended to change the effect of the statute from which it was derived but has been reformatted to conform with the structure of these rules. It is not intended to create a new procedure or modify and existing procedure.

Rule History

1977 Revision: Editorial change in subdivision (c) of prior rule.

1984 Revision: Extensive changes. Committee notes revised.

1988 Revision: Rule rewritten to conform to statute. Committee notes expanded. Citation form change in committee notes.

1992 Revision: Committee notes revised. Citation form changes in committee notes.

2002 Revision: Subdivision (d) added to implement procedure formerly found in section 733.207(3), Florida Statutes. Committee notes revised.

2003 Revision: Committee notes revised.

2012 Revision: Committee notes revised.

Statutory Reference

§ 733.207, Fla. Stat. Establishment and probate of lost or destroyed will.

Rule References

Fla. Prob. R. 5.020 Pleadings; verification; motions.

Fla. Prob. R. 5.025 Adversary proceedings.

Fla. Prob. R. 5.040 Notice.

Fla. Prob. R. 5.041 Notice of pleadings and documents.

Fla. Prob. R. 5.042 Time.

Fla. Prob. R. 5.200 Petition for administration.

Fla. R. Jud. Admin. 2.516 Service of pleadings and documents.

RULE 5.530. SUMMARY ADMINISTRATION

(a) Petition. The petition shall be verified as required by law and shall contain:

(1) a statement of the interest of each petitioner, each petitioner's name and address, and the name and office address of each petitioner's attorney;

(2) the name and last known address of the decedent, last 4 digits of the decedent's social security number, date and place of death of the decedent, and state and county of the decedent's domicile;

(3) so far as is known, the names and addresses of the surviving spouse, if any, and the beneficiaries and their relationship to the decedent and the date of birth of any who are minors;

(4) a statement showing venue;

(5) a statement whether domiciliary or principal proceedings are pending in another state or country, if known, and the name and address of the foreign personal representative and the court issuing letters;

(6) a statement that the decedent's will, if any, does not direct administration as required by chapter 733, Florida Statutes;

(7) a statement that the value of the entire estate subject to administration in this state, less the value of property exempt from the claims of creditors, does not exceed $75,000 or that the decedent has been dead for more than 2 years;

(8) a description of all assets in the estate and the estimated value of each, and a separate description of any protected homestead and exempt property;

(9) a statement either that all creditors' claims are barred or that a diligent search and reasonable inquiry for any known or reasonably ascertainable creditors has been made and one of the following:

(A) A statement that the estate is not indebted.

(B) The name and address of each creditor, the nature of the debt, the amount of the debt and whether the amount is estimated or exact, and when the debt is due. If provision for payment of the debt has been made other than for full payment in the proposed order of distribution, the following information shall be shown:

(i) The name of the person who will pay the debt.

(ii) The creditor's written consent for substitution or assumption of the debt by another person.

(iii) The amount to be paid if the debt has been compromised.

(iv) The terms for payment and any limitations on the liability of the person paying the debt;

(10) in an intestate estate, a statement that after the exercise of reasonable diligence each petitioner is unaware of any unrevoked wills or codicils;

(11) in a testate estate, a statement identifying all unrevoked wills and codicils being presented for probate, and a statement that each petitioner is unaware of any other unrevoked will or codicil; and

(12) a schedule of proposed distribution of all probate assets and the person to whom each asset is to be distributed.

(b) Service. The joinder in, or consent to, a petition for summary administration is not required of a beneficiary who will receive full distributive share under the proposed distribution. Any beneficiary and any known or reasonably ascertainable creditor not joining or consenting shall receive formal notice of the petition.

(c) Testate Estate. In a testate estate, on the filing of the petition for summary administration, the decedent's will shall be proved and admitted to probate.

(d) Order. If the court determines that the decedent's estate qualifies for summary administration, it shall enter an order distributing the probate assets and specifically designating the person to whom each asset is to be distributed.

Committee Notes

Verification and service of a petition for summary administration are governed by rules 5.020, 5.040, and 5.041. Section 735.206(2), Florida Statutes, relating to diligent search for, and service of the petition for summary administration on, reasonably ascertainable creditors is substantive. Nothing in this rule is intended to change the effect of the statutory amendments.

Rule History

1977 Revision: Changes to conform to 1975 statutory revision. Established the requirements of a petition for summary administration and provided for the hearing thereon and the entry of the order of distribution of the assets.

1984 Revision: Extensive revisions and editorial changes. Committee notes revised.

1988 Revision: Editorial change in caption of (a). Committee notes revised.

1992 Revision: Editorial changes. Committee notes revised. Citation form changes in committee notes.

2002 Revision: Replaces "homestead" with "protected homestead" in (a)(2) to conform to addition of term in section 731.201(29), Florida Statutes. Committee notes revised.

2003 Revision: Committee notes revised.

2005 Revision: Subdivision (a)(3) amended to include requirements of section 735.206(2), Florida Statutes.

2007 Revision: Rule substantially rewritten to require petition to include essentially the same information required to be stated in a petition for administration and to require the petitioners to specify facts showing they are entitled to summary administration. New subdivision (b) added to provide for formal notice of the petition, and subsequent subdivisions relettered.

2011 Revision: Subdivision (a)(2) amended to limit listing of decedent's social security number to last four digits.

2012 Revision: Committee notes revised.

Statutory References

§ 731.104, Fla. Stat. Verification of documents.

§§ 735.201-735.2063, Fla. Stat. Summary administration.

Rule References

Fla. Prob. R. 5.020 Pleadings; verification; motions.

Fla. Prob. R. 5.040 Notice.

Fla. Prob. R. 5.041 Service of pleadings and documents.

Fla. Prob. R. 5.205(a)(3) Filing evidence of death.

Fla. R. Jud. Admin. 2.516 Service of pleadings and documents.

PART III. GUARDIANSHIP

RULE 5.540. HEARINGS.

(a) Application. All hearings under chapter 744 and under section 393.12, Florida Statutes, shall be open unless the alleged incapacitated person, adjudicated ward, or person alleged to have a developmental disability elects to have the hearing closed.

(b) Election. An election to close a hearing may be made before the hearing by filing a written notice. Subject to the court's approval, an election to close or reopen a hearing may be made at any time during the hearing by oral or written motion.

Committee Notes

This rule permits an alleged incapacitated person, adjudicated ward, or person alleged to have a developmental disability to elect to have all hearings open or closed at any time by oral or written election.

Rule History

1991 Revision: New rule.

1992 Revision: Committee notes revised.

2008 Revision: Subdivision (1) amended to include persons with a developmental disability. Committee notes revised.

Statutory References

§ 393.12, Fla. Stat. Capacity; appointment of guardian advocate.

§ 744.1095, Fla. Stat. Hearings.

§ 744.3085, Fla. Stat. Guardian advocates.

Rule Reference

Fla. Prob. R. 5.541 Recording of hearings.

RULE 5.541. RECORDING OF HEARINGS

Electronic or stenographic recordings shall be made of all hearings on the:

(a) adjudication of incapacity;

(b) appointment of a guardian;

(c) modification, termination, or revocation of the adjudication of incapacity;

(d) restoration of capacity; or

(e) restoration of rights.

Committee Notes

This rule represents a rule implementation of the procedure found in sections 744.109 and 744.3031, Florida Statutes. It is not intended to change the effect of the statutes from which it is derived, or to create a new procedure or modify an existing procedure.

Rule History

1991 Revision: New rule.

1992 Revision: Editorial changes. Committee notes revised. Citation form change in committee notes.

2003 Revision: Committee notes revised.

2008 Revision: New subdivision (e) added for proceedings involving guardian advocates. Committee notes revised.

Statutory References

§ 393.12, Fla. Stat. Capacity; appointment of guardian advocate.

§ 744.109, Fla. Stat. Records.

§ 744.3031, Fla. Stat. Emergency temporary guardianship.

§ 744.3085, Fla. Stat. Guardian advocates.

§ 744.3371, Fla. Stat. Notice of petition for appointment of guardian and hearing.

RULE 5.550. PETITION TO DETERMINE INCAPACITY

(a) **Contents.** The petition to determine incapacity shall be verified by the petitioner, and shall state:

(1) the name, age, and present address of the petitioner and the petitioner's relationship to the alleged incapacitated person;

(2) the name, age, county of residence, and present address of the alleged incapacitated person, and specify the primary language spoken by the alleged incapacitated person, if known;

(3) that the petitioner believes the alleged incapacitated person to be incapacitated, the facts on which such belief is based, and the names and addresses of all persons known to the petitioner who have knowledge of such facts through personal observation;

(4) the name and address of the alleged incapacitated person's attending or family physician, if known;

(5) which rights the alleged incapacitated person is incapable of exercising to the best of the petitioner's knowledge; and, if the petitioner has insufficient experience to make that judgment, the petitioner shall so indicate;

(6) whether plenary or limited guardianship is sought for the alleged incapacitated person; and

(7) the names, relationships, and addresses of the next of kin of the alleged incapacitated person, specifying the dates of birth of any who are minors, to the extent known to the petitioner.

(b) **Notice.**

(1) **Contents.** The notice of filing the petition to determine incapacity shall state:

(A) the time and place of the hearing to inquire into the capacity of the alleged incapacitated person;

(B) that an attorney has been appointed to represent such person; and

(C) that if the court determines that such person is incapable of exercising any of the rights enumerated in the petition a guardian may be appointed.

(2) **Service on Alleged Incapacitated Person.** The notice and a copy of the petition to determine incapacity shall be personally served by an elisor appointed by the court, who may be the court appointed counsel for the alleged incapacitated person. The elisor shall read the notice to the alleged incapacitated person, but need not read the petition. A return of service shall be filed by the elisor certifying that the notice and petition have been served on and the notice read to the alleged incapacitated person. No responsive pleading is required and no default may be entered for failure to file a responsive pleading. The allegations of the petition are deemed denied.

(3) **Service on Others.** A copy of the petition and the notice shall also be served on counsel for the alleged incapacitated person, and on all next of kin.

(c) **Verified Statement.** An interested person may file a verified statement that shall state:

(1) that he or she has a good faith belief that the alleged incapacitated person's trust, trust amendment, or durable power of attorney is invalid; and

(2) facts constituting a reasonable basis for that belief.

(d) **Order.** When an order determines that a person is incapable of exercising delegable rights, it shall specify whether there is an alternative to guardianship that will sufficiently address the problems of the incapacitated person.

Committee Notes

Rule History

1980 Revision: Implements 1979 amendments to section 744.331, Florida Statutes.

1984 Revision: Change in title of rule. Editorial changes and adds a provision for service of petition. Committee notes revised.

1988 Revision: Committee notes revised. Citation form changes in committee notes.

1989 Revision by Ad Hoc Committee: The committee realized that formal notice as defined in rule 5.040(a)(1) requires the recipient of notice to file a responsive pleading within 20 days after the service of the notice. The committee believed that to impose such a requirement on the alleged incapacitated person would contravene the legislative intent of the 1989 revisions to chapter 744, Florida Statutes. The committee observed that the time required for appointment of mandatory appointed counsel might render a responsive pleading within 20 days impossible for the alleged incapacitated person. The committee concluded that, procedurally, notice upon the alleged incapacitated person should occur in the same manner as formal notice in rule 5.040, but the required response under that rule should not be imposed upon the alleged incapacitated person.

1991 Revision: Implements 1989 amendments to sections 744.3201 and 744.331, Florida Statutes, and 1990 technical amendments.

1992 Revision: Citation form changes in committee notes.

2006 Revision: Subdivisions (c) and (d) added to incorporate 2006 amendment to section 744.441 and creation of section 744.462, Florida Statutes. Committee notes revised.

Statutory References

§ 744.3201, Fla. Stat. Petition to determine incapacity.

§ 744.331, Fla. Stat. Procedures to determine incapacity.

§ 744.3371, Fla. Stat. Notice of petition for appointment of guardian and hearing.

§ 744.441(11), Fla. Stat. Powers of guardian upon court approval.

§ 744.462, Fla. Stat. Determination regarding alternatives to guardianship.

Rule References

Fla. Prob. R. 5.020 Pleadings; verification; motions.

Fla. Prob. R. 5 040(a)(3) Notice.

Fla. Prob. R. 5 800(a) Application of revised chapter 744 to existing guardianships.

RULE 5.552. VOLUNTARY GUARDIANSHIP OF PROPERTY

(a) **Petition for Appointment of Guardian.** The petition for voluntary guardianship shall be verified by the petitioner and shall state:

(1) the facts to establish venue;

(2) the petitioner's residence and post office address;

(3) that the petitioner although mentally competent is incapable of the care, custody, and management of the petitioner's estate by reason of age or physical infirmity, and is voluntarily petitioning to have a guardian of the petitioner's property appointed;

(4) whether the guardianship shall apply to all of the petitioner's property or less than all of the petitioner's property; and if less than all of the petitioner's property, the specific property to which the guardianship is to apply;

(5) the name and residence and post office address of any proposed guardian;

(6) that the proposed guardian is qualified to serve or that a willing and qualified proposed guardian has not been located; and

(7) the names and post office addresses of persons to whom the petitioner requests that notice of the hearing for the appointment of the guardian, and any petition for authority to act, be given.

(b) **Certificate of Licensed Physician.** The petition shall be accompanied by a certificate of a licensed physician as required by law.

(c) **Notice of Hearing.** Notice of hearing on the petition for appointment, and any petition for authority to act, shall be given to the ward and any person to whom the ward requests notice be given, which request can be made in the petition for appointment or a subsequent written request for notice signed by the ward.

(d) **Annual Report.** The annual report shall be accompanied by a certificate from a licensed physician as required by law.

(e) **Termination.** The ward may terminate a voluntary guardianship by filing a notice of termination. Copies of the notice shall be served on all interested persons. The guardian shall file a petition for discharge in accordance with these rules.

Committee Notes

Rule History

2003 Revision: New rule.

2006 Revision: New (d) added to incorporate 2006 amendment to section 744.341, Florida Statutes, requiring inclusion of physician's certificate in annual report, and subsequent subdivision relettered. Committee notes revised.

Statutory References

§ 744.341, Fla. Stat. Voluntary guardianship.

Rule References

Fla. Prob. R. 5.680 Termination of Guardianship.

Fla. Prob. R. 5.695 Annual guardianship report.

RULE 5.555. GUARDIANSHIPS OF MINORS

(a) Application. This rule shall apply to any guardianship for a minor.

(b) Petition to Determine Incapacity. No petition to determine incapacity need be filed.

(c) Petition for Appointment of Guardian. The petition shall be verified by the petitioner and shall state:

(1) the facts to establish venue;

(2) the petitioner's residence and post office address;

(3) the name, age, and residence and post office address of the minor;

(4) the names and addresses of the parents of the minor and if none, the next of kin known to the petitioner;

(5) the name and residence and post office address of the proposed guardian, and that the proposed guardian is qualified to serve; or, that a willing and qualified guardian has not been located;

(6) the proposed guardian's relationship to and any previous association with the minor;

(7) the reasons why the proposed guardian should be appointed; and

(8) the nature and value of the property subject to the guardianship.

(d) Notice. Formal notice of the petition for appointment of guardian shall be served on any parent who is not a petitioner or, if there is no parent, on the persons with whom the minor resides and on such other persons as the court may direct.

(e) Initial and Annual Guardianship Reports.

(1) The initial guardianship report shall consist only of the verified inventory. The annual guardianship report shall consist only of the annual accounting.

(2) The guardian shall file an initial and annual guardianship plan as required by law.

(3) Unless otherwise ordered by the court or required by law, the guardian need not serve a copy of the initial guardianship report and the annual guardianship reports on the ward.

(f) Inspection of Inventory or Accounting. Unless otherwise ordered by the court for good cause shown, any inventory, amended or supplementary inventory, or accounting is subject to inspection only by the clerk, the ward or the ward's attorney, and the guardian or the guardian's attorney.

Committee Notes

The provisions of chapter 744, Florida Statutes, and the guardianship rules enacted in 1989 leave some uncertainty with respect to the procedural requirements in guardianships for minors who are not incapacitated persons. This rule is intended to address only certain procedures with respect to the establishment and administration of guardianships over minors. The committee believes that certain provisions of the guardianship law and rules apply to both guardianships of minors as well as guardianships of incapacitated persons and no change has been suggested with respect to such rules. Because no adjudication of a minor is required by statute, it is contemplated that appointment of a guardian for a minor may be accomplished without a hearing. Initial and annual guardianship reports for minors have been simplified where all assets are on deposit with a designated financial institution under applicable Florida law.

Rule History

1991 Revision: New rule adopted to apply to guardianship over minors who are not incapacitated persons.

1992 Revision: Committee notes revised. Citation form changes in committee notes.

1996 Revision: Committee notes revised.

2000 Revision: Deletes requirement in subdivision (c) to report social security number of proposed guardian.

2003 Revision: Deletes requirement in subdivision (c) to report social security number of minor. Committee notes revised.

2006 Revision: Subdivision (e)(2) amended to conform to requirement in sections 744.362(1) and 744.3675, Florida Statutes, to file initial and annual guardianship plans. Subdivision (e)(3) amended to eliminate requirement of service on ward unless ordered by court or required by statute.

Statutory References

§ 69.031, Fla. Stat. Designated financial institutions for assets in hands of guardians, curators, administrators, trustees, receivers, or other officers.

§ 744.3021, Fla. Stat. Guardians of minors.

§ 744.334, Fla. Stat. Petition for appointment of guardian or professional guardian; contents.

§ 744.3371(2), Fla. Stat. Notice of petition for appointment of guardian and hearing.

§ 744.342, Fla. Stat. Minors; guardianship.

§ 744.362, Fla. Stat. Initial guardianship report.

§ 744.363, Fla. Stat. Initial guardianship plan.

§ 744.365, Fla. Stat. Verified inventory.

§ 744.367, Fla. Stat. Duty to file annual guardianship report.

§ 744.3675, Fla. Stat. Annual guardianship plan.

§ 744.3678, Fla. Stat. Annual accounting.

§ 744.3679, Fla. Stat. Simplified accounting procedures in certain cases.

Rule References

Fla. Prob. R. 5.040 Notice.

Fla. Prob. R. 5.541 Recording of hearings.

Fla. Prob. R. 5.560 Petition for appointment of a guardian of an incapacitated person.

Fla. Prob. R. 5.620 Inventory.

Fla. Prob. R. 5.636 Settlement of minors' claims.

Fla. Prob. R. 5.690 Initial guardianship report.

RULE 5.560. PETITION FOR APPOINTMENT OF A GUARDIAN OF AN INCAPACITATED PERSON

(a) **Contents.** The petition shall be verified by the petitioner and shall state:

(1) the facts to establish venue;

(2) the petitioner's residence and post office address;

(3) the name, age, residence and post office address of the alleged incapacitated person;

(4) the nature of the incapacity, the extent of guardianship, either limited or plenary, requested for the alleged incapacitated person, and the nature and value of property subject to the guardianship;

(5) the names and addresses of the next of kin of the alleged incapacitated person known to the petitioner;

(6) the name and residence and post office address of the proposed guardian, and that the proposed guardian is qualified to serve, or that a willing and qualified guardian has not been located;

(7) the proposed guardian's relationship to and any previous association with the alleged incapacitated person;

(8) the reasons why the proposed guardian should be appointed;

(9) whether there are alternatives to guardianship known to the petitioner that may sufficiently address the problems of the alleged incapacitated person in whole or in part; and

(10) if the proposed guardian is a professional guardian, a statement that the proposed guardian has complied with the registration requirements of section 744.1083, Florida Statutes.

(b) **Notice.** Notice of filing the petition for appointment of guardian may be served as a part of the notice of filing the petition to determine incapacity, but shall be served a reasonable time before the hearing on the petition or other pleading seeking appointment of a guardian.

(c) **Service on Public Guardian.** If the petitioner requests appointment of the public guardian, a copy of the petition and the notice shall be served on the public guardian.

Committee Notes

Rule History

1975 Revision: Substantially the same as section 744.334, Florida Statutes, expanded to include provisions of section 744.302, Florida Statutes, and section 744.312, Florida Statutes, by reference.

1977 Revision: Change in committee notes to conform to statutory renumbering.

1980 Revision: Implements 1979 amendment to section 744.334, Florida Statutes.

1984 Revision: Combines rule 5.560 and part of prior rule 5.570. Editorial changes and committee notes revised.

1988 Revision: Editorial changes. Committee notes revised. Citation form changes in committee notes.

1989 Revision by Ad Hoc Committee: Subsection (a)(4) of the former rule has been deleted altogether because the date and court of adjudication will probably not be known at the time of filing the petition for the appointment since petition for appointment will henceforth be filed contemporaneously with the petition to determine incapacity.

1991 Revision: Implements 1989 amendments to sections 744.334 and 744.331(1), Florida Statutes, and 1990 technical amendments. Subdivision (c)(1) deleted because rule 5.555(d) addresses service on parents.

1992 Revision: Citation form changes in committee notes.

1996 Revision: Deletes requirement in subdivision (a) to report social security number of alleged incapacitated person. Adds provision to subdivision (b) for notice before hearing when petition is not served simultaneously with petition to determine incapacity.

2000 Revision: Deletes requirement in subdivision (a) to report social security number of proposed guardian.

2003 Revision: Committee notes revised.

2006 Revision: New (a)(9) added to incorporate 2006 passage of section 744.462, Florida Statutes. Subdivision (a)(10) added to implement section 744.1083, Florida Statutes. Committee notes revised.

Statutory References

§ 744.1083, Fla. Stat. Professional guardian registration.

§ 744.309, Fla. Stat. Who may be appointed guardian of a resident ward.

§ 744.312, Fla. Stat. Considerations in appointment of guardian.

§ 744.331, Fla. Stat. Procedures to determine incapacity.

§ 744.334, Fla. Stat. Petition for appointment of guardian or professional guardian; contents.

§ 744.3371(1), Fla. Stat. Notice of petition for appointment of guardian and hearing.

§ 744.341, Fla. Stat. Voluntary guardianship.

§ 744.344, Fla. Stat. Order of appointment.

§ 744.462, Fla. Stat. Determination regarding alternatives to guardianship.

§ 744.703, Fla. Stat. Office of public guardian; appointment; notification.

Rule References

Fla. Prob. R. 5.020 Pleadings; verification; motions.

Fla. Prob. R. 5.040 Notice.

Fla. Prob. R. 5.550 Petition to determine incapacity.

RULE 5.590. APPLICATION FOR APPOINTMENT AS GUARDIAN; DISCLOSURE STATEMENT; FILING

(a) Individual Applicants.

(1) The application for appointment shall contain:

(A) the applicant's qualifications to serve as a guardian; and

(B) the names of all wards for whom the applicant is then acting as guardian, the court file number and circuit court in which each case is pending, and a statement as to whether the applicant is acting as a limited or plenary guardian of the person or property, or both, of each ward.

(2) The application for appointment shall be filed and served a reasonable time before the hearing on the appointment of a guardian.

(b) Nonprofit Corporate Guardians.

(1) No application for appointment shall be required of a nonprofit corporate guardian.

(2) A disclosure statement shall contain:

(A) the corporation's qualifications to serve as a guardian; and

(B) the names of all wards for whom the corporation is then acting as guardian, the court file number and circuit court in which each case is pending, and a statement as to whether the corporation is acting as a limited or plenary guardian of the person or property, or both, of each ward.

(3) The disclosure statement of a nonprofit corporate guardian shall be filed quarterly with the clerk of the court for each circuit in which the corporation has been appointed, or is seeking appointment, as guardian.

(c) For Profit Corporations and Associations. No application for appointment or disclosure statement shall be required of any for profit corporation or association authorized to exercise fiduciary powers under Florida law.

(d) Public Guardians. No application for appointment or disclosure statement shall be required of a public guardian.

Committee Notes

Rule History

1988 Revision: Prior rule deleted; text of rule moved to rule 5.650.

1989 Revision: Rule reactivated with different title and text.

1991 Revision: Implements 1989 and 1990 amendments to section 744.3125, Florida Statutes.

1992 Revision: Citation form change in committee notes.

1996 Revision: Adds filing and service provisions consistent with rule 5.560. Corrects reference to corporations qualified to exercise fiduciary powers. Editorial changes. Adds statutory references.

2003 Revision: Committee notes revised.

2006 Revision: Committee notes revised.

2008 Revision: Committee notes revised.

Statutory References

§ 393.063(17), Fla Stat. Definitions.

§ 393.12, Fla. Stat. Capacity; appointment of guardian advocate.

§ 744.102(4), (9), (11), (14), (22) Fla. Stat. Definitions.

§ 744.3085, Fla. Stat. Guardian advocates.

§ 744.309, Fla. Stat. Who may be appointed guardian of a resident ward.

§ 744.3125, Fla. Stat. Application for appointment.

§ 744.331(1), Fla. Stat. Procedures to determine incapacity.

§ 744.3371, Fla. Stat. Notice of petition for appointment of guardian and hearing.

RULE 5.600. OATH

Every guardian or emergency temporary guardian shall take an oath to perform faithfully the duties of guardian or emergency temporary guardian before exercising such authority. The oath may be incorporated in the petition for appointment of guardian, or petition for appointment of emergency temporary guardian, if verified by the prospective guardian.

Committee Notes

Rule History

1977 Revision: Change in committee notes to conform to statutory renumbering. Rule permits oath of guardian to be incorporated in petition for appointment and in designation of resident agent.

1984 Revision: Editorial change and deletes genders.

1989 Revision: Prior rule adopted as temporary emergency rule.

1991 Revision: Permits oath to be incorporated in application for appointment of guardian, adds reference to temporary emergency guardian, and makes editorial change.

1992 Revision: Editorial changes.

2008 Revision: Committee notes revised.

Statutory References

§ 393.12, Fla. Stat. Capacity; appointment of guardian advocate.

§ 744.347, Fla. Stat. Oath of guardian.

RULE 5.610. EXECUTION BY GUARDIAN

The guardian shall sign the:

(a) initial guardianship plan;

(b) inventory, amended inventory, or supplemental inventory;

(c) annual guardianship plan;

(d) annual accounting;

(e) guardian's petition for court approval required by law;

(f) petition for discharge;

(g) final report; and

(h) resignation of guardian.

Committee Notes

Rule History

1975 Revision: Rule lists what guardian shall sign and includes any petition for court approval required by F.S. 744.441. The rule requires that the guardian have actual knowledge of the more important steps and acts of administration.

1977 Revision: Change in statutory reference in rule and in committee note to conform to statutory renumbering.

1988 Revision: Editorial changes. Committee notes revised. Citation form changes in rule and committee notes.

1989 Revision: Follows statutory requirements. See 549 So. 2d665, 668 (effective October 1, 1989).

1991 Revision: Changes to conform to 1989 and 1990 revisions to guardianship law. Adds additional documents to be signed by the guardian. Statutory references added.

2003 Revision: Committee notes revised.

2008 Revision: Committee notes revised.

Statutory References

§ 393.12, Fla. Stat. Capacity; appointment of guardian advocate.

§ 744.362, Fla. Stat. Initial guardianship report.

§ 744.363, Fla. Stat. Initial guardianship plan.

§ 744.365, Fla. Stat. Verified inventory.

§ 744.367, Fla. Stat. Duty to file annual guardianship report.

§ 744.3675, Fla. Stat. Annual guardianship plan.

§ 744.3678, Fla. Stat. Annual accounting.

§ 744.387, Fla. Stat. Settlement of claims.

§ 744.441, Fla. Stat. Powers of guardian upon court approval.

§ 744.446, Fla. Stat. Conflicts of interest; prohibited activities; court approval; breach of fiduciary duty.

§ 744.447, Fla. Stat. Petition for authorization to act.

§ 744.451, Fla. Stat. Order.

§ 744.467, Fla. Stat. Resignation of guardian.

§ 744.511, Fla. Stat. Accounting upon removal.

§ 744.521, Fla. Stat. Termination of guardianship.

§ 744.524, Fla. Stat. Termination of guardianship on change of domicile of resident ward.

§ 744.527(1), Fla. Stat. Final reports and application for discharge; hearing.

§ 744.534, Fla. Stat. Disposition of unclaimed funds held by guardian.

RULE 5.620. INVENTORY

(a) Inventory. Within 60 days after issuance of letters, the guardian of the property shall file a verified inventory as required by law. All property not in the guardian's possession as of the date the inventory is filed shall be so identified.

(b) Amended or Supplemental Inventory. If the guardian of the property learns of any property not included in the inventory, or learns that the description in the inventory is inaccurate, the guardian shall, within 30 days of this discovery, file a verified amended or supplemental inventory showing the change.

(c) Substantiating Papers. Unless ordered by the court, the guardian need not file the papers substantiating the inventory. Upon reasonable written request, the guardian of the property shall make the substantiating papers available for examination to those persons entitled to receive or inspect the inventory.

(d) Safe-Deposit Box Inventory. If the ward has a safe-deposit box, a copy of the safe-deposit box inventory shall be filed as part of the verified inventory.

(e) Guardian Advocates. This rule shall apply to a guardian advocate to the extent that the guardian advocate was granted authority over the property of the person with a developmental disability.

Committee Notes

Rule History

1977 Revision: Change in committee notes to conform to statutory renumbering.

1984 Revision: Change to require inventory to be filed within 60 days after issuance of letters, rather than after appointment. Committee notes revised.

1988 Revision: Editorial changes. Committee notes revised. Citation form change in committee notes.

1989 Revision: Prior rule deleted and replaced by temporary emergency rule.

1991 Revision: Former rule 5.620(b) has been deleted as partly substantive and addressed in section 744.381, Florida Statutes, and the procedural part is unnecessary.

The committee recognizes the conflict between this rule and section 744.362, Florida Statutes, which requires the filing of the initial guardianship report (which includes the inventory) within 60 days after appointment. The committee believes this provision, which attempts to regulate when a paper must be filed with the court, is procedural and that a guardian may not receive letters of guardianship empowering the guardian to act contemporaneously with the appointment. Therefore, the issuance of letters is a more practical time from which to measure the beginning of the time period for the accomplishment of this act.

1992 Revision: Citation form changes in committee notes.

2005 Revision: Editorial changes in (d).

2007 Revision: Committee notes revised.

2008 Revision: Adds reference to guardian advocate in new (e). Committee notes revised.

2012 Revision: Committee notes revised.

Statutory References

§ 393.12, Fla. Stat. Capacity; appointment of guardian advocate.

§ 744.362, Fla. Stat. Initial guardianship report.

§ 744.365, Fla. Stat. Verified inventory.

§ 744.3701, Fla. Stat. Inspection of report.

§ 744.381, Fla. Stat. Appraisals.

§ 744.384, Fla. Stat. Subsequently discovered or acquired property.

Rule References

Fla. Prob. R. 5.020 Pleadings; verification; motions.

Fla. Prob. R. 5.041 Service of pleadings and documents.

Fla. Prob. R. 5.060 Request for notices and copies of pleadings.

Fla. Prob. R. 5.610 Execution by guardian.

Fla. Prob. R. 5.649 Guardian advocate.

Fla. Prob. R. 5.690 Initial guardianship report.

Fla. Prob. R. 5.700 Objection to guardianship reports.

Fla. R. Jud. Admin. 2.516 Service of pleadings and documents.

RULE 5.625. NOTICE OF COMPLETION OF GUARDIAN EDUCATION REQUIREMENTS

(a) Filing. Unless the guardian education requirement is waived by the court, each guardian, other than a professional guardian, shall file with the court within 4 months after the issuance of letters of guardianship or letters of guardian advocacy a notice of completion of guardian education requirements.

(b) Content. The notice shall state:

(1) that the guardian has completed the required number of hours of course instruction and training covering the legal duties and responsibilities of a guardian, the rights of a ward, the availability of local resources to aid a ward, and the preparation of habilitation plans and annual guardianship reports, including accountings;

(2) the date the course was completed;

(3) the name of the course completed; and

(4) the name of the entity or instructor that taught the course.

(c) Verification. The notice shall be verified by the guardian.

Committee Notes

Rule History.

2005 Revision: New rule.

2006 Revision: Subdivision (a) amended to conform to 2006 amendment to section 744.3145(4), Florida Statutes.

2008 Revision: Adds reference in (a) to guardian advocacy. Committee notes revised.

Statutory References.

§ 393.12, Fla. Stat. Capacity; appointment of guardian advocate.

§ 744.3145, Fla. Stat. Guardian education requirements.

RULE 5.630. PETITION FOR APPROVAL OF ACTS

(a) Contents. When authorization or confirmation of any act of the guardian is required, application shall be made by verified petition stating the facts showing:

(1) the expediency or necessity for the action;

(2) a description of any property involved;

(3) the price and terms of any sale, mortgage, or other contract;

(4) whether the ward has been adjudicated incapacitated to act with respect to the rights to be exercised;

(5) whether the action requested conforms to the guardianship plan; and

(6) the basis for the relief sought.

(b) Notice. No notice of a petition to authorize sale of perishable personal property or of property rapidly deteriorating shall be required. Notice of a petition to perform any other act requiring a court order shall be given to the ward, to the next of kin, if any, and to those persons who have filed requests for notices and copies of pleadings.

(c) Order.

(1) If the act is authorized or confirmed, the order shall describe the permitted act and authorize the guardian to perform it or confirm its performance.

(2) If a sale or mortgage is authorized or confirmed, the order shall describe the property. If a sale is to be private, the order shall specify the price and the terms of the sale. If a sale is to be public, the order

shall state that the sale shall be made to the highest bidder and that the court reserves the right to reject all bids.

(3) If the guardian is authorized to bring an action to contest the validity of all or part of a revocable trust, the order shall contain a finding that the action appears to be in the ward's best interests during the ward's probable lifetime. If the guardian is not authorized to bring such an action, the order shall contain a finding concerning the continued need for a guardian and the extent of the need for delegation of the ward's rights.

Committee Notes

Rule History

1975 Revision: Substantially the same as sections 744.503, 744.447, and 744.451, Florida Statutes, with editorial changes.

1977 Revision: Change in statutory reference in rule and in committee note to conform to statutory renumbering.

1980 Revision: Implements 1979 Amendments to section 744.447(2), Florida Statutes.

1988 Revision: Editorial changes; captions added to subdivisions. Committee notes revised. Citation form changes in rule and committee notes.

1989 Revision: Prior rule deleted and replaced by temporary emergency rule.

1991 Revision: Changes to conform to 1989 revised guardianship law.

1992 Revision: Committee notes revised. Citation form changes in committee notes.

2006 Revision: New (a)(6) added to incorporate 2006 amendment to section 744.441, Florida Statutes. New (c)(3) added to reflect passage of 2006 amendment to section 737.2065, Florida Statutes. Committee notes revised.

2007 Revision: Committee notes revised.

2008 Revision: Committee notes revised.

2012 Revision: Committee notes revised.

Statutory References

§ 393.12, Fla. Stat. Capacity; appointment of guardian advocate.

§ 736.0207, Fla. Stat. Trust contests.

§ 744.3215, Fla. Stat. Rights of persons determined incapacitated.

§ 744.441, Fla. Stat. Powers of guardian upon court approval.

§ 744.447, Fla. Stat. Petition for authorization to act.

§ 744.451, Fla. Stat. Order.

Rule References

Fla. Prob. R. 5.020 Pleadings; verification; motions.

Fla. Prob. R. 5.025 Adversary proceedings.

Fla. Prob. R. 5.040 Notice.

Fla. Prob. R. 5.041 Service of pleadings and documents.

Fla. Prob. R. 5.060 Request for notices and copies of pleadings.

Fla. Prob. R. 5.610 Execution by guardian.

Fla. Prob. R. 5.636 Settlement of minors' claims.

Fla. Prob. R. 5.649 Guardian advocate.

Fla. R. Jud. Admin. 2.516 Service of pleadings and documents.

RULE 5.635. PETITION FOR EXTRAORDINARY AUTHORITY

(a) Contents. When authorization for extraordinary authority is sought as permitted by law, application shall be made by verified petition stating:

(1) the petitioner's interest in the proceeding;

(2) the specific authority requested; and

(3) the facts constituting the basis for the relief sought and that the authority being requested is in the best interest of the ward.

(b) Notice.

(1) The petition shall be served by formal notice. For good cause shown, the court may shorten the time for response to the formal notice and may set an expedited hearing.

(2) The petition shall be served on the guardian of the person, if the guardian is not the petitioner, the ward, the next of kin, if any, those interested persons who have filed requests for notices and copies of pleadings, and such other persons as the court may direct.

(c) Hearing. The hearing shall be at a time and place that will enable the ward to express the ward's views to the court.

Committee Notes

Rule History

1991 Revision: New rule.

1992 Revision: Committee notes revised.

2008 Revision: Committee notes revised.

Statutory References

§ 393.12, Fla. Stat. Capacity; appointment of guardian advocate.

§ 744.3215(4), Fla. Stat. Rights of persons determined incapacitated.

§ 744.3725, Fla. Stat. Procedure for extraordinary authority.

RULE 5.636. SETTLEMENT OF MINORS' CLAIMS

(a) Time of Settlement. Claims on behalf of minors may be settled either before or after an action is filed.

(b) Petition. The petition for approval of a settlement shall contain:

(1) the name, residence address, and date of birth of the minor;

(2) the name and address of any guardian appointed for the minor;

(3) the name and residence address of the natural guardians or other persons having legal custody of the minor;

(4) a statement disclosing the interests of any natural or court-appointed guardian whose interest may be in conflict with that of the minor;

(5) a description of the cause of action in which the minor's interest arises;

(6) a summary of the terms of the proposed settlement; and

(7) copies of all agreements, releases, or other documents to be executed on behalf of the minor.

(c) Notice. Notice of the petition shall be given to the court-appointed guardians for the minor, to the natural guardians or other persons with legal custody of the minor, to the minor if age 14 or older, and to the minor's next of kin if required by the court.

(d) Guardian Ad Litem. The court shall appoint a guardian ad litem on behalf of a minor, without bond or notice, with respect to any proposed settlement that exceeds $50,000 and affects the interests of the minor, if:

(1) there is no court-appointed guardian of the minor;

(2) the court-appointed guardian may have an interest adverse to the minor; or

(3) the court determines that representation of the minor's interest is otherwise inadequate.

(e) Valuation of Proposed Settlement. A proposed settlement is deemed to exceed $50,000 if the gross amount payable exceeds $50,000, without reduction to reflect present value or fees and costs.

(f) Report. A guardian ad litem appointed with respect to a proposed settlement affecting the interests of a minor shall, not later than 5 days prior to the hearing on a petition for order authorizing settlement, file and serve a report indicating the guardian ad litem's determination regarding whether the proposed settlement will be in the best interest of the minor. The report shall include:

(1) a statement of the facts of the minor's claim and the terms of the proposed settlement, including any benefits to any persons or parties with related claims;

(2) a list of the persons interviewed and documents reviewed by the guardian ad litem in evaluating the minor's claim and proposed settlement; and

(3) the guardian ad litem's analysis of whether the proposed settlement will be in the best interest of the minor.

A copy of the report shall be served on those persons on whom service is required in subdivision (c) of this rule.

Committee Notes

When a civil action is pending, the petition for approval of settlement should be filed in that civil action. In all other circumstances, the petition for approval of settlement should be filed in the same court and assigned to a judge who would preside over a petition for appointment of guardian of a minor.

The total settlement to be considered under subdivisions (d) and (e) is not limited to the amounts received only by the minor, but includes all settlement payments or proceeds received by all parties to the claim or action. For example, the proposed settlement may have a gross value of $60,000, with $30,000 payable to the minor and $30,000 payable to another party. In that instance the total proposed settlement exceeds $50,000. Further, the "gross amount payable" under subdivision (e) is the total sum payable, without reducing the settlement amount by fees and costs that might be paid from the proceeds of the settlement. For example, if the proposed settlement is $60,000 but $20,000 of that sum will be paid to the attorneys representing the minor's interest in the action, the "gross amount payable" still exceeds $50,000. Likewise, the "gross amount payable" cannot be reduced to reflect the present value of the proposed settlement on behalf of the minor.

Rule History

1992 Revision: New Rule.

2003 Revision: Committee notes revised.

2006 Revision: Amended to reflect 2006 passage of new section 744.3025, Claims of Minors, increasing dollar figure from $25,000 to $50,000 as threshold amount requiring appointment of guardian ad litem if interests of minor are not otherwise adequately represented. Committee notes revised.

Statutory References

§ 744.3025, Fla. Stat. Claims of minors.

§ 744.387, Fla. Stat. Settlement of claims.

§ 744.391, Fla. Stat. Actions by and against guardian or ward.

§ 744.441, Fla. Stat. Powers of guardian upon court approval.

§ 744.446, Fla. Stat. Conflicts of interest; prohibited activities; court approval; breach of fiduciary duty.

§ 744.447, Fla. Stat. Petition for authorization to act.

§ 744.23, Fla. Stat. Protection of minors and incompetents.

§ 768.25, Fla. Stat. Court approval of settlements.

Rule References

Fla. Prob. R. 5.040 Notice.

Fla. Prob. R. 5.042 Time.

Fla. Prob. R. 5.120 Administrator ad litem and guardian ad litem.

Fla. Prob. R. 5.610 Execution by guardian.

Fla. Prob. R. 5.630 Petition for approval of acts.

RULE 5.640. CONTINUANCE OF UNINCORPORATED BUSINESS OR VENTURE OF WARD

(a) Continuance of Business. When the ward is adjudicated incapacitated while engaged in any unincorporated business or venture, or the court finds that a person with a developmental disability lacks capacity to manage an unincorporated business or venture, the court may authorize the guardian to continue the business or venture for a reasonable time under the supervision of the court.

(b) Petition. Before an order is made under subdivision (a), the guardian shall file a verified petition,

alleging sufficient facts to make it appear that it is in the best interest of the ward's estate to continue the business or venture.

(c) Order. The order authorizing the continuance of the business or venture may empower the guardian to make contracts necessary to conduct the business or venture and to incur debts and pay out money in the proper conduct of the business or venture. The net profits only of the business or venture are to be added to the assets of the ward's estate.

(d) Accounts and Reports. In the conduct of the business or venture, the guardian shall keep full and accurate accounts of all receipts and expenditures and make reports as the court requires.

(e) Discontinuance of business. Any person interested in the ward's estate may at any time petition the court for an order requiring the guardian to discontinue and to wind up the business or venture, and the court, after notice to the guardian, shall enter such order thereon as is in the best interest of the ward's estate.

Committee Notes

Rule History

1975 Revision: Implements section 744.441(16), Florida Statutes. The rule is patterned after rule 5.350 pertaining to the continuance of a business of a decedent by a personal representative.

1977 Revision: No change in rule. Change in committee note to conform to statutory renumbering.

1988 Revision: Change in title of rule; captions added to subdivisions. Committee notes revised. Citation form changes in committee notes.

1989 Revision: Prior rule deleted and replaced by temporary emergency rule.

1991 Revision: Editorial changes in (a), (b), and (e).

1992 Revision: Citation form changes in committee notes.

2008 Revision: Subdivision (a) amended to include persons with a developmental disability. Committee notes revised.

Statutory References

§ 393.12, Fla. Stat. Capacity; appointment of guardian advocate.

§ 744.3085, Fla. Stat. Guardian advocates.

§ 744.441(13), Fla. Stat. Powers of guardian upon court approval.

§ 744.447, Fla. Stat. Petition for authorization to act.

Rule Reference

Fla. Prob. R. 5.350 Continuance of unincorporated business or venture.

RULE 5.645. MANAGEMENT OF PROPERTY OF NONRESIDENT WARD BY FOREIGN GUARDIAN

(a) Petition. A guardian of the property of a nonresident ward, duly appointed by a court of another state, territory, or country, who desires to manage any part or all of the property of the ward located in this state, may file a verified petition for authority to manage the property. The petition shall state:

(1) the circumstances of the guardian's appointment;

(2) a description of the property and its estimated value; and

(3) the indebtedness, if any, existing against the ward in this state.

(b) Designation of Resident Agent. The guardian shall designate a resident agent as required by these rules.

(c) Oath. The guardian shall file an oath as required by these rules.

(d) Filing of Authenticated Copies. The guardian shall file authenticated copies of:

(1) letters of guardianship or other authority to act as guardian; and

(2) bond or other security, if any.

(e) Order. The court shall determine if the foreign bond or other security is sufficient to guarantee the faithful management of the ward's property in this state. The court may require a new guardian's bond in this state in an amount it deems necessary. The order shall authorize the guardian to manage the property and shall specifically describe the property.

Committee Notes

Rule History

2007 Revision: New rule.

Statutory References

§ 744.306, Fla. Stat. Foreign guardians.

§ 744.307, Fla. Stat. Foreign guardian may manage the property of nonresident ward.

Rule References

Fla. Prob. R. 5.110 Address designation for personal representative or guardian; designation of resident agent and acceptance.

Fla. Prob. R. 5.600 Oath.

RULE 5.646. STANDBY GUARDIANS

(a) Petition for Appointment of Standby Guardian for Minor.

(1) Contents. A minor's guardian or the natural guardians of a minor may petition for the appointment of a standby guardian of the person or property of the minor. The petition shall be verified by the petitioner and shall state:

(A) the facts to establish venue;

(B) the petitioner's residence and post office address;

(C) the name, age, and residence and post office address of the minor;

(D) the names and addresses of the parents of the minor and, if none, the next of kin known to the petitioner;

(E) the name and residence and post office address of the proposed standby guardian, and that the proposed standby guardian is qualified to serve;

(F) the proposed standby guardian's relationship to and any previous association with the minor;

(G) the reasons why the proposed standby guardian should be appointed; and

(H) the nature and value of the property subject to the guardianship.

(2) Notice and Waiver of Notice. Notice of the hearing on the petition must be served on the parents, natural or adoptive, of the minor and on any guardian for the minor. Notice may be waived by those required to receive notice or by the court for good cause.

(b) Petition for Appointment of Standby Guardian for Incapacitated Person.

(1) Contents. A currently serving guardian may petition for the appointment of a standby guardian of the person or property of an incapacitated person. The petition shall be verified by the petitioner and shall state:

(A) the petitioner's residence and post office address;

(B) the name, age, and residence and post office address of the incapacitated person;

(C) the nature of the incapacity, the extent of guardianship, either limited or plenary, and the nature and value of property subject to the guardianship;

(D) the names and addresses of the next of kin of the incapacitated person known to the petitioner;

(E) the name and residence and post office address of the proposed standby guardian, and that the proposed standby guardian is qualified to serve;

(F) the proposed standby guardian's relationship to and any previous association with the incapacitated person; and

(G) the reasons why the proposed standby guardian should be appointed.

(2) Notice. Notice of the hearing on the petition must be served on the incapacitated person's next of kin.

(c) Petition for Confirmation.

(1) Contents. A standby guardian, not later than 20 days after the assumption of duties as guardian, shall petition for confirmation of appointment. The petition shall be verified by the petitioner and shall state:

(A) the petitioner's residence and post office address;

(B) the name, age, and residence and post office address of the incapacitated person or minor;

(C) the nature of the incapacity, the extent of guardianship, either limited or plenary, and the nature and value of property subject to the guardianship;

(D) the names and addresses of the next of kin of the incapacitated person or minor known to the petitioner;

(E) the name and residence and post office address of the proposed guardian, and that the proposed guardian is qualified to serve;

(F) the proposed guardian's relationship to and any previous association with the incapacitated person or minor;

(G) the reasons why appointment of the proposed guardian should be confirmed; and

(H) if the proposed guardian is a professional guardian, a statement that the proposed guardian has complied with the educational requirements of section 744.1083, Florida Statutes.

(2) Service. The petition for confirmation and notice of hearing shall be served on the incapacitated person's next of kin a reasonable time before the hearing on the petition or other pleading seeking confirmation of the guardian.

Committee Notes

The standby guardian must file an oath pursuant to rule 5.600 before commencing the exercise of authority as guardian. Prior to appointment, the standby guardian must file an application pursuant to rule 5.590.

Section 393.12(10), Florida Statutes, provides that a guardian advocate shall have all of the duties, responsibilities, and powers of a guardian under Chapter 744, Florida Statutes. However, section 744.304 authorizes the appointment of a standby guardian only for a minor or incapacitated person.

Rule History

2006 Revision: New rule.

2008 Revision: Committee notes revised.

Statutory Reference

§ 744.304, Fla. Stat. Standby guardianship.

Rule References

Fla. Prob. R. 5.590 Application for appointment as guardian; disclosure statement; filing.

Fla. Prob. R. 5.600 Oath.

RULE 5.647. SURROGATE GUARDIAN

(a) Petition for Designation of Surrogate Guardian. A guardian may file a petition to designate a surrogate guardian to exercise the powers of the guardian if the guardian is unavailable to act. The surrogate must be a professional guardian. The petition shall state:

(1) the name and business address of the surrogate guardian;

(2) the requested duration of the appointment; and

(3) the powers to be exercised by the surrogate guardian.

(b) Service. The petition for appointment of a surrogate guardian shall be served on all interested persons and the ward, unless the ward is a minor.

(c) Oath. The surrogate guardian must file with the court an oath swearing or affirming that the surrogate guardian will faithfully perform the duties delegated.

(d) Termination. Prior to the expiration of the period granted by court order, the guardian may terminate the authority of the surrogate guardian by filing a written notice of the termination with the court and serving it on the surrogate guardian.

Committee Notes

Rule History

2006 Revision: New rule.

2008 Revision: Committee notes revised.

Statutory References

§ 393.12, Fla. Stat. Capacity; appointment of guardian advocate.

§ 744.442, Fla. Stat. Delegation of authority.

RULE 5.648. EMERGENCY TEMPORARY GUARDIAN

(a) Petition for Appointment of Emergency Temporary Guardian. Prior to appointment of a guardian but after a petition for determination of incapacity has been filed, the alleged incapacitated person or any adult interested in the welfare of that person may petition for the appointment of an emergency temporary guardian of the person or property. The petition shall be verified and shall state:

(1) the petitioner's residence and post office address;

(2) the name, age, and residence and post office address of the alleged incapacitated person;

(3) that there appears to be imminent danger that the physical or mental health or safety of the alleged incapacitated person will be seriously impaired or that the alleged incapacitated person's property is in danger of being wasted, misappropriated, or lost unless immediate action is taken;

(4) the nature of the emergency and the reason immediate action must be taken;

(5) the extent of the emergency temporary guardianship, either limited or plenary, requested for the alleged incapacitated person, and, if known, the nature and value of the property to be subject to the emergency temporary guardianship;

(6) the names and addresses of the next of kin of the alleged incapacitated person known to the petitioner;

(7) the name and residence and post office address of the proposed emergency temporary guardian, and that the proposed emergency temporary guardian is qualified to serve, or that a willing and qualified emergency temporary guardian has not been located, and;

(8) the proposed emergency temporary guardian's relationship to or any previous association with the alleged incapacitated person.

(b) Notice. Unless the court orders otherwise, notice of filing of the petition for appointment of an emergency temporary guardian and any hearing on the petition shall be served before the hearing on the petition on the alleged incapacitated person and on the alleged incapacitated person's attorney.

(c) Service on Public Guardian. If the petitioner requests appointment of the public guardian as emergency temporary guardian, a copy of the petition and notice shall be served on the public guardian.

(d) Order. The order appointing the emergency temporary guardian shall specify the powers and duties of the emergency temporary guardian.

(e) Extension of Authority. Prior to the expiration of the authority of the emergency temporary guardian, any interested person may file a verified petition for extension of authority of the emergency temporary guardian. The petition must show that the conditions that warranted the initial appointment of the emergency temporary guardian still exist. The petition shall be served on the ward's attorney and on the emergency guardian.

(f) Final Report. An emergency temporary guardian shall file a final report no later than 30 days after the expiration of the emergency temporary guardianship. A copy of the final report shall be served on the successor guardian, if any, the ward, and the ward's attorney. With approval of the court, service on the ward may be accomplished by serving the attorney for the ward.

(1) If the emergency temporary guardian is a guardian of the property, the final report shall consist of a verified inventory of the ward's property as of the date letters of emergency temporary guardianship were issued, a final accounting that gives a full and correct account of the receipts and disbursements of all the ward's property over which the guardian had control, and a statement of the property on hand at the end of the emergency temporary guardianship.

(2) If the emergency temporary guardian is a guardian of the person, the final report shall summarize the activities of the guardian with regard to residential placement, medical condition, mental health and rehabilitative services, and the social condition of the ward to the extent of the authority granted to the emergency temporary guardian.

(3) If the emergency temporary guardian becomes the successor guardian of the property or person of the ward, the final report must satisfy the requirements of, and shall serve as, the initial report of the guardian of the property or person of the ward, as the case may be, as set forth in rule 5.690.

Committee Notes

Rule History

2007 Revision: New rule.

Statutory References

§ 744.3031, Fla. Stat. Emergency temporary guardianship.

§ 744.344(4), Fla. Stat. Order of appointment.

Rule References

Fla. Prob. R. 5.600 Oath.

Fla. Prob. R. 5.690 Initial Guardianship Report.

RULE 5.649. GUARDIAN ADVOCATE

(a) Petition for Appointment of Guardian Advocate. A petition to appoint a guardian advocate for a person with a developmental disability may be executed by an adult person who is a resident of this state. The petition must be verified by the petitioner and must state:

(1) the name, age, and present address of the petitioner and the petitioner's relationship to the person with a developmental disability;

(2) the name, age, county of residence, and present address of the person with a developmental disability;

(3) that the petitioner believes that the person needs a guardian advocate and the factual information on which such belief is based;

(4) the exact areas in which the person lacks the ability to make informed decisions about the person's care and treatment services or to meet the essential requirements for the person's physical health or safety;

(5) the legal disabilities to which the person is subject;

(6) the name of the proposed guardian advocate, the relationship of that person to the person with a

developmental disability, the relationship of the proposed guardian advocate with the providers of health care services, residential services, or other services to the person with developmental disabilities, and the reason why this person should be appointed. If a willing and qualified guardian advocate cannot be located, the petition shall so state; and

(7) whether the petitioner has knowledge, information, or belief that the person with a developmental disability has executed an advance directive under chapter 765, Florida Statutes or a durable power of attorney under chapter 709, Florida Statutes.

(b) Notice.

(1) Notice of the filing of the petition must be given to the person with a developmental disability, both verbally and in writing, in the language of the person and in English. Notice must also be given to the person with a developmental disability's next of kin, any designated health care surrogate, an attorney-in-fact designated in a durable power of attorney, and such other persons as the court may direct. A copy of the petition to appoint a guardian advocate must be served with the notice.

(2) The notice must state that a hearing will be held to inquire into the capacity of the person with a developmental disability to exercise the rights enumerated in the petition. The notice must also state the date of the hearing on the petition.

(3) The notice must state that the person with a developmental disability has the right to be represented by counsel of the person's own choice and that if the person cannot afford an attorney, the court shall appoint one.

(c) Counsel. Within 3 days after a petition has been filed, the court shall appoint an attorney to represent a person with a developmental disability who is the subject of a petition to appoint a guardian advocate. The person with a developmental disability may substitute his or her own attorney for the attorney appointed by the court.

(d) Order. If the court finds the person with a developmental disability requires the appointment of a guardian advocate, the order appointing the guardian advocate shall contain findings of facts and conclusions of law, including:

(1) the nature and scope of the person's inability to make decisions;

(2) the exact areas in which the individual lacks ability to make informed decisions about care and treatment services or to meet the essential requirements for the individual's physical health and safety;

(3) if the person has executed an advance directive or durable power of attorney, a determination as to whether the documents sufficiently address the needs of the person and a finding that the advance directive or durable power of attorney does not provide an alternative to the appointment of a guardian advocate that sufficiently addresses the needs of the person with a developmental disability;

(4) if a durable power of attorney exists, the powers of the attorney-in-fact, if any, that are suspended and granted to the guardian advocate;

(5) if an advance directive exists and the court determines that the appointment of a guardian advocate is necessary, the authority, if any, the guardian advocate shall exercise over the health care surrogate;

(6) the specific legal disabilities to which the person with a developmental disability is subject;

(7) the name of the person selected as guardian advocate; and

(8) the powers, duties, and responsibilities of the guardian advocate, including bonding of the guardian advocate as provided by law.

Committee Notes

Rule History

2008 Revision: New rule.

Statutory References

§ 393.063(9), Fla. Stat. Definitions.

§ 393.12, Fla. Stat. Capacity; appointment of guardian advocate.

§ 709.08, Fla. Stat. Durable power of attorney.

§ 765.101, Fla. Stat. Definitions.

§ 765.104, Fla. Stat. Amendment or revocation.

§ 765.202, Fla. Stat. Designation of a health care surrogate.

§ 765.204, Fla. Stat. Capacity of principal; procedure.

§ 765.205(3), Fla. Stat. Responsibility of the surrogate.

§ 765.302, Fla. Stat. Procedure for making a living will; notice to physician.

§ 765.401, Fla. Stat. The proxy.

Rule References

Fla. Prob. R. 5.020 Pleadings; verification; motions.

Fla. Prob. R. 5.540 Hearings.

Fla. Prob. R. 5.681 Restoration of rights of person with developmental disability.

RULE 5.650. RESIGNATION OR DISQUALIFICATION OF GUARDIAN; APPOINTMENT OF SUCCESSOR

(a) **Resignation and Petition for Discharge.** A guardian seeking to resign shall file a resignation and petition for discharge.

(b) **Contents.** The resignation and petition for discharge shall state:

(1) that the guardian wishes to resign and be relieved of all duties as guardian;

(2) the amount of compensation to be paid to the guardian and to the attorneys, accountants, or other agents employed by the guardian; and

(3) the names and addresses of the successor guardian and the successor guardian's attorney, or that a successor guardian has not yet been appointed or duly qualified.

(c) **Final Report.** A resigning guardian of the property shall file a final report showing receipts, disbursements, amounts reserved for unpaid and anticipated costs and fees, and other relevant financial information from the date of the previous annual accounting, and a list of assets to be turned over to the successor guardian.

(d) **Notice.** A notice shall be served stating that:

(1) any objection shall be in writing and shall state with particularity each item to which the objection is directed and the grounds on which the objection is based;

(2) any objection to the resignation, petition for discharge, or final report shall be filed within 30 days from the date of service of the petition for discharge; and

(3) within 90 days after filing of the objection, a notice of hearing thereon shall be served or the objection is abandoned.

(e) **Service.** A copy of the resignation, petition for discharge, final report, and notice of resignation and petition for discharge shall be served on the ward, any surety on the guardian's bond, any successor guardian, and such other persons as the court may direct.

(f) **Objections.** Objections shall be in the form and be filed within the time set forth in the notice of resignation and petition for discharge. A copy of the objections shall be served by the objector on the ward, all guardians, any surety on the guardian's bond, and any successor guardian.

(g) **Disposition of Objections.** Any interested person may set a hearing on the objections. Notice of the hearing shall be served on the guardian, the successor guardian, if any, and any other interested persons. If a notice of hearing on the objections is not served within 90 days of filing of the objections, the objections will be deemed abandoned.

(h) **Discharge.** The guardian's resignation shall not be accepted and the guardian shall not be discharged until all objections have been withdrawn, abandoned, or judicially resolved and a successor guardian has been appointed and duly qualified. After all objections have been withdrawn, abandoned, or judicially resolved, if the court is satisfied that the resigning guardian has faithfully discharged the duties of the guardianship and the interests of the ward are protected, and the resigning guardian of the property has delivered the assets of the ward, all guardianship records, and all money due to the ward from the guardian to the remaining or successor guardian, the court shall enter an order accepting resignation of guardian and granting discharge.

(i) Disqualification. Any guardian who is improperly appointed, or who becomes disqualified to act after appointment, shall immediately file a resignation and petition for discharge and proceed in accordance with this rule.

(j) Nonresident Guardians. Nonresident guardians appointed before October 1, 1989, shall not be automatically disqualified to serve and shall not be required to resign and initiate their own removal.

(k) Guardian Advocates. This rule shall apply to guardian advocates, except that a final report shall be required of a guardian advocate only if the guardian advocate's authority included the management of the property of the person with a developmental disability.

Committee Notes

Rule History

1975 Revision: Substantially the same as sections 744.467 and 744.471, Florida Statutes, with editorial changes.

1977 Revision: No change in rule. Change in committee note to conform to statutory renumbering.

1988 Revision: Editorial changes in (a). Text of rule 5.590 inserted in (b). Editorial change in (c). Captions added to subdivisions. Committee notes revised. Citation form changes in committee notes.

1989 Revision: Prior rule deleted and replaced by temporary emergency rule.

1991 Revision: Substantial revision of entire rule to harmonize with procedure for termination of guardianship under rules 5.670 and 5.680. Subdivision (k) transferred from temporary emergency rule 5.800.

1992 Revision: Committee notes revised. Citation form changes in committee notes.

2007 Revision: Subdivision (i) deleted because right of waiver is substantive. Subsequent subdivisions relettered.

2008 Revision: Subdivision (k) added to include guardian advocates. Committee notes revised.

2012 Revision: Committee notes revised.

Statutory References

§ 393.12, Fla. Stat. Capacity; appointment of guardian advocate.

§ 744.102(11), Fla. Stat. Definitions.

§ 744.3085, Fla. Stat. Guardian advocates.

§ 744.467, Fla. Stat. Resignation of guardian.

§ 744.471, Fla. Stat. Appointment of successor.

Rule References

Fla. Prob. R. 5.040 Notice.

Fla. Prob. R. 5.041 Service of pleadings and documents.

Fla. Prob. R. 5.180 Waiver and consent.

Fla. Prob. R. 5.610 Execution by guardian.

Fla. Prob. R. 5.649 Guardian advocate.

Fla. Prob. R. 5.681 Restoration of rights of person with developmental disability.

Fla. R. Jud. Admin. 2.516 Service of pleadings and documents.

RULE 5.660. PROCEEDINGS FOR REMOVAL OF GUARDIAN

(a) Notice. Proceedings for removal of a guardian may be instituted by a court, by any surety or other interested person, or by the ward, and formal notice of the petition for removal of a guardian shall be served on all guardians, other interested persons, any next of kin, and the ward. The pleading shall state with particularity the reasons why the guardian should be removed.

(b) Accounting. A removed guardian shall file with the court an accounting for the guardianship within 20 days after the guardian's removal. A copy of the accounting shall be served on the successor guardian and the ward, unless the ward is a minor.

(c) Transfer of Property and Records. The removed guardian (or the guardian's heirs, personal representative, or surety) shall turn over all the property of the ward in the removed guardian's control and all guardianship records to the duly qualified successor. The successor guardian shall, or the ward may, demand of the removed guardian (or the guardian's heirs, personal representative, or surety) all of those items.

(d) Failure to Comply. If a removed guardian fails to file a true, complete, and final accounting for the guardianship or to turn over to the successor all property of the ward in the removed guardian's control and all guardianship records, the court shall issue a show-cause order.

(e) Guardian Advocates. Subdivisions (b) through (d) of this rule shall apply to guardian advocates only to the extent that the guardian advocate was granted authority over the property of the person with a developmental disability.

Committee Notes

Rule History

1977 Revision: No change in rule. Change in committee notes to conform to statutory renumbering.

1980 Revision: Subdivision (a) amended to specifically authorize any guardian or next of kin to file the petition and to require formal notice in conformity with rule 5.630(b).

1984 Revision: Subdivision (b) amended to conform to statute. Editorial changes and committee notes revised.

1988 Revision: Subdivision (a) rewritten for clarity. Language in (b) deleted as surplusage. Editorial change in caption of (c). Committee notes revised. Citation form change in committee notes.

1989 Revision: Prior rule deleted and replaced by temporary emergency rule.

1991 Revision: Subdivision (a) amended to require that the petition allege specific reasons why the guardian should be removed and to require service of the petition on the ward. Otherwise, editorial changes in all subdivisions.

1992 Revision: Citation form changes in committee notes.

2006 Revision: Requirement in (b) to serve minors deleted to conform to 2006 amendment to section 744.511, Florida Statutes.

2008 Revision: Subdivision (e) added to include guardian advocates. Committee notes revised.

2012 Revision: Committee notes revised.

Statutory References

§ 393.12, Fla. Stat. Capacity; appointment of guardian advocate.

§ 744.3085, Fla. Stat. Guardian advocates.

§ 744.474, Fla. Stat. Reasons for removal of guardian.

§ 744.477, Fla. Stat. Proceedings for removal of a guardian.

§ 744.511, Fla. Stat. Accounting upon removal.

§ 744.514, Fla. Stat. Surrender of assets upon removal.

§ 744.517, Fla. Stat. Proceedings for contempt.

Rule References

Fla. Prob. R. 5.025 Adversary proceedings.

Fla. Prob. R. 5.040 Notice.

Fla. Prob. R. 5.041 Service of pleadings and documents.

Fla. Prob. R. 5.649 Guardian advocate.

Fla. R. Jud. Admin. 2.516 Service of pleadings and documents.

RULE 5.670. TERMINATION OF GUARDIANSHIP ON CHANGE OF DOMICILE OF RESIDENT WARD

(a) Petition for Discharge. The Florida guardian may file a petition for discharge when the domicile of a resident ward has changed to a foreign jurisdiction, the foreign court having jurisdiction over the ward at the ward's new domicile has appointed a foreign guardian, and the foreign guardian has qualified and posted a bond in the amount required by the foreign court.

(b) Contents of Petition. The petition for discharge shall state:

(1) that the grounds set forth in subdivision (a) have occurred;

(2) that the guardian has fully administered the Florida guardianship; and

(3) the amount of compensation to be paid to the guardian and to the attorneys, accountants, or other agents employed by the guardian.

(c) Final Report. The Florida guardian of the property shall file a final report showing receipts, disbursements, amounts reserved for unpaid and anticipated costs and fees, and other relevant financial information from the date of the previous annual accounting, and a list of the assets to be turned over to the foreign guardian.

(d) Notice. The Florida guardian of the property shall publish a notice as required by law, which shall state:

(1) the name of the ward;

(2) the file number of the guardianship;

(3) the designation and address of the court;

(4) the name and address of the guardian and the guardian's attorney;

(5) the name and address of the foreign guardian and the foreign guardian's attorney, if any;

(6) the date of first publication;

(7) that a petition for discharge has been filed upon the grounds of change of domicile of the ward;

(8) the date the guardian will apply for discharge;

(9) that the jurisdiction of the ward will be transferred to the foreign jurisdiction;

(10) that any objection shall be in writing and shall state with particularity each item to which the objection is directed and the grounds on which the objection is based;

(11) that any objection to the final report or the petition for discharge shall be filed within the later of 30 days from the date of service of the petition for discharge or the date of first publication of the notice; and

(12) that within 90 days after filing of the objection, a notice of hearing thereon shall be served or the objection is abandoned.

(e) Service. A copy of the petition for discharge and of the notice of petition for discharge shall be served on the foreign guardian and such other persons as the court may direct.

(f) Objections. Objections shall be in the form and be filed within the time set forth in the notice of petition for discharge. A copy of the objections shall be served by the objector on the Florida guardian and the foreign guardian.

(g) Disposition of Objections. Any interested person may set a hearing on the objections. Notice of the hearing shall be served on the Florida guardian, the foreign guardian, and any other interested persons. If a notice of hearing on the objections is not served within 90 days of filing of the objections, the objections will be deemed abandoned.

(h) Discharge. The Florida guardian may not be discharged until all objections have been withdrawn, abandoned, or judicially resolved. After all objections have been withdrawn, abandoned, or judicially resolved, if the court is satisfied that the Florida guardian has faithfully discharged the duties of the guardianship and the interests of the ward are protected, and the Florida guardian of the property has delivered the assets of the ward to the foreign guardian, the court shall enter an order of discharge.

Committee Notes

Rule History

1977 Revision: Change in committee notes to conform to statutory renumbering.

1984 Revision: Adds 30-day requirement for filing objections. Editorial changes and committee notes revised.

1988 Revision: Editorial change in (c). First and last sentences of (d) deleted and clarifying word added.

1989 Revision: Prior rule adopted as temporary emergency rule.

1991 Revision: Substantial revision of entire rule to harmonize with procedure for discharge of guardian under rule 5.680 and to conform to section 744.524, Florida Statutes.

1992 Revision: Committee notes revised. Citation form changes in committee notes.

2007 Revision: Subdivision (i) deleted because right of waiver is substantive. Committee notes revised.

2008 Revision: Committee notes revised.

2012 Revision: Committee notes revised.

Statutory References

§ 393.12, Fla. Stat. Capacity; appointment of guardian advocate.

§ 744.102(8), (9), Fla. Stat. Definitions.

§ 744.201, Fla. Stat. Domicile of ward.

§ 744.202, Fla. Stat. Venue.

§ 744.2025, Fla. Stat. Change of ward's residence.

§ 744.524, Fla. Stat. Termination of guardianship on change of domicile of resident ward.

§ 744.531, Fla. Stat. Order of discharge.

Rule References

Fla. Prob. R. 5.041 Service of pleadings and documents.

Fla. Prob. R. 5.180 Waiver and consent.

Fla. Prob. R. 5.610 Execution by guardian.

Fla. Prob. R. 5.680 Termination of guardianship.

Fla. R. Jud. Admin. 2.516 Service of pleadings and documents.

RULE 5.680. TERMINATION OF GUARDIANSHIP

(a) Petition for Discharge. When the ward has become sui juris, has terminated a voluntary guardianship, has been restored to capacity, has had all rights restored, or has died, or when the guardian has been unable to locate the ward after diligent search, or, for a guardian of the property, when the property subject to the guardianship has been exhausted, the guardian shall file a petition for discharge. A guardian of the person is discharged without further proceeding upon filing a certified copy of the ward's death certificate.

(b) Contents of Petition. The petition for discharge shall state:

(1) the reason for termination of the guardianship;

(2) that the guardian has fully administered the guardianship; and

(3) the amount of unpaid and anticipated costs and fees to be paid to the guardian and to the attorneys, accountants, or other agents employed by the guardian.

(c) Final Report. The guardian of the property shall promptly file a final report. If the ward has died, the guardian must file the report no later than 45 days after he or she has been served with letters of administration, letters of curatorship, or an order of summary administration. The report shall show receipts, disbursements, amounts reserved for unpaid and anticipated disbursements, costs, and fees, including the amounts set forth in subdivision (b)(3), and other relevant financial information from the date of the previous annual accounting, and a list of the assets to be turned over to the person entitled to them.

(d) Notice. A notice shall be served stating:

(1) that any objection shall be in writing and shall state with particularity each item to which the objection is directed and the grounds on which the objection is based;

(2) that any objection to the final report or the petition for discharge shall be filed within 30 days from the date of service of the petition for discharge; and

(3) that within 90 days after filing of the objection, a notice of hearing thereon shall be served or the objection is abandoned.

(e) Service. The guardian applying for discharge shall serve a copy of the petition for discharge and final report on the ward, on the personal representative of a deceased ward, or if there are no assets justifying qualification of a personal representative for the estate of a deceased ward, on the known next of kin of the deceased ward, or such other persons as the court may direct; provided, however, that a guardian of the property who is subsequently appointed personal representative shall serve a copy of the petition for discharge and final report on all beneficiaries of the ward's estate.

(f) Objections. All persons served shall have 30 days to file objections to the petition for discharge and final report. The objections shall state with particularity the items to which the objections are directed and shall state the grounds on which the objections are based. Copies of the objections shall be served by the objector on the guardian. Any interested person may set a hearing on the objections. Notice of the hearing shall be served on the guardian and any other interested persons. If a notice of hearing on the objections is not served within 90 days of filing of the objections, the objections will be deemed abandoned. The guardian may not be discharged until all objections have been withdrawn, abandoned, or judicially resolved, and the petition for discharge of the guardian is granted by the court.

(g) Discharge. The guardian may not be discharged until all objections are withdrawn, abandoned, or judicially resolved. After all objections are withdrawn, abandoned, or judicially resolved, and if it appears that the guardian has paid all amounts reserved to the persons entitled to them and has made full and complete distribution of the ward's assets to the persons entitled to them and has otherwise faithfully discharged the duties of the guardian, the court shall grant the petition for discharge and enter an order of discharge. If objections are filed and are not withdrawn, abandoned, or judicially resolved, the court shall conduct a hearing in the same manner as for a hearing on objections to annual guardianship plans. After hearing, if the court is satisfied that the guardian has faithfully discharged the duties of the guardianship and the interests of the ward are protected, and the guardian has rendered a complete and accurate final report and has delivered the assets of the ward to the person entitled to them, the court shall enter an order of discharge.

Committee Notes

Rule History

1975 Revision: Implements sections 744.527 and 744.531, Florida Statutes, and also requires the guardian applying for discharge to do so by filing a petition for discharge and provides the procedure pertaining thereto.

1977 Revision: No change in rule. Change in committee note to conform to statutory renumbering.

1988 Revision: Captions added to subdivisions. Committee notes revised. Citation form changes in committee notes.

1989 Revision: Prior rule deleted and replaced by temporary emergency rule.

1991 Revision: Substantial revision of entire rule to harmonize with procedure for discharge of personal representatives under rules 5.400 and 5.401.

1992 Revision: Committee notes revised. Citation form changes in committee notes.

1996 Revision: Editorial changes to clarify that all anticipated costs and fees should be shown on final report and thereafter paid prior to transfer of assets and discharge of guardian.

2003 Revision: Subdivision (a) amended to reflect addition of rule 5.552 dealing with voluntary guardianship of property. Committee notes revised.

2006 Revision: Subdivision (c) amended to conform to 2006 amendments to section 744.527, Florida Statutes. Subdivision (h) deleted as unnecessary because substantive right of waiver is provided by section 731.302, Florida Statutes.

2008 Revision: Reference to restoration of rights added in subdivision (a). Committee notes revised.

2012 Revision: Committee notes revised.

Statutory References

§ 393.12, Fla. Stat. Capacity; appointment of guardian advocate.

§ 744.521, Fla. Stat. Termination of guardianship.

§ 744.527, Fla. Stat. Final reports and application for discharge; hearing.

§ 744.528, Fla. Stat. Discharge of guardian named as personal representative.

§ 744.531, Fla. Stat. Order of discharge.

§ 744.534, Fla. Stat. Disposition of unclaimed funds held by guardian.

Rule References

Fla. Prob. R. 5.040 Notice.

Fla. Prob. R. 5.041 Service of pleadings and documents.

Fla. Prob. R. 5.180 Waiver and consent.

Fla. Prob. R. 5.552 Voluntary guardianship of property.

Fla. Prob. R. 5.610 Execution by guardian.

Fla. Prob. R. 5.681 Restoration of rights of person with developmental disability.

Fla. R. Jud. Admin. 2.516 Service of pleadings and documents.

RULE 5.681. RESTORATION OF RIGHTS OF PERSON WITH DEVELOPMENTAL DISABILITY

(a) Contents of Petition. A petition for restoration of rights of a person with a developmental disability shall contain:

(1) facts that support the suggestion that restoration is feasible and would not pose a detriment to the health or welfare of the ward; and

(2) a statement that the person with a developmental disability is capable of exercising some or all of the rights that were granted to the guardian advocate.

(b) Counsel. Within 3 days after filing the petition, counsel shall be appointed for the person for whom a guardian advocate has been appointed as provided by law.

(c) Notice. Upon the appointment of counsel, the clerk shall immediately send notice of the filing of the petition, together with a copy of the petition, to the person for whom a guardian advocate was appointed, the person's guardian advocate, the person's attorney, and any other interested person as directed by the court. The notice must contain a statement that all objections to the petition must be filed within 20 days after service of the notice. Formal notice shall be served on the guardian advocate. Informal notice may be served on the other persons. The clerk shall file proof of service. Notice need not be served on the petitioner.

(d) Objections. Any objection shall be in writing and shall state with particularity each item to which the objection is directed and the grounds on which the objection is based. The objector shall serve a copy of the objection on the person with the developmental disability, the person's attorney, the person's guardian advocate, and any other interested persons as directed by the court.

(e) Order.

(1) With Hearing. The court shall enter an order denying the petition or restoring all or some of the rights that were granted to the guardian advocate. If only some rights are restored to the person with a developmental disability, the order must state which rights are restored and amend the letters of guardian advocacy accordingly.

(2) Without Hearing. If the petitioner has attached evidence supporting the petition and if no objection is filed, the court may restore all or some of the person's rights that were granted to a guardian advocate.

(f) Amended Plan. Within 60 days after the order restoring rights is entered, the guardian advocate shall file an amended plan. A copy of the amended plan and accounting shall be served on the person with a developmental disability and the person's attorney.

Committee Notes

Rule History

2008 Revision: New rule.

Statutory References

§ 393.063(9), Fla. Stat. Definitions.

§ 393.12, Fla. Stat. Capacity; appointment of guardian advocate.

§ 709.08, Fla. Stat. Durable power of attorney.

§ 765.101, Fla. Stat. Definitions.

§ 765.104, Fla. Stat. Amendment or revocation.

§ 765.202, Fla. Stat. Designation of a health care surrogate.

§ 765.204, Fla. Stat. Capacity of principal; procedure.

§ 765.205(3), Fla. Stat. Responsibility of the surrogate.

§ 765.302, Fla. Stat. Procedure for making a living will; notice to physician.

§ 765.401, Fla. Stat. The proxy.

Rule References

Fla. Prob. R. 5.020 Pleadings; verification; motions.

Fla. Prob. R. 5.540 Hearings.

Fla. Prob. R. 5.541 Recording of hearings.

Fla. Prob. R. 5.680 Termination of guardianship.

RULE 5.685. DETERMINATION REGARDING ALTERNATIVES TO GUARDIANSHIP

(a) Reporting by Guardian. The guardian shall promptly file a report attaching a copy of a final order or judgment that determines the validity of a ward's durable power of attorney, trust, or trust amendment.

(b) Petition. At any time after the appointment of a guardian, the guardian, the ward, the ward's attorney, if any, or any other interested person may file a verified petition stating that there is an alternative to guardianship that will sufficiently address the problems of the ward.

(c) Contents of Petition. The petition to determine alternatives to guardianship shall state:

(1) the petitioner's interest in the proceeding; and

(2) the facts constituting the basis for the relief sought and that the proposed alternative to guardian-

ship will sufficiently address the problems of the ward and is in the ward's best interest.

(d) Service. The petition shall be served on the guardian, the ward, the ward's attorney, if any, those interested persons who have filed requests for notices and copies of pleadings, and such other persons as the court may direct.

(e) Order. The order shall specify whether there is an alternative to guardianship that will sufficiently address the problems of the ward, the continued need for a guardian, and the extent of the need for delegation of the ward's rights.

Committee Notes

Rule History

2006 Revision: New rule.

Statutory References

§ 744.331, Fla. Stat. Procedures to determine incapacity.

§ 744.462, Fla. Stat. Determination regarding alternatives to guardianship.

RULE 5.690. INITIAL GUARDIANSHIP REPORT

(a) Contents and Filing. An initial guardianship report shall be filed within 60 days after the issuance of letters of guardianship. The guardian of the property shall file the initial guardianship report consisting of the verified inventory. The guardian of the person shall file the initial guardianship report consisting of the guardianship plan.

(b) Service. Copies of the initial guardianship report shall be served on the ward, unless the ward is a minor under the age of 14 years or is totally incapacitated, and the attorney for the ward, if any. With approval of the court, service on the ward may be accomplished by serving the attorney for the ward.

Committee Notes

The committee recognizes the conflict between this rule and section 744.362, Florida Statutes, which requires the filing of the initial guardianship report (which includes the inventory) within 60 days after appointment. The committee believes this provision, which attempts to regulate when a paper must be filed with the court, is procedural and that a guardian may not receive letters of guardianship empowering the guardian to act contemporaneously with the appointment. Therefore, the issuance of letters is a more practical time from which to measure the beginning of the time period for the accomplishment of this act.

In the event the guardian of the property and the guardian of the person are not the same entity or person, they shall make a good faith effort to jointly file the initial guardianship report.

Rule History

1991 Revision: New rule.

1992 Revision: Addition of phrase in subdivision (b) to conform to 1992 amendment to section 744.362(1), Florida Statutes. Citation form changes in committee notes.

2012 Revision: Committee notes revised.

Statutory References

§ 744.362, Fla. Stat. Initial guardianship report.

§ 744.363, Fla. Stat. Initial guardianship plan.

§ 744.365, Fla. Stat. Verified inventory.

§ 744.3701, Fla. Stat. Inspection of report.

§ 744.384, Fla. Stat. Subsequently discovered or acquired property.

Rule References

Fla. Prob. R. 5.020 Pleadings; verification; motions.

Fla. Prob. R. 5.041 Service of pleadings and documents.

Fla. Prob. R. 5.060 Request for notices and copies of pleadings.

Fla. Prob. R. 5.180 Waiver and consent.

Fla. Prob. R. 5.610 Execution by guardian.

Fla. Prob. R. 5.620 Inventory.

Fla. Prob. R. 5.700 Objection to guardianship reports.

Fla. R. Jud. Admin. 2.516 Service of pleadings and documents.

RULE 5.695. ANNUAL GUARDIANSHIP REPORTS

(a) Contents and Filing.

(1) Guardian of the Person. Unless the court requires reporting on a calendar year basis, the guardian of the person shall file an annual guardianship plan within 90 days after the last day of the anniversary month in which the letters of guardianship were issued. The plan shall be for the year ending on the last day of such anniversary month. If the court requires reporting on a calendar year basis, the guardianship plan shall be filed on or before April 1 of each year.

(2) Guardian of the Property. Unless the court requires or authorizes reporting on a fiscal year basis, the guardian of the property shall file an annual accounting on or before April 1 of each year. The annual accounting shall cover the preceding annual accounting period. If the court requires or authorizes reporting on a fiscal year basis, the annual accounting shall be filed on or before the first day of the fourth month after the end of the fiscal year.

(b) Service. Copies of the annual plan and accounting shall be served on the ward, unless the ward is a minor or is totally incapacitated, and the attorney for the ward, if any. With the approval of the court, service on the ward may be accomplished by serving the attorney for the ward. The guardian shall serve copies on such other persons as the court may direct.

Committee Notes

The annual guardianship report consists of the annual plan for the guardian of the person and the annual accounting for the guardian of the property.

For annual guardianship reports regarding minors, see rule 5.555.

With approval of the court, service on the ward may be accomplished by service on the attorney for the ward, if any. The committee was concerned that actual service on a ward of the accounting or guardianship plan may give uninterested persons access to financial or personal information to the detriment of the ward. The committee believes that under such circumstances, the guardian of the property could seek an order under section 744.371(5), Florida Statutes, even if the ward's circumstances were set out in detail in a pleading other than the annual guardianship report. Such court order may be sought in appropriate circumstances at the time of the initial hearing to determine incapacity.

Rule History

1975 Revision: Substantially the same as section 744.427(1), (2), and (4), Florida Statutes, and section 744.437, Florida Statutes, with editorial changes and providing for the waiving, by a ward who has become sui juris or by the personal representative of a deceased ward, of the filing of an annual accounting. The rule requires the guardian of the property of a ward to appear before the court at the time he files his annual accounting or at such time the court shall determine in order that the court may inquire as to any matter relating to the physical and financial well-being of the ward. This appears to be in conflict with section 744.437, Florida Statutes, which refers to "every guardian" but in the same sentence it refers to "at the time the guardian files his annual return" and only the guardian of the property is required to file an annual accounting.

1977 Revision: No change in rule. Change in committee note to conform to statutory renumbering.

1980 Revision: Subdivision (e) amended to avoid conflict with statutory changes in section 744.437, Florida Statutes (1979).

1988 Revision: Matter in (b) deleted; covered in sections 744.427(2) and 744.434, Florida Statutes. Subdivision (c) deleted; covered in section 744.427(4), Florida Statutes. Captions added to subdivisions. Committee notes revised. Citation form changes in committee notes.

1989 Revision: Prior rule deleted and replaced by temporary emergency rule.

1991 Revision: Substantial changes and rule renumbered.

1992 Revision: Addition of language in subdivisions (a)(1) and (a)(2) to implement 1992 amendments to sections 744.367(1) and (2), Florida Statutes. Committee notes revised. Citation form changes in committee notes.

2006 Revision: Requirement in (b) to serve minors age 14 and above deleted to conform to amendment to section 744.367(3), Florida Statutes. Committee notes revised.

2012 Revision: Committee notes revised.

Statutory References

§ 744.367, Fla. Stat. Duty to file annual guardianship report.

§ 744.3675, Fla. Stat. Annual guardianship plan.

§ 744.3678, Fla. Stat. Annual accounting.

§ 744.3685, Fla. Stat. Order requiring guardianship report; contempt.

§ 744.3701, Fla. Stat. Inspection of report.

§ 744.371, Fla. Stat. Relief to be granted.

§ 744.3735, Fla. Stat. Annual appearance of the guardian.

Rule References

Fla. Prob. R. 5.020 Pleadings; verification; motions.

Fla. Prob. R. 5.041 Service of pleadings and documents.

Fla. Prob. R. 5.060 Request for notices and copies of pleadings.

Fla. Prob. R. 5.180 Waiver and consent.

Fla. Prob. R. 5.552 Voluntary guardianship of property.

Fla. Prob. R. 5.555 Guardianships of minors.

Fla. Prob. R. 5.610 Execution by guardian.

Fla. Prob. R. 5.700 Objection to guardianship reports.

Fla. Prob. R. 5.800(b) Application of revised chapter 744 to existing guardianships.

Fla. R. Jud. Admin. 2.516 Service of pleadings and documents.

RULE 5.696. ANNUAL ACCOUNTING

(a) **Contents and Filing.** The guardian of the property shall file an annual accounting as required by law. The annual accounting shall include:

(1) a full and correct account of the receipts and disbursements of all of the ward's property over which the guardian has control and a statement of the ward's property on hand at the end of the accounting period; and

(2) a copy of the statements of all of the ward's cash accounts as of the end of the accounting period from each institution where the cash is deposited.

(b) **Substantiating Papers.** Unless otherwise ordered by the court, the guardian need not file the papers substantiating the annual accounting. Upon reasonable written request, the guardian of the property shall make the substantiating papers available for examination to persons entitled to receive or inspect the annual accounting.

(c) **Interim Inspection of Records.** Upon reasonable written request and notice, the guardian of the property shall make all material financial records pertaining to the guardianship available for inspections to those persons entitled to receive or inspect the annual accounting.

Committee Notes

Rule History

1991 Revision: New rule.

1992 Revision: Citation form changes in committee notes.

2010 Revision: Editorial change in (b) to delete redundant language.

2012 Revision: Committee notes revised.

Statutory References

§ 744.367, Fla. Stat. Duty to file annual guardianship report.

§ 744.3678, Fla. Stat. Annual accounting.

§ 744.3701, Fla. Stat. Inspection of report.

§ 744.3735, Fla. Stat. Annual appearance of the guardian.

Rule References

Fla. Prob. R. 5.020 Pleadings; verification; motions.

Fla. Prob. R. 5.041 Service of pleadings and documents.

Fla. Prob. R. 5.060 Request for notices and copies of pleadings.

Fla. Prob. R. 5.610 Execution by guardian.

Fla. Prob. R. 5.695 Annual guardianship report.

Fla. Prob. R. 5.700 Objection to guardianship reports.

Fla. R. Jud. Admin. 2.516 Service of pleadings and documents.

RULE 5.697. MAGISTRATES' REVIEW OF GUARDIANSHIP INVENTORIES, ACCOUNTINGS, AND PLANS

(a) **General Magistrates.** The court may appoint general magistrates to review guardianship inventories, accountings, and plans. General magistrates shall be members of The Florida Bar and shall continue in office until removed by the court. The order appointing a general magistrate shall be recorded. Each general magistrate shall take the oath required of officers of the court by the Florida Constitution. The oath shall be recorded before the magistrate begins to act.

(b) Special Magistrates. In connection with the court's review of guardianship inventories, accountings, and plans, the court may appoint members of The Florida Bar as special magistrates for any particular service required by the court. Special magistrates shall be governed by all laws and rules relating to general magistrates except special magistrates shall not be required to take an oath unless specifically required by the court. For good cause shown, the court may appoint a person other than a member of The Florida Bar as a special magistrate.

(c) General Powers and Duties. Every magistrate shall act under the direction of the court. Process issued by a magistrate shall be directed as provided by law. All grounds for disqualification of a judge shall apply to magistrates.

(d) Hearings. Hearings before any magistrate may be held in the county where the action is pending, or at any other place by order of the court for the convenience of the witnesses or the parties. A magistrate shall give notice of hearings to all parties. If any party fails to appear, the magistrate may proceed ex parte or may continue the hearing to a future day, with notice to the absent party. The magistrate shall proceed with reasonable diligence and the least practicable delay. Any party may apply to the court for an order directing the magistrate to accelerate the proceedings and to make a report promptly. Evidence shall be taken in writing or by electronic recording by the magistrate or by some other person under the magistrate's authority in the magistrate's presence and shall be filed with the magistrate's report. The magistrate may examine and take testimony from the parties and their witnesses under oath, on all matters authorized by the court for review by the magistrate and may require production of all books, papers, writings, vouchers, and other documents applicable to those matters. The magistrate shall admit only evidence that would be admissible in court. The magistrate may take all actions concerning evidence that may be taken by the court.

(e) Magistrate's Report. The magistrate's report shall contain a description of the matters considered and the magistrate's conclusions and any recommendations. No part of any statement of facts, account, charge, deposition, examination, or answer used before the magistrate shall be recited. The magistrate shall be required to file a report only if a hearing is held pursuant to subdivision (d) of this rule or if specifically directed to do so by the court.

(f) Filing Report; Service; Exceptions. The magistrate shall file a report with the court and serve copies on the parties. The parties may serve exceptions to the report within 10 days from the date the report is served on them. If no exceptions are timely filed, the court shall take appropriate action on the report. All timely filed exceptions may shall be heard by the court on reasonable notice by any party.

Committee Notes

Rule History

1991 Revision: This is a new rule, patterned after Florida Rule of Civil Procedure 1.490.

1992 Revision: Editorial change. Citation form change in committee notes.

2007 Revision: Title of rule and subdivisions (a) and (b) amended to include inventories. "Shall" substituted for "may" in last sentence of subdivision (f). Committee notes revised.

Statutory Reference

§ 744.369(2), Fla. Stat. Judicial review of guardianship reports.

Rule Reference

Fla. Prob. R. 5.095 General and special magistrates.

Fla. R. Civ. P. 1.490 Magistrates.

RULE 5.700. OBJECTION TO GUARDIANSHIP REPORTS

(a) Objections. The ward, or any other interested person, may file an objection to any part of a guardianship report within the time provided by law.

(b) Contents. Any objection shall be in writing and shall state with particularity each item to which the objection is directed and the grounds on which the objection is based.

(c) Service. The objector shall serve a copy of the objection on each guardian and on any other person as directed by the court.

Committee Notes

Rule History

1975 Revision: Substantially the same as section 744.427(3), (5), and (6), Florida Statutes, with editorial changes.

1977 Revision: No change in rule. Change in committee note to conform to statutory renumbering.

1988 Revision: Captions added to subdivisions. Committee notes revised. Citation form change in committee notes.

1989 Revision: Prior rule deleted and replaced by temporary emergency rule.

1991 Revision: Revised to conform with new statutory requirements.

1992 Revision: Citation form changes in committee notes.

2008 Revision: Committee notes revised.

2012 Revision: Committee notes revised.

Statutory References

§ 393.12, Fla. Stat. Capacity; appointment of guardian advocate.

§ 744.362, Fla. Stat. Initial guardianship report.

§ 744.363, Fla. Stat. Initial guardianship plan.

§ 744.365, Fla. Stat. Verified inventory.

§ 744.367, Fla. Stat. Duty to file annual guardianship report.

§ 744.3675, Fla. Stat. Annual guardianship plan.

§ 744.3678, Fla. Stat. Annual accounting.

Rule References

Fla. Prob. R. 5.020 Pleadings; verification; motions.

Fla. Prob. R. 5.041 Service of pleadings and documents.

Fla. Prob. R. 5.060 Request for notices and copies of pleadings.

Fla. Prob. R. 5.180 Waiver and consent.

Fla. Prob. R. 5.610 Execution by guardian.

Fla. R. Jud. Admin. 2.516 Service of pleadings and documents.

RULE 5.705. PETITION FOR INTERIM JUDICIAL REVIEW

(a) Contents. A petition for interim judicial review shall be verified, state the petitioner's interest in the proceeding, state with particularity the manner in which the guardian's action or proposed action does not comply with or exceeds the guardian's authority under the guardian plan, and state why the action or proposed action of the guardian is not in the best interest of the ward.

(b) Service. The petition shall be served by formal notice.

(c) Hearing. The petitioner or any interested person may set the matter for hearing.

(d) Expedited Proceedings. For good cause shown, the court may shorten the time for response to the formal notice and may set an expedited hearing.

Committee Notes

Rule History

1991 Revision: New rule.

2000 Revision: Subdivision (d) added to permit expedited proceedings.

2008 Revision: Committee notes revised.

Statutory References

§ 393.12, Fla. Stat. Capacity; appointment of guardian advocate.

§ 744.3715 Petition for interim judicial review.

RULE 5.710. REPORTS OF PUBLIC GUARDIAN

The public guardian, as the guardian of a ward, shall file:

(a) an initial report as required by law;

(b) annual guardianship reports, which shall include the dates of quarterly visits to the ward, as required by law;

(c) a report within 6 months of his or her appointment as guardian of a ward, which shall also be filed with the executive director of the Statewide Public Guardianship Office, stating:

(1) the public guardian's efforts to locate a family member or friend, other person, bank, or corporation to act as guardian of the ward; and

(2) the ward's potential to be restored to capacity;

(d) an annual report, filed with the Statewide Public Guardianship Office, by September 1 for the preceding fiscal year, on the operations of the office of public guardian; and

(e) a report of an independent audit by a qualified certified public accountant, to be filed with the Statewide Public Guardianship Office every 2 years.

Committee Notes

Rule History

1987 Revision: This is a new rule and was promulgated to establish procedures to accommodate the Public Guardian Act. See § 744.701, et seq., Fla. Stat. See also Fla. Prob. R. 5.560.

1989 Revision: Prior rule adopted as temporary emergency rule.

1991 Revision: Editorial changes.

1992 Revision: Citation form changes in committee notes.

2007 Revision: Rule extensively amended to specify reports a public guardian is required to file.

2010 Revision: Editorial change in (e).

Statutory Reference

§§ 744.701-744.709, Fla. Stat. Public Guardianship Act.

Rule Reference

Fla. Prob. R. 5.560 Petition for appointment of guardian of an incapacitated person.

RULE 5.720. COURT MONITOR

(a) Appointment. Upon motion or inquiry by any interested person or upon its own motion, the court may appoint a court monitor in any proceeding over which it has jurisdiction.

(b) Order of Appointment. The order of appointment shall state the name, address, and phone number of the monitor and shall set forth the matters to be investigated. The order may authorize the monitor to investigate, seek information, examine documents, or interview the ward. The order of appointment shall be served upon the guardian, the ward, and such other persons as the court may determine.

(c) Report. The monitor shall file a verified written report with the court setting forth the monitor's findings. The report shall be served on the guardian, the ward, and such other persons as the court may determine.

(d) Protection of Ward. If it appears from the monitor's report that further action by the court to protect the interests of the ward is necessary, the court shall, after a hearing with notice, enter any order necessary to protect the ward or the ward's property, including amending the plan, requiring an accounting, ordering production of assets, or initiating proceedings to remove a guardian. Notice of the hearing shall be served on the guardian, the ward, and such other persons as the court may determine.

Committee Notes

This rule applies to the non-emergency appointment of court monitors.

Rule History

2006 Revision: New rule.

2008 Revision: Editorial change in (d). Committee notes revised.

Statutory References

§ 393.12, Fla. Stat. Capacity; appointment of guardian advocate.

§ 744.107, Fla. Stat. Court monitors.

§ 744.3701, Fla. Stat. Inspection of report.

RULE 5.725. EMERGENCY COURT MONITOR

(a) Appointment. Upon motion or inquiry by any interested person or upon its own motion, the court may appoint a court monitor on an emergency basis without notice in any proceeding over which it has jurisdiction.

(b) Order of Appointment. The order of appointment shall specifically find that there appears to be imminent danger that the physical or mental health or safety of the ward will be seriously impaired or that the ward's property is in danger of being wasted, misappropriated, or lost unless immediate action is taken. The scope of the matters to be investigated and the powers and duties of the monitor must be specifically enumerated in the order.

(c) Duration of Authority. The authority of a monitor expires 60 days after the date of appointment or upon a finding of no probable cause, whichever occurs first. The court may enter an order extending the authority of the monitor for an additional 30 days upon a showing that an emergency condition still exists.

(d) Report. Within 15 days after the entry of an order of appointment, the monitor shall file a verified written report setting forth the monitor's findings and recommendations. The report may be supported by documents or other evidence. The time for filing the report may be extended by the court for good cause.

(e) Review. Upon review of the report, the court shall enter an order determining whether there is probable cause to take further action to protect the person or property of the ward.

(1) If the court finds no probable cause, the court shall enter an order finding no probable cause and discharging the monitor.

(2) If the court finds probable cause, the court shall enter an order directed to the respondent stating the essential facts constituting the conduct charged and requiring the respondent to appear before the court to show cause why the court should not take further action. The order shall specify the time and place of the hearing with a reasonable time to allow for the preparation of a defense after service of the order. A copy of the order to show cause together with the order of appointment and report of the monitor shall be served upon the guardian, the ward, the ward's attorney, if any, and the respondent.

(f) Protecting Ward. If at any time prior to the hearing on the order to show cause the court enters a temporary injunction, a restraining order, an order freezing assets, an order suspending the guardian or appointing a guardian ad litem, or any other order to protect the physical or mental health, safety, or property of the ward, the order or injunction shall be served on the guardian, the ward, the ward's attorney, if any, and such other persons as the court may determine.

Committee Notes

Rule History

2006 Revision: New rule.

2008 Revision: Committee notes revised.

2010 Revision: Editorial change in (c).

Statutory references

§ 393.12, Fla. Stat. Capacity; appointment of guardian advocate.

§ 744.1075, Fla. Stat. Emergency court monitor.

RULE 5.800. APPLICATION OF REVISED CHAPTER 744 TO EXISTING GUARDIANSHIPS

(a) Prior Adjudication of Incompetency. When an adjudication of incompetency has taken place under chapter 744, Florida Statutes, before October 1, 1989, no readjudication of incapacity shall be required.

(b) Annual Guardianship Reports. Guardians appointed before October 1, 1989, shall file annual guardianship reports as required by law.

Committee Notes

Rule History

1989 Revision by Ad Hoc Committee: The committee adopted a position that guardians appointed before the effective date of the 1989 revisions to chapter 744, Florida Statutes, should comply with all sections of the law that apply to future acts of the guardian. For example, all guardians will in the future file annual reports and will be responsible for the continuing well-being of their wards. The committee recognized a distinction between those actions that will necessarily occur on a continuing basis throughout the guardianship and those actions that happen at a particular moment in time but are not necessarily ongoing duties. There are two and only two specific examples to which the statutory reforms would not apply retrospectively if the above distinction is adopted. First, the initial adjudication of incapacity occurs only once in any guardianship. Although guardianships are reevaluated annually, the statute does not contemplate a complete readjudication procedure every year. Therefore, the committee concluded that the initial adjudicatory hearing need not be repeated for wards adjudicated incompetent before October 1, 1989. Second, as concerns nonresident guardians appointed before October 1, 1989, normally, a guardian is appointed only once at the beginning of the guardianship. While these nonresident guardians would be expected to obey all provisions of the law prospectively, they would not be required to initiate their own removal.

1991 Revision: Editorial changes in first sentence of (a), and rest of subdivision deleted as unnecessary. Subdivision (b) has been transferred to rule 5.650. Date reference no longer required in (c), and modified to make filing requirement of preexisting guardianships consistent with the current statutory provisions.

1992 Revision: Citation form changes in committee notes.

Statutory References

§ 744.367, Fla. Stat. Duty to file annual guardianship report.

§ 744.3675, Fla. Stat. Annual guardianship plan.

§ 744.3678, Fla. Stat. Annual accounting.

Rule References

Fla. Prob. R. 5.695 Annual guardianship report.

Fla. Prob. R. 5.696 Annual accounting.

PART IV. EXPEDITED JUDICIAL INTERVENTION CONCERNING MEDICAL TREATMENT PROCEDURES

RULE 5.900. EXPEDITED JUDICIAL INTERVENTION CONCERNING MEDICAL TREATMENT PROCEDURES

(a) Petition. Any proceeding for expedited judicial intervention concerning medical treatment procedures may be brought by any interested adult person and shall be commenced by the filing of a verified petition which states:

(1) the name and address of the petitioner;

(2) the name and location of the person who is the subject of the petition (hereinafter referred to as the "patient");

(3) the relationship of the petitioner to the patient;

(4) the names, relationship to the patient, and addresses if known to the petitioner, of:

(A) the patient's spouse and adult children;

(B) the patient's parents (if the patient is a minor);

(C) if none of the above, the patient's next of kin;

(D) any guardian and any court-appointed health care decision-maker;

(E) any person designated by the patient in a living will or other document to exercise the patient's health care decision in the event of the patient's incapacity;

(F) the administrator of the hospital, nursing home, or other facility where the patient is located;

(G) the patient's principal treating physician and other physicians known to have provided any medical opinion or advice about any condition of the patient relevant to this petition; and

(H) all other persons the petitioner believes may have information concerning the expressed wishes of the patient; and

(5) facts sufficient to establish the need for the relief requested, including, but not limited to, facts to support the allegation that the patient lacks the capacity to make the requisite medical treatment decision.

(b) Supporting Documentation. Any affidavits and supporting documentation, including any living will or designation of health care decision-maker, shall be attached to the petition.

(c) Notice. Unless waived by the court, notice of the petition and the preliminary hearing shall be served on the following persons who have not joined in the petition or otherwise consented to the proceedings:

(1) the patient;

(2) the patient's spouse and the patient's parents, if the patient is a minor;

(3) the patient's adult children;

(4) any guardian and any court-appointed health care decision-maker;

(5) any person designated by the patient in a living will or other document to exercise the patient's health care decision in the event of the patient's incapacity;

(6) the administrator of the hospital, nursing home, or other facility where the patient is located;

(7) the patient's principal treating physician and other physicians believed to have provided any medical opinion or advice about any condition of the patient relevant to this petition;

(8) all other persons the petitioner believes may have information concerning the expressed wishes of the patient; and

(9) such other persons as the court may direct.

(d) Hearing. A preliminary hearing on the petition shall be held within 72 hours after the filing of the petition. At that time the court shall review the petition and supporting documentation. In its discretion the court shall either:

(1) rule on the relief requested immediately after the preliminary hearing; or

(2) conduct an evidentiary hearing not later than 4 days after the preliminary hearing and rule on the relief requested immediately after the evidentiary hearing.

Committee Notes

This rule was submitted by the committee in response to the request contained in footnote 17 of *In re Guardianship of Browning*,

568 So. 2d 4 (Fla. 1990). See also *Cruzan by Cruzan v. Director, Missouri Department of Health*, U.S., 110 S. Ct. 2841, 111 L. Ed. 2d 224 (1990).

The promulgation of this rule is not intended to imply that judicial intervention is required to terminate life-prolonging procedures.

Practitioners should note that the criteria and standards of proof contained in Browning differ from the criteria and standards of proof presently existing in chapter 765, Florida Statutes.

Rule History.

1991 Revision: New rule.

1992 Revision: This rule was created on an emergency basis and on further review, the committee decided it needed to clarify that the petition should include an allegation that the patient lacks capacity to make the requisite medical treatment decision, and that the patient should receive notice of the petition and hearing. Committee notes revised. Citation form changes in committee notes.

2008 Revision: Committee notes revised.

Constitutional Reference.

Art. I, § 23, Fla. Const.

Statutory References

§ 393.12, Fla. Stat. Capacity; appointment of guardian advocate.

§ 709.08, Fla. Stat. Durable power of attorney.

§ 731.302, Fla. Stat. Waiver and consent by interested person.

§ 744.102, Fla. Stat. Definitions.

§ 744.104, Fla. Stat. Verification of documents.

§ 744.3115, Fla. Stat. Advanced directives for health care.

ch. 765, Fla. Stat. Health care advance directives.

Rule References

Fla. Prob. R. 5.020 Pleadings; verification; motions.

Fla. Prob. R. 5.040 Notice.

FLORIDA STATUTES

———

TITLE VI
CIVIL PRACTICE AND PROCEDURE.

CHAPTER 69
MISCELLANEOUS PROCEDURAL MATTERS.

CHAPTER 86
DECLARATORY JUDGMENTS.

TITLE XIV
TAXATION AND FINANCE

CHAPTER 198
ESTATE TAXES.

TITLE XV
HOMESTEAD AND EXEMPTIONS.

CHAPTER 222
METHOD OF SETTING APART HOMESTEAD AND EXEMPTIONS.

TITLE XXIX
PUBLIC HEALTH.

CHAPTER 393
DEVELOPMENTAL DISABILITIES.

TITLE XXX
SOCIAL WELFARE.

CHAPTER 409
SOCIAL AND ECONOMIC ASSISTANCE.

TITLE XXXIII
REGULATION OF TRADE, COMMERCE, INVESTMENTS, AND SOLICITATIONS.

CHAPTER 518
INVESTMENT OF FIDUCIARY FUNDS.

TITLE XXXVIII
BANKS AND BANKING.

CHAPTER 655
FINANCIAL INSTITUTIONS GENERALLY.

TITLE XL
REAL AND PERSONAL PROPERTY.

CHAPTER 689
CONVEYANCES OF LAND AND DECLARATIONS OF TRUST.

CHAPTER 695
RECORD OF CONVEYANCES OF REAL ESTATE.

CHAPTER 709
POWERS OF ATTORNEY AND SIMILAR INSTRUMENTS.

PART I. POWERS OF APPOINTMENT.

CHAPTER 710
TRANSFERS TO MINORS.

CHAPTER 711
FLORIDA UNIFORM TRANSFER-ON-DEATH SECURITY REGISTRATION ACT.

CHAPTER 716
ESCHEATS.

CHAPTER 717
DISPOSITION OF UNCLAIMED PROPERTY.

TITLE XLII
ESTATES AND TRUSTS.

CHAPTER 731
PROBATE CODE: GENERAL PROVISIONS.

PART I. SHORT TITLE; CONSTRUCTION.

CHAPTER 732
PROBATE CODE: INTESTATE SUCCESSION AND WILLS.

CHAPTER 733
PROBATE CODE: ADMINISTRATION OF ESTATES.

CHAPTER 734
PROBATE CODE: FOREIGN PERSONAL REPRESENTATIVES; ANCILLARY ADMINISTRATION

CHAPTER 735
PROBATE CODE: SMALL ESTATES

CHAPTER 736
FLORIDA TRUST CODE

PART XI. RULES OF CONSTRUCTION.

PART XII. CHARITABLE TRUSTS.

PART XIII. MISCELLANEOUS.

CHAPTER 737
TRUST ADMINISTRATION
[NOTE: CHAPTER 737 WAS REPEALED JULY 1, 2007]

PART I. TRUST REGISTRATION.

PART VI. RULES OF CONSTRUCTION.

CHAPTER 738
PRINCIPAL AND INCOME

CHAPTER 739
FLORIDA UNIFORM DISCLAIMER OF PROPERTY INTERESTS ACT

TITLE XLIII
DOMESTIC RELATIONS.

CHAPTER 744
GUARDIANSHIP

PART I. GENERAL PROVISIONS.

PART II. VENUE.

PART III. TYPES OF GUARDIANSHIP.

CHAPTER 747
CONSERVATORSHIP

TITLE XLIV
CIVIL RIGHTS.

CHAPTER 765
HEALTH CARE ADVANCE DIRECTIVES

PART I. GENERAL PROVISIONS.

TITLE VI.

CIVIL PRACTICE AND PROCEDURE

CHAPTER 69.
MISCELLANEOUS PROCEDURAL MATTERS

69.031. Designated financial institutions for assets in hands of guardians, curators, administrators, trustees, receivers, or other officers.

(1) When it is expedient in the judgment of any court having jurisdiction of any estate in process of administration by any guardian, curator, executor, administrator, trustee, receiver, or other officer, because the size of the bond required of the officer is burdensome or for other cause, the court may order part or all of the personal assets of the estate placed with a bank, trust company, or savings and loan association (which savings and loan association is a member of the Federal Savings and Loan Insurance Corporation and doing business in this state) designated by the court, consideration being given to any bank, trust company or savings and loan association proposed by the officer. When the assets are placed with the designated financial institution, it shall file a receipt therefor in the name of the estate and give the officer a copy. Such receipt shall acknowledge the assets received by the financial institution. All interest, dividends, principal and other debts collected by the financial institution on account thereof shall be held by the financial institution in safekeeping, subject to the instructions of the officer authorized by order of the court directed to the financial institution.

(2) Accountings shall be made to the officer at reasonably frequent intervals. After the receipt for the original assets has been filed by the financial institution, the court shall waive the bond given or to be given or reduce it so that it shall apply only to the estate remaining in the hands of the officer, whichever the court deems proper.

(3) When the court has ordered any assets of an estate to be placed with a designated financial institution, any person or corporation having possession or control of any of the assets, or owing interest, dividends, principal or other debts on account thereof, shall pay and deliver such assets, interest, dividends, principal and other debts to the financial institution on its demand whether the officer has duly qualified or not, and the receipt of the financial institution relieves the person or corporation from further responsibility therefor.

(4) Any bank, trust company, or savings and loan association which is designated under this section, may accept or reject the designation in any instance, and shall file its acceptance or rejection with the court making the designation within 15 days after actual knowledge of the designation comes to the attention of the financial institution, and if the financial institution accepts, it shall be allowed a reasonable amount for its services and expenses which the court may allow as a charge against the assets placed with the financial institution.

History.
SS. 1, 2, 3, ch. 21980, 1943; s. 1, ch. 57-198; s. 23, ch. 67-254.
Editor's Notes.
Former s. 69.15.

CHAPTER 86.
DECLARATORY JUDGMENTS

86.041. Actions by executors, administrators, trustees, etc.

Any person interested as or through an executor, administrator, trustee, guardian, or other fiduciary, creditor, devisee, legatee, heir, next of kin, or cestui que trust, in the administration of a trust, a guardianship, or of the estate of a decedent, an infant, a mental incompetent, or insolvent may have a declaration of rights or equitable or legal relations in respect thereto:

(1) To ascertain any class of creditors, devisees, legatees, heirs, next of kin, or others; or

(2) To direct the executor, administrator, or trustee to refrain from doing any particular act in his or her fiduciary capacity; or

(3) To determine any question arising in the administration of the guardianship, estate, or trust, including questions of construction of wills and other writings.

For the purpose of this section, a "mental incompetent" is one who, because of mental illness, mental retardation, senility, excessive use of drugs or alcohol, or other mental incapacity, is incapable of either managing his or her property or caring for himself or herself, or both.

History.
S. 4, ch. 21820, 1943; s. 38, ch. 67-254; s. 1, ch. 88-33; s. 459, ch. 95-147.

Editor's Notes.
Former s. 87.04.

TITLE XIV.
TAXATION AND FINANCE

CHAPTER 198.
ESTATE TAXES

198.01. Definitions.

When used in this chapter the term, phrase or word:

(1) "Department" means the Department of Revenue.

(2) "Personal representative" means the executor, administrator, or curator of the decedent, or, if there is no executor, administrator, or curator appointed, qualified, and acting, then any person who is in the actual or constructive possession of any property included in the gross estate of the decedent or any other person who is required to file a return or pay the taxes due under any provision of this chapter.

(3) "Person" means persons, corporations, associations, joint stock companies, and business trusts.

(4) "Transfer" shall be taken to include the passing of property or any interest therein, in possession or enjoyment, present or future, by inheritance, descent, devise, succession, bequest, grant, deed, bargain, sale, gift, or appointment in the manner herein described.

(5) "Decedent" shall include the testator, intestate, grantor, bargainor, vendor, or donor.

(6) "Resident" means a natural person domiciled in the state.

(7) "Nonresident" means a natural person domiciled without the state.

(8) "Gross estate" means the gross estate as determined under the provisions of the applicable federal revenue act.

(9) "Net estate" means the net estate as determined under the provisions of the applicable federal revenue act.

(10) "Tangible personal property" means corporeal personal property, including money.

(11) "Intangible personal property" means incorporeal personal property including deposits in banks, negotiable instruments, mortgages, debts, receivables, shares of stock, bonds, notes, credits, evidences of an interest in property, evidences of debt and choses in action generally.

(12) "United States" when used in a geographical sense includes only the 50 states and the District of Columbia.

(13) "Generation-skipping transfer" means every transfer subject to the federal generation-skipping transfer tax in which transfer the original transferor is a resident of this state at the date of original transfer

or the property transferred is real or personal property in this state.

(14) "Original transferor" means any grantor, donor, trustor, or testator who by grant, gift, trust, or will makes a transfer of real or personal property that results in a federal generation-skipping transfer tax.

(15) "Federal generation-skipping transfer tax" means the tax imposed by chapter 13 of the Internal Revenue Code of 1986, as amended.

History.

S. 2, ch. 16015, 1933; CGL 1936 Supp. 1342(81); ss. 21, 35, ch. 69-106; s. 44, ch. 71-377; s. 1, ch. 80-153; s. 3, ch. 89-356.

198.015. Domicile of decedent.

(1) For the purposes of this chapter, every person shall be presumed to have died a resident and not a nonresident of the state:

(a) If such person has dwelt or lodged in the state during and for the greater part of any period of 12 consecutive months in the 24 months next preceding death, notwithstanding the fact that from time to time during such 24 months such person may have sojourned outside of this state, and without regard to whether or not such person may have voted, may have been entitled to vote, or may have been assessed for taxes in this state; or

(b) If such person has been a resident of Florida, sojourning outside of this state.

(2) The burden of proof in an estate tax proceeding shall be upon any person claiming exemption by reason of alleged nonresidency. Domicile shall be determined exclusively in the proceedings provided in this chapter, and orders relating to domicile previously entered in the probate proceedings shall not be conclusive for the purposes of this chapter.

History.

S. 1, ch. 77-411; s. 1031, ch. 95-147.

198.02. Tax upon estates of resident decedents.

A tax is imposed upon the transfer of the estate of every person who, at the time of death, was a resident of this state, the amount of which shall be a sum equal to the amount by which the credit allowable under the applicable federal revenue act for estate, inheritance, legacy, and succession taxes actually paid to the several states exceeds the aggregate amount of all constitutionally valid estate, inheritance, legacy, and succession taxes actually paid to the several states of the United States (other than this state) in respect of any property owned by such decedent or subject to such taxes as a part of or in connection with his or her estate. All values shall be as finally determined for federal estate tax purposes.

History.
S. 3, ch. 16015, 1933; CGL 1936 Supp. 1342(83); s. 1, ch. 71-202;
s. 3, ch. 82-38; s. 1032, ch. 95-147.

198.021. Tax upon generation-skipping transfers of residents.

A tax is hereby imposed upon every generation-skipping transfer in which the original transferor is a resident of this state at the date of original transfer, in an amount equal to the amount allowable as a credit for state legacy taxes under s. 2604 of the Internal Revenue Code of 1986, as amended, to the extent such credit exceeds the aggregate amount of all constitutionally valid taxes on the same transfer actually paid to the several states of the United States other than this state.

History.
S. 2, ch. 80-153; s. 4, ch. 89-356.
Editor's Notes.
Section 2604 of the Internal Revenue Code of 1986, referred to in this section, is codified as 26 U.S.C.S. § 2604.

198.03. Tax upon estates of nonresident decedents.

A tax is imposed upon the transfer of real property situate in this state, upon tangible personal property having an actual situs in this state, upon intangible personal property having a business situs in this state and upon stocks, bonds, debentures, notes, and other securities or obligations of corporations organized under the laws of this state, of every person who at the time of death was not a resident of this state but was a resident of the United States, the amount of which shall be a sum equal to such proportion of the amount of the credit allowable under the applicable federal revenue act for estate, inheritance, legacy, and succession taxes actually paid to the several states, as the value of the property taxable in this state bears to the value of the entire gross estate wherever situate.

History.
S. 4, ch. 16015, 1933; CGL 1936 Supp. 1342(84); s. 1, ch. 28031, 1953.

198.031. Tax upon generation-skipping transfers of nonresidents.

A tax is hereby imposed upon every generation-skipping transfer in which the original transferor is not a resident of this state at the date of the original transfer but in which the property transferred includes real or personal property in this state, in an amount equal to the amount allowable as a credit for state legacy taxes under s. 2604 of the Internal Revenue Code of 1986, as amended, reduced by an amount which bears the same ratio to the total state tax credit allowable for federal generation-skipping transfer tax purposes as the value of the transferred property taxable by all other states bears to the value of the gross generation-skipping transfer for federal generation-skipping transfer tax purposes.

History.
S. 3, ch. 80-153; s. 5, ch. 89-356.
Editor's Notes.
Section 2604 of the Internal Revenue Code of 1986, referred to in this section, is codified as 26 U.S.C.S. § 2604.

198.04. Tax upon estates of alien decedents.

A tax is imposed upon the transfer of real property situate and tangible personal property having an actual situs in this state and upon intangible personal property physically present within this state of every person who at the time of death was not a resident of the United States, the amount of which shall be a sum equal to such proportion of the credit allowable under the applicable federal revenue act for estate, inheritance, legacy, and succession taxes actually paid to the several states, as the value of the property taxable in this state bears to the value of the estate taxable by the United States wherever situate. For the purpose of this section, stock in a corporation organized under the laws of this state shall be deemed physically present within this state. The amount receivable as insurance upon the life of a decedent who at the time of death was not a resident of the United States, and any moneys deposited with any person carrying on the banking business by or for such decedent who was not engaged in business in the United States at the time of death, shall not, for the purpose of this section, be deemed to be physically present in this state.

History.
S. 5, ch. 16015, 1933; CGL 1936 Supp. 1342(85); s. 1033, ch. 95-147.

198.05. Administration of law by Department of Revenue.

The Department of Revenue shall, except as otherwise provided, have jurisdiction and be charged with the administration and enforcement of the provisions of this chapter.

History.
S. 6, ch. 16015, 1933; CGL 1936 Supp. 1342(86); ss. 21, 35, ch. 69-106.

198.06. Examination of books, papers, records, or memoranda by the department.

(1) The department, for the purpose of ascertaining the correctness of any return, or for the purpose of making a return where none has been made, may examine any books, papers, records, or memoranda, bearing upon the matter required to be included in the return; may require the attendance of persons rendering return or of any officer or employee of such persons, or of any person having knowledge in the premises, at any convenient place in the county in which such person resides, and may take his or her testimony with reference to the matter required by law to be included in such return, and may administer oaths to such persons.

(2) If any person summoned to appear under this chapter to testify, or to produce books, papers, or other data, shall refuse to do so, the circuit court for the

county in which such person resides shall have jurisdiction by appropriate process to compel such attendance, testimony, or production of books, papers, or other data.

History.
S. 6, ch. 16015, 1933; CGL 1936 Supp. 1342(86); ss. 21, 35, ch. 69-106; s. 1034, ch. 95-147.

198.07. Appointment of agents by department; bonds of agents; may administer oaths; credentials.

(1) The department may appoint and remove such examiners, appraisers, attorneys and employees as it may deem necessary, such persons to have such duties and powers as the department may from time to time prescribe. The salaries of all examiners, appraisers, attorneys and employees employed by the department shall be such as it may prescribe, and such examiners, appraisers, attorneys and employees shall be reimbursed for travel expenses as provided in s. 112.061.

(2) The department may require such of the examiners, appraisers, attorneys and employees as it may designate to give bond payable to the state for the faithful performance of their duties in such form and with such sureties as it may determine, and all premiums on such bonds shall be paid by the state.

(3) All officers empowered by law to administer oaths and the examiners, appraisers and attorneys appointed by the department may administer an oath to all persons giving any testimony before them or to take the acknowledgment of any person in respect to any return or report required under this chapter.

(4) All examiners, appraisers and attorneys appointed by the department shall have for identification purpose proper credentials issued by the department and exhibit the same upon demand.

History.
S. 6, ch. 16015, 1933; CGL 1936 Supp. 1342(86); s. 19, ch. 63-400; ss. 21, 35, ch. 69-106.

198.08. Rules.

The department has authority to adopt rules pursuant to ss. 120.536(1) and 120.54 to enforce the provisions of this chapter and may adopt, as rules, such rules and regulations as are promulgated with respect to the estate tax or generation-skipping transfer tax provisions of the Revenue Act of the United States insofar as they are applicable hereto. The department may from time to time prescribe such forms as it shall deem proper for the administration of this chapter.

History.
S. 6, ch. 16015, 1933; CGL 1936 Supp. 1342(86); ss. 21, 35, ch. 69-106; s. 4, ch. 80-153; s. 14, ch. 98-200.

198.11. Appointment of special appraisers.

The department may employ special appraisers for the purpose of determining the value of any property which is, or is believed by the department to be, subject to the tax imposed by this chapter, and such special appraisers shall be paid such compensation as said department shall deem proper.

History.
S. 6, ch. 16015, 1933; CGL 1936 Supp. 1342(86); ss. 21, 35, ch. 69-106.

198.13. Tax return to be made in certain cases; certificate of nonliability.

(1) The personal representative of every estate required by the laws of the United States to file a federal estate tax return shall file with the department, on or before the last day prescribed by law for filing the initial federal estate tax return for such estate, a return consisting of an executed copy of the federal estate tax return and shall file with such return all supplemental data, if any, as may be necessary to determine and establish the correct tax under this chapter. Such return shall be made in the case of every decedent who at the time of death was not a resident of the United States and whose gross estate includes any real property situate in the state, tangible personal property having an actual situs in the state, and intangible personal property physically present within the state.

(2) Whenever it is made to appear to the department that an estate that has filed a return owes no taxes under this chapter, the department shall issue to the personal representative a certificate in writing to that effect, which certificate shall have the same force and effect as a receipt showing payment. The certificate shall be subject to record and admissible in evidence in like manner as a receipt showing payment of taxes. A fee of $5 shall be paid to the department for each certificate so issued.

(3) Every person required to file a return reporting a generation-skipping transfer under applicable federal statutes and regulations shall file with the Department of Revenue, on or before the last day prescribed for filing the federal return, a return consisting of a duplicate copy of the federal return.

(4) Notwithstanding any other provisions of this section and applicable to the estate of a decedent who dies after December 31, 2004, if, upon the death of the decedent, a state death tax credit or a generation-skipping transfer credit is not allowable pursuant to the Internal Revenue Code of 1986, as amended:

(a) The personal representative of the estate is not required to file a return under subsection (1) in connection with the estate.

(b) The person who would otherwise be required to file a return reporting a generation-skipping transfer under subsection (3) is not required to file such a return in connection with the estate.

The provisions of this subsection do not apply to estates of decedents dying after December 31, 2012.

History.
S. 7, ch. 16015, 1933; CGL 1936 Supp. 1342(87); s. 2, ch. 28031, 1953; s. 2, ch. 29718, 1955; ss. 21, 35, ch. 69-106; s. 2, ch. 71-202; s. 7, ch. 80-153; s. 1, ch. 84-325; s. 38, ch. 85-342; s. 1035, ch. 95-147;

s. 4, ch. 99-208; s. 7, ch. 2007-106, eff. July 1, 2007; s. 35, ch. 2008-4, eff. July 1, 2008; s. 1, ch. 2011-86, eff. May 31, 2011.

Editor's Notes.

The introductory language of ch. 2011-86, s. 1 states that the amendment of subsection (4) is retroactive to January 1, 2011.

198.14. Failure to make return; extension of time for filing.

To obtain an extension for filing a Florida return, the personal representative shall file with the department a copy of the federal extension request within 30 days after filing such request with the federal taxing authorities. If the federal taxing authorities grant an extension of time for filing a return, the department shall allow a like extension of time for filing if the personal representative files a copy of such federal extension with the department within 30 days after receiving an approved federal extension. An extension of time for filing a return shall not operate to extend the time for payment of the tax. If any person fails to file a return at the time prescribed by law or files, willfully or otherwise, a false or fraudulent return, the department shall make the return from its own knowledge and from such information as it can obtain through testimony or otherwise. Any such return so made by the department shall be prima facie good and sufficient for all legal purposes.

History.

S. 7, ch. 16015, 1933; CGL 1936 Supp. 1342(87); s. 3, ch. 29718, 1955; ss. 21, 35, ch. 69-106; s. 2, ch. 87-102.

198.15. When tax due; extension; interest; penalty.

(1) The tax imposed by this chapter is due and payable on or before the last day prescribed by law for paying the federal estate tax pursuant to the initial estate tax return and shall be paid by the personal representative to the department. The department shall extend the time for payment of the tax or any part of the tax if the time for paying the federal estate tax is extended, provided the personal representative files with the department a copy of the approved federal extension notice within 30 days after receiving such notice. No extension shall be for more than 1 year, and the aggregate of extensions with respect to any estate shall not exceed 10 years from the due date. In such case, the amount in respect of which the extension is granted shall be paid on or before the date of the expiration of the period of the extension, unless a further extension is granted. If the time for the payment is thus extended, there shall be collected, as part of such amount, interest thereon at the rate of 1 percent per month of the amount due from the due date of the tax to the date the same is paid.

(2) For any tax that is due on or after July 1, 1991, and that is not paid by the due date or by the due date of any extension granted by the department, in addition to any other penalties, a specific penalty shall be added to the tax in the amount of 10 percent of any unpaid tax if the failure is for not more than 30 days, or 20 percent of the aggregate of any unpaid tax if the failure is for more than 30 days.

History.

S. 8, ch. 16015, 1933; CGL 1936 Supp. 1342(88); s. 3, ch. 28031, 1953; ss. 21, 35, ch. 69-106; s. 3, ch. 71-202; s. 1, ch. 76-261; s. 2, ch. 77-411; s. 1, ch. 80-24; s. 8, ch. 80-153; s. 2, ch. 84-325; s. 39, ch. 85-342; s. 3, ch. 87-102; s. 8, ch. 91-112; s. 3, ch. 92-320.

198.155. Payment of tax on generation-skipping transfers.

(1) The person liable for payment of the federal generation-skipping transfer tax shall be liable for the tax imposed by ss. 198.021 and 198.031.

(2) The tax imposed by ss. 198.021 and 198.031 is due upon a taxable distribution or taxable termination as determined under applicable provisions of the federal generation-skipping transfer tax.

(3) The tax becomes delinquent the day after the last day allowed for filing a return for the generation-skipping transfer.

(4) The tax shall be paid to the Department of Revenue.

(5) If the tax, or any portion thereof, is not paid before it becomes delinquent, it shall bear interest at the rate of 1 percent per month for each month or fraction thereof that it is delinquent.

History.

S. 21, ch. 80-153.

198.16. Notice of determination of deficiency in federal tax to be filed with department.

(1) It shall be the duty of the personal representative to file with the department within 60 days after a final determination of any deficiency in federal estate tax has been made, written notice thereof.

(2) If, after a duplicate federal return of a generation-skipping transfer has been filed with the Department of Revenue, the federal authorities increase or decrease the amount of the federal generation-skipping transfer tax, an amended return shall be filed with the department showing all changes made in the original return and the amount of increase or decrease in the federal generation-skipping transfer tax.

(3) If, based upon any deficiency and the ground therefor, it shall appear that the amount of tax previously paid is less than the amount of tax owing, the difference, together with interest at the rate of 1 percent per month from the due date of the tax, shall be paid upon notice and demand by the department. In the event the personal representative or person required to return and pay such tax shall fail to give the notice required by this section, any additional tax which shall be owing may be assessed, or a proceeding in court for the collection of such tax may be begun without assessment at any time prior to the filing of such notice or within 30 days after the delinquent filing of such notice, notwithstanding the provisions of s. 198.28.

History.

S. 9, ch. 16015, 1933; CGL 1936 Supp. 1342(89); s. 4, ch. 28031,

1953; s. 4, ch. 29718, 1955; ss. 21, 35, ch. 69-106; s. 3, ch. 77-411; s. 9, ch. 80-153.

198.17. Deficiency; hearing by department.

If upon examination of any return a tax or a deficiency in tax is disclosed, the department shall proceed to determine all questions involving such tax or deficiency. Such tax or deficiency in tax shall be assessed and paid together with the penalty and interest, if any, applicable thereto, within 60 days after such demand as may be included in the department's order.

History.
S. 10, ch. 16015, 1933; CGL 1936 Supp. 1342(90); s. 5, ch. 29718, 1955; s. 19, ch. 63-559; ss. 21, 35, ch. 69-106; s. 54, ch. 78-95.

198.18. Failure to pay tax; penalties; delinquent or deficient taxes, interest.

(1) If any part of a deficiency in tax due under the provisions of this chapter is due to negligence or intentional disregard of the provisions of this chapter or the rules and regulations issued pursuant hereto, with knowledge thereof but without intent to defraud, there shall be added as a penalty 10 percent per month of the total amount of the deficiency in tax to a maximum of 50 percent of the tax due; and, if any part of such deficiency is willfully made with intent to defraud, there shall be added as a penalty 100 percent of the total amount of such deficiency, which penalty shall become due and payable upon notice and demand by the department. The personal representative shall be liable to the state personally and on his or her official bond, if any, for any loss to the state accruing under the provisions of this section through the personal representative's negligence or willful neglect. No interest shall be collected upon the amount of any penalty. The department may settle or compromise such penalties pursuant to s. 213.21.

(2) Any deficiency in tax or any tax payment not received by the department on or before the due date as provided in s. 198.15, in addition to any other penalties, shall bear interest at the rate of 1 percent per month of the amount due from the due date until paid. The department may settle or compromise such interest pursuant to s. 213.21.

History.
S. 11, ch. 16015, 1933; CGL 1936 Supp. 1342(91); s. 6, ch. 29718, 1955; ss. 21, 35, ch. 69-106; s. 2, ch. 76-261; s. 1, ch. 77-174; s. 10, ch. 80-153; s. 2, ch. 81-178; s. 50, ch. 87-6; s. 30, ch. 87-101; s. 4, ch. 92-320; s. 1036, ch. 95-147.

198.19. Receipts for taxes.

The department shall issue to the personal representative, upon payment of the tax imposed by this chapter, receipts in triplicate, any of which shall be sufficient evidence of such payment and shall entitle the personal representative to be credited and allowed the amount thereof by any court having jurisdiction to audit or settle his or her accounts. If the personal representative files a complete return and makes written application to the department for determination of the amount of the tax and discharge from personal liability therefor, the department as soon as possible, and in any event within 1 year after receipt of such application, shall notify the personal representative of the amount of the tax; and upon payment thereof the personal representative shall be discharged from personal liability for any additional tax thereafter found to be due and shall be entitled to receive from the department a receipt in writing showing such discharge; however, such discharge shall not operate to release the gross estate of the lien of any additional tax that may thereafter be found to be due, while the title to the gross estate remains in the personal representative or in the heirs, devisees, or distributees thereof; but after such discharge is given, no part of the gross estate shall be subject to such lien or to any claim or demand for any such tax after the title thereto has passed to a bona fide purchaser for value.

History.
S. 12, ch. 16015, 1933; CGL 1936 Supp. 1342(92); ss. 21, 35, ch. 69-106; s. 11, ch. 80-153; s. 1037, ch. 95-147.

198.20. Failure to pay tax when due, department's warrant, etc.

If any tax imposed by this chapter or any portion of such tax be unpaid within 90 days after the same becomes due, and the time for payment be not extended, the department shall issue a warrant directed to the sheriff of any county of the state in which the estate or any part thereof may be situated, commanding the sheriff to levy upon and sell the real and personal property of such estate found within his or her county, for the payment of the amount thereof, with such interest and penalties, if any, as may have accrued thereon or been assessed against the same, together with the cost of executing the warrant, and to return such warrant, to the department and pay to it the money collected by virtue thereof, by a time to be therein specified, not less than 60 days from the date of the warrant. The sheriff thereupon shall proceed upon the same in all respects, with like effect, and in the same manner prescribed by law in respect to executions issued against property upon judgments of a court of record, and shall be entitled to the same fees for services in executing the warrant as are now allowed by law for like services to be collected in the same manner as now provided by law. Alias and pluries warrants may issue from time to time as said department may deem proper until the entire amount of the tax, deficiency, interest, penalties, and costs have been recovered.

History.
S. 13, ch. 16015, 1933; CGL 1936 Supp. 1342(93); ss. 21, 35, ch. 69-106; s. 1038, ch. 95-147.

198.21. Tax due payable from entire estate; third persons.

If the tax or any part thereof is paid or collected out of that part of the estate passing to or in possession of any person other than the personal representative in his or her capacity as such, such person shall be entitled to a reimbursement out of any part of the estate still undistributed or by a just and equitable contribution by the person whose interest in the estate of the decedent would have been reduced if the tax had been paid before the distribution of the estate or whose interest in the estate is subject to an equal or prior liability for the payment of tax, debts, or other charges against the estate, it being the purpose and intent of this section that, so far as is practical and unless otherwise directed by the will of the decedent, the tax shall be paid out of the estate before its distribution; but the department shall not be charged with enforcing contribution from any person.

History.
S. 14, ch. 16015, 1933; CGL 1936 Supp. 1342(94); ss. 21, 35, ch. 69-106; s. 12, ch. 80-153; s. 1039, ch. 95-147.

198.22. Lien for unpaid taxes.

Unless the tax is sooner paid in full, it shall be a lien for 12 years upon the gross estate of the decedent, except that such part of the gross estate as is used for the payment of charges against the estate and expenses of its administration, allowed by any court having jurisdiction thereof, shall be divested of such lien, and except that such part of the gross estate of a resident decedent as is transferred to a bona fide purchaser, mortgagee, or pledgee, for an adequate and full consideration in money or money's worth shall be divested of such lien and such lien shall then attach to the consideration received for such property from such purchaser, mortgagee, or pledgee. If the department is satisfied that no tax liability exists or that the tax liability of an estate has been fully discharged or provided for, it may issue a waiver releasing any or all property of such estate from the lien herein imposed.

History.
S. 15, ch. 16015, 1933; CGL 1936 Supp. 1342(95); s. 1, ch. 57-108; s. 13, ch. 59-1; ss. 21, 35, ch. 69-106; s. 4, ch. 77-411.

198.23. Personal liability of personal representative.

If any personal representative shall make distribution either in whole or in part of any of the property of an estate to the heirs, next of kin, distributees, legatees, or devisees without having paid or secured the tax due the state under this chapter, or having obtained the release of such property from the lien of such tax either by the department or pursuant to s. 198.32(2), he or she shall become personally liable for the tax so due the state, or so much thereof as may remain due and unpaid, to the full extent of the full value of any property belonging to such person or estate which may come into the personal representative's hands, custody, or control.

History.
S. 16, ch. 16015, 1933; CGL 1936 Supp. 1342(96); s. 13, ch. 80-153; s. 1040, ch. 95-147; s. 5, ch. 99-208.

198.24. Sale of real estate by personal representative to pay tax.

Every personal representative shall have the same right and power to take possession of or sell, convey, and dispose of real estate, as assets of the estate, for the payment of the tax imposed by this chapter as he or she may have for the payment of the debts of the decedent.

History.
S. 17, ch. 16015, 1933; CGL 1936 Supp. 1342(97); s. 14, ch. 80-153; s. 1041, ch. 95-147.

198.25. Actions to enforce payment of tax.

Actions may be brought within the time or times herein specified by the department to recover the amount of any taxes, penalties and interest due under this chapter. Every such action shall be brought in the county where the estate is being or has been administered, or if no administration be had in this state, then in any county where any of the property of the estate shall be situate.

History.
S. 18, ch. 16015, 1933; CGL 1936 Supp. 1342(98); ss. 21, 35, ch. 69-106.

198.26. No discharge of personal representative until tax is paid.

No final account of a personal representative shall be allowed by any court unless and until such account shows, and the judge of said court finds, that the tax imposed by the provisions of this chapter upon the personal representative, which has become payable, has been paid. The certificate of the department of nonliability for the tax or its receipt for the amount of tax therein certified shall be conclusive in such proceedings as to the liability or the payment of the tax to the extent of said certificate. In the case of a nontaxable estate, the court may consider the affidavit prepared pursuant to s. 198.32(2) as evidence of the nonliability for tax.

History.
S. 19, ch. 16015, 1933; CGL 1936 Supp. 1342(99); s. 7, ch. 29718, 1955; ss. 21, 35, ch. 69-106; s. 15, ch. 80-153; s. 6, ch. 99-208.

198.28. Time for assessment of tax.

The amount of estate tax due under this chapter shall be determined and assessed within 4 years from the date the return was filed, or within a period expiring 90 days after the last day on which the assessment of a deficiency in federal estate tax may lawfully be made under applicable provisions of the Internal Revenue Laws of the United States, whichever date last occurs, and no suit or other proceedings for the collection of any tax due under this chapter shall be begun after such date; provided, however, that in the case of a false or fraudulent return or of a failure to file a return, the tax may be assessed, or a proceeding in court for the collection of such tax may be begun without assessment, at any time.

History.
S. 21, ch. 16015, 1933; CGL 1936 Supp. 1342(101); s. 5, ch. 28031, 1953; s. 8, ch. 29718, 1955.

198.29. Refunds of excess tax paid.

(1) Whenever it appears, upon the examination of any return made under this chapter or upon proof submitted to the department by the personal representative, that an amount of estate tax has been paid in excess of the tax legally due under this chapter, the amount of such overpayment, together with any overpayment of interest thereon shall be refunded to the personal representative and paid by the Chief Financial Officer; such refund shall be made by the department as a matter of course regardless of whether or not the personal representative has filed a written claim therefor, except that upon request of the department, the personal representative shall file with the department a conformed copy of any written claim for refund of federal estate tax which has theretofore been filed with the United States.

(2) Notwithstanding the foregoing provisions, no refund of estate tax shall be made nor shall any personal representative be entitled to bring any action for refund of estate tax after the expiration of 4 years from the date of payment of the tax to be refunded, unless there shall have been filed with the department written notice of any administrative or judicial determination of the federal estate tax liability of the estate, whichever shall last occur, and such notice shall have been so filed not later than 60 days after the determination shall have become final.

(3) For the purpose of this section, an administrative determination shall be deemed to have become final on the date of receipt by the personal representative or other interested party of the final payment to be made refunding federal estate tax or upon the last date on which the personal representative or any other interested party shall receive notice from the United States that an overpayment of federal estate tax has been credited by the United States against any liability other than federal estate tax of said estate. A final judicial determination shall be deemed to have occurred on the date on which any judgment entered by a court of competent jurisdiction and determining that there has been an overpayment of federal estate tax becomes final.

(4) Nothing herein contained shall be construed to prevent a personal representative from bringing or maintaining an action in any court of competent jurisdiction, within any period otherwise prescribed by law, to determine any question bearing upon the taxable situs of property, the domicile of a decedent, or otherwise affecting the jurisdiction of the state to impose an inheritance or estate tax with respect to a particular item or items of property.

(5) Notwithstanding any other provision of this section, estate tax may not be refunded pursuant to any allegation that the decedent was a resident of another state unless this state is a party to any compromise agreement between the decedent's estate and the other state or unless this state is allowed to intervene as a party in any action in the other state in which the residency of the decedent is at issue.

History.
S. 22, ch. 16015, 1933; CGL 1936 Supp. 1342(102); s. 8-A, ch. 29718, 1955; ss. 21, 35, ch. 69-106; s. 17, ch. 80-153; s. 2, ch. 89-356; s. 176, ch. 2003-261.

198.30. Circuit judge to report names of decedents, etc.

Each circuit judge of this state shall, on or before the 10th day of every month, notify the department of the names of all decedents; the names and addresses of the respective personal representatives, administrators, or curators appointed; the amount of the bonds, if any, required by the court; and the probable value of the estates, in all estates of decedents whose wills have been probated or propounded for probate before the circuit judge or upon which letters testamentary or upon whose estates letters of administration or curatorship have been sought or granted, during the preceding month; and such report shall contain any other information which the circuit judge may have concerning the estates of such decedents. In addition, a copy of this report shall be provided to the Agency for Health Care Administration. A circuit judge shall also furnish forthwith such further information, from the records and files of the circuit court in regard to such estates, as the department may from time to time require.

History.
S. 23, ch. 16015, 1933; CGL 1936 Supp. 1342(103); s. 9, ch. 29718, 1955; ss. 21, 35, ch. 69-106; s. 20, ch. 73-334; s. 18, ch. 80-153; s. 1042, ch. 95-147; s. 14, ch. 98-191.

198.31. Duties and powers of corporate personal representatives of nonresident decedents.

If the personal representative of the estate of a nonresident is a corporation duly authorized, qualified, and acting as personal representative in the jurisdiction of the domicile of the decedent, it shall be under the duties and obligations as to the giving of notices and filing of returns required by this chapter, and may bring and defend actions and suits as may be authorized or permitted by this chapter, to the same extent as an individual personal representative, notwithstanding that such corporation may be prohibited from exercising, in this state, any powers as personal representative; but nothing herein contained shall be taken or construed as authorizing a corporation not authorized to do business in this state to qualify or act as a personal representative, an administrator, or in any other fiduciary capacity, if otherwise prohibited by the laws of this state, except to the extent herein expressly provided.

History.
S. 24, ch. 16015, 1933; CGL 1936 Supp. 1342(104); s. 19, ch. 80-153.

198.32. Prima facie liability for tax.

(1) The estate of each decedent whose property is subject to the laws of the state shall be deemed prima facie liable for estate taxes under this chapter and shall be subject to a lien therefor in such amount as may be later determined to be due and payable on the estate as provided in this chapter. This presumption of liability shall begin on the date of the death of the decedent and shall continue until the full settlement of all taxes which may be found to be due under this chapter, the settlement to be shown by receipts for all taxes due to be issued by the department as provided for in this chapter.

(2) Whenever an estate is not subject to tax under this chapter and is not required to file a return, the personal representative may execute an affidavit attesting that the estate is not taxable. The form of the affidavit shall be prescribed by the department, and shall include, but not be limited to, statements regarding the decedent's domicile and whether a federal estate tax return will be filed, and acknowledgment of the personal representative's personal liability under s. 198.23. This affidavit shall be subject to record and admissible in evidence to show nonliability for tax. This subsection applies to all estates, regardless of the date of death of the decedent.

History.
S. 25, ch. 16015, 1933; CGL 1936 Supp. 1342(105); ss. 21, 35, ch. 69-106; s. 4, ch. 71-202; s. 20, ch. 80-153; s. 7, ch. 99-208; s. 2, ch. 2005-280.

198.33. Discharge of estate, notice of lien, limitation on lien, etc.

(1) Where no receipt for the payment of taxes, or no affidavit or certificate of nonliability for taxes has been issued or recorded as provided for in this chapter, the property constituting the estate of the decedent in this state shall be deemed fully acquitted and discharged of all liability for estate and inheritance taxes under this chapter after a lapse of 10 years from the date of the filing with the department of an estate tax return, unless the department shall make out and file and have recorded in the public records of the county wherein any part of the estate of the decedent may be situated in this state, a notice of lien against the property of the estate, specifying the amount or approximate amount of taxes claimed to be due to the state under this chapter, which notice of lien shall continue said lien in force for an additional period of 5 years or until payment is made. Such notice of lien shall be filed and recorded in the book of deeds in the office of the clerk of the circuit court; provided, where no receipt for the payment of taxes, or no affidavit or certificate of nonliability for taxes, has been issued or recorded as provided for in this chapter, the property constituting the estate of the decedent in this state, if said decedent was a resident of this state at the time of death, shall be deemed fully acquitted and discharged of all liability for tax under this chapter after a lapse of 10 years from the date of the death of the decedent, unless the department shall make out and file and have recorded notice of lien as herein provided, which notice shall continue said lien in force against such property of the estate as is situate in the county wherein said notice of lien was recorded for an additional period of 5 years or until payment is made.

(2) Notwithstanding anything to the contrary in this section or this chapter, no lien for estate and inheritance taxes under this chapter shall continue for more than 20 years from the date of death of the decedent, whether the decedent be a resident or nonresident of this state.

History.
S. 26, ch. 16015, 1933; CGL 1936 Supp. 1342(106); s. 6, ch. 28031, 1953; s. 10, ch. 29718, 1955; s. 2, ch. 57-108; ss. 21, 35, ch. 69-106; s. 1043, ch. 95-147; s. 8, ch. 99-208.

198.34. Disposition of proceeds from taxes.

All taxes and fees levied and collected under this chapter shall be paid into the Treasury of the state to the credit of the General Revenue Fund.

History.
S. 28, ch. 16015, 1933; CGL 1936 Supp. 1342(108); s. 10, ch. 26869, 1951.

198.35. Interpretation and construction.

When not otherwise provided for in this chapter, the rules of interpretation and construction applicable to the estate and inheritance tax laws of the United States shall apply to and be followed in the interpretation of this chapter.

History.
S. 32, ch. 16015, 1933; CGL 1936 Supp. 1342(111); s. 5, ch. 77-411; s. 1, ch. 79-34; s. 1, ch. 80-16; s. 1, ch. 82-38.

198.36. Failure to produce records; penalty.

Whoever fails to comply with any duty imposed upon him or her by this law, or having in his or her possession or control any record, file, or paper, containing or supposed to contain any information concerning the estate of the decedent, or, having in his or her possession or control any property comprised in the gross estate of the decedent, fails to exhibit the same upon request to the department or any examiner, appraiser, or attorney appointed pursuant to this chapter, who desires to examine the same in the performance of his or her duties under this chapter, shall be liable to a penalty of not exceeding $500 to be recovered, with costs of suit, in a civil action in the name of the state.

History.
S. 27, ch. 16015, 1933; CGL 1936 Supp. 1342(107); ss. 21, 35, ch. 69-106; s. 1044, ch. 95-147.

198.37. Failure to make return; penalty.

Any person required under this chapter to pay any tax, or required by law or regulations made under authority thereof to make a return, keep any records, or supply any information for the purposes of the computation, assessment, or collection of any tax imposed by this chapter, who willfully fails to pay such tax, make such return, keep such records, or supply such information, at the time or times required by law or regulations, is, in addition to other penalties provided by law, guilty of a misdemeanor of the first degree, punishable as provided in s. 775.082 or s. 775.083.

History.
S. 27, ch. 16015, 1933; CGL 1936 Supp. 7473(3-a); s. 97, ch. 71-136; s. 62, ch. 87-6; s. 36, ch. 87-101; s. 11, ch. 91-224.

198.38. False return; penalty.

Any person who willfully aids or assists in, or procures, counsels, or advises, the preparation or presentation under, or in connection with any matter arising under, this chapter of a false or fraudulent return, affidavit, claim, or document shall (whether or not such falsity or fraud is with the knowledge or consent of the person authorized or required to present such return, affidavit, claim or document) be guilty of a felony of the third degree, punishable as provided in s. 775.082, s. 775.083, or s. 775.084.

History.
S. 27, ch. 16015, 1933; CGL 1936 Supp. 7473(3-a); s. 98, ch. 71-136.

198.39. False statement in return; penalty.

Whoever knowingly makes any false statement in any notice, affidavit, or return required to be filed or made under this chapter is guilty of a misdemeanor of the first degree, punishable as provided in s. 775.082 or s. 775.083.

History.
S. 27, ch. 16015, 1933; CGL 1936 Supp. 7473(3-a); s. 99, ch. 71-136; s. 63, ch. 87-6; s. 37, ch. 87-101; s. 12, ch. 91-224; s. 9, ch. 99-208.

198.40. Failure to pay tax, evasion of tax, etc.; penalty.

Any person required under this chapter to collect, account for, and pay over any tax imposed by this chapter who willfully fails to collect or truthfully account for and pay over such tax, and any person who willfully attempts in any manner to evade or defeat any tax imposed by this chapter or the payment thereof, shall, in addition to other penalties provided by law, be guilty of a felony of the third degree, punishable as provided in s. 775.082, s. 775.083, or s. 775.084.

History.
S. 27, ch. 16015, 1933; CGL 1936 Supp. 7473(3-a); s. 100, ch. 71-136.

198.41. Effectiveness of this chapter, etc.

This chapter shall remain in force and effect so long as the Government of the United States retains in full force and effect as a part of the Revenue Laws of the United States a Federal Estate Tax, and this chapter shall cease to be operative as and when the Government of the United States ceases to impose any Estate Tax of the United States.

History.
S. 29, ch. 16015, 1933; CGL 1936 Supp. 1342(109).

198.42. Short title.

This chapter may be cited as the "Estate Tax Law of Florida."

History.
S. 1, ch. 16015, 1933; CGL 1936 Supp. 1342(80).

198.44. Certain exemptions from inheritance and estate taxes.

The tax imposed under the inheritance and estate tax laws of this state in respect to personal property (except tangible property having an actual situs in this state) shall not be payable:

(1) If the transferor at the time of death was a resident of a state or territory of the United States, or the District of Columbia, which at the time of death did not impose a death tax of any character in respect to property of residents of this state (except tangible personal property having an actual situs in such state, territory, or district); or

(2) If the laws of the state, territory, or district of the residence of the transferor at the time of death contained a reciprocal exemption provision under which nonresidents were exempted from said death taxes of every character in respect to personal property (except tangible personal property having an actual situs therein), and provided that the state, territory, or district of the residence of such nonresident decedent allowed a similar exemption to residents of the state, territory, or district of residence of such decedent.

History.
S. 1, ch. 15747, 1931; CGL 1936 Supp. 1342(70); s. 1045, ch. 95-147.

TITLE XV.
HOMESTEAD AND EXEMPTIONS

CHAPTER 222.
METHOD OF SETTING APART HOMESTEAD AND EXEMPTIONS

222.01. Designation of homestead by owner before levy.

(1) Whenever any natural person residing in this state desires to avail himself or herself of the benefit of the provisions of the constitution and laws exempting property as a homestead from forced sale under any process of law, he or she may make a statement, in writing, containing a description of the real property, mobile home, or modular home claimed to be exempt and declaring that the real property, mobile home, or modular home is the homestead of the party in whose behalf such claim is being made. Such statement shall be signed by the person making it and shall be recorded in the circuit court.

(2) When a certified copy of a judgment has been filed in the public records of a county pursuant to chapter 55, a person who is entitled to the benefit of the provisions of the State Constitution exempting real property as homestead and who has a contract to sell or a commitment from a lender for a mortgage on the homestead may file a notice of homestead in the public records of the county in which the homestead property is located in substantially the following form:

NOTICE OF HOMESTEAD

To: (Name and address of judgment creditor as shown on recorded judgment and name and address of any other person shown in the recorded judgment to receive a copy of the Notice of Homestead).

You are notified that the undersigned claims as homestead exempt from levy and execution under Section 4, Article X of the State Constitution, the following described property:

(Legal description)

The undersigned certifies, under oath, that he or she has applied for and received the homestead tax exemption as to the above-described property, that _____ is the tax identification parcel number of this property, and that the undersigned has resided on this property continuously and uninterruptedly from (date) to the date of this Notice of Homestead. Further, the undersigned will either convey or mortgage the above-described property pursuant to the following:

(Describe the contract of sale or loan commitment by date, names of parties, date of anticipated closing, and amount. The name, address, and telephone number of the person conducting the anticipated closing must be set forth.)

The undersigned also certifies, under oath, that the judgment lien filed by you on (date) and recorded in Official Records Book _____, Page _____ , of the Public Records of _____ County, Florida, does not constitute a valid lien on the described property.

YOU ARE FURTHER NOTIFIED, PURSUANT TO SECTION 222.01 ET SEQ., FLORIDA STATUTES, THAT WITHIN 45 DAYS AFTER THE MAILING OF THIS NOTICE YOU MUST FILE AN ACTION IN THE CIRCUIT COURT OF _____ COUNTY, FLORIDA, FOR A DECLARATORY JUDGMENT TO DETERMINE THE CONSTITUTIONAL HOMESTEAD STATUS OF THE SUBJECT PROPERTY OR TO FORECLOSE YOUR JUDGMENT LIEN ON THE PROPERTY AND RECORD A LIS PENDENS IN THE PUBLIC RECORDS OF THE COUNTY WHERE THE HOMESTEAD IS LOCATED. YOUR FAILURE TO SO ACT WILL RESULT IN ANY BUYER OR LENDER, OR HIS OR HER SUCCESSORS AND ASSIGNS, UNDER THE ABOVE-DESCRIBED CONTRACT OF SALE OR LOAN COMMITMENT TO TAKE FREE AND CLEAR OF ANY JUDGMENT LIEN YOU MAY HAVE ON THE PROPERTY.

This _____ day of _____, 2 _____.

_____
(Signature of Owner)

_____
(Printed Name of Owner)

_____
(Owner's Address)

Sworn to and subscribed before me by _____ who is personally known to me or produced _____ as identification, this _____ day of _____, 2 _____.

_____
Notary Public

(3) The clerk shall mail a copy of the notice of homestead to the judgment lienor, by certified mail, return receipt requested, at the address shown in the most recent recorded judgment or accompanying affidavit, and to any other person designated in the most recent recorded judgment or accompanying affidavit to receive the notice of homestead, and shall certify to such service on the face of such notice and record the notice. Notwithstanding the use of certified mail, return receipt requested, service shall be deemed complete upon mailing.

(4) A lien pursuant to chapter 55 of any lienor upon whom such notice is served, who fails to institute an action for a declaratory judgment to determine the constitutional homestead status of the property described in the notice of homestead or to file an action to foreclose the judgment lien, together with the filing of a lis pendens in the public records of the county in which the homestead is located, within 45 days after service of such notice shall be deemed as not attaching to the property by virtue of its status as homestead property as to the interest of any buyer or lender, or his or her successors or assigns, who takes under the contract of sale or loan commitment described above within 180 days after the filing in the public records of the notice of homestead. This subsection shall not act to prohibit a lien from attaching to the real property described in the notice of homestead at such time as the property loses its homestead status.

(5) As provided in s. 4, Art. X of the State Constitution, this subsection shall not apply to:

(a) Liens and judgments for the payment of taxes and assessments on real property.

(b) Liens and judgments for obligations contracted for the purchase of real property.

(c) Liens and judgments for labor, services, or materials furnished to repair or improve real property.

(d) Liens and judgments for other obligations contracted for house, field, or other labor performed on real property.

History.
S. 1, ch. 1715, 1869; RS 1998; GS 2520; RGS 3875; CGL 5782; s. 20, ch. 73-334; s. 2, ch. 77-299; s. 1, ch. 83-40; s. 1195, ch. 95-147; s. 25, ch. 2000-258; s. 17, ch. 2005-241.

222.02.　Designation of homestead after levy.

Whenever a levy is made upon the lands, tenements, mobile home, or modular home of such person whose homestead has not been set apart and selected, such person, or the person's agent or attorney, may in writing notify the officer making such levy, by notice under oath made before any officer of this state duly authorized to administer oaths, at any time before the day appointed for the sale thereof, of what such person regards as his or her homestead, with a description thereof; and the remainder only shall be subject to sale under such levy.

History.
S. 2, ch. 1715, 1869; RS 1999; GS 2521; RGS 3876; CGL 5783; s. 3, ch. 77-299; s. 2, ch. 83-40; s. 1196, ch. 95-147.

222.03.　Survey at instance of dissatisfied creditor.

If the creditor in any execution or process sought to be levied is dissatisfied with the quantity of land selected and set apart, and shall himself or herself, or by his or her agent or attorney, notify the officer levying, the officer shall at the creditor's request cause the same to be surveyed, and when the homestead is not within the corporate limits of any town or city, the person claiming said exemption shall have the right to set apart that portion of land belonging to him or her which includes the residence, or not, at the person's option, and if the first tract or parcel does not contain 160 acres, the said officer shall set apart the remainder from any other tract or tracts claimed by the debtor, but in every case taking all the land lying contiguous until the whole quantity of 160 acres is made up. The person claiming the exemption shall not be forced to take as his or her homestead any tract or portion of a tract, if any defect exists in the title, except at the person's option. The expense of such survey shall be chargeable on the execution as costs; but if it shall appear that the person claiming such exemption does not own more than 160 acres in the state, the expenses of said survey shall be paid by the person directing the same to be made.

History.
S. 3, ch. 1715, 1869; s. 1, ch. 1944, 1873; RS 2000; GS 2522; RGS 3877; CGL 5784; s. 1197, ch. 95-147.

222.04.　Sale after survey.

After such survey has been made, the officer making the levy may sell the property levied upon not included in such property set off in such manner.

History.
S. 4, ch. 1715, 1869; RS 2001; GS 2523; RGS 3878; CGL 5785.

222.05.　Setting apart leasehold.

Any person owning and occupying any dwelling house, including a mobile home used as a residence, or modular home, on land not his or her own which he or she may lawfully possess, by lease or otherwise, and claiming such house, mobile home, or modular home as his or her homestead, shall be entitled to the exemption of such house, mobile home, or modular home from levy and sale as aforesaid.

History.
S. 5, ch. 1715, 1869; RS 2002; GS 2524; RGS 3879; CGL 5786; s. 1, ch. 77-299; s. 1198, ch. 95-147.

222.061.　Method of exempting personal property; inventory.

(1) When a levy is made by writ of execution, writ of attachment, or writ of garnishment upon personal property which is allowed by law or by the State Constitution to be exempt from levy and sale, the debtor may claim such personal property to be exempt from sale by making, within 15 days after the date of the levy, an inventory of his or her personal property. The inventory shall show the fair market valuation of the property listed and shall have an affidavit attached certifying that the inventory contains a correct list of all personal property owned by the debtor in this state and that the value shown is the fair market value of the property. The debtor shall designate the property listed in the schedule which he or she claims to be exempt from levy and sale.

(2) The original inventory and affidavit shall be filed with the court which issued the writ. The debtor, by mail or hand delivery, shall promptly serve one copy on the judgment creditor and furnish one copy to the sheriff who executed the writ. If the creditor desires to object to the inventory, he or she shall file an objection with the court which issued the writ within 5 days after service of the inventory, or he or she shall be deemed to admit the inventory as true. If the creditor does not file an objection, the clerk of the court shall immediately send the case file to the court issuing the writ, and the court shall promptly issue an order exempting the items claimed. Such order shall be sent by the court to the sheriff directing him or her to promptly redeliver to the debtor any exempt property under the levy and to sell any nonexempt property under the levy according to law.

(3) If the creditor files an objection, he or she shall promptly serve, by mail or hand delivery, one copy on the debtor and furnish one copy to the sheriff who executed the writ. Upon the filing of an objection, the clerk shall immediately send the case file to the court issuing the writ, and the court shall automatically schedule a prompt evidentiary hearing to determine the validity of the objection and shall enter its order therein describing the exempt and nonexempt property. Upon its issuance, the order shall be sent by the court to the sheriff directing him or her to promptly redeliver to the debtor any exempt property under the levy and to sell the nonexempt property under the levy according to law.

(4) The court shall appoint a disinterested appraiser to assist in its evidentiary hearing unless the debtor and creditor mutually waive the appointment of such appraiser. The appraiser shall take and file an oath that he or she will faithfully appraise the property at its fair market value and that he or she will file a signed and sworn appraisal with the court as required by law. Notice of the time and place of the inspection of the property for the purpose of its appraisal shall be given by the appraiser to the debtor, creditor, and sheriff, at least 24 hours before the inspection is made. The appraiser shall be entitled to a reasonable fee as determined by the court for his or her services. The appraiser's fee shall be taxed as costs, but no costs shall be assessed against the debtor for the proceedings under this section if the debtor prevails on his or her claim of exemption. The court may require the creditor to deposit a cash bond, a surety bond, or other security, conditioned on the creditor's obligation to pay reasonable appraisal expenses, not to exceed $100.

(5) During the pendency of proceedings under this section, the sheriff shall safeguard the property seized under the writ, and the creditor shall deposit sufficient moneys with the sheriff to pay the cost of such safeguarding until the property is sold or redelivered to the debtor. When the sheriff receives a copy of a court order identifying which property has been declared exempt and which property has been declared not exempt and ordering the sale of the property not exempt from levy, he or she shall sell the property.

(6) The party who successfully maintains his or her claim at the time of the evidentiary hearing may be entitled to reasonable attorney's fees and shall be entitled to costs. The costs shall include, but not be limited to, appraisal fees, storage fees, and such other costs incurred as a result of the levy.

(7) No inventory or schedule to exempt personal property from sale shall be accepted prior to a levy on the property.

History.
S. 5, ch. 85-272; s. 61, ch. 87-224; s. 1199, ch. 95-147.

222.07. Defendant's rights of selection.

Upon the completion of the inventory the person entitled to the exemption, or the person's agent or attorney, may select from such an inventory an amount of property not exceeding, according to such appraisal, the amount of value exempted; but if the person so entitled, or the person's agent or attorney, does not appear and make such selection, the officer shall make the selection for him or her, and the property not so selected as exempt may be sold.

History.
S. 8, ch. 1715, 1869; RS 2004; GS 2526; RGS 3881; CGL 5788; s. 1200, ch. 95-147.

222.08. Jurisdiction to set apart homestead and exemption.

The circuit courts have equity jurisdiction to order and decree the setting apart of homesteads and of exemptions of personal property from forced sales.

History.
S. 2, ch. 3246, 1881; RS 2005; GS 2527; RGS 3882; CGL 5789.

222.09. Injunction to prevent sale.

The circuit courts have equity jurisdiction to enjoin the sale of all property, real and personal, that is exempt from forced sale.

History.
S. 1, ch. 3246, 1881; RS 2006; GS 2528; RGS 3883; CGL 5790.

222.10. Jurisdiction to subject property claimed to be exempt.

The circuit courts have equity jurisdiction upon bill filed by a creditor or other person interested in enforcing any unsatisfied judgment or decree, to determine whether any property, real or personal, claimed to be exempt, is so exempt, and in case it be not exempt, the court shall, by its decree subject it, or so much thereof as may be necessary, to the satisfaction of said judgment or decree and may enjoin the sheriff or other officer from setting apart as exempt property, real or personal, which is not exempt, and may annul all exemptions made and set apart by the sheriff or other officer.

History.
S. 3, ch. 3246, 1881; RS 2007; GS 2529; RGS 3884; CGL 5791.

222.11.   Exemption of wages from garnishment.

(1) As used in this section, the term:

(a) "Earnings" includes compensation paid or payable, in money of a sum certain, for personal services or labor whether denominated as wages, salary, commission, or bonus.

(b) "Disposable earnings" means that part of the earnings of any head of family remaining after the deduction from those earnings of any amounts required by law to be withheld.

(c) "Head of family" includes any natural person who is providing more than one-half of the support for a child or other dependent.

(2)(a) All of the disposable earnings of a head of family whose disposable earnings are less than or equal to $750 a week are exempt from attachment or garnishment.

(b) Disposable earnings of a head of a family, which are greater than $750 a week, may not be attached or garnished unless such person has agreed otherwise in writing. The agreement to waive the protection provided by this paragraph must:

1. Be written in the same language as the contract or agreement to which the waiver relates;

2. Be contained in a separate document attached to the contract or agreement; and

3. Be in substantially the following form in at least 14-point type:

IF YOU PROVIDE MORE THAN ONE-HALF OF THE SUPPORT FOR A CHILD OR OTHER DEPENDENT, ALL OR PART OF YOUR INCOME IS EXEMPT FROM GARNISHMENT UNDER FLORIDA LAW. YOU CAN WAIVE THIS PROTECTION ONLY BY SIGNING THIS DOCUMENT. BY SIGNING BELOW, YOU AGREE TO WAIVE THE PROTECTION FROM GARNISHMENT.

_____
(Consumer's Signature)   (Date Signed)

I have fully explained this document to the consumer.

_____
(Creditor's Signature)   (Date Signed)

The amount attached or garnished may not exceed the amount allowed under the Consumer Credit Protection Act, 15 U.S.C. s. 1673.

(c) Disposable earnings of a person other than a head of family may not be attached or garnished in excess of the amount allowed under the Consumer Credit Protection Act, 15 U.S.C. s. 1673.

(3) Earnings that are exempt under subsection (2) and are credited or deposited in any financial institution are exempt from attachment or garnishment for 6 months after the earnings are received by the financial institution if the funds can be traced and properly identified as earnings. Commingling of earnings with other funds does not by itself defeat the ability of a head of family to trace earnings.

History.
S. 1, ch. 2065, 1875; RS 2008; GS 2530; RGS 3885; CGL 5792; s. 1, ch. 81-301; s. 6, ch. 85-272; s. 2, ch. 93-256; s. 1, ch. 2010-97, eff. Oct. 1, 2010.

222.12.   Proceedings for exemption.

Whenever any money or other thing due for labor or services as aforesaid is attached by such process, the person to whom the same is due and owing may make oath before the officer who issued the process or before a notary public that the money attached is due for the personal labor and services of such person, and she or he is the head of a family residing in said state. When such an affidavit is made, notice of same shall be forthwith given to the party, or her or his attorney, who sued out the process, and if the facts set forth in such affidavit are not denied under oath within 2 business days after the service of said notice, the process shall be returned, and all proceedings under the same shall cease. If the facts stated in the affidavit are denied by the party who sued out the process within the time above set forth and under oath, then the matter shall be tried by the court from which the writ or process issued, in like manner as claims to property levied upon by writ of execution are tried, and the money or thing attached shall remain subject to the process until released by the judgment of the court which shall try the issue.

History.
S. 2, ch. 2065, 1875; RS 2009; GS 2531; RGS 3886; CGL 5793; s. 1201, ch. 95-147; s. 26, ch. 2000-258.

222.13.   Life insurance policies; disposition of proceeds.

(1) Whenever any person residing in the state shall die leaving insurance on his or her life, the said insurance shall inure exclusively to the benefit of the person for whose use and benefit such insurance is designated in the policy, and the proceeds thereof shall be exempt from the claims of creditors of the insured unless the insurance policy or a valid assignment thereof provides otherwise. Notwithstanding the foregoing, whenever the insurance, by designation or otherwise, is payable to the insured or to the insured's estate or to his or her executors, administrators, or assigns, the insurance proceeds shall become a part of the insured's estate for all purposes and shall be administered by the personal representative of the estate of the insured in accordance with the probate laws of the state in like manner as other assets of the insured's estate.

(2) Payments as herein directed shall, in every such case, discharge the insurer from any further liability

under the policy, and the insurer shall in no event be responsible for, or be required to see to, the application of such payments.

History.
S. 1, ch. 1864, 1872; RS 2347; s. 1, ch. 4555, 1897; s. 1, ch. 5165, 1903; GS 3154; RGS 4977; CGL 7065; s. 1, ch. 29861, 1955; s. 1, ch. 59-333; s. 1, ch. 63-230; s. 1, ch. 70-376; s. 51, ch. 71-355; s. 1202, ch. 95-147.

222.14. Exemption of cash surrender value of life insurance policies and annuity contracts from legal process.

The cash surrender values of life insurance policies issued upon the lives of citizens or residents of the state and the proceeds of annuity contracts issued to citizens or residents of the state, upon whatever form, shall not in any case be liable to attachment, garnishment or legal process in favor of any creditor of the person whose life is so insured or of any creditor of the person who is the beneficiary of such annuity contract, unless the insurance policy or annuity contract was effected for the benefit of such creditor.

History.
S. 1, ch. 10154, 1925; CGL 7066; s. 1, ch. 78-76.

222.15. Wages or reemployment assistance or unemployment compensation payments due deceased employee may be paid spouse or certain relatives.

(1) It is lawful for any employer, in case of the death of an employee, to pay to the wife or husband, and in case there is no wife or husband, then to the child or children, provided the child or children are over the age of 18 years, and in case there is no child or children, then to the father or mother, any wages or travel expenses that may be due such employee at the time of his or her death.

(2) It is also lawful for the Department of Economic Opportunity, in case of death of any unemployed individual, to pay to those persons referred to in subsection (1) any reemployment assistance or unemployment compensation payments that may be due to the individual at the time of his or her death.

History.
S. 1, ch. 7366, 1917; RGS 4979; CGL 7068; s. 1, ch. 20407, 1941; s. 1, ch. 63-165; ss. 17, 35, ch. 69-106; s. 1, ch. 73-283; s. 10, ch. 79-7; s. 5, ch. 83-174; s. 1203, ch. 95-147; s. 7, ch. 2003-36; s. 96, ch. 2011-142, eff. July 1, 2011; s. 52, ch. 2012-30, eff. July 1, 2012.

Editor's Notes.
Section 93, ch. 2012-30, provides: "If any provision of this act or its application to any person or circumstance is held invalid, the invalidity does not affect other provisions or applications of the act which can be given effect without the invalid provision or application, and to this end the provisions of the act are severable."

222.16. Wages or reemployment assistance or unemployment compensation payments so paid not subject to administration.

Any wages, travel expenses, or reemployment assistance or unemployment compensation payments so paid under the authority of s. 222.15 shall not be considered as assets of the estate and subject to administration; provided, however, that the travel expenses so exempted from administration shall not exceed the sum of $300.

History.
S. 2, ch. 7366, 1917; RGS 4980; CGL 7069; s. 2, ch. 20407, 1941; s. 2, ch. 63-165; s. 53, ch. 2012-30, eff. July 1, 2012.

Editor's Notes.
Section 93, ch. 2012-30, provides: "If any provision of this act or its application to any person or circumstance is held invalid, the invalidity does not affect other provisions or applications of the act which can be given effect without the invalid provision or application, and to this end the provisions of the act are severable."

222.17. Manifesting and evidencing domicile in Florida.

(1) Any person who shall have established a domicile in this state may manifest and evidence the same by filing in the office of the clerk of the circuit court for the county in which the said person shall reside, a sworn statement showing that he or she resides in and maintains a place of abode in that county which he or she recognizes and intends to maintain as his or her permanent home.

(2) Any person who shall have established a domicile in the State of Florida, but who shall maintain another place or places of abode in some other state or states, may manifest and evidence his or her domicile in this state by filing in the office of the clerk of the circuit court for the county in which he or she resides, a sworn statement that his or her place of abode in Florida constitutes his or her predominant and principal home, and that he or she intends to continue it permanently as such.

(3) Such sworn statement shall contain, in addition to the foregoing, a declaration that the person making the same is, at the time of making such statement, a bona fide resident of the state, and shall set forth therein his or her place of residence within the state, the city, county and state wherein he or she formerly resided, and the place or places, if any, where he or she maintains another or other place or places of abode.

(4) Any person who shall have been or who shall be domiciled in a state other than the State of Florida, and who has or who may have a place of abode within the State of Florida, or who has or may do or perform other acts within the State of Florida, which independently of the actual intention of such person respecting his or her domicile might be taken to indicate that such person is or may intend to be or become domiciled in the State of Florida, and if such person desires to maintain or continue his or her domicile in such state other than the State of Florida, the person may manifest and evidence his or her permanent domicile and intention to permanently maintain and continue his or her domicile in such state other than the State of Florida, by filing in the office of the clerk of the circuit court in any county in the State of Florida in which the person may have a place of abode or in which the

person may have done or performed such acts which independently may indicate that he or she is or may intend to be or become domiciled in the State of Florida, a sworn statement that the person's domicile is in such state other than the State of Florida, as the case may be, naming such state where he or she is domiciled and stating that he or she intends to permanently continue and maintain his or her domicile in such other state so named in said sworn statement. Such sworn statement shall also contain a declaration that the person making the same is at the time of the making of such statement a bona fide resident of such state other than the State of Florida, and shall set forth therein his or her place of abode within the State of Florida, if any. Such sworn statement may contain such other and further facts with reference to any acts done or performed by such person which such person desires or intends not to be construed as evidencing any intention to establish his or her domicile within the State of Florida.

(5) The sworn statement permitted by this section shall be signed under oath before an official authorized to take affidavits. Upon the filing of such declaration with the clerk of the circuit court, it shall be the duty of the clerk in whose office such declaration is filed to record the same in a book to be provided for that purpose. For the performance of the duties herein prescribed, the clerk of the circuit court shall collect a service charge for each declaration as provided in s. 28.24.

(6) It shall be the duty of the Department of Legal Affairs to prescribe a form for the declaration herein provided for, and to furnish the same to the several clerks of the circuit courts of the state.

(7) Nothing herein shall be construed to repeal or abrogate other existing methods of proving and evidencing domicile except as herein specifically provided.

History.
SS. 1, 2, 3, 4, 5, 6, ch. 20412, 1941; s. 1, ch. 26896, 1951; ss. 11, 35, ch. 69-106; s. 15, ch. 70-134; s. 1204, ch. 95-147.

222.18. Exempting disability income benefits from legal processes.

Disability income benefits under any policy or contract of life, health, accident, or other insurance of whatever form, shall not in any case be liable to attachment, garnishment, or legal process in the state, in favor of any creditor or creditors of the recipient of such disability income benefits, unless such policy or contract of insurance was effected for the benefit of such creditor or creditors.

History.
S. 1, ch. 20741, 1941.

222.20. Nonavailability of federal bankruptcy exemptions.

In accordance with the provision of s. 522(b) of the Bankruptcy Code of 1978 (11 U.S.C. s. 522(b)), resi-

dents of this state shall not be entitled to the federal exemptions provided in s. 522(d) of the Bankruptcy Code of 1978 (11 U.S.C. s. 522(d)). Nothing herein shall affect the exemptions given to residents of this state by the State Constitution and the Florida Statutes.

History.
S. 1, ch. 79-363.

222.201. Availability of federal bankruptcy exemptions.

(1) Notwithstanding s. 222.20, an individual debtor under the federal Bankruptcy Reform Act of 1978 may exempt, in addition to any other exemptions allowed under state law, any property listed in subsection (d)(10) of s. 522 of that act.

(2) The provisions of this section apply to any bankruptcy action that is filed on or after October 1, 1987.

History.
S. 2, ch. 87-375.

222.21. Exemption of pension money and certain tax-exempt funds or accounts from legal processes.

(1) Money received by any debtor as pensioner of the United States within 3 months next preceding the issuing of an execution, attachment, or garnishment process may not be applied to the payment of the debts of the pensioner when it is made to appear by the affidavit of the debtor or otherwise that the pension money is necessary for the maintenance of the debtor's support or a family supported wholly or in part by the pension money. The filing of the affidavit by the debtor, or the making of such proof by the debtor, is prima facie evidence; and it is the duty of the court in which the proceeding is pending to release all pension moneys held by such attachment or garnishment process, immediately, upon the filing of such affidavit or the making of such proof.

(2)(a) Except as provided in paragraph (d), any money or other assets payable to an owner, a participant, or a beneficiary from, or any interest of any owner, participant, or beneficiary in, a fund or account is exempt from all claims of creditors of the owner, beneficiary, or participant if the fund or account is:

1. Maintained in accordance with a master plan, volume submitter plan, prototype plan, or any other plan or governing instrument that has been preapproved by the Internal Revenue Service as exempt from taxation under s. 401(a), s. 403(a), s. 403(b), s. 408, s. 408A, s. 409, s. 414, s. 457(b), or s. 501(a) of the Internal Revenue Code of 1986, as amended, unless it has been subsequently determined that the plan or governing instrument is not exempt from taxation in a proceeding that has become final and nonappealable;

2. Maintained in accordance with a plan or governing instrument that has been determined by the Internal Revenue Service to be exempt from taxation under s. 401(a), s. 403(a), s. 403(b), s. 408, s. 408A, s. 409, s. 414, s. 457(b), or s. 501(a) of the Internal Revenue Code of 1986, as amended, unless it has been subsequently determined that the plan or governing instrument is not exempt from taxation in a proceeding that has become final and nonappealable; or

3. Not maintained in accordance with a plan or governing instrument described in subparagraph 1. or subparagraph 2. if the person claiming exemption under this paragraph proves by a preponderance of the evidence that the fund or account is maintained in accordance with a plan or governing instrument that:

a. Is in substantial compliance with the applicable requirements for tax exemption under s. 401(a), s. 403(a), s. 403(b), s. 408, s. 408A, s. 409, s. 414, s. 457(b), or s. 501(a) of the Internal Revenue Code of 1986, as amended; or

b. Would have been in substantial compliance with the applicable requirements for tax exemption under s. 401(a), s. 403(a), s. 403(b), s. 408, s. 408A, s. 409, s. 414, s. 457(b), or s. 501(a) of the Internal Revenue Code of 1986, as amended, but for the negligent or wrongful conduct of a person or persons other than the person who is claiming the exemption under this section.

(b) It is not necessary that a fund or account that is described in paragraph (a) be maintained in accordance with a plan or governing instrument that is covered by any part of the Employee Retirement Income Security Act for money or assets payable from or any interest in that fund or account to be exempt from claims of creditors under that paragraph.

(c) Any money or other assets or any interest in any fund or account that is exempt from claims of creditors of the owner, beneficiary, or participant under paragraph (a) does not cease to be exempt after the owner's death by reason of a direct transfer or eligible rollover that is excluded from gross income under the Internal Revenue Code of 1986, including, but not limited to, a direct transfer or eligible rollover to an inherited individual retirement account as defined in s. 408(d)(3) of the Internal Revenue Code of 1986, as amended. This paragraph is intended to clarify existing law, is remedial in nature, and shall have retroactive application to all inherited individual retirement accounts without regard to the date an account was created.

(d) Any fund or account described in paragraph (a) is not exempt from the claims of an alternate payee under a qualified domestic relations order or from the claims of a surviving spouse pursuant to an order determining the amount of elective share and contribution as provided in part II of chapter 732. However, the interest of any alternate payee under a qualified domestic relations order is exempt from all claims of any creditor, other than the Department of Revenue, of the alternate payee. As used in this paragraph, the terms "alternate payee" and "qualified domestic relations order" have the meanings ascribed to them in s. 414(p) of the Internal Revenue Code of 1986.

(e) This subsection applies to any proceeding that is filed on or after the effective date of this act.

History.
S. 1, ch. 87-375; s. 1, ch. 98-159; s. 25, ch. 99-8; s. 5, ch. 2005-82; s. 1, ch. 2005-101; s. 1, ch. 2007-74, eff. July 1, 2007; s. 1, ch. 2011-84, eff. May 31, 2011.

Editor's Notes.
Sections 401(a), 402(c), 403(a), 403(b), 408, 408A, 409, 414, 457(b), and 501(a) of the Internal Revenue Code of 1986, referred to in this section, are codified as 26 U.S.C.S. §§ 401(a), 402(c), 403(a), 403(b), 408, 408A, 409, 414, 457(b), and 501(a).

The introductory language of ch. 2011-84 provided in part: "WHEREAS, many residents of this state have individual retirement accounts, relying upon the Legislature's intent that individual retirement accounts be exempt from claims of creditors, and WHEREAS, the Legislature clearly intended in s. 222.21(2)(c), Florida Statutes, that inherited individual retirement accounts included in s. 402(c) of the Internal Revenue Code of 1986, as amended, be exempt from claims of creditors of the owner, beneficiary, or participant of the inherited individual retirement account, and WHEREAS, in Robertson v. Deeb, 16 So. 3d 936 (Fla. 2d DCA 2009) the appellate court, contrary to the Legislature's intent, held that an inherited individual retirement account was not exempt from the beneficiaries' creditors because such an account was not included in property described in s. 222.21, Florida Statutes, a decision that was followed in the Bankruptcy Court of the Middle District of Florida, In re: Ard, 435 B.R. 719 (Bkrtcy. M.D. Fla. 2010)."

222.22. Exemption of assets in qualified tuition programs, medical savings accounts, Coverdell education savings accounts, and hurricane savings accounts from legal process.

(1) Moneys paid into or out of, the assets of, and the income of any validly existing qualified tuition program authorized by s. 529 of the Internal Revenue Code of 1986, as amended, including, but not limited to, the Florida Prepaid College Trust Fund advance payment contracts under s. 1009.98 and Florida Prepaid College Trust Fund participation agreements under s. 1009.981, are not liable to attachment, levy, garnishment, or legal process in the state in favor of any creditor of or claimant against any program participant, purchaser, owner or contributor, or program beneficiary.

(2) Moneys paid into or out of, the assets of, and the income of a health savings account or medical savings account authorized under ss. 220 and 223 of the Internal Revenue Code of 1986, as amended, are not liable to attachment, levy, garnishment, or legal process in this state in favor of any creditor of or claimant against any account participant, purchaser, owner or contributor, or account beneficiary.

(3) Moneys paid into or out of, the assets of, and the income of any Coverdell education savings account, also known as an educational IRA, established or existing in accordance with s. 530 of the Internal Revenue Code of 1986, as amended, are not liable to attachment, levy, garnishment, or legal process in this state in favor of any creditor of or claimant against any account participant, purchaser, owner or contributor, or account beneficiary.

(4)(a) Moneys paid into or out of, the assets of, and the income of any hurricane savings account established by an insurance policyholder for residential property in this state equal to twice the deductible sum of such insurance to cover an insurance deductible or other uninsured portion of the risks of loss from a hurricane, rising flood waters, or other catastrophic windstorm event are not liable to attachment, levy, garnishment, or legal process in this state in favor of any creditor of or claimant against any account participant, purchaser, owner or contributor, or account beneficiary.

(b) As used in this subsection, the term "hurricane savings account" means an account established by the owner of residential real estate in this state, which meets the requirements of homestead exemption under s. 4, Art. X of the State Constitution, who specifies that the purpose of the account is to cover the amount of insurance deductibles and other uninsured portions of risks of loss from hurricanes, rising flood waters, or other catastrophic windstorm events.

(c) This subsection shall take effect only when the federal government provides tax-exempt or tax-deferred status to a hurricane savings account, disaster savings account, or other similar account created to cover an insurance deductible or other uninsured portion of the risks of loss from a hurricane, rising flood waters, or other catastrophic windstorm event.

History.
S. 2, ch. 88-313; s. 2, ch. 89-296; s. 5, ch. 91-429; s. 2, ch. 98-159; s. 50, ch. 98-421; s. 2, ch. 99-220; s. 926, ch. 2002-387; s. 2, ch. 2005-101.

Editor's Notes.
Sections 529, 220, 223, and 530 of the Internal Revenue Code of 1986, referred to in this section, are codified as 26 U.S.C.S. §§ 529, 220, 223, and 530, respectively.

222.25. Other individual property of natural persons exempt from legal process.

The following property is exempt from attachment, garnishment, or other legal process:

(1) A debtor's interest, not to exceed $1,000 in value, in a single motor vehicle as defined in s. 320.01.

(2) A debtor's interest in any professionally prescribed health aids for the debtor or a dependent of the debtor.

(3) A debtor's interest in a refund or a credit received or to be received, or the traceable deposits in a financial institution of a debtor's interest in a refund or credit, pursuant to s. 32 of the Internal Revenue Code of 1986, as amended. This exemption does not apply to a debt owed for child support or spousal support.

(4) A debtor's interest in personal property, not to exceed $4,000, if the debtor does not claim or receive the benefits of a homestead exemption under s. 4, Art. X of the State Constitution. This exemption does not apply to a debt owed for child support or spousal support.

History.
S. 3, ch. 93-256; s. 1, ch. 2001-129; s. 1, ch. 2007-185, eff. July 1, 2007; s. 43, ch. 2008-4, eff. July 1, 2008.

Editor's Notes.
Section 32 of the Internal Revenue Code of 1986, referred to in this section, is codified as 26 U.S.C.S. § 32.

222.29. No exemption for fraudulent transfers.

An exemption from attachment, garnishment, or legal process provided by this chapter is not effective if it results from a fraudulent transfer or conveyance as provided in chapter 726.

History.
S. 4, ch. 93-256.

222.30. Fraudulent asset conversions.

(1) As used in this section, "conversion" means every mode, direct or indirect, absolute or conditional, of changing or disposing of an asset, such that the products or proceeds of the asset become immune or exempt by law from claims of creditors of the debtor and the products or proceeds of the asset remain property of the debtor. The definitions of chapter 726 apply to this section unless the application of a definition would be unreasonable.

(2) Any conversion by a debtor of an asset that results in the proceeds of the asset becoming exempt by law from the claims of a creditor of the debtor is a fraudulent asset conversion as to the creditor, whether the creditor's claim to the asset arose before or after the conversion of the asset, if the debtor made the conversion with the intent to hinder, delay, or defraud the creditor.

(3) In an action for relief against a fraudulent asset conversion, a creditor may obtain:

(a) Avoidance of the fraudulent asset conversion to the extent necessary to satisfy the creditor's claim.

(b) An attachment or other provisional remedy against the asset converted in accordance with applicable law.

(c) Subject to applicable principles of equity and in accordance with applicable rules of civil procedure:

1. An injunction against further conversion by the debtor of the asset or of other property.

2. Any other relief the circumstances may require.

(4) If a creditor has obtained a judgment on a claim against the debtor, the creditor, if the court so orders,

may levy execution on the asset converted or its proceeds.

(5) A cause of action with respect to a fraudulent asset conversion is extinguished unless an action is brought within 4 years after the fraudulent asset conversion was made.

(6) If an asset is converted and the converted asset is subsequently transferred to a third party, the provisions of chapter 726 apply to the transfer to the third party.

History.

S. 5, ch. 93-256.

TITLE XXIX.
PUBLIC HEALTH

CHAPTER 393.
DEVELOPMENTAL DISABILITIES

393.063. Definitions.

For the purposes of this chapter, the term:

(1) "Agency" means the Agency for Persons with Disabilities.

(2) "Adult day training" means training services which take place in a nonresidential setting, separate from the home or facility in which the client resides; are intended to support the participation of clients in daily, meaningful, and valued routines of the community; and may include work-like settings that do not meet the definition of supported employment.

(3) "Autism" means a pervasive, neurologically based developmental disability of extended duration which causes severe learning, communication, and behavior disorders with age of onset during infancy or childhood. Individuals with autism exhibit impairment in reciprocal social interaction, impairment in verbal and nonverbal communication and imaginative ability, and a markedly restricted repertoire of activities and interests.

(4) "Cerebral palsy" means a group of disabling symptoms of extended duration which results from damage to the developing brain that may occur before, during, or after birth and that results in the loss or impairment of control over voluntary muscles. For the purposes of this definition, cerebral palsy does not include those symptoms or impairments resulting solely from a stroke.

(5) "Client" means any person determined eligible by the agency for services under this chapter.

(6) "Client advocate" means a friend or relative of the client, or of the client's immediate family, who advocates for the best interests of the client in any proceedings under this chapter in which the client or his or her family has the right or duty to participate.

(7) "Comprehensive assessment" means the process used to determine eligibility for services under this chapter.

(8) "Comprehensive transitional education program" means the program established in s. 393.18.

(9) "Developmental disability" means a disorder or syndrome that is attributable to retardation, cerebral palsy, autism, spina bifida, or Prader-Willi syndrome; that manifests before the age of 18; and that constitutes a substantial handicap that can reasonably be expected to continue indefinitely.

(10) "Developmental disabilities center" means a state-owned and state-operated facility, formerly known as a "Sunland Center," providing for the care, habilitation, and rehabilitation of clients with developmental disabilities.

(11) "Direct service provider" means a person 18 years of age or older who has direct face-to-face contact with a client while providing services to the client or has access to a client's living areas or to a client's funds or personal property.

(12) "Domicile" means the place where a client legally resides, which place is his or her permanent home. Domicile may be established as provided in s. 222.17. Domicile may not be established in Florida by a minor who has no parent domiciled in Florida, or by a minor who has no legal guardian domiciled in Florida, or by any alien not classified as a resident alien.

(13) "Down syndrome" means a disorder caused by the presence of an extra chromosome 21.

(14) "Express and informed consent" means consent voluntarily given in writing with sufficient knowledge and comprehension of the subject matter to enable the person giving consent to make a knowing decision without any element of force, fraud, deceit, duress, or other form of constraint or coercion.

(15) "Family care program" means the program established in s. 393.068.

(16) "Foster care facility" means a residential facility licensed under this chapter which provides a family living environment including supervision and care necessary to meet the physical, emotional, and social needs of its residents. The capacity of such a facility may not be more than three residents.

(17) "Group home facility" means a residential facility licensed under this chapter which provides a family living environment including supervision and care necessary to meet the physical, emotional, and social needs of its residents. The capacity of such a facility shall be at least 4 but not more than 15 residents.

(18) "Guardian advocate" means a person appointed by a written order of the court to represent a person with developmental disabilities under s. 393.12.

(19) "Habilitation" means the process by which a client is assisted to acquire and maintain those life skills which enable the client to cope more effectively with the demands of his or her condition and environment and to raise the level of his or her physical, mental, and social efficiency. It includes, but is not limited to, programs of formal structured education and treatment.

(20) "High-risk child" means, for the purposes of this chapter, a child from 3 to 5 years of age with one or more of the following characteristics:

(a) A developmental delay in cognition, language, or physical development.

(b) A child surviving a catastrophic infectious or traumatic illness known to be associated with developmental delay, when funds are specifically appropriated.

(c) A child with a parent or guardian with developmental disabilities who requires assistance in meeting the child's developmental needs.

(d) A child who has a physical or genetic anomaly associated with developmental disability.

(21) "Intermediate care facility for the developmentally disabled" or "ICF/DD" means a residential facility licensed and certified pursuant to part VIII of chapter 400.

(22) "Medical/dental services" means medically necessary services which are provided or ordered for a client by a person licensed under chapter 458, chapter 459, or chapter 466. Such services may include, but are not limited to, prescription drugs, specialized therapies, nursing supervision, hospitalization, dietary services, prosthetic devices, surgery, specialized equipment and supplies, adaptive equipment, and other services as required to prevent or alleviate a medical or dental condition.

(23) "Personal care services" means individual assistance with or supervision of essential activities of daily living for self-care, including ambulation, bathing, dressing, eating, grooming, and toileting, and other similar services that are incidental to the care furnished and essential to the health, safety, and welfare of the client when there is no one else available to perform those services.

(24) "Prader-Willi syndrome" means an inherited condition typified by neonatal hypotonia with failure to thrive, hyperphagia or an excessive drive to eat which leads to obesity usually at 18 to 36 months of age, mild to moderate mental retardation, hypogonadism, short stature, mild facial dysmorphism, and a characteristic neurobehavior.

(25) "Relative" means an individual who is connected by affinity or consanguinity to the client and who is 18 years of age or older.

(26) "Resident" means any person with developmental disabilities residing at a residential facility, whether or not such person is a client of the agency.

(27) "Residential facility" means a facility providing room and board and personal care for persons with developmental disabilities.

(28) "Residential habilitation" means supervision and training with the acquisition, retention, or improvement in skills related to activities of daily living, such as personal hygiene skills, homemaking skills, and the social and adaptive skills necessary to enable the individual to reside in the community.

(29) "Residential habilitation center" means a community residential facility licensed under this chapter which provides habilitation services. The capacity of such a facility shall not be fewer than nine residents. After October 1, 1989, new residential habilitation centers may not be licensed and the licensed capacity for any existing residential habilitation center may not be increased.

(30) "Respite service" means appropriate, short-term, temporary care that is provided to a person with developmental disabilities to meet the planned or emergency needs of the person or the family or other direct service provider.

(31) "Restraint" means a physical device, method, or drug used to control dangerous behavior.

(a) A physical restraint is any manual method or physical or mechanical device, material, or equipment attached or adjacent to the individual's body so that he or she cannot easily remove the restraint and which restricts freedom of movement or normal access to one's body.

(b) A drug used as a restraint is a medication used to control the person's behavior or to restrict his or her freedom of movement and is not a standard treatment for the person's medical or psychiatric condition. Physically holding a person during a procedure to forcibly administer psychotropic medication is a physical restraint.

(c) Restraint does not include physical devices, such as orthopedically prescribed appliances, surgical dressings and bandages, supportive body bands, or other physical holding when necessary for routine physical examinations and tests; for purposes of orthopedic, surgical, or other similar medical treatment; when used to provide support for the achievement of functional body position or proper balance; or when used to protect a person from falling out of bed.

(32) "Retardation" means significantly subaverage general intellectual functioning existing concurrently with deficits in adaptive behavior that manifests before the age of 18 and can reasonably be expected to continue indefinitely. "Significantly subaverage general intellectual functioning," for the purpose of this definition, means performance which is two or more standard deviations from the mean score on a standardized intelligence test specified in the rules of the agency. "Adaptive behavior," for the purpose of this definition, means the effectiveness or degree with which an individual meets the standards of personal independence and social responsibility expected of his or her age, cultural group, and community.

(33) "Seclusion" means the involuntary isolation of a person in a room or area from which the person is prevented from leaving. The prevention may be by physical barrier or by a staff member who is acting in a manner, or who is physically situated, so as to

prevent the person from leaving the room or area. For the purposes of this chapter, the term does not mean isolation due to the medical condition or symptoms of the person.

(34) "Self-determination" means an individual's freedom to exercise the same rights as all other citizens, authority to exercise control over funds needed for one's own support, including prioritizing these funds when necessary, responsibility for the wise use of public funds, and self-advocacy to speak and advocate for oneself in order to gain independence and ensure that individuals with a developmental disability are treated equally.

(35) "Specialized therapies" means those treatments or activities prescribed by and provided by an appropriately trained, licensed, or certified professional or staff person and may include, but are not limited to, physical therapy, speech therapy, respiratory therapy, occupational therapy, behavior therapy, physical management services, and related specialized equipment and supplies.

(36) "Spina bifida" means, for purposes of this chapter, a person with a medical diagnosis of spina bifida cystica or myelomeningocele.

(37) "Support coordinator" means a person who is designated by the agency to assist individuals and families in identifying their capacities, needs, and resources, as well as finding and gaining access to necessary supports and services; coordinating the delivery of supports and services; advocating on behalf of the individual and family; maintaining relevant records; and monitoring and evaluating the delivery of supports and services to determine the extent to which they meet the needs and expectations identified by the individual, family, and others who participated in the development of the support plan.

(38) "Supported employment" means employment located or provided in an integrated work setting, with earnings paid on a commensurate wage basis, and for which continued support is needed for job maintenance.

(39) "Supported living" means a category of individually determined services designed and coordinated in such a manner as to provide assistance to adult clients who require ongoing supports to live as independently as possible in their own homes, to be integrated into the community, and to participate in community life to the fullest extent possible.

(40) "Training" means a planned approach to assisting a client to attain or maintain his or her maximum potential and includes services ranging from sensory stimulation to instruction in skills for independent living and employment.

(41) "Treatment" means the prevention, amelioration, or cure of a client's physical and mental disabilities or illnesses.

History.

S. 1, ch. 77-335; s. 1, ch. 79-148; s. 153, ch. 79-400; s. 3, ch. 81-23; s. 4, ch. 85-54; s. 1, ch. 85-147; s. 5, ch. 87-238; s. 5, ch. 88-398; s. 7, ch. 89-308; ss. 2, 4, ch. 89-339; s. 27, ch. 90-306; s. 1, ch. 90-333; s. 17, ch. 91-158; s. 3, ch. 94-154; s. 1045, ch. 95-148; s. 53, ch. 95-228; s. 1, ch. 95-293; s. 13, ch. 96-417; s. 23, ch. 98-171; s. 140, ch. 98-403; s. 80, ch. 99-8; s. 203, ch. 99-13; s. 3, ch. 2000-338; s. 35, ch. 2002-400; s. 7, ch. 2004-260; s. 71, ch. 2004-267; s. 15, ch. 2006-197, eff. July 1, 2006; s. 10, ch. 2006-227, eff. July 1, 2006; s. 2, ch. 2008-244, eff. July 1, 2008; s. 2, ch. 2011-135, eff. July 1, 2011.

Editor's Notes.

Section 36, ch. 2011-135 provides: "If any provision of this act or its application to any person or circumstance is held invalid, the invalidity does not affect other provisions or applications of the act which can be given effect without the invalid provision or application, and to this end the provisions of this act are severable."

393.12. Capacity; appointment of guardian advocate.

(1) Capacity.

(a) A person with a developmental disability may not be presumed incapacitated solely by reason of his or her acceptance in nonresidential services or admission to residential care and may not be denied the full exercise of all legal rights guaranteed to citizens of this state and of the United States.

(b) The determination of incapacity of a person with a developmental disability and the appointment of a guardian must be conducted in a separate proceeding according to the procedures and requirements of chapter 744 and the Florida Probate Rules.

(2) Appointment of a guardian advocate.

(a) A circuit court may appoint a guardian advocate, without an adjudication of incapacity, for a person with developmental disabilities, if the person lacks the decisionmaking ability to do some, but not all, of the decisionmaking tasks necessary to care for his or her person or property or if the person has voluntarily petitioned for the appointment of a guardian advocate. Except as otherwise specified, the proceeding shall be governed by the Florida Rules of Probate Procedure.

(b) A person who is being considered for appointment or is appointed as a guardian advocate need not be represented by an attorney unless required by the court or if the guardian advocate is delegated any rights regarding property other than the right to be the representative payee for government benefits. This paragraph applies only to proceedings relating to the appointment of a guardian advocate and the court's supervision of a guardian advocate and is not an exercise of the Legislature's authority pursuant to s. 2(a), Art. V of the State Constitution.

(3) Petition. — A petition to appoint a guardian advocate for a person with a developmental disability may be executed by an adult person who is a resident of this state. The petition must be verified and must:

(a) State the name, age, and present address of the petitioner and his or her relationship to the person with a developmental disability;

(b) State the name, age, county of residence, and present address of the person with a developmental disability;

(c) Allege that the petitioner believes that the person needs a guardian advocate and specify the factual information on which such belief is based;

(d) Specify the exact areas in which the person lacks the decisionmaking ability to make informed decisions about his or her care and treatment services or to meet the essential requirements for his or her physical health or safety;

(e) Specify the legal disabilities to which the person is subject; and

(f) State the name of the proposed guardian advocate, the relationship of that person to the person with a developmental disability; the relationship that the proposed guardian advocate had or has with a provider of health care services, residential services, or other services to the person with a developmental disability; and the reason why this person should be appointed. If a willing and qualified guardian advocate cannot be located, the petition shall so state.

(4) Notice.

(a) Notice of the filing of the petition must be given to the person with a developmental disability, verbally and in writing in the language of the person and in English. Notice must also be given to the next of kin of the person with a developmental disability as defined in chapter 744, a health care surrogate designated pursuant to an advance directive under chapter 765, an agent under a durable power of attorney, and such other persons as the court may direct. A copy of the petition to appoint a guardian advocate must be served with the notice.

(b) The notice must state that a hearing will be held to inquire into the capacity of the person with a developmental disability to exercise the rights enumerated in the petition. The notice must also state the date of the hearing on the petition.

(c) The notice shall state that the person with a developmental disability has the right to be represented by counsel of his or her own choice and the court shall initially appoint counsel.

(5) Counsel. — Within 3 days after a petition has been filed, the court shall appoint an attorney to represent a person with a developmental disability who is the subject of a petition to appoint a guardian advocate. The person with a developmental disability may substitute his or her own attorney for the attorney appointed by the court.

(a) The court shall initially appoint a private attorney who shall be selected from the attorney registry compiled pursuant to s. 27.40. Such attorney must have completed a minimum of 8 hours of education in guardianship. The court may waive this requirement for an attorney who has served as a court-appointed attorney in guardian advocate proceedings or as an attorney of record for guardian advocates for at least 3 years.

(b) An attorney representing a person with a developmental disability may not also serve as the guardian advocate of the person, as counsel for the guardian advocate, or as counsel for the person petitioning for the appointment of a guardian advocate.

(6) Hearing.

(a) Upon the filing of the petition to appoint a guardian advocate, the court shall set a date for holding a hearing on the petition. The hearing must be held as soon as practicable after the petition is filed, but reasonable delay for the purpose of investigation, discovery, or procuring counsel or witnesses may be granted.

(b) The hearing must be held at the time and place specified in the notice of hearing and must be conducted in a manner consistent with due process.

(c) The person with a developmental disability has the right to be present at the hearing and shall be present unless good cause to exclude the individual can be shown. The person has the right to remain silent, to present evidence, to call and cross-examine witnesses, and to have the hearing open or closed, as the person may choose.

(d) At the hearing, the court shall receive and consider all reports relevant to the person's disability, including, but not limited to, the person's current individual family or individual support plan, the individual education plan, and other professional reports documenting the condition and needs of the person.

(e) The Florida Evidence Code, chapter 90, applies at the hearing. The burden of proof must be by clear and convincing evidence.

(7) Advance directives for health care and durable power of attorney. — In each proceeding in which a guardian advocate is appointed under this section, the court shall determine whether the person with a developmental disability has executed any valid advance directive under chapter 765 or a durable power of attorney under chapter 709.

(a) If the person with a developmental disability has executed an advance directive or durable power of attorney, the court must consider and find whether the documents will sufficiently address the needs of the person with a developmental disability for whom the guardian advocate is sought. A guardian advocate may not be appointed if the court finds that the advance directive or durable power of attorney provides an alternative to the appointment of a guardian advocate which will sufficiently address the needs of the person with a developmental disability.

(b) If an interested person seeks to contest an advance directive or durable power of attorney executed by a person with a developmental disability, the interested person shall file a verified statement. The verified statement shall include the factual basis for the belief that the advance directive or durable power of attorney is invalid or does not sufficiently address the needs of the person for whom a guardian advocate is sought or that the person with authority under the advance directive or durable power of attorney is abusing his or her power.

(c) If an advance directive exists, the court shall specify in its order and letters of guardian advocacy what authority, if any, the guardian advocate shall exercise over the person's health care surrogate. Pursuant to the grounds listed in s. 765.105, the court, upon its own motion, may, with notice to the health care surrogate and any other appropriate parties, modify or revoke the authority of the health care surrogate to make health care decisions for the person with a developmental disability. For purposes of this section, the term "health care decision" has the same meaning as in s. 765.101.

(d) If any durable power of attorney exists, the court shall specify in its order and letters of guardian advocacy what powers of the agent, if any, are suspended and granted to the guardian advocate. The court, however, may not suspend any powers of the agent unless the court determines the durable power of attorney is invalid or there is an abuse by the agent of the powers granted.

(8) Court order. — If the court finds the person with a developmental disability requires the appointment of a guardian advocate, the court shall enter a written order appointing the guardian advocate and containing the findings of facts and conclusions of law on which the court made its decision, including:

(a) The nature and scope of the person's lack of decisionmaking ability;

(b) The exact areas in which the individual lacks decisionmaking ability to make informed decisions about care and treatment services or to meet the essential requirements for his or her physical health and safety;

(c) The specific legal disabilities to which the person with a developmental disability is subject;

(d) The name of the person selected as guardian advocate and the reasons for the court's selection; and

(e) The powers, duties, and responsibilities of the guardian advocate, including bonding of the guardian advocate, as provided in s. 744.351.

(9) Legal rights. — A person with a developmental disability for whom a guardian advocate has been appointed retains all legal rights except those that have been specifically granted to the guardian advocate.

(10) Powers and duties of guardian advocate. — A guardian advocate for a person with a developmental disability shall be a person or corporation qualified to act as guardian, with the same powers, duties, and responsibilities required of a guardian under chapter 744 or those defined by court order under this section. However, a guardian advocate may not be required to file an annual accounting under s. 744.3678 if the court determines that the person with a developmental disability receives income only from Social Security ben-

efits and the guardian advocate is the person's representative payee for the benefits.

(11) Court costs. — In all proceedings under this section, court costs may not be charged against the agency.

(12) Suggestion of restoration of rights. — Any interested person, including the person with a developmental disability, may file a suggestion of restoration of rights with the court in which the guardian advocacy is pending. The suggestion must state that the person with a developmental disability is currently capable of exercising some or all of the rights that were delegated to the guardian advocate and provide evidentiary support for the filing of the suggestion. Evidentiary support includes, but is not limited to, a signed statement from a medical, psychological, or psychiatric practitioner by whom the person with a developmental disability was evaluated and which supports the suggestion for the restoration. If the petitioner is unable to provide evidentiary support due to the lack of access to such information or reports, the petitioner may state a good faith basis for the suggestion for the restoration of rights without attaching evidentiary support. The court shall immediately set a hearing if no evidentiary support is attached to inquire of the petitioner and guardian advocate as to the reason and enter such orders as are appropriate to secure the required documents. The person with a disability and the person's attorney shall be provided notice of the hearing.

(a) Within 3 days after the filing of the suggestion, counsel shall be appointed for the person with a developmental disability as set forth in subsection (5).

(b) The clerk of the court shall immediately send notice of the filing of the suggestion to the person with a developmental disability, the guardian advocate, the attorney for the person with a developmental disability, the attorney for the guardian advocate, if any, and any other interested person designated by the court. Formal notice shall be served on the guardian advocate. Informal notice may be served on other persons. Notice need not be served on the person who filed the suggestion.

(c) Any objections to the suggestion must be filed within 20 days after service of the notice. If an objection is timely filed, or if the evidentiary support suggests that restoration of rights is not appropriate, the court shall set the matter for hearing. The hearing shall be conducted as set forth in s. 744.1095. The court, at the hearing, shall consider all reports and testimony relevant to the person's decisionmaking abilities at the hearing, including, but not limited to, the person's current individual family plan or individual support plan, the individual education plan, and other professional reports that document the condition and needs of the person.

(d) Notice of the hearing and copies of the objections shall be served upon the person with a developmental disability, the attorney for the person with a developmental disability, the guardian advocate, the attorney for the guardian advocate, the next of kin of the person with a developmental disability, and any other interested person as directed by the court.

(e) If no objections are filed and the court is satisfied with the evidentiary support for restoration, the court shall enter an order of restoration of rights which were delegated to a guardian advocate and which the person with a developmental disability may now exercise.

(f) At the conclusion of a hearing, the court shall enter an order denying the suggestion or restoring all or some of the rights that were delegated to the guardian advocate. If only some rights are restored to the person with a developmental disability, the court shall enter amended letters of guardian advocacy.

(g) If only some rights are restored to the person with a developmental disability, the order must state which rights are restored and amended letters of guardian advocacy shall be issued by the court. The guardian advocate shall amend the current plan as required under chapter 744 if personal rights are restored to the person with a developmental disability. The guardian advocate shall file a final accounting as required under chapter 744 if all property rights are restored to the person with a developmental disability. The guardian advocate must file the amended plan or final accounting within 60 days after the order restoring rights and amended letters of guardian advocacy are issued. A copy of the reports shall be served upon the person with a developmental disability and the attorney for the person with a developmental disability.

History.

S. 1, ch. 29853, 1955; s. 1, ch. 61-426; s. 26, ch. 63-559; s. 1, ch. 70-343; s. 5, ch. 73-308; s. 25, ch. 73-334; s. 4, ch. 77-335; s. 2, ch. 80-171; s. 10, ch. 88-398; s. 109, ch. 89-96; s. 15, ch. 94-154; s. 96, ch. 95-143; s. 1049, ch. 95-148; s. 8, ch. 2004-260; s. 108, ch. 2004-267; s. 1, ch. 2008-124, eff. July 1, 2008.

TITLE XXX.
SOCIAL WELFARE

CHAPTER 409.
SOCIAL AND ECONOMIC ASSISTANCE

409.910. Responsibility for payments on behalf of Medicaid-eligible persons when other parties are liable.

(1) It is the intent of the Legislature that Medicaid be the payor of last resort for medically necessary goods and services furnished to Medicaid recipients. All other sources of payment for medical care are primary to medical assistance provided by Medicaid. If benefits of a liable third party are discovered or become available after medical assistance has been provided by Medicaid, it is the intent of the Legislature that Medicaid be repaid in full and prior to any other person, program, or entity. Medicaid is to be repaid in full from, and to the extent of, any third-party benefits, regardless of whether a recipient is made whole or other creditors paid. Principles of common law and equity as to assignment, lien, and subrogation are abrogated to the extent necessary to ensure full recovery by Medicaid from third-party resources. It is intended that if the resources of a liable third party become available at any time, the public treasury should not bear the burden of medical assistance to the extent of such resources.

(2) This section may be cited as the "Medicaid Third-Party Liability Act."

(3) Third-party benefits for medical services shall be primary to medical assistance provided by Medicaid.

(4) After the agency has provided medical assistance under the Medicaid program, it shall seek recovery of reimbursement from third-party benefits to the limit of legal liability and for the full amount of third-party benefits, but not in excess of the amount of medical assistance paid by Medicaid, as to:

(a) Claims for which the agency has a waiver pursuant to federal law; or

(b) Situations in which the agency learns of the existence of a liable third party or in which third-party benefits are discovered or become available after medical assistance has been provided by Medicaid.

(5) An applicant, recipient, or legal representative shall inform the agency of any rights the applicant or recipient has to third-party benefits and shall inform the agency of the name and address of any person that is or may be liable to provide third-party benefits. When the agency provides, pays for, or becomes liable for medical services provided by a hospital, the recipient receiving such medical services or his or her legal representative shall also provide the information as to third-party benefits, as defined in this section, to the hospital, which shall provide notice thereof to the agency in a manner specified by the agency.

(6) When the agency provides, pays for, or becomes liable for medical care under the Medicaid program, it has the following rights, as to which the agency may assert independent principles of law, which shall nevertheless be construed together to provide the greatest recovery from third-party benefits:

(a) The agency is automatically subrogated to any rights that an applicant, recipient, or legal representative has to any third-party benefit for the full amount of medical assistance provided by Medicaid. Recovery pursuant to the subrogation rights created hereby shall not be reduced, prorated, or applied to only a portion of a judgment, award, or settlement, but is to provide full recovery by the agency from any and all third-party benefits. Equities of a recipient, his or her legal representative, a recipient's creditors, or health care providers shall not defeat, reduce, or prorate recovery by the agency as to its subrogation rights granted under this paragraph.

(b) By applying for or accepting medical assistance, an applicant, recipient, or legal representative automatically assigns to the agency any right, title, and interest such person has to any third-party benefit, excluding any Medicare benefit to the extent required to be excluded by federal law.

1. The assignment granted under this paragraph is absolute, and vests legal and equitable title to any such right in the agency, but not in excess of the amount of medical assistance provided by the agency.

2. The agency is a bona fide assignee for value in the assigned right, title, or interest, and takes vested legal and equitable title free and clear of latent equities in a third person. Equities of a recipient, the recipient's legal representative, his or her creditors, or health care providers shall not defeat or reduce recovery by the agency as to the assignment granted under this paragraph.

3. By accepting medical assistance, the recipient grants to the agency the limited power of attorney to act in his or her name, place, and stead to perform specific acts with regard to third-party benefits, the recipient's assent being deemed to have been given, including:

a. Endorsing any draft, check, money order, or other negotiable instrument representing third-party benefits that are received on behalf of the recipient as a third-party benefit.

b. Compromising claims to the extent of the rights assigned, provided that the recipient is not otherwise represented by an attorney as to the claim.

(c) The agency is entitled to, and has, an automatic lien for the full amount of medical assistance provided by Medicaid to or on behalf of the recipient for medical care furnished as a result of any covered injury or illness for which a third party is or may be liable, upon the collateral, as defined in s. 409.901.

1. The lien attaches automatically when a recipient first receives treatment for which the agency may be obligated to provide medical assistance under the Medicaid program. The lien is perfected automatically at the time of attachment.

2. The agency is authorized to file a verified claim of lien. The claim of lien shall be signed by an authorized employee of the agency, and shall be verified as to the employee's knowledge and belief. The claim of lien may be filed and recorded with the clerk of the circuit court in the recipient's last known county of residence or in any county deemed appropriate by the agency. The claim of lien, to the extent known by the agency, shall contain:

a. The name and last known address of the person to whom medical care was furnished.

b. The date of injury.

c. The period for which medical assistance was provided.

d. The amount of medical assistance provided or paid, or for which Medicaid is otherwise liable.

e. The names and addresses of all persons claimed by the recipient to be liable for the covered injuries or illness.

3. The filing of the claim of lien pursuant to this section shall be notice thereof to all persons.

4. If the claim of lien is filed within 1 year after the later of the date when the last item of medical care relative to a specific covered injury or illness was paid, or the date of discovery by the agency of the liability of any third party, or the date of discovery of a cause of action against a third party brought by a recipient or his or her legal representative, record notice shall relate back to the time of attachment of the lien.

5. If the claim of lien is filed after 1 year after the later of the events specified in subparagraph 4., notice shall be effective as of the date of filing.

6. Only one claim of lien need be filed to provide notice as set forth in this paragraph and shall provide sufficient notice as to any additional or after-paid amount of medical assistance provided by Medicaid for any specific covered injury or illness. The agency may, in its discretion, file additional, amended, or substitute claims of lien at any time after the initial filing, until the agency has

been repaid the full amount of medical assistance provided by Medicaid or otherwise has released the liable parties and recipient.

7. No release or satisfaction of any cause of action, suit, claim, counterclaim, demand, judgment, settlement, or settlement agreement shall be valid or effectual as against a lien created under this paragraph, unless the agency joins in the release or satisfaction or executes a release of the lien. An acceptance of a release or satisfaction of any cause of action, suit, claim, counterclaim, demand, or judgment and any settlement of any of the foregoing in the absence of a release or satisfaction of a lien created under this paragraph shall prima facie constitute an impairment of the lien, and the agency is entitled to recover damages on account of such impairment. In an action on account of impairment of a lien, the agency may recover from the person accepting the release or satisfaction or making the settlement the full amount of medical assistance provided by Medicaid. Nothing in this section shall be construed as creating a lien or other obligation on the part of an insurer which in good faith has paid a claim pursuant to its contract without knowledge or actual notice that the agency has provided medical assistance for the recipient related to a particular covered injury or illness. However, notice or knowledge that an insured is, or has been a Medicaid recipient within 1 year from the date of service for which a claim is being paid creates a duty to inquire on the part of the insurer as to any injury or illness for which the insurer intends or is otherwise required to pay benefits.

8. The lack of a properly filed claim of lien shall not affect the agency's assignment or subrogation rights provided in this subsection, nor shall it affect the existence of the lien, but only the effective date of notice as provided in subparagraph 5.

9. The lien created by this paragraph is a first lien and superior to the liens and charges of any provider, and shall exist for a period of 7 years, if recorded, after the date of recording; and shall exist for a period of 7 years after the date of attachment, if not recorded. If recorded, the lien may be extended for one additional period of 7 years by rerecording the claim of lien within the 90-day period preceding the expiration of the lien.

10. The clerk of the circuit court for each county in the state shall endorse on a claim of lien filed under this paragraph the date and hour of filing and shall record the claim of lien in the official records of the county as for other records received for filing. The clerk shall receive as his or her fee for filing and recording any claim of lien or release of lien under this paragraph the total sum of $2. Any fee required to be paid by the agency shall not be required to be paid in advance of filing and

recording, but may be billed to the agency after filing and recording of the claim of lien or release of lien.

11. After satisfaction of any lien recorded under this paragraph, the agency shall, within 60 days after satisfaction, either file with the appropriate clerk of the circuit court or mail to any appropriate party, or counsel representing such party, if represented, a satisfaction of lien in a form acceptable for filing in Florida.

(7) The agency shall recover the full amount of all medical assistance provided by Medicaid on behalf of the recipient to the full extent of third-party benefits.

(a) Recovery of such benefits shall be collected directly from:

1. Any third party;

2. The recipient or legal representative, if he or she has received third-party benefits;

3. The provider of a recipient's medical services if third-party benefits have been recovered by the provider; notwithstanding any provision of this section, to the contrary, however, no provider shall be required to refund or pay to the agency any amount in excess of the actual third-party benefits received by the provider from a third-party payor for medical services provided to the recipient; or

4. Any person who has received the third-party benefits.

(b) Upon receipt of any recovery or other collection pursuant to this section, the agency shall distribute the amount collected as follows:

1. To itself, an amount equal to the state Medicaid expenditures for the recipient plus any incentive payment made in accordance with paragraph (14)(a).

2. To the Federal Government, the federal share of the state Medicaid expenditures minus any incentive payment made in accordance with paragraph (14)(a) and federal law, and minus any other amount permitted by federal law to be deducted.

3. To the recipient, after deducting any known amounts owed to the agency for any related medical assistance or to health care providers, any remaining amount. This amount shall be treated as income or resources in determining eligibility for Medicaid.

The provisions of this subsection do not apply to any proceeds received by the state, or any agency thereof, pursuant to a final order, judgment, or settlement agreement, in any matter in which the state asserts claims brought on its own behalf, and not as a subrogee of a recipient, or under other theories of liability. The provisions of this subsection do not apply to any proceeds received by the state, or an agency thereof, pursuant to a final order, judgment, or settlement agreement, in any matter in which the state asserted

both claims as a subrogee and additional claims, except as to those sums specifically identified in the final order, judgment, or settlement agreement as reimbursements to the recipient as expenditures for the named recipient on the subrogation claim.

(8) The agency shall require an applicant or recipient, or the legal representative thereof, to cooperate in the recovery by the agency of third-party benefits of a recipient and in establishing paternity and support of a recipient child born out of wedlock. As a minimal standard of cooperation, the recipient or person able to legally assign a recipient's rights shall:

(a) Appear at an office designated by the agency to provide relevant information or evidence.

(b) Appear as a witness at a court or other proceeding.

(c) Provide information, or attest to lack of information, under penalty of perjury.

(d) Pay to the agency any third-party benefit received.

(e) Take any additional steps to assist in establishing paternity or securing third-party benefits, or both.

(f) Paragraphs (a)-(e) notwithstanding, the agency shall have the discretion to waive, in writing, the requirement of cooperation for good cause shown and as required by federal law.

(9) The department shall deny or terminate eligibility for any applicant or recipient who refuses to cooperate as required in subsection (8), unless cooperation has been waived in writing by the department as provided in paragraph (8)(f). However, any denial or termination of eligibility shall not reduce medical assistance otherwise payable by the department to a provider for medical care provided to a recipient prior to denial or termination of eligibility.

(10) An applicant or recipient shall be deemed to have provided to the agency the authority to obtain and release medical information and other records with respect to such medical care, for the sole purpose of obtaining reimbursement for medical assistance provided by Medicaid.

(11) The agency may, as a matter of right, in order to enforce its rights under this section, institute, intervene in, or join any legal or administrative proceeding in its own name in one or more of the following capacities: individually, as subrogee of the recipient, as assignee of the recipient, or as lienholder of the collateral.

(a) If either the recipient, or his or her legal representative, or the agency brings an action against a third party, the recipient, or the recipient's legal representative, or the agency, or their attorneys, shall, within 30 days after filing the action, provide to the other written notice, by personal delivery or registered mail, of the action, the name of the court in which the case is brought, the case number of such action, and a copy of the pleadings. If an action is brought by either the agency, or the recipient or the recipient's legal representative, the other may, at any time before trial on the merits, become a party to, or shall consolidate his or her action with the other if brought independently. Unless waived by the other, the recipient, or his or her legal representative, or the agency shall provide notice to the other of the intent to dismiss at least 21 days prior to voluntary dismissal of an action against a third party. Notice to the agency shall be sent to an address set forth by rule. Notice to the recipient or his or her legal representative, if represented by an attorney, shall be sent to the attorney, and, if not represented, then to the last known address of the recipient or his or her legal representative.

(b) An action by the agency to recover damages in tort under this subsection, which action is derivative of the rights of the recipient or his or her legal representative, shall not constitute a waiver of sovereign immunity pursuant to s. 768.14.

(c) In the event of judgment, award, or settlement in a claim or action against a third party, the court shall order the segregation of an amount sufficient to repay the agency's expenditures for medical assistance, plus any other amounts permitted under this section, and shall order such amounts paid directly to the agency.

(d) No judgment, award, or settlement in any action by a recipient or his or her legal representative to recover damages for injuries or other third-party benefits, when the agency has an interest, shall be satisfied without first giving the agency notice and a reasonable opportunity to file and satisfy its lien, and satisfy its assignment and subrogation rights or proceed with any action as permitted in this section.

(e) Except as otherwise provided in this section, notwithstanding any other provision of law, the entire amount of any settlement of the recipient's action or claim involving third-party benefits, with or without suit, is subject to the agency's claims for reimbursement of the amount of medical assistance provided and any lien pursuant thereto.

(f) Notwithstanding any provision in this section to the contrary, in the event of an action in tort against a third party in which the recipient or his or her legal representative is a party which results in a judgment, award, or settlement from a third party, the amount recovered shall be distributed as follows:

1. After attorney's fees and taxable costs as defined by the Florida Rules of Civil Procedure, one-half of the remaining recovery shall be paid to the agency up to the total amount of medical assistance provided by Medicaid.

2. The remaining amount of the recovery shall be paid to the recipient.

3. For purposes of calculating the agency's recovery of medical assistance benefits paid, the fee for services of an attorney retained by the recipient or his or her legal representative shall be calculated at 25 percent of the judgment, award, or settlement.

4. Notwithstanding any provision of this section to the contrary, the agency shall be entitled to all medical coverage benefits up to the total amount of medical assistance provided by Medicaid. For purposes of this paragraph, "medical coverage" means any benefits under health insurance, a health maintenance organization, a preferred provider arrangement, or a prepaid health clinic, and the portion of benefits designated for medical payments under coverage for workers' compensation, personal injury protection, and casualty.

(g) In the event that the recipient, his or her legal representative, or the recipient's estate brings an action against a third party, notice of institution of legal proceedings, notice of settlement, and all other notices required by this section or by rule shall be given to the agency, in Tallahassee, in a manner set forth by rule. All such notices shall be given by the attorney retained to assert the recipient's or legal representative's claim, or, if no attorney is retained, by the recipient, the recipient's legal representative, or his or her estate.

(h) Except as otherwise provided in this section, actions to enforce the rights of the agency under this section shall be commenced within 5 years after the date a cause of action accrues, with the period running from the later of the date of discovery by the agency of a case filed by a recipient or his or her legal representative, or of discovery of any judgment, award, or settlement contemplated in this section, or of discovery of facts giving rise to a cause of action under this section. Nothing in this paragraph affects or prevents a proceeding to enforce a lien during the existence of the lien as set forth in subparagraph (6)(c)9.

(i) Upon the death of a recipient, and within the time prescribed by ss. 733.702 and 733.710, the agency, in addition to any other available remedy, may file a claim against the estate of the recipient for the total amount of medical assistance provided by Medicaid for the benefit of the recipient. Claims so filed shall take priority as class 3 claims as provided by s. 733.707(1)(c). The filing of a claim pursuant to this paragraph shall neither reduce nor diminish the general claims of the agency under s. 414.28, except that the agency may not receive double recovery for the same expenditure. Claims under this paragraph shall be superior to those under s. 414.28. The death of the recipient shall neither extinguish nor diminish any right of the agency to recover third-party benefits from a third party or provider. Nothing in this paragraph affects or prevents a proceeding to enforce a lien created pursuant to this section or a proceeding to set aside a fraudulent conveyance as defined in subsection (16).

(12) No action taken by the agency shall operate to deny the recipient's recovery of that portion of benefits

not assigned or subrogated to the agency, or not secured by the agency's lien. The agency's rights of recovery created by this section, however, shall not be limited to some portion of recovery from a judgment, award, or settlement. Only the following benefits are not subject to the rights of the agency: benefits not related in any way to a covered injury or illness; proceeds of life insurance coverage on the recipient; proceeds of insurance coverage, such as coverage for property damage, which by its terms and provisions cannot be construed to cover personal injury, death, or a covered injury or illness; proceeds of disability coverage for lost income; and recovery in excess of the amount of medical benefits provided by Medicaid after repayment in full to the agency.

(13) No action of the recipient shall prejudice the rights of the agency under this section. No settlement, agreement, consent decree, trust agreement, annuity contract, pledge, security arrangement, or any other device, hereafter collectively referred to in this subsection as a "settlement agreement," entered into or consented to by the recipient or his or her legal representative shall impair the agency's rights. However, in a structured settlement, no settlement agreement by the parties shall be effective or binding against the agency for benefits accrued without the express written consent of the agency or an appropriate order of a court having personal jurisdiction over the agency.

(14) The agency is authorized to enter into agreements to enforce or collect medical support and other third-party benefits.

(a) If a cooperative agreement is entered into with any agency, program, or subdivision of the state, or any agency, program, or legal entity of or operated by a subdivision of the state, or with any other state, the agency is authorized to make an incentive payment of up to 15 percent of the amount actually collected and reimbursed to the agency, to the extent of medical assistance paid by Medicaid. Such incentive payment is to be deducted from the federal share of that amount, to the extent authorized by federal law. The agency may pay such person an additional percentage of the amount actually collected and reimbursed to the agency as a result of the efforts of the person, but no more than a maximum percentage established by the agency. In no case shall the percentage exceed the lesser of a percentage determined to be commercially reasonable or 15 percent, in addition to the 15-percent incentive payment, of the amount actually collected and reimbursed to the agency as a result of the efforts of the person under contract.

(b) If an agreement to enforce or collect third-party benefits is entered into by the agency with any person other than those described in paragraph (a), including any attorney retained by the agency who is not an employee or agent of any person named in paragraph (a), then the agency may pay such person a percentage of the amount actually collected and reimbursed to the agency as a result of the efforts of the person, to the extent of medical assistance paid by Medicaid. In no case shall the percentage exceed a maximum established by the agency, which shall not exceed the lesser of a percentage determined to be commercially reasonable or 30 percent of the amount actually collected and reimbursed to the agency as a result of the efforts of the person under contract.

(c) An agreement pursuant to this subsection may permit reasonable litigation costs or expenses to be paid from the agency's recovery to a person under contract with the agency.

(d) Contingency fees and costs incurred in recovery pursuant to an agreement under this subsection may, for purposes of determining state and federal share, be deemed to be administrative expenses of the state. To the extent permitted by federal law, such administrative expenses shall be shared with, or fully paid by, the Federal Government.

(15) Insurance and other third-party benefits may not contain any term or provision which purports to limit or exclude payment or provisions of benefits for an individual if the individual is eligible for, or a recipient of, medical assistance from Medicaid, and any such term or provision shall be void as against public policy.

(16) Any transfer or encumbrance of any right, title, or interest to which the agency has a right pursuant to this section, with the intent, likelihood, or practical effect of defeating, hindering, or reducing recovery by the agency for reimbursement of medical assistance provided by Medicaid, shall be deemed to be a fraudulent conveyance, and such transfer or encumbrance shall be void and of no effect against the claim of the agency, unless the transfer was for adequate consideration and the proceeds of the transfer are reimbursed in full to the agency, but not in excess of the amount of medical assistance provided by Medicaid.

(17) A recipient or his or her legal representative or any person representing, or acting as agent for, a recipient or the recipient's legal representative, who has notice, excluding notice charged solely by reason of the recording of the lien pursuant to paragraph (6)(c), or who has actual knowledge of the agency's rights to third-party benefits under this section, who receives any third-party benefit or proceeds therefrom for a covered illness or injury, is required either to pay the agency, within 60 days after receipt of settlement proceeds, the full amount of the third-party benefits, but not in excess of the total medical assistance provided by Medicaid, or to place the full amount of the third-party benefits in a trust account for the benefit of the agency pending judicial or administrative determination of the agency's right thereto. Proof that any such person had notice or knowledge that the recipient had received medical assistance from Medicaid, and that third-party benefits or proceeds therefrom were in any

way related to a covered illness or injury for which Medicaid had provided medical assistance, and that any such person knowingly obtained possession or control of, or used, third-party benefits or proceeds and failed either to pay the agency the full amount required by this section or to hold the full amount of third-party benefits or proceeds in trust pending judicial or administrative determination, unless adequately explained, gives rise to an inference that such person knowingly failed to credit the state or its agent for payments received from social security, insurance, or other sources, pursuant to s. 414.39(4)(b), and acted with the intent set forth in s. 812.014(1).

(a) In cases of suspected criminal violations or fraudulent activity, the agency may take any civil action permitted at law or equity to recover the greatest possible amount, including, without limitation, treble damages under ss. 772.11 and 812.035(7).

(b) The agency is authorized to investigate and to request appropriate officers or agencies of the state to investigate suspected criminal violations or fraudulent activity related to third-party benefits, including, without limitation, ss. 414.39 and 812.014. Such requests may be directed, without limitation, to the Medicaid Fraud Control Unit of the Office of the Attorney General, or to any state attorney. Pursuant to s. 409.913, the Attorney General has primary responsibility to investigate and control Medicaid fraud.

(c) In carrying out duties and responsibilities related to Medicaid fraud control, the agency may subpoena witnesses or materials within or outside the state and, through any duly designated employee, administer oaths and affirmations and collect evidence for possible use in either civil or criminal judicial proceedings.

(d) All information obtained and documents prepared pursuant to an investigation of a Medicaid recipient, the recipient's legal representative, or any other person relating to an allegation of recipient fraud or theft is confidential and exempt from s. 119.07(1):

1. Until such time as the agency takes final agency action;

2. Until such time as the Department of Legal Affairs refers the case for criminal prosecution;

3. Until such time as an indictment or criminal information is filed by a state attorney in a criminal case; or

4. At all times if otherwise protected by law.

(18) In recovering any payments in accordance with this section, the agency is authorized to make appropriate settlements.

(19) Notwithstanding any provision in this section to the contrary, the agency shall not be required to seek reimbursement from a liable third party on claims for which the agency determines that the amount it rea-sonably expects to recover will be less than the cost of recovery, or that recovery efforts will otherwise not be cost-effective.

(20) Entities providing health insurance as defined in s. 624.603, health maintenance organizations and prepaid health clinics as defined in chapter 641, and, on behalf of their clients, third-party administrators and pharmacy benefits managers as defined in s. 409.901(27) shall provide such records and information as are necessary to accomplish the purpose of this section, unless such requirement results in an unreasonable burden.

(a) The director of the agency and the Director of the Office of Insurance Regulation of the Financial Services Commission shall enter into a cooperative agreement for requesting and obtaining information necessary to effect the purpose and objective of this section.

1. The agency shall request only that information necessary to determine whether health insurance as defined pursuant to s. 624.603, or those health services provided pursuant to chapter 641, could be, should be, or have been claimed and paid with respect to items of medical care and services furnished to any person eligible for services under this section.

2. All information obtained pursuant to subparagraph 1. is confidential and exempt from s. 119.07(1). The agency shall provide the information obtained pursuant to subparagraph 1. to the Department of Revenue for purposes of administering the state Title IV-D program. The agency and the Department of Revenue shall enter into a cooperative agreement for purposes of implementing this requirement.

3. The cooperative agreement or rules adopted under this subsection may include financial arrangements to reimburse the reporting entities for reasonable costs or a portion thereof incurred in furnishing the requested information. Neither the cooperative agreement nor the rules shall require the automation of manual processes to provide the requested information.

(b) The agency and the Financial Services Commission jointly shall adopt rules for the development and administration of the cooperative agreement. The rules shall include the following:

1. A method for identifying those entities subject to furnishing information under the cooperative agreement.

2. A method for furnishing requested information.

3. Procedures for requesting exemption from the cooperative agreement based on an unreasonable burden to the reporting entity.

(21) Entities providing health insurance as defined in s. 624.603, and health maintenance organizations as defined in chapter 641, requiring tape or electronic

billing formats from the agency shall accept Medicaid billings that are prepared using the current Medicare standard billing format. If the insurance entity or health maintenance organization is unable to use the agency format, the entity shall accept paper claims from the agency in lieu of tape or electronic billing, provided that these claims are prepared using current Medicare standard billing formats.

(22) The agency is authorized to adopt rules to implement the provisions of this section and federal requirements.

History.
S. 4, ch. 90-232; s. 33, ch. 90-295; s. 38, ch. 91-282; s. 4, ch. 92-79; s. 4, ch. 94-251; s. 98, ch. 96-175; s. 3, ch. 96-331; s. 259, ch. 96-406; s. 1023, ch. 97-103; s. 32, ch. 98-191; s. 1, ch. 98-411; s. 184, ch. 99-8; s. 1, ch. 99-231; s. 1, ch. 99-323; s. 8, ch. 99-356; s. 9, ch. 99-393; s. 67, ch. 99-397; s. 58, ch. 2000-153; s. 449, ch. 2003-261; s. 3, ch. 2005-140; s. 13, ch. 2008-246, eff. July 1, 2008; s. 13, ch. 2010-187, eff. June 3, 2010.

409.9101. Recovery for payments made on behalf of Medicaid-eligible persons.

(1) This section may be cited as the "Medicaid Estate Recovery Act."

(2) It is the intent of the Legislature by this section to supplement Medicaid funds that are used to provide medical services to eligible persons. Medicaid estate recovery shall be accomplished by the agency filing a statement of claim against the estate of a deceased Medicaid recipient as provided in part VII of chapter 733. Recovery shall be made pursuant to federal authority in s. 13612 of the Omnibus Budget Reconciliation Act of 1993, which amends s. 1917(b)(1) of the Social Security Act, 42 U.S.C. s. 1396p(b)(1).

(3) The acceptance of public medical assistance, as defined by Title XIX (Medicaid) of the Social Security Act, including mandatory and optional supplemental payments under the Social Security Act, shall create a debt to the agency in the total amount paid to or for the benefit of the recipient for medical assistance after the recipient reached 55 years of age. Payment of benefits to a person under the age of 55 years does not create a debt. Upon filing of a statement of claim in the probate proceeding, the agency shall be an interested person as defined in s. 731.201 to the same extent as other estate claimants.

(4) The agency may amend the claim as a matter of right up to 1 year after the last date medical services were rendered to the decedent.

(5) The agency's provider processing system reports shall be admissible as prima facie evidence in substantiating the agency's claim.

(6) The debt created under this section shall not be enforced if the recipient is survived by:

(a) A spouse;

(b) A child or children under 21 years of age; or

(c) A child or children who are blind or permanently and totally disabled pursuant to the eligibility requirements of Title XIX of the Social Security Act.

(7) No debt under this section shall be enforced against any property that is determined to be exempt from the claims of creditors under the constitution or laws of this state.

(8) The agency shall not recover from an estate if doing so would cause undue hardship for the qualified heirs, as defined in s. 731.201. The personal representative of an estate and any heir may request that the agency waive recovery of any or all of the debt when recovery would create a hardship. A hardship does not exist solely because recovery will prevent any heirs from receiving an anticipated inheritance. The following criteria shall be considered by the agency in reviewing a hardship request:

(a) The heir:

1. Currently resides in the residence of the decedent;

2. Resided there at the time of the death of the decedent;

3. Has made the residence his or her primary residence for the 12 months immediately preceding the death of the decedent; and

4. Owns no other residence;

(b) The heir would be deprived of food, clothing, shelter, or medical care necessary for the maintenance of life or health;

(c) The heir can document that he or she provided full-time care to the recipient which delayed the recipient's entry into a nursing home. The heir must be either the decedent's sibling or the son or daughter of the decedent and must have resided with the recipient for at least 1 year prior to the recipient's death; or

(d) The cost involved in the sale of the property would be equal to or greater than the value of the property.

(9) Instances arise in Medicaid estate-recovery cases where the assets include a settlement of a claim against a liable third party. The agency's claim under s. 409.910 must be satisfied prior to including the settlement proceeds as estate assets. The remaining settlement proceeds shall be included in the estate and be available to satisfy the Medicaid estate-recovery claim. The Medicaid estate-recovery share shall be one-half of the settlement proceeds included in the estate. Nothing in this subsection is intended to limit the agency's rights against other assets in the estate not related to the settlement. However, in no circumstances shall the agency's recovery exceed the total amount of Medicaid medical assistance provided to the recipient.

(10) In instances where there are no liquid assets to satisfy the Medicaid estate-recovery claim, if there is nonexempt personal property or real property which is not protected homestead and the costs of sale will not exceed the proceeds, the property shall be sold to satisfy the Medicaid estate-recovery claim. Real prop-

erty shall not be transferred to the agency in any instance.

(11) The agency is authorized to adopt rules to implement the provisions of this section.

History.
S. 68, ch. 99-397; s. 2, ch. 2001-226.

TITLE XXXIII.

REGULATION OF TRADE, COMMERCE, INVESTMENTS, AND SOLICITATIONS

CHAPTER 518.

INVESTMENT OF FIDUCIARY FUNDS

518.01. Investments of funds received from United States Department of Veterans Affairs.

Subject to the conditions herein contained, and except as otherwise authorized by law, guardians holding funds received from, or currently in receipt of funds from, the United States Department of Veterans Affairs, to the extent of those funds alone, may invest such funds only in the following:

(1) United States government obligations. — In bonds or other obligations, either bearing interest or sold on a discount basis, of the United States, or the United States Treasury, or those for the payment of the principal and interest of which the faith and credit of the United States is pledged, including such bonds or obligations of the District of Columbia.

(2) Bonds and obligations of states and territories. — In bonds or other interest-bearing obligations of any state of the United States, or the Territory of Puerto Rico; provided such state or territory has not, within 10 years previous to the date of making such investment, defaulted for more than 90 days in the payment of any part of the principal or interest of any of its bonded indebtedness.

(3) Bonds and other obligations of political subdivisions within the state of Florida. — In bonds or other interest-bearing obligations of any incorporated county, city, town, school district, or road and bridge district located within the state and which has according to the federal census next preceding the date of making the investment, a population of not less than 2,000 inhabitants and for which the full faith and credit of such political subdivision has been pledged; provided, that such political subdivision or its successor through merger, consolidation, or otherwise, has not within 5 years previous to the making of such investment, defaulted for more than 6 months in the payment of any part of the principal or interest of its bonded indebtedness.

(4) Bonds and obligations of political subdivisions located outside the state of Florida. — In bonds or other interest-bearing obligations of any incorporated county, city, or town located outside of the state, but within another state of the United States, which county, city, or town has, according to the federal census next preceding the date of making the investment a population of not less than 40,000 inhabitants and the indebtedness of which does not exceed 7 percent of the last preceding valuation of property for the purposes of taxation; provided, that the full faith and credit of such political subdivision shall have been pledged for the payment of the principal and interest of such bonds or obligations, and provided further, that such political subdivision or its successor, through merger, consolidation, or otherwise, has not within 15 years previous to the making of such investment, defaulted for more than 90 days in the payment of any part of the principal or interest of its bonded indebtedness.

(5) Bonds or obligations of federal land banks and farm credit institutions. — In the bonds or other interest-bearing obligations of any federal land bank organized under any Act of Congress enacted prior to June 14, 1937, provided such bank is not in default in the payment of principal or interest on any of its obligations at the time of making the investment; and on any notes, bonds, debentures, or other similar obligations, consolidated or otherwise, issued by farm credit institutions pursuant to the Farm Credit Act of 1971, Pub. L. No. 92-181.

(6) Bonds of railroad companies.

(a) Bonds bearing a fixed rate of interest secured by first mortgage, general mortgage, refunding mortgage, or consolidated mortgage which is a lien on real estate, rights or interest therein, leaseholds, right-of-way, trackage, or other fixed assets; provided, that such bonds have been issued or assumed by a qualified railroad company or guaranteed as to principal and interest by indorsement by a qualified railroad company or guaranteed as to principal and interest by indorsement, which guaranty has been assumed by a qualified railroad company.

(b) In bonds secured by first mortgage upon terminal, depot, or tunnel property, including buildings and appurtenances used in the service or transportation by one or more qualified railroad companies; provided that such bonds have been issued or assumed by a qualified railroad company or guaranteed as to principal and interest by indorsement by a qualified railroad company, or guaranteed as to principal and interest by indorsement, which guaranty has been assumed by a qualified railroad company.

(c) As used in this subsection, the words "qualified railroad company" means a railroad corporation other than a street railroad corporation which, at the date of the investment by the fiduciary, meets the following requirements:

1. It shall be a railroad corporation incorporated under the laws of the United States or of

any state or commonwealth thereof or of the District of Columbia.

2. It shall own and operate within the United States not less than 500 miles of standard gauge railroad lines, exclusive of sidings.

3. Its railroad operating revenues derived from the operation of all railroad lines operated by it, including leased lines and lines owned or leased by a subsidiary corporation, all of the voting stock of which, except directors' qualifying shares, is owned by it, for its fiscal year next preceding the date of the investment, shall have been not less than $10 million.

4. At no time during its fiscal year in which the investment is made, and its 5 fiscal years immediately prior thereto, shall it have been in default in the payment of any part of the principal or interest owing by it upon any part of its funded indebtedness.

5. In at least 4 of its 5 fiscal years immediately preceding the date of investment, its net income available for fixed charges shall have been at least equal to its fixed charges, and in its fiscal year immediately preceding the date of investment, its net income available for fixed charges shall have been not less than 1 times its fixed charges.

(d) As used in this subsection, the words "income available for fixed charges" mean the amount obtained by deducting from gross income all items deductible in ascertaining the net income other than contingent income interest and those constituting fixed charges as used in the accounting reports of common carriers as prescribed by the accounting regulations of the Interstate Commerce Commission.

(e) As used in this subsection, the words "fixed charges" mean rent for leased roads, miscellaneous rents, funded debt interest, and amortization of discount on funded debt.

(7) Bonds of gas, water, or electric companies. — In bonds issued by, or guaranteed as to principal and interest by, or assumed by, any gas, water, or electric company, subject to the following conditions:

(a) Gas, water, or electric companies by which such bonds are issued, guaranteed, or assumed, shall be incorporated under the laws of the United States or any state or commonwealth thereof or of the District of Columbia.

(b) The company shall be an operating company transacting the business of supplying water, electrical energy, artificial gas, or natural gas for light, heat, power, and other purposes, and provided that at least 75 percent of its gross operating revenue shall be derived from such business and not more than 15 percent of its gross operating revenues shall be derived from any other one kind of business.

(c) The company shall be subject to regulation by a public service commission, a public utility commission, or any other similar regulatory body duly established by the laws of the United States or any state or commonwealth or of the District of Columbia in which such company operates.

(d) The company shall have all the franchises necessary to operate in the territory in which at least 75 percent of its gross revenues are obtained, which franchises shall either be indeterminate permits of, or agreements with, or subject to the jurisdiction of, a public service commission or other duly constituted regulatory body, or shall extend at least 5 years beyond the maturity of the bonds.

(e) The company shall have been in existence for a period of not less than 8 fiscal years, and at no time within the period of 8 fiscal years immediately preceding the date of such investment shall such company have failed to pay punctually and regularly the matured principal and interest of all its indebtedness, direct, assumed, or guaranteed, but the period of life of the company, together with the period of life of any predecessor company, or company from which a major portion of its property was acquired by consolidation, merger, or purchase, shall be considered together in determining such required period.

(f) For a period of 5 fiscal years immediately preceding the date of the investment, net earnings shall have averaged per year not less than 2 times the average annual interest charges on its entire funded debt, applicable to that period and for the last fiscal year preceding the date of investment, such net earnings shall have been not less than 2 times such interest charges for that year.

(g) The bonds of any such company must be part of an issue of not less than $1 million and must be mortgage bonds secured by a first or refunding mortgage upon property owned and operated by the company issuing or assuming them or must be underlying mortgage bonds secured by property owned and operated by the companies issuing or assuming them. The aggregate principal amount of bonds secured by such first or refunding mortgage, plus the principal amount of all the underlying outstanding bonds, shall not exceed 60 percent of the value of the physical property owned, which shall be book value less such reserves for depreciation or retirement, as the company may have established, and subject to the lien of such mortgage or mortgages securing the total mortgage debt. If such mortgage is a refunding mortgage, it must provide for the retirement on or before the date of maturity of all bonds secured by prior liens on the property.

(h) As used in this subsection, the words "gross operating revenues and expenses" mean, respectively, the total amount earned from the operation of, and the total expenses of maintaining and operating, all property owned and operated by, or leased and operated by, such companies, as determined by the system of accounts prescribed by the Public Service Commission or other similar regulatory body having jurisdiction.

(i) As used in this subsection, the words "net earnings" mean the balance obtained by deducting from its gross operating revenues, its operating and maintenance expenses, taxes, other than federal and state income taxes, rentals, and provisions for depreciation, renewals and retirements of the physical assets of the company, and by adding to such balance its income from securities and miscellaneous sources, but not, however, exceeding 15 percent of such balance.

(8) Bonds of telephone companies. — In bonds issued by, or guaranteed as to principal and interest by, or assumed by, any telephone company, subject to the following conditions:

(a) The telephone company by which such bonds are issued shall be incorporated under the laws of the United States or of any state or commonwealth thereof or of the District of Columbia and shall be engaged in the business of supplying telephone service in the United States and shall be subject to regulations by the Federal Communications Commission, a public service commission, a public utility commission, or any similar regulatory body duly established by the laws of the United States or of any state or commonwealth or of the District of Columbia in which such company operates.

(b) The company by which such bonds are issued, guaranteed, or assumed shall have been in existence for a period of not less than 8 fiscal years, and at no time within the period of 8 fiscal years immediately preceding the date of such investment shall such company have failed to pay punctually and regularly the matured principal and interest of all its indebtedness, direct, assumed, or guaranteed, but the period of life of the company, together with the period of life of any predecessor company, or company from which a major portion of its property was acquired by consolidation, merger, or purchase, shall be considered together in determining such required period. The company shall file with the Federal Communications Commission, or a public service commission or similar regulatory body having jurisdiction over it, and make public in each year a statement and a report giving the income account covering the previous fiscal year, and a balance sheet showing in reasonable detail the assets and liabilities at the end of the year.

(c) For a period of 5 fiscal years immediately preceding the investment, the net earnings of such telephone company shall have averaged per year not less than twice the average annual interest charges on its outstanding obligations applicable to that period, and for the last fiscal year preceding such investment, such net earnings shall have been not less than twice such interest charges for that year.

(d) The bonds must be part of an issue of not less than $5 million and must be mortgage bonds secured by a first or refunding mortgage upon property owned and operated by the company issuing or assuming them, or must be underlying mortgage bonds similarly secured. As of the close of the fiscal year preceding the date of the investment by the fiduciary, the aggregate principal amount of bonds secured by such first or refunding mortgage, plus the principal amount of all the underlying outstanding bonds, shall not exceed 60 percent of the value of the real estate and tangible personal property owned absolutely, which value shall be book value less such reserves for depreciation or retirement as the company may have established, and subject to the lien of such mortgage, or mortgages, securing the total mortgage debt. If such mortgage is a refunding mortgage, it must provide for the retirement, on or before the date of their maturity, of all bonds secured by prior liens on the property.

(e) As used in this subsection, the words "gross operating revenues and expenses" mean, respectively, the total amount earned from the operation of, and the total expenses of maintaining and operating all property owned and operated by, or leased and operated by, such company as determined by the system of accounts prescribed by the Federal Communications Commission, or any other similar federal or state regulatory body having jurisdiction in the matter.

(f) As used in this subsection, the words "net earnings" mean the balance obtained by deducting from the telephone company's gross operating revenues its operating and maintenance expenses, provision for depreciation of the physical assets of the company, taxes, other than federal and state income taxes, rentals, and miscellaneous charges, and by adding to such balance its income from securities and miscellaneous sources but not, however, to exceed 15 percent of such balance.

(9) First mortgages. — In mortgages signed by one or more individuals or corporations, subject to the following conditions:

(a) If the taking of the mortgages as an investment for any particular trust, estate, or guardianship will not result in more than 40 percent of the then value of the principal of such trust, estate, or guardianship being invested in mortgages.

(b) Within 30 days preceding the taking of a mortgage as an investment, the property encumbered or to be encumbered thereby shall be appraised by two or more reputable persons especially familiar with real estate values. The fair market value of the property as disclosed by the appraisal of such persons shall be set forth in a writing dated and signed by them and in such writing they shall certify that their valuation of the property was made after an inspection of the same, including all buildings and other improvements.

(c) The mortgage shall encumber improved real estate located in the state and in or within 5 miles of the corporate limits of a city or town having a population of 2,000 or more, according to the federal census next preceding the date of making any such investment.

(d) The mortgage shall be or become, through the recordation of documents simultaneously filed for record, a first lien upon the property described therein prior to all other liens, except taxes previously levied or assessed but not due and payable at the time the mortgage is taken as an investment.

(e) The mortgage shall secure no indebtedness other than that owing to the executor, administrator, trustee, or guardian taking the same as an investment.

(f) The amount of the indebtedness secured by the mortgage shall not exceed 60 percent of the fair market value, as determined in accordance with the provisions of paragraph (b), of the property encumbered or to be encumbered by said mortgage.

(g) If the amount of the indebtedness secured by the mortgage is in excess of 50 percent of the fair market value, as determined in accordance with the provisions of paragraph (b), of the property encumbered or to be encumbered by said mortgage, then the mortgage shall require principal payments, at annual or more frequent intervals, sufficient to reduce by or before the expiration of 3 years from the date the mortgage is taken as an investment, the unpaid principal balance secured thereby to an amount not in excess of 50 percent of the fair market value of said property, as determined in accordance with the provisions of paragraph (b).

(h) The mortgage shall contain a covenant of the mortgagor to keep insured at all times the improvements on the real estate encumbered by said mortgage, with loss payable to the mortgagee, against loss and damage by fire, in an amount not less than the unpaid principal secured by said mortgage.

(i) Provided, however, that the foregoing limitations and requirements shall not apply to notes or bonds secured by mortgage or trust deed insured by the Federal Housing Administrator, and that notes or bonds secured by mortgage or trust deed insured by the Federal Housing Administrator are declared to be eligible for investment under the provisions of this chapter.

(10) Life insurance. — Annuity or endowment contracts with any life insurance company which is qualified to do business in the state under the laws thereof.

(11) Savings and loan associations. — In savings share or investment share accounts of any federal savings and loan association chartered under the laws of the United States, and doing business in this state, and in the shares of any Florida building and loan association which is a member of the Federal Home Loan Bank System.

(12) Savings accounts, certificates of deposit; state and national banks. — In savings accounts and certificates of deposit in any bank chartered under the laws of the United States and doing business in this state, and in savings accounts and certificates of deposit in any bank chartered under the laws of this state.

(13) Savings share accounts, credit unions. — In savings share accounts of any credit union chartered under the laws of the United States and doing business in this state, and savings share accounts of any credit union chartered under the laws of this state, provided the credit union is insured under the federal share insurance program or an approved state share insurance program.

In determining the qualification of investments under the requirements of this section, published statements of corporations or statements of reliable companies engaged in the business of furnishing statistical information on bonds may be used.

History.
S. 1, ch. 17949, 1937; CGL 1940 Supp. 7100(9); s. 1, ch. 28154, 1953; s. 1, ch. 63-111; s. 1, ch. 73-41; s. 2, ch. 74-92; s. 24, ch. 93-268.
Editor's Notes.
The Interstate Commerce Commission, referred to in paragraph (6)(d), was abolished by s. 101, Pub. L. No. 104-88.

518.06. Investment of fiduciary funds in loans insured by Federal Housing Administrator.

Banks, savings banks, trust companies, building and loan associations, insurance companies, and guardians holding funds received from or currently in receipt of funds from the United States Department of Veterans Affairs to the extent of those funds alone, may:

(1) Make such loans and advances of credit, and purchases of obligations representing loans and advances of credit, as are insured by the Federal Housing Administrator, and obtain such insurance;

(2) Make such loans secured by real property or leasehold as the Federal Housing Administrator insures or makes a commitment to insure, and obtain such insurance.

History.
S. 1, ch. 17130, 1935; CGL 1936 Supp. 7100(1); s. 1, ch. 17980, 1937; s. 2, ch. 28154, 1953; s. 25, ch. 93-268.

518.07. Investment of fiduciary funds in bonds, etc., issued by Federal Housing Administrator.

(1) Banks, savings banks, trust companies, building and loan associations, insurance companies, guardians holding funds received from or currently in receipt of funds from the United States Department of Veterans Affairs to the extent of those funds alone, the state and its political subdivisions, all institutions and agencies thereof, with the approval of the officials or boards having supervision or management of same, may invest their funds and moneys in their custody or possession, eligible for investment, in notes or bonds secured by mortgage or trust deed insured by the Federal Housing Administrator, in debentures issued by the Federal Housing Administrator, and in securities issued by national mortgage associations.

(2) Such notes, bonds, debentures, and securities made eligible for investment may be used wherever, by statute of this state, collateral is required as security for the deposit of public or other funds; or deposits are required to be made with any public official or departments, or an investment of capital or surplus, or a reserve or other fund, is required to be maintained consisting of designated securities.

History.
S. 2, ch. 17130, 1935; CGL 1936 Supp. 7100(2); s. 2, ch. 17980, 1937; s. 3, ch. 28154, 1953; s. 26, ch. 93-268.

518.08. Applicability of laws requiring security, etc.

No law of this state requiring security upon which loans or investments may be made, prescribing the nature, amount, or form of such security, prescribing or limiting interest rates upon loans or investments, limiting investments of capital or deposits, or prescribing or limiting the period for which loans or investments may be made, shall be deemed to apply to loans or investments made pursuant to ss. 518.06 and 518.07.

History.
S. 3, ch. 17130, 1935; CGL 1936 Supp. 7100(3).

518.09. Housing bonds legal investments and security.

The state and all public officers, municipal corporations, political subdivisions, and public bodies, all banks, bankers, trust companies, savings banks and institutions, building and loan associations, savings and loan associations, investment companies, all insurance companies, insurance associations, and other persons carrying on an insurance business, and guardians holding funds received from or currently in receipt of funds from the United States Department of Veterans Affairs to the extent of those funds alone may legally invest any sinking funds, moneys, or other funds belonging to them or within their control in any bonds or other obligations issued by a housing authority pursuant to the Housing Authorities Law of this state (chapter 421), or issued by any public housing authority or agency in the United States, when such bonds or

other obligations are secured by a pledge of annual contributions to be paid by the United States Government or any agency thereof, and such bonds and other obligations shall be authorized security for all public deposits; it being the purpose of this section to authorize any person, associations, political subdivisions, bodies, and officers, public or private, to use any funds owned or controlled by them, including, but not limited to, sinking, insurance, investment, retirement, compensation, pension, and trust funds, and funds held on deposit, for the purchase of any bonds or other obligations; provided, however, that nothing contained in this section shall be construed as relieving any person from any duty of exercising reasonable care in selecting securities.

History.
SS. 1, 2, 3, ch. 19512, 1939; CGL 1940 Supp. 7100(3-nn); s. 4, ch. 28154, 1953; s. 27, ch. 93-268.

518.10. Fiduciary defined as used in ss. 518.11-518.14.

For the purpose of ss. 518.11-518.14, a "fiduciary" is defined as an executor, administrator, trustee, guardian (except any guardian holding funds received from or currently in receipt of funds from the United States Department of Veterans Affairs, to the extent of those funds alone), or other person, whether individual or corporate, who by reason of a written agreement, will, court order, or other instrument has the responsibility for the acquisition, investment, reinvestment, exchange, retention, sale, or management of money or property of another.

History.
S. 5, ch. 28154, 1953; s. 28, ch. 93-268.

518.11. Investments by fiduciaries; prudent investor rule.

(1) A fiduciary has a duty to invest and manage investment assets as follows:

(a) The fiduciary has a duty to invest and manage investment assets as a prudent investor would considering the purposes, terms, distribution requirements, and other circumstances of the trust. This standard requires the exercise of reasonable care and caution and is to be applied to investments not in isolation, but in the context of the investment portfolio as a whole and as a part of an overall investment strategy that should incorporate risk and return objectives reasonably suitable to the trust, guardianship, or probate estate. If the fiduciary has special skills, or is named fiduciary on the basis of representations of special skills or expertise, the fiduciary is under a duty to use those skills.

(b) No specific investment or course of action is, taken alone, prudent or imprudent. The fiduciary may invest in every kind of property and type of investment, subject to this section. The fiduciary's investment decisions and actions are to be judged in terms of the fiduciary's reasonable business judgment regarding the anticipated effect on the investment portfolio as a whole under the facts and circumstances prevailing at the time of the decision or action. The prudent investor rule is a test of conduct and not of resulting performance.

(c) The fiduciary has a duty to diversify the investments unless, under the circumstances, the fiduciary believes reasonably it is in the interests of the beneficiaries and furthers the purposes of the trust, guardianship, or estate not to diversify.

(d) The fiduciary has a duty, within a reasonable time after acceptance of the trust, estate, or guardianship, to review the investment portfolio and to make and implement decisions concerning the retention and disposition of original preexisting investments in order to conform to the provisions of this section. The fiduciary's decision to retain or dispose of an asset may be influenced properly by the asset's special relationship or value to the purposes of the trust, estate, or guardianship, or to some or all of the beneficiaries, consistent with the trustee's duty of impartiality, or to the ward.

(e) The fiduciary has a duty to pursue an investment strategy that considers both the reasonable production of income and safety of capital, consistent with the fiduciary's duty of impartiality and the purposes of the trust, estate, or guardianship. Whether investments are underproductive or overproductive of income shall be judged by the portfolio as a whole and not as to any particular asset.

(f) The circumstances that the fiduciary may consider in making investment decisions include, without limitation, the general economic conditions, the possible effect of inflation, the expected tax consequences of investment decisions or strategies, the role each investment or course of action plays within the overall portfolio, the expected total return, including both income yield and appreciation of capital, and the duty to incur only reasonable and appropriate costs. The fiduciary may, but need not, consider related trusts, estates, and guardianships, and the income available from other sources to, and the assets of, beneficiaries when making investment decisions.

(2) The provisions of this section may be expanded, restricted, eliminated, or otherwise altered by express provisions of the governing instrument, whether the instrument was executed before or after the effective date of this section. An express provision need not refer specifically to this statute. The fiduciary is not liable to any person for the fiduciary's reasonable reliance on those express provisions.

(3) Nothing in this section abrogates or restricts the power of an appropriate court in proper cases:

(a) To direct or permit the trustee to deviate from the terms of the governing instrument; or

(b) To direct or permit the fiduciary to take, or to restrain the fiduciary from taking, any action regarding the making or retention of investments.

(4) The following terms or comparable language in the investment powers and related provisions of a governing instrument shall be construed as authorizing any investment or strategy permitted under this section: "investments permissible by law for investment of trust funds," "legal investments," "authorized investments," "using the judgment and care under the circumstances then prevailing that persons of prudence, discretion, and intelligence exercise in the management of their own affairs, not in regard to speculation but in regard to the permanent disposition of their funds, considering the probable income as well as the probable safety of their capital," "prudent trustee rule," "prudent person rule," and "prudent investor rule."

(5) This section applies to all existing and future fiduciary relationships subject to this section, but only as to acts or omissions occurring after October 1, 1993.

History.
S. 6, ch. 28154, 1953; s. 2, ch. 93-257; s. 26, ch. 97-98; s. 686, ch. 97-103.

518.112. Delegation of investment functions.

(1) A fiduciary may delegate any part or all of the investment functions, with regard to acts constituting investment functions that a prudent investor of comparable skills might delegate under the circumstances, to an investment agent as provided in subsection (3), if the fiduciary exercises reasonable care, judgment, and caution in selecting the investment agent, in establishing the scope and specific terms of any delegation, and in reviewing periodically the agent's actions in order to monitor overall performance and compliance with the scope and specific terms of the delegation.

(2)(a) The requirements of subsection (1) notwithstanding, a fiduciary that administers an insurance contract on the life or lives of one or more persons may delegate without any continuing obligation to review the agent's actions, certain investment functions with respect to any such contract as provided in subsection (3), to any one or more of the following persons as investment agents:

1. The trust's settlor if the trust is one described in s. 733.707(3);

2. Beneficiaries of the trust or estate, regardless of the beneficiary's interest therein, whether vested or contingent;

3. The spouse, ancestor, or descendant of any person described in subparagraph 1. or subparagraph 2.;

4. Any person or entity nominated by a majority of the beneficiaries entitled to receive notice under paragraph (3)(b); or

5. An investment agent if the fiduciary exercises reasonable care, judgment, and caution in selecting the investment agent and in establishing the scope and specific terms of any delegation.

(b) The delegable investment functions under this subsection include:

1. A determination of whether the insurance contract was procured or effected in compliance with s. 627.404;

2. A determination of whether any insurance contract is or remains a proper investment;

3. The investigation of the financial strength of the life insurance company;

4. A determination of whether or not to exercise any policy option available under any insurance contracts;

5. A determination of whether or not to diversify such contracts relative to one another or to other assets, if any, administered by the fiduciary; or

6. An inquiry about changes in the health or financial condition of the insured or insureds relative to any such contract.

(c) Until the contract matures and the policy proceeds are received, a fiduciary that administers insurance contracts under this subsection is not obligated to diversify nor allocate other assets, if any, relative to such insurance contracts.

(3) A fiduciary may delegate investment functions to an investment agent under subsection (1) or subsection (2), if:

(a) In the case of a guardianship, the fiduciary has obtained court approval.

(b) In the case of a trust or estate, the fiduciary has given written notice, of its intention to begin delegating investment functions under this section, to all beneficiaries, or their legal representative, eligible to receive distributions from the trust or estate within 30 days of the delegation unless such notice is waived by the eligible beneficiaries entitled to receive such notice. This notice shall thereafter, until or unless the beneficiaries eligible to receive income from the trust or distributions from the estate at the time are notified to the contrary, authorize the trustee or legal representative to delegate investment functions pursuant to this subsection. This discretion to revoke the delegation does not imply under subsection (2) any continuing obligation to review the agent's actions.

1. Notice to beneficiaries eligible to receive distributions from the trust from the estate, or their legal representatives shall be sufficient notice to all persons who may join the eligible class of beneficiaries in the future.

2. Additionally, as used herein, legal representative includes one described in s. 731.303, without any requirement of a court order, an attorney-in-fact under a durable power of attorney sufficient to grant such authority, a legally appointed guardian, or equivalent under applicable law, any living, natural guardian of a minor child, or a guardian ad litem.

3. Written notice shall be given as provided in part III of chapter 731 as to an estate, and as provided in s. 736.0109 and part III of chapter 736 as to a trust.

(4) If all requirements of subsection (3) are satisfied, the fiduciary shall not be responsible otherwise for the investment decisions nor actions or omissions of the investment agent to which the investment functions are delegated.

(5) The investment agent shall, by virtue of acceptance of its appointment, be subject to the jurisdiction of the courts of this state.

(6) In performing a delegated function, the investment agent shall be subject to the same standards as the fiduciary.

History.

S. 3, ch. 93-257; s. 8, ch. 97-240; s. 2, ch. 2010-172, eff. July 1, 2010.

518.115. Power of fiduciary or custodian to deposit securities in a central depository.

(1)(a) Notwithstanding any other provision of law, any fiduciary, as defined in s. 518.10, holding securities, as defined in s. 678.102(1), in its fiduciary capacity, and any bank or trust company holding securities as a custodian, managing agent, or custodian for a fiduciary, is authorized to deposit or arrange for the deposit of such securities in a clearing corporation, as defined in s. 678.102(3). When such securities are so deposited, certificates representing securities of the same class of the same issuer may be merged and held in bulk in the name of the nominee of such clearing corporation with any other such securities deposited in such clearing corporation by any person, regardless of the ownership of such securities, and certificates of small denomination may be merged into one or more certificates of larger denomination.

(b) A bank or a trust company so depositing securities with a clearing corporation shall be subject to such rules and regulations with respect to the making and maintenance of such deposit as, in the case of state-chartered institutions, the Financial Services Commission and, in the case of national banking associations, the Comptroller of the Currency may from time to time issue.

(c) Notwithstanding any other provisions of law, ownership of, and other interests in, the securities credited to such account may be transferred by entries on the books of said clearing corporation without physical delivery of any securities. The records of such fiduciary and the records of such bank or trust company acting as custodian, managing agent, or custodian for a fiduciary shall at all times show the name of the party for whose account the securities are so deposited. A bank or trust company acting as custodian for a fiduciary shall, on demand by the fiduciary, certify in writing to the fiduciary the securities so deposited by such bank or trust company in such clearing corporation for the account of such fiduciary. A fiduciary shall, on demand by any party to a judicial proceeding for the settlement of such fiduciary's account or on demand by the attorney for such party, certify in writing to such party the securities deposited by such fiduciary in such clearing corporation for its account as such fiduciary.

(2) This section shall apply to any fiduciary holding securities in its fiduciary capacity, and to any bank or trust company holding securities as a custodian, managing agent, or custodian for a fiduciary, acting on June 18, 1974, or who thereafter may act regardless of the date of the agreement, instrument, or court order by which it is appointed and regardless of whether or not such fiduciary, custodian, managing agent, or custodian for a fiduciary owns capital stock of such clearing corporation.

History.
S. 1, ch. 74-224; s. 613, ch. 2003-261.

Editor's Notes.
Section 678.102, referred to in two places in paragraph (1)(a), was repealed by s. 25, ch. 98-11.

518.116. Power of certain fiduciaries and custodians to deposit United States Government and agency securities with a Federal Reserve bank.

(1)(a) Notwithstanding any other provision of law, any fiduciary, as defined in s. 518.10, which is a bank or trust company holding securities in its fiduciary capacity, and any bank or trust company holding securities as a custodian, managing agent, or custodian for a fiduciary, is authorized to deposit or arrange for the deposit with the Federal Reserve Bank in its district of any securities, the principal and interest of which the United States Government or any department, agency, or instrumentality thereof has agreed to pay or has guaranteed payment, to be credited to one or more accounts on the books of said Federal Reserve Bank in the name of such bank or trust company to be designated fiduciary or safekeeping accounts, to which account other similar securities may be credited.

(b) A bank or trust company so depositing securities with a Federal Reserve Bank shall be subject to such rules and regulations with respect to the making and maintenance of such deposits as, in the case of state-chartered institutions, the Financial Services Commission and, in the case of national banking associations, the Comptroller of the Currency may from time to time issue. The records of such bank or trust company shall at all times show the ownership of the securities held in such account.

(c) Notwithstanding any other provision of law, ownership of, and other interests in, the securities credited to such account may be transferred by entries on the books of said Federal Reserve Bank without physical delivery of any securities. The records of such fiduciary and the records of such bank or trust company acting as custodian, managing agent, or custodian for a fiduciary shall at all times show the name of the party for whose account the

securities are so deposited. A bank or a trust company acting as custodian for a fiduciary shall, on demand by the fiduciary, certify in writing to the fiduciary the securities so deposited by such bank or trust company with such Federal Reserve Bank for the account of such fiduciary. A fiduciary shall, on demand by any party to a judicial proceeding for the settlement of such fiduciary's account or on demand by the attorney for such party, certify in writing to such party the securities deposited by such fiduciary with such Federal Reserve bank for its account as such fiduciary.

(2) This section shall apply to any fiduciary and to any bank or trust company holding securities as custodian, managing agent, or custodian for a fiduciary, acting on June 18, 1974, or who thereafter may act regardless of the date of the instrument or court order by which it is appointed.

History.
S. 2, ch. 74-224; s. 1, ch. 77-174; s. 614, ch. 2003-261.

518.117. Permissible investments of fiduciary funds.

A fiduciary that is authorized by lawful authority to engage in trust business as defined in s. 658.12(20) may invest fiduciary funds in accordance with s. 660.417 so long as the investment otherwise complies with this chapter.

History.
S. 15, ch. 2006-217, eff. July 1, 2007.

518.12. Instrument creating or defining powers, duties of fiduciary not affected.

Nothing contained in ss. 518.10-518.14 shall be construed as conferring a power of sale upon any fiduciary not possessing such power or as authorizing any departure from, or variation of, the express terms or limitations set forth in any will, agreement, court order, or other instrument creating or defining the fiduciary's duties and powers, but the terms "legal investment" or "authorized investment" or words of similar import, as used in any such instrument, shall be taken to mean any investment which is permitted by the terms of s. 518.11.

History.
S. 7, ch. 28154, 1953; s. 1, ch. 57-120.

518.13. Authority of court to permit deviation from terms of instrument creating trust not affected.

Nothing contained in ss. 518.10-518.14 shall be construed as restricting the power of a court of proper jurisdiction to permit a fiduciary to deviate from the terms of any will, agreement, or other instrument relating to the acquisition, investment, reinvestment, exchange, retention, sale, or management of fiduciary property.

History.
S. 8, ch. 28154, 1953.

518.14. Scope of ss. 518.10-518.13.

The provisions of ss. 518.10-518.13 shall govern fiduciaries acting under wills, agreements, court orders, and other instruments now existing or hereafter made.

History.
S. 9, ch. 28154, 1953.

518.15. Bonds or motor vehicle tax anticipation certificates, legal investments and security.

Notwithstanding any restrictions on investments contained in any law of this state, the state and all public officers, municipal corporations, political subdivisions, and public bodies, all banks, bankers, trust companies, savings banks, building and loan associations, savings and loan associations, investment companies, and all persons carrying on an insurance business, and all executors, administrators, guardians, trustees, and other fiduciaries may legally invest any sinking funds, moneys or other funds belonging to them or within their control in bonds or motor vehicle anticipation certificates issued under authority of s. 18, Art. XII of the State Constitution of 1885 as adopted by s. 9(d) of Art. XII, 1968 revised constitution, and the additional provisions of s. 9(d), and such bonds or certificates shall be authorized security for all public deposits, including, but not restricted to, deposits as authorized in s. 17.57, it being the purpose of this act to authorize any person, firm or corporation, association, political subdivision, body, and officer, public or private, to use any funds owned or controlled by them, including, but not limited to, sinking, insurance, investment, retirement, compensation, pension, and trust funds, and funds held on deposit, for the purchase of any such bonds or anticipation certificates, up to the amount as authorized by law to be invested in any type of security, including United States Government Bonds.

History.
S. 1, ch. 27990, 1953; s. 31, ch. 69-216; s. 615, ch. 2003-261.

518.151. Higher education bonds or certificates, legal investments and security.

Notwithstanding any restrictions on investments contained in any law of this state, the state and all public officers, municipal corporations, political subdivisions, and public bodies, all banks, bankers, trust companies, savings banks, building and loan associations, savings and loan associations, investment companies, and all persons carrying on an insurance business, and all executors, administrators, guardians, trustees, and other fiduciaries may legally invest any sinking funds, moneys or other funds belonging to them or within their control in higher education bonds or certificates issued under authority of s. 19, Art. XII of the State Constitution of 1885 or of s. 9(a), Art. XII of the constitution as revised in 1968, as amended, and such bonds or certificates shall be authorized security for all public deposits, including, but not restricted to,

deposits as authorized in s. 17.57, it being the purpose of this act to authorize any person, firm or corporation, association, political subdivision, body, and officer, public or private, to use any funds owned or controlled by them, including, but not limited to, sinking, insurance, investment, retirement, compensation, pension, and trust funds, and funds held on deposit, for the purchase of any such bonds or certificates, up to the amount as authorized by law to be invested in any type of security, including United States Government Bonds.

History.
S. 1, ch. 65-443; s. 140, ch. 71-355; s. 616, ch. 2003-261.

518.152. Puerto Rican bonds or obligations, legal investments and securities.

Notwithstanding any restrictions on investments contained in any law of this state, all public officers and public bodies of the state, counties, municipal corporations, and other political subdivisions; all banks, bankers, trust companies, savings banks, building and loan associations, savings and loan associations, investment companies, and other persons carrying on a banking business; all insurance companies, insurance associations and other persons carrying on an insurance business; all persons holding in trust any pension, health and welfare, and vacation funds; all administrators, executors, guardians, trustees, and other fiduciaries of any public, quasi-public, or private fund or estate; and all other persons authorized to invest in bonds or other obligations may legally invest any sinking funds, moneys, or other funds belonging to them or within their control in bonds or other obligations issued by the Commonwealth of Puerto Rico, its agencies, authorities, instrumentalities, municipalities, or political subdivisions, provided such agency, authority, instrumentality, municipality, or political subdivision has not, within 5 years prior to the making of such investment, defaulted for more than 90 days in the payment of any part of the principal or interest of its bonded indebtedness. Such bonds or obligations shall be authorized security for all public deposits, including, but not restricted to, deposits as authorized in s. 17.57, it being the purpose of this section to authorize any person, firm, corporation, association, political subdivision, body, and officer, public or private, to use any funds owned or controlled by them, including, but not limited to, sinking, insurance, investment, retirement, compensation, pension and trust funds, and funds held on deposit, for the purchase of any such bonds or obligations up to the amount as authorized by law to be invested in any type of security, including United States Government Bonds. However, nothing contained in this section shall be construed as relieving any person from any duty of exercising reasonable care in selecting securities.

History.
S. 1, ch. 72-136; s. 617, ch. 2003-261.

518.16. Chapter cumulative.

This chapter shall be cumulative to any other law providing for investments and security for public deposits.

History.
S. 2, ch. 27990, 1953; s. 11, ch. 28154, 1953.

TITLE XXXVIII.
BANKS AND BANKING

CHAPTER 655.
FINANCIAL INSTITUTIONS GENERALLY

655.769. Definitions of terms used in ss. 655.77-655.91.

As used in ss. 655.77-655.91, the term:

(1) "Check" includes a share draft of a credit union.

(2) "Deposit" includes a share of a credit union.

(3) "Depositor" includes a member of a credit union.

(4) "Institution" means any state or national bank, state or federal association, or state or federal credit union.

History.
S. 45, ch. 92-303.

655.77. Deposits by minors.

Deposits made by a minor, or made in the minor's name by other than a court-appointed guardian, may be withdrawn by the minor in the absence of an agreement to the contrary made between the institution and the depositor at the time the account is opened. In case of any such agreement, such moneys, until the minor's disabilities are removed, may be withdrawn by the person or persons designated in such agreement.

History.
S. 46, ch. 92-303; s. 526, ch. 97-102.

655.78. Deposit accounts in two or more names.

(1) Unless otherwise expressly provided in a contract, agreement, or signature card executed in connection with the opening or maintenance of an account, including a certificate of deposit, a deposit account in the names of two or more persons may be paid to, or on the order of, either or any of such persons or to, or on the order of, the guardian of the property of any such person who is incompetent, whether the other or others are competent. The check or other order for payment to any such person or guardian is a valid and sufficient release and discharge of the obligation of the institution for funds transferred thereby.

(2) In the case of a credit union, a member may designate any person or persons to hold deposits with the member in joint tenancy with the right of survivorship; but a joint tenant, unless he or she is a member in his or her own right, may not be permitted to vote, obtain a loan, or hold office or be required to pay an entrance or membership fee.

History.
S. 47, ch. 92-303; s. 527, ch. 97-102.

655.79. Deposits and accounts in two or more names; presumption as to vesting on death.

(1) Unless otherwise expressly provided in a contract, agreement, or signature card executed in connection with the opening or maintenance of an account, including a certificate of deposit, a deposit account in the names of two or more persons shall be presumed to have been intended by such persons to provide that, upon the death of any one of them, all rights, title, interest, and claim in, to, and in respect of such deposit account, less all proper setoffs and charges in favor of the institution, vest in the surviving person or persons. Any deposit or account made in the name of two persons who are husband and wife shall be considered a tenancy by the entirety unless otherwise specified in writing.

(2) The presumption created in this section may be overcome only by proof of fraud or undue influence or clear and convincing proof of a contrary intent. In the absence of such proof, all rights, title, interest, and claims in, to, and in respect of such deposits and account and the additions thereto, and the obligation of the institution created thereby, less all proper setoffs and charges in favor of the institution against any one or more of such persons, upon the death of any such person, vest in the surviving person or persons, notwithstanding the absence of proof of any donative intent or delivery, possession, dominion, control, or acceptance on the part of any person and notwithstanding that the provisions hereof may constitute or cause a vesting or disposition of property or rights or interests therein, testamentary in nature, which, except for the provisions of this section, would or might otherwise be void or voidable.

(3) This section does not abridge, impair, or affect the validity, effectiveness, or operation of any of the provisions of ss. 655.78 and 674.405 or the rights of institutions to make payments as therein provided.

History.
S. 48, ch. 92-303; s. 8, ch. 2008-75, eff. Oct. 1, 2008.

655.80. Convenience accounts.

(1) A convenience account is a deposit account, other than a certificate of deposit, in the name of one individual (principal), in which one or more other individuals have been designated as agents with the right to make deposits to and to withdraw funds from or draw checks on such account. The designation of agents, the substitution or removal of agents, or any other change in the contractual terms or provisions governing a convenience account may be made only by the principal. Except as otherwise provided in this section,

the agency relationship created under this account is not affected by the subsequent death or incompetence of the principal.

(2) All rights, interests, and claims in, to, and in respect of, such deposits and convenience account and the additions thereto shall be those of the principal only.

(3) Any balance standing to the credit of a convenience account shall be paid to the guardian of the property of the principal, to any person designated in a court order entered pursuant to s. 735.206, to any person designated by letter or other writing as authorized by s. 735.301, or to the personal representative of the deceased principal's estate, upon presentation of effective written notice and, if applicable, proof of judicial appointment of such guardian or personal representative by a court of competent jurisdiction. No such court order or letter, written notice, or proof of judicial appointment is effective until it is served upon and received by an officer of the institution during regular banking hours and in such time and in such manner as to afford the institution a reasonable opportunity to act on it prior to the happening of any of the events described in s. 674.303. No other notice, knowledge, or other information shown to have been available to an institution affects its right to the protection provided by this section.

(4) Payment by an institution pursuant to this section is a valid and sufficient release and discharge to the institution from all claims for payments so paid.

(5) Without qualifying any other right to setoff or lien, and subject to any contractual provision, if the principal is indebted to the institution, the institution has a right to setoff against the account.

History.
S. 49, ch. 92-303.

655.82. Pay-on-death accounts.

(1) As used in this section:

(a) "Account" means a contract of deposit between a depositor and an institution, including, but not limited to, a checking account, savings account, certificate of deposit, and share account.

(b) "Beneficiary" means a person named as one to whom sums on deposit in an account are payable on request after death of all parties or for whom a party is named as trustee.

(c) "Devisee" means any person designated in a will to receive a testamentary disposition of real or personal property.

(d) "Heirs" means those persons, including a surviving spouse, who are entitled, under the laws of this state regarding intestate succession, to the property of a decedent.

(e) "Multiple-party account" means an account payable on request to one or more of two or more parties, whether or not a right of survivorship is mentioned.

(f) "Party" means a person who, by the terms of an account, has a present right, subject to request, to payment from the account other than as a beneficiary.

(g) "Payment" means disbursement of sums on deposit, and includes withdrawal, payment to a party or third person pursuant to check or other request, and a pledge of sums on deposit by a party, or a setoff, reduction, or other disposition of all or part of an account pursuant to a pledge.

(h) "Pay-on-death designation" means the designation of:

1. A beneficiary in an account payable on request to one party during the party's lifetime and on the party's death to one or more beneficiaries, or to one or more parties during their lifetimes and on death of all of them to one or more beneficiaries; or

2. A beneficiary in an account in the name of one or more parties as trustee for one or more beneficiaries if the relationship is established by the terms of the account and there is no subject of the trust other than the sums on deposit in the account, whether or not payment to the beneficiary is mentioned.

(i) "Personal representative" means an executor, administrator, curator, successor personal representative, special administrator, or any other person who performs substantially the same function under the law governing their status.

(j) "Receive," as it relates to notice to an institution, means receipt in the office or branch office of the institution in which the account is established, but if the terms of the account require notice at a particular place, in the place required.

(k) "Request" means a request for payment complying with all terms of the account, including special requirements concerning necessary signatures and regulations of the institution; but, for purposes of this section, if terms of the account condition payment on advance notice, a request for payment is treated as immediately effective and a notice of intent to withdraw is treated as a request for payment.

(l) "Successor" means any person, other than a creditor, who is entitled to property of a decedent under the decedent's will or otherwise.

(m) "Sums on deposit" means the balance payable on an account, including interest and dividends earned, whether or not included in the current balance, and any deposit of life insurance proceeds added to the account by reason of death of a party.

(n) "Terms of the account" means the deposit agreement and other terms and conditions, including the form, of the contract of deposit.

(2) A beneficiary in an account having a pay-on-death designation has no right to sums on deposit during the lifetime of any party.

(3) In an account with a pay-on-death designation:

(a) On the death of one of two or more parties, sums on deposit in the account belong to the surviving party or parties.

(b) On the death of the sole party or the last survivor of two or more parties, sums on deposit belong to the surviving beneficiary or beneficiaries. If two or more beneficiaries survive, sums on deposit belong to them in equal and undivided shares, and, unless otherwise provided in a depository agreement written between December 31, 1994, and July 1, 2001, there is no right of survivorship in the event of death of a beneficiary thereafter. If no beneficiary survives, sums on deposit belong to the estate of the last surviving party.

(4) A pay-on-death designation in a multiple-party account without right of survivorship is ineffective. For purposes of this section, designation of an account as a tenancy in common establishes that the account is without right of survivorship.

(5) The ownership right of a surviving party or beneficiary, or of the decedent's estate, in sums on deposit is subject to requests for payment made by a party before the party's death, whether paid by the institution before or after death, or unpaid. The surviving party or beneficiary, or the decedent's estate, is liable to the payee of an unpaid request for payment. The liability is limited to a proportionate share of the amount transferred under this section, to the extent necessary to discharge the request for payment.

(6) An institution, on request, may pay sums on deposit in an account with a pay-on-death designation to:

(a) One or more of the parties, whether or not another party is disabled, incapacitated, or deceased when the payment is requested and whether or not a party survives another party;

(b) The beneficiary or beneficiaries, if proof of death is presented to the institution showing that the beneficiary or beneficiaries survived all persons named as parties; or

(c) The personal representative, if any, or, if there is none, the heirs or devisees of a deceased party, if proof of death is presented to the institution showing that the deceased party was the survivor of all other persons named on the account either as a party or beneficiary.

(7) Payment made pursuant to this section discharges the institution from all claims for amounts so paid, whether or not the payment is consistent with the beneficial ownership of the account as between parties, beneficiaries, or their successors. Payment may be made whether or not a party or beneficiary is disabled, incapacitated, or deceased when payment is requested, received, or made.

(8) A beneficiary in an account at a credit union having a pay-on-death designation, unless the beneficiary is a member in her or his own right, may not be permitted to vote, obtain an extension of credit, or hold office or be required to pay an entrance or membership fee.

(9) The following is an example of the form of a contract of deposit that may be used to select a pay-on-death account for use by one or more parties:

SINGLE-PARTY ACCOUNT OR MULTIPLE-PARTY ACCOUNT WITH PAY-ON-DEATH DESIGNATION

PARTIES (Name each party): _____

OWNERSHIP (Select one and initial):
_____ SINGLE-PARTY ACCOUNT
_____ MULTIPLE-PARTY ACCOUNT

RIGHTS AT DEATH (Select one and initial):
_____ SINGLE-PARTY ACCOUNT
At death of the party, ownership passes as part of the party's estate.
_____ SINGLE-PARTY ACCOUNT WITH A PAY-ON-DEATH DESIGNATION

(Name one or more beneficiaries):

_____

At death of the party, ownership passes to the designated pay-on-death beneficiaries and is not part of the party's estate.
_____ MULTIPLE-PARTY ACCOUNT WITH RIGHT OF SURVIVORSHIP
At death of a party, ownership passes to the surviving party or parties.
_____ MULTIPLE-PARTY ACCOUNT WITH RIGHT OF SURVIVORSHIP AND A PAY-ON-DEATH DESIGNATION
(Name one or more beneficiaries):

_____

At death of the last surviving party, ownership passes to the designated pay-on-death beneficiaries and is not part of the last surviving party's estate.

History.
S. 1, ch. 94-216; s. 529, ch. 97-102; s. 21, ch. 2001-243.

655.825. Deposits in trust; applicability of s. 655.82 in place of former s. 655.81.

(1) Because deposits in trust are also accounts with a pay-on-death designation as described in s. 655.82, it is the intent of the Legislature that the provisions of s. 655.82 shall apply to and govern deposits in trust. References to s. 655.81 in any depository agreement shall be interpreted after the effective date of this act as references to s. 655.82.

(2) This section shall take effect July 1, 2001, and shall apply to deposits made to a depository account created after December 31, 1994.

History.
S. 3, ch. 2001-243.

655.83. Adverse claim to a deposit or fiduciary account.

Notice to any institution of an adverse claim to a deposit or fiduciary account standing on its books to the credit of any person does not obligate the institution to recognize the adverse claimant unless the adverse claimant also either:

(1) Procures a restraining order, injunction, or other appropriate process having specific application to the institution issued by a court of competent jurisdiction in a cause therein instituted by such claimant wherein the person to whose credit the deposit or fiduciary account stands is made a party and served with process; or

(2) Obtains in favor of the institution, in a form, amount, and with sureties acceptable to it, a bond indemnifying the institution from any and all liability (including liabilities for penalties), loss, damage, costs, and expenses should it act to give effect to the adverse claim, including the decision not to honor the check or other order of the person to whose credit the deposit or fiduciary account stands on the books of the institution. Upon receipt of such bond, the institution shall hold the account pending agreement between the claimant and the person to whose credit the deposit or fiduciary account stands on the books of the institution or pending receipt of a restraining order, injunction, or other process pursuant to subsection (1).

History.
S. 51, ch. 92-303.

655.84. Limitations; statements as correct.

(1) Unless written objection thereto has been theretofore delivered by the depositor to the institution, a statement of account rendered by any institution in this state to a depositor, with a description of the amount and type (such as deposit, withdrawal, debit, credit, or any similar designation) of entries to such account, which description may be on accompanying documents or on the statement itself, shall, after the expiration of 2 years from the date rendered, be conclusively presumed to be correct; and the depositor is thereafter barred from questioning same.

(2) In the absence of a written contract between an institution and a depositor providing otherwise, the statement of account is deemed to have been rendered to the depositor within the meaning of this section when prepared and lodged by the institution at its statement window or other customary place for delivery to the depositor. Any such statement of account which is not demanded by the depositor within 3 years may be destroyed by the institution without accountability or liability therefor to anyone.

(3) This section does not relieve a depositor from any duty or obligation imposed by law or by contract heretofore or hereafter made to examine such statement of account and to report any disputed debits, credits, errors, or irregularities within a shorter period of time than mentioned in this section, or from the legal consequences of the depositor's failure to perform any such duty or obligation.

History.
S. 52, ch. 92-303.

655.85. Settlement of checks.

Whenever any check is forwarded or presented to an institution for payment, except when presented by the payee in person, the paying institution or remitting institution may pay or remit the same, at its option, either in money or in exchange drawn on its reserve agent or agents in the City of New York or in any reserve city within the Sixth Federal Reserve District; however, an institution may not settle any check drawn on it otherwise than at par. The provisions of this section do not apply with respect to the settlement of a check sent to such institution as a special collection item.

History.
S. 53, ch. 92-303.

655.851. Unclaimed credit balances.

Credit balances held by a financial institution, credit union, or participant as defined in 12 U.S.C. s. 4001(19) which result from the performance of or participation in check-clearing functions, whether pursuant to a contractual relationship between financial institutions, credit unions, or participants; through a clearinghouse as defined by s. 674.104; or through a clearinghouse association as defined by 12 U.S.C. s. 4001(8), are not subject to s. 717.117. This section is intended to clarify existing law and to be remedial in nature and applies to credit balances held before, on, or after July 1, 2007.

History.
S. 1, ch. 2007-142, eff. July 1, 2007.

655.86. Issuance of postdated checks.

It is the duty of the person drawing a postdated check to notify, in writing, the separate office or branch of the institution upon which such check is drawn, giving a complete description thereof, including the name of the payee, the date, the number, and the amount thereof; otherwise, the institution is not liable for paying such check.

History.
S. 54, ch. 92-303.

655.89. Legal holidays; business days; business and transactions.

(1) In this section, the term:

(a) "Business day" means that part of any day on which an institution is open to the public for carrying on substantially all its banking functions, trust functions, or transactions. A financial institution is deemed to be "closed" on any day, or any part of a day, when it is not open to the public for carrying on substantially all its banking functions, trust functions, and transactions.

(b) "Legal holiday" means a statutory holiday or a permissive holiday. A "statutory holiday" is any day which, by the laws of this state or the United States, is designated or recognized as a legal or public holiday. A "permissive holiday" is any one day, other than a statutory holiday, in each week on which an institution is customarily closed.

(c) "Transaction" means any one or more of the functions and elements of the business of an institution and includes, but is not limited to, the receipt or giving of any notice; the receipt or acceptance of deposits; the transmission, acceptance, payment, dishonor, and giving notice of dishonor of items; and its obligations and duties with respect to all thereof; and the word "transact" means to take action or nonaction the result of which is a transaction.

(2) Any institution may, but unless otherwise required by law is not required to, be closed or be open only for limited transactions and functions or purposes on any legal holiday. When an institution is closed as provided or permitted by law, it is not under any obligation or duty to conduct any of its business or effectuate any transaction. An institution is open only for limited transactions and functions or purposes when one or more, but fewer than all, of its branches, separate or other offices, departments, sections, or other functional elements of its business, which customarily are open to the public for carrying on the banking or trust business and transactions, are not open to the public for such purposes. When, as provided or permitted by law, an institution is open only for limited transactions and functions or purposes, it is not under any obligation or duty to conduct or transact, at or from such of its branches, separate or other offices, departments, sections, or other functional elements of its business which are not open to the public for such purposes, any of the business or transactions customarily conducted or transacted therefrom or thereat.

(3) When any statutory holiday occurs on a Sunday or on a day when an institution customarily is closed, such institution may, but unless otherwise required by law is not required to, elect to be closed or to be open only for limited transactions and functions or purposes on the next preceding or the next following day which, except for the provisions of this section, would not be a legal holiday, and such day so elected is, with respect to such institution, a legal holiday as to all transactions and for all purposes and laws.

(4) Any legal holiday on which an institution is closed or is open only for limited transactions and functions or purposes may, if the institution elects, be deemed and treated with respect to all transactions and for all purposes and laws, including, but not limited to, the Uniform Commercial Code, as not a business day; and any notice, item, or deposit of money received on any such day may be treated as being received at the opening of the next business day, and any transaction or other business which would or should have occurred or been transacted on any such legal holiday may be treated as postponed by law to the next business day.

(5) An institution may establish the regular and customary hours of each day during which each of its branches, separate or other offices, departments, sections, or functional elements of its business will be operated for the transaction of the business customarily conducted or transacted at or from each such branch, office, department, section, or functional element of business, and the regular and customary hours during which each thereof will be open to the public for the conduct of such business and transactions, and it is not necessary that the same hours be established for all thereof or that the hours so established for any thereof be the same on every day.

(6) With prior written approval of the office, an institution may designate another day or other days on which the institution may be closed and which day or days will not be considered business days.

(7) An institution may, but unless otherwise required by law is not under or subject to any obligation or duty to, effectuate any transaction or transact any business on any legal holiday; at any time before the beginning, or after the close, of its business day; or outside the regular and customary hours established as provided in subsection (5) or subsection (6) of any separate or other office or branch or any department, section, or functional element of business. If the institution elects to do so, it has all the rights provided by law with respect to such transaction or business, and, at its election, any such transactions or business shall be treated as having occurred or as having been transacted on that day or on its next following business day, except that any transaction or business occurring before the beginning of its regular business day shall be treated as occurring at the beginning of that business day.

(8) No liability or loss of rights of any kind on the part of any institution accrues or results by reason of any institution being closed or open only for limited functions or purposes, or by reason of any branch, separate or other office, department, section, or functional element of business being operated or open for the transaction of business only during the regular and customary hours established by the institution, as provided in this section.

History.
S. 55, ch. 92-303; s. 1732, ch. 2003-261.

655.90. Closing during emergencies and other special days.

(1) Definitions. — As used in this section, the term:

(a) "Commissioner" means the director of the Office of Financial Regulation and any other person lawfully exercising such powers.

(b) "Emergency" means any condition or occurrence, actual or threatened, which may interfere physically with the conduct of normal business operations of an institution or of one or more or all of the departments, sections, functions, offices, or facilities of an institution, or which poses an imminent or existing threat to the safety or security of persons or property, or both. Without limiting the generality of the foregoing, an emergency may exist, arise, or be imminent as the result of any one or more, actual or threatened, of the following: fires; floods; earthquakes; tornadoes; hurricanes; wind, rain, or other storms; labor disputes and strikes; power failures; transportation failures; interruption of communication facilities; shortages of fuel, food, transportation, or labor; robberies or burglaries or attempted robberies or burglaries; actual or threatened enemy attacks; epidemics or other catastrophes; explosions; and riots, civil commotions, and other acts of lawlessness or violence, actual or threatened.

(c) "Office" means any place at which an institution transacts its business or conducts operations relating to its business. However, this section does not authorize an institution to conduct its banking business at any place or places not otherwise authorized or permitted by law.

(d) "Officers" means the person or persons designated by the board of directors, board of trustees, or other governing body of an institution to act for the institution in carrying out the provisions of this section or, in the absence of any such designation or in the absence of the officers so designated, the president or any other officer currently in charge of the institution or of the office or offices in question.

(e) The authorizations herein provided for an institution "to close" in case of an emergency means and includes the authority not to open on any business or banking day and, if having opened, to close and suspend business.

(2) Powers of commissioner. — Whenever the commissioner is of the opinion that an emergency exists, or is impending, in this state or in any part of this state, he or she may, by proclamation, authorize state and nationally or federally chartered institutions, if not inconsistent with, and if it does not infringe upon, paramount federal law, located in the affected area or areas to close or to close any or all the departments, sections, functions, offices, or facilities thereof. In addition, if the commissioner is of the opinion that an emergency exists, or is impending, which affects, or may affect, a particular institution or institutions, or one or more particular departments, sections, functions, offices, or facilities thereof, but not institutions located in the area generally, he or she may authorize the particular institution or institutions to close or to close one or more of the departments, sections, functions, offices, or facilities thereof. The institution or institutions affected by any such proclamation or authorization may close in accordance therewith. Such institutions and such of the departments, sections, functions, offices, or facilities thereof so closed may remain closed until the commissioner proclaims that the emergency has ended, or until such earlier time as the officers of the institution determine that the institution or any of its departments, sections, functions, offices, or facilities, theretofore closed because of the emergency, should reopen, and, in either event, for such further time thereafter as may reasonably be required to reopen.

(3) Powers of officers.

(a) Whenever the officers of an institution are of the opinion that an emergency exists, or is impending, which affects, or may affect, the institution or one or more or all of its departments, sections, functions, offices, or facilities, they shall have the authority, in the reasonable exercise of their discretion, to close the institution or any one or more or all of the departments, sections, functions, offices, or facilities thereof on any business day or days during the continuation of such business emergency, even if the commissioner has not issued and does not issue a proclamation of emergency. The office or offices so closed may remain closed until such time as the officers determine that the emergency has ended and for such further time thereafter as may reasonably be required to reopen. However, in no case may such institution or any department, section, function, office, or facility thereof remain closed pursuant to this paragraph for more than 48 consecutive hours, excluding other legal holidays, without requesting the approval of the commissioner.

(b) The officers of an institution may close the institution or any one or more or all of the institution's departments, sections, functions, offices, or facilities on any day or days designated, by proclamation of the President of the United States or the Governor of this state, as a day or days of mourning, rejoicing, or other special observance.

(4) Notice to be given.

(a) An institution chartered under the laws of this state closing, or closing any of its departments, sections, functions, offices, or facilities, pursuant to the authority granted under subsection (3) shall give notice of its action to the commissioner as promptly as conditions reasonably permit and by any means reasonably available.

(b) A national or federal institution closing, or closing any of its departments, sections, functions, offices, or facilities, pursuant to the authority granted by this section shall give notice of its action to the appropriate federal regulatory agency as promptly as conditions reasonably permit and by any means reasonably available.

(5) Effect of closing and partial closing.

(a) Any day on which an institution, or any one or more of its departments, sections, functions, offices, or facilities, is closed during all or any part of its normal banking hours pursuant to the authorization granted in this section is, with respect to such institution or, if not all its departments, sections, functions, offices, or facilities are closed, then with respect to any of its departments, sections, functions, offices, or facilities which are closed, a legal holiday for all purposes with respect to any business of any kind or character of the institution, or of any of its departments, sections, functions, offices, or facilities, so closed, including, but without limiting the generality of the foregoing, matters relating to the time payable, the presenting for payment or acceptance, and the protesting and giving notice of protest and notice of dishonor of bills of exchange, checks, promissory notes, and other items drawn on or payable at such institution and relating to any other banking business of any kind or character. No liability or loss of rights of any kind on the part of any institution or director, officer, or employee thereof accrues or results by virtue of any closing authorized by this section.

(b) On any day which by the provisions of this section is deemed or declared to be a legal holiday with respect to any institution or institutions or office or offices thereof, the officers thereof may, in the exercise of their discretion, cause such institution or any office thereof to open its doors or facilities for the transaction or conduct of a limited business by the operation of one or more, but less than all, of its departments, sections, offices, functions, or facilities. On any day when, pursuant to the provisions of this section, less than all the departments, sections, functions, offices, or facilities are open, at the election of such institution the limited business transacted or conducted on such day is deemed for all purposes as transacted or conducted on the next following business day which is not deemed or declared as a legal holiday pursuant to the provisions of this section or of any other provision of law.

(6) Provisions cumulative. — The provisions of this section shall be construed and applied as being in addition to, and not in substitution for or limitation of, any other law of this state or of the United States authorizing the closing of an institution or excusing the delay by an institution in the performance of its duties and obligations because of emergencies or conditions beyond the institution's control or otherwise.

History.
S. 56, ch. 92-303; s. 530, ch. 97-102; s. 31, ch. 99-155; s. 1733, ch. 2003-261.

655.91. Records of institutions and copies thereof; retention and destruction.

(1) In this section, "records" of an institution means and includes all books of account and other books of every kind, journals, ledgers, statements, instruments, documents, files, messages, writings of every kind, and other internal or other data and other information of every description, made or received by an institution in the regular course of its business or otherwise, regardless of the mode in which it is recorded.

(2) Institutions need not preserve or retain any of their records or copies thereof for a period longer than is expressly required by an applicable statute or rule or regulation of this state or the United States which identifies, either specifically or by type or category, the relevant records or copies thereof or, if there is no such statute or rule or regulation which specifies a retention period applicable to the records or copies thereof, for a period longer than 5 years. An institution may destroy any of its records or copies thereof after the expiration of the retention period determined as provided in this subsection.

(3) No liability shall accrue against any institution because of the destruction of any of its records or copies thereof as permitted by subsection (2), and in any judicial or other action or proceeding in which any such records or copies thereof may be called in question or be demanded of the institution or any officer or employee thereof, a showing that such records or copies thereof have been destroyed in accordance with the provisions of subsection (2) is a sufficient excuse for the failure to produce them.

(4) Any institution may at any time make, or cause to be made, a copy or copies of any or all of its records, and any such copy duly certified, authenticated, or identified by a responsible officer or agent of the institution under whose supervision the records or copies are kept shall, in all cases and in all courts and places, be admitted and received as evidence with a like force and effect as the original record, whether or not the original is in existence.

(5) The original of any record of an institution includes the data or other information comprising a record stored or transmitted in or by means of any electronic, computerized, mechanized, or other information storage or retrieval or transmission system or device which can upon request generate, regenerate, or transmit the precise data or other information comprising the record; and an original also includes the visible data or other information so generated, regenerated, or transmitted if it is legible or can be made legible by enlargement or other process.

(6) Copies of records of an institution, heretofore or hereafter made, include duplicates or counterparts of an original produced from the same impression or process as the original by carbon or other chemical or substance or process; negative and positive film and prints of an original or copy and reproductions and facsimiles of an original or copy, whether or not the same size, produced by photographic, microphotographic, photostatic, xerographic, electronic, computerized, or mechanized process, or by any other process, and enlargements and reductions thereof; and the data or other information comprising a record stored or transmitted as provided in subsection (5), and the visible data or other information generated or

regenerated or transmitted by such information storage or retrieval or transmission system or device, if it is legible or can be made legible by enlargement or other process.

History.
S. 57, ch. 92-303.

655.921. Transaction of business by out-of-state financial institutions; exempt transactions in the financial institutions codes.

(1) Nothing in the financial institutions codes shall be construed to prohibit a financial institution having its principal place of business outside this state and not operating branches in this state from:

(a) Contracting in this state with any person to acquire from such person a part, or the entire, interest in a loan that such person proposes to make, has heretofore made, or hereafter makes, together with a like interest in any security instrument covering real or personal property in the state proposed to be given or hereafter or heretofore given to such person to secure or evidence such loan.

(b) Entering into mortgage servicing contracts with persons authorized to transact business in this state and enforcing in this state the obligations heretofore or hereafter acquired by it in the transaction of business outside this state or in the transaction of any business authorized by this section.

(c) Acquiring, holding, leasing, mortgaging, contracting with respect to, or otherwise protecting, managing, or conveying property in this state which has heretofore or may hereafter be assigned, transferred, mortgaged, or conveyed to it as security for, or in whole or in part in satisfaction of, a loan or loans made by it or obligations acquired by it in the transaction of any business authorized by this section.

(d) Making loans or committing to make loans to any person located in this state and soliciting compensating deposit balances in connection therewith.

(2) No such financial institution shall be deemed to be transacting business in this state, or be required to qualify so to do, solely by reason of the performance of any of the acts or business authorized in this section.

History.
S. 58, ch. 92-303; s. 10, ch. 2004-340; s. 93, ch. 2004-390.

655.922. Banking business by unauthorized persons; use of name.

(1) No person other than a financial institution authorized to do business in this state pursuant to the financial institutions codes of any state or federal law shall, in this state, engage in the business of soliciting or receiving funds for deposit or of issuing certificates of deposit or of paying checks; and no person shall establish or maintain a place of business in this state for any of the functions, transactions, or purposes mentioned in this subsection. Any person who violates the provisions of this subsection is guilty of a felony of the third degree, punishable as provided in s. 775.082, s. 775.083, or s. 775.084. This subsection does not prohibit the issuance or sale by a financial institution of traveler's checks, money orders, or other instruments for the transmission or payment of money, by or through employees or agents of the financial institution off the financial institution's premises.

(2) No person other than a financial institution shall, in this state:

(a) Transact business under any name or title that contains the words "bank," "banco," "banque," "banker," "banking," "trust company," "savings and loan association," "savings bank," or "credit union," or words of similar import, in any context or in any manner;

(b) Use any name, word, sign, symbol, or device in any context or in any manner; or

(c) Circulate or use any letterhead, billhead, circular, paper, or writing of any kind or otherwise advertise or represent in any manner,

which indicates or reasonably implies that the business being conducted or advertised is the kind or character of business transacted or conducted by a financial institution or which is likely to lead any person to believe that such business is that of a financial institution; however, the words "bank," "banker," "banking," "trust company," "savings and loan association," "savings bank," or "credit union," or the plural of any thereof, may be used by, and in the corporate or other name or title of, any company which is or becomes a financial institution holding company pursuant to federal law; any subsidiary of any such financial institution holding company which includes as a part of its name or title all or any part, or abbreviations, of the name or title of the financial institution holding company of which it is a subsidiary; any trade organization or association, whether or not incorporated, functioning for the purpose of promoting the interests of financial institutions or financial institution holding companies, the active members of which are financial institutions or financial institution holding companies; and any international development bank chartered pursuant to part II of chapter 663.

(3) No person may use the name or logo of any financial institution or an affiliate or subsidiary thereof, or use a name similar to that of a financial institution or an affiliate or subsidiary thereof, to market or solicit business from a customer or prospective customer of such institution if:

(a) The solicitation is done without the written consent of the financial institution or its affiliate or subsidiary; and

(b) A reasonable person would believe that the materials originated from, are endorsed by, or are connected with the financial institution or its affiliates or subsidiaries.

(4) Any court, in a proceeding brought by the office, by any financial institution the principal place of busi-

ness of which is in this state, or by any other person residing, or whose principal place of business is located, in this state and whose interests are substantially affected thereby, may enjoin any person from violating any of the provisions of this section. For the purposes of this subsection, the interests of a trade organization or association are deemed to be substantially affected if the interests of any of its members are so affected. In addition, the office may issue and serve upon any person who violates any of the provisions of this section a complaint seeking a cease and desist order in accordance with the procedures and in the manner prescribed by s. 655.033.

(5) Nothing in this section shall be construed to prohibit the lawful establishment or the lawful operations of a financial institution and nothing in this code shall be construed to prohibit any advertisement or other activity in this state by any person if such prohibition would contravene any applicable federal law which preempts the law of this state.

(6) The commission shall adopt rules to administer this section.

History.
S. 59, ch. 92-303; s. 12, ch. 96-168; s. 1734, ch. 2003-261; s. 11, ch. 2004-340; s. 94, ch. 2004-390.

655.93. Definitions for ss. 655.93-655.94.

As used in ss. 655.93-655.94, the term:

(1) "Lessee" means a person who contracts with a lessor for the use of a safe-deposit box.

(2) "Lessor" means a financial institution that rents safe-deposit facilities.

(3) "Safe-deposit box" means a safe-deposit box, vault, or other safe-deposit receptacle maintained by a lessor, and the rules relating thereto apply to property or documents kept in safekeeping in the financial institution's vault.

History.
S. 60, ch. 92-303.

655.931. Authority to engage in safe-deposit business.

A financial institution may maintain and lease safe-deposit boxes and may accept property or documents for safekeeping if, except in the case of property or documents accepted through night depositories, it issues a receipt therefor.

History.
S. 61, ch. 92-303.

655.932. Lease to minor.

A lessor may lease a safe-deposit box to, and in connection therewith deal with, a minor with the same effect as if leasing to and dealing with a person of full legal capacity.

History.
S. 62, ch. 92-303.

655.933. Access by fiduciaries.

If a safe-deposit box is made available by a lessor to one or more persons acting as fiduciaries, the lessor may, except as otherwise expressly provided in the lease or the writings pursuant to which such fiduciaries are acting, allow access thereto as follows:

(1) By any one or more of the persons acting as personal representatives.

(2) By any one or more of the persons otherwise acting as fiduciaries if authorized in writing, which writing is signed by all other persons so acting.

(3) By any agent authorized in writing, which writing is signed by all persons acting as fiduciaries.

History.
S. 63, ch. 92-303.

655.934. Effect of lessee's death or incapacity.

If a lessor without knowledge of the death or an order determining the incapacity of the lessee deals with the lessee's agent in accordance with a written power of attorney or a durable power of attorney signed by such lessee, the transaction binds the lessee's estate and the lessee.

History.
S. 64, ch. 92-303; s. 1, ch. 2010-132, eff. Oct. 1, 2010.

655.935. Search procedure on death of lessee.

If satisfactory proof of the death of the lessee is presented, a lessor shall permit the person named in a court order for that purpose, or if no order has been served upon the lessor, the spouse, a parent, an adult descendant, or a person named as a personal representative in a copy of a purported will produced by such person, to open and examine the contents of a safe-deposit box leased or coleased by a decedent, or any documents delivered by a decedent for safekeeping, in the presence of an officer of the lessor.

(1) If requested by such person, the lessor shall remove and deliver only:

(a) Any writing purporting to be a will of the decedent, to the court having probate jurisdiction in the county in which the financial institution is located.

(b) Any writing purporting to be a deed to a burial plot or to give burial instructions, to the person making the request for a search.

(c) Any document purporting to be an insurance policy on the life of the decedent, to the beneficiary named therein.

(2) The officer of the lessor shall make a complete copy of any document removed and delivered pursuant to this section and place that copy, together with a memorandum of delivery identifying the name of the officer, the person to whom the document was delivered, the purported relationship of the person to whom the document was delivered, and the date of delivery, in the safe-deposit box leased or coleased by the decedent.

(3) The lessor may charge reasonable fees to cover costs incurred pursuant to this section.

(4) Access granted pursuant to this section is not considered the initial opening of the safe-deposit box pursuant to s. 733.6065.

History.

S. 65, ch. 92-303; s. 1, ch. 2006-134, eff. July 1, 2006; s. 67, ch. 2006-213, eff. October 1, 2006; s. 2, ch. 2010-132, eff. Oct. 1, 2010.

655.936. Delivery of safe-deposit box contents or property held in safekeeping to personal representative.

(1) Subject to the provisions of subsection (3), the lessor shall immediately deliver to a personal representative appointed by a court in this state, upon presentation of a certified copy of his or her letters of authority, all property deposited with it by the decedent for safekeeping, and shall grant the personal representative access to any safe-deposit box in the decedent's name and permit him or her to remove from such box any part or all of the contents thereof.

(2) If a personal representative of a deceased lessee has been appointed by a court of any other state, a lessor may, at its discretion, after 3 months from the issuance to such personal representative of his or her letters of authority, deliver to such personal representative all properties deposited with it for safekeeping and the contents of any safe-deposit box in the name of the decedent if at such time the lessor has not received written notice of the appointment of a personal representative in this state, and such delivery is a valid discharge of the lessor for all property or contents so delivered. A personal representative appointed by a court of any other state shall furnish the lessor with an affidavit setting forth facts showing the domicile of the deceased lessee to be other than this state and stating that there are no unpaid creditors of the deceased lessee in this state, together with a certified copy of his or her letters of authority. A lessor making delivery pursuant to this subsection shall maintain in its files a receipt executed by such personal representative which itemizes in detail all property so delivered.

(3) Notwithstanding the provisions of subsection (1), after the death of a lessee of a safe-deposit box, the lessor shall permit the initial opening of the safe-deposit box and the removal of the contents of the safe-deposit box in accordance with s. 733.6065.

(4) A lessor is not liable for damages or penalty by reason of any delivery made pursuant to this section.

History.

S. 66, ch. 92-303; s. 531, ch. 97-102; s. 12, ch. 97-240; s. 3, ch. 2001-226; s. 2, ch. 2006-134, eff. July 1, 2006; s. 68, ch. 2006-213, eff. October 1, 2006.

655.937. Access to safe-deposit boxes leased in two or more names.

(1) Unless specifically provided in the lease or rental agreement to the contrary, if a safe-deposit box is rented or leased in the names of two or more lessees, access to the safe-deposit box will be granted to:

(a) Either or any of such lessees, regardless of whether or not the other lessee or lessees or any of them are living or competent.

(b) Subject to s. 655.933, those persons named in s. 655.933.

(c) Subject to s. 655.935, those persons named in s. 655.935.

(d) Subject to s. 733.6065, the personal representative of the estate of either or any of such lessees who is deceased, or the guardian of the property of either or any of such lessees who is incapacitated.

(2) In all cases described in subsection (1), the signature on the safe-deposit entry or access record, or the receipt or acquittance, in the case of property or documents otherwise held for safekeeping, is a valid and sufficient release and discharge to the lessor for granting access to such safe-deposit box or for the delivery of such property or documents otherwise held for safekeeping.

(3) A lessor may not be held liable for damages or penalty by reason of any access granted or delivery made pursuant to this section.

(4) The right of access by a colessee is separate from the rights and responsibilities of other persons who may be granted access to a safe-deposit box after the death or incapacity of another colessee, and such right of access is not subject to the provisions of s. 655.935, s. 733.6065, or other requirements imposed upon personal representatives, guardians, or other fiduciaries.

(5) After the death of a colessee, the surviving colessee or any other person who is granted access to the safe-deposit box pursuant to this section may make a written inventory of the box, which must be conducted by the person making the request in the presence of one other person as specified in this subsection. Each person present shall verify the contents of the box by signing a copy of the inventory under penalty of perjury.

(a) If the person making the written inventory is a surviving colessee, the other person may be any other person granted access pursuant to this section, an employee of the institution where the box is located, or an attorney licensed in this state.

(b) If the person making the written inventory is not a surviving colessee, the other person may be a surviving colessee, an employee of the institution where the box is located, or an attorney licensed in this state.

History.

S. 67, ch. 92-303; s. 3, ch. 2006-134, eff. July 1, 2006; s. 69, ch. 2006-213, eff. October 1, 2006.

655.938. Adverse claims to contents of safe-deposit box.

(1) An adverse claim to the contents of a safe-deposit box, or to property held in safekeeping, is not sufficient to require the lessor to deny access to its lessee unless:

(a) The lessor is directed to do so by a court order issued in an action in which the lessee is served with process and named as a party by a name which identifies the lessee with the name in which the safe-deposit box is leased or the property held; or

(b) The safe-deposit box is leased or the property is held in the name of a lessee with the addition of words indicating that the contents or property are held in a fiduciary capacity, and the adverse claim is supported by a written statement of facts disclosing that it is made by, or on behalf of, a beneficiary and that there is reason to know that the fiduciary will misappropriate the trust property.

(2) A claim is also an adverse claim if one of several lessees claims, contrary to the terms of the lease, an exclusive right of access, or if one or more persons claim a right of access as agents or officers of a lessee to the exclusion of others as agents or officers, or if it is claimed that a lessee is the same person as one using another name.

History.
S. 68, ch. 92-303.

655.939. Limiting right of access for failure to comply with security procedures.

If any individual who has a right of access to a safe-deposit box is unwilling or unable for any reason or cause to comply with any of the lessor's normal requirements or procedures in connection with such access relating to security, safety, or protection, the lessor has the right to limit or deny access to the safe-deposit box by such individual unless all lessees of such safe-deposit box take such action as is necessary to ensure reasonable compliance with such security, safety, or protection requirements or procedures.

History.
S. 69, ch. 92-303.

655.94. Special remedies for nonpayment of rent.

(1) If the rental due on a safe-deposit box has not been paid for 3 months, the lessor may send a notice by certified mail to the last known address of the lessee stating that the safe-deposit box will be opened and its contents stored at the expense of the lessee unless payment of the rental is made within 30 days. If the rental is not paid within 30 days from the mailing of the notice, the box may be opened in the presence of an officer of the lessor and of a notary public. The contents shall be sealed in a package by a notary public who shall write on the outside the name of the lessee and the date of the opening. The notary public shall execute a certificate reciting the name of the lessee, the date of the opening of the box, and a list of its contents. The certificate shall be included in the package, and a copy of the certificate shall be sent by certified mail to the last known address of the lessee. The package shall then be placed in the general vaults of the lessor at a rental not exceeding the rental previously charged for the box. The lessor has a lien on the package and its contents to the extent of any rental due and owing plus the actual, reasonable costs of removing the contents from the safe-deposit box.

(2) If the contents of the safe-deposit box have not been claimed within 1 year after the mailing of the certificate, the lessor may send a further notice to the last known address of the lessee stating that, unless the accumulated charges are paid within 30 days, the contents of the box will be sold at public auction at a specified time and place or, in the case of securities listed on a stock exchange, will be sold upon the exchange on or after a specified date and unsalable items will be destroyed. The time, place, and manner of sale shall also be posted conspicuously on the premises of the lessor and advertised once in a newspaper of general circulation in the community. If the articles are not claimed, they may then be sold in accordance with the notice. The balance of the proceeds, after deducting accumulated charges, including the expenses of advertising and conducting the sale, shall be deposited to the credit of the lessee in any account maintained by the lessee, or, if none, shall be deemed a deposit account with the financial institution operating the safe-deposit facility, and shall be identified on the books of the financial institution as arising from the sale of contents of a safe-deposit box.

(3) Any documents or writings of a private nature, and having little or no apparent value, need not be offered for sale, but shall be retained, unless claimed by the owner, for the period specified for unclaimed contents, after which they may be destroyed.

History.
S. 70, ch. 92-303; s. 12, ch. 2004-340; s. 95, ch. 2004-390.

TITLE XL.
REAL AND PERSONAL PROPERTY

CHAPTER 689.
CONVEYANCES OF LAND AND DECLARATIONS OF TRUST

689.01. How real estate conveyed.

No estate or interest of freehold, or for a term of more than 1 year, or any uncertain interest of, in or out of any messuages, lands, tenements or hereditaments shall be created, made, granted, transferred or released in any other manner than by instrument in writing, signed in the presence of two subscribing witnesses by the party creating, making, granting, conveying, transferring or releasing such estate, interest, or term of more than 1 year, or by the party's lawfully authorized agent, unless by will and testament, or other testamentary appointment, duly made according to law; and no estate or interest, either of freehold, or of term of more than 1 year, or any uncertain interest of, in, to, or out of any messuages, lands, tenements or hereditaments, shall be assigned or surrendered unless it be by instrument signed in the presence of two subscribing witnesses by the party so assigning or surrendering, or by the party's lawfully authorized agent, or by the act and operation of law. No seal shall be necessary to give validity to any instrument executed in conformity with this section. Corporations may execute any and all conveyances in accordance with the provisions of this section or ss. 692.01 and 692.02.

History.
S. 1, Nov. 15, 1828; RS 1950; GS 2448; RGS 3787; CGL 5660; s. 4, ch. 20954, 1941; s. 751, ch. 97-102; s. 2, ch. 2008-35, eff. July 1, 2008.

689.02. Form of warranty deed prescribed.

(1) Warranty deeds of conveyance to land may be in the following form, viz.:

"This indenture, made this _____ day of _____ A.D. _____, between _____, of the County of _____ in the State of _____, party of the first part, and _____ , of the County of _____, in the State of _____, party of the second part, witnesseth: That the said party of the first part, for and in consideration of the sum of _____ dollars, to her or him in hand paid by the said party of the second part, the receipt whereof is hereby acknowledged, has granted, bargained and sold to the said party of the second part, her or his heirs and assigns forever, the following described land, to wit:

And the said party of the first part does hereby fully warrant the title to said land, and will defend the same against the lawful claims of all persons whomsoever."

(2) The form for warranty deeds of conveyance to land shall include a blank space for the property appraiser's parcel identification number describing the property conveyed, which number, if available, shall be entered on the deed before it is presented for recording, and blank spaces for the social security numbers of the grantees named in the deed, if available, which numbers may be entered on the deed before it is presented for recording. The failure to include such blank spaces, or the parcel identification number, or any social security number, or the inclusion of an incorrect parcel identification number or social security number, shall not affect the validity of the conveyance or the recordability of the deed. Such parcel identification number shall not constitute a part of the legal description of the property otherwise set forth in the deed and shall not be used as a substitute for the legal description of the property being conveyed, nor shall a social security number serve as a designation of the grantee named in the deed.

History.
S. 1, ch. 4038, 1891; GS 2449; RGS 3788; CGL 5661; s. 1, ch. 87-66; s. 17, ch. 88-176; s. 60, ch. 89-356; s. 752, ch. 97-102.

689.03. Effect of such deed.

A conveyance executed substantially in the foregoing form shall be held to be a warranty deed with full common-law covenants, and shall just as effectually bind the grantor, and the grantor's heirs, as if said covenants were specifically set out therein. And this form of conveyance when signed by a married woman shall be held to convey whatever interest in the property conveyed which she may possess.

History.
S. 2, ch. 4038, 1891; GS 2450; RGS 3789; CGL 5662; s. 5, ch. 20954, 1941; s. 753, ch. 97-102.

689.04. How executed.

Such deeds shall be executed and acknowledged as is now or may hereafter be provided by the law regulating conveyances of realty by deed.

History.
S. 3, ch. 4038, 1891; GS 2451; RGS 3790; CGL 5663.

689.045. Conveyances to or by partnership.

(1) Any estate in real property may be acquired in the name of a limited partnership. Title so acquired must be conveyed or encumbered in the partnership name. Unless otherwise provided in the certificate of limited partnership, a conveyance or encumbrance of real property held in the partnership name, and any other instrument affecting title to real property in which

the partnership has an interest, must be executed in the partnership name by one of the general partners.

(2) Every conveyance to a limited partnership in its name recorded before January 1, 1972, as required by law while the limited partnership was in existence is validated and is deemed to convey the title to the real property described in the conveyance to the partnership named as grantee.

(3) When title to real property is held in the name of a limited partnership or a general partnership, one of the general partners may execute and record, in the public records of the county in which such partnership's real property is located, an affidavit stating the names of the general partners then existing and the authority of any general partner to execute a conveyance, encumbrance, or other instrument affecting such partnership's real property. The affidavit shall be conclusive as to the facts therein stated as to purchasers without notice.

History.
S. 2, ch. 71-9; s. 71, ch. 86-263; s. 23, ch. 95-242.
Editor's Notes.
Former s. 620.081.

689.05. How declarations of trust proved.

All declarations and creations of trust and confidence of or in any messuages, lands, tenements or hereditaments shall be manifested and proved by some writing, signed by the party authorized by law to declare or create such trust or confidence, or by the party's last will and testament, or else they shall be utterly void and of none effect; provided, always, that where any conveyance shall be made of any lands, messuages or tenements by which a trust or confidence shall or may arise or result by the implication or construction of law, or be transferred or extinguished by the act and operation of law, then, and in every such case, such trust or confidence shall be of the like force and effect as the same would have been if this section had not been made, anything herein contained to the contrary in anywise notwithstanding.

History.
S. 2, Nov. 15, 1828; RS 1951; GS 2452; RGS 3791; CGL 5664; s. 754, ch. 97-102.

689.06. How trust estate conveyed.

All grants, conveyances, or assignments of trust or confidence of or in any lands, tenements, or hereditaments, or of any estate or interest therein, shall be by deed signed and delivered, in the presence of two subscribing witnesses, by the party granting, conveying, or assigning, or by the party's attorney or agent thereunto lawfully authorized, or by last will and testament duly made and executed, or else the same shall be void and of no effect.

History.
S. 3, Nov. 15, 1828; RS 1952; GS 2453; RGS 3792; CGL 5665; s. 1, ch. 80-219; s. 755, ch. 97-102.

689.07. "Trustee" or "as trustee" added to name of grantee, transferee, assignee, or mortgagee

transfers interest or creates lien as if additional word or words not used.

(1) Every deed or conveyance of real estate heretofore or hereafter made or executed in which the words "trustee" or "as trustee" are added to the name of the grantee, and in which no beneficiaries are named, the nature and purposes of the trust, if any, are not set forth, and the trust is not identified by title or date, shall grant and is hereby declared to have granted a fee simple estate with full power and authority in and to the grantee in such deed to sell, convey, and grant and encumber both the legal and beneficial interest in the real estate conveyed, unless a contrary intention shall appear in the deed or conveyance; provided, that there shall not appear of record among the public records of the county in which the real property is situate at the time of recording of such deed or conveyance, a declaration of trust by the grantee so described declaring the purposes of such trust, if any, declaring that the real estate is held other than for the benefit of the grantee.

(2) Every instrument heretofore or hereafter made or executed transferring or assigning an interest in real property in which the words "trustee" or "as trustee" are added to the name of the transferee or assignee, and in which no beneficiaries are named, the nature and purposes of the trust, if any, are not set forth, and the trust is not identified by title or date, shall transfer and assign, and is hereby declared to have transferred and assigned, the interest of the transferor or assign or to the transferee or assignee with full power and authority to transfer, assign, and encumber such interest, unless a contrary intention shall appear in the instrument; provided that there shall not appear of record among the public records of the county in which the real property is situate at the time of the recording of such instrument, a declaration of trust by the assignee or transferee so described declaring the purposes of such trust, if any, or declaring that the interest in real property is held other than for the benefit of the transferee or assignee.

(3) Every mortgage of any interest in real estate or assignment thereof heretofore or hereafter made or executed in which the words "trustee" or "as trustee" are added to the name of the mortgagee or assignee, and in which no beneficiaries are named, the nature and purposes of the trust, if any, are not set forth, and the trust is not identified by title or date, shall vest and is hereby declared to have vested full rights of ownership to such mortgage or assignment and the lien created thereby with full power in such mortgagee or assignee to assign, hypothecate, release, satisfy, or foreclose such mortgage unless a contrary intention shall appear in the mortgage or assignment; provided that there shall not appear of record among the public records of the county in which the property constituting security is situate at the time of recording of such mortgage or assignment, a declaration of trust by such

mortgagee or assignee declaring the purposes of such trust, if any, or declaring that such mortgage is held other than for the benefit of the mortgagee or assignee.

(4) Nothing herein contained shall prevent any person from causing any declaration of trust to be recorded before or after the recordation of the instrument evidencing title or ownership of property in a trustee; nor shall this section be construed as preventing any beneficiary under an unrecorded declaration of trust from enforcing the terms thereof against the trustee; provided, however, that any grantee, transferee, assignee, or mortgagee, or person obtaining a release or satisfaction of mortgage from such trustee for value prior to the placing of record of such declaration of trust among the public records of the county in which such real property is situate, shall take such interest or hold such previously mortgaged property free and clear of the claims of the beneficiaries of such declaration of trust and of anyone claiming by, through or under such beneficiaries, and such person need not see to the application of funds furnished to obtain such transfer of interest in property or assignment or release or satisfaction of mortgage thereon.

(5) In all cases in which tangible personal property is or has been sold, transferred, or mortgaged in a transaction in conjunction with and subordinate to the transfer or mortgage of real property, and the personal property so transferred or mortgaged is physically located on and used in conjunction with such real property, the prior provisions of this section are applicable to the transfer or mortgage of such personal property, and, where the prior provisions of this section in fact apply to a transfer or mortgage of personal property, then any transferee or mortgagee of such tangible personal property shall take such personal property free and clear of the claims of the beneficiaries under such declaration of trust (if any), and of the claims of anyone claiming by, through, or under such beneficiaries, and the release or satisfaction of a mortgage on such personal property by such trustee shall release or satisfy such personal property from the claims of the beneficiaries under such declaration of trust, if any, and from the claims of anyone claiming by, through, or under such beneficiaries.

History.
S. 1, ch. 6925, 1915; s. 10, ch. 7838, 1919; RGS 3793; CGL 5666; s. 1, ch. 59-251; s. 1, ch. 2004-19.

Editor's Notes.
Section 2, ch. 2004-19 provides: "The amendments to section 689.07, Florida Statutes, provided by this act are intended to clarify existing law and shall apply retroactively."

689.071. Florida Land Trust Act.

(1) Short title. — This section may be cited as the "Florida Land Trust Act."

(2) Definitions. — As used in this section, the term:

(a) "Beneficial interest" means any interest, vested or contingent and regardless of how small or minimal such interest may be, in a land trust which is held by a beneficiary.

(b) "Beneficiary" means any person or entity having a beneficial interest in a land trust. A trustee may be a beneficiary of the land trust for which such trustee serves as trustee.

(c) "Holder of the power of direction" means any person or entity having the authority to direct the trustee to convey property or interests, execute a mortgage, distribute proceeds of a sale or financing, and execute documents incidental to the administration of a land trust.

(d) "Land trust" means any express written agreement or arrangement by which a use, confidence, or trust is declared of any land, or of any charge upon land, under which the title to real property, both legal and equitable, is vested in a trustee by a recorded instrument that confers on the trustee the power and authority prescribed in subsection (3). The recorded instrument does not itself create an entity, regardless of whether the relationship among the beneficiaries and the trustee is deemed to be an entity under other applicable law.

(e) "Trustee" means the person or entity designated in a trust instrument to hold legal and equitable title to property of a land trust.

(3) Ownership vests in trustee. — Every conveyance, deed, mortgage, lease assignment, or other instrument heretofore or hereafter made, hereinafter referred to as the "recorded instrument," transferring any interest in real property in this state, including, but not limited to, a leasehold or mortgagee interest, to any person or any corporation, bank, trust company, or other entity duly formed under the laws of its state of qualification, in which recorded instrument the person, corporation, bank, trust company, or other entity is designated "trustee" or "as trustee," whether or not reference is made in the recorded instrument to the beneficiaries of such trust or to any separate collateral unrecorded declarations or agreements, is effective to vest, and is hereby declared to have vested, in such trustee both legal and equitable title, and full rights of ownership, over the real property or interest therein, with full power and authority as granted and provided in the recorded instrument to deal in and with the property or interest therein or any part thereof; provided, the recorded instrument confers on the trustee the power and authority to protect, to conserve, to sell, to lease, to encumber, or otherwise to manage and dispose of the real property described in the recorded instrument.

(4) No duty to inquire. — Any grantee, mortgagee, lessee, transferee, assignee, or person obtaining satisfactions or releases or otherwise in any way dealing with the trustee with respect to the real property or any interest in such property held in trust under the recorded instrument, as hereinabove provided for, is not obligated to inquire into the identification or status of any named or unnamed beneficiaries, or their heirs or assigns to whom a trustee may be accountable under the terms of the recorded instrument, or under any

unrecorded separate declarations or agreements collateral to the recorded instrument, whether or not such declarations or agreements are referred to therein; or to inquire into or ascertain the authority of such trustee to act within and exercise the powers granted under the recorded instrument; or to inquire into the adequacy or disposition of any consideration, if any is paid or delivered to such trustee in connection with any interest so acquired from such trustee; or to inquire into any of the provisions of any such unrecorded declarations or agreements.

(5) Beneficiary claims. — All persons dealing with the trustee under the recorded instrument as hereinabove provided take any interest transferred by the trustee thereunder, within the power and authority as granted and provided therein, free and clear of the claims of all the named or unnamed beneficiaries of such trust, and of any unrecorded declarations or agreements collateral thereto whether referred to in the recorded instrument or not, and of anyone claiming by, through, or under such beneficiaries. However, this section does not prevent a beneficiary of any such unrecorded collateral declarations or agreements from enforcing the terms thereof against the trustee.

(6) Personal property. — In all cases in which the recorded instrument, as hereinabove provided, contains a provision defining and declaring the interests of beneficiaries thereunder to be personal property only, such provision shall be controlling for all purposes when such determination becomes an issue under the laws or in the courts of this state.

(7) Trustee liability. — In addition to any other limitation on personal liability existing pursuant to statute or otherwise, the provisions of ss. 736.08125 and 736.1013 apply to the trustee of a land trust created pursuant to this section.

(8) Land trust beneficiaries.

(a) Except as provided in this section, the beneficiaries of a land trust are not liable, solely by being beneficiaries, under a judgment, decree, or order of court or in any other manner for a debt, obligation, or liability of the land trust.

(b) Any beneficiary acting under the trust agreement of a land trust is not liable to the land trust's trustee or to any other beneficiary for the beneficiary's good faith reliance on the provisions of the trust agreement.

(c) Chapter 679 applies to the perfection of any security interest in a beneficial interest in a land trust. The perfection of a security interest in a beneficial interest in a land trust does not impair or diminish the authority of the trustee under the recorded instrument, and parties dealing with the trustee are not required to inquire into the terms of the unrecorded trust agreement.

(d) A beneficiary's duties and liabilities may be expanded or restricted in a trust agreement or beneficiary agreement.

(e) Any subsequent document appearing of record in which a beneficiary of a trust transfers or encumbers the beneficial interest in the trust does not diminish or impair the authority of the trustee under the terms of the recorded instrument. Parties dealing with the trustee are not required to inquire into the terms of the unrecorded trust agreement.

(f) An unrecorded trust agreement giving rise to a recorded instrument for a land trust may provide that one or more persons or entities have the power to direct the trustee to convey property or interests, execute a mortgage, distribute proceeds of a sale or financing, and execute documents incidental to administration of the land trust. The power of direction, unless provided otherwise in the land trust agreement, is conferred upon the holders of the power for the use and benefit of all holders of any beneficial interest in the land trust. In the absence of a provision in the land trust agreement to the contrary, the power of direction shall be in accordance with the percentage of individual ownership. In exercising the power of direction, the holders of the power of direction are presumed to act in a fiduciary capacity for the benefit of all holders of any beneficial interest in the trust, unless otherwise provided in the land trust agreement. A beneficial interest is indefeasible, and the power of direction may not be exercised so as to alter, amend, revoke, terminate, defeat, or otherwise affect or change the enjoyment of any beneficial interest.

(g) A trust relating to real estate does not fail, and any use relating to real estate may not be defeated, because beneficiaries are not specified by name in the recorded deed of conveyance to the trustee or because duties are not imposed upon the trustee. The power conferred by any recorded deed of conveyance on a trustee to sell, lease, encumber, or otherwise dispose of property described in the deed is effective, and a person dealing with the trustee is not required to inquire any further into the right of the trustee to act or the disposition of any proceeds.

(h) The principal residence of a beneficiary shall be entitled to the homestead tax exemption even if the homestead is held by a trustee in a land trust, provided the beneficiary qualifies for the homestead exemption under chapter 196.

(9) Successor trustee.

(a) The provisions of s. 736.0705 relating to the resignation of a trustee do not apply to the appointment of a successor trustee under this section.

(b) If the recorded instrument and the unrecorded land trust agreement are silent as to the appointment of a successor trustee in the event of the death, incapacity, resignation, or termination due to dissolution of a land trustee or if a land trustee is unable to serve as trustee, one or more persons or entities having the power of direction of the land trust agreement may appoint a successor trustee or trustees of the land trust by filing a declaration of appointment of a successor trustee or trustees in the office of the recorder of deeds in the county in which the trust property is located. The declaration must be signed by a beneficiary or beneficiaries of the trust and by each successor trustee, must be acknowledged in the manner provided for acknowledgment of deeds, and must contain:

1. The legal description of the trust property.

2. The name and address of the former trustee.

3. The name and address of each successor trustee.

4. A statement that each successor trustee has been appointed by one or more persons or entities having the power of direction of the land trust, together with an acceptance of appointment by each successor trustee.

(c) If the recorded instrument is silent as to the appointment of a successor trustee or trustees but an unrecorded land trust agreement provides for the appointment of a successor trustee or trustees in the event of the death, incapacity, resignation, or termination due to dissolution of the land trustee, upon the appointment of any successor trustee pursuant to the terms of the unrecorded land trust agreement, each successor trustee shall file a declaration of appointment of a successor trustee in the office of the recorder of deeds in the county in which the trust property is located. The declaration must be signed by both the former trustee and each successor trustee, must be acknowledged in the manner provided for acknowledgment of deeds, and must contain:

1. The legal description of the trust property.

2. The name and address of the former trustee.

3. The name and address of the successor trustee.

4. A statement of resignation by the former trustee and a statement of acceptance of appointment by each successor trustee.

5. A statement that each successor trustee was duly appointed under the terms of the unrecorded land trust agreement.

If the appointment of any successor trustee is due to the death or incapacity of the former trustee, the declaration need not be signed by the former trustee and a copy of the death certificate or a statement that the former trustee is incapacitated or unable to serve must be attached to or included in the declaration, as applicable.

(d) If the recorded instrument provides for the appointment of any successor trustee and any successor trustee is appointed in accordance with the recorded instrument, no additional declarations of appointment of any successor trustee are required under this section.

(e) Each successor land trustee appointed is fully vested with all the estate, properties, rights, powers, trusts, duties, and obligations of the predecessor land trustee, except that any successor land trustee is not under any duty to inquire into the acts or omissions of a predecessor trustee and is not liable for any act or failure to act of a predecessor trustee. A person dealing with any successor trustee pursuant to a declaration filed under this section is not obligated to inquire into or ascertain the authority of the successor trustee to act within or exercise the powers granted under the recorded instruments or any unrecorded declarations or agreements.

(f) A land trust agreement may provide that the trustee, when directed to do so by the beneficiaries of the land trust or legal representatives of the beneficiaries, may convey the trust property directly to another trustee on behalf of the beneficiaries or others named by the beneficiaries.

(10) Trustee as creditor.

(a) If a debt is secured by a security interest in a beneficial interest in a land trust or by a mortgage on land trust property, the validity or enforceability of the debt, security interest, or mortgage and the rights, remedies, powers, and duties of the creditor with respect to the debt or the security are not affected by the fact that the creditor and the trustee are the same person or entity, and the creditor may extend credit, obtain any necessary security interest or mortgage, and acquire and deal with the property comprising the security as though the creditor were not the trustee.

(b) A trustee of a land trust does not breach a fiduciary duty to the beneficiaries, and it is not evidence of a breach of any fiduciary duty owed by the trustee to the beneficiaries for a trustee to be or become a secured or unsecured creditor of the land trust, the beneficiary of the land trust, or a third party whose debt to such creditor is guaranteed by a beneficiary of the land trust.

(11) Remedial act. — This act is remedial in nature and shall be given a liberal interpretation to effectuate the intent and purposes hereinabove expressed.

(12) Exclusion. — This act does not apply to any deed, mortgage, or other instrument to which s. 689.07 applies.

History.

SS. 1, 2, 3, 4, 5, 6, ch. 63-468; s. 1, ch. 84-31; s. 2, ch. 2002-233; s. 21, ch. 2006-217, eff. July 1, 2007; s. 1, ch. 2006-274, eff. October 1, 2006; s. 7, ch. 2007-153, eff. July 1, 2007.

689.072.   Real estate interests transferred to or by a custodian or trustee of an individual retirement account or qualified plan.

(1)(a) A conveyance, deed, mortgage, lease assignment, or other recorded instrument that transfers an interest in real property in this state, including a leasehold or mortgagee interest, to a person who is qualified to act as a custodian or trustee for an individual retirement account under 26 U.S.C. s. 408(a)(2), as amended, in which instrument the transferee is designated "custodian," "as custodian," "trustee," or "as trustee" and the account owner or beneficiary of the custodianship in the individual retirement account is named, creates custodial property and transfers title to the custodian or trustee when an interest in real property is recorded in the name of the custodian or trustee, followed by the words "as custodian or trustee for the benefit of (name of individual retirement account owner or beneficiary) individual retirement account."

(b) This section also applies to a qualified stock bonus, pension, or profit-sharing plan created under 26 U.S.C. s. 401(a), as amended, in which instrument a person is designated "custodian," "as custodian," "trustee," or "as trustee" and the plan, plan participant, or plan beneficiary of the custodianship in the plan also creates custodial property and transfers title to the custodian or trustee when an interest in real property is recorded in the name of the custodian or trustee, followed by the words "as custodian, or trustee of the (name of plan) for the benefit of (name of plan participant or beneficiary)."

(2) A transfer to a custodian or trustee of an individual retirement account or qualified plan pursuant to this section incorporates the provisions of this section into the disposition and grants to the custodian or trustee the power to protect, conserve, sell, lease, encumber, or otherwise manage and dispose of the real property described in the recorded instrument without joinder of the named individual retirement account owner, plan participant, or beneficiary, except as provided in subsection (5).

(3) A person dealing with the custodian or trustee does not have a duty to inquire as to the qualifications of the custodian or trustee and may rely on the powers of the custodian or trustee for the custodial property created under this section regardless of whether such powers are specified in the recorded instrument. A grantee, mortgagee, lessee, transferee, assignee, or person obtaining a satisfaction or release or otherwise dealing with the custodian or trustee regarding such custodial property is not required to inquire into:

(a) The identification or status of any named individual retirement account owner, plan participant, or beneficiary of the individual retirement account or qualified plan or his or her heirs or assigns to whom a custodian or trustee may be accountable under the terms of the individual retirement account agreement or qualified plan document;

(b) The authority of the custodian or trustee to act within and exercise the powers granted under the individual retirement account agreement or qualified plan document;

(c) The adequacy or disposition or any consideration provided to the custodian or trustee in connection with any interest acquired from such custodian or trustee; or

(d) Any provision of an individual retirement account agreement or qualified plan document.

(4) A person dealing with the custodian or trustee under the recorded instrument takes any interest transferred by such custodian or trustee, within the authority provided under this section, free of claims of the named owner, plan participant, or beneficiary of the individual retirement account or qualified plan or of anyone claiming by, through, or under such owner, plan participant, or beneficiary.

(5) If notice of the revocation or termination of the individual retirement account agreement, qualified plan, or custodianship established under such individual retirement account agreement or qualified plan is recorded, any disposition or encumbrance of the custodial property must be by an instrument executed by the custodian or trustee or the successor and the respective owner, plan participant, or beneficiary of the individual retirement account or qualified plan.

(6) In dealing with custodial property created under this section, a custodian or trustee shall observe the standard of care of a prudent person dealing with property of another person. This section does not relieve the custodian or trustee from liability for breach of the individual retirement account agreement, custodial agreement, or qualified plan document.

(7) A provision of the recorded instrument that defines and declares the interest of the owner, plan participant, or beneficiary of the individual retirement account or qualified plan to be personal property controls only if a determination becomes an issue in any legal proceeding.

(8) As used in this section, the term "beneficiary" applies only when the individual retirement account owner or qualified plan participant is deceased.

(9)(a) This section does not apply to any deed, mortgage, or instrument to which s. 689.071 applies.

(b) Section 689.09 does not apply to transfers of real property interests to a custodian or trustee under this section.

(10) This section is remedial and shall be liberally construed to effectively carry out its purposes.

History.

S. 1, ch. 2006-147, eff. July 1, 2006.

689.075. Inter vivos trusts; powers retained by settlor.

(1) A trust which is otherwise valid and which complies with s. 736.0403, including, but not limited to, a trust the principal of which is composed of real property, intangible personal property, tangible personal property, the possible expectancy of receiving as a named beneficiary death benefits as described in s. 733.808, or any combination thereof, and which has been created by a written instrument shall not be held invalid or an attempted testamentary disposition for any one or more of the following reasons:

(a) Because the settlor or another person or both possess the power to revoke, amend, alter, or modify the trust in whole or in part;

(b) Because the settlor or another person or both possess the power to appoint by deed or will the persons and organizations to whom the income shall be paid or the principal distributed;

(c) Because the settlor or another person or both possess the power to add to, or withdraw from, the trust all or any part of the principal or income at one time or at different times;

(d) Because the settlor or another person or both possess the power to remove the trustee or trustees and appoint a successor trustee or trustees;

(e) Because the settlor or another person or both possess the power to control the trustee or trustees in the administration of the trust;

(f) Because the settlor has retained the right to receive all or part of the income of the trust during her or his life or for any part thereof; or

(g) Because the settlor is, at the time of the execution of the instrument, or thereafter becomes, sole trustee.

(2) Nothing contained herein shall affect the validity of those accounts, including but not limited to bank accounts, share accounts, deposits, certificates of deposit, savings certificates, and other similar arrangements, heretofore or hereafter established at any bank, savings and loan association, or credit union by one or more persons, in trust for one or more other persons, which arrangements are, by their terms, revocable by the person making the same until her or his death or incompetency.

(3) The fact that any one or more of the powers specified in subsection (1) are in fact exercised once, or more than once, shall not affect the validity of the trust or its nontestamentary character.

(4) This section shall be applicable to trusts executed before or after July 1, 1969, by persons who are living on or after said date.

(5) The amendment of this section, by chapter 75-74, Laws of Florida, is intended to clarify the legislative intent of this section at the time of its original enactment that it apply to all otherwise valid trusts which are created by written instrument and which are not expressly excluded by the terms of this section and that no such trust shall be declared invalid for any of the reasons stated in subsections (1) and (3) regardless of whether the trust involves or relates to an interest in real property.

History.
SS. 1, 2, ch. 69-192; s. 1, ch. 69-1747; ss. 1, 2, ch. 71-126; s. 169, ch. 73-333; s. 1, ch. 74-78; ss. 1, 2, ch. 75-74; s. 5, ch. 95-401; s. 756, ch. 97-102; s. 22, ch. 2006-217, eff. July 1, 2007.

689.08. Fines and common recoveries.

Conveyance by fine or by common recovery shall never be used in this state.

History.
S. 2, Feb. 4, 1835; RS 1953; GS 2454; RGS 3794; CGL 5667.

689.09. Deeds under statute of uses.

By deed of bargain and sale, or by deed of lease and release, or of covenant to stand seized to the use of any other person, or by deed operating by way of covenant to stand seized to the use of another person, of or in any lands or tenements in this state, the possession of the bargainor, releasor or covenantor shall be deemed and adjudged to be transferred to the bargainee, releasee or person entitled to the use as perfectly as if such bargainee, releasee or person entitled to the use had been enfeoffed by livery of seizin of the land conveyed by such deed of bargain and sale, release or covenant to stand seized; provided, that livery of seizin can be lawfully made of the lands or tenements at the time of the execution of the said deeds or any of them.

History.
S. 12, Nov. 15, 1828; RS 1954; GS 2455; RGS 3795; CGL 5668.

689.10. Words of limitation and the words "fee simple" dispensed with.

Where any real estate has heretofore been conveyed or granted or shall hereafter be conveyed or granted without there being used in the said deed or conveyance or grant any words of limitation, such as heirs or successors, or similar words, such conveyance or grant, whether heretofore made or hereafter made, shall be construed to vest the fee simple title or other whole estate or interest which the grantor had power to dispose of at that time in the real estate conveyed or granted, unless a contrary intention shall appear in the deed, conveyance or grant.

History.
S. 1, ch. 5145, 1903; GS 2456; RGS 3796; s. 1, ch. 10170, 1925; CGL 5669.

689.11. Conveyances between husband and wife direct; homestead.

(1) A conveyance of real estate, including homestead, made by one spouse to the other shall convey the legal title to the grantee spouse in all cases in which it would be effectual if the parties were not married, and the grantee need not execute the conveyance. An estate by the entirety may be created by the action of the spouse holding title:

(a) Conveying to the other by a deed in which the purpose to create the estate is stated; or

(b) Conveying to both spouses.

(2) All deeds heretofore made by a husband direct to his wife or by a wife direct to her husband are hereby validated and made as effectual to convey the title as they would have been were the parties not married;

(3) Provided, that nothing herein shall be construed as validating any deed made for the purpose, or that operates to defraud any creditor or to avoid payment of any legal debt or claim; and

(4) Provided further that this section shall not apply to any conveyance heretofore made, the validity of which shall be contested by suit commenced within 1 year of the effective date of this law.

History.
S. 1, ch. 5147, 1903; GS 2457; RGS 3797; CGL 5670; s. 6, ch. 20954, 1941; s. 1, ch. 23964, 1947; s. 1, ch. 71-54.

689.111. Conveyances of homestead; power of attorney.

(1) A deed or mortgage of homestead realty owned by an unmarried person may be executed by virtue of a power of attorney executed in the same manner as a deed.

(2) A deed or mortgage of homestead realty owned by a married person, or owned as an estate by the entirety, may be executed by virtue of a power of attorney executed solely by one spouse to the other, or solely by one spouse or both spouses to a third party, provided the power of attorney is executed in the same manner as a deed. Nothing in this section shall be construed as dispensing with the requirement that husband and wife join in the conveyance or mortgage of homestead realty, but the joinder may be accomplished through the exercise of a power of attorney.

History.
S. 1, ch. 71-27.

689.115. Estate by the entirety in mortgage made or assigned to husband and wife.

Any mortgage encumbering real property, or any assignment of a mortgage encumbering real property, made to two persons who are husband and wife, heretofore or hereafter made, creates an estate by the entirety in such mortgage and the obligation secured thereby unless a contrary intention appears in such mortgage or assignment.

History.
S. 1, ch. 86-29; s. 21, ch. 91-110.

689.12. How state lands conveyed for educational purposes.

(1) The title to all lands granted to or held by the state for educational purposes shall be conveyed by deed executed by the members of the State Board of Education, with an impression of the seal of the Board of Trustees of the Internal Improvement Trust Fund of the state thereon and when so impressed by this seal deeds shall be entitled to be recorded in the public records and to be received in evidence in all courts and judicial proceedings.

(2) Lands held for any tuberculosis hospital and declared to be surplus to the needs of such hospital may be conveyed to the district school board in which said lands are located for educational purposes.

History.
S. 1, ch. 4999, 1901; GS 2458; RGS 3798; CGL 5671; ss. 1, 2, ch. 67-191; ss. 27, 35, ch. 69-106; s. 1, ch. 69-300.

689.13. Rule against perpetuities not applicable to dispositions of property for private cemeteries, etc.

No disposition of property, or the income thereof, hereafter made for the maintenance or care of any public or private burying ground, churchyard, or other place for the burial of the dead, or any portion thereof, or grave therein, or monument or other erection in or about the same, shall fail by reason of such disposition having been made in perpetuity; but such disposition shall be held to be made for a charitable purpose or purposes.

History.
S. 1, ch. 14655, 1931; CGL 1936 Supp. 5671(1).

No fee tails!

689.14. Entailed estates.

No property, real or personal, shall be entailed in this state. Any instrument purporting to create an estate tail, express or implied, shall be deemed to create an estate for life in the first taker with remainder per stirpes to the lineal descendants of the first taker in being at the time of her or his death. If the remainder fails for want of such remainderman, then it shall vest in any other remaindermen designated in such instrument, or, if there is no such designation, then it shall revert to the original donor or to her or his heirs.

History.
S. 20, Nov. 17, 1829; RS 1818; GS 2293; RGS 3616; CGL 5481; s. 2, ch. 20954, 1941; s. 1, ch. 23126, 1945; s. 757, ch. 97-102.

689.15. Estates by survivorship.

The doctrine of the right of survivorship in cases of real estate and personal property held by joint tenants shall not prevail in this state; that is to say, except in cases of estates by entirety, a devise, transfer or conveyance heretofore or hereafter made to two or more shall create a tenancy in common, unless the instrument creating the estate shall expressly provide for the right of survivorship; and in cases of estates by entirety, the tenants, upon dissolution of marriage, shall become tenants in common.

History.
S. 20, Nov. 17, 1829; RS 1819; GS 2294; RGS 3617; CGL 5482; s. 3, ch. 20954, 1941; s. 1, ch. 73-300.

689.17. Rule in Shelley's Case abolished.

The rule in Shelley's Case is hereby abolished. Any instrument purporting to create an estate for life in a person with remainder to her or his heirs, lawful heirs, heirs of her or his body or to her or his heirs described by words of similar import, shall be deemed to create an estate for life with remainder per stirpes to the life tenant's lineal descendants in being at the time said life estate commences, but said remainder shall be subject to open and to take in per stirpes other lineal descendants of the life tenant who come into being during the continuance of said life estate.

History.
S. 2, ch. 23126, 1945; s. 758, ch. 97-102.

689.175. Worthier title doctrine abolished.

The doctrine of worthier title is abolished as a rule of law and as a rule of construction. Language in a governing instrument describing the beneficiaries of a disposition as the transferor's "heirs," "heirs at law," "next of kin," "distributees," "relatives," or "family," or language of similar import, does not create or presumptively create a reversionary interest in the transferor.

History.
S. 23, ch. 2006-217, eff. July 1, 2007.

689.18. Reverter or forfeiture provisions, limitations; exceptions.

(1) It is hereby declared by the Legislature of the state that reverter or forfeiture provisions of unlimited duration in the conveyance of real estate or any interest therein in the state constitute an unreasonable restraint on alienation and are contrary to the public policy of the state.

(2) All reverter or forfeiture provisions of unlimited duration embodied in any plat or deed executed more than 21 years prior to the passage of this law conveying real estate or any interest therein in the state, be and the same are hereby canceled and annulled and declared to be of no further force and effect.

(3) All reverter provisions in any conveyance of real estate or any interest therein in the state, now in force, shall cease and terminate and become null, void, and unenforceable 21 years from the date of the conveyance embodying such reverter or forfeiture provision.

(4) No reverter or forfeiture provision contained in any deed conveying real estate or any interest therein in the state, executed on and after July 1, 1951, shall be valid and binding more than 21 years from the date of such deed, and upon the expiration of such period of 21 years, the reverter or forfeiture provision shall become null, void, and unenforceable.

(5) Any and all conveyances of real property in this state heretofore or hereafter made to any governmental, educational, literary, scientific, religious, public utility, public transportation, charitable or nonprofit corporation or association are hereby excepted from the provisions of this section.

(6) Any holder of a possibility of reverter who claims title to any real property in the state, or any interest therein by reason of a reversion or forfeiture under the terms or provisions of any deed heretofore executed and delivered containing such reverter or forfeiture provision shall have 1 year from July 1, 1951, to institute suit in a court of competent jurisdiction in this state to establish or enforce such right, and failure to institute such action within said time shall be conclusive evidence of the abandonment of any such right, title, or interest, and all right of forfeiture or reversion shall thereupon cease and determine, and become null, void, and unenforceable.

(7) This section shall not vary, alter, or terminate the restrictions placed upon said real estate, contained either in restrictive covenants or reverter or forfeiture clauses, and all said restrictions may be enforced and violations thereof restrained by a court of competent jurisdiction whenever any one of said restrictions or conditions shall be violated, or threat to violate the same be made by owners or parties in possession or control of said real estate, by an injunction which may be issued upon petition of any person adversely affected, mandatorily requiring the abatement of such violations or threatened violation and restraining any future violation of said restrictions and conditions.

History.
SS. 1, 2, 3, 4, 5, 6, 7, ch. 26927, 1951; s. 218, ch. 77-104.

689.19. Variances of names in recorded instruments.

(1) The word "instrument" as used in this section shall be construed to mean and include not only instruments voluntarily executed but also papers filed or issued in or in connection with actions and other proceedings in court and orders, judgments and decrees entered therein and transcripts of such judgments and proceedings in foreclosure of mortgage or other liens.

(2) Variances between any two instruments affecting the title to the same real property both of which shall have been spread on the record for the period of more than 10 years among the public records of the county in which such real property is situated, with respect to the names of persons named in the respective instruments or in acknowledgments thereto arising from the full Christian name appearing in one and only the initial letter of that Christian name appearing in the other or from a full middle name appearing in one and only the initial letter of that middle name appearing in the other or from the initial letter of a middle name appearing in one and not appearing in the other, irrespective of which one of the two instruments in which any such variance occurred was prior in point of time to the other and irrespective of whether the instruments were executed or originated before or after August 5, 1953, shall not destroy or impair the presumption that the person so named in one of said instruments was the same person as the one so named in the other of said instruments which would exist if the names in the two instruments were identical; and, in spite of any such variance, the person so named in one of said instruments shall be presumed to be the same person as the one so named in the other until such time as the contrary appears and, until such time, either or both of such instruments or the record thereof or certified copy or copies of the record thereof shall be admissible in evidence in the same manner as though the names in the two instruments were identical.

History.
S. 1, ch. 28208, 1953.

689.20. Limitation on use of word "minerals."

Whenever the word "minerals" is hereafter used in any deed, lease, or other contract in writing, said word or term shall not include any of the following: topsoil, muck, peat, humus, sand, and common clay, unless expressly provided in said deed, lease, or other contract in writing.

History.
S. 1, ch. 59-375.

689.21.　Disclaimer of interests in property passing under certain nontestamentary instruments or under certain powers of appointment [Repealed.]

Repealed by s. 5, ch. 2005-108, effective July 1, 2005.

History.
S. 1, ch. 71-31; s. 26, ch. 73-334; s. 759, ch. 97-102; s. 3, ch. 2002-233.

689.225.　Statutory rule against perpetuities.

(1) Short title. — This section may be cited as the "Florida Uniform Statutory Rule Against Perpetuities."

(2) Statement of the rule.

(a) A nonvested property interest in real or personal property is invalid unless:

1. When the interest is created, it is certain to vest or terminate no later than 21 years after the death of an individual then alive; or

2. The interest either vests or terminates within 90 years after its creation.

(b) A general power of appointment not presently exercisable because of a condition precedent is invalid unless:

1. When the power is created, the condition precedent is certain to be satisfied or become impossible to satisfy no later than 21 years after the death of an individual then alive; or

2. The condition precedent either is satisfied or becomes impossible to satisfy within 90 years after its creation.

(c) A nongeneral power of appointment or a general testamentary power of appointment is invalid unless:

1. When the power is created, it is certain to be irrevocably exercised or otherwise to terminate no later than 21 years after the death of an individual then alive; or

2. The power is irrevocably exercised or otherwise terminates within 90 years after its creation.

(d) In determining whether a nonvested property interest or a power of appointment is valid under subparagraph (a)1., subparagraph (b)1., or subparagraph (c)1., the possibility that a child will be born to an individual after the individual's death is disregarded.

(e) If, in measuring a period from the creation of a trust or other property arrangement, language in a governing instrument (i) seeks to disallow the vesting or termination of any interest or trust beyond, (ii) seeks to postpone the vesting or termination of any interest or trust until, or (iii) seeks to operate in effect in any similar fashion upon, the later of:

1. The expiration of a period of time not exceeding 21 years after the death of a specified life or the survivor of specified lives, or upon the death of a specified life or the death of the survivor of specified lives in being at the creation of the trust or other property arrangement, or

2. The expiration of a period of time that exceeds or might exceed 21 years after the death of the survivor of lives in being at the creation of the trust or other property arrangement,

that language is inoperative to the extent it produces a period of time that exceeds 21 years after the death of the survivor of the specified lives.

(f) As to any trust created after December 31, 2000, this section shall apply to a nonvested property interest or power of appointment contained in a trust by substituting 360 years in place of "90 years" in each place such term appears in this section unless the terms of the trust require that all beneficial interests in the trust vest or terminate within a lesser period.

(3) When nonvested property interest or power of appointment created.

(a) Except as provided in paragraphs (b), (d), and (e) of this subsection and in paragraph (a) of subsection (6), the time of creation of a nonvested property interest or a power of appointment is determined under general principles of property law.

(b) For purposes of this section, if there is a person who alone can exercise a power created by a governing instrument to become the unqualified beneficial owner of a nonvested property interest or a property interest subject to a power of appointment described in paragraph (b) or paragraph (c) of subsection (2), the nonvested property interest or power of appointment is created when the power to become the unqualified beneficial owner terminates.

(c) For purposes of this section, a joint power with respect to community property or to marital property under the Uniform Marital Property Act held by individuals married to each other is a power exercisable by one person alone.

(d) For purposes of this section, a nonvested property interest or a power of appointment arising from a transfer of property to a previously funded trust or other existing property arrangement is created when the nonvested property interest or power of appointment in the original contribution was created.

(e) For purposes of this section, if a nongeneral or testamentary power of appointment is exercised to create another nongeneral or testamentary power of appointment, every nonvested property interest or power of appointment created through the exercise of such other nongeneral or testamentary power is considered to have been created at the time of the creation of the first nongeneral or testamentary power of appointment.

(4) Reformation. — Upon the petition of an interested person, a court shall reform a disposition in the manner that most closely approximates the transferor's manifested plan of distribution and is within the 90 years allowed by subparagraph (2)(a)2., subparagraph (2)(b)2., or subparagraph (2)(c)2. if:

(a) A nonvested property interest or a power of appointment becomes invalid under subsection (2);

(b) A class gift is not but might become invalid under subsection (2) and the time has arrived when the share of any class member is to take effect in possession or enjoyment; or

(c) A nonvested property interest that is not validated by subparagraph (2)(a)1. can vest but not within 90 years after its creation.

(5) Exclusions from statutory rule against perpetuities. — Subsection (2) does not apply to:

(a) A nonvested property interest or a power of appointment arising out of a nondonative transfer, except a nonvested property interest or a power of appointment arising out of:

1. A premarital or postmarital agreement;

2. A separation or divorce settlement;

3. A spouse's election;

4. A similar arrangement arising out of a prospective, existing, or previous marital relationship between the parties;

5. A contract to make or not to revoke a will or trust;

6. A contract to exercise or not to exercise a power of appointment;

7. A transfer in satisfaction of a duty of support; or

8. A reciprocal transfer;

(b) A fiduciary's power relating to the administration or management of assets, including the power of a fiduciary to sell, lease, or mortgage property, and the power of a fiduciary to determine principal and income;

(c) A power to appoint a fiduciary;

(d) A discretionary power of a trustee to distribute principal before termination of a trust to a beneficiary having an indefeasibly vested interest in the income and principal;

(e) A nonvested property interest held by a charity, government, or governmental agency or subdivision, if the nonvested property interest is preceded by an interest held by another charity, government, or governmental agency or subdivision;

(f) A nonvested property interest in, or a power of appointment with respect to, a trust or other property arrangement forming part of a pension, profit-sharing, stock bonus, health, disability, death benefit, income deferral, or other current or deferred benefit plan for one or more employees, independent contractors, or their beneficiaries or spouses, to which contributions are made for the purpose of distributing to or for the benefit of the participants, or their beneficiaries or spouses, the property, income, or principal in the trust or other property arrangement, except a nonvested property interest or a power of appointment that is created by an election of a participant or a beneficiary or spouse; or

(g) A property interest, power of appointment, or arrangement that was not subject to the common-law rule against perpetuities or is excluded by another statute of this state.

(6) Application.

(a) Except as extended by paragraph (c), this section applies to a nonvested property interest or a power of appointment that is created on or after October 1, 1988. For purposes of this subsection, a nonvested property interest or a power of appointment created by the exercise of a power of appointment is created when the power is irrevocably exercised or when a revocable exercise becomes irrevocable.

(b) This section also applies to a power of appointment that was created before October 1, 1988, but only to the extent that it remains unexercised on October 1, 1988.

(c) If a nonvested property interest or a power of appointment was created before October 1, 1988, and is determined in a judicial proceeding commenced on or after October 1, 1988, to violate this state's rule against perpetuities as that rule existed before October 1, 1988, a court, upon the petition of an interested person, may reform the disposition in the manner that most closely approximates the transferor's manifested plan of distribution and is within the limits of the rule against perpetuities applicable when the nonvested property interest or power of appointment was created.

(7) Rule of construction. — With respect to any matter relating to the validity of an interest within the rule against perpetuities, unless a contrary intent appears, it shall be presumed that the transferor of the interest intended that the interest be valid. This section is the sole expression of any rule against perpetuities or remoteness in vesting in this state. No common-law rule against perpetuities or remoteness in vesting shall exist with respect to any interest or power regardless of whether such interest or power is governed by this section.

(8) Uniformity of application and construction. — This section shall be applied and construed to effectuate its general purpose to make uniform the law with respect to the subject of this act among states enacting it.

History.

S. 1, ch. 88-40; s. 1, ch. 97-240; s. 1, ch. 2000-245.

689.25. Failure to disclose homicide, suicide, deaths, or diagnosis of HIV or AIDS infection in an occupant of real property.

(1)(a) The fact that an occupant of real property is infected or has been infected with human immunodeficiency virus or diagnosed with acquired immune deficiency syndrome is not a material fact that must be disclosed in a real estate transaction.

(b) The fact that a property was, or was at any time suspected to have been, the site of a homicide, suicide, or death is not a material fact that must be disclosed in a real estate transaction.

(2) A cause of action shall not arise against an owner of real property, his or her agent, an agent of a transferee of real property, or a person licensed under chapter 475 for the failure to disclose to the transferee that the property was or was suspected to have been the site of a homicide, suicide, or death or that an occupant of that property was infected with human immunodeficiency virus or diagnosed with acquired immune deficiency syndrome.

History.
S. 46, ch. 88-380; s. 51, ch. 2003-164.

689.26. Prospective purchasers subject to association membership requirement; disclosure required; covenants; assessments; contract voidability [Transferred.]

Transferred to s. 720.401.

689.261. Sale of residential property; disclosure of ad valorem taxes to prospective purchaser.

(1) A prospective purchaser of residential property must be presented a disclosure summary at or before execution of the contract for sale. Unless a substantially similar disclosure summary is included in the contract for sale, a separate disclosure summary must be attached to the contract for sale. The disclosure summary, whether separate or included in the contract, must be in a form substantially similar to the following:
PROPERTY TAX
DISCLOSURE SUMMARY
BUYER SHOULD NOT RELY ON THE SELLER'S CURRENT PROPERTY TAXES AS THE AMOUNT OF PROPERTY TAXES THAT THE BUYER MAY BE OBLIGATED TO PAY IN THE YEAR SUBSEQUENT TO PURCHASE. A CHANGE OF OWNERSHIP OR PROPERTY IMPROVEMENTS TRIGGERS REASSESSMENTS OF THE PROPERTY THAT COULD RESULT IN HIGHER PROPERTY TAXES. IF YOU HAVE ANY QUESTIONS CONCERNING VALUATION, CONTACT THE COUNTY PROPERTY APPRAISER'S OFFICE FOR INFORMATION.

(2) Unless included in the contract, the disclosure summary must be provided by the seller. If the disclosure summary is not included in the contract for sale, the contract for sale must refer to and incorporate by reference the disclosure summary and include, in prominent language, a statement that the potential purchaser should not execute the contract until he or she has read the disclosure summary required by this section.

History.
S. 5, ch. 2004-349.

689.262. Sale of residential property; disclosure of windstorm mitigation rating [Repealed.]

Repealed by s. 1, ch. 2010-275, effective November 17, 2010.
History.
S. 15, ch. 2008-66, eff. Jan. 1, 2011.

689.265. Financial report [Transferred.]

Transferred to s. 720.3086.

689.27. Termination by servicemember of agreement to purchase real property.

(1) Notwithstanding any other provisions of law and for the purposes of this section:

(a) "Closing" means the finalizing of the sale of property, upon which title to the property is transferred from the seller to the buyer.

(b) "Contract" means an instrument purporting to contain an agreement to purchase real property.

(c) "Property" means a house, condominium, or mobile home that a servicemember intends to purchase to serve as his or her primary residence.

(d) "Servicemember" shall have the same meaning as provided in s. 250.01.

(2) Any servicemember may terminate a contract to purchase property, prior to closing on such property, by providing the seller or mortgagor of the property with a written notice of termination to be effective immediately, if any of the following criteria are met:

(a) The servicemember is required, pursuant to permanent change of station orders received after entering into a contract for the property and prior to closing, to move 35 miles or more from the location of the property;

(b) The servicemember is released from active duty or state active duty after having agreed to purchase the property and prior to closing while serving on active duty or state active duty status, and the property is 35 miles or more from the servicemember's home of record prior to entering active duty or state active duty;

(c) Prior to closing, the servicemember receives military orders requiring him or her to move into government quarters or the servicemember becomes eligible to live in and opts to move into government quarters; or

(d) Prior to closing, the servicemember receives temporary duty orders, temporary change of station orders, or active duty or state active duty orders to an area 35 miles or more from the location of the property, provided such orders are for a period exceeding 90 days.

(3) The notice to the seller or mortgagor canceling the contract must be accompanied by either a copy of the official military orders or a written verification signed by the servicemember's commanding officer.

(4) Upon termination of a contract under this section, the seller or mortgagor or his or her agent shall refund any funds provided by the servicemember under the contract within 7 days. The servicemember is not liable for any other fees due to the termination of the contract as provided for in this section.

(5) The provisions of this section may not be waived or modified by the agreement of the parties under any circumstances.

History.
S. 19, ch. 2003-72.

689.28. Prohibition against transfer fee covenants.

(1) Intent. — The Legislature finds and declares that the public policy of this state favors the marketability of real property and the transferability of interests in real property free of title defects or unreasonable restraints on alienation. The Legislature further finds and declares that transfer fee covenants violate this public policy by impairing the marketability and transferability of real property and by constituting an unreasonable restraint on alienation regardless of the duration of such covenants or the amount of such transfer fees, and do not run with the title to the property or bind subsequent owners of the property under common law or equitable principles.

(2) Definitions. — As used in this section, the term:

(a) "Environmental covenant" means a covenant or servitude that imposes limitations on the use of real property pursuant to an environmental remediation project pertaining to the property. An environmental covenant is not a transfer fee covenant.

(b) "Transfer" means the sale, gift, conveyance, assignment, inheritance, or other transfer of an ownership interest in real property located in this state.

(c) "Transfer fee" means a fee or charge required by a transfer fee covenant and payable upon the transfer of an interest in real property, or payable for the right to make or accept such transfer, regardless of whether the fee or charge is a fixed amount or is determined as a percentage of the value of the property, the purchase price, or other consideration given for the transfer. The following are not transfer fees for purposes of this section:

1. Any consideration payable by the grantee to the grantor for the interest in real property being transferred, including any subsequent additional consideration for the property payable by the grantee based upon any subsequent appreciation, development, or sale of the property. For the purposes of this subparagraph, an interest in real property may include a separate mineral estate and its appurtenant surface access rights.

2. Any commission payable to a licensed real estate broker for the transfer of real property pursuant to an agreement between the broker and the grantor or the grantee, including any subsequent additional commission for that transfer payable by the grantor or the grantee based upon any subsequent appreciation, development, or sale of the property.

3. Any interest, charges, fees, or other amounts payable by a borrower to a lender pursuant to a loan secured by a mortgage against real property, including, but not limited to, any fee payable to the lender for consenting to an assumption of the loan or a transfer of the real property subject to the mortgage, any fees or charges payable to the lender for estoppel letters or certificates, and any shared appreciation interest or profit participation or other consideration described in s. 687.03(4) and payable to the lender in connection with the loan.

4. Any rent, reimbursement, charge, fee, or other amount payable by a lessee to a lessor under a lease, including, but not limited to, any fee payable to the lessor for consenting to an assignment, subletting, encumbrance, or transfer of the lease.

5. Any consideration payable to the holder of an option to purchase an interest in real property or the holder of a right of first refusal or first offer to purchase an interest in real property for waiving, releasing, or not exercising the option or right upon the transfer of the property to another person.

6. Any tax, fee, charge, assessment, fine, or other amount payable to or imposed by a governmental authority.

7. Any fee, charge, assessment, fine, or other amount payable to a homeowners', condominium, cooperative, mobile home, or property owners' association pursuant to a declaration or covenant or law applicable to such association, including, but not limited to, fees or charges payable for estoppel letters or certificates issued by the association or its authorized agent.

8. Any fee, charge, assessment, dues, contribution, or other amount imposed by a declaration or covenant encumbering four or more parcels in a community, as defined in s. 720.301, and payable to a nonprofit or charitable organization for the purpose of supporting cultural, educational, charitable, recreational, environmental, conservation, or other similar activities benefiting the community that is subject to the declaration or covenant.

9. Any fee, charge, assessment, dues, contribution, or other amount pertaining to the purchase or transfer of a club membership relating to real property owned by the member, including, but not limited to, any amount determined by reference to the value, purchase price, or other consideration given for the transfer of the real property.

10. Any payment required pursuant to an environmental covenant.

(d) "Transfer fee covenant" means a declaration or covenant recorded against the title to real property which requires or purports to require the payment of a transfer fee to the declarant or other person specified in the declaration or covenant or to their successors or assigns upon a subsequent transfer of an interest in the real property.

(3) Prohibition. — A transfer fee covenant recorded in this state on or after July 1, 2008, does not run with the title to real property and is not binding on or enforceable at law or in equity against any subsequent owner, purchaser, or mortgagee of any interest in real property as an equitable servitude or otherwise. Any liens purporting to secure the payment of a transfer fee under a transfer fee covenant that is recorded in this state on or after July 1, 2008, are void and unenforceable. This subsection does not mean that transfer fee covenants or liens recorded in this state before July 1, 2008, are presumed valid and enforceable.

History.
S. 1, ch. 2008-35, eff. July 1, 2008.

CHAPTER 695.
RECORD OF CONVEYANCES OF REAL ESTATE

695.01. Conveyances to be recorded.

(1) No conveyance, transfer, or mortgage of real property, or of any interest therein, nor any lease for a term of 1 year or longer, shall be good and effectual in law or equity against creditors or subsequent purchasers for a valuable consideration and without notice, unless the same be recorded according to law; nor shall any such instrument made or executed by virtue of any power of attorney be good or effectual in law or in equity against creditors or subsequent purchasers for a valuable consideration and without notice unless the power of attorney be recorded before the accruing of the right of such creditor or subsequent purchaser.

(2) Grantees by quitclaim, heretofore or hereafter made, shall be deemed and held to be bona fide purchasers without notice within the meaning of the recording acts.

History.
SS. 4, 9, Nov. 15, 1828; RS 1972; GS 2480; RGS 3822; CGL 5698; s. 10, ch. 20954, 1941; s. 8, ch. 85-63.

695.015. Conveyances by law between governmental agencies, recording.

All laws which purport to convey title to real property from one governmental agency or political subdivision to another shall be recorded in the public records of the county or counties in which the property is located, and such laws shall contain a provision requiring such recording.

History.
S. 1, ch. 70-103.

695.02. Blank or master form of instruments may be recorded.

(1) Any person may have a blank or master form of mortgage or other instrument conveying, transferring or reserving an interest in, or creating a lien on, real or personal property, filed, indexed and recorded in the office of the clerk of the circuit court.

(2) When any such blank or master form is filed with the clerk of the circuit court, she or he shall record and index the same in the manner provided by law for recording and indexing mortgages and such other instruments respectively, except that the name of the person whose name appears on such blank or master form shall be inserted in the indexes as grantor and also as grantee.

(3) When any instrument conveying, transferring or reserving an interest in, or creating a lien on, real or personal property, incorporates by reference the provisions, terms, covenants, conditions, obligations, powers and other contents, or any of them, set forth in any such recorded blank or master form, such incorporation by reference, for all purposes, shall be equivalent to setting forth in extenso in such instrument that which is incorporated by reference.

History.
SS. 1, 2, 3, 4, ch. 17109, 1935; CGL 1936 Supp. 5698(1); s. 219, ch. 77-104; s. 762, ch. 97-102.

695.03. Acknowledgment and proof; validation of certain acknowledgments; legalization or authentication before foreign officials.

To entitle any instrument concerning real property to be recorded, the execution must be acknowledged by the party executing it, proved by a subscribing witness to it, or legalized or authenticated by a civil-law notary or notary public who affixes her or his official seal, before the officers and in the form and manner following:

(1) Within this state. — An acknowledgment or proof made within this state may be made before a judge, clerk, or deputy clerk of any court; a United States commissioner or magistrate; or a notary public or civil-law notary of this state, and the certificate of acknowledgment or proof must be under the seal of the court or officer, as the case may be. All affidavits and acknowledgments heretofore made or taken in this manner are hereby validated.

(2) Without this state but within the united states. — An acknowledgment or proof made out of this state but within the United States may be made before a civil-law notary of this state or a commissioner of deeds appointed by the Governor of this state; a judge or clerk of any court of the United States or of any state, territory, or district; a United States commissioner or magistrate; or a notary public, justice of the peace, master in chancery, or registrar or recorder of deeds of any state, territory, or district having a seal, and the certificate of acknowledgment or proof must be under the seal of the court or officer, as the case may be. If the acknowledgment or proof is made before a notary public who does not affix a seal, it is sufficient for the notary public to type, print, or write by hand on the instrument, "I am a Notary Public of the State of (state), and my commission expires on (date)."

(3) Within foreign countries. — If the acknowledgment, legalization, authentication, or proof is made in a foreign country, it may be made before a commissioner of deeds appointed by the Governor of this state to act in such country; before a notary public of such foreign country or a civil-law notary of this state or of such foreign country who has an official seal; before an ambassador, envoy extraordinary, minister plenipotentiary, minister, commissioner, charge d'affaires, consul general, consul, vice consul, consular agent, or other diplomatic or consular officer of the United States appointed to reside in such country; or before a military or naval officer authorized by the Laws or Articles of War of the United States to perform the duties of notary public, and the certificate of acknowledgment, legalization, authentica-

tion, or proof must be under the seal of the officer. A certificate legalizing or authenticating the signature of a person executing an instrument concerning real property and to which a civil-law notary or notary public of that country has affixed her or his official seal is sufficient as an acknowledgment. For the purposes of this section, the term "civil-law notary" means a civil-law notary as defined in chapter 118 or an official of a foreign country who has an official seal and who is authorized to make legal or lawful the execution of any document in that jurisdiction, in which jurisdiction the affixing of her or his official seal is deemed proof of the execution of the document or deed in full compliance with the laws of that jurisdiction.

All affidavits, legalizations, authentications, and acknowledgments heretofore made or taken in the manner set forth above are hereby validated.

History.
RS 1973; ch. 5404, 1905; GS 2481; ss. 1, 2, ch. 7849, 1919; RGS 3823; CGL 5699; s. 7, ch. 22858, 1945; s. 1, ch. 28225, 1953; s. 1, ch. 69-79; s. 1, ch. 71-53; s. 26, ch. 73-334; s. 3, ch. 80-173; s. 1, ch. 84-97; s. 763, ch. 97-102; s. 21, ch. 98-246.

695.031. Affidavits and acknowledgments by members of armed forces and their spouses.

(1) In addition to the manner, form and proof of acknowledgment of instruments as now provided by law, any person serving in or with the Armed Forces of the United States, including the Army, Navy, Marine Corps, Coast Guard, or any component or any arm or service of any thereof, including any female auxiliary of any thereof, and any person whose duties require his or her presence with the Armed Forces of the United States, as herein designated, or otherwise designated by law or military or naval command, may acknowledge any instrument, wherever located, either within or without the state, or without the United States, before any commissioned officer in active service of the Armed Forces of the United States, as herein designated, or otherwise designated by law, or military or naval command, or order, with the rank of second lieutenant or higher in the Army or Marine Corps, or of any component or any arm or service of either thereof, including any female auxiliary of any thereof, or ensign or higher in the Navy or United States Coast Guard, or of any component or any arm or service of either thereof, including any female auxiliary of any thereof.

(2) The instrument shall not be rendered invalid by the failure to state therein the place of execution or acknowledgment. No authentication of the officer's certificate of acknowledgment or otherwise shall be required, and no seal shall be necessary, but the officer taking the acknowledgment shall endorse thereon or attach thereto a certificate substantially in the following form:

On this _____ day of _____, (year), before me _____, the undersigned officer, personally ap-

peared _____, known to me (or satisfactorily proven) to be serving in or with, or whose duties require her or his presence with the Armed Forces of the United States, and to be the person whose name is subscribed to the within instrument, and acknowledged that she or he executed the same for the purposes therein contained, and the undersigned does further certify that she or he is at the date of this certificate a commissioned officer of the rank stated below and is in the active service of the Armed Forces of the United States.

(Signature of commissioned officer.)
(Rank of commissioned officer and command or branch of service to which officer is attached.)

(3) Such acknowledgments by a married woman, who is a member of the Armed Forces of the United States, shall be sufficient in all respects to bar the dower, homestead rights or separate property rights of such married woman in any real estate described in the instrument thus acknowledged by her, as fully and completely as though such married woman had acknowledged such instrument as now required by other statutes.

(4) An acknowledgment by the spouse of a member of the Armed Forces of the United States shall be sufficient in all respects if it is acknowledged in the manner and form herein provided and shall have the same force and effect as though the instrument had been acknowledged as now required by other statutes and such acknowledgment by a married woman who is a spouse of a member of the Armed Forces of the United States shall be sufficient in all respects to bar the dower, homestead rights or separate property rights of such married woman in any real estate described in the instrument thus acknowledged by her as fully and completely as though such married woman had acknowledged such instrument as now required by other statutes.

(5) Any instrument or document acknowledged in the manner and form herein provided shall be entitled to be recorded and shall be recorded as in the case of other instruments or documents properly acknowledged.

(6) This section is to be liberally construed in favor of the validity of any such acknowledgments by any such member of the Armed Forces of the United States and any acknowledgments heretofore taken, containing words of similar import, are hereby confirmed and declared to be valid and binding. This section shall be construed as an enabling act and as an exception to existing laws rather than, inferentially or otherwise, as a repeal of the same or any part of the same.

History.
S. 7, ch. 22858, 1945; s. 1, ch. 57-40; s. 764, ch. 97-102; s. 28, ch. 99-6.

Editor's Notes.
Former s. 120.08.

695.032. Provisions not applicable to transactions under chapter 679, Uniform Commercial Code.

Section 695.03 shall not apply to any of the transactions within the scope of chapter 679 of the Uniform Commercial Code.

History.
S. 1, ch. 65-254.

695.04. Requirements of certificate.

The certificate of the officer before whom the acknowledgment or proof is taken, except for a certificate legalizing or authenticating the signature of a person executing an instrument concerning real property pursuant to s. 695.03(3), shall contain and set forth substantially the matter required to be done or proved to make such acknowledgment or proof effectual.

History.
RS 1974; GS 2482; RGS 3824; CGL 5700; s. 2, ch. 84-97.

695.05. Certain defects cured as to acknowledgments and witnesses.

All deeds, conveyances, bills of sale, mortgages or other transfers of real or personal property within the limits of this state, heretofore or hereafter made and received bona fide and upon good consideration by any corporation, and acknowledged for record before some officer, stockholder or other person interested in the corporation, grantee, or mortgagee as a notary public or other officer authorized to take acknowledgments of instruments for record within this state, shall be held, deemed and taken as valid as if acknowledged by the proper notary public or other officer authorized to take acknowledgments of instruments for record in this state not so interested in said corporation, grantee or mortgagee; and said instrument whenever recorded shall be deemed notice to all persons; provided, however, that this section shall not apply to any instrument heretofore made, the validity of which shall be contested by suit commenced within 1 year of the effective date of this law.

History.
S. 1, ch. 4953, 1901; GS 2483; RGS 3825; s. 1, ch. 11991, 1927; CGL 5701, 5702; s. 1, ch. 14706, 1931; CGL 1936 Supp. 5702(1); s. 11, ch. 20954, 1941.

695.06. Certain irregularities as to venue validated.

Whenever, in the acknowledgment to any deed or other instrument relating to real estate, heretofore recorded in this state, it shall appear, either from the recitals in such acknowledgment, or following the signature of the officer taking the same, or from the seal of such officer that the said acknowledgment was not taken, or may not have been taken, in the place as stated in the caption or venue thereof, said deed or other instrument shall, notwithstanding such irregularity or defect, be deemed and taken as properly acknowledged and of record.

History.
S. 1, ch. 11990, 1927; CGL 5703.

695.07. Use of scrawl as seal.

A scrawl or scroll, printed or written, affixed as a seal to any written instrument shall be as effectual as a seal.

History.
S. 1, ch. 4148, 1893; GS 2484; RGS 3826; CGL 5704.

695.08. Prior use of scrawl as seal.

All written instruments heretofore or hereafter made with a scrawl or scroll, printed or written, affixed as a seal are declared to be sealed instruments, and shall be construed and received in evidence as such in all the courts of this state.

History.
S. 2, ch. 4148, 1893; GS 2485; RGS 3827; CGL 5705.

695.09. Identity of grantor.

No acknowledgment or proof shall be taken, except as set forth in s. 695.03(3), by any officer within or without the United States unless the officer knows, or has satisfactory proof, that the person making the acknowledgment is the individual described in, and who executed, such instrument or that the person offering to make proof is one of the subscribing witnesses to such instrument.

History.
RS 1975; GS 2486; RGS 3828; CGL 5706; s. 3, ch. 84-97; s. 765, ch. 97-102.

695.10. Proof by others.

Where the grantors and witnesses of any instrument which may be recorded are dead, or cannot be had, the judge of the circuit court, or the county court judge for the county wherein the real property is situated, may take the examination of any competent witness or witnesses, on oath, to prove the handwriting of the witness or witnesses, or where such proof cannot be had, then to prove the handwriting of the grantor or grantors, which shall be certified by the judge, and the instrument being thus proved may be recorded.

History.
RS 1976; GS 2487; RGS 3829; CGL 5707; s. 26, ch. 73-334.

695.11. Instruments deemed to be recorded from time of filing.

All instruments which are authorized or required to be recorded in the office of the clerk of the circuit court of any county in the State of Florida, and which are to be recorded in the "Official Records" as provided for under s. 28.222, and which are filed for recording on or after the effective date of this act, shall be deemed to have been officially accepted by the said officer, and officially recorded, at the time she or he affixed thereon the consecutive official register numbers required under s. 28.222, and at such time shall be notice to all persons. The sequence of such official numbers shall determine the priority of recordation. An instrument bearing the lower number in the then-current series of numbers shall have priority over any instrument bearing a higher number in the same series.

History.
S. 1, ch. 3592, 1885; RS 1977; GS 2488; RGS 3830; CGL 5708; s. 1, ch. 17217, 1935; s. 1, ch. 67-442; s. 766, ch. 97-102.

695.12. Imperfect record.

Whenever any instrument authorized or required by law to be recorded in any county either has been or may be so imperfectly or erroneously recorded as to require a new record thereof, if the officer who so recorded the same be still in office, she or he shall, upon demand of the owner of such instrument, or person controlling the same, record it anew free of any charge or fee than the fee allowed by law for one perfect record thereof.

History.
S. 1, ch. 3896, 1889; RS 1978; GS 2489; RGS 3831; CGL 5709; s. 767, ch. 97-102.

695.13. Want of certificate of record.

Whenever any instrument authorized or required by law to be recorded shall appear to be recorded in the appropriate record book in the proper office, whether the record shall be in the handwriting of the officer whose duty it was to record such instrument, or in the handwriting of any other person, the record shall be presumed to have been made by the officer whose duty it was to make it, and the absence of a certificate of such officer that such instrument was recorded by her or him shall in no wise affect the validity of the record.

History.
S. 1, ch. 3894, 1889; RS 1979; GS 2490; RGS 3832; CGL 5710; s. 768, ch. 97-102.

695.14. Unsigned certificate of record.

Whenever any unsigned certificate on such record of the instruments mentioned in s. 695.13 shall contain the date of filing or of recording such instrument, it shall be prima facie evidence of the time of filing or of recording such instrument.

History.
S. 2, ch. 3894, 1889; RS 1980; GS 2491; RGS 3833; CGL 5711.

695.15. Recording conveyances lost by fire.

Whenever the record in the office of the clerk of the circuit court of any county in this state of any deed, conveyance, contract, mortgage, deed of trust, map or plat or other instrument in writing affecting real estate in such county has been heretofore destroyed by fire, any such instrument, or a copy thereof from such former record duly certified, may be rerecorded in such county, and in rerecording the same the officer shall record the certificate of the previous record, and the date of filing for record appearing in said original certificate so recorded shall be deemed and taken as the date of the record thereof. And copies of such record so authorized to be made hereunder, duly

certified by said officer, under the seal of said court, shall be received in evidence under the same circumstances and conditions under which a certified copy of the original record would be so received, and shall have the same force and effect as a certified copy of the original record.

History.
S. 1, ch. 4950, 1901; GS 2492; RGS 3834; CGL 5712; s. 7, ch. 22858, 1945.

695.16. When mortgage or lien is destroyed.

Whenever any mortgage or other lien required by law to be recorded, to be good and effectual against creditors or subsequent purchasers for a valuable consideration and without notice, has been heretofore recorded, and the record thereof has been destroyed by fire prior to May 30, 1901, such mortgage or other lien or a certified copy thereof, as aforesaid, shall be rerecorded within 9 months from said date, or such mortgage or other lien shall not be good or effectual in law or equity against a creditor or subsequent purchaser for valuable consideration and without notice; provided, however, that if the original instrument of mortgage or other lien has been lost or destroyed, the foregoing provision of this section shall not apply thereto, but such mortgage or other lien shall not be good or effectual in law or equity against creditors, or subsequent purchasers for a valuable consideration and without notice, unless legal proceedings to reestablish the same were begun in the proper court prior to March 3, 1902.

History.
S. 2, ch. 4950, 1901; GS 2493; RGS 3835; CGL 5713.

695.17. United States deeds and patents may be recorded.

Deeds and patents issued by the United States Government and photographic copies made by authority of said government from its records thereof in the general land office, embracing lands within the state, shall be admitted to record in this state in the county or counties where the land lies, when presented to the clerk of the court of the county where same is to be recorded, and when said deeds, patents or photographic copies shall appear to her or him to be genuine.

History.
S. 1, ch. 8565, 1921; CGL 5714; s. 769, ch. 97-102.

695.18. Indorsement by clerk.

Upon recording said deed, patent or certified copy, the clerk of the court shall indorse thereon and also upon the record made by her or him the following:

"This deed and patent (or certified copy as the case may be) having been presented to me on the _____ day of _____ for record, and same appearing to me to be genuine and to have been made and issued by the authority of the United States

Government, I have duly recorded same in _____ on page _____ of the public records of my office.

Witness my hand and official seal at _____ Florida, this _____ day of _____.

(Clerk.) "

History.
S. 2, ch. 8565, 1921; CGL 5715; s. 770, ch. 97-102.

695.19. Certified copies of recorded instruments may be recorded.

Certified copies of deeds, mortgages, powers of attorney and all other instruments of any kind which have been or may hereafter be duly recorded or filed among the public records of any county in this state may be recorded or rerecorded among the public records of any other county in this state as fully and in the same manner and with like effect as if such certified copy were the original instrument.

History.
S. 1, ch. 11989, 1927; CGL 5717.

695.20. Unperformed contracts of record.

Whenever anyone shall have contracted to purchase real estate in the state, prior to January 1, 1930, by written agreement requiring all payments to be made within 10 years from the date of the contract, or has accepted an assignment of such an agreement, and the fact of the existence of such a contract of purchase, or assignment, appears of record from the instrument itself or by reference in some other recorded instrument, and shall not have obtained and placed of record a deed to the property or a decree of a court of competent jurisdiction recognizing her or his rights thereunto, and is not in actual possession of the property covered by the contract or by the assignment, as defined in s. 95.17, she or he, her or his surviving spouse, heirs, personal representatives, successors, and assigns, shall have no further interest in the property described in the contract, or the assignment, by virtue thereof, and the record of such contract, assignment or other record reference thereto, shall no longer constitute either actual or constructive notice to a purchaser, mortgagee, or other person acquiring an interest in the property, unless within 6 months after this law shall take effect, (approved April 26, 1941) she or he or some one claiming under her or him shall:

(1) Place on record a deed or other conveyance of the property from the holder of the record title; or

(2) Place on record a written instrument executed by the holder of the record title evidencing an extension or modification of the original contract and showing that the original contract remains in force and effect; or

(3) Institute, or have pending, in a court of competent jurisdiction a suit for the enforcement of her or his rights under such contract.

History.
S. 1, ch. 20235, 1941; s. 771, ch. 97-102.

Editor's Notes.
Section 95.17, referred to in the middle of this section, was transferred to s. 95.16(2) by the reviser incident to compiling the 1974 Supplement to the Florida Statutes 1973.

695.22. Daily schedule of deeds and conveyances filed for record to be furnished property appraiser.

After October 1, 1945, the several clerks of the circuit courts shall keep and furnish to the respective county property appraisers in the counties where such instruments are recorded a daily schedule of the aforesaid deeds and conveyances so filed for recordation, in which schedule shall be set forth the name of the grantor or grantors, the names and addresses of each grantee and a description of the land as specified in each instrument so filed.

History.
S. 2, ch. 23114, 1945; s. 1, ch. 77-102.

695.25. Short form of acknowledgment.

The forms of acknowledgment set forth in this section may be used, and are sufficient for their respective purposes, under any law of this state. The forms shall be known as "Statutory Short Forms of Acknowledgment" and may be referred to by that name. The authorization of the forms in this section does not preclude the use of other forms.

(1) For an individual acting in his or her own right:

STATE OF _____
COUNTY OF _____

The foregoing instrument was acknowledged before me this (date) by (name of person acknowledging), who is personally known to me or who has produced (type of identification) as identification.

(Signature of person taking acknowledgment)
(Name typed, printed or stamped)
(Title or rank)
(Serial number, if any)

(2) For a corporation:

STATE OF _____
COUNTY OF _____

The foregoing instrument was acknowledged before me this (date) by (name of officer or agent, title of officer or agent) of (name of corporation acknowledging), a (state or place of incorporation) corporation, on behalf of the corporation. He/she is personally known to me or has produced (type of identification) as identification.

(Signature of person taking acknowledgment)
(Name typed, printed or stamped)
(Title or rank)
(Serial number, if any)

(3) For a partnership:

STATE OF _____
COUNTY OF _____

The foregoing instrument was acknowledged before me this (date) by (name of acknowledging partner or agent), partner (or agent) on behalf of (name of partnership), a partnership. He/she is personally known to me or has produced (type of identification) as identification.

(Signature of person taking acknowledgment)
(Name typed, printed or stamped)
(Title or rank)
(Serial number, if any)

(4) For an individual acting as principal by an attorney in fact:

STATE OF _____
COUNTY OF _____

The foregoing instrument was acknowledged before me this (date) by (name of attorney in fact) as attorney in fact, who is personally known to me or who has produced (type of identification) as identification on behalf of (name of principal).

(Signature of person taking acknowledgment)
(Name typed, printed or stamped)
(Title or rank)
(Serial number, if any)

(5) By any public officer, trustee, or personal representative:

STATE OF _____
COUNTY OF _____

The foregoing instrument was acknowledged before me this (date) by (name and title of position), who is personally known to me or who has produced (type of identification) as identification.

(Signature of person taking acknowledgment)

(Name typed, printed or stamped) :
(Title or rank)
(Serial number, if any).

History.
S. 1, ch. 73-62; s. 10, ch. 91-291; s. 7, ch. 93-62; s. 772, ch. 97-102.

695.26. Requirements for recording instruments affecting real property.

(1) No instrument by which the title to real property or any interest therein is conveyed, assigned, encumbered, or otherwise disposed of shall be recorded by the clerk of the circuit court unless:

(a) The name of each person who executed such instrument is legibly printed, typewritten, or stamped upon such instrument immediately beneath the signature of such person and the post-office address of each such person is legibly printed, typewritten, or stamped upon such instrument;

(b) The name and post-office address of the natural person who prepared the instrument or under whose supervision it was prepared are legibly printed, typewritten, or stamped upon such instrument;

(c) The name of each witness to the instrument is legibly printed, typewritten, or stamped upon such instrument immediately beneath the signature of such witness;

(d) The name of any notary public or other officer authorized to take acknowledgments or proofs whose signature appears upon the instrument is legibly printed, typewritten, or stamped upon such instrument immediately beneath the signature of such notary public or other officer authorized to take acknowledgment or proofs;

(e) A 3-inch by 3-inch space at the top right-hand corner on the first page and a 1-inch by 3-inch space at the top right-hand corner on each subsequent page are reserved for use by the clerk of the court; and

(f) In any instrument other than a mortgage conveying or purporting to convey any interest in real property, the name and post-office address of each grantee in such instrument are legibly printed, typewritten, or stamped upon such instrument.

(2) If a name or address is printed, typewritten, or stamped on an instrument in a position other than the position required by subsection (1), the clerk of the circuit court may, in her or his discretion, accept the instrument for recordation if she or he determines that the connection between the signature and the name or the name and the address is apparent.

(3) This section does not apply to:

(a) An instrument executed before July 1, 1991.

(b) A decree, order, judgment, or writ of any court.

(c) An instrument executed, acknowledged, or proved outside of this state.

(d) A will.

(e) A plat.

(f) An instrument prepared or executed by any public officer other than a notary public.

(4) The failure of the clerk of the circuit court to comply with this section does not impair the validity of the recordation or of the constructive notice imparted by recordation.

History.
S. 1, ch. 90-183; ss. 8, 22, ch. 94-348; s. 773, ch. 97-102.

695.27. Uniform Real Property Electronic Recording Act.

(1) Short title. — This section may be cited as the "Uniform Real Property Electronic Recording Act."

(2) Definitions. — As used in this section:

(a) "Document" means information that is:

1. Inscribed on a tangible medium or that is stored in an electronic or other medium and is retrievable in perceivable form; and

2. Eligible to be recorded in the Official Records, as defined in s. 28.222, and maintained by a county recorder.

(b) "Electronic" means relating to technology having electrical, digital, magnetic, wireless, optical, electromagnetic, or similar capabilities.

(c) "Electronic document" means a document that is received by a county recorder in an electronic form.

(d) "Electronic signature" means an electronic sound, symbol, or process that is executed or adopted by a person with the intent to sign the document and is attached to or logically associated with a document such that, when recorded, it is assigned the same document number or a consecutive page number immediately following such document.

(e) "Person" means an individual, corporation, business trust, estate, trust, partnership, limited liability company, association, joint venture, public corporation, government or governmental subdivision, agency, instrumentality, or any other legal or commercial entity.

(f) "State" means a state of the United States, the District of Columbia, Puerto Rico, the United States Virgin Islands, or any territory or insular possession subject to the jurisdiction of the United States.

(3) Validity of electronic documents.

(a) If a law requires, as a condition for recording, that a document be an original, be on paper or another tangible medium, or be in writing, the requirement is satisfied by an electronic document satisfying the requirements of this section.

(b) If a law requires, as a condition for recording, that a document be signed, the requirement is satisfied by an electronic signature.

(c) A requirement that a document or a signature associated with a document be notarized, acknowledged, verified, witnessed, or made under oath is satisfied if the electronic signature of the person authorized to perform that act, and all other information required to be included, is attached to or logically associated with the document or signature. A physical or electronic image of a stamp, impression, or seal need not accompany an electronic signature.

(4) Recording of documents.

(a) In this subsection, the term "paper document" means a document that is received by the county recorder in a form that is not electronic.

(b) A county recorder:

1. Who implements any of the functions listed in this section shall do so in compliance with standards established by rule by the Department of State.

2. May receive, index, store, archive, and transmit electronic documents.

3. May provide for access to, and for search and retrieval of, documents and information by electronic means.

4. Who accepts electronic documents for recording shall continue to accept paper documents as authorized by state law and shall place entries for both types of documents in the same index.

5. May convert paper documents accepted for recording into electronic form.

6. May convert into electronic form information recorded before the county recorder began to record electronic documents.

7. May agree with other officials of a state or a political subdivision thereof, or of the United States, on procedures or processes to facilitate the electronic satisfaction of prior approvals and conditions precedent to recording.

(5) Administration and standards.

(a) The Department of State, by rule pursuant to ss. 120.536(1) and 120.54, shall prescribe standards to implement this section in consultation with the Electronic Recording Advisory Committee, which is hereby created. The Florida Association of Court Clerks and Comptrollers shall provide administrative support to the committee and technical support to the Department of State and the committee at no charge. The committee shall consist of nine members, as follows:

1. Five members appointed by the Florida Association of Court Clerks and Comptrollers, one of whom must be an official from a large urban charter county where the duty to maintain official records exists in a county office other than the clerk of court or comptroller.

2. One attorney appointed by the Real Property, Probate and Trust Law Section of The Florida Bar Association.

3. Two members appointed by the Florida Land Title Association.

4. One member appointed by the Florida Bankers Association.

(b) Appointed members shall serve a 1-year term. All initial terms shall commence on the effective date of this act. Members shall serve until their successors are appointed. An appointing authority may reappoint a member for successive terms. A vacancy on the committee shall be filled in the same manner in which the original appointment was made, and the term shall be for the balance of the unexpired term.

(c) The first meeting of the committee shall be within 60 days of the effective date of this act. Thereafter, the committee shall meet at the call of the chair, but at least annually.

(d) The members of the committee shall serve without compensation and shall not claim per diem and travel expenses from the Secretary of State.

(e) To keep the standards and practices of county recorders in this state in harmony with the standards and practices of recording offices in other jurisdictions that enact substantially this section and to keep the technology used by county recorders in this state compatible with technology used by recording offices in other jurisdictions that enact substantially this section, the Department of State, in consultation with the committee, so far as is consistent with the purposes, policies, and provisions of this section, in adopting, amending, and repealing standards, shall consider:

1. Standards and practices of other jurisdictions.

2. The most recent standards adopted by national standard-setting bodies, such as the Property Records Industry Association.

3. The views of interested persons and governmental officials and entities.

4. The needs of counties of varying size, population, and resources.

5. Standards requiring adequate information security protection to ensure that electronic documents are accurate, authentic, adequately preserved, and resistant to tampering.

(f) The committee shall terminate on July 1, 2010.

(6) Uniformity of application and construction. — In applying and construing this section, consideration must be given to the need to promote uniformity of the law with respect to its subject matter among states that enact it.

(7) Relation to electronic signatures in global and national commerce act. — This section modifies, limits, and supersedes the federal Electronic Signatures in Global and National Commerce Act, 15 U.S.C. ss. 7001 et seq., but this section does not modify, limit, or supersede s. 101(c) of that act, 15 U.S.C. s. 7001(c), or authorize electronic delivery of any of the notices described in s. 103(b) of that act, 15 U.S.C. s. 7003(b).

History.
S. 1, ch. 2007-233, eff. June 27, 2007.

695.28. Validity of recorded electronic documents.

(1) A document that is otherwise entitled to be recorded and that was or is submitted to the clerk of the court or county recorder by electronic means and accepted for recordation is deemed validly recorded and provides notice to all persons notwithstanding:

(a) That the document was received and accepted for recordation before the Department of State adopted standards implementing s. 695.27; or

(b) Any defects in, deviations from, or the inability to demonstrate strict compliance with any statute, rule, or procedure to submit or record an electronic document in effect at the time the electronic document was submitted for recording.

(2) This section does not alter the duty of the clerk or recorder to comply with s. 695.27 or rules adopted pursuant to that section.

History.
S. 1, ch. 2011-173, eff. June 17, 2011.

Editor's Notes.
Section 2, ch. 2011-173 provides: "This act is intended to clarify existing law and applies prospectively and retroactively."

CHAPTER 709.
POWERS OF ATTORNEY AND SIMILAR INSTRUMENTS

PART I.
POWERS OF APPOINTMENT.

709.01. Power of attorney; authority of nominee when principal dead [Repealed].

Repealed by s. 33, ch. 2011-210, effective October 1, 2011.

History.
S. 1, ch. 23011, 1945; s. 1, ch. 67-453; s. 793, ch. 97-102.

709.015. Power of attorney; authority of agent when principal listed as missing [Repealed].

Repealed by s. 33, ch. 2011-210, effective October 1, 2011.

History.
S. 1, ch. 70-33; s. 794, ch. 97-102.

709.02. Power of appointment; method of release.

Powers of appointment over any property, real, personal, intangible or mixed, may be released, in whole or in part, by a written instrument signed by the donee or donees of such powers. Such written releases shall be signed in the presence of two witnesses but need not be sealed, acknowledged or recorded in order to be valid, nor shall it be necessary to the validity of such releases for spouses of married donees to join such donees in the execution of releases, in whole or part, of powers of appointment.

History.
S. 1, ch. 23007, 1945; s. 795, ch. 97-102.

709.03. Power of appointment; property held in trust.

If property subject to a power of appointment is held in trust by a person, firm or corporation other than the donee or donees of the power, a written release, in whole or in part, of a power to appoint the same shall be delivered to such trustee or trustees before the written release becomes legally effective. In no other instance shall a delivery of a release, in whole or in part, of a power of appointment be necessary to the validity of such release.

History.
S. 2, ch. 23007, 1945.

709.04. Power of appointment; effect of release.

Any power of appointment wholly released by a written instrument signed by the donee or donees of such power shall be, in legal effect, completely revoked, and shall not, after such release, be subject to being exercised in any manner whatsoever. Any power of appointment partially released by a written instrument signed by the donee or donees of such power shall be, in legal effect, as to such released part, completely revoked, and shall not after such release be subject to being exercised in any manner whatsoever as to such released part.

History.
S. 3, ch. 23007, 1945.

709.05. Powers of appointment; validation of prior releases.

All releases, in whole or in part, of powers of appointment heretofore executed in a manner that conforms with the provisions of this law be and they are hereby validated and shall be given the same force and effect as if executed subsequently to the effective date of this law.

History.
S. 4, ch. 23007, 1945.

709.06. Powers of appointment included in law.

Powers of appointment referred to in this law shall include not only those recognized as such by general law but also those designated as such under the tax law of the United States.

History.
S. 5, ch. 23007, 1945.

709.07. Power of appointment; effect of release on title to property.

No such release, in whole or in part, of a power of appointment shall affect the title to property of any bona fide purchaser for value who does not have notice or knowledge of such release.

History.
S. 7, ch. 23007, 1945.

709.08. Durable power of attorney [Repealed].

Repealed by s. 33, ch. 2011-210, effective October 1, 2011.

History.
S. 1, ch. 74-245; s. 1, ch. 77-272; s. 1, ch. 83-139; s. 1, ch. 88-36; s. 24, ch. 90-232; s. 1, ch. 92-71; s. 8, ch. 92-199; s. 17, ch. 95-401; s. 796, ch. 97-102; s. 2, ch. 97-240; s. 29, ch. 99-6; s. 1, ch. 2001-241; s. 104, ch. 2002-1; s. 22, ch. 2003-154; s. 16, ch. 2004-260; s. 31, ch. 2006-178, eff. July 1, 2006; s. 24, ch. 2006-217, eff. July 1, 2007.

709.11. Deployment-contingent power of attorney [Repealed].

Repealed by s. 33, ch. 2011-210, effective October 1, 2011.

History.
S. 1, ch. 88-62.

PART II.
POWERS OF ATTORNEY.

709.2101. Short title.

This part may be cited as the "Florida Power of Attorney Act."

History.
S. 3, ch. 2011-210, eff. Oct. 1, 2011.

709.2102. Definitions.

As used in this part, the term:

(1) "Agent" means a person granted authority to act for a principal under a power of attorney, whether denominated an agent, attorney in fact, or otherwise. The term includes an original agent, co-agent, and successor agent.

(2) "Durable" means, with respect to a power of attorney, not terminated by the principal's incapacity.

(3) "Electronic" means technology having electrical, digital, magnetic, wireless, optical, electromagnetic, or similar capabilities.

(4) "Financial institution" has the same meaning as in s. 655.005.

(5) "Incapacity" means the inability of an individual to take those actions necessary to obtain, administer, and dispose of real and personal property, intangible property, business property, benefits, and income.

(6) "Knowledge" means a person has actual knowledge of the fact, has received a notice or notification of the fact, or has reason to know the fact from all other facts and circumstances known to the person at the time in question. An organization that conducts activities through employees has notice or knowledge of a fact involving a power of attorney only from the time information was received by an employee having responsibility to act on matters involving the power of attorney, or would have had if brought to the employee's attention if the organization had exercised reasonable diligence. An organization exercises reasonable diligence if the organization maintains reasonable routines for communicating significant information to the employee having responsibility to act on matters involving the power of attorney and there is reasonable compliance with the routines. Reasonable diligence does not require an employee to communicate information unless the communication is part of the individual's regular duties or the individual knows that a matter involving the power of attorney would be materially affected by the information.

(7) "Power of attorney" means a writing that grants authority to an agent to act in the place of the principal, whether or not the term is used in that writing.

(8) "Presently exercisable general power of appointment" means, with respect to property or a property interest subject to a power of appointment, power exercisable at the time in question to vest absolute ownership in the principal individually, the principal's estate, the principal's creditors, or the creditors of the principal's estate. The term includes a power of appointment not exercisable until the occurrence of a specified event, the satisfaction of an ascertainable standard, or the passage of a specified period only after the occurrence of the specified event, the satisfaction of the ascertainable standard, or the passage of the specified period. The term does not include a power exercisable in a fiduciary capacity or only by will.

(9) "Principal" means an individual who grants authority to an agent in a power of attorney.

(10) "Property" means anything that may be the subject of ownership, whether real or personal, legal or equitable, or any interest or right therein.

(11) "Record" means information that is inscribed on a tangible medium or that is stored in an electronic or other medium and is retrievable in perceivable form.

(12) "Sign" means having present intent to authenticate or adopt a record to:

(a) Execute or adopt a tangible symbol; or

(b) Attach to, or logically associate with the record an electronic sound, symbol, or process.

(13) "Third person" means any person other than the principal, or the agent in the agent's capacity as agent.

History.
S. 4, ch. 2011-210, eff. Oct. 1, 2011.

709.2103. Applicability.

This part applies to all powers of attorney except:

(1) A proxy or other delegation to exercise voting rights or management rights with respect to an entity;

(2) A power created on a form prescribed by a government or governmental subdivision, agency, or instrumentality for a governmental purpose;

(3) A power to the extent it is coupled with an interest in the subject of the power, including a power given to or for the benefit of a creditor in connection with a credit transaction; and

(4) A power created by a person other than an individual.

History.
S. 5, ch. 2011-210, eff. Oct. 1, 2011.

709.2104. Durable power of attorney.

Except as otherwise provided under this part, a power of attorney is durable if it contains the words: "This durable power of attorney is not terminated by subsequent incapacity of the principal except as provided in chapter 709, Florida Statutes," or similar words that show the principal's intent that the authority conferred is exercisable notwithstanding the principal's subsequent incapacity.

History.
S. 6, ch. 2011-210, eff. Oct. 1, 2011.

709.2105. Qualifications of agent; execution of power of attorney.

(1) The agent must be a natural person who is 18 years of age or older or a financial institution that has

trust powers, has a place of business in this state, and is authorized to conduct trust business in this state.

(2) A power of attorney must be signed by the principal and by two subscribing witnesses and be acknowledged by the principal before a notary public or as otherwise provided in s. 695.03.

History.
S. 7, ch. 2011-210, eff. Oct. 1, 2011.

709.2106. Validity of power of attorney.

(1) A power of attorney executed on or after October 1, 2011, is valid if its execution complies with s. 709.2105.

(2) A power of attorney executed before October 1, 2011, is valid if its execution complied with the law of this state at the time of execution.

(3) A power of attorney executed in another state which does not comply with the execution requirements of this part is valid in this state if, when the power of attorney was executed, the power of attorney and its execution complied with the law of the state of execution. A third person who is requested to accept a power of attorney that is valid in this state solely because of this subsection may in good faith request, and rely upon, without further investigation, an opinion of counsel as to any matter of law concerning the power of attorney, including the due execution and validity of the power of attorney. An opinion of counsel requested under this subsection must be provided at the principal's expense. A third person may accept a power of attorney that is valid in this state solely because of this subsection if the agent does not provide the requested opinion of counsel, and in such case, a third person has no liability for refusing to accept the power of attorney. This subsection does not affect any other rights of a third person who is requested to accept the power of attorney under this part, or any other provisions of applicable law.

(4) A military power of attorney is valid if it is executed in accordance with 10 U.S.C. s. 1044b, as amended. A deployment-contingent power of attorney may be signed in advance, is effective upon the deployment of the principal, and shall be afforded full force and effect by the courts of this state.

(5) Except as otherwise provided in the power of attorney, a photocopy or electronically transmitted copy of an original power of attorney has the same effect as the original.

History.
S. 8, ch. 2011-210, eff. Oct. 1, 2011.

709.2107. Meaning and effectiveness of power of attorney.

The meaning and effectiveness of a power of attorney is governed by this part if the power of attorney:

(1) Is used in this state; or

(2) States that it is to be governed by the laws of this state.

History.
S. 9, ch. 2011-210, eff. Oct. 1, 2011.

709.2108. When power of attorney is effective.

(1) Except as provided in this section, a power of attorney is exercisable when executed.

(2) If a power of attorney executed before October 1, 2011, is conditioned on the principal's lack of capacity and the power of attorney has not become exercisable before that date, the power of attorney is exercisable upon the delivery of the affidavit of a physician who has primary responsibility for the treatment and care of the principal and who is licensed to practice medicine or osteopathic medicine pursuant to chapter 458 or chapter 459 as of the date of the affidavit. The affidavit executed by the physician must state that the physician is licensed to practice medicine or osteopathic medicine pursuant to chapter 458 or chapter 459, that the physician is the primary physician who has responsibility for the treatment and care of the principal, and that the physician believes that the principal lacks the capacity to manage property.

(3) Except as provided in subsection (2) and s. 709.2106(4), a power of attorney is ineffective if the power of attorney provides that it is to become effective at a future date or upon the occurrence of a future event or contingency.

History.
S. 10, ch. 2011-210, eff. Oct. 1, 2011.

709.2109. Termination or suspension of power of attorney or agent's authority.

(1) A power of attorney terminates when:

(a) The principal dies;

(b) The principal becomes incapacitated, if the power of attorney is not durable;

(c) The principal is adjudicated totally or partially incapacitated by a court, unless the court determines that certain authority granted by the power of attorney is to be exercisable by the agent;

(d) The principal revokes the power of attorney;

(e) The power of attorney provides that it terminates;

(f) The purpose of the power of attorney is accomplished; or

(g) The agent's authority terminates and the power of attorney does not provide for another agent to act under the power of attorney.

(2) An agent's authority is exercisable until the authority terminates. An agent's authority terminates when:

(a) The agent dies, becomes incapacitated, resigns, or is removed by a court;

(b) An action is filed for the dissolution or annulment of the agent's marriage to the principal or for their legal separation, unless the power of attorney otherwise provides; or

(c) The power of attorney terminates.

(3) If any person initiates judicial proceedings to determine the principal's incapacity or for the appointment of a guardian advocate, the authority granted under the power of attorney is suspended until the petition is dismissed or withdrawn or the court enters an order authorizing the agent to exercise one or more powers granted under the power of attorney.

(a) If an emergency arises after initiation of proceedings to determine incapacity and before adjudication regarding the principal's capacity, the agent may petition the court in which the proceeding is pending for authorization to exercise a power granted under the power of attorney. The petition must set forth the nature of the emergency, the property or matter involved, and the power to be exercised by the agent.

(b) Notwithstanding the provisions of this section, unless otherwise ordered by the court, a proceeding to determine incapacity does not affect the authority of the agent to make health care decisions for the principal, including, but not limited to, those provided in chapter 765. If the principal has executed a health care advance directive designating a health care surrogate, the terms of the directive control if the directive and the power of attorney are in conflict unless the power of attorney is later executed and expressly states otherwise.

(4) Termination or suspension of an agent's authority or of a power of attorney is not effective as to an agent who, without knowledge of the termination or suspension, acts in good faith under the power of attorney. An act so performed, unless otherwise invalid or unenforceable, binds the principal and the principal's successors in interest.

History.
S. 11, ch. 2011-210, eff. Oct. 1, 2011.

709.2110. Revocation of power of attorney.

(1) A principal may revoke a power of attorney by expressing the revocation in a subsequently executed power of attorney or other writing signed by the principal. The principal may give notice of the revocation to an agent who has accepted authority under the revoked power of attorney.

(2) Except as provided in subsection (1), the execution of a power of attorney does not revoke a power of attorney previously executed by the principal.

History.
S. 12, ch. 2011-210, eff. Oct. 1, 2011.

709.2111. Co-agents and successor agents.

(1) A principal may designate two or more persons to act as co-agents. Unless the power of attorney otherwise provides, each co-agent may exercise its authority independently.

(2) A principal may designate one or more successor agents to act if an agent resigns, dies, becomes incapacitated, is not qualified to serve, or declines to serve. Unless the power of attorney otherwise provides, a successor agent:

(a) Has the same authority as that granted to the original agent; and

(b) May not act until the predecessor agents have resigned, have died, have become incapacitated, are no longer qualified to serve, or have declined to serve.

(3) Except as otherwise provided in the power of attorney and subsection (4), an agent who does not participate in or conceal a breach of fiduciary duty committed by another agent, including a predecessor agent, is not liable for the actions or omissions of the other agent.

(4) An agent who has actual knowledge of a breach or imminent breach of fiduciary duty by another agent, including a predecessor agent, must take any action reasonably appropriate in the circumstances to safeguard the principal's best interests. If the agent in good faith believes that the principal is not incapacitated, giving notice to the principal is a sufficient action. An agent who fails to take action as required by this subsection is liable to the principal for the principal's reasonably foreseeable damages that could have been avoided if the agent had taken such action.

(5) A successor agent does not have a duty to review the conduct or decisions of a predecessor agent. Except as provided in subsection (4), a successor agent does not have a duty to institute any proceeding against a predecessor agent, or to file any claim against a predecessor agent's estate, for any of the predecessor agent's actions or omissions as agent.

(6) If a power of attorney requires that two or more persons act together as co-agents, notwithstanding the requirement that they act together, one or more of the agents may delegate to a co-agent the authority to conduct banking transactions as provided in s. 709.2208(1), whether the authority to conduct banking transactions is specifically enumerated or incorporated by reference to that section in the power of attorney.

History.
S. 13, ch. 2011-210, eff. Oct. 1, 2011.

709.2112. Reimbursement and compensation of agent.

(1) Unless the power of attorney otherwise provides, an agent is entitled to reimbursement of expenses reasonably incurred on behalf of the principal.

(2) Unless the power of attorney otherwise provides, a qualified agent is entitled to compensation that is reasonable under the circumstances.

(3) Notwithstanding any provision in the power of attorney, an agent may not be paid compensation unless the agent is a qualified agent.

(4) For purposes of this section, the term "qualified agent" means an agent who is the spouse of the principal, an heir of the principal within the meaning of s. 732.103, a financial institution that has trust powers

and a place of business in this state, an attorney or certified public accountant who is licensed in this state, or a natural person who is a resident of this state and who has never been an agent for more than three principals at the same time.

History.
S. 14, ch. 2011-210, eff. Oct. 1, 2011.

709.2113. Agent's acceptance of appointment.

Except as otherwise provided in the power of attorney, a person accepts appointment as an agent by exercising authority or performing duties as an agent or by any other assertion or conduct indicating acceptance. The scope of an agent's acceptance is limited to those aspects of the power of attorney for which the agent's assertions or conduct reasonably manifests acceptance.

History.
S. 15, ch. 2011-210, eff. Oct. 1, 2011.

709.2114. Agent's duties.

(1) An agent is a fiduciary. Notwithstanding the provisions in the power of attorney, an agent who has accepted appointment:

(a) Must act only within the scope of authority granted in the power of attorney. In exercising that authority, the agent:

1. May not act contrary to the principal's reasonable expectations actually known by the agent;

2. Must act in good faith;

3. May not act in a manner that is contrary to the principal's best interest, except as provided in paragraph (2)(d) and s. 709.2202; and

4. Must attempt to preserve the principal's estate plan, to the extent actually known by the agent, if preserving the plan is consistent with the principal's best interest based on all relevant factors, including:

  a. The value and nature of the principal's property;

  b. The principal's foreseeable obligations and need for maintenance;

  c. Minimization of taxes, including income, estate, inheritance, generation-skipping transfer, and gift taxes;

  d. Eligibility for a benefit, a program, or assistance under a statute or rule; and

  e. The principal's personal history of making or joining in making gifts;

(b) May not delegate authority to a third person except as provided in s. 518.112;

(c) Must keep a record of all receipts, disbursements, and transactions made on behalf of the principal; and

(d) Must create and maintain an accurate inventory each time the agent accesses the principal's safe-deposit box, if the power of attorney authorizes the agent to access the box.

(2) Except as otherwise provided in the power of attorney, an agent who has accepted appointment shall:

(a) Act loyally for the sole benefit of the principal;

(b) Act so as not to create a conflict of interest that impairs the agent's ability to act impartially in the principal's best interest;

(c) Act with the care, competence, and diligence ordinarily exercised by agents in similar circumstances; and

(d) Cooperate with a person who has authority to make health care decisions for the principal in order to carry out the principal's reasonable expectations to the extent actually known by the agent and, otherwise, act in the principal's best interest.

(3) An agent who acts in good faith is not liable to any beneficiary of the principal's estate plan for failure to preserve the plan.

(4) If an agent is selected by the principal because of special skills or expertise possessed by the agent or in reliance on the agent's representation that the agent has special skills or expertise, the special skills or expertise must be considered in determining whether the agent has acted with care, competence, and diligence under the circumstances.

(5) Absent a breach of duty to the principal, an agent is not liable if the value of the principal's property declines.

(6) Except as otherwise provided in the power of attorney, an agent is not required to disclose receipts, disbursements, transactions conducted on behalf of the principal, or safe-deposit box inventories, unless ordered by a court or requested by the principal, a court-appointed guardian, another fiduciary acting for the principal, a governmental agency having authority to protect the welfare of the principal, or, upon the death of the principal, by the personal representative or successor in interest of the principal's estate. If requested, the agent must comply with the request within 60 days or provide a writing or other record substantiating why additional time is needed and comply with the request within an additional 60 days.

History.
S. 16, ch. 2011-210, eff. Oct. 1, 2011.

709.2115. Exoneration of agent.

A power of attorney may provide that the agent is not liable for any acts or decisions made by the agent in good faith and under the power of attorney, except to the extent the provision:

(1) Relieves the agent of liability for breach of a duty committed dishonestly, with improper motive, or with reckless indifference to the purposes of the power of attorney or the best interest of the principal; or

(2) Was inserted as a result of an abuse of a confidential or fiduciary relationship with the principal.

History.
S. 17, ch. 2011-210, eff. Oct. 1, 2011.

709.2116. Judicial relief; conflicts of interests.

(1) A court may construe or enforce a power of attorney, review the agent's conduct, terminate the agent's authority, remove the agent, and grant other appropriate relief.

(2) The following persons may petition the court:

(a) The principal or the agent, including any nominated successor agent.

(b) A guardian, conservator, trustee, or other fiduciary acting for the principal or the principal's estate.

(c) A person authorized to make health care decisions for the principal if the health care of the principal is affected by the actions of the agent.

(d) Any other interested person if the person demonstrates to the court's satisfaction that the person is interested in the welfare of the principal and has a good faith belief that the court's intervention is necessary.

(e) A governmental agency having regulatory authority to protect the welfare of the principal.

(f) A person asked to honor the power of attorney.

(3) In any proceeding commenced by filing a petition under this section, including, but not limited to, the unreasonable refusal of a third person to allow an agent to act pursuant to the power of attorney, and in challenges to the proper exercise of authority by the agent, the court shall award reasonable attorney's fees and costs.

(4) If an agent's exercise of a power is challenged in a judicial proceeding brought by or on behalf of the principal on the grounds that the exercise of the power was affected by a conflict of interest, and evidence is presented that the agent or an affiliate of the agent had a personal interest in the exercise of the power, the agent or affiliate has the burden of proving, by clear and convincing evidence that the agent acted:

(a) Solely in the interest of the principal; or

(b) In good faith in the principal's best interest, and the conflict of interest was expressly authorized in the power of attorney.

(5) For purposes of subsection (4):

(a) A provision authorizing an agent to engage in a transaction affected by a conflict of interest which is inserted into a power of attorney as the result of the abuse of a fiduciary or confidential relationship with the principal by the agent or the agent's affiliate is invalid.

(b) Affiliates of an agent include:

1. The agent's spouse;

2. The agent's descendants, siblings, parents, or their spouses;

3. A corporation or other entity in which the agent, or a person who owns a significant interest in the agent, has an interest that might affect the agent's best judgment;

4. A person or entity that owns a significant interest in the agent; or

5. The agent acting in a fiduciary capacity for someone other than the principal.

History.
S. 18, ch. 2011-210, eff. Oct. 1, 2011.

709.2117. Agent's liability.

An agent who violates this part is liable to the principal or the principal's successors in interest for the amount required to:

(1) Restore the value of the principal's property to what it would have been had the violation not occurred; and

(2) Reimburse the principal or the principal's successors in interest for the attorney's fees and costs paid from the principal's funds on the agent's behalf in defense of the agent's actions.

History.
S. 19, ch. 2011-210, eff. Oct. 1, 2011.

709.2118. Agent's resignation.

Unless the power of attorney provides a different method for an agent's resignation, an agent may resign by giving notice to the principal, to the guardian if the principal is incapacitated and one has been appointed for the principal, and to any co-agent, or if none, the next successor agent.

History.
S. 20, ch. 2011-210, eff. Oct. 1, 2011.

709.2119. Acceptance of and reliance upon power of attorney.

(1)(a) A third person who in good faith accepts a power of attorney that appears to be executed in the manner required by law at the time of its execution may rely upon the power of attorney and the actions of the agent which are reasonably within the scope of the agent's authority and may enforce any obligation created by the actions of the agent as if:

1. The power of attorney were genuine, valid, and still in effect;

2. The agent's authority were genuine, valid, and still in effect; and

3. The authority of the officer executing for or on behalf of a financial institution that has trust powers and acting as agent is genuine, valid, and still in effect.

(b) For purposes of this subsection, and without limiting what constitutes good faith, a third person does not accept a power of attorney in good faith if the third person has notice that:

1. The power of attorney is void, invalid, or terminated; or

2. The purported agent's authority is void, invalid, suspended, or terminated.

(2) A third person may require:

(a) An agent to execute an affidavit stating where the principal is domiciled; that the principal is not deceased; that there has been no revocation, or partial or complete termination by adjudication of incapacity or by the occurrence of an event referenced in the power of attorney; that there has been no suspension by initiation of proceedings to determine incapacity, or to appoint a guardian, of the principal; and, if the affiant is a successor agent, the reasons for the unavailability of the predecessor agents, if any, at the time the authority is exercised.

(b) An officer of a financial institution acting as agent to execute a separate affidavit, or include in the form of the affidavit, the officer's title and a statement that the officer has full authority to perform all acts and enter into all transactions authorized by the power of attorney for and on behalf of the financial institution in its capacity as agent. A written affidavit executed by the agent under this subsection may, but need not, be in the following form:

STATE OF_____
COUNTY OF_____

Before me, the undersigned authority, personally appeared (attorney in fact) ("Affiant"), who swore or affirmed that:

    1. Affiant is the attorney in fact named in the Durable Power of Attorney executed by (principal) ("Principal") on (date) .

    2. This Power of Attorney is currently exercisable by Affiant. The principal is domiciled in (insert name of state, territory, or foreign country) .

    3. To the best of Affiant's knowledge after diligent search and inquiry:

       a. The Principal is not deceased;

       b. Affiant's authority has not been suspended by initiation of proceedings to determine incapacity or to appoint a guardian or a guardian advocate; and

       c. There has been no revocation, or partial or complete termination, of the power of attorney or of Affiant's authority.

    4. Affiant is acting within the scope of authority granted in the power of attorney.

    5. Affiant is the successor to (insert name of predecessor agent), who has resigned, died, become incapacitated, is no longer qualified to serve, has declined to serve as agent, or is otherwise unable to act, if applicable.

    6. Affiant agrees not to exercise any powers granted by the Durable Power of Attorney if Affiant attains knowledge that it has been revoked, has been partially or completely terminated or suspended, or is no longer valid because of the death or adjudication of incapacity of the Principal.

_____
                            (Affiant)

Sworn to (or affirmed) and subscribed before me this _____ day of (month), (year), by (name of person making statement)

(Signature of Notary Public-State of Florida)

(Print, Type, or Stamp Commissioned Name of Notary Public)

Personally Known OR Produced Identification (Type of Identification Produced)

(3) A third person who is asked to accept a power of attorney that appears to be executed in accordance with s. 709.2103 may in good faith request, and rely upon, without further investigation:

(a) A verified English translation of the power of attorney if the power of attorney contains, in whole or in part, language other than English;

(b) An opinion of counsel as to any matter of law concerning the power of attorney if the third person making the request provides in a writing or other record the reason for the request; or

(c) The affidavit described in subsection (2).

(4) An English translation or an opinion of counsel requested under this section must be provided at the principal's expense unless the request is made after the time specified in s. 709.2120(1) for acceptance or rejection of the power of attorney.

(5) Third persons who act in reliance upon the authority granted to an agent and in accordance with the instructions of the agent shall be held harmless by the principal from any loss suffered or liability incurred as a result of actions taken before the receipt of notice as provided in s. 709.2121. A third person who acts in good faith upon any representation, direction, decision, or act of the agent is not liable to the principal or the principal's estate, beneficiaries, or joint owners for those acts.

(6) The acts of an agent under a power of attorney are as valid and binding on the principal or the principal's estate as if the principal were alive and competent if, in connection with any activity pertaining to hostilities in which the United States is then engaged, the principal is officially listed or reported by a branch of the United States Armed Forces in a missing status as defined in 37 U.S.C. s. 551 or 5 U.S.C. s. 5561, regardless of whether the principal is dead, alive, or incompetent. Homestead property held as tenants by the entireties may not be conveyed by a power of attorney regulated under this provision until 1 year after the first official report or listing of the principal as missing or missing in action. An affidavit of an officer of the Armed Forces having maintenance and control of the records pertaining to those missing or missing in action that the principal has been in that status for a given period is conclusive presumption of the fact.

History.
S. 21, ch. 2011-210, eff. Oct. 1, 2011.

709.2120. Refusal to accept power of attorney.

(1) Except as provided in subsection (2):

(a) A third person must accept or reject a power of attorney within a reasonable time. A third person who rejects a power of attorney must state in writing the reason for the rejection.

(b) Four days, excluding Saturdays, Sundays, and legal holidays, are presumed to be a reasonable time for a financial institution to accept or reject a power of attorney with respect to:

1. A banking transaction, if the power of attorney expressly contains authority to conduct banking transactions pursuant to s. 709.2208(1); or

2. A security transaction, if the power of attorney expressly contains authority to conduct security transactions pursuant to s. 709.2208(2).

(c) A third person may not require an additional or different form of power of attorney for authority granted in the power of attorney presented.

(2) A third person is not required to accept a power of attorney if:

(a) The third person is not otherwise required to engage in a transaction with the principal in the same circumstances;

(b) The third person has knowledge of the termination or suspension of the agent's authority or of the power of attorney before exercising the power;

(c) A timely request by the third person for an affidavit, English translation, or opinion of counsel under s. 709.2119(4) is refused by the agent;

(d) Except as provided in paragraph (b), the third person believes in good faith that the power is not valid or that the agent does not have authority to perform the act requested; or

(e) The third person makes, or has knowledge that another person has made, a report to the local adult protective services office stating a good faith belief that the principal may be subject to physical or financial abuse, neglect, exploitation, or abandonment by the agent or a person acting for or with the agent.

(3) A third person who, in violation of this section, refuses to accept a power of attorney is subject to:

(a) A court order mandating acceptance of the power of attorney; and

(b) Liability for damages, including reasonable attorney's fees and costs, incurred in any action or proceeding that confirms, for the purpose tendered, the validity of the power of attorney or mandates acceptance of the power of attorney.

History.
S. 22, ch. 2011-210, eff. Oct. 1, 2011.

709.2121.   Notice.

(1) A notice, including a notice of revocation, notice of partial or complete termination by adjudication of incapacity or by the occurrence of an event referenced in the power of attorney, notice of death of the principal, notice of suspension by initiation of proceedings to determine incapacity or to appoint a guardian, or other notice, is not effective until written notice is provided to the agent or any third persons relying upon a power of attorney.

(2) Notice must be in writing and must be accomplished in a manner reasonably suitable under the circumstances and likely to result in receipt of the notice or document. Permissible methods of notice or for sending a document include first-class mail, personal delivery, delivery to the person's last known place of residence or place of business, or a properly directed facsimile or other electronic message.

(3) Notice to a financial institution must contain the name, address, and the last four digits of the principal's taxpayer identification number and be directed to an officer or a manager of the financial institution in this state.

(4) Notice is effective when given, except that notice upon a financial institution, brokerage company, or title insurance company is not effective until 5 days, excluding Saturdays, Sundays, and legal holidays, after it is received.

History.
S. 23, ch. 2011-210, eff. Oct. 1, 2011.

709.2201.   Authority of agent.

(1) Except as provided in this section or other applicable law, an agent may only exercise authority specifically granted to the agent in the power of attorney and any authority reasonably necessary to give effect to that express grant of specific authority. General provisions in a power of attorney which do not identify the specific authority granted, such as provisions purporting to give the agent authority to do all acts that the principal can do, are not express grants of specific authority and do not grant any authority to the agent. Court approval is not required for any action of the agent in furtherance of an express grant of specific authority.

(2) As a confirmation of the law in effect in this state when this part became effective, such authorization may include, without limitation, authority to:

(a) Execute stock powers or similar documents on behalf of the principal and delegate to a transfer agent or similar person the authority to register any stocks, bonds, or other securities into or out of the principal's or nominee's name.

(b) Convey or mortgage homestead property. However, if the principal is married, the agent may not mortgage or convey homestead property without joinder of the principal's spouse or the spouse's guardian. Joinder by a spouse may be accomplished by the exercise of authority in a power of attorney executed by the joining spouse, and either spouse may appoint the other as his or her agent.

(c) If such authority is specifically granted in a durable power of attorney, make all health care decisions on behalf of the principal, including, but not limited to, those set forth in chapter 765.

(3) Notwithstanding the provisions of this section, an agent may not:

(a) Perform duties under a contract that requires the exercise of personal services of the principal;

(b) Make any affidavit as to the personal knowledge of the principal;

(c) Vote in any public election on behalf of the principal;

(d) Execute or revoke any will or codicil for the principal; or

(e) Exercise powers and authority granted to the principal as trustee or as court-appointed fiduciary.

(4) Subject to s. 709.2202, if the subjects over which authority is granted in a power of attorney are similar or overlap, the broadest authority controls.

(5) Authority granted in a power of attorney is exercisable with respect to property that the principal has when the power of attorney is executed and to property that the principal acquires later, whether or not the property is located in this state and whether or not the authority is exercised or the power of attorney is executed in this state.

(6) An act performed by an agent pursuant to a power of attorney has the same effect and inures to the benefit of and binds the principal and the principal's successors in interest as if the principal had performed the act.

History.
S. 24, ch. 2011-210, eff. Oct. 1, 2011.

709.2202. Authority that requires separate signed enumeration.

(1) Notwithstanding s. 709.2201, an agent may exercise the following authority only if the principal signed or initialed next to each specific enumeration of the authority, the exercise of the authority is consistent with the agent's duties under s. 709.2114, and the exercise is not otherwise prohibited by another agreement or instrument:

(a) Create an inter vivos trust;

(b) With respect to a trust created by or on behalf of the principal, amend, modify, revoke, or terminate the trust, but only if the trust instrument explicitly provides for amendment, modification, revocation, or termination by the settlor's agent;

(c) Make a gift, subject to subsection (3);

(d) Create or change rights of survivorship;

(e) Create or change a beneficiary designation;

(f) Waive the principal's right to be a beneficiary of a joint and survivor annuity, including a survivor benefit under a retirement plan; or

(g) Disclaim property and powers of appointment.

(2) Notwithstanding a grant of authority to do an act described in subsection (1), unless the power of attorney otherwise provides, an agent who is not an ancestor, spouse, or descendant of the principal may not exercise authority to create in the agent, or in an individual to whom the agent owes a legal obligation of support, an interest in the principal's property, whether by gift, right of survivorship, beneficiary designation, disclaimer, or otherwise.

(3) Unless the power of attorney otherwise provides, a provision in a power of attorney granting general authority with respect to gifts authorizes the agent to only:

(a) Make outright to, or for the benefit of, a person a gift of any of the principal's property, including by the exercise of a presently exercisable general power of appointment held by the principal, in an amount per donee not to exceed the annual dollar limits of the federal gift tax exclusion under 26 U.S.C. s. 2503(b), as amended, without regard to whether the federal gift tax exclusion applies to the gift, or if the principal's spouse agrees to consent to a split gift pursuant to 26 U.S.C. s. 2513, as amended, in an amount per donee not to exceed twice the annual federal gift tax exclusion limit; and

(b) Consent, pursuant to 26 U.S.C. s. 2513, as amended, to the splitting of a gift made by the principal's spouse in an amount per donee not to exceed the aggregate annual gift tax exclusions for both spouses.

(4) Notwithstanding subsection (1), if a power of attorney is otherwise sufficient to grant an agent authority to conduct banking transactions, as provided in s. 709.2208(1), conduct investment transactions as provided in s. 709.2208(2), or otherwise make additions to or withdrawals from an account of the principal, making a deposit to or withdrawal from an insurance policy, retirement account, individual retirement account, benefit plan, bank account, or any other account held jointly or otherwise held in survivorship or payable on death, is not considered to be a change to the survivorship feature or beneficiary designation, and no further specific authority is required for the agent to exercise such authority. A bank or other financial institution does not have a duty to inquire as to the appropriateness of the agent's exercise of that authority and is not liable to the principal or any other person for actions taken in good faith reliance on the appropriateness of the agent's actions. This subsection does not eliminate the agent's fiduciary duties to the principal with respect to any exercise of the power of attorney.

(5) This section does not apply to a power of attorney executed before October 1, 2011.

History.
S. 25, ch. 2011-210, eff. Oct. 1, 2011.

709.2208. Banks and other financial institutions.

(1) A power of attorney that includes the statement that the agent has "authority to conduct banking transactions as provided in section 709.2208(1), Florida Statutes" grants general authority to the agent to engage in the following transactions with financial institutions without additional specific enumeration in the power of attorney:

(a) Establish, continue, modify, or terminate an account or other banking arrangement with a financial institution.

(b) Contract for services available from a financial institution, including renting a safe-deposit box or space in a vault.

(c) Withdraw, by check, order, electronic funds transfer, or otherwise, money or property of the principal deposited with or left in the custody of a financial institution.

(d) Receive statements of account, vouchers, notices, and similar documents from a financial institution and act with respect to them.

(e) Purchase cashier's checks, official checks, counter checks, bank drafts, money orders, and similar instruments.

(f) Endorse and negotiate checks, cashier's checks, official checks, drafts, and other negotiable paper of the principal or payable to the principal or the principal's order, transfer money, receive the cash or other proceeds of those transactions, and accept a draft drawn by a person upon the principal and pay it when due.

(g) Apply for, receive, and use debit cards, electronic transaction authorizations, and traveler's checks from a financial institution.

(h) Use, charge, or draw upon any line of credit, credit card, or other credit established by the principal with a financial institution.

(i) Consent to an extension of the time of payment with respect to commercial paper or a financial transaction with a financial institution.

(2) A power of attorney that specifically includes the statement that the agent has "authority to conduct investment transactions as provided in section 709.2208(2), Florida Statutes" grants general authority to the agent with respect to securities held by financial institutions to take the following actions without additional specific enumeration in the power of attorney:

(a) Buy, sell, and exchange investment instruments.

(b) Establish, continue, modify, or terminate an account with respect to investment instruments.

(c) Pledge investment instruments as security to borrow, pay, renew, or extend the time of payment of a debt of the principal.

(d) Receive certificates and other evidences of ownership with respect to investment instruments.

(e) Exercise voting rights with respect to investment instruments in person or by proxy, enter into voting trusts, and consent to limitations on the right to vote.

(f) Sell commodity futures contracts and call and put options on stocks and stock indexes.

For purposes of this subsection, the term "investment instruments" means stocks, bonds, mutual funds, and all other types of securities and financial instruments, whether held directly, indirectly, or in any other manner, including shares or interests in a private investment fund, including, but not limited to, a private investment fund organized as a limited partnership, a limited liability company, a statutory or common law business trust, a statutory trust, or a real estate investment trust, joint venture, or any other general or limited partnership; derivatives or other interests of any nature in securities such as options, options on futures, and variable forward contracts; mutual funds; common trust funds; money market funds; hedge funds; private equity or venture capital funds; insurance contracts; and other entities or vehicles investing in securities or interests in securities whether registered or otherwise, except commodity futures contracts and call and put options on stocks and stock indexes.

History.
S. 26, ch. 2011-210, eff. Oct. 1, 2011.

709.2301. Principles of law and equity.

The common law of agency and principles of equity supplement this part, except as modified by this part or other state law.

History.
S. 27, ch. 2011-210, eff. Oct. 1, 2011.

709.2302. Laws applicable to financial institutions and entities.

This part does not supersede any other law applicable to financial institutions or other entities, and that law controls if inconsistent with this part.

History.
S. 28, ch. 2011-210, eff. Oct. 1, 2011.

709.2303. Remedies under other law.

The remedies under this part are not exclusive and do not abrogate any right or remedy under any other law other than this part.

History.
S. 29, ch. 2011-210, eff. Oct. 1, 2011.

709.2401. Relation to electronic signatures in federal law.

This part modifies, limits, and supersedes the federal Electronic Signatures in Global and National Commerce Act, 15 U.S.C. s. 7001 et seq., but does not modify, limit, or supersede s. 101(c) of that act, or authorize electronic delivery of any of the notices described in s. 103(b) of that act.

History.
S. 30, ch. 2011-210, eff. Oct. 1, 2011.

709.2402. Effect on existing powers of attorney.

Except as otherwise provided in this part:

(1) With respect to formalities of execution, this part applies to a power of attorney created on or after October 1, 2011.

(2) With respect to all matters other than formalities of execution, this part applies to a power of attorney regardless of the date of creation.

(3) With respect to a power of attorney existing on October 1, 2011, this part does not invalidate such power of attorney and it shall remain in effect. If a right was acquired under any other law before October 1, 2011, that law continues to apply to the right even if it has been repealed or superseded.

(4) An act of an agent occurring before October 1, 2011, is not affected by this part.

History.
S. 31, ch. 2011-210, eff. Oct. 1, 2011.

CHAPTER 710.
TRANSFERS TO MINORS

710.101. Short title.

This act may be cited as the "Florida Uniform Transfers to Minors Act."

History.
S. 1, ch. 85-95.

710.102. Definitions.

As used in this act, the term:

(1) "Adult" means an individual who has attained the age of 21 years.

(2) "Benefit plan" means a retirement plan and may include, but is not limited to, any pension, profit-sharing, stock-bonus, or stock-ownership plan or individual retirement account.

(3) "Broker" means a person lawfully engaged in the business of effecting transactions in securities or commodities for the person's own account or for the account of others.

(4) "Conservator" means a person appointed or qualified by a court to act as general, limited, or temporary guardian of a minor's property or a person legally authorized to perform substantially the same functions.

(5) "Court" means the circuit court.

(6) "Custodial property" means any interest in property transferred to a custodian under this act and the income from and proceeds of that interest in property.

(7) "Custodian" means a person so designated under s. 710.111 or a successor or substitute custodian designated under s. 710.121.

(8) "Financial institution" means a bank, trust company, savings institution, or credit union, chartered and supervised under state or federal law.

(9) "Legal representative" means an individual's personal representative or conservator.

(10) "Member of the minor's family" means the minor's parent, stepparent, spouse, grandparent, brother, sister, uncle, or aunt, whether of the whole or half blood or by adoption.

(11) "Minor" means an individual who has not attained the age of 21 years.

(12) "Person" means an individual, corporation, organization, or other legal entity.

(13) "Personal representative" means an executor, administrator, successor personal representative, or special administrator of a decedent's estate or a person legally authorized to perform substantially the same functions.

(14) "Qualified minor's trust" means a trust that meets the requirements of s. 2503(c) of the Internal Revenue Code of 1986, as amended.

(15) "State" includes any state of the United States, the District of Columbia, the Commonwealth of Puerto Rico, and any territory or possession subject to the legislative authority of the United States.

(16) "Transfer" means a transaction that creates custodial property under s. 710.111.

(17) "Transferor" means a person who makes a transfer under this act.

(18) "Trust company" means a financial institution, corporation, or other legal entity, authorized to exercise general trust powers.

History.
S. 1, ch. 85-95; s. 3, ch. 2005-101.
Editor's Notes.
Section 2503(c) of the Internal Revenue Code of 1986, referred to in this section, is codified as 26 U.S.C.S. § 2503(c).

710.103. Scope and jurisdiction.

(1) This act applies to a transfer that refers to this act in the designation under s. 710.111(1) by which the transfer is made if at the time of the transfer, the transferor, the minor, or the custodian is a resident of this state or the custodial property is located in this state. The custodianship so created remains subject to this act despite a subsequent change in residence of a transferor, the minor, or the custodian, or the removal of custodial property from this state.

(2) A person designated as custodian under this act is subject to personal jurisdiction in this state with respect to any matter relating to the custodianship.

(3) A transfer that purports to be made and which is valid under the Uniform Transfers to Minors Act, the Uniform Gifts to Minors Act, or a substantially similar act, of another state is governed by the law of the designated state and may be executed and is enforceable in this state if, at the time of the transfer, the transferor, the minor, or the custodian is a resident of the designated state or the custodial property is located in the designated state.

History.
S. 1, ch. 85-95.

710.104. Nomination of custodian.

(1) A person having the right to designate the recipient of property transferable upon the occurrence of a future event may revocably nominate a custodian to receive the property for a minor beneficiary upon the occurrence of the event by naming the custodian followed in substance by the words: "as custodian for (name of minor) under the Florida Uniform Transfers to Minors Act." The nomination may name one or more persons as substitute custodians to whom the property must be transferred, in the order named, if the first nominated custodian dies before the transfer or is unable, declines, or is ineligible to serve. The nomination may be made in a will, a trust, a deed, an instrument exercising a power of appointment, or in a writing designating a beneficiary of contractual rights, including, but not limited to, the right to a benefit plan, which is registered with or delivered to the payor, issuer, or other obligor of the contractual rights.

(2) A custodian nominated under this section must be a person to whom a transfer of property of that kind may be made under s. 710.111(1).

(3) The nomination of a custodian under this section does not create custodial property until the nominating instrument becomes irrevocable or a transfer to the nominated custodian is completed under s. 710.111. Unless the nomination of a custodian has been revoked, upon the occurrence of the future event the custodianship becomes effective and the custodian shall enforce a transfer of the custodial property pursuant to s. 710.111.

History.
S. 1, ch. 85-95; s. 4, ch. 2005-101.

710.105. Transfer by gift or exercise of power of appointment.

A person may make a transfer by irrevocable gift to, or the irrevocable exercise of a power of appointment in favor of, a custodian for the benefit of a minor pursuant to s. 710.111.

History.
S. 1, ch. 85-95.

710.106. Transfer authorized by will or trust.

(1) A personal representative or trustee may make an irrevocable transfer pursuant to s. 710.111 to a custodian for the benefit of a minor as authorized in the governing will or trust.

(2) If the testator or settlor has nominated a custodian under s. 710.104 to receive the custodial property, the transfer must be made to that person.

(3) If the testator or settlor has not nominated a custodian under s. 710.104, or all persons so nominated as custodian die before the transfer or are unable, decline, or are ineligible to serve, the personal representative or the trustee, as the case may be, shall designate the custodian from among those eligible to serve as custodian for property of that kind under s. 710.111(1).

History.
S. 1, ch. 85-95.

710.107. Other transfer by fiduciary.

(1) Subject to subsection (3), a personal representative or trustee may make an irrevocable transfer to another adult or trust company as custodian for the benefit of a minor pursuant to s. 710.111, in the absence of a will or under a will or trust that does not contain an authorization to do so.

(2) Subject to subsection (3), a conservator may make an irrevocable transfer to another adult or trust company as custodian for the benefit of the minor pursuant to s. 710.111.

(3) A transfer under subsection (1) or subsection (2) may be made only if:

(a) The personal representative, trustee, or conservator considers the transfer to be in the best interest of the minor;

(b) The transfer is not prohibited by or inconsistent with provisions of the applicable will, trust agreement, or other governing instrument; and

(c) The transfer is authorized by the court if it exceeds $10,000 in value.

History.
S. 1, ch. 85-95.

710.108. Transfer by obligor.

(1) Subject to subsections (2) and (3), a person not subject to s. 710.106 or s. 710.107 who holds property, including, but not limited to, a benefit plan, of a minor not having a conservator, or who owes a liquidated debt to a minor not having a conservator, may make an irrevocable transfer to a custodian for the benefit of the minor pursuant to s. 710.111.

(2) If a person having the right to do so under s. 710.104 has nominated a custodian under that section to receive the custodial property, the transfer must be made to that person.

(3) If no custodian has been nominated under s. 710.104, or all persons so nominated as custodian die before the transfer or are unable, decline, or are ineligible to serve, a transfer under this section may be made to an adult member of the minor's family or to a trust company unless the property exceeds $15,000 in value.

History.
S. 1, ch. 85-95; s. 61, ch. 87-226; s. 5, ch. 2005-101.

710.109. Receipt for custodial property.

A written acknowledgment of delivery by a custodian constitutes a sufficient receipt and discharge for custodial property transferred to the custodian pursuant to this act.

History.
S. 1, ch. 85-95.

710.111. Manner of creating custodial property and effecting transfer; designation of initial custodian; control.

(1) Custodial property is created and a transfer is made whenever:

(a) An uncertificated security or a certificated security in registered form is either:

1. Registered in the name of the transferor, an adult other than the transferor, or a trust company, followed in substance by the words: "as custodian for (name of minor) under the Florida Uniform Transfers to Minors Act"; or

2. Delivered if in certificated form, or any document necessary for the transfer of an uncertificated security is delivered, together with any necessary endorsement to an adult other than the transferor or to a trust company as custodian, accompanied by an instrument in substantially the form set forth in subsection (2);

(b) Money is paid or delivered to a broker or financial institution for credit to an account in the name of the transferor, an adult other than the transferor, or a trust company, followed in substance by the words: "as custodian for (name of minor) under the Florida Uniform Transfers to Minors Act";

(c) The ownership of a life or endowment insurance policy or annuity contract is either:

1. Registered with the issuer in the name of the transferor, an adult other than the transferor, or a trust company, followed in substance by the words: "as custodian for (name of minor) under the Florida Uniform Transfers to Minors Act"; or

2. Assigned in a writing delivered to an adult other than the transferor or to a trust company whose name in the assignment is followed in substance by the words: "as custodian for (name of minor) under the Florida Uniform Transfers to Minors Act";

(d) An irrevocable exercise of a power of appointment or an irrevocable present right to future payment under a contract is the subject of a written notification delivered to the payor, issuer, or other obligor that the right is transferred to the transferor, an adult other than the transferor, or a trust company, whose name in the notification is followed in substance by the words: "as custodian for (name of minor) under the Florida Uniform Transfers to Minors Act";

(e) An interest in real property is recorded in the name of the transferor, an adult other than the transferor, or a trust company, followed in substance by the words: "as custodian for (name of minor) under the Florida Uniform Transfers to Minors Act";

(f) A certificate of title issued by a department or agency of a state or of the United States which evidences title to tangible personal property is either:

1. Issued in the name of the transferor, an adult other than the transferor, or a trust company, followed in substance by the words: "as custodian for (name of minor) under the Florida Uniform Transfers to Minors Act"; or

2. Delivered to an adult other than the transferor or to a trust company, endorsed to that person followed in substance by the words: "as custodian for (name of minor) under the Florida Uniform Transfers to Minors Act"; or

(g) An interest in any property not described in paragraphs (a)-(f) is transferred to an adult other than the transferor or to a trust company by a written instrument in substantially the form set forth in subsection (2).

(2) An instrument in the following form satisfies the requirements of subparagraph (1)(a)2. and paragraph (1)(g):

"TRANSFER UNDER THE FLORIDA UNIFORM TRANSFERS TO MINORS ACT

I, (name of transferor or name and representative capacity if a fiduciary) hereby transfer to (name of custodian), as custodian for (name of minor) under the Florida Uniform Transfers to Minors Act, the following: (insert a description of the custodial property sufficient to identify it).

Dated: _____

(signature)

(name of custodian) acknowledges receipt of the property described above as custodian for the minor named above under the Florida Uniform Transfers to Minors Act.

Dated: _____

(signature of custodian)."

(3) A transferor shall place the custodian in control of the custodial property as soon as practicable.

History.
S. 1, ch. 85-95.

710.112.   Single custodianship.

A transfer may be made only for one minor, and only one person may be the custodian. All custodial property held under this act by the same custodian for the benefit of the same minor constitutes a single custodianship.

History.
S. 1, ch. 85-95.

710.113.   Validity and effect of transfer.

(1) The validity of a transfer made in a manner prescribed in this act is not affected by:

(a) Failure of the transferor to comply with s. 710.111(3) concerning possession and control;

(b) Designation of an ineligible custodian, except designation of the transferor in the case of property for which the transferor is ineligible to serve as custodian under s. 710.111(1); or

(c) Death or incapacity of a person nominated under s. 710.104 or designated under s. 710.111 as custodian or the disclaimer of the office by that person.

(2) A transfer made pursuant to s. 710.111 is irrevocable, and the custodial property is indefeasibly vested in the minor, but the custodian has all the rights, powers, duties, and authority provided in this act, and neither the minor nor the minor's legal representative has any right, power, duty, or authority with respect to the custodial property except as provided in this act.

(3) By making a transfer, the transferor incorporates in the disposition all the provisions of this act and grants to the custodian, and to any third person dealing with a person designated as custodian, the respective powers, rights, and immunities provided in this act.

History.
S. 1, ch. 85-95.

710.114.   Care of custodial property.

(1) A custodian shall:

(a) Take control of custodial property;

(b) Register or record title to custodial property if appropriate; and

(c) Collect, hold, manage, invest, and reinvest custodial property.

(2) In dealing with custodial property, a custodian shall observe the standard of care that would be observed by a prudent person dealing with property of another and is not limited by any other statute restricting investments by fiduciaries. If a custodian has a special skill or expertise or is named custodian on the basis of representations of a special skill or expertise, the custodian shall use that skill or expertise. However, a custodian, in the custodian's discretion and without liability to the minor or the minor's estate, may retain any custodial property received from a transferor.

(3) A custodian may invest in or pay premiums on life insurance or endowment policies on the life of the minor only if the minor or the minor's estate is the sole beneficiary, or on the life of another person in whom the minor has an insurable interest only to the extent that the minor, the minor's estate, or the custodian in the capacity of custodian is the irrevocable beneficiary.

(4) A custodian at all times shall keep custodial property separate and distinct from all other property in a manner sufficient to identify it clearly as custodial property of the minor. Custodial property consisting of an undivided interest is so identified if the minor's interest is held as a tenant in common and is fixed. Custodial property subject to recordation is so identified if it is recorded, and custodial property subject to registration is so identified if it is either registered, or held in an account designated, in the name of the custodian, followed in substance by the words: "as a custodian for (name of minor) under the Florida Uniform Transfers to Minors Act."

(5) A custodian shall keep records of all transactions with respect to custodial property, including information necessary for the preparation of the minor's tax returns, and shall make them available for inspection at reasonable intervals by a parent or legal representative of the minor or by the minor if the minor has attained the age of 14 years.

History.
S. 1, ch. 85-95.

710.115. Powers of custodian.

(1) A custodian, acting in a custodial capacity, has all the rights, powers, and authority over custodial property that unmarried adult owners have over their own property, but a custodian may exercise those rights, powers, and authority in that capacity only.

(2) This section does not relieve a custodian from liability for breach of s. 710.114.

History.
S. 1, ch. 85-95.

710.116. Use of custodial property.

(1) A custodian may deliver or pay to the minor or expend for the minor's benefit so much of the custodial property as the custodian considers advisable for the use and benefit of the minor, without court order and without regard to the duty or ability of the custodian personally or of any other person to support the minor, or to any other income or property of the minor which may be applicable or available for that purpose.

(2) A custodian may, without court order, transfer all or part of the custodial property to a qualified minor's trust. A transfer of property pursuant to this subsection terminates the custodianship to the extent of the property transferred.

(3) On petition of an interested person or the minor if the minor has attained the age of 14 years, the court may order the custodian to deliver or pay to the minor or expend for the minor's benefit so much of the custodial property as the court considers advisable for the use and benefit of the minor.

(4) A delivery, payment, or expenditure under this section is in addition to, not in substitution for, and does not affect any obligation of a person to support the minor.

History.
S. 1, ch. 85-95; s. 6, ch. 2005-101.

710.117. Custodian's expenses, compensation, and bond.

(1) A custodian is entitled to reimbursement from custodial property for reasonable expenses incurred in the performance of the custodian's duties.

(2) Except for one who is a transferor under s. 710.105, a custodian has a noncumulative election during each calendar year to charge reasonable compensation for services performed during that year.

(3) Except as provided in s. 710.121(6), a custodian need not give a bond.

History.
S. 1, ch. 85-95.

710.118. Exemption of third person from liability.

A third person in good faith and without court order may act on the instructions of or otherwise deal with any person purporting to make a transfer or purporting to act in the capacity of a custodian and, in the absence of knowledge, is not responsible for determining:

(1) The validity of the purported custodian's designation;

(2) The propriety of, or the authority under this act for, any act of the purported custodian;

(3) The validity or propriety under this act of any instrument or instructions executed or given either by the person purporting to make a transfer or by the purported custodian; or

(4) The propriety of the application of any property of the minor delivered to the purported custodian.

History.
S. 1, ch. 85-95.

710.119. Liability to third persons.

(1) A claim based on:

(a) A contract entered into by a custodian acting in a custodial capacity;

(b) An obligation arising from the ownership or control of custodial property; or

(c) A tort committed during the custodianship, may be asserted against the custodial property by proceeding against the custodian in the custodial capacity, whether or not the custodian or the minor is personally liable therefor.

(2) A custodian is not personally liable:

(a) On a contract properly entered into in the custodial capacity unless the custodian fails to reveal that capacity and to identify the custodianship in the contract; or

(b) For an obligation arising from control of custodial property or for a tort committed during the custodianship unless the custodian is personally at fault.

(3) A minor is not personally liable for an obligation arising from ownership of custodial property or for a tort committed during the custodianship unless the minor is personally at fault.

History.
S. 1, ch. 85-95.

710.121. Renunciation, resignation, death, or removal of custodian; designation of successor custodian.

(1) A person nominated under s. 710.104 or designated under s. 710.111 as custodian may decline to serve by delivering a valid disclaimer under chapter 739 to the person who made the nomination or to the transferor or the transferor's legal representative. If the event giving rise to a transfer has not occurred and no substitute custodian able, willing, and eligible to serve was nominated under s. 710.104, the person who made the nomination may nominate a substitute custodian under s. 710.104; otherwise, the transferor or the transferor's legal representative shall designate a substitute custodian at the time of the transfer, in either case from among the persons eligible to serve as custodian for that kind of property under s. 710.111(1). The custodian so designated has the rights of a successor custodian.

(2) A custodian at any time may designate a trust company or an adult other than a transferor under s. 710.105 as successor custodian by executing and dating an instrument of designation before a subscribing witness other than the successor. If the instrument of designation does not contain or is not accompanied by the resignation of the custodian, the designation of the successor does not take effect until the custodian resigns, dies, becomes incapacitated, or is removed.

(3) A custodian may resign at any time by delivering written notice to the minor if the minor has attained the age of 14 years and to the successor custodian and by delivering the custodial property to the successor custodian.

(4) If a custodian is ineligible, dies, or becomes incapacitated without having effectively designated a successor and the minor has attained the age of 14 years, the minor may designate as successor custodian, in the manner prescribed in subsection (2), an adult member of the minor's family, a conservator of the minor, or a trust company. If the minor has not attained the age of 14 years or fails to act within 60 days after the ineligibility, death, or incapacity, the conservator of the minor becomes successor custodian. If the minor has no conservator or the conservator declines to act, the transferor, the legal representative of the transferor or of the custodian, an adult member of the minor's family, or any other interested person may petition the court to designate a successor custodian.

(5) A custodian who declines to serve under subsection (1) or resigns under subsection (3), or the legal representative of a deceased or incapacitated custodian, as soon as practicable, shall put the custodial property and records in the possession and control of the successor custodian. The successor custodian by action may enforce the obligation to deliver custodial property and records and becomes responsible for each item as received.

(6) A transferor, the legal representative of a transferor, an adult member of the minor's family, a guardian of the person of the minor, the conservator of the minor, or the minor if the minor has attained the age of 14 years may petition the court to remove the custodian for cause and designate a successor custodian other than a transferor under s. 710.105 or to require the custodian to give appropriate bond.

History.
S. 1, ch. 85-95; s. 4, ch. 2005-108.

710.122. Accounting by and determination of liability of custodian.

(1) A minor who has attained the age of 14 years, the minor's guardian of the person or legal representative, an adult member of the minor's family, a transferor, or a transferor's legal representative may petition the court for an accounting by the custodian or the custodian's legal representative or for a determination of responsibility, as between the custodial property and the custodian personally, for claims against the custodial property unless the responsibility has been adjudicated in an action under s. 710.119 to which the minor or the minor's legal representative was a party.

(2) A successor custodian may petition the court for an accounting by the predecessor custodian.

(3) The court, in a proceeding under this act or in any other proceeding, may require or permit the custodian or the custodian's legal representative to account.

(4) If a custodian is removed under s. 710.121(6), the court shall require an accounting and order delivery

of the custodial property and records to the successor custodian and the execution of all instruments required for transfer of the custodial property.

History.
S. 1, ch. 85-95.

710.123. Termination of custodianship.

The custodian shall transfer in an appropriate manner the custodial property to the minor or to the minor's estate upon the earlier of:

(1) The minor's attainment of 21 years of age with respect to custodial property transferred under s. 710.105 or s. 710.106;

(2) The minor's attainment of age 18 with respect to custodial property transferred under s. 710.107 or s. 710.108; or

(3) The minor's death.

History.
S. 1, ch. 85-95.

710.124. Applicability.

This act applies to a transfer within the scope of s. 710.103 made after October 1, 1985, if:

(1) The transfer purports to have been made under the Florida Gifts to Minors Act (former ss. 710.01-710.10); or

(2) The instrument by which the transfer purports to have been made uses in substance the designation "as custodian under the Uniform Gifts to Minors Act" or "as custodian under the Uniform Transfers to Minors Act" of any other state, and the application of this act is necessary to validate the transfer.

History.

S. 1, ch. 85-95; s. 62, ch. 87-226.

710.125. Effect on existing custodianships.

(1) Any transfer of custodial property as now defined in this act made before October 1, 1985, is validated notwithstanding that there was no specific authority in the Florida Gifts to Minors Act for the coverage of custodial property of that kind or for a transfer from that source at the time the transfer was made.

(2) This act applies to all transfers made before October 1, 1985, in a manner and form prescribed in the Florida Gifts to Minors Act, except insofar as the application impairs constitutionally vested rights or extends the duration of custodianships in existence on October 1, 1985.

(3) Sections 710.102-710.123 with respect to the age of a minor for whom custodial property is held under this act do not apply to custodial property held in a custodianship that terminated because of the minor's attainment of the age of 18 after January 1, 1975, and before October 1, 1985.

History.
S. 1, ch. 85-95.

710.126. Uniformity of application and construction.

This act shall be applied and construed to effectuate its general purpose to make uniform the law with respect to the subject of this act among states enacting it.

History.
S. 1, ch. 85-95.

CHAPTER 711.
FLORIDA UNIFORM TRANSFER-ON-DEATH SECURITY REGISTRATION ACT

711.50. Short title.

Sections 711.50-711.512 may be cited as the "Florida Uniform Transfer-on-Death Security Registration Act."

History.
S. 3, ch. 94-216.

711.501. Definitions.

In ss. 711.50-711.512, unless the context otherwise requires, the term:

(1) "Beneficiary form" means a registration of a security which indicates the present owner of the security and the intention of the owner regarding the person who will become the owner of the security upon the death of the owner.

(2) "Devisee" means any person designated in a will to receive a disposition of real or personal property.

(3) "Heirs" means those persons, including the surviving spouse, who are entitled under the statutes of intestate succession to the property of a decedent.

(4) "Person" means an individual, a corporation, an organization, or other legal entity.

(5) "Personal representative" includes an executor, administrator, successor personal representative, special administrator, and persons who perform substantially the same function under the law governing their status.

(6) "Property" includes both real and personal property or any interest therein and means anything that may be the subject of ownership.

(7) "Register," including its derivatives, means to issue a certificate showing the ownership of a certificated security or, in the case of an uncertificated security, to initiate or transfer an account showing ownership of securities.

(8) "Registering entity" means a person who originates or transfers a security title by registration, and includes a broker maintaining security accounts for customers and a transfer agent or other person acting for or as an issuer of securities.

(9) "Security" means a share, participation, or other interest in property, in a business, or in an obligation of an enterprise or other issuer, and includes a certificated security, an uncertificated security, and a security account.

(10) "Security account" means:

(a) A reinvestment account associated with a security, a securities account with a broker, a cash balance in a brokerage account, cash, interest, earnings, or dividends earned or declared on a security in an account, a reinvestment account, or a brokerage account, whether or not credited to the account before the owner's death;

(b) An investment management account, investment advisory account, investment agency account, custody account, or any other type of account with a bank or trust company, including the securities in the account, the cash balance in the account, and cash equivalents, and any interest, earnings, or dividends earned or declared on a security in the account, whether or not credited to the account before the owner's death; or

(c) A cash balance or other property held for or due to the owner of a security as a replacement for or product of an account security, whether or not credited to the account before the owner's death.

(11) "State" includes any state of the United States, the District of Columbia, the Commonwealth of Puerto Rico, and any territory or possession subject to the legislative authority of the United States.

History.
S. 3, ch. 94-216; s. 1, ch. 2005-85.

711.502. Registration in beneficiary form; sole or joint tenancy ownership.

Only individuals whose registration of a security shows sole ownership by one individual or multiple ownership by two or more with right of survivorship, rather than as tenants in common, may obtain registration in beneficiary form. Multiple owners of a security registered in beneficiary form hold as joint tenants with right of survivorship, as tenants by the entireties, or as owners of community property held in survivorship form, and not as tenants in common.

History.
S. 3, ch. 94-216.

711.503. Registration in beneficiary form; applicable law.

A security may be registered in beneficiary form if the form is authorized by this or a similar statute of the state of organization of the issuer or registering entity, the location of the registering entity's principal office, the office of its transfer agent or its office making the registration, or by this or a similar statute of the law of the state listed as the owner's address at the time of registration. A registration governed by the law of a jurisdiction in which this or similar legislation is not in force or was not in force when a registration in beneficiary form was made is nevertheless presumed to be valid and authorized as a matter of contract law.

History.
S. 3, ch. 94-216.

711.504. Origination of registration in beneficiary form.

A security, whether evidenced by certificate or account, is registered in beneficiary form when the registration includes a designation of a beneficiary to take the ownership at the death of the owner or the deaths of all multiple owners.

History.
S. 3, ch. 94-216.

711.505. Form of registration in beneficiary form.

Registration in beneficiary form may be shown by the words "transfer on death" or the abbreviation "TOD," or by the words "pay on death" or the abbreviation "POD," after the name of the registered owner and before the name of a beneficiary.

History.
S. 3, ch. 94-216.

711.506. Effect of registration in beneficiary form.

The designation of a transfer-on-death beneficiary on a registration in beneficiary form has no effect on ownership until the owner's death. A registration of a security in beneficiary form may be canceled or changed at any time by the sole owner or all then-surviving owners without the consent of the beneficiary.

History.
S. 3, ch. 94-216.

711.507. Ownership on death of owner.

On death of a sole owner or the last to die of all multiple owners, ownership of securities registered in beneficiary form passes to the beneficiary or beneficiaries who survive all owners. On proof of death of all owners and compliance with any applicable requirements of the registering entity, a security registered in beneficiary form may be reregistered in the name of the beneficiary or beneficiaries who survived the death of all owners. Until division of the security after the death of all owners, multiple beneficiaries surviving the death of all owners hold their interests as tenants in common. If no beneficiary survives the death of all owners, the security belongs to the estate of the deceased sole owner or the estate of the last to die of all multiple owners.

History.
S. 3, ch. 94-216.

711.508. Protection of registering entity.

(1) A registering entity is not required to offer or to accept a request for security registration in beneficiary form. If a registration in beneficiary form is offered by a registering entity, the owner requesting registration in beneficiary form assents to the protections given to the registering entity by ss. 711.50-711.512.

(2) By accepting a request for registration of a security in beneficiary form, the registering entity agrees that the registration will be implemented on death of the deceased owner as provided in ss. 711.50-711.512.

(3) A registering entity is discharged from all claims to a security by the estate, creditors, heirs, or devisees of a deceased owner if it registers a transfer of the security in accordance with s. 711.507 and does so in good faith reliance on the registration, on ss. 711.50-

711.512, and on information provided to it by affidavit of the personal representative of the deceased owner, or by the surviving beneficiary or by the surviving beneficiary's representatives, or other information available to the registering entity. The protections of ss. 711.50-711.512 do not extend to a reregistration or payment made after a registering entity has received written notice from any claimant to any interest in the security objecting to implementation of a registration in beneficiary form. No other notice or other information available to the registering entity affects its right to protection under ss. 711.50-711.512.

(4) The protection provided by ss. 711.50-711.512 to the registering entity of a security does not affect the rights of beneficiaries in disputes between themselves and other claimants to ownership of the security transferred or its value or proceeds.

History.
S. 3, ch. 94-216.

711.509. Nontestamentary transfer on death.

(1) A transfer on death resulting from a registration in beneficiary form is effective by reason of the contract regarding the registration between the owner and the registering entity and ss. 711.50-711.512 and is not testamentary.

(2) Sections 711.50-711.512 do not limit the rights of creditors of security owners against beneficiaries and other transferees under other laws of this state.

History.
S. 3, ch. 94-216.

711.51. Terms, conditions, and forms for registration.

(1) A registering entity offering to accept registrations in beneficiary form may establish the terms and conditions under which it will receive requests for registrations in beneficiary form, and requests for implementation of registrations in beneficiary form, including requests for cancellation of previously registered transfer-on-death beneficiary designations and requests for reregistration to effect a change of beneficiary. The terms and conditions so established may provide for proving death, avoiding or resolving any problems concerning fractional shares, designating primary and contingent beneficiaries, and substituting a named beneficiary's descendants to take in the place of the named beneficiary in the event of the beneficiary's death. Substitution may be indicated by appending to the name of the primary beneficiary the letters "LDPS," standing for "lineal descendants per stirpes." This designation substitutes a deceased beneficiary's descendants who survive the owner for a beneficiary who fails to so survive, the descendants to be identified and to share in accordance with the law of the beneficiary's domicile at the owner's death governing inheritance by descendants of an intestate. Other forms of identifying beneficiaries who are to take on one or more contingencies, and rules for providing proofs and

assurances needed to satisfy reasonable concerns by registering entities regarding conditions and identities relevant to accurate implementation of registrations in beneficiary form, may be contained in a registering entity's terms and conditions.

(2) The following are illustrations of registrations in beneficiary form which a registering entity may authorize:

(a) Sole owner-sole beneficiary: John S Brown TOD (or POD) John S Brown Jr.

(b) Multiple owners-sole beneficiary: John S Brown Mary B Brown JT TEN TOD John S Brown Jr.

(c) Multiple owners-primary and secondary (substituted) beneficiaries:

1. John S Brown Mary B Brown JT TEN TOD John S Brown Jr SUB BENE Peter Q Brown; or

2. John S Brown Mary B Brown JT TEN TOD John S Brown Jr LDPS.

History.
S. 3, ch. 94-216.

711.511. Rules of construction.

(1) Sections 711.50-711.512 shall be liberally construed and applied to promote their underlying purposes and policy and to make uniform the laws with respect to the subject of these sections among states enacting them.

(2) Unless displaced by the particular provisions of ss. 711.50-711.512, the principles of law and equity supplement the provisions of these sections.

History.
S. 3, ch. 94-216.

711.512. Application of ss. 711.50-711.512.

Sections 711.50-711.512 apply to registrations of securities in beneficiary form made before, on, or after January 1, 1995, by decedents dying on or after January 1, 1995.

History.
S. 3, ch. 94-216.

CHAPTER 716.
ESCHEATS

716.01. Declaration of policy.

It is hereby declared to be the policy of the state, while protecting the interests of the owners thereof, to possess all unclaimed and abandoned money and property for the benefit of all the people of the state, and this law shall be liberally construed to accomplish such purpose.

History.
S. 1, ch. 24333, 1947.

716.02. Escheat of funds in the possession of federal agencies.

All property within the provisions of subsections (1), (2), (3), (4) and (5), are declared to have escheated, or to escheat, including all principal and interest accruing thereon, and to have become the property of the state.

(1) All money or other property which has remained in, or has been deposited in the custody of, or under the control of, any court of the United States, in and for any district within this state, or which has been deposited with and is in the custody of any depository, registry, clerk or other officer of such court, or the United States treasury, which money or other property the rightful owner or owners thereof, either:

(a) Has been unknown for a period of 5 or more consecutive years; or,

(b) Has died, without having disposed thereof, and without having left heirs, next of kin or distributees, or

(c) Has made no demand for such money or other property for 5 years;

are declared to have escheated, or to escheat, together with all interest accrued thereon, and to have become the property of the state.

(2) After June 16, 1947, all money or other property which has remained in, or has been deposited in the custody of, or under the control of, any court of the United States, in and for any district within this state, for a period of 4 years, the rightful owner or owners of which, either:

(a) Shall have been unknown for a period of 4 years; or,

(b) Shall have died without having disposed thereof, and without having left or without leaving heirs, next of kin or distributees; or,

(c) Shall have failed within 4 years to demand the payment or delivery of such funds or other property;

is hereby declared to have escheated, or to escheat, together with all interest accrued thereon, and to have become the property of the state.

(3) All money or other property which has remained in, or has been deposited in the custody of, or under the control of any officer, department or agency of the United States for 5 or more consecutive years, which money or other property had its situs or source in this state, except as hereinafter provided in subsection (4), the sender of which is unknown, or who sent the money or other property for an unknown purpose, or money which is credited as "unknown," and which said governmental agency is unable to credit to any particular account, or the sender of which has been unknown for a period of 5 or more consecutive years; or when known, has died without having disposed thereof, and without leaving heirs, next of kin or distributees, or for any reason is unclaimed from such governmental agency.

(4) In the event any money is due to any resident of this state as a refund, rebate or tax rebate from the United States Commissioner of Internal Revenue, the United States Treasurer, or other governmental agency or department, which said resident will, or is likely to have her or his rights to apply for and secure such refund or rebate barred by any statute of limitations or, in any event, has failed for a period of 1 year after said resident could have filed a claim for said refund or rebate, the Department of Financial Services is appointed agent of such resident to demand, file and apply for said refund or rebate, and is appointed to do any act which a natural person could do to recover such money, and it is hereby declared that when the department files such application or any other proceeding to secure such refund or rebate, its agency is coupled with an interest in the money sought and money recovered.

(5) It is the purpose of this chapter to include all funds or other property in the possession of the government of the United States, and of its departments, officers, and agencies, which property has its situs in this state or belonged to a resident thereof, and not to limit the application of this chapter by the naming of any particular agency. This chapter shall include all funds held in the United States Department of Veterans Affairs, Comptroller of Currency, United States Treasury, Department of Internal Revenue, federal courts, registry of federal courts, and such evidences of indebtedness as adjusted service bonds, old matured debts issued prior to 1917, unclaimed and interest thereon, postal savings bonds, liberty bonds, victory notes, treasury bonds, treasury notes, certificates of indebtedness, treasury bills, treasurer's savings certificates, bonuses and adjusted compensation, allotments, and all unclaimed refunds or rebates of whatever kind or nature, which are subjects of escheat, under the terms of this chapter. Provided, however, that nothing in this chapter shall be construed to mean that any refunds due ratepayers under order of any court of the United States shall become the property of the state.

History.
S. 2, ch. 24333, 1947; s. 11, ch. 25035, 1949; ss. 12, 35, ch. 69-106;

s. 1, ch. 70-405; s. 36, ch. 93-268; s. 847, ch. 97-102; s. 1881, ch. 2003-261.

716.03. Department to institute proceedings to recover escheated property.

When there exists, or may exist, escheated funds or property under this chapter, the Department of Financial Services shall demand or institute proceedings in the name of the state for an adjudication that an escheat to the state of such funds or property has occurred; and shall take appropriate action to recover such funds or property.

History.
S. 3, ch. 24333, 1947; s. 11, ch. 25035, 1949; ss. 12, 35, ch. 69-106; s. 1882, ch. 2003-261.

716.04. Jurisdiction.

Whenever the Department of Financial Services is of the opinion an escheat has occurred, or shall occur, of any money or other property deposited in the custody of, or under the control of, any court of the United States, in and for any district within the state, or in the custody of any depository, registry or clerk or other officer of such court, or the treasury of the United States, it shall cause to be filed a complaint in the Circuit Court of Leon County, or in any other court of competent jurisdiction, to ascertain if any escheat has occurred, and to cause said court to enter a judgment or decree of escheat in favor of the state, with costs, disbursements, and attorney fee.

History.
S. 4, ch. 24333, 1947; ss. 12, 35, ch. 69-106; s. 1883, ch. 2003-261.

716.05. Money recovered to be paid into State Treasury.

When any funds or property which has escheated within the meaning of this chapter has been recovered by the Department of Financial Services, the department shall first pay all costs incident to the collection and recovery of such funds or property and shall promptly deposit the remaining balance of such funds or property with the Chief Financial Officer, to be distributed in accordance with law.

History.
S. 5, ch. 24333, 1947; ss. 12, 35, ch. 69-106; s. 153, ch. 83-216; s. 1884, ch. 2003-261.

716.06. Public records.

All records in the office of the Chief Financial Officer or the Department of Financial Services relating to federal funds, pursuant to this chapter, shall be public records.

History.
S. 6, ch. 24333, 1947; ss. 12, 35, ch. 69-106; s. 1885, ch. 2003-261.

716.07. Recovery of escheated property by claimant.

(1) Any person who claims any property, funds, or money delivered to the Treasurer or Chief Financial Officer under this chapter, shall, within 5 years from the date of receipt of such property, funds, or money, file a verified claim with the Chief Financial Officer, setting forth the facts upon which such party claims to be entitled to recover such money or property. All claims made for recovery of property, funds, or money, not filed within 5 years from the date that such property, funds, or money is received by the Chief Financial Officer, shall be forever barred, and the Chief Financial Officer shall be without power to consider or determine any claims so made by any claimant after 5 years from the date that the property, funds, or money was received by the Chief Financial Officer.

(2) The Chief Financial Officer shall approve or disapprove the claim. If the claim is approved, the funds, money, or property of the claimant, less any expenses and costs which shall have been incurred by the state in securing the possession of said property, as provided by this chapter, shall be delivered to the claimant by the Chief Financial Officer upon warrant issued according to law and her or his receipt taken therefor. If the court finds, upon any judicial review, that the claimant is entitled to the property, money, or funds claimed, and shall render judgment in her or his or its favor, declaring that the claimant is entitled to such property, funds, or money, then upon presentation of said judgment or a certified copy thereof to the Chief Financial Officer, the Chief Financial Officer shall draw her or his warrant for the amount of money stated in such judgment, without interest or cost to the state, less any sum paid by the state as costs or expenses in securing possession of such property, funds, or money. When payment has been made to any claimant, no action thereafter shall be maintained by any other claimant against the state or any officer thereof, for or on account of such money, property, or funds.

History.
S. 7, ch. 24333, 1947; s. 30, ch. 63-559; ss. 12, 35, ch. 69-106; s. 7, ch. 78-95; s. 848, ch. 97-102; s. 1886, ch. 2003-261.

CHAPTER 717.
DISPOSITION OF UNCLAIMED PROPERTY

717.001. Short title.

This chapter may be cited as the "Florida Disposition of Unclaimed Property Act."

History.
S. 1, ch. 87-105.

717.101. Definitions.

As used in this chapter, unless the context otherwise requires:

(1) "Aggregate" means the amounts reported for owners of unclaimed property of less than $50 or where there is no name for the individual or entity listed on the holder's records, regardless of the amount to be reported.

(2) "Apparent owner" means the person whose name appears on the records of the holder as the person entitled to property held, issued, or owing by the holder.

(3) "Banking organization" means any state or national bank, international banking entity or similar entity, trust company, savings bank, industrial savings bank, land bank, safe-deposit company, private bank, or any organization otherwise defined by law as a bank or banking organization.

(4) "Business association" means any corporation (other than a public corporation), joint stock company, investment company, business trust, partnership, or association for business purposes of two or more individuals, whether or not for profit, including a banking organization, financial organization, insurance company, dissolved pension plan, or utility.

(5) "Claimant" means the person on whose behalf a claim is filed.

(6) "Credit balance" means an account balance in the customer's favor.

(7) "Department" means the Department of Financial Services.

(8) "Domicile" means the state of incorporation, in the case of a corporation incorporated under the laws of a state, and the state of the principal place of business, in the case of a person not incorporated under the laws of a state.

(9) "Due diligence" means the use of reasonable and prudent methods under particular circumstances to locate apparent owners of inactive accounts using the taxpayer identification number or social security number, if known, which may include, but are not limited to, using a nationwide database, cross-indexing with other records of the holder, mailing to the last known address unless the last known address is known to be inaccurate, or engaging a licensed agency or company capable of conducting such search and providing updated addresses.

(10) "Financial organization" means a state or federal savings association, savings and loan association, bank, trust company, international bank agency, cooperative bank, building and loan association, or credit union.

(11) "Health care provider" means any state-licensed entity that provides and receives payment for health care services. These entities include, but are not limited to, hospitals, outpatient centers, physician practices, and skilled nursing facilities.

(12) "Holder" means a person, wherever organized or domiciled, who is:

(a) In possession of property belonging to another;

(b) A trustee in case of a trust; or

(c) Indebted to another on an obligation.

(13) "Insurance company" means an association, corporation, or fraternal or mutual benefit organization, whether or not for profit, which is engaged in providing insurance coverage, including, by way of illustration and not limitation, accident, burial, casualty, credit life, contract performance, dental, fidelity, fire, health, hospitalization, illness, life (including endowments and annuities), malpractice, marine, mortgage, surety, and wage protection insurance.

(14) "Intangible property" includes, by way of illustration and not limitation:

(a) Moneys, checks, drafts, deposits, interest, dividends, and income.

(b) Credit balances, customer overpayments, security deposits and other instruments as defined by chapter 679, refunds, unpaid wages, unused airline tickets, and unidentified remittances.

(c) Stocks, and other intangible ownership interests in business associations.

(d) Moneys deposited to redeem stocks, bonds, bearer bonds, original issue discount bonds, coupons, and other securities, or to make distributions.

(e) Amounts due and payable under the terms of insurance policies.

(f) Amounts distributable from a trust or custodial fund established under a plan to provide any health, welfare, pension, vacation, severance, retirement, death, stock purchase, profit sharing, employee savings, supplemental unemployment insurance, or similar benefit.

(15) "Last known address" means a description of the location of the apparent owner sufficient for the purpose of the delivery of mail. For the purposes of identifying, reporting, and remitting property to the department which is presumed to be unclaimed, "last known address" includes any partial description of the location of the apparent owner sufficient to establish the apparent owner was a resident of this state at the time of last contact with the apparent owner or at the time the property became due and payable.

(16) "Lawful charges" means charges against dormant accounts that are authorized by statute for the purpose of offsetting the costs of maintaining the dormant account.

(17) "Managed care payor" means a health care plan that has a defined system of selecting and limiting health care providers as evidenced by a managed care contract with the health care providers. These plans include, but are not limited to, managed care health insurance companies and health maintenance organizations.

(18) "Owner" means a depositor in the case of a deposit, a beneficiary in the case of a trust or a deposit in trust, or a payee in the case of other intangible property, or a person having a legal or equitable interest in property subject to this chapter or his or her legal representative.

(19) "Public corporation" means a corporation created by the state, founded and owned in the public interest, supported by public funds, and governed by those deriving their power from the state.

(20) "Reportable period" means the calendar year ending December 31 of each year.

(21) "State," when applied to a part of the United States, includes any state, district, commonwealth, territory, insular possession, and any other area subject to the legislative authority of the United States.

(22) "Ultimate equitable owner" means a natural person who, directly or indirectly, owns or controls an ownership interest in a corporation, a foreign corporation, an alien business organization, or any other form of business organization, regardless of whether such natural person owns or controls such ownership interest through one or more natural persons or one or more proxies, powers of attorney, nominees, corporations, associations, partnerships, trusts, joint stock companies, or other entities or devices, or any combination thereof.

(23) "Utility" means a person who owns or operates, for public use, any plant, equipment, property, franchise, or license for the transmission of communications or the production, storage, transmission, sale, delivery, or furnishing of electricity, water, steam, or gas.

History.
S. 2, ch. 87-105; s. 23, ch. 91-110; s. 1, ch. 96-301; s. 1770, ch. 97-102; s. 1, ch. 2001-36; s. 1, ch. 2003-21; s. 1887, ch. 2003-261; s. 110, ch. 2004-390; s. 1, ch. 2005-163.

717.102. Property presumed unclaimed; general rule.

(1) All intangible property, including any income or increment thereon less any lawful charges, that is held, issued, or owing in the ordinary course of the holder's business and the owner fails to claim such property for more than 5 years after the property becomes payable or distributable is presumed unclaimed, except as otherwise provided by this chapter.

(2) Property is payable or distributable for the purpose of this chapter notwithstanding the owner's failure to make demand or to present any instrument or document required to receive payment.

History.
S. 3, ch. 87-105; s. 2, ch. 2001-36.

717.103. General rules for taking custody of intangible unclaimed property.

Unless otherwise provided in this chapter or by other statute of this state, intangible property is subject to the custody of the department as unclaimed property if the conditions leading to a presumption that the property is unclaimed as described in ss. 717.102 and 717.105-717.116 are satisfied and:

(1) The last known address, as shown on the records of the holder, of the apparent owner is in this state;

(2) The records of the holder do not reflect the identity of the person entitled to the property, and it is established that the last known address of the person entitled to the property is in this state;

(3) The records of the holder do not reflect the last known address of the apparent owner, and it is established that:

(a) The last known address of the person entitled to the property is in this state; or

(b) The holder is a domiciliary or a government or governmental subdivision or agency of this state and has not previously paid the property to the state of the last known address of the apparent owner or other person entitled to the property;

(4) The last known address, as shown on the records of the holder, of the apparent owner or other person entitled to the property is in a state that does not provide by law for the escheat or custodial taking of the property, or its escheat or unclaimed property law is not applicable to the property, and the holder is a domiciliary or a government or governmental subdivision or agency of this state;

(5) The last known address, as shown on the records of the holder, of the apparent owner is in a foreign nation and the holder is a domiciliary or a government or governmental subdivision or agency of this state; or

(6) The transaction out of which the property arose occurred in this state, and;

(a)1. The last known address of the apparent owner or other person entitled to the property is unknown; or

2. The last known address of the apparent owner or other person entitled to the property is in a state that does not provide by law for the escheat or custodial taking of the property, or its escheat or unclaimed property law is not applicable to the property; and

(b) The holder is a domiciliary of a state that does not provide by law for the escheat or custodial taking of the property, or its escheat or unclaimed property law is not applicable to the property.

History.
S. 4, ch. 87-105; s. 3, ch. 2001-36.

717.1035. Property originated or issued by this state, any political subdivision of this state, or any entity incorporated, organized, created, or otherwise located in the state.

(1) All intangible property, including, but not limited to, any interest, dividend, or other earnings thereon, less any lawful charges, held by a business association, federal, state, or local government or governmental subdivision, agency, or entity, or any other person or entity, regardless of where the holder may be found, if the owner has not claimed or corresponded in writing concerning the property within 3 years after the date prescribed for payment or delivery, is presumed to be unclaimed property and subject to the custody of this state as such if:

(a) The last known address of the owner is unknown; and

(b) The person or entity originating or issuing the intangible property is this state or any political subdivision of this state, or the person or entity is incorporated, organized, created, or otherwise located in this state.

(2) The provisions of subsection (1) shall not apply to property which is or may be presumed unclaimed and subject to the custody of this state pursuant to any other provision of law containing a dormancy period different than that prescribed in subsection (1).

(3) The provisions of subsection (1) shall apply to all property held at the time of enactment, or at any time thereafter, regardless of when such property became or becomes presumptively unclaimed.

History.
S. 1, ch. 90-113; s. 2, ch. 92-169; s. 4, ch. 2001-36.

717.104. Traveler's checks and money orders.

(1) Subject to subsection (4), any sum payable on a traveler's check that has been outstanding for more than 15 years after its issuance is presumed unclaimed unless the owner, within 15 years, has communicated in writing with the issuer concerning it or otherwise indicated an interest as evidenced by a memorandum or other record on file with the issuer.

(2) Subject to subsection (4), any sum payable on a money order or similar written instrument, other than a third party bank check, that has been outstanding for more than 7 years after its issuance is presumed unclaimed unless the owner, within 7 years, has communicated in writing with the issuer concerning it or otherwise indicated an interest as evidenced by a memorandum or other record on file with the issuer.

(3) No holder may deduct from the amount of any traveler's check or money order any charges imposed by reason of the failure to present those instruments for payment unless there is a valid and enforceable written contract between the issuer and the owner of the property pursuant to which the issuer may impose those charges and the issuer regularly imposes those charges and does not regularly reverse or otherwise cancel those charges with respect to the property.

(4) No sum payable on a traveler's check, money order, or similar written instrument, other than a third party bank check, described in subsections (1) and (2) may be subjected to the custody of this state as unclaimed property unless:

(a) The records of the issuer show that the traveler's check, money order, or similar written instrument was purchased in this state;

(b) The issuer has its principal place of business in this state and the records of the issuer do not show the state in which the traveler's check, money order, or similar written instrument was purchased; or

(c) The issuer has its principal place of business in this state; the records of the issuer show the state in which the traveler's check, money order, or similar written instrument was purchased; and the laws of the state of purchase do not provide for the escheat or custodial taking of the property, or its escheat or unclaimed property law is not applicable to the property.

(5) Notwithstanding any other provision of this chapter, subsection (4) applies to sums payable on traveler's checks, money orders, and similar written instruments presumed unclaimed on or after February 1, 1965, except to the extent that those sums have been paid over to a state prior to January 1, 1974.

History.
S. 5, ch. 87-105; s. 5, ch. 2001-36.

717.1045. Gift certificates and similar credit items.

Notwithstanding s. 717.117, an unredeemed gift certificate or credit memo as defined in s. 501.95 is not required to be reported as unclaimed property.

(1) The consideration paid for an unredeemed gift certificate or credit memo is the property of the issuer of the unredeemed gift certificate or credit memo.

(2) An unredeemed gift certificate or credit memo is subject only to any rights of a purchaser or owner thereof and is not subject to a claim made by any state acting on behalf of a purchaser or owner.

(3) It is the intent of the Legislature that this section apply to the custodial holding of unredeemed gift certificates and credit memos.

(4) However, a gift certificate or credit memo described in s. 501.95(2)(b) shall be reported as unclaimed property. The consideration paid for such a gift certificate or credit memo is the property of the owner of the gift certificate or credit memo.

History.
S. 2, ch. 2007-256, eff. June 28, 2007.

717.105. Checks, drafts, and similar instruments issued or certified by banking and financial organizations.

(1) Any sum payable on a check, draft, or similar instrument, except those subject to ss. 717.104 and 717.115, on which a banking or financial organization is directly liable, including, but not limited to, a cashier's check or a certified check, which has been outstanding for more than 5 years after it was payable or after its issuance if payable on demand, is presumed unclaimed unless the owner, within 5 years, has communicated in writing with the banking or financial organization concerning it or otherwise indicated an interest as evidenced by a memorandum or other record on file with the banking or financial organization.

(2) No holder may deduct from the amount of any instrument subject to this section any charges imposed by reason of the failure to present the instrument for encashment unless there is a valid and enforceable written contract between the holder and the owner of the instrument pursuant to which the holder may impose those charges and does not regularly reverse or otherwise cancel those charges with respect to the instrument.

History.
S. 6, ch. 87-105; s. 2, ch. 96-301; s. 6, ch. 2001-36.

717.106. Bank deposits and funds in financial organizations.

(1) Any demand, savings, or matured time deposit with a banking or financial organization, including deposits that are automatically renewable, and any funds paid toward the purchase of shares, a mutual investment certificate, or any other interest in a banking or financial organization is presumed unclaimed unless the owner has, within 5 years:

(a) Increased or decreased the amount of the deposit or presented the passbook or other similar evidence of the deposit for the crediting of interest;

(b) Communicated in writing or by documented telephone contact with the banking or financial organization concerning the property;

(c) Otherwise indicated an interest in the property as evidenced by a memorandum or other record on file with the banking or financial organization;

(d) Owned other property to which paragraph (a), paragraph (b), or paragraph (c) is applicable and if the banking or financial organization communicates in writing with the owner with regard to the property that would otherwise be presumed unclaimed under this subsection at the address to which communications regarding the other property regularly are sent; or

(e) Had another relationship with the banking or financial organization concerning which the owner has:

1. Communicated in writing with the banking or financial organization; or

2. Otherwise indicated an interest as evidenced by a memorandum or other record on file with the banking or financial organization and if the banking or financial organization communicates in writing with the owner with regard to the property that would otherwise be unclaimed under this subsection at the address to which communications regarding the other relationship regularly are sent.

(2) For purpose of paragraph (1)(a), property includes any interest or dividends thereon.

(3) No holder may impose with respect to property described in subsection (1) any charges due to dormancy or inactivity or cease payment of interest unless:

(a) There is an enforceable written contract between the holder and the owner of the property pursuant to which the holder may impose those charges or cease payment of interest.

(b) For property in excess of $2, the holder, no more than 3 months prior to the initial imposition of those charges or cessation of interest, has given written notice to the owner of the amount of those charges at the last known address of the owner stating that those charges shall be imposed or that interest shall cease, but the notice provided in this section need not be given with respect to charges imposed or interest ceased before July 1, 1987.

(c) The holder regularly imposes those charges or ceases payment of interest and does not regularly reverse or otherwise cancel those charges or retroactively credit interest with respect to such property.

(4) Any property described in subsection (1) that is automatically renewable is matured for purposes of subsection (1) upon the expiration of its initial time period except that, in the case of any renewal to which the owner consents at or about the time of renewal by communicating in writing with the banking or financial organization or otherwise indicating consent as evidenced by a memorandum or other record on file prepared by an employee of the organization, the property is matured upon the expiration of the last time period for which consent was given. If, at the time provided for delivery in s. 717.119, a penalty or forfeiture in the payment of interest would result from the delivery of the property, the time for delivery is extended until the time when no penalty or forfeiture would result.

(5) If the documents establishing a deposit described in subsection (1) state the address of a beneficiary of the deposit, and the account has a value of at least $50, notice shall be given to the beneficiary as provided for notice to the apparent owner under s. 717.117(4). This subsection shall apply to accounts opened on or after October 1, 1990.

History.
S. 7, ch. 87-105; s. 2, ch. 90-113; s. 63, ch. 91-110; s. 3, ch. 96-301; s. 7, ch. 2001-36; s. 111, ch. 2004-390; s. 2, ch. 2005-163.

717.107. Funds owing under life insurance policies.

(1) Funds held or owing under any life or endowment insurance policy or annuity contract which has matured or terminated are presumed unclaimed if unclaimed for more than 5 years after the funds became due and payable as established from the records of the insurance company holding or owing the funds, but property described in paragraph (3)(b) is presumed unclaimed if such property is not claimed for more than 2 years. The amount presumed unclaimed shall include any amount due and payable under s. 627.4615.

(2) If a person other than the insured or annuitant is entitled to the funds and no address of the person is known to the company or it is not definite and certain from the records of the company who is entitled to the funds, it is presumed that the last known address of the person entitled to the funds is the same as the last known address of the insured or annuitant according to the records of the company.

(3) For purposes of this chapter, a life or endowment insurance policy or annuity contract not matured by actual proof of the death of the insured or annuitant according to the records of the company is deemed matured and the proceeds due and payable if:

(a) The company knows that the insured or annuitant has died; or

(b)1. The insured has attained, or would have attained if he or she were living, the limiting age under the mortality table on which the reserve is based;

2. The policy was in force at the time the insured attained, or would have attained, the limiting age specified in subparagraph 1.; and

3. Neither the insured nor any other person appearing to have an interest in the policy within the preceding 2 years, according to the records of the company, has assigned, readjusted, or paid premiums on the policy; subjected the policy to a loan; corresponded in writing with the company concerning the policy; or otherwise indicated an interest as evidenced by a memorandum or other record on file prepared by an employee of the company.

(4) For purposes of this chapter, the application of an automatic premium loan provision or other nonforfeiture provision contained in an insurance policy does not prevent the policy from being matured or terminated under subsection (1) if the insured has died or the insured or the beneficiaries of the policy otherwise have become entitled to the proceeds thereof before the depletion of the cash surrender value of a policy by the application of those provisions.

(5) If the laws of this state or the terms of the life insurance policy require the company to give notice to the insured or owner that an automatic premium loan provision or other nonforfeiture provision has been exercised and the notice, given to an insured or owner whose last known address according to the records of the company is in this state, is undeliverable, the company shall make a reasonable search to ascertain the policyholder's correct address to which the notice must be mailed.

(6) Notwithstanding any other provision of law, if the company learns of the death of the insured or annuitant and the beneficiary has not communicated with the insurer within 4 months after the death, the company shall take reasonable steps to pay the proceeds to the beneficiary.

(7) Commencing 2 years after July 1, 1987, every change of beneficiary form issued by an insurance company under any life or endowment insurance policy or annuity contract to an insured or owner who is a resident of this state must request the following information:

(a) The name of each beneficiary, or if a class of beneficiaries is named, the name of each current beneficiary in the class.

(b) The address of each beneficiary.

(c) The relationship of each beneficiary to the insured.

History.
S. 8, ch. 87-105; s. 849, ch. 97-102; s. 8, ch. 2001-36; s. 112, ch. 2004-390.

717.1071. Lost owners of unclaimed demutualization, rehabilitation, or related reorganization proceeds.

(1) Property distributable in the course of a demutualization, rehabilitation, or related reorganization of an insurance company is deemed abandoned 2 years after the date the property is first distributable if, at the time of the first distribution, the last known address of the owner on the books and records of the holder is known to be incorrect or the distribution or statements are returned by the post office as undeliverable; and the owner has not communicated in writing with the holder or its agent regarding the interest or otherwise communicated with the holder regarding the interest as evidenced by a memorandum or other record on file with the holder or its agent.

(2) Property distributable in the course of demutualization, rehabilitation, or related reorganization of a mutual insurance company that is not subject to subsection (1) shall be reportable as otherwise provided by this chapter.

(3) Property subject to this section shall be reported and delivered no later than May 1 as of the preceding December 31; however, the initial report under this section shall be filed no later than November 1, 2003, as of December 31, 2002.

History.
S. 2, ch. 2003-21; s. 75, ch. 2003-281.

Editor's Notes.
This section is set out as enacted by s. 75, ch. 2003-281. Section 717.1071 was also enacted by s. 2, ch. 2003-21, and that version read: "717.1071 Unclaimed demutualization proceeds. — Unclaimed

property payable or distributable in the course of a demutualization of an insurance company is presumed unclaimed 5 years after the earlier of the date of last contact with the policyholder or the date the property became payable or distributable."

717.108. Deposits held by utilities.

Any deposit, including any interest thereon, made by a subscriber with a utility to secure payment or any sum paid in advance for utility services to be furnished, less any lawful charges, that remains unclaimed by the owner for more than 1 year after termination of the services for which the deposit or advance payment was made is presumed unclaimed.

History.
S. 9, ch. 87-105; s. 4, ch. 96-301; s. 9, ch. 2001-36.

717.109. Refunds held by business associations.

Except as otherwise provided by law, any sum that a business association has been ordered to refund by a court or administrative agency which has been unclaimed by the owner for more than 1 year after it became payable in accordance with the final determination or order providing for the refund, regardless of whether the final determination or order requires any person entitled to a refund to make a claim for it, is presumed unclaimed.

History.
S. 10, ch. 87-105; s. 10, ch. 2001-36; s. 113, ch. 2004-390.

717.1101. Unclaimed equity and debt of business associations.

(1)(a) Stock or other equity interest in a business association is presumed unclaimed 3 years after the earliest of:

1. The date of the most recent dividend, stock split, or other distribution unclaimed by the apparent owner;

2. The date of a statement of account or other notification or communication that was returned as undeliverable; or

3. The date the holder discontinued mailings, notifications, or communications to the apparent owner.

(b) Unmatured or unredeemed debt, other than a bearer bond or an original issue discount bond, is presumed unclaimed 3 years after the date of the most recent interest payment unclaimed by the owner.

(c) Matured or redeemed debt is presumed unclaimed 3 years after the date of maturity or redemption.

(d) At the time property is presumed unclaimed under paragraph (a) or paragraph (b), any other property right accrued or accruing to the owner as a result of the property interest and not previously presumed unclaimed is also presumed unclaimed.

(2) The running of such 3-year period ceases if the person:

(a)1. Communicates in writing with the association or its agent regarding the interest or a dividend, distribution, or other sum payable as a result of the interest; or

2. Otherwise communicates with the association regarding the interest or a dividend, distribution, or other sum payable as a result of the interest, as evidenced by a memorandum or other record on file with the association or its agent.

(b) Presents an instrument issued to pay interest or a dividend or other cash distribution. If any future dividend, distribution, or other sum payable to the owner as a result of the interest is subsequently not claimed by the owner, a new period in which the property is presumed unclaimed commences and relates back only to the time a subsequent dividend, distribution, or other sum became due and payable.

(3) At the same time any interest is presumed unclaimed under this section, any dividend, distribution, or other sum then held for or owing to the owner as a result of the interest, is presumed unclaimed.

(4) Any dividend, profit, distribution, interest redemption, payment on principal, or other sum held or owing by a business association for or to a shareholder, certificateholder, member, bondholder, or other security holder, who has not claimed such amount or corresponded in writing with the business association concerning such amount, within 3 years after the date prescribed for payment or delivery, is presumed unclaimed.

History.
S. 11, ch. 87-105; s. 5, ch. 96-301; s. 11, ch. 2001-36; s. 3, ch. 2003-21; s. 3, ch. 2005-163.

717.111. Property of business associations held in course of dissolution.

All intangible property distributable in the course of a voluntary or involuntary dissolution of a business association which is not claimed by the owner for more than 6 months after the date specified for final distribution is presumed unclaimed.

History.
S. 12, ch. 87-105; s. 12, ch. 2001-36.

717.112. Property held by agents and fiduciaries.

(1) All intangible property and any income or increment thereon held in a fiduciary capacity for the benefit of another person is presumed unclaimed unless the owner has within 5 years after it has become payable or distributable increased or decreased the principal, accepted payment of principal or income, communicated concerning the property, or otherwise indicated an interest as evidenced by a memorandum or other record on file with the fiduciary.

(2) Funds in an individual retirement account or a retirement plan for self-employed individuals or similar account or plan established pursuant to the Internal Revenue laws of the United States are not payable or distributable within the meaning of subsection (1) un-

less, under the terms of the account or plan, distribution of all or part of the funds would then be mandatory.

(3) For the purpose of this section, a person who holds property as an agent for a business association is deemed to hold the property in a fiduciary capacity for that business association alone, unless the agreement between said person and the business association provides otherwise.

(4) For the purposes of this chapter, a person who is deemed to hold property in a fiduciary capacity for a business association alone is the holder of the property only insofar as the interest of the business association in the property is concerned, and the business association is the holder of the property insofar as the interest of any other person in the property is concerned.

(5) All intangible property, and any income or increment thereon, issued by a government or governmental subdivision or agency, public corporation, or public authority and held in an agency capacity for the governmental subdivision, agency, public corporation, or public authority for the benefit of the owner of record, is presumed unclaimed unless the owner has, within 1 year after such property has become payable or distributable, increased or decreased the principal, accepted payment of the principal or income, communicated concerning the property, or otherwise indicated an interest in the property as evidenced by a memorandum or other record on file with the fiduciary.

History.
S. 13, ch. 87-105; s. 6, ch. 96-301; s. 13, ch. 2001-36.

717.113. Property held by courts and public agencies.

All intangible property held for the owner by any court, government or governmental subdivision or agency, public corporation, or public authority that has not been claimed by the owner for more than 1 year after it became payable or distributable is presumed unclaimed. Notwithstanding the provisions of this section, funds deposited in the Minerals Trust Fund pursuant to s. 377.247 are presumed unclaimed only if the funds have not been claimed by the owner for more than 5 years after the date of first production from the well.

History.
S. 14, ch. 87-105; s. 4, ch. 94-193; s. 71, ch. 96-321; s. 14, ch. 2001-36.

717.115. Wages.

Unpaid wages, including wages represented by unpresented payroll checks, owing in the ordinary course of the holder's business that have not been claimed by the owner for more than 1 year after becoming payable are presumed unclaimed.

History.
S. 16, ch. 87-105; s. 15, ch. 2001-36.

717.116. Contents of safe-deposit box or other safekeeping repository.

All tangible and intangible property held by a banking or financial organization in a safe-deposit box or any other safekeeping repository in this state in the ordinary course of the holder's business, and proceeds resulting from the sale of the property permitted by law, that has not been claimed by the owner for more than 3 years after the lease or rental period on the box or other repository has expired are presumed unclaimed.

History.
S. 17, ch. 87-105; s. 8, ch. 96-301; s. 16, ch. 2001-36; s. 114, ch. 2004-390.

717.117. Report of unclaimed property.

(1) Every person holding funds or other property, tangible or intangible, presumed unclaimed and subject to custody as unclaimed property under this chapter shall report to the department on such forms as the department may prescribe by rule. In lieu of forms, a report identifying 25 or more different apparent owners must be submitted by the holder via electronic medium as the department may prescribe by rule. The report must include:

(a) Except for traveler's checks and money orders, the name, social security number or taxpayer identification number, and date of birth, if known, and last known address, if any, of each person appearing from the records of the holder to be the owner of any property which is presumed unclaimed and which has a value of $50 or more.

(b) For unclaimed funds which have a value of $50 or more held or owing under any life or endowment insurance policy or annuity contract, the full name, taxpayer identification number or social security number, date of birth, if known, and last known address of the insured or annuitant and of the beneficiary according to records of the insurance company holding or owing the funds.

(c) For all tangible property held in a safe-deposit box or other safekeeping repository, a description of the property and the place where the property is held and may be inspected by the department, and any amounts owing to the holder. Contents of a safe-deposit box or other safekeeping repository which consist of documents or writings of a private nature and which have little or no apparent value shall not be presumed unclaimed.

(d) The nature and identifying number, if any, or description of the property and the amount appearing from the records to be due. Items of value under $50 each may be reported in the aggregate.

(e) The date the property became payable, demandable, or returnable, and the date of the last transaction with the apparent owner with respect to the property.

(f) Any person or business association or public corporation holding funds presumed unclaimed and having a total value of $10 or less may file a zero balance report for that reporting period. The balance brought forward to the new reporting period is zero.

(g) Such other information as the department may prescribe by rule as necessary for the administration of this chapter.

(h) Credit balances, customer overpayments, security deposits, and refunds having a value of less than $10 shall not be presumed unclaimed.

(2) If the holder of property presumed unclaimed and subject to custody as unclaimed property is a successor holder or if the holder has changed the holder's name while in possession of the property, the holder shall file with the holder's report all known names and addresses of each prior holder of the property. Compliance with this subsection means the holder exercises reasonable and prudent efforts to determine the names of all prior holders.

(3) The report must be filed before May 1 of each year. The report shall apply to the preceding calendar year. The department may impose and collect a penalty of $10 per day up to a maximum of $500 for the failure to timely report or the failure to include in a report information required by this chapter. The penalty shall be remitted to the department within 30 days after the date of the notification to the holder that the penalty is due and owing. As necessary for proper administration of this chapter, the department may waive any penalty due with appropriate justification. On written request by any person required to file a report and upon a showing of good cause, the department may postpone the reporting date. The department must provide information contained in a report filed with the department to any person requesting a copy of the report or information contained in a report, to the extent the information requested is not confidential, within 45 days after the report has been processed and added to the unclaimed property database subsequent to a determination that the report is accurate and that the reported property is the same as the remitted property.

(4) Holders of inactive accounts having a value of $50 or more shall use due diligence to locate apparent owners. Not more than 120 days and not less than 60 days prior to filing the report required by this section, the holder in possession of property presumed unclaimed and subject to custody as unclaimed property under this chapter shall send written notice to the apparent owner at the apparent owner's last known address informing the apparent owner that the holder is in possession of property subject to this chapter, if the holder has in its records an address for the apparent owner which the holder's records do not disclose to be inaccurate.

(5) Any holder of intangible property may file with the department a petition for determination that the property is unclaimed requesting the department to accept custody of the property. The petition shall state any special circumstances that exist, contain the information required by subsection (2), and show that a diligent search has been made to locate the owner. If the department finds that the proof of diligent search is satisfactory, it shall give notice as provided in s. 717.118 and accept custody of the property.

(6) Upon written request by any entity or person required to file a report, stating such entity's or person's justification for such action, the department may place that entity or person in an inactive status as an unclaimed property "holder."

(7)(a) This section does not apply to the unclaimed patronage refunds as provided for by contract or through bylaw provisions of entities organized under chapter 425.

(b) This section does not apply to intangible property held, issued, or owing by a business association subject to the jurisdiction of the United States Surface Transportation Board or its successor federal agency if the apparent owner of such intangible property is a business association. The holder of such property does not have any obligation to report, to pay, or to deliver such property to the department.

(c) This section does not apply to credit balances, overpayments, refunds, or outstanding checks owed by a health care provider to a managed care payor with whom the health care provider has a managed care contract, provided that the credit balances, overpayments, refunds, or outstanding checks become due and owing pursuant to the managed care contract.

(8)(a) As used in this subsection, the term "property identifier" means the descriptor used by the holder to identify the unclaimed property.

(b) Social security numbers and property identifiers contained in reports required under this section, held by the department, are confidential and exempt from s. 119.07(1) and s. 24(a), Art. I of the State Constitution.

(c) This exemption applies to social security numbers and property identifiers held by the department before, on, or after the effective date of this exemption.

(d) This subsection is subject to the Open Government Sunset Review Act in accordance with s. 119.15, and shall stand repealed October 2, 2017, unless reviewed and saved from repeal through reenactment by the Legislature.

History.

S. 18, ch. 87-105; s. 1, ch. 92-169; s. 30, ch. 92-319; s. 1, ch. 93-280; s. 9, ch. 96-301; s. 1771, ch. 97-102; s. 17, ch. 2001-36; s. 1, ch. 2002-64; s. 1888, ch. 2003-261; s. 115, ch. 2004-390; s. 4, ch. 2005-163; s. 1, ch. 2007-69, eff. Oct. 1, 2007; s. 1, ch. 2012-227, eff. May 4, 2012.

Editor's Notes.

Section 2, ch. 2007-69, provides: "The Legislature finds that it is a public necessity that property identifiers contained in reports of unclaimed property be made confidential and exempt from public-records requirements. Property identifiers, which are descriptors used by a holder to identify unclaimed property, could be used to obtain fraudulently unclaimed funds or property. Protection of property identifiers is a public necessity in order to prevent the fraudulent use of such information for purposes of creating falsified or forged documents that appear to demonstrate entitlement to unclaimed property. Such use defrauds the rightful property owner or the State School Fund. Furthermore, the release of property identifiers contained in reports of unclaimed property hinders the effective and efficient administration of the unclaimed property program."

Section 2, ch. 2012-227 provides: "The Legislature finds that it is a public necessity that social security numbers contained in reports of unclaimed property remain confidential and exempt from public records requirements. Social security numbers, which are used by a holder of unclaimed property to identify such property, could be used to fraudulently obtain unclaimed property. The release of social security numbers could also place owners of unclaimed property at risk of identity theft. Therefore, the protection of social security numbers is a public necessity in order to prevent the fraudulent use of such information by creating falsified or forged documents that appear to demonstrate entitlement to unclaimed property and to prevent opportunities for identify theft. Such use defrauds the rightful owner or the State School Fund, which is the depository for all remaining unclaimed funds."

717.118. Notification of apparent owners of unclaimed property.

(1) It is specifically recognized that the state has an obligation to make an effort to notify owners of unclaimed property in a cost-effective manner. In order to provide all the citizens of this state an effective and efficient program for the recovery of unclaimed property, the department shall use cost-effective means to make at least one active attempt to notify owners of unclaimed property accounts valued at more than $250 with a reported address or taxpayer identification number. Such active attempt to notify apparent owners shall include any attempt by the department to directly contact the owner. Other means of notification, such as publication of the names of owners in the newspaper, on television, on the Internet, or through other promotional efforts and items in which the department does not directly attempt to contact the owner are expressly declared to be passive attempts. Nothing in this subsection precludes other agencies or entities of state government from notifying owners of the existence of unclaimed property or attempting to notify apparent owners of unclaimed property.

(2) Notification provided directly to individual apparent owners shall consist of a description of the property and information regarding recovery of unclaimed property from the department.

(3) This section is not applicable to sums payable on traveler's checks, money orders, and other written instruments presumed unclaimed under s. 717.104.

History.
S. 19, ch. 87-105; s. 2, ch. 88-256; s. 31, ch. 92-319; s. 2, ch. 93-280; s. 10, ch. 96-301; s. 18, ch. 2001-36; s. 116, ch. 2004-390; s. 5, ch. 2005-163.

717.119. Payment or delivery of unclaimed property.

(1) Every person who is required to file a report under s. 717.117 shall simultaneously pay or deliver to the department all unclaimed property required to be reported. Such payment or delivery shall accompany the report as required in this chapter for the preceding calendar year.

(2) Payment of unclaimed funds may be made to the department by electronic funds transfer.

(3) If the owner establishes the right to receive the unclaimed property to the satisfaction of the holder before the property has been delivered to the department or it appears that for some other reason the presumption that the property is unclaimed is erroneous, the holder need not pay or deliver the property to the department. In lieu of delivery, the holder shall file a verified written explanation of the proof of claim or of the error in the presumption that the property was unclaimed.

(4) All stock or other intangible ownership interest reported under this chapter on the annual report filing required in s. 717.117 shall be remitted to the department with the report. Upon delivery of the stock or other intangible ownership interest to the department, the holder and any transfer agent, registrar, or other person acting for or on behalf of a holder is relieved of all liability of every kind in accordance with the provisions of s. 717.1201 to every person for any losses or damages resulting to the person by the delivery to the department of the stock or other intangible ownership interest.

(5) All intangible and tangible property held in a safe-deposit box or any other safekeeping repository reported under s. 717.117 shall not be delivered to the department until 120 days after the report due date. The delivery of the property, through the United States mail or any other carrier, shall be insured by the holder at an amount equal to the estimated value of the property. Each package shall be clearly marked on the outside "Deliver Unopened." A holder's safe-deposit box contents shall be delivered to the department in a single shipment. In lieu of a single shipment, holders may provide the department with a single detailed shipping schedule that includes package tracking information for all packages being sent pursuant to this section.

(a) Holders may remit the value of cash and coins found in unclaimed safe-deposit boxes to the department by cashier's check or by electronic funds transfer, unless the cash or coins have a value above face value. The department shall identify by rule those cash and coin items having a numismatic value. Cash and coin items identified as having a numismatic value shall be remitted to the department in their original form.

(b) Any firearm or ammunition found in an unclaimed safe-deposit box or any other safekeeping repository shall be delivered by the holder to a law enforcement agency for disposal pursuant to s. 705.103(2)(b) with the balance of the proceeds deposited into the State School Fund if the firearm is sold. However, the department is authorized to make a reasonable attempt to ascertain the historical value to collectors of any firearm that has been delivered to the department. Any firearm appearing to have historical value to collectors may be sold by the department pursuant to s. 717.122 to a person having a federal firearms license. Any firearm which is not sold pursuant to s. 717.122 shall be delivered by the department to a law enforcement agency in this state for disposal pursuant to s. 705.103(2)(b) with the balance of the proceeds deposited into the State School Fund if the firearm is sold. The department shall not be administratively, civilly, or criminally liable for any firearm delivered by the department to a law enforcement agency in this state for disposal.

(c) If such property is not paid or delivered to the department on or before the applicable payment or delivery date, the holder shall pay to the department a penalty for each safe-deposit box shipment received late. The penalty shall be $100 for a safe-deposit box shipment container that is late 30 days or less. Thereafter, the penalty shall be $500 for a safe-deposit box shipment container that is late for each additional successive 30-day period. The penalty assessed against a holder for a late safe-deposit box shipment container shall not exceed $4,000 annually. The penalty shall be remitted to the department within 30 days after the date of the notification to the holder that the penalty is due and owing.

(d) The department may waive any penalty due with appropriate justification, as provided by rule.

(6) Any holder may request an extension in writing of up to 60 days for the delivery of property if extenuating circumstances exist for the late delivery of the property. Any such extension the department may grant shall be in writing.

History.
S. 20, ch. 87-105; s. 11, ch. 96-301; s. 19, ch. 2001-36; s. 4, ch. 2003-21; s. 117, ch. 2004-390; s. 6, ch. 2005-163.

717.1201. Custody by state; holder relieved from liability; reimbursement of holder paying claim; reclaiming for owner; defense of holder; payment of safe-deposit box or repository charges.

(1) Upon the payment or delivery of property to the department, the state assumes custody and responsibility for the safekeeping of property. Any person who pays or delivers property to the department in good faith is relieved of all liability to the extent of the value of the property paid or delivered for any claim then existing or which thereafter may arise or be made in respect to the property.

(2) Any holder who has paid money to the department pursuant to this chapter may make payment to any person appearing to be entitled to payment and, upon filing proof that the payee is entitled thereto, the department shall forthwith repay the holder without deduction of any fee or other charges. If repayment is sought for a payment made on a negotiable instrument, including a traveler's check or money order, the holder must be repaid under this subsection upon filing proof that the instrument was duly presented and that the payee is entitled to payment. The holder shall be repaid for payment made under this subsection even if the payment was made to a person whose claim was barred under s. 717.129(1).

(3) Any holder who has delivered property, including a certificate of any interest in a business association, other than money to the department pursuant to this chapter may reclaim the property if still in the possession of the department, without payment of any fee or other charges, upon filing proof that the owner has claimed the property from the holder.

(4) The department may accept an affidavit of the holder stating the facts that entitle the holder to recover money and property under this section as sufficient proof.

(5) If the holder pays or delivers property to the department in good faith and thereafter any other person claims the property from the holder paying or delivering, or another state claims the money or property under that state's laws relating to escheat or abandoned or unclaimed property, the department, upon written notice of the claim, shall defend the holder against the claim and indemnify the holder against any liability on the claim.

(6) For the purposes of this section, "good faith" means that:

(a) Payment or delivery was made in a reasonable attempt to comply with this chapter.

(b) The person delivering the property was not a fiduciary then in breach of trust in respect to the property and had a reasonable basis for believing, based on the facts then known to that person, that the property was unclaimed for the purposes of this chapter.

(c) There is no showing that the records pursuant to which the delivery was made did not meet reasonable commercial standards of practice in the industry.

(7) Property removed from a safe-deposit box or other safekeeping repository is received by the department subject to the holder's right under this subsection to be reimbursed for the actual cost of the opening and to any valid lien or contract providing for the holder to be reimbursed for unpaid rent or storage charges. The department shall make the reimbursement to the holder out of the proceeds remaining after the deduction of the department's selling cost.

History.
S. 21, ch. 87-105; s. 20, ch. 2001-36; s. 118, ch. 2004-390.

717.121. Crediting of dividends, interest, or increments to owner's account.

Whenever property other than money is paid or delivered to the department under this chapter, the owner is entitled to receive from the department any dividends, interest, or other increments realized or accruing on the property at or before liquidation or conversion thereof into money.

History.
S. 22, ch. 87-105.

717.122. Public sale of unclaimed property.

(1) Except as provided in paragraph (2)(a), the department after the receipt of unclaimed property shall sell it to the highest bidder at public sale on the Internet or at a specified physical location wherever in the judgment of the department the most favorable market for the property involved exists. The department may decline the highest bid and reoffer the property for sale if in the judgment of the department the bid is insufficient. The department shall have the discretion to withhold from sale any unclaimed property that the department deems to be of benefit to the people of the state. If in the judgment of the department the probable cost of sale exceeds the value of the property, it need not be offered for sale and may be disposed of as the department determines appropriate. Any sale at a specified physical location held under this section must be preceded by a single publication of notice, at least 3 weeks in advance of sale, in a newspaper of general circulation in the county in which the property is to be sold. The department shall proportionately deduct auction fees, preparation costs, and expenses from the amount posted to the owner's account when safe-deposit box contents are sold. No action or proceeding may be maintained against the department for or on account of any decision to decline the highest bid or withhold any unclaimed property from sale.

(2)(a) Securities listed on an established stock exchange must be sold at prices prevailing at the time of sale on the exchange. Other securities may be sold over the counter at prices prevailing at the time of sale or by any other method the department deems advisable. The department may authorize the agent or broker acting on behalf of the department to deduct fees from the proceeds of these sales at a rate agreed upon in advance by the agent or broker and the department. The department shall reimburse owners' accounts for these brokerage fees from the State School Fund unless the securities are sold at the owner's request.

(b) Unless the department deems it to be in the public interest to do otherwise, all securities presumed unclaimed and delivered to the department may be sold upon receipt. Any person making a claim pursuant to this chapter is entitled to receive either the securities delivered to the department by the holder, if they still remain in the hands of the department, or the proceeds received from sale, but no person has any claim under this chapter against the state, the holder, any transfer agent, any registrar, or any other person acting for or on behalf of a holder for any appreciation in the value of the property occurring after delivery by the holder to the state.

(c) Certificates for unclaimed stock or other equity interest of business associations that cannot be canceled and registered in the department's name or that cannot be readily liquidated and converted into the currency of the United States may be sold for the value of the certificate, if any, in accordance with subsection (1) or may be destroyed in accordance with s. 717.128.

(3) The purchaser of property at any sale conducted by the department pursuant to this chapter is entitled to ownership of the property purchased free from all claims of the owner or previous holder thereof and of all persons claiming through or under them. The department shall execute all documents necessary to complete the transfer of ownership.

(4) The sale of unclaimed tangible personal property is not subject to tax under chapter 212 when such property is sold by or on behalf of the department pursuant to this section.

History.
S. 23, ch. 87-105; s. 3, ch. 90-113; s. 12, ch. 96-301; s. 21, ch. 2001-36; s. 119, ch. 2004-390; s. 7, ch. 2005-163.

717.123. Deposit of funds.

(1) All funds received under this chapter, including the proceeds from the sale of unclaimed property under s. 717.122, shall forthwith be deposited by the department in the Unclaimed Property Trust Fund. The department shall retain, from funds received under this chapter, an amount not exceeding $15 million from which the department shall make prompt payment of claims allowed by the department and shall pay the costs incurred by the department in administering and enforcing this chapter. All remaining funds received by the department under this chapter shall be deposited by the department into the State School Fund.

(2) The department shall record the name and last known address of each person appearing from the holder's reports to be entitled to the unclaimed property in the total amounts of $5 or greater; the name and the last known address of each insured person or annuitant; and with respect to each policy or contract listed in the report of an insurance corporation, its number, the name of the corporation, and the amount due.

History.
S. 24, ch. 87-105; s. 13, ch. 96-301; s. 22, ch. 2001-36; s. 120, ch. 2004-390.

717.124. Unclaimed property claims.

(1) Any person, excluding another state, claiming an interest in any property paid or delivered to the department under this chapter may file with the department a claim on a form prescribed by the department and verified by the claimant or the claimant's representative. The claimant's representative must be an attorney licensed to practice law in this state, a licensed Florida-certified public accountant, or a private investigator licensed under chapter 493. The claimant's representative must be registered with the department under this chapter. The claimant, or the claimant's representative, shall provide the department with a legible copy of a valid driver's license of the claimant at the time the

original claim form is filed. If the claimant has not been issued a valid driver's license at the time the original claim form is filed, the department shall be provided with a legible copy of a photographic identification of the claimant issued by the United States, a state or territory of the United States, a foreign nation, or a political subdivision or agency thereof or other evidence deemed acceptable by the department by rule. In lieu of photographic identification, a notarized sworn statement by the claimant may be provided which affirms the claimant's identity and states the claimant's full name and address. The claimant must produce to the notary photographic identification of the claimant issued by the United States, a state or territory of the United States, a foreign nation, or a political subdivision or agency thereof or other evidence deemed acceptable by the department by rule. The notary shall indicate the notary's full address on the notarized sworn statement. Any claim filed without the required identification or the sworn statement with the original claim form and the original power of attorney or purchase agreement, if applicable, is void.

(a) Within 90 days after receipt of a claim, the department may return any claim that provides for the receipt of fees and costs greater than that permitted under this chapter or that contains any apparent errors or omissions. The department may also request that the claimant or the claimant's representative provide additional information. The department shall retain a copy or electronic image of the claim.

(b) A claimant or the claimant's representative shall be deemed to have withdrawn a claim if no response to the department's request for additional information is received by the department within 60 days after the notification of any apparent errors or omissions.

(c) Within 90 days after receipt of the claim, or the response of the claimant or the claimant's representative to the department's request for additional information, whichever is later, the department shall determine each claim. Such determination shall contain a notice of rights provided by ss. 120.569 and 120.57. The 90-day period shall be extended by 60 days if the department has good cause to need additional time or if the unclaimed property:

1. Is owned by a person who has been a debtor in bankruptcy;

2. Was reported with an address outside of the United States;

3. Is being claimed by a person outside of the United States; or

4. Contains documents filed in support of the claim that are not in the English language and have not been accompanied by an English language translation.

(d) The department shall deny any claim under which the claimant's representative has refused to authorize the department to reduce the fees and costs to the maximum permitted under this chapter.

(2) A claim for a cashier's check or a stock certificate without the original instrument may require an indemnity bond equal to the value of the claim to be provided prior to issue of the stock or payment of the claim by the department.

(3) The department may require an affidavit swearing to the authenticity of the claim, lack of documentation, and an agreement to allow the department to provide the name and address of the claimant to subsequent claimants coming forward with substantiated proof to claim the account. This shall apply to claims equal to or less than $250. The exclusive remedy of a subsequent claimant to the property shall be against the person who received the property from the department.

(4)(a) Except as otherwise provided in this chapter, if a claim is determined in favor of the claimant, the department shall deliver or pay over to the claimant the property or the amount the department actually received or the proceeds if it has been sold by the department, together with any additional amount required by s. 717.121.

(b) If an owner authorizes an attorney licensed to practice law in this state, Florida-certified public accountant, or private investigator licensed under chapter 493, and registered with the department under this chapter, to claim the unclaimed property on the owner's behalf, the department is authorized to make distribution of the property or money in accordance with such power of attorney. The original power of attorney must be executed by the owner and must be filed with the department.

(c)1. Payments of approved claims for unclaimed cash accounts shall be made to the owner after deducting any fees and costs authorized pursuant to a written power of attorney. The contents of a safe-deposit box shall be delivered directly to the claimant notwithstanding any power of attorney or agreement to the contrary.

2. Payments of fees and costs authorized pursuant to a written power of attorney for approved claims shall be made or issued to the law firm of the designated attorney licensed to practice law in this state, the public accountancy firm of the licensed Florida-certified public accountant, or the designated employing private investigative agency licensed by this state. Such payments shall be made by electronic funds transfer and may be made on such periodic schedule as the department may define by rule, provided the payment intervals do not exceed 31 days. Payment made to an attorney licensed in this state, a Florida-certified public accountant, or a private investigator licensed under chapter 493, operating individually or as a sole practitioner, shall be to the attorney, certified public accountant, or private investigator.

(5) The department shall not be administratively, civilly, or criminally liable for any property or funds distributed pursuant to this section, provided such distribution is made in good faith.

(6) This section does not supersede the licensing requirements of chapter 493.

History.
S. 25, ch. 87-105; s. 3, ch. 89-291; s. 8, ch. 89-299; s. 4, ch. 90-113; s. 14, ch. 96-301; s. 295, ch. 96-410; s. 31, ch. 97-93; s. 1772, ch. 97-102; s. 23, ch. 2001-36; s. 121, ch. 2004-390; s. 8, ch. 2005-163.

717.12403. Unclaimed demand, savings, or checking account in a financial institution held in the name of more than one person.

(1)(a) If an unclaimed demand, savings, or checking account in a financial institution is reported as an "and" account in the name of two or more persons who are not beneficiaries, it is presumed that each person must claim the account in order for the claim to be approved by the department. This presumption may be rebutted by showing that entitlement to the account has been transferred to another person or by clear and convincing evidence demonstrating that the account should have been reported by the financial institution as an "or" account.

(b) If an unclaimed demand, savings, or checking account in a financial institution is reported as an "and" account and one of the persons on the account is deceased, it is presumed that the account is a survivorship account. This presumption may be rebutted by showing that entitlement to the account has been transferred to another person or by clear and convincing evidence demonstrating that the account is not a survivorship account.

(2) If an unclaimed demand, savings, or checking account in a financial institution is reported as an "or" account in the name of two or more persons who are not beneficiaries, it is presumed that either person listed on the account may claim the entire amount held in the account. This presumption may be rebutted by showing that entitlement to the account has been transferred to another person or by clear and convincing evidence demonstrating that the account should have been reported by the financial institution as an "and" account.

(3) If an unclaimed demand, savings, or checking account in a financial institution is reported in the name of two or more persons who are not beneficiaries without identifying whether the account is an "and" account or an "or" account, it is presumed that the account is an "or" account. This presumption may be rebutted by showing that entitlement to the account has been transferred to another person or by clear and convincing evidence demonstrating that the account should have been reported by the financial institution as an "and" account.

(4) The department shall be deemed to have made a distribution in good faith if the department remits funds consistent with this section.

History.
S. 122, ch. 2004-390.

717.12404. Claims on behalf of a business entity or trust.

(1)(a) Claims on behalf of an active or dissolved corporation, for which the last annual report is not available from the Department of State through the Internet, must be accompanied by a microfiche copy of the records on file with the Department of State or, if the corporation has not made a corporate filing with the Department of State, the claim must be accompanied by a uniform resource locator for the address of a free Internet site operated by the state of incorporation of the corporation that provides access to the last corporate filing identifying the officers and directors of the corporation. If available, the claim must be accompanied by a printout of the officers and directors from the Department of State Internet site or the free Internet site operated by the state of incorporation of the corporation. If the free Internet site is not available, the claim must be accompanied by an authenticated copy of the last corporate filing identifying the officers and directors from the appropriate authorized official of the state of incorporation.

(b) A claim on behalf of a corporation must be made by an officer or director identified on the last corporate filing.

(2) Claims on behalf of a dissolved corporation, a business entity other than an active corporation, or a trust must include a legible copy of a valid driver's license of the person acting on behalf of the dissolved corporation, business entity other than an active corporation, or trust. If the person has not been issued a valid driver's license, the department shall be provided with a legible copy of a photographic identification of the person issued by the United States, a foreign nation, or a political subdivision or agency thereof. In lieu of photographic identification, a notarized sworn statement by the person may be provided which affirms the person's identity and states the person's full name and address. The person must produce his or her photographic identification issued by the United States, a state or territory of the United States, a foreign nation, or a political subdivision or agency thereof or other evidence deemed acceptable by the department by rule. The notary shall indicate the notary's full address on the notarized sworn statement. Any claim filed without the required identification or the sworn statement with the original claim form and the original power of attorney, if applicable, is void.

History.
S. 123, ch. 2004-390; s. 9, ch. 2005-163.

717.12405. Claims by estates.

An estate or any person representing an estate or acting on behalf of an estate may claim unclaimed property only after the heir or legatee of the decedent entitled to the property has been located. Any estate, or any person representing an estate or acting on behalf of an estate, that receives unclaimed property before the heir or legatee of the decedent entitled to the property has been located, is personally liable for the unclaimed property and must immediately return the full amount of the unclaimed property or the value thereof to the department in accordance with s. 717.1341.

History.
S. 124, ch. 2004-390.

717.12406.　Joint ownership of unclaimed securities or dividends.

For the purpose of determining joint ownership of unclaimed securities or dividends, the term:

(1) "TEN COM" means tenants in common.

(2) "TEN ENT" means tenants by the entireties.

(3) "JT TEN" or "JT" means joint tenants with the right of survivorship and not as tenants in common.

(4) "And" means tenants in common with each person entitled to an equal pro rata share.

(5) "Or" means that each person listed on the account is entitled to all of the funds.

History.
S. 10, ch. 2005-163.

717.1241.　Conflicting claims.

(1) When conflicting claims have been received by the department for the same unclaimed property account or accounts, the property shall be remitted in accordance with the claim filed by the person as follows, notwithstanding the withdrawal of a claim:

(a) To the person submitting the first claim received by the Bureau of Unclaimed Property of the department that is complete or made complete.

(b) If a claimant's claim and a claimant's representative's claim are received by the Bureau of Unclaimed Property of the department on the same day and both claims are complete, to the claimant.

(c) If a buyer's claim and a claimant's claim or a claimant's representative's claim are received by the Bureau of Unclaimed Property of the department on the same day and the claims are complete, to the buyer.

(d) As between two or more claimant's representative's claims received by the Bureau of Unclaimed Property of the department that are complete or made complete on the same day, to the claimant's representative who has agreed to receive the lowest fee. If the two or more claimant's representatives whose claims received by the Bureau of Unclaimed Property of the department were complete or made complete on the same day are charging the same lowest fee, the fee shall be divided equally between the claimant's representatives.

(e) If more than one buyer's claim received by the Bureau of Unclaimed Property of the department is complete or made complete on the same day, the department shall remit the unclaimed property to the buyer who paid the highest amount to the seller. If the buyers paid the same amount to the seller, the department shall remit the unclaimed property to the buyers divided in equal amounts.

(2) The purpose of this section is solely to provide guidance to the department regarding to whom it should remit the unclaimed property and is not intended to extinguish or affect any private cause of action that any person may have against another person for breach of contract or other statutory or common-law remedy. A buyer's sole remedy, if any, shall be against the claimant's representative or the seller, or both. A claimant's representative's sole remedy, if any, shall be against the buyer or the seller, or both. A claimant's or seller's sole remedy, if any, shall be against the buyer or the claimant's representative, or both. Nothing in this section forecloses the right of a person to challenge the department's determination of completeness in a proceeding under ss. 120.569 and 120.57.

(3) A claim is complete when entitlement to the unclaimed property has been established.

History.
S. 15, ch. 96-301; s. 24, ch. 2001-36; s. 125, ch. 2004-390; s. 11, ch. 2005-163.

717.1242.　Restatement of jurisdiction of the circuit court sitting in probate and the department.

(1) It is and has been the intent of the Legislature that, pursuant to s. 26.012(2)(b), circuit courts have jurisdiction of proceedings relating to the settlement of the estates of decedents and other jurisdiction usually pertaining to courts of probate. It is and has been the intent of the Legislature that, pursuant to s. 717.124, the department determines the merits of claims for property paid or delivered to the department under this chapter. Consistent with this legislative intent, any estate or beneficiary, as defined in s. 731.201, of an estate seeking to obtain property paid or delivered to the department under this chapter must file a claim with the department as provided in s. 717.124.

(2) If any estate or heir of an estate seeks or obtains an order from a circuit court sitting in probate directing the department to pay or deliver to any person property paid or delivered to the department under this chapter, the estate or heir shall be ordered to pay the department reasonable costs and attorney's fees in any proceeding brought by the department to oppose, appeal, or collaterally attack the order if the department is the prevailing party in any such proceeding.

History.
S. 16, ch. 96-301; s. 126, ch. 2004-390; s. 12, ch. 2005-163.

717.1243.　Small estate accounts.

(1) A claim for unclaimed property made by a beneficiary, as defined in s. 731.201, of a deceased owner need not be accompanied by an order of a probate court if the claimant files with the department an affidavit, signed by all beneficiaries, stating that all the

beneficiaries have amicably agreed among themselves upon a division of the estate and that all funeral expenses, expenses of the last illness, and any other lawful claims have been paid, and any additional information reasonably necessary to make a determination of entitlement. If the owner died testate, the claim shall be accompanied by a copy of the will.

(2) Each person receiving property under this section shall be personally liable for all lawful claims against the estate of the owner, but only to the extent of the value of the property received by such person under this section, exclusive of the property exempt from claims of creditors under the constitution and laws of this state.

(3) Any heir or devisee of the owner, who was lawfully entitled to share in the property but did not receive his or her share of the property, may enforce his or her rights in appropriate proceedings against those who received the property and shall be awarded taxable costs as in chancery actions, including attorney's fees.

(4) This section only applies if all of the unclaimed property held by the department on behalf of the owner has an aggregate value of $5,000 or less and no probate proceeding is pending.

(5) Nothing in this section shall be interpreted as precluding the use of live testimony in order to establish entitlement.

History.
S. 17, ch. 96-301; s. 25, ch. 2001-36; s. 23, ch. 2003-154; s. 13, ch. 2005-163.

Editor's Notes.
Section 23, ch. 2003-154 renacted (1) without change to incorporate amendments to statutory sections referenced therein.

717.1244. Determinations of unclaimed property claims.

In rendering a determination regarding the merits of an unclaimed property claim, the department shall rely on the applicable statutory, regulatory, common, and case law. Agency statements applying the statutory, regulatory, common, and case law to unclaimed property claims are not agency statements subject to s. 120.56(4).

History.
S. 127, ch. 2004-390.

717.1245. Garnishment of unclaimed property.

If any person files a petition for writ of garnishment seeking to obtain property paid or delivered to the department under this chapter, the petitioner shall be ordered to pay the department reasonable costs and attorney's fees in any proceeding brought by the department to oppose, appeal, or collaterally attack the petition or writ if the department is the prevailing party in any such proceeding.

History.
S. 14, ch. 2005-163.

717.125. Claim of another state to recover property; procedure.

(1) At any time after property has been paid or delivered to the department under this chapter, another state may recover the property if:

(a) The property was subjected to custody by this state because the records of the holder did not reflect the last known address of the apparent owner when the property was presumed unclaimed under this chapter, and the other state establishes that the last known address of the apparent owner or other person entitled to the property was in that state and under the laws of that state the property escheated to or was subject to a claim of abandonment or being unclaimed by that state;

(b) The last known address of the apparent owner or other person entitled to the property, as reflected by the records of the holder, is in the other state and under the laws of that state the property has escheated to or become subject to a claim of abandonment by that state;

(c) The records of the holder were erroneous in that they did not accurately reflect the actual owner of the property and the last known address of the actual owner is in the other state and under laws of that state the property escheated to or was subject to a claim of abandonment by that state;

(d) The property was subject to custody by this state under s. 717.103(6) and under the laws of the state of domicile of the holder the property has escheated to or become subject to a claim of abandonment by that state; or

(e) The property is the sum payable on a traveler's check, money order, or other similar instrument that was subjected to custody by this state under s. 717.104, and the instrument was purchased in the other state, and under the laws of that state the property escheated to or became subject to a claim of abandonment by that state.

(2) The claim of another state to recover escheated or unclaimed property under this section must be presented in a form prescribed by the department, and the department shall determine the claim within 90 days after it is presented. Such determination shall contain a notice of rights provided by ss. 120.569 and 120.57.

(3) The department shall require a state, prior to recovery of property under this section, to indemnify this state and its officers and employees against any liability on a claim for the property.

History.
S. 26, ch. 87-105; s. 296, ch. 96-410; s. 26, ch. 2001-36.

717.126. Administrative hearing; burden of proof; proof of entitlement; venue.

(1) Any person aggrieved by a decision of the department may petition for a hearing as provided in ss. 120.569 and 120.57. In any proceeding for determination of a claim to property paid or delivered to the department under this chapter, the burden shall be

upon the claimant to establish entitlement to the property by a preponderance of evidence. Having the same name as that reported to the department is not sufficient, in the absence of other evidence, to prove entitlement to unclaimed property.

(2) Unless otherwise agreed by the parties, venue shall be in Tallahassee, Leon County, Florida. However, upon the request of a party, the presiding officer may, in the presiding officer's discretion, conduct the hearing at an alternative remote video location.

History.
S. 27, ch. 87-105; s. 297, ch. 96-410; s. 128, ch. 2004-390.

717.1261.　Death certificates.

Any person who claims entitlement to unclaimed property by means of the death of one or more persons shall file a copy of the death certificate of the decedent or decedents that has been certified as being authentic by the issuing governmental agency.

History.
S. 129, ch. 2004-390.

717.1262.　Court documents.

Any person who claims entitlement to unclaimed property by reason of a court document shall file a certified copy of the court document with the department.

History.
S. 130, ch. 2004-390.

717.127.　Election to take payment or delivery.

The department may decline to receive any property reported under this chapter that the department considers to have a value less than the expense of giving notice and of sale. If the department elects not to receive custody of the property, the holder shall be notified within 120 days after filing the report required under s. 717.117 or remitting the property required under s. 717.119.

History.
S. 28, ch. 87-105; s. 18, ch. 96-301.

717.128.　Destruction or disposition of property having insubstantial commercial value; immunity from liability.

If the department after investigation finds that any property delivered under this chapter has insubstantial commercial value, the department may destroy or otherwise dispose of the property. No action or proceeding may be maintained against the state or any officer or against the holder for or on account of any action taken by the department pursuant to this section with respect to the property.

History.
S. 29, ch. 87-105.

717.129.　Periods of limitation.

(1) The expiration before or after July 1, 1987, of any period of time specified by contract, statute, or court order, during which a claim for money or property may be made or during which an action or proceeding may be commenced or enforced to obtain payment of a claim for money or to recover property, does not prevent the money or property from being presumed unclaimed or affect any duty to file a report or to pay or deliver unclaimed property to the department as required by this chapter.

(2) No action or proceeding may be commenced by the department with respect to any duty of a holder under this chapter more than 10 years after the duty arose.

History.
S. 30, ch. 87-105; s. 27, ch. 2001-36.

717.1301.　Investigations; examinations; subpoenas.

(1) The department may make investigations and examinations within or outside this state of claims, reports, and other records as it deems necessary to administer and enforce the provisions of this chapter. In such investigations and examinations the department may administer oaths, examine witnesses, issue subpoenas, and otherwise gather evidence. The department may request any person who has not filed a report under s. 717.117 to file a verified report stating whether or not the person is holding any unclaimed property reportable or deliverable under this chapter.

(2) Subpoenas for witnesses whose evidence is deemed material to any investigation or examination under this section may be issued by the department under seal of the department, or by any court of competent jurisdiction, commanding such witnesses to appear before the department at a time and place named and to bring such books, records, and documents as may be specified or to submit such books, records, and documents to inspection. Such subpoenas may be served by an authorized representative of the department.

(3) If any person shall refuse to testify, produce books, records, and documents, or otherwise refuse to obey a subpoena issued under this section, the department may present its petition to a court of competent jurisdiction in or for the county in which such person resides or has its principal place of business, whereupon the court shall issue its rule nisi requiring such person to obey forthwith the subpoena issued by the department or show cause for failing to obey said subpoena. Unless said person shows sufficient cause for failing to obey the subpoena, the court shall forthwith direct such person to obey the same subject to such punishment as the court may direct including, but not limited to, the restraint, by injunction or by appointment of a receiver, of any transfer, pledge, assignment, or other disposition of such person's assets or any concealment, alteration, destruction, or other disposition of subpoenaed books, records, or documents as the court deems appropriate, until such person has

fully complied with such subpoena and the department has completed its investigation or examination. The department is entitled to the summary procedure provided in s. 51.011, and the court shall advance the cause on its calendar. Costs incurred by the department to obtain an order granting, in whole or in part, its petition shall be taxed against the subpoenaed person, and failure to comply with such order shall be a contempt of court.

(4) Witnesses shall be entitled to the same fees and mileage as they may be entitled by law for attending as witnesses in the circuit court, except where such examination or investigation is held at the place of business or residence of the witness.

(5) The material compiled by the department in an investigation or examination under this chapter is confidential until the investigation or examination is complete. The material compiled by the department in an investigation or examination under this chapter remains confidential after the department's investigation or examination is complete if the department has submitted the material or any part of it to any law enforcement agency or other administrative agency for further investigation or for the filing of a criminal or civil prosecution and such investigation has not been completed or become inactive.

(6) If an investigation or an examination of the records of any person results in the disclosure of property reportable and deliverable under this chapter, the department may assess the cost of investigation or the examination against the holder at the rate of $100 per 8-hour day for each investigator or examiner. Such fee shall be calculated on an hourly basis and shall be rounded to the nearest hour. The person shall also pay the travel expense and per diem subsistence allowance provided for state employees in s. 112.061. The person shall not be required to pay a per diem fee and expenses of an examination or investigation which shall consume more than 30 worker-days in any one year unless such examination or investigation is due to fraudulent practices of the person, in which case such person shall be required to pay the entire cost regardless of time consumed. The fee shall be remitted to the department within 30 days after the date of the notification that the fee is due and owing. Any person who fails to pay the fee within 30 days after the date of the notification that the fee is due and owing shall pay to the department interest at the rate of 12 percent per annum on such fee from the date of the notification.

History.
S. 31, ch. 87-105; s. 1, ch. 94-262; s. 131, ch. 2004-390.

717.1311.   Retention of records.

(1) Every holder required to file a report under s. 717.117 shall maintain a record of the specific type of property, amount, name, and last known address of the owner for 5 years after the property becomes reportable, except to the extent that a shorter time is provided in subsection (2) or by rule of the department.

(2) Any business association that sells in this state its traveler's checks, money orders, or other similar written instruments, other than third-party bank checks on which the business association is directly responsible, or that provides such instruments to others for sale in this state, shall maintain a record of those instruments while they remain outstanding, indicating the state and date of issue for 3 years after the date the property is reportable.

History.
S. 32, ch. 87-105; s. 24, ch. 91-110; s. 19, ch. 96-301; s. 15, ch. 2005-163.

717.1315.   Retention of records by claimant's representatives and buyers of unclaimed property.

(1) Every claimant's representative and buyer of unclaimed property shall keep and use in his or her business such books, accounts, and records of the business conducted under this chapter to enable the department to determine whether such person is complying with this chapter and the rules adopted by the department under this chapter. Every claimant's representative and buyer of unclaimed property shall preserve such books, accounts, and records, including every power of attorney or agreement between the owner and such claimant's representative or buyer, for at least 3 years after the date of the initial power of attorney or agreement.

(2) A claimant's representative or buyer of unclaimed property, operating at two or more places of business in this state, may maintain the books, accounts, and records of all such offices at any one of such offices, or at any other office maintained by such claimant's representative or buyer of unclaimed property, upon the filing of a written notice with the department designating in the written notice the office at which such records are maintained.

(3) A claimant's representative or buyer of unclaimed property shall make all books, accounts, and records available at a convenient location in this state upon request of the department.

History.
S. 28, ch. 2001-36; s. 132, ch. 2004-390; s. 16, ch. 2005-163.

717.132.   Enforcement; cease and desist orders; fines.

(1) The department may bring an action in any court of competent jurisdiction to enforce or administer any provision of this chapter, any rule or order promulgated under this chapter, or any written agreement entered into with the department.

(2) In addition to any other powers conferred upon it to enforce and administer the provisions of this chapter, the department may issue and serve upon a person an order to cease and desist and to take corrective action whenever the department finds that such person is violating, has violated, or is about to violate any provision of this chapter, any rule or order promulgated under this chapter, or any written agreement entered

into with the department. For purposes of this subsection, the term "corrective action" includes refunding excessive charges, requiring a person to return unclaimed property, requiring a holder to remit unclaimed property, and requiring a holder to correct a report that contains errors or omissions. Any such order shall contain a notice of rights provided by ss. 120.569 and 120.57.

(3) In addition to any other powers conferred upon it to enforce and administer the provisions of this chapter, the department or a court of competent jurisdiction may impose fines against any person found to have violated any provision of this chapter, any rule or order promulgated under this chapter, or any written agreement entered into with the department in an amount not to exceed $2,000 for each violation. All fines collected under this subsection shall be deposited as received in the Unclaimed Property Trust Fund.

History.
S. 33, ch. 87-105; s. 4, ch. 93-280; s. 20, ch. 96-301; s. 298, ch. 96-410; s. 29, ch. 2001-36; s. 133, ch. 2004-390; s. 17, ch. 2005-163.

717.1322. Administrative and civil enforcement.
(1) The following acts are violations of this chapter and constitute grounds for an administrative enforcement action by the department in accordance with the requirements of chapter 120 and for civil enforcement by the department in a court of competent jurisdiction:

(a) Failure to comply with any provision of this chapter, any rule or order adopted under this chapter, or any written agreement entered into with the department.

(b) Fraud, misrepresentation, deceit, or gross negligence in any matter within the scope of this chapter.

(c) Fraudulent misrepresentation, circumvention, or concealment of any matter required to be stated or furnished to an owner or apparent owner under this chapter, regardless of reliance by or damage to the owner or apparent owner.

(d) Willful imposition of illegal or excessive charges in any unclaimed property transaction.

(e) False, deceptive, or misleading solicitation or advertising within the scope of this chapter.

(f) Failure to maintain, preserve, and keep available for examination all books, accounts, or other documents required by this chapter, by any rule or order adopted under this chapter, or by any agreement entered into with the department under this chapter.

(g) Refusal to permit inspection of books and records in an investigation or examination by the department or refusal to comply with a subpoena issued by the department under this chapter.

(h) Criminal conduct in the course of a person's business.

(i) Failure to timely pay any fine imposed or assessed under this chapter or any rule adopted under this chapter.

(j) Requesting or receiving compensation for notifying a person of his or her unclaimed property or assisting another person in filing a claim for unclaimed property, unless the person is an attorney licensed to practice law in this state, a Florida-certified public accountant, or a private investigator licensed under chapter 493, or entering into, or making a solicitation to enter into, a power of attorney to file a claim for unclaimed property owned by another, or a contract or agreement to purchase unclaimed property, unless such person is registered with the department pursuant to this chapter and an attorney licensed to practice law in this state in the regular practice of her or his profession, a Florida-certified public accountant who is acting within the scope of the practice of public accounting as defined in chapter 473, or a private investigator licensed under chapter 493. This subsection does not apply to a person who has been granted a durable power of attorney to convey and receive all of the real and personal property of the owner, is the court-appointed guardian of the owner, has been employed as an attorney or qualified representative to contest the department's denial of a claim, or has been employed as an attorney to probate the estate of the owner or an heir or legatee of the owner.

(k) Failure to authorize the release of records in the possession of a third party after being requested to do so by the department regarding a pending examination or investigation.

(l) Receipt or solicitation of consideration to be paid in advance of the approval of a claim under this chapter.

(2) Upon a finding by the department that any person has committed any of the acts set forth in subsection (1), the department may enter an order:

(a) Revoking for a minimum of 5 years or suspending for a maximum of 5 years a registration previously granted under this chapter during which time the registrant may not reapply for a registration under this chapter;

(b) Placing a registrant or an applicant for a registration on probation for a period of time and subject to such conditions as the department may specify;

(c) Placing permanent restrictions or conditions upon issuance or maintenance of a registration under this chapter;

(d) Issuing a reprimand;

(e) Imposing an administrative fine not to exceed $2,000 for each such act; or

(f) Prohibiting any person from being a director, officer, agent, employee, or ultimate equitable owner of a 10-percent or greater interest in an employer of a registrant.

(3) A registrant is subject to civil enforcement and the disciplinary actions specified in subsection (2) for violations of subsection (1) by an agent or employee of

the registrant's employer if the registrant knew or should have known that such agent or employee was violating any provision of this chapter.

(4)(a) The department shall adopt, by rule, and periodically review the disciplinary guidelines applicable to each ground for disciplinary action which may be imposed by the department under this chapter.

(b) The disciplinary guidelines shall specify a meaningful range of designated penalties based upon the severity or repetition of specific offenses, or both. It is the legislative intent that minor violations be distinguished from more serious violations; that such guidelines consider the amount of the claim involved, the complexity of locating the owner, the steps taken to ensure the accuracy of the claim by the person filing the claim, the acts of commission and omission of the ultimate owners in establishing themselves as rightful owners of the funds, the acts of commission or omission of the agent or employee of an employer in the filing of the claim, the actual knowledge of the agent, employee, employer, or owner in the filing of the claim, the departure, if any, by the agent or employee from the internal controls and procedures established by the employer with regard to the filing of a claim, the number of defective claims previously filed by the agent, employee, employer, or owner; that such guidelines provide reasonable and meaningful notice of likely penalties that may be imposed for proscribed conduct; and that such penalties be consistently applied by the department.

(c) A specific finding of mitigating or aggravating circumstances shall allow the department to impose a penalty other than that provided for in such guidelines. The department shall adopt by rule disciplinary guidelines to designate possible mitigating and aggravating circumstances and the variation and range of penalties permitted for such circumstances. Such mitigating and aggravating circumstances shall also provide for consideration of, and be consistent with, the legislative intent expressed in paragraph (b).

(d) In any proceeding brought under this chapter, the administrative law judge, in recommending penalties in any recommended order, shall follow the penalty guidelines established by the department and shall state in writing any mitigating or aggravating circumstances upon which the recommended penalty is based.

(5) The department may seek any appropriate civil legal remedy available to it by filing a civil action in a court of competent jurisdiction against any person who has, directly or through a claimant's representative, wrongfully submitted a claim as the ultimate owner of property and improperly received funds from the department in violation of this chapter.

History.
S. 134, ch. 2004-390; s. 18, ch. 2005-163.

717.1323. Prohibited practice.

No person may knowingly enter false information onto the Internet website of the Bureau of Unclaimed Property.

History.
S. 19, ch. 2005-163.

717.133. Interstate agreements and cooperation; joint and reciprocal actions with other states.

(1) The department may enter into agreements with other states to exchange information needed to enable this or another state to audit or otherwise determine unclaimed property that it or another state may be entitled to subject to a claim of custody. The department may require the reporting of information needed to enable compliance with agreements made pursuant to this section and prescribe the form.

(2) The department may join with other states to seek enforcement of this chapter against any person.

(3) At the request of another state, the department may bring an action in the name of the other state in any court of competent jurisdiction to enforce the unclaimed property laws of the other state against a holder in this state of property subject to escheat or a claim of abandonment by the other state, if the other state has agreed to pay expenses incurred in bringing the action.

(4) The department may request that the attorney general of another state or any other person bring an action in the name of the department in the other state. The department may pay all expenses including attorneys' fees in any action under this subsection.

(5) As necessary for proper administration of this chapter, the department may enter into contracts for the location or collection of property subject to payment or delivery to the department under this chapter.

History.
S. 34, ch. 87-105.

717.1331. Actions against holders.

The department may initiate, or cause to be initiated, an action against a holder to enforce a subpoena or recover unclaimed property. If the department prevails in a civil or administrative action to enforce a subpoena or recover unclaimed property initiated by or on behalf of the department, the holder shall be ordered to pay the department reasonable costs and attorney's fees.

History.
S. 135, ch. 2004-390; s. 20, ch. 2005-163.

717.1333. Evidence; estimations; audit reports, examiner's worksheets, investigative reports, other related documents.

(1) In any proceeding involving a holder under ss. 120.569 and 120.57 in which an auditor, examiner, or investigator acting under authority of this chapter is available for cross-examination, any official written report, worksheet, or other related paper, or copy thereof, compiled, prepared, drafted, or otherwise

made or received by the auditor, examiner, or investigator, after being duly authenticated by the auditor, examiner, or investigator, may be admitted as competent evidence upon the oath of the auditor, examiner, or investigator that the report, worksheet, or related paper was prepared or received as a result of an audit, examination, or investigation of the books and records of the person audited, examined, or investigated, or the agent thereof.

(2) If the records of the holder that are available for the periods subject to this chapter are insufficient to permit the preparation of a report of the unclaimed property due and owing by a holder, the amount due may be reasonably estimated.

History.
S. 136, ch. 2004-390; s. 21, ch. 2005-163.

717.134. Penalties and interest.

(1) The department may impose and collect a penalty of $500 per day up to a maximum of $5,000 and 25 percent of the value of property not reported until a report is rendered for any person who willfully fails to render any report required under this chapter. Upon a holder's showing of good cause, the department may waive said penalty or any portion thereof. If the holder acted in good faith and without negligence, the department shall waive the penalty provided herein.

(2) The department may impose and collect a penalty of $500 per day up to a maximum of $5,000 and 25 percent of the value of property not paid or delivered until the property is paid or delivered for any person who willfully refuses to pay or deliver abandoned property to the department as required under this chapter.

(3) Any person who willfully or fraudulently conceals, destroys, damages, or makes unlawful disposition of any property or of the books, records, or accounts pertaining to property which is subject to the provisions of this chapter is guilty of a misdemeanor of the second degree, punishable as provided in s. 775.082 or s. 775.083.

(4) In addition to any damages, penalties, or fines for which a person may be liable under any other provision of law, any person who fails to report or pay or deliver unclaimed property within the time prescribed by this chapter shall pay to the department interest at the rate of 12 percent per annum on such property, or value thereof, from the date such property shall have been paid or delivered. The department may waive any penalty due under this subsection with appropriate justification.

(5) The department may impose and collect a penalty of $500 per day up to a maximum of $5,000 and 25 percent of the value of property willfully not reported with all of the information required by this chapter. Upon a holder's showing of good cause, the department may waive the penalty or any portion thereof. If the holder acted in good faith and without negligence,

the department shall waive the penalty provided herein.

History.
S. 35, ch. 87-105; s. 21, ch. 96-301; s. 137, ch. 2004-390.

717.1341. Invalid claims, recovery of property, interest and penalties.

(1)(a) No person shall receive unclaimed property that the person is not entitled to receive. Any person who receives, or assists another person to receive, unclaimed property that the person is not entitled to receive is strictly, jointly, personally, and severally liable for the unclaimed property and shall immediately return the property, or the reasonable value of the property if the property has been damaged or disposed of, to the department plus interest at the rate set in accordance with s. 55.03(1). Assisting another person to receive unclaimed property includes executing a claim form on the person's behalf.

(b)1. In the case of stocks or bonds which have been sold, the proceeds from the sale shall be returned to the department plus any dividends or interest received thereon plus an amount equal to the brokerage fee plus interest at a rate set in accordance with s. 55.03(1) on the proceeds from the sale of the stocks or bonds, the dividends or interest received, and the brokerage fee.

2. In the case of stocks or bonds which have not been sold, the stocks or bonds and any dividends or interest received thereon shall be returned to the department, together with interest on the dividends or interest received, at a rate set in accordance with s. 55.03(1) of the value of the property.

(2) The department may maintain a civil or administrative action:

(a) To recover unclaimed property that was paid or remitted to a person who was not entitled to the unclaimed property or to offset amounts owed to the department against amounts owed to an owner representative;

(b) Against a person who assists another person in receiving, or attempting to receive, unclaimed property that the person is not entitled to receive; or

(c) Against a person who attempts to receive unclaimed property that the person is not entitled to receive.

(3) If the department prevails in any proceeding under subsection (2), a fine not to exceed three times the value of the property received or sought to be received may be imposed on any person who knowingly, or with reckless disregard or deliberate ignorance of the truth, violated this section. If the department prevails in a civil or administrative proceeding under subsection (2), the person who violated subsection (1) shall be ordered to pay the department reasonable costs and attorney's fees.

(4) No person shall knowingly file, knowingly conspire to file, or knowingly assist in filing, a claim for unclaimed property the person is not entitled to receive. Any person who violates this subsection regarding unclaimed property of an aggregate value:

(a) Greater than $50,000, is guilty of a felony of the first degree, punishable as provided in s. 775.082, s. 775.083, or s. 775.084;

(b) Greater than $10,000 up to $50,000, is guilty of a felony of the second degree, punishable as provided in s. 775.082, s. 775.083, or s. 775.084;

(c) Greater than $250 up to $10,000, is guilty of a felony of the third degree, punishable as provided in s. 775.082, s. 775.083, or s. 775.084;

(d) Greater than $50 up to $250, is guilty of a misdemeanor of the first degree, punishable as provided in s. 775.082 or s. 775.083; or

(e) Up to $50, is guilty of a misdemeanor of the second degree, punishable as provided in s. 775.082 or s. 775.083.

History.
S. 138, ch. 2004-390; s. 2, ch. 2011-169, eff. July 1, 2011.

717.135. Power of attorney to recover reported property in the custody of the department.

(1) A power of attorney executed by a claimant to a claimant's representative for compensation to recover or assist in the recovery of property reported to the department under s. 717.117 shall be in 10-point type or greater.

(2) A power of attorney described in subsection (1) must:

(a) Limit the fees and costs for services to 20 percent per unclaimed property account held by the department. Fees and costs for cash accounts shall be based on the value of the property at the time the power of attorney is signed by the claimant. Fees and costs for accounts containing securities or other intangible ownership interests, which securities or interests are not converted to cash, shall be based on the purchase price of the security as quoted on a national exchange or other market on which the property is regularly traded at the time the securities or other ownership interest is remitted to the claimant or the claimant's representative. Fees and costs for tangible property or safe-deposit box accounts shall be based on the value of the tangible property or contents of the safe-deposit box at the time the ownership interest is transferred or remitted to the claimant. Total fees and costs on any single account owned by a natural person residing in this country must not exceed $1,000; or

(b) Fully disclose that the property is held by the Bureau of Unclaimed Property of the Department of Financial Services pursuant to this chapter, the mailing address of the bureau, the Internet address of the bureau, the person or name of the entity that held the property prior to the property becoming unclaimed, the date of the holder's last contact with the owner, if known, and the approximate value of the property, and identify which of the following categories of unclaimed property the claimant's representative is seeking to recover, as reported by the holder:

1. Cash accounts.
2. Stale dated checks.
3. Life insurance or annuity contract assets.
4. Utility deposits.
5. Securities or other interests in business associations.
6. Wages.
7. Accounts receivable.
8. Contents of safe-deposit boxes.

This subsection shall not apply if probate proceedings must be initiated on behalf of the claimant for an estate that has never been probated or if the unclaimed property is being claimed by a person outside of the United States.

(3)(a) A power of attorney described in paragraph (2)(b) must state in 12-point type or greater in the order indicated with the blank spaces accurately completed:

FULL DISCLOSURE STATEMENT

The property is currently held by the State of Florida Department of Financial Services, Bureau of Unclaimed Property, pursuant to chapter 717, Florida Statutes. The mailing address of the Bureau of Unclaimed Property is _____. The Internet address of the Bureau of Unclaimed Property is

_____.

The property was Remitted by: _____.

Date of last contact: _____.

Property category: _____.

(b) Immediately above the signature line for the claimant, a power of attorney described in paragraph (2)(b) must state in 12-point type or greater:

Claimant agrees, by signing below, that the FULL DISCLOSURE STATEMENT has been read and fully understood.

(4)(a) Powers of attorney for recovery of cash accounts shall state the value of the unclaimed property, the unclaimed property account number, and the percentage value of the unclaimed property account to be paid to the claimant and shall also state the percentage value of compensation to be paid to the claimant's representative, if applicable.

(b) Powers of attorney for recovery of accounts containing securities, safe-deposit box accounts, other intangible or tangible ownership interests, or other types of accounts, except cash accounts, shall state the unclaimed property account number, the number of shares of stock, if applicable, the approximate value of the unclaimed property, and the percentage value of compensation to be paid to the claimant's representative, if applicable.

(c) All powers of attorney shall include:

1. The name and professional license number of the claimant's representative.

2. The name, address, and telephone number of the claimant's representative's firm or employer.

3. The name, address, and telephone number of the claimant.

4. If applicable, the taxpayer identification number or social security number, address, and telephone number of the claimant.

5. The name and address to whom the warrant is to be issued, if different than the claimant's name and address.

(d) The original of all such disclosures and powers of attorney shall be signed and dated by the claimant of the property and shall be filed with the claim form.

(e) All powers of attorney executed by a claimant to a claimant's representative for compensation to recover or assist in the recovery of property reported to the department under s. 717.117 must use the following form on 8 and -inch by 11-inch paper or on 8 and -inch by 14-inch paper with all of the text on one side of the paper and with the other side of the paper left blank. The power of attorney must be accurately completed and executed. The title of the power of attorney shall be in bold 14-point type or greater and underlined. Except as otherwise provided in this section, the rest of the power of attorney shall be in 10-point type or greater. All unclaimed property accounts claimed must be identified on the power of attorney by account number. The power of attorney must state in bold 12-point type or greater at the top of the power of attorney in the order indicated:

LIMITED POWER OF ATTORNEY

$ _____ = Approximate Dollar Value of the Property

_____ = Number of Shares of Stock to be Recovered (If Applicable)

_____ Percent to be Paid as Compensation to the Claimant's Representative

$ _____ = Amount to be Paid to Claimant's Representative

$ _____ = Net Amount to be Paid to Claimant

Property Account Numbers: _____

(f) All fees, whether expressed as a percentage or as a flat fee, are subject to the limitations and requirements of subsection (2).

(g) This section does not prohibit the:

1. Use of bolding, italics, print of different colors, and text borders as a means of highlighting or stressing certain selected items within the text.

2. Placement of the name, address, and telephone number of the representative's firm or company in the top margin above the words "POWER OF ATTORNEY." No additional writing of any kind may be placed in the top margin including, but not limited to, logos, license numbers, Internet addresses, or slogans.

3. Placement of the word "pending" prior to the words "NET AMOUNT TO BE PAID TO CLAIMANT," if it is not yet possible to determine the percentage interest of an heir or legatee prior to a determination on the issue by the probate court.

4. Deletion of the words "Number of Shares of Stock (If Applicable)" if the agreement does not relate to the recovery of securities.

5. Deletion of the words "Percent to Be Paid as Compensation to Claimant's Representative" if the power of attorney provides for a flat fee to be paid as compensation to the claimant's representative.

(5) As used in this section, "claimant" means the person on whose behalf a claim is filed.

(6) This section does not supersede the licensing requirements of chapter 493.

History.
S. 36, ch. 87-105; s. 1, ch. 91-261; s. 2, ch. 94-191; s. 22, ch. 96-301; s. 30, ch. 2001-36; s. 1889, ch. 2003-261; s. 139, ch. 2004-390; s. 22, ch. 2005-163.

717.1351. Acquisition of unclaimed property.

(1) A person desiring to acquire ownership of or entitlement to property reported to the department under s. 717.117 must be an attorney licensed to practice law in this state, a licensed Florida-certified public accountant, a private investigator licensed under chapter 493, or an employer of a licensed private investigator which employer possesses a Class "A" license under chapter 493 and must be registered with the department under this chapter.

(2) All contracts to acquire ownership of or entitlement to unclaimed property from the person or persons entitled to the unclaimed property must be in 10-point type or greater and must:

(a) Have a purchase price that discounts the value of the unclaimed property at the time the agreement is executed by the seller at no greater than 20 percent per account held by the department. An unclaimed property account must not be discounted in excess of $1,000. However, the $1,000 discount limitation does not apply if probate proceedings must be initiated on behalf of the seller for an estate that has never been probated or if the seller of the unclaimed property is not a natural person or is a person outside the United States; or

(b) Fully disclose that the property is held by the Bureau of Unclaimed Property of the Department of Financial Services pursuant to this chapter, the mailing address of the bureau, the Internet address of the bureau, the person or name of the entity that held the property prior to the property becoming unclaimed, the date of the holder's last contact with the owner, if known, and the approximate value of the property, and identify which of the following categories of unclaimed property the buyer is seeking to purchase as reported by the holder:

    1. Cash accounts.

    2. Stale dated checks.

    3. Life insurance or annuity contract assets.

    4. Utility deposits.

    5. Securities or other interests in business associations.

    6. Wages.

    7. Accounts receivable.

    8. Contents of safe-deposit boxes.

The purchase agreement described in this paragraph must state in 12-point type or greater in the order indicated with the blank spaces accurately completed:

FULL DISCLOSURE STATEMENT

The property is currently held by the State of Florida Department of Financial Services, Bureau of Unclaimed Property, pursuant to chapter 717, Florida Statutes. The mailing address of the Bureau of Unclaimed Property is _____. The Internet address of the Bureau of Unclaimed Property is _____.

The property was remitted by: _____.

Date of last contact: _____.

Property category: _____.

Immediately above the signature line for the seller, the purchase agreement described in this paragraph must state in 12-point type or greater:

Seller agrees, by signing below, that the FULL DISCLOSURE STATEMENT has been read and fully understood.

(3) The originals of all such disclosures and agreements to transfer ownership of or entitlement to unclaimed property shall be signed and dated by the seller and shall be filed with the claim form. The claimant shall provide the department with a legible copy of a valid driver's license of the seller at the time the original claim form is filed. If a seller has not been issued a valid driver's license at the time the original claim form is filed, the department shall be provided with a legible copy of a photographic identification of the seller issued by the United States or a foreign nation, a state or territory of the United States or a foreign nation, or a political subdivision or agency thereof. In lieu of photographic identification, a notarized sworn statement by the seller may be provided which affirms the seller's identity and states the seller's full name and address. The seller must produce to the

notary his or her photographic identification issued by the United States, a state or territory of the United States, a foreign nation, or a political subdivision or agency thereof or other evidence deemed acceptable by department rule. The notary shall indicate the notary's full address on the notarized sworn statement. If a claim is filed without the required identification or the sworn statement with the original claim form and the original agreement to acquire ownership of or entitlement to the unclaimed property, the claim is void.

(4) Any contract to acquire ownership of or entitlement to unclaimed property from the person or persons entitled to the unclaimed property must provide for the purchase price to be remitted to the seller or sellers within 10 days after the execution of the contract by the seller or sellers. The contract must specify the unclaimed property account number, the name of the holder who reported the property to the department, the category of unclaimed property, the value of the unclaimed property account, and the number of shares of stock, if applicable. Proof of payment by check must be filed with the department with the claim.

(5) All agreements to purchase unclaimed property from an owner must use the following form on 8 and -inch by 11-inch paper or on 8 and -inch by 14-inch paper with all of the text on one side of the paper and with the other side of the paper left blank. The agreement must be accurately completed and executed. The title of the agreement shall be in bold 14-point type or greater and underlined. Except as otherwise provided in this section, the rest of the agreement shall be in 10-point type or greater. All unclaimed property accounts to be purchased must be identified on the agreement by account number. The agreement must state, in bold 12-point type or greater at the top of the agreement in the order indicated:

PURCHASE AGREEMENT

$ _____ = Approximate Dollar Value of the Property

_____ = Number of Shares of Stock (If Applicable)

_____ = Percent of Property to be Paid to the Buyer

$ _____ = Amount to be Paid to Buyer

$ _____ = Net Amount to be Paid to Seller

Property Account Number(s): _____

    (6) All agreements shall include:

      (a) The name and professional license number of the registrant.

      (b) The name, address, and telephone number of the registrant's firm or employer.

      (c) The name, address, and telephone number of the seller.

      (d) The taxpayer identification number or social security number of the seller, if available.

      (e) The name and address to whom the warrant is to be issued if it is different from the seller's name and address.

(f) The original signature of the registrant and the date signed by the registrant.

(7) This section does not prohibit the:

(a) Use of bolding, italics, print of different colors, or text borders as a means of highlighting or stressing certain selected items within the text.

(b) Placement of the name, address, and telephone number of the registrant's firm or company in the top margin above the words "PURCHASE AGREEMENT." No additional writing of any kind may be placed in the top margin, including, but not limited to, logos, license numbers, Internet addresses, or slogans.

(c) Deletion of the words "Number of Shares of Stock (If Applicable)" if the agreement does not relate to the recovery of securities.

(d) Deletion of the words "Percent of Property to be Paid to Buyer," if the purchase agreement provides for a flat fee to be paid as compensation to the buyer.

(8) This section does not supersede the licensing requirements of chapter 493.

History.
S. 140, ch. 2004-390; s. 23, ch. 2005-163.

717.1355. Theme park and entertainment complex tickets.

This chapter does not apply to any tickets for admission to a theme park or entertainment complex as defined in s. 509.013(9), or to any tickets to a permanent exhibition or recreational activity within such theme park or entertainment complex.

History.
S. 23, ch. 96-301.

717.136. Foreign transactions.

This chapter does not apply to any property held, due, and owing in a foreign country and arising out of foreign transaction.

History.
S. 37, ch. 87-105.

717.138. Rulemaking authority.

The department shall administer and provide for the enforcement of this chapter. The department has authority to adopt rules pursuant to ss. 120.536(1) and 120.54 to implement the provisions of this chapter. The department may adopt rules to allow for electronic filing of fees, forms, and reports required by this chapter.

History.
S. 39, ch. 87-105; s. 220, ch. 98-200; s. 31, ch. 2001-36; s. 1890, ch. 2003-261.

717.1381. Void unclaimed property powers of attorney and purchase agreements.

(1) Protecting the interests of owners of unclaimed property is declared to be the public policy of this state. It is in the best interests of the owners of unclaimed property that they have the opportunity to receive the full amount of the unclaimed property returned to them without deduction of any fees. Further, it is specifically recognized that the Legislature has mandated and the state has an obligation to make a meaningful and active effort to notify owners concerning their unclaimed property. The state recognizes that this policy and obligation cannot be fulfilled without providing the state with the first opportunity to notify the owners of unclaimed property that they may file a claim for their property with the department. In furtherance of this policy and obligation:

(a) Any oral or written agreement or power of attorney for compensation or gain or in the expectation of compensation or gain, that includes an unclaimed property account valued at more than $250 which was made on or before 45 days after the holder or examination report was processed and added to the unclaimed property database, subsequent to a determination that the report was accurate and that the reported property was the same as the remitted property, is void as contrary to public policy.

(b) Any oral or written purchase agreement that includes an unclaimed property account valued at more than $250, owned by another and made on or before 45 days after the holder or examination report was processed and added to the unclaimed property database, subsequent to a determination that the report was accurate and that the reported property was the same as the remitted property, is void as contrary to public policy.

(2) A person may not enter into a power of attorney or an agreement, or make a solicitation to enter into a power of attorney or an agreement, that is void under this section.

History.
S. 24, ch. 2005-163.

717.139. Uniformity of application and construction.

This chapter shall be applied and construed as to effectuate its general purpose of protecting the interest of missing owners of property, while providing that the benefit of all unclaimed and abandoned property shall go to all the people of the state, and to make uniform the law with respect to the subject of this chapter among states enacting it.

History.
S. 40, ch. 87-105.

717.1400. Registration.

(1) In order to file claims as a claimant's representative, acquire ownership of or entitlement to unclaimed property, receive a distribution of fees and costs from the department, and obtain unclaimed property dollar amounts, numbers of reported shares of stock, and social security numbers held by the department, a private investigator holding a Class "C" individual license under chapter 493 must register with the department on such form as the department shall

prescribe by rule, and must be verified by the applicant. To register with the department, a private investigator must provide:

(a) A legible copy of the applicant's Class "A" business license under chapter 493 or that of the applicant's firm or employer which holds a Class "A" business license under chapter 493.

(b) A legible copy of the applicant's Class "C" individual license issued under chapter 493.

(c) The business address and telephone number of the applicant's private investigative firm or employer.

(d) The names of agents or employees, if any, who are designated to act on behalf of the private investigator, together with a legible copy of their photo identification issued by an agency of the United States, or a state, or a political subdivision thereof.

(e) Sufficient information to enable the department to disburse funds by electronic funds transfer.

(f) The tax identification number of the private investigator's firm or employer which holds a Class "A" business license under chapter 493.

(2) In order to file claims as a claimant's representative, acquire ownership of or entitlement to unclaimed property, receive a distribution of fees and costs from the department, and obtain unclaimed property dollar amounts, numbers of reported shares of stock, and social security numbers held by the department, a Florida-certified public accountant must register with the department on such form as the department shall prescribe by rule, and must be verified by the applicant. To register with the department a Florida-certified public accountant must provide:

(a) The applicant's Florida Board of Accountancy number.

(b) A legible copy of the applicant's current driver's license showing the full name and current address of such person. If a current driver's license is not available, another form of identification showing the full name and current address of such person or persons shall be filed with the department.

(c) The business address and telephone number of the applicant's public accounting firm or employer.

(d) The names of agents or employees, if any, who are designated to act on behalf of the Florida-certified public accountant, together with a legible copy of their photo identification issued by an agency of the United States, or a state, or a political subdivision thereof.

(e) Sufficient information to enable the department to disburse funds by electronic funds transfer.

(f) The tax identification number of the accountant's public accounting firm employer.

(3) In order to file claims as a claimant's representative, acquire ownership of or entitlement to unclaimed property, receive a distribution of fees and costs from the department, and obtain unclaimed property dollar amounts, numbers of reported shares of stock, and social security numbers held by the department, an attorney licensed to practice in this state must register with the department on such form as the department shall prescribe by rule, and must be verified by the applicant. To register with the department, such attorney must provide:

(a) The applicant's Florida Bar number.

(b) A legible copy of the applicant's current driver's license showing the full name and current address of such person. If a current driver's license is not available, another form of identification showing the full name and current address of such person or persons shall be filed with the department.

(c) The business address and telephone number of the applicant's firm or employer.

(d) The names of agents or employees, if any, who are designated to act on behalf of the attorney, together with a legible copy of their photo identification issued by an agency of the United States, or a state, or a political subdivision thereof.

(e) Sufficient information to enable the department to disburse funds by electronic funds transfer.

(f) The tax identification number of the attorney's firm or employer.

(4) Information and documents already on file with the department prior to the effective date of this provision need not be resubmitted in order to complete the registration.

(5) If a material change in the status of a registration occurs, a registrant must, within 30 days, provide the department with the updated documentation and information in writing. Material changes include, but are not limited to: a designated agent or employee ceasing to act on behalf of the designating person, a surrender, suspension, or revocation of a license, or a license renewal.

(a) If a designated agent or employee ceases to act on behalf of the person who has designated the agent or employee to act on such person's behalf, the designating person must, within 30 days, inform the Bureau of Unclaimed Property in writing of the termination of agency or employment.

(b) If a registrant surrenders the registrant's license or the license is suspended or revoked, the registrant must, within 30 days, inform the bureau in writing of the surrender, suspension, or revocation.

(c) If a private investigator's Class "C" individual license under chapter 493 or a private investigator's employer's Class "A" business license under chapter 493 is renewed, the private investigator must provide a copy of the renewed license to the department within 30 days after the receipt of the renewed license by the private investigator or the private investigator's employer.

(6) A registrant's firm or employer may not have a name that might lead another person to conclude that the registrant's firm or employer is affiliated or associ-

ated with the United States, or an agency thereof, or a state or an agency or political subdivision of a state. The department shall deny an application for registration or revoke a registration if the applicant's or registrant's firm or employer has a name that might lead another person to conclude that the firm or employer is affiliated or associated with the United States, or an agency thereof, or a state or an agency or political subdivision of a state. Names that might lead another person to conclude that the firm or employer is affiliated or associated with the United States, or an agency thereof, or a state or an agency or political subdivision of a state, include, but are not limited to, the words United States, Florida, state, bureau, division, department, or government.

(7) The licensing and other requirements of this section must be maintained as a condition of registration with the department.

History.
S. 141, ch. 2004-390; s. 133, ch. 2005-2; s. 25, ch. 2005-163.

717.1401. Repeal.

This chapter shall not repeal, but shall be additional and supplemental to the existing provisions of ss. 43.18, 43.19, and 402.17 and chapter 716.

History.
S. 41, ch. 87-105; s. 62, ch. 92-348.

TITLE XLII.

ESTATES AND TRUSTS

CHAPTER 731.
PROBATE CODE: GENERAL PROVISIONS

PART I.
SHORT TITLE; CONSTRUCTION.

731.005. Short title.

Chapters 731-735 shall be known and may be cited as the Florida Probate Code and referred to as the "code."

History.
S. 1, ch. 74-106; s. 1, ch. 75-220; s. 4, ch. 2001-226.

731.011. Determination of substantive rights; procedures.

The code became effective on January 1, 1976. The substantive rights of all persons that vested prior to January 1, 1976, shall be determined as provided in former chapters 731-737 and 744-746. The procedures for the enforcement of vested substantive rights shall be as provided in the Florida Probate Rules.

History.
S. 4, ch. 74-106; ss. 2, 113, ch. 75-220; s. 5, ch. 2001-226.

731.102. Construction against implied repeal.

This code is intended as unified coverage of its subject matter. No part of it shall be impliedly repealed by subsequent legislation if that construction can reasonably be avoided.

History.
S. 1, ch. 74-106; s. 2, ch. 75-220.

731.103. Evidence as to death or status.

In proceedings under this code and under chapter 736, the following additional rules relating to determination of death and status are applicable:

(1) An authenticated copy of a death certificate issued by an official or agency of the place where the death purportedly occurred is prima facie proof of the fact, place, date, and time of death and the identity of the decedent.

(2) A copy of any record or report of a governmental agency, domestic or foreign, that a person is alive, missing, detained, or, from the facts related, presumed dead is prima facie evidence of the status and of the dates, circumstances, and places disclosed by the record or report.

(3) A person who is absent from the place of his or her last known domicile for a continuous period of 5 years and whose absence is not satisfactorily explained after diligent search and inquiry is presumed to be dead. The person's death is presumed to have occurred at the end of the period unless there is evidence establishing that death occurred earlier. Evidence showing that the absent person was exposed to a specific peril of death may be a sufficient basis for the court determining at any time after such exposure that he or she died less than 5 years after the date on which his or her absence commenced. A petition for this determination shall be filed in the county in Florida where the decedent maintained his or her domicile or in any county of this state if the decedent was not a resident of Florida at the time his or her absence commenced.

(4) This section does not preclude the establishment of death by direct or circumstantial evidence prior to expiration of the 5-year time period set forth in subsection (3).

History.
S. 1, ch. 74-106; s. 2, ch. 75-220; s. 946, ch. 97-102; s. 1, ch. 2003-154; s. 27, ch. 2006-217, eff. July 1, 2007.
Editor's Notes.
Created from former s. 734.34.

731.1035. Applicable rules of evidence.

In proceedings under this code, the rules of evidence in civil actions are applicable unless specifically changed by the code.

History.
S. 28, ch. 2006-217, eff. July 1, 2007.

731.104. Verification of documents.

When verification of a document is required in this code or by rule, the document filed shall include an oath or affirmation as provided in the Florida Probate Rules. Any person who willfully includes a false statement in the document shall be guilty of perjury.

History.
S. 1, ch. 74-106; s. 2, ch. 75-220; s. 6, ch. 2001-226.

731.105. In rem proceeding.

Probate proceedings are in rem proceedings.

History.
S. 3, ch. 75-220.

731.106. Assets of nondomiciliaries.

(1) A debt in favor of a nondomiciliary, other than one evidenced by investment or commercial paper or other instrument, is located in the county where the debtor resides or, if the debtor is not an individual, at

the place where the debtor has its principal office. Commercial paper, investment paper, and other instruments are located where the instrument is at the time of death.

(2) When a nonresident decedent, whether or not a citizen of the United States, provides by will that the testamentary disposition of tangible or intangible personal property having a situs within this state, or of real property in this state, shall be construed and regulated by the laws of this state, the validity and effect of the dispositions shall be determined by Florida law. The court may, and in the case of a decedent who was at the time of death a resident of a foreign country the court shall, direct the personal representative appointed in this state to make distribution directly to those designated by the decedent's will as beneficiaries of the tangible or intangible property or to the persons entitled to receive the decedent's personal estate under the laws of the decedent's domicile.

History.
S. 3, ch. 75-220; s. 1, ch. 77-174; s. 947, ch. 97-102; s. 7, ch. 2001-226.

731.109. Seal of the court.

For the purposes of this code, the seal of the clerk of the circuit court is the seal of the court.

History.
S. 3, ch. 75-220.

731.110. Caveat; proceedings.

(1) Any interested person who is apprehensive that an estate, either testate or intestate, will be administered or that a will may be admitted to probate without that person's knowledge may file a caveat with the court. The caveat of the interested person, other than a creditor, may be filed before or after the death of the person for whom the estate will be, or is being, administered. The caveat of a creditor may be filed only after the person's death.

(2) If the caveator is a nonresident and is not represented by an attorney admitted to practice in this state who has signed the caveat, the caveator must designate some person residing in the county in which the caveat is filed as the agent of the caveator, upon whom service may be made; however, if the caveator is represented by an attorney admitted to practice in this state who has signed the caveat, it is not necessary to designate a resident agent.

(3) If a caveat has been filed by an interested person other than a creditor, the court may not admit a will of the decedent to probate or appoint a personal representative until formal notice of the petition for administration has been served on the caveator or the caveator's designated agent and the caveator has had the opportunity to participate in proceedings on the petition, as provided by the Florida Probate Rules.

(4) A caveat filed before the death of the person for whom the estate will be administered expires 2 years after filing.

History.
S. 3, ch. 75-220; s. 2, ch. 77-87; s. 1, ch. 85-79; s. 2, ch. 92-200; s. 948, ch. 97-102; s. 9, ch. 2001-226; s. 2, ch. 2007-74, eff. July 1, 2007; s. 3, ch. 2010-132, eff. Oct. 1, 2010.

731.155. Applicability.

This act shall take effect January 1, 2002. The substantive rights of all persons that have vested prior to January 1, 2002, shall be determined as provided in former chapters 63, 215, 409, 660, and 731-737 as they existed prior to January 1, 2002. The procedures for the enforcement of substantive rights which have vested prior to January 1, 2002, shall be as provided in this act, except that any Family Administration filed before January 1, 2002, may be completed as a Family Administration.

History.
S. 195, ch. 2001-226.

PART II.
DEFINITIONS.

731.201. General definitions.

Subject to additional definitions in subsequent chapters that are applicable to specific chapters or parts, and unless the context otherwise requires, in this code, in s. 409.9101, and in chapters 736, 738, 739, and 744, the term:

(1) "Authenticated," when referring to copies of documents or judicial proceedings required to be filed with the court under this code, means a certified copy or a copy authenticated according to the Federal Rules of Civil Procedure.

(2) "Beneficiary" means heir at law in an intestate estate and devisee in a testate estate. The term "beneficiary" does not apply to an heir at law or a devisee after that person's interest in the estate has been satisfied. In the case of a devise to an existing trust or trustee, or to a trust or trustee described by will, the trustee is a beneficiary of the estate. Except as otherwise provided in this subsection, the beneficiary of the trust is not a beneficiary of the estate of which that trust or the trustee of that trust is a beneficiary. However, if each trustee is also a personal representative of the estate, each qualified beneficiary of the trust as defined in s. 736.0103(14) shall be regarded as a beneficiary of the estate.

(3) "Child" includes a person entitled to take as a child under this code by intestate succession from the parent whose relationship is involved, and excludes any person who is only a stepchild, a foster child, a grandchild, or a more remote descendant.

(4) "Claim" means a liability of the decedent, whether arising in contract, tort, or otherwise, and funeral expense. The term does not include an expense of administration or estate, inheritance, succession, or other death taxes.

(5) "Clerk" means the clerk or deputy clerk of the court.

(6) "Collateral heir" means an heir who is related to the decedent through a common ancestor but who is not an ancestor or descendant of the decedent.

(7) "Court" means the circuit court.

(8) "Curator" means a person appointed by the court to take charge of the estate of a decedent until letters are issued.

(9) "Descendant" means a person in any generational level down the applicable individual's descending line and includes children, grandchildren, and more remote descendants. The term "descendant" is synonymous with the terms "lineal descendant" and "issue" but excludes collateral heirs.

(10) "Devise," when used as a noun, means a method testamentary disposition of real or personal property and, when used as a verb, means to dispose of real or personal property by will or trust. The term includes "gift," "give," "bequeath," "bequest," and "legacy." A devise is subject to charges for debts, expenses, and taxes as provided in this code, the will, or the trust.

(11) "Devisee" means a person designated in a will or trust to receive a devise. Except as otherwise provided in this subsection, in the case of a devise to an existing trust or trustee, or to a trust or trustee of a trust described by will, the trust or trustee, rather than the beneficiaries of the trust, is the devisee. However, if each trustee is also a personal representative of the estate, each qualified beneficiary of the trust as defined in s. 736.0103(14) shall be regarded as a devisee.

(12) "Distributee" means a person who has received estate property from a personal representative or other fiduciary other than as a creditor or purchaser. A testamentary trustee is a distributee only to the extent of distributed assets or increments to them remaining in the trustee's hands. A beneficiary of a testamentary trust to whom the trustee has distributed property received from a personal representative is a distributee. For purposes of this provision, "testamentary trustee" includes a trustee to whom assets are transferred by will, to the extent of the devised assets.

(13) "Domicile" means a person's usual place of dwelling and shall be synonymous with residence.

(14) "Estate" means the property of a decedent that is the subject of administration.

(15) "Exempt property" means the property of a decedent's estate which is described in s. 732.402.

(16) "File" means to file with the court or clerk.

(17) "Foreign personal representative" means a personal representative of another state or a foreign country.

(18) "Formal notice" means a form of notice that is described in and served by a method of service provided under rule 5.040(a) of the Florida Probate Rules.

(19) "Grantor" means one who creates or adds to a trust and includes "settlor" or "trustor" and a testator who creates or adds to a trust.

(20) "Heirs" or "heirs at law" means those persons, including the surviving spouse, who are entitled under the statutes of intestate succession to the property of a decedent.

(21) "Incapacitated" means a judicial determination that a person lacks the capacity to manage at least some of the person's property or to meet at least some of the person's essential health and safety requirements. A minor shall be treated as being incapacitated.

(22) "Informal notice" or "notice" means a method of service for pleadings or papers as provided under rule 5.040(b) of the Florida Probate Rules.

(23) "Interested person" means any person who may reasonably be expected to be affected by the outcome of the particular proceeding involved. In any proceeding affecting the estate or the rights of a beneficiary in the estate, the personal representative of the estate shall be deemed to be an interested person. In any proceeding affecting the expenses of the administration and obligations of a decedent's estate, or any claims described in s. 733.702(1), the trustee of a trust described in s. 733.707(3) is an interested person in the administration of the grantor's estate. The term does not include a beneficiary who has received complete distribution. The meaning, as it relates to particular persons, may vary from time to time and must be determined according to the particular purpose of, and matter involved in, any proceedings.

(24) "Letters" means authority granted by the court to the personal representative to act on behalf of the estate of the decedent and refers to what has been known as letters testamentary and letters of administration. All letters shall be designated "letters of administration."

(25) "Minor" means a person under 18 years of age whose disabilities have not been removed by marriage or otherwise.

(26) "Other state" means any state of the United States other than Florida and includes the District of Columbia, the Commonwealth of Puerto Rico, and any territory or possession subject to the legislative authority of the United States.

(27) "Parent" excludes any person who is only a stepparent, foster parent, or grandparent.

(28) "Personal representative" means the fiduciary appointed by the court to administer the estate and refers to what has been known as an administrator, administrator cum testamento annexo, administrator de bonis non, ancillary administrator, ancillary executor, or executor.

(29) "Petition" means a written request to the court for an order.

(30) "Power of appointment" means an authority, other than as an incident of the beneficial ownership of property, to designate recipients of beneficial interests in property.

(31) "Probate of will" means all steps necessary to establish the validity of a will and to admit a will to probate.

(32) "Property" means both real and personal property or any interest in it and anything that may be the subject of ownership.

(33) "Protected homestead" means the property described in s. 4(a)(1), Art. X of the State Constitution on which at the death of the owner the exemption inures to the owner's surviving spouse or heirs under s. 4(b), Art. X of the State Constitution. For purposes of the code, real property owned in tenancy by the entireties or in joint tenancy with rights of survivorship is not protected homestead.

(34) "Residence" means a person's place of dwelling.

(35) "Residuary devise" means a devise of the assets of the estate which remain after the provision for any devise which is to be satisfied by reference to a specific property or type of property, fund, sum, or statutory amount. If the will contains no devise which is to be satisfied by reference to a specific property or type of property, fund, sum, or statutory amount, "residuary devise" or "residue" means a devise of all assets remaining after satisfying the obligations of the estate.

(36) "Security" means a security as defined in s. 517.021.

(37) "Security interest" means a security interest as defined in s. 671.201.

(38) "Trust" means an express trust, private or charitable, with additions to it, wherever and however created. It also includes a trust created or determined by a judgment or decree under which the trust is to be administered in the manner of an express trust. "Trust" excludes other constructive trusts, and it excludes resulting trusts; conservatorships; custodial arrangements pursuant to the Florida Uniform Transfers to Minors Act; business trusts providing for certificates to be issued to beneficiaries; common trust funds; land trusts under s. 689.071, except to the extent provided in s. 689.071(7); trusts created by the form of the account or by the deposit agreement at a financial institution; voting trusts; security arrangements; liquidation trusts; trusts for the primary purpose of paying debts, dividends, interest, salaries, wages, profits, pensions, or employee benefits of any kind; and any arrangement under which a person is nominee or escrowee for another.

(39) "Trustee" includes an original, additional, surviving, or successor trustee, whether or not appointed or confirmed by court.

(40) "Will" means an instrument, including a codicil, executed by a person in the manner prescribed by this code, which disposes of the person's property on or after his or her death and includes an instrument which merely appoints a personal representative or revokes or revises another will.

History.

S. 1, ch. 74-106; s. 4, ch. 75-220; s. 1, ch. 77-174; s. 2, ch. 85-79; s. 66, ch. 87-226; s. 1, ch. 88-340; s. 7, ch. 93-257; s. 6, ch. 95-401; s. 949, ch. 97-102; s. 52, ch. 98-421; s. 11, ch. 2001-226; s. 106, ch. 2002-1; s. 2, ch. 2003-154; s. 2, ch. 2005-108; s. 29, ch. 2006-217, eff. July 1, 2007; s. 3, ch. 2007-74, eff. July 1, 2007; s. 1, ch. 2009-115, eff. July 1, 2009; s. 4, ch. 2010-132, eff. Oct. 1, 2010; s. 1, ch. 2012-109, eff. July 1, 2012.

Editor's Notes.

Created from former s. 731.03.

The introductory language of s. 1, ch. 2012-109 provides: "Effective July 1, 2012, and applicable to proceedings pending before or commenced on or after July 1, 2012, subsection (33) of section 731.201, Florida Statutes, is amended to read."

PART III.
NOTICE AND REPRESENTATION.

731.301. Notice.

(1) If notice to an interested person of a petition or other proceeding is required, the notice shall be given to the interested person or that person's attorney as provided in the code or the Florida Probate Rules.

(2) In a probate proceeding, formal notice is sufficient to acquire jurisdiction over the person receiving formal notice to the extent of the person's interest in the estate or in the decedent's protected homestead.

(3) Persons given proper notice of a proceeding are bound by all orders entered in that proceeding.

History.

S. 1, ch. 74-106; s. 5, ch. 75-220; s. 3, ch. 77-87; s. 1, ch. 77-174; s. 1, ch. 93-257; s. 64, ch. 95-211; s. 950, ch. 97-102; s. 12, ch. 2001-226; s. 5, ch. 2010-132, eff. Oct. 1, 2010.

Editor's Notes.

Created from former s. 732.28.

731.302. Waiver and consent by interested person.

Subsequent to the filing of a petition for administration, an interested person, including a guardian ad litem, administrator ad litem, guardian of the property, personal representative, trustee, or other fiduciary, or a sole holder or all coholders of a power of revocation or a power of appointment, may waive, to the extent of that person's interest or the interest which that person represents, subject to the provisions of ss. 731.303 and 733.604, any right or notice or the filing of any document, exhibit, or schedule required to be filed and may consent to any action or proceeding which may be required or permitted by this code.

History.

S. 1, ch. 74-106; s. 6, ch. 75-220; s. 4, ch. 77-87; s. 267, ch. 79-400; s. 3, ch. 84-106; s. 25, ch. 2003-154.

Editor's Notes.

Section 25, ch. 2003-154 reenacted 731.302 without change to incorporate amendments to statutory sections referenced therein.

Created from former s. 732.28.

731.303. Representation.

In the administration of or in judicial proceedings involving estates of decedents, the following apply:

(1) Persons are bound by orders binding others in the following cases:

(a)1. Orders binding the sole holder or all coholders of a power of revocation or a general, special, or limited power of appointment, including one in the form of a power of amendment or revocation to the extent that the power has not become unexercisable in fact, bind all persons to the extent that their interests, as persons who may take by virtue of the exercise or nonexercise of the power, are subject to the power.

2. Subparagraph 1. does not apply to:

a. Any matter determined by the court to involve fraud or bad faith by the trustee;

b. A power of a trustee to distribute trust property; or

c. A power of appointment held by a person while the person is the sole trustee.

(b) To the extent there is no conflict of interest between them or among the persons represented:

1. Orders binding a guardian of the property bind the ward.

2. Orders binding a trustee bind beneficiaries of the trust in proceedings to probate a will, in establishing or adding to a trust, in reviewing the acts or accounts of a prior fiduciary, and in proceedings involving creditors or other third parties. However, for purposes of this section, a conflict of interest shall be deemed to exist when each trustee of a trust that is a beneficiary of the estate is also a personal representative of the estate.

3. Orders binding a personal representative bind persons interested in the undistributed assets of a decedent's estate, in actions or proceedings by or against the estate.

(c) An unborn or unascertained person, or a minor or any other person under a legal disability, who is not otherwise represented is bound by an order to the extent that person's interest is represented by another party having the same or greater quality of interest in the proceeding.

(2) Orders binding a guardian of the person shall not bind the ward.

(3) In proceedings involving the administration of estates, notice is required as follows:

(a) Notice as prescribed by law shall be given to every interested person, or to one who can bind the interested person as described in paragraph (1)(a) or paragraph (1)(b). Notice may be given both to the interested person and to another who can bind him or her.

(b) Notice is given to unborn or unascertained persons who are not represented pursuant to paragraph (1)(a) or paragraph (1)(b) by giving notice to all known persons whose interests in the proceedings are the same as, or of a greater quality than, those of the unborn or unascertained persons.

(4) If the court determines that representation of the interest would otherwise be inadequate, the court may, at any time, appoint a guardian ad litem to represent the interests of an incapacitated person, an unborn or unascertained person, a minor or any other person otherwise under a legal disability, or a person whose identity or address is unknown. If not precluded by conflict of interest, a guardian ad litem may be appointed to represent several persons or interests.

(5) The holder of a power of appointment over property not held in trust may represent and bind persons whose interests, as permissible appointees, takers in default, or otherwise, are subject to the power. Representation under this subsection does not apply to:

(a) Any matter determined by the court to involve fraud or bad faith by the trustee;

(b) A power of a trustee to distribute trust property; or

(c) A power of appointment held by a person while the person is the sole trustee.

History.
S. 1, ch. 74-106; s. 7, ch. 75-220; s. 5, ch. 77-87; s. 1, ch. 77-174; s. 1, ch. 88-217; s. 3, ch. 92-200; s. 951, ch. 97-102; s. 13, ch. 2001-226; s. 3, ch. 2002-82; s. 3, ch. 2003-154; s. 30, ch. 2006-217, eff. July 1, 2007; s. 9, ch. 2007-153, eff. July 1, 2007.

731.401. Arbitration of disputes.

(1) A provision in a will or trust requiring the arbitration of disputes, other than disputes of the validity of all or a part of a will or trust, between or among the beneficiaries and a fiduciary under the will or trust, or any combination of such persons or entities, is enforceable.

(2) Unless otherwise specified in the will or trust, a will or trust provision requiring arbitration shall be presumed to require binding arbitration under s. 44.104.

History.
S. 4, ch. 2007-74, eff. July 1, 2007.

CHAPTER 732.
PROBATE CODE: INTESTATE SUCCESSION AND WILLS

PART I.
INTESTATE SUCCESSION.

* FL only goes as far as grand-parents and aunts/uncles

732.101. Intestate estate.

(1) Any part of the estate of a decedent not effectively disposed of by will passes to the decedent's heirs as prescribed in the following sections of this code.

(2) The decedent's death is the event that vests the heirs' right to the decedent's intestate property.

History.
S. 1, ch. 74-106; s. 8, ch. 75-220; s. 14, ch. 2001-226.
Editor's Notes.
Created from former s. 731.23.

732.102. Spouse's share of intestate estate.

The intestate share of the surviving spouse is:

(1) If there is no surviving descendant of the decedent, the entire intestate estate.

(2) If the decedent is survived by one or more descendants, all of whom are also descendants of the surviving spouse, and the surviving spouse has no other descendant, the entire intestate estate.

(3) If there are one or more surviving descendants of the decedent who are not lineal descendants of the surviving spouse, one-half of the intestate estate.

(4) If there are one or more surviving descendants of the decedent, all of whom are also descendants of the surviving spouse, and the surviving spouse has one or more descendants who are not descendants of the decedent, one-half of the intestate estate.

History.
S. 1, ch. 74-106; s. 8, ch. 75-220; s. 15, ch. 2001-226; s. 5, ch. 2007-74, eff. July 1, 2007; s. 2, ch. 2011-183, eff. Oct. 1, 2011.
Editor's Notes.
Created from former s. 731.23.
Section 14, ch. 2011-183 provides: "Except as otherwise expressly provided in this act, this act shall take effect upon becoming a law and shall apply to all proceedings pending before such date and all cases commenced on or after the effective date."
Section 2, ch. 2012-109 provides: "Notwithstanding section 2 or section 14 of chapter 2011-183, Laws of Florida, the amendments to section 732.102, Florida Statutes, made by section 2 of that act apply only to the estates of decedents dying on or after October 1, 2011."

732.103. Share of other heirs.

The part of the intestate estate not passing to the surviving spouse under s. 732.102, or the entire intestate estate if there is no surviving spouse, descends as follows:

(1) To the descendants of the decedent.

(2) If there is no descendant, to the decedent's father and mother equally, or to the survivor of them.

(3) If there is none of the foregoing, to the decedent's brothers and sisters and the descendants of deceased brothers and sisters.

(4) If there is none of the foregoing, the estate shall be divided, one-half of which shall go to the decedent's paternal, and the other half to the decedent's maternal, kindred in the following order:

(a) To the grandfather and grandmother equally, or to the survivor of them.

(b) If there is no grandfather or grandmother, to uncles and aunts and descendants of deceased uncles and aunts of the decedent.

(c) If there is either no paternal kindred or no maternal kindred, the estate shall go to the other kindred who survive, in the order stated above.

(5) If there is no kindred of either part, the whole of the property shall go to the kindred of the last deceased spouse of the decedent as if the deceased spouse had survived the decedent and then died intestate entitled to the estate.

(6) If none of the foregoing, and if any of the descendants of the decedent's great-grandparents were Holocaust victims as defined in s. 626.9543(3)(a), including such victims in countries cooperating with the discriminatory policies of Nazi Germany, then to the descendants of the great-grandparents. The court shall allow any such descendant to meet a reasonable, not unduly restrictive, standard of proof to substantiate his or her lineage. This subsection only applies to escheated property and shall cease to be effective for proceedings filed after December 31, 2004.

History.
S. 1, ch. 74-106; s. 8, ch. 75-220; s. 1, ch. 77-174; s. 16, ch. 2001-226; s. 145, ch. 2004-390; s. 102, ch. 2006-1, eff. July 4, 2006; s. 6, ch. 2007-74, eff. July 1, 2007.
Editor's Notes.
Created from former s. 731.23.

732.104. Inheritance per stirpes.

Descent shall be per stirpes, whether to descendants or to collateral heirs.

History.
S. 1, ch. 74-106; s. 9, ch. 75-220; s. 7, ch. 2007-74, eff. July 1, 2007.
Editor's Notes.
Created from former s. 731.25.

732.105. Half blood.

When property descends to the collateral kindred of the intestate and part of the collateral kindred are of the whole blood to the intestate and the other part of the half blood, those of the half blood shall inherit only half as much as those of the whole blood; but if all are of the half blood they shall have whole parts.

History.
S. 1, ch. 74-106; s. 10, ch. 75-220.
Editor's Notes.
Created from former s. 731.24.

732.106. Afterborn heirs.

Heirs of the decedent conceived before his or her death, but born thereafter, inherit intestate property as if they had been born in the decedent's lifetime.

History.
S. 1, ch. 74-106; s. 10, ch. 75-220; s. 6, ch. 77-87; s. 952, ch. 97-102.
Editor's Notes.
Created from former s. 731.11.

732.107. Escheat.

(1) When a person dies leaving an estate without being survived by any person entitled to a part of it, that part shall escheat to the state.

(2) Property that escheats shall be sold as provided in the Florida Probate Rules and the proceeds paid to the Chief Financial Officer of the state and deposited in the State School Fund.

(3) At any time within 10 years after the payment to the Chief Financial Officer, a person claiming to be entitled to the proceeds may reopen the administration to assert entitlement to the proceeds. If no claim is timely asserted, the state's rights to the proceeds shall become absolute.

(4) The Department of Legal Affairs shall represent the state in all proceedings concerning escheated estates.

(5)(a) If a person entitled to the proceeds assigns the rights to receive payment to an attorney, Florida-certified public accountant, or private investigative agency which is duly licensed to do business in this state pursuant to a written agreement with that person, the Department of Financial Services is authorized to make distribution in accordance with the assignment.

(b) Payments made to an attorney, Florida-certified public accountant, or private investigative agency shall be promptly deposited into a trust or escrow account which is regularly maintained by the attorney, Florida-certified public accountant, or private investigative agency in a financial institution authorized to accept such deposits and located in this state.

(c) Distribution by the attorney, Florida-certified public accountant, or private investigative agency to the person entitled to the proceeds shall be made within 10 days following final credit of the deposit into the trust or escrow account at the financial institution, unless a party to the agreement protests the distribution in writing before it is made.

(d) The department shall not be civilly or criminally liable for any proceeds distributed pursuant to this subsection, provided such distribution is made in good faith.

History.
S. 1, ch. 74-106; s. 10, ch. 75-220; s. 4, ch. 89-291; s. 9, ch. 89-299; s. 953, ch. 97-102; s. 32, ch. 2001-36; s. 17, ch. 2001-226; s. 1896, ch. 2003-261.
Editor's Notes.
Created from former s. 731.33.

732.108. Adopted persons and persons born out of wedlock.

(1) For the purpose of intestate succession by or from an adopted person, the adopted person is a descendant of the adopting parent and is one of the natural kindred of all members of the adopting parent's family, and is not a descendant of his or her natural parents, nor is he or she one of the kindred of any member of the natural parent's family or any prior adoptive parent's family, except that:

(a) Adoption of a child by the spouse of a natural parent has no effect on the relationship between the child and the natural parent or the natural parent's family.

(b) Adoption of a child by a natural parent's spouse who married the natural parent after the death of the other natural parent has no effect on the relationship between the child and the family of the deceased natural parent.

(c) Adoption of a child by a close relative, as defined in s. 63.172(2), has no effect on the relationship between the child and the families of the deceased natural parents.

(2) For the purpose of intestate succession in cases not covered by subsection (1), a person born out of wedlock is a descendant of his or her mother and is one of the natural kindred of all members of the mother's family. The person is also a descendant of his or her father and is one of the natural kindred of all members of the father's family, if:

(a) The natural parents participated in a marriage ceremony before or after the birth of the person born out of wedlock, even though the attempted marriage is void.

(b) The paternity of the father is established by an adjudication before or after the death of the father. Chapter 95 shall not apply in determining heirs in a probate proceeding under this paragraph.

(c) The paternity of the father is acknowledged in writing by the father.

History.
S. 1, ch. 74-106; s. 11, ch. 75-220; s. 7, ch. 77-87; s. 1, ch. 77-174; s. 2, ch. 87-27; s. 954, ch. 97-102; s. 8, ch. 2007-74, eff. July 1, 2007; s. 2, ch. 2009-115, eff. July 1, 2009.
Editor's Notes.
Created from former ss. 731.29, 731.30.

732.1081. Termination of parental rights.

For the purpose of intestate succession by a natural or adoptive parent, a natural or adoptive parent is barred from inheriting from or through a child if the natural or adoptive parent's parental rights were terminated pursuant to chapter 39 prior to the death of the child, and the natural or adoptive parent shall be treated as if the parent predeceased the child.

History.
S. 4, ch. 2012-109, eff. July 1, 2012.
Editor's Notes.
The introductory language of s. 4, ch. 2012-109 provides: "Effective July 1, 2012, and applicable only to estates of persons dying on or after July 1, 2012, section 732.1081, Florida Statutes, is created to read."

732.109. Debts to decedent.

A debt owed to the decedent shall not be charged against the intestate share of any person except the debtor. If the debtor does not survive the decedent, the debt shall not be taken into account in computing the intestate share of the debtor's heirs.

History.
S. 1, ch. 74-106; s. 11, ch. 75-220.
Editor's Notes.
Created from former s. 736.01.

732.1101. Aliens.

Aliens shall have the same rights of inheritance as citizens.

History.
S. 1, ch. 74-106; s. 113, ch. 75-220; s. 955, ch. 97-102; s. 18, ch. 2001-226.
Editor's Notes.
Created from former s. 731.28.

732.111. Dower and curtesy abolished.

Dower and curtesy are abolished.

History.
S. 1, ch. 74-106; s. 113, ch. 75-220.

PART II.
ELECTIVE SHARE OF SURVIVING SPOUSE; RIGHTS IN COMMUNITY PROPERTY.

732.201. Right to elective share.

The surviving spouse of a person who dies domiciled in Florida has the right to a share of the elective estate of the decedent as provided in this part, to be designated the elective share.

History.
S. 1, ch. 74-106; s. 13, ch. 75-220; s. 1, ch. 99-343.
Editor's Notes.
Created from former s. 731.34.

732.2025. Definitions.

As used in ss. 732.2025-732.2155, the term:

(1) "Direct recipient" means the decedent's probate estate and any other person who receives property included in the elective estate by transfer from the decedent, including transfers described in s. 732.2035(8), by right of survivorship, or by beneficiary designation under a governing instrument. For this purpose, a beneficiary of an insurance policy on the decedent's life, the net cash surrender value of which is included in the elective estate, is treated as having received property included in the elective estate. In the case of property held in trust, "direct recipient" includes the trustee but excludes the beneficiaries of the trust.

(2) "Elective share trust" means a trust under which:

(a) The surviving spouse is entitled for life to the use of the property or to all of the income payable at least as often as annually;

(b) The surviving spouse has the right under the terms of the trust or state law to require the trustee either to make the property productive or to convert it within a reasonable time; and

(c) During the spouse's life, no person other than the spouse has the power to distribute income or principal to anyone other than the spouse.

As used in this subsection, the term "income" has the same meaning as that provided in s. 643(b) of the Internal Revenue Code, as amended, and regulations adopted under that section.

(3) "General power of appointment" means a power of appointment under which the holder of the power, whether or not the holder has the capacity to exercise it, has the power to create a present or future interest in the holder, the holder's estate, or the creditors of either. The term includes a power to consume or invade the principal of a trust, but only if the power is not limited by an ascertainable standard relating to the holder's health, education, support, or maintenance.

(4) "Governing instrument" means a deed; will; trust; insurance or annuity policy; account with payable-on-death designation; security registered in beneficiary form (TOD); pension, profit-sharing, retirement, or similar benefit plan; an instrument creating or exercising a power of appointment or a power of attorney; or a dispositive, appointive, or nominative instrument of any similar type.

(5) "Payor" means an insurer, business entity, employer, government, governmental agency or subdivision, or any other person, other than the decedent's personal representative or a trustee of a trust created by the decedent, authorized or obligated by law or a governing instrument to make payments.

(6) "Person" includes an individual, trust, estate, partnership, association, company, or corporation.

(7) "Probate estate" means all property wherever located that is subject to estate administration in any state of the United States or in the District of Columbia.

(8) "Qualifying special needs trust" or "supplemental needs trust" means a trust established for an ill or disabled surviving spouse with court approval before or after a decedent's death, if, commencing on the decedent's death:

(a) The income and principal are distributable to or for the benefit of the spouse for life in the discretion of one or more trustees less than half of whom are ineligible family trustees. For purposes of this paragraph, ineligible family trustees include the decedent's grandparents and any descendants of the decedent's grandparents who are not also descendants of the surviving spouse; and

(b) During the spouse's life, no person other than the spouse has the power to distribute income or principal to anyone other than the spouse.

The requirement for court approval shall not apply if the aggregate value of all property in all qualifying special needs trusts for the spouse is less than $100,000. For purposes of this subsection, value is determined on the "applicable valuation date" as defined in s. 732.2095(1)(a).

(9) "Revocable trust" means a trust that is includable in the elective estate under s. 732.2035(4).

(10) "Transfer in satisfaction of the elective share" means an irrevocable transfer by the decedent during life to an elective share trust.

(11) "Transfer tax value" means the value the interest would have for purposes of the United States estate and gift tax laws if it passed without consideration to an unrelated person on the applicable valuation date.

History.
S. 2, ch. 99-343; s. 19, ch. 2001-226; s. 2, ch. 2002-82; s. 151, ch. 2004-5; s. 9, ch. 2007-74, eff. July 1, 2007; s. 3, ch. 2009-115, eff. July 1, 2009.

Editor's Notes.
Section 643(b) of the Internal Revenue Code, referred to in this section, is codified as 26 U.S.C.S. § 643(b).

732.2035. Property entering into elective estate.

Except as provided in s. 732.2045, the elective estate consists of the sum of the values as determined under s. 732.2055 of the following property interests:

(1) The decedent's probate estate.

(2) The decedent's ownership interest in accounts or securities registered in "Pay On Death," "Transfer On Death," "In Trust For," or coownership with right of survivorship form. For this purpose, "decedent's ownership interest" means, in the case of accounts or securities held in tenancy by the entirety, one-half of the value of the account or security, and in all other cases, that portion of the accounts or securities which the decedent had, immediately before death, the right to withdraw or use without the duty to account to any person.

(3) The decedent's fractional interest in property, other than property described in subsection (2) or subsection (7), held by the decedent in joint tenancy with right of survivorship or in tenancy by the entirety. For this purpose, "decedent's fractional interest in property" means the value of the property divided by the number of tenants.

(4) That portion of property, other than property described in subsection (2), transferred by the decedent to the extent that at the time of the decedent's death the transfer was revocable by the decedent alone or in conjunction with any other person. This subsection does not apply to a transfer that is revocable by the decedent only with the consent of all persons having a beneficial interest in the property.

(5)(a) That portion of property, other than property described in subsection (3), subsection (4), or subsection (7), transferred by the decedent to the extent that at the time of the decedent's death:

1. The decedent possessed the right to, or in fact enjoyed the possession or use of, the income or principal of the property; or

2. The principal of the property could, in the discretion of any person other than the spouse of the decedent, be distributed or appointed to or for the benefit of the decedent.

In the application of this subsection, a right to payments under a commercial or private annuity, an annuity trust, a unitrust, or a similar arrangement shall be treated as a right to that portion of the income of the property necessary to equal the annuity, unitrust, or other payment.

(b) The amount included under this subsection is:

1. With respect to subparagraph (a)1., the value of the portion of the property to which the decedent's right or enjoyment related, to the extent the portion passed to or for the benefit of any person other than the decedent's probate estate; and

2. With respect to subparagraph (a)2., the value of the portion subject to the discretion, to the extent the portion passed to or for the benefit of any person other than the decedent's probate estate.

(c) This subsection does not apply to any property if the decedent's only interests in the property are that:

1. The property could be distributed to or for the benefit of the decedent only with the consent of all persons having a beneficial interest in the property; or

2. The income or principal of the property could be distributed to or for the benefit of the decedent only through the exercise or in default of an exercise of a general power of appointment held by any person other than the decedent; or

3. The income or principal of the property is or could be distributed in satisfaction of the decedent's obligation of support; or

4. The decedent had a contingent right to receive principal, other than at the discretion of any person, which contingency was beyond the

control of the decedent and which had not in fact occurred at the decedent's death.

(6) The decedent's beneficial interest in the net cash surrender value immediately before death of any policy of insurance on the decedent's life.

(7) The value of amounts payable to or for the benefit of any person by reason of surviving the decedent under any public or private pension, retirement, or deferred compensation plan, or any similar arrangement, other than benefits payable under the federal Railroad Retirement Act or the federal Social Security System. In the case of a defined contribution plan as defined in s. 414(i) of the Internal Revenue Code of 1986, as amended, this subsection shall not apply to the excess of the proceeds of any insurance policy on the decedent's life over the net cash surrender value of the policy immediately before the decedent's death.

(8) Property that was transferred during the 1-year period preceding the decedent's death as a result of a transfer by the decedent if the transfer was either of the following types:

(a) Any property transferred as a result of the termination of a right or interest in, or power over, property that would have been included in the elective estate under subsection (4) or subsection (5) if the right, interest, or power had not terminated until the decedent's death.

(b) Any transfer of property to the extent not otherwise included in the elective estate, made to or for the benefit of any person, except:

1. Any transfer of property for medical or educational expenses to the extent it qualifies for exclusion from the United States gift tax under s. 2503(e) of the Internal Revenue Code, as amended; and

2. After the application of subparagraph 1., the first annual exclusion amount of property transferred to or for the benefit of each donee during the 1-year period, but only to the extent the transfer qualifies for exclusion from the United States gift tax under s. 2503(b) or (c) of the Internal Revenue Code, as amended. For purposes of this subparagraph, the term "annual exclusion amount" means the amount of one annual exclusion under s. 2503(b) or (c) of the Internal Revenue Code, as amended.

(c) Except as provided in paragraph (d), for purposes of this subsection:

1. A "termination" with respect to a right or interest in property occurs when the decedent transfers or relinquishes the right or interest, and, with respect to a power over property, a termination occurs when the power terminates by exercise, release, lapse, default, or otherwise.

2. A distribution from a trust the income or principal of which is subject to subsection (4), subsection (5), or subsection (9) shall be treated as a transfer of property by the decedent and not as a termination of a right or interest in, or a power over, property.

(d) Notwithstanding anything in paragraph (c) to the contrary:

1. A "termination" with respect to a right or interest in property does not occur when the right or interest terminates by the terms of the governing instrument unless the termination is determined by reference to the death of the decedent and the court finds that a principal purpose for the terms of the instrument relating to the termination was avoidance of the elective share.

2. A distribution from a trust is not subject to this subsection if the distribution is required by the terms of the governing instrument unless the event triggering the distribution is determined by reference to the death of the decedent and the court finds that a principal purpose of the terms of the governing instrument relating to the distribution is avoidance of the elective share.

(9) Property transferred in satisfaction of the elective share.

History.
S. 15, ch. 75-220; s. 3, ch. 99-343; s. 20, ch. 2001-226; s. 10, ch. 2007-74, eff. July 1, 2007.

Editor's Notes.
Former s. 732.206.
Sections 414(i) and 2503 of the Internal Revenue Code, referred to in this section, are codified as 26 U.S.C.S. §§n 414(i) and 2503, respectively.

732.2045. Exclusions and overlapping application.

(1) Exclusions. — Section 732.2035 does not apply to:

(a) Except as provided in s. 732.2155(4), any transfer of property by the decedent to the extent the transfer is irrevocable before the effective date of this subsection or after that date but before the date of the decedent's marriage to the surviving spouse.

(b) Any transfer of property by the decedent to the extent the decedent received adequate consideration in money or money's worth for the transfer.

(c) Any transfer of property by the decedent made with the written consent of the decedent's spouse. For this purpose, spousal consent to split-gift treatment under the United States gift tax laws does not constitute written consent to the transfer by the decedent.

(d) The proceeds of any policy of insurance on the decedent's life in excess of the net cash surrender value of the policy whether payable to the decedent's estate, a trust, or in any other manner.

(e) Any policy of insurance on the decedent's life maintained pursuant to a court order.

(f) The decedent's one-half of the property to which ss. 732.216-732.228, or any similar provisions of law of another state, apply and real property that is community property under the laws of the jurisdiction where it is located.

(g) Property held in a qualifying special needs trust on the date of the decedent's death.

(h) Property included in the gross estate of the decedent for federal estate tax purposes solely because the decedent possessed a general power of appointment.

(i) Property which constitutes the protected homestead of the decedent whether held by the decedent or by a trust at the decedent's death.

(2) Overlapping application. — If s. 732.2035(1) and any other subsection of s. 732.2035 apply to the same property interest, the amount included in the elective estate under other subsections is reduced by the amount included under subsection (1). In all other cases, if more than one subsection of s. 732.2035 applies to a property interest, only the subsection resulting in the largest elective estate shall apply.

History.
S. 4, ch. 99-343; s. 21, ch. 2001-226; s. 4, ch. 2009-115, eff. July 1, 2009.

732.2055.   Valuation of the elective estate.

For purposes of s. 732.2035, "value" means:

(1) In the case of any policy of insurance on the decedent's life includable under s. 732.2035(4), (5), or (6), the net cash surrender value of the policy immediately before the decedent's death.

(2) In the case of any policy of insurance on the decedent's life includable under s. 732.2035(8), the net cash surrender value of the policy on the date of the termination or transfer.

(3) In the case of amounts includable under s. 732.2035(7), the transfer tax value of the amounts on the date of the decedent's death.

(4) In the case of other property included under s. 732.2035(8), the fair market value of the property on the date of the termination or transfer, computed after deducting any mortgages, liens, or security interests on the property as of that date.

(5) In the case of all other property, the fair market value of the property on the date of the decedent's death, computed after deducting from the total value of the property:

(a) All claims paid or payable from the elective estate; and

(b) To the extent they are not deducted under paragraph (a), all mortgages, liens, or security interests on the property.

History.
S. 5, ch. 99-343; s. 22, ch. 2001-226.

732.2065.   Amount of the elective share.

The elective share is an amount equal to 30 percent of the elective estate.

History.
S. 15, ch. 75-220; s. 1, ch. 81-27; s. 6, ch. 99-343.

Editor's Notes.
Former s. 732.207.

732.2075.   Sources from which elective share payable; abatement.

(1) Unless otherwise provided in the decedent's will or, in the absence of a provision in the decedent's will, in a trust referred to in the decedent's will, the following are applied first to satisfy the elective share:

(a) Property interests included in the elective estate that pass or have passed to or for the benefit of the surviving spouse, including interests that are contingent upon making the election, but only to the extent that such contingent interests do not diminish other property interests that would be applied to satisfy the elective share in the absence of the contingent interests.

(b) To the extent paid to or for the benefit of the surviving spouse, amounts payable under any plan or arrangement described in s. 732.2035(7).

(c) To the extent paid to or for the benefit of the surviving spouse, the decedent's one-half of any property described in s. 732.2045(1)(f).

(d) To the extent paid to or for the benefit of the surviving spouse, the proceeds of any term or other policy of insurance on the decedent's life if, at the time of decedent's death, the policy was owned by any person other than the surviving spouse.

(e) Property held for the benefit of the surviving spouse in a qualifying special needs trust.

(f) Property interests that would have satisfied the elective share under any preceding paragraph of this subsection but were disclaimed.

(2) If, after the application of subsection (1), the elective share is not fully satisfied, the unsatisfied balance shall be allocated entirely to one class of direct recipients of the remaining elective estate and apportioned among those recipients, and if the elective share amount is not fully satisfied, to the next class of direct recipients, in the following order of priority, until the elective share amount is satisfied:

(a) Class 1. — The decedent's probate estate and revocable trusts.

(b) Class 2. — Recipients of property interests, other than protected charitable interests, included in the elective estate under s. 732.2035(2), (3), or (6) and, to the extent the decedent had at the time of death the power to designate the recipient of the property, property interests, other than protected charitable interests, included under s. 732.2035(5) and (7).

(c) Class 3. — Recipients of all other property interests, other than protected charitable interests, included in the elective estate.

For purposes of this subsection, a protected charitable interest is any interest for which a charitable deduction with respect to the transfer of the property was allowed or allowable to the decedent or the decedent's spouse under the United States gift or income tax laws.

(3) If, after the application of subsections (1) and (2), the elective share amount is not fully satisfied, the additional amount due to the surviving spouse shall be determined and satisfied as follows:

(a) The remaining unsatisfied balance shall be satisfied from property described in paragraphs (1)(a) and (b) which passes or which has passed in a trust in which the surviving spouse has a beneficial interest, other than an elective share trust or a qualified special needs trust.

(b) In determining the amount of the remaining unsatisfied balance, the effect, if any, of any change caused by the operation of this subsection in the value of the spouse's beneficial interests in property described in paragraphs (1)(a) and (b) shall be taken into account, including, if necessary, further recalculations of the value of those beneficial interests.

(c) If there is more than one trust to which this subsection could apply, unless otherwise provided in the decedent's will or, in the absence of a provision in the decedent's will, in a trust referred to in the decedent's will, the unsatisfied balance shall be apportioned pro rata to all such trusts in proportion to the value, as determined under s. 732.2095(2)(d), of the surviving spouse's beneficial interests in the trusts.

(4) If, after the application of subsections (1), (2), and (3), the elective share is not fully satisfied, any remaining unsatisfied balance shall be satisfied from direct recipients of protected charitable lead interests, but only to the extent and at such times that contribution is permitted without disqualifying the charitable interest in that property for a deduction under the United States gift tax laws. For purposes of this subsection, a protected charitable lead interest is a protected charitable interest as defined in subsection (2) in which one or more deductible interests in charity precede some other nondeductible interest or interests in the property.

(5) The contribution required of the decedent's probate estate and revocable trusts may be made in cash or in kind. In the application of this subsection, subsections (6) and (7) are to be applied to charge contribution for the elective share to the beneficiaries of the probate estate and revocable trusts as if all beneficiaries were taking under a common governing instrument.

(6) Unless otherwise provided in the decedent's will or, in the absence of a provision in the decedent's will, in a trust referred to in the decedent's will, any amount to be satisfied from the decedent's probate estate, other than from property passing to an inter vivos trust, shall be paid from the assets of the probate estate in the order prescribed in s. 733.805.

(7) Unless otherwise provided in the trust instrument or, in the decedent's will if there is no provision in the trust instrument, any amount to be satisfied from trust property shall be paid from the assets of the trust

in the order provided for claims under s. 736.05053(2) and (3). A direction in the decedent's will is effective only for revocable trusts.

History.
S. 15, ch. 75-220; s. 7, ch. 99-343; s. 23, ch. 2001-226; s. 4, ch. 2002-82; s. 31, ch. 2006-217, eff. July 1, 2007; s. 11, ch. 2007-74, eff. July 1, 2007; s. 5, ch. 2009-115, eff. July 1, 2009.
Editor's Notes.
Former s. 732.209.

732.2085. Liability of direct recipients and beneficiaries.

(1) Only direct recipients of property included in the elective estate and the beneficiaries of the decedent's probate estate or of any trust that is a direct recipient, are liable to contribute toward satisfaction of the elective share.

(a) Within each of the classes described in s. 732.2075(2)(b) and (c), each direct recipient is liable in an amount equal to the value, as determined under s. 732.2055, of the proportional part of the liability for all members of the class.

(b) Trust and probate estate beneficiaries who receive a distribution of principal after the decedent's death are liable in an amount equal to the value of the principal distributed to them multiplied by the contribution percentage of the distributing trust or estate. For this purpose, "contribution percentage" means the remaining unsatisfied balance of the trust or estate at the time of the distribution divided by the value of the trust or estate as determined under s. 732.2055. "Remaining unsatisfied balance" means the amount of liability initially apportioned to the trust or estate reduced by amounts or property previously contributed by any person in satisfaction of that liability.

(2) In lieu of paying the amount for which they are liable, beneficiaries who have received a distribution of property included in the elective estate and direct recipients other than the decedent's probate estate or revocable trusts, may:

(a) Contribute a proportional part of all property received; or

(b) With respect to any property interest received before the date of the court's order of contribution:

1. Contribute all of the property; or

2. If the property has been sold or exchanged prior to the date on which the spouse's election is filed, pay an amount equal to the value of the property, less reasonable costs of sale, on the date it was sold or exchanged.

In the application of paragraph (a), the "proportional part of all property received" is determined separately for each class of priority under s. 732.2075(2).

(3) If a person pays the value of the property on the date of a sale or exchange or contributes all of the property received, as provided in paragraph (2)(b):

(a) No further contribution toward satisfaction of the elective share shall be required with respect to that property.

(b) Any unsatisfied contribution is treated as additional unsatisfied balance and reapportioned to other recipients as provided in s. 732.2075 and this section.

(4) If any part of s. 732.2035 or s. 732.2075 is preempted by federal law with respect to a payment, an item of property, or any other benefit included in the elective estate, a person who, not for value, receives the payment, item of property, or any other benefit is obligated to return the payment, item of property, or benefit, or is personally liable for the amount of the payment or the value of that item of property or benefit, as provided in ss. 732.2035 and 732.2075, to the person who would have been entitled to it were that section or part of that section not preempted.

History.

S. 8, ch. 99-343; s. 24, ch. 2001-226; s. 6, ch. 2009-115, eff. July 1, 2009.

732.2095. Valuation of property used to satisfy elective share.

(1) Definitions. — As used in this section, the term:

(a) "Applicable valuation date" means:

1. In the case of transfers in satisfaction of the elective share, the date of the decedent's death.

2. In the case of property held in a qualifying special needs trust on the date of the decedent's death, the date of the decedent's death.

3. In the case of other property irrevocably transferred to or for the benefit of the surviving spouse during the decedent's life, the date of the transfer.

4. In the case of property distributed to the surviving spouse by the personal representative, the date of distribution.

5. Except as provided in subparagraphs 1., 2., and 3., in the case of property passing in trust for the surviving spouse, the date or dates the trust is funded in satisfaction of the elective share.

6. In the case of property described in s. 732.2035(2) or (3), the date of the decedent's death.

7. In the case of proceeds of any policy of insurance payable to the surviving spouse, the date of the decedent's death.

8. In the case of amounts payable to the surviving spouse under any plan or arrangement described in s. 732.2035(7), the date of the decedent's death.

9. In all other cases, the date of the decedent's death or the date the surviving spouse first comes into possession of the property, whichever occurs later.

(b) "Qualifying power of appointment" means a general power of appointment that is exercisable alone and in all events by the decedent's spouse in favor of the spouse or the spouse's estate. For this purpose, a general power to appoint by will is a qualifying power of appointment if the power may be exercised by the spouse in favor of the spouse's estate without the consent of any other person.

(c) "Qualifying invasion power" means a power held by the surviving spouse or the trustee of an elective share trust to invade trust principal for the health, support, and maintenance of the spouse. The power may, but need not, provide that the other resources of the spouse are to be taken into account in any exercise of the power.

(2) Except as provided in this subsection, the value of property for purposes of s. 732.2075 is the fair market value of the property on the applicable valuation date.

(a) If the surviving spouse has a life interest in property not in trust that entitles the spouse to the use of the property for life, the value of the spouse's interest is one-half of the value of the property on the applicable valuation date.

(b) If the surviving spouse has an interest in a trust, or portion of a trust, which meets the requirements of an elective share trust, the value of the spouse's interest is a percentage of the value of the principal of the trust, or trust portion, on the applicable valuation date as follows:

1. One hundred percent if the trust instrument includes both a qualifying invasion power and a qualifying power of appointment.

2. Eighty percent if the trust instrument includes a qualifying invasion power but no qualifying power of appointment.

3. Fifty percent in all other cases.

(c) If the surviving spouse is a beneficiary of a trust, or portion of a trust, which meets the requirements of a qualifying special needs trust, the value of the principal of the trust, or trust portion, on the applicable valuation date.

(d) If the surviving spouse has an interest in a trust that does not meet the requirements of either an elective share trust or a qualifying special needs trust, the value of the spouse's interest is the transfer tax value of the interest on the applicable valuation date; however, the aggregate value of all of the spouse's interests in the trust shall not exceed one-half of the value of the trust principal on the applicable valuation date.

(e) In the case of any policy of insurance on the decedent's life the proceeds of which are payable outright or to a trust described in paragraph (b), paragraph (c), or paragraph (d), the value of the policy for purposes of s. 732.2075 and paragraphs (b), (c), and (d) is the net proceeds.

(f) In the case of a right to one or more payments from an annuity or under a similar contractual arrangement or under any plan or arrangement described in s. 732.2035(7), the value of the right to payments for purposes of s. 732.2075 and paragraphs (b), (c), and (d) is the transfer tax value of the right on the applicable valuation date.

History.
S. 9, ch. 99-343; s. 25, ch. 2001-226.

732.2105. Effect of election on other interests.

The elective share shall be in addition to homestead, exempt property, and allowances as provided in part IV.

History.
S. 15, ch. 75-220; s. 10, ch. 99-343; s. 26, ch. 2001-226.
Editor's Notes.
Former s. 732.208.

732.2115. Protection of payors and other third parties.

Although a property interest is included in the decedent's elective estate under s. 732.2035(2)-(8), a payor or other third party is not liable for paying, distributing, or transferring the property to a beneficiary designated in a governing instrument, or for taking any other action in good faith reliance on the validity of a governing instrument.

History.
S. 11, ch. 99-343.

732.2125. Right of election; by whom exercisable.

The right of election may be exercised:

(1) By the surviving spouse.

(2) With approval of the court having jurisdiction of the probate proceeding by an attorney in fact or a guardian of the property of the surviving spouse. Before approving the election, the court shall determine that the election is in the best interests of the surviving spouse during the spouse's probable lifetime.

History.
S. 15, ch. 75-220; s. 12, ch. 99-343; s. 27, ch. 2001-226; s. 6, ch. 2010-132, eff. Oct. 1, 2010.
Editor's Notes.
Former s. 732.210.

732.2135. Time of election; extensions; withdrawal.

(1) Except as provided in subsection (2), the election must be filed on or before the earlier of the date that is 6 months after the date of service of a copy of the notice of administration on the surviving spouse, or an attorney in fact or guardian of the property of the surviving spouse, or the date that is 2 years after the date of the decedent's death.

(2) Within the period provided in subsection (1), the surviving spouse or an attorney in fact or guardian of the property of the surviving spouse may petition the court for an extension of time for making an election. For good cause shown, the court may extend the time for election. If the court grants the petition for an extension, the election must be filed within the time allowed by the extension.

(3) The surviving spouse or an attorney in fact, guardian of the property, or personal representative of the surviving spouse may withdraw an election at any time within 8 months after the decedent's death and before the court's order of contribution.

(4) A petition for an extension of the time for making the election or for approval to make the election shall toll the time for making the election.

(5) If the court determines that an election is made or pursued in bad faith, the court may assess attorney's fees and costs against the surviving spouse or the surviving spouse's estate.

History.
S. 15, ch. 75-220; s. 13, ch. 99-343; s. 28, ch. 2001-226; s. 4, ch. 2006-134, eff. July 1, 2006; s. 7, ch. 2009-115, eff. July 1, 2009.
Editor's Notes.
Former s. 732.212.

732.2145. Order of contribution; personal representative's duty to collect contribution.

(1) The court shall determine the elective share and contribution. Contributions shall bear interest at the statutory rate beginning 90 days after the order of contribution. The order is prima facie correct in proceedings in any court or jurisdiction.

(2) Except as provided in subsection (3), the personal representative shall collect contribution from the recipients of the elective estate as provided in the court's order of contribution.

(a) If property within the possession or control of the personal representative is distributable to a beneficiary or trustee who is required to contribute in satisfaction of the elective share, the personal representative shall withhold from the distribution the contribution required of the beneficiary or trustee.

(b) If, after the order of contribution, the personal representative brings an action to collect contribution from property not within the personal representative's control, the judgment shall include the personal representative's costs and reasonable attorney's fees. The personal representative is not required to seek collection of any portion of the elective share from property not within the personal representative's control until after the entry of the order of contribution.

(3) A personal representative who has the duty under this section of enforcing contribution may be relieved of that duty by an order of the court finding that it is impracticable to enforce contribution in view of the improbability of obtaining a judgment or the improbability of collection under any judgment that might be obtained, or otherwise. The personal representative shall not be liable for failure to attempt collection if the attempt would have been economically impracticable.

(4) Nothing in this section limits the independent right of the surviving spouse to collect the elective share as provided in the order of contribution, and that right is hereby conferred. If the surviving spouse brings an action to enforce the order, the judgment shall include the surviving spouse's costs and reasonable attorney's fees.

History.
S. 14, ch. 99-343; s. 29, ch. 2001-226.

732.2155. Effective date; effect of prior waivers; transition rules.

(1) Sections 732.201-732.2155 are effective on October 1, 1999, for all decedents dying on or after October 1, 2001. The law in effect prior to October 1, 1999, applies to decedents dying before October 1, 2001.

(2) Nothing in ss. 732.201-732.2155 modifies or applies to the rights of spouses under chapter 61.

(3) A waiver of elective share rights before the effective date of this section which is otherwise in compliance with the requirements of s. 732.702 is a waiver of all rights under ss. 732.201-732.2145.

(4) Notwithstanding anything in s. 732.2045(1)(a) to the contrary, any trust created by the decedent before the effective date of ss. 732.201-732.2145 that meets the requirements of an elective share trust is treated as if the decedent created the trust after the effective date of these sections and in satisfaction of the elective share.

(5) Sections 732.201-732.2155 do not affect any interest in contracts entered into for adequate consideration in money or money's worth before October 1, 1999, to the extent that the contract was irrevocable at all times from October 1, 1999, until the date of the decedent's death.

(6) Sections 732.201-732.2155 do not affect any interest in property held, as of the decedent's death, in a trust, whether revocable or irrevocable, if:

(a) The property was an asset of the trust at all times between October 1, 1999, and the date of the decedent's death;

(b) The decedent was not married to the decedent's surviving spouse when the property was transferred to the trust; and

(c) The property was a nonmarital asset as defined in s. 61.075 immediately prior to the decedent's death.

History.
S. 15, ch. 99-343; s. 30, ch. 2001-226.

732.216. Short title.

Sections 732.216-732.228 may be cited as the "Florida Uniform Disposition of Community Property Rights at Death Act."

History.
S. 4, ch. 92-200.

732.217. Application.

Sections 732.216-732.228 apply to the disposition at death of the following property acquired by a married person:

(1) Personal property, wherever located, which:

(a) Was acquired as, or became and remained, community property under the laws of another jurisdiction;

(b) Was acquired with the rents, issues, or income of, or the proceeds from, or in exchange for, community property; or

(c) Is traceable to that community property.

(2) Real property, except real property held as tenants by the entirety, which is located in this state, and which:

(a) Was acquired with the rents, issues, or income of, the proceeds from, or in exchange for, property acquired as, or which became and remained, community property under the laws of another jurisdiction; or

(b) Is traceable to that community property.

History.
S. 5, ch. 92-200; s. 4, ch. 2003-154.

732.218. Rebuttable presumptions.

In determining whether ss. 732.216-732.228 apply to specific property, the following rebuttable presumptions apply:

(1) Property acquired during marriage by a spouse of that marriage while domiciled in a jurisdiction under whose laws property could then be acquired as community property is presumed to have been acquired as, or to have become and remained, property to which these sections apply.

(2) Real property located in this state, other than homestead and real property held as tenants by the entirety, and personal property wherever located acquired by a married person while domiciled in a jurisdiction under whose laws property could not then be acquired as community property and title to which was taken in a form which created rights of survivorship are presumed to be property to which these sections do not apply.

History.
S. 6, ch. 92-200; s. 31, ch. 2001-226.

732.219. Disposition upon death.

Upon the death of a married person, one-half of the property to which ss. 732.216-732.228 apply is the property of the surviving spouse and is not subject to testamentary disposition by the decedent or distribution under the laws of succession of this state. One-half of that property is the property of the decedent and is subject to testamentary disposition or distribution under the laws of succession of this state. The decedent's one-half of that property is not in the elective estate.

History.
S. 7, ch. 92-200; s. 32, ch. 2001-226; s. 107, ch. 2002-1.

732.221. Perfection of title of personal representative or beneficiary.

If the title to any property to which ss. 732.216-732.228 apply is held by the surviving spouse at the time of the decedent's death, the personal representative or a beneficiary of the decedent may institute an action to perfect title to the property. The personal representative has no duty to discover whether any property held by the surviving spouse is property to which ss. 732.216-732.228 apply, unless a written demand is made by a beneficiary within 3 months after service of a copy of the notice of administration on the beneficiary or by a creditor within 3 months after the first publication of the notice to creditors.

History.
S. 8, ch. 92-200; s. 33, ch. 2001-226.

732.222.   Purchaser for value or lender.

(1) If a surviving spouse has apparent title to property to which ss. 732.216-732.228 apply, a purchaser for value or a lender taking a security interest in the property takes the interest in the property free of any rights of the personal representative or a beneficiary of the decedent.

(2) If a personal representative or a beneficiary of the decedent has apparent title to property to which ss. 732.216-732.228 apply, a purchaser for value or a lender taking a security interest in the property takes that interest in the property free of any rights of the surviving spouse.

(3) A purchaser for value or a lender need not inquire whether a vendor or borrower acted properly.

(4) The proceeds of a sale or creation of a security interest must be treated as the property transferred to the purchaser for value or a lender.

History.
S. 9, ch. 92-200; s. 956, ch. 97-102; s. 34, ch. 2001-226.

732.223.   Perfection of title of surviving spouse.

If the title to any property to which ss. 732.216-732.228 apply was held by the decedent at the time of the decedent's death, title of the surviving spouse may be perfected by an order of the probate court or by execution of an instrument by the personal representative or the beneficiaries of the decedent with the approval of the probate court. The probate court in which the decedent's estate is being administered has no duty to discover whether property held by the decedent is property to which ss. 732.216-732.228 apply. The personal representative has no duty to discover whether property held by the decedent is property to which ss. 732.216-732.228 apply unless a written demand is made by the surviving spouse or the spouse's successor in interest within 3 months after service of a copy of the notice of administration on the surviving spouse or the spouse's successor in interest.

History.
S. 10, ch. 92-200; s. 957, ch. 97-102; s. 35, ch. 2001-226.

732.224.   Creditor's rights.

Sections 732.216-732.228 do not affect rights of creditors with respect to property to which ss. 732.216-732.228 apply.

History.
S. 11, ch. 92-200.

732.225.   Acts of married persons.

Sections 732.216-732.228 do not prevent married persons from severing or altering their interests in property to which these sections apply. The reinvestment of any property to which these sections apply in real property located in this state which is or becomes homestead property creates a conclusive presumption that the spouses have agreed to terminate the community property attribute of the property reinvested.

History.
S. 12, ch. 92-200.

732.226.   Limitations on testamentary disposition.

Sections 732.216-732.228 do not authorize a person to dispose of property by will if it is held under limitations imposed by law preventing testamentary disposition by that person.

History.
S. 13, ch. 92-200.

732.227.   Homestead defined.

For purposes of ss. 732.216-732.228, the term "homestead" refers only to property the descent and devise of which is restricted by s. 4(c), Art. X of the State Constitution.

History.
S. 14, ch. 92-200.

732.228.   Uniformity of application and construction.

Sections 732.216-732.228 are to be so applied and construed as to effectuate their general purpose to make uniform the law with respect to the subject of these sections among those states which enact them.

History.
S. 15, ch. 92-200.

PART III.
PRETERMITTED SPOUSE AND CHILDREN.

732.301.   Pretermitted spouse.

When a person marries after making a will and the spouse survives the testator, the surviving spouse shall receive a share in the estate of the testator equal in value to that which the surviving spouse would have received if the testator had died intestate, unless:

(1) Provision has been made for, or waived by, the spouse by prenuptial or postnuptial agreement;

(2) The spouse is provided for in the will; or

(3) The will discloses an intention not to make provision for the spouse.

The share of the estate that is assigned to the pretermitted spouse shall be obtained in accordance with s. 733.805.

History.
S. 1, ch. 74-106; s. 16, ch. 75-220; s. 9, ch. 77-87.
Editor's Notes.
Created from former s. 731.10.

732.302. Pretermitted children.

When a testator omits to provide by will for any of his or her children born or adopted after making the will and the child has not received a part of the testator's property equivalent to a child's part by way of advancement, the child shall receive a share of the estate equal in value to that which the child would have received if the testator had died intestate, unless:

(1) It appears from the will that the omission was intentional; or

(2) The testator had one or more children when the will was executed and devised substantially all the estate to the other parent of the pretermitted child and that other parent survived the testator and is entitled to take under the will.

The share of the estate that is assigned to the pretermitted child shall be obtained in accordance with s. 733.805.

History.
S. 1, ch. 74-106; s. 16, ch. 75-220; s. 958, ch. 97-102; s. 36, ch. 2001-226.

Editor's Notes.
Created from former s. 731.11.

PART IV.
EXEMPT PROPERTY AND ALLOWANCES.

732.401. Descent of homestead.

(1) If not devised as authorized by law and the constitution, the homestead shall descend in the same manner as other intestate property; but if the decedent is survived by a spouse and one or more descendants, the surviving spouse shall take a life estate in the homestead, with a vested remainder to the descendants in being at the time of the decedent's death per stirpes.

(2) In lieu of a life estate under subsection (1), the surviving spouse may elect to take an undivided one-half interest in the homestead as a tenant in common, with the remaining undivided one-half interest vesting in the decedent's descendants in being at the time of the decedent's death, per stirpes.

(a) The right of election may be exercised:

1. By the surviving spouse; or

2. With the approval of a court having jurisdiction of the real property, by an attorney in fact or guardian of the property of the surviving spouse. Before approving the election, the court shall determine that the election is in the best interests of the surviving spouse during the spouse's probable lifetime.

(b) The election must be made within 6 months after the decedent's death and during the surviving spouse's lifetime. The time for making the election may not be extended except as provided in paragraph (c).

(c) A petition by an attorney in fact or by a guardian of the property of the surviving spouse for approval to make the election must be filed within 6 months after the decedent's death and during the surviving spouse's lifetime. If the petition is timely filed, the time for making the election shall be extended for at least 30 days after the rendition of the order allowing the election.

(d) Once made, the election is irrevocable.

(e) The election shall be made by filing a notice of election containing the legal description of the homestead property for recording in the official record books of the county or counties where the homestead property is located. The notice must be in substantially the following form:

ELECTION OF SURVIVING SPOUSE TO TAKE A ONE-HALF INTEREST OF DECEDENT'S INTEREST IN HOMESTEAD PROPERTY

STATE OF _____
COUNTY OF _____

1. The decedent, _____, died on _____. On the date of the decedent's death, The decedent was married to _____, who survived the decedent.

2. At the time of the decedent's death, the decedent owned an interest in real property that the affiant believes to be homestead property described in s. 4, Article X of the State Constitution, which real property being in _____ County, Florida, and described as: (description of homestead property).

3. Affiant elects to take one-half of decedent's interest in the homestead as a tenant in common in lieu of a life estate.

4. If affiant is not the surviving spouse, affiant is the surviving spouse's attorney in fact or guardian of the property, and an order has been rendered by a court having jurisdiction of the real property authorizing the undersigned to make this election.

_____
(Affiant)

Sworn to (or affirmed) and subscribed before me this _____ day of (month), (year), by (affiant)

(Signature of Notary Public-State of Florida)

(Print, Type, or Stamp Commissioned Name of Notary Public)

Personally Known OR Produced Identification

(Type of Identification Produced)

(3) Unless and until an election is made under subsection (2), expenses relating to the ownership of the homestead shall be allocated between the surviving spouse, as life tenant, and the decedent's descen-

dants, as remaindermen, in accordance with chapter 738. If an election is made, expenses relating to the ownership of the homestead shall be allocated between the surviving spouse and the descendants as tenants in common in proportion to their respective shares, effective as of the date the election is filed for recording.

(4) If the surviving spouse's life estate created in subsection (1) is disclaimed pursuant to chapter 739, the interests of the decedent's descendants may not be divested.

(5) This section does not apply to property that the decedent owned in tenancy by the entireties or in joint tenancy with rights of survivorship.

History.
S. 1, ch. 74-106; s. 17, ch. 75-220; s. 37, ch. 2001-226; s. 12, ch. 2007-74, eff. July 1, 2007; s. 7, ch. 2010-132, eff. Oct. 1, 2010; s. 3, ch. 2012-109, eff. July 1, 2012.

Editor's Notes.
Created from former s. 731.27.
The introductory language of s. 3, ch. 2012-109 provides: "Effective July 1, 2012, and applicable only to estates of persons dying on or after July 1, 2012, section 732.401, Florida Statutes, is amended to read."

732.4015. Devise of homestead.

(1) As provided by the Florida Constitution, the homestead shall not be subject to devise if the owner is survived by a spouse or a minor child or minor children, except that the homestead may be devised to the owner's spouse if there is no minor child or minor children.

(2) For the purposes of subsection (1), the term:

(a) "Owner" includes the grantor of a trust described in s. 733.707(3) that is evidenced by a written instrument which is in existence at the time of the grantor's death as if the interest held in trust was owned by the grantor.

(b) "Devise" includes a disposition by trust of that portion of the trust estate which, if titled in the name of the grantor of the trust, would be the grantor's homestead.

(3) If an interest in homestead has been devised to the surviving spouse as authorized by law and the constitution, and the surviving spouse's interest is disclaimed, the disclaimed interest shall pass in accordance with chapter 739.

History.
S. 1, ch. 74-106; ss. 18, 30, ch. 75-220; s. 16, ch. 92-200; s. 959, ch. 97-102; s. 38, ch. 2001-226; s. 13, ch. 2007-74, eff. July 1, 2007; s. 8, ch. 2010-132, eff. Oct. 1, 2010.

732.4017. Inter vivos transfer of homestead property.

(1) If the owner of homestead property transfers an interest in that property, including a transfer in trust, with or without consideration, to one or more persons during the owner's lifetime, the transfer is not a devise for purposes of s. 731.201(10) or s. 732.4015, and the interest transferred does not descend as provided in s. 732.401 if the transferor fails to retain a power, held in

any capacity, acting alone or in conjunction with any other person, to revoke or revest that interest in the transferor.

(2) As used in this section, the term "transfer in trust" refers to a trust under which the transferor of the homestead property, alone or in conjunction with another person, does not possess a right of revocation as that term is defined in s. 733.707(3)(e). A power possessed by the transferor which is exercisable during the transferor's lifetime to alter the beneficial use and enjoyment of the interest within a class of beneficiaries identified only in the trust instrument is not a right of revocation if the power may not be exercised in favor of the transferor, the transferor's creditors, the transferor's estate, or the creditors of the transferor's estate or exercised to discharge the transferor's legal obligations. This subsection does not create an inference that a power not described in this subsection is a power to revoke or revest an interest in the transferor.

(3) The transfer of an interest in homestead property described in subsection (1) may not be treated as a devise of that interest even if:

(a) The transferor retains a separate legal or equitable interest in the homestead property, directly or indirectly through a trust or other arrangement such as a term of years, life estate, reversion, possibility of reverter, or fractional fee interest;

(b) The interest transferred does not become a possessory interest until a date certain or upon a specified event, the occurrence or nonoccurrence of which does not constitute a power held by the transferor to revoke or revest the interest in the transferor, including, without limitation, the death of the transferor; or

(c) The interest transferred is subject to divestment, expiration, or lapse upon a date certain or upon a specified event, the occurrence or nonoccurrence of which does not constitute a power held by the transferor to revoke or revest the interest in the transferor, including, without limitation, survival of the transferor.

(4) It is the intent of the Legislature that this section clarify existing law.

History.
S. 9, ch. 2010-132, eff. Oct. 1, 2010.

732.402. Exempt property.

(1) If a decedent was domiciled in this state at the time of death, the surviving spouse, or, if there is no surviving spouse, the children of the decedent shall have the right to a share of the estate of the decedent as provided in this section, to be designated "exempt property."

(2) Exempt property shall consist of:

(a) Household furniture, furnishings, and appliances in the decedent's usual place of abode up to a net value of $20,000 as of the date of death.

(b) Two motor vehicles as defined in s. 316.003(21), which do not, individually as to either such motor vehicle, have a gross vehicle weight in excess of 15,000 pounds, held in the decedent's name and regularly used by the decedent or members of the decedent's immediate family as their personal motor vehicles.

(c) All qualified tuition programs authorized by s. 529 of the Internal Revenue Code of 1986, as amended, including, but not limited to, the Florida Prepaid College Trust Fund advance payment contracts under s. 1009.98 and the Florida Prepaid College Trust Fund participation agreements under s. 1009.981.

(d) All benefits paid pursuant to s. 112.1915.

(3) Exempt property shall be exempt from all claims against the estate except perfected security interests thereon.

(4) Exempt property shall be in addition to protected homestead, statutory entitlements, and property passing under the decedent's will or by intestate succession.

(5) Property specifically or demonstratively devised by the decedent's will to any devisee shall not be included in exempt property. However, persons to whom property has been specifically or demonstratively devised and who would otherwise be entitled to it as exempt property under this section may have the court determine the property to be exempt from claims, except for perfected security interests thereon, after complying with the provisions of subsection (6).

(6) Persons entitled to exempt property shall be deemed to have waived their rights under this section unless a petition for determination of exempt property is filed by or on behalf of the persons entitled to the exempt property on or before the later of the date that is 4 months after the date of service of the notice of administration or the date that is 40 days after the date of termination of any proceeding involving the construction, admission to probate, or validity of the will or involving any other matter affecting any part of the estate subject to this section.

(7) Property determined as exempt under this section shall be excluded from the value of the estate before residuary, intestate, or pretermitted or elective shares are determined.

History.
S. 1, ch. 74-106; s. 19, ch. 75-220; s. 10, ch. 77-87; s. 1, ch. 77-174; s. 1, ch. 81-238; s. 3, ch. 85-79; s. 67, ch. 87-226; s. 51, ch. 98-421; s. 3, ch. 99-220; s. 3, ch. 2001-180; s. 39, ch. 2001-226; s. 1036, ch. 2002-387; s. 5, ch. 2006-134, eff. July 1, 2006; s. 5, ch. 2006-303, eff. July 1, 2006; s. 8, ch. 2009-115, eff. July 1, 2009.

Editor's Notes.
Created from former s. 734.08.

Section 8, ch. 85-79, provides in pertinent part that with respect to s. 3, ch. 85-79, "the substantive rights of all persons which have vested prior to October 1, 1985, shall be determined as provided in s. 732.402, Florida Statutes, 1983."

Section 529 of the Internal Revenue Code, referred to in this section, is codified as 26 U.S.C.S. § 529.

732.403. Family allowance.

In addition to protected homestead and statutory entitlements, if the decedent was domiciled in Florida at the time of death, the surviving spouse and the decedent's lineal heirs the decedent was supporting or was obligated to support are entitled to a reasonable allowance in money out of the estate for their maintenance during administration. The court may order this allowance to be paid as a lump sum or in periodic installments. The allowance shall not exceed a total of $18,000. It shall be paid to the surviving spouse, if living, for the use of the spouse and dependent lineal heirs. If the surviving spouse is not living, it shall be paid to the lineal heirs or to the persons having their care and custody. If any lineal heir is not living with the surviving spouse, the allowance may be made partly to the lineal heir or guardian or other person having the heir's care and custody and partly to the surviving spouse, as the needs of the dependent heir and the surviving spouse appear. The family allowance is not chargeable against any benefit or share otherwise passing to the surviving spouse or to the dependent lineal heirs, unless the will otherwise provides. The death of any person entitled to a family allowance terminates the right to that part of the allowance not paid. For purposes of this section, the term "lineal heir" or "lineal heirs" means lineal ascendants and lineal descendants of the decedent.

History.
S. 1, ch. 74-106; s. 19, ch. 75-220; s. 960, ch. 97-102; s. 40, ch. 2001-226.

Editor's Notes.
Created from former s. 733.20.

PART V.
WILLS.

732.501. Who may make a will.

Any person who is of sound mind and who is either 18 or more years of age or an emancipated minor may make a will.

History.
S. 1, ch. 74-106; s. 113, ch. 75-220; s. 41, ch. 2001-226.

Editor's Notes.
Created from former s. 731.04.

732.502. Execution of wills.

Every will must be in writing and executed as follows:

(1)(a) *Testator's signature.*

1. The testator must sign the will at the end; or

2. The testator's name must be subscribed at the end of the will by some other person in the testator's presence and by the testator's direction.

(b) *Witnesses.* — The testator's:

1. Signing, or

2. Acknowledgment:

a. That he or she has previously signed the will, or

b. That another person has subscribed the testator's name to it,

must be in the presence of at least two attesting witnesses.

(c) *Witnesses' signatures.* — The attesting witnesses must sign the will in the presence of the testator and in the presence of each other.

(2) Any will, other than a holographic or nuncupative will, executed by a nonresident of Florida, either before or after this law takes effect, is valid as a will in this state if valid under the laws of the state or country where the will was executed. A will in the testator's handwriting that has been executed in accordance with subsection (1) shall not be considered a holographic will.

(3) Any will executed as a military testamentary instrument in accordance with 10 U.S.C. s. 1044d, Chapter 53, by a person who is eligible for military legal assistance is valid as a will in this state.

(4) No particular form of words is necessary to the validity of a will if it is executed with the formalities required by law.

(5) A codicil shall be executed with the same formalities as a will.

History.
S. 1, ch. 74-106; s. 21, ch. 75-220; s. 11, ch. 77-87; s. 961, ch. 97-102; s. 42, ch. 2001-226; s. 5, ch. 2003-154.

Editor's Notes.
Created from former s. 731.07.

732.503. Self-proof of will.

(1) A will or codicil executed in conformity with s. 732.502 may be made self-proved at the time of its execution or at any subsequent date by the acknowledgment of it by the testator and the affidavits of the witnesses, made before an officer authorized to administer oaths and evidenced by the officer's certificate attached to or following the will, in substantially the following form:

STATE OF FLORIDA
COUNTY OF _____

I, _____, declare to the officer taking my acknowledgment of this instrument, and to the subscribing witnesses, that I signed this instrument as my will.

_____

Testator

We, _____ and _____, have been sworn by the officer signing below, and declare to that officer on our oaths that the testator declared the instrument to be the testator's will and signed it in our presence and that we each signed the instrument as a witness in the presence of the testator and of each other.

_____

Witness

_____

Witness

Acknowledged and subscribed before me by the testator, (type or print testator's name), who is personally known to me or who has produced (state type of identification—see s. 117.05(5)(b)2.) as identification, and sworn to and subscribed before me by the witnesses, (type or print name of first witness) who is personally known to me or who has produced (state type of identification—see s. 117.05(5)(b)2.) as identification and (type or print name of second witness) who is personally known to me or who has produced (state type of identification—see s. 117.05(5)(b)2.) as identification, and subscribed by me in the presence of the testator and the subscribing witnesses, all on (date).

_____

(Signature of Officer)

_____

(Print, type, or stamp commissioned name and affix official seal)

(2) A will or codicil made self-proved under former law, or executed in another state and made self-proved under the laws of that state, shall be considered as self-proved under this section.

History.
S. 1, ch. 74-106; s. 21, ch. 75-220; s. 12, ch. 77-87; s. 8, ch. 93-62; s. 962; ch. 97-102; s. 18, ch. 98-246; s. 43, ch. 2001-226.

Editor's Notes.
Created from former s. 731.071.

732.504. Who may witness.

(1) Any person competent to be a witness may act as a witness to a will.

(2) A will or codicil, or any part of either, is not invalid because the will or codicil is signed by an interested witness.

History.
S. 1, ch. 74-106; s. 22, ch. 75-220; s. 1, ch. 77-174; s. 268, ch. 79-400.

732.505. Revocation by writing.

A will or codicil, or any part of either, is revoked:

(1) By a subsequent inconsistent will or codicil, even though the subsequent inconsistent will or codicil does not expressly revoke all previous wills or codicils, but the revocation extends only so far as the inconsistency.

(2) By a subsequent will, codicil, or other writing executed with the same formalities required for the execution of wills declaring the revocation.

History.
S. 1, ch. 74-106; s. 23, ch. 75-220; s. 13, ch. 77-87; s. 269, ch. 79-400; s. 44, ch. 2001-226.
Editor's Notes.
Created from former ss. 731.12, 731.13.

732.506.   Revocation by act.

A will or codicil is revoked by the testator, or some other person in the testator's presence and at the testator's direction, by burning, tearing, canceling, defacing, obliterating, or destroying it with the intent, and for the purpose, of revocation.

History.
S. 1, ch. 74-106; s. 23, ch. 75-220; s. 963, ch. 97-102.
Editor's Notes.
Created from former s. 731.14.

732.507.   Effect of subsequent marriage, birth, adoption, or dissolution of marriage.

(1) Neither subsequent marriage, birth, nor adoption of descendants shall revoke the prior will of any person, but the pretermitted child or spouse shall inherit as set forth in ss. 732.301 and 732.302, regardless of the prior will.

(2) Any provision of a will executed by a married person that affects the spouse of that person shall become void upon the divorce of that person or upon the dissolution or annulment of the marriage. After the dissolution, divorce, or annulment, the will shall be administered and construed as if the former spouse had died at the time of the dissolution, divorce, or annulment of the marriage, unless the will or the dissolution or divorce judgment expressly provides otherwise.

History.
S. 1, ch. 74-106; s. 113, ch. 75-220; s. 3, ch. 90-23; s. 45, ch. 2001-226; s. 14, ch. 2007-74, eff. July 1, 2007.
Editor's Notes.
Created from former ss. 731.10, 731.101, 731.11.

732.508.   Revival by revocation.

(1) The revocation by the testator of a will that revokes a former will shall not revive the former will, even though the former will is in existence at the date of the revocation of the subsequent will.

(2) The revocation of a codicil to a will does not revoke the will, and, in the absence of evidence to the contrary, it shall be presumed that in revoking the codicil the testator intended to reinstate the provisions of a will or codicil that were changed or revoked by the revoked codicil, as if the revoked codicil had never been executed.

History.
S. 1, ch. 74-106; s. 25, ch. 75-220.
Editor's Notes.
Created from former s. 731.15.

732.509.   Revocation of codicil.

The revocation of a will revokes all codicils to that will.

History.
S. 1, ch. 74-106; s. 113, ch. 75-220.
Editor's Notes.
Created from former s. 731.16.

732.5105.   Republication of wills by codicil.

The execution of a codicil referring to a previous will has the effect of republishing the will as modified by the codicil.

History.
S. 1, ch. 74-106; s. 113, ch. 75-220.
Editor's Notes.
Created from former s. 731.17.

732.511.   Republication of wills by reexecution.

If a will has been revoked or if it is invalid for any other reason, it may be republished and made valid by its reexecution or the execution of a codicil republishing it with the formalities required by this law for the execution of wills.

History.
S. 1, ch. 74-106; s. 113, ch. 75-220.
Editor's Notes.
Created from former s. 731.18.

732.512.   Incorporation by reference.

(1) A writing in existence when a will is executed may be incorporated by reference if the language of the will manifests this intent and describes the writing sufficiently to permit its identification.

(2) A will may dispose of property by reference to acts and events which have significance apart from their effect upon the dispositions made by the will, whether they occur before or after the execution of the will or before or after the testator's death. The execution or revocation of a will or trust by another person is such an event.

History.
S. 1, ch. 74-106; s. 27, ch. 75-220.

732.513.   Devises to trustee.

(1) A valid devise may be made to the trustee of a trust that is evidenced by a written instrument in existence at the time of making the will, or by a written instrument subscribed concurrently with making of the will, if the written instrument is identified in the will.

(2) The devise shall not be invalid for any or all of the following reasons:

    (a) Because the trust is amendable or revocable, or both, by any person.

    (b) Because the trust has been amended or revoked in part after execution of the will or a codicil to it.

    (c) Because the only res of the trust is the possible expectancy of receiving, as a named beneficiary, a devise under a will or death benefits as described in s. 733.808, and even though the testator or other person has reserved any or all rights of ownership in the death benefit policy, contract, or plan, including the right to change the beneficiary.

(d) Because of any of the provisions of s. 689.075.

(3) The devise shall dispose of property under the terms of the instrument that created the trust as previously or subsequently amended.

(4) An entire revocation of the trust by an instrument in writing before the testator's death shall invalidate the devise or bequest.

(5) Unless the will provides otherwise, the property devised shall not be held under a testamentary trust of the testator but shall become a part of the principal of the trust to which it is devised.

History.
S. 1, ch. 74-106; s. 3, ch. 75-74; s. 113, ch. 75-220; s. 2, ch. 88-340; s. 46, ch. 2001-226; s. 32, ch. 2006-217, eff. July 1, 2007.

Editor's Notes.
Created from former s. 736.17.

732.514. Vesting of devises.

The death of the testator is the event that vests the right to devises unless the testator in the will has provided that some other event must happen before a devise vests.

History.
S. 1, ch. 74-106; ss. 28, 113, ch. 75-220; s. 964, ch. 97-102; s. 47, ch. 2001-226.

Editor's Notes.
Created from former ss. 731.21 and 733.102.

• 732.515. Separate writing identifying devises of tangible property.

A written statement or list referred to in the decedent's will shall dispose of items of tangible personal property, other than property used in trade or business, not otherwise specifically disposed of by the will. To be admissible under this section as evidence of the intended disposition, the writing must be signed by the testator and must describe the items and the devisees with reasonable certainty. The writing may be prepared before or after the execution of the will. It may be altered by the testator after its preparation. It may be a writing that has no significance apart from its effect upon the dispositions made by the will. If more than one otherwise effective writing exists, then, to the extent of any conflict among the writings, the provisions of the most recent writing revoke the inconsistent provisions of each prior writing.

History.
S. 1, ch. 74-106; s. 29, ch. 75-220; s. 48, ch. 2001-226.

732.5165. Effect of fraud, duress, mistake, and undue influence.

A will is void if the execution is procured by fraud, duress, mistake, or undue influence. Any part of the will is void if so procured, but the remainder of the will not so procured shall be valid if it is not invalid for other reasons. If the revocation of a will, or any part thereof, is procured by fraud, duress, mistake, or undue influence, such revocation is void.

History.
S. 31, ch. 75-220; s. 6, ch. 2011-183, eff. June 21, 2011.

Editor's Notes.
Section 14, ch. 2011-183 provides: "Except as otherwise expressly provided in this act, this act shall take effect upon becoming a law and shall apply to all proceedings pending before such date and all cases commenced on or after the effective date."

732.517. Penalty clause for contest.

A provision in a will purporting to penalize any interested person for contesting the will or instituting other proceedings relating to the estate is unenforceable.

History.
S. 1, ch. 74-106; s. 113, ch. 75-220.

732.518. Will contests.

An action to contest the validity of all or part of a will or the revocation of all or part of a will may not be commenced before the death of the testator.

History.
S. 17, ch. 92-200; s. 7, ch. 2011-183, eff. June 21, 2011.

Editor's Notes.
Section 14, ch. 2011-183 provides: "Except as otherwise expressly provided in this act, this act shall take effect upon becoming a law and shall apply to all proceedings pending before such date and all cases commenced on or after the effective date."

PART VI.
RULES OF CONSTRUCTION.

732.6005. Rules of construction and intention.

(1) The intention of the testator as expressed in the will controls the legal effect of the testator's dispositions. The rules of construction expressed in this part shall apply unless a contrary intention is indicated by the will.

(2) Subject to the foregoing, a will is construed to pass all property which the testator owns at death, including property acquired after the execution of the will.

History.
S. 1, ch. 74-106; ss. 33, 35, ch. 75-220; s. 965, ch. 97-102; s. 49, ch. 2001-226.

Editor's Notes.
Created from former ss. 732.41 and 732.602.

732.601. Simultaneous Death Law.

Unless a contrary intention appears in the governing instrument:

(1) When title to property or its devolution depends on priority of death and there is insufficient evidence that the persons have died otherwise than simultaneously, the property of each person shall be disposed of as if that person survived.

(2) When two or more beneficiaries are designated to take successively by reason of survivorship under another person's disposition of property and there is insufficient evidence that the beneficiaries

died otherwise than simultaneously, the property thus disposed of shall be divided into as many equal parts as there are successive beneficiaries and the parts shall be distributed to those who would have taken if each designated beneficiary had survived.

(3) When there is insufficient evidence that two joint tenants or tenants by the entirety died otherwise than simultaneously, the property so held shall be distributed one-half as if one had survived and one-half as if the other had survived. If there are more than two joint tenants and all of them so died, the property thus distributed shall be in the proportion that one bears to the number of joint tenants.

(4) When the insured and the beneficiary in a policy of life or accident insurance have died and there is insufficient evidence that they died otherwise than simultaneously, the proceeds of the policy shall be distributed as if the insured had survived the beneficiary.

History.
S. 1, ch. 74-106; s. 34, ch. 75-220; s. 966, ch. 97-102; s. 50, ch. 2001-226.
Editor's Notes.
Created from former s. 736.05.

732.603. Antilapse; deceased devisee; class gifts.

(1) Unless a contrary intent appears in the will, if a devisee who is a grandparent, or a descendant of a grandparent, of the testator:

(a) Is dead at the time of the execution of the will;

(b) Fails to survive the testator; or

(c) Is required by the will or by operation of law to be treated as having predeceased the testator,

a substitute gift is created in the devisee's surviving descendants who take per stirpes the property to which the devisee would have been entitled had the devisee survived the testator.

(2) When a power of appointment is exercised by will, unless a contrary intent appears in the document creating the power of appointment or in the testator's will, if an appointee who is a grandparent, or a descendant of a grandparent, of the donor of the power:

(a) Is dead at the time of the execution of the will or the creation of the power;

(b) Fails to survive the testator; or

(c) Is required by the will, the document creating the power, or by operation of law to be treated as having predeceased the testator,

a substitute gift is created in the appointee's surviving descendants who take per stirpes the property to which the appointee would have been entitled had the appointee survived the testator. Unless the language creating a power of appointment expressly excludes the substitution of the descendants of an object of a power for the object, a surviving descendant of a deceased object of a power of appointment may be substituted for the object whether or not the descendant is an object of the power.

(3) In the application of this section:

(a) Words of survivorship in a devise or appointment to an individual, such as "if he survives me," or to "my surviving children," are a sufficient indication of an intent contrary to the application of subsections (1) and (2). Words of survivorship used by the donor of the power in a power to appoint to an individual, such as the term "if he survives the donee," or in a power to appoint to the donee's "then surviving children," are a sufficient indication of an intent contrary to the application of subsection (2).

(b) The term:

1. "Appointment" includes an alternative appointment and an appointment in the form of a class gift.

2. "Appointee" includes:

a. A class member if the appointment is in the form of a class gift.

b. An individual or class member who was deceased at the time the testator executed his or her will as well as an individual or class member who was then living but who failed to survive the testator.

3. "Devise" also includes an alternative devise and a devise in the form of a class gift.

4. "Devisee" also includes:

a. A class member if the devise is in the form of a class gift.

b. An individual or class member who was deceased at the time the testator executed his or her will as well as an individual or class member who was then living but who failed to survive the testator.

(4) This section applies only to outright devises and appointments. Devises and appointments in trust, including to a testamentary trust, are subject to s. 736.1106.

History.
S. 1, ch. 74-106; s. 36, ch. 75-220; s. 967, ch. 97-102; s. 51, ch. 2001-226; s. 6, ch. 2003-154; s. 33, ch. 2006-217, eff. July 1, 2007.
Editor's Notes.
Created from former s. 731.20.

732.604. Failure of testamentary provision.

(1) Except as provided in s. 732.603, if a devise other than a residuary devise fails for any reason, it becomes a part of the residue.

(2) Except as provided in s. 732.603, if the residue is devised to two or more persons, the share of a residuary devisee that fails for any reason passes to the other residuary devisee, or to the other residuary devisees in proportion to the interests of each in the remaining part of the residue.

History.
S. 1, ch. 74-106; s. 113, ch. 75-220; s. 968, ch. 97-102; s. 52, ch. 2001-226; s. 29, ch. 2003-154; s. 34, ch. 2006-217, eff. July 1, 2007.
Editor's Notes.
Section 29, ch. 2003-154 reenacted 732.604 without change to incorporate amendments to statutory sections referenced therein.

732.605. Change in securities; accessions; nonademption.

(1) If the testator intended a specific devise of certain securities rather than their equivalent value, the specific devisee is entitled only to:

(a) As much of the devised securities as is a part of the estate at the time of the testator's death.

(b) Any additional or other securities of the same entity owned by the testator because of action initiated by the entity, excluding any acquired by exercise of purchase options.

(c) Securities of another entity owned by the testator as a result of a merger, consolidation, reorganization, or other similar action initiated by the entity.

(d) Securities of the same entity acquired as a result of a plan of reinvestment.

(2) Distributions before death with respect to a specifically devised security, whether in cash or otherwise, which are not provided for in subsection (1) are not part of the specific devise.

History.
S. 1, ch. 74-106; s. 113, ch. 75-220; s. 53, ch. 2001-226.

732.606. Nonademption of specific devises in certain cases; sale by guardian of the property; unpaid proceeds of sale, condemnation, or insurance.

(1) If specifically devised property is sold by a guardian of the property or if a condemnation award or insurance proceeds are paid to a guardian of the property, the specific devisee has the right to a general pecuniary devise equal to the net sale price, the condemnation award, or the insurance proceeds. This subsection does not apply if, subsequent to the sale, condemnation, or casualty, it is adjudicated that the disability of the testator has ceased and the testator survives the adjudication by 1 year. The right of the specific devisee under this subsection is reduced by any right described in subsection (2).

(2) A specific devisee has the right to the remaining specifically devised property and:

(a) Any balance of the purchase price owing from a purchaser to the testator at death because of sale of the property plus any security interest.

(b) Any amount of a condemnation award for the taking of the property unpaid at death.

(c) Any proceeds unpaid at death on fire or casualty insurance on the property.

(d) Property owned by the testator at death as a result of foreclosure, or obtained instead of foreclosure, of the security for the specifically devised obligation.

History.
S. 1, ch. 74-106; s. 38, ch. 75-220; s. 969, ch. 97-102; s. 54, ch. 2001-226.

732.607. Exercise of power of appointment.

A general residuary clause in a will, or a will making general disposition of all the testator's property, does not exercise a power of appointment held by the testator unless specific reference is made to the power or there is some other indication of intent to include the property subject to the power.

History.
S. 1, ch. 74-106; s. 38, ch. 75-220.

732.608. Construction of terms.

The laws used to determine paternity and relationships for the purposes of intestate succession apply when determining whether class gift terminology and terms of relationship include adopted persons and persons born out of wedlock.

History.
S. 1, ch. 74-106; s. 38, ch. 75-220; s. 10, ch. 2010-132, eff. Oct. 1, 2010.

732.609. Ademption by satisfaction.

Property that a testator gave to a person in the testator's lifetime is treated as a satisfaction of a devise to that person, in whole or in part, only if the will provides for deduction of the lifetime gift, the testator declares in a contemporaneous writing that the gift is to be deducted from the devise or is in satisfaction of the devise, or the devisee acknowledges in writing that the gift is in satisfaction. For purposes of part satisfaction, property given during the testator's lifetime is valued at the time the devisee came into possession or enjoyment of the property or at the time of the death of the testator, whichever occurs first.

History.
S. 1, ch. 74-106; s. 38, ch. 75-220.

732.611. Devises to multigeneration classes to be per stirpes.

Unless the will provides otherwise, all devises to descendants, issue, and other multigeneration classes shall be per stirpes.

History.
S. 1, ch. 74-106; s. 38, ch. 75-220; s. 35, ch. 2006-217, eff. July 1, 2007.

732.615. Reformation to correct mistakes.

Upon application of any interested person, the court may reform the terms of a will, even if unambiguous, to conform the terms to the testator's intent if it is proved by clear and convincing evidence that both the accomplishment of the testator's intent and the terms of the will were affected by a mistake of fact or law, whether in expression or inducement. In determining the testator's original intent, the court may consider evidence relevant to the testator's intent even though the evidence contradicts an apparent plain meaning of the will.

(1) and (2) → 2 seperate exceptions

History.
S. 3, ch. 2011-183, eff. July 1, 2011.
Editor's Notes.
Section 14, ch. 2011-183 provides: "Except as otherwise expressly provided in this act, this act shall take effect upon becoming a law and shall apply to all proceedings pending before such date and all cases commenced on or after the effective date."

732.616. Modification to achieve testator's tax objectives.

Upon application of any interested person, to achieve the testator's tax objectives the court may modify the terms of a will in a manner that is not contrary to the testator's probable intent. The court may provide that the modification has retroactive effect.

History.
S. 4, ch. 2011-183, eff. July 1, 2011.
Editor's Notes.
Section 14, ch. 2011-183 provides: "Except as otherwise expressly provided in this act, this act shall take effect upon becoming a law and shall apply to all proceedings pending before such date and all cases commenced on or after the effective date."

PART VII.
CONTRACTUAL ARRANGEMENTS RELATING TO DEATH.

732.701. Agreements concerning succession.

(1) No agreement to make a will, to give a devise, not to revoke a will, not to revoke a devise, not to make a will, or not to make a devise shall be binding or enforceable unless the agreement is in writing and signed by the agreeing party in the presence of two attesting witnesses. Such an agreement executed by a nonresident of Florida, either before or after this law takes effect, is valid in this state if valid when executed under the laws of the state or country where the agreement was executed, whether or not the agreeing party is a Florida resident at the time of death.

(2) The execution of a joint will or mutual wills neither creates a presumption of a contract to make a will nor creates a presumption of a contract not to revoke the will or wills.

History.
S. 1, ch. 74-106; s. 39, ch. 75-220; s. 55, ch. 2001-226.
Editor's Notes.
Created from former s. 731.051.

732.702. Waiver of spousal rights.

(1) The rights of a surviving spouse to an elective share, intestate share, pretermitted share, homestead, exempt property, family allowance, and preference in appointment as personal representative of an intestate estate or any of those rights, may be waived, wholly or partly, before or after marriage, by a written contract, agreement, or waiver, signed by the waiving party in the presence of two subscribing witnesses. The requirement of witnesses shall be applicable only to contracts, agreements, or waivers signed by Florida residents after the effective date of this law. Any contract, agreement, or waiver executed by a nonresident of Florida, either before or after this law takes effect, is valid in this state if valid when executed under the laws of the state or country where it was executed, whether or not he or she is a Florida resident at the time of death. Unless the waiver provides to the contrary, a waiver of "all rights," or equivalent language, in the property or estate of a present or prospective spouse, or a complete property settlement entered into after, or in anticipation of, separation, dissolution of marriage, or divorce, is a waiver of all rights to elective share, intestate share, pretermitted share, homestead, exempt property, family allowance, and preference in appointment as personal representative of an intestate estate, by the waiving party in the property of the other and a renunciation by the waiving party of all benefits that would otherwise pass to the waiving party from the other by intestate succession or by the provisions of any will executed before the written contract, agreement, or waiver.

(2) Each spouse shall make a fair disclosure to the other of that spouse's estate if the agreement, contract, or waiver is executed after marriage. No disclosure shall be required for an agreement, contract, or waiver executed before marriage.

(3) No consideration other than the execution of the agreement, contract, or waiver shall be necessary to its validity, whether executed before or after marriage.

History.
S. 1, ch. 74-106; s. 39, ch. 75-220; s. 14, ch. 77-87; s. 56, ch. 2001-226.

732.703. Effect of divorce, dissolution, or invalidity of marriage on disposition of certain assets at death.

(1) As used in this section, unless the context requires otherwise, the term:

(a) "Asset," when not modified by other words or phrases, means an asset described in subsection (3), except as provided in paragraph (4)(j).

(b) "Beneficiary" means any person designated in a governing instrument to receive an interest in an asset upon the death of the decedent.

(c) "Death certificate" means a certified copy of a death certificate issued by an official or agency for the place where the decedent's death occurred.

(d) "Employee benefit plan" means any funded or unfunded plan, program, or fund established by an employer to provide an employee's beneficiaries with benefits that may be payable on the employee's death.

(e) "Governing instrument" means any writing or contract governing the disposition of all or any part of an asset upon the death of the decedent.

(f) "Payor" means any person obligated to make payment of the decedent's interest in an asset upon the death of the decedent, and any other person who is in control or possession of an asset.

(g) "Primary beneficiary" means a beneficiary designated under the governing instrument to receive an interest in an asset upon the death of the decedent who is not a secondary beneficiary. A person who receives an interest in the asset upon the death of the decedent due to the death of another beneficiary prior to the decedent's death is also a primary beneficiary.

(h) "Secondary beneficiary" means a beneficiary designated under the governing instrument who will receive an interest in an asset if the designation of the primary beneficiary is revoked or otherwise cannot be given effect.

(2) A designation made by or on behalf of the decedent providing for the payment or transfer at death of an interest in an asset to or for the benefit of the decedent's former spouse is void as of the time the decedent's marriage was judicially dissolved or declared invalid by court order prior to the decedent's death, if the designation was made prior to the dissolution or court order. The decedent's interest in the asset shall pass as if the decedent's former spouse predeceased the decedent. An individual retirement account described in s. 408 or s. 408A of the Internal Revenue Code of 1986, or an employee benefit plan, may not be treated as a trust for purposes of this section.

(3) Subsection (2) applies to the following assets in which a resident of this state has an interest at the time of the resident's death:

(a) A life insurance policy, qualified annuity, or other similar tax-deferred contract held within an employee benefit plan.

(b) An employee benefit plan.

(c) An individual retirement account described in s. 408 or s. 408A of the Internal Revenue Code of 1986, including an individual retirement annuity described in s. 408(b) of the Internal Revenue Code of 1986.

(d) A payable-on-death account.

(e) A security or other account registered in a transfer-on-death form.

(f) A life insurance policy, annuity, or other similar contract that is not held within an employee benefit plan or a tax-qualified retirement account.

(4) Subsection (2) does not apply:

(a) To the extent that controlling federal law provides otherwise;

(b) If the governing instrument is signed by the decedent, or on behalf of the decedent, after the order of dissolution or order declaring the marriage invalid and such governing instrument expressly provides that benefits will be payable to the decedent's former spouse;

(c) To the extent a will or trust governs the disposition of the assets and s. 732.507(2) or s. 736.1005 applies;

(d) If the order of dissolution or order declaring the marriage invalid requires that the decedent acquire or maintain the asset for the benefit of a former spouse or children of the marriage, payable upon the death of the decedent either outright or in trust, only if other assets of the decedent fulfilling such a requirement for the benefit of the former spouse or children of the marriage do not exist upon the death of the decedent;

(e) If, under the terms of the order of dissolution or order declaring the marriage invalid, the decedent could not have unilaterally terminated or modified the ownership of the asset, or its disposition upon the death of the decedent;

(f) If the designation of the decedent's former spouse as a beneficiary is irrevocable under applicable law;

(g) If the instrument directing the disposition of the asset at death is governed by the laws of a state other than this state;

(h) To an asset held in two or more names as to which the death of one coowner vests ownership of the asset in the surviving coowner or coowners;

(i) If the decedent remarries the person whose interest would otherwise have been revoked under this section and the decedent and that person are married to one another at the time of the decedent's death; or

(j) To state-administered retirement plans under chapter 121.

(5) In the case of an asset described in paragraph (3)(a), paragraph (3)(b), or paragraph (3)(c), unless payment or transfer would violate a court order directed to, and served as required by law on, the payor:

(a) If the governing instrument does not explicitly specify the relationship of the beneficiary to the decedent or if the governing instrument explicitly provides that the beneficiary is not the decedent's spouse, the payor is not liable for making any payment on account of, or transferring any interest in, the asset to the beneficiary.

(b) As to any portion of the asset required by the governing instrument to be paid after the decedent's death to a primary beneficiary explicitly designated in the governing instrument as the decedent's spouse:

1. If the death certificate states that the decedent was married at the time of his or her death to that spouse, the payor is not liable for making a payment on account of, or for transferring an interest in, that portion of the asset to such primary beneficiary.

2. If the death certificate states that the decedent was not married at the time of his or her death, or if the death certificate states that the decedent was married to a person other than the spouse designated as the primary beneficiary at the time of his or her death, the payor is not liable

for making a payment on account of, or for transferring an interest in, that portion of the asset to a secondary beneficiary under the governing instrument.

3. If the death certificate is silent as to the decedent's marital status at the time of his or her death, the payor is not liable for making a payment on account of, or for transferring an interest in, that portion of the asset to the primary beneficiary upon delivery to the payor of an affidavit validly executed by the primary beneficiary in substantially the following form:
STATE OF _____.
COUNTY OF _____
Before me, the undersigned authority, personally appeared (type or print affiant's name) ("Affiant"), who swore or affirmed that:
  1. (Type or print name of decedent) ("Decedent") died on (type or print the date of the Decedent's death)
  2. Affiant is a "primary beneficiary" as that term is defined in Section 732.703, Florida Statutes. Affiant and Decedent were married on (type or print the date of marriage) , and were legally married to one another on the date of the Decedent's death.

_____ (Affiant)_____
Sworn to or affirmed before me by the affiant who is personally known to me or who has produced (state type of identification) as identification this ____ day of (month)_____,____ (year)
(Signature of Officer)
(Print, Type, or Stamp Commissioned name of Notary Public)
  4. If the death certificate is silent as to the decedent's marital status at the time of his or her death, the payor is not liable for making a payment on account of, or for transferring an interest in, that portion of the asset to the secondary beneficiary upon delivery to the payor of an affidavit validly executed by the secondary beneficiary affidavit in substantially the following form:
STATE OF _____
COUNTY OF _____.
Before me, the undersigned authority, personally appeared _____ (type or print affiant's name) _____ ("Affiant"), who swore or affirmed that:
  1. _____ (Type or print name of decedent) _____ ("Decedent") died on _____ (type or print the date of the Decedent's death) _____
  2. Affiant is a "secondary beneficiary" as that term is defined in Section 732.703, Florida Statutes. On the date of the Decedent's death, the Decedent was not legally married to the spouse designated as the "primary beneficiary" as that term is defined in Section 732.703, Florida Statutes.

Sworn to or affirmed before me by the affiant who is personally known to me or who has produced _____ (state type of identification) _____ as identification this _____ day of _____ (month) _____,_____ (year) _____
_____ (Signature of Officer)_____
(Print, Type, or Stamp Commissioned name of Notary Public)
  (6) In the case of an asset described in paragraph (3)(d), paragraph (3)(e), or paragraph (3)(f), the payor is not liable for making any payment on account of, or transferring any interest in, the asset to any beneficiary.
  (7) Subsections (5) and (6) apply notwithstanding the payor's knowledge that the person to whom the asset is transferred is different from the person who would own the interest pursuant to subsection (2).
  (8) This section does not affect the ownership of an interest in an asset as between the former spouse and any other person entitled to such interest by operation of this section, the rights of any purchaser for value of any such interest, the rights of any creditor of the former spouse or any other person entitled to such interest, or the rights and duties of any insurance company, financial institution, trustee, administrator, or other third party.
  (9) This section applies to all designations made by or on behalf of decedents dying on or after July 1, 2012, regardless of when the designation was made.
History.
S. 1, ch. 2012-148, eff. July 1, 2012.

PART VIII.
GENERAL PROVISIONS.

732.801. Disclaimer of interests in property passing by will or intestate succession or under certain powers of appointment [Repealed.]
  Repealed by s. 5, ch. 2005-108, effective July 1, 2005.
History.
S. 1, ch. 74-106; s. 40, ch. 75-220; s. 15, ch. 77-87; s. 970, ch. 97-102; s. 57, ch. 2001-226; s. 30, ch. 2003-154.

732.802. Killer not entitled to receive property or other benefits by reason of victim's death.
  (1) A surviving person who unlawfully and intentionally kills or participates in procuring the death of the decedent is not entitled to any benefits under the will or under the Florida Probate Code, and the estate of the decedent passes as if the killer had predeceased the decedent. Property appointed by the will of the decedent to or for the benefit of the killer passes as if the killer had predeceased the decedent.
  (2) Any joint tenant who unlawfully and intentionally kills another joint tenant thereby effects a severance of the interest of the decedent so that the share of the decedent passes as the decedent's property and the

killer has no rights by survivorship. This provision applies to joint tenancies with right of survivorship and tenancies by the entirety in real and personal property; joint and multiple-party accounts in banks, savings and loan associations, credit unions, and other institutions; and any other form of coownership with survivorship incidents.

(3) A named beneficiary of a bond, life insurance policy, or other contractual arrangement who unlawfully and intentionally kills the principal obligee or the person upon whose life the policy is issued is not entitled to any benefit under the bond, policy, or other contractual arrangement; and it becomes payable as though the killer had predeceased the decedent.

(4) Any other acquisition of property or interest by the killer, including a life estate in homestead property, shall be treated in accordance with the principles of this section.

(5) A final judgment of conviction of murder in any degree is conclusive for purposes of this section. In the absence of a conviction of murder in any degree, the court may determine by the greater weight of the evidence whether the killing was unlawful and intentional for purposes of this section.

(6) This section does not affect the rights of any person who, before rights under this section have been adjudicated, purchases from the killer for value and without notice property which the killer would have acquired except for this section, but the killer is liable for the amount of the proceeds or the value of the property. Any insurance company, bank, or other obligor making payment according to the terms of its policy or obligation is not liable by reason of this section unless prior to payment it has received at its home office or principal address written notice of a claim under this section.

History.
S. 1, ch. 74-106; s. 113, ch. 75-220; s. 1, ch. 82-71.
Editor's Notes.
Created from former s. 731.31.

732.804. Provisions relating to disposition of the body.

Before issuance of letters, any person may carry out written instructions of the decedent relating to the decedent's body and funeral and burial arrangements. The fact that cremation occurred pursuant to a written direction signed by the decedent that the body be cremated is a complete defense to a cause of action against any person acting or relying on that direction.

History.
S. 1, ch. 74-106; s. 43, ch. 75-220; s. 971, ch. 97-102; s. 58, ch. 2001-226.

732.805. Spousal rights procured by fraud, duress, or undue influence.

(1) A surviving spouse who is found to have procured a marriage to the decedent by fraud, duress, or undue influence is not entitled to any of the following

rights or benefits that inure solely by virtue of the marriage or the person's status as surviving spouse of the decedent unless the decedent and the surviving spouse voluntarily cohabited as husband and wife with full knowledge of the facts constituting the fraud, duress, or undue influence or both spouses otherwise subsequently ratified the marriage:

(a) Any rights or benefits under the Florida Probate Code, including, but not limited to, entitlement to elective share or family allowance; preference in appointment as personal representative; inheritance by intestacy, homestead, or exempt property; or inheritance as a pretermitted spouse.

(b) Any rights or benefits under a bond, life insurance policy, or other contractual arrangement if the decedent is the principal obligee or the person upon whose life the policy is issued, unless the surviving spouse is provided for by name, whether or not designated as the spouse, in the bond, life insurance policy, or other contractual arrangement.

(c) Any rights or benefits under a will, trust, or power of appointment, unless the surviving spouse is provided for by name, whether or not designated as the spouse, in the will, trust, or power of appointment.

(d) Any immunity from the presumption of undue influence that a surviving spouse may have under state law.

(2) Any of the rights or benefits listed in paragraphs (1)(a)-(c) which would have passed solely by virtue of the marriage to a surviving spouse who is found to have procured the marriage by fraud, duress, or undue influence shall pass as if the spouse had predeceased the decedent.

(3) A challenge to a surviving spouse's rights under this section may be maintained as a defense, objection, or cause of action by any interested person after the death of the decedent in any proceeding in which the fact of marriage may be directly or indirectly material.

(4) The contestant has the burden of establishing, by a preponderance of the evidence, that the marriage was procured by fraud, duress, or undue influence. If ratification of the marriage is raised as a defense, the surviving spouse has the burden of establishing, by a preponderance of the evidence, the subsequent ratification by both spouses.

(5) In all actions brought under this section, the court shall award taxable costs as in chancery actions, including attorney's fees. When awarding taxable costs and attorney's fees, the court may direct payment from a party's interest, if any, in the estate, or enter a judgment that may be satisfied from other property of the party, or both.

(6) An insurance company, financial institution, or other obligor making payment according to the terms of its policy or obligation is not liable by reason of this

section unless, before payment, it received written notice of a claim pursuant to this section.

(a) The notice required by this subsection must be in writing and must be accomplished in a manner reasonably suitable under the circumstances and likely to result in receipt of the notice. Permissible methods of notice include first-class mail, personal delivery, delivery to the person's last known place of residence or place of business, or a properly directed facsimile or other electronic message.

(b) To be effective, notice to a financial institution or insurance company must contain the name, address, and the taxpayer identification number, or the account or policy number, of the principal obligee or person whose life is insured and shall be directed to an officer or a manager of the financial institution or insurance company in this state. If the financial institution or insurance company has no offices in this state, the notice shall be directed to the principal office of the financial institution or insurance company.

(c) Notice shall be effective when given, except that notice to a financial institution or insurance company is not effective until 5 business days after being given.

(7) The rights and remedies granted in this section are in addition to any other rights or remedies a person may have at law or equity.

(8) Unless sooner barred by adjudication, estoppel, or a provision of the Florida Probate Code or Florida Probate Rules, an interested person is barred from bringing an action under this section unless the action is commenced within 4 years after the decedent's date of death. A cause of action under this section accrues on the decedent's date of death.

History.
S. 11, ch. 2010-132, eff. Oct. 1, 2010.

PART IX.
PRODUCTION OF WILLS.

732.901.   Production of wills.

(1) The custodian of a will must deposit the will with the clerk of the court having venue of the estate of the decedent within 10 days after receiving information that the testator is dead. The custodian must supply the testator's date of death or social security number to the clerk upon deposit.

(2) Upon petition and notice, the custodian of any will may be compelled to produce and deposit the will as provided in subsection (1). All costs, damages, and a reasonable attorney's fee shall be adjudged to petitioner against the delinquent custodian if the court finds that the custodian had no just or reasonable cause for failing to deposit the will.

History.
S. 1, ch. 74-106; s. 44, ch. 75-220; s. 18, ch. 92-200; s. 972, ch. 97-102; s. 59, ch. 2001-226.

Editor's Notes.
Created from former s. 732.22.

CHAPTER 733.
PROBATE CODE: ADMINISTRATION OF ESTATES

PART I.
GENERAL PROVISIONS.

733.101. Venue of probate proceedings.

(1) The venue for probate of wills and granting letters shall be:

(a) In the county in this state where the decedent was domiciled.

(b) If the decedent had no domicile in this state, then in any county where the decedent's property is located.

(c) If the decedent had no domicile in this state and possessed no property in this state, then in the county where any debtor of the decedent resides.

(2) For the purpose of this section, a married woman whose husband is an alien or a nonresident of Florida may establish or designate a separate domicile in this state.

(3) Whenever a proceeding is filed laying venue in an improper county, the court may transfer the action in the same manner as provided in the Florida Rules of Civil Procedure. Any action taken by the court or the parties before the transfer is not affected by the improper venue.

History.
S. 1, ch. 74-106; s. 46, ch. 75-220; s. 981, ch. 97-102; s. 78, ch. 2001-226.

Editor's Notes.
Created from former s. 732.06.

733.103. Effect of probate.

(1) Until admitted to probate in this state or in the state where the decedent was domiciled, the will shall be ineffective to prove title to, or the right to possession of, property of the testator.

(2) In any collateral action or proceeding relating to devised property, the probate of a will in Florida shall be conclusive of its due execution; that it was executed by a competent testator, free of fraud, duress, mistake, and undue influence; and that the will was unrevoked on the testator's death.

History.
S. 1, ch. 74-106; s. 48, ch. 75-220; s. 17, ch. 77-87; s. 1, ch. 77-174; s. 79, ch. 2001-226.

Editor's Notes.
Created from former s. 732.26.

733.104. Suspension of statutes of limitation in favor of the personal representative.

(1) If a person entitled to bring an action dies before the expiration of the time limited for the commencement of the action and the cause of action survives, the action may be commenced by that person's personal representative before the later of the expiration of the time limited for the commencement of the action or 12 months after the decedent's death.

(2) If a person against whom a cause of action exists dies before the expiration of the time limited for commencement of the action and the cause of action survives, if a claim is timely filed, the expiration of the time limited for commencement of the action shall not apply.

History.
S. 1, ch. 74-106; s. 48, ch. 75-220; s. 1, ch. 77-174; s. 982, ch. 97-102; s. 80, ch. 2001-226.

Editor's Notes.
Created from former s. 734.27.

733.105. Determination of beneficiaries.

(1) When property passes by intestate succession or the will is unclear and there is doubt about:

(a) Who is entitled to receive any part of the property, or

(b) The shares and amounts that any person is entitled to receive,

any interested person may petition the court to determine beneficiaries or their shares.

(2) Any personal representative who makes distribution or takes any other action pursuant to an order determining beneficiaries shall be fully protected.

(3) A separate civil action to determine beneficiaries may be brought when an estate has not been administered.

History.
S. 1, ch. 74-106; s. 48, ch. 75-220; s. 226, ch. 77-104; s. 1, ch. 77-174; s. 983, ch. 97-102; s. 81, ch. 2001-226.

Editor's Notes.
Created from former s. 734.25.

733.1051. Limited judicial construction of will with federal tax provisions.

(1) Upon the application of a personal representative or a person who is or may be a beneficiary who is affected by the outcome of the construction, a court at any time may construe the terms of a will to define the respective shares or determine beneficiaries, in accordance with the intention of a testator, if a disposition occurs during the applicable period and the will contains a provision that:

(a) Includes a disposition formula referring to the

terms "unified credit," "estate tax exemption," "applicable exemption amount," "applicable credit amount," "applicable exclusion amount," "generation-skipping transfer tax exemption," "GST exemption," "marital deduction," "maximum marital deduction," "unlimited marital deduction," or "maximum charitable deduction";

(b) Measures a share of an estate based on the amount that may pass free of federal estate tax or the amount that may pass free of federal generation-skipping transfer tax;

(c) Otherwise makes a disposition referring to a charitable deduction, marital deduction, or another provision of federal estate tax or generation-skipping transfer tax law; or

(d) Appears to be intended to reduce or minimize the federal estate tax or generation-skipping transfer tax.

(2) For purposes of this section:

(a) The term "applicable period" means a period beginning January 1, 2010, and ending on the end of the day on the earlier of December 31, 2010, or the day before the date that an act becomes law that repeals or otherwise modifies or has the effect of repealing or modifying s. 901 of the Economic Growth and Tax Relief Reconciliation Act of 2001.

(b) A "disposition occurs" when the testator dies.

(3) In construing the will, the court shall consider the terms and purposes of the will, the facts and circumstances surrounding the creation of the will, and the testator's probable intent. In determining the testator's probable intent, the court may consider evidence relevant to the testator's intent even though the evidence contradicts an apparent plain meaning of the will.

(4) This section does not apply to a disposition that is specifically conditioned upon no federal estate or generation-skipping transfer tax being imposed.

(5)(a) Unless otherwise ordered by the court, during the applicable period and without court order, the personal representative administering a will containing one or more provisions described in subsection (1) may:

1. Delay or refrain from making any distribution.

2. Incur and pay fees and costs reasonably necessary to determine its duties and obligations, including compliance with provisions of existing and reasonably anticipated future federal tax laws.

3. Establish and maintain reserves for the payment of these fees and costs and federal taxes.

(b) The personal representative shall not be liable for its actions as provided in this subsection made or taken in good faith.

(6) The provisions of this section are in addition to, and not in derogation of, rights under the common law to construe a will.

(7) This section is remedial in nature and intended to provide a new or modified legal remedy. This section shall operate retroactively to January 1, 2010.

History.
S. 12, ch. 2010-132, eff. May 27, 2010.

733.106. Costs and attorney's fees.

(1) In all probate proceedings costs may be awarded as in chancery actions.

(2) A person nominated as personal representative, or any proponent of a will if the person so nominated does not act within a reasonable time, if in good faith justified in offering the will in due form for probate, shall receive costs and attorney's fees from the estate even though probate is denied or revoked.

(3) Any attorney who has rendered services to an estate may be awarded reasonable compensation from the estate.

(4) When costs and attorney's fees are to be paid from the estate, the court may direct from what part of the estate they shall be paid.

History.
S. 1, ch. 74-106; s. 49, ch. 75-220; s. 984, ch. 97-102; s. 82, ch. 2001-226.
Editor's Notes.
Created from former s. 732.14.

733.1061. Fees and costs; will reformation and modification.

(1) In a proceeding arising under s. 732.615 or s. 732.616, the court shall award taxable costs as in chancery actions, including attorney's fees and guardian ad litem fees.

(2) When awarding taxable costs, including attorney's fees and guardian ad litem fees, under this section, the court in its discretion may direct payment from a party's interest, if any, in the estate or enter a judgment which may be satisfied from other property of the party, or both.

History.
S. 5, ch. 2011-183, eff. July 1, 2011.
Editor's Notes.
Section 14, ch. 2011-183 provides: "Except as otherwise expressly provided in this act, this act shall take effect upon becoming a law and shall apply to all proceedings pending before such date and all cases commenced on or after the effective date."

733.107. Burden of proof in contests; presumption of undue influence.

(1) In all proceedings contesting the validity of a will, the burden shall be upon the proponent of the will to establish prima facie its formal execution and attestation. A self-proving affidavit executed in accordance with s. 732.503 or an oath of an attesting witness executed as required in s. 733.201(2) is admissible and establishes prima facie the formal execution and attestation of the will. Thereafter, the contestant shall have the burden of establishing the grounds on which the probate of the will is opposed or revocation is sought.

(2) The presumption of undue influence implements public policy against abuse of fiduciary or confidential

relationships and is therefore a presumption shifting the burden of proof under ss. 90.301-90.304.

History.
S. 1, ch. 74-106; s. 50, ch. 75-220; s. 83, ch. 2001-226; s. 5, ch. 2002-82; s. 13, ch. 2010-132, eff. Oct. 1, 2010.

Editor's Notes.
Created from former s. 732.31.

733.109. Revocation of probate.

(1) A proceeding to revoke the probate of a will shall be brought in the court having jurisdiction over the administration. Any interested person, including a beneficiary under a prior will, unless barred under s. 733.212 or s. 733.2123, may commence the proceeding before final discharge of the personal representative.

(2) Pending the determination of any petition for revocation of probate, the personal representative shall proceed with the administration of the estate as if no revocation proceeding had been commenced, except that no distribution may be made to beneficiaries in contravention of the rights of those who, but for the will, would be entitled to the property disposed of.

(3) Revocation of probate of a will shall not affect or impair the title to property purchased in good faith for value from the personal representative prior to an order of revocation.

History.
S. 1, ch. 74-106; s. 50, ch. 75-220; s. 18, ch. 77-87; s. 227, ch. 77-104; s. 84, ch. 2001-226.

Editor's Notes.
Created from former s. 732.30.

PART II.
COMMENCING ADMINISTRATION.

733.201. Proof of wills.

(1) Self-proved wills executed in accordance with this code may be admitted to probate without further proof.

(2) A will may be admitted to probate upon the oath of any attesting witness taken before any circuit judge, commissioner appointed by the court, or clerk.

(3) If it appears to the court that the attesting witnesses cannot be found or that they have become incapacitated after the execution of the will or their testimony cannot be obtained within a reasonable time, a will may be admitted to probate upon the oath of the personal representative nominated by the will as provided in subsection (2), whether or not the nominated personal representative is interested in the estate, or upon the oath of any person having no interest in the estate under the will stating that the person believes the writing exhibited to be the true last will of the decedent.

History.
S. 1, ch. 74-106; s. 51, ch. 75-220; s. 985, ch. 97-102; s. 85, ch. 2001-226; s. 9, ch. 2009-115, eff. July 1, 2009.

Editor's Notes.
Created from former s. 732.24.

733.202. Petition.

Any interested person may petition for administration.

History.
S. 1, ch. 74-106; s. 52, ch. 75-220; s. 19, ch. 77-87; s. 19, ch. 92-200; s. 986, ch. 97-102; s. 86, ch. 2001-226.

Editor's Notes.
Created from former s. 732.43.

733.204. Probate of a will written in a foreign language.

(1) No will written in a foreign language shall be admitted to probate unless it is accompanied by a true and complete English translation.

(2) No personal representative who complies in good faith with the English translation of the will as established by the court shall be liable for doing so.

History.
S. 1, ch. 74-106; s. 54, ch. 75-220; s. 1, ch. 77-174; s. 88, ch. 2001-226.

Editor's Notes.
Created from former s. 732.34.

733.205. Probate of notarial will.

(1) When a copy of a notarial will in the possession of a notary entitled to its custody in a foreign state or country, the laws of which state or country require that the will remain in the custody of the notary, duly authenticated by the notary, whose official position, signature, and seal of office are further authenticated by an American consul, vice consul, or other American consular officer within whose jurisdiction the notary is a resident, or whose official position, signature, and seal of office have been authenticated according to the requirements of the Hague Convention of 1961, is presented to the court, it may be admitted to probate if the original could have been admitted to probate in this state.

(2) The duly authenticated copy shall be prima facie evidence of its purported execution and of the facts stated in the certificate in compliance with subsection (1).

(3) Any interested person may oppose the probate of such a notarial will or may petition for revocation of probate of such a notarial will, as in the original probate of a will in this state.

History.
S. 1, ch. 74-106; s. 55, ch. 75-220; s. 89, ch. 2001-226; s. 7, ch. 2003-154.

Editor's Notes.
Created from former s. 732.37.

733.206. Probate of will of resident after foreign probate.

(1) If a will of any person who dies a resident of this state is admitted to probate in any other state or country through inadvertence, error, or omission before probate in this state, the will may be admitted to probate in this state if the original could have been admitted to probate in this state.

(2) An authenticated copy of the will, foreign proof of the will, the foreign order of probate, and any letters issued shall be filed instead of the original will and shall be prima facie evidence of its execution and admission to foreign probate.

(3) Any interested person may oppose the probate of the will or may petition for revocation of the probate of the will, as in the original probate of a will in this state.

History.
S. 1, ch. 74-106; s. 56, ch. 75-220; s. 90, ch. 2001-226.
Editor's Notes.
Created from former s. 732.35.

733.207. Establishment and probate of lost or destroyed will.

Any interested person may establish the full and precise terms of a lost or destroyed will and offer the will for probate. The specific content of the will must be proved by the testimony of two disinterested witnesses, or, if a correct copy is provided, it shall be proved by one disinterested witness.

History.
S. 1, ch. 74-106; s. 57, ch. 75-220; s. 91, ch. 2001-226.
Editor's Notes.
Created from former s. 732.27.

733.208. Discovery of later will.

On the discovery of a later will or codicil, any interested person may petition to revoke the probate of the earlier will or to probate the later will or codicil. No will or codicil may be offered after the testate or intestate estate has been completely administered and the personal representative discharged.

History.
S. 1, ch. 74-106; s. 58, ch. 75-220; s. 92, ch. 2001-226.
Editor's Notes.
Created from former s. 732.32.

733.209. Estates of missing persons.

Any interested person may petition to administer the estate of a missing person; however, no personal representative shall be appointed until the court determines the missing person is dead.

History.
S. 1, ch. 74-106; s. 93, ch. 2001-226.
Editor's Notes.
Created from former s. 732.53.

733.212. Notice of administration; filing of objections.

(1) The personal representative shall promptly serve a copy of the notice of administration on the following persons who are known to the personal representative:

(a) The decedent's surviving spouse;

(b) Beneficiaries;

(c) The trustee of any trust described in s. 733.707(3) and each qualified beneficiary of the trust as defined in s. 736.0103(14), if each trustee is also a personal representative of the estate; and

(d) Persons who may be entitled to exempt property

in the manner provided for service of formal notice, unless served under s. 733.2123. The personal representative may similarly serve a copy of the notice on any devisees under a known prior will or heirs or others who claim or may claim an interest in the estate.

(2) The notice shall state:

(a) The name of the decedent, the file number of the estate, the designation and address of the court in which the proceedings are pending, whether the estate is testate or intestate, and, if testate, the date of the will and any codicils.

(b) The name and address of the personal representative and the name and address of the personal representative's attorney, and that the fiduciary lawyer-client privilege in s. 90.5021 applies with respect to the personal representative and any attorney employed by the personal representative.

(c) That any interested person on whom a copy of the notice of administration is served must file on or before the date that is 3 months after the date of service of a copy of the notice of administration on that person any objection that challenges the validity of the will, the qualifications of the personal representative, the venue, or the jurisdiction of the court.

(d) That persons who may be entitled to exempt property under s. 732.402 will be deemed to have waived their rights to claim that property as exempt property unless a petition for determination of exempt property is filed by such persons or on their behalf on or before the later of the date that is 4 months after the date of service of a copy of the notice of administration on such persons or the date that is 40 days after the date of termination of any proceeding involving the construction, admission to probate, or validity of the will or involving any other matter affecting any part of the exempt property.

(e) That an election to take an elective share must be filed on or before the earlier of the date that is 6 months after the date of service of a copy of the notice of administration on the surviving spouse, or an attorney in fact or a guardian of the property of the surviving spouse, or the date that is 2 years after the date of the decedent's death.

(3) Any interested person on whom a copy of the notice of administration is served must object to the validity of the will, the qualifications of the personal representative, the venue, or the jurisdiction of the court by filing a petition or other pleading requesting relief in accordance with the Florida Probate Rules on or before the date that is 3 months after the date of service of a copy of the notice of administration on the objecting person, or those objections are forever barred.

(4) The appointment of a personal representative or a successor personal representative shall not extend

or renew the period for filing objections under this section, unless a new will or codicil is admitted.

(5) The personal representative is not individually liable to any person for giving notice under this section, regardless of whether it is later determined that notice was not required by this section. The service of notice in accordance with this section shall not be construed as conferring any right.

(6) If the personal representative in good faith fails to give notice required by this section, the personal representative is not liable to any person for the failure. Liability, if any, for the failure is on the estate.

(7) If a will or codicil is subsequently admitted to probate, the personal representative shall promptly serve a copy of a new notice of administration as required for an initial will admission.

(8) For the purpose of determining deadlines established by reference to the date of service of a copy of the notice of administration in cases in which such service has been waived, service shall be deemed to occur on the date the waiver is filed.

History.
S. 1, ch. 74-106; s. 60, ch. 75-220; s. 227, ch. 77-104; s. 3, ch. 88-340; s. 2, ch. 89-340; s. 2, ch. 90-23; s. 8, ch. 93-257; s. 7, ch. 95-401; s. 191, ch. 99-397; s. 94, ch. 2001-226; s. 8, ch. 2003-154; s. 6, ch. 2006-134, eff. July 1, 2006; s. 36, ch. 2006-217, eff. July 1, 2007; s. 8, ch. 2011-183, eff. June 21, 2011.

Editor's Notes.
Created from former s. 732.28.
Section 14, ch. 2011-183 provides: "Except as otherwise expressly provided in this act, this act shall take effect upon becoming a law and shall apply to all proceedings pending before such date and all cases commenced on or after the effective date."

733.2121. Notice to creditors; filing of claims.

(1) Unless creditors' claims are otherwise barred by s. 733.710, the personal representative shall promptly publish a notice to creditors. The notice shall contain the name of the decedent, the file number of the estate, the designation and address of the court in which the proceedings are pending, the name and address of the personal representative, the name and address of the personal representative's attorney, and the date of first publication. The notice shall state that creditors must file claims against the estate with the court during the time periods set forth in s. 733.702, or be forever barred.

(2) Publication shall be once a week for 2 consecutive weeks, in a newspaper published in the county where the estate is administered or, if there is no newspaper published in the county, in a newspaper of general circulation in that county.

(3)(a) The personal representative shall promptly make a diligent search to determine the names and addresses of creditors of the decedent who are reasonably ascertainable, even if the claims are unmatured, contingent, or unliquidated, and shall promptly serve a copy of the notice on those creditors. Impracticable and extended searches are not required. Service is not required on any creditor who has filed a claim as provided in this part, whose claim has been paid in full, or whose claim is listed in a personal representative's timely filed proof of claim.

(b) The personal representative is not individually liable to any person for giving notice under this section, even if it is later determined that notice was not required. The service of notice to creditors in accordance with this section shall not be construed as admitting the validity or enforceability of a claim.

(c) If the personal representative in good faith fails to give notice required by this section, the personal representative is not liable to any person for the failure. Liability, if any, for the failure is on the estate.

(d) If a decedent at the time of death was 55 years of age or older, the personal representative shall promptly serve a copy of the notice to creditors and provide a copy of the death certificate on the Agency for Health Care Administration within 3 months after the first publication of the notice to creditors, unless the agency has already filed a statement of claim in the estate proceedings.

(e) If the Department of Revenue has not previously been served with a copy of the notice to creditors, then service of the inventory on the Department of Revenue shall be the equivalent of service of a copy of the notice to creditors.

(4) Claims are barred as provided in ss. 733.702 and 733.710.

History.
S. 95, ch. 2001-226; s. 9, ch. 2003-154; s. 4, ch. 2005-140.

733.2123. Adjudication before issuance of letters.

A petitioner may serve formal notice of the petition for administration on interested persons. A person who is served with such notice before the issuance of letters or who has waived notice may not challenge the validity of the will, testacy of the decedent, qualifications of the personal representative, venue, or jurisdiction of the court, except in the proceedings before issuance of letters.

History.
S. 60, ch. 75-220; s. 2, ch. 81-27; s. 987, ch. 97-102; s. 96, ch. 2001-226; s. 14, ch. 2010-132, eff. Oct. 1, 2010.

733.213. Probate as prerequisite to judicial construction of will.

A will may not be construed until it has been admitted to probate.

History.
S. 1, ch. 74-106; s. 61, ch. 75-220; s. 97, ch. 2001-226.
Editor's Notes.
Created from former s. 732.42.

PART III.

PREFERENCE IN APPOINTMENT AND QUALIFICATIONS OF PERSONAL REPRESENTATIVE.

733.301. Preference in appointment of personal representative.

(1) In granting letters of administration, the following order of preference shall be observed:

(a) In testate estates:

1. The personal representative, or his or her successor, nominated by the will or pursuant to a power conferred in the will.

2. The person selected by a majority in interest of the persons entitled to the estate.

3. A devisee under the will. If more than one devisee applies, the court may select the one best qualified.

(b) In intestate estates:

1. The surviving spouse.

2. The person selected by a majority in interest of the heirs.

3. The heir nearest in degree. If more than one applies, the court may select the one best qualified.

(2) A guardian of the property of a ward who if competent would be entitled to appointment as, or to select, the personal representative may exercise the right to select the personal representative.

(3) In either a testate or an intestate estate, if no application is made by any of the persons described in subsection (1), the court shall appoint a capable person; but no person may be appointed under this subsection:

(a) Who works for, or holds public office under, the court.

(b) Who is employed by, or holds office under, any judge exercising probate jurisdiction.

(4) After letters have been granted in either a testate or an intestate estate, if a person who was entitled to, and has not waived, preference over the person appointed at the time of the appointment and on whom formal notice was not served seeks the appointment, the letters granted may be revoked and the person entitled to preference may have letters granted after formal notice and hearing.

(5) After letters have been granted in either a testate or an intestate estate, if any will is subsequently admitted to probate, the letters shall be revoked and new letters granted.

History.
S. 1, ch. 74-106; s. 62, ch. 75-220; s. 21, ch. 77-87; s. 1, ch. 77-174; s. 988, ch. 97-102; s. 98, ch. 2001-226.
Editor's Notes.
Created from former s. 732.44.

733.302. Who may be appointed personal representative.

Subject to the limitations in this part, any person who is sui juris and is a resident of Florida at the time of the death of the person whose estate is to be administered is qualified to act as personal representative in Florida.
History.
S. 1, ch. 74-106; s. 63, ch. 75-220; s. 5, ch. 79-343; s. 989, ch. 97-102; s. 99, ch. 2001-226.
Editor's Notes.
Created from former s. 732.45.

733.303. Persons not qualified.

(1) A person is not qualified to act as a personal representative if the person:

(a) Has been convicted of a felony.

(b) Is mentally or physically unable to perform the duties.

(c) Is under the age of 18 years.

(2) If the person named as personal representative in the will is not qualified, letters shall be granted as provided in s. 733.301.
History.
S. 1, ch. 74-106; s. 63, ch. 75-220; s. 22, ch. 77-87; s. 990, ch. 97-102.
Editor's Notes.
Created from former s. 732.46.

733.304. Nonresidents.

A person who is not domiciled in the state cannot qualify as personal representative unless the person is:

(1) A legally adopted child or adoptive parent of the decedent;

(2) Related by lineal consanguinity to the decedent;

(3) A spouse or a brother, sister, uncle, aunt, nephew, or niece of the decedent, or someone related by lineal consanguinity to any such person; or

(4) The spouse of a person otherwise qualified under this section.
History.
S. 1, ch. 74-106; s. 63, ch. 75-220; s. 6, ch. 79-343.
Editor's Notes.
Created from former s. 732.47.

733.305. Trust companies and other corporations and associations.

(1) All trust companies incorporated under the laws of Florida, all state banking corporations and state savings associations authorized and qualified to exercise fiduciary powers in Florida, and all national banking associations and federal savings and loan associations authorized and qualified to exercise fiduciary powers in Florida shall be entitled to act as personal representatives and curators of estates.

(2) When a qualified corporation has been named as a personal representative in a will and subsequently transfers its business and assets to, consolidates or

merges with, or is in any manner provided by law succeeded by, another qualified corporation, on the death of the testator, the successor corporation may qualify as personal representative unless the will provides otherwise.

(3) A corporation authorized and qualified to act as a personal representative as a result of merger or consolidation shall succeed to the rights and duties of all predecessor corporations as the personal representative of estates upon filing proof in the court, and without a new appointment. A purchase of substantially all the assets and the assumption of substantially all the liabilities shall be deemed a merger for the purpose of this section.

History.
S. 1, ch. 74-106; s. 63, ch. 75-220; s. 1, ch. 77-174; s. 3, ch. 81-27; s. 100, ch. 2001-226.
Editor's Notes.
Created from former s. 732.49.

733.306. Effect of appointment of debtor.

The appointment of a debtor as personal representative shall not extinguish the debt due the decedent.

History.
S. 1, ch. 74-106; s. 63, ch. 75-220; s. 101, ch. 2001-226.
Editor's Notes.
Created from former s. 732.51.

733.307. Succession of administration.

The personal representative of the estate of a deceased personal representative is not authorized to administer the estate of the first decedent. On the death of a sole or surviving personal representative, the court shall appoint a successor personal representative to complete the administration of the estate.

History.
S. 1, ch. 74-106; s. 64, ch. 75-220; s. 102, ch. 2001-226.
Editor's Notes.
Created from former s. 732.52.

733.308. Administrator ad litem.

When an estate must be represented and the personal representative is unable to do so, the court shall appoint an administrator ad litem without bond to represent the estate in that proceeding. The fact that the personal representative is seeking reimbursement for claims against the decedent does not require appointment of an administrator ad litem.

History.
S. 1, ch. 74-106; s. 65, ch. 75-220; s. 103, ch. 2001-226.
Editor's Notes.
Created from former s. 732.55.

733.309. Executor de son tort.

No person shall be liable to a creditor of a decedent as executor de son tort, but any person taking, converting, or intermeddling with the property of a decedent shall be liable to the personal representative or curator, when appointed, for the value of all the property so taken or converted and for all damages to the estate caused by the wrongful action. This section shall not be construed to prevent a creditor of a decedent from suing anyone in possession of property fraudulently conveyed by the decedent to set aside the fraudulent conveyance.

History.
S. 1, ch. 74-106; s. 65, ch. 75-220; s. 991, ch. 97-102; s. 104, ch. 2001-226.

733.3101. Personal representative not qualified.

Any time a personal representative knows or should have known that he or she would not be qualified for appointment if application for appointment were then made, the personal representative shall promptly file and serve a notice setting forth the reasons. A personal representative who fails to comply with this section shall be personally liable for costs, including attorney's fees, incurred in any removal proceeding, if the personal representative is removed. This liability shall be cumulative to any other provided by law.

History.
S. 105, ch. 2001-226.

PART IV.
FIDUCIARY BONDS.

733.402. Bond of fiduciary; when required; form.

(1) Unless the bond requirement has been waived by the will or by the court, every fiduciary to whom letters are granted shall execute and file a bond with surety, as defined in s. 45.011, to be approved by the clerk without a service fee. The bond shall be payable to the Governor and the Governor's successors in office, conditioned on the performance of all duties as personal representative according to law. The bond must be joint and several.

(2) No bond shall be void or invalid because of an informality in it or an informality or illegality in the appointment of the fiduciary. The bond shall have the same force as if the appointment had been legally made and the bond executed in proper form.

(3) The requirements of this section shall not apply to banks and trust companies authorized by law to act as personal representative.

(4) On petition by any interested person or on the court's own motion, the court may waive the requirement of filing a bond, require a bond, increase or decrease the bond, or require additional surety.

History.
S. 1, ch. 74-106; s. 67, ch. 75-220; s. 24, ch. 77-87; s. 1, ch. 77-174; s. 992, ch. 97-102; s. 107, ch. 2001-226.
Editor's Notes.
Created from former s. 732.61.

733.403. Amount of bond.

All bonds required by this part shall be in the penal

sum that the court deems sufficient after consideration of the gross value of the estate, the relationship of the personal representative to the beneficiaries, exempt property and any family allowance, the type and nature of assets, known creditors, and liens and encumbrances on the assets.

History.
S. 1, ch. 74-106; s. 67, ch. 75-220; s. 108, ch. 2001-226.
Editor's Notes.
Created from former ss. 732.63, 732.64, 732.66.

733.404. Liability of surety.

No surety for any personal representative or curator shall be charged beyond the value of the assets of an estate because of any omission or mistake in pleading or of false pleading of the personal representative or curator.

History.
S. 1, ch. 74-106; s. 68, ch. 75-220; s. 109, ch. 2001-226.
Editor's Notes.
Created from former s. 732.65.

733.405. Release of surety.

(1) Subject to the limitations of this section, on the petition of any interested person, the surety is entitled to be released from liability for the future acts and omissions of the fiduciary.

(2) Pending the hearing of the petition, the court may restrain the fiduciary from acting, except to preserve the estate.

(3) On hearing, the court shall enter an order prescribing the amount of the new bond for the fiduciary and the date when the bond shall be filed. If the fiduciary fails to give the new bond, the fiduciary shall be removed at once, and further proceedings shall be had as in cases of removal.

(4) The original surety shall remain liable in accordance with the terms of its original bond for all acts and omissions of the fiduciary that occur prior to the approval of the new surety and filing and approval of the bond. The new surety shall be liable on its bond only after the filing and approval of the new bond.

History.
S. 1, ch. 74-106; s. 68, ch. 75-220; s. 993, ch. 97-102; s. 110, ch. 2001-226.
Editor's Notes.
Created from former s. 732.68.

733.406. Bond premium allowable as expense of administration.

A personal representative or other fiduciary required to give bond shall pay the reasonable premium as an expense of administration.

History.
S. 613, ch. 59-205; s. 3, ch. 76-168; s. 1, ch. 77-457; ss. 2, 3, ch. 81-318; ss. 253, 566, ch. 82-243; s. 994, ch. 97-102; s. 111, ch. 2001-226.
Editor's Notes.
Former s. 627.753.

PART V.
CURATORS; RESIGNATION AND REMOVAL OF PERSONAL REPRESENTATIVES.

733.501. Curators.

(1) When it is necessary, the court may appoint a curator after formal notice to the person apparently entitled to letters of administration. The curator may be authorized to perform any duty or function of a personal representative. If there is great danger that any of the decedent's property is likely to be wasted, destroyed, or removed beyond the jurisdiction of the court and if the appointment of a curator would be delayed by giving notice, the court may appoint a curator without giving notice.

(2) Bond shall be required of the curator as the court deems necessary. No bond shall be required of banks and trust companies as curators.

(3) Curators shall be allowed reasonable compensation for their services, and the court may consider the provisions of s. 733.617.

(4) Curators shall be subject to removal and surcharge.

History.
S. 1, ch. 74-106; s. 69, ch. 75-220; s. 1, ch. 77-174; s. 995, ch. 97-102; s. 112, ch. 2001-226; s. 108, ch. 2002-1.
Editor's Notes.
Created from former s. 732.21.

733.502. Resignation of personal representative.

A personal representative may resign. After notice to all interested persons, the court may accept the resignation and then revoke the letters of the resigning personal representative if the interests of the estate are not jeopardized by the resignation. The acceptance of the resignation shall not exonerate the personal representative or the surety from liability.

History.
S. 1, ch. 74-106; s. 69, ch. 75-220; s. 25, ch. 77-87; s. 996, ch. 97-102; s. 113, ch. 2001-226.
Editor's Notes.
Created from former s. 734.09.

733.503. Appointment of successor upon resignation.

When the personal representative's resignation is accepted, the court shall appoint a personal representative or shall appoint a curator to serve until a successor personal representative is appointed.

History.
S. 1, ch. 74-106; s. 69, ch. 75-220; s. 997, ch. 97-102; s. 114, ch. 2001-226.
Editor's Notes.
Created from former s. 734.10.

733.5035. Surrender of assets after resignation.

When the resignation has been accepted by the court, all estate assets, records, documents, papers, and other property of or concerning the estate in the resigning personal representative's possession or control shall immediately be surrendered to the successor fiduciary. The court may establish the conditions and specify the assets and records, if any, that the resigning personal representative may retain until the final accounting of the resigning personal representative has been approved.

History.
S. 115, ch. 2001-226.

733.5036. Accounting and discharge following resignation.

(1) A resigning personal representative shall file and serve a final accounting of the personal representative's administration.

(2) After determination and satisfaction of the liability, if any, of the resigning personal representative, after compensation of the personal representative and the attorney and other persons employed by the personal representative, and upon receipt of evidence that undistributed estate assets have been delivered to the successor fiduciary, the personal representative shall be discharged, the bond released, and the surety discharged.

History.
S. 116, ch. 2001-226.

733.504. Removal of personal representative; causes for removal.

A personal representative may be removed and the letters revoked for any of the following causes, and the removal shall be in addition to any penalties prescribed by law:

(1) Adjudication that the personal representative is incapacitated.

(2) Physical or mental incapacity rendering the personal representative incapable of the discharge of his or her duties.

(3) Failure to comply with any order of the court, unless the order has been superseded on appeal.

(4) Failure to account for the sale of property or to produce and exhibit the assets of the estate when so required.

(5) Wasting or maladministration of the estate.

(6) Failure to give bond or security for any purpose.

(7) Conviction of a felony.

(8) Insolvency of, or the appointment of a receiver or liquidator for, any corporate personal representative.

(9) Holding or acquiring conflicting or adverse interests against the estate that will or may interfere with the administration of the estate as a whole. This cause of removal shall not apply to the surviving spouse because of the exercise of the right to the elective share, family allowance, or exemptions, as provided elsewhere in this code.

(10) Revocation of the probate of the decedent's will that authorized or designated the appointment of the personal representative.

(11) Removal of domicile from Florida, if domicile was a requirement of initial appointment.

(12) The personal representative would not now be entitled to appointment.

History.
S. 1, ch. 74-106; s. 69, ch. 75-220; s. 1, ch. 77-174; s. 998, ch. 97-102; s. 117, ch. 2001-226; s. 10, ch. 2009-115, eff. July 1, 2009.
Editor's Notes.
Created from former s. 734.11.

733.505. Jurisdiction in removal proceedings.

A petition for removal shall be filed in the court having jurisdiction of the administration.

History.
S. 1, ch. 74-106; s. 118, ch. 2001-226.
Editor's Notes.
Created from former s. 734.12.

733.506. Proceedings for removal.

Proceedings for removal of a personal representative may be commenced by the court or upon the petition of an interested person. The court shall revoke the letters of a removed personal representative. The removal of a personal representative shall not exonerate the removed personal representative or the removed personal representative's surety from any liability.

History.
S. 1, ch. 74-106; s. 71, ch. 75-220; s. 119, ch. 2001-226.
Editor's Notes.
Created from former s. 734.13.

733.5061. Appointment of successor upon removal.

When a personal representative is removed, the court shall appoint a personal representative or shall appoint a curator to serve until a successor personal representative is appointed.

History.
S. 120, ch. 2001-226.

733.508. Accounting and discharge of removed personal representatives upon removal.

(1) A removed personal representative shall file and serve a final accounting of that personal representative's administration.

(2) After determination and satisfaction of the liability, if any, of the removed personal representative, after compensation of that personal representative and the attorney and other persons employed by that personal representative, and upon receipt of evidence that the estate assets have been delivered to the successor fiduciary, the removed personal representative shall be discharged, the bond released, and the surety discharged.

History.
S. 1, ch. 74-106; s. 999, ch. 97-102; s. 122, ch. 2001-226.
Editor's Notes.
Created from former s. 734.15.

733.509. Surrender of assets upon removal.

Upon entry of an order removing a personal representative, the removed personal representative shall immediately deliver all estate assets, records, documents, papers, and other property of or concerning the estate in the removed personal representative's possession or control to the remaining personal representative or successor fiduciary.

History.
S. 1, ch. 74-106; s. 73, ch. 75-220; s. 123, ch. 2001-226.
Editor's Notes.
Created from former s. 734.16.

PART VI.
DUTIES AND POWERS OF PERSONAL REPRESENTATIVE.

733.601. Time of accrual of duties and powers.

The duties and powers of a personal representative commence upon appointment. The powers of a personal representative relate back in time to give acts by the person appointed, occurring before appointment and beneficial to the estate, the same effect as those occurring after appointment. A personal representative may ratify and accept acts on behalf of the estate done by others when the acts would have been proper for a personal representative.

History.
S. 1, ch. 74-106; s. 74, ch. 75-220; s. 1000, ch. 97-102; s. 124, ch. 2001-226.

733.602. General duties.

(1) A personal representative is a fiduciary who shall observe the standards of care applicable to trustees. A personal representative is under a duty to settle and distribute the estate of the decedent in accordance with the terms of the decedent's will and this code as expeditiously and efficiently as is consistent with the best interests of the estate. A personal representative shall use the authority conferred by this code, the authority in the will, if any, and the authority of any order of the court, for the best interests of interested persons, including creditors.

(2) A personal representative shall not be liable for any act of administration or distribution if the act was authorized at the time. Subject to other obligations of administration, a probated will is authority to administer and distribute the estate according to its terms. An order of appointment of a personal representative is authority to distribute apparently intestate assets to the heirs of the decedent if, at the time of distribution, the personal representative is not aware of a proceeding challenging intestacy or a proceeding questioning the appointment or fitness to continue. Nothing in this section affects the duty of the personal representative to administer and distribute the estate in accordance with the rights of interested persons.

History.
S. 1, ch. 74-106; s. 74, ch. 75-220; s. 27, ch. 77-87; s. 1, ch. 77-174; s. 270, ch. 79-400; s. 3, ch. 89-340; s. 1001, ch. 97-102; s. 125, ch. 2001-226; s. 37, ch. 2006-217, eff. July 1, 2007; s. 11, ch. 2009-115, eff. July 1, 2009.

733.603. Personal representative to proceed without court order.

A personal representative shall proceed expeditiously with the settlement and distribution of a decedent's estate and, except as otherwise specified by this code or ordered by the court, shall do so without adjudication, order, or direction of the court. A personal representative may invoke the jurisdiction of the court to resolve questions concerning the estate or its administration.

History.
S. 1, ch. 74-106; s. 1002, ch. 97-102; s. 126, ch. 2001-226.

733.604. Inventories and accountings; public records exemptions.

(1)(a) Unless an inventory has been previously filed, a personal representative shall file a verified inventory of property of the estate, listing it with reasonable detail and including for each listed item its estimated fair market value at the date of the decedent's death.

(b)1. Any inventory of an estate, whether initial, amended, or supplementary, filed with the clerk of the court in conjunction with the administration of an estate is confidential and exempt from s. 119.07(1) and s. 24(a), Art. I of the State Constitution.

2. Any inventory of an elective estate, whether initial, amended, or supplementary, filed with the clerk of the court in conjunction with an election made in accordance with part II of chapter 732 is confidential and exempt from s. 119.07(1) and s. 24(a), Art. I of the State Constitution.

3. Any accounting, whether interim, final, amended, or supplementary, filed in an estate proceeding is confidential and exempt from s. 119.07(1) and s. 24(a), Art. I of the State Constitution.

4. Any inventory or accounting made confidential and exempt by subparagraph 1., subparagraph 2., or subparagraph 3. shall be disclosed by the custodian for inspection or copying:

a. To the personal representative;

b. To the personal representative's attorney;

c. To an interested person as defined in s. 731.201; or

d. By court order upon a showing of good cause.

5. These exemptions apply to any inventory or accounting filed before, on, or after July 1, 2009.

6. This paragraph is subject to the Open Government Sunset Review Act in accordance with s. 119.15 and shall stand repealed on October 2, 2014, unless reviewed and saved from repeal through reenactment by the Legislature.

(2) If the personal representative learns of any property not included in the original inventory, or learns that the estimated value or description indicated in the original inventory for any item is erroneous or misleading, the personal representative shall file a verified amended or supplementary inventory showing any new items and their estimated value at the date of the decedent's death, or the revised estimated value or description.

(3) Upon written request to the personal representative, a beneficiary shall be furnished a written explanation of how the inventory value for an asset was determined, or, if an appraisal was obtained, a copy of the appraisal, as follows:

    (a) To a residuary beneficiary or heir in an intestate estate, regarding all inventoried assets.

    (b) To any other beneficiary, regarding all assets distributed or proposed to be distributed to that beneficiary.

The personal representative must notify each beneficiary of that beneficiary's rights under this subsection. Neither a request nor the failure to request information under this subsection affects any rights of a beneficiary in subsequent proceedings concerning any accounting of the personal representative or the propriety of any action of the personal representative.

History.
S. 1, ch. 74-106; s. 76, ch. 75-220; s. 1, ch. 80-127; s. 4, ch. 84-106; s. 1, ch. 85-72; s. 29, ch. 85-342; s. 68, ch. 87-226; s. 28, ch. 95-401; s. 1003, ch. 97-102; s. 13, ch. 97-240; s. 127, ch. 2001-226; s. 1, ch. 2009-230, eff. July 1, 2009.

Editor's Notes.
Section 2, ch. 2009-230 provides: "The Legislature finds that it is a public necessity to exempt from public records requirements all inventories of property of estates of decedents, including amended and supplementary inventories, and all inventories of elective estates of surviving spouses, whether initial, amended, or supplementary. In addition, in order to preserve the privacy of information that would otherwise be available in an accounting filed in an estate proceeding, the Legislature finds that it is a public necessity that all accountings, whether interim, final, amended, or supplementary, filed in the estate proceeding be made exempt from public records requirements. The Legislature finds that the public disclosure of estate inventories and accountings would make public financial information of the decedent that would produce undue harm to the heirs of the decedent or beneficiaries of the decedent's estate."

Created from former s. 733.03.

733.6065. Opening safe-deposit box.

(1) Subject to the provisions of s. 655.936(2), the initial opening of a safe-deposit box that is leased or coleased by the decedent shall be conducted in the presence of any two of the following persons: an employee of the institution where the box is located, the personal representative, or the personal representative's attorney of record. Each person who is present must verify the contents of the box by signing a copy of the inventory under penalties of perjury. The personal representative shall file the safe-deposit box inventory, together with a copy of the box entry record from a date which is 6 months prior to the date of death to the date of inventory, with the court within 10 days after the box

is opened. Unless otherwise ordered by the court, this inventory and the attached box entry record is subject to inspection only by persons entitled to inspect an inventory under s. 733.604(1). The personal representative may remove the contents of the box.

(2) The right to open and examine the contents of a safe-deposit box leased by a decedent, or any documents delivered by a decedent for safekeeping, and to receive items as provided for in s. 655.935 is separate from the rights provided for in subsection (1).

History.
S. 129, ch. 2001-226; s. 7, ch. 2006-134, eff. July 1, 2006; s. 71, ch. 2006-213, eff. October 1, 2006.

733.607. Possession of estate.

(1) Except as otherwise provided by a decedent's will, every personal representative has a right to, and shall take possession or control of, the decedent's property, except the protected homestead, but any real property or tangible personal property may be left with, or surrendered to, the person presumptively entitled to it unless possession of the property by the personal representative will be necessary for purposes of administration. The request by a personal representative for delivery of any property possessed by a beneficiary is conclusive evidence that the possession of the property by the personal representative is necessary for the purposes of administration, in any action against the beneficiary for possession of it. The personal representative shall take all steps reasonably necessary for the management, protection, and preservation of the estate until distribution and may maintain an action to recover possession of property or to determine the title to it.

(2) If, after providing for statutory entitlements and all devises other than residuary devises, the assets of the decedent's estate are insufficient to pay the expenses of the administration and obligations of the decedent's estate, the personal representative is entitled to payment from the trustee of a trust described in s. 733.707(3), in the amount the personal representative certifies in writing to be required to satisfy the insufficiency, subject to the exclusions and preferences under s. 736.05053. The provisions of s. 733.805 shall apply in determining the amount of any payment required by this section.

History.
S. 1, ch. 74-106; s. 28, ch. 77-87; s. 9, ch. 93-257; s. 9, ch. 95-401; s. 1005, ch. 97-102; s. 130, ch. 2001-226; s. 1, ch. 2010-122, eff. July 1, 2010.

Editor's Notes.
Created from former s. 733.01.

733.608. General power of the personal representative.

(1) All real and personal property of the decedent, except the protected homestead, within this state and the rents, income, issues, and profits from it shall be assets in the hands of the personal representative:

(a) For the payment of devises, family allowance, elective share, estate and inheritance taxes, claims, charges, and expenses of the administration and obligations of the decedent's estate.

(b) To enforce contribution and equalize advancement.

(c) For distribution.

(2) If property that reasonably appears to the personal representative to be protected homestead is not occupied by a person who appears to have an interest in the property, the personal representative is authorized, but not required, to take possession of that property for the limited purpose of preserving, insuring, and protecting it for the person having an interest in the property, pending a determination of its homestead status. If the personal representative takes possession of that property, any rents and revenues may be collected by the personal representative for the account of the heir or devisee, but the personal representative shall have no duty to rent or otherwise make the property productive.

(3) If the personal representative expends funds or incurs obligations to preserve, maintain, insure, or protect the property referenced in subsection (2), the personal representative shall be entitled to a lien on that property and its revenues to secure repayment of those expenditures and obligations incurred. These expenditures and obligations incurred, including, but not limited to, fees and costs, shall constitute a debt owed to the personal representative that is charged against and which may be secured by a lien on the protected homestead, as provided in this section. The debt shall include any amounts paid for these purposes after the decedent's death and prior to the personal representative's appointment to the extent later ratified by the personal representative in the court proceeding provided for in this section.

(a) On the petition of the personal representative or any interested person, the court having jurisdiction of the administration of the decedent's estate shall adjudicate the amount of the debt after formal notice to the persons appearing to have an interest in the property.

(b) The persons having an interest in the protected homestead shall have no personal liability for the repayment of the above noted debt. The personal representative may enforce payment of the debt through any of the following methods:

1. By foreclosure of the lien as provided in this section;

2. By offset of the debt against any other property in the personal representative's possession that otherwise would be distributable to any person having an interest in the protected homestead, but only to the extent of the fraction of the total debt owed to the personal representative the numerator of which is the value of that person's interest in the protected homestead and the de-

nominator of which is the total value of the protected homestead; or

3. By offset of the debt against the revenues from the protected homestead received by the personal representative.

(4) The personal representative's lien shall attach to the property and take priority as of the date and time a notice of that lien is recorded in the official records of the county where that property is located, and the lien may secure expenditures and obligations incurred, including, but not limited to, fees and costs made before or after recording the notice. The notice of lien may be recorded before adjudicating the amount of the debt. The notice of lien shall also be filed in the probate proceeding, but failure to do so does not affect the validity of the lien. A copy of the notice of lien shall be served in the manner provided for service of formal notice upon each person appearing to have an interest in the property. The notice of lien must state:

(a) The name and address of the personal representative and the personal representative's attorney;

(b) The legal description of the property;

(c) The name of the decedent and also, to the extent known to the personal representative, the name and address of each person appearing to have an interest in the property; and

(d) That the personal representative has expended or is obligated to expend funds to preserve, maintain, insure, and protect the property and that the lien stands as security for recovery of those expenditures and obligations incurred, including, but not limited to, fees and costs.

Substantial compliance with the foregoing provisions renders the notice in comportment with this section.

(5) The lien shall terminate upon the earliest of:

(a) Recording a satisfaction or release signed by the personal representative in the official records of the county where the property is located;

(b) The discharge of the personal representative when the estate administration is complete;

(c) One year from the recording of the lien in the official records unless a proceeding to determine the debt or enforce the lien has been filed; or

(d) The entry of an order releasing the lien.

(6) Within 14 days after receipt of the written request of any interested person, the personal representative shall deliver to the requesting person at a place designated in the written request an estoppel letter setting forth the unpaid balance of the debt secured by the lien referred to in this section. After complete satisfaction of the debt secured by the lien, the personal representative shall record within 30 days after complete payment, a satisfaction of the lien in the official records of the county where the property is located. If a judicial proceeding is necessary to compel compliance with the provisions of this subsection, the prevailing party shall be entitled to an award of attorney's fees and costs.

(7) The lien created by this section may be foreclosed in the manner of foreclosing a mortgage under the provisions of chapter 702.

(8) In any action for enforcement of the debt described in this section, the court shall award taxable costs as in chancery actions, including reasonable attorney's fees.

(9) A personal representative entitled to recover a debt for expenditures and obligations incurred, including, but not limited to, fees and costs, under this section may be relieved of the duty to enforce collection by an order of the court finding:

(a) That the estimated court costs and attorney's fees in collecting the debt will approximate or exceed the amount of the recovery; or

(b) That it is impracticable to enforce collection in view of the improbability of collection.

(10) A personal representative shall not be liable for failure to attempt to enforce collection of the debt if the personal representative reasonably believes it would have been economically impracticable.

(11) The personal representative shall not be liable for failure to take possession of the protected homestead or to expend funds on its behalf. In the event that the property is determined by the court not to be protected homestead, subsections (2)-(10) shall not apply and any liens previously filed shall be deemed released upon recording of the order in the official records of the county where the property is located.

(12) Upon the petition of an interested party to accommodate a sale or the encumbrance of the protected homestead, the court may transfer the lien provided for in this section from the property to the proceeds of the sale or encumbrance by requiring the deposit of the proceeds into a restricted account subject to the lien. The court shall have continuing jurisdiction over the funds deposited. The transferred lien shall attach only to the amount asserted by the personal representative, and any proceeds in excess of that amount shall not be subject to the lien or otherwise restricted under this section. Alternatively, the personal representative and the apparent owners of the protected homestead may agree to retain in escrow the amount demanded as reimbursement by the personal representative, to be held there under the continuing jurisdiction of the court pending a final determination of the amount properly reimbursable to the personal representative under this section.

(13) This act shall apply to estates of decedents dying after the date on which this act becomes a law.

History.
S. 1, ch. 74-106; s. 29, ch. 77-87; s. 131, ch. 2001-226; s. 10, ch. 2003-154; s. 15, ch. 2010-132, eff. Oct. 1, 2010.

Editor's Notes.
Created from former s. 733.01(1).

733.609. Improper exercise of power; breach of fiduciary duty.

(1) A personal representative's fiduciary duty is the same as the fiduciary duty of a trustee of an express trust, and a personal representative is liable to interested persons for damage or loss resulting from the breach of this duty. In all actions for breach of fiduciary duty or challenging the exercise of or failure to exercise a personal representative's powers, the court shall award taxable costs as in chancery actions, including attorney's fees.

(2) When awarding taxable costs, including attorney's fees, under this section, the court in its discretion may direct payment from a party's interest, if any, in the estate or enter a judgment which may be satisfied from other property of the party, or both.

(3) This section shall apply to all proceedings commenced hereunder after the effective date, without regard to the date of the decedent's death.

History.
S. 1, ch. 74-106; s. 78, ch. 75-220; s. 1006, ch. 97-102; s. 132, ch. 2001-226; s. 11, ch. 2003-154.

733.610. Sale, encumbrance, or transaction involving conflict of interest.

Any sale or encumbrance to the personal representative or the personal representative's spouse, agent, or attorney, or any corporation or trust in which the personal representative has a substantial beneficial interest, or any transaction that is affected by a conflict of interest on the part of the personal representative, is voidable by any interested person except one who has consented after fair disclosure, unless:

(1) The will or a contract entered into by the decedent expressly authorized the transaction; or

(2) The transaction is approved by the court after notice to interested persons.

History.
S. 1, ch. 74-106; s. 78, ch. 75-220; s. 1007, ch. 97-102; s. 133, ch. 2001-226.

733.611. Persons dealing with the personal representative; protection.

Except as provided in s. 733.613(1), a person who in good faith either assists or deals for value with a personal representative is protected as if the personal representative acted properly. The fact that a person knowingly deals with the personal representative does not require the person to inquire into the authority of the personal representative. A person is not bound to see to the proper application of estate assets paid or delivered to the personal representative. This protection extends to instances in which a procedural irregularity or jurisdictional defect occurred in proceedings leading to the issuance of letters, including a case in which the alleged decedent is alive. This protection is in addition to any protection afforded by comparable provisions of the laws relating to commercial transactions and laws simplifying transfers of securities by fiduciaries.

History.
S. 1, ch. 74-106; s. 78, ch. 75-220; s. 30, ch. 77-87; s. 1, ch. 77-174; s. 1008, ch. 97-102; s. 134, ch. 2001-226.

733.612. Transactions authorized for the personal representative; exceptions.

Except as otherwise provided by the will or court order, and subject to the priorities stated in s. 733.805, without court order, a personal representative, acting reasonably for the benefit of the interested persons, may properly:

(1) Retain assets owned by the decedent, pending distribution or liquidation, including those in which the personal representative is personally interested or that are otherwise improper for fiduciary investments.

(2) Perform or compromise, or, when proper, refuse to perform, the decedent's contracts. In performing the decedent's enforceable contracts to convey or lease real property, among other possible courses of action, the personal representative may:

(a) Convey the real property for cash payment of all sums remaining due or for the purchaser's note for the sum remaining due, secured by a mortgage on the property.

(b) Deliver a deed in escrow, with directions that the proceeds, when paid in accordance with the escrow agreement, be paid as provided in the escrow agreement.

(3) Receive assets from fiduciaries or other sources.

(4) Invest funds as provided in ss. 518.10-518.14, considering the amount to be invested, liquidity needs of the estate, and the time until distribution will be made.

(5) Acquire or dispose of an asset, excluding real property in this or another state, for cash or on credit and at public or private sale, and manage, develop, improve, exchange, partition, or change the character of an estate asset.

(6) Make ordinary or extraordinary repairs or alterations in buildings or other structures; demolish improvements; or erect new party walls or buildings.

(7) Enter into a lease, as lessor or lessee, for a term within, or extending beyond, the period of administration, with or without an option to renew.

(8) Enter into a lease or arrangement for exploration and removal of minerals or other natural resources or enter into a pooling or unitization agreement.

(9) Abandon property when it is valueless or so encumbered, or in a condition, that it is of no benefit to the estate.

(10) Vote, or refrain from voting, stocks or other securities in person or by general or limited proxy.

(11) Pay calls, assessments, and other sums chargeable or accruing against, or on account of, securities, unless barred by the provisions relating to claims.

(12) Hold property in the name of a nominee or in other form without disclosure of the interest of the estate, but the personal representative is liable for any act of the nominee in connection with the property so held.

(13) Insure the assets of the estate against damage or loss and insure against personal and fiduciary liability to third persons.

(14) Borrow money, with or without security, to be repaid from the estate assets or otherwise, other than real property, and advance money for the protection of the estate.

(15) Extend, renew, or in any manner modify any obligation owing to the estate. If the personal representative holds a mortgage, security interest, or other lien upon property of another person, he or she may accept a conveyance or transfer of encumbered assets from the owner in satisfaction of the indebtedness secured by its lien instead of foreclosure.

(16) Pay taxes, assessments, and other expenses incident to the administration of the estate.

(17) Sell or exercise stock subscription or conversion rights or consent, directly or through a committee or other agent, to the reorganization, consolidation, merger, dissolution, or liquidation of a corporation or other business enterprise.

(18) Allocate items of income or expense to either estate income or principal, as permitted or provided by law.

(19) Employ persons, including, but not limited to, attorneys, accountants, auditors, appraisers, investment advisers, and others, even if they are one and the same as the personal representative or are associated with the personal representative, to advise or assist the personal representative in the performance of administrative duties; act upon the recommendations of those employed persons without independent investigation; and, instead of acting personally, employ one or more agents to perform any act of administration, whether or not discretionary. Any fees and compensation paid to a person who is the same as, associated with, or employed by, the personal representative shall be taken into consideration in determining the personal representative's compensation.

(20) Prosecute or defend claims or proceedings in any jurisdiction for the protection of the estate and of the personal representative.

(21) Sell, mortgage, or lease any personal property of the estate or any interest in it for cash, credit, or for part cash or part credit, and with or without security for the unpaid balance.

(22) Continue any unincorporated business or venture in which the decedent was engaged at the time of death:

(a) In the same business form for a period of not more than 4 months from the date of appointment, if continuation is a reasonable means of preserving the value of the business, including good will.

(b) In the same business form for any additional period of time that may be approved by court order.

(23) Provide for exoneration of the personal representative from personal liability in any contract entered into on behalf of the estate.

(24) Satisfy and settle claims and distribute the estate as provided in this code.

(25) Enter into agreements with the proper officer or department head, commissioner, or agent of any department of the government of the United States, waiving the statute of limitations concerning the assessment and collection of any federal tax or any deficiency in a federal tax.

(26) Make partial distribution to the beneficiaries of any part of the estate not necessary to satisfy claims, expenses of administration, taxes, family allowance, exempt property, and an elective share, in accordance with the decedent's will or as authorized by operation of law.

(27) Execute any instruments necessary in the exercise of the personal representative's powers.

History.
S. 1, ch. 74-106; s. 78, ch. 75-220; s. 3, ch. 76-172; s. 31, ch. 77-87; s. 1, ch. 77-174; s. 271, ch. 79-400; s. 1009, ch. 97-102; s. 135, ch. 2001-226.

733.6121. Personal representative; powers as to environmental issues relating to property subject to administration; liability.

(1) Except as otherwise provided by the will or by court order, and subject to s. 733.805, the personal representative has, without court authorization, the powers specified in subsection (2).

(2) A personal representative has the power, acting reasonably and for the benefit of the interested persons:

(a) To inspect or investigate, or cause to be inspected or investigated, property subject to administration, including interests in sole proprietorships, partnerships, or corporations and any assets owned by such a business entity for the purpose of determining compliance with an environmental law affecting that property or to respond to an actual or threatened violation of an environmental law affecting that property;

(b) To take, on behalf of the estate, any action necessary to prevent, abate, or otherwise remedy an actual or potential violation of an environmental law affecting property subject to administration, either before or after initiation of an enforcement action by a governmental body;

(c) To settle or compromise at any time any claim against the estate or the personal representative that may be asserted by a governmental body or private party which involves the alleged violation of an environmental law affecting property subject to administration over which the personal representative has responsibility;

(d) To disclaim any power granted by any document, statute, or rule of law which, in the sole judgment of the personal representative, could cause the personal representative to incur personal liability, or the estate to incur liability, under any environmental law;

(e) To decline to serve as a personal representative, or having undertaken to serve, to resign at any time, if the personal representative believes that there is or could be a conflict of interest because of potential claims or liabilities that could be asserted on behalf of the estate by reason of the type or condition of the assets held; or

(f) To charge against the assets of the estate the cost of any inspection, investigation, review, abatement, response, cleanup, or remedial action considered reasonable by the personal representative; and, in the event of the closing or termination of the estate or the transfer of the estate property to another personal representative, to hold moneys sufficient to cover the cost of cleaning up any known environmental problem.

(3) A personal representative is not personally liable to any beneficiary or any other party for a decrease in value of assets in an estate by reason of the personal representative's compliance or efforts to comply with an environmental law, specifically including any reporting requirement under that law.

(4) A personal representative who acquires ownership or control of a vessel or other property without having owned, operated, or materially participated in the management of that vessel or property before assuming ownership or control as personal representative is not considered an owner or operator for purposes of liability under chapter 376, chapter 403, or any other environmental law. A personal representative who willfully, knowingly, or recklessly causes or exacerbates a release or threatened release of a hazardous substance is personally liable for the cost of the response, to the extent that the release or threatened release is attributable to the personal representative's activities. This subsection does not preclude the filing of claims against the assets that constitute the estate held by the personal representative or the filing of actions against the personal representative as representative of the estate. In such an action, an award or judgment against the personal representative must be satisfied only from the assets of the estate.

(5) Neither the acceptance by the personal representative of the property or a failure by the personal representative to inspect or investigate the property creates any inference of liability under an environmental law with respect to that property.

(6) For the purposes of this section, the term "environmental law" means a federal, state, or local law, rule, regulation, or ordinance that relates to protection of the environment or human health, and the term "hazardous substance" means a substance, material, or waste defined as hazardous or toxic, or any contaminant, pollutant, or constituent thereof, or otherwise regulated by an environmental law.

(7) This section applies to any estate admitted to probate on or after July 1, 1995.

History.
S. 18, ch. 95-401; s. 1010, ch. 97-102; s. 136, ch. 2001-226.

733.613. Personal representative's right to sell real property.

(1) When a personal representative of an intestate estate, or whose testator has not conferred a power of sale or whose testator has granted a power of sale but the power is so limited by the will or by operation of law that it cannot be conveniently exercised, shall consider that it is for the best interest of the estate and of those interested in it that real property be sold, the personal representative may sell it at public or private sale. No title shall pass until the court authorizes or confirms the sale. No bona fide purchaser shall be required to examine any proceedings before the order of sale.

(2) When a decedent's will confers specific power to sell or mortgage real property or a general power to sell any asset of the estate, the personal representative may sell, mortgage, or lease, without authorization or confirmation of court, any real property of the estate or any interest therein for cash or credit, or for part cash and part credit, and with or without security for unpaid balances. The sale, mortgage, or lease need not be justified by a showing of necessity, and the sale pursuant to power of sale shall be valid.

(3) In a sale or mortgage which occurs under a specific power to sell or mortgage real property, or under a court order authorizing or confirming that act, the purchaser or lender takes title free of claims of creditors of the estate and entitlements of estate beneficiaries, except existing mortgages or other liens against real property are not affected.

History.
S. 1, ch. 74-106; s. 78, ch. 75-220; s. 1011, ch. 97-102; s. 137, ch. 2001-226.

Editor's Notes.
Created from former s. 733.23.

733.614. Powers and duties of successor personal representative.

A successor personal representative has the same power and duty as the original personal representative to complete the administration and distribution of the estate as expeditiously as possible, but shall not exercise any power made personal to the personal representative named in the will without court approval.

History.
S. 1, ch. 74-106; s. 78, ch. 75-220; s. 1012, ch. 97-102; s. 138, ch. 2001-226.

Editor's Notes.
Created from former s. 734.10.

733.615. Joint personal representatives; when joint action required.

(1) If two or more persons are appointed joint personal representatives, and unless the will provides otherwise, the concurrence of all joint personal representatives appointed pursuant to a will or codicil executed prior to October 1, 1987, or appointed to administer an intestate estate of a decedent who died prior to October 1, 1987, or of a majority of joint personal representatives appointed pursuant to a will or codicil executed on or after October 1, 1987, or appointed to administer an intestate estate of a decedent dying on or after October 1, 1987, is required on all acts connected with the administration and distribution of the estate. This restriction does not apply when any joint personal representative receives and receipts for property due the estate, when the concurrence required under this subsection cannot readily be obtained in the time reasonably available for emergency action necessary to preserve the estate, or when a joint personal representative has been delegated to act for the others.

(2) Where action by a majority of the joint personal representatives appointed is authorized, a joint personal representative who has not joined in exercising a power is not liable to the beneficiaries or to others for the consequences of the exercise, and a dissenting joint personal representative is not liable for the consequences of an action in which the dissenting personal representative joins at the direction of the majority of the joint personal representatives, if the dissent is expressed in writing to the other joint personal representatives at or before the time of the action.

(3) A person dealing with a joint personal representative without actual knowledge that joint personal representatives have been appointed, or if advised by a joint personal representative that the joint personal representative has authority to act alone for any of the reasons mentioned in subsection (1), is as fully protected in dealing with that joint personal representative as if that joint personal representative possessed and properly exercised the power.

History.
S. 1, ch. 74-106; s. 1, ch. 87-317; s. 4, ch. 88-340; s. 1013, ch. 97-102; s. 139, ch. 2001-226.

Editor's Notes.
Created from former s. 732.50.

733.616. Powers of surviving personal representatives.

Unless otherwise provided by the terms of the will or a court order, every power exercisable by joint personal representatives may be exercised by the one or more remaining after the appointment of one or more is terminated. If one or more, but not all, nominated as joint personal representatives are not appointed, those appointed may exercise all powers granted to those nominated.

History.
S. 1, ch. 74-106; s. 140, ch. 2001-226.
Editor's Notes.
Created from former s. 732.52.

733.617. Compensation of personal representative.

(1) A personal representative shall be entitled to a commission payable from the estate assets without court order as compensation for ordinary services. The commission shall be based on the compensable value of the estate, which is the inventory value of the probate estate assets and the income earned by the estate during administration.

(2) A commission computed on the compensable value of the estate is presumed to be reasonable compensation for a personal representative in formal administration as follows:

(a) At the rate of 3 percent for the first $1 million.

(b) At the rate of 2.5 percent for all above $1 million and not exceeding $5 million.

(c) At the rate of 2 percent for all above $5 million and not exceeding $10 million.

(d) At the rate of 1.5 percent for all above $10 million.

(3) In addition to the previously described commission, a personal representative shall be allowed further compensation as is reasonable for any extraordinary services including, but not limited to:

(a) The sale of real or personal property.

(b) The conduct of litigation on behalf of or against the estate.

(c) Involvement in proceedings for the adjustment or payment of any taxes.

(d) The carrying on of the decedent's business.

(e) Dealing with protected homestead.

(f) Any other special services which may be necessary for the personal representative to perform.

(4) If the will provides that a personal representative's compensation shall be based upon specific criteria, other than a general reference to commissions allowed by law or words of similar import, including, but not limited to, rates, amounts, commissions, or reference to the personal representative's regularly published schedule of fees in effect at the decedent's date of death, or words of similar import, then a personal representative shall be entitled to compensation in accordance with that provision. However, except for references in the will to the personal representative's regularly published schedule of fees in effect at the decedent's date of death, or words of similar import, if there is no written contract with the decedent regarding compensation, a personal representative may renounce the provisions contained in the will and be entitled to compensation under this section. A personal representative may also renounce the right to all or any part of the compensation.

(5) If the probate estate's compensable value is $100,000 or more, and there are two representatives, each personal representative is entitled to the full commission allowed to a sole personal representative. If there are more than two personal representatives and the probate estate's compensable value is $100,000 or more, the compensation to which two would be entitled must be apportioned among the personal representatives. The basis for apportionment shall be one full commission allowed to the personal representative who has possession of and primary responsibility for administration of the assets and one full commission among the remaining personal representatives according to the services rendered by each of them respectively. If the probate estate's compensable value is less than $100,000 and there is more than one personal representative, then one full commission must be apportioned among the personal representatives according to the services rendered by each of them respectively.

(6) If the personal representative is a member of The Florida Bar and has rendered legal services in connection with the administration of the estate, then in addition to a fee as personal representative, there also shall be allowed a fee for the legal services rendered.

(7) Upon petition of any interested person, the court may increase or decrease the compensation for ordinary services of the personal representative or award compensation for extraordinary services if the facts and circumstances of the particular administration warrant. In determining reasonable compensation, the court shall consider all of the following factors, giving weight to each as it determines to be appropriate:

(a) The promptness, efficiency, and skill with which the administration was handled by the personal representative;

(b) The responsibilities assumed by and the potential liabilities of the personal representative;

(c) The nature and value of the assets that are affected by the decedent's death;

(d) The benefits or detriments resulting to the estate or interested persons from the personal representative's services;

(e) The complexity or simplicity of the administration and the novelty of the issues presented;

(f) The personal representative's participation in tax planning for the estate and the estate's beneficiaries and in tax return preparation, review, or approval;

(g) The nature of the probate, nonprobate, and exempt assets, the expenses of administration, the liabilities of the decedent, and the compensation paid to other professionals and fiduciaries;

(h) Any delay in payment of the compensation after the services were furnished; and

(i) Any other relevant factors.

History.
S. 1, ch. 74-106; s. 80, ch. 75-220; s. 1, ch. 76-172; s. 5, ch. 88-340;

s. 1, ch. 90-129; s. 10, ch. 93-257; s. 1, ch. 95-401; s. 141, ch. 2001-226; s. 109, ch. 2002-1.

Editor's Notes.
Created from former s. 734.01.

733.6171. Compensation of attorney for the personal representative.

(1) Attorneys for personal representatives shall be entitled to reasonable compensation payable from the estate assets without court order.

(2) The attorney, the personal representative, and persons bearing the impact of the compensation may agree to compensation determined in a different manner than provided in this section. Compensation may also be determined in a different manner than provided in this section if the manner is disclosed to the parties bearing the impact of the compensation and if no objection is made as provided for in the Florida Probate Rules.

(3) Compensation for ordinary services of attorneys in formal estate administration is presumed to be reasonable if based on the compensable value of the estate, which is the inventory value of the probate estate assets and the income earned by the estate during the administration as provided in the following schedule:

(a) One thousand five hundred dollars for estates having a value of $40,000 or less.

(b) An additional $750 for estates having a value of more than $40,000 and not exceeding $70,000.

(c) An additional $750 for estates having a value of more than $70,000 and not exceeding $100,000.

(d) For estates having a value in excess of $100,000, at the rate of 3 percent on the next $900,000.

(e) At the rate of 2.5 percent for all above $1 million and not exceeding $3 million.

(f) At the rate of 2 percent for all above $3 million and not exceeding $5 million.

(g) At the rate of 1.5 percent for all above $5 million and not exceeding $10 million.

(h) At the rate of 1 percent for all above $10 million.

(4) In addition to fees for ordinary services, the attorney for the personal representative shall be allowed further reasonable compensation for any extraordinary service. What is an extraordinary service may vary depending on many factors, including the size of the estate. Extraordinary services may include, but are not limited to:

(a) Involvement in a will contest, will construction, a proceeding for determination of beneficiaries, a contested claim, elective share proceeding, apportionment of estate taxes, or any adversarial proceeding or litigation by or against the estate.

(b) Representation of the personal representative in audit or any proceeding for adjustment, determination, or collection of any taxes.

(c) Tax advice on postmortem tax planning, including, but not limited to, disclaimer, renunciation of fiduciary commission, alternate valuation date, allocation of administrative expenses between tax returns, the QTIP or reverse QTIP election, allocation of GST exemption, qualification for Internal Revenue Code ss. 6166 and 303 privileges, deduction of last illness expenses, fiscal year planning, distribution planning, asset basis considerations, handling income or deductions in respect of a decedent, valuation discounts, special use and other valuation, handling employee benefit or retirement proceeds, prompt assessment request, or request for release of personal liability for payment of tax.

(d) Review of estate tax return and preparation or review of other tax returns required to be filed by the personal representative.

(e) Preparation of the estate's federal estate tax return. If this return is prepared by the attorney, a fee of one-half of 1 percent up to a value of $10 million and one-fourth of 1 percent on the value in excess of $10 million of the gross estate as finally determined for federal estate tax purposes, is presumed to be reasonable compensation for the attorney for this service. These fees shall include services for routine audit of the return, not beyond the examining agent level, if required.

(f) Purchase, sale, lease, or encumbrance of real property by the personal representative or involvement in zoning, land use, environmental, or other similar matters.

(g) Legal advice regarding carrying on of the decedent's business or conducting other commercial activity by the personal representative.

(h) Legal advice regarding claims for damage to the environment or related procedures.

(i) Legal advice regarding homestead status of real property or proceedings involving that status and services related to protected homestead.

(j) Involvement in fiduciary, employee, or attorney compensation disputes.

(k) Proceedings involving ancillary administration of assets not subject to administration in this state.

(5) Upon petition of any interested person, the court may increase or decrease the compensation for ordinary services of the attorney or award compensation for extraordinary services if the facts and circumstances of the particular administration warrant. In determining reasonable compensation, the court shall consider all of the following factors, giving weight to each as it determines to be appropriate:

(a) The promptness, efficiency, and skill with which the administration was handled by the attorney.

(b) The responsibilities assumed by and the potential liabilities of the attorney.

(c) The nature and value of the assets that are affected by the decedent's death.

(d) The benefits or detriments resulting to the estate or interested persons from the attorney's services.

(e) The complexity or simplicity of the administration and the novelty of issues presented.

(f) The attorney's participation in tax planning for the estate and the estate's beneficiaries and tax return preparation, review, or approval.

(g) The nature of the probate, nonprobate, and exempt assets, the expenses of administration, the liabilities of the decedent, and the compensation paid to other professionals and fiduciaries.

(h) Any delay in payment of the compensation after the services were furnished.

(i) Any other relevant factors.

(6) If a separate written agreement regarding compensation exists between the attorney and the decedent, the attorney shall furnish a copy to the personal representative prior to commencement of employment, and, if employed, shall promptly file and serve a copy on all interested persons. Neither a separate agreement nor a provision in the will suggesting or directing that the personal representative retain a specific attorney will obligate the personal representative to employ the attorney or obligate the attorney to accept the representation, but if the attorney who is a party to the agreement or who drafted the will is employed, the compensation paid shall not exceed the compensation provided in the agreement or in the will.

History.
S. 4, ch. 93-257; s. 2, ch. 95-401; s. 142, ch. 2001-226.

Editor's Notes.
Sections 6166 and 303 of the Internal Revenue Code, referred to in this section, are codified as 26 U.S.C.S. §§ 6166 and 303, respectively.

733.6175. Proceedings for review of employment of agents and compensation of personal representatives and employees of estate.

(1) The court may review the propriety of the employment of any person employed by the personal representative and the reasonableness of any compensation paid to that person or to the personal representative.

(2) Court proceedings to determine reasonable compensation of the personal representative or any person employed by the personal representative, if required, are a part of the estate administration process, and the costs, including attorneys' fees, of the person assuming the burden of proof of propriety of the employment and reasonableness of the compensation shall be determined by the court and paid from the assets of the estate unless the court finds the requested compensation to be substantially unreasonable. The court shall direct from which part of the estate the compensation shall be paid.

(3) The burden of proof of propriety of the employment and the reasonableness of the compensation shall be upon the personal representative and the person employed. Any person who is determined to have received excessive compensation from an estate for services rendered may be ordered to make appropriate refunds.

(4) The court may determine reasonable compensation for the personal representative or any person employed by the personal representative without receiving expert testimony. Any party may offer expert testimony after notice to interested persons. If expert testimony is offered, a reasonable expert witness fee shall be awarded by the court and paid from the assets of the estate. The court shall direct from what part of the estate the fee shall be paid.

History.
S. 2, ch. 76-172; s. 1014, ch. 97-102; s. 143, ch. 2001-226.

733.619. Individual liability of personal representative.

(1) Unless otherwise provided in the contract, a personal representative is not individually liable on a contract, except a contract for attorney's fee, properly entered into as fiduciary unless the personal representative fails to reveal that representative capacity and identify the estate in the contract.

(2) A personal representative is individually liable for obligations arising from ownership or control of the estate or for torts committed in the course of administration of the estate only if personally at fault.

(3) Claims based on contracts, except a contract for attorney's fee, entered into by a personal representative as a fiduciary, on obligations arising from ownership or control of the estate, or on torts committed in the course of estate administration, may be asserted against the estate by proceeding against the personal representative in that capacity, whether or not the personal representative is individually liable.

(4) Issues of liability as between the estate and the personal representative individually may be determined in a proceeding for accounting, surcharge, or indemnification, or other appropriate proceeding.

History.
S. 82, ch. 75-220; s. 32, ch. 77-87; s. 228, ch. 77-104; s. 1015, ch. 97-102; s. 144, ch. 2001-226.

733.620. Exculpation of personal representative.

(1) A term of a will relieving a personal representative of liability to a beneficiary for breach of fiduciary duty is unenforceable to the extent that the term:

(a) Relieves the personal representative of liability for breach of fiduciary duty committed in bad faith or with reckless indifference to the purposes of the will or the interests of interested persons; or

(b) Was inserted into the will as the result of an abuse by the personal representative of a fiduciary or confidential relationship with the testator.

(2) An exculpatory term drafted or caused to be drafted by the personal representative is invalid as an abuse of a fiduciary or confidential relationship unless:

(a) The personal representative proves that the exculpatory term is fair under the circumstances.

(b) The term's existence and contents were adequately communicated directly to the testator or to the independent attorney of the testator. This paragraph applies only to wills created on or after July 1, 2007.

History.
S. 15, ch. 2007-74, eff. July 1, 2007.

PART VII.
CREDITORS' CLAIMS.

733.701.   Notifying creditors.

Unless creditors' claims are otherwise barred by s. 733.710, every personal representative shall cause notice to creditors to be published and served under s. 733.2121.

History.
S. 1, ch. 74-106; s. 83, ch. 75-220; s. 33, ch. 77-87; s. 4, ch. 89-340; s. 145, ch. 2001-226; s. 31, ch. 2003-154.

Editor's Notes.
Section 31, ch. 2003-154 reenacted 733.701 without change to incorporate amendments to statutory sections referenced therein.

Created from former s. 733.15.

733.702.   Limitations on presentation of claims.

(1) If not barred by s. 733.710, no claim or demand against the decedent's estate that arose before the death of the decedent, including claims of the state and any of its political subdivisions, even if the claims are unmatured, contingent, or unliquidated; no claim for funeral or burial expenses; no claim for personal property in the possession of the personal representative; and no claim for damages, including, but not limited to, an action founded on fraud or another wrongful act or omission of the decedent, is binding on the estate, on the personal representative, or on any beneficiary unless filed in the probate proceeding on or before the later of the date that is 3 months after the time of the first publication of the notice to creditors or, as to any creditor required to be served with a copy of the notice to creditors, 30 days after the date of service on the creditor, even though the personal representative has recognized the claim or demand by paying a part of it or interest on it or otherwise. The personal representative may settle in full any claim without the necessity of the claim being filed when the settlement has been approved by the interested persons.

(2) No cause of action, including, but not limited to, an action founded upon fraud or other wrongful act or omission, shall survive the death of the person against whom the claim may be made, whether or not an action is pending at the death of the person, unless a claim is filed within the time periods set forth in this part.

(3) Any claim not timely filed as provided in this section is barred even though no objection to the claim is filed unless the court extends the time in which the claim may be filed. An extension may be granted only upon grounds of fraud, estoppel, or insufficient notice of the claims period. No independent action or declaratory action may be brought upon a claim which was not timely filed unless an extension has been granted by the court. If the personal representative or any other interested person serves on the creditor a notice to file a petition for an extension, the creditor shall be limited to a period of 30 days from the date of service of the notice in which to file a petition for extension.

(4) Nothing in this section affects or prevents:

(a) A proceeding to enforce any mortgage, security interest, or other lien on property of the decedent.

(b) To the limits of casualty insurance protection only, any proceeding to establish liability that is protected by the casualty insurance.

(c) The filing of a cross-claim or counterclaim against the estate in an action instituted by the estate; however, no recovery on a cross-claim or counterclaim shall exceed the estate's recovery in that action.

(5) Nothing in this section shall extend the limitations period set forth in s. 733.710.

History.
S. 1, ch. 74-106; s. 84, ch. 75-220; s. 2, ch. 80-127; s. 4, ch. 81-27; s. 160, ch. 83-216; s. 5, ch. 84-106; s. 4, ch. 85-79; s. 6, ch. 88-340; s. 5, ch. 89-340; s. 4, ch. 90-23; s. 1016, ch. 97-102; s. 146, ch. 2001-226; s. 6, ch. 2002-82; s. 26, ch. 2006-312, eff. January 1, 2007; s. 21, ch. 2010-4, eff. June 29, 2010.

Editor's Notes.
Created from former s. 733.16.

Section 23, ch. 2010-4 provides: "This act shall take effect on the 60th day after adjournment sine die of the session of the Legislature in which enacted."

733.703.   Form and manner of presenting claim.

(1) A creditor shall file a written statement of the claim. No additional charge may be imposed by a claimant who files a claim against the estate.

(2) Within the time allowed by s. 733.702, the personal representative may file a proof of claim of all claims he or she has paid or intends to pay. A claimant whose claim is listed in a personal representative's proof of claim shall be deemed to have filed a statement of the claim listed. Except as provided otherwise in this part, the claim shall be treated as if the claimant had filed it.

History.
S. 1, ch. 74-106; s. 84, ch. 75-220; s. 5, ch. 81-27; s. 5, ch. 85-79; s. 6, ch. 89-340; s. 147, ch. 2001-226.

Editor's Notes.
Created from former s. 733.16.

733.704.   Amendment of claims.

If a bona fide attempt to file a claim is made but the claim is defective as to form, the court may permit the amendment of the claim at any time.

History.
S. 1, ch. 74-106; s. 1, ch. 77-174; s. 148, ch. 2001-226.

Editor's Notes.
Created from former s. 733.17.

733.705. Payment of and objection to claims.

(1) The personal representative shall pay all claims within 1 year from the date of first publication of notice to creditors, provided that the time shall be extended with respect to claims in litigation, unmatured claims, and contingent claims for the period necessary to dispose of those claims pursuant to subsections (5), (6), (7), and (8). The court may extend the time for payment of any claim upon a showing of good cause. No personal representative shall be compelled to pay the debts of the decedent until after the expiration of 5 months from the first publication of notice to creditors. If any person brings an action against a personal representative within the 5 months on any claim to which the personal representative has not filed an objection, the plaintiff shall not receive any costs or attorneys' fees, nor shall the judgment change the class of the claim for payment under this code.

(2) On or before the expiration of 4 months from the first publication of notice to creditors or within 30 days from the timely filing or amendment of a claim, whichever occurs later, a personal representative or other interested person may file a written objection to a claim. If an objection is filed, the person filing it shall serve a copy of the objection as provided by the Florida Probate Rules. The failure to serve a copy of the objection constitutes an abandonment of the objection. For good cause, the court may extend the time for filing or serving an objection to any claim. Objection to a claim constitutes an objection to an amendment of that claim unless the objection is withdrawn.

(3) If the objection is filed by a person other than the personal representative, the personal representative may apply to the court for an order relieving him or her from the obligation to defend the estate in an independent action or for the appointment of the objector as administrator ad litem to defend the action. Fees for the attorney for the administrator ad litem may be awarded as provided in s. 733.106(3). If costs or attorney's fees are awarded from or against the estate, the probate court may charge or apportion that award as provided in s. 733.106(4).

(4) An objection by an interested person to a personal representative's proof of claim shall state the particular item or items to which the interested person objects and shall be filed and served as provided in subsection (2). Issues of liability as between the estate and the personal representative individually for items listed in a personal representative's proof of claim shall be determined in the estate administration, in a proceeding for accounting or surcharge, or in another appropriate proceeding, whether or not an objection has been filed. If an objection to an item listed as to be paid in a personal representative's proof of claim is filed and served, and the personal representative has not paid the item, the other subsections of this section shall apply as if a claim for the item had been filed by the claimant; but if the personal representative has paid the claim after listing it as to be paid, issues of liability as between the estate and the personal representative individually shall be determined in the manner provided for an item listed as paid.

(5) The claimant is limited to a period of 30 days from the date of service of an objection within which to bring an independent action upon the claim, or a declaratory action to establish the validity and amount of an unmatured claim which is not yet due but which is certain to become due in the future, or a declaratory action to establish the validity of a contingent claim upon which no cause of action has accrued on the date of service of an objection and that may or may not become due in the future, unless an extension of this time is agreed to by the personal representative in writing before it expires. For good cause, the court may extend the time for filing an action or proceeding after objection is filed. No action or proceeding on the claim may be brought against the personal representative after the time limited above, and the claim is barred without court order. If an objection is filed to the claim of any creditor and the creditor brings an action to establish the claim, a judgment establishing the claim shall give it no priority over claims of the same class to which it belongs.

(6) A claimant may bring an independent action or declaratory action upon a claim which was not timely filed pursuant to s. 733.702(1) only if the claimant has been granted an extension of time to file the claim pursuant to s. 733.702(3).

(7) If an unmatured claim has not become due before the time for distribution of an estate, the personal representative may prepay the full amount of principal plus accrued interest due on the claim, without discount and without penalty, regardless of any prohibition against prepayment or provision for penalty in any instrument on which the claim is founded. If the claim is not prepaid, no order of discharge may be entered until the creditor and personal representative have filed an agreement disposing of the claim, or in the absence of an agreement until the court provides for payment by one of the following methods:

(a) Requiring the personal representative to reserve such assets as the court determines to be adequate to pay the claim when it becomes due; in fixing the amount to be reserved, the court may determine the value of any security or collateral to which the creditor may resort for payment of the claim and may direct the reservation, if necessary, of sufficient assets to pay the claim or to pay the difference between the value of any security or collateral and the amount necessary to pay the claim. If the estate is insolvent, the court may direct a proportionate amount to be reserved. The court shall direct that the amount reserved be retained by the personal representative until the time that the claim becomes due, and that so much of the reserved amount as is not used for payment be distributed according to law;

(b) Requiring that the claim be adequately secured by a mortgage, pledge, bond, trust, guaranty, or other security, as may be determined by the court, the security to remain in effect until the time the claim becomes due, and so much of the security or collateral as is not needed for payment be distributed according to law; or

(c) Making provisions for the disposition or satisfaction of the claim as are equitable, and in a manner so as not to delay unreasonably the closing of the estate.

(8) If no cause of action has accrued on a contingent claim before the time for distribution of an estate, no order of discharge may be entered until the creditor and the personal representative have filed an agreement disposing of the claim or, in the absence of an agreement, until:

(a) The court determines that the claim is adequately secured or that it has no value,

(b) Three months from the date on which a cause of action accrues upon the claim, provided that no action on the claim is then pending,

(c) Five years from the date of first publication of notice to creditors, or

(d) The court provides for payment of the claim upon the happening of the contingency by one of the methods described in paragraph (a), paragraph (b), or paragraph (c) of subsection (7),

whichever occurs first. No action or proceeding on the claim may be brought against the personal representative after the time limited above, and the claim is barred without court order. If an objection is filed to the claim of any creditor and the creditor brings an action to establish the claim, a judgment establishing the claim shall give it no priority over claims of the same class to which it belongs.

(9) Interest shall be paid by the personal representative on written obligations of the decedent providing for the payment of interest. On all other claims, interest shall be allowed and paid beginning 5 months from the first publication of the notice to creditors.

(10) The court may determine all issues concerning claims or matters not requiring trial by jury.

(11) An order for extension of time authorized under this section may be entered only in the estate administration proceeding.

History.
S. 1, ch. 74-106; s. 86, ch. 75-220; s. 34, ch. 77-87; s. 1, ch. 77-174; s. 1, ch. 84-25; s. 1, ch. 86-249; s. 7, ch. 88-340; s. 7, ch. 89-340; s. 2, ch. 91-61; s. 1017, ch. 97-102; s. 149, ch. 2001-226.
Editor's Notes.
Created from former s. 733.18.

733.706.   Executions and levies.

Except upon approval by the court, no execution or other process shall issue on or be levied against property of the estate. An order approving execution or other process to be levied against property of the estate may be entered only in the estate administration

proceeding. Claims on all judgments against a decedent shall be filed in the same manner as other claims against estates of decedents. This section shall not be construed to prevent the enforcement of mortgages, security interests, or liens encumbering specific property.

History.
S. 1, ch. 74-106; s. 86, ch. 75-220; s. 8, ch. 89-340.
Editor's Notes.
Created from former s. 733.19.

733.707.   Order of payment of expenses and obligations.

(1) The personal representative shall pay the expenses of the administration and obligations of the decedent's estate in the following order:

(a) *Class 1.* — Costs, expenses of administration, and compensation of personal representatives and their attorneys fees and attorneys fees awarded under s. 733.106(3).

(b) *Class 2.* — Reasonable funeral, interment, and grave marker expenses, whether paid by a guardian, the personal representative, or any other person, not to exceed the aggregate of $6,000.

(c) *Class 3.* — Debts and taxes with preference under federal law, claims pursuant to ss. 409.9101 and 414.28, and claims in favor of the state for unpaid court costs, fees, or fines.

(d) *Class 4.* — Reasonable and necessary medical and hospital expenses of the last 60 days of the last illness of the decedent, including compensation of persons attending the decedent.

(e) *Class 5.* — Family allowance.

(f) *Class 6.* — Arrearage from court-ordered child support.

(g) *Class 7.* — Debts acquired after death by the continuation of the decedent's business, in accordance with s. 733.612(22), but only to the extent of the assets of that business.

(h) *Class 8.* — All other claims, including those founded on judgments or decrees rendered against the decedent during the decedent's lifetime, and any excess over the sums allowed in paragraphs (b) and (d).

(2) After paying any preceding class, if the estate is insufficient to pay all of the next succeeding class, the creditors of the latter class shall be paid ratably in proportion to their respective claims.

(3) Any portion of a trust with respect to which a decedent who is the grantor has at the decedent's death a right of revocation, as defined in paragraph (e), either alone or in conjunction with any other person, is liable for the expenses of the administration and obligations of the decedent's estate to the extent the decedent's estate is insufficient to pay them as provided in ss. 733.607(2) and 736.05053.

(a) For purposes of this subsection, any trusts established as part of, and all payments from, either an employee annuity described in s. 403 of the

Internal Revenue Code of 1986, as amended, an Individual Retirement Account, as described in s. 408 of the Internal Revenue Code of 1986, as amended, a Keogh (HR-10) Plan, or a retirement or other plan established by a corporation which is qualified under s. 401 of the Internal Revenue Code of 1986, as amended, shall not be considered a trust over which the decedent has a right of revocation.

(b) For purposes of this subsection, any trust described in s. 664 of the Internal Revenue Code of 1986, as amended, shall not be considered a trust over which the decedent has a right of revocation.

(c) This subsection shall not impair any rights an individual has under a qualified domestic relations order as that term is defined in s. 414(p) of the Internal Revenue Code of 1986, as amended.

(d) For purposes of this subsection, property held or received by a trust to the extent that the property would not have been subject to claims against the decedent's estate if it had been paid directly to a trust created under the decedent's will or other than to the decedent's estate, or assets received from any trust other than a trust described in this subsection, shall not be deemed assets of the trust available to the decedent's estate.

(e) For purposes of this subsection, a "right of revocation" is a power retained by the decedent, held in any capacity, to:

1. Amend or revoke the trust and revest the principal of the trust in the decedent; or

2. Withdraw or appoint the principal of the trust to or for the decedent's benefit.

History.
S. 1, ch. 74-106; s. 86, ch. 75-220; s. 35, ch. 77-87; s. 7, ch. 85-79; s. 69, ch. 87-226; s. 20, ch. 93-208; s. 11, ch. 93-257; s. 10, ch. 95-401; s. 1018, ch. 97-102; s. 3, ch. 97-240; s. 150, ch. 2001-226; s. 2, ch. 2010-122, eff. July 1, 2010; s. 17, ch. 2012-100, eff. July 1, 2012.

Editor's Notes.
Created from former s. 733.20.

Sections 401, 403, 408, 414, and 664 of the Internal Revenue Code, referred to in this section, are codified as 26 U.S.C.S. §§ 401, 403, 408, 414, and 664.

733.708. Compromise.

When a proposal is made to compromise any claim, whether in suit or not, by or against the estate of a decedent or to compromise any question concerning the distribution of a decedent's estate, the court may enter an order authorizing the compromise if satisfied that the compromise will be for the best interest of the interested persons. The order shall relieve the personal representative of liability or responsibility for the compromise. Claims against the estate may not be compromised until after the time for filing objections to claims has expired.

History.
S. 1, ch. 74-106; s. 86, ch. 75-220; s. 151, ch. 2001-226.
Editor's Notes.
Created from former s. 733.21.

733.710. Limitations on claims against estates.

(1) Notwithstanding any other provision of the code, 2 years after the death of a person, neither the decedent's estate, the personal representative, if any, nor the beneficiaries shall be liable for any claim or cause of action against the decedent, whether or not letters of administration have been issued, except as provided in this section.

(2) This section shall not apply to a creditor who has filed a claim pursuant to s. 733.702 within 2 years after the person's death, and whose claim has not been paid or otherwise disposed of pursuant to s. 733.705.

(3) This section shall not affect the lien of any duly recorded mortgage or security interest or the lien of any person in possession of personal property or the right to foreclose and enforce the mortgage or lien.

History.
S. 1, ch. 74-106; s. 50, ch. 75-220; s. 36, ch. 77-87; s. 9, ch. 89-340; s. 152, ch. 2001-226.
Editor's Notes.
Created from former s. 734.29(1).

PART VIII.
SPECIAL PROVISIONS FOR DISTRIBUTION.

733.801. Delivery of devises and distributive shares.

(1) No personal representative shall be required to pay or deliver any devise or distributive share or to surrender possession of any land to any beneficiary until the expiration of 5 months from the granting of letters.

(2) Except as otherwise provided in the will, the personal representative shall pay as an expense of administration the reasonable expenses of storage, insurance, packing, and delivery of tangible personal property to a beneficiary.

History.
S. 1, ch. 74-106; s. 86, ch. 75-220; s. 153, ch. 2001-226.
Editor's Notes.
Created from former s. 734.02.

733.802. Proceedings for compulsory payment of devises or distributive interest.

(1) Before final distribution, no personal representative shall be compelled:

(a) To pay a devise in money before the final settlement of the personal representative's accounts,

(b) To deliver specific personal property devised, unless the personal property is exempt personal property,

(c) To pay all or any part of a distributive share in the personal estate of a decedent, or

(d) To surrender land to any beneficiary,

unless the beneficiary establishes that the property will not be required for the payment of debts, family allowance, estate and inheritance taxes, claims, elective share of the surviving spouse, charges, or expenses of administration or to provide funds for contribution or to enforce equalization in case of advancements.

(2) An order directing the surrender of real property or the delivery of personal property by the personal representative to the beneficiary shall be conclusive in favor of bona fide purchasers for value from the beneficiary or distributee as against the personal representative and all other persons claiming by, through, under, or against the decedent or the decedent's estate.

(3) If the administration of the estate has not been completed before the entry of an order of partial distribution, the court may require the person entitled to distribution to give a bond with sureties as prescribed in s. 45.011, conditioned on the making of due contribution for the payment of devises, family allowance, estate and inheritance taxes, claims, elective share of the spouse, charges, expenses of administration, and equalization in case of advancements, plus any interest on them.

History.
S. 1, ch. 74-106; s. 86, ch. 75-220; s. 37, ch. 77-87; s. 1, ch. 77-174; s. 272, ch. 79-400; s. 1019, ch. 97-102; s. 154, ch. 2001-226.
Editor's Notes.
Created from former s. 734.03.

733.803. Encumbered property; liability for payment.

The specific devisee of any encumbered property shall be entitled to have the encumbrance on devised property paid at the expense of the residue of the estate only when the will shows that intent. A general direction in the will to pay debts does not show that intent.

History.
S. 1, ch. 74-106; s. 86, ch. 75-220; s. 155, ch. 2001-226.
Editor's Notes.
Created from former s. 734.051.

733.805. Order in which assets abate.

(1) Funds or property designated by the will shall be used to pay debts, family allowance, exempt property, elective share charges, expenses of administration, and devises, to the extent the funds or property is sufficient. If no provision is made or the designated fund or property is insufficient, the funds and property of the estate shall be used for these purposes, and to raise the shares of a pretermitted spouse and children, except as otherwise provided in subsections (3) and (4), in the following order:

(a) Property passing by intestacy.

(b) Property devised to the residuary devisee or devisees.

(c) Property not specifically or demonstratively devised.

(d) Property specifically or demonstratively devised.

(2) Demonstrative devises shall be classed as general devises upon the failure or insufficiency of funds or property out of which payment should be made, to the extent of the insufficiency. Devises to the decedent's surviving spouse, given in satisfaction of, or instead of, the surviving spouse's statutory rights in the estate, shall not abate until other devises of the same class are exhausted. Devises given for a valuable consideration shall abate with other devises of the same class only to the extent of the excess over the amount of value of the consideration until all others of the same class are exhausted. Except as herein provided, devises shall abate equally and ratably and without preference or priority as between real and personal property. When property that has been specifically devised or charged with a devise is sold or used by the personal representative, other devisees shall contribute according to their respective interests to the devisee whose devise has been sold or used. The amounts of the respective contributions shall be determined by the court and shall be paid or withheld before distribution is made.

(3) Section 733.817 shall be applied before this section is applied.

(4) In determining the contribution required under s. 733.607(2), subsections (1)-(3) of this section and s. 736.05053(2) shall be applied as if the beneficiaries of the estate and the beneficiaries of a trust described in s. 733.707(3), other than the estate or trust itself, were taking under a common instrument.

History.
S. 1, ch. 74-106; s. 88, ch. 75-220; s. 1, ch. 77-174; s. 1020, ch. 97-102; s. 156, ch. 2001-226; s. 38, ch. 2006-217, eff. July 1, 2007.
Editor's Notes.
Created from former s. 734.05.

733.806. Advancement.

If a person dies intestate, property that the decedent gave during lifetime to an heir is treated as an advancement against the heir's share of the estate only if declared in a contemporaneous writing by the decedent or acknowledged in writing by the heir. The property advanced shall be valued at the time the heir came into possession or enjoyment of the property or at the time of the death of the decedent, whichever first occurs. If the recipient of the property does not survive the decedent, the property shall not be taken into account in computing the intestate share to be received by the recipient's descendants unless the declaration or acknowledgment provides otherwise.

History.
S. 1, ch. 74-106; s. 1021, ch. 97-102; s. 157, ch. 2001-226.
Editor's Notes.
Created from former s. 734.07.

733.808. Death benefits; disposition of proceeds.

(1) Death benefits of any kind, including, but not limited to, proceeds of:

(a) An individual life insurance policy;

(b) A group life insurance policy;

(c) A benefit plan as defined by s. 710.102;

(d) An annuity or endowment contract; and

(e) A health or accident policy,

may be made payable to the trustee under a trust agreement or declaration of trust in existence at the time of the death of the insured, employee, or annuitant or the owner of or participant in the benefit plan. The death benefits shall be held and disposed of by the trustee in accordance with the terms of the trust as they appear in writing on the date of the death of the insured, employee, annuitant, owner, or participant. It shall not be necessary to the validity of the trust agreement or declaration of trust, whether revocable or irrevocable, that it have a trust corpus other than the right of the trustee to receive death benefits.

(2) Death benefits of any kind, including, but not limited to, proceeds of:

(a) An individual life insurance policy;

(b) A group life insurance policy;

(c) A benefit plan as defined in s. 710.102;

(d) An annuity or endowment contract; and

(e) A health or accident policy,

may be made payable to the trustee named, or to be named, in a written instrument that is admitted to probate as the last will of the insured, the owner of the policy, the employee, owner, or participant covered by the plan or contract, or any other person, whether or not the will is in existence at the time of designation. Upon the admission of the will to probate, the death benefits shall be paid to the trustee, to be held, administered, and disposed of in accordance with the terms of the trust or trusts created by the will.

(3) In the event no trustee makes proper claim to the proceeds from the insurance company or other obligor within a period of 6 months after the date of the death of the insured, employee, annuitant, owner, or participant, or if satisfactory evidence is furnished to the insurance company or obligor within that period that there is, or will be, no trustee to receive the proceeds, payment shall be made by the insurance company or obligor to the personal representative of the person making the designation, unless otherwise provided by agreement with the insurer or obligor during the lifetime of the insured, employee, annuitant, owner, or participant.

(4) Death benefits payable as provided in subsection (1), subsection (2), or subsection (3), unless paid to a personal representative under the provisions of subsection (3), shall not be deemed to be part of the decedent's estate, and shall not be subject to any obligation to pay the expenses of the administration and obligations of the decedent's estate or for contribution required from a trust under s. 733.607(2) to any greater extent than if the proceeds were payable directly to the beneficiaries named in the trust.

(5) The death benefits held in trust may be commingled with any other assets that may properly come into the trust.

(6) This section does not affect the validity of any designation of a beneficiary of proceeds previously made that designates as beneficiary the trustee of any trust established under a trust agreement or declaration of trust or by will.

History.
S. 1, ch. 74-106; s. 38, ch. 77-87; s. 158, ch. 2001-226; s. 7, ch. 2005-101.
Editor's Notes.
Created from former s. 736.172.

733.809.　Right of retainer.

The amount of a noncontingent indebtedness due from a beneficiary to the estate or its present value, if not due, may be offset against that beneficiary's interest. However, that beneficiary shall have the benefit of any defense that would be available in a direct proceeding for recovery of the debt.

History.
S. 1, ch. 74-106; s. 39, ch. 77-87; s. 1022, ch. 97-102; s. 159, ch. 2001-226.

733.810.　Distribution in kind; valuation.

(1) Assets shall be distributed in kind unless:

(a) A general power of sale is conferred;

(b) A contrary intention is indicated by the will or trust; or

(c) Disposition is made otherwise under the provisions of this code.

(2) Any pecuniary devise, family allowance, or other pecuniary share of the estate or trust may be satisfied in kind if:

(a) The person entitled to payment has not demanded cash;

(b) The property is distributed at fair market value as of its distribution date; and

(c) No residuary devisee has requested that the asset remain a part of the residuary estate.

(3) When not practicable to distribute undivided interests in a residuary asset, the asset may be sold.

(4) When the fiduciary under a will or trust is required, or has an option, to satisfy a pecuniary devise or transfer in trust, to or for the benefit of the surviving spouse, with an in-kind distribution, at values as finally determined for federal estate tax purposes, the fiduciary shall, unless the governing instrument otherwise provides, satisfy the devise or transfer in trust by distribution of assets, including cash, fairly representative of the appreciated or depreciated value of all property available for that distribution, taking into consideration any gains and losses realized from a prior sale of any property not devised specifically, generally, or demonstratively.

(5) A personal representative or a trustee is authorized to distribute any distributable assets, non-pro rata among the beneficiaries subject to the fiduciary's duty of impartiality.

History.
S. 1, ch. 74-106; s. 92, ch. 75-220; s. 40, ch. 77-87; s. 160, ch. 2001-226.
Editor's Notes.
Created from former s. 734.031.

733.811. Distribution; right or title of distributee.

If a distributee receives from a fiduciary an instrument transferring assets in kind, payment in distribution, or possession of specific property, the distributee has succeeded to the estate's interest in the assets as against all persons interested in the estate. However, the fiduciary may recover the assets or their value if the distribution was improper.

History.
S. 1, ch. 74-106; s. 161, ch. 2001-226.

733.812. Improper distribution or payment; liability of distributee or payee.

A distributee or a claimant who was paid improperly must return the assets or funds received, and the income from those assets or interest on the funds since distribution or payment, unless the distribution or payment cannot be questioned because of adjudication, estoppel, or limitations. If the distributee or claimant does not have the property, its value at the date of disposition, income thereon, and gain received by the distributee or claimant must be returned.

History.
S. 1, ch. 74-106; s. 92, ch. 75-220; s. 1023, ch. 97-102; s. 162, ch. 2001-226.

733.813. Purchasers from distributees protected.

If property distributed in kind, or a security interest in that property, is acquired by a purchaser or lender for value from a distributee, the purchaser or lender takes title free of any claims of the estate and incurs no personal liability to the estate, whether or not the distribution was proper. The purchaser or lender need not inquire whether a personal representative acted properly in making the distribution in kind.

History.
S. 1, ch. 74-106; s. 163, ch. 2001-226.

733.814. Partition for purpose of distribution.

When two or more beneficiaries are entitled to distribution of undivided interests in any property, the personal representative or any beneficiary may petition the court before the estate is closed to partition the property in the same manner as provided by law for civil actions of partition. The court may direct the personal representative to sell any property that cannot be partitioned without prejudice to the owners and that cannot be allotted equitably and conveniently.

History.
S. 1, ch. 74-106; s. 164, ch. 2001-226.

733.815. Private contracts among interested persons.

Subject to the rights of creditors and taxing authorities, interested persons may agree among themselves to alter the interests, shares, or amounts to which they are entitled in a written contract executed by them. The personal representative shall abide by the terms of the contract, subject to the personal representative's obligation to administer the estate for the benefit of interested persons who are not parties to the contract, and to pay costs of administration. Trustees of a testamentary trust are interested persons for the purposes of this section. Nothing in this section relieves trustees of any duties owed to beneficiaries of trusts.

History.
S. 1, ch. 74-106; s. 94, ch. 75-220; s. 1024, ch. 97-102; s. 165, ch. 2001-226.

733.816. Disposition of unclaimed property held by personal representatives.

(1) In all cases in which there is unclaimed property in the hands of a personal representative that cannot be distributed or paid because of the inability to find the lawful owner or because no lawful owner is known or because the lawful owner refuses to accept the property after a reasonable attempt to distribute it and after notice to that lawful owner, the court shall order the personal representative to sell the property and deposit the proceeds and cash already in hand, after retaining those amounts provided for in subsection (4), with the clerk and receive a receipt, and the clerk shall deposit the funds in the registry of the court to be disposed of as follows:

(a) If the value of the funds is $500 or less, the clerk shall post a notice for 30 days at the courthouse door giving the amount involved, the name of the personal representative, and the other pertinent information that will put interested persons on notice.

(b) If the value of the funds is over $500, the clerk shall publish the notice once a month for 2 consecutive months in a newspaper of general circulation in the county.

After the expiration of 6 months from the posting or first publication, the clerk shall deposit the funds with the Chief Financial Officer after deducting the clerk's fees and the costs of publication.

(2) Upon receipt of the funds, the Chief Financial Officer shall deposit them to the credit of the State School Fund, to become a part of the school fund. All interest and all income that may accrue from the money while so deposited shall belong to the fund. The funds so deposited shall constitute and be a permanent appropriation for payments by the Chief Financial Officer in obedience to court orders entered as provided by subsection (3).

(3) Within 10 years from the date of deposit with the Chief Financial Officer, on written petition to the court that directed the deposit of the funds and informal notice to the Department of Legal Affairs, and after proof of entitlement, any person entitled to the funds before or after payment to the Chief Financial Officer and deposit as provided by subsection (1) may obtain a court order directing the payment of the funds to that person. All funds deposited with the Chief Financial Officer and not claimed within 10 years from the date of deposit shall escheat to the state for the benefit of the State School Fund.

(4) The personal representative depositing assets with the clerk is permitted to retain from the funds a sufficient amount to pay final costs of administration chargeable to the assets accruing between the deposit of the funds with the clerk of the court and the order of discharge. Any funds so retained which are surplus shall be deposited with the clerk prior to discharge of the personal representative.

(5)(a) If a person entitled to the funds assigns the right to receive payment or part payment to an attorney or private investigative agency which is duly licensed to do business in this state pursuant to a written agreement with that person, the Department of Financial Services is authorized to make distribution in accordance with the assignment.

(b) Payments made to an attorney or private investigative agency shall be promptly deposited into a trust or escrow account which is regularly maintained by the attorney or private investigative agency in a financial institution located in this state and authorized to accept these deposits.

(c) Distribution by the attorney or private investigative agency to the person entitled to the funds shall be made within 10 days following final credit of the deposit into the trust or escrow account at the financial institution, unless a party to the agreement protests the distribution in writing before it is made.

(d) The department shall not be civilly or criminally liable for any funds distributed pursuant to this subsection, provided the distribution is made in good faith.

History.
S. 1, ch. 74-106; s. 95, ch. 75-220; s. 6, ch. 85-79; s. 5, ch. 89-291; s. 10, ch. 89-299; s. 21, ch. 95-401; s. 1025, ch. 97-102; s. 166, ch. 2001-226; s. 1897, ch. 2003-261.

Editor's Notes.
Created from former s. 734.221.

733.817. Apportionment of estate taxes.

(1) For purposes of this section:

(a) "Fiduciary" means a person other than the personal representative in possession of property included in the measure of the tax who is liable to the applicable taxing authority for payment of the entire tax to the extent of the value of the property in possession.

(b) "Governing instrument" means a will, trust agreement, or any other document that controls the transfer of an asset on the occurrence of the event with respect to which the tax is being levied.

(c) "Gross estate" means the gross estate, as determined by the Internal Revenue Code with respect to the federal estate tax and the Florida estate tax, and as that concept is otherwise determined by the estate, inheritance, or death tax laws of the particular state, country, or political subdivision whose tax is being apportioned.

(d) "Included in the measure of the tax" means that for each separate tax that an interest may incur, only interests included in the measure of that particular tax are considered. The term "included in the measure of the tax" does not include any interest, whether passing under the will or not, to the extent the interest is initially deductible from the gross estate, without regard to any subsequent reduction of the deduction by reason of the charge of any part of the applicable tax to the interest. The term "included in the measure of the tax" does not include interests or amounts that are not included in the gross estate but are included in the amount upon which the applicable tax is computed, such as adjusted taxable gifts with respect to the federal estate tax. If an election is required for deductibility, an interest is not "initially deductible" unless the election for deductibility is allowed.

(e) "Internal Revenue Code" means the Internal Revenue Code of 1986, as amended from time to time.

(f) "Net tax" means the net tax payable to the particular state, country, or political subdivision whose tax is being apportioned, after taking into account all credits against the applicable tax except as provided in this section. With respect to the federal estate tax, "net tax" is determined after taking into account all credits against the tax except for the credit for foreign death taxes.

(g) "Nonresiduary devise" means any devise that is not a residuary devise.

(h) "Nonresiduary interest" in connection with a trust means any interest in a trust which is not a residuary interest.

(i) "Recipient" means, with respect to property or an interest in property included in the gross estate, an heir at law in an intestate estate, devisee in a testate estate, beneficiary of a trust, beneficiary of an insurance policy, annuity, or other contractual right, surviving tenant, taker as a result of the exercise or in default of the exercise of a general power of appointment, person who receives or is to receive the property or an interest in the property, or person in possession of the property, other than a creditor.

(j) "Residuary devise" has the meaning set forth in s. 731.201.

(k) "Residuary interest," in connection with a trust, means an interest in the assets of a trust which remain after provision for any distribution that is to be satisfied by reference to a specific property or type of property, fund, sum, or statutory amount.

(*l*) "Revocable trust" means a trust as described in s. 733.707(3).

(m) "State" means any state, territory, or possession of the United States, the District of Columbia, and the Commonwealth of Puerto Rico.

(n) "Tax" means any estate tax, inheritance tax, generation skipping transfer tax, or other tax levied or assessed under the laws of this or any other state, the United States, any other country, or any political subdivision of the foregoing, as finally determined, which is imposed as a result of the death of the decedent, including, without limitation, the tax assessed pursuant to s. 4980A of the Internal Revenue Code. The term also includes any interest and penalties imposed in addition to the tax. Unless the context indicates otherwise, the term "tax" means each separate tax.

(o) "Temporary interest" means an interest in income or an estate for a specific period of time or for life or for some other period controlled by reference to extrinsic events, whether or not in trust.

(p) "Tentative Florida tax" with respect to any property means the net Florida estate tax that would have been attributable to that property if no tax were payable to any other state in respect of that property.

(q) "Value" means the pecuniary worth of the interest involved as finally determined for purposes of the applicable tax after deducting any debt, expense, or other deduction chargeable to it for which a deduction was allowed in determining the amount of the applicable tax. A lien or other encumbrance is not regarded as chargeable to a particular interest to the extent that it will be paid from other interests. The value of an interest shall not be reduced by reason of the charge against it of any part of the tax.

(2) An interest in protected homestead shall be exempt from the apportionment of taxes.

(3) The net tax attributable to the interests included in the measure of each tax shall be determined by the proportion that the value of each interest included in the measure of the tax bears to the total value of all interests included in the measure of the tax. Notwithstanding the foregoing:

(a) The net tax attributable to interests included in the measure of the tax by reason of s. 2044 of the Internal Revenue Code shall be determined in the manner provided for the federal estate tax in s. 2207A of the Internal Revenue Code, and the amount so determined shall be deducted from the tax to determine the net tax attributable to all remaining interests included in the measure of the tax.

(b) The foreign tax credit allowed with respect to the federal estate tax shall be allocated among the recipients of interests finally charged with the payment of the foreign tax in reduction of any federal estate tax chargeable to the recipients of the foreign interests, whether or not any federal estate tax is attributable to the foreign interests. Any excess of the foreign tax credit shall be applied to reduce proportionately the net amount of federal estate tax chargeable to the remaining recipients of the interests included in the measure of the federal estate tax.

(c) The reduction in the Florida tax on the estate of a Florida resident for tax paid to other states shall be allocated as follows:

1. If the net tax paid to another state is greater than or equal to the tentative Florida tax attributable to the property subject to tax in the other state, none of the Florida tax shall be attributable to that property.

2. If the net tax paid to another state is less than the tentative Florida tax attributable to the property subject to tax in the other state, the net Florida tax attributable to the property subject to tax in the other state shall be the excess of the amount of the tentative Florida tax attributable to the property over the net tax payable to the other state with respect to the property.

3. Any remaining net Florida tax shall be attributable to property included in the measure of the Florida tax exclusive of property subject to tax in other states.

4. The net federal tax attributable to the property subject to tax in the other state shall be determined as if it were located in the state.

(d) The net tax attributable to a temporary interest, if any, shall be regarded as attributable to the principal that supports the temporary interest.

(4)(a) Except as otherwise effectively directed by the governing instrument, if the Internal Revenue Code, including, but not limited to, ss. 2032A(c)(5), 2206, 2207, 2207A, 2207B, and 2603, applies to apportion federal tax against recipients of certain interests, all net taxes, including taxes levied by the state attributable to each type of interest, shall be apportioned against the recipients of all interests of that type in the proportion that the value of each interest of that type included in the measure of the tax bears to the total of all interests of that type included in the measure of the tax.

(b) The provisions of this subsection do not affect allocation of the reduction in the Florida tax as provided in this section with respect to estates of Florida residents which are also subject to tax in other states.

(5) Except as provided above or as otherwise directed by the governing instrument, the net tax attributable to each interest shall be apportioned as follows:

(a) For property passing under the decedent's will:

1. The net tax attributable to nonresiduary devises shall be charged to and paid from the residuary estate whether or not all interests in the residuary estate are included in the measure of the tax. If the residuary estate is insufficient to pay the net tax attributable to all nonresiduary devises, the balance of the net tax attributable to nonresiduary devises shall be apportioned among the recipients of the nonresiduary devises in the proportion that the value of each nonresiduary devise included in the measure of the tax bears to the total of all nonresiduary devises included in the measure of the tax.

2. The net tax attributable to residuary devises shall be apportioned among the recipients of the residuary devises included in the measure of tax in the proportion that the value of each residuary devise included in the measure of the tax bears to the total of all residuary devises included in the measure of the tax.

(b) For property passing under the terms of any trust other than a trust created in the decedent's will:

1. The net tax attributable to nonresiduary interests shall be charged to and paid from the residuary portion of the trust, whether or not all interests in the residuary portion are included in the measure of the tax. If the residuary portion of the trust is insufficient to pay the net tax attributable to all nonresiduary interests, the balance of the net tax attributable to nonresiduary interests shall be apportioned among the recipients of the nonresiduary interests in the proportion that the value of each nonresiduary interest included in the measure of the tax bears to the total of all nonresiduary interests included in the measure of the tax.

2. The net tax attributable to residuary interests shall be apportioned among the recipients of the residuary interests included in the measure of the tax in the proportion that the value of each residuary interest included in the measure of the tax bears to the total of all residuary interests included in the measure of the tax.

(c) The net tax attributable to an interest in protected homestead shall be apportioned against the recipients of other interests in the estate or passing under any revocable trust in the following order:

1. Class I: Recipients of interests not disposed of by the decedent's will or revocable trust that are included in the measure of the federal estate tax.

2. Class II: Recipients of residuary devises and residuary interests that are included in the measure of the federal estate tax.

3. Class III: Recipients of nonresiduary devises and nonresiduary interests that are included in the measure of the federal estate tax.

The net tax apportioned to a class, if any, pursuant to this paragraph shall be apportioned among the recipients in the class in the proportion that the value of the interest of each bears to the total value of all interests included in that class.

(d) In the application of this subsection, paragraphs (a), (b), and (c) shall be applied to apportion the net tax to the recipients of the estate and the recipients of the decedent's revocable trust as if all recipients, other than the estate or trusts themselves, were taking under a common instrument.

(e) The net tax imposed under s. 4980A of the Internal Revenue Code shall be apportioned among the recipients of the interests included in the measure of that tax in the proportion that the value of the interest of each bears to the total value of all interests included in the measure of that tax.

(f) The net tax that is not apportioned under paragraphs (a), (b), and (c), including, but not limited to, the net tax attributable to interests passing by intestacy, jointly held interests passing by survivorship, insurance, properties in which the decedent held a reversionary or revocable interest, and annuities, shall be apportioned among the recipients of the remaining interests that are included in the measure of the tax in the proportion that the value of each such interest bears to the total value of all the remaining interests included in the measure of the tax.

(g) If the court finds that it is inequitable to apportion interest, penalties, or both, in the manner provided in paragraphs (a)-(f), the court may assess liability for the payment thereof in the manner it finds equitable.

(h)1. To be effective as a direction for payment of tax in a manner different from that provided in this section, the governing instrument must direct that the tax be paid from assets that pass pursuant to that governing instrument, except as provided in this section.

2. If the decedent's will provides that the tax shall be apportioned as provided in the decedent's revocable trust by specific reference to the trust, the direction in the revocable trust shall be deemed to be a direction contained in the will and shall control with respect to payment of taxes from assets passing under both the will and the revocable trust.

3. A direction in the decedent's will to pay tax from the decedent's revocable trust is effective if a contrary direction is not contained in the trust agreement.

4. For a direction in a governing instrument to be effective to direct payment of taxes attributable to property not passing under the governing instrument from property passing under the governing instrument, the governing instrument must expressly refer to this section, or expressly indicate that the property passing under the governing instrument is to bear the burden of taxation for property not passing under the governing instrument. A direction in the governing instrument to the effect that all taxes are to be paid from property passing under the governing instrument whether attributable to property passing under the governing instrument or otherwise shall be effective to direct the payment from property passing under the governing instrument of taxes attributable to property not passing under the governing instrument.

5. If there is a conflict as to payment of taxes between the decedent's will and the governing instrument, the decedent's will controls, except as follows:

a. The governing instrument shall be given effect with respect to any tax remaining unpaid after the application of the decedent's will.

b. A direction in a governing instrument to pay the tax attributable to assets that pass pursuant to the governing instrument from assets that pass pursuant to that governing instrument shall be effective notwithstanding any conflict with the decedent's will, unless the tax provision in the decedent's will expressly overrides the conflicting provision in the governing instrument.

(6) The personal representative or fiduciary shall not be required to transfer to a recipient any property reasonably anticipated to be necessary for the payment of taxes. Further, the personal representative or fiduciary shall not be required to transfer any property to the recipient until the amount of the tax due from the recipient is paid by the recipient. If property is transferred before final apportionment of the tax, the recipient shall provide a bond or other security for his or her apportioned liability in the amount and form prescribed by the personal representative or fiduciary.

(7)(a) The personal representative may petition at any time for an order of apportionment. If no administration has been commenced at any time after 90 days from the decedent's death, any fiduciary may petition for an order of apportionment in the court in which venue would be proper for administration of the decedent's estate. Formal notice of the petition for order of apportionment shall be given to all interested persons. At any time after 6 months from the decedent's death, any recipient may petition the court for an order of apportionment.

(b) The court shall determine all issues concerning apportionment. If the tax to be apportioned has not been finally determined, the court shall determine the probable tax due or to become due from all interested persons, apportion the probable tax, and retain jurisdiction over the parties and issues to modify the order of apportionment as appropriate until after the tax is finally determined.

(8)(a) If the personal representative or fiduciary does not have possession of sufficient property otherwise distributable to the recipient to pay the tax apportioned to the recipient, whether under this section, the Internal Revenue Code, or the governing instrument, if applicable, the personal representative or fiduciary shall recover the deficiency in tax so apportioned to the recipient:

1. From the fiduciary in possession of the property to which the tax is apportioned, if any; and

2. To the extent of any deficiency in collection from the fiduciary, or to the extent collection from the fiduciary is excused pursuant to subsection (9) and in all other cases, from the recipient of the property to which the tax is apportioned, unless relieved of this duty as provided in subsection (9).

(b) In any action to recover the tax apportioned, the order of apportionment shall be prima facie correct.

(c) In any action for the enforcement of an order of apportionment, the court shall award taxable costs as in chancery actions, including reasonable attorney's fees, and may award penalties and interest on the unpaid tax in accordance with equitable principles.

(d) This subsection shall not authorize the recovery of any tax from any company issuing insurance included in the gross estate, or from any bank, trust company, savings and loan association, or similar institution with respect to any account in the name of the decedent and any other person which passed by operation of law on the decedent's death.

(9)(a) A personal representative or fiduciary who has the duty under this section of collecting the apportioned tax from recipients may be relieved of the duty to collect the tax by an order of the court finding:

1. That the estimated court costs and attorney's fees in collecting the apportioned tax from a person against whom the tax has been apportioned will approximate or exceed the amount of the recovery;

2. That the person against whom the tax has been apportioned is a resident of a foreign country other than Canada and refuses to pay the apportioned tax on demand; or

3. That it is impracticable to enforce contribution of the apportioned tax against a person against whom the tax has been apportioned in view of the improbability of obtaining a judgment or the improbability of collection under any judgment that might be obtained, or otherwise.

(b) A personal representative or fiduciary shall not be liable for failure to attempt to enforce collection if the personal representative or fiduciary reasonably believes it would have been economically impracticable.

(10) Any apportioned tax that is not collected shall be reapportioned in accordance with this section as if the portion of the property to which the uncollected tax had been apportioned had been exempt.

(11) Nothing in this section shall limit the right of any person who has paid more than the amount of the tax apportionable to that person, calculated as if all apportioned amounts would be collected, to obtain contribution from those who have not paid the full amount of the tax apportionable to them, calculated as if all apportioned amounts would be collected, and that right is hereby conferred. In any action to enforce contribution, the court shall award taxable costs as in chancery actions, including reasonable attorney's fees.

(12) Nothing herein contained shall be construed to require the personal representative or fiduciary to pay any tax levied or assessed by any foreign country,

unless specific directions to that effect are contained in the will or other instrument under which the personal representative or fiduciary is acting.

History.

S. 1, ch. 74-106; s. 95, ch. 75-220; s. 41, ch. 77-87; s. 273, ch. 79-400; s. 20, ch. 92-200; s. 1026, ch. 97-102; s. 9, ch. 97-240; s. 13, ch. 2000-159; s. 167, ch. 2001-226; s. 39, ch. 2006-217, eff. July 1, 2007; s. 122, ch. 2010-5, eff. June 29, 2010.

Editor's Notes.

Created from former s. 734.041.

The references to sections of the Internal Revenue Code, referred to in this section, are codified throughout Title 26 of the U.S.C.S.

PART IX.
CLOSING ESTATES.

733.901.   Final discharge.

(1) After administration has been completed, the personal representative shall be discharged.

(2) The discharge of the personal representative shall release the personal representative and shall bar any action against the personal representative, as such or individually, and the surety.

History.

S. 1, ch. 74-106; s. 96, ch. 75-220; s. 42, ch. 77-87; s. 1, ch. 77-174; s. 6, ch. 81-27; s. 29, ch. 95-401; s. 1027, ch. 97-102; s. 168, ch. 2001-226.

Editor's Notes.

Created from former s. 734.22.

733.903.   Subsequent administration.

The final settlement of an estate and the discharge of the personal representative shall not prevent further administration. The order of discharge may not be revoked based upon the discovery of a will or later will.

History.

S. 1, ch. 74-106; s. 96, ch. 75-220; s. 1, ch. 88-110; s. 169, ch. 2001-226.

Editor's Notes.

Created from former s. 734.26.

CHAPTER 734.
PROBATE CODE: FOREIGN PERSONAL REPRESENTATIVES; ANCILLARY ADMINISTRATION

PART I.
GENERAL PROVISIONS.

734.101. Foreign personal representative.

(1) Personal representatives who produce authenticated copies of probated wills or letters of administration duly obtained in any state or territory of the United States may maintain actions in the courts of this state.

(2) Personal representatives appointed in any state or country may be sued in this state concerning property in this state and may defend actions or proceedings brought in this state.

(3) Debtors who have not received a written demand for payment from a personal representative or curator appointed in this state within 90 days after appointment of a personal representative in any other state or country, and whose property in Florida is subject to a mortgage or other lien securing the debt held by the foreign personal representative, may pay the foreign personal representative after the expiration of 90 days from the date of appointment of the foreign personal representative. Thereafter, a satisfaction of the mortgage or lien executed by the foreign personal representative, with an authenticated copy of the letters or other evidence of authority attached, may be recorded in the public records. The satisfaction shall be an effective discharge of the mortgage or lien, irrespective of whether the debtor making payment had received a written demand before paying the debt.

(4) Except as provided in s. 655.936, all persons indebted to the estate of a decedent, or having possession of personal property belonging to the estate, who have received no written demand from a personal representative or curator appointed in this state for payment of the debt or the delivery of the property are authorized to pay the debt or to deliver the personal property to the foreign personal representative after the expiration of 90 days from the date of appointment of the foreign personal representative.

History.
S. 1, ch. 74-106; s. 98, ch. 75-220; s. 1028, ch. 97-102; s. 170, ch. 2001-226; s. 110, ch. 2002-1; s. 16, ch. 2007-74, eff. July 1, 2007.

Editor's Notes.
Created from former s. 734.30.

734.102. Ancillary administration.

(1) If a nonresident of this state dies leaving assets in this state, credits due from residents in this state, or liens on property in this state, a personal representa-

tive specifically designated in the decedent's will to administer the Florida property shall be entitled to have ancillary letters issued, if qualified to act in Florida. Otherwise, the foreign personal representative of the decedent's estate shall be entitled to have letters issued, if qualified to act in Florida. If the foreign personal representative is not qualified to act in Florida and the will names an alternate or successor who is qualified to act in Florida, the alternate or successor shall be entitled to have letters issued. Otherwise, those entitled to a majority interest of the Florida property may have letters issued to a personal representative selected by them who is qualified to act in Florida. If the decedent dies intestate and the foreign personal representative is not qualified to act in Florida, the order of preference for appointment of a personal representative as prescribed in this code shall apply. If ancillary letters are applied for by other than the domiciliary personal representative, prior notice shall be given to any domiciliary personal representative.

(2) Ancillary administration shall be commenced as provided by the Florida Probate Rules.

(3) If the will and any codicils are executed as required by the code, they shall be admitted to probate.

(4) The ancillary personal representative shall give bond as do personal representatives generally. All proceedings for appointment and administration of the estate shall be as similar to those in original administrations as possible.

(5) Unless creditors' claims are otherwise barred by s. 733.710, the ancillary personal representative shall cause a notice to creditors to be served and published according to the requirements of chapter 733. Claims not filed in accordance with chapter 733 shall be barred as provided in s. 733.702.

(6) After the payment of all expenses of administration and claims against the estate, the court may order the remaining property held by the ancillary personal representative transferred to the foreign personal representative or distributed to the beneficiaries.

(7) Ancillary personal representatives shall have the same rights, powers, and authority as other personal representatives in Florida to manage and settle estates; to sell, lease, or mortgage local property; and to raise funds for the payment of debts, claims, and devises in the domiciliary jurisdiction. No property shall be sold, leased, or mortgaged to pay a debt or claim that is barred by any statute of limitation or of nonclaim of this state.

History.
S. 1, ch. 74-106; s. 98, ch. 75-220; s. 43, ch. 77-87; s. 1, ch. 77-174; s. 1029, ch. 97-102; s. 171, ch. 2001-226.

Editor's Notes.
Created from former s. 734.31.

734.1025. Nonresident decedent's testate estate

with property not exceeding $50,000 in this state; determination of claims.

(1) When a nonresident decedent dies testate and leaves property subject to administration in this state the gross value of which does not exceed $50,000 at the date of death, the foreign personal representative of the estate before the expiration of 2 years after the decedent's death may file in the circuit court of the county where any property is located an authenticated transcript of so much of the foreign proceedings as will show the will and beneficiaries of the estate, as provided in the Florida Probate Rules. The court shall admit the will and any codicils to probate if they comply with s. 732.502(1), (2), or (3).

(2) The foreign personal representative may cause a notice to creditors to be served and published according to the relevant requirements of chapter 733. Claims not filed in accordance with chapter 733 shall be barred as provided in s. 733.702. If any claim is filed, a personal representative shall be appointed as provided in the Florida Probate Rules.

History.
S. 1, ch. 80-203; s. 10, ch. 89-340; s. 1030, ch. 97-102; s. 79, ch. 99-3; s. 172, ch. 2001-226; s. 12, ch. 2003-154.

734.104. Foreign wills; admission to record; effect on title.

(1) An authenticated copy of the will of a nonresident that devises real property in this state, or any right, title, or interest in the property, may be admitted to record in any county of this state where the property is located at any time after 2 years from the death of the decedent or at any time after the domiciliary personal representative has been discharged if there has been no proceeding to administer the estate of the decedent in this state, provided:

(a) The will was executed as required by chapter 732; and

(b) The will has been admitted to probate in the proper court of any other state, territory, or country.

(2) A petition to admit a foreign will to record may be filed by any person and shall be accompanied by authenticated copies of the foreign will, the petition for probate, and the order admitting the will to probate. If no petition is required as a prerequisite to the probate of a will in the jurisdiction where the will of the nonresident was probated, upon proof by affidavit or certificate that no petition is required, an authenticated copy of the will may be admitted to record without an authenticated copy of a petition for probate, and the order admitting the will to record in this state shall recite that no petition was required in the jurisdiction of original probate.

(3) If the court finds that the requirements of this section have been met, it shall enter an order admitting the foreign will to record.

(4) When admitted to record, the foreign will shall be as valid and effectual to pass title to real property and any right, title, or interest therein as if the will had been admitted to probate in this state.

History.
S. 3, ch. 74-106; s. 98, ch. 75-220; s. 45, ch. 77-87; s. 229, ch. 77-104; s. 15, ch. 79-221; s. 274, ch. 79-400; s. 11, ch. 89-340; s. 173, ch. 2001-226.

Editor's Notes.
Created from former s. 736.06.

PART II.
JURISDICTION OVER FOREIGN PERSONAL REPRESENTATIVES.

734.201. Jurisdiction by act of foreign personal representative.

A foreign personal representative submits personally to the jurisdiction of the courts of this state in any proceeding concerning the estate by:

(1) Filing authenticated copies of the domiciliary proceedings under s. 734.104;

(2) Receiving payment of money or taking delivery of personal property, under s. 734.101; or

(3) Doing any act as a personal representative in this state that would have given the state jurisdiction over that person as an individual.

History.
S. 1, ch. 74-106; s. 99, ch. 75-220; s. 1031, ch. 97-102; s. 174, ch. 2001-226.

734.202. Jurisdiction by act of decedent.

In addition to jurisdiction conferred by s. 734.201, a foreign personal representative is subject to the jurisdiction of the courts of this state to the same extent that the decedent was subject to jurisdiction immediately before death.

History.
S. 1, ch. 74-106; s. 1032, ch. 97-102; s. 175, ch. 2001-226.

CHAPTER 735.
PROBATE CODE: SMALL ESTATES

PART I.
SUMMARY ADMINISTRATION.

735.201. Summary administration; nature of proceedings.

Summary administration may be had in the administration of either a resident or nonresident decedent's estate, when it appears:

(1) In a testate estate, that the decedent's will does not direct administration as required by chapter 733.

(2) That the value of the entire estate subject to administration in this state, less the value of property exempt from the claims of creditors, does not exceed $75,000 or that the decedent has been dead for more than 2 years.

History.
S. 1, ch. 74-106; s. 105, ch. 75-220; s. 2, ch. 80-203; s. 13, ch. 89-340; s. 179, ch. 2001-226.

735.202. May be administered in the same manner as other estates.

The estate may be administered in the same manner as the administration of any other estate, or it may be administered as provided in this part.

History.
S. 1, ch. 74-106.
Editor's Notes.
Created from former s. 735.02.

735.203. Petition for summary administration.

(1) A petition for summary administration may be filed by any beneficiary or person nominated as personal representative in the decedent's will offered for probate. The petition must be signed and verified by the surviving spouse, if any, and any beneficiaries except that the joinder in a petition for summary administration is not required of a beneficiary who will receive a full distributive share under the proposed distribution. However, formal notice of the petition must be served on a beneficiary not joining in the petition.

(2) If a person named in subsection (1) has died, is incapacitated, or is a minor, or has conveyed or transferred all interest in the property of the estate, then, as to that person, the petition must be signed and verified by:

(a) The personal representative, if any, of a deceased person or, if none, the surviving spouse, if any, and the beneficiaries;

(b) The guardian of an incapacitated person or a minor; or

(c) The grantee or transferee of any of them shall be authorized to sign and verify the petition instead of the beneficiary or surviving spouse.

(3) If each trustee of a trust that is a beneficiary of the estate of the deceased person is also a petitioner, formal notice of the petition for summary administration shall be served on each qualified beneficiary of the trust as defined in s. 736.0103 unless joinder in, or consent to, the petition is obtained from each qualified beneficiary of the trust.

History.
S. 1, ch. 74-106; s. 107, ch. 75-220; s. 1, ch. 77-174; s. 180, ch. 2001-226; s. 12, ch. 2009-115, eff. July 1, 2009; s. 16, ch. 2010-132, eff. Oct. 1, 2010.
Editor's Notes.
Created from former s. 735.05.

735.2055. Filing of petition.

The petition for summary administration may be filed at any stage of the administration of an estate if it appears that at the time of filing the estate would qualify.

History.
S. 47, ch. 77-87.

735.206. Summary administration distribution.

(1) Upon the filing of the petition for summary administration, the will, if any, shall be proved in accordance with chapter 733 and be admitted to probate.

(2) Prior to entry of the order of summary administration, the petitioner shall make a diligent search and reasonable inquiry for any known or reasonably ascertainable creditors, serve a copy of the petition on those creditors, and make provision for payment for those creditors to the extent that assets are available.

(3) The court may enter an order of summary administration allowing immediate distribution of the assets to the persons entitled to them.

(4) The order of summary administration and distribution so entered shall have the following effect:

(a) Those to whom specified parts of the decedent's estate, including exempt property, are assigned by the order shall be entitled to receive and collect the parts and to have the parts transferred to them. They may maintain actions to enforce the right.

(b) Debtors of the decedent, those holding property of the decedent, and those with whom securities or other property of the decedent are registered are authorized and empowered to comply with the order by paying, delivering, or transferring to those specified in the order the parts of the decedent's estate assigned to them by the order, and the persons so paying, delivering, or transferring shall not be accountable to anyone else for the property.

(c) After the entry of the order, bona fide purchasers for value from those to whom property of the decedent may be assigned by the order shall take the property free of all claims of creditors of the decedent and all rights of the surviving spouse and all other beneficiaries.

(d) Property of the decedent that is not exempt from claims of creditors and that remains in the hands of those to whom it may be assigned by the order shall continue to be liable for claims against the decedent until barred as provided in the code. Any known or reasonably ascertainable creditor who did not receive notice and for whom provision for payment was not made may enforce the claim and, if the creditor prevails, shall be awarded reasonable attorney's fees as an element of costs against those who joined in the petition.

(e) The recipients of the decedent's property under the order of summary administration shall be personally liable for a pro rata share of all lawful claims against the estate of the decedent, but only to the extent of the value of the estate of the decedent actually received by each recipient, exclusive of the property exempt from claims of creditors under the constitution and statutes of Florida.

(f) After 2 years from the death of the decedent, neither the decedent's estate nor those to whom it may be assigned shall be liable for any claim against the decedent, unless proceedings have been taken for the enforcement of the claim.

(g) Any heir or devisee of the decedent who was lawfully entitled to share in the estate but who was not included in the order of summary administration and distribution may enforce all rights in appropriate proceedings against those who procured the order and, if successful, shall be awarded reasonable attorney's fees as an element of costs.

History.
S. 1, ch. 74-106; s. 108, ch. 75-220; s. 48, ch. 77-87; s. 1, ch. 77-174; s. 14, ch. 89-340; s. 1035, ch. 97-102; s. 181, ch. 2001-226.
Editor's Notes.
Created from former s. 735.07.

735.2063.   Notice to creditors.

(1) Any person who has obtained an order of summary administration may publish a notice to creditors according to the relevant requirements of s. 733.2121, notifying all persons having claims or demands against the estate of the decedent that an order of summary administration has been entered by the court. The notice shall specify the total value of the estate and the names and addresses of those to whom it has been assigned by the order.

(2) If proof of publication of the notice is filed with the court, all claims and demands of creditors against the estate of the decedent who are not known or are not reasonably ascertainable shall be forever barred unless the claims and demands are filed with the court within 3 months after the first publication of the notice.

History.
S. 3, ch. 80-203; s. 182, ch. 2001-226; s. 13, ch. 2003-154.

PART II.
DISPOSITION OF PERSONAL PROPERTY WITHOUT ADMINISTRATION.

735.301.   Disposition without administration.

(1) No administration shall be required or formal proceedings instituted upon the estate of a decedent leaving only personal property exempt under the provisions of s. 732.402, personal property exempt from the claims of creditors under the Constitution of Florida, and nonexempt personal property the value of which does not exceed the sum of the amount of preferred funeral expenses and reasonable and necessary medical and hospital expenses of the last 60 days of the last illness.

(2) Upon informal application by affidavit, letter, or otherwise by any interested party, and if the court is satisfied that subsection (1) is applicable, the court, by letter or other writing under the seal of the court, may authorize the payment, transfer, or disposition of the personal property, tangible or intangible, belonging to the decedent to those persons entitled.

(3) Any person, firm, or corporation paying, delivering, or transferring property under the authorization shall be forever discharged from liability thereon.
History.
S. 1, ch. 74-106; s. 111, ch. 75-220; s. 50, ch. 77-87; s. 1, ch. 77-174; s. 275, ch. 79-400; s. 52, ch. 98-421; s. 184, ch. 2001-226.

735.302.   Income tax refunds in certain cases.

(1) In any case when the United States Treasury Department determines that an overpayment of federal income tax exists and the person in whose favor the overpayment is determined is dead at the time the overpayment of tax is to be refunded, and irrespective of whether the decedent had filed a joint and several or separate income tax return, the amount of the overpayment, if not in excess of $2,500, may be refunded as follows:

(a) Directly to the surviving spouse on his or her verified application; or

(b) If there is no surviving spouse, to one of the decedent's children who is designated in a verified application purporting to be executed by all of the decedent's children over the age of 14 years.

In either event, the application must show that the decedent was not indebted, that provision has been made for the payment of the decedent's debts, or that the entire estate is exempt from the claims of creditors under the constitution and statutes of the state, and that no administration of the estate, including summary administration, has been initiated and that none is planned, to the knowledge of the applicant.

(2) If a refund is made to the surviving spouse or designated child pursuant to the application, the refund shall operate as a complete discharge to the United

States from liability from any action, claim, or demand by any beneficiary of the decedent or other person. This section shall be construed as establishing the ownership or rights of the payee in the refund.

History.
S. 1, ch. 74-106; s. 112, ch. 75-220; s. 51, ch. 77-87; s. 1, ch. 77-174; s. 185, ch. 2001-226.
Editor's Notes.
Created from former s. 735.15.

CHAPTER 736.
FLORIDA TRUST CODE

PART I.
GENERAL PROVISIONS AND DEFINITIONS.

736.0101.   Short title.

This chapter may be cited as the "Florida Trust Code" and for purposes of this chapter is referred to as the "code."

History.
S. 1, ch. 2006-217, eff. July 1, 2007.

736.0102.   Scope.

This code applies to express trusts, charitable or noncharitable, and trusts created pursuant to a law, judgment, or decree that requires the trust to be administered in the manner of an express trust. This code does not apply to constructive or resulting trusts; conservatorships; custodial arrangements pursuant to the Florida Uniform Transfers to Minors Act; business trusts providing for certificates to be issued to beneficiaries; common trust funds; land trusts under s. 689.071, except to the extent provided in s. 689.071(7); trusts created by the form of the account or by the deposit agreement at a financial institution; voting trusts; security arrangements; liquidation trusts; trusts for the primary purpose of paying debts, dividends, interest, salaries, wages, profits, pensions, or employee benefits of any kind; and any arrangement under which a person is nominee or escrowee for another.

History.
S. 1, ch. 2006-217, eff. July 1, 2007; s. 10, ch. 2007-153, eff. July 1, 2007.

736.0103.   Definitions.

Unless the context otherwise requires, in this code:

(1) "Action," with respect to an act of a trustee, includes a failure to act.

(2) "Affiliate" means any person or entity that directly or indirectly through one or more intermediaries owns or controls, is owned or controlled by, or is under common control or ownership with, the fiduciary. An affiliate may include, but is not limited to, an investment adviser, administrator, broker, transfer agent, placement agent, servicing agent, registrar, custodian, underwriter, sponsor, distributor, or manager.

(3) "Ascertainable standard" means a standard relating to an individual's health, education, support, or maintenance within the meaning of s. 2041(b)(1)(A) or s. 2514(c)(1) of the Internal Revenue Code of 1986, as amended.

(4) "Beneficiary" means a person who has a present or future beneficial interest in a trust, vested or contingent, or who holds a power of appointment over trust property in a capacity other than that of trustee. An interest as a permissible appointee of a power of appointment, held by a person in a capacity other than that of trustee, is not a beneficial interest for purposes of this subsection. Upon an irrevocable exercise of a power of appointment, the interest of a person in whose favor the appointment is made shall be considered a present or future beneficial interest in a trust in the same manner as if the interest had been included in the trust instrument.

(5) "Charitable trust" means a trust, or portion of a trust, created for a charitable purpose as described in s. 736.0405(1).

(6) "Environmental law" means a federal, state, or local law, rule, regulation, or ordinance that relates to protection of the environment or human health.

(7) "General power of appointment" means a power of appointment exercisable in favor of the holder of the power, the power holder's creditors, the power holder's estate, or the creditors of the power holder's estate.

(8) "Guardian of the person" means a person appointed by the court to make decisions regarding the support, care, education, health, and welfare of a minor or an incapacitated adult. The term does not include a guardian ad litem.

(9) "Guardian of the property" means a person appointed by the court to administer the estate of a minor or incapacitated adult.

(10) "Interests of the beneficiaries" means the beneficial interests provided in the terms of the trust.

(11) "Jurisdiction" with respect to a geographic area, includes a state or country.

(12) "Power of withdrawal" means a presently exercisable general power of appointment other than a power:

(a) Exercisable by a trustee and limited by an ascertainable standard; or

(b) Exercisable by another person only upon consent of the trustee or a person holding an adverse interest.

(13) "Property" means anything that may be the subject of ownership, real or personal, legal or equitable, or any interest therein.

(14) "Qualified beneficiary" means a living beneficiary who, on the date the beneficiary's qualification is determined:

(a) Is a distributee or permissible distributee of trust income or principal;

(b) Would be a distributee or permissible distributee of trust income or principal if the interests of the distributees described in paragraph (a) terminated on that date without causing the trust to terminate; or

(c) Would be a distributee or permissible distributee of trust income or principal if the trust terminated in accordance with its terms on that date.

(15) "Revocable," as applied to a trust, means revocable by the settlor without the consent of the trustee or a person holding an adverse interest.

(16) "Settlor" means a person, including a testator, who creates or contributes property to a trust. If more than one person creates or contributes property to a trust, each person is a settlor of the portion of the trust property attributable to that person's contribution except to the extent another person has the power to revoke or withdraw that portion.

(17) "Spendthrift provision" means a term of a trust that restrains both voluntary and involuntary transfer of a beneficiary's interest.

(18) "State" means any state of the United States and includes the District of Columbia, the Commonwealth of Puerto Rico, and any territory or possession subject to the legislative authority of the United States.

(19) "Terms of a trust" means the manifestation of the settlor's intent regarding a trust's provisions as expressed in the trust instrument or as may be established by other evidence that would be admissible in a judicial proceeding.

(20) "Trust instrument" means an instrument executed by a settlor that contains terms of the trust, including any amendments to the trust.

(21) "Trustee" means the original trustee and includes any additional trustee, any successor trustee, and any cotrustee.

History.
S. 1, ch. 2006-217, eff. July 1, 2007; s. 1, ch. 2009-117, eff. July 1, 2009.

Editor's Notes.
Sections 2041(b)(1)(A) and 2514(c)(1) of the Internal Revenue Code, referred to in this section, are codified as 26 U.S.C.S. §§ 2041(b)(1)(A) and 2514(c)(1), respectively.

736.0104.　Knowledge.

(1) Subject to subsection (2), a person has knowledge of a fact if the person:

(a) Has actual knowledge of the fact;

(b) Has received a notice or notification of the fact; or

(c) Has reason to know the fact from all the other facts and circumstances known to the person at the time in question.

(2) An organization that conducts activities through employees has notice or knowledge of a fact involving a trust only from the time the information was received by an employee having responsibility to act on matters involving the trust, or would have been brought to the employee's attention if the organization had exercised reasonable diligence. An organization exercises reasonable diligence if the organization maintains reasonable routines for communicating significant information to the employee having responsibility to act on matters involving the trust and there is reasonable compliance with the routines. Reasonable diligence does not require an employee of the organization to communicate information unless the communication is part of the individual's regular duties or the individual knows a matter involving the trust would be materially affected by the information.

History.
S. 1, ch. 2006-217, eff. July 1, 2007.

736.0105.　Default and mandatory rules.

(1) Except as otherwise provided in the terms of the trust, this code governs the duties and powers of a trustee, relations among trustees, and the rights and interests of a beneficiary.

(2) The terms of a trust prevail over any provision of this code except:

(a) The requirements for creating a trust.

(b) The duty of the trustee to act in good faith and in accordance with the terms and purposes of the trust and the interests of the beneficiaries.

(c) The requirement that a trust and its terms be for the benefit of the trust's beneficiaries, and that the trust have a purpose that is lawful, not contrary to public policy, and possible to achieve.

(d) The periods of limitation for commencing a judicial proceeding.

(e) The power of the court to take such action and exercise such jurisdiction as may be necessary in the interests of justice.

(f) The requirements under s. 736.0108(1) for the designation of a principal place of administration of the trust and the requirements under s. 736.0107 for the designation of a jurisdiction the law of which determines the meaning and effect of the terms of a trust.

(g) The jurisdiction and venue provisions in ss. 736.0202, 736.0203, and 736.0204.

(h) The restrictions on the designation of representative under s. 736.0306.

(i) The formalities required under s. 736.0403(2) for the execution of a trust.

(j) The power of the court to modify or terminate a trust under ss. 736.0410-736.04115, except as provided in s. 736.04115(3)(b), and under ss. 736.0413, 736.0415, and 736.0416.

(k) The ability to modify a trust under s. 736.0412, except as provided in s. 736.0412(4)(b).

(*l*) The effect of a spendthrift provision and the rights of certain creditors and assignees to reach a trust as provided in part V.

(m) The trustee's duty under s. 736.05053 to pay expenses and obligations of the settlor's estate.

(n) The trustee's duty under s. 736.05055 to file a notice of trust at the settlor's death.

(o) The right of a trustee under s. 736.0701 to decline a trusteeship and the right of a trustee under s. 736.0705 to resign a trusteeship.

(p) The power of the court under s. 736.0702 to require, dispense with, modify, or terminate a bond.

(q) The power of the court under s. 736.0708(2) to adjust a trustee's compensation specified in the terms of the trust that is unreasonably low or high.

(r) The duty under s. 736.0813(1)(a) and (b) to notify qualified beneficiaries of an irrevocable trust of the existence of the trust, of the identity of the trustee, and of their rights to trust accountings.

(s) The duty under s. 736.0813(1)(c) and (d) to provide a complete copy of the trust instrument and to account to qualified beneficiaries.

(t) The duty under s. 736.0813(1)(e) to respond to the request of a qualified beneficiary of an irrevocable trust for relevant information about the assets and liabilities of the trust and the particulars relating to trust administration.

(u) The effect of an exculpatory term under s. 736.1011.

(v) The rights under ss. 736.1013-736.1017 of a person other than a trustee or beneficiary.

(w) The effect of a penalty clause for contesting a trust under s. 736.1108.

History.
S. 1, ch. 2006-217, eff. July 1, 2007; s. 2, ch. 2009-117, eff. July 1, 2009.

736.0106. Common law of trusts; principles of equity.

The common law of trusts and principles of equity supplement this code, except to the extent modified by this code or another law of this state.

History.
S. 1, ch. 2006-217, eff. July 1, 2007.

736.0107. Governing law.

The meaning and effect of the terms of a trust are determined by:

(1) The law of the jurisdiction designated in the terms of the trust, provided there is a sufficient nexus to the designated jurisdiction at the time of the creation of the trust or during the trust administration, including, but not limited to, the location of real property held by the trust or the residence or location of an office of the settlor, trustee, or any beneficiary; or

(2) In the absence of a controlling designation in the terms of the trust, the law of the jurisdiction where the settlor resides at the time the trust is first created.

Notwithstanding subsection (1) or subsection (2), a designation in the terms of a trust is not controlling as to any matter for which the designation would be contrary to a strong public policy of this state.

History.
S. 1, ch. 2006-217, eff. July 1, 2007.

736.0108. Principal place of administration.

(1) Terms of a trust designating the principal place of administration of the trust are valid only if there is a sufficient connection with the designated jurisdiction. Without precluding other means for establishing a sufficient connection, terms of a trust designating the principal place of administration are valid and controlling if:

(a) A trustee's principal place of business is located in or a trustee is a resident of the designated jurisdiction; or

(b) All or part of the administration occurs in the designated jurisdiction.

(2) Unless otherwise validly designated in the trust instrument, the principal place of administration of a trust is the trustee's usual place of business where the records pertaining to the trust are kept or, if the trustee has no place of business, the trustee's residence. In the case of cotrustees, the principal place of administration is:

(a) The usual place of business of the corporate trustee, if there is only one corporate cotrustee;

(b) The usual place of business or residence of the individual trustee who is a professional fiduciary, if there is only one such person and no corporate cotrustee; or otherwise

(c) The usual place of business or residence of any of the cotrustees as agreed on by the cotrustees.

(3) Notwithstanding any other provision of this section, the principal place of administration of a trust, for which a bank, association, or trust company organized under the laws of this state or bank or savings association organized under the laws of the United States with its main office in this state has been appointed trustee, shall not be moved or otherwise affected solely because the trustee engaged in an interstate merger transaction with an out-of-state bank pursuant to s. 658.2953 in which the out-of-state bank is the resulting bank.

(4) A trustee is under a continuing duty to administer the trust at a place appropriate to its purposes and its administration.

(5) Without precluding the right of the court to order, approve, or disapprove a transfer, the trustee, in furtherance of the duty prescribed by subsection (4), may transfer the trust's principal place of administration to another state or to a jurisdiction outside of the United States.

(6) The trustee shall notify the qualified beneficiaries of a proposed transfer of a trust's principal place of administration not less than 60 days before initiating the transfer. The notice of proposed transfer must include:

(a) The name of the jurisdiction to which the principal place of administration is to be transferred.

(b) The address and telephone number at the new location at which the trustee can be contacted.

(c) An explanation of the reasons for the proposed transfer.

(d) The date on which the proposed transfer is anticipated to occur.

(e) The date, not less than 60 days after the notice is provided, by which the qualified beneficiary must notify the trustee of an objection to the proposed transfer.

(7) The authority of a trustee to act under this section without court approval to transfer a trust's principal place of administration is suspended if a qualified beneficiary files a lawsuit objecting to the proposed transfer on or before the date specified in the notice. The suspension is effective until the lawsuit is dismissed or withdrawn.

(8) In connection with a transfer of the trust's principal place of administration, the trustee may transfer any of the trust property to a successor trustee designated in the terms of the trust or appointed pursuant to s. 736.0704.

History.
S. 1, ch. 2006-217, eff. July 1, 2007.

736.0109. Methods and waiver of notice.

(1) Notice to a person under this code or the sending of a document to a person under this code must be accomplished in a manner reasonably suitable under the circumstances and likely to result in receipt of the notice or document. Permissible methods of notice or for sending a document include first-class mail, personal delivery, delivery to the person's last known place of residence or place of business, or a properly directed facsimile or other electronic message.

(2) Notice otherwise required under this code or a document otherwise required to be sent under this code need not be provided to a person whose identity or location is unknown to and not reasonably ascertainable by the trustee.

(3) Notice under this code or the sending of a document under this code may be waived by the person to be notified or to whom the document is to be sent.

(4) Notice of a judicial proceeding must be given as provided in the Florida Rules of Civil Procedure.

History.
S. 1, ch. 2006-217, eff. July 1, 2007.

736.0110. Others treated as qualified beneficiaries.

(1) A charitable organization expressly designated to receive distributions under the terms of a charitable trust has the rights of a qualified beneficiary under this code if the charitable organization, on the date the charitable organization's qualification is being determined:

(a) Is a distributee or permissible distributee of trust income or principal;

(b) Would be a distributee or permissible distributee of trust income or principal on termination of the interests of other distributees or permissible distributees then receiving or eligible to receive distributions; or

(c) Would be a distributee or permissible distributee of trust income or principal if the trust terminated on that date.

(2) A person appointed to enforce a trust created for the care of an animal or another noncharitable purpose as provided in s. 736.0408 or s. 736.0409 has the rights of a qualified beneficiary under this code.

(3) The Attorney General may assert the rights of a qualified beneficiary with respect to a charitable trust having its principal place of administration in this state.

History.
S. 1, ch. 2006-217, eff. July 1, 2007.

736.0111. Nonjudicial settlement agreements.

(1) For purposes of this section, the term "interested persons" means persons whose interest would be affected by a settlement agreement.

(2) Except as otherwise provided in subsection (3), interested persons may enter into a binding nonjudicial settlement agreement with respect to any matter involving a trust.

(3) A nonjudicial settlement agreement among the trustee and trust beneficiaries is valid only to the extent the terms and conditions could be properly approved by the court. A nonjudicial settlement may not be used to produce a result not authorized by other provisions of this code, including, but not limited to, terminating or modifying a trust in an impermissible manner.

(4) Matters that may be resolved by a nonjudicial settlement agreement include:

(a) The interpretation or construction of the terms of the trust.

(b) The approval of a trustee's report or accounting.

(c) The direction to a trustee to refrain from performing a particular act or the grant to a trustee of any necessary or desirable power.

(d) The resignation or appointment of a trustee and the determination of a trustee's compensation.

(e) The transfer of a trust's principal place of administration.

(f) The liability of a trustee for an action relating to the trust.

(5) Any interested person may request the court to approve or disapprove a nonjudicial settlement agreement.

History.
S. 1, ch. 2006-217, eff. July 1, 2007.

736.0112. Qualification of foreign trustee.

Unless otherwise doing business in this state, local qualification by a foreign trustee is not required for the trustee to receive distribution from a local estate. Nothing in this chapter shall affect the provisions of s. 660.41.

History.
S. 1, ch. 2006-217, eff. July 1, 2007.

PART II.
JUDICIAL PROCEEDINGS.

736.0201. Role of court in trust proceedings.

(1) Except as provided in subsections (5) and (6) and s. 736.0206, judicial proceedings concerning trusts shall be commenced by filing a complaint and shall be governed by the Florida Rules of Civil Procedure.

(2) The court may intervene in the administration of a trust to the extent the court's jurisdiction is invoked by an interested person or as provided by law.

(3) A trust is not subject to continuing judicial supervision unless ordered by the court.

(4) A judicial proceeding involving a trust may relate to the validity, administration, or distribution of a trust, including proceedings to:

(a) Determine the validity of all or part of a trust;

(b) Appoint or remove a trustee;

(c) Review trustees' fees;

(d) Review and settle interim or final accounts;

(e) Ascertain beneficiaries; determine any question arising in the administration or distribution of any trust, including questions of construction of trust instruments; instruct trustees; and determine the existence or nonexistence of any immunity, power, privilege, duty, or right;

(f) Obtain a declaration of rights; or

(g) Determine any other matters involving trustees and beneficiaries.

(5) A proceeding for the construction of a testamentary trust may be filed in the probate proceeding for the testator's estate. The proceeding shall be governed by the Florida Probate Rules.

(6) Rule 1.525, Florida Rules of Civil Procedure, shall apply to judicial proceedings concerning trusts, except that the following do not constitute taxation of costs or attorney's fees even if the payment is for services rendered or costs incurred in a judicial proceeding:

(a) A trustee's payment of compensation or reimbursement of costs to persons employed by the trustee from assets of the trust.

(b) A determination by the court directing from what part of the trust fees or costs shall be paid, unless the determination is made under s. 736.1004 in an action for breach of fiduciary duty or challenging the exercise of, or failure to exercise, a trustee's powers.

History.
S. 2, ch. 2006-217, eff. July 1, 2007; s. 13, ch. 2011-183, eff. June 21, 2011.

Editor's Notes.
Section 14, ch. 2011-183 provides: "Except as otherwise expressly provided in this act, this act shall take effect upon becoming a law and shall apply to all proceedings pending before such date and all cases commenced on or after the effective date."

736.0202. Jurisdiction over trustee and beneficiary.

(1) By accepting the trusteeship of a trust having its principal place of administration in this state or by moving the principal place of administration to this state, the trustee submits personally to the jurisdiction of the courts of this state regarding any matter involving the trust.

(2) With respect to their interests in the trust, the beneficiaries of a trust having its principal place of administration in this state are subject to the jurisdiction of the courts of this state regarding any matter involving the trust. By accepting a distribution from such a trust, the recipient submits personally to the jurisdiction of the courts of this state regarding any matter involving the distribution.

(3) This section does not preclude other methods of obtaining jurisdiction over a trustee, beneficiary, or other person receiving property from the trust.

History.
S. 2, ch. 2006-217, eff. July 1, 2007.

736.0203. Subject matter jurisdiction.

The circuit court has original jurisdiction in this state of all proceedings arising under this code.

History.
S. 2, ch. 2006-217, eff. July 1, 2007.

736.0204. Venue.

Venue for actions and proceedings concerning trusts, including those under s. 736.0201, may be laid in:

(1) Any county where the venue is proper under chapter 47;

(2) Any county where the beneficiary suing or being sued resides or has its principal place of business; or

(3) The county where the trust has its principal place of administration.

History.
S. 2, ch. 2006-217, eff. July 1, 2007.

736.0205. Trust proceedings; dismissal of matters relating to foreign trusts.

Over the objection of a party, the court shall not entertain proceedings under s. 736.0201 for a trust registered, or having its principal place of administration, in another state unless all interested parties could not be bound by litigation in the courts of the state where the trust is registered or has its principal place of administration. The court may condition a stay or dismissal of a proceeding under this section on the consent of any party to jurisdiction of the state where the trust is registered or has its principal place of business, or the court may grant a continuance or enter any other appropriate order.

History.
S. 2, ch. 2006-217, eff. July 1, 2007.

736.0206. Proceedings for review of employment of agents and review of compensation of trustee and employees of trust.

(1) The court may review the propriety of the employment by a trustee of any person, including any attorney, auditor, investment adviser, or other specialized agent or assistant, and the reasonableness of any compensation paid to that person or to the trustee.

(2) If the settlor's estate is being probated, and the settlor's trust or the trustee of the settlor's trust is a beneficiary under the settlor's will, the trustee, any person employed by the trustee, or any interested person may have the propriety of employment and the reasonableness of the compensation of the trustee or any person employed by the trustee determined in the probate proceeding.

(3) The burden of proof of the propriety of the employment and the reasonableness of the compensation shall be on the trustee and the person employed by the trustee. Any person who is determined to have received excessive compensation from a trust for services rendered may be ordered to make appropriate refunds.

(4) Court proceedings to determine reasonable compensation of a trustee or any person employed by a trustee, if required, are a part of the trust administration process. The costs, including attorney's fees, of the person assuming the burden of proof of propriety of the employment and reasonableness of the compensation shall be determined by the court and paid from the assets of the trust unless the court finds the compensation paid or requested to be substantially unreasonable. The court shall direct from which part of the trust assets the compensation shall be paid.

(5) The court may determine reasonable compensation for a trustee or any person employed by a trustee without receiving expert testimony. Any party may offer expert testimony after notice to interested persons. If expert testimony is offered, a reasonable expert witness fee may be awarded by the court and paid from the assets of the trust unless the court finds that the expert testimony did not assist the court. The court shall direct from which part of the trust assets the fee shall be paid.

(6) In a proceeding pursuant to subsection (2), the petitioner may serve formal notice as provided in the Florida Probate Rules, and such notice shall be sufficient for the court to acquire jurisdiction over the person receiving the notice to the extent of the person's interest in the trust.

History.
S. 2, ch. 2006-217, eff. July 1, 2007; s. 3, ch. 2010-122, eff. July 1, 2010.

736.0207. Trust contests.

An action to contest the validity of all or part of a revocable trust, or the revocation of part of a revocable trust, may not be commenced until the trust becomes irrevocable by its terms or by the settlor's death. If all of a revocable trust has been revoked, an action to contest the revocation may not be commenced until after the settlor's death. This section does not prohibit such action by the guardian of the property of an incapacitated settlor.

History.
S. 2, ch. 2006-217, eff. July 1, 2007; s. 9, ch. 2011-183, eff. June 21, 2011.

Editor's Notes.
Section 14, ch. 2011-183 provides: "Except as otherwise expressly provided in this act, this act shall take effect upon becoming a law and shall apply to all proceedings pending before such date and all cases commenced on or after the effective date."

PART III.
REPRESENTATION.

736.0301. Representation; basic effect.

(1) Notice, information, accountings, or reports given to a person who may represent and bind another person under this part may serve as a substitute for and have the same effect as notice, information, accountings, or reports given directly to the other person.

(2) Actions taken by a person who represents the interests of another person under this part are binding on the person whose interests are represented to the same extent as if the actions had been taken by the person whose interests are represented.

(3) Except as otherwise provided in s. 736.0602, a person under this part who represents a settlor lacking capacity may receive notice and give a binding consent on the settlor's behalf.

(4) A trustee is not liable for giving notice, information, accountings, or reports to a beneficiary who is represented by another person under this part, and nothing in this part prohibits the trustee from giving notice, information, accountings, or reports to the person represented.

History.
S. 3, ch. 2006-217, eff. July 1, 2007.

736.0302. Representation by holder of power of appointment.

(1) The holder of a power of appointment may represent and bind persons whose interests, as permissible appointees, takers in default, or otherwise, are subject to the power.

(2) The takers in default of the exercise of a power of appointment may represent and bind persons whose interests, as permissible appointees, are subject to the power.

(3) Subsection (1) does not apply to:

(a) Any matter determined by the court to involve fraud or bad faith by the trustee; or

(b) A power of appointment held by a person while the person is the sole trustee.

(4) As used in this section, the term "power of appointment" does not include a power of a trustee to make discretionary distributions of trust property.

History.
S. 3, ch. 2006-217, eff. July 1, 2007; s. 3, ch. 2009-117, eff. July 1, 2009.

736.0303. Representation by fiduciaries and parents.

To the extent there is no conflict of interest between the representative and the person represented or among those being represented with respect to a particular question or dispute:

(1) A guardian of the property may represent and bind the estate that the guardian of the property controls.

(2) An agent having authority to act with respect to the particular question or dispute may represent and bind the principal.

(3) A trustee may represent and bind the beneficiaries of the trust.

(4) A personal representative of a decedent's estate may represent and bind persons interested in the estate.

(5) A parent may represent and bind the parent's unborn child, or the parent's minor child if a guardian of the property for the minor child has not been appointed.

History.
S. 3, ch. 2006-217, eff. July 1, 2007.

736.0304. Representation by person having substantially identical interest.

Unless otherwise represented, a minor, incapacitated, or unborn individual, or a person whose identity or location is unknown and not reasonably ascertainable, may be represented by and bound by another person having a substantially identical interest with respect to the particular question or dispute, but only to the extent there is no conflict of interest between the representative and the person represented.

History.
S. 3, ch. 2006-217, eff. July 1, 2007.

736.0305. Appointment of representative.

(1) If the court determines that an interest is not represented under this part, or that the otherwise available representation might be inadequate, the court may appoint a representative to receive notice, give consent, and otherwise represent, bind, and act on behalf of a minor, incapacitated, or unborn individual, or a person whose identity or location is unknown. If not precluded by a conflict of interest, a representative may be appointed to represent several persons or interests.

(2) A representative may act on behalf of the individual represented with respect to any matter arising under this code, whether or not a judicial proceeding concerning the trust is pending.

(3) In making decisions, a representative may consider general benefits accruing to the living members of the represented individual's family.

History.
S. 3, ch. 2006-217, eff. July 1, 2007.

736.0306. Designated representative.

(1) If specifically nominated in the trust instrument, one or more persons may be designated to represent and bind a beneficiary and receive any notice, information, accounting, or report. The trust instrument may also authorize any person or persons, other than a trustee of the trust, to designate one or more persons to represent and bind a beneficiary and receive any notice, information, accounting, or report.

(2) Except as otherwise provided in this code, a person designated, as provided in subsection (1) may not represent and bind a beneficiary while that person is serving as trustee.

(3) Except as otherwise provided in this code, a person designated, as provided in subsection (1) may not represent and bind another beneficiary if the person designated also is a beneficiary, unless:

(a) That person was named by the settlor; or

(b) That person is the beneficiary's spouse or a grandparent or descendant of a grandparent of the beneficiary or the beneficiary's spouse.

(4) No person designated, as provided in subsection (1), is liable to the beneficiary whose interests are represented, or to anyone claiming through that beneficiary, for any actions or omissions to act made in good faith.

History.
S. 3, ch. 2006-217, eff. July 1, 2007; s. 4, ch. 2009-117, eff. July 1, 2009.

PART IV.
CREATION, VALIDITY, MODIFICATION, AND TERMINATION.

736.0401. Methods of creating trust.

A trust may be created by:

(1) Transfer of property to another person as trustee during the settlor's lifetime or by will or other disposition taking effect on the settlor's death;

(2) Declaration by the owner of property that the owner holds identifiable property as trustee; or

(3) Exercise of a power of appointment in favor of a trustee.

History.
S. 4, ch. 2006-217, eff. July 1, 2007.

736.0402. Requirements for creation.

(1) A trust is created only if:

(a) The settlor has capacity to create a trust.

(b) The settlor indicates an intent to create the trust.

(c) The trust has a definite beneficiary or is:

1. A charitable trust;

2. A trust for the care of an animal, as provided in s. 736.0408; or

3. A trust for a noncharitable purpose, as provided in s. 736.0409.

(d) The trustee has duties to perform.

(e) The same person is not the sole trustee and sole beneficiary.

(2) A beneficiary is definite if the beneficiary can be ascertained now or in the future, subject to any applicable rule against perpetuities.

(3) A power of a trustee to select a beneficiary from an indefinite class is valid. If the power is not exercised within a reasonable time, the power fails and the property subject to the power passes to the persons who would have taken the property had the power not been conferred.

History.
S. 4, ch. 2006-217, eff. July 1, 2007.

736.0403. Trusts created in other jurisdictions; formalities required for revocable trusts.

(1) A trust not created by will is validly created if the creation of the trust complies with the law of the jurisdiction in which the trust instrument was executed or the law of the jurisdiction in which, at the time of creation, the settlor was domiciled.

(2) Notwithstanding subsection (1):

(a) No trust or confidence of or in any messuages, lands, tenements, or hereditaments shall arise or result unless the trust complies with the provisions of s. 689.05.

(b) The testamentary aspects of a revocable trust, executed by a settlor who is a domiciliary of this state at the time of execution, are invalid unless the trust instrument is executed by the settlor with the formalities required for the execution of a will in this state. For purposes of this subsection, the term "testamentary aspects" means those provisions of the trust instrument that dispose of the trust property on or after the death of the settlor other than to the settlor's estate.

(3) Paragraph (2)(b) does not apply to trusts established as part of an employee annuity described in s. 403 of the Internal Revenue Code of 1986, as amended, an individual retirement account as described in s. 408 of the Internal Revenue Code of 1986, as amended, a Keogh (HR-10) Plan, or a retirement or other plan that is qualified under s. 401 of the Internal Revenue Code of 1986, as amended.

(4) Paragraph (2)(b) applies to trusts created on or after the effective date of this code. Section 737.111, as in effect prior to the effective date of this code, continues to apply to trusts created before the effective date of this code.

History.
S. 4, ch. 2006-217, eff. July 1, 2007.

Editor's Notes.
Sections 401, 403, and 408 of the Internal Revenue Code, referred to in this section, are codified as 26 U.S.C.S. §§ 401, 403, and 408, respectively.

736.0404. Trust purposes.

A trust may be created only to the extent the purposes of the trust are lawful, not contrary to public policy, and possible to achieve. A trust and its terms must be for the benefit of its beneficiaries.

History.
S. 4, ch. 2006-217, eff. July 1, 2007.

736.0405. Charitable purposes; enforcement.

(1) A trust may be created for charitable purposes. Charitable purposes include, but are not limited to, the relief of poverty; the advancement of arts, sciences, education, or religion; and the promotion of health, governmental, or municipal purposes.

(2) If the terms of a charitable trust do not indicate a particular charitable purpose or beneficiary, the court may select one or more charitable purposes or beneficiaries. The selection must be consistent with the settlor's intent to the extent such intent can be ascertained.

(3) The settlor of a charitable trust, among others, has standing to enforce the trust.

History.
S. 4, ch. 2006-217, eff. July 1, 2007.

736.0406. Effect of fraud, duress, mistake, or undue influence.

If the creation, amendment, or restatement of a trust is procured by fraud, duress, mistake, or undue influence, the trust or any part so procured is void. The remainder of the trust not procured by such means is valid if the remainder is not invalid for other reasons. If the revocation of a trust, or any part thereof, is procured by fraud, duress, mistake, or undue influence, such revocation is void.

History.
S. 4, ch. 2006-217, eff. July 1, 2007; s. 10, ch. 2011-183, eff. June 21, 2011.

Editor's Notes.
Section 14, ch. 2011-183 provides: "Except as otherwise expressly provided in this act, this act shall take effect upon becoming a law and

shall apply to all proceedings pending before such date and all cases commenced on or after the effective date."

736.0407. Evidence of oral trust.

Except as required by s. 736.0403 or a law other than this code, a trust need not be evidenced by a trust instrument but the creation of an oral trust and its terms may be established only by clear and convincing evidence.

History.
S. 4, ch. 2006-217, eff. July 1, 2007.

736.0408. Trust for care of an animal.

(1) A trust may be created to provide for the care of an animal alive during the settlor's lifetime. The trust terminates on the death of the animal or, if the trust was created to provide for the care of more than one animal alive during the settlor's lifetime, on the death of the last surviving animal.

(2) A trust authorized by this section may be enforced by a person appointed in the terms of the trust or, if no person is appointed, by a person appointed by the court. A person having an interest in the welfare of the animal may request the court to appoint a person to enforce the trust or to remove a person appointed.

(3) Property of a trust authorized by this section may be applied only to the intended use of the property, except to the extent the court determines that the value of the trust property exceeds the amount required for the intended use. Except as otherwise provided in the terms of the trust, property not required for the intended use must be distributed to the settlor, if then living, otherwise as part of the settlor's estate.

History.
S. 4, ch. 2006-217, eff. July 1, 2007.

736.0409. Noncharitable trust without ascertainable beneficiary.

Except as otherwise provided in s. 736.0408 or by another provision of law, the following rules apply:

(1) A trust may be created for a noncharitable purpose without a definite or definitely ascertainable beneficiary or for a noncharitable but otherwise valid purpose to be selected by the trustee. The trust may not be enforced for more than 21 years.

(2) A trust authorized by this section may be enforced by a person appointed in the terms of the trust or, if no person is appointed, by a person appointed by the court.

(3) Property of a trust authorized by this section may be applied only to the intended use of the property, except to the extent the court determines that the value of the trust property exceeds the amount required for the intended use. Except as otherwise provided in the terms of the trust, property not required for the intended use must be distributed to the settlor, if then living, otherwise as part of the settlor's estate.

History.
S. 4, ch. 2006-217, eff. July 1, 2007.

736.0410. Modification or termination of trust; proceedings for disapproval of nonjudicial acts.

(1) In addition to the methods of termination prescribed by ss. 736.04113-736.0414, a trust terminates to the extent the trust expires or is revoked or is properly distributed pursuant to the terms of the trust.

(2) A proceeding to disapprove a proposed modification or termination under s. 736.0412 or a trust combination or division under s. 736.0417 may be commenced by any beneficiary.

(3) A proceeding to disapprove a proposed termination under s. 736.0414(1) may be commenced by any qualified beneficiary.

History.
S. 4, ch. 2006-217, eff. July 1, 2007.

736.04113. Judicial modification of irrevocable trust when modification is not inconsistent with settlor's purpose.

(1) Upon the application of a trustee of the trust or any qualified beneficiary, a court at any time may modify the terms of a trust that is not then revocable in the manner provided in subsection (2), if:

(a) The purposes of the trust have been fulfilled or have become illegal, impossible, wasteful, or impracticable to fulfill;

(b) Because of circumstances not anticipated by the settlor, compliance with the terms of the trust would defeat or substantially impair the accomplishment of a material purpose of the trust; or

(c) A material purpose of the trust no longer exists.

(2) In modifying a trust under this section, a court may:

(a) Amend or change the terms of the trust, including terms governing distribution of the trust income or principal or terms governing administration of the trust;

(b) Terminate the trust in whole or in part;

(c) Direct or permit the trustee to do acts that are not authorized or that are prohibited by the terms of the trust; or

(d) Prohibit the trustee from performing acts that are permitted or required by the terms of the trust.

(3) In exercising discretion to modify a trust under this section:

(a) The court shall consider the terms and purposes of the trust, the facts and circumstances surrounding the creation of the trust, and extrinsic evidence relevant to the proposed modification.

(b) The court shall consider spendthrift provisions as a factor in making a decision, but the court is not precluded from modifying a trust because the trust contains spendthrift provisions.

(4) The provisions of this section are in addition to, and not in derogation of, rights under the common law to modify, amend, terminate, or revoke trusts.

History.
S. 4, ch. 2006-217, eff. July 1, 2007.

736.04114. Limited judicial construction of irrevocable trust with federal tax provisions.

(1) Upon the application of a trustee or any qualified beneficiary of a trust, a court at any time may construe the terms of a trust that is not then revocable to define the respective shares or determine beneficiaries, in accordance with the intention of the settlor, if a disposition occurs during the applicable period and the trust contains a provision that:

(a) Includes a formula disposition referring to the "unified credit," "estate tax exemption," "applicable exemption amount," "applicable credit amount," "applicable exclusion amount," "generation-skipping transfer tax exemption," "GST exemption," "marital deduction," "maximum marital deduction," "unlimited marital deduction," or "maximum charitable deduction";

(b) Measures a share of a trust based on the amount that can pass free of federal estate tax or the amount that can pass free of federal generation-skipping transfer tax;

(c) Otherwise makes a disposition referring to a charitable deduction, marital deduction, or another provision of federal estate tax or generation-skipping transfer tax law; or

(d) Appears to be intended to reduce or minimize federal estate tax or generation-skipping transfer tax.

(2) For the purpose of this section:

(a) "Applicable period" means a period beginning January 1, 2010, and ending on the end of the day on the earlier of:

1. December 31, 2010; or

2. The day before the date that an act becomes law which repeals or otherwise modifies or has the effect of repealing or modifying s. 901 of the Economic Growth and Tax Relief Reconciliation Act of 2001.

(b) A "disposition occurs" when an interest takes effect in possession or enjoyment.

(3) In construing the trust, the court shall consider the terms and purposes of the trust, the facts and circumstances surrounding the creation of the trust, and the settlor's probable intent. In determining the settlor's probable intent, the court may consider evidence relevant to the settlor's intent even though the evidence contradicts an apparent plain meaning of the trust instrument.

(4) This section does not apply to a disposition that is specifically conditioned upon no federal estate or generation-skipping transfer tax being imposed.

(5) Unless otherwise ordered by the court, during the applicable period and without court order, the trustee administering a trust containing one or more provisions described in subsection (1) may:

(a) Delay or refrain from making any distribution;

(b) Incur and pay fees and costs reasonably necessary to determine its duties and obligations, including compliance with provisions of existing and reasonably anticipated future federal tax laws; and

(c) Establish and maintain reserves for the payment of these fees and costs and federal taxes.

The trustee is not liable for its actions as provided in this subsection which are made or taken in good faith.

(6) The provisions of this section are in addition to, and not in derogation of, rights under this code or the common law to construe a trust.

(7) This section is remedial in order to provide a new or modified legal remedy. This section applies retroactively and is effective as of January 1, 2010.

History.
S. 4, ch. 2010-122, eff. May 27, 2010.

Editor's Notes.
Section 901 of the Economic Growth and Tax Relief Reconciliation Act of 2001, referred to in this section, is carried as a note to 26 U.S.C.S. § 1.

736.04115. Judicial modification of irrevocable trust when modification is in best interests of beneficiaries.

(1) Without regard to the reasons for modification provided in s. 736.04113, if compliance with the terms of a trust is not in the best interests of the beneficiaries, upon the application of a trustee or any qualified beneficiary, a court may at any time modify a trust that is not then revocable as provided in s. 736.04113(2).

(2) In exercising discretion to modify a trust under this section:

(a) The court shall exercise discretion in a manner that conforms to the extent possible with the intent of the settlor, taking into account the current circumstances and best interests of the beneficiaries.

(b) The court shall consider the terms and purposes of the trust, the facts and circumstances surrounding the creation of the trust, and extrinsic evidence relevant to the proposed modification.

(c) The court shall consider spendthrift provisions as a factor in making a decision, but the court is not precluded from modifying a trust because the trust contains spendthrift provisions.

(3) This section shall not apply to:

(a) Any trust created prior to January 1, 2001.

(b) Any trust created after December 31, 2000, if:

1. Under the terms of the trust, all beneficial interests in the trust must vest or terminate within the period prescribed by the rule against perpetuities in s. 689.225(2), notwithstanding s. 689.225(2)(f).

2. The terms of the trust expressly prohibit judicial modification.

(4) For purposes of subsection (3), a revocable trust shall be treated as created when the right of revocation terminates.

(5) The provisions of this section are in addition to, and not in derogation of, rights under the common law to modify, amend, terminate, or revoke trusts.

History.
S. 4, ch. 2006-217, eff. July 1, 2007.

736.04117. Trustee's power to invade principal in trust.

(1)(a) Unless the trust instrument expressly provides otherwise, a trustee who has absolute power under the terms of a trust to invade the principal of the trust, referred to in this section as the "first trust," to make distributions to or for the benefit of one or more persons may instead exercise the power by appointing all or part of the principal of the trust subject to the power in favor of a trustee of another trust, referred to in this section as the "second trust," for the current benefit of one or more of such persons under the same trust instrument or under a different trust instrument; provided:

    1. The beneficiaries of the second trust may include only beneficiaries of the first trust;

    2. The second trust may not reduce any fixed income, annuity, or unitrust interest in the assets of the first trust; and

    3. If any contribution to the first trust qualified for a marital or charitable deduction for federal income, gift, or estate tax purposes under the Internal Revenue Code of 1986, as amended, the second trust shall not contain any provision which, if included in the first trust, would have prevented the first trust from qualifying for such a deduction or would have reduced the amount of such deduction.

(b) For purposes of this subsection, an absolute power to invade principal shall include a power to invade principal that is not limited to specific or ascertainable purposes, such as health, education, maintenance, and support, whether or not the term "absolute" is used. A power to invade principal for purposes such as best interests, welfare, comfort, or happiness shall constitute an absolute power not limited to specific or ascertainable purposes.

(2) The exercise of a power to invade principal under subsection (1) shall be by an instrument in writing, signed and acknowledged by the trustee, and filed with the records of the first trust.

(3) The exercise of a power to invade principal under subsection (1) shall be considered the exercise of a power of appointment, other than a power to appoint to the trustee, the trustee's creditors, the trustee's estate, or the creditors of the trustee's estate, and shall be subject to the provisions of s. 689.225 covering the time at which the permissible period of the rule against perpetuities begins and the law that determines the permissible period of the rule against perpetuities of the first trust.

(4) The trustee shall notify all qualified beneficiaries of the first trust, in writing, at least 60 days prior to the effective date of the trustee's exercise of the trustee's power to invade principal pursuant to subsection (1), of the manner in which the trustee intends to exercise the power. A copy of the proposed instrument exercising the power shall satisfy the trustee's notice obligation under this subsection. If all qualified beneficiaries waive the notice period by signed written instrument delivered to the trustee, the trustee's power to invade principal shall be exercisable immediately. The trustee's notice under this subsection shall not limit the right of any beneficiary to object to the exercise of the trustee's power to invade principal except as provided in other applicable provisions of this code.

(5) The exercise of the power to invade principal under subsection (1) is not prohibited by a spendthrift clause or by a provision in the trust instrument that prohibits amendment or revocation of the trust.

(6) Nothing in this section is intended to create or imply a duty to exercise a power to invade principal, and no inference of impropriety shall be made as a result of a trustee not exercising the power to invade principal conferred under subsection (1).

(7) The provisions of this section shall not be construed to abridge the right of any trustee who has a power of invasion to appoint property in further trust that arises under the terms of the first trust or under any other section of this code or under another provision of law or under common law.

History.
S. 2, ch. 2007-153, eff. July 1, 2007.

736.0412. Nonjudicial modification of irrevocable trust.

(1) After the settlor's death, a trust may be modified at any time as provided in s. 736.04113(2) upon the unanimous agreement of the trustee and all qualified beneficiaries.

(2) Modification of a trust as authorized in this section is not prohibited by a spendthrift clause or by a provision in the trust instrument that prohibits amendment or revocation of the trust.

(3) An agreement to modify a trust under this section is binding on a beneficiary whose interest is represented by another person under part III of this code.

(4) This section shall not apply to:

    (a) Any trust created prior to January 1, 2001.

    (b) Any trust created after December 31, 2000, if, under the terms of the trust, all beneficial interests in the trust must vest or terminate within the period prescribed by the rule against perpetuities in s. 689.225(2), notwithstanding s. 689.225(2)(f), unless the terms of the trust expressly authorize nonjudicial modification.

    (c) Any trust for which a charitable deduction is allowed or allowable under the Internal Revenue Code until the termination of all charitable interests in the trust.

(5) For purposes of subsection (4), a revocable trust shall be treated as created when the right of revocation terminates.

(6) The provisions of this section are in addition to, and not in derogation of, rights under the common law to modify, amend, terminate, or revoke trusts.

History.
S. 4, ch. 2006-217, eff. July 1, 2007.

736.0413. Cy pres.

(1) If a particular charitable purpose becomes unlawful, impracticable, impossible to achieve, or wasteful, the court may apply the doctrine of cy pres to modify or terminate the trust by directing that the trust property be applied or distributed, in whole or in part, in a manner consistent with the settlor's charitable purposes.

(2) A proceeding to modify or terminate a trust under this section may be commenced by a settlor, a trustee, or any qualified beneficiary.

History.
S. 4, ch. 2006-217, eff. July 1, 2007.

736.0414. Modification or termination of uneconomic trust.

(1) After notice to the qualified beneficiaries, the trustee of a trust consisting of trust property having a total value less than $50,000 may terminate the trust if the trustee concludes that the value of the trust property is insufficient to justify the cost of administration.

(2) Upon application of a trustee or any qualified beneficiary, the court may modify or terminate a trust or remove the trustee and appoint a different trustee if the court determines that the value of the trust property is insufficient to justify the cost of administration.

(3) Upon termination of a trust under this section, the trustee shall distribute the trust property in a manner consistent with the purposes of the trust. The trustee may enter into agreements or make such other provisions that the trustee deems necessary or appropriate to protect the interests of the beneficiaries and the trustee and to carry out the intent and purposes of the trust.

(4) The existence of a spendthrift provision in the trust does not make this section inapplicable unless the trust instrument expressly provides that the trustee may not terminate the trust pursuant to this section.

(5) This section does not apply to an easement for conservation or preservation.

History.
S. 4, ch. 2006-217, eff. July 1, 2007.

736.0415. Reformation to correct mistakes.

Upon application of a settlor or any interested person, the court may reform the terms of a trust, even if unambiguous, to conform the terms to the settlor's intent if it is proved by clear and convincing evidence that both the accomplishment of the settlor's intent and the terms of the trust were affected by a mistake of fact or law, whether in expression or inducement. In determining the settlor's original intent, the court may consider evidence relevant to the settlor's intent even though the evidence contradicts an apparent plain meaning of the trust instrument.

History.
S. 4, ch. 2006-217, eff. July 1, 2007.

736.0416. Modification to achieve settlor's tax objectives.

Upon application of any interested person, to achieve the settlor's tax objectives the court may modify the terms of a trust in a manner that is not contrary to the settlor's probable intent. The court may provide that the modification has retroactive effect.

History.
S. 4, ch. 2006-217, eff. July 1, 2007.

736.0417. Combination and division of trusts.

(1) After notice to the qualified beneficiaries, a trustee may combine two or more trusts into a single trust or divide a trust into two or more separate trusts, if the result does not impair rights of any beneficiary or adversely affect achievement of the purposes of the trusts or trust, respectively.

(2) Subject to the terms of the trust, the trustee may take into consideration differences in federal tax attributes and other pertinent factors in administering the trust property of any separate account or trust, in making applicable tax elections, and in making distributions. A separate trust created by severance must be treated as a separate trust for all purposes from the date on which the severance is effective. The effective date of the severance may be retroactive to a date before the date on which the trustee exercises such power.

History.
S. 4, ch. 2006-217, eff. July 1, 2007.

PART V.
CREDITORS' CLAIMS; SPENDTHRIFT AND DISCRETIONARY TRUSTS.

736.0501. Rights of beneficiary's creditor or assignee.

Except as provided in s. 736.0504, to the extent a beneficiary's interest is not subject to a spendthrift provision, the court may authorize a creditor or assignee of the beneficiary to reach the beneficiary's interest by attachment of present or future distributions to or for the benefit of the beneficiary or by other means. The court may limit the award to such relief as is appropriate under the circumstances.

History.
S. 5, ch. 2006-217, eff. July 1, 2007; s. 11, ch. 2007-153, eff. July 1, 2007.

736.0502.   Spendthrift provision.

(1) A spendthrift provision is valid only if the provision restrains both voluntary and involuntary transfer of a beneficiary's interest. This subsection does not apply to any trust the terms of which are included in an instrument executed before the effective date of this code.

(2) A term of a trust providing that the interest of a beneficiary is held subject to a spendthrift trust, or words of similar import, is sufficient to restrain both voluntary and involuntary transfer of the beneficiary's interest.

(3) A beneficiary may not transfer an interest in a trust in violation of a valid spendthrift provision and, except as otherwise provided in this part, a creditor or assignee of the beneficiary may not reach the interest or a distribution by the trustee before receipt of the interest or distribution by the beneficiary.

(4) A valid spendthrift provision does not prevent the appointment of interests through the exercise of a power of appointment.

History.
S. 5, ch. 2006-217, eff. July 1, 2007; s. 12, ch. 2007-153, eff. July 1, 2007.

736.0503.   Exceptions to spendthrift provision.

(1) As used in this section, the term "child" includes any person for whom an order or judgment for child support has been entered in this or any other state.

(2) To the extent provided in subsection (3), a spendthrift provision is unenforceable against:

(a) A beneficiary's child, spouse, or former spouse who has a judgment or court order against the beneficiary for support or maintenance.

(b) A judgment creditor who has provided services for the protection of a beneficiary's interest in the trust.

(c) A claim of this state or the United States to the extent a law of this state or a federal law so provides.

(3) Except as otherwise provided in this subsection and in s. 736.0504, a claimant against which a spendthrift provision may not be enforced may obtain from a court, or pursuant to the Uniform Interstate Family Support Act, an order attaching present or future distributions to or for the benefit of the beneficiary. The court may limit the award to such relief as is appropriate under the circumstances. Notwithstanding this subsection, the remedies provided in this subsection apply to a claim by a beneficiary's child, spouse, former spouse, or a judgment creditor described in paragraph (2)(a) or paragraph (2)(b) only as a last resort upon an initial showing that traditional methods of enforcing the claim are insufficient.

History.
S. 5, ch. 2006-217, eff. July 1, 2007; s. 13, ch. 2007-153, eff. July 1, 2007.

736.0504.   Discretionary trusts; effect of standard.

(1) As used in this section, the term "discretionary distribution" means a distribution that is subject to the trustee's discretion whether or not the discretion is expressed in the form of a standard of distribution and whether or not the trustee has abused the discretion.

(2) Whether or not a trust contains a spendthrift provision, if a trustee may make discretionary distributions to or for the benefit of a beneficiary, a creditor of the beneficiary, including a creditor as described in s. 736.0503(2), may not:

(a) Compel a distribution that is subject to the trustee's discretion; or

(b) Attach or otherwise reach the interest, if any, which the beneficiary might have as a result of the trustee's authority to make discretionary distributions to or for the benefit of the beneficiary.

(3) If the trustee's discretion to make distributions for the trustee's own benefit is limited by an ascertainable standard, a creditor may not reach or compel distribution of the beneficial interest except to the extent the interest would be subject to the creditor's claim were the beneficiary not acting as trustee.

(4) This section does not limit the right of a beneficiary to maintain a judicial proceeding against a trustee for an abuse of discretion or failure to comply with a standard for distribution.

History.
S. 5, ch. 2006-217, eff. July 1, 2007; s. 14, ch. 2007-153, eff. July 1, 2007.

736.0505.   Creditors' claims against settlor.

(1) Whether or not the terms of a trust contain a spendthrift provision, the following rules apply:

(a) The property of a revocable trust is subject to the claims of the settlor's creditors during the settlor's lifetime to the extent the property would not otherwise be exempt by law if owned directly by the settlor.

(b) With respect to an irrevocable trust, a creditor or assignee of the settlor may reach the maximum amount that can be distributed to or for the settlor's benefit. If a trust has more than one settlor, the amount the creditor or assignee of a particular settlor may reach may not exceed the settlor's interest in the portion of the trust attributable to that settlor's contribution.

(c) Notwithstanding the provisions of paragraph (b), the assets of an irrevocable trust may not be subject to the claims of an existing or subsequent creditor or assignee of the settlor, in whole or in part, solely because of the existence of a discretionary power granted to the trustee by the terms of the trust, or any other provision of law, to pay directly to the taxing authorities or to reimburse the settlor for any tax on trust income or principal which is payable by the settlor under the law imposing such tax.

(2) For purposes of this section:

(a) During the period the power may be exercised, the holder of a power of withdrawal is treated in the same manner as the settlor of a revocable trust to the extent of the property subject to the power.

(b) Upon the lapse, release, or waiver of the power, the holder is treated as the settlor of the trust only to the extent the value of the property affected by the lapse, release, or waiver exceeds the greater of the amount specified in:

    1. Section 2041(b)(2) or s. 2514(e); or

    2. Section 2503(b) and, if the donor was married at the time of the transfer to which the power of withdrawal applies, twice the amount specified in s. 2503(b),

of the Internal Revenue Code of 1986, as amended.

(3) Subject to the provisions of s. 726.105, for purposes of this section, the assets in:

(a) A trust described in s. 2523(e) of the Internal Revenue Code of 1986, as amended, or a trust for which the election described in s. 2523(f) of the Internal Revenue Code of 1986, as amended, has been made; and

(b) Another trust, to the extent that the assets in the other trust are attributable to a trust described in paragraph (a),

shall, after the death of the settlor's spouse, be deemed to have been contributed by the settlor's spouse and not by the settlor.

History.
S. 5, ch. 2006-217, eff. July 1, 2007; s. 5, ch. 2010-122, eff. July 1, 2010.

Editor's Notes.
Sections 2041(b)(2), 2503(b), 2514(e), and 2523 of the Internal Revenue Code, referred to in this section, are codified as 26 U.S.C.S. §§ 2041(b)(2), 2503(b), 2514(e), and 2523, respectively.

736.05053. Trustee's duty to pay expenses and obligations of settlor's estate.

(1) A trustee of a trust described in s. 733.707(3) shall pay to the personal representative of a settlor's estate any amounts that the personal representative certifies in writing to the trustee are required to pay the expenses of the administration and obligations of the settlor's estate. Payments made by a trustee, unless otherwise provided in the trust instrument, must be charged as expenses of the trust without a contribution from anyone. The interests of all beneficiaries of such a trust are subject to the provisions of this subsection; however, the payments must be made from assets, property, or the proceeds of the assets or property, other than assets proscribed in s. 733.707(3), that are included in the settlor's gross estate for federal estate tax purposes.

(2) Unless a settlor provides by will, or designates in a trust described in s. 733.707(3) funds or property passing under the trust to be used as designated, the expenses of the administration and obligations of the settlor's estate must be paid from the trust in the following order:

(a) Property of the residue of the trust remaining after all distributions that are to be satisfied by reference to a specific property or type of property, fund, or sum.

(b) Property that is not to be distributed from specified or identified property or a specified or identified item of property.

(c) Property that is to be distributed from specified or identified property or a specified or identified item of property.

(3) Trust distributions that are to be satisfied from specified or identified property must be classed as distributions to be satisfied from the general assets of the trust and not otherwise disposed of in the trust instrument on the failure or insufficiency of funds or property from which payment should be made, to the extent of the insufficiency. Trust distributions given for valuable consideration abate with other distributions of the same class only to the extent of the excess over the value of the consideration until all others of the same class are exhausted. Except as provided in this section, trust distributions abate equally and ratably and without preference or priority between real and personal property. When a specified or identified item of property that has been designated for distribution in the trust instrument or that is charged with a distribution is sold or taken by the trustee, other beneficiaries shall contribute according to their respective interests to the beneficiary whose property has been sold or taken. Before distribution, the trustee shall determine the amounts of the respective contributions and such amounts must be paid or withheld before distribution is made.

(4) The trustee shall pay the expenses of trust administration, including compensation of trustees and attorneys of the trustees, before and in preference to the expenses of the administration and obligations of the settlor's estate.

(5) Nonresiduary trust dispositions shall abate pro rata with nonresiduary devises pursuant to the priorities specified in this section and s. 733.805, determined as if the beneficiaries of the will and trust, other than the estate or trust itself, were taking under a common instrument.

History.
S. 5, ch. 2006-217, eff. July 1, 2007; s. 6, ch. 2010-122, eff. July 1, 2010.

736.05055. Notice of trust.

(1) Upon the death of a settlor of a trust described in s. 733.707(3), the trustee must file a notice of trust with the court of the county of the settlor's domicile and the court having jurisdiction of the settlor's estate.

(2) The notice of trust must contain the name of the settlor, the settlor's date of death, the title of the trust, if any, the date of the trust, and the name and address of the trustee.

(3) If the settlor's probate proceeding has been commenced, the clerk shall notify the trustee in writing of the date of the commencement of the probate proceeding and the file number.

(4) The clerk shall file and index the notice of trust in the same manner as a caveat unless there exists a probate proceeding for the settlor's estate, in which case the notice of trust must be filed in the probate proceeding and the clerk shall send a copy to the personal representative.

(5) The clerk shall send a copy of any caveat filed regarding the settlor to the trustee, and the notice of trust to any caveator, unless there is a probate proceeding pending and the personal representative and the trustee are the same.

(6) Any proceeding affecting the expenses of the administration or obligations of the settlor's estate prior to the trustee filing a notice of trust are binding on the trustee.

(7) The trustee's failure to file the notice of trust does not affect the trustee's obligation to pay expenses of administration and obligations of the settlor's estate as provided in s. 733.607(2).

History.
S. 5, ch. 2006-217, eff. July 1, 2007.

736.0506.   Overdue distribution.

(1) As used in this section, the term "mandatory distribution" means a distribution of income or principal the trustee is required to make to a beneficiary under the terms of the trust, including a distribution on termination of the trust. The term does not include a distribution subject to the exercise of the trustee's discretion, even if:

(a) The discretion is expressed in the form of a standard of distribution; or

(b) The terms of the trust authorizing a distribution couple language of discretion with language of direction.

(2) A creditor or assignee of a beneficiary may reach a mandatory distribution of income or principal, including a distribution upon termination of the trust, if the trustee has not made the distribution to the beneficiary within a reasonable time after the designated distribution date, whether or not a trust contains a spendthrift provision.

History.
S. 5, ch. 2006-217, eff. July 1, 2007.

736.0507.   Personal obligations of trustee.

Except to the extent of the trustee's interest in the trust other than as a trustee, trust property is not subject to personal obligations of the trustee, even if the trustee becomes insolvent or bankrupt.

History.
S. 5, ch. 2006-217, eff. July 1, 2007.

PART VI.
REVOCABLE TRUSTS.

736.0601.   Capacity of settlor of revocable trust.

The capacity required to create, amend, revoke, or add property to a revocable trust, or to direct the actions of the trustee of a revocable trust, is the same as that required to make a will.

History.
S. 6, ch. 2006-217, eff. July 1, 2007.

736.0602.   Revocation or amendment of revocable trust.

(1) Unless the terms of a trust expressly provide that the trust is irrevocable, the settlor may revoke or amend the trust. This subsection does not apply to a trust created under an instrument executed before the effective date of this code.

(2) If a revocable trust is created or funded by more than one settlor:

(a) To the extent the trust consists of community property, the trust may be revoked by either spouse acting alone but may be amended only by joint action of both spouses.

(b) To the extent the trust consists of property other than community property, each settlor may revoke or amend the trust with regard to the portion of the trust property attributable to that settlor's contribution.

(c) Upon the revocation or amendment of the trust by fewer than all of the settlors, the trustee shall promptly notify the other settlors of the revocation or amendment.

(3) Subject to s. 736.0403(2), the settlor may revoke or amend a revocable trust:

(a) By substantial compliance with a method provided in the terms of the trust; or

(b) If the terms of the trust do not provide a method, by:

1. A later will or codicil that expressly refers to the trust or specifically devises property that would otherwise have passed according to the terms of the trust; or

2. Any other method manifesting clear and convincing evidence of the settlor's intent.

(4) Upon revocation of a revocable trust, the trustee shall deliver the trust property as the settlor directs.

(5) A settlor's powers with respect to revocation, amendment, or distribution of trust property may be exercised by an agent under a power of attorney only as authorized by s. 709.2202.

(6) A guardian of the property of the settlor may exercise a settlor's powers with respect to revocation, amendment, or distribution of trust property only as provided in s. 744.441.

(7) A trustee who does not know that a trust has been revoked or amended is not liable for distributions

made and other actions taken on the assumption that the trust had not been amended or revoked.

History.
S. 6, ch. 2006-217, eff. July 1, 2007; s. 32, ch. 2011-210, eff. Oct. 1, 2011.

736.0603. Settlor's powers; powers of withdrawal.

(1) While a trust is revocable, the duties of the trustee are owed exclusively to the settlor.

(2) During the period the power may be exercised, the holder of a power of withdrawal has the rights of a settlor of a revocable trust under this section to the extent of the property subject to the power.

History.
S. 6, ch. 2006-217, eff. July 1, 2007.

736.0604. Limitation on action contesting validity of revocable trust.

An action to contest the validity of a trust that was revocable at the settlor's death is barred, if not commenced within the earlier of:

(1) The time as provided in chapter 95; or

(2) Six months after the trustee sent the person a copy of the trust instrument and a notice informing the person of the trust's existence, of the trustee's name and address, and of the time allowed for commencing a proceeding.

History.
S. 6, ch. 2006-217, eff. July 1, 2007.

PART VII.
OFFICE OF TRUSTEE.

736.0701. Accepting or declining trusteeship.

(1) Except as otherwise provided in subsection (3), a person designated as trustee accepts the trusteeship:

(a) By substantially complying with a method of acceptance provided in the terms of the trust; or

(b) If the terms of the trust do not provide a method or the method provided in the terms is not expressly made exclusive, by accepting delivery of the trust property, exercising powers or performing duties as trustee, or otherwise indicating acceptance of the trusteeship.

(2) A person designated as trustee who has not accepted the trusteeship may decline the trusteeship. A designated trustee who does not accept the trusteeship within a reasonable time after knowing of the designation is deemed to have declined the trusteeship.

(3) A person designated as trustee may, without accepting the trusteeship:

(a) Act to preserve the trust property if, within a reasonable time after acting, the person sends to a qualified beneficiary a written statement declining the trusteeship.

(b) Inspect or investigate trust property to determine potential liability under environmental or other law or for any other purpose.

History.
S. 7, ch. 2006-217, eff. July 1, 2007.

736.0702. Trustee's bond.

(1) A trustee shall give bond to secure performance of the trustee's duties only if the court finds that a bond is needed to protect the interests of the beneficiaries or is required by the terms of the trust and the court has not dispensed with the requirement.

(2) The court may specify the amount of a bond, the trustee's liabilities under the bond, and whether sureties are necessary. The court may modify or terminate a bond at any time.

History.
S. 7, ch. 2006-217, eff. July 1, 2007.

736.0703. Cotrustees.

(1) Cotrustees who are unable to reach a unanimous decision may act by majority decision.

(2) If a vacancy occurs in a cotrusteeship, the remaining cotrustees or a majority of the remaining cotrustees may act for the trust.

(3) A cotrustee must participate in the performance of a trustee's function unless the cotrustee is unavailable to perform the function because of absence, illness, disqualification under other provision of law, or other temporary incapacity or the cotrustee has properly delegated the performance of the function to another cotrustee.

(4) If a cotrustee is unavailable to perform duties because of absence, illness, disqualification under other law, or other temporary incapacity, and prompt action is necessary to achieve the purposes of the trust or to avoid injury to the trust property, the remaining cotrustee or a majority of the remaining cotrustees may act for the trust.

(5) A cotrustee may not delegate to another cotrustee the performance of a function the settlor reasonably expected the cotrustees to perform jointly, except that a cotrustee may delegate investment functions to a cotrustee pursuant to and in compliance with s. 518.112. A cotrustee may revoke a delegation previously made.

(6) Except as otherwise provided in subsection (7), a cotrustee who does not join in an action of another cotrustee is not liable for the action.

(7) Except as otherwise provided in subsection (9), each cotrustee shall exercise reasonable care to:

(a) Prevent a cotrustee from committing a breach of trust.

(b) Compel a cotrustee to redress a breach of trust.

(8) A dissenting cotrustee who joins in an action at the direction of the majority of the cotrustees and who notifies any cotrustee of the dissent at or before the time of the action is not liable for the action.

(9) If the terms of a trust instrument provide for the appointment of more than one trustee but confer upon one or more of the trustees, to the exclusion of the others, the power to direct or prevent specified actions of the trustees, the excluded trustees shall act in accordance with the exercise of the power. Except in cases of willful misconduct on the part of the trustee with the authority to direct or prevent actions of the trustees of which the excluded trustee has actual knowledge, an excluded trustee is not liable, individually or as a fiduciary, for any consequence that results from compliance with the exercise of the power, regardless of the information available to the excluded trustees. The excluded trustees are relieved of any obligation to review, inquire, investigate, or make recommendations or evaluations with respect to the exercise of the power. The trustee or trustees having the power to direct or prevent actions of the trustees shall be liable to the beneficiaries with respect to the exercise of the power as if the excluded trustees were not in office and shall have the exclusive obligation to account to and to defend any action brought by the beneficiaries with respect to the exercise of the power.

History.
S. 7, ch. 2006-217, eff. July 1, 2007; s. 1, ch. 2008-76, eff. July 1, 2008; s. 5, ch. 2009-117, eff. July 1, 2009.

736.0704.　Vacancy in trusteeship; appointment of successor.

(1) A vacancy in a trusteeship occurs if:

(a) A person designated as trustee declines the trusteeship;

(b) A person designated as trustee cannot be identified or does not exist;

(c) A trustee resigns;

(d) A trustee is disqualified or removed;

(e) A trustee dies; or

(f) A trustee is adjudicated to be incapacitated.

(2) If one or more cotrustees remain in office, a vacancy in a trusteeship need not be filled. A vacancy in a trusteeship must be filled if the trust has no remaining trustee.

(3) A vacancy in a trusteeship of a noncharitable trust that is required to be filled must be filled in the following order of priority:

(a) By a person named or designated pursuant to the terms of the trust to act as successor trustee.

(b) By a person appointed by unanimous agreement of the qualified beneficiaries.

(c) By a person appointed by the court.

(4) A vacancy in a trusteeship of a charitable trust that is required to be filled must be filled in the following order of priority:

(a) By a person named or designated pursuant to the terms of the trust to act as successor trustee.

(b) By a person selected by unanimous agreement of the charitable organizations expressly designated to receive distributions under the terms of the trust.

(c) By a person appointed by the court.

(5) The court may appoint an additional trustee or special fiduciary whenever the court considers the appointment necessary for the administration of the trust, whether or not a vacancy in a trusteeship exists or is required to be filled.

History.
S. 7, ch. 2006-217, eff. July 1, 2007.

736.0705.　Resignation of trustee.

(1) A trustee may resign:

(a) Upon at least 30 days' notice to the qualified beneficiaries, the settlor, if living, and all cotrustees; or

(b) With the approval of the court.

(2) In approving a resignation, the court may issue orders and impose conditions reasonably necessary for the protection of the trust property.

(3) Any liability of a resigning trustee or of any sureties on the trustee's bond for acts or omissions of the trustee is not discharged or affected by the trustee's resignation.

History.
S. 7, ch. 2006-217, eff. July 1, 2007.

736.0706.　Removal of trustee.

(1) The settlor, a cotrustee, or a beneficiary may request the court to remove a trustee, or a trustee may be removed by the court on the court's own initiative.

(2) The court may remove a trustee if:

(a) The trustee has committed a serious breach of trust;

(b) The lack of cooperation among cotrustees substantially impairs the administration of the trust;

(c) Due to the unfitness, unwillingness, or persistent failure of the trustee to administer the trust effectively, the court determines that removal of the trustee best serves the interests of the beneficiaries; or

(d) There has been a substantial change of circumstances or removal is requested by all of the qualified beneficiaries, the court finds that removal of the trustee best serves the interests of all of the beneficiaries and is not inconsistent with a material purpose of the trust, and a suitable cotrustee or successor trustee is available.

(3) Pending a final decision on a request to remove a trustee, or in lieu of or in addition to removing a trustee, the court may order such appropriate relief under s. 736.1001(2) as may be necessary to protect the trust property or the interests of the beneficiaries.

History.
S. 7, ch. 2006-217, eff. July 1, 2007.

736.0707.　Delivery of property by former trustee.

(1) Unless a cotrustee remains in office or the court otherwise orders and until the trust property is delivered to a successor trustee or other person entitled to the property, a trustee who has resigned or been

removed has the duties of a trustee and the powers necessary to protect the trust property.

(2) A trustee who has resigned or been removed shall within a reasonable time deliver the trust property within the trustee's possession to the cotrustee, successor trustee, or other person entitled to the property, subject to the right of the trustee to retain a reasonable reserve for the payment of debts, expenses, and taxes. The provisions of this subsection are in addition to and are not in derogation of the rights of a removed or resigning trustee under the common law.

History.
S. 7, ch. 2006-217, eff. July 1, 2007.

736.0708. Compensation of trustee.

(1) If the terms of a trust do not specify the trustee's compensation, a trustee is entitled to compensation that is reasonable under the circumstances.

(2) If the terms of a trust specify the trustee's compensation, the trustee is entitled to be compensated as specified, but the court may allow more or less compensation if:

(a) The duties of the trustee are substantially different from those contemplated when the trust was created; or

(b) The compensation specified by the terms of the trust would be unreasonably low or high.

(3) If the trustee has rendered other services in connection with the administration of the trust, the trustee shall also be allowed reasonable compensation for the other services rendered in addition to reasonable compensation as trustee.

History.
S. 7, ch. 2006-217, eff. July 1, 2007.

736.0709. Reimbursement of expenses.

(1) A trustee is entitled to be reimbursed out of the trust property, with interest as appropriate, for reasonable expenses that were properly incurred in the administration of the trust.

(2) An advance by the trustee of money for the protection of the trust gives rise to a lien against trust property to secure reimbursement with reasonable interest.

History.
S. 7, ch. 2006-217, eff. July 1, 2007.

PART VIII.
DUTIES AND POWERS OF TRUSTEE.

736.0801.   Duty to administer trust.

Upon acceptance of a trusteeship, the trustee shall administer the trust in good faith, in accordance with its terms and purposes and the interests of the beneficiaries, and in accordance with this code.

History.
S. 8, ch. 2006-217, eff. July 1, 2007.

736.0802.   Duty of loyalty.

(1) As between a trustee and the beneficiaries, a trustee shall administer the trust solely in the interests of the beneficiaries.

(2) Subject to the rights of persons dealing with or assisting the trustee as provided in s. 736.1016, a sale, encumbrance, or other transaction involving the investment or management of trust property entered into by the trustee for the trustee's own personal account or which is otherwise affected by a conflict between the trustee's fiduciary and personal interests is voidable by a beneficiary affected by the transaction unless:

(a) The transaction was authorized by the terms of the trust;

(b) The transaction was approved by the court;

(c) The beneficiary did not commence a judicial proceeding within the time allowed by s. 736.1008;

(d) The beneficiary consented to the trustee's conduct, ratified the transaction, or released the trustee in compliance with s. 736.1012;

(e) The transaction involves a contract entered into or claim acquired by the trustee when that person had not become or contemplated becoming trustee;

(f) The transaction was consented to in writing by a settlor of the trust while the trust was revocable; or

(g) The transaction is one by a corporate trustee that involves a money market mutual fund, mutual fund, or a common trust fund described in s. 736.0816(3).

(3) A sale, encumbrance, or other transaction involving the investment or management of trust property is presumed to be affected by a conflict between personal and fiduciary interests if the sale, encumbrance, or other transaction is entered into by the trustee with:

(a) The trustee's spouse;

(b) The trustee's descendants, siblings, parents, or their spouses;

(c) An officer, director, employee, agent, or attorney of the trustee; or

(d) A corporation or other person or enterprise in which the trustee, or a person that owns a significant interest in the trustee, has an interest that might affect the trustee's best judgment.

(4) A transaction not concerning trust property in which the trustee engages in the trustee's individual capacity involves a conflict between personal and fiduciary interests if the transaction concerns an opportunity properly belonging to the trust.

(5)(a) An investment by a trustee authorized by lawful authority to engage in trust business, as defined in s. 658.12(20), in investment instruments, as defined in s. 660.25(6), that are owned or controlled by the trustee or its affiliate, or from which the trustee or its affiliate receives compensation for providing services in a capacity other than as trustee, is not presumed to be affected by a conflict between personal and fiduciary interests provided the investment otherwise complies with chapters 518 and 660 and the trustee complies with the requirements of this subsection.

(b) A trustee who, pursuant to this subsection, invests trust funds in investment instruments that are owned or controlled by the trustee or its affiliate shall disclose the following to all qualified beneficiaries:

1. Notice that the trustee has invested trust funds in investment instruments owned or controlled by the trustee or its affiliate.

2. The identity of the investment instruments.

3. The identity and relationship to the trustee of any affiliate that owns or controls the investment instruments.

(c) A trustee who, pursuant to this subsection, invests trust funds in investment instruments with respect to which the trustee or its affiliate receives compensation for providing services in a capacity other than as trustee shall disclose to all qualified beneficiaries, the nature of the services provided by the trustee or its affiliate, and all compensation, including, but not limited to, fees or commissions paid or to be paid by the account and received or to be received by an affiliate arising from such affiliated investment.

(d) Disclosure required by this subsection shall be made at least annually unless there has been no change in the method or increase in the rate at which such compensation is calculated since the most recent disclosure. The disclosure may be given in a trust disclosure document as defined in s. 736.1008, in a copy of the prospectus for the investment instrument, in any other written disclosure prepared for the investment instrument under applicable federal or state law, or in a written summary that includes all compensation received or to be received by the trustee and any affiliate of the trustee and an explanation of the manner in which such compensation is calculated, either as a percentage of the assets invested or by some other method.

(e) This subsection shall apply as follows:

1. This subsection does not apply to qualified investment instruments or to a trust for which a right of revocation exists.

2. For investment instruments other than qualified investment instruments, paragraphs (a), (b), (c), and (d) shall apply to irrevocable trusts created on or after July 1, 2007, which expressly authorize the trustee, by specific reference to this subsection, to invest in investment instruments owned or controlled by the trustee or its affiliate.

3. For investment instruments other than qualified investment instruments, paragraphs (a), (b), (c), and (d) shall apply to irrevocable trusts created on or after July 1, 2007, that are not described in subparagraph 2. and to irrevocable trusts created prior to July 1, 2007, only as follows:

a. Such paragraphs shall not apply until the statement required in paragraph (f) is provided and a majority of the qualified beneficiaries have provided written consent. All consents must be obtained within 90 days after the date of delivery of the written request. Once given, consent shall be valid as to all investment instruments acquired pursuant to the consent prior to the date of any withdrawal of the consent.

(I) Any qualified beneficiary may petition the court for an order to prohibit, limit, or restrict a trustee's authority to make investments under this subsection. The burden shall be upon the petitioning beneficiary to show good cause for the relief sought.

(II) The court may award costs and attorney's fees relating to any petition under this subparagraph in the same manner as in chancery actions. When costs and attorney's fees are to be paid out of the trust, the court, in its discretion, may direct from which part of the trust such costs and fees shall be paid.

b. The consent of a majority of the qualified beneficiaries under this subparagraph may be withdrawn prospectively by written notice of a majority of any one of the class or classes of the qualified beneficiaries.

(f)1. The trustee of a trust as defined in s. 731.201 may request authority to invest in investment instruments described in this subsection other than a qualified investment instrument, by providing to all qualified beneficiaries a written request containing the following:

a. The name, telephone number, street address, and mailing address of the trustee and of any individuals who may be contacted for further information.

b. A statement that the investment or investments cannot be made without the consent of a majority of each class of the qualified beneficiaries.

c. A statement that, if a majority of each class of qualified beneficiaries consent, the trustee will have the right to make investments in investment instruments, as defined in s. 660.25(6), which are owned or controlled by the trustee or its affiliate, or from which the trustee or its affiliate receives compensation for providing services in a capacity other than as trustee, that such investment instruments may include investment instruments sold primarily to trust accounts, and that the trustee or its affiliate may receive fees in addition to the trustee's compensation for administering the trust.

d. A statement that the consent may be withdrawn prospectively at any time by written notice given by a majority of any class of the qualified beneficiaries.

A statement by the trustee is not delivered if the statement is accompanied by another written communication other than a written communication by the trustee that refers only to the statement.

2. For purposes of paragraph (e) and this paragraph:

a. "Majority of the qualified beneficiaries" means:

(I) If at the time the determination is made there are one or more beneficiaries as described in s. 736.0103(14)(c), at least a majority in interest of the beneficiaries described in s. 736.0103(14)(a), at least a majority in interest of the beneficiaries described in s. 736.0103(14)(b), and at least a majority in interest of the beneficiaries described in s. 736.0103(14)(c), if the interests of the beneficiaries are reasonably ascertainable; otherwise, a majority in number of each such class; or

(II) If there is no beneficiary as described in s. 736.0103(14)(c), at least a majority in interest of the beneficiaries described in s. 736.0103(14)(a) and at least a majority in interest of the beneficiaries described in s. 736.0103(14)(b), if the interests of the beneficiaries are reasonably ascertainable; otherwise, a majority in number of each such class.

b. "Qualified investment instrument" means a mutual fund, common trust fund, or money market fund described in and governed by s. 736.0816(3).

c. An irrevocable trust is created upon execution of the trust instrument. If a trust that was revocable when created thereafter becomes irrevocable, the irrevocable trust is created when the right of revocation terminates.

(g) Nothing in this chapter is intended to create or imply a duty for the trustee to seek the application of this subsection to invest in investment instruments described in paragraph (a), and no inference of impropriety may be made as a result of a trustee electing not to invest trust assets in investment instruments described in paragraph (a).

(h) This subsection is not the exclusive authority under this code for investing in investment instruments described in paragraph (a). A trustee who invests trust funds in investment instruments described in paragraph (a) is not required to comply with paragraph (b), paragraph (c), or paragraph (f) if the trustee is permitted to invest in such investment instruments pursuant to subsection (2).

(6) In voting shares of stock or in exercising powers of control over similar interests in other forms of enterprise, the trustee shall act in the best interests of the beneficiaries. If the trust is the sole owner of a corporation or other form of enterprise, the trustee shall elect or appoint directors or other managers who will manage the corporation or enterprise in the best interests of the beneficiaries.

(7) This section does not preclude the following transactions, if fair to the beneficiaries:

(a) An agreement between a trustee and a beneficiary relating to the appointment or compensation of the trustee;

(b) A payment of reasonable compensation to the trustee;

(c) A transaction between a trust and another trust, the decedent's estate, or a guardian of the property of which the trustee is a fiduciary or in which a beneficiary has an interest;

(d) A deposit of trust money in a regulated financial service institution operated by the trustee; or

(e) An advance by the trustee of money for the protection of the trust.

(8) This section does not preclude the employment of persons, including, but not limited to, attorneys, accountants, investment advisers, or agents, even if they are the trustee, an affiliate of the trustee, or otherwise associated with the trustee, to advise or assist the trustee in the exercise of any of the trustee's powers and to pay reasonable compensation and costs incurred in connection with such employment from the assets of the trust; to act without independent investigation on their recommendations; and, instead of acting personally, to employ one or more agents to perform any act of administration, whether or not discretionary.

(9) The court may appoint a special fiduciary to act with respect to any proposed transaction that might violate this section if entered into by the trustee.

(10) Payment of costs or attorney's fees incurred in any proceeding from the assets of the trust may be made by the trustee without the approval of any person and without court authorization, unless the court orders otherwise as provided in paragraph (b).

(a) If a claim or defense based upon a breach of trust is made against a trustee in a proceeding, the trustee shall provide written notice to each qualified beneficiary of the trust whose share of the trust may be affected by the payment of attorney's fees and costs of the intention to pay costs or attorney's fees incurred in the proceeding from the trust prior to making payment. The written notice shall be delivered by sending a copy by any commercial delivery service requiring a signed receipt, by any form of mail requiring a signed receipt, or as provided in the Florida Rules of Civil Procedure for service of process. The written notice shall inform each qualified beneficiary of the trust whose share of the trust may be affected by the payment of attorney's fees and costs of the right to apply to the court for an order prohibiting the trustee from paying attorney's fees or costs from trust assets. If a trustee is served with a motion for an order prohibiting the trustee from paying attorney's fees or costs in the proceeding and the trustee pays attorney's fees or costs before an order is entered on the motion, the trustee and the trustee's attorneys who have been paid attorney's fees or costs from trust assets to defend against the claim or defense are subject to the remedies in paragraphs (b) and (c).

(b) If a claim or defense based upon breach of trust is made against a trustee in a proceeding, a party must obtain a court order to prohibit the trustee from paying costs or attorney's fees from trust assets. To obtain an order prohibiting payment of costs or attorney's fees from trust assets, a party must make a reasonable showing by evidence in the record or by proffering evidence that provides a reasonable basis for a court to conclude that there has been a breach of trust. The trustee may proffer evidence to rebut the evidence submitted by a party. The court in its discretion may defer ruling on the motion, pending discovery to be taken by the parties. If the court finds that there is a reasonable basis to conclude that there has been a breach of trust, unless the court finds good cause, the court shall enter an order prohibiting the payment of further attorney's fees and costs from the assets of the trust and shall order attorney's fees or costs previously paid from assets of the trust to be refunded. An order entered under this paragraph shall not limit a trustee's right to seek an order permitting the payment of some or all of the attorney's fees or costs incurred in the proceeding from trust assets, including any fees required to be refunded, after the claim or defense is finally determined by the court. If a claim or defense based upon a breach of trust is withdrawn, dismissed, or resolved without a determination by the court that the trustee committed a breach of trust after the entry of an order prohibiting payment of attorney's fees and costs pursuant to this paragraph, the trustee may pay costs or attorney's fees incurred in the proceeding from the assets of the trust without further court authorization.

(c) If the court orders a refund under paragraph (b), the court may enter such sanctions as are appropriate if a refund is not made as directed by the court, including, but not limited to, striking defenses or pleadings filed by the trustee. Nothing in this subsection limits other remedies and sanctions the court may employ for the failure to refund timely.

(d) Nothing in this subsection limits the power of the court to review fees and costs or the right of any interested persons to challenge fees and costs after payment, after an accounting, or after conclusion of the litigation.

(e) Notice under paragraph (a) is not required if the action or defense is later withdrawn or dismissed by the party that is alleging a breach of trust or resolved without a determination by the court that the trustee has committed a breach of trust.

History.

S. 8, ch. 2006-217, eff. July 1, 2007; s. 3, ch. 2007-153, eff. July 1, 2007; s. 159, ch. 2008-4, eff. July 1, 2008; s. 2, ch. 2008-76, eff. July 1, 2008; s. 20, ch. 2009-115, eff. July 1, 2009.

736.0803. Impartiality.

If a trust has two or more beneficiaries, the trustee shall act impartially in administering the trust property, giving due regard to the beneficiaries' respective interests.

History.

S. 8, ch. 2006-217, eff. July 1, 2007.

736.0804. Prudent administration.

A trustee shall administer the trust as a prudent person would, by considering the purposes, terms, distribution requirements, and other circumstances of the trust. In satisfying this standard, the trustee shall exercise reasonable care, skill, and caution.

History.

S. 8, ch. 2006-217, eff. July 1, 2007.

736.0805. Expenses of administration.

In administering a trust, the trustee shall only incur expenses that are reasonable in relation to the trust property, the purposes of the trust, and the skills of the trustee.

History.

S. 8, ch. 2006-217, eff. July 1, 2007.

736.0806. Trustee's skills.

A trustee who has special skills or expertise, or is named trustee in reliance on the trustee's representation that the trustee has special skills or expertise, shall use those special skills or expertise.

History.

S. 8, ch. 2006-217, eff. July 1, 2007.

736.0807. Delegation by trustee.

(1) A trustee may delegate duties and powers that a prudent trustee of comparable skills could properly delegate under the circumstances, including investment functions pursuant to s. 518.112. The trustee shall exercise reasonable care, skill, and caution in:

(a) Selecting an agent.

(b) Establishing the scope and terms of the delegation, consistent with the purposes and terms of the trust.

(c) Reviewing the agent's actions periodically, in order to monitor the agent's performance and compliance with the terms of the delegation.

(2) In performing a delegated function, an agent owes a duty to the trust to exercise reasonable care to comply with the terms of the delegation.

(3) A trustee who complies with subsection (1) and, when investment functions are delegated, s. 518.112 is not liable to the beneficiaries or to the trust for an action of the agent to whom the function was delegated.

(4) By accepting a delegation of powers or duties from the trustee of a trust that is subject to the law of

this state, an agent submits to the jurisdiction of the courts of this state.

History.
S. 8, ch. 2006-217, eff. July 1, 2007; s. 6, ch. 2009-117, eff. July 1, 2009.

736.0808. Powers to direct.

(1) Subject to ss. 736.0403(2) and 736.0602(3)(a), the trustee may follow a direction of the settlor that is contrary to the terms of the trust while a trust is revocable.

(2) If the terms of a trust confer on a person other than the settlor of a revocable trust the power to direct certain actions of the trustee, the trustee shall act in accordance with an exercise of the power unless the attempted exercise is manifestly contrary to the terms of the trust or the trustee knows the attempted exercise would constitute a serious breach of a fiduciary duty that the person holding the power owes to the beneficiaries of the trust.

(3) The terms of a trust may confer on a trustee or other person a power to direct the modification or termination of the trust.

(4) A person, other than a beneficiary, who holds a power to direct is presumptively a fiduciary who, as such, is required to act in good faith with regard to the purposes of the trust and the interests of the beneficiaries. The holder of a power to direct is liable for any loss that results from breach of a fiduciary duty.

History.
S. 8, ch. 2006-217, eff. July 1, 2007.

736.0809. Control and protection of trust property.

A trustee shall take reasonable steps to take control of and protect the trust property.

History.
S. 8, ch. 2006-217, eff. July 1, 2007.

736.0810. Recordkeeping and identification of trust property.

(1) A trustee shall keep clear, distinct, and accurate records of the administration of the trust.

(2) A trustee shall keep trust property separate from the trustee's own property.

(3) Except as otherwise provided in subsection (4), a trustee shall cause the trust property to be designated so that the interest of the trust, to the extent feasible, appears in records maintained by a party other than a trustee or beneficiary.

(4) If the trustee maintains records clearly indicating the respective interests, a trustee may invest as a whole the property of two or more separate trusts.

History.
S. 8, ch. 2006-217, eff. July 1, 2007.

736.08105. Duty to ascertain marketable title of trust real property.

A trustee holding title to real property received from a settlor or estate shall not be required to obtain title insurance or proof of marketable title until a marketable title is required for a sale or conveyance of the real property.

History.
S. 8, ch. 2006-217, eff. July 1, 2007.

736.0811. Enforcement and defense of claims.

A trustee shall take reasonable steps to enforce claims of the trust and to defend claims against the trust.

History.
S. 8, ch. 2006-217, eff. July 1, 2007.

736.0812. Collecting trust property.

A trustee shall take reasonable steps to compel a former trustee or other person to deliver trust property to the trustee and, except as provided in s. 736.08125, to redress a breach of trust known to the trustee to have been committed by a former trustee.

History.
S. 8, ch. 2006-217, eff. July 1, 2007.

736.08125. Protection of successor trustees.

(1) A successor trustee is not personally liable for actions taken by any prior trustee, nor does any successor trustee have a duty to institute any proceeding against any prior trustee, or file any claim against any prior trustee's estate, for any of the prior trustee's actions as trustee under any of the following circumstances:

(a) As to a successor trustee who succeeds a trustee who was also the settlor of a trust that was revocable during the time that the settlor served as trustee;

(b) As to any beneficiary who has waived any accounting required by s. 736.0813, but only as to the periods included in the waiver;

(c) As to any beneficiary who has released the successor trustee from the duty to institute any proceeding or file any claim;

(d) As to any person who is not an eligible beneficiary; or

(e) As to any eligible beneficiary:

1. If a super majority of the eligible beneficiaries have released the successor trustee;

2. If the eligible beneficiary has not delivered a written request to the successor trustee to institute an action or file a claim against the prior trustee within 6 months after the date of the successor trustee's acceptance of the trust, if the successor trustee has notified the eligible beneficiary in writing of acceptance by the successor trustee in accordance with s. 736.0813(1)(a) and that writing advises the beneficiary that, unless the beneficiary

delivers the written request within 6 months after the date of acceptance, the right to proceed against the successor trustee will be barred pursuant to this section; or

3. For any action or claim that the eligible beneficiary is barred from bringing against the prior trustee.

(2) For the purposes of this section, the term:

(a) "Eligible beneficiaries" means:

1. At the time the determination is made, if there are one or more beneficiaries as described in s. 736.0103(14)(c), the beneficiaries described in s. 736.0103(14)(a) and (c); or

2. If there is no beneficiary as described in s. 736.0103(14)(c), the beneficiaries described in s. 736.0103(14)(a) and (b).

(b) "Super majority of eligible beneficiaries" means at least two-thirds in interest of the eligible beneficiaries if the interests of the eligible beneficiaries are reasonably ascertainable, otherwise, at least two-thirds in number of the eligible beneficiaries.

(3) Nothing in this section affects any liability of the prior trustee or the right of the successor trustee or any beneficiary to pursue an action or claim against the prior trustee.

History.
S. 8, ch. 2006-217, eff. July 1, 2007.

736.0813. Duty to inform and account.

The trustee shall keep the qualified beneficiaries of the trust reasonably informed of the trust and its administration.

(1) The trustee's duty to inform and account includes, but is not limited to, the following:

(a) Within 60 days after acceptance of the trust, the trustee shall give notice to the qualified beneficiaries of the acceptance of the trust, the full name and address of the trustee, and that the fiduciary lawyer-client privilege in s. 90.5021 applies with respect to the trustee and any attorney employed by the trustee.

(b) Within 60 days after the date the trustee acquires knowledge of the creation of an irrevocable trust, or the date the trustee acquires knowledge that a formerly revocable trust has become irrevocable, whether by the death of the settlor or otherwise, the trustee shall give notice to the qualified beneficiaries of the trust's existence, the identity of the settlor or settlors, the right to request a copy of the trust instrument, the right to accountings under this section, and that the fiduciary lawyer-client privilege in s. 90.5021 applies with respect to the trustee and any attorney employed by the trustee.

(c) Upon reasonable request, the trustee shall provide a qualified beneficiary with a complete copy of the trust instrument.

(d) A trustee of an irrevocable trust shall provide a trust accounting, as set forth in s.

736.08135, to each qualified beneficiary annually and on termination of the trust or on change of the trustee.

(e) Upon reasonable request, the trustee shall provide a qualified beneficiary with relevant information about the assets and liabilities of the trust and the particulars relating to administration.

Paragraphs (a) and (b) do not apply to an irrevocable trust created before the effective date of this code, or to a revocable trust that becomes irrevocable before the effective date of this code. Paragraph (a) does not apply to a trustee who accepts a trusteeship before the effective date of this code.

(2) A qualified beneficiary may waive the trustee's duty to account under paragraph (1)(d). A qualified beneficiary may withdraw a waiver previously given. Waivers and withdrawals of prior waivers under this subsection must be in writing. Withdrawals of prior waivers are effective only with respect to accountings for future periods.

(3) The representation provisions of part III apply with respect to all rights of a qualified beneficiary under this section.

(4) As provided in s. 736.0603(1), the trustee's duties under this section extend only to the settlor while a trust is revocable.

(5) This section applies to trust accountings rendered for accounting periods beginning on or after July 1, 2007.

History.
S. 8, ch. 2006-217, eff. July 1, 2007; s. 15, ch. 2007-153, eff. July 1, 2007; s. 11, ch. 2011-183, eff. June 21, 2011.
Editor's Notes.
Section 14, ch. 2011-183 provides: "Except as otherwise expressly provided in this act, this act shall take effect upon becoming a law and shall apply to all proceedings pending before such date and all cases commenced on or after the effective date."

736.08135. Trust accountings.

(1) A trust accounting must be a reasonably understandable report from the date of the last accounting or, if none, from the date on which the trustee became accountable, that adequately discloses the information required in subsection (2).

(2)(a) The accounting must begin with a statement identifying the trust, the trustee furnishing the accounting, and the time period covered by the accounting.

(b) The accounting must show all cash and property transactions and all significant transactions affecting administration during the accounting period, including compensation paid to the trustee and the trustee's agents. Gains and losses realized during the accounting period and all receipts and disbursements must be shown.

(c) To the extent feasible, the accounting must identify and value trust assets on hand at the close of the accounting period. For each asset or class of assets reasonably capable of valuation, the accounting shall contain two values, the asset acquisition value or carrying value and the estimated current value. The accounting must identify each known noncontingent liability with an estimated current amount of the liability if known.

(d) To the extent feasible, the accounting must show significant transactions that do not affect the amount for which the trustee is accountable, including name changes in investment holdings, adjustments to carrying value, a change of custodial institutions, and stock splits.

(e) The accounting must reflect the allocation of receipts, disbursements, accruals, or allowances between income and principal when the allocation affects the interest of any beneficiary of the trust.

(f) The trustee shall include in the final accounting a plan of distribution for any undistributed assets shown on the final accounting.

(3) This section applies to all trust accountings rendered for any accounting periods beginning on or after January 1, 2003.

History.
S. 8, ch. 2006-217, eff. July 1, 2007.

736.0814. Discretionary powers; tax savings.

(1) Notwithstanding the breadth of discretion granted to a trustee in the terms of the trust, including the use of such terms as "absolute," "sole," or "uncontrolled," the trustee shall exercise a discretionary power in good faith and in accordance with the terms and purposes of the trust and the interests of the beneficiaries. A court shall not determine that a trustee abused its discretion merely because the court would have exercised the discretion in a different manner or would not have exercised the discretion.

(2) Subject to subsection (3) and unless the terms of the trust expressly indicate that a rule in this subsection does not apply, a person who is a beneficiary and a trustee may not:

(a) Make discretionary distributions of either principal or income to or for the benefit of that trustee, except to provide for that trustee's health, education, maintenance, or support as described in ss. 2041 and 2514 of the Internal Revenue Code;

(b) Make discretionary allocations of receipts or expenses as between principal and income, unless the trustee acts in a fiduciary capacity whereby the trustee has no power to enlarge or shift any beneficial interest except as an incidental consequence of the discharge of the trustee's fiduciary duties;

(c) Make discretionary distributions of either principal or income to satisfy any of the trustee's legal support obligations; or

(d) Exercise any other power, including, but not limited to, the right to remove or to replace any trustee, so as to cause the powers enumerated in paragraph (a), paragraph (b), or paragraph (c) to be exercised on behalf of, or for the benefit of, a beneficiary who is also a trustee.

(3) Subsection (2) does not apply to:

(a) A power held by the settlor of the trust;

(b) A power held by the settlor's spouse who is the trustee of a trust for which a marital deduction, as defined in s. 2056(a) or s. 2523(a) of the Internal Revenue Code of 1986, as amended, was previously allowed;

(c) Any trust during any period that the trust may be revoked or amended by its settlor; or

(d) A trust if contributions to the trust qualify for the annual exclusion under s. 2503(c) of the Internal Revenue Code of 1986, as amended.

(4) A power whose exercise is limited or prohibited by subsection (2) may be exercised by the remaining trustees whose exercise of the power is not so limited or prohibited. If there is no trustee qualified to exercise the power, on petition by any qualified beneficiary, the court may appoint an independent trustee with authority to exercise the power.

(5) A person who has the right to remove or to replace a trustee does not possess nor may that person be deemed to possess, by virtue of having that right, the powers of the trustee that is subject to removal or to replacement.

History.
S. 8, ch. 2006-217, eff. July 1, 2007.

Editor's Notes.
Sections 2041, 2056(a), 2503(c), 2514, and 2523(a) of the Internal Revenue Code, referred to in this section, are codified as 26 U.S.C.S. §§ 2041, 2056(a), 2503(c), 2514, and 2523(a), respectively.

736.08147. Duty to distribute trust income.

If a will or trust instrument granting income to the settlor's or testator's spouse for life is silent as to the time of distribution of income and the frequency of distributions, the trustee shall distribute all net income, as defined in chapter 738, to the spouse no less frequently than annually. This provision shall apply to any trust established before, on, or after July 1, 2007, unless the trust instrument expressly directs or permits net income to be distributed less frequently than annually.

History.
S. 8, ch. 2006-217, eff. July 1, 2007.

736.0815. General powers of trustee.

(1) A trustee, without authorization by the court, may, except as limited or restricted by this code, exercise:

(a) Powers conferred by the terms of the trust.

(b) Except as limited by the terms of the trust:

1. All powers over the trust property that an unmarried competent owner has over individually owned property.

2. Any other powers appropriate to achieve the proper investment, management, and distribution of the trust property.

3. Any other powers conferred by this code.

(2) The exercise of a power is subject to the fiduciary duties prescribed by this code.

History.
S. 8, ch. 2006-217, eff. July 1, 2007.

736.0816. Specific powers of trustee.

Except as limited or restricted by this code, a trustee may:

(1) Collect trust property and accept or reject additions to the trust property from a settlor, including an asset in which the trustee is personally interested, and hold property in the name of a nominee or in other form without disclosure of the trust so that title to the property may pass by delivery but the trustee is liable for any act of the nominee in connection with the property so held.

(2) Acquire or sell property, for cash or on credit, at public or private sale.

(3) Acquire an undivided interest in a trust asset, including, but not limited to, a money market mutual fund, mutual fund, or common trust fund, in which asset the trustee holds an undivided interest in any trust capacity, including any money market or other mutual fund from which the trustee or any affiliate or associate of the trustee is entitled to receive reasonable compensation for providing necessary services as an investment adviser, portfolio manager, or servicing agent. A trustee or affiliate or associate of the trustee may receive compensation for such services in addition to fees received for administering the trust provided such compensation is fully disclosed in writing to all qualified beneficiaries. As used in this subsection, the term "mutual fund" includes an open-end or closed-end management investment company or investment trust registered under the Investment Company Act of 1940, 15 U.S.C. ss. 80a-1 et seq., as amended.

(4) Exchange, partition, or otherwise change the character of trust property.

(5) Deposit trust money in an account in a regulated financial service institution.

(6) Borrow money, with or without security, and mortgage or pledge trust property for a period within or extending beyond the duration of the trust and advance money for the protection of the trust.

(7) With respect to an interest in a proprietorship, partnership, limited liability company, business trust, corporation, or other form of business or enterprise, continue the business or other enterprise and take any action that may be taken by shareholders, members, or property owners, including, but not limited to, merging, dissolving, or otherwise changing the form of business organization or contributing additional capital.

(8) With respect to stocks or other securities, exercise the rights of an absolute owner, including, but not limited to, the right to:

(a) Vote, or give proxies to vote, with or without power of substitution, or enter into or continue a voting trust agreement.

(b) Hold a security in the name of a nominee or in other form without disclosure of the trust so that title may pass by delivery.

(c) Pay calls, assessments, and other sums chargeable or accruing against the securities, and sell or exercise stock subscription or conversion rights.

(d) Deposit the securities with a depositary or other regulated financial service institution.

(9) With respect to an interest in real property, construct, or make ordinary or extraordinary repairs to, alterations to, or improvements in, buildings or other structures, demolish improvements, raze existing or erect new party walls or buildings, subdivide or develop land, dedicate land to public use or grant public or private easements, and make or vacate plats and adjust boundaries.

(10) Enter into a lease for any purpose as lessor or lessee, including a lease or other arrangement for exploration and removal of natural resources, with or without the option to purchase or renew, for a period within or extending beyond the duration of the trust.

(11) Grant an option involving a sale, lease, or other disposition of trust property or acquire an option for the acquisition of property, including an option exercisable beyond the duration of the trust, and exercise an option so acquired.

(12) Insure the property of the trust against damage or loss and insure the trustee, trustee's agents, and beneficiaries against liability arising from the administration of the trust.

(13) Abandon or decline to administer property of no value or of insufficient value to justify the collection or continued administration of such property.

(14) Pay or contest any claim, settle a claim by or against the trust, and release, in whole or in part, a claim belonging to the trust.

(15) Pay taxes, assessments, compensation of the trustee and of employees and agents of the trust, and other expenses incurred in the administration of the trust.

(16) Allocate items of income or expense to trust income or principal, as provided by law.

(17) Exercise elections with respect to federal, state, and local taxes.

(18) Select a mode of payment under any employee benefit or retirement plan, annuity, or life insurance payable to the trustee, exercise rights under such plan, annuity, or insurance, including exercise of the right to indemnification for expenses and against liabilities, and take appropriate action to collect the proceeds.

(19) Make loans out of trust property, including, but not limited to, loans to a beneficiary on terms and conditions that are fair and reasonable under the circumstances, and the trustee has a lien on future distributions for repayment of those loans.

(20) Employ persons, including, but not limited to, attorneys, accountants, investment advisers, or agents, even if they are the trustee, an affiliate of the trustee, or otherwise associated with the trustee, to advise or assist the trustee in the exercise of any of the trustee's powers and pay reasonable compensation and costs incurred in connection with such employment from the assets of the trust and act without independent investigation on the recommendations of such persons.

(21) Pay an amount distributable to a beneficiary who is under a legal disability or who the trustee reasonably believes is incapacitated, by paying the amount directly to the beneficiary or applying the amount for the beneficiary's benefit, or by:

(a) Paying the amount to the beneficiary's guardian of the property or, if the beneficiary does not have a guardian of the property, the beneficiary's guardian of the person;

(b) Paying the amount to the beneficiary's custodian under a Uniform Transfers to Minors Act or custodial trustee under a Uniform Custodial Trust Act, and, for that purpose, creating a custodianship or custodial trust;

(c) Paying the amount to an adult relative or other person having legal or physical care or custody of the beneficiary, to be expended on the beneficiary's behalf, if the trustee does not know of a guardian of the property, guardian of the person, custodian, or custodial trustee; or

(d) Managing the amount as a separate fund on the beneficiary's behalf, subject to the beneficiary's continuing right to withdraw the distribution.

(22) On distribution of trust property or the division or termination of a trust, make distributions in divided or undivided interests, allocate particular assets in proportionate or disproportionate shares, value the trust property for those purposes, and adjust for resulting differences in valuation.

(23) Prosecute or defend, including appeals, an action, claim, or judicial proceeding in any jurisdiction to protect trust property or the trustee in the performance of the trustee's duties.

(24) Sign and deliver contracts and other instruments that are useful to achieve or facilitate the exercise of the trustee's powers.

(25) On termination of the trust, exercise the powers appropriate to wind up the administration of the trust and distribute the trust property to the persons entitled to the property, subject to the right of the trustee to retain a reasonable reserve for the payment of debts, expenses, and taxes.

History.

S. 8, ch. 2006-217, eff. July 1, 2007; s. 4, ch. 2007-153, eff. July 1, 2007.

736.08163. Powers of trustees relating to environmental or human health laws or to trust property contaminated with hazardous or toxic substances; liability.

(1) From the creation of a trust until final distribution of the assets from the trust, the trustee has, without court authorization, the powers specified in subsection (2).

(2) Unless otherwise provided in the trust instrument, a trustee has the power, acting reasonably, to:

(a) Inspect or investigate, or cause to be inspected or investigated, property held by the trustee, including interests in sole proprietorships, partnerships, or corporations and any assets owned by any such business entity for the purpose of determining compliance with an environmental law affecting that property or to respond to an actual or threatened violation of an environmental law affecting that property;

(b) Take, on behalf of the trust, any action necessary to prevent, abate, or otherwise remedy an actual or potential violation of an environmental law affecting property held by the trustee, before or after initiation of an enforcement action by a governmental body;

(c) Refuse to accept property in trust if the trustee determines that any property to be donated or conveyed to the trustee is contaminated with a hazardous substance or is being used or has been used for an activity directly or indirectly involving a hazardous substance, which circumstance could result in liability to the trust or trustee or otherwise impair the value of the assets to be held;

(d) Settle or compromise at any time any claim against the trust or trustee that may be asserted by a governmental body or private party that involves the alleged violation of an environmental law affecting property of any trust over which the trustee has responsibility;

(e) Disclaim any power granted by any document, law, or rule of law that, in the sole judgment of the trustee, may cause the trustee to incur personal liability, or the trust to incur liability, under any environmental law;

(f) Decline to serve as a trustee, or having undertaken to serve as a trustee, resign at any time, if the trustee believes there is or may be a conflict of interest in its fiduciary capacity and in its individual capacity because of potential claims or liabilities that may be asserted against the trustee on behalf of the trust by reason of the type or condition of the assets held; or

(g) Charge against the income and principal of the trust the cost of any inspection, investigation, review, abatement, response, cleanup, or remedial action that this section authorizes the trustee to take and, if the trust terminates or closes or the trust property is transferred to another trustee, hold assets sufficient to cover the cost of cleaning up any known environmental problem.

(3) A trustee is not personally liable to any beneficiary or any other person for a decrease in value of assets in a trust by reason of the trustee's compliance or efforts to comply with an environmental law, specifically including any reporting requirement under that law.

(4) A trustee that acquires ownership or control of a vessel or other property, without having owned, operated, or materially participated in the management of that vessel or property before assuming ownership or control as trustee, is not considered an owner or operator for purposes of liability under chapter 376, chapter 403, or any other environmental law. A trustee that willfully, knowingly, or recklessly causes or exacerbates a release or threatened release of a hazardous substance is personally liable for the cost of the response, to the extent that the release or threatened release is attributable to the trustee's activities. This subsection does not preclude the filing of claims against the assets that constitute the trust held by the trustee or the filing of actions against the trustee in its representative capacity and in any such action, an award or judgment against the trustee must be satisfied only from the assets of the trust.

(5) The acceptance by the trustee of the property or a failure by the trustee to inspect or investigate the property does not create any inference as to whether there is liability under an environmental law with respect to that property.

(6) For the purposes of this section, the term "hazardous substance" means a substance defined as hazardous or toxic, or any contaminant, pollutant, or constituent thereof, or otherwise regulated, by an environmental law.

(7) This section does not apply to any trust created under a document executed before July 1, 1995, unless the trust is amendable and the settlor amends the trust at any time to incorporate the provisions of this section.

History.
S. 8, ch. 2006-217, eff. July 1, 2007.

736.08165. Administration pending outcome of contest or other proceeding.

(1) Pending the outcome of a proceeding filed to determine the validity of all or part of a trust or the beneficiaries of all or part of a trust, the trustee shall proceed with the administration of the trust as if no proceeding had been commenced, except no action may be taken and no distribution may be made to a beneficiary in contravention of the rights of those persons who may be affected by the outcome of the proceeding.

(2) Upon motion of a party and after notice to interested persons, a court, on good cause shown, may make an exception to the prohibition under subsection (1) and authorize the trustee to act or to distribute trust assets to a beneficiary subject to any conditions the court, in the court's discretion, may impose, including the posting of bond by the beneficiary.

History.
S. 8, ch. 2006-217, eff. July 1, 2007.

736.0817. Distribution on termination.

Upon the occurrence of an event terminating or partially terminating a trust, the trustee shall proceed expeditiously to distribute the trust property to the persons entitled to the property, subject to the right of the trustee to retain a reasonable reserve for the payment of debts, expenses, and taxes. The provisions of this section are in addition to and are not in derogation of the rights of a trustee under the common law with respect to final distribution of a trust.

History.
S. 8, ch. 2006-217, eff. July 1, 2007.

PART IX.
TRUST INVESTMENTS.

736.0901. Applicability of chapter 518.

A trustee shall invest trust property in accordance with chapter 518.

History.
S. 9, ch. 2006-217, eff. July 1, 2007.

736.0902. Nonapplication of prudent investor rule.

(1) Notwithstanding the provisions of s. 518.11 or s. 736.0804, with respect to any contract for life insurance acquired or retained on the life of a qualified person, a trustee has no duty to:

(a) Determine whether the contract of life insurance is or was procured or effected in compliance with s. 627.404;

(b) Determine whether any contract of life insurance is, or remains, a proper investment;

(c) Investigate the financial strength of the life insurance company;

(d) Determine whether to exercise any policy option available under the contract for life insurance;

(e) Diversify any such contract for life insurance or the assets of the trust with respect to the contract for life insurance; or

(f) Inquire about or investigate the health or financial condition of any insureds.

(2) For purposes of this section, a "qualified person" is a person who is insured or a proposed insured, or the spouse of that person, who has provided the trustee with the funds used to acquire or pay premiums with respect to a policy of insurance on the life of that person or the spouse of that person, or on the lives of that person and the spouse of that person.

(3) The trustee is not liable to the beneficiaries of the trust or any other person for any loss sustained with

respect to a contract for life insurance to which this section applies.

(4) Unless otherwise provided in the trust instrument, paragraph (1)(a) applies to any contract for life insurance on the life of a qualified person.

(5) Unless otherwise provided in the trust instrument, paragraphs (1)(b)-(f) apply if:

(a) The trust instrument, by reference to this section, makes this section applicable to contracts for life insurance held by the trust; or

(b) The trustee gives notice that this section applies to a contract for life insurance held by the trust.

1. The notice of the application of this section shall be given to the qualified beneficiaries and shall contain a copy or restatement of this section.

2. Notice given pursuant to any of the provisions of part III of this chapter to a person who represents the interests of any of the persons set forth in subparagraph 1. shall be treated as notice to the person so represented.

3. Notice shall be given in the manner provided in s. 736.0109.

4. If any person notified pursuant to this paragraph delivers a written objection to the application of this section to the trustee within 30 days after the date on which the objector received such notice, paragraphs (1)(b)-(f) shall not apply until the objection is withdrawn.

5. There shall exist a rebuttable presumption that any notice sent by United States mail is received 3 days after depositing the notice in the United States mail system with proper postage prepaid.

(6) This section does not apply to any contract for life insurance purchased from any affiliate of the trustee, or with respect to which the trustee or any affiliate of the trustee receives any commission unless the duties have been delegated to another person in accordance with s. 518.112. For purposes of this subsection, an "affiliate" is any person who controls, is controlled by, or is under common control with the trustee.

(7) Paragraph (1)(a) does not apply if the trustee applied for or accepted ownership of a contract of life insurance and the trustee had knowledge that:

(a) The benefits were not payable to a person specified in s. 627.404 when the contract of life insurance was issued; or

(b) The contract of life insurance is or was purchased with resources or guarantees directly or indirectly provided by a person who, at the time of the inception of such contract, did not have an insurable interest in the insured as defined by s. 627.404, and, at the time of the inception of such contract, there is a verbal or written arrangement, agreement, or plan with a third party to transfer ownership of the policy or policy benefits in a manner that would be in violation of state law.

(8) A trustee who performs fiduciary or advisory services related to a policy of life insurance to which subsection (1) applies shall not be compensated for performing the applicable service to which subsection (1) applies.

History.
S. 1, ch. 2010-172, eff. July 1, 2010.

PART X.
LIABILITY OF TRUSTEE AND RIGHTS OF PERSONS DEALING WITH TRUSTEE.

736.1001.   Remedies for breach of trust.

(1) A violation by a trustee of a duty the trustee owes to a beneficiary is a breach of trust.

(2) To remedy a breach of trust that has occurred or may occur, the court may:

(a) Compel the trustee to perform the trustee's duties;

(b) Enjoin the trustee from committing a breach of trust;

(c) Compel the trustee to redress a breach of trust by paying money or restoring property or by other means;

(d) Order a trustee to account;

(e) Appoint a special fiduciary to take possession of the trust property and administer the trust;

(f) Suspend the trustee;

(g) Remove the trustee as provided in s. 736.0706;

(h) Reduce or deny compensation to the trustee;

(i) Subject to s. 736.1016, void an act of the trustee, impose a lien or a constructive trust on trust property, or trace trust property wrongfully disposed of and recover the property or its proceeds; or

(j) Order any other appropriate relief.

(3) As an illustration of the remedies available to the court and without limiting the court's discretion as provided in subsection (2), if a breach of trust results in the favoring of any beneficiary to the detriment of any other beneficiary or consists of an abuse of the trustee's discretion:

(a) To the extent the breach of trust has resulted in no distribution to a beneficiary or a distribution that is too small, the court may require the trustee to pay from the trust to the beneficiary an amount the court determines will restore the beneficiary, in whole or in part, to his or her appropriate position.

(b) To the extent the breach of trust has resulted in a distribution to a beneficiary that is too large, the court may restore the beneficiaries, the trust, or both, in whole or in part, to their appropriate positions by requiring the trustee to withhold an amount from one or more future distributions to the beneficiary who received the distribution that was too large or by requiring that beneficiary to return some or all of the distribution to the trust.

History.
S. 10, ch. 2006-217, eff. July 1, 2007; s. 147, ch. 2007-5, eff. July 1, 2007; s. 19, ch. 2007-153, eff. July 1, 2007.

736.1002. Damages for breach of trust.

(1) A trustee who commits a breach of trust is liable for the greater of:

(a) The amount required to restore the value of the trust property and trust distributions to what they would have been if the breach had not occurred, including lost income, capital gain, or appreciation that would have resulted from proper administration; or

(b) The profit the trustee made by reason of the breach.

(2) Except as otherwise provided in this subsection, if more than one person, including a trustee or trustees, is liable to the beneficiaries for a breach of trust, each liable person is entitled to pro rata contribution from the other person or persons. A person is not entitled to contribution if the person committed the breach of trust in bad faith. A person who received a benefit from the breach of trust is not entitled to contribution from another person to the extent of the benefit received.

(3) In determining the pro rata shares of liable persons in the entire liability for a breach of trust:

(a) Their relative degrees of fault shall be the basis for allocation of liability.

(b) If equity requires, the collective liability of some as a group shall constitute a single share.

(c) Principles of equity applicable to contribution generally shall apply.

(4) The right of contribution shall be enforced as follows:

(a) Contribution may be enforced by separate action, whether or not judgment has been entered in an action against two or more liable persons for the same breach of trust.

(b) When a judgment has been entered in an action against two or more liable persons for the same breach of trust, contribution may be enforced in that action by judgment in favor of one judgment defendant against any other judgment defendants by motion upon notice to all parties to the action.

(c) If there is a judgment for breach of trust against the liable person seeking contribution, any separate action by that person to enforce contribution must be commenced within 1 year after the judgment has become final by lapse of time for appeal or after appellate review.

(d) If there is no judgment for the breach of trust against the liable person seeking contribution, the person's right of contribution is barred unless the person has:

1. Discharged by payment the common liability within the period of the statute of limitations applicable to the beneficiary's right of action against the liable person and the person has commenced an action for contribution within 1 year after payment, or

2. Agreed, while action is pending against the liable person, to discharge the common liability and has within 1 year after the agreement paid the liability and commenced the person's action for contribution.

(5) The beneficiary's recovery of a judgment for breach of trust against one liable person does not of itself discharge other liable persons from liability for the breach of trust unless the judgment is satisfied. The satisfaction of the judgment does not impair any right of contribution.

(6) The judgment of the court in determining the liability of several defendants to the beneficiary for breach of trust is binding upon such defendants in determining the right of such defendants to contribution.

(7) Subsection (2) applies to all causes of action for breach of trust pending on July 1, 2007, under which causes of action the right of contribution among persons jointly and severally liable is involved and to all causes of action filed after July 1, 2007.

History.
S. 10, ch. 2006-217, eff. July 1, 2007.

736.1003. Damages in absence of breach.

Absent a breach of trust, a trustee is not liable to a beneficiary for a loss or depreciation in the value of trust property or for not having made a profit.

History.
S. 10, ch. 2006-217, eff. July 1, 2007.

736.1004. Attorney's fees and costs.

(1)(a) In all actions for breach of fiduciary duty or challenging the exercise of, or failure to exercise, a trustee's powers; and

(b) In proceedings arising under ss. 736.0410-736.0417,

the court shall award taxable costs as in chancery actions, including attorney fees and guardian ad litem fees.

(2) When awarding taxable costs under this section, including attorney fees and guardian ad litem fees, the court, in its discretion, may direct payment from a party's interest, if any, in the trust or enter a judgment that may be satisfied from other property of the party, or both.

History.
S. 10, ch. 2006-217, eff. July 1, 2007.

736.1005. Attorney's fees for services to the trust.

(1) Any attorney who has rendered services to a trust may be awarded reasonable compensation from the trust. The attorney may apply to the court for an order awarding attorney's fees and, after notice and service on the trustee and all beneficiaries entitled to an accounting under s. 736.0813, the court shall enter an order on the fee application.

(2) Whenever attorney's fees are to be paid out of the trust, the court, in its discretion, may direct from what part of the trust the fees shall be paid.

(3) Except when a trustee's interest may be adverse in a particular matter, the attorney shall give reasonable notice in writing to the trustee of the attorney's retention by an interested person and the attorney's entitlement to fees pursuant to this section. A court may reduce any fee award for services rendered by the attorney prior to the date of actual notice to the trustee, if the actual notice date is later than a date of reasonable notice. In exercising this discretion, the court may exclude compensation for services rendered after the reasonable notice date but prior to the date of actual notice.

History.
S. 10, ch. 2006-217, eff. July 1, 2007.

736.1006. Costs in trust proceedings.

(1) In all trust proceedings, costs may be awarded as in chancery actions.

(2) Whenever costs are to be paid out of the trust, the court, in its discretion, may direct from what part of the trust the costs shall be paid.

History.
S. 10, ch. 2006-217, eff. July 1, 2007.

736.1007. Trustee's attorney's fees.

(1) If the trustee of a revocable trust retains an attorney to render legal services in connection with the initial administration of the trust, the attorney is entitled to reasonable compensation for those legal services, payable from the assets of the trust without court order. The trustee and the attorney may agree to compensation that is determined in a manner or amount other than the manner or amount provided in this section. The agreement is not binding on a person who bears the impact of the compensation unless that person is a party to or otherwise consents to be bound by the agreement. The agreement may provide that the trustee is not individually liable for the attorney's fees and costs.

(2) Unless otherwise agreed, compensation based on the value of the trust assets immediately following the settlor's death and the income earned by the trust during initial administration at the rate of 75 percent of the schedule provided in s. 733.6171(3)(a)-(h) is presumed to be reasonable total compensation for ordinary services of all attorneys employed generally to advise a trustee concerning the trustee's duties in initial trust administration.

(3) An attorney who is retained to render only limited and specifically defined legal services shall be compensated as provided in the retaining agreement. If the amount or method of determining compensation is not provided in the agreement, the attorney is entitled to a reasonable fee, taking into account the factors set forth in subsection (6).

(4) Ordinary services of the attorney in an initial trust administration include legal advice and representation concerning the trustee's duties relating to:

(a) Review of the trust instrument and each amendment for legal sufficiency and interpretation.

(b) Implementation of substitution of the successor trustee.

(c) Persons who must or should be served with required notices and the method and timing of such service.

(d) The obligation of a successor to require a former trustee to provide an accounting.

(e) The trustee's duty to protect, insure, and manage trust assets and the trustee's liability relating to these duties.

(f) The trustee's duty regarding investments imposed by the prudent investor rule.

(g) The trustee's obligation to inform and account to beneficiaries and the method of satisfaction of such obligations, the liability of the trust and trustee to the settlor's creditors, and the advisability or necessity for probate proceedings to bar creditors.

(h) Contributions due to the personal representative of the settlor's estate for payment of expenses of administration and obligations of the settlor's estate.

(i) Identifying tax returns required to be filed by the trustee, the trustee's liability for payment of taxes, and the due date of returns.

(j) Filing a nontaxable affidavit, if not filed by a personal representative.

(k) Order of payment of expenses of administration of the trust and order and priority of abatement of trust distributions.

(l) Distribution of income or principal to beneficiaries or funding of further trusts provided in the governing instrument.

(m) Preparation of any legal documents required to effect distribution.

(n) Fiduciary duties, avoidance of self-dealing, conflicts of interest, duty of impartiality, and obligations to beneficiaries.

(o) If there is a conflict of interest between a trustee who is a beneficiary and other beneficiaries of the trust, advice to the trustee on limitations of certain authority of the trustee regarding discretionary distributions or exercise of certain powers and alternatives for appointment of an independent trustee and appropriate procedures.

(p) Procedures for the trustee's discharge from liability for administration of the trust on termination or resignation.

(5) In addition to the attorney's fees for ordinary services, the attorney for the trustee shall be allowed further reasonable compensation for any extraordinary service. What constitutes an extraordinary service may vary depending on many factors, including the size of the trust. Extraordinary services may include, but are not limited to:

(a) Involvement in a trust contest, trust construction, a proceeding for determination of beneficiaries, a contested claim, elective share proceedings, apportionment of estate taxes, or other adversary proceedings or litigation by or against the trust.

(b) Representation of the trustee in an audit or any proceeding for adjustment, determination, or collection of any taxes.

(c) Tax advice on postmortem tax planning, including, but not limited to, disclaimer, renunciation of fiduciary commission, alternate valuation date, allocation of administrative expenses between tax returns, the QTIP or reverse QTIP election, allocation of GST exemption, qualification for Internal Revenue Code ss. 303 and 6166 privileges, deduction of last illness expenses, distribution planning, asset basis considerations, throwback rules, handling income or deductions in respect of a decedent, valuation discounts, special use and other valuation, handling employee benefit or retirement proceeds, prompt assessment request, or request for release from personal liability for payment of tax.

(d) Review of an estate tax return and preparation or review of other tax returns required to be filed by the trustee.

(e) Preparation of decedent's federal estate tax return. If this return is prepared by the attorney, a fee of one-half of 1 percent up to a value of $10 million and one-fourth of 1 percent on the value in excess of $10 million, of the gross estate as finally determined for federal estate tax purposes, is presumed to be reasonable compensation for the attorney for this service. These fees shall include services for routine audit of the return, not beyond the examining agent level, if required.

(f) Purchase, sale, lease, or encumbrance of real property by the trustee or involvement in zoning, land use, environmental, or other similar matters.

(g) Legal advice regarding carrying on of decedent's business or conducting other commercial activity by the trustee.

(h) Legal advice regarding claims for damage to the environment or related procedures.

(i) Legal advice regarding homestead status of trust real property or proceedings involving the status.

(j) Involvement in fiduciary, employee, or attorney compensation disputes.

(k) Considerations of special valuation of trust assets, including discounts for blockage, minority interests, lack of marketability, and environmental liability.

(6) Upon petition of any interested person in a proceeding to review the compensation paid or to be paid to the attorney for the trustee, the court may increase or decrease the compensation for ordinary services of the attorney for the trustee or award compensation for extraordinary services if the facts and circumstances of the particular administration warrant. In determining reasonable compensation, the court shall consider all of the following factors giving such weight to each as the court may determine to be appropriate:

(a) The promptness, efficiency, and skill with which the initial administration was handled by the attorney.

(b) The responsibilities assumed by, and potential liabilities of, the attorney.

(c) The nature and value of the assets that are affected by the decedent's death.

(d) The benefits or detriments resulting to the trust or the trust's beneficiaries from the attorney's services.

(e) The complexity or simplicity of the administration and the novelty of issues presented.

(f) The attorney's participation in tax planning for the estate, the trust, and the trust's beneficiaries and tax return preparation or review and approval.

(g) The nature of the trust assets, the expenses of administration, and the claims payable by the trust and the compensation paid to other professionals and fiduciaries.

(h) Any delay in payment of the compensation after the services were furnished.

(i) Any other relevant factors.

(7) If a separate written agreement regarding compensation exists between the attorney and the settlor, the attorney shall furnish a copy to the trustee prior to commencement of employment and, if employed, shall promptly file and serve a copy on all interested persons. A separate agreement or a provision in the trust suggesting or directing the trustee to retain a specific attorney does not obligate the trustee to employ the attorney or obligate the attorney to accept the representation but, if the attorney who is a party to the agreement or who drafted the trust is employed, the compensation paid shall not exceed the compensation provided in the agreement.

(8) As used in this section, the term "initial trust administration" means administration of a revocable trust during the period that begins with the death of the settlor and ends on the final distribution of trust assets outright or to continuing trusts created under the trust agreement but, if an estate tax return is required, not until after issuance of an estate tax closing letter or other evidence of termination of the estate tax proceeding. This initial period is not intended to include continued regular administration of the trust.

History.

S. 10, ch. 2006-217, eff. July 1, 2007; s. 7, ch. 2010-122, eff. July 1, 2010.

Editor's Notes.

Sections 303 and 6166 of the Internal Revenue Code, referred to in this section, are codified as 26 U.S.C.S. §§ 303 and 6166, respectively.

736.1008. Limitations on proceedings against trustees.

(1) Except as provided in subsection (2), all claims by a beneficiary against a trustee for breach of trust are barred as provided in chapter 95 as to:

(a) All matters adequately disclosed in a trust disclosure document issued by the trustee, with the limitations period beginning on the date of receipt of adequate disclosure.

(b) All matters not adequately disclosed in a trust disclosure document if the trustee has issued a final trust accounting and has given written notice to the beneficiary of the availability of the trust records for examination and that any claims with respect to matters not adequately disclosed may be barred unless an action is commenced within the applicable limitations period provided in chapter 95. The limitations period begins on the date of receipt of the final trust accounting and notice.

(2) Unless sooner barred by adjudication, consent, or limitations, a beneficiary is barred from bringing an action against a trustee for breach of trust with respect to a matter that was adequately disclosed in a trust disclosure document unless a proceeding to assert the claim is commenced within 6 months after receipt from the trustee of the trust disclosure document or a limitation notice that applies to that disclosure document, whichever is received later.

(3) When a trustee has not issued a final trust accounting or has not given written notice to the beneficiary of the availability of the trust records for examination and that claims with respect to matters not adequately disclosed may be barred, a claim against the trustee for breach of trust based on a matter not adequately disclosed in a trust disclosure document is barred as provided in chapter 95 and accrues when the beneficiary has actual knowledge of:

(a) The facts upon which the claim is based if such actual knowledge is established by clear and convincing evidence; or

(b) The trustee's repudiation of the trust or adverse possession of trust assets.

Paragraph (a) applies to claims based upon acts or omissions occurring on or after July 1, 2008.

(4) As used in this section, the term:

(a) "Trust disclosure document" means a trust accounting or any other written report of the trustee. A trust disclosure document adequately discloses a matter if the document provides sufficient information so that a beneficiary knows of a claim or reasonably should have inquired into the existence of a claim with respect to that matter.

(b) "Trust accounting" means an accounting that adequately discloses the information required by and that substantially complies with the standards set forth in s. 736.08135.

(c) "Limitation notice" means a written statement of the trustee that an action by a beneficiary against the trustee for breach of trust based on any matter adequately disclosed in a trust disclosure document may be barred unless the action is commenced within 6 months after receipt of the trust disclosure document or receipt of a limitation notice that applies to that trust disclosure document, whichever is later. A limitation notice may but is not required to be in the following form: "An action for breach of trust based on matters disclosed in a trust accounting or other written report of the trustee may be subject to a 6-month statute of limitations from the receipt of the trust accounting or other written report. If you have questions, please consult your attorney."

(5) For purposes of this section, a limitation notice applies to a trust disclosure document when the limitation notice is:

(a) Contained as a part of the trust disclosure document or as a part of another trust disclosure document received within 1 year prior to the receipt of the latter trust disclosure document;

(b) Accompanied concurrently by the trust disclosure document or by another trust disclosure document that was received within 1 year prior to the receipt of the latter trust disclosure document;

(c) Delivered separately within 10 days after the delivery of the trust disclosure document or of another trust disclosure document that was received within 1 year prior to the receipt of the latter trust disclosure document. For purposes of this paragraph, a limitation notice is not delivered separately if the notice is accompanied by another written communication, other than a written communication that refers only to the limitation notice; or

(d) Received more than 10 days after the delivery of the trust disclosure document, but only if the limitation notice references that trust disclosure document and:

1. Offers to provide to the beneficiary on request another copy of that trust disclosure document if the document was received by the beneficiary within 1 year prior to receipt of the limitation notice; or

2. Is accompanied by another copy of that trust disclosure document if the trust disclosure document was received by the beneficiary 1 year or more prior to the receipt of the limitation notice.

(6)(a) Notwithstanding subsections (1), (2), and (3), all claims by a beneficiary against a trustee are barred:

1. Upon the later of:

a. Ten years after the date the trust terminates, the trustee resigns, or the fiduciary relationship between the trustee and the beneficiary otherwise ends if the beneficiary had actual knowledge of the existence of the trust and the beneficiary's status as a beneficiary throughout the 10-year period; or

b. Twenty years after the date of the act or omission of the trustee that is complained of if the beneficiary had actual knowledge of the existence of the trust and the beneficiary's status as a beneficiary throughout the 20-year period; or

2. Forty years after the date the trust terminates, the trustee resigns, or the fiduciary relationship between the trustee and the beneficiary otherwise ends.

(b) When a beneficiary shows by clear and convincing evidence that a trustee actively concealed facts supporting a cause of action, any existing applicable statute of repose shall be extended by 30 years.

(c) For purposes of sub-subparagraph (a)1.b., the failure of the trustee to take corrective action is not a separate act or omission and does not extend the period of repose established by this subsection.

(d) This subsection applies to claims based upon acts or omissions occurring on or after July 1, 2008.

(7) This section applies to trust accountings for accounting periods beginning on or after July 1, 2007, and to written reports, other than trust accountings, received by a beneficiary on or after July 1, 2007.

History.
S. 10, ch. 2006-217, eff. July 1, 2007; s. 5, ch. 2007-153, eff. July 1, 2007; s. 3, ch. 2008-76, eff. July 1, 2008.

736.1009. Reliance on trust instrument.

A trustee who acts in reasonable reliance on the terms of the trust as expressed in the trust instrument is not liable to a beneficiary for a breach of trust to the extent the breach resulted from the reliance.

History.
S. 10, ch. 2006-217, eff. July 1, 2007.

736.1010. Event affecting administration or distribution.

If the happening of an event, including marriage, divorce, performance of educational requirements, or death, affects the administration or distribution of a trust, a trustee who has exercised reasonable care to ascertain the happening of the event is not liable for a loss resulting from the trustee's lack of knowledge.

History.
S. 10, ch. 2006-217, eff. July 1, 2007.

736.1011. Exculpation of trustee.

(1) A term of a trust relieving a trustee of liability for breach of trust is unenforceable to the extent that the term:

(a) Relieves the trustee of liability for breach of trust committed in bad faith or with reckless indifference to the purposes of the trust or the interests of the beneficiaries; or

(b) Was inserted into the trust instrument as the result of an abuse by the trustee of a fiduciary or confidential relationship with the settlor.

(2) An exculpatory term drafted or caused to be drafted by the trustee is invalid as an abuse of a fiduciary or confidential relationship unless:

(a) The trustee proves that the exculpatory term is fair under the circumstances.

(b) The term's existence and contents were adequately communicated directly to the settlor or the independent attorney of the settlor. This paragraph applies only to trusts created on or after July 1, 2007.

History.
S. 10, ch. 2006-217, eff. July 1, 2007; s. 6, ch. 2007-153, eff. July 1, 2007.

736.1012. Beneficiary's consent, release, or ratification.

A trustee is not liable to a beneficiary for breach of trust if the beneficiary consented to the conduct constituting the breach, released the trustee from liability for the breach, or ratified the transaction constituting the breach, unless:

(1) The consent, release, or ratification of the beneficiary was induced by improper conduct of the trustee; or

(2) At the time of the consent, release, or ratification, the beneficiary did not know of the beneficiary's rights or of the material facts relating to the breach.

History.
S. 10, ch. 2006-217, eff. July 1, 2007.

736.1013. Limitation on personal liability of trustee.

(1) Except as otherwise provided in the contract, a trustee is not personally liable on a contract properly entered into in the trustee's fiduciary capacity in the course of administering the trust if the trustee in the contract disclosed the fiduciary capacity.

(2) A trustee is personally liable for torts committed in the course of administering a trust or for obligations arising from ownership or control of trust property only if the trustee is personally at fault.

(3) A claim based on a contract entered into by a trustee in the trustee's fiduciary capacity, on an obligation arising from ownership or control of trust property, or on a tort committed in the course of administering a trust may be asserted in a judicial proceeding against the trustee in the trustee's fiduciary capacity, whether or not the trustee is personally liable for the claim.

(4) Issues of liability between the trust estate and the trustee individually may be determined in a proceeding for accounting, surcharge, or indemnification or in any other appropriate proceeding.

History.
S. 10, ch. 2006-217, eff. July 1, 2007.

736.1014. Limitations on actions against certain trusts.

(1) After the death of a settlor, no creditor of the settlor may bring, maintain, or continue any direct action against a trust described in s. 733.707(3), the

trustee of the trust, or any beneficiary of the trust that is dependent on the individual liability of the settlor. Such claims and causes of action against the settlor shall be presented and enforced against the settlor's estate as provided in part VII of chapter 733, and the personal representative of the settlor's estate may obtain payment from the trustee of a trust described in s. 733.707(3) as provided in ss. 733.607(2), 733.707(3), and 736.05053.

(2) This section does not preclude a direct action against a trust described in s. 733.707(3), the trustee of the trust, or a beneficiary of the trust that is not dependent on the individual liability of the settlor.

(3) This section does not affect the lien of any duly recorded mortgage or security interest or the lien of any person in possession of personal property or the right to foreclose and enforce the mortgage or lien.

History.
S. 10, ch. 2006-217, eff. July 1, 2007.

736.1015. Interest as general partner.

(1) Unless personal liability is imposed in the contract, a trustee who holds an interest as a general partner in a general or limited partnership is not personally liable on a contract entered into by the partnership after the trust's acquisition of the interest if the fiduciary capacity was disclosed in the contract or in a statement previously filed pursuant to a Uniform Partnership Act or Uniform Limited Partnership Act.

(2) A trustee who holds an interest as a general partner is not personally liable for torts committed by the partnership or for obligations arising from ownership or control of the interest unless the trustee is personally at fault.

(3) If the trustee of a revocable trust holds an interest as a general partner, the settlor is personally liable for contracts and other obligations of the partnership as if the settlor were a general partner.

History.
S. 10, ch. 2006-217, eff. July 1, 2007.

736.1016. Protection of person dealing with trustee.

(1) A person other than a beneficiary who in good faith assists a trustee or who in good faith and for value deals with a trustee, without knowledge that the trustee is exceeding or improperly exercising the trustee's powers, is protected from liability as if the trustee properly exercised the power.

(2) A person other than a beneficiary who in good faith deals with a trustee is not required to inquire into the extent of the trustee's powers or the propriety of their exercise.

(3) A person who in good faith delivers assets to a trustee need not ensure their proper application.

(4) A person other than a beneficiary who in good faith assists a former trustee or who in good faith and for value deals with a former trustee, without knowl-

edge that the trusteeship has terminated, is protected from liability as if the former trustee were still a trustee.

(5) Comparable protective provisions of other laws relating to commercial transactions or transfer of securities by fiduciaries prevail over the protection provided by this section.

History.
S. 10, ch. 2006-217, eff. July 1, 2007.

736.1017. Certification of trust.

(1) Instead of furnishing a copy of the trust instrument to a person other than a beneficiary, the trustee may furnish to the person a certification of trust containing the following information:

(a) The trust exists and the date the trust instrument was executed.

(b) The identity of the settlor.

(c) The identity and address of the currently acting trustee.

(d) The powers of the trustee.

(e) The revocability or irrevocability of the trust and the identity of any person holding a power to revoke the trust.

(f) The authority of cotrustees to sign or otherwise authenticate and whether all or less than all are required in order to exercise powers of the trustee.

(g) The manner of taking title to trust property.

(2) A certification of trust may be signed or otherwise authenticated by any trustee.

(3) A certification of trust must state that the trust has not been revoked, modified, or amended in any manner that would cause the representations contained in the certification of trust to be incorrect.

(4) A certification of trust need not contain the dispositive terms of a trust.

(5) A recipient of a certification of trust may require the trustee to furnish copies of any excerpts from the original trust instrument and later amendments that designate the trustee and confer upon the trustee the power to act in the pending transaction.

(6) A person who acts in reliance on a certification of trust without knowledge that the representations contained in the certification are incorrect is not liable to any person for so acting and may assume without inquiry the existence of the facts contained in the certification. Knowledge of the terms of the trust may not be inferred solely from the fact that a copy of all or part of the trust instrument is held by the person relying on the certification.

(7) A person who in good faith enters into a transaction in reliance on a certification of trust may enforce the transaction against the trust property as if the representations contained in the certification were correct.

(8) This section does not limit the right of a person to obtain a copy of the trust instrument when required to be furnished by law or in a judicial proceeding concerning the trust.

History.
S. 10, ch. 2006-217, eff. July 1, 2007.

736.1018. Improper distribution or payment; liability of distributee.

Any person who received a distribution or was paid improperly from a trust shall return the assets or funds received and the income from those assets or interest on the funds from the date of distribution or payment unless the distribution or payment cannot be questioned because of adjudication, estoppel, or limitations. If the person does not have the assets or funds, the value of the assets or funds at the date of disposition, income from the assets or funds, and gain received by the person from the assets or funds shall be returned.

History.
S. 10, ch. 2006-217, eff. July 1, 2007.

PART XI.
RULES OF CONSTRUCTION.

736.1101. Rules of construction; general provisions.

Except as provided in s. 736.0105(2):

(1) The intent of the settlor as expressed in the terms of the trust controls the legal effect of the dispositions made in the trust.

(2) The rules of construction as expressed in this part shall apply unless a contrary intent is indicated by the terms of the trust.

History.
S. 11, ch. 2006-217, eff. July 1, 2007.

736.1102. Construction of terms.

The laws used to determine paternity and relationships for the purposes of intestate succession apply when determining whether class gift terminology and terms of relationship include adopted persons and persons born out of wedlock.

History.
S. 11, ch. 2006-217, eff. July 1, 2007; s. 17, ch. 2010-132, eff. Oct. 1, 2010.

736.1103. Gifts to multigeneration classes to be per stirpes.

Class gifts to descendants, issue, and other multigeneration classes shall be per stirpes.

History.
S. 11, ch. 2006-217, eff. July 1, 2007.

736.1104. Killer not entitled to receive property or other benefits by reason of victim's death.

(1) A beneficiary of a trust who unlawfully and intentionally kills or unlawfully and intentionally participates in procuring the death of the settlor or another person on whose death such beneficiary's interest depends, is not entitled to any trust interest, including homestead, dependent on the victim's death, and such interest shall devolve as though the killer had predeceased the victim.

(2) A final judgment of conviction of murder in any degree is conclusive for the purposes of this section. In the absence of a murder conviction in any degree, the court may determine by the greater weight of the evidence whether the killing was unlawful and intentional for purposes of this section.

History.
S. 11, ch. 2006-217, eff. July 1, 2007.

736.1105. Dissolution of marriage; effect on revocable trust.

Unless the trust instrument or the judgment for dissolution of marriage or divorce expressly provides otherwise, if a revocable trust is executed by a husband or wife as settlor prior to annulment of the marriage or entry of a judgment for dissolution of marriage or divorce of the settlor from the settlor's spouse, any provision of the trust that affects the settlor's spouse will become void upon annulment of the marriage or entry of the judgment of dissolution of marriage or divorce and any such trust shall be administered and construed as if the settlor's spouse had died on the date of the annulment or on entry of the judgment for dissolution of marriage or divorce.

History.
S. 11, ch. 2006-217, eff. July 1, 2007.

736.1106. Antilapse; survivorship with respect to future interests under terms of inter vivos and testamentary trusts; substitute takers.

(1) As used in this section, the term:

(a) "Beneficiary" means the beneficiary of a future interest and includes a class member if the future interest is in the form of a class gift.

(b) "Distribution date," with respect to a future interest, means the time when the future interest is to take effect. The distribution date need not occur at the beginning or end of a calendar day, but can occur at a time during the course of a day. The distribution date refers to the time that the right to possession or enjoyment arises and is not necessarily the time that any benefit of the right is realized.

(c) "Future interest" includes an alternative future interest and a future interest in the form of a class gift.

(d) "Future interest under the terms of a trust" means a future interest created by an inter vivos or testamentary transfer to an existing trust or creating a trust or by an exercise of a power of appointment to an existing trust directing the continuance of an existing trust, designating a beneficiary of an existing trust, or creating a trust.

(e) "Surviving beneficiary" or "surviving descendant" means a beneficiary or a descendant who did not predecease the distribution date or is not deemed to have predeceased the distribution date by operation of law.

(2) A future interest under the terms of a trust is contingent upon the beneficiary surviving the distribution date. Unless a contrary intent appears in the trust instrument, if a beneficiary of a future interest under the terms of a trust fails to survive the distribution date, and the deceased beneficiary leaves surviving descendants, a substitute gift is created in the beneficiary's surviving descendants. They take per stirpes the property to which the beneficiary would have been entitled if the beneficiary had survived the distribution date.

(3) In the application of this section:

(a) Words of survivorship attached to a future interest are a sufficient indication of an intent contrary to the application of this section.

(b) A residuary clause in a will is not a sufficient indication of an intent contrary to the application of this section, whether or not the will specifically provides that lapsed or failed devises are to pass under the residuary clause.

(4) If, after the application of subsections (2) and (3), there is no surviving taker, the property passes in the following order:

(a) If the future interest was created by the exercise of a power of appointment, the property passes under the donor's gift-in-default clause, if any, which clause is treated as creating a future interest under the terms of a trust.

(b) If no taker is produced by the application of paragraph (a) and the trust was created in a nonresiduary devise or appointment in the transferor's will, the property passes under the residuary clause in the transferor's will. For purposes of this section, the residuary clause is treated as creating a future interest under the terms of a trust.

(c) If no taker is produced by the application of paragraph (a) or paragraph (b), the property passes to those persons, including the state, and in such shares as would succeed to the transferor's intestate estate under the intestate succession law of the transferor's domicile if the transferor died when the disposition is to take effect in possession or enjoyment.

For purposes of paragraphs (b) and (c), the term "transferor" with respect to a future interest created by the exercise of a power of appointment, means the donor if the power was a nongeneral power and the donee if the power was a general power.

(5) Subsections (1)-(4) apply to all trusts other than trusts that were irrevocable before the effective date of this code. Sections 732.603, 732.604, and 737.6035, as they exist on June 30, 2007, continue to apply to other trusts executed on or after June 12, 2003.

History.
S. 11, ch. 2006-217, eff. July 1, 2007; s. 16, ch. 2007-153, eff. July 1, 2007; s. 7, ch. 2009-117, eff. July 1, 2009.

736.1107. Change in securities; accessions; nonademption.

A gift of specific securities, rather than their equivalent value, entitles the beneficiary only to:

(1) As much of the gifted securities of the same issuer held by the trust estate at the time of the occurrence of the event entitling the beneficiary to distribution.

(2) Any additional or other securities of the same issuer held by the trust estate because of action initiated by the issuer, excluding any acquired by exercise of purchase options.

(3) Securities of another issuer held by the trust estate as a result of a merger, consolidation, reorganization, or other similar action initiated by the original issuer.

History.
S. 11, ch. 2006-217, eff. July 1, 2007.

736.1108. Penalty clause for contest.

(1) A provision in a trust instrument purporting to penalize any interested person for contesting the trust instrument or instituting other proceedings relating to a trust estate or trust assets is unenforceable.

(2) This section applies to trusts created on or after October 1, 1993. For purposes of this subsection, a revocable trust shall be treated as created when the right of revocation terminates.

History.
S. 11, ch. 2006-217, eff. July 1, 2007.

PART XII.
CHARITABLE TRUSTS.

736.1201. Definitions.

As used in this part:

(1) "Charitable organization" means an organization described in s. 501(c)(3) of the Internal Revenue Code and exempt from tax under s. 501(a) of the Internal Revenue Code.

(2) "Internal Revenue Code" means the Internal Revenue Code of 1986, as amended.

(3) "Private foundation trust" means a trust, including a trust described in s. 4947(a)(1) of the Internal Revenue Code, as defined in s. 509(a) of the Internal Revenue Code.

(4) "Split interest trust" means a trust for individual and charitable beneficiaries that is subject to the provisions of s. 4947(a)(2) of the Internal Revenue Code.

(5) "State attorney" means the state attorney for the judicial circuit of the principal place of administration of the trust pursuant to s. 736.0108.

History.
S. 12, ch. 2006-217, eff. July 1, 2007.
Editor's Notes.
Sections 501(a), 501(c)(3), 509(a), and 4947 of the Internal Revenue Code, are codified as 26 U.S.C.S. §§ 501(a), 501(c)(3), 509(a), and 4947, respectively.

736.1202. Application of this part.

Except as otherwise provided in the trust, the provisions of this part apply to all private foundation trusts and split interest trusts, whether created or established before or after November 1, 1971, and to all trust assets acquired by the trustee before or after November 1, 1971.

History.
S. 12, ch. 2006-217, eff. July 1, 2007.

736.1203. Trustee of a private foundation trust or a split interest trust.

Except as provided in s. 736.1205, the trustee of a private foundation trust or a split interest trust has the duties and powers conferred on the trustee by this part.

History.
S. 12, ch. 2006-217, eff. July 1, 2007.

736.1204. Powers and duties of trustee of a private foundation trust or a split interest trust.

(1) In the exercise of a trustee's powers, including the powers granted by this part, a trustee has a duty to act with due regard to the trustee's obligation as a fiduciary, including a duty not to exercise any power in such a way as to:

(a) Deprive the trust of an otherwise available tax exemption, deduction, or credit for tax purposes;

(b) Deprive a donor of a trust asset or tax deduction or credit; or

(c) Operate to impose a tax on a donor, trust, or other person.

For purposes of this subsection, the term "tax" includes, but is not limited to, any federal, state, or local excise, income, gift, estate, or inheritance tax.

(2) Except as provided in s. 736.1205, a trustee of a private foundation trust shall make distributions at such time and in such manner as not to subject the trust to tax under s. 4942 of the Internal Revenue Code.

(3) Except as provided in subsection (4) and in s. 736.1205, a trustee of a private foundation trust, or a split interest trust to the extent that the split interest trust is subject to the provisions of s. 4947(a)(2) of the Internal Revenue Code, in the exercise of the trustee's powers shall not:

(a) Engage in any act of self-dealing as defined in s. 4941(d) of the Internal Revenue Code;

(b) Retain any excess business holdings as defined in s. 4943(c) of the Internal Revenue Code;

(c) Make any investments in a manner that subjects the foundation to tax under s. 4944 of the Internal Revenue Code; or

(d) Make any taxable expenditures as defined in s. 4945(d) of the Internal Revenue Code.

(4) Paragraphs (3)(b) and (c) shall not apply to a split interest trust if:

(a) All the income interest, and none of the remainder interest, of the trust is devoted solely to one or more of the purposes described in s. 170(c)(2)(B)

of the Internal Revenue Code, and all amounts in the trust for which a deduction was allowed under s. 170, s. 545(b)(2), s. 556(b)(2), s. 642(c), s. 2055, s. 2106(a)(2), or s. 2522 of the Internal Revenue Code have an aggregate fair market value of not more than 60 percent of the aggregate fair market value of all amounts in the trust; or

(b) A deduction was allowed under s. 170, s. 545(b)(2), s. 556(b)(2), s. 642(c), s. 2055, s. 2106(a)(2), or s. 2522 of the Internal Revenue Code for amounts payable under the terms of the trust to every remainder beneficiary but not to any income beneficiary.

History.
S. 12, ch. 2006-217, eff. July 1, 2007; s. 17, ch. 2007-153, eff. July 1, 2007.

Editor's Notes.
The references to sections of the Internal Revenue Code, referred to in this section, are codified throughout Title 26 of the U.S.C.S.

736.1205. Notice that this part does not apply.

In the case of a power to make distributions, if the trustee determines that the governing instrument contains provisions that are more restrictive than s. 736.1204(2), or if the trust contains other powers, inconsistent with the provisions of s. 736.1204(3) that specifically direct acts by the trustee, the trustee shall notify the state attorney when the trust becomes subject to this part. Section 736.1204 does not apply to any trust for which notice has been given pursuant to this section unless the trust is amended to comply with the terms of this part.

History.
S. 12, ch. 2006-217, eff. July 1, 2007.

736.1206. Power to amend trust instrument.

(1) In the case of a trust that is solely for a named charitable organization or organizations and for which the trustee does not possess any discretion concerning the distribution of income or principal among two or more such organizations, the trustee may amend the governing instrument to comply with the provisions of s. 736.1204(2) with the consent of the named charitable organization or organizations.

(2) In the case of a charitable trust that is not subject to the provisions of subsection (1), the trustee may amend the governing instrument to comply with the provisions of s. 736.1204(2) with the consent of the state attorney.

History.
S. 12, ch. 2006-217, eff. July 1, 2007.

736.1207. Power of court to permit deviation.

This part does not affect the power of a court to relieve a trustee from any restrictions on the powers and duties that are placed on the trustee by the governing instrument or applicable law for cause shown and on complaint of the trustee, state attorney, or an affected beneficiary and notice to the affected parties.

History.
S. 12, ch. 2006-217, eff. July 1, 2007.

736.1208. Release; property and persons affected; manner of effecting.

(1) The trustee of a trust, all of the unexpired interests in which are devoted to one or more charitable purposes, may release a power to select charitable donees unless the creating instrument provides otherwise.

(2) The release of a power to select charitable donees may apply to all or any part of the property subject to the power and may reduce or limit the charitable organizations, or classes of charitable organizations, in whose favor the power is exercisable.

(3) A release shall be effected by a duly acknowledged written instrument signed by the trustee and delivered as provided in subsection (4).

(4) Delivery of a release shall be accomplished as follows:

(a) If the release is accomplished by specifying a charitable organization or organizations as beneficiary or beneficiaries of the trust, by delivery of a copy of the release to each designated charitable organization.

(b) If the release is accomplished by reducing the class of permissible charitable organizations, by delivery of a copy of the release to the state attorney.

(5) If a release is accomplished by specifying a public charitable organization or organizations as beneficiary or beneficiaries of the trust, the trust at all times thereafter shall be operated exclusively for the benefit of, and be supervised by, the specified public charitable organization or organizations.

History.
S. 12, ch. 2006-217, eff. July 1, 2007.

736.1209. Election to come under this part.

With the consent of that organization or organizations, a trustee of a trust for the benefit of a public charitable organization or organizations may come under s. 736.1208(5) by filing with the state attorney an election, accompanied by the proof of required consent. Thereafter the trust shall be subject to s. 736.1208(5).

History.
S. 12, ch. 2006-217, eff. July 1, 2007; s. 148, ch. 2007-5, eff. July 1, 2007; s. 18, ch. 2007-153, eff. July 1, 2007.

736.1210. Interpretation.

This part shall be interpreted to effectuate the intent of the state to preserve, foster, and encourage gifts to, or for the benefit of, charitable organizations.

History.
S. 12, ch. 2006-217, eff. July 1, 2007.

736.1211. Protections afforded to certain charitable trusts and organizations.

(1) A charitable organization, private foundation trust, split interest trust, or a private foundation as defined in s. 509(a) of the Internal Revenue Code may not be required by a state agency or a local government to disclose the race, religion, gender, national origin, socioeconomic status, age, ethnicity, disability, marital status, sexual orientation, or political party registration of its employees, officers, directors, trustees, members, or owners, without the prior written consent of the individual or individuals in question.

(2) A private foundation as defined in s. 509(a) of the Internal Revenue Code, a private foundation trust, a split interest trust, or a grant-making organization may not be required by the state or any local government to disclose the race, religion, gender, national origin, socioeconomic status, age, ethnicity, disability, marital status, sexual orientation, or political party registration of any person, or of the employees, officers, directors, trustees, members, or owners of any entity that has received monetary or in-kind contributions from or contracted with the organization, trust, or foundation, without the prior written consent of the individual or individuals in question. For purposes of this subsection, a "grant-making organization" is an organization that makes grants to charitable organizations but is not a private foundation, private foundation trust, or split interest trust.

(3) A state agency or a local government may not require that the governing board or officers of a charitable organization, private foundation trust, split interest trust, or a private foundation as defined in s. 509(a) of the Internal Revenue Code include an individual or individuals of any particular race, religion, gender, national origin, socioeconomic status, age, ethnicity, disability, marital status, sexual orientation, or political party registration. Further, a state agency or a local government may not prohibit service as a board member or officer by an individual or individuals based upon their familial relationship to each other or to a donor or require that the governing board or officers include one or more individuals who do not share a familial relationship with each other or with a donor.

(4) A charitable organization, private foundation trust, split interest trust, or any private foundation as defined in s. 509(a) of the Internal Revenue Code may not be required by a state agency or a local government to distribute its funds to or contract with any person or entity based upon the race, religion, gender, national origin, socioeconomic status, age, ethnicity, disability, marital status, sexual orientation, or political party registration of the person or of the employees, officers, directors, trustees, members, or owners of the entity, or based upon the populations, locales, or communities served by the person or entity, except as a lawful condition on the expenditure of particular funds imposed by the donor of such funds.

History.
S. 8, ch. 2010-122, eff. July 1, 2010.
Editor's Notes.
Section 9, ch. 2010-122 provides: "Section 8 of this act does not invalidate contracts in effect before the effective date of this act."
Section 509(a) of the Internal Revenue Code, referred to in this section, is codified as 26 U.S.C.S. § 509(a).

PART XIII.
MISCELLANEOUS.

736.1301.   Electronic records and signatures.

Any provisions of this code governing the legal effect, validity, or enforceability of electronic records or electronic signatures, and of contracts formed or performed with the use of such records or signatures, are deemed to conform to the requirements of s. 102 of the Electronic Signatures in Global and National Commerce Act, 15 U.S.C. s. 7002, and supersede, modify, and limit the requirements of the Electronic Signatures in Global and National Commerce Act.

History.
S. 13, ch. 2006-217, eff. July 1, 2007.

736.1302.   Severability clause.

If any provision of this code or its application to any person or circumstances is held invalid, the invalidity does not affect other provisions or applications of this code that can be given effect without the invalid provision or application, and to this end the provisions of this code are severable.

History.

S. 13, ch. 2006-217, eff. July 1, 2007.

736.1303.   Application to existing relationships.

(1) Except as otherwise provided in this code, on July 1, 2007:

(a) This code applies to all trusts created before, on, or after such date.

(b) This code applies to all judicial proceedings concerning trusts commenced on or after such date.

(c) This code applies to judicial proceedings concerning trusts commenced before such date, unless the court finds that application of a particular provision of this code would substantially interfere with the effective conduct of the judicial proceedings or prejudice the rights of the parties, in which case the particular provision of this code does not apply and the superseded law applies.

(d) Any rule of construction or presumption provided in this code applies to trust instruments executed before the effective date of this code unless there is a clear indication of a contrary intent in the terms of the trust.

(e) An act done before such date is not affected by this code.

(2) If a right is acquired, extinguished, or barred on the expiration of a prescribed period that has commenced to run under any other law before July 1, 2007, that law continues to apply to the right even if it has been repealed or superseded.

History.
S. 13, ch. 2006-217, eff. July 1, 2007.

CHAPTER 737
TRUST ADMINISTRATION

[NOTE: CHAPTER 737 WAS REPEALED
JULY 1, 2007]

PART I.
TRUST REGISTRATION.

[1]737.101. Principal place of administration of trust.

(1) Unless otherwise designated in the trust agreement, the principal place of administration of a trust is the trustee's usual place of business where the records pertaining to the trust are kept or, if he or she has no place of business, the trustee's residence.

(2) If not otherwise designated in the trust instrument in the case of cotrustees, the principal place of administration is:

(a) The usual place of business of the corporate trustee, if there is but one corporate cotrustee;

(b) The usual place of business or residence of the individual trustee who is a professional fiduciary, if there is but one such person and no corporate cotrustee; or otherwise,

(c) The usual place of business or residence of any of the cotrustees as agreed upon by them.

(3) Unless otherwise designated in the trust agreement and notwithstanding any other provision of this section, the principal place of administration of a trust, for which a bank, association, or trust company organized under the laws of this state or bank or savings association organized under the laws of the United States with its main office in this state has been appointed trustee, shall not be moved or otherwise affected solely because the trustee engaged in an interstate merger transaction with an out-of-state bank pursuant to s. 658.2953 in which the out-of-state bank is the resulting bank.

History: s. 1, ch. 74-106; s. 1, ch. 75-221; s. 1, ch. 77-344; s. 16, ch. 97-30; s. 1037, ch. 97-102; s. 48, ch. 2006-217.

[1]Note.—Repealed July 1, 2007, by s. 48, ch. 2006-217.

[1]737.105. Qualification of foreign trustee.

Unless otherwise doing business in this state, local qualification by a foreign trustee is not required in order for the trustee to receive distribution from a local estate. Nothing in this chapter shall affect the provisions of s. 660.41.

History: s. 1, ch. 74-106; s. 1, ch. 75-221; s. 150, ch. 80-260; s. 48, ch. 2006-217.

[1]Note.—Repealed July 1, 2007, by s. 48, ch. 2006-217.

[1]737.106. Revocable trust prior to dissolution of marriage.

Unless the trust instrument or the judgment for dissolution of marriage or divorce expressly provides otherwise, if a revocable trust is executed by a husband or wife as settlor prior to annulment of the marriage or entry of a judgment for dissolution of marriage or divorce of settlor from settlor's spouse, then any provision of the trust which affects the settlor's spouse will become void upon annulment of the marriage or entry of the judgment of dissolution of marriage or divorce, and any such trust will be administered and construed as if the settlor's spouse had died on the date of the annulment or upon entry of the judgment for dissolution of marriage or divorce.

History: s. 1, ch. 89-39; s. 14, ch. 2003-154; s. 48, ch. 2006-217.

[1]Note.—Repealed July 1, 2007, by s. 48, ch. 2006-217.

[1]737.111. Execution requirements for express trusts.

(1) The testamentary aspects of a trust defined in s. 731.201(34), are invalid unless the trust instrument is executed by the grantor with the formalities required for the execution of a will.

(2) The testamentary aspects of a trust created by a nonresident of Florida, either before or after this law takes effect, are not invalid because the trust does not meet the requirements of this section, if the trust is valid under the laws of the state or country where the settlor was at the time of execution.

(3) The testamentary aspects of an amendment to a trust are invalid unless the amendment is executed by the settlor with the same formalities as a will.

(4) For the purposes of this section, the term "testamentary aspects" means those provisions of the trust that dispose of the trust property on or after the death of the settlor other than to the settlor's estate.

(5) This section shall not apply to trusts established as part of an employee annuity described in s. 403 of the Internal Revenue Code of 1986, as amended, an Individual Retirement Account as described in s. 408 of the Internal Revenue Code of 1986, as amended, a Keogh (HR-10) Plan, or a retirement or other plan that is qualified under s. 401 of the Internal Revenue Code of 1986, as amended.

(6) This section shall not apply to trust instruments executed prior to October 1, 1995.

History: s. 11, ch. 95-401; s. 4, ch. 97-240; s. 193, ch. 2001-226; s. 48, ch. 2006-217.

[1]Note.—Repealed July 1, 2007, by s. 48, ch. 2006-217.

[1]737.115. Notice of trustee duties.

(1) A trust described in s. 733.707(3) must contain a notice that the trustee may have duties and responsibilities in addition to those described in the instrument creating the trust. The notice may, but need not, read as follows:

"The trustee of a trust may have duties and responsibilities in addition to those described in the instrument creating the trust. If you have questions you should obtain legal advice."

(2) The absence of the notice described in this section in the trust instrument does not affect the validity of the trust. A trustee is not relieved of any duty if the notice is not contained in the trust instrument. No person is liable for the failure to include the notice in the trust instrument.

(3) This section applies to all trusts described in s. 733.707(3) and amendments to those trusts executed on or after January 1, 2003.

History: s. 7, ch. 2002-82; s. 48, ch. 2006-217.

[1]Note.—Repealed July 1, 2007, by s. 48, ch. 2006-217.

[1]737.116. Trust for care of animal.

(1) A trust may be created to provide for the care of an animal alive during the settlor's lifetime. The trust terminates upon the death of the animal or, if the trust was created to provide for the care of more than one animal alive during the settlor's lifetime, upon the death of the last surviving animal.

(2) Except as provided in this section, the law of this state regarding the creation and administration of express trusts applies to a trust for the care of an animal.

(3) A trust authorized by this section may be enforced by a person appointed in the terms of the trust or, if no person is so appointed, by a person appointed by the court. A person having an interest in the welfare of the animal may request the court to appoint a person to enforce the trust or to remove a person appointed. The appointed person shall have the rights of a trust beneficiary for the purpose of enforcing the trust, including receiving accountings, notices, and other information from the trustee and providing consents.

(4) Property of a trust authorized by this section may be applied only to its intended use, except to the extent the court determines that the value of the trust property exceeds the amount required for the intended use. Property not required for the intended use, including the trust property remaining upon its termination, shall be distributed in the following order of priority:

(a) As directed by the terms of the trust;

(b) To the settlor, if then living;

(c) Pursuant to the residuary clause of the settlor's will if the trust for the animal was created in a preresiduary clause in the settlor's will;

(d) If the settlor is deceased, pursuant to the residuary provisions of the inter vivos trust if the trust for the animal was created in a preresiduary clause in the trust instrument; or

(e) To the settlor's heirs.

(5) This section applies to trusts created on or after January 1, 2003.

History: s. 8, ch. 2002-82; s. 48, ch. 2006-217.

[1]Note.—Repealed July 1, 2007, by s. 48, ch. 2006-217.

PART II.
JURISDICTION OF COURTS.

[1]737.201. Court powers over trusts.

(1) The proceedings that may be maintained under this section are those concerning the administration and distribution of trusts, the declaration of rights, and the determination of any other matters involving trustees and beneficiaries of trusts. These include, but are not limited to, proceedings to:

(a) Appoint or remove a trustee.

(b) Review trustees' fees and to review and settle interim or final accounts.

(c) Ascertain beneficiaries; determine any question arising in the administration or distribution of any trust, including questions of construction of trust instruments; instruct trustees; and determine the existence or nonexistence of any immunity, power, privilege, duty, or right.

(2) A proceeding under this section does not result in continuing supervisory proceedings. The management and distribution of a trust estate, submission of accounts and reports to beneficiaries, payment of trustee's fees and other obligations of a trust, acceptance and change of trusteeship, and other aspects of the administration of a trust shall proceed expeditiously, consistent with the terms of the trust, free of judicial intervention and without order, approval, or other action of any court, subject to the jurisdiction of the court invoked by interested parties or otherwise exercised as provided by law.

History: s. 1, ch. 74-106; s. 2, ch. 75-221; s. 3, ch. 77-344; s. 48, ch. 2006-217.

[1]Note.—Repealed July 1, 2007, by s. 48, ch. 2006-217.

[1]737.202. Trust proceedings; venue.

Venue for actions and proceedings concerning trusts, including those under s. 737.201, may be laid in:

(1) Any county where the venue is proper under chapter 47.

(2) Any county where the beneficiary suing or being sued resides or has its principal place of business.

(3) The county where the trust has its principal place of administration.

History: s. 1, ch. 74-106; s. 4, ch. 77-344; s. 48, ch. 2006-217.

[1]Note.—Repealed July 1, 2007, by s. 48, ch. 2006-217.

[1]737.203. Trust proceedings; dismissal of matters relating to foreign trusts.

Over the objection of a party, the court shall not entertain proceedings under s. 737.201 for a trust registered, or having its principal place of administration, in another state unless all interested parties could not be bound by litigation in the courts of the state where the trust is registered or has its principal place of administration. The court may condition a stay or dismissal of a proceeding under this section on the consent of any party to jurisdiction of the state where the trust is registered or has its principal place of business, or the court may grant a continuance or enter any other appropriate order.

History: s. 1, ch. 74-106; s. 48, ch. 2006-217.

[1]Note.—Repealed July 1, 2007, by s. 48, ch. 2006-217.

[1]737.2035. Costs and attorney's fees in trust proceedings.

(1) In all trust proceedings, costs may be awarded as in chancery actions.

(2) Any attorney who has rendered services to a trust may be awarded reasonable compensation from the trust. The attorney may apply to the court for an order awarding attorney's fees, and, after notice and service upon the trustee and all beneficiaries entitled to an accounting under s. 737.303, the court shall enter its order on the fee application.

(3) When costs and attorney's fees are to be paid out of the trust, the court may, in its discretion, direct from what part of the trust they shall be paid.

(4) The provisions of this section shall apply only to services of an attorney rendered on or after July 1, 1999.

(5) Except when a trustee's interest may be adverse in a particular matter, the attorney shall give reasonable notice in writing to the trustee of the attorney's retention by an interested person and the attorney's entitlement to fees pursuant to this section. A court may reduce any fee award for services rendered by the attorney prior to the date

of actual notice to the trustee, if the actual notice date is later than a date of reasonable notice. In exercising this discretion, the court may exclude compensation for services rendered after the reasonable notice date but prior to the date of actual notice.

History: s. 1, ch. 99-352; s. 15, ch. 2003-154; s. 48, ch. 2006-217.

[1]Note.—Repealed July 1, 2007, by s. 48, ch. 2006-217.

[1]737.204. Proceedings for review of employment of agents and review of compensation of trustee and employees of trust.

(1) After notice to all interested persons, the court may review the propriety of the employment by a trustee of any person, including any attorney, auditor, investment adviser, or other specialized agent or assistant, and the reasonableness of any compensation paid to that person or to the trustee.

(2) If the settlor's estate is being probated, and the settlor's trust or the trustee of the settlor's trust is a beneficiary under the settlor's will, the trustee, any person employed by the trustee, or any interested person may have the propriety of employment and the reasonableness of the compensation of the trustee or any person employed by the trustee determined in the probate proceeding.

(3) The burden of proof of propriety of the employment and the reasonableness of the compensation shall be upon the trustee and the person employed by the trustee. Any person who is determined to have received excessive compensation from a trust for services rendered may be ordered to make appropriate refunds.

(4) Court proceedings to determine reasonable compensation of a trustee or any person employed by a trustee, if required, are a part of the trust administration process. The costs, including attorney's fees, of the person assuming the burden of proof of propriety of the employment and reasonableness of the compensation shall be determined by the court and paid from the assets of the trust unless the court finds the compensation paid or requested to be substantially unreasonable. The court shall direct from which part of the trust assets the compensation shall be paid.

(5) The court may determine reasonable compensation for a trustee or any person employed by a trustee without receiving expert testimony. Any party may offer expert testimony after notice to interested persons. If expert testimony is offered, a reasonable expert witness fee shall be awarded by the court and paid from the assets of the trust. The court shall direct from which part of the trust assets the fee shall be paid.

(6) Persons given notice as provided in this section shall be bound by all orders entered on the petition.

(7) In a proceeding pursuant to subsection (2), the petitioner may serve formal notice as provided in the Florida Probate Rules, and such notice shall be sufficient for the court to acquire jurisdiction over the person receiving it to the extent of the person's interest in the trust.

History: s. 1, ch. 74-106; s. 4, ch. 75-221; s. 3, ch. 95-401; s. 1038, ch. 97-102; s. 16, ch. 2003-154; s. 48, ch. 2006-217.

[1]Note.—Repealed July 1, 2007, by s. 48, ch. 2006-217.

[1]737.2041. Trustee's attorney's fees.

(1) If the trustee of a trust described in s. 733.707(3) retains an attorney to render legal services in connection with the initial administration of the trust, the attorney is entitled to reasonable compensation for those legal services, payable from the assets of the trust without court order. If the trustee of a trust described in s. 733.707(3) retains an attorney to render legal services in connection with the initial administration of a trust, the trustee and the attorney may agree to compensation that is determined in a manner or amount other than the manner or amount provided in this section. The agreement is not binding upon a person who bears the impact of the compensation unless that person is a party to or otherwise consents to be bound by the agreement. The agreement may provide that the trustee is not individually liable for the attorney's fees and costs.

(2) Unless otherwise agreed, compensation based upon the value of the trust assets immediately following the settlor's death and the income earned by the trust during initial administration at the rate of 75 percent of the schedule provided in s. 733.6171(3)(a)-(h) is presumed to be reason-

able total compensation for ordinary services of all attorneys employed generally to advise trustees concerning their duties in initial trust administration.

(3) An attorney who is retained to render only limited and specifically defined legal services shall be compensated as provided in the retaining agreement. If the amount or method of determining compensation is not provided in the agreement, the attorney is entitled to a reasonable fee, taking into account the factors set forth in subsection (6).

(4) Ordinary services of the attorney in an initial trust administration include legal advice and representation concerning the trustee's duties relating to:

(a) Review of the trust instrument and each amendment for legal sufficiency and interpretation.

(b) Implementation of substitution of the successor trustee.

(c) Persons who must or should be served with required notices and the method and timing of such service.

(d) The obligation of a successor to require a former trustee to account.

(e) The trustee's duty to protect, insure, and manage trust assets and the trustee's liability relating to these duties.

(f) The trustee's duty regarding investments imposed by the prudent investor rule.

(g) Contributions due to the personal representative of settlor's estate for payment of administrative expenses or creditor claims and estate taxes.

(h) The trustee's obligation to inform and account to beneficiaries and the method of satisfaction of these obligations; the liability of the trust and trustee to the settlor's creditors; the advisability or necessity for probate proceedings to bar creditors; and the contribution requirements to the settlor's probate estate.

(i) Identifying tax returns required to be filed by the trustee, the trustee's liability for payment of taxes, and the due date of returns.

(j) Obtaining nontaxable certificate and receipt, if not done by a personal representative.

(k) Order of payment of expenses of administration of the trust and order and priority of abatement of bequests and legacies in the trust.

(l) Distribution of income or principal to beneficiaries or funding of further trusts provided in the governing instrument.

(m) Preparation of any legal documents required to effect distribution.

(n) Fiduciary duties, avoidance of self-dealing, conflicts of interest, duty of impartiality, and obligations to beneficiaries.

(o) If there is a conflict of interest between a trustee who is a beneficiary and other beneficiaries of the trust, advice to the trustee on limitations of certain authority of the trustee regarding discretionary distributions or exercise of certain powers and alternatives for appointment of an independent trustee and appropriate procedures.

(p) Procedures for trustee's discharge from liability for administration of trust upon termination or resignation.

(5) In addition to the attorney's fees for ordinary services, the attorney for the trustee shall be allowed further reasonable compensation for any extraordinary service. What is an extraordinary service may vary depending on many factors, including the size of the trust. Extraordinary services may include, but are not limited to:

(a) Involvement in a trust contest, trust construction, a proceeding for determination of beneficiaries, a contested claim, elective share proceedings, apportionment of estate taxes, or other adversary proceedings or litigation by or against the trust.

(b) Representation of the trustee in audit or any proceeding for adjustment, determination, or collection of any taxes.

(c) Tax advice on postmortem tax planning, including, but not limited to, disclaimer, renunciation of fiduciary commission, alternate valuation date, allocation of administrative expenses between tax returns, the QTIP or reverse QTIP election, allocation of GST exemption, qualification for Internal Revenue Code ss. 303 and 6166 privileges, deduction of last illness expenses, distribution planning, asset basis considerations, throwback rules, handling income or deductions in respect of a decedent, valuation discounts, special use and other valuation, handling employee benefit or retirement proceeds, prompt assessment request, or request for release of personal liability for payment of tax.

(d) Review of estate tax return and preparation or review of other tax returns required to be filed by the trustee.

(e) Preparation of decedent's federal estate tax return. If this return is prepared by the attorney, a fee of one-half of 1 percent up to a value of $10 million and one-fourth of 1 percent on the value in excess of $10 million, of the gross estate as finally determined for federal estate tax purposes, is presumed to be reasonable compensation for the attorney for this service. These fees shall include services for routine audit of the return, not beyond the examining agent level, if required.

(f) Purchase, sale, lease, or encumbrance of real property by the trustee or involvement in zoning, land use, environmental, or other similar matters.

(g) Legal advice regarding carrying on of decedent's business or conducting other commercial activity by the trustee.

(h) Legal advice regarding claims for damage to the environment or related procedures.

(i) Legal advice regarding homestead status of trust real property or proceedings involving the status.

(j) Involvement in fiduciary, employee, or attorney compensation disputes.

(k) Considerations of special valuation of trust assets, including discounts for blockage, minority interests, lack of marketability, and environmental liability.

(6) Upon petition of any interested person in a proceeding to review the compensation paid or to be paid to the attorney for the trustee, the court may increase or decrease the compensation for ordinary services of the attorney for the trustee or award compensation for extraordinary services if the facts and circumstances of the particular administration warrant. In determining reasonable compensation, the court shall consider all of the following factors giving such weight to each as it may determine to be appropriate:

(a) The promptness, efficiency, and skill with which the initial administration was handled by the attorney.

(b) The responsibilities assumed by, and potential liabilities of, the attorney.

(c) The nature and value of the assets that are affected by the decedent's death.

(d) The benefits or detriments resulting to the trust or its beneficiaries from the attorney's services.

(e) The complexity or simplicity of the administration and the novelty of issues presented.

(f) The attorney's participation in tax planning for the estate, the trust, and the trust's beneficiaries and tax return preparation or review and approval.

(g) The nature of the trust assets, the expenses of administration, and the claims payable by the trust and the compensation paid to other professionals and fiduciaries.

(h) Any delay in payment of the compensation after the services were furnished.

(i) Any other relevant factors.

(7) The court may determine reasonable attorney's compensation without receiving expert testimony. Any party may offer expert testimony after notice to interested persons. If expert testimony is offered, an expert witness fee may be awarded by the court and paid from the assets of the trust. The court may, in its discretion, direct from what part of the trust it shall be paid.

(8) If a separate written agreement regarding compensation exists between the attorney and the settlor, the attorney shall furnish a copy to the trustee prior to commencement of employment and, if employed, shall promptly file and serve a copy on all interested persons. Neither a separate agreement nor a provision in the trust suggesting or directing the trustee to retain a specific attorney will obligate the trustee to employ the attorney or obligate the attorney to accept the representation, but if the attorney who is a party to the agreement or who drafted the trust is employed, the compensation paid shall not exceed the compensation provided in the agreement.

(9) Court proceedings to determine compensation, if required, are a part of the trust administration process, and the costs, including fees for

the trustee's attorney, shall be determined by the court and paid from the assets of the trust unless the court finds the attorney's fees request to be substantially unreasonable. The court shall direct from which part of the trust they shall be paid.

(10) "Initial trust administration" as used in this section means administration of a trust described in s. 733.707(3) during the period which begins with the death of the settlor and ends upon the final distribution of trust assets outright or to continuing trusts created under the trust agreement, but if an estate tax return is required, not until after issuance of an estate tax closing letter or other evidence of termination of the estate tax proceeding. This initial period is not intended to include continued regular administration of the trust.

(11) This section shall apply to trusts of settlors who die on or after July 1, 1995.

History: s. 4, ch. 95-401; s. 5, ch. 97-240; s. 48, ch. 2006-217.

[1]Note.—Repealed July 1, 2007, by s. 48, ch. 2006-217.

[1]737.205. Trust proceedings; commencement.

Proceedings concerning trusts shall be commenced by filing a complaint and shall be governed by the Florida Rules of Civil Procedure.

History: s. 1, ch. 74-106; s. 4, ch. 75-221; s. 48, ch. 2006-217.

[1]Note.—Repealed July 1, 2007, by s. 48, ch. 2006-217.

[1]737.206. Effect of fraud, duress, mistake, and undue influence.

A trust is void if the execution is procured by fraud, duress, mistake, or undue influence. Any part of the trust is void if so procured, but the remainder of the trust not so procured is valid if it is not invalid for other reasons.

History: s. 21, ch. 92-200; s. 2, ch. 2000-245; s. 48, ch. 2006-217.

[1]Note.—Repealed July 1, 2007, by s. 48, ch. 2006-217.

[1]737.2065. Trust contests.

An action to contest the validity of all or part of a trust may not be commenced until the trust becomes irrevocable, except this section does not prohibit such action by the guardian of the property of an incapacitated settlor.

History: s. 3, ch. 2000-245; s. 1, ch. 2006-77; s. 48, ch. 2006-217.

[1]Note.—Repealed July 1, 2007, by s. 48, ch. 2006-217.

[1]737.207. Penalty clause for contest.

A provision in a trust instrument purporting to penalize any interested person for contesting the trust instrument or instituting other proceedings relating to a trust estate or trust assets is unenforceable.

History: s. 12, ch. 93-257; s. 48, ch. 2006-217.

[1]Note.—Repealed July 1, 2007, by s. 48, ch. 2006-217.

[1]737.208. Administration pending outcome of contest or other proceeding.

(1) Pending the outcome of a proceeding filed to determine the validity of all or part of a trust or the beneficiaries of all or part of a trust, the trustee shall proceed with the administration of the trust as if no proceeding had been commenced, except that no distribution may be made to a beneficiary in contravention of the rights of those persons that may be affected by the outcome of the proceeding.

(2) Upon motion of a party and after notice to interested persons, a court may, upon good cause shown, make an exception to the prohibition under subsection (1) and authorize the trustee to distribute trust assets to a beneficiary subject to any conditions the court, in its discretion, may impose, including the posting of bond by the beneficiary.

History: s. 186, ch. 2001-226; s. 48, ch. 2006-217.

[1]Note.—Repealed July 1, 2007, by s. 48, ch. 2006-217.

[1]737.209. Improper distribution or payment; liability of distributee.

A distributee who was paid improperly must return the assets or funds received and the income from those assets or interest on the funds since distribution or payment, unless the distribution or payment cannot be questioned because of adjudication, estoppel, or limitations. If the distributee does not have the property, its value at the date of disposition, income thereon, and gain received by the distributee must be returned.

History: s. 9, ch. 2002-82; s. 48, ch. 2006-217.

[1]Note.—Repealed July 1, 2007, by s. 48, ch. 2006-217.

PART III.
DUTIES AND LIABILITIES OF TRUSTEES.

[1]737.301. General duties not limited.

Except as specifically provided, the general duty of the trustee to administer a trust diligently for the benefit of the beneficiaries is not altered by this part.

History: s. 1, ch. 74-106; s. 48, ch. 2006-217.

[1]Note.—Repealed July 1, 2007, by s. 48, ch. 2006-217.

[1]737.302. Trustee's standard of care and performance.

Except as otherwise provided by the trust instrument, the trustee shall observe the standards in s. 518.11 regarding investments by fiduciaries when dealing with the trust assets. If the trustee has special skills, or is named trustee on the basis of representations of special skills or expertise, the trustee is under a duty to use those skills.

History: s. 1, ch. 74-106; s. 6, ch. 75-221; s. 13, ch. 93-257; s. 48, ch. 2006-217.

[1]Note.—Repealed July 1, 2007, by s. 48, ch. 2006-217.

[1]737.303. Duty to inform and account to beneficiaries.

The trustee shall keep the beneficiaries of the trust reasonably informed of the trust and its administration. The trustee's duty to inform and account includes, but is not limited to, the following:

(1) Within 30 days after acceptance of the trust, the trustee shall inform the beneficiaries in writing of the acceptance of the trust and the full name and address of the trustee.

(2) Upon reasonable request, the trustee shall provide a beneficiary with a complete copy of the trust instrument, including amendments.

(3) Upon reasonable request, the trustee shall provide a beneficiary with relevant information about the assets of the trust and the particulars relating to administration.

(4) (a) A beneficiary is entitled to a trust accounting, as set forth in s. 737.3035, annually and upon termination of the trust or upon change of the trustee except as provided under paragraph (c).

(b) For purposes of this section, the term "beneficiary" means:

1. All current income or principal beneficiaries, whether discretionary or mandatory; and

2. All reasonably ascertainable remainder beneficiaries who would take if all income interests immediately terminated.

(c) In the case of a trust described in s. 733.707(3), during the grantor's lifetime, the trustee's duties under this section extend only to the grantor or the legal representative of the grantor.

(d) A beneficiary or the beneficiary's representative, as defined in s. 731.303, may waive, in writing, the trustee's duty to account under paragraph (a).

(e) All rights provided a beneficiary under this section may be asserted by a legal representative or natural guardian of the beneficiary. Notice under subsection (1) and a trust accounting under paragraph (a) provided to a representative of the beneficiary as defined in s. 731.303 shall bind the beneficiary, and the trustee shall not be required to provide such notice or trust accounting to any beneficiary who would be bound by an order binding on a representative of the beneficiary under s. 731.303, if such notice or trust accounting, respectively, is provided to that representative.

(5) This section applies to trust accountings rendered for accounting periods beginning on or after January 1, 2003.

History: s. 1, ch. 74-106; s. 6, ch. 75-221; s. 5, ch. 77-344; s. 12, ch. 95-401; s. 6, ch. 97-240; s. 4, ch. 2000-245; s. 10, ch. 2002-82; s. 26, ch. 2003-154; s. 48, ch. 2006-217.

[1]Note.—Repealed July 1, 2007, by s. 48, ch. 2006-217.

[1]737.3035. Trust accountings.

(1) A trust accounting must be a reasonably understandable report from the date of the last accounting or, if none, from the date upon which the trustee became accountable, which adequately discloses the information required in subsection (2).

(2) (a) The accounting must begin with a statement identifying the trust, the trustee furnishing the accounting, and the time period covered by the accounting.

(b) The accounting must show all cash and property transactions and all significant transactions affecting administration during the accounting period, including compensation paid to the trustee and the trustee's agents.

Gains and losses realized during the accounting period, and all receipts and disbursements must be shown.

(c) The accounting must, to the extent feasible, identify and value trust assets on hand at the close of the accounting period. For each asset or class of assets reasonably capable of valuation, the accounting shall contain two values, the asset acquisition value or carrying value and the estimated current value. The accounting must identify each known noncontingent liability with an estimated current amount of the liability if known.

(d) To the extent feasible, the accounting must show significant transactions that do not affect the amount for which the trustee is accountable, including name changes in investment holdings, adjustments to carrying value, a change of custodial institutions, and stock splits.

(e) The accounting must reflect the allocation of receipts, disbursements, accruals, or allowances between income and principal when the allocation affects the interest of any beneficiary of the trust.

(3) This section applies to all trust accountings rendered for any accounting periods beginning on or after January 1, 2003.

History: s. 11, ch. 2002-82; s. 48, ch. 2006-217.

[1]Note.—Repealed July 1, 2007, by s. 48, ch. 2006-217.

[1]737.304. Duty to provide bond.

A trustee need not provide bond to secure performance of his or her duties unless this is required by the trust instrument, reasonably requested by a beneficiary, or found by the court to be necessary to protect the interests of beneficiaries who are not able to protect themselves and whose interests otherwise are not adequately represented. On application of the trustee or other interested person, the court may excuse a requirement of bond, increase or reduce the amount of the bond, release the surety, or permit the substitution of another bond with the same or different sureties. If bond is required, it shall be filed in the clerk's office in the county where the trust has its principal place of business, in amounts and with surety as provided in s. 45.011 and conditioned on the faithful performance of the trust.

History: s. 1, ch. 74-106; s. 6, ch. 75-221; s. 6, ch. 77-344; s. 1039, ch. 97-102; s. 48, ch. 2006-217.

[1]Note.—Repealed July 1, 2007, by s. 48, ch. 2006-217.

[1]737.305. Trustee's duty concerning location of trust.

A trustee is under a continuing duty to administer the trust at a place appropriate to the purposes of the trust and its sound, efficient management. If the principal place of administration becomes inappropriate for any reason, the court may enter an order for the purposes of furthering efficient administration and the interests of beneficiaries, including, if appropriate, removal of the trustee and appointment of a trustee in another state. Trust provisions relating to the place of administration and to changes in the place of administration or of trustee shall control, unless compliance would be contrary to efficient administration or the purposes of the trust. Views of adult beneficiaries shall be given weight in determining the suitability of the trustee and the place of administration.

History: s. 1, ch. 74-106; s. 7, ch. 75-221; s. 7, ch. 77-344; s. 48, ch. 2006-217.

[1]Note.—Repealed July 1, 2007, by s. 48, ch. 2006-217.

[1]737.3053. Trustee's duty to distribute trust income.

If a will or trust instrument granting income to the grantor's or testator's spouse for life is silent as to the time of distribution of income and the frequency thereof, the trustee shall distribute all net income to the income beneficiary, as defined in chapter 738, no less frequently than annually. This provision shall apply to any trust established before, on, or after the effective date hereof unless the trust instrument expressly directs or permits net income to be distributed less frequently than annually.

History: s. 3, ch. 79-343; s. 1, ch. 86-248; s. 48, ch. 2006-217.

[1]Note.—Repealed July 1, 2007, by s. 48, ch. 2006-217.

[1]737.3054. Trustee's duty to pay expenses and obligations of grantor's estate.

(1) A trustee of a trust described in s. 733.707(3) shall pay to the personal representative of a grantor's estate any amounts that the personal representative certifies in writing to the trustee are

required to pay the expenses of the administration and obligations of the grantor's estate. Payments made by a trustee, unless otherwise provided in the trust instrument, must be charged as expenses of the trust without a contribution from anyone. The interests of all beneficiaries of such a trust are subject to the provisions of this subsection; however, the payments must be made from assets or property or the proceeds thereof, other than assets proscribed in s. 733.707(3), which are included in the grantor's gross estate for federal estate tax purposes.

(2) Unless a grantor provides by will, or designates in a trust described in s. 733.707(3) funds or property passing under the trust to be so used, the expenses of the administration and obligations of the grantor's estate must be paid from the trust in the following order:

(a) Property of the residue of the trust remaining after all distributions that are to be satisfied by reference to a specific property or type of property, fund, or sum;

(b) Property that is not to be distributed from specified or identified property or a specified or identified item of property; and

(c) Property that is to be distributed from specified or identified property or a specified or identified item of property.

(3) Trust distributions that are to be satisfied from specified or identified property must be classed as distributions to be satisfied from the general assets of the trust and not otherwise disposed of in the trust instrument upon the failure or insufficiency of funds or property from which payment should be made, to the extent of the insufficiency. Trust distributions given for valuable consideration abate with other distributions of the same class only to the extent of the excess over the value of the consideration until all others of the same class are exhausted. Except as provided in this section, trust distributions abate equally and ratably and without preference or priority between real and personal property. When a specified or identified item of property that has been designated for distribution in the trust instrument or that is charged with a distribution is sold or taken by the trustee, other beneficiaries shall contribute according to their respective interests to the ben-

eficiary whose property has been sold or taken, and before distribution the trustee shall determine the amounts of the respective contributions, and they must be paid or withheld before distribution is made.

(4) The trustee shall pay the expenses of trust administration, including compensation of trustees and their attorneys, before and in preference to the expenses of the administration and obligations of the grantor's estate.

History: s. 13, ch. 95-401; s. 187, ch. 2001-226; s. 48, ch. 2006-217.

[1]Note.—Repealed July 1, 2007, by s. 48, ch. 2006-217.

[1]737.3055. Trustee's duty to ascertain marketable title of trust real property.

A trustee holding title to real property received from a settlor or estate shall not be required to obtain title insurance or proof of marketable title until a marketable title is required for a sale or conveyance of the real property.

History: s. 4, ch. 79-343; s. 48, ch. 2006-217.

[1]Note.—Repealed July 1, 2007, by s. 48, ch. 2006-217.

[1]737.306. Personal liability of trustee.

(1) (a) Unless otherwise provided in the contract, a trustee is not personally liable on contracts, except contracts for attorneys' fees, properly entered into in the trustee's fiduciary capacity in the course of administration of the trust estate unless the trustee fails to reveal that representative capacity and identify the trust estate in the contract.

(b) A trustee is personally liable for obligations arising from ownership or control of property of the trust estate or for torts committed in the course of administration of the trust estate only if the trustee is personally at fault.

(c) Claims based on contracts, except contracts for attorneys' fees, entered into by a trustee in his or her fiduciary capacity, on obligations arising from ownership or control of the trust estate, or on torts committed in the course of trust administration may be asserted against the trust estate by proceeding against the trustee in the trustee's fiduciary capacity, whether or not the trustee is personally liable.

(2) Issues of liability between the trust estate and the trustee individually may be determined in a proceeding for accounting, surcharge, or indemnification, or in any other appropriate proceeding.

(3) A successor trustee is not personally liable for any action taken or omitted to be taken by any prior trustee; nor does any successor trustee have a duty to institute any action against any prior trustee, or file any claim against any prior trustee's estate, for any of the prior trustee's acts or omissions as trustee under any of the following circumstances:

(a) The successor trustee succeeds a trustee who was also the grantor of a trust that was revocable during the time that the grantor served as trustee;

(b) As to any beneficiary who has waived any accounting required by s. 737.303, but only as to the periods included in the waiver;

(c) As to any beneficiary who has released the successor trustee from the duty to institute any action or file any claim;

(d) As to any person who is not a beneficiary within the meaning of s. 737.303(4)(b); or

(e) As to any beneficiary described in s. 737.303(4)(b):

1. If a super majority of the reasonably ascertainable current income or principal beneficiaries described in s. 737.303(4)(b)1. and a super majority of the reasonably ascertainable remainder beneficiaries described in s. 737.303(4)(b)2. have released the successor trustee;

2. If the beneficiary has not delivered a written request to the successor trustee to institute an action or file a claim against the prior trustee within 6 months after the date of the successor trustee's acceptance of the trust, if the successor trustee has notified the beneficiary in writing of its acceptance in accordance with s. 737.303(1) and that writing advises the beneficiary that, unless the beneficiary delivers the written request within 6 months after the date of acceptance, the right to proceed against the successor trustee will be barred pursuant to this section; or

3. For any action or claim that the beneficiary is barred from bringing against the prior trustee.

(f) For the purposes of this section, a super majority of beneficiaries means at least two-thirds in interest of the beneficiaries if the interests of the beneficiaries are reasonably ascertainable; otherwise, it means at least two-thirds in number of the beneficiaries. A release or waiver under this section may be exercised by a legal representative or natural guardian of the beneficiary without the filing of any proceeding or approval of any court. Nothing in this subsection affects any liability of the prior trustee or the right of the successor trustee or any beneficiary to pursue an action or claim against the prior trustee.

History: s. 1, ch. 74-106; s. 7, ch. 75-221; s. 8, ch. 77-344; s. 2, ch. 86-248; s. 8, ch. 95-401; s. 1040, ch. 97-102; s. 2, ch. 99-352; s. 188, ch. 2001-226; s. 48, ch. 2006-217.

[1]Note.—Repealed July 1, 2007, by s. 48, ch. 2006-217.

[1]737.3061. Limitations on actions against certain trusts.

(1) After the death of a grantor, no creditor of the grantor may bring, maintain, or continue any direct action against a trust described in s. 733.707(3), the trustee of the trust, or any beneficiary of the trust that is dependent on the individual liability of the grantor. Those claims and causes of action against the grantor shall be presented and enforced against the grantor's estate as provided in part VII of chapter 733, and the personal representative of the grantor's estate may obtain payment from the trustee of a trust described in s. 733.707(3) as provided in ss. 733.607(2), 733.707(3), and 737.3054(1).

(2) This section shall not preclude a direct action against a trust described in s. 733.707(3), the trustee of the trust, or a beneficiary of the trust that is not dependent on the individual liability of the grantor.

(3) This section does not affect the lien of any duly recorded mortgage or security interest or the lien of any person in possession of personal property or the right to foreclose and enforce the mortgage or lien.

History: s. 189, ch. 2001-226; s. 48, ch. 2006-217.

[1]Note.—Repealed July 1, 2007, by s. 48, ch. 2006-217.

[1]737.307. Limitations on proceedings against trustees after beneficiary receives trust disclosure documents.

(1) Unless previously barred by adjudication, consent, or limitations, an action against a trustee

for breach of trust is barred for any beneficiary who has received a trust disclosure document adequately disclosing the matter unless a proceeding to assert the claim is commenced within 6 months after receipt from the trustee of the trust disclosure document or the limitation notice that applies to the trust disclosure document, whichever is received later. All claims against a trustee who has issued a trust disclosure document adequately disclosing a matter but who has not delivered a limitation notice that applies to that trust disclosure document are barred as provided in chapter 95 as to the matters disclosed in the trust disclosure document. In any event, and notwithstanding lack of adequate disclosure or delivery of a limitation notice, all claims against a trustee who has issued a final trust accounting received by the beneficiary and has informed the beneficiary of the location and availability of records for his or her examination are barred as provided in chapter 95.

(2) As used in this section, the term "trust disclosure document" means a trust accounting as defined in s. 737.3035 or any other written report of the trustee. A trust disclosure document adequately discloses a matter if it provides sufficient information so that a beneficiary knows of a claim or reasonably should have inquired into the existence of a claim with respect to that matter. An accounting that adequately discloses the information required by and that substantially complies with the standards set forth in s. 737.3035 is a trust accounting under this section.

(3) As used in this section, the term "limitation notice" means a written statement of the trustee that an action by a beneficiary against the trustee for breach of trust based on any matter adequately disclosed in a trust disclosure document may be barred unless the action is commenced within 6 months after receipt of the trust disclosure document or receipt of a limitation notice that applies to that trust disclosure document, whichever is later.

(a) A limitation notice may be contained as a part of the trust disclosure document, may be accompanied concurrently by the trust disclosure document, or may be delivered separately from the trust disclosure document.

(b) A limitation notice may, but is not required to be, in the following form: "An action for breach of trust based on matters disclosed in a trust accounting or other written report of the trustee may be subject to a 6-month statute of limitations from the receipt of the trust accounting or other written report. If you have questions, please consult your attorney."

(c) For purposes of this section, a limitation notice applies to a trust disclosure document when the limitation notice:

1. Is contained as a part of the trust disclosure document;

2. Is accompanied concurrently by the trust disclosure document or is delivered separately within 10 days of the delivery of the trust disclosure document;

3. Is contained as a part of another trust disclosure document received within 1 year prior to the receipt of the latter trust disclosure document;

4. Is accompanied concurrently by another trust disclosure document that was received within 1 year prior to the receipt of the latter trust disclosure document or that was delivered separately within 10 days of the earlier trust disclosure document to the beneficiary; or

5. Is received after the trust disclosure document, but only if the limitation notice references that trust disclosure document and:

a. Offers to provide to the beneficiary upon request another copy of that trust disclosure document if it was received by the beneficiary within 1 year prior to receipt of the limitation notice; or

b. Is accompanied by another copy of that trust disclosure document if the trust disclosure document was received by the beneficiary 1 year or more prior to the receipt of the limitation notice.

(d) A limitation notice is not delivered separately if it is accompanied by another written communication, other than a written communication which refers only to the limitation notice.

(4) A beneficiary has received a trust disclosure document or a limitation notice if, being an adult, it is received by the beneficiary or if, being a minor, disabled person, or person who may take by virtue of the exercise or nonexercise of a power of appointment, it is received by the beneficiary's representative as defined in s. 731.303.

(5) This section applies to trust accountings for accounting periods beginning on or after January 1, 2003, and to written reports, other than trust accountings, received by a beneficiary on or after January 1, 2003.

History: s. 1, ch. 74-106; s. 7, ch. 75-221; s. 2, ch. 88-217; s. 1041, ch. 97-102; s. 12, ch. 2002-82; s. 27, ch. 2003-154; s. 48, ch. 2006-217.

[1]Note.—Repealed July 1, 2007, by s. 48, ch. 2006-217.

[1]737.308. Notice of trust.

(1) Upon the death of a grantor of a trust described in s. 733.707(3), the trustee must file a notice of trust with the court of the county of the grantor's domicile and the court having jurisdiction of the grantor's estate.

(2) The notice of trust must contain the name of the grantor, the grantor's date of death, the title of the trust, if any, the date of the trust, and the name and address of the trustee.

(3) If the grantor's probate proceeding has been commenced, the clerk must notify the trustee in writing of the date of the commencement of the probate proceeding and the file number.

(4) The clerk shall file and index the notice of trust in the same manner as a caveat, unless there exists a probate proceeding for the grantor's estate in which case the notice of trust must be filed in the probate proceeding and the clerk shall send a copy to the personal representative.

(5) The clerk shall send a copy of any caveat filed regarding the grantor to the trustee, and the notice of trust to any caveator, unless there is a probate proceeding pending and the personal representative and the trustee are the same.

(6) Any proceeding affecting the expenses of the administration or obligations of the grantor's estate prior to the trustee filing a notice of trust are binding upon the trustee.

(7) The trustee's failure to file the notice of trust does not affect the trustee's obligation to pay expenses of administration and obligations of the grantor's estate as provided in s. 733.607(2).

History: s. 14, ch. 95-401; s. 7, ch. 97-240; s. 190, ch. 2001-226; s. 48, ch. 2006-217.

[1]Note.—Repealed July 1, 2007, by s. 48, ch. 2006-217.

[1]737.309. Resignation of trustee.

(1) A trustee may resign:

(a) Upon at least 30 days' written notice to the settlor, if living, all cotrustees, and all persons entitled to a trust accounting pursuant to s. 737.303, as qualified by s. 731.303; or

(b) With approval of the court. In approving a resignation, the court may issue orders and impose conditions reasonably necessary for the protection of the trust property.

(2) Any liability of a resigning trustee or of any sureties on the trustee's bond for acts or omissions of the trustee is not discharged or affected by the trustee's resignation.

(3) If the resignation of a trustee would require the vacancy to be filled by a successor trustee, a trustee that resigns shall continue to serve until the successor assumes the trusteeship. The resigning trustee shall deliver copies of all notices and other records pertaining to the resignation to the successor trustee or, if none, to a cotrustee.

(4) Notice of resignation shall be served in the manner provided in the Florida Rules of Civil Procedure relating to service of pleadings subsequent to the initial pleading. The notice may be served on a legal representative or natural guardian of a beneficiary without the filing of any proceeding or approval of any court.

History: s. 2, ch. 2005-85; s. 48, ch. 2006-217.

[1]Note.—Repealed July 1, 2007, by s. 48, ch. 2006-217.

PART IV.
POWERS OF TRUSTEES.

[1]737.401. Powers of trustee conferred by trust or by law.

The trustee has all powers conferred upon him or her by this part, unless limited in the trust instrument.

History: s. 1, ch. 74-106; s. 8, ch. 75-221; s. 9, ch. 77-344; s. 1042, ch. 97-102; s. 48, ch. 2006-217.

[1]Note.—Repealed July 1, 2007, by s. 48, ch. 2006-217.

[1]737.402. Powers of trustees conferred by this part.

(1) From the creation of the trust until final distribution of the assets from the trust, a trustee has the power to perform every act that a prudent trustee would perform for the purposes of the

trust, without court authorization, including, but not limited to, the powers specified in subsections (2) and (3) but subject to the limitations of subsection (4).

(2) Unless otherwise provided in the trust instrument, a trustee has the power:

(a) To collect, hold, and retain trust assets received from a settlor until disposition of the assets should be made. The assets may be retained even though they include an asset in which the trustee is personally interested.

(b) To hold without liability, other than that involved in holding property legal for investment of trust funds, any and all property received from or through the settlor of the trust, whether or not permissible for investment of funds of that particular trust, and any property lawfully coming into the hands of the trustees instead of or in substitution therefor, including the power to exchange capital stock of any bank or trust company, including capital stock of the corporate trustee, for capital stock in any registered bank holding company if the bank holding company is subject to the provisions of 12 U.S.C. ss. 1841 et seq., as amended, commonly known as the Bank Holding Company Act of 1956. This provision does not cover reinvestments of cash made by the trustee except for the purchase of fractional shares and the exercise of rights acquired in the exchange.

(c) To receive additions to the assets of the trust and, unless expressly provided to the contrary in the trust instrument, to incorporate those additions as part of the trust or hold the additions as a separate trust having terms identical to the terms of the existing trust.

(d) To continue or participate in the operation of any business or other enterprise and to effect incorporation, dissolution, or other change in the form of the organization of the business or enterprise.

(e) To acquire an undivided interest in a trust asset, including, but not limited to, a money market mutual fund, mutual fund, or common trust fund, in which asset the trustee holds an undivided interest in any trust capacity, including any money market or other mutual fund from which the trustee, any cotrustee, or any affiliate or associate of the trustee or cotrustee is entitled to receive reasonable compensation for providing necessary services as an investment adviser, portfolio manager, or servicing agent. A trustee, cotrustee, or affiliate or associate of the trustee or cotrustee may receive compensation for such services in addition to fees received for administering the trust, provided such compensation is fully disclosed in writing to all current income beneficiaries of the trust.

(f) To invest and reinvest trust assets in accordance with the provisions of the trust or as provided by law.

(g) If a bank, to deposit trust funds in another department of the same entity or in a bank that is affiliated with the trustee bank.

(h) To acquire or dispose of an asset for cash or on credit at a public or private sale; to manage, develop, improve, exchange, partition, change the character of, or abandon a trust asset or any interest in it; and to encumber, mortgage, or pledge a trust asset for a term within or extending beyond the term of the trust in connection with the exercise of any power vested in the trustee.

(i) To make ordinary or extraordinary repairs or alterations in buildings or other structures; to demolish any improvements; or to raze existing, or erect new, party walls or buildings.

(j) To subdivide, develop, or dedicate land to public use; to make, or obtain the vacation of, plats and adjust boundaries; to adjust differences in valuation on exchange or partition by giving or receiving consideration; or to dedicate easements to public use without consideration.

(k) To enter for any purpose into a lease as lessor or lessee with or without option to purchase or renew for a term within or extending beyond the term of the trust.

(l) To enter into a lease or arrangement for exploration and removal of minerals or other natural resources or enter into a pooling or unitization agreement.

(m) To grant an option involving disposition of a trust asset or to take an option for the acquisition of any asset.

(n) To vote a security, in person or by general or limited proxy, or not to vote a security.

(o) To pay calls, assessments, and any other sums chargeable or accruing against, or on account of, securities.

(p) To sell or exercise stock subscription or conversion rights and consent, directly or through a committee or other agent, to the reorganization, consolidation, merger, dissolution, or liquidation of a corporation or other business enterprise.

(q) To hold property in the name of a nominee or in other form without disclosure of the trust so that title to the property may pass by delivery, but the trustee is liable for any act of the nominee in connection with the property so held.

(r) To insure the assets of the trust against damage or loss and insure the trustee against liability with respect to third persons.

(s) To borrow money to be repaid from trust assets or otherwise, and to advance money for the protection of the trust and for all expenses, losses, and liabilities sustained in the administration of the trust or because of the holding or ownership of any trust assets, for which advances, with any interest, the trustee has a lien on the trust assets as against the beneficiary.

(t) To pay or contest any claim; to settle a claim by or against the trust by compromise, arbitration, or otherwise; and to release any claim belonging to the trust in whole or in part to the extent that the claim is uncollectible.

(u) To pay taxes, assessments, compensation of the trustee, and other expenses incurred in the collection, care, administration, and protection of the trust.

(v) To allocate items of income or expense to either trust income or principal, as provided by law.

(w) To pay any sum distributable to a beneficiary under legal disability to the beneficiary or by paying the sum for the use of the beneficiary either to a legal representative appointed by the court or, if none, to a relative; and, when income is directed to be paid to minors, apply and expend it for their benefit either with or without the intervention of a guardian.

(x) To effect distribution of property and money in divided or undivided interests and to adjust resulting differences in valuation.

(y) To employ persons, including attorneys, auditors, investment advisers, or agents, even if they are the trustee or associated with the trustee, to advise or assist the trustee in the performance of his or her administrative duties and to pay compensation and costs incurred in connection with such employment from the assets of the trust; to act without independent investigation upon their recommendations; and, instead of acting personally, to employ one or more agents to perform any act of administration, whether or not discretionary.

(z) 1. To prosecute or defend actions, claims, or proceedings, including appeals, for the protection of trust assets and of the trustee in the performance of his or her duties.

2. To employ attorneys and other agents to advise and assist the trustee in the exercise of any of the trustee's powers and to pay compensation and costs incurred in connection with such employment from the assets of the trust.

(aa) To execute and deliver all instruments that will accomplish or facilitate the exercise of the powers vested in the trustee.

(bb) To sever any trust on a fractional basis into two or more separate and identical trusts for any reason or to segregate by allocation to a separate account or trust a specific amount from, a portion of, or specific assets included in, the trust property of any trust, unless expressly provided to the contrary in the trust instrument. Income earned on a segregated amount, portion, or specific asset after the segregation is effective passes with the amount, portion, or asset segregated. Each separate trust must be held and administered upon the identical terms and conditions of the trust from which it was severed. Subject to the terms of the trust, the trustee may take into consideration differences in federal tax attributes and other pertinent factors in administering the trust property of any separate account or trust, in making applicable tax elections, and in making distributions. A separate trust created by severance must be treated as a separate trust for all purposes from the date on which the severance is effective. The effective date of the severance may be retroactive to a date before the date on which the trustee exercises such power.

(3) If a trustee has determined that the market value of a trust is less than $50,000 and that, relative to the costs of administering the trust, continuance pursuant to its existing terms will defeat or substantially impair the accomplishment of its purposes, the trustee may, in the trustee's sole discretion, terminate the trust and distribute the trust property, including principal and undistributed income, to the beneficiaries in a manner which conforms as nearly as possible to the intention of the settlor. The trustee may enter into agreements or make such other provisions that it deems necessary or appropriate to protect the interests of the beneficiaries and the trustee and to carry out the intent and purpose of the trust. The existence of a spendthrift or similar protective provision in the trust does not make this subsection inapplicable unless the trust instrument expressly provides that the trustee may not terminate the trust pursuant to this subsection.

(4) (a) Due to the inherent conflict of interest that exists between a trustee who is a beneficiary and other beneficiaries of the trust, unless the terms of a trust refer specifically to this subsection and provide expressly to the contrary, any power conferred upon a trustee (other than the settlor of a revocable or amendable trust or a decedent's or settlor's spouse who is the trustee of a testamentary or an inter vivos trust for which a marital deduction has been allowed):

1. To make discretionary distributions of either principal or income to or for the benefit of such trustee, except to provide for that trustee's health, education, maintenance, or support as described under Internal Revenue Code ss. 2041 and 2514;

2. To make discretionary allocations of receipts or expenses as between principal and income, unless such trustee acts in a fiduciary capacity whereby such trustee has no power to enlarge or shift any beneficial interest except as an incidental consequence of the discharge of such trustee's fiduciary duties;

3. To make discretionary distributions of either principal or income to satisfy any legal support obligations of such trustee; or

4. To exercise any other power, including the right to remove or to replace any trustee, so as to cause the powers enumerated in subparagraph 1., subparagraph 2., or subparagraph 3. to be exercised on behalf of, or for the benefit of, a beneficiary who is also a trustee, cannot be exercised by such trustee. Any of the foregoing proscribed powers that are conferred upon two or more trustees may be exercised by the trustees who are not so disqualified. If there is no trustee qualified to exercise such power, any party in interest, as defined in paragraph (c), may apply to a court of competent jurisdiction to appoint an independent trustee and such power may be exercised by the independent trustee appointed by the court.

(b) This subsection applies to:

1. Any trust executed after June 30, 1991, unless the terms of the trust refer specifically to this subsection and provide expressly to the contrary;

2. Any testamentary trust created under a will executed after June 30, 1991, unless the terms of the trust refer specifically to this subsection and provide expressly to the contrary; and

3. Any trust created under a document executed before July 1, 1991, unless:

a. If the trust is revocable or amendable, the settlor revokes or amends the trust at any time to provide otherwise; or

b. If the trust is irrevocable, all parties in interest, as defined in paragraph (c), elect affirmatively, in the manner prescribed in paragraph (d), not to be subject to the application of this subsection. Such election must be made on or before the later of July 1, 1994, or 3 years after the date on which the trust becomes irrevocable.

However, the provisions of this subsection neither create a new cause of action nor impair any existing cause of action which, in either case, relates to any power proscribed by paragraph (a) that was exercised before July 1, 1991.

(c) For the purpose of paragraph (a) or paragraph (b):

1. If the trust is revocable or amendable and the settlor is not incapacitated, the party in interest is the settlor.

2. If the trust is revocable or amendable and the settlor is incapacitated, the party in interest is the settlor's legal representative under applicable law or the settlor's donee under a durable power of attorney that is sufficient to grant such authority.

3. If the trust is not revocable or amendable, the parties in interest are:

a. Each trustee then serving;

b. Each income beneficiary then in existence or, if any such beneficiary has not attained majority or is otherwise incapacitated, the beneficiary's legal representative under applicable law or the beneficiary's donee under a durable power of attorney that is sufficient to grant such authority; and

c. Each remainder beneficiary then in existence or, if any such remainder beneficiary has not attained majority or is otherwise incapacitated, the beneficiary's legal representative under applicable law or the beneficiary's donee under a durable power of attorney that is sufficient to grant such authority.

(d) The affirmative election required under paragraph (b) must be made:

1. If the settlor is not incapacitated and the trust is revocable or amendable, through a revocation of or an amendment to the trust;

2. If the settlor is incapacitated and the trust is revocable or amendable, through a written declaration executed in the manner prescribed for the recordation of deeds in this state and delivered to the trustee; or

3. If the trust is not revocable or amendable, through a written declaration executed in the manner prescribed for the recordation of deeds in this state and delivered to the trustee.

(e) A person who has the right to remove or to replace a trustee does not possess nor may that person be deemed to possess, by virtue of having that right, the powers of the trustee that is subject to removal or to replacement.

History: s. 1, ch. 74-106; s. 8, ch. 75-221; s. 3, ch. 84-31; s. 1, ch. 84-179; s. 2, ch. 89-39; s. 3, ch. 91-61; s. 27, ch. 92-200; s. 15, ch. 95-401; s. 1043, ch. 97-102; s. 3, ch. 2005-85; s. 48, ch. 2006-217.

[1]Note.—Repealed July 1, 2007, by s. 48, ch. 2006-217.

Note.—Created from former s. 691.03.

[1]**737.4025. Powers of trustees conferred by this part in relation to environmental or human health laws affecting trust property or to trust property contaminated with hazardous or toxic substances; liability.**

(1) From the creation of a trust until final distribution of the assets from the trust, the trustee has, without court authorization, the powers specified in subsection (2).

(2) Unless otherwise provided in the trust instrument, a trustee has the power, acting reasonably and for the benefit of the beneficiaries:

(a) To inspect or investigate, or cause to be inspected or investigated, property held by the trustee, including interests in sole proprietorships, partnerships, or corporations and any assets owned by any such business entity for the purpose of determining compliance with an environmental law affecting that property or to respond to an actual or threatened violation of an environmental law affecting that property;

(b) To take, on behalf of the trust, any action necessary to prevent, abate, or otherwise remedy an actual or potential violation of an environmental law affecting property held by the trustee, either before or after initiation of an enforcement action by a governmental body;

(c) To refuse to accept property in trust if the trustee determines that any property to be donated or conveyed to the trustee either is contaminated with a hazardous substance or is being used or has been used for an activity directly or indirectly involving a hazardous substance, which circumstance could result in liability to the trust or trustee or otherwise impair the value of the assets to be held;

(d) To settle or compromise at any time any claim against the trust or trustee that may be asserted by a governmental body or private party which involves the alleged violation of an environmental law affecting property of any trust over which the trustee has responsibility;

(e) To disclaim any power granted by any document, statute, or rule of law which, in the sole judgment of the trustee, may cause the trustee to incur personal liability, or the trust to incur liability, under any environmental law;

(f) To decline to serve as a trustee, or having undertaken to serve as a trustee, to resign at any time, if the trustee believes that there is or may be a conflict of interest in its fiduciary capacity and in its individual capacity because of potential claims or liabilities that may be asserted against it on behalf of the trust by reason of the type or condition of the assets held; or

(g) To charge against the income and principal of the trust the cost of any inspection, investigation, review, abatement, response, cleanup, or remedial action that this section authorizes the trustee to take; and, in the event of the closing or termination of the trust or the transfer of the trust property to another trustee, to hold assets sufficient to cover the cost of cleaning up any known environmental problem.

(3) A trustee is not personally liable to any beneficiary or any other party for a decrease in value of assets in a trust by reason of the trustee's compliance or efforts to comply with an environmental law, specifically including any reporting requirement under that law.

(4) A trustee that acquires ownership or control of a vessel or other property without having owned, operated, or materially participated in the management of that vessel or property before assuming ownership or control as trustee is not considered an owner or operator for purposes of liability under chapter 376, chapter 403, or any other environmental law. A trustee that willfully, knowingly, or recklessly causes or exacerbates a release or threatened release of a hazardous substance is personally liable for the cost of the response, to the extent that the release or threatened release is attributable to the trustee's activities. This subsection does not preclude the filing of claims against the assets that constitute the trust held by the trustee or the filing of actions against the trustee in its representative capacity. In any such action, an award or judgment against the trustee must be satisfied only from the assets of the trust.

(5) Neither the acceptance by the trustee of the property nor a failure by the trustee to inspect or investigate the property creates any inference as to whether there is liability under an environmental law with respect to that property.

(6) For the purposes of this section, the term "environmental law" means a federal, state, or local law, rule, regulation, or ordinance that relates to protection of the environment or human health, and the term "hazardous substance" means a substance defined as hazardous or toxic, or any contaminant, pollutant, or constituent thereof, or otherwise regulated by an environmental law.

(7) This section does not apply to any trust created under a document executed before July 1, 1995, unless the trust is amendable and the settlor amends the trust at any time to incorporate the provisions of this section.

History: s. 19, ch. 95-401; s. 48, ch. 2006-217.

[1]Note.—Repealed July 1, 2007, by s. 48, ch. 2006-217.

[1]737.403. Power of court to permit deviation or to approve transactions involving conflict of interest.

(1) This part does not affect the power of the court to relieve a trustee for cause from any restrictions on the trustee's power that would otherwise be placed upon the trustee by the trust or by this part.

(a) Unless expressly provided to the contrary in the trust instrument, the court may permit a trustee:

1. To consolidate two or more trusts having similar terms into a single trust; or

2. To sever any trust on a fractional basis into two or more separate trusts for any reason, and to segregate by allocation to a separate account or trust a specific amount from, a portion of, or a specific asset included in the trust property of any trust to reflect a disclaimer, to reflect or result in differences in federal tax attributes, to satisfy any federal tax requirement, to make federal tax elections, to reduce potential generation-skipping transfer tax liability, or for any other tax planning purposes or other reasons. a. A separate trust created by severance must be treated as a separate trust for all purposes from the effective date on which the severance is effective. The effective date of the severance may be retroactive to a date before the date on which the court approves the severance.

b. A trustee who acts in good faith is not liable to any person for taking into consideration differences in federal tax attributes and other pertinent factors in administering the trust property of any separate account or trust, in making applicable tax elections, and making distributions pursuant to the terms of the separate trust.

(b) A trust created by consolidation or severance under this section must be held on terms and conditions identical to those before the consolidation or severance, or upon such terms or conditions that the aggregate interests of each beneficiary after the consolidation or severance will be reasonably equivalent to that beneficiary's aggregate interests before the consolidation or severance. In determining whether a beneficiary's aggregate interests are reasonably equivalent, the court shall consider the economic value of those interests to the extent that they can be valued, considering such actuarial factors as may be appropriate. If a beneficiary's interest cannot be valued with any reasonable degree of certainty because of the nature of the trust property, the terms of the trust, or other reasons, the court shall base the determination upon such other factors as are reasonable and appropriate under the facts and circumstances applicable to that particular trust, including the purposes of the trust.

(c) The terms of any trust before consolidation or a severance under paragraph (a) which permit qualification of that trust for an applicable federal tax deduction, exclusion, election, exemption, or other special federal tax status must remain identical in the consolidated trust or in each of the separate trusts created by severance.

(d) Income earned on a consolidated or severed amount, portion, or specific asset after the consolidation or severance is effective passes with that amount, portion, or specific asset.

(2) If the duty of the trustee and the trustee's individual interest or his or her interest as trustee of another trust conflict in the exercise of a trust power, the power may be exercised only by court authorization. Under this section, personal profit or advantage to an affiliated or subsidiary company or association is personal profit to any corporate trustee. Court authorization is not required for any of the following:

(a) The exercise of any power described in s. 737.402(2)(a), (e), (g), (s), or (y);

(b) The exercise of any power for which the trust instrument acknowledges the trustee's conflict of interest and expressly authorizes the exercise of that power notwithstanding the conflict;

(c) The exercise of any power consented to in writing by a settlor of the trust while the settlor holds the right of revocation of the trust;

(d) The exercise of any power consented to in writing by each of the beneficiaries to whom the trustee is required to provide any annual or periodic accounting. Consent under this paragraph may be given by a person who represents the interest of the beneficiary under s. 731.303 or by the legal guardian of the beneficiary or, if there is no legal guardian, by the natural guardian of the beneficiary; or

(e) Payment of costs or attorney's fees incurred in any trust proceeding from the assets of the trust unless an action has been filed or defense asserted against the trustee based upon a breach of trust. Court authorization is not required if the action or defense is later withdrawn or dismissed by the party that is alleging a breach of trust or resolved without a determination by the court that the trustee has committed a breach of trust.

History: s. 1, ch. 74-106; s. 8, ch. 75-221; s. 16, ch. 95-401; s. 1044, ch. 97-102; s. 4, ch. 2005-85; s. 48, ch. 2006-217.

[1]Note.—Repealed July 1, 2007, by s. 48, ch. 2006-217.

[1]737.4031. Judicial modification of trusts.

(1) If the purposes of a trust have been fulfilled or have become illegal or impossible to fulfill or, if because of circumstances not known to or anticipated by the settlor, compliance with the terms of the trust would defeat or substantially impair the accomplishment of a material purpose of the trust or, if a material purpose of the trust no longer exists, upon the application of a trustee of the trust or any beneficiary a court at any time may modify the terms of a trust which is not then revocable to:

(a) Amend or change the terms of the trust, including terms governing distribution of the trust income or principal, or terms governing administration of the trust;

(b) Terminate the trust in whole or in part;

(c) Direct or permit the trustee to do acts that are not authorized or that are prohibited by the terms of the trust; or

(d) Prohibit the trustee from performing acts that are permitted or required by the terms of the trust.

(2) Upon the application of a trustee of the trust or any beneficiary, a trust which is not then revocable may be modified at any time by a court as provided in subsection (1), and without regard to the reasons for modification provided in subsection (1), if compliance with the terms of the trust is not in the best interest of the persons having a beneficial interest in the trust. (a) The court shall exercise its discretion to order a modification of the trust under this subsection in a manner that conforms to the extent possible with the intention of the settlor, taking into account the current circumstances and best interests of the beneficiaries.

(b) This subsection shall not apply to a trust created prior to January 1, 2001.

(c) This subsection shall not apply to a trust created after December 31, 2000, if:

1. Under the terms of the trust, all beneficial interests in the trust must vest or terminate within the period prescribed by the rule against perpetuities in s. 689.225(2), notwithstanding s. 689.225(2)(f).

2. The terms of the trust expressly prohibit judicial modification.

(d) Modification of a trust, as authorized in this subsection, is not prohibited by a provision in the trust instrument that prohibits amendment or revocation of the trust if the provision does not expressly prohibit judicial modification.

(3) In exercising its discretion to order a modification of a trust under this section, the court shall consider the terms and purposes of the trust, the facts and circumstances surrounding the creation of the trust, and extrinsic evidence relevant to the proposed modification.

(4) To the extent the interests of any person with a beneficial interest in the trust who is unborn or unascertained, whose identity is not then known for any reason, or who is a minor or under a legal disability are not represented by another beneficiary, such person shall be represented by the person's legal guardian, if any, or, if none, by a guardian ad litem appointed by the court upon the court's own motion or upon application by the trustee or any beneficiary.

(5) The court shall consider spendthrift provisions as a factor in making a decision whether to modify a trust under this section, but the court is not precluded from exercising authority to modify the trust because the trust contains spendthrift provisions.

(6) For purposes of this section:

(a) "Beneficiary" means:

1. All current income or principal beneficiaries, whether the beneficiaries' beneficial interests are discretionary or mandatory.

2. All reasonably ascertainable beneficiaries if all current income interests immediately terminated, determined as if any power of appointment over the trust assets were not exercised.

(b) "Trust" means trust as defined in s. 731.201.

(c) A trust is revocable if revocable by the settlor alone or in conjunction with any other person. A trust is not revocable for purposes of this section if revocable by the settlor only with the consent of all persons having a beneficial interest in the property.

(d) A trust which is revocable shall be treated as created when the right of revocation terminates.

(7) The provisions of this section are in addition to, and not in derogation of, rights under the common law to modify, amend, or revoke trusts.

History: s. 7, ch. 2000-245; s. 48, ch. 2006-217.

¹Note.—Repealed July 1, 2007, by s. 48, ch. 2006-217.

¹737.4032. Nonjudicial modification of trusts.

(1) A trust which is not revocable may be modified at any time after the settlor's death, upon the unanimous agreement of the trustee and all beneficiaries of the trust, to:

(a) Amend or change the terms of the trust, including terms governing distribution of the trust income or principal or terms governing administration of the trust;

(b) Terminate the trust in whole or in part;

(c) Direct or permit the trustee to do acts that are not authorized or that are prohibited by the terms of the trust; or

(d) Prohibit the trustee from performing acts that are permitted or required by the terms of the trust.

(2) This section shall not apply to any trust for which a charitable deduction is allowed or allow-

able under the Internal Revenue Code until the termination of all charitable interests in the trust.

(3) An agreement to modify a trust under this section shall be binding upon a person with a beneficial interest in the trust who is unborn or unascertained, whose identity is not then known for any reason, or who is a minor or under a legal disability, to the extent that his or her interest is represented by another beneficiary having the same or greater quality of beneficial interest in the trust, but only to the extent there is no conflict of interest between such person and such beneficiary or among the persons represented.

(4) To the extent the interests of any person having a beneficial interest in a trust who is unborn or unascertained, whose identity is not then known for any reason, or who is a minor or under a legal disability are not represented by a beneficiary under subsection (3), such person shall be represented by the person's legal guardian if there is one or, if the person does not have a legal guardian, such person shall be represented by a guardian ad litem appointed by the court upon application by the trustee or any beneficiary. Unless the court requires otherwise, the guardian ad litem's decision whether to consent to modify the trust shall be binding upon any person represented by the guardian ad litem without seeking court approval.

(5) This section shall not apply to a trust created prior to January 1, 2001.

(6) This section shall not apply to a trust created after December 31, 2000, if, under the terms of the trust, all beneficial interests in the trust must vest or terminate within the period prescribed by the rule against perpetuities in s. 689.225(2), notwithstanding s. 689.225(2)(f), unless the terms of the trust expressly permit modification under this section.

(7) Modification of a trust as authorized in this section is not prohibited by a spendthrift clause, or by a provision in the trust instrument that prohibits amendment or revocation of the trust.

(8) For purposes of this section:

(a) "Beneficiary" means:

1. All current income or principal beneficiaries, whether the beneficiaries' beneficial interests are discretionary or mandatory.

2. All reasonably ascertainable beneficiaries if all current income interests immediately terminated, determined as if any power of appointment over the trust assets were not exercised.

(b) "Trust" means trust as defined in s. 731.201.

(c) A trust is revocable if revocable by the settlor alone or in conjunction with any other person. A trust is not revocable for purposes of this section if revocable by the settlor only with the consent of all persons having a beneficial interest in the property.

(d) A trust which is revocable shall be treated as created when the right of revocation terminates.

(9) The provisions of this section are in addition to, and not in derogation of, rights under the common law to modify, amend, or revoke trusts.

History: s. 7, ch. 2000-245; s. 48, ch. 2006-217.

¹Note.—Repealed July 1, 2007, by s. 48, ch. 2006-217.

¹737.4033. Costs and attorney's fees.

In all proceedings under s. 737.4031 or s. 737.4032, the court shall award taxable costs as in chancery actions, including attorney's fees and guardian ad litem fees, and such costs may be paid from the trust or as otherwise directed by the court.

History: s. 7, ch. 2000-245; s. 48, ch. 2006-217.

¹Note.—Repealed July 1, 2007, by s. 48, ch. 2006-217.

¹737.404. Powers exercisable by joint trustees; liability.

(1) Any power vested in three or more trustees may be exercised by a majority, but a trustee who has not joined in exercising a power is not liable to the beneficiaries or to others for the consequences of the exercise, and a dissenting trustee is not liable for the consequences of an action in which the dissenting trustee joins at the direction of the majority of the trustees if the dissent is expressed in writing to the other cotrustees at or before the time of the action.

(2) If two or more trustees are appointed to perform a trust and any of them is unable or refuses to accept the appointment or, having accepted, ceases to be a trustee, the surviving or remaining trustees shall perform the trust and succeed to all the powers, duties, and discretionary authority given to the trustees jointly.

(3) This section does not excuse a cotrustee from liability for failure either to participate in the administration of the trust or to attempt to prevent a breach of trust.

History: s. 1, ch. 74-106; s. 1045, ch. 97-102; s. 17, ch. 2003-154; s. 48, ch. 2006-217.

¹Note.—Repealed July 1, 2007, by s. 48, ch. 2006-217.

Note.—Created from former s. 691.04.

¹737.405. Third persons protected.

With respect to a third person dealing with a trustee or assisting a trustee in the conduct of a transaction, the existence of trust powers and their proper exercise by the trustee may be assumed without inquiry. The third person is not bound to inquire whether the trustee has power to act or is properly exercising the power. A third person without actual knowledge that the trustee is exceeding his or her powers or improperly exercising them is as fully protected in dealing with the trustee as if the trustee possessed and properly exercised the powers he or she purports to exercise. A third person is not bound to assure the proper application of trust assets paid or delivered to the trustee.

History: s. 1, ch. 74-106; s. 10, ch. 75-221; s. 10, ch. 77-344; s. 1046, ch. 97-102; s. 48, ch. 2006-217.

¹Note.—Repealed July 1, 2007, by s. 48, ch. 2006-217.

¹737.406. Application of this part.

Except as specifically provided in the trust, the provisions of this part apply to any trust established before or after the effective date of this part.

History: s. 1, ch. 74-106; s. 48, ch. 2006-217.

¹Note.—Repealed July 1, 2007, by s. 48, ch. 2006-217.

PART V.
CHARITABLE TRUSTS.

¹737.501. Definitions.

As used in this part:

(1) Unless otherwise indicated, section references relate to the Internal Revenue Code of 1954, in effect on January 1, 1971, and the references are to sections of Title 26 of the United States Code as in effect on that date.

(2) "Charitable organization" means an organization described in s. 501(c)(3) and exempt from tax under s. 501(a).

(3) "Private foundation trust" means a trust, including a trust described in s. 4947(a)(1), as defined in s. 509(a).

(4) "Split interest trust" means a trust for individual and charitable beneficiaries that is subject to the provisions of s. 4947(a)(2).

(5) "State attorney" means:

(a) The state attorney for the judicial circuit having original jurisdiction of the trust if the trust is registered.

(b) The state attorney for the judicial circuit where the trustee is domiciled or has his or her principal place of business if the trust is not registered.

(6) "Trust" means an express trust created by a trust instrument, including a will.

(7) "Trustee" means the trustee, trustees, person, or persons possessing a power or powers referred to in this part concerning a private foundation trust or a split interest trust.

History: s. 1, ch. 74-106; s. 12, ch. 75-221; s. 1047, ch. 97-102; s. 48, ch. 2006-217.

¹Note.—Repealed July 1, 2007, by s. 48, ch. 2006-217.

Note.—Created from former s. 691.11.

¹737.502. Application of this part.

Except as otherwise provided in the trust, the provisions of this part apply to all private foundation trusts and split interest trusts, whether created or established before or after November 1, 1971, and to all trust assets acquired by the trustee before or after November 1, 1971.

History: s. 1, ch. 74-106; s. 12, ch. 75-221; s. 48, ch. 2006-217.

¹Note.—Repealed July 1, 2007, by s. 48, ch. 2006-217.

Note.—Created from former s. 691.12.

¹737.503. Trustee of a private foundation trust or a split interest trust.

Except as provided in s. 737.505, the trustee of a private foundation trust or a split interest trust has the duties and powers conferred on him or her by this part.

History: s. 1, ch. 74-106; s. 12, ch. 75-221; s. 1048, ch. 97-102; s. 48, ch. 2006-217.

¹737.504. Powers and duties of trustee of a private foundation trust or a split interest trust.

(1) In the exercise of his or her powers, including the powers granted by this part, a trustee has a duty to act with due regard to his or her obligation as a fiduciary, including a duty not to exercise any power in such a way as to:

(a) Deprive the trust of an otherwise available tax exemption, deduction, or credit for tax purposes.

(b) Deprive a donor of a trust asset or tax deduction or credit.

(c) Operate to impose a tax upon a donor, trust, or other person.

"Tax" includes, but is not limited to, any federal, state, or local excise, income, gift, estate, or inheritance tax.

(2) Except as provided in s. 737.505, a trustee of a private foundation trust shall make distributions at such time and in such manner as not to subject the trust to tax under s. 4942.

(3) Except as provided in subsection (4) and in s. 737.505, a trustee of a private foundation trust, or a split interest trust to the extent that the split interest trust is subject to the provisions of s. 4947(a)(2), in the exercise of his or her powers shall not:

(a) Engage in any act of self-dealing as defined in s. 4941(d).

(b) Retain any excess business holdings as defined in s. 4943(c).

(c) Make any investments in a manner that subjects the foundation to tax under s. 4944.

(d) Make any taxable expenditures as defined in s. 4945(d).

(4) Paragraphs (3)(b) and (c) shall not apply to a split interest trust if:

(a) All the income interest, and none of the remainder interest, of the trust is devoted solely to one or more of the purposes described in s. 170(c)(2)(B), and all amounts in the trust for which a deduction was allowed under s. 170, s. 545(b)(2), s. 556(b)(2), s. 642(c), s. 2055, s. 2106(a)(2), or s. 2522 have an aggregate fair market value of not more than 60 percent of the aggregate fair market value of all amounts in the trust; or

(b) A deduction was allowed under s. 170, s. 545(b)(2), s. 556(b)(2), s. 642(c), s. 2055, s. 2106(a)(2), or s. 2522 for amounts payable under the terms of the trust to every remainder beneficiary, but not to any income beneficiary.

History: s. 1, ch. 74-106; s. 12, ch. 75-221; s. 1, ch. 77-174; s. 1049, ch. 97-102; s. 48, ch. 2006-217.

¹737.505. Notice that this part does not apply.

In the case of a power to make distributions, if the trustee determines that the governing instrument contains provisions that are more restrictive than s. 737.504(2), or if the trust contains other powers, inconsistent with the provisions of s. 737.504(3) that specifically direct acts by the trustee, the trustee shall notify the state attorney within 6 months after November 1, 1971, or when the trust becomes subject to this part, whichever last occurs. Section 737.504 shall not apply to any trust for which notice has been given unless the trust is amended to comply with the terms of this part.

History: s. 1, ch. 74-106; s. 12, ch. 75-221; s. 48, ch. 2006-217.

¹737.506. Power to amend trust instrument.

(1) In the case of a trust that is solely for a named charitable organization or organizations and for which the trustee does not possess any discretion concerning the distribution of income or principal among two or more such organizations, the trustee may amend the governing instrument to comply with the provisions of s. 737.504(2) with the consent of the named charitable organization or organizations.

(2) In the case of a charitable trust that is not subject to the provisions of subsection (1), the trustee may amend the governing instrument to comply with the provisions of s. 737.504(2) with the consent of the state attorney.

History: s. 1, ch. 74-106; s. 12, ch. 75-221; s. 48, ch. 2006-217.

[1]Note.—Repealed July 1, 2007, by s. 48, ch. 2006-217.

Note.—Created from former s. 691.16.

[1]737.507. Power of court to permit deviation.

This part does not affect the power of a court to relieve a trustee from any restrictions on his or her powers and duties that are placed upon him or her by the governing instrument or applicable law for cause shown and upon complaint of the trustee, state attorney, or an affected beneficiary and notice to the affected parties.

History: s. 1, ch. 74-106; s. 12, ch. 75-221; s. 1050, ch. 97-102; s. 48, ch. 2006-217.

[1]Note.—Repealed July 1, 2007, by s. 48, ch. 2006-217.

Note.—Created from former s. 691.17.

[1]737.508. Release; property and persons affected; manner of effecting.

(1) The trustee of a trust, all of the unexpired interests in which are devoted to one or more charitable purposes, may release a power to select charitable donees unless the creating instrument provides otherwise.

(2) The release of a power to select charitable donees may apply to all or any part of the property subject to the power and may reduce or limit the charitable organizations, or classes of charitable organizations, in whose favor the power is exercisable.

(3) A release shall be effected by a duly acknowledged written instrument signed by the trustee and delivered as provided in subsection (4).

(4) Delivery of a release shall be accomplished as follows:

(a) If the release is accomplished by specifying a charitable organization or organizations as beneficiary or beneficiaries of the trust, by delivery of a copy of the release to each designated charitable organization.

(b) If the release is accomplished by reducing the class of permissible charitable organizations, by delivery of a copy of the release to the state attorney.

(5) If a release is accomplished by specifying a public charitable organization or organizations as beneficiary or beneficiaries of the trust, the trust at all times thereafter shall be operated exclusively for the benefit of, and be supervised by, the specified public charitable organization or organizations.

History: s. 1, ch. 74-106; s. 12, ch. 75-221; s. 48, ch. 2006-217.

[1]Note.—Repealed July 1, 2007, by s. 48, ch. 2006-217.

Note.—Created from former s. 691.18.

[1]737.509. Election to come under this part.

With the consent of that organization or organizations, a trustee of a trust for the benefit of a public charitable organization or organizations may come under s. 737.508(5) by filing with the state attorney an election, accompanied by the proof of required consent. Thereafter the trust shall be subject to ss. 737.508(5) and 737.510.

History: s. 1, ch. 74-106; s. 12, ch. 75-221; s. 48, ch. 2006-217.

[1]Note.—Repealed July 1, 2007, by s. 48, ch. 2006-217.

Note.—Created from former s. 691.19.

[1]737.510. Supervision by public charitable organization.

(1) The trustee of a trust subject to the supervision by a specified public charitable organization or organizations, as provided in s. 737.508(5) shall file with each specified charitable organization:

(a) A true copy of the governing instrument with a verified written report setting forth complete information concerning the nature of the assets and liabilities at the delivery of the release pursuant to s. 737.508(4), or the filing of the election under s. 737.509.

(b) An annual report within 4 ½ months following the close of each year setting forth a complete statement of receipts, disbursements, assets with cost and market value of each asset, and liabilities.

(c) Such other information as may be necessary to compel proper administration of the trust.

(2) By delivery of the release or execution of the election, as the case may be, the trustee and each specified public charitable organization, by accepting delivery of the release as provided in s. 737.508(4), or by consenting to the election in

s. 737.509, agree that the public charitable organization or organizations shall have:

(a) The power and duty to compel the proper administration of the trust.

(b) The power to inspect the books, records, memoranda, papers, documents of title, and evidence of assets, liabilities, receipts, or disbursements in the possession or control of the trustee or other person having custody of the books and records.

(c) The power to require such other information as may be necessary to compel proper administration of the trust.

History: s. 1, ch. 74-106; s. 12, ch. 75-221; s. 48, ch. 2006-217.

[1]Note.—Repealed July 1, 2007, by s. 48, ch. 2006-217.

Note.—Created from former s. 691.20.

[1]737.511. Interpretation.

This part shall be interpreted to effectuate the intent of the state to preserve, foster, and encourage gifts to, or for the benefit of, charitable organizations.

History: s. 1, ch. 74-106; s. 12, ch. 75-221; s. 48, ch. 2006-217.

[1]Note.—Repealed July 1, 2007, by s. 48, ch. 2006-217.

Note.—Created from former s. 691.21.

[1]737.512. Inapplicability to certain trusts.

This part shall not apply to any trust to the extent that a court shall determine, in a proceeding initiated before November 1, 1971, that the application would be contrary to the terms of the instrument governing the trust and that it may not properly be changed to conform to the provisions of this part, but nothing herein shall be construed as creating or imposing on the trustee of any trust any obligation to initiate a proceeding to obtain any court determination with respect to the application of the provisions of this part.

History: s. 1, ch. 74-106; s. 12, ch. 75-221; s. 48, ch. 2006-217.

[1]Note.—Repealed July 1, 2007, by s. 48, ch. 2006-217.

Note.—Created from former s. 691.22.

PART VI.
RULES OF CONSTRUCTION.

[1]737.6035. Antilapse; deceased trust beneficiary; class gifts.

Unless a contrary intention appears in the inter vivos trust:

(1) If a beneficiary of an inter vivos trust who is a grandparent, or a lineal descendant of a grandparent, of the grantor:

(a) Is dead at the time of the execution of the inter vivos trust or at the termination of a trust interest created by an inter vivos trust;

(b) Fails to survive the grantor; or

(c) Is required by the inter vivos trust or by operation of law to be treated as having predeceased the grantor;

then the descendants of the trust beneficiary take per stirpes in place of the deceased beneficiary. A person who would have been a trust beneficiary under a class gift if that person had survived the grantor shall be a trust beneficiary for purposes of this section regardless of whether that person died before or after the execution of the inter vivos trust.

(2) If a trust beneficiary of an inter vivos trust who is not a grandparent, or a descendant of a grandparent, of the grantor:

(a) Is dead at the time of the execution of the inter vivos trust or at the termination of a trust interest created in an inter vivos trust;

(b) Fails to survive the grantor; or

(c) Is required by the inter vivos trust or by operation of law to be treated as having predeceased the grantor;

then the trust disposition to the trust beneficiary shall lapse unless an intention to substitute another appears in the inter vivos trust.

(3) This section shall apply to all inter vivos trusts and amendments to those trusts executed on or after the effective date of this section.

History: s. 18, ch. 2003-154; s. 48, ch. 2006-217.

[1]Note.—Repealed July 1, 2007, by s. 48, ch. 2006-217.

[1]737.621. Rules of construction; general provisions.

The intention of the grantor as expressed in the trust controls the legal effect of the dispositions therein made. The rules of construction as expressed in this part shall apply unless a contrary intention is indicated by the terms of the trust.

History: s. 16, ch. 93-257; s. 48, ch. 2006-217.

[1]Note.—Repealed July 1, 2007, by s. 48, ch. 2006-217.

[1]737.622. Change in securities; accessions; nonademption.

A gift of specific securities, rather than their equivalent value, shall entitle the beneficiary only to:

(1) As much of the gifted securities of the same issuer held by the trust estate at the time of the occurrence of the event entitling the beneficiary to distribution.

(2) Any additional or other securities of the same issuer held by the trust estate because of action initiated by the issuer, excluding any acquired by exercise of purchase options.

(3) Securities of another issuer held by the trust estate as a result of a merger, consolidation, reorganization, or other similar action initiated by the original issuer.

History: s. 16, ch. 93-257; s. 48, ch. 2006-217.

[1]Note.—Repealed July 1, 2007, by s. 48, ch. 2006-217.

[1]737.623. Construction of generic terms.

Adopted persons and persons born out of wedlock are included in class gift terminology and terms of relationship, in accordance with rules for determining relationships for purposes of intestate succession.

History: s. 16, ch. 93-257; s. 48, ch. 2006-217.

[1]Note.—Repealed July 1, 2007, by s. 48, ch. 2006-217.

[1]737.624. Gifts to be per stirpes.

Unless the trust instrument provides otherwise, all class gifts shall be per stirpes.

History: s. 16, ch. 93-257; s. 48, ch. 2006-217.

[1]Note.—Repealed July 1, 2007, by s. 48, ch. 2006-217.

[1]737.625. Killer not entitled to receive property or other benefits by reason of victim's death.

(1) A beneficiary of a trust who unlawfully and intentionally kills or unlawfully and intentionally participates in procuring the death of the grantor or another person upon whose death such ben-eficiary's interest depends, shall not be entitled to any trust interest, including homestead, dependent upon the victim's death, and such interest shall devolve as though the killer had predeceased the victim.

(2) A final judgment of conviction of murder in any degree is conclusive for the purposes of this section. In the absence of a murder conviction in any degree, the court may determine by the greater weight of the evidence whether the killing was unlawful and intentional for purposes of this section.

History: s. 16, ch. 93-257; s. 5, ch. 2000-245; s. 48, ch. 2006-217.

[1]Note.—Repealed July 1, 2007, by s. 48, ch. 2006-217.

[1]737.626. Evidence as to death or status.

In proceedings concerning trusts, this section relating to determination of death and status is applicable:

(1) An authenticated copy of a death certificate issued by an official or agency of the place where the death purportedly occurred is prima facie evidence of the fact, place, date, and time of death and the identity of the decedent.

(2) A copy of any record or report of a governmental agency, domestic or foreign, that a person is alive, missing, detained, or, from the facts related, presumed dead is prima facie evidence of the status and of the dates, circumstances, and places disclosed by the record or report.

(3) A person who is absent from the place of his or her last known domicile for a continuous period of 5 years and whose absence is not satisfactorily explained after diligent search and inquiry is presumed to be dead. The person's death is presumed to have occurred at the end of the period unless there is evidence establishing that death occurred earlier.

(4) This section does not preclude the establishment of death by direct or circumstantial evidence prior to expiration of the 5-year time period set forth in subsection (3).

History: s. 6, ch. 2000-245; s. 48, ch. 2006-217.

[1]Note.—Repealed July 1, 2007, by s. 48, ch. 2006-217.

[1]737.627. Costs and attorney's fees.

(1) In all actions for breach of fiduciary duty or challenging the exercise of, or failure to exercise, a trustee's powers, the court shall award taxable costs as in chancery actions, including attorney's fees.

(2) When awarding taxable costs, including attorney's fees, under this section, the court, in its discretion, may direct payment from a party's interest, if any, in the trust or enter a judgment which may be satisfied from other property of the party, or both.

(3) This section shall apply to all proceedings described in subsection (1) commenced after the effective date of this act, without regard to the date the trust was created or the date of the settlor's death.

History: s. 16, ch. 93-257; s. 19, ch. 2003-154; s. 48, ch. 2006-217.

[1]Note.—Repealed July 1, 2007, by s. 48, ch. 2006-217.

CHAPTER 738.
PRINCIPAL AND INCOME

738.101. Short title.

This chapter may be cited as the "Florida Uniform Principal and Income Act."

History.
S. 1, ch. 2002-42.

738.102. Definitions.

As used in this chapter, the term:

(1) "Accounting period" means a calendar year unless another 12-month period is selected by a fiduciary. The term includes a portion of a calendar year or other 12-month period that begins when an income interest begins or ends when an income interest ends.

(2) "Beneficiary" means, in the case of a decedent's estate, an heir or devisee and, in the case of a trust, an income beneficiary or a remainder beneficiary.

(3) "Carrying value" means the fair market value at the time the assets are received by the fiduciary. For the estates of decedents and trusts described in s. 733.707(3), after the grantor's death, the assets are considered received as of the date of death. If there is a change in fiduciaries, a majority of the continuing fiduciaries may elect to adjust the carrying values to reflect the fair market value of the assets at the beginning of their administration. If such election is made, it must be reflected on the first accounting filed after the election. For assets acquired during the administration of the estate or trust, the carrying value is equal to the acquisition costs of the asset.

(4) "Fiduciary" means a personal representative or a trustee. The term includes an executor, administrator, successor personal representative, special administrator, or a person performing substantially the same function.

(5) "Income" means money or property that a fiduciary receives as current return from a principal asset. The term includes a portion of receipts from a sale, exchange, or liquidation of a principal asset, to the extent provided in ss. 738.401-738.403 and s. 738.503.

(6) "Income beneficiary" means a person to whom net income of a trust is or may be payable.

(7) "Income interest" means the right of an income beneficiary to receive all or part of net income, whether the terms of the trust require the net income to be distributed or authorize the net income to be distributed in the trustee's discretion.

(8) "Mandatory income interest" means the right of an income beneficiary to receive net income that the terms of the trust require the fiduciary to distribute.

(9) "Net income" means the total receipts allocated to income during an accounting period minus the disbursements made from income during the period, plus or minus transfers under this chapter to or from income during the period.

(10) "Person" means an individual, corporation, business trust, estate, trust, partnership, limited liability company, association, joint venture, public corporation, or any other legal or commercial entity or a government or governmental subdivision, agency, or instrumentality.

(11) "Principal" means property held in trust for distribution to a remainder beneficiary when the trust terminates.

(12) "Remainder beneficiary" means a person entitled to receive principal when an income interest ends.

(13) "Terms of a trust" means the manifestation of the intent of a grantor or decedent with respect to the trust, expressed in a manner that admits of its proof in a judicial proceeding, whether by written or spoken words or by conduct.

(14) "Trustee" includes an original, additional, or successor trustee, whether or not appointed or confirmed by a court.

History.
S. 1, ch. 2002-42; s. 2, ch. 2012-49, eff. Jan. 1, 2013.

738.103. Fiduciary duties; general principles.

(1) In allocating receipts and disbursements to or between principal and income, and with respect to any matter within the scope of ss. 738.201 and 738.202 and ss. 738.301-738.303, a fiduciary:

(a) Shall administer a trust or estate in accordance with the terms of the trust or the will, even if there is a different provision in this chapter.

(b) May administer a trust or estate by the exercise of a discretionary power of administration given to the fiduciary by the terms of the trust or the will, even if the exercise of the power produces a result different from a result required or permitted by this chapter.

(c) Shall administer a trust or estate in accordance with this chapter if the terms of the trust or the will do not contain a different provision or do not give the fiduciary a discretionary power of administration.

(d) Shall add a receipt or charge a disbursement to principal to the extent the terms of the trust and this chapter do not provide a rule for allocating the receipt or disbursement to or between principal and income.

(2) In exercising the power to adjust under s. 738.104(1) or a discretionary power of administration regarding a matter within the scope of this chapter, whether granted by the terms of a trust, a will, or this chapter, a fiduciary shall administer a trust or estate impartially, based on what is fair and reasonable to all of the beneficiaries, except to the extent the terms of

the trust or the will clearly manifest an intention that the fiduciary shall or may favor one or more of the beneficiaries. A determination in accordance with this chapter is presumed to be fair and reasonable to all of the beneficiaries.

(3) Except as provided in s. 738.1041(9), this chapter pertains to the administration of a trust and is applicable to any trust that is administered in this state or under its law. This chapter also applies to any estate that is administered in this state unless the provision is limited in application to a trustee, rather than a fiduciary.

History.
S. 1, ch. 2002-42; s. 3, ch. 2012-49, eff. Jan. 1, 2013.

738.104. Trustee's power to adjust.

(1) A trustee may adjust between principal and income to the extent the trustee considers necessary if the trustee invests and manages trust assets as a prudent investor, the terms of the trust describe the amount that may or shall be distributed to a beneficiary by referring to the trust's income, and the trustee determines, after applying the rules in s. 738.103(1), that the trustee is unable to comply with s. 738.103(2).

(2) In deciding whether and to what extent to exercise the power conferred by subsection (1), a trustee shall consider all factors relevant to the trust and its beneficiaries, including the following factors to the extent they are relevant:

(a) The nature, purpose, and expected duration of the trust.

(b) The intent of the grantor.

(c) The identity and circumstances of the beneficiaries.

(d) The needs for liquidity, regularity of income, and preservation and appreciation of capital.

(e) The assets held in the trust; the extent to which the assets consist of financial assets, interests in closely held enterprises, tangible and intangible personal property, or real property; the extent to which an asset is used by a beneficiary; and whether an asset was purchased by the trustee or received from the grantor.

(f) The net amount allocated to income under the other sections of this chapter and the increases or decreases in the value of the principal assets, which the trustee may estimate as to assets for which market values are not readily available.

(g) Whether and to what extent the terms of the trust give the trustee the power to invade principal or accumulate income or prohibit the trustee from invading principal or accumulating income and the extent to which the trustee has exercised a power from time to time to invade principal or accumulate income.

(h) The actual and anticipated effect of economic conditions on principal and income and effects of inflation and deflation.

(i) The anticipated tax consequences of an adjustment.

(3) A trustee may not make an adjustment:

(a) That reduces the actuarial value of the income interest in a trust to which a person transfers property with the intent to qualify for a gift tax exclusion;

(b) That changes the amount payable to a beneficiary as a fixed annuity or a fixed fraction of the value of the trust assets;

(c) From any amount that is permanently set aside for charitable purposes under a will or the terms of a trust unless both income and principal are so set aside;

(d) If possessing or exercising the power to adjust causes an individual to be treated as the owner of all or part of the trust for income tax purposes and the individual would not be treated as the owner if the trustee did not possess the power to adjust;

(e) If possessing or exercising the power to adjust causes all or part of the trust assets to be included for estate tax purposes in the estate of an individual who has the power to remove a trustee or appoint a trustee, or both, and the assets would not be included in the estate of the individual if the trustee did not possess the power to adjust;

(f) If the trustee is a beneficiary of the trust; or

(g) If the trustee is not a beneficiary of the trust but the adjustment would benefit the trustee directly or indirectly, except that in the case of a trustee whose compensation for acting as trustee is based upon the value of trust assets, an adjustment that affects the value of trust assets shall not be deemed to benefit the trustee.

(4) If paragraph (3)(d), paragraph (3)(e), paragraph (3)(f), or paragraph (3)(g) applies to a trustee and there is more than one trustee, a cotrustee to whom the provision does not apply may make the adjustment unless the exercise of the power by the remaining trustee is not permitted by the terms of the trust.

(5) A trustee may release the entire power to adjust conferred by subsection (1) or may release only the power to adjust from income to principal or the power to adjust from principal to income if the trustee is uncertain about whether possessing or exercising the power will cause a result described in paragraphs (3)(a)-(e) or paragraph (3)(g) or if the trustee determines that possessing or exercising the power will or may deprive the trust of a tax benefit or impose a tax burden not described in subsection (3). A release under this subsection may be permanent or for a specified period, including a period measured by the life of an individual.

(6) Terms of a trust that limit a trustee's power to adjust between principal and income do not affect the application of this section unless it is clear from the terms of the trust that the terms are intended to deny the trustee the power to adjust conferred by subsection (1).

(7) Nothing in this chapter is intended to create or imply a duty to make an adjustment and no inference of impropriety shall be made as a result of a trustee not exercising the power to adjust conferred by subsection (1).

(8) With respect to a trust in existence on January 1, 2003:

(a) A trustee shall not have the power to adjust under this section until the statement required in subsection (9) is provided and either no objection is made or any objection which is made has been terminated.

1. An objection is made if, within 60 days after the date of the statement required in subsection (9), a super majority of the eligible beneficiaries deliver to the trustee a written objection to the application of this section to such trust. An objection shall be deemed to be delivered to the trustee on the date the objection is mailed to the mailing address listed in the notice provided in subsection (9).

2. An objection is terminated upon the earlier of the receipt of consent from a super majority of eligible beneficiaries of the class that made the objection, or the resolution of the objection pursuant to paragraph (c).

(b) An objection or consent under this section may be executed by a legal representative or natural guardian of a beneficiary without the filing of any proceeding or approval of any court.

(c) If an objection is delivered to the trustee, then the trustee may petition the circuit court for an order quashing the objection and vesting in such trustee the power to adjust under this section. The burden will be on the objecting beneficiaries to prove that the power to adjust would be inequitable, illegal, or otherwise in contravention of the grantor's intent. The court may award costs and attorney's fees relating to the trustee's petition in the same manner as in chancery actions. When costs and attorney's fees are to be paid out of the trust, the court may, in its discretion, direct from which part of the trust they shall be paid.

(d) If no timely objection is made or if the trustee is vested with the power to adjust by court order, the trustee may thereafter exercise the power to adjust without providing notice of its intent to do so unless, in vesting the trustee with the power to adjust, the court determines that unusual circumstances require otherwise.

(e)1. If a trustee makes a good faith effort to comply with the notice provisions of subsection (9), but fails to deliver notice to one or more beneficiaries entitled to such notice, neither the validity of the notice required under this subsection nor the trustee's power to adjust under this section shall be affected until the trustee has actual notice that one or more beneficiaries entitled to notice were not notified. Until the trustee has actual notice of the notice deficiency, the trustee shall have all of the powers and protections granted a trustee with the power to adjust under this chapter.

2. When the trustee has actual notice that one or more beneficiaries entitled to notice under subsection (9) were not notified, the trustee's power to adjust under this section shall cease until all beneficiaries who are entitled to such notice, including those who were previously provided with such notice, are notified and given the opportunity to object as provided for under this subsection.

(f) The objection of a super majority of eligible beneficiaries under this subsection shall be valid for a period of 1 year after the date of the notice set forth in subsection (9). Upon expiration of the objection, the trustee may thereafter give a new notice under subsection (9).

(g) Nothing in this section is intended to create or imply a duty of the trustee of a trust existing on January 1, 2003, to seek a power to adjust pursuant to this subsection or to give the notice described in subsection (9) if the trustee does not desire to have a power to adjust under this section, and no inference of impropriety shall be made as the result of a trustee not seeking a power to adjust pursuant to this subsection.

(9)(a) A trustee of a trust in existence on January 1, 2003, that is not prohibited under subsection (3) from exercising the power to adjust shall, any time prior to initially exercising the power, provide to all eligible beneficiaries a statement containing the following:

1. The name, telephone number, street address, and mailing address of the trustee and of any individuals who may be contacted for further information;

2. A statement that unless a super majority of the eligible beneficiaries objects to the application of this section to the trust within 60 days after the date the statement pursuant to this subsection was served, s. 738.104 shall apply to the trust; and

3. A statement that, if s. 738.104 applies to the trust, the trustee will have the power to adjust between income and principal and that such a power may have an effect on the distributions to such beneficiary from the trust.

(b) The statement may contain information regarding a trustee's fiduciary obligations with respect to the power to adjust between income and principal under this section.

(c) The statement referred to in this subsection shall be served informally, in the manner provided in the Florida Rules of Civil Procedure relating to service of pleadings subsequent to the initial pleading. The statement may be served on a legal representative or natural guardian of a beneficiary without the filing of any proceeding or approval of any court.

(d) For purposes of subsection (8) and this subsection, the term: .

1. "Eligible beneficiaries" means:

a. If at the time the determination is made there are one or more beneficiaries described in s. 736.0103(14)(c), the beneficiaries described in s. 736.0103(14)(a) and (c); or

b. If there is no beneficiary described in s. 736.0103(14)(c), the beneficiaries described in s. 736.0103(14)(a) and (b).

2. "Super majority of the eligible beneficiaries" means:

a. If at the time the determination is made there are one or more beneficiaries described in s. 736.0103(14)(c), at least two-thirds in interest of the beneficiaries described in s. 736.0103(14)(a) or two-thirds in interest of the beneficiaries described in s. 736.0103(14)(c), if the interests of the beneficiaries are reasonably ascertainable; otherwise, it means two-thirds in number of either such class; or

b. If there is no beneficiary described in s. 736.0103(14)(c), at least two-thirds in interest of the beneficiaries described in s. 736.0103(14)(a) or two-thirds in interest of the beneficiaries described in s. 736.0103(14)(b), if the interests of the beneficiaries are reasonably ascertainable, otherwise, two-thirds in number of either such class.

(10) A trust exists on January 1, 2003, if it is not revocable on January 1, 2003. A trust is revocable if revocable by the grantor alone or in conjunction with any other person. A trust is not revocable for purposes of this section if revocable by the grantor only with the consent of all persons having a beneficial interest in the property.

History.
S. 1, ch. 2002-42; s. 1, ch. 2003-43; s. 5, ch. 2005-85; s. 40, ch. 2006-217, eff. July 1, 2007; s. 4, ch. 2012-49, eff. Jan. 1, 2013.

738.1041.   Total return unitrust.

(1) For purposes of this section, the term:

(a) "Average fair market value" means the average of the fair market values of assets held by the trust at the beginning of the current and each of the 2 preceding years, or for the entire term of the trust if there are less than 2 preceding years, and adjusted as follows:

1. If assets have been added to the trust during the years used to determine the average, the amount of each addition is added to all years in which such addition was not included.

2. If assets have been distributed from the trust during the years used to determine the average, other than in satisfaction of the unitrust amount, the amount of each distribution is subtracted from all years in which such distribution was not included.

(b) "Disinterested person" means a person who is not a related or subordinate party with respect to the person acting as trustee of the trust and excludes the grantor and any interested trustee.

(c) "Fair market value" means the fair market value of the assets held by the trust as otherwise determined under this chapter, reduced by all known noncontingent liabilities.

(d) "Income trust" means a trust, created by an inter vivos or a testamentary instrument, which directs or permits the trustee to distribute the net income of the trust to one or more persons, in fixed proportions or in amounts or proportions determined by the trustee and regardless of whether the trust directs or permits the trustee to distribute the principal of the trust to one or more such persons.

(e) "Interested distributee" means a person to whom distributions of income or principal can currently be made and who has the power to remove the existing trustee and designate as successor a person who may be a related or subordinate party with respect to such distributee.

(f) "Interested trustee" means an individual trustee to whom the net income or principal of the trust can currently be distributed or would be distributed if the trust were then to terminate and be distributed, any trustee whom an interested distributee has the power to remove and replace with a related or subordinate party, or an individual trustee whose legal obligation to support a beneficiary may be satisfied by distributions of income and principal of the trust.

(g) "Related or subordinate party" has the same meaning as provided in the Internal Revenue Code, 26 U.S.C. s. 672(c) or any successor provision thereof.

(h) "Unitrust amount" means the amount determined by multiplying the average fair market value of the assets as calculated in paragraph (a) by the percentage calculated under paragraph (2)(b).

(2) A trustee may, without court approval, convert an income trust to a total return unitrust, reconvert a total return unitrust to an income trust, or change the percentage used to calculate the unitrust amount or the method used to determine the fair market value of the trust if:

(a) The trustee adopts a written statement regarding trust distributions which provides:

1. In the case of a trust being administered as an income trust, that future distributions from the trust will be unitrust amounts rather than net income, and indicates the manner in which the unitrust amount will be calculated and the method in which the fair market value of the trust will be determined.

2. In the case of a trust being administered as a total return unitrust, that:

a. Future distributions from the trust will be net income rather than unitrust amounts; or

b. The percentage used to calculate the unitrust amount or the method used to determine the fair market value of the trust will be changed, and indicates the manner in which the new unitrust amount will be calculated and the method in which the new fair market value of the trust will be determined;

(b) The trustee determines the terms of the unitrust under one of the following methods:

1. A disinterested trustee determines, or if there is no trustee other than an interested trustee, the interested trustee appoints a disinterested person who, in its sole discretion but acting in a fiduciary capacity, determines for the interested trustee:

a. The percentage to be used to calculate the unitrust amount, provided the percentage used is not greater than 5 percent nor less than 3 percent;

b. The method to be used in determining the fair market value of the trust; and

c. Which assets, if any, are to be excluded in determining the unitrust amount; or

2. The interested trustee or disinterested trustee administers the trust such that:

a. The percentage used to calculate the unitrust amount is 50 percent of the rate as defined in the Internal Revenue Code, 26 U.S.C. s. 7520, in effect for the month the conversion under this section becomes effective and for each January thereafter; however, if the percentage calculated exceeds 5 percent, the unitrust percentage is 5 percent and if the percentage calculated is less than 3 percent, the unitrust percentage is 3 percent; and

b. The fair market value of the trust shall be determined at least annually on an asset-by-asset basis, reasonably and in good faith, in accordance with s. 738.202(5), except the following property shall not be included in determining the value of the trust:

(I) Any residential property or any tangible personal property that, as of the first business day of the current valuation year, one or more current beneficiaries of the trust have or have had the right to occupy, or have or have had the right to possess or control, other than in his or her capacity as trustee of the trust, and instead the right of occupancy or the right to possession and control is the unitrust amount with respect to such property; however, the unitrust amount must be adjusted to take into account partial distributions from or receipt into the trust of such property during the valuation year;

(II) Any asset specifically given to a beneficiary and the return on investment on such property, which return on investment shall be distributable to the beneficiary; or

(III) Any asset while held in a decedent's estate;

(c) The trustee sends written notice of its intention to take such action, along with copies of the written statement regarding trust distributions and this section, and, if applicable, the determinations of the trustee or the disinterested person to:

1. The grantor of the trust, if living.

2. All living persons who are currently receiving or eligible to receive distributions of income from the trust.

3. All living persons who would receive distributions of principal of the trust if the trust were to terminate at the time of giving such notice without regard to the exercise of any power of appointment, or, if the trust does not provide for its termination, all living persons who would receive or be eligible to receive distributions of income or principal of the trust if the persons identified in subparagraph 2. were deceased.

4. All persons acting as advisers or protectors of the trust.

Notice under this paragraph shall be served informally in the manner provided in the Florida Rules of Civil Procedure relating to service of pleadings subsequent to the initial pleading. Notice may be served on a legal representative or natural guardian of a person without filing any proceeding or approval of any court;

(d) At least one person receiving notice under each of subparagraphs (c)2. and 3. is legally competent; and

(e) No person receiving such notice objects, by written instrument delivered to the trustee, to the proposed action of the trustee or the determinations of the disinterested person within 60 days after service of such notice. An objection may be executed by a legal representative or natural guardian of a person without filing any proceeding or approval of any court.

(3) If a trustee desires to convert an income trust to a total return unitrust, reconvert a total return unitrust to an income trust, or change the percentage used to calculate the unitrust amount or the method used to determine a fair market value of the trust but does not have the ability to or elects not to do it under subsection (2), the trustee may petition the circuit court for such order as the trustee deems appropriate. In that event, the court, in its own discretion or on the petition of such trustee or any person having an income or remainder interest in the trust, may appoint a disinterested person who, acting in a fiduciary capacity, shall present such information to the court as is necessary for the court to make a determination hereunder.

(4) Following the conversion of an income trust to a total return unitrust, the trustee:

(a) Shall treat the unitrust amount as if it were net income of the trust for purposes of determining the amount available, from time to time, for distribution from the trust.

(b) May allocate to trust income for each taxable year of the trust, or portion thereof:

1. Net short-term capital gain described in the Internal Revenue Code, 26 U.S.C. s. 1222(5), for such year, or portion thereof, but only to the extent that the amount so allocated together with all other amounts allocated to trust income, as determined under the provisions of this chapter without regard to this section and s. 738.104, for such year, or portion thereof, does not exceed the unitrust amount for such year, or portion thereof.

2. Net long-term capital gain described in the Internal Revenue Code, 26 U.S.C. s. 1222(7), for such year, or portion thereof, but only to the extent that the amount so allocated together with all other amounts, including amounts described in subparagraph 1., allocated to trust income for such year, or portion thereof, does not exceed the unitrust amount for such year, or portion thereof.

(5) In administering a total return unitrust, the trustee may, in its sole discretion but subject to the provisions of the governing instrument, determine:

(a) The effective date of the conversion.

(b) The timing of distributions, including provisions for prorating a distribution for a short year in which a beneficiary's right to payments commences or ceases.

(c) Whether distributions are to be made in cash or in kind or partly in cash and partly in kind.

(d) If the trust is reconverted to an income trust, the effective date of such reconversion.

(e) Such other administrative issues as may be necessary or appropriate to carry out the purposes of this section.

(6) Conversion to a total return unitrust under this section does not affect any other provision of the governing instrument, if any, regarding distributions of principal.

(7) Any trustee or disinterested person who in good faith takes or fails to take any action under this section is not liable to any person affected by such action or inaction, regardless of whether such person received written notice as provided in this section or such person was under a legal disability at the time of the delivery of such notice. Such person's exclusive remedy is to obtain, under subsection (8), an order of the court directing the trustee to convert an income trust to a total return unitrust, to reconvert from a total return unitrust to an income trust, or to change the percentage used to calculate the unitrust amount. If a court determines that the trustee or disinterested person has not acted in good faith in taking or failing to take any action under this section, s. 738.105(3) applies.

(8) If a majority in interest of the income or remainder beneficiaries of an income trust has delivered to the trustee a written objection to the amount of the income distributions of the trust, and, if the trustee has failed to resolve the objection to the satisfaction of the objecting beneficiaries within 6 months after receipt of such written objection, the objecting beneficiaries may petition the court in accordance with subsection (3).

(9) This section pertains to the administration of a trust and is applicable to any trust that is administered in this state or under Florida law unless:

(a) The governing instrument reflects an intention that the current beneficiary or beneficiaries are to receive an amount other than a reasonable current return from the trust;

(b) The trust is a trust described in the Internal Revenue Code, 26 U.S.C. s. 170(f)(2)(B), s. 642(c)(5), s. 664(d), s. 2702(a)(3), or s. 2702(b);

(c) One or more persons to whom the trustee could distribute income have a power of withdrawal over the trust:

1. That is not subject to an ascertainable standard under the Internal Revenue Code, 26 U.S.C. s. 2041 or s. 2514, and exceeds in any calendar year the amount set forth in the Internal Revenue Code, 26 U.S.C. s. 2041(b)(2) or s. 2514(e); or

2. A power of withdrawal over the trust that can be exercised to discharge a duty of support he or she possesses; or

(d) The governing instrument expressly prohibits use of this section by specific reference to the section. A provision in the governing instrument that, "The provisions of section 738.1041, Florida Statutes, as amended, or any corresponding provision of future law, may not be used in the administration of this trust," or similar words reflecting such intent are sufficient to preclude the use of this section.

(10) The grantor of a trust may create an express total return unitrust that will be effective as provided in the trust instrument without requiring a conversion under this section.

(a) An express total return unitrust created by the grantor of the trust is treated as a unitrust only if the terms of the trust instrument contain all of the following provisions:

1. That distributions from the trust will be unitrust amounts and the manner in which the unitrust amount will be calculated; and

2. The percentage to be used to calculate the unitrust amount, provided the percentage used is not greater than 5 percent nor less than 3 percent.

(b) The trust instrument may also contain provisions specifying:

1. The method to be used in determining the fair market value of the trust, including whether to use an average fair market value or the fair market value of the assets held by the trust at the beginning of the current year; or

2. Which assets, if any, are to be excluded in determining the unitrust amount.

(c) This section establishes the method of determining the fair market value of the trust if the trust instrument is silent as to subparagraph (b)1., and to specify those assets, if any, which are to be excluded in determining the unitrust amount if the trust instrument is silent as to subparagraph (b)2.

History.
S. 1, ch. 2002-42; s. 2, ch. 2003-43; s. 6, ch. 2005-85; s. 41, ch. 2006-217, eff. July 1, 2007; s. 5, ch. 2012-49, eff. Jan. 1, 2013.

Editor's Notes.
The references to sections of the Internal Revenue Code, referred to in this section, are codified throughout Title 26 of the U.S.C.S.

738.105. Judicial control of discretionary powers.

(1) A court may not change a trustee's decision to exercise or not to exercise a discretionary power conferred by this chapter unless the court determines that the decision was an abuse of the trustee's discretion. A court may not determine that a trustee abused its discretion merely because the court would have exercised the discretion in a different manner or would not have exercised the discretion.

(2) The decisions to which subsection (1) applies include:

(a) A determination under s. 738.104(1) of whether and to what extent an amount should be transferred from principal to income or from income to principal.

(b) A determination of the factors that are relevant to the trust and trust beneficiaries, the extent to which such factors are relevant, and the weight, if any, to be given to the relevant factors, in deciding whether and to what extent to exercise the power conferred by s. 738.104(1).

(3) If a court determines that a trustee has abused its discretion, the remedy is to restore the income and remainder beneficiaries to the positions they would have occupied if the trustee had not abused its discretion, in accordance with the following:

(a) To the extent the abuse of discretion has resulted in no distribution to a beneficiary or a distribution that is too small, the court shall require the trustee to distribute from the trust to the beneficiary an amount the court determines will restore the beneficiary, in whole or in part, to his or her appropriate position.

(b) To the extent the abuse of discretion has resulted in a distribution to a beneficiary that is too large, the court shall restore the beneficiaries, the trust, or both, in whole or in part, to their appropriate positions by requiring the trustee to withhold an amount from one or more future distributions to the beneficiary who received the distribution that was too large or requiring that beneficiary to return some or all of the distribution to the trust.

(c) To the extent the court is unable, after applying paragraphs (a) and (b), to restore the beneficiaries

or the trust, or both, to the positions they would have occupied if the trustee had not abused its discretion, the court may require the trustee to pay an appropriate amount from its own funds to one or more of the beneficiaries or the trust or both.

(4) Upon the filing of a petition by the trustee, the court having jurisdiction over the trust shall determine whether a proposed exercise or nonexercise by the trustee of a discretionary power conferred by this chapter will result in an abuse of the trustee's discretion. If the petition describes the proposed exercise or nonexercise of the power and contains sufficient information to inform the beneficiaries of the reasons for the proposal, the facts upon which the trustee relies, and an explanation of how the income and remainder beneficiaries will be affected by the proposed exercise or nonexercise of the power, a beneficiary who challenges the proposed exercise or nonexercise has the burden of establishing that such exercise or nonexercise will result in an abuse of discretion.

(5) If an action is instituted alleging an abuse of discretion in the exercise or nonexercise of the power of adjustment conferred by s. 738.104(1) and the court determines that no abuse of discretion has occurred, the trustee's costs and attorney's fees incurred in defending the action shall be paid from the trust assets.

History.
S. 1, ch. 2002-42; s. 6, ch. 2012-49, eff. Jan. 1, 2013.

738.201. Determination and distribution of net income.

After a decedent dies, in the case of an estate, or after an income interest in a trust ends, the following rules apply:

(1) A fiduciary of an estate or of a terminating income interest shall determine the amount of net income and net principal receipts received from property specifically given to a beneficiary under ss. 738.301-738.706 and subsection (5). The fiduciary shall distribute the net income and net principal receipts to the beneficiary who is to receive the specific property.

(2) A fiduciary shall determine the remaining net income of a decedent's estate or a terminating income interest under ss. 738.301-738.706 and by:

(a) Including in net income all income from property used to discharge liabilities.

(b) Paying from income or principal, in the fiduciary's discretion, fees of attorneys, accountants, and fiduciaries; court costs and other expenses of administration; and interest on death taxes. The fiduciary may pay those expenses from income of property passing to a trust for which the fiduciary claims an estate tax marital or charitable deduction under the Internal Revenue Code or comparable law of any state only to the extent the payment of those expenses from income will not cause the reduction or loss of the deduction.

(c) Paying from principal all other disbursements made or incurred in connection with the settlement of a decedent's estate or the winding up of a terminating income interest, including debts, funeral expenses, disposition of remains, family allowances, and death taxes and related penalties that are apportioned to the estate or terminating income interest by the will, the terms of the trust, or applicable law.

(3) If a beneficiary who receives a pecuniary devise outright is also entitled to receive interest or any other amount on the devise under the terms of the will or trust, the fiduciary shall distribute the interest or other amount from net income determined under subsection (2) or from principal to the extent net income is insufficient.

(4) A fiduciary shall distribute the net income remaining after distributions required under subsections (1)-(3) in the manner described in s. 738.202 to all other beneficiaries, including a beneficiary who receives a pecuniary amount in trust, even if the beneficiary holds an unqualified power to withdraw assets from the trust or other presently exercisable general power of appointment over the trust.

(5) A fiduciary may not reduce principal or income receipts from property described in subsection (1) because of a payment described in s. 738.701 or s. 738.702 to the extent the will, the terms of the trust, or applicable law requires the fiduciary to make the payment from assets other than the property or to the extent the fiduciary recovers or expects to recover the payment from a third party. The net income and principal receipts from the property are determined by including all of the amounts the fiduciary receives or pays with respect to the property, whether those amounts accrued or became due before, on, or after the date of a decedent's death or an income interest's terminating event, and by making a reasonable provision for amounts the fiduciary believes the estate or terminating income interest may become obligated to pay after the property is distributed.

History.
S. 1, ch. 2002-42; s. 7, ch. 2012-49, eff. Jan. 1, 2013.

738.202. Distribution to residuary and remainder beneficiaries.

(1) Each beneficiary described in s. 738.201(4) is entitled to receive a portion of the net income remaining after the application of s. 738.201(1)-(3), which is equal to the beneficiary's fractional interest in undistributed principal assets, using carrying values as of the distribution date. If a fiduciary makes more than one distribution of assets to beneficiaries to whom this section applies, each beneficiary, including one who does not receive part of the distribution, is entitled, as of each distribution date, to the net income the fiduciary received after the date of death or terminating event or

earlier distribution date but has not distributed as of the current distribution date.

(2) In determining a beneficiary's share of net income, the following applies:

(a) The beneficiary is entitled to receive a portion of the net income equal to the beneficiary's fractional interest in the carrying value of the undistributed principal assets immediately before the distribution date, excluding the amount of unpaid liabilities.

(b) The beneficiary's fractional interest in the undistributed principal assets shall be calculated:

1. At the time the interest began and adjusted for any disproportionate distributions since the interest began;

2. By excluding any liabilities of the estate or trust from the calculation;

3. By also excluding property specifically given to a beneficiary and property required to pay pecuniary amounts not in trust; and

4. On the basis of the aggregate carrying value of those assets determined under subsection (1) as of the distribution date.

(c) If a disproportionate distribution of principal is made to any beneficiary, the respective fractional interests of all beneficiaries in the remaining underlying assets shall be recomputed by:

1. Adjusting the carrying value of the principal assets to their fair market value before the distribution;

2. Reducing the fractional interest of the recipient of the disproportionate distribution in the remaining principal assets by the fair market value of the principal distribution; and

3. Recomputing the fractional interests of all beneficiaries in the remaining principal assets based upon the now restated carrying values.

(3) If a fiduciary does not distribute all of the collected but undistributed net income to each person as of a distribution date, the fiduciary shall maintain appropriate records showing the interest of each beneficiary in that net income.

(4) A fiduciary may apply the provisions of this section, to the extent the fiduciary considers appropriate, to net gain or loss realized after the date of death or terminating event or earlier distribution date from the disposition of a principal asset if this section applies to the income from the asset.

(5) The carrying value or fair market value of trust assets shall be determined on an asset-by-asset basis and is conclusive if reasonable and determined in good faith. Determinations of fair market value based on appraisals performed within 2 years before or after the valuation date are presumed reasonable. The values of trust assets are conclusively presumed to be reasonable and determined in good faith unless proven otherwise in a proceeding commenced by or on behalf of a person interested in the trust within the time provided in s. 736.1008.

(6) All distributions to a beneficiary shall be valued based on their fair market value on the date of distribution.

History.
S. 1, ch. 2002-42; s. 3, ch. 2003-43; s. 42, ch. 2006-217, eff. July 1, 2007; s. 8, ch. 2012-49, eff. Jan. 1, 2013.

738.301. When right to income begins and ends.

An income beneficiary is entitled to net income from the date on which the income interest begins.

(1) An income interest begins on the date specified in the terms of the trust or, if no date is specified, on the date an asset becomes subject to a trust or successive income interest.

(2) An asset becomes subject to a trust:

(a) On the date the asset is transferred to the trust in the case of an asset that is transferred to a trust during the transferor's life;

(b) On the date of a testator's death in the case of an asset that becomes subject to a trust by reason of a will, even if there is an intervening period of administration of the testator's estate; or

(c) On the date of an individual's death in the case of an asset that is transferred to a fiduciary by a third party because of the individual's death.

(3) An asset becomes subject to a successive income interest on the day after the preceding income interest ends, as determined under subsection (4), even if there is an intervening period of administration to wind up the preceding income interest.

(4) An income interest ends on the day before an income beneficiary dies or another terminating event occurs, or on the last day of a period during which there is no beneficiary to whom a fiduciary may distribute income.

History.
S. 1, ch. 2002-42; s. 9, ch. 2012-49, eff. Jan. 1, 2013.

738.302. Apportionment of receipts and disbursements when decedent dies or income interest begins.

(1) A fiduciary shall allocate an income receipt or disbursement other than one to which s. 738.201(1) applies to principal if the due date of the receipt or disbursement occurs before a decedent dies in the case of an estate or before an income interest begins in the case of a trust or successive income interest.

(2) A fiduciary shall allocate an income receipt or disbursement to income if the due date of the receipt or disbursement occurs on or after the date on which a decedent dies or an income interest begins and the due date is a periodic due date. An income receipt or disbursement shall be treated as accruing from day to day if the due date of the receipt or disbursement is not periodic or the receipt or disbursement has no due date. The portion of the receipt or disbursement accruing before the date on which a decedent dies or an income interest begins shall be allocated to principal and the balance shall be allocated to income.

(3) An item of income or an obligation is due on the date the payor is required to make a payment. If a payment date is not stated, there is no due date for the purposes of this chapter. Distributions to shareholders or other owners from an entity to which s. 738.401 applies are deemed to be due on the date fixed by the entity for determining who is entitled to receive the distribution or, if no date is fixed, on the declaration date for the distribution. A due date is periodic for receipts or disbursements that shall be paid at regular intervals under a lease or an obligation to pay interest or if an entity customarily makes distributions at regular intervals.

(4) Nothing in this section shall prevent the application of s. 733.817 to apportion tax to the income recipient under this section.

History.
S. 1, ch. 2002-42; s. 10, ch. 2012-49, eff. Jan. 1, 2013.

738.303. Apportionment when income interest ends.

(1) For purposes of this section, "undistributed income" means net income received on or before the date on which an income interest ends. The term does not include an item of income or expense that is due or accrued or net income that has been added or is required to be added to principal under the terms of the trust. In the case of a trust being administered as a unitrust under s. 738.1041, the term "undistributed income" means the prorated unitrust amount computed on a daily basis through the date on which the income interest ends.

(2) When a mandatory income interest ends, the fiduciary shall pay to a mandatory income beneficiary who survives that date, or the estate of a deceased mandatory income beneficiary whose death causes the interest to end, the beneficiary's share of the undistributed income that is not disposed of under the terms of the trust unless the beneficiary has an unqualified power to revoke more than 5 percent of the trust immediately before the income interest ends. In the latter case, the undistributed income from the portion of the trust that may be revoked shall be added to principal.

(3) When a fiduciary's obligation to pay a fixed annuity or a fixed fraction of the value of the trust's assets ends, the fiduciary shall prorate the final payment if and to the extent required by applicable law to accomplish a purpose of the trust or its grantor relating to income, gift, estate, or other tax requirements.

History.
S. 1, ch. 2002-42; s. 7, ch. 2005-85; s. 11, ch. 2012-49, eff. Jan. 1, 2013.

738.401. Character of receipts.

(1) For purposes of this section, the term "entity" means a corporation, partnership, limited liability com-

pany, regulated investment company, real estate investment trust, common trust fund, or any other organization in which a fiduciary has an interest other than a trust or estate to which s. 738.402 applies, a business or activity to which s. 738.403 applies, or an asset-backed security to which s. 738.608 applies.

(2) Except as otherwise provided in this section, a fiduciary shall allocate to income money received from an entity.

(3) Except as otherwise provided in this section, a fiduciary shall allocate the following receipts from an entity to principal:

(a) Property other than money.

(b) Money received in one distribution or a series of related distributions in exchange for part or all of a trust's or estate's interest in the entity.

(c) Money received in total or partial liquidation of the entity.

(d) Money received from an entity that is a regulated investment company or a real estate investment trust if the money received represents short-term or long-term capital gain realized within the entity.

(e) Money received from an entity listed on a public stock exchange during any year of the trust or estate which exceeds 10 percent of the fair market value of the trust's or estate's interest in the entity on the first day of that year. The amount to be allocated to principal must be reduced to the extent that the cumulative distributions from the entity to the trust or estate allocated to income do not exceed a cumulative annual return of 3 percent of the fair market value of the interest in the entity at the beginning of each year or portion of a year for the number of years or portion of years in the period that the interest in the entity has been held by the trust or estate. If a trustee has exercised a power to adjust under s. 738.104 during any period the interest in the entity has been held by the trust, the trustee, in determining the total income distributions from that entity, must take into account the extent to which the exercise of that power resulted in income to the trust from that entity for that period. If the income of the trust for any period has been computed under s. 738.1041, the trustee, in determining the total income distributions from that entity for that period, must take into account the portion of the unitrust amount paid as a result of the ownership of the trust's interest in the entity for that period.

(4) If a fiduciary elects, or continues an election made by its predecessor, to reinvest dividends in shares of stock of a distributing corporation or fund, whether evidenced by new certificates or entries on the books of the distributing entity, the new shares retain their character as income.

(5) Money is received in partial liquidation:

(a) To the extent the entity, at or near the time of a distribution, indicates that such money is a distribution in partial liquidation; or

(b) To the extent the total amount of money and property received in a distribution or series of related distributions from an entity that is not listed on a public stock exchange exceeds 20 percent of the trust's or estate's pro rata share of the entity's gross assets, as shown by the entity's year-end financial statements immediately preceding the initial receipt. This subsection does not apply to an entity to which subsection (7) applies.

(6) Money may not be taken into account in determining any excess under paragraph (5)(b), to the extent that the cumulative distributions from the entity to the trust or the estate allocated to income do not exceed the greater of:

(a) A cumulative annual return of 3 percent of the entity's carrying value computed at the beginning of each period for the number of years or portion of years that the entity was held by the fiduciary. If a trustee has exercised a power to adjust under s. 738.104 during any period the interest in the entity has been held by the trust, the trustee, in determining the total income distributions from that entity, must take into account the extent to which exercise of the power resulted in income to the trust from that entity for that period. If the income of a trust for any period has been computed pursuant to s. 738.1041, the trustee, in determining the total income distributions from the entity for that period, must take into account the portion of the unitrust amount paid as a result of the ownership of the trust's interest in the entity for that period; or

(b) If the entity is treated as a partnership, subchapter S corporation, or a disregarded entity pursuant to the Internal Revenue Code of 1986, as amended, the amount of income tax attributable to the trust's or estate's ownership share of the entity, based on its pro rata share of the taxable income of the entity that distributes the money, for the number of years or portion of years that the interest in the entity was held by the fiduciary, calculated as if all of that tax was incurred by the fiduciary.

(7) The following applies to money or property received by a private trustee as a distribution from an investment entity described in this subsection:

(a) The trustee shall first treat as income of the trust all of the money or property received from the investment entity in the current year which would be considered income under this chapter if the trustee had directly held the trust's pro rata share of the assets of the investment entity. For this purpose, all distributions received in the current year must be aggregated.

(b) The trustee shall next treat as income of the trust any additional money or property received in the current year which would have been considered income in the prior 2 years under paragraph (a) if additional money or property had been received from the investment entity in any of those prior 2 years. The amount to be treated as income shall be reduced by any distributions of money or property made by the investment entity to the trust during the current and prior 2 years which were treated as income under this paragraph.

(c) The remainder of the distribution, if any, is treated as principal.

(d) As used in this subsection, the term:

1. "Investment entity" means an entity, other than a business activity conducted by the trustee described in s. 738.403 or an entity that is listed on a public stock exchange, which is treated as a partnership, subchapter S corporation, or disregarded entity pursuant to the Internal Revenue Code of 1986, as amended, and which normally derives 50 percent or more of its annual cumulative net income from interest, dividends, annuities, royalties, rental activity, or other passive investments, including income from the sale or exchange of such passive investments.

2. "Private trustee" means a trustee who is a natural person, but only if the trustee is unable to use the power to adjust between income and principal with respect to receipts from entities described in this subsection pursuant to s. 738.104. A bank, trust company, or other commercial trustee is not considered a private trustee.

(8) This section shall be applied before ss. 738.705 and 738.706 and does not modify or change any of the provisions of those sections.

History.
S. 1, ch. 2002-42; s. 4, ch. 2003-43; s. 8, ch. 2005-85; s. 12, ch. 2012-49, eff. Jan. 1, 2013.

738.402. Distribution from trust or estate.

A fiduciary shall allocate to income an amount received as a distribution of income from a trust or an estate in which the trust has an interest other than a purchased interest and allocate to principal an amount received as a distribution of principal from such a trust or estate. If a fiduciary purchases an interest in a trust that is an investment entity, or a decedent or donor transfers an interest in such a trust to a fiduciary, s. 738.401 or s. 738.608 applies to a receipt from the trust.

History.
S. 1, ch. 2002-42; s. 13, ch. 2012-49, eff. Jan. 1, 2013.

738.403. Business and other activities conducted by fiduciary.

(1) If a fiduciary who conducts a business or other activity determines that it is in the best interest of all the beneficiaries to account separately for the business or activity instead of accounting for the business or activity as part of the trust's or estate's general accounting records, the fiduciary may maintain separate accounting records for the transactions of the business or other activity, whether or not the assets of such business or activity are segregated from other trust or estate assets.

(2) A fiduciary who accounts separately for a business or other activity may determine the extent to which the net cash receipts of the business or activity must be retained for working capital, the acquisition or replacement of fixed assets, and other reasonably foreseeable needs of the business or activity, and the extent to which the remaining net cash receipts are accounted for as principal or income in the trust's or estate's general accounting records. If a fiduciary sells assets of the business or other activity, other than in the ordinary course of the business or activity, the fiduciary must account for the net amount received as principal in the trust's or estate's general accounting records to the extent the fiduciary determines that the amount received is no longer required in the conduct of the business.

(3) Activities for which a fiduciary may maintain separate accounting records include:

(a) Retail, manufacturing, service, and other traditional business activities.

(b) Farming.

(c) Raising and selling livestock and other animals.

(d) Management of rental properties.

(e) Extraction of minerals and other natural resources.

(f) Timber operations.

(g) Activities to which s. 738.607 applies.

History.
S. 1, ch. 2002-42; s. 14, ch. 2012-49, eff. Jan. 1, 2013.

738.501. Principal receipts.

A fiduciary shall allocate to principal:

(1) To the extent not allocated to income under this chapter, assets received from a donor during the donor's lifetime, a decedent's estate, a trust with a terminating income interest, or a payor under a contract naming the trust, estate, or fiduciary as beneficiary.

(2) Money or other property received from the sale, exchange, liquidation, or change in form of a principal asset, including realized profit, subject to this section.

(3) Amounts recovered from third parties to reimburse the trust or estate because of disbursements described in s. 738.702(1)(g) or for other reasons to the extent not based on the loss of income.

(4) Proceeds of property taken by eminent domain; however, a separate award made for the loss of income with respect to an accounting period during which a current income beneficiary had a mandatory income interest is income.

(5) Net income received in an accounting period during which there is no beneficiary to whom a fiduciary may or shall distribute income.

(6) Other receipts as provided in ss. 738.601-738.608.

History.
S. 1, ch. 2002-42; s. 15, ch. 2012-49, eff. Jan. 1, 2013.

738.502. Rental property.

If a fiduciary accounts for receipts from rental property pursuant to this section, the fiduciary shall allocate to income an amount received as rent of real or personal property, including an amount received for cancellation or renewal of a lease. An amount received as a refundable deposit, including a security deposit or a deposit that is to be applied as rent for future periods, must be added to principal and held subject to the terms of the lease and is not available for distribution to a beneficiary until the fiduciary's contractual obligations have been satisfied with respect to that amount.

History.
S. 1, ch. 2002-42; s. 16, ch. 2012-49, eff. Jan. 1, 2013.

738.503. Obligation to pay money.

(1) An amount received as interest, whether determined at a fixed, variable, or floating rate, on an obligation to pay money to the fiduciary, including an amount received as consideration for prepaying principal, shall be allocated to income without any provision for amortization of premium.

(2) Except as otherwise provided herein, a fiduciary shall allocate to principal an amount received from the sale, redemption, or other disposition of an obligation to pay money to the fiduciary.

(3) The increment in value of a bond or other obligation for the payment of money bearing no stated interest but payable at a future time in excess of the price at which it was issued or purchased, if purchased after issuance, is distributable as income. If the increment in value accrues and becomes payable pursuant to a fixed schedule of appreciation, it may be distributed to the beneficiary who was the income beneficiary at the time of increment from the first principal cash available or, if none is available, when the increment is realized by sale, redemption, or other disposition. If unrealized increment is distributed as income but out of principal, the principal must be reimbursed for the increment when realized. If, in the reasonable judgment of the fiduciary, exercised in good faith, the ultimate payment of the bond principal is in doubt, the fiduciary may withhold the payment of incremental interest to the income beneficiary.

(4) This section does not apply to an obligation to which s. 738.602, s. 738.603, s. 738.604, s. 738.605, s. 738.607, or s. 738.608 applies.

History.
S. 1, ch. 2002-42; s. 17, ch. 2012-49, eff. Jan. 1, 2013.

738.504. Insurance policies and similar contracts.

(1) Except as otherwise provided in subsection (2), a fiduciary shall allocate to principal the proceeds of a life insurance policy or other contract in which the trust, estate, or fiduciary is named as beneficiary, including a contract that insures the trust, estate, or fiduciary against loss for damage to, destruction of, or loss of title to a trust or estate asset. The fiduciary shall allocate dividends on an insurance policy to income if the premiums on the policy are paid from income and to principal if the premiums are paid from principal.

(2) A fiduciary shall allocate to income the proceeds of a contract that insures the fiduciary against loss of occupancy or other use by an income beneficiary, loss of income, or, subject to s. 738.403, loss of profits from a business.

(3) This section does not apply to a contract to which s. 738.602 applies.

History.
S. 1, ch. 2002-42; s. 18, ch. 2012-49, eff. Jan. 1, 2013.

738.601. Insubstantial allocations not required.

If a fiduciary determines that an allocation between principal and income required by s. 738.602, s. 738.603, s. 738.604, s. 738.605, or s. 738.608 is insubstantial, the fiduciary may allocate the entire amount to principal unless one of the circumstances described in s. 738.104(3) applies to the allocation. This power may be exercised by a cofiduciary under the circumstances described in s. 738.104(4) and may be released for the reasons and in the manner described in s. 738.104(5). An allocation is presumed to be insubstantial if:

(1) The amount of the allocation would increase or decrease net income in an accounting period, as determined before the allocation, by less than 10 percent; or

(2) The value of the asset producing the receipt for which the allocation would be made is less than 10 percent of the total value of the trust or estate assets at the beginning of the accounting period.

History.
S. 1, ch. 2002-42; s. 19, ch. 2012-49, eff. Jan. 1, 2013.

738.602. Payments from deferred compensation plans, annuities, and retirement plans or accounts.

(1) As used in this section, the term:

(a) "Fund" means a private or commercial annuity, an individual retirement account, an individual retirement annuity, a deferred compensation plan, a pension plan, a profit-sharing plan, a stock-bonus plan, an employee stock-ownership plan, or another similar arrangement in which federal income tax is deferred.

(b) "Income of the fund" means income that is determined according to subsection (2) or subsection (3).

(c) "Nonseparate account" means a fund for which the value of the participant's or account owner's right to receive benefits can be determined only by the occurrence of a date or event as defined in the instrument governing the fund.

(d) "Payment" means a distribution from a fund that a fiduciary may receive over a fixed number of years or during the life of one or more individuals because of services rendered or property transferred to the payor in exchange for future payments. The term includes a distribution made in money or property from the payor's general assets or from a fund created by the payor or payee.

(e) "Separate account" means a fund holding assets exclusively for the benefit of a participant or account owner and:

1. The value of such assets or the value of the separate account is ascertainable at any time; or

2. The administrator of the fund maintains records that show receipts and disbursements associated with such assets.

(2)(a) For a fund that is a separate account, income of the fund shall be determined:

1. As if the fund were a trust subject to the provisions of ss. 738.401-738.706; or

2. As a unitrust amount calculated by multiplying the fair market value of the fund as of the first day of the first accounting period and, thereafter, as of the last day of the accounting period that immediately precedes the accounting period during which a payment is received by the percentage determined in accordance with s. 738.1041(2)(b)2.a. The fiduciary shall determine such percentage as of the first month that the fiduciary's election to treat the income of the fund as a unitrust amount becomes effective. For purposes of this subparagraph, "fair market value" means the fair market value of the assets held in the fund as of the applicable valuation date determined as provided in this subparagraph. The fiduciary is not liable for good faith reliance upon any valuation supplied by the person or persons in possession of the fund. If the fiduciary makes or terminates an election under this subparagraph, the fiduciary shall make such disclosure in a trust disclosure document that satisfies the requirements of s. 736.1008(4)(a).

(b) The fiduciary may elect the method of determining the income of the fund pursuant to this subsection and may change the method of determining income of the fund for any future accounting period.

(3) For a fund that is a nonseparate account, income of the fund is a unitrust amount determined by calculating the present value of the right to receive the remaining payments under the Internal Revenue Code, 26 U.S.C. s. 7520, as of the first day of the accounting period and multiplying it by the percentage determined in accordance with s. 738.1041(2)(b)2.a. The fiduciary shall determine the unitrust amount as of the first month that the fiduciary's election to treat the income of the fund as a unitrust amount becomes effective.

(4) Except for those trusts described in subsection (5), the fiduciary shall allocate to income the lesser of the payment received from a fund or the income determined under subsection (2) or subsection (3). Any remaining amount of the payment shall be allocated to principal.

(5) For a trust that, in order to qualify for the estate or gift tax marital deduction under the Internal Revenue Code or comparable law of any state, entitles the spouse to all of the income of the trust, and the terms of the trust are silent as to the time and frequency for distribution of the income of the fund:

(a) For a fund that is a separate account, unless the spouse directs the fiduciary to leave the income of the fund in the fund, the fiduciary shall withdraw and pay to the spouse, at least annually:

1. All of the income of the fund determined in accordance with subparagraph (2)(a)1.; or

2. The income of the fund as a unitrust amount determined in accordance with subparagraph (2)(a)2.

(b) For a fund that is a nonseparate account, the fiduciary shall withdraw and pay to the spouse, at least annually, the income of the fund as a unitrust amount determined in accordance with subsection (3).

(6) This section does not apply to payments to which s. 738.603 applies.

History.
S. 1, ch. 2002-42; s. 1, ch. 2009-207, eff. July 1, 2009; s. 20, ch. 2012-49, eff. Jan. 1, 2013.

Editor's Notes.
Section 7520 of the Internal Revenue Code, referred to in this section, is codified as 26 U.S.C.S. § 7520.

738.603. Liquidating asset.

(1) For purposes of this section, the term "liquidating asset" means an asset the value of which will diminish or terminate because the asset is expected to produce receipts for a period of limited duration. The term includes a leasehold, patent, copyright, royalty right, and right to receive payments for more than 1 year under an arrangement that does not provide for the payment of interest on the unpaid balance. The term does not include a payment subject to s. 738.602, resources subject to s. 738.604, timber subject to s. 738.605, an activity subject to s. 738.607, an asset subject to s. 738.608, or any asset for which the fiduciary establishes a reserve for depreciation under s. 738.703.

(2) A fiduciary shall allocate to income 5 percent of the receipts from the carrying value of a liquidating asset and the balance to principal. Amounts allocated to principal shall reduce the carrying value of the liquidating asset, but not below zero. Amounts received in excess of the remaining carrying value must be allocated to principal.

History.
S. 1, ch. 2002-42; s. 21, ch. 2012-49, eff. Jan. 1, 2013.

738.604. Minerals, water, and other natural resources.

(1) If a fiduciary accounts for receipts from an interest in minerals or other natural resources pursuant to this section, the fiduciary shall allocate such receipts as follows:

(a) If received as nominal delay rental or nominal annual rent on a lease, a receipt shall be allocated to income.

(b) If received from a production payment, a receipt shall be allocated to income if and to the extent the agreement creating the production payment provides a factor for interest or its equivalent. The balance shall be allocated to principal.

(c) If an amount received as a royalty, shut-in-well payment, take-or-pay payment, bonus, or delay rental is more than nominal, 90 percent shall be allocated to principal and the balance to income.

(d) If an amount is received from a working interest or any other interest not provided for in paragraph (a), paragraph (b), or paragraph (c), 90 percent of the net amount received shall be allocated to principal and the balance to income.

(2) An amount received on account of an interest in water that is renewable shall be allocated to income. If the water is not renewable, 90 percent of the amount shall be allocated to principal and the balance to income.

(3) This chapter applies whether or not a decedent or donor was extracting minerals, water, or other natural resources before the interest became subject to the trust or estate.

(4) If a trust or estate owns an interest in minerals, water, or other natural resources on January 1, 2003, the fiduciary may allocate receipts from the interest as provided in this chapter or in the manner used by the fiduciary before January 1, 2003. If the trust or estate acquires an interest in minerals, water, or other natural resources after January 1, 2003, the fiduciary shall allocate receipts from the interest as provided in this chapter.

History.
S. 1, ch. 2002-42; s. 22, ch. 2012-49, eff. Jan. 1, 2013.

738.605. Timber.

(1) If a fiduciary accounts for receipts from the sale of timber and related products pursuant to this section, the fiduciary shall allocate such net receipts as follows:

(a) To income to the extent the amount of timber removed from the land does not exceed the rate of growth of the timber during the accounting periods in which a beneficiary has a mandatory income interest;

(b) To principal to the extent the amount of timber removed from the land exceeds the rate of growth of the timber or the net receipts are from the sale of standing timber;

(c) To or between income and principal if the net receipts are from the lease of timberland or from a contract to cut timber from land owned by a trust or estate by determining the amount of timber removed from the land under the lease or contract and applying the rules in paragraphs (a) and (b); or

(d) To principal to the extent advance payments, bonuses, and other payments are not allocated pursuant to paragraph (a), paragraph (b), or paragraph (c).

(2) In determining net receipts to be allocated pursuant to subsection (1), a fiduciary shall deduct and transfer to principal a reasonable amount for depletion.

(3) This chapter applies whether or not a decedent or donor was harvesting timber from the property before the property became subject to the trust or estate.

(4) If a trust or estate owns an interest in timberland on January 1, 2003, the fiduciary may allocate net receipts from the sale of timber and related products as provided in this chapter or in the manner used by the fiduciary before January 1, 2003. If the trust or estate acquires an interest in timberland after January 1, 2003, the fiduciary shall allocate net receipts from the sale of timber and related products as provided in this chapter.

History.
S. 1, ch. 2002-42; s. 23, ch. 2012-49, eff. Jan. 1, 2013.

738.606. Property not productive of income.

(1) If a marital deduction under the Internal Revenue Code or comparable law of any state is allowed for all or part of a trust the income of which must be distributed to the grantor's spouse and the assets of which consist substantially of property that does not provide the spouse with sufficient income from or use of the trust assets, and if the amounts the trustee transfers from principal to income under s. 738.104 and distributes to the spouse from principal pursuant to the terms of the trust are insufficient to provide the spouse with the beneficial enjoyment required to obtain the marital deduction, the spouse may require the trustee to make property productive of income, convert property within a reasonable time, or exercise the power conferred by ss. 738.104 and 738.1041. The trustee may decide which action or combination of actions to take.

(2) In cases not governed by subsection (1), proceeds from the sale or other disposition of an asset are principal without regard to the amount of income the asset produces during any accounting period.

History.
S. 1, ch. 2002-42; s. 24, ch. 2012-49, eff. Jan. 1, 2013.

738.607. Derivatives and options.

(1) For purposes of this section, "derivative" means a contract or financial instrument or a combination of contracts and financial instruments which gives a trust the right or obligation to participate in some or all changes in the price of a tangible or intangible asset or group of assets, or changes in a rate, an index of prices

or rates, or other market indicator for an asset or a group of assets.

(2) To the extent a fiduciary does not account under s. 738.403 for transactions in derivatives, the fiduciary shall allocate to principal receipts from and disbursements made in connection with those transactions.

(3) If a fiduciary grants an option to buy property from the trust or estate whether or not the trust or estate owns the property when the option is granted, grants an option that permits another person to sell property to the trust or estate, or acquires an option to buy property for the trust or estate or an option to sell an asset owned by the trust or estate, and the fiduciary or other owner of the asset is required to deliver the asset if the option is exercised, an amount received for granting the option shall be allocated to principal. An amount paid to acquire the option shall be paid from principal. A gain or loss realized upon the exercise of an option, including an option granted to a grantor of the trust or estate for services rendered, shall be allocated to principal.

History.
S. 1, ch. 2002-42; s. 25, ch. 2012-49, eff. Jan. 1, 2013.

738.608. Asset-backed securities.

(1) For purposes of this section, "asset-backed security" means an asset the value of which is based upon the right given the owner to receive distributions from the proceeds of financial assets that provide collateral for the security. The term includes an asset that gives the owner the right to receive from the collateral financial assets only the interest or other current return or only the proceeds other than interest or current return. The term does not include an asset to which s. 738.401 or s. 738.602 applies.

(2) If a trust or estate receives a payment from interest or other current return and from other proceeds of the collateral financial assets, the fiduciary shall allocate to income the portion of the payment which the payor identifies as being from interest or other current return and allocate the balance of the payment to principal.

(3) If a trust or estate receives one or more payments in exchange for the trust's or estate's entire interest in an asset-backed security during a single accounting period, the fiduciary shall allocate the payments to principal. If a payment is one of a series of payments that will result in the liquidation of the trust's or estate's interest in the security over more than a single accounting period, the fiduciary shall allocate 10 percent of the payment to income and the balance to principal.

History.
S. 1, ch. 2002-42; s. 26, ch. 2012-49, eff. Jan. 1, 2013.

738.701. Disbursements from income.

A fiduciary shall make the following disbursements from income to the extent they are not disbursements to which s. 738.201(2) applies:

(1) One-half of the regular compensation of the fiduciary and of any person providing investment advisory or custodial services to the fiduciary.

(2) One-half of all expenses for accountings, judicial proceedings, or other matters that involve both the income and remainder interests.

(3) All of the other ordinary expenses incurred in connection with the administration, management, or preservation of trust property and the distribution of income, including interest, ordinary repairs, regularly recurring taxes assessed against principal, and expenses of a proceeding or other matter that concerns primarily the income interest.

(4) Recurring premiums on insurance covering the loss of a principal asset or the loss of income from or use of the asset.

History.
S. 1, ch. 2002-42; s. 27, ch. 2012-49, eff. Jan. 1, 2013.

738.702. Disbursements from principal.

(1) A fiduciary shall make the following disbursements from principal:

(a) The remaining one-half of the disbursements described in s. 738.701(1) and (2).

(b) All of the trustee's compensation calculated on principal as a fee for acceptance, distribution, or termination and disbursements made to prepare property for sale.

(c) Payments on the principal of a trust debt.

(d) Expenses of a proceeding that concerns primarily principal, including a proceeding to construe the trust or will, or to protect the trust, estate, or its property.

(e) Premiums paid on a policy of insurance not described in s. 738.701(4) of which the trust or estate is the owner and beneficiary.

(f) Estate, inheritance, and other transfer taxes, including penalties, apportioned to the trust.

(g) Disbursements related to environmental matters, including reclamation, assessing environmental conditions, remedying and removing environmental contamination, monitoring remedial activities and the release of substances, preventing future releases of substances, collecting amounts from persons liable or potentially liable for the costs of such activities, penalties imposed under environmental laws or regulations and other payments made to comply with those laws or regulations, statutory or common law claims by third parties, and defending claims based on environmental matters.

(h) Payments representing extraordinary repairs or expenses incurred in making a capital improvement to principal, including special assessments; however, a fiduciary may establish an allowance for depreciation out of income to the extent permitted by s. 738.703.

(2) If a principal asset is encumbered with an obligation that requires income from that asset to be paid

directly to the creditor, the trustee shall transfer from principal to income an amount equal to the income paid to the creditor in reduction of the principal balance of the obligation.

History.

S. 1, ch. 2002-42; s. 28, ch. 2012-49, eff. Jan. 1, 2013.

738.703. Transfers from income to principal for depreciation.

(1) For purposes of this section, "depreciation" means a reduction in value due to wear, tear, decay, corrosion, or gradual obsolescence of a fixed asset having a useful life of more than 1 year.

(2) A fiduciary may transfer to principal a reasonable amount of the net cash receipts from a principal asset that is subject to depreciation but may not transfer any amount for depreciation:

　(a) Of that portion of real property used or available for use by a beneficiary as a residence or of tangible personal property held or made available for the personal use or enjoyment of a beneficiary;

　(b) During the administration of a decedent's estate; or

　(c) Under this section if the fiduciary is accounting under s. 738.403 for the business or activity in which the asset is used.

(3) The amount of depreciation taken for tax purposes with respect to an asset shall be presumed to be a reasonable amount of depreciation. An amount taken for depreciation shall not be considered unreasonable solely because it is greater or less than the amount taken for tax purposes.

(4) An amount transferred to principal need not be held as a separate fund.

History.

S. 1, ch. 2002-42; s. 29, ch. 2012-49, eff. Jan. 1, 2013.

738.704. Transfers from income to reimburse principal.

(1) If a fiduciary makes or expects to make a principal disbursement described in this section, the fiduciary may transfer an appropriate amount from income to principal in one or more accounting periods to reimburse principal or to provide a reserve for future principal disbursements.

(2) Principal disbursements to which subsection (1) applies include the following, but only to the extent the fiduciary has not been and does not expect to be reimbursed by a third party:

　(a) An amount chargeable to income but paid from principal because the amount is unusually large.

　(b) Disbursements made to prepare property for rental, including tenant allowances, leasehold improvements, and broker's commissions.

　(c) Disbursements described in s. 738.702(1)(g).

(3) If the asset the ownership of which gives rise to the disbursements becomes subject to a successive income interest after an income interest ends, a fiduciary may continue to transfer amounts from income to principal as provided in subsection (1).

(4) To the extent principal cash is not sufficient to pay the principal balance of payments due on mortgaged property, income may be applied to such payment in order to avoid a default on any mortgage or security interest securing the property. Income shall be reimbursed for such payments out of the first available principal cash. If the asset the ownership of which gives rise to the disbursements described in this subsection becomes subject to a successive income interest after an income interest ends, all rights of the initial income interest shall lapse, and amounts remaining due from principal shall not be a lien on the assets of the trust.

History.

S. 1, ch. 2002-42; s. 30, ch. 2012-49, eff. Jan. 1, 2013.

738.705. Income taxes.

(1) A tax required to be paid by a fiduciary based on receipts allocated to income shall be paid from income.

(2) A tax required to be paid by a fiduciary based on receipts allocated to principal shall be paid from principal, even if the tax is called an income tax by the taxing authority.

(3) A tax required to be paid by a fiduciary on the trust's or estate's share of an entity's taxable income shall be paid proportionately:

　(a) From income to the extent receipts from the entity are allocated to income.

　(b) From principal to the extent receipts from the entity are allocated to principal.

　(c) From principal to the extent that the income taxes payable by the trust or estate exceed the total receipts from the entity.

(4) After applying subsections (1)-(3), the fiduciary shall adjust income or principal receipts to the extent that the trust's or estate's income taxes are reduced, but not eliminated, because the trust or estate receives a deduction for payments made to a beneficiary. The amount distributable to that beneficiary as income as a result of this adjustment shall be equal to the cash received by the trust or estate, reduced, but not below zero, by the entity's taxable income allocable to the trust or estate multiplied by the trust's or estate's income tax rate. The reduced amount shall be divided by the difference between 1 and the trust's or estate's income tax rate in order to determine the amount distributable to that beneficiary as income before giving effect to other receipts or disbursements allocable to that beneficiary's interest.

History.

S. 1, ch. 2002-42; s. 31, ch. 2012-49, eff. Jan. 1, 2013.

738.706. Adjustments between principal and income because of taxes.

(1) A fiduciary may make adjustments between principal and income to offset the shifting of economic

interests or tax benefits between income beneficiaries and remainder beneficiaries which arise from:

(a) Elections and decisions, other than those described in paragraph (b), that the fiduciary makes from time to time regarding tax matters;

(b) An income tax or any other tax that is imposed upon the fiduciary or a beneficiary as a result of a transaction involving or a distribution from the estate or trust; or

(c) The ownership by an estate or trust of an interest in an entity whose taxable income, whether or not distributed, is includable in the taxable income of the estate, trust, or a beneficiary.

(2) If the amount of an estate tax marital deduction or charitable contribution deduction is reduced because a fiduciary deducts an amount paid from principal for income tax purposes instead of deducting such amount for estate tax purposes, and as a result estate taxes paid from principal are increased and income taxes paid by an estate, trust, or beneficiary are decreased, each estate, trust, or beneficiary that benefits from the decrease in income tax shall reimburse the principal from which the increase in estate tax is paid. The total reimbursement shall equal the increase in the estate tax to the extent the principal used to pay the increase would have qualified for a marital deduction or charitable contribution deduction but for the payment. The proportionate share of the reimbursement for each estate, trust, or beneficiary whose income taxes are reduced shall be the same as such estate's, trust's, or beneficiary's proportionate share of the total decrease in income tax. An estate or trust shall reimburse principal from income.

History.
S. 1, ch. 2002-42.

738.801. Apportionment of expenses; improvements.

(1) For purposes of this section, the term:

(a) "Remainderman" means the holder of the remainder interests after the expiration of a tenant's estate in property.

(b) "Tenant" means the holder of an estate for life or term of years in real property or personal property, or both.

(2) If a trust has not been created, expenses shall be apportioned between the tenant and remainderman as follows:

(a) The following expenses are allocated to and shall be paid by the tenant:

1. All ordinary expenses incurred in connection with the administration, management, or preservation of the property, including interest, ordinary repairs, regularly recurring taxes assessed against the property, and expenses of a proceeding or other matter that concerns primarily the tenant's estate or use of the property.

2. Recurring premiums on insurance covering the loss of the property or the loss of income from or use of the property.

3. Any of the expenses described in subparagraph (b)3. which are attributable to the use of the property by the tenant.

(b) The following expenses are allocated to and shall be paid by the remainderman:

1. Payments on the principal of a debt secured by the property, except to the extent the debt is for expenses allocated to the tenant.

2. Expenses of a proceeding or other matter that concerns primarily the title to the property, other than title to the tenant's estate.

3. Except as provided in subparagraph (a)3., expenses related to environmental matters, including reclamation, assessing environmental conditions, remedying and removing environmental contamination, monitoring remedial activities and the release of substances, preventing future releases of substances, collecting amounts from persons liable or potentially liable for the costs of such activities, penalties imposed under environmental laws or regulations and other payments made to comply with those laws or regulations, statutory or common law claims by third parties, and defending claims based on environmental matters.

4. Extraordinary repairs.

(c) If the tenant or remainderman incurred an expense for the benefit of his or her own estate without consent or agreement of the other, he or she must pay such expense in full.

(d) Except as provided in paragraph (c), the cost of, or special taxes or assessments for, an improvement representing an addition of value to property forming part of the principal shall be paid by the tenant if the improvement is not reasonably expected to outlast the estate of the tenant. In all other cases, only a part shall be paid by the tenant while the remainder shall be paid by the remainderman. The part payable by the tenant is ascertainable by taking that percentage of the total that is found by dividing the present value of the tenant's estate by the present value of an estate of the same form as that of the tenant, except that it is limited for a period corresponding to the reasonably expected duration of the improvement. The computation of present values of the estates shall be made by using the rate defined in 26 U.S.C. s. 7520, then in effect and, in the case of an estate for life, the official mortality tables then in effect under 26 U.S.C. s. 7520. Other evidence of duration or expectancy may not be considered.

(3) This section does not apply to the extent it is inconsistent with the instrument creating the estates, the agreement of the parties, or the specific direction of the taxing or other statutes.

(4) The common law applicable to tenants and remaindermen supplements this section, except as modified by this section or other laws.

History.
S. 1, ch. 2002-42; s. 32, ch. 2012-49, eff. Jan. 1, 2013.

738.802. Uniformity of application and construction.

In applying and construing this act, consideration shall be given to the need to promote uniformity of the law with respect to the act's subject matter among states that enact such act.

History.
S. 1, ch. 2002-42.

738.803. Severability.

If any provision of this chapter or its application to any person or circumstance is held invalid, the invalidity shall not affect other provisions or applications of this chapter which can be given effect without the invalid provision or application, and to this end the provisions of this chapter are severable.

History.

S. 1, ch. 2002-42.

738.804. Application.

Except as provided in the trust instrument, the will, or this chapter, this chapter shall apply to any receipt or expense received or incurred and any disbursement made after January 1, 2003, by any trust or decedent's estate, whether established before or after January 1, 2003, and whether the asset involved was acquired by the trustee or personal representative before or after January 1, 2003. Receipts or expenses received or incurred and disbursements made before January 1, 2003, shall be governed by the law of this state in effect at the time of the event, except as otherwise expressly provided in the will or terms of the trust or in this chapter.

History.
S. 1, ch. 2002-42.

CHAPTER 739.
FLORIDA UNIFORM DISCLAIMER OF PROPERTY INTERESTS ACT

739.101. Short title.

This chapter may be cited as the "Florida Uniform Disclaimer of Property Interests Act."

History.
S. 1, ch. 2005-108.

739.102. Definitions.

As used in this chapter, the term:

(1) "Benefactor" means the creator of the interest that is subject to a disclaimer.

(2) "Beneficiary designation" means an instrument, other than an instrument creating or amending a trust, naming the beneficiary of:

(a) An annuity or insurance policy;

(b) An account with a designation for payment on death;

(c) A security registered in beneficiary form;

(d) A pension, profit-sharing, retirement, or other employment-related benefit plan; or

(e) Any other nonprobate transfer at death.

(3) "Disclaimant" means the person to whom a disclaimed interest or power would have passed had the disclaimer not been made.

(4) "Disclaimed interest" means the interest that would have passed to the disclaimant had the disclaimer not been made.

(5) "Disclaimer" means the refusal to accept an interest in or power over property. The term includes a renunciation.

(6) "Fiduciary" means a personal representative, trustee, agent acting under a power of attorney, guardian, or other person authorized to act as a fiduciary with respect to the property of another person.

(7) "Future interest" means an interest that takes effect in possession or enjoyment, if at all, later than the time of its creation.

(8) "Insolvent" means, solely for purposes of this chapter, that the sum of a person's debts is greater than all of the person's assets at fair valuation and that the person is generally not paying his or her debts as they become due. For purposes of this subsection, the term "assets" has the same meaning as that provided in s. 726.102.

(9) "Jointly held property" means property held in the names of two or more persons under an arrangement in which all holders have concurrent interests and under which the last surviving holder is entitled to the whole of the property. Jointly held property does not include property held as tenants by the entirety.

(10) "Person" includes individuals, ascertained and unascertained, living or not living, whether entitled to an interest by right of intestacy or otherwise;

a government, governmental subdivision, agency, or instrumentality; and a public corporation.

(11) "Time of distribution" means the time when a disclaimed interest would have taken effect in possession or enjoyment.

(12) "Trust" means:

(a) An express trust (including an honorary trust or a trust under s. 736.0408), charitable or noncharitable, with additions thereto, whenever and however created; and

(b) A trust created pursuant to a statute, judgment, or decree which requires the trust be administered in the manner of an express trust.

As used in this chapter, the term "trust" does not include a constructive trust or a resulting trust.

History.
S. 1, ch. 2005-108; s. 43, ch. 2006-217, eff. July 1, 2007; s. 13, ch. 2009-115, eff. July 1, 2009.

739.103. Scope.

This chapter applies to disclaimers of any interest in or power over property, whenever created. Except as provided in s. 739.701, this chapter is the exclusive means by which a disclaimer may be made under Florida law.

History.
S. 1, ch. 2005-108.

739.104. Power to disclaim; general requirements; when irrevocable.

(1) A person may disclaim, in whole or in part, conditionally or unconditionally, any interest in or power over property, including a power of appointment. A person may disclaim the interest or power even if its creator imposed a spendthrift provision or similar restriction on transfer or a restriction or limitation on the right to disclaim. A disclaimer shall be unconditional unless the disclaimant explicitly provides otherwise in the disclaimer.

(2) With court approval, a fiduciary may disclaim, in whole or part, any interest in or power over property, including a power of appointment, except that a disclaimer of a power arising under s. 739.201(4) does not require court approval. Without court approval, a fiduciary may disclaim, in whole or in part, any interest in or power over property, including a power of appointment, if and to the extent that the instrument creating the fiduciary relationship explicitly grants the fiduciary the right to disclaim. In the absence of a court-appointed guardian, notwithstanding anything in chapter 744 to the contrary, without court approval, a natural guardian under s. 744.301 may disclaim on behalf of a minor child of the natural guardian, in whole or in part, any interest in or power over property, including a power of appointment, which the minor child is to receive solely as a result of another disclaimer, but only if the disclaimed interest or power does not pass to or for the benefit of the natural guardian as a result of the disclaimer.

(3) To be effective, a disclaimer must be in writing, declare the writing as a disclaimer, describe the interest or power disclaimed, and be signed by the person making the disclaimer and witnessed and acknowledged in the manner provided for deeds of real estate to be recorded in this state. In addition, for a disclaimer to be effective, an original of the disclaimer must be delivered or filed in the manner provided in s. 739.301.

(4) A partial disclaimer may be expressed as a fraction, percentage, monetary amount, term of years, limitation of a power, or any other interest or estate in the property.

(5) A disclaimer becomes irrevocable when any conditions to which the disclaimant has made the disclaimer subject are satisfied and when the disclaimer is delivered or filed pursuant to s. 739.301 or it becomes effective as provided in ss. 739.201-739.207, whichever occurs later.

(6) A disclaimer made under this chapter is not a transfer, assignment, or release.

History.
S. 1, ch. 2005-108; s. 103, ch. 2006-1, eff. July 4, 2006; s. 14, ch. 2009-115, eff. July 1, 2009.

739.201. Disclaimer of interest in property.

Except for a disclaimer governed by s. 739.202, s. 739.203, or s. 739.204, the following rules apply to a disclaimer of an interest in property:

(1) The disclaimer takes effect as of the time the instrument creating the interest becomes irrevocable or, if the interest arose under the law of intestate succession, as of the time of the intestate's death.

(2) The disclaimed interest passes according to any provision in the instrument creating the interest providing explicitly for the disposition of the interest, should it be disclaimed, or of disclaimed interests in general.

(3) If the instrument does not contain a provision described in subsection (2), the following rules apply:

    (a) If the disclaimant is an individual, the disclaimed interest passes as if the disclaimant had died immediately before the interest was created, unless under the governing instrument or other applicable law the disclaimed interest is contingent on surviving to the time of distribution, in which case the disclaimed interest passes as if the disclaimant had died immediately before the time for distribution. However, if, by law or under the governing instrument, the descendants of the disclaimant would share in the disclaimed interest by any method of representation had the disclaimant died before the time of distribution, the disclaimed interest passes only to the descendants of the disclaimant who survive the time of distribution. For purposes of this subsection, a disclaimed interest is created at the death of the benefactor or such earlier time, if any, that the benefactor's transfer of the interest is a completed gift for federal gift tax purposes. Also for purposes of this subsection, a disclaimed interest in a trust described in s. 733.707(3) shall pass as if the interest had been created under a will.

    (b) If the disclaimant is not an individual, the disclaimed interest passes as if the disclaimant did not exist.

    (c) Upon the disclaimer of a preceding interest, a future interest held by a person other than the disclaimant takes effect as if the disclaimant had died or ceased to exist immediately before the time of distribution, but a future interest held by the disclaimant is not accelerated in possession or enjoyment as a result of the disclaimer.

(4) In the case of a disclaimer of property over which the disclaimant has a power, in a fiduciary or nonfiduciary capacity, to direct the beneficial enjoyment of the disclaimed property, unless the disclaimer specifically provides to the contrary with reference to this subsection, the disclaimant shall also be deemed to have disclaimed that power unless the power is limited by an ascertainable standard, as defined in s. 736.0103, as in effect when the disclaimer becomes irrevocable.

History.
S. 1, ch. 2005-108; s. 15, ch. 2009-115, eff. July 1, 2009.

739.202. Disclaimer of rights of survivorship in jointly held property.

(1) Upon the death of a holder of jointly held property:

    (a) If, during the deceased holder's lifetime, the deceased holder could have unilaterally regained a portion of the property attributable to the deceased holder's contributions without the consent of any other holder, another holder may disclaim, in whole or in part, a fractional share of that portion of the property attributable to the deceased holder's contributions determined by dividing the number one by the number of joint holders alive immediately after the death of the holder to whose death the disclaimer relates.

    (b) For all other jointly held property, another holder may disclaim, in whole or in part, a fraction of the whole of the property the numerator of which is one and the denominator of which is the product of the number of joint holders alive immediately before the death of the holder to whose death the disclaimer relates multiplied by the number of joint holders alive immediately after the death of the holder to whose death the disclaimer relates.

(2) A disclaimer under subsection (1) takes effect as of the death of the holder of jointly held property to whose death the disclaimer relates.

(3) An interest in jointly held property disclaimed by a surviving holder of the property passes as if the disclaimant predeceased the holder to whose death the disclaimer relates.

History.
S. 1, ch. 2005-108.

739.203. Disclaimer of property held as tenancy by the entirety.

(1) The survivorship interest in property held as a tenancy by the entirety to which the survivor succeeds by operation of law upon the death of the cotenant may be disclaimed as provided in this chapter. For purposes of this chapter only, the deceased tenant's interest in property held as a tenancy by the entirety shall be deemed to be an undivided one-half interest.

(2) A disclaimer under subsection (1) takes effect as of the death of the deceased tenant to whose death the disclaimer relates.

(3) The survivorship interest in property held as a tenancy by the entirety disclaimed by the surviving tenant passes as if the disclaimant had predeceased the tenant to whose death the disclaimer relates.

(4) A disclaimer of an interest in real property held as tenants by the entirety does not cause the disclaimed interest to be homestead property for purposes of descent and distribution under ss. 732.401 and 732.4015.

History.
S. 1, ch. 2005-108.

739.204. Disclaimer of interest by trustee.

If a trustee having the power to disclaim under the instrument creating the fiduciary relationship or pursuant to court order disclaims an interest in property that otherwise would have become trust property, the interest does not become trust property.

History.
S. 1, ch. 2005-108.

739.205. Disclaimer of power of appointment or other power not held in a fiduciary capacity.

If a holder disclaims a power of appointment or other power not held in a fiduciary capacity, the following rules apply:

(1) If the holder has not exercised the power, the disclaimer takes effect as of the time the instrument creating the power becomes irrevocable.

(2) If the holder has exercised the power and the disclaimer is of a power other than a presently exercisable general power of appointment, the disclaimer takes effect immediately after the last exercise of the power.

(3) The instrument creating the power is construed as if the power expired when the disclaimer became effective.

History.
S. 1, ch. 2005-108.

739.206. Disclaimer by appointee, object, or taker in default of exercise of power of appointment.

(1) A disclaimer of an interest in property by an appointee of a power of appointment takes effect as of the time the instrument by which the holder exercises the power becomes irrevocable.

(2) A disclaimer of an interest in property by an object, or taker in default of an exercise of a power of appointment, takes effect as of the time the instrument creating the power becomes irrevocable.

History.
S. 1, ch. 2005-108.

739.207. Disclaimer of power held in fiduciary capacity.

(1) If a fiduciary disclaims a power held in a fiduciary capacity which has not been exercised, the disclaimer takes effect as of the time the instrument creating the power becomes irrevocable.

(2) If a fiduciary disclaims a power held in a fiduciary capacity which has been exercised, the disclaimer takes effect immediately after the last exercise of the power.

(3) A disclaimer under this section is effective as to another fiduciary if the disclaimer so provides and the fiduciary disclaiming has the authority to bind the estate, trust, or other person for whom the fiduciary is acting, except that a disclaimer of a fiduciary power arising under s. 739.201(4) shall bind only the disclaiming fiduciary.

History.
S. 1, ch. 2005-108; s. 16, ch. 2009-115, eff. July 1, 2009.

739.301. Delivery or filing.

(1) Subject to subsections (2) through (12), delivery of a disclaimer may be effected by personal delivery, first-class mail, or any other method that results in its receipt. A disclaimer sent by first-class mail shall be deemed to have been delivered on the date it is postmarked. Delivery by any other method shall be effective upon receipt by the person to whom the disclaimer is to be delivered under this section.

(2) In the case of a disclaimer of an interest created under the law of intestate succession or an interest created by will, other than an interest in a testamentary trust:

(a) The disclaimer must be delivered to the personal representative of the decedent's estate; or

(b) If no personal representative is serving when the disclaimer is sought to be delivered, the disclaimer must be filed with the clerk of the court in any county where venue of administration would be proper.

(3) In the case of a disclaimer of an interest in a testamentary trust:

(a) The disclaimer must be delivered to the trustee serving when the disclaimer is delivered or, if no trustee is then serving, to the personal representative of the decedent's estate; or

(b) If no personal representative is serving when the disclaimer is sought to be delivered, the disclaimer must be filed with the clerk of the court in any county where venue of administration of the decedent's estate would be proper.

(4) In the case of a disclaimer of an interest in an inter vivos trust:

(a) The disclaimer must be delivered to the trustee serving when the disclaimer is delivered;

(b) If no trustee is then serving, it must be filed with the clerk of the court in any county where the filing of a notice of trust would be proper; or

(c) If the disclaimer is made before the time the instrument creating the trust becomes irrevocable, the disclaimer must be delivered to the grantor of the revocable trust or the transferor of the interest or to such person's legal representative.

(5) In the case of a disclaimer of an interest created by a beneficiary designation made before the time the designation becomes irrevocable, the disclaimer must be delivered to the person making the beneficiary designation or to such person's legal representative.

(6) In the case of a disclaimer of an interest created by a beneficiary designation made after the time the designation becomes irrevocable, the disclaimer must be delivered to the person obligated to distribute the interest.

(7) In the case of a disclaimer by a surviving holder of jointly held property, or by the surviving tenant in property held as a tenancy by the entirety, the disclaimer must be delivered to the person to whom the disclaimed interest passes or, if such person cannot reasonably be located by the disclaimant, the disclaimer must be delivered as provided in subsection (2).

(8) In the case of a disclaimer by an object, or taker in default of exercise, of a power of appointment at any time after the power was created:

(a) The disclaimer must be delivered to the holder of the power or to the fiduciary acting under the instrument that created the power; or

(b) If no fiduciary is serving when the disclaimer is sought to be delivered, the disclaimer must be filed with a court having authority to appoint the fiduciary.

(9) In the case of a disclaimer by an appointee of a nonfiduciary power of appointment:

(a) The disclaimer must be delivered to the holder, the personal representative of the holder's estate, or the fiduciary under the instrument that created the power; or

(b) If no fiduciary is serving when the disclaimer is sought to be delivered, the disclaimer must be filed with a court having authority to appoint the fiduciary.

(10) In the case of a disclaimer by a fiduciary of a power over a trust or estate, the disclaimer must be delivered as provided in subsection (2), subsection (3), or subsection (4) as if the power disclaimed were an interest in property.

(11) In the case of a disclaimer of a power exercisable by an agent, other than a power exercisable by a fiduciary over a trust or estate, the disclaimer must be delivered to the principal or the principal's representative.

(12) Notwithstanding subsection (1), delivery of a disclaimer of an interest in or relating to real estate shall be presumed upon the recording of the disclaimer in the office of the clerk of the court of the county or counties where the real estate is located.

(13) A fiduciary or other person having custody of the disclaimed interest is not liable for any otherwise proper distribution or other disposition made without actual notice of the disclaimer or, if the disclaimer is barred under s. 739.402, for any otherwise proper distribution or other disposition made in reliance on the disclaimer, if the distribution or disposition is made without actual knowledge of the facts constituting the bar of the right to disclaim.

History.
S. 1, ch. 2005-108.

739.401.   When disclaimer is permitted.

A disclaimer may be made at any time unless barred under s. 739.402.

History.
S. 1, ch. 2005-108.

739.402.   When disclaimer is barred or limited.

(1) A disclaimer is barred by a written waiver of the right to disclaim.

(2) A disclaimer of an interest in property is barred if any of the following events occur before the disclaimer becomes effective:

(a) The disclaimant accepts the interest sought to be disclaimed;

(b) The disclaimant voluntarily assigns, conveys, encumbers, pledges, or transfers the interest sought to be disclaimed or contracts to do so;

(c) The interest sought to be disclaimed is sold pursuant to a judicial sale; or

(d) The disclaimant is insolvent when the disclaimer becomes irrevocable.

(3) A disclaimer, in whole or in part, of the future exercise of a power held in a fiduciary capacity is not barred by its previous exercise.

(4) A disclaimer, in whole or in part, of the future exercise of a power not held in a fiduciary capacity is not barred by its previous exercise unless the power is exercisable in favor of the disclaimant.

(5) A disclaimer of an interest in, or a power over, property which is barred by this section is ineffective.

History.
S. 1, ch. 2005-108; s. 17, ch. 2009-115, eff. July 1, 2009.

739.501.   Tax-qualified disclaimer.

Notwithstanding any provision of this chapter other than s. 739.402, if, as a result of a disclaimer or transfer, the disclaimed or transferred interest is treated pursuant to the provisions of s. 2518 of the Internal Revenue Code of 1986 as never having been transferred to the disclaimant, the disclaimer or transfer is effective as a disclaimer under this chapter.

History.

S. 1, ch. 2005-108; s. 18, ch. 2009-115, eff. July 1, 2009.

Editor's Notes.

Section 2518 of the Internal Revenue Code, referred to in this section, is codified as 26 U.S.C.S. § 2518.

739.601. Recording of disclaimer relating to real estate.

(1) A disclaimer of an interest in or relating to real estate does not provide constructive notice to all persons unless the disclaimer contains a legal description of the real estate to which the disclaimer relates and unless the disclaimer is filed for recording in the office of the clerk of the court in the county or counties where the real estate is located.

(2) An effective disclaimer meeting the requirements of subsection (1) constitutes constructive notice to all persons from the time of filing. Failure to record the disclaimer does not affect its validity as between the disclaimant and persons to whom the property interest or power passes by reason of the disclaimer.

History.

S. 1, ch. 2005-108.

739.701. Application to existing relationships.

Except as otherwise provided in s. 739.402, an interest in or power over property existing on July 1, 2005, as to which the time for delivering or filing a disclaimer under laws superseded by this chapter has not expired, may be disclaimed after July 1, 2005.

History.

S. 1, ch. 2005-108.

TITLE XLIII.

DOMESTIC RELATIONS

CHAPTER 744.
GUARDIANSHIP

PART I.
GENERAL PROVISIONS.

744.101.   Short title.

This chapter may be cited as the "Florida Guardianship Law."

History.
S. 1, ch. 74-106; s. 1, ch. 89-96.
Editor's Notes.
Created from former s. 744.01.

744.1012.   Legislative intent.

The Legislature finds that adjudicating a person totally incapacitated and in need of a guardian deprives such person of all her or his civil and legal rights and that such deprivation may be unnecessary. The Legislature further finds that it is desirable to make available the least restrictive form of guardianship to assist persons who are only partially incapable of caring for their needs. Recognizing that every individual has unique needs and differing abilities, the Legislature declares that it is the purpose of this act to promote the public welfare by establishing a system that permits incapacitated persons to participate as fully as possible in all decisions affecting them; that assists such persons in meeting the essential requirements for their physical health and safety, in protecting their rights, in managing their financial resources, and in developing or regaining their abilities to the maximum extent possible; and that accomplishes these objectives through providing, in each case, the form of assistance that least interferes with the legal capacity of a person to act in her or his own behalf. This act shall be liberally construed to accomplish this purpose.

History.
S. 3, ch. 89-96; s. 1, ch. 90-271; s. 1067, ch. 97-102.

744.102.   Definitions.

As used in this chapter, the term:

(1) "Attorney for the alleged incapacitated person" means an attorney who represents the alleged incapacitated person. The attorney shall represent the expressed wishes of the alleged incapacitated person to the extent it is consistent with the rules regulating The Florida Bar.

(2) "Audit" means a systematic review of financial and all other documents to ensure compliance with s. 744.368, rules of court, and local procedures using generally accepted accounting principles.

(3) "Clerk" means the clerk or deputy clerk of the court.

(4) "Corporate guardian" means a corporation authorized to exercise fiduciary or guardianship powers in this state and includes a nonprofit corporate guardian.

(5) "Court" means the circuit court.

(6) "Court monitor" means a person appointed by the court under s. 744.107 to provide the court with information concerning a ward.

(7) "Estate" means the property of a ward subject to administration.

(8) "Foreign guardian" means a guardian appointed in another state or country.

(9) "Guardian" means a person who has been appointed by the court to act on behalf of a ward's person or property, or both.

(a) "Limited guardian" means a guardian who has been appointed by the court to exercise the legal rights and powers specifically designated by court order entered after the court has found that the ward lacks the capacity to do some, but not all, of the tasks necessary to care for his or her person or property, or after the person has voluntarily petitioned for appointment of a limited guardian.

(b) "Plenary guardian" means a person who has been appointed by the court to exercise all delegable legal rights and powers of the ward after the court has found that the ward lacks the capacity to perform all of the tasks necessary to care for his or her person or property.

(10) "Guardian ad litem" means a person who is appointed by the court having jurisdiction of the guardianship or a court in which a particular legal matter is pending to represent a ward in that proceeding.

(11) "Guardian advocate" means a person appointed by a written order of the court to represent a person with developmental disabilities under s. 393.12. As used in this chapter, the term does not apply to a guardian advocate appointed for a person

determined incompetent to consent to treatment under s. 394.4598.

(12) "Incapacitated person" means a person who has been judicially determined to lack the capacity to manage at least some of the property or to meet at least some of the essential health and safety requirements of the person.

(a) To "manage property" means to take those actions necessary to obtain, administer, and dispose of real and personal property, intangible property, business property, benefits, and income.

(b) To "meet essential requirements for health or safety" means to take those actions necessary to provide the health care, food, shelter, clothing, personal hygiene, or other care without which serious and imminent physical injury or illness is more likely than not to occur.

(13) "Minor" means a person under 18 years of age whose disabilities have not been removed by marriage or otherwise.

(14) "Next of kin" means those persons who would be heirs at law of the ward or alleged incapacitated person if the person were deceased and includes the lineal descendants of the ward or alleged incapacitated person.

(15) "Nonprofit corporate guardian" means a nonprofit corporation organized for religious or charitable purposes and existing under the laws of this state.

(16) "Preneed guardian" means a person named in a written declaration to serve as guardian in the event of the incapacity of the declarant as provided in s. 744.3045.

(17) "Professional guardian" means any guardian who has at any time rendered services to three or more wards as their guardian. A person serving as a guardian for two or more relatives as defined in s. 744.309(2) is not considered a professional guardian. A public guardian shall be considered a professional guardian for purposes of regulation, education, and registration.

(18) "Property" means both real and personal property or any interest in it and anything that may be the subject of ownership.

(19) "Standby guardian" means a person empowered to assume the duties of guardianship upon the death or adjudication of incapacity of the last surviving natural or appointed guardian.

(20) "Surrogate guardian" means a guardian designated according to s. 744.442.

(21) "Totally incapacitated" means incapable of exercising any of the rights enumerated in s. 744.3215(2) and (3).

(22) "Ward" means a person for whom a guardian has been appointed.

History.
S. 1, ch. 74-106; s. 2, ch. 75-222; s. 231, ch. 77-104; s. 1, ch. 79-221; s. 3, ch. 80-171; s. 4, ch. 89-96; s. 2, ch. 90-271; s. 1, ch.

96-354; s. 1780, ch. 97-102; s. 6, ch. 2003-57; s. 9, ch. 2004-260; s. 1, ch. 2006-178, eff. July 1, 2006.
Editor's Notes.
Created from former s. 744.03.

744.1025. Additional definitions.

The definitions contained in the Florida Probate Code shall be applicable to the Florida Guardianship Law, unless the context requires otherwise, insofar as such definitions do not conflict with definitions contained in this law.
History.
S. 2, ch. 79-221; s. 5, ch. 89-96.

744.103. Guardians of incapacitated world war veterans [Repealed.]

Repealed by s. 1, ch. 2012-40, effective July 1, 2012.
History.
S. 1, ch. 74-106; s. 2, ch. 75-222; s. 1, ch. 77-174; s. 6, ch. 89-96.

744.104. Verification of documents.

When verification of a document is required in this chapter or by rule, the document filed shall include an oath or affirmation or the following statement: "Under penalties of perjury, I declare that I have read the foregoing, and the facts alleged are true to the best of my knowledge and belief." Any person who shall willfully include a false statement in the document shall be guilty of perjury and upon conviction shall be punished accordingly.
History.
S. 1, ch. 74-106; s. 2, ch. 75-222; s. 7, ch. 89-96.
Editor's Notes.
Created from former s. 744.37.

744.105. Costs.

In all guardianship proceedings, costs may be awarded. When the costs are to be paid out of the property of the ward, the court may direct from what part of the property the costs shall be paid.
History.
S. 1, ch. 74-106; s. 8, ch. 89-96; s. 3, ch. 90-271.
Editor's Notes.
Created from former s. 744.47.

744.106. Notice.

The requirements for notice under this chapter are those provided for in the Florida Probate Rules except as provided in s. 744.331(1).
History.
S. 4, ch. 75-222; s. 9, ch. 89-96; s. 65, ch. 95-211.

744.107. Court monitors.

(1) The court may, upon inquiry from any interested person or upon its own motion in any proceeding over which it has jurisdiction, appoint a monitor. The court shall not appoint as a monitor a family member or any person with a personal interest in the proceedings. The order of appointment shall be served upon the guardian, the ward, and such other persons as the court may determine.

(2) The monitor may investigate, seek information, examine documents, or interview the ward and shall report to the court his or her findings. The report shall be verified and shall be served on the guardian, the ward, and such other persons as the court may determine.

(3) If it appears from the monitor's report that further action by the court to protect the interests of the ward is necessary, the court shall, after a hearing with notice, enter any order necessary to protect the ward or the ward's estate, including amending the plan, requiring an accounting, ordering production of assets, freezing assets, suspending a guardian, or initiating proceedings to remove a guardian.

(4) Unless otherwise prohibited by law, a monitor may be allowed a reasonable fee as determined by the court and paid from the property of the ward. No full-time state, county, or municipal employee or officer shall be paid a fee for such investigation and report. If the court finds the motion for court monitor to have been filed in bad faith, the costs of the proceeding, including attorney's fees, may be assessed against the movant.

History.
SS. 18, 26, ch. 75-222; s. 10, ch. 89-96; s. 4, ch. 90-271; s. 1068, ch. 97-102; s. 2, ch. 2006-77, eff. June 6, 2006.

744.1075. Emergency court monitor.

(1)(a) A court, upon inquiry from any interested person or upon its own motion, in any proceeding over which the court has jurisdiction, may appoint a court monitor on an emergency basis without notice. The court must specifically find that there appears to be imminent danger that the physical or mental health or safety of the ward will be seriously impaired or that the ward's property is in danger of being wasted, misappropriated, or lost unless immediate action is taken. The scope of the matters to be investigated and the powers and duties of the monitor must be specifically enumerated by court order.

(b) The authority of a monitor appointed under this section expires 60 days after the date of appointment or upon a finding of no probable cause, whichever occurs first. The authority of the monitor may be extended for an additional 30 days upon a showing that the emergency conditions still exist.

(2) Within 15 days after the entry of the order of appointment, the monitor shall file his or her report of findings and recommendations to the court. The report shall be verified and may be supported by documents or other evidence.

(3) Upon review of the report, the court shall determine whether there is probable cause to take further action to protect the person or property of the ward. If the court finds no probable cause, the court shall issue an order finding no probable cause and discharging the monitor.

(4)(a) If the court finds probable cause, the court shall issue an order to show cause directed to the guardian or other respondent stating the essential facts constituting the conduct charged and requiring the respondent to appear before the court to show cause why the court should not take further action. The order shall specify the time and place of the hearing with a reasonable time to allow for the preparation of a defense after service of the order.

(b) At any time prior to the hearing on the order to show cause, the court may issue a temporary injunction, a restraining order, or an order freezing assets; may suspend the guardian or appoint a guardian ad litem; or may issue any other appropriate order to protect the physical or mental health or safety or property of the ward. A copy of all such orders or injunctions shall be transmitted by the court or under its direction to all parties at the time of entry of the order or injunction.

(c) Following a hearing on the order to show cause, the court may impose sanctions on the guardian or his or her attorney or other respondent or take any other action authorized by law, including entering a judgment of contempt; ordering an accounting; freezing assets; referring the case to local law enforcement agencies or the state attorney; filing an abuse, neglect, or exploitation complaint with the Department of Children and Family Services; or initiating proceedings to remove the guardian. Nothing in this subsection shall be construed to preclude the mandatory reporting requirements of chapter 39.

(5) Unless otherwise prohibited by law, a monitor may be allowed a reasonable fee as determined by the court and paid from the property of the ward. No full-time state, county, or municipal employee or officer shall be paid a fee for such investigation and report. If the court finds the motion for a court monitor to have been filed in bad faith, the costs of the proceeding, including attorney's fees, may be assessed against the movant.

History.
S. 3, ch. 2006-77, eff. June 6, 2006.

744.1076. Court orders appointing court monitors and emergency court monitors; reports of court monitors; orders finding no probable cause; public records exemptions.

(1)(a) The order of any court appointing a court monitor pursuant to s. 744.107 or an emergency court monitor pursuant to s. 744.1075 is exempt from s. 24(a), Art. I of the State Constitution.

(b) The reports of an appointed court monitor or emergency court monitor relating to the medical condition, financial affairs, or mental health of the ward are confidential and exempt from s. 24(a), Art. I of the State Constitution. Such reports may be subject to inspection as determined by the court or upon a showing of good cause.

(c) The public records exemptions provided in this subsection expire if a court makes a finding of probable cause, except that information otherwise made confidential or exempt shall retain its confidential or exempt status.

(2) Court orders finding no probable cause pursuant to s. 744.107 or s. 744.1075 are confidential and exempt from s. 24(a), Art. I of the State Constitution; however, such orders may be subject to inspection as determined by the court or upon a showing of good cause.

History.
S. 1, ch. 2006-129, eff. June 6, 2006; s. 161, ch. 2008-4, eff. July 1, 2008; s. 1, ch. 2011-204, eff. Oct. 1, 2011.

744.108. Guardian's and attorney's fees and expenses.

(1) A guardian, or an attorney who has rendered services to the ward or to the guardian on the ward's behalf, is entitled to a reasonable fee for services rendered and reimbursement for costs incurred on behalf of the ward.

(2) When fees for a guardian or an attorney are submitted to the court for determination, the court shall consider the following criteria:

(a) The time and labor required;

(b) The novelty and difficulty of the questions involved and the skill required to perform the services properly;

(c) The likelihood that the acceptance of the particular employment will preclude other employment of the person;

(d) The fee customarily charged in the locality for similar services;

(e) The nature and value of the incapacitated person's property, the amount of income earned by the estate, and the responsibilities and potential liabilities assumed by the person;

(f) The results obtained;

(g) The time limits imposed by the circumstances;

(h) The nature and length of the relationship with the incapacitated person; and

(i) The experience, reputation, diligence, and ability of the person performing the service.

(3) In awarding fees to attorney guardians, the court must clearly distinguish between fees and expenses for legal services and fees and expenses for guardian services and must have determined that no conflict of interest exists.

(4) Fees for legal services may include customary and reasonable charges for work performed by legal assistants employed by and working under the direction of the attorney.

(5) All petitions for guardian's and attorney's fees and expenses must be accompanied by an itemized description of the services performed for the fees and expenses sought to be recovered.

(6) A petition for fees or expenses may not be approved without prior notice to the guardian and to the ward, unless the ward is a minor or is totally incapacitated.

(7) A petition for fees shall include the period covered and the total amount of all prior fees paid or costs awarded to the petitioner in the guardianship proceeding currently before the court.

(8) When court proceedings are instituted to review or determine a guardian's or an attorney's fees under subsection (2), such proceedings are part of the guardianship administration process and the costs, including fees for the guardian's attorney, shall be determined by the court and paid from the assets of the guardianship estate unless the court finds the requested compensation under subsection (2) to be substantially unreasonable.

History.
SS. 18, 26, ch. 75-222; s. 11, ch. 89-96; s. 5, ch. 90-271; s. 2, ch. 96-354; s. 7, ch. 2003-57.

744.1083. Professional guardian registration.

(1) A professional guardian must register with the Statewide Public Guardianship Office established in part IX of this chapter.

(2) Annual registration shall be made on forms furnished by the Statewide Public Guardianship Office and accompanied by the applicable registration fee as determined by rule. The fee may not exceed $100.

(3) Registration must include the following:

(a) Sufficient information to identify the professional guardian, as follows:

1. If the professional guardian is a natural person, the name, address, date of birth, and employer identification or social security number of the person.

2. If the professional guardian is a partnership or association, the name, address, and employer identification number of the entity.

(b) Documentation that the bonding and educational requirements of s. 744.1085 have been met.

(c) Sufficient information to distinguish a guardian providing guardianship services as a public guardian, individually, through partnership, corporation, or any other business organization.

(4) Prior to registering a professional guardian, the Statewide Public Guardianship Office must receive and review copies of the credit and criminal investigations conducted under s. 744.3135. The credit and criminal investigations must have been completed within the previous 2 years.

(5) The executive director of the office may deny registration to a professional guardian if the executive director determines that the guardian's proposed registration, including the guardian's credit or criminal investigations, indicates that registering the professional guardian would violate any provision of this chapter. If a guardian who is currently registered with the office violates a provision of this chapter, the executive director of the office may suspend or revoke the guardian's registration. If the executive director denies registration to a professional guardian or suspends or revokes a professional guardian's registra-

tion, the Statewide Public Guardianship Office must send written notification of the denial, suspension, or revocation to the chief judge of each judicial circuit in which the guardian was serving on the day of the office's decision to deny, suspend, or revoke the registration.

(6) The Department of Elderly Affairs may adopt rules necessary to administer this section.

(7) A trust company, a state banking corporation or state savings association authorized and qualified to exercise fiduciary powers in this state, or a national banking association or federal savings and loan association authorized and qualified to exercise fiduciary powers in this state, may, but is not required to, register as a professional guardian under this section. If a trust company, state banking corporation, state savings association, national banking association, or federal savings and loan association described in this subsection elects to register as a professional guardian under this subsection, the requirements of subsections (3) and (4) do not apply and the registration must include only the name, address, and employer identification number of the registrant, the name and address of its registered agent, if any, and the documentation described in paragraph (3)(b).

(8) The Department of Elderly Affairs may contract with the Florida Guardianship Foundation or other not-for-profit entity to register professional guardians.

(9) The department or its contractor shall ensure that the clerks of the court and the chief judge of each judicial circuit receive information about each registered professional guardian.

(10) A state college or university or an independent college or university that is located and chartered in Florida, that is accredited by the Commission on Colleges of the Southern Association of Colleges and Schools or the Accrediting Council for Independent Colleges and Schools, and that confers degrees as defined in s. 1005.02(7) may, but is not required to, register as a professional guardian under this section. If a state college or university or independent college or university elects to register as a professional guardian under this subsection, the requirements of subsections (3) and (4) do not apply and the registration must include only the name, address, and employer identification number of the registrant.

History.

S. 3, ch. 2002-195; s. 8, ch. 2003-57; s. 10, ch. 2004-260; s. 2, ch. 2006-178, eff. July 1, 2006; s. 2, ch. 2009-175, eff. July 1, 2009.

744.1085. Regulation of professional guardians; application; bond required; educational requirements.

(1) The provisions of this section are in addition to and supplemental to any other provision of the Florida Guardianship Law, except s. 744.3145.

(2) Each professional guardian who files a petition for appointment after October 1, 1997, shall post a blanket fiduciary bond with the clerk of the circuit court in the county in which the guardian's primary place of business is located. The guardian shall provide proof of the fiduciary bond to the clerks of each additional circuit court in which he or she is serving as a professional guardian. The bond shall be maintained by the guardian in an amount not less than $50,000. The bond must cover all wards for whom the guardian has been appointed at any given time. The liability of the provider of the bond is limited to the face amount of the bond, regardless of the number of wards for whom the professional guardian has been appointed. The act or omissions of each employee of a professional guardian who has direct contact with the ward or access to the ward's assets is covered by the terms of such bond. The bond must be payable to the Governor of the State of Florida and his or her successors in office and conditioned on the faithful performance of all duties by the guardian. In form, the bond must be joint and several. The bond is in addition to any bonds required under s. 744.351. This subsection does not apply to any attorney who is licensed to practice law in this state and who is in good standing, to any financial institution as defined in s. 744.309(4), or a public guardian. The expenses incurred to satisfy the bonding requirements prescribed in this section may not be paid with the assets of any ward.

(3) Each professional guardian defined in s. 744.102(17) and public guardian must receive a minimum of 40 hours of instruction and training. Each professional guardian must receive a minimum of 16 hours of continuing education every 2 calendar years after the year in which the initial 40-hour educational requirement is met. The instruction and education must be completed through a course approved or offered by the Statewide Public Guardianship Office. The expenses incurred to satisfy the educational requirements prescribed in this section may not be paid with the assets of any ward. This subsection does not apply to any attorney who is licensed to practice law in this state.

(4) Each professional guardian must allow, at the guardian's expense, an investigation of the guardian's credit history, and the credit history of employees of the guardian, in a manner prescribed by the Department of Elderly Affairs.

(5) As required in s. 744.3135, each professional guardian shall allow a level 2 background screening of the guardian and employees of the guardian in accordance with the provisions of s. 435.04.

(6) After July 1, 2005, each professional guardian shall be required to demonstrate competency to act as a professional guardian by taking an examination approved by the Department of Elderly Affairs.

(a) The Department of Elderly Affairs shall determine the minimum examination score necessary for passage of guardianship examinations.

(b) The Department of Elderly Affairs shall determine the procedure for administration of the examination.

(c) The Department of Elderly Affairs or its contractor shall charge an examination fee for the actual costs of the development and the administration of the examination, not to exceed $500.

(d) The Department of Elderly Affairs may recognize passage of a national guardianship examination in lieu of all or part of the examination approved by the Department of Elderly Affairs, except that all professional guardians must take and pass an approved examination section related to Florida law and procedure.

(7) The Department of Elderly Affairs shall set the minimum score necessary to demonstrate professional guardianship competency.

(8) The Department of Elderly Affairs shall waive the examination requirement in subsection (6) if a professional guardian can provide:

(a) Proof that the guardian has actively acted as a professional guardian for 5 years or more; and

(b) A letter from a circuit judge before whom the professional guardian practiced at least 1 year which states that the professional guardian had demonstrated to the court competency as a professional guardian.

(9) After July 1, 2004, the court shall not appoint any professional guardian who has not met the requirements of this section and s. 744.1083.

(10) This section does not apply to a professional guardian or the employees of that professional guardian when that guardian is a trust company, a state banking corporation, state savings association authorized and qualified to exercise fiduciary powers in this state, or a national banking association or federal savings and loan association authorized and qualified to exercise fiduciary powers in this state.

History.
S. 1, ch. 97-161; s. 9, ch. 99-277; s. 9, ch. 2003-57; s. 17, ch. 2004-260; s. 62, ch. 2004-267; s. 32, ch. 2006-178, eff. July 1, 2006.
Editor's Notes.
Section 62, ch. 2004-267, reenacted (5) without change to incorporate amendments to statutory sections referenced therein.

744.109. Records.

(1) All hearings on appointment of a guardian; adjudication of incapacity; modification, termination, or revocation of the adjudication of incapacity; or restoration of capacity must be electronically or stenographically recorded.

(2) If an appeal is taken from any of these proceedings, a transcript must be furnished to an indigent ward at public expense.

History.
S. 12, ch. 89-96.

744.1095. Hearings.

At any hearing under this chapter, the alleged incapacitated person or the adjudicated ward has the right to:

(1) Remain silent and refuse to testify at the hearing. The person may not be held in contempt of court or otherwise penalized for refusing to testify. Refusal to testify may not be used as evidence of incapacity;

(2) Testify;

(3) Present evidence;

(4) Call witnesses;

(5) Confront and cross-examine all witnesses; and

(6) Have the hearing open or closed as she or he may choose.

History.
S. 13, ch. 89-96; s. 6, ch. 90-271; s. 1069, ch. 97-102.

PART II.
VENUE.

744.201. Domicile of ward.

The domicile of a resident ward is the county where the ward resides.

History.
S. 1, ch. 74-106; s. 5, ch. 75-222; s. 14, ch. 89-96.
Editor's Notes.
Created from former s. 744.10.

744.202. Venue.

(1) The venue in proceedings for declaration of incapacity shall be where the alleged incapacitated person resides or is found. The provisions of this section do not apply to veterans.

(2) The venue in proceedings for the appointment of a guardian shall be:

(a) If the incapacitated person is a resident of this state, in the county where the incapacitated person resides.

(b) If the incapacitated person is not a resident of this state, in any county in this state where property of the incapacitated person is located.

(c) If the incapacitated person is not a resident of this state and owns no property in this state, in the county where any debtor of the incapacitated person resides.

(3) When the residence of an incapacitated person is changed to another county, the guardian shall petition to have the venue of the guardianship changed to the county of the acquired residence, except as provided in s. 744.2025.

(4) If an incapacitated person is a resident of this state and is found in a county other than the county of residence, the venue for declaration of incapacity and for the appointment of a guardian may be the county where the incapacitated person is found. Upon transfer of the incapacitated person to the county of residence, the guardian may have the venue of the guardianship changed to the county of residence and a successor guardian may be appointed.

History.
S. 1, ch. 74-106; s. 5, ch. 75-222; s. 15, ch. 89-96; s. 7, ch. 90-271; s. 33, ch. 95-401; s. 3, ch. 96-354.
Editor's Notes.
Created from former s. 744.11.

744.2025. Change of ward's residence.

(1) Prior court approval required. — A guardian who has power pursuant to this chapter to determine the residence of the ward may not, without court approval, change the residence of the ward from this state to another, or from one county of this state to another county of this state, unless such county is adjacent to the county of the ward's current residence. Any guardian who wishes to remove the ward from the ward's current county of residence to another county which is not adjacent to the ward's current county of residence must obtain court approval prior to removal of the ward. In granting its approval, the court shall, at a minimum, consider the reason for such relocation and the longevity of such relocation.

(2) Immediate court notification required. — Any guardian who wishes to remove the ward from the ward's current county of residence to another county adjacent to the ward's county of residence shall notify the court having jurisdiction of the guardianship within 15 days after relocation of the ward. Such notice shall state the compelling reasons for relocation of the ward and how long the guardian expects the ward to remain in such other county.
History.
S. 16, ch. 89-96; s. 8, ch. 90-271; s. 4, ch. 96-354.

PART III.
TYPES OF GUARDIANSHIP.

744.301. Natural guardians.

(1) The parents jointly are the natural guardians of their own children and of their adopted children, during minority. If one parent dies, the surviving parent remains the sole natural guardian even if he or she remarries. If the marriage between the parents is dissolved, the natural guardianship belongs to the parent to whom sole parental responsibility has been granted, or if the parents have been granted shared parental responsibility, both continue as natural guardians. If the marriage is dissolved and neither parent is given parental responsibility for the child, neither may act as natural guardian of the child. The mother of a child born out of wedlock is the natural guardian of the child and is entitled to primary residential care and custody of the child unless the court enters an order stating otherwise.

(2) Except as otherwise provided in this chapter, on behalf of any of their minor children, and without appointment, authority, or bond if the amounts received in the aggregate do not exceed $15,000, natural guardians may:

(a) Settle and consummate a settlement of any claim or cause of action accruing to any of their minor children for damages to the person or property of any minor children;

(b) Collect, receive, manage, and dispose of the proceeds of any settlement;

(c) Collect, receive, manage, and dispose of any real or personal property distributed from an estate or trust;

(d) Collect, receive, manage, and dispose of and make elections regarding the proceeds from a life insurance policy or annuity contract payable to, or otherwise accruing to the benefit of, the child; and

(e) Collect, receive, manage, dispose of, and make elections regarding the proceeds of any benefit plan as defined in s. 710.102, of which the minor is a beneficiary, participant, or owner.

(3) In addition to the authority granted in subsection (2), natural guardians are authorized, on behalf of any of their minor children, to waive and release, in advance, any claim or cause of action against a commercial activity provider, or its owners, affiliates, employees, or agents, which would accrue to a minor child for personal injury, including death, and property damage resulting from an inherent risk in the activity.

(a) As used in this subsection, the term "inherent risk" means those dangers or conditions, known or unknown, which are characteristic of, intrinsic to, or an integral part of the activity and which are not eliminated even if the activity provider acts with due care in a reasonably prudent manner. The term includes, but is not limited to:

1. The failure by the activity provider to warn the natural guardian or minor child of an inherent risk; and

2. The risk that the minor child or another participant in the activity may act in a negligent or intentional manner and contribute to the injury or death of the minor child. A participant does not include the activity provider or its owners, affiliates, employees, or agents.

(b) To be enforceable, a waiver or release executed under this subsection must, at a minimum, include the following statement in uppercase type that is at least 5 points larger than, and clearly distinguishable from, the rest of the text of the waiver or release:

NOTICE TO THE MINOR CHILD'S NATURAL GUARDIAN

READ THIS FORM COMPLETELY AND CAREFULLY. YOU ARE AGREEING TO LET YOUR MINOR CHILD ENGAGE IN A POTENTIALLY DANGEROUS ACTIVITY. YOU ARE AGREEING THAT, EVEN IF (name of released party or parties) USES REASONABLE CARE IN PROVIDING THIS ACTIVITY,

THERE IS A CHANCE YOUR CHILD MAY BE SERIOUSLY INJURED OR KILLED BY PARTICIPATING IN THIS ACTIVITY BECAUSE THERE ARE CERTAIN DANGERS INHERENT IN THE ACTIVITY WHICH CANNOT BE AVOIDED OR ELIMINATED. BY SIGNING THIS FORM YOU ARE GIVING UP YOUR CHILD'S RIGHT AND YOUR RIGHT TO RECOVER FROM (name of released party or parties) IN A LAWSUIT FOR ANY PERSONAL INJURY, INCLUDING DEATH, TO YOUR CHILD OR ANY PROPERTY DAMAGE THAT RESULTS FROM THE RISKS THAT ARE A NATURAL PART OF THE ACTIVITY. YOU HAVE THE RIGHT TO REFUSE TO SIGN THIS FORM, AND (name of released party or parties) HAS THE RIGHT TO REFUSE TO LET YOUR CHILD PARTICIPATE IF YOU DO NOT SIGN THIS FORM.

(c) If a waiver or release complies with paragraph (b) and waives no more than allowed under this subsection, there is a rebuttable presumption that the waiver or release is valid and that any injury or damage to the minor child arose from the inherent risk involved in the activity.

1. To rebut the presumption that the waiver or release is valid, a claimant must demonstrate by a preponderance of the evidence that the waiver or release does not comply with this subsection.

2. To rebut the presumption that the injury or damage to the minor child arose from an inherent risk involved in the activity, a claimant must demonstrate by clear and convincing evidence that the conduct, condition, or other cause resulting in the injury or damage was not an inherent risk of the activity.

3. If a presumption under this paragraph is rebutted, liability and compensatory damages must be established by a preponderance of the evidence.

(d) Nothing in this subsection limits the ability of natural guardians, on behalf of any of their minor children, to waive and release, in advance, any claim or cause of action against a noncommercial activity provider, or its owners, affiliates, employees, or agents, to the extent authorized by common law.

(4) All instruments executed by a natural guardian for the benefit of the ward under the powers specified in this section are binding on the ward. The natural guardian may not, without a court order, use the property of the ward for the guardian's benefit or to satisfy the guardian's support obligation to the ward.

History.
S. 1, ch. 74-106; s. 8, ch. 75-166; s. 7, ch. 75-222; s. 1, ch. 77-190; s. 3, ch. 79-221; s. 17, ch. 89-96; s. 22, ch. 92-200; s. 66, ch. 95-211; s. 73, ch. 97-170; s. 11, ch. 2002-195; s. 8, ch. 2005-101; s. 3, ch. 2006-178, eff. July 1, 2006; s. 2, ch. 2010-27, eff. Apr. 27, 2010; s. 1, ch. 2012-48, eff. July 1, 2012.

Editor's Notes.
Created from former s. 744.13.

744.3021. Guardians of minors.

(1) Upon petition of a parent, brother, sister, next of kin, or other person interested in the welfare of a minor, a guardian for a minor may be appointed by the court without the necessity of adjudication pursuant to s. 744.331. A guardian appointed for a minor, whether of the person or property, has the authority of a plenary guardian.

(2) A minor is not required to attend the hearing on the petition for appointment of a guardian, unless otherwise directed by the court.

(3) In its discretion, the court may appoint an attorney to represent the interests of a minor at the hearing on the petition for appointment of a guardian.

History.
S. 9, ch. 90-271.

744.3025. Claims of minors.

(1)(a) The court may appoint a guardian ad litem to represent the minor's interest before approving a settlement of the minor's portion of the claim in any case in which a minor has a claim for personal injury, property damage, wrongful death, or other cause of action in which the gross settlement of the claim exceeds $15,000.

(b) The court shall appoint a guardian ad litem to represent the minor's interest before approving a settlement of the minor's claim in any case in which the gross settlement involving a minor equals or exceeds $50,000.

(c) The appointment of the guardian ad litem must be without the necessity of bond or notice.

(d) The duty of the guardian ad litem is to protect the minor's interests as described in the Florida Probate Rules.

(e) A court need not appoint a guardian ad litem for the minor if a guardian of the minor has previously been appointed and that guardian has no potential adverse interest to the minor. A court may appoint a guardian ad litem if the court believes a guardian ad litem is necessary to protect the interests of the minor.

(2) Unless waived, the court shall award reasonable fees and costs to the guardian ad litem to be paid out of the gross proceeds of the settlement.

History.
S. 4, ch. 2006-178, eff. July 1, 2006.

744.3031. Emergency temporary guardianship.

(1) A court, prior to appointment of a guardian but after a petition for determination of incapacity has been filed pursuant to this chapter, may appoint an emergency temporary guardian for the person or property, or both, of an alleged incapacitated person. The court must specifically find that there appears to be imminent

danger that the physical or mental health or safety of the person will be seriously impaired or that the person's property is in danger of being wasted, misappropriated, or lost unless immediate action is taken. The subject of the proceeding or any adult interested in the welfare of that person may apply to the court in which the proceeding is pending for the emergency appointment of a temporary guardian. The powers and duties of the emergency temporary guardian must be specifically enumerated by court order. The court shall appoint counsel to represent the alleged incapacitated person during any such summary proceedings, and such appointed counsel may request that the proceeding be recorded and transcribed.

(2) The court may appoint an emergency temporary guardian on its own motion if no petition for appointment of guardian has been filed at the time of entry of an order determining incapacity.

(3) The authority of an emergency temporary guardian expires 90 days after the date of appointment or when a guardian is appointed, whichever occurs first. The authority of the emergency temporary guardian may be extended for an additional 90 days upon a showing that the emergency conditions still exist.

(4) The court may issue an injunction, restraining order, or other appropriate writ to protect the physical or mental health or safety of the person who is the ward of the emergency temporary guardianship.

(5) The emergency temporary guardian shall take an oath to faithfully perform the duties of a guardian before letters of emergency temporary guardianship are issued.

(6) Before exercising authority as guardian, the emergency temporary guardian of the property may be required to file a bond in accordance with s. 744.351.

(7) An emergency temporary guardian's authority and responsibility begins upon issuance of letters of emergency temporary guardianship in accordance with s. 744.345.

(8)(a) An emergency temporary guardian shall file a final report no later than 30 days after the expiration of the emergency temporary guardianship.

(b) If an emergency temporary guardian is a guardian for the property, the final report must consist of a verified inventory of the property, as provided in s. 744.365, as of the date the letters of emergency temporary guardianship were issued, a final accounting that gives a full and correct account of the receipts and disbursements of all the property of the ward over which the guardian had control, and a statement of the property of the ward on hand at the end of the emergency temporary guardianship. If the emergency temporary guardian becomes the successor guardian of the property, the final report must satisfy the requirements of the initial guardianship report for the guardian of the property as provided in s. 744.362.

(c) If the emergency temporary guardian is a guardian of the person, the final report must summarize the activities of the temporary guardian with regard to residential placement, medical condition, mental health and rehabilitative services, and the social condition of the ward to the extent of the authority granted to the temporary guardian in the letters of guardianship. If the emergency temporary guardian becomes the successor guardian of the person, the report must satisfy the requirements of the initial report for a guardian of the person as stated in s. 744.362.

(d) A copy of the final report of the emergency temporary guardianship shall be served on the successor guardian and the ward.

History.

S. 19, ch. 89-96; s. 10, ch. 90-271; s. 1070, ch. 97-102; s. 5, ch. 2006-178, eff. July 1, 2006.

744.304. Standby guardianship.

(1) Upon a petition by the natural guardians or a guardian appointed under s. 744.3021, the court may appoint a standby guardian of the person or property of a minor. The court may also appoint an alternate to the guardian to act if the standby guardian does not serve or ceases to serve after appointment. Notice of a hearing on the petition must be served on the parents, natural or adoptive, and on any guardian currently serving unless the notice is waived in writing by them or waived by the court for good cause shown.

(2) Upon petition of a currently serving guardian, a standby guardian of the person or property of an incapacitated person may be appointed by the court. Notice of the hearing shall be served on the ward's next of kin.

(3) The standby guardian or alternate shall be empowered to assume the duties of guardianship immediately on the death, removal, or resignation of the guardian of a minor, or on the death or adjudication of incapacity of the last surviving natural guardian of a minor, or upon the death, removal, or resignation of the guardian for an adult. The guardian of the ward's property may not be empowered to deal with the ward's property, other than to safeguard it, before issuance of letters of guardianship. If the ward is over the age of 18 years, the court shall conduct a hearing as provided in s. 744.331 before confirming the appointment of the standby guardian, unless the ward has previously been found to be incapacitated.

(4) Within 20 days after assumption of duties as guardian, a standby guardian shall petition for confirmation of appointment. If the court finds the standby guardian to be qualified to serve as guardian under ss. 744.309 and 744.312, appointment of the guardian must be confirmed. Each guardian so confirmed shall file an oath in accordance with s. 744.347, shall file a bond, and shall submit to a credit and a criminal history record check as set forth in s. 744.3135, if required.

Letters of guardianship must then be issued in the manner provided in s. 744.345.

(5) After the assumption of duties by a standby guardian, the court shall have jurisdiction over the guardian and the ward.

History.
S. 1, ch. 74-106; s. 7, ch. 75-222; s. 1, ch. 77-174; s. 20, ch. 89-96; s. 11, ch. 90-271; s. 1071, ch. 97-102; s. 6, ch. 2006-178, eff. July 1, 2006.

Editor's Notes.
Created from former s. 744.72.

744.3045. Preneed guardian.

(1) A competent adult may name a preneed guardian by making a written declaration that names such guardian to serve in the event of the declarant's incapacity.

(2) The written declaration must reasonably identify the declarant and preneed guardian and be signed by the declarant in the presence of at least two attesting witnesses present at the same time.

(3) The declarant may file the declaration with the clerk of the court. When a petition for incapacity is filed, the clerk shall produce the declaration.

(4) Production of the declaration in a proceeding for incapacity shall constitute a rebuttable presumption that the preneed guardian is entitled to serve as guardian. The court shall not be bound to appoint the preneed guardian if the preneed guardian is found to be unqualified to serve as guardian.

(5) The preneed guardian shall assume the duties of guardian immediately upon an adjudication of incapacity.

(6) If the preneed guardian refuses to serve, a written declaration appointing an alternate preneed guardian constitutes a rebuttable presumption that such preneed guardian is entitled to serve as guardian. The court is not bound to appoint the alternate preneed guardian if the alternate preneed guardian is found to be unqualified to serve as guardian.

(7) Within 20 days after assumption of duties as guardian, a preneed guardian shall petition for confirmation of appointment. If the court finds the preneed guardian to be qualified to serve as guardian pursuant to ss. 744.309 and 744.312, appointment of the guardian must be confirmed. Each guardian so confirmed shall file an oath in accordance with s. 744.347 and shall file a bond, if required. Letters of guardianship must then be issued in the manner provided in s. 744.345.

History.
S. 21, ch. 89-96; s. 12, ch. 90-271.

744.3046. Preneed guardian for minor.

(1) Both parents, natural or adoptive, if living, or the surviving parent, may nominate a preneed guardian of the person or property or both of the parent's minor child by making a written declaration that names such guardian to serve if the minor's last surviving parent becomes incapacitated or dies. The declarant or declarants may also name an alternate to the guardian to act if the designated preneed guardian refuses to serve, renounces the appointment, dies, or becomes incapacitated after the death of the last surviving parent of the minor.

(2) The written declaration must reasonably identify the declarant or declarants and the designated preneed guardian and must be signed by the declarant or declarants in the presence of at least two attesting witnesses present at the same time. The written declaration must also provide the following information for each minor child named in such declaration: the full name as it appears on the birth certificate or as ordered by a court, date of birth, and social security number, if any.

(3) The declarant must file the declaration with the clerk of the court. When a petition for incapacity of the last surviving parent or the appointment of a guardian upon the death of the last surviving parent is filed, the clerk shall produce the declaration.

(4) Production of the declaration in a proceeding to determine incapacity of the last surviving parent, or in a proceeding to appoint a guardian upon the death of the last surviving parent, constitutes a rebuttable presumption that the designated preneed guardian is entitled to serve as guardian. The court is not bound to appoint the designated preneed guardian if the designated preneed guardian is found to be unqualified to serve as guardian.

(5) The preneed guardian shall assume the duties of guardian immediately upon an adjudication of incapacity of the last surviving parent or the death of the last surviving parent.

(6) If the preneed guardian refuses to serve, a written declaration appointing an alternate preneed guardian constitutes a rebuttable presumption that the alternate preneed guardian is entitled to serve as guardian. The court is not bound to appoint the alternate preneed guardian if the alternate preneed guardian is found to be unqualified to serve as guardian.

(7) Within 20 days after assumption of duties as guardian, a preneed guardian shall petition for confirmation of appointment. If the court finds the preneed guardian to be qualified to serve as guardian, appointment of the guardian must be confirmed. Each guardian so confirmed shall file an oath in accordance with s. 744.347 and shall file a bond, if the court requires a bond. Letters of guardianship must then be issued in the manner provided in s. 744.345.

(8) The clerk shall maintain all declarations filed pursuant to this section until:

(a) A petition for incapacity of the last surviving parent is filed or petition for the appointment of a guardian upon the death of the last surviving parent is filed as provided in subsection (3); or

(b) All minor children named in the declaration have reached the age of majority.

The clerk may dispose of such written declaration in accordance with law.

History.
S. 23, ch. 92-200.

744.306. Foreign guardians.

(1) When the residence of a ward of a foreign guardian is moved to this state, the guardian shall, within 60 days after such change of residence, file the authenticated order of her or his appointment with the clerk of the court in the county where the ward resides. Such order shall be recognized and given full faith and credit in the courts of this state. The guardian and the ward are subject to this chapter.

(2) A guardian appointed in any state, territory, or country may maintain or defend any action in this state as a representative of her or his ward.

(3) Debtors who have received no written demand for payment from a guardian appointed in this state within 60 days after the appointment of a guardian, curator, conservator, or committee in any state, territory, or country other than this state, and whose property in this state is subject to a mortgage or other lien securing the debt held by the foreign guardian, curator, conservator, or committee, may pay the debt to the foreign guardian, curator, conservator, or committee after the expiration of 60 days from the date of her or his appointment. A satisfaction of the mortgage or lien, executed after the 60 days have expired by the foreign guardian, curator, conservator, or committee, with an authenticated copy of the letters or other evidence of authority of the foreign guardian, curator, conservator, or committee attached, may be recorded in the public records of this state and shall constitute an effective discharge of the mortgage or lien, irrespective of whether the debtor had received written demand before paying the debt.

(4) All persons indebted to a ward, or having possession of personal property belonging to a ward, who have received no written demand for payment of the indebtedness or the delivery of the property from a guardian appointed in this state are authorized to pay the indebtedness or to deliver the personal property to the foreign guardian, curator, conservator, or committee after the expiration of the 60 days from the date of her or his appointment.

History.
S. 1, ch. 74-106; s. 7, ch. 75-222; s. 23, ch. 89-96; s. 1072, ch. 97-102.
Editor's Notes.
Created from former s. 744.15.

744.307. Foreign guardian may manage the property of nonresident ward.

(1) A guardian of the property of a nonresident ward, duly appointed by a court of another state, territory, or country, who desires to manage any part or all of the property of the ward located in this state, may file a petition showing his or her appointment, describing the property, stating its estimated value, and showing the indebtedness, if any, existing against the ward in this state, to the best of the guardian's knowledge and belief.

(2) The guardian shall designate a resident agent as required by the Florida Probate Rules.

(3) The guardian shall file authenticated copies of his or her letters of guardianship or other authority and of his or her bond or other security. The court shall determine if the foreign bond or other security is sufficient to guarantee the faithful management of the ward's property in this state. The court may require a new guardian's bond in this state in the amount it deems necessary and conditioned for the proper management and application of the property of the ward coming into the custody of the guardian in this state.

(4) Thereafter, the guardianship shall be governed by the law concerning guardianships.

History.
S. 1, ch. 74-106; s. 7, ch. 75-222; s. 24, ch. 89-96; s. 67, ch. 95-211; s. 1073, ch. 97-102.
Editor's Notes.
Created from former s. 744.16.

744.308. Resident guardian of the property of nonresident ward.

(1) The court may appoint a person qualified under s. 744.309 as guardian of a nonresident ward's property upon the petition of a foreign guardian, next of kin, or creditor of the ward, regardless of whether he or she has a foreign guardian or not.

(2) The petition for the appointment of a guardian for the property of a nonresident ward shall be in writing and shall be prepared in accordance with the requirements of s. 744.334.

(3) If it is alleged that the incapacity is due to mental or physical incapacity, the petition shall be accompanied by an authenticated copy of the adjudication of incapacity from the qualified authorities in the state, territory, or country where the incapacitated person is domiciled and shall state whether the incapacitated person is in the custody of any person or institution and, if so, the name and post office address of the custodian. The adjudication shall constitute prima facie proof of the incapacity.

(4) If the question about the mental or physical incapacity of a nonresident is presented while the nonresident is temporarily residing in this state and he or she is not under an adjudication of incapacity made in some other state, territory, or country, the procedure for the appointment of a guardian of the nonresident's property shall be the same as though he or she were a resident of this state.

(5) When the ground for the appointment of a guardian is incapacity for which the person has been adjudicated in another state, territory, or country, notice of the hearing shall be served personally or by registered mail on the ward and the ward's next of kin and legal custodian, if any, at least 20 days before the hearing.

(6) In the appointment of the guardian, the court shall be governed by s. 744.312.

(7) The duties, powers, and liabilities for the custody, control, management, and disposition of the ward's property and removal, accounting, and discharge shall be governed by the law applicable to guardians of property of resident wards.

History.
S. 1, ch. 74-106; s. 7, ch. 75-222; s. 1, ch. 77-174; s. 25, ch. 89-96; s. 13, ch. 90-271; s. 1074, ch. 97-102.

Editor's Notes.
Created from former ss. 744.18, 744.19, 744.21, 744.25, 744.26.

744.3085. Guardian advocates.

A circuit court may appoint a guardian advocate, without an adjudication of incapacity, for a person with developmental disabilities if the person lacks the capacity to do some, but not all, of the tasks necessary to care for his or her person, property, or estate, or if the person has voluntarily petitioned for the appointment of a guardian advocate. Unless otherwise specified, the proceeding shall be governed by the Florida Probate Rules. In accordance with the legislative intent of this chapter, courts are encouraged to consider appointing a guardian advocate, when appropriate, as a less restrictive form of guardianship.

History.
S. 11, ch. 2004-260.

PART IV.
GUARDIANS.

744.309. Who may be appointed guardian of a resident ward.

(1) Resident.

(a) Any resident of this state who is sui juris and is 18 years of age or older is qualified to act as guardian of a ward.

(b) No judge shall act as guardian after this law becomes effective, except when he or she is related to the ward by blood, marriage, or adoption, or has maintained a close relationship with the ward or the ward's family, and serves without compensation.

(2) Nonresident. — A nonresident of the state may serve as guardian of a resident ward if he or she is:

(a) Related by lineal consanguinity to the ward;

(b) A legally adopted child or adoptive parent of the ward;

(c) A spouse, brother, sister, uncle, aunt, niece, or nephew of the ward, or someone related by lineal consanguinity to any such person; or

(d) The spouse of a person otherwise qualified under this section.

(3) Disqualified persons. — No person who has been convicted of a felony or who, from any incapacity or illness, is incapable of discharging the duties of a guardian, or who is otherwise unsuitable to perform the duties of a guardian, shall be appointed to act as guardian. Further, no person who has been judicially determined to have committed abuse, abandonment, or neglect against a child as defined in s. 39.01 or s. 984.03(1), (2), and (37), or who has been found guilty of, regardless of adjudication, or entered a plea of nolo contendere or guilty to, any offense prohibited under s. 435.04 or similar statute of another jurisdiction, shall be appointed to act as a guardian. Except as provided in subsection (5) or subsection (6), a person who provides substantial services to the proposed ward in a professional or business capacity, or a creditor of the proposed ward, may not be appointed guardian and retain that previous professional or business relationship. A person may not be appointed a guardian if he or she is in the employ of any person, agency, government, or corporation that provides service to the proposed ward in a professional or business capacity, except that a person so employed may be appointed if he or she is the spouse, adult child, parent, or sibling of the proposed ward or the court determines that the potential conflict of interest is insubstantial and that the appointment would clearly be in the proposed ward's best interest. The court may not appoint a guardian in any other circumstance in which a conflict of interest may occur.

(4) Trust company, state bank or savings association, or national bank or federal savings and loan association. — A trust company, a state banking corporation or state savings association authorized and qualified to exercise fiduciary powers in this state, or a national banking association or federal savings and loan association authorized and qualified to exercise fiduciary powers in this state may act as guardian of the property of the ward.

(5) Nonprofit corporate guardian. — A nonprofit corporation organized for religious or charitable purposes and existing under the laws of this state may be appointed guardian for a ward. If the nonprofit corporate guardian charges fees against the assets or property of the ward for its services, the corporation must employ at least one professional guardian.

(6) Health care provider. — A provider of health care services to the ward, whether direct or indirect, may not be appointed the guardian of the ward, unless the court specifically finds that there is no conflict of interest with the ward's best interests.

History.
S. 1, ch. 74-106; s. 8, ch. 75-222; s. 4, ch. 79-221; s. 7, ch. 81-27; s. 2, ch. 83-139; s. 26, ch. 89-96; s. 14, ch. 90-271; s. 6, ch. 96-184; s. 5, ch. 96-354; s. 1781, ch. 97-102; s. 48, ch. 98-280; s. 159, ch. 98-403; s. 8, ch. 2000-135; s. 110, ch. 2000-349; s. 4, ch. 2002-195; s. 31, ch. 2004-267; s. 53, ch. 2010-114, eff. Aug. 1, 2010.

Editor's Notes.
Section 31, ch. 2004-267, reenacted (3) without change to incorporate amendments to statutory sections referenced therein.

Created from former s. 744.27.

Section 58, ch. 2010-114 provides: "The changes made by this act are intended to be prospective in nature. It is not intended that persons who are employed or licensed on the effective date of this act be rescreened until such time as they are otherwise required to be rescreened pursuant to law, at which time they must meet the requirements for screening as set forth in this act."

744.3115. Advance directives for health care.

In each proceeding in which a guardian is appointed under this chapter, the court shall determine whether the ward, prior to incapacity, has executed any valid advance directive under chapter 765. If any advance directive exists, the court shall specify in its order and letters of guardianship what authority, if any, the guardian shall exercise over the surrogate. Pursuant to the grounds listed in s. 765.105, the court, upon its own motion, may, with notice to the surrogate and any other appropriate parties, modify or revoke the authority of the surrogate to make health care decisions for the ward. For purposes of this section, the term "health care decision" has the same meaning as in s. 765.101.

History.

S. 6, ch. 92-199; s. 1, ch. 94-183; s. 7, ch. 2006-178, eff. July 1, 2006.

744.312. Considerations in appointment of guardian.

(1) Subject to the provisions of subsection (4), the court may appoint any person who is fit and proper and qualified to act as guardian, whether related to the ward or not.

(2) The court shall give preference to the appointment of a person who:

(a) Is related by blood or marriage to the ward;

(b) Has educational, professional, or business experience relevant to the nature of the services sought to be provided;

(c) Has the capacity to manage the financial resources involved; or

(d) Has the ability to meet the requirements of the law and the unique needs of the individual case.

(3) The court shall also:

(a) Consider the wishes expressed by an incapacitated person as to who shall be appointed guardian;

(b) Consider the preference of a minor who is age 14 or over as to who should be appointed guardian;

(c) Consider any person designated as guardian in any will in which the ward is a beneficiary.

(4) If the person designated is qualified to serve pursuant to s. 744.309, the court shall appoint any standby guardian or preneed guardian, unless the court determines that appointing such person is contrary to the best interests of the ward.

History.

S. 1, ch. 74-106; s. 12, ch. 75-222; s. 1, ch. 77-174; s. 5, ch. 79-221; s. 27, ch. 89-96; s. 15, ch. 90-271.

Editor's Notes.

Created from former s. 744.35.

744.3125. Application for appointment.

(1) Every prospective guardian must complete an application for appointment as guardian. The application must list the person's qualifications to serve as a guardian.

(2) A person may not be appointed a guardian unless the person discloses in the application form the names of all wards for whom the person is currently acting as a guardian. The application must identify each ward by court file number and circuit court in which the case is pending and must state whether the person is acting as the limited or plenary guardian of the person or property or both.

(3) This section does not apply to corporate guardians other than nonprofit corporate guardians or to public guardians.

(4) Nonprofit corporate guardians must file quarterly with the clerk of court disclosure statements that contain the information required under subsections (1) and (2), rather than filing a guardianship application with each petition to be appointed guardian.

History.

S. 29, ch. 89-96; s. 16, ch. 90-271; s. 1075, ch. 97-102.

744.3135. Credit and criminal investigation.

(1) The court may require a nonprofessional guardian and shall require a professional or public guardian, and all employees of a professional guardian who have a fiduciary responsibility to a ward, to submit, at their own expense, to an investigation of the guardian's credit history and to undergo level 2 background screening as required under s. 435.04. If a credit or criminal history record check is required, the court must consider the results of any investigation before appointing a guardian. At any time, the court may require a guardian or the guardian's employees to submit to an investigation of the person's credit history and complete a level 1 background screening as set forth in s. 435.03. The court shall consider the results of any investigation when reappointing a guardian. The clerk of the court shall maintain a file on each guardian appointed by the court and retain in the file documentation of the result of any investigation conducted under this section. A professional guardian must pay the clerk of the court a fee of up to $7.50 for handling and processing professional guardian files.

(2) For nonprofessional guardians, the court shall accept the satisfactory completion of a criminal history record check as described in this subsection. A nonprofessional guardian satisfies the requirements of this section by undergoing a state and national criminal history record check using a fingerprint card. The clerk of the court shall obtain fingerprint cards from the Federal Bureau of Investigation and make them available to nonprofessional guardians. Any nonprofessional guardian who is so required shall have his or her fingerprints taken and forward the completed fingerprint card along with the necessary fee to the Department of Law Enforcement for processing. The results of the fingerprint card criminal history record check shall be forwarded to the clerk of the court, who shall maintain the results in the nonprofessional guardian's file and make the results available to the court.

(3) For professional guardians, the court and the Statewide Public Guardianship Office shall accept the satisfactory completion of a criminal history record check by any method described in this subsection. A professional guardian satisfies the requirements of this section by undergoing:

(a) An electronic fingerprint criminal history record check. A professional guardian may use any electronic fingerprinting equipment used for criminal history record checks. The Statewide Public Guardianship Office shall adopt a rule detailing the acceptable methods for completing an electronic fingerprint criminal history record check under this section. The professional guardian shall pay the actual costs incurred by the Federal Bureau of Investigation and the Department of Law Enforcement for the criminal history record check. The entity completing the record check must immediately send the results of the criminal history record check to the clerk of the court and the Statewide Public Guardianship Office. The clerk of the court shall maintain the results in the professional guardian's file and shall make the results available to the court; or

(b) A criminal history record check using a fingerprint card. The clerk of the court shall obtain fingerprint cards from the Federal Bureau of Investigation and make them available to guardians. Any guardian who is so required shall have his or her fingerprints taken and forward the proper fingerprint card along with the necessary fee to the Department of Law Enforcement for processing. The results of the fingerprint card criminal history record checks shall be forwarded to the clerk of the court, who shall maintain the results in the guardian's file and make the results available to the court and the Statewide Public Guardianship Office.

(4)(a) A professional guardian, and each employee of a professional guardian who has a fiduciary responsibility to a ward, must complete, at his or her own expense, a level 2 background screening as set forth in s. 435.04 before and at least once every 5 years after the date the guardian is registered. A professional guardian, and each employee of a professional guardian who has a fiduciary responsibility to a ward, must complete, at his or her own expense, a level 1 background screening as set forth in s. 435.03 at least once every 2 years after the date the guardian is registered. However, a professional guardian is not required to resubmit fingerprints for a criminal history record check if he or she has been screened using electronic fingerprinting equipment and the fingerprints are retained by the Department of Law Enforcement in order to notify the clerk of the court of any crime charged against the person in this state or elsewhere, as appropriate.

(b) All fingerprints electronically submitted to the Department of Law Enforcement under this section shall be retained by the Department of Law Enforce-

ment in a manner provided by rule and entered in the statewide automated fingerprint identification system authorized by s. 943.05(2)(b). The fingerprints shall thereafter be available for all purposes and uses authorized for arrest fingerprint cards entered in the Criminal Justice Information Program under s. 943.051.

(c) The Department of Law Enforcement shall search all arrest fingerprint cards received under s. 943.051 against the fingerprints retained in the statewide automated fingerprint identification system under paragraph (b). Any arrest record that is identified with the fingerprints of a person described in this paragraph must be reported to the clerk of court. The clerk of court must forward any arrest record received for a professional guardian to the Statewide Public Guardianship Office within 5 days. Each professional guardian who elects to submit fingerprint information electronically shall participate in this search process by paying an annual fee to the Statewide Public Guardianship Office of the Department of Elderly Affairs and by informing the clerk of court and the Statewide Public Guardianship Office of any change in the status of his or her guardianship appointment. The amount of the annual fee to be imposed for performing these searches and the procedures for the retention of professional guardian fingerprints and the dissemination of search results shall be established by rule of the Department of Law Enforcement. At least once every 5 years, the Statewide Public Guardianship Office must request that the Department of Law Enforcement forward the fingerprints maintained under this section to the Federal Bureau of Investigation.

(5)(a) A professional guardian, and each employee of a professional guardian who has a fiduciary responsibility to a ward, must complete, at his or her own expense, an investigation of his or her credit history before and at least once every 2 years after the date of the guardian's registration with the Statewide Public Guardianship Office.

(b) The Statewide Public Guardianship Office shall adopt a rule detailing the acceptable methods for completing a credit investigation under this section. If appropriate, the Statewide Public Guardianship Office may administer credit investigations. If the office chooses to administer the credit investigation, the office may adopt a rule setting a fee, not to exceed $25, to reimburse the costs associated with the administration of a credit investigation.

(6) The Statewide Public Guardianship Office may inspect at any time the results of any credit or criminal history record check of a public or professional guardian conducted under this section. The office shall maintain copies of the credit or criminal history record check results in the guardian's registration file. If the results of a credit or criminal investigation of a public or professional guardian have not been forwarded to the

Statewide Public Guardianship Office by the investigating agency, the clerk of the court shall forward copies of the results of the investigations to the office upon receiving them.

(7) The requirements of this section do not apply to a professional guardian, or to the employees of a professional guardian, that is a trust company, a state banking corporation or state savings association authorized and qualified to exercise fiduciary powers in this state, or a national banking association or federal savings and loan association authorized and qualified to exercise fiduciary powers in this state.

History.
S. 30, ch. 89-96; s. 1076, ch. 97-102; s. 2, ch. 97-161; s. 10, ch. 99-277; s. 5, ch. 2002-195; s. 10, ch. 2003-57; s. 114, ch. 2003-402; s. 12, ch. 2004-260; s. 22, ch. 2004-267; s. 8, ch. 2006-178, eff. July 1, 2006; s. 1, ch. 2007-127, eff. July 1, 2007.

Editor's Notes.
Section 22, ch. 2004-267, reenacted this section without change to incorporate amendments to statutory sections referenced therein.

744.3145. Guardian education requirements.

(1) Each ward is entitled to a guardian competent to perform the duties of a guardian necessary to protect the interests of the ward.

(2) Each person appointed by the court to be a guardian, other than a parent who is the guardian of the property of a minor child, must receive a minimum of 8 hours of instruction and training which covers:

(a) The legal duties and responsibilities of the guardian;

(b) The rights of the ward;

(c) The availability of local resources to aid the ward; and

(d) The preparation of habilitation plans and annual guardianship reports, including financial accounting for the ward's property.

(3) Each person appointed by the court to be the guardian of the property of his or her minor child must receive a minimum of 4 hours of instruction and training that covers:

(a) The legal duties and responsibilities of the guardian of the property;

(b) The preparation of the initial inventory and annual guardianship accountings for the ward's property; and

(c) Use of guardianship assets.

(4) Each person appointed by the court to be a guardian must complete the required number of hours of instruction and education within 4 months after his or her appointment as guardian. The instruction and education must be completed through a course approved by the chief judge of the circuit court and taught by a court-approved organization. Court-approved organizations may include, but are not limited to, community or junior colleges, guardianship organizations, and the local bar association or The Florida Bar.

(5) Expenses incurred by the guardian to satisfy the education requirement may be paid from the ward's estate, unless the court directs that such expenses be paid by the guardian individually.

(6) The court may, in its discretion, waive some or all of the requirements of this section or impose additional requirements. The court shall make its decision on a case-by-case basis and, in making its decision, shall consider the experience and education of the guardian, the duties assigned to the guardian, and the needs of the ward.

(7) The provisions of this section do not apply to professional guardians.

History.
S. 31, ch. 89-96; s. 17, ch. 90-271; s. 1077, ch. 97-102; s. 3, ch. 97-161; s. 11, ch. 2003-57; s. 9, ch. 2006-178, eff. July 1, 2006.

PART V.
ADJUDICATION OF INCAPACITY AND APPOINTMENT OF GUARDIANS.

744.3201. Petition to determine incapacity.

(1) A petition to determine incapacity of a person may be executed by an adult person.

(2) The petition must be verified and must:

(a) State the name, age, and present address of the petitioner and his or her relationship to the alleged incapacitated person;

(b) State the name, age, county of residence, and present address of the alleged incapacitated person;

(c) Specify the primary language spoken by the alleged incapacitated person, if known;

(d) Allege that the petitioner believes the alleged incapacitated person to be incapacitated and specify the factual information on which such belief is based and the names and addresses of all persons known to the petitioner who have knowledge of such facts through personal observations;

(e) State the name and address of the alleged incapacitated person's attending or family physician, if known;

(f) State which rights enumerated in s. 744.3215 the alleged incapacitated person is incapable of exercising, to the best of petitioner's knowledge. If the petitioner has insufficient experience to make such judgments, the petition must so state; and

(g) State the names, relationships, and addresses of the next of kin of the alleged incapacitated person, so far as are known, specifying the dates of birth of any who are minors.

(3) A copy of any petition for appointment of guardian or emergency temporary guardian, if applicable, shall be filed with the petition to determine incapacity.

History.
S. 33, ch. 89-96; s. 18, ch. 90-271; s. 22, ch. 95-401; s. 1078, ch. 97-102.

744.3215. Rights of persons determined incapacitated.

(1) A person who has been determined to be incapacitated retains the right:

(a) To have an annual review of the guardianship report and plan.

(b) To have continuing review of the need for restriction of his or her rights.

(c) To be restored to capacity at the earliest possible time.

(d) To be treated humanely, with dignity and respect, and to be protected against abuse, neglect, and exploitation.

(e) To have a qualified guardian.

(f) To remain as independent as possible, including having his or her preference as to place and standard of living honored, either as he or she expressed or demonstrated his or her preference prior to the determination of his or her incapacity or as he or she currently expresses his or her preference, insofar as such request is reasonable.

(g) To be properly educated.

(h) To receive prudent financial management for his or her property and to be informed how his or her property is being managed, if he or she has lost the right to manage property.

(i) To receive services and rehabilitation necessary to maximize the quality of life.

(j) To be free from discrimination because of his or her incapacity.

(k) To have access to the courts.

(*l*) To counsel.

(m) To receive visitors and communicate with others.

(n) To notice of all proceedings related to determination of capacity and guardianship, unless the court finds the incapacitated person lacks the ability to comprehend the notice.

(o) To privacy.

(2) Rights that may be removed from a person by an order determining incapacity but not delegated to a guardian include the right:

(a) To marry. If the right to enter into a contract has been removed, the right to marry is subject to court approval.

(b) To vote.

(c) To personally apply for government benefits.

(d) To have a driver's license.

(e) To travel.

(f) To seek or retain employment.

(3) Rights that may be removed from a person by an order determining incapacity and which may be delegated to the guardian include the right:

(a) To contract.

(b) To sue and defend lawsuits.

(c) To apply for government benefits.

(d) To manage property or to make any gift or disposition of property.

(e) To determine his or her residence.

(f) To consent to medical and mental health treatment.

(g) To make decisions about his or her social environment or other social aspects of his or her life.

(4) Without first obtaining specific authority from the court, as described in s. 744.3725, a guardian may not:

(a) Commit the ward to a facility, institution, or licensed service provider without formal placement proceeding, pursuant to chapter 393, chapter 394, or chapter 397.

(b) Consent on behalf of the ward to the performance on the ward of any experimental biomedical or behavioral procedure or to the participation by the ward in any biomedical or behavioral experiment. The court may permit such performance or participation only if:

1. It is of direct benefit to, and is intended to preserve the life of or prevent serious impairment to the mental or physical health of the ward; or

2. It is intended to assist the ward to develop or regain his or her abilities.

(c) Initiate a petition for dissolution of marriage for the ward.

(d) Consent on behalf of the ward to termination of the ward's parental rights.

(e) Consent on behalf of the ward to the performance of a sterilization or abortion procedure on the ward.

History.

S. 34, ch. 89-96; s. 19, ch. 90-271; s. 36, ch. 93-39; s. 13, ch. 94-183; s. 44, ch. 96-169; s. 6, ch. 96-354; s. 1782, ch. 97-102; s. 10, ch. 2006-178, eff. July 1, 2006.

744.331. Procedures to determine incapacity.

(1) Notice of petition to determine incapacity. — Notice of the filing of a petition to determine incapacity and a petition for the appointment of a guardian if any and copies of the petitions must be served on and read to the alleged incapacitated person. The notice and copies of the petitions must also be given to the attorney for the alleged incapacitated person, and served upon all next of kin identified in the petition. The notice must state the time and place of the hearing to inquire into the capacity of the alleged incapacitated person and that an attorney has been appointed to represent the person and that, if she or he is determined to be incapable of exercising certain rights, a guardian will be appointed to exercise those rights on her or his behalf.

(2) Attorney for the alleged incapacitated person.

(a) When a court appoints an attorney for an alleged incapacitated person, the court must appoint the office of criminal conflict and civil regional counsel or a private attorney as prescribed in s. 27.511(6). A private attorney must be one who is included in the attorney registry compiled pursuant to s. 27.40. Appointments of private attorneys must be made on a rotating basis, taking into consideration conflicts arising under this chapter.

(b) The court shall appoint an attorney for each person alleged to be incapacitated in all cases involving a petition for adjudication of incapacity. The alleged incapacitated person may substitute her or his own attorney for the attorney appointed by the court.

(c) Any attorney representing an alleged incapacitated person may not serve as guardian of the alleged incapacitated person or as counsel for the guardian of the alleged incapacitated person or the petitioner.

(d) Effective January 1, 2007, an attorney seeking to be appointed by a court for incapacity and guardianship proceedings must have completed a minimum of 8 hours of education in guardianship. A court may waive the initial training requirement for an attorney who has served as a court-appointed attorney in incapacity proceedings or as an attorney of record for guardians for not less than 3 years. The education requirement of this paragraph does not apply to the office of criminal conflict and civil regional counsel until July 1, 2008.

(3) Examining committee.

(a) Within 5 days after a petition for determination of incapacity has been filed, the court shall appoint an examining committee consisting of three members. One member must be a psychiatrist or other physician. The remaining members must be either a psychologist, gerontologist, another psychiatrist, or other physician, a registered nurse, nurse practitioner, licensed social worker, a person with an advanced degree in gerontology from an accredited institution of higher education, or other person who by knowledge, skill, experience, training, or education may, in the court's discretion, advise the court in the form of an expert opinion. One of three members of the committee must have knowledge of the type of incapacity alleged in the petition. Unless good cause is shown, the attending or family physician may not be appointed to the committee. If the attending or family physician is available for consultation, the committee must consult with the physician. Members of the examining committee may not be related to or associated with one another, with the petitioner, with counsel for the petitioner or the proposed guardian, or with the person alleged to be totally or partially incapacitated. A member may not be employed by any private or governmental agency that has custody of, or furnishes, services or subsidies, directly or indirectly, to the person or the family of the person alleged to be incapacitated or for whom a guardianship is sought. A petitioner may not serve as a member of the examining committee. Members of the examining committee must be able to communicate, either directly or through an interpreter, in the language that the alleged incapacitated person speaks or to communicate in a medium understandable to the alleged incapacitated person if she or he is able to communicate. The clerk of the court shall send notice of the appointment to each person appointed no later than 3 days after the court's appointment.

(b) A person who has been appointed to serve as a member of an examining committee to examine an alleged incapacitated person may not thereafter be appointed as a guardian for the person who was the subject of the examination.

(c) Each person appointed to an examining committee must file an affidavit with the court stating that he or she has completed the required courses or will do so no later than 4 months after his or her initial appointment. Each year, the chief judge of the circuit must prepare a list of persons qualified to be members of an examining committee.

(d) A member of an examining committee must complete a minimum of 4 hours of initial training. The person must complete 2 hours of continuing education during each 2-year period after the initial training. The initial training and continuing education program must be developed under the supervision of the Statewide Public Guardianship Office, in consultation with the Florida Conference of Circuit Court Judges; the Elder Law and the Real Property, Probate and Trust Law sections of The Florida Bar; the Florida State Guardianship Association; and the Florida Guardianship Foundation. The court may waive the initial training requirement for a person who has served for not less than 5 years on examining committees. If a person wishes to obtain his or her continuing education on the Internet or by watching a video course, the person must first obtain the approval of the chief judge before taking an Internet or video course.

(e) Each member of the examining committee shall examine the person. Each examining committee member must determine the alleged incapacitated person's ability to exercise those rights specified in s. 744.3215. In addition to the examination, each examining committee member must have access to, and may consider, previous examinations of the person, including, but not limited to, habilitation plans, school records, and psychological and psychosocial reports voluntarily offered for use by the alleged incapacitated person. Each member of the examining committee must submit a report within 15 days after appointment.

(f) The examination of the alleged incapacitated person must include a comprehensive examination, a report of which shall be filed by each examining committee member as part of his or her written report. The comprehensive examination report should be an essential element, but not necessarily the only element, used in making a capacity and guardianship decision. The comprehensive examination must include, if indicated:

1. A physical examination;

2. A mental health examination; and

3. A functional assessment. If any of these three aspects of the examination is not indicated or cannot be accomplished for any reason, the written report must explain the reasons for its omission.

(g) Each committee member's written report must include:

1. To the extent possible, a diagnosis, prognosis, and recommended course of treatment.

2. An evaluation of the alleged incapacitated person's ability to retain her or his rights, including, without limitation, the rights to marry; vote; contract; manage or dispose of property; have a driver's license; determine her or his residence; consent to medical treatment; and make decisions affecting her or his social environment.

3. The results of the comprehensive examination and the committee member's assessment of information provided by the attending or family physician, if any.

4. A description of any matters with respect to which the person lacks the capacity to exercise rights, the extent of that incapacity, and the factual basis for the determination that the person lacks that capacity.

5. The names of all persons present during the time the committee member conducted his or her examination. If a person other than the person who is the subject of the examination supplies answers posed to the alleged incapacitated person, the report must include the response and the name of the person supplying the answer.

6. The signature of the committee member and the date and time the member conducted his or her examination.

(h) A copy of each committee member's report must be served on the petitioner and on the attorney for the alleged incapacitated person within 3 days after the report is filed and at least 5 days before the hearing on the petition.

(4) Dismissal of petition. — If a majority of the examining committee members conclude that the alleged incapacitated person is not incapacitated in any respect, the court shall dismiss the petition.

(5) Adjudicatory hearing.

(a) Upon appointment of the examining committee, the court shall set the date upon which the petition will be heard. The date for the adjudicatory hearing must be set no more than 14 days after the filing of the reports of the examining committee members, unless good cause is shown. The adjudicatory hearing must be conducted at the time and place specified in the notice of hearing and in a manner consistent with due process.

(b) The alleged incapacitated person must be present at the adjudicatory hearing, unless waived by the alleged incapacitated person or the person's attorney or unless good cause can be shown for her or his absence. Determination of good cause rests in the sound discretion of the court.

(c) In the adjudicatory hearing on a petition alleging incapacity, the partial or total incapacity of the person must be established by clear and convincing evidence.

(6) Order determining incapacity. — If, after making findings of fact on the basis of clear and convincing evidence, the court finds that a person is incapacitated with respect to the exercise of a particular right, or all rights, the court shall enter a written order determining such incapacity. A person is determined to be incapacitated only with respect to those rights specified in the order.

(a) The court shall make the following findings:

1. The exact nature and scope of the person's incapacities;

2. The exact areas in which the person lacks capacity to make informed decisions about care and treatment services or to meet the essential requirements for her or his physical or mental health or safety;

3. The specific legal disabilities to which the person is subject; and

4. The specific rights that the person is incapable of exercising.

(b) When an order determines that a person is incapable of exercising delegable rights, the court must consider and find whether there is an alternative to guardianship that will sufficiently address the problems of the incapacitated person. A guardian must be appointed to exercise the incapacitated person's delegable rights unless the court finds there is an alternative. A guardian may not be appointed if the court finds there is an alternative to guardianship which will sufficiently address the problems of the incapacitated person.

(c) In determining that a person is totally incapacitated, the order must contain findings of fact demonstrating that the individual is totally without capacity to care for herself or himself or her or his property.

(d) An order adjudicating a person to be incapacitated constitutes proof of such incapacity until further order of the court.

(e) After the order determining that the person is incapacitated has been filed with the clerk, it must be served on the incapacitated person. The person is deemed incapacitated only to the extent of the findings of the court. The filing of the order is notice of the incapacity. An incapacitated person retains all rights not specifically removed by the court.

(f) Upon the filing of a verified statement by an interested person stating:

1. That he or she has a good faith belief that the alleged incapacitated person's trust, trust amendment, or durable power of attorney is invalid; and

2. A reasonable factual basis for that belief,

the trust, trust amendment, or durable power of attorney shall not be deemed to be an alternative to the appointment of a guardian. The appointment of a guardian does not limit the court's power to determine that certain authority granted by a durable power of attorney is to remain exercisable by the attorney in fact.

(7) Fees.

(a) The examining committee and any attorney appointed under subsection (2) are entitled to reasonable fees to be determined by the court.

(b) The fees awarded under paragraph (a) shall be paid by the guardian from the property of the ward or, if the ward is indigent, by the state. The state shall have a creditor's claim against the guardianship property for any amounts paid under this section. The state may file its claim within 90 days after the entry of an order awarding attorney ad litem fees. If the state does not file its claim within the 90-day period, the state is thereafter barred from asserting the claim. Upon petition by the state for payment of the claim, the court shall enter an order authorizing immediate payment out of the property of the ward. The state shall keep a record of the payments.

(c) If the petition is dismissed, costs and attorney's fees of the proceeding may be assessed against the petitioner if the court finds the petition to have been filed in bad faith.

History.
SS. 9, 26, ch. 75-222; s. 4, ch. 77-328; s. 1, ch. 78-342; s. 6, ch. 79-221; s. 35, ch. 89-96; s. 20, ch. 90-271; s. 4, ch. 91-303; s. 5, ch. 91-306; s. 7, ch. 96-354; s. 1783, ch. 97-102; s. 76, ch. 2004-265; s. 4, ch. 2006-77, eff. June 6, 2006; s. 11, ch. 2006-178, eff. July 1, 2006; s. 44, ch. 2006-217, eff. July 1, 2007; s. 28, ch. 2007-62, eff. Oct. 1, 2007.

744.334. Petition for appointment of guardian or professional guardian; contents.

(1) Every petition for the appointment of a guardian shall be verified by the petitioner and shall contain statements, to the best of petitioner's knowledge and belief, showing the name, age, residence, and post office address of the alleged incapacitated person or minor; the nature of her or his incapacity, if any; the extent of guardianship desired, either plenary or limited; the residence and post office address of the petitioner; the names and addresses of the next of kin of the incapacitated person or minor, if known to the petitioner; the name of the proposed guardian; the relationship and previous relationship of the proposed guardian to the ward; the nature and value of property subject to the guardianship; and the reasons why this person should be appointed guardian. If a willing and qualified guardian cannot be located, the petition must so state.

(2) The petition for appointment of a professional guardian must comply with the provisions of subsection (1), and must state that the petitioner is a professional guardian.

History.
SS. 11, 26, ch. 75-222; s. 7, ch. 79-221; s. 36, ch. 89-96; s. 21, ch. 90-271; s. 8, ch. 96-354; s. 1784, ch. 97-102.

744.3371. Notice of petition for appointment of guardian and hearing.

(1) When the petition for appointment of a guardian for an incapacitated person is heard upon the conclusion of the hearing in which the person is determined to be incapacitated, the court shall hear the petition without further notice. If the petition is heard on a later date, reasonable notice of the hearing must be served on the incapacitated person, the person's attorney, if any, any guardian then serving, the person's next of kin, and such other interested persons as the court may direct.

(2) When a petition for appointment of a guardian for a minor is filed, formal notice must be served on the minor's parents. If the petitioner has custody of the minor and the petition alleges that, after diligent search, the parents cannot be found, the parents may be served by informal notice, delivered to their last known address or addresses. When a parent petitions for appointment as guardian for his or her minor child, no notice is necessary unless the other parent is living and does not consent to the appointment.

History.
S. 22, ch. 90-271; s. 1079, ch. 97-102.

744.341. Voluntary guardianship.

(1) Without adjudication of incapacity, the court shall appoint a guardian of the property of a resident or nonresident person who, though mentally competent, is incapable of the care, custody, and management of his or her estate by reason of age or physical infirmity and who has voluntarily petitioned for the appointment. The petition shall be accompanied by a certificate of a licensed physician specifying that he or she has examined the petitioner and that the petitioner is competent to understand the nature of the guardianship and his or her delegation of authority. Notice of hearing on any petition for appointment and for authority to act shall be given to the petitioner and to any person to whom the petitioner requests that notice be given. Such request may be made in the petition for appointment of guardian or in a subsequent written request for notice signed by the petitioner.

(2) If requested in the petition for appointment of a guardian brought under this section, the court may direct the guardian to take possession of less than all of the ward's property and of the rents, income, issues, and profits from it. In such case, the court shall specify in its order the property to be included in the guardianship estate, and the duties and responsibilities of the guardian appointed under this section will extend only to such property.

(3) Unless the voluntary guardianship is limited pursuant to subsection (2), any guardian appointed under this section has the same duties and responsibilities as

are provided by law for plenary guardians of the property, generally.

(4) A guardian must include in the annual report filed with the court a certificate from a licensed physician who examined the ward not more than 90 days before the annual report is filed with the court. The certificate must certify that the ward is competent to understand the nature of the guardianship and of the ward's authority to delegate powers to the voluntary guardian.

(5) A voluntary guardianship may be terminated by the ward by filing a notice with the court that the voluntary guardianship is terminated. A copy of the notice must be served on all interested persons.

History.
SS. 11, 26, ch. 75-222; s. 9, ch. 79-221; s. 4, ch. 84-31; s. 38, ch. 89-96; s. 23, ch. 90-271; s. 1080, ch. 97-102; s. 12, ch. 2006-178, eff. July 1, 2006.

744.342.　Minors; guardianship.

Upon petition, the court may appoint a guardian for a minor without appointing an examining committee or conducting an adjudicatory hearing pursuant to s. 744.331.

History.
S. 71, ch. 90-271.

744.344.　Order of appointment.

(1) The court may hear testimony on the question of who is entitled to preference in the appointment of a guardian. Any interested person may intervene in the proceedings. The order appointing a guardian must state the nature of the guardianship as either plenary or limited. If limited, the order must state that the guardian may exercise only those delegable rights which have been removed from the incapacitated person and specifically delegated to the guardian. The order shall state the specific powers and duties of the guardian.

(2) The order appointing a guardian must be consistent with the incapacitated person's welfare and safety, must be the least restrictive appropriate alternative, and must reserve to the incapacitated person the right to make decisions in all matters commensurate with the person's ability to do so.

(3) If a petition for appointment of guardian has been filed, an order appointing a guardian must be issued contemporaneously with the order adjudicating the person incapacitated. The order must specify the amount of the bond to be given by the guardian and must state specifically whether the guardian must place all, or part, of the property of the ward in a restricted account in a financial institution designated pursuant to s. 69.031.

(4) If a petition for the appointment of a guardian has not been filed at the time of the hearing on the petition to determine capacity, the court may appoint an emergency temporary guardian in the manner and for the purposes specified in s. 744.3031.

(5) A plenary guardian shall exercise all delegable rights and powers of the incapacitated person.

(6) A person for whom a limited guardian has been appointed retains all legal rights except those which have been specifically granted to the guardian in the court's written order.

History.
S. 1, ch. 74-106; ss. 12, 26, ch. 75-222; s. 39, ch. 89-96; s. 24, ch. 90-271; s. 1081, ch. 97-102.

Editor's Notes.
Created from former s. 744.34.

744.345.　Letters of guardianship.

Letters of guardianship shall be issued to the guardian and shall specify whether the guardianship pertains to the person, or the property, or both, of the ward. The letters must state whether the guardianship is plenary or limited, and, if limited, the letters must state the powers and duties of the guardian. If the guardianship is limited, the letters shall state whether or not and to what extent the guardian is authorized to act on behalf of the ward with regard to any advance directive previously executed by the ward.

History.
S. 1, ch. 74-106; s. 12, ch. 75-222; s. 28, ch. 89-96; s. 25, ch. 90-271; s. 7, ch. 92-199; s. 2, ch. 94-183.

Editor's Notes.
Created from former s. 744.40; former s. 744.313.

744.347.　Oath of guardian.

Before exercising his or her authority as guardian, every guardian shall take an oath that he or she will faithfully perform his or her duties as guardian. This oath is not jurisdictional.

History.
S. 1, ch. 74-106; ss. 19, 26, ch. 75-222; s. 40, ch. 89-96; s. 1082, ch. 97-102.

Editor's Notes.
Created from former s. 744.36.

744.351.　Bond of guardian.

(1) Before exercising his or her authority as guardian, every person appointed a guardian of the property of a ward in this state shall file a bond with surety as prescribed in s. 45.011 to be approved by the clerk. The bond shall be payable to the Governor of the state and the Governor's successors in office, conditioned on the faithful performance of all duties by the guardian. In form the bond shall be joint and several. When the petitioner or guardian presents compelling reasons, the court may waive a bond or require the use of a designated financial institution as defined in s. 655.005(1).

(2) When the sureties on a bond are natural persons, the guardian shall be required to file with the annual guardianship report proof satisfactory to the court that the sureties are alive and solvent.

(3) The penal sum of a guardian's bond shall be fixed by the court, and it must be in an amount not less than the full amount of the cash on hand and on deposit belonging to the ward and subject to the control

of the guardian, plus the value of the notes and bonds owned by the ward that are payable to bearer, and plus the value of all other intangible personal property, in whatever form, owned by the ward which has a market value which readily can be fixed and which intangible personal property readily can be traded for cash or its equivalent.

(4) For good cause, the court may require, or increase or reduce the amount of, bond or change or release the surety.

(5) Financial institutions as defined in s. 744.309(4) and public guardians authorized by law to be guardians shall not be required to file bonds.

(6) When it is expedient in the judgment of any court having jurisdiction of any guardianship property, because the size of the bond required of the guardian is burdensome, or for other cause, the court may order, in lieu of a bond or in addition to a lesser bond, that the guardian place all or part of the property of the ward in a designated financial institution under the same conditions and limitations as are contained in s. 69.031. A designated financial institution shall also include a dealer, as defined in s. 517.021(6), if the dealer is a member of the Security Investment Protection Corporation and is doing business in the state.

History.
S. 1, ch. 74-106; ss. 19, 26, ch. 75-222; s. 1, ch. 77-174; s. 2, ch. 78-342; s. 2, ch. 86-120; s. 41, ch. 89-96; s. 26, ch. 90-271; s. 30, ch. 95-401; s. 9, ch. 96-354; s. 1785, ch. 97-102.
Editor's Notes.
Created from former s. 744.38.

744.354. Validity of bond.

No bond executed by any guardian shall be invalid because of an informality in it or because of an informality or illegality in the appointment of the guardian. The bond shall have the same force and effect as if the bond had been executed in proper form and the appointment had been legally made.

History.
S. 1, ch. 74-106; ss. 19, 26, ch. 75-222; s. 42, ch. 89-96.
Editor's Notes.
Created from former s. 744.42.

744.357. Liability of surety.

No surety for a guardian shall be charged beyond the property of the ward.

History.
S. 1, ch. 74-106; ss. 19, 26, ch. 75-222; s. 43, ch. 89-96; s. 27, ch. 90-271.
Editor's Notes.
Created from former s. 744.43.

744.358. Liability of a guardian.

(1) A guardian is not liable, solely because of the guardianship, for the debts, contracts, or torts of her or his ward.

(2) In dealing with the ward's property, a guardian is subject to the standards set forth in s. 518.11.

History.
S. 44, ch. 89-96; s. 28, ch. 90-271; s. 1083, ch. 97-102.

PART VI.
POWERS AND DUTIES.

744.361. Powers and duties of guardian.

(1) The guardian of an incapacitated person may exercise only those rights that have been removed from the ward and delegated to the guardian. The guardian of a minor shall exercise the powers of a plenary guardian.

(2) The guardian shall file an initial guardianship report in accordance with s. 744.362.

(3) The guardian shall file a guardianship report annually in accordance with s. 744.367.

(4) The guardian of the person shall implement the guardianship plan.

(5) When two or more guardians have been appointed, the guardians shall consult with each other.

(6) A guardian who is given authority over any property of the ward shall:

(a) Protect and preserve the property and invest it prudently as provided in chapter 518, apply it as provided in s. 744.397, and account for it faithfully.

(b) Perform all other duties required of him or her by law.

(c) At the termination of the guardianship, deliver the property of the ward to the person lawfully entitled to it.

(7) The guardian shall observe the standards in dealing with the guardianship property that would be observed by a prudent person dealing with the property of another, and, if the guardian has special skills or is named guardian on the basis of representations of special skills or expertise, he or she is under a duty to use those skills.

(8) The guardian, if authorized by the court, shall take possession of all of the ward's property and of the rents, income, issues, and profits from it, whether accruing before or after the guardian's appointment, and of the proceeds arising from the sale, lease, or mortgage of the property or of any part. All of the property and the rents, income, issues, and profits from it are assets in the hands of the guardian for the payment of debts, taxes, claims, charges, and expenses of the guardianship and for the care, support, maintenance, and education of the ward or the ward's dependents, as provided for under the terms of the guardianship plan or by law.

(9) A professional guardian must ensure that each of the guardian's wards is personally visited by the guardian or one of the guardian's professional staff at least once each calendar quarter. During the personal visit, the guardian or the guardian's professional staff person shall assess:

(a) The ward's physical appearance and condition.

(b) The appropriateness of the ward's current living situation.

(c) The need for any additional services and the necessity for continuation of existing services, taking into consideration all aspects of social, psychological, educational, direct service, health, and personal care needs. This subsection does not apply to a professional guardian who has been appointed only as guardian of the property.

History.
S. 1, ch. 74-106; ss. 6, 26, ch. 75-222; s. 45, ch. 89-96; s. 29, ch. 90-271; s. 1084, ch. 97-102; s. 13, ch. 2006-178, eff. July 1, 2006; s. 45, ch. 2006-217, eff. July 1, 2007.

Editor's Notes.
Created from former ss. 744.48, 744.49.

744.362. Initial guardianship report.

(1) Each guardian shall file with the court an initial guardianship report within 60 days after her or his letters of guardianship are signed. The initial guardianship report for a guardian of the property must consist of a verified inventory. The initial report for a guardian of the person must consist of an initial guardianship plan. The initial report shall be served on the ward, unless the ward is a minor under the age of 14 years or is totally incapacitated, and the attorney for the ward. Either the ward or the ward's attorney may request a hearing concerning the adequacy of the report.

(2) Review of the initial guardianship report and representation of the ward during an objection thereto, if any, shall be the appointed attorney's final official action on behalf of the ward. Thereafter, the court-appointed attorney is no longer obligated to represent the ward.

History.
S. 46, ch. 89-96; s. 30, ch. 90-271; s. 24, ch. 92-200; s. 23, ch. 95-401; s. 1085, ch. 97-102.

744.363. Initial guardianship plan.

(1) The initial guardianship plan shall include the following:

(a) The provision of medical, mental, or personal care services for the welfare of the ward;

(b) The provision of social and personal services for the welfare of the ward;

(c) The place and kind of residential setting best suited for the needs of the ward;

(d) The application of health and accident insurance and any other private or governmental benefits to which the ward may be entitled to meet any part of the costs of medical, mental health, or related services provided to the ward; and

(e) Any physical and mental examinations necessary to determine the ward's medical and mental health treatment needs.

(2) The initial guardianship plan for an incapacitated person must be based on the recommendations of the examining committee's examination, as incorporated into the order determining incapacity.

(3) Unless the ward has been found to be totally incapacitated or is a minor under the age of 14 years, the initial guardianship plan must contain an attestation that the guardian has consulted with the ward and, to the extent reasonable, has honored the ward's wishes consistent with the rights retained by the ward under the plan. To the maximum extent reasonable, the plan must be in accordance with the wishes of the ward.

(4) The guardianship plan may not restrict the physical liberty of the ward more than reasonably necessary to protect the ward or others from serious physical injury, illness, or disease and to provide the ward with medical care and mental health treatment for the ward's physical and mental health.

(5) An initial guardianship plan continues in effect until it is amended or replaced by the approval of an annual guardianship plan, until the restoration of capacity or death of the ward, or until the ward, if a minor, reaches the age of 18 years. If there are significant changes in the capacity of the ward to meet the essential requirements for his or her health or safety, the guardian may file a petition to modify the guardianship plan and shall serve notice on all persons who received notice of the plan. At the hearing on such petition, the court may modify the guardianship plan and specify the effective date of such amendment.

(6) In exercising his or her powers, the guardian shall recognize any rights retained by the ward.

History.
S. 47, ch. 89-96; s. 31, ch. 90-271; s. 1086, ch. 97-102.

744.365. Verified inventory.

(1) Filing. — A guardian of the property shall file a verified inventory of the ward's property.

(2) Contents. — The verified inventory must include the following:

(a) All property of the ward, real and personal, that has come into the guardian's possession or knowledge, including a statement of all encumbrances, liens, and other secured claims on any item, any claims against the property, any cause of action accruing to the ward, and any trusts of which the ward is a beneficiary.

(b) The location of the real and personal property in sufficient detail so that it may be clearly identified or located.

(c) A description of all sources of income, including, without limitation, social security benefits and pensions.

(3) Cash assets. — Along with the verified inventory, the guardian must file a copy of the most current statement of all of the ward's cash assets from all institutions where the cash is on deposit.

(4) Safe-deposit box.

(a) The initial opening of any safe-deposit box of the ward must be conducted in the presence of an employee of the institution where the box is located. The inventory of the contents of the box also must be conducted in the presence of the employee, who must verify the contents of the box by signing a copy of the inventory. This safe-deposit box inventory shall be filed with the court within 10 days after the box is opened.

(b) The guardian shall provide the ward with a copy of each signed safe-deposit box inventory unless the ward is a minor or has been adjudicated totally incapacitated or unless the order appointing the guardian states otherwise.

(c) Nothing may be removed from the ward's safe-deposit box without specific court approval.

(5) Records retention.

(a) The guardian shall maintain substantiating papers and records sufficient to demonstrate the accuracy of the initial inventory for a period of 3 years after her or his discharge. The substantiating papers need not be filed with the court but must be made available for inspection and review at such time and place and before such persons as the court may order.

(b) As part of the substantiating papers, the guardian must identify by name, address, and occupation, the witness or witnesses, if any, who were present during the initial inventory of the ward's personal property.

(6) Audit fee.

(a) Where the value of the ward's property exceeds $25,000, a guardian shall pay from the ward's property to the clerk of the circuit court a fee of up to $85, upon the filing of the verified inventory, for the auditing of the inventory. Upon petition by the guardian, the court may waive the auditing fee upon a showing of insufficient funds in the ward's estate. Any guardian unable to pay the auditing fee may petition the court for waiver of the fee. The court may waive the fee after it has reviewed the documentation filed by the guardian in support of the waiver.

(b) An audit fee may not be charged to any ward whose property has a value of less than $25,000.

History.

S. 49, ch. 89-96; s. 32, ch. 90-271; s. 1087, ch. 97-102; s. 115, ch. 2003-402; s. 77, ch. 2004-265; s. 14, ch. 2006-178, eff. July 1, 2006; s. 40, ch. 2008-111, eff. July 1, 2008.

744.367. Duty to file annual guardianship report.

(1) Unless the court requires filing on a calendar-year basis, each guardian of the person shall file with the court an annual guardianship plan within 90 days after the last day of the anniversary month the letters of guardianship were signed, and the plan must cover the coming fiscal year, ending on the last day in such anniversary month. If the court requires calendar-year filing, the guardianship plan must be filed on or before April 1 of each year.

(2) Unless the court requires or authorizes filing on a fiscal-year basis, each guardian of the property shall file with the court an annual accounting on or before April 1 of each year. The annual accounting must cover the preceding calendar year. If the court authorizes or directs filing on a fiscal-year basis, the annual account-

ing must be filed on or before the first day of the fourth month after the end of the fiscal year.

(3) The annual guardianship report of a guardian of the property must consist of an annual accounting, and the annual report of a guardian of the person must consist of an annual guardianship plan. The annual report shall be served on the ward, unless the ward is a minor or is totally incapacitated, and on the attorney for the ward, if any. The guardian shall provide a copy to any other person as the court may direct.

(4) Unless the ward is a minor or has been determined to be totally incapacitated, the guardian shall review a copy of the annual report with the ward, to the extent possible. Within 30 days after the annual report has been filed, any interested person, including the ward, may file written objections to any element of the report, specifying the nature of the objection.

(5) If the guardian fails to timely file the annual guardianship report, the judge may impose sanctions which may include contempt, removal of the guardian, or other sanctions provided by law in s. 744.3685.

(6) Notwithstanding any other requirement of this section or unless otherwise directed by the court, the guardian of the property may file the first annual accounting on either a fiscal-year or calendar-year basis. Unless the court directs otherwise, the guardian shall notify the court as to the guardian's filing intention within 30 days from the date the guardian was issued the letter of guardianship. All subsequent annual accountings must be filed on the same accounting period as the first annual accounting unless the court authorizes or directs otherwise. The first accounting period must end within 1 year after the end of the month in which the letters of guardianship were issued to the guardian of the property.

History.

S. 1, ch. 74-106; ss. 6, 26, ch. 75-222; s. 50, ch. 89-96; s. 33, ch. 90-271; s. 25, ch. 92-200; s. 68, ch. 95-211; s. 24, ch. 95-401; s. 10, ch. 96-354; s. 15, ch. 2006-178, eff. July 1, 2006.

Editor's Notes.

Created from former s. 744.482.

744.3675. Annual guardianship plan.

Each guardian of the person must file with the court an annual guardianship plan which updates information about the condition of the ward. The annual plan must specify the current needs of the ward and how those needs are proposed to be met in the coming year.

(1) Each plan for an adult ward must, if applicable, include:

(a) Information concerning the residence of the ward, including:

1. The ward's address at the time of filing the plan.

2. The name and address of each place where the ward was maintained during the preceding year.

3. The length of stay of the ward at each place.

4. A statement of whether the current residential setting is best suited for the current needs of the ward.

5. Plans for ensuring during the coming year that the ward is in the best residential setting to meet his or her needs.

(b) Information concerning the medical and mental health conditions and treatment and rehabilitation needs of the ward, including:

1. A resume of any professional medical treatment given to the ward during the preceding year.

2. The report of a physician who examined the ward no more than 90 days before the beginning of the applicable reporting period. The report must contain an evaluation of the ward's condition and a statement of the current level of capacity of the ward.

3. The plan for providing medical, mental health, and rehabilitative services in the coming year.

(c) Information concerning the social condition of the ward, including:

1. The social and personal services currently used by the ward.

2. The social skills of the ward, including a statement of how well the ward communicates and maintains interpersonal relationships.

3. The social needs of the ward.

(2) Each plan filed by the legal guardian of a minor must include:

(a) Information concerning the residence of the minor, including:

1. The minor's address at the time of filing the plan.

2. The name and address of each place the minor lived during the preceding year.

(b) Information concerning the medical and mental health conditions and treatment and rehabilitation needs of the minor, including:

1. A resume of any professional medical treatment given to the minor during the preceding year.

2. A report from the physician who examined the minor no more than 180 days before the beginning of the applicable reporting period that contains an evaluation of the minor's physical and mental conditions.

3. The plan for providing medical services in the coming year.

(c) Information concerning the education of the minor, including:

1. A summary of the school progress report.

2. The social development of the minor, including a statement of how well the minor communicates and maintains interpersonal relationships.

3. The social needs of the minor.

(3) Each plan for an adult ward must address the issue of restoration of rights to the ward and include:

(a) A summary of activities during the preceding year that were designed to enhance the capacity of the ward.

(b) A statement of whether the ward can have any rights restored.

(c) A statement of whether restoration of any rights will be sought.

(4) The court, in its discretion, may require reexamination of the ward by a physician at any time.

History.

S. 51, ch. 89-96; s. 34, ch. 90-271; s. 11, ch. 96-354; s. 1786, ch. 97-102; s. 4, ch. 97-161; s. 16, ch. 2006-178, eff. July 1, 2006.

744.3678. Annual accounting.

(1) Each guardian of the property must file an annual accounting with the court.

(2) The annual accounting must include:

(a) A full and correct account of the receipts and disbursements of all of the ward's property over which the guardian has control and a statement of the ward's property on hand at the end of the accounting period. This paragraph does not apply to any property or any trust of which the ward is a beneficiary but which is not under the control or administration of the guardian.

(b) A copy of the annual or year-end statement of all of the ward's cash accounts from each of the institutions where the cash is deposited.

(3) The guardian must obtain a receipt, canceled check, or other proof of payment for all expenditures and disbursements made on behalf of the ward. The guardian must preserve all evidence of payment, along with other substantiating papers, for a period of 3 years after his or her discharge. The receipts, proofs of payment, and substantiating papers need not be filed with the court but shall be made available for inspection and review at the time and place and before the persons as the court may order.

(4) The guardian shall pay from the ward's estate to the clerk of the circuit court a fee based upon the following graduated fee schedule, upon the filing of the annual financial return, for the auditing of the return:

(a) For estates with a value of $25,000 or less the clerk of the court may charge a fee of up to $20.

(b) For estates with a value of more than $25,000 up to and including $100,000 the clerk of the court may charge a fee of up to $85.

(c) For estates with a value of more than $100,000 up to and including $500,000 the clerk of the court may charge a fee of up to $170.

(d) For estates with a value in excess of $500,000 the clerk of the court may charge a fee of up to $250. Upon petition by the guardian, the court may waive the auditing fee upon a showing of insufficient funds in the ward's estate. Any guardian unable to pay the auditing fee may petition the court for a waiver of the fee. The court may waive the fee after it has reviewed the documentation filed by the guardian in support of the waiver.

(5) This section does not apply if the court determines that the ward receives income only from social security benefits and the guardian is the ward's representative payee for the benefits.

History.
S. 52, ch. 89-96; ss. 35, 72, ch. 90-271; s. 1088, ch. 97-102; s. 116, ch. 2003-402; s. 13, ch. 2004-260; s. 78, ch. 2004-265; s. 139, ch. 2005-2; s. 17, ch. 2006-178, eff. July 1, 2006; s. 41, ch. 2008-111, eff. July 1, 2008.

744.3679. Simplified accounting procedures in certain cases.

(1) In a guardianship of property, when all assets of the estate are in designated depositories under s. 69.031 and the only transactions that occur in that account are interest accrual, deposits from a settlement, or financial institution service charges, the guardian may elect to file an accounting consisting of:

(a) The original or a certified copy of the year-end statement of the ward's account from the financial institution; and

(b) A statement by the guardian under penalty of perjury that the guardian has custody and control of the ward's property as shown in the year-end statement.

(2) The accounting allowed by subsection (1) is in lieu of the accounting and auditing procedures under s. 744.3678(2). However, any interested party may seek judicial review as provided in s. 744.3685.

(3) The guardian need not be represented by an attorney in order to file the annual accounting allowed by subsection (1).

History.
S. 1, ch. 93-102; s. 18, ch. 2006-178, eff. July 1, 2006.

744.368. Responsibilities of the clerk of the circuit court.

(1) In addition to the duty to serve as the custodian of the guardianship files, the clerk shall review each initial and annual guardianship report to ensure that it contains information about the ward addressing, as appropriate:

(a) Physical and mental health care;

(b) Personal and social services;

(c) The residential setting;

(d) The application of insurance, private benefits, and government benefits;

(e) The physical and mental health examinations; and

(f) The initial verified inventory or the annual accounting.

(2) The clerk shall, within 30 days after the date of filing of the initial or annual report of the guardian of the person, complete his or her review of the report.

(3) Within 90 days after the filing of the verified inventory and accountings by a guardian of the property, the clerk shall audit the verified inventory and the accountings. The clerk shall advise the court of the results of the audit.

(4) The clerk shall report to the court when a report is not timely filed.

History.
S. 53, ch. 89-96; s. 36, ch. 90-271; s. 1089, ch. 97-102; s. 19, ch. 2006-178, eff. July 1, 2006.

744.3685. Order requiring guardianship report; contempt.

When a guardian fails to file the guardianship report, the court shall order the guardian to file the report within 15 days after the service of the order upon her or him or show cause why she or he should not be compelled to do so. A copy of the order shall be served on the guardian or on the guardian's resident agent. If the guardian fails to file her or his report within the time specified by the order without good cause, the court may cite the guardian for contempt of court and may fine her or him. The fine may not be paid out of the ward's property.

History.
S. 1, ch. 74-106; ss. 17, 26, ch. 75-222; s. 70, ch. 89-96; s. 37, ch. 90-271; s. 1090, ch. 97-102.

Editor's Notes.
Created from former s. 745.29; former s. 744.431.

744.369. Judicial review of guardianship reports.

(1) The court shall review the initial guardianship report within 60 days after the filing of the clerk's report of findings to the court. The court shall review the annual guardianship report within 30 days after the filing of the clerk's report of findings to the court.

(2) The court may appoint a general or special magistrate to assist the court in its review function. The court may require the general or special magistrate to conduct random field audits.

(3) If an initial or annual report is not timely filed, the court shall order the guardian to file the report or to show cause why the report has not been filed within the prescribed time. Service of the order and subsequent proceedings shall be governed by s. 744.3685.

(4) The court must review the initial and annual guardianship report to determine that the report:

(a) Meets the needs of the ward;

(b) Authorizes the guardian to act only in areas in which an adult ward has been declared incapacitated; and

(c) Conforms to all other requirements of the law.

(5) Upon examining the initial or annual guardianship report, the court shall enter an order approving or disapproving the report. If the court disapproves the report, the court shall order the guardian to provide a revised report or proof of any item in the report to the court. The guardian shall do so within a reasonable amount of time set by court.

(6) If the guardian fails to comply with the court order entered pursuant to subsection (5), the court shall take immediate action to compel compliance or to sanction the guardian after a hearing with appropriate notice to the ward, the ward's counsel, if any, the guardian, and the ward's next of kin.

(7) If an objection has been filed to a report, the court shall set the matter for hearing and shall conduct the hearing within 30 days after the filing of the objection. After the hearing, the court shall enter a written order either approving, or ordering modifications to, the report. If an objection is found to be without merit, the court may assess costs and attorney's fees against the person who made the objection.

(8) The approved report constitutes the authority for the guardian to act in the forthcoming year. The powers of the guardian are limited by the terms of the report. The annual report may not grant additional authority to the guardian without a hearing, as provided for in s. 744.331, to determine that the ward is incapacitated to act in that matter.

History.
S. 54, ch. 89-96; s. 38, ch. 90-271; s. 1, ch. 99-277; s. 96, ch. 2004-11.

744.3701.　Inspection of report.

(1) Unless otherwise ordered by the court, any initial, annual, or final guardianship report or amendment thereto is subject to inspection only by the court, the clerk or the clerk's representative, the guardian and the guardian's attorney, and the ward, unless he or she is a minor or has been determined to be totally incapacitated, and the ward's attorney.

(2) The court may direct disclosure and recording of parts of an initial, annual, or final report in connection with any real property transaction or for such other purpose as the court allows, in its discretion.

History.
S. 39, ch. 90-271; s. 1091, ch. 97-102.

744.371.　Relief to be granted.

If it appears from the annual guardianship report that:

(1) The condition of the ward requires further examination;

(2) Any change in the proposed care, maintenance, or treatment is needed;

(3) The ward is qualified for restoration of some or all rights;

(4) The condition or maintenance of the ward requires the performance or doing of any other thing for the best interest of the ward which is not indicated in the plan; or

(5) There is any other matter necessary to protect the interests of the ward,

the court shall, after a hearing with appropriate notice, amend the plan or enter any other order necessary to protect the ward.

History.
S. 1, ch. 74-106; ss. 6, 26, ch. 75-222; s. 55, ch. 89-96; s. 40, ch. 90-271.

Editor's Notes.
Created from former s. 744.484.

744.3715.　Petition for interim judicial review.

(1) At any time, any interested person, including the ward, may petition the court for review alleging that the guardian is not complying with the guardianship plan or is exceeding his or her authority under the guardianship plan and the guardian is not acting in the best interest of the ward. The petition for review must state the nature of the objection to the guardian's action or proposed action. Upon the filing of any such petition, the court shall review the petition and act upon it expeditiously.

(2) If the petition for review is found to be without merit, the court may assess costs and attorney's fees against the petitioner.

History.
S. 56, ch. 89-96; s. 41, ch. 90-271; s. 1092, ch. 97-102.

744.372.　Judicial review of guardianships.

The court retains jurisdiction over all guardianships. The court shall review the appropriateness and extent of a guardianship annually and:

(1) If an objection to the terms of the guardianship report has been filed pursuant to s. 744.367;

(2) If interim review has been requested under s. 744.3715;

(3) If a person, including the ward, has filed a suggestion of increased capacity; or

(4) If the guardianship report has not been received and the guardian has failed to respond to a show cause order.

History.
S. 57, ch. 89-96; s. 42, ch. 90-271.

744.3725.　Procedure for extraordinary authority.

Before the court may grant authority to a guardian to exercise any of the rights specified in s. 744.3215(4), the court must:

(1) Appoint an independent attorney to act on the incapacitated person's behalf, and the attorney must have the opportunity to meet with the person and to present evidence and cross-examine witnesses at any hearing on the petition for authority to act;

(2) Receive as evidence independent medical, psychological, and social evaluations with respect to the incapacitated person by competent professionals or appoint its own experts to assist in the evaluations;

(3) Personally meet with the incapacitated person to obtain its own impression of the person's capacity, so as to afford the incapacitated person the full opportunity to express his or her personal views or desires with respect to the judicial proceeding and issue before the court;

(4) Find by clear and convincing evidence that the person lacks the capacity to make a decision about the issue before the court and that the incapacitated person's capacity is not likely to change in the foreseeable future;

(5) Be persuaded by clear and convincing evidence that the authority being requested is in the best interests of the incapacitated person; and

(6) In the case of dissolution of marriage, find that the ward's spouse has consented to the dissolution. The provisions of this section and s. 744.3215(4) are procedural and do not establish any new or independent right to or authority over the termination of parental rights, dissolution of marriage, sterilization, abortion, or the termination of life support systems.

History.
S. 58, ch. 89-96; s. 43, ch. 90-271; s. 25, ch. 95-401; s. 1093, ch. 97-102.

744.373. Production of property.

On the petition of a creditor or other interested person, including the ward, or on its own motion, the court may require a guardian of the property to produce satisfactory evidence that the property of the ward for which the guardian is responsible is in the guardian's possession or under her or his control. If it deems it necessary or proper, the court may order the guardian to produce the property for the inspection of the creditor, another interested person, the ward, or the court.

History.
S. 1, ch. 74-106; ss. 17, 26, ch. 75-222; s. 71, ch. 89-96; s. 44, ch. 90-271; s. 1094, ch. 97-102.
Editor's Notes.
Created from former s. 745.30; former s. 744.434.

744.3735. Annual appearance of the guardian.

The court may require the guardian to appear before the court at the time the guardian files the annual guardianship report or at such other time as the court determines, in order for the court to inquire as to any matter relating to the well-being of the ward.

History.
S. 1, ch. 74-106; ss. 17, 26, ch. 75-222; s. 11, ch. 79-221; s. 72, ch. 89-96.
Editor's Notes.
Former s. 744.437.

744.374. Payments to guardian.

If there is more than one guardian, either guardian may petition for an order directing the guardian of the property to pay to the guardian of the person periodic amounts for the support, care, maintenance, education, and other needs of the ward if not otherwise provided for in the guardianship plan. The amount may be increased or decreased from time to time. If an order is entered, the receipt of the guardian for payments made shall be a sufficient discharge of the guardian who makes the payments. The guardian shall not be bound to see to the application of the payments.

History.
S. 1, ch. 74-106; ss. 6, 26, ch. 75-222; s. 59, ch. 89-96; s. 45, ch. 90-271; s. 1095, ch. 97-102.
Editor's Notes.
Created from former s. 744.50.

744.381. Appraisals.

When the court deems it necessary, appraisers may be appointed to appraise the property of the ward that is subject to the guardianship.

History.
S. 1, ch. 74-106; s. 61, ch. 89-96; s. 46, ch. 90-271.
Editor's Notes.
Created from former s. 744.54.

744.384. Subsequently discovered or acquired property.

(1) If a plenary guardian of the property of the ward learns of any property that is not included in previous inventories, the property shall be inventoried within 30 days after the discovery or acquisition.

(2) If a limited guardian of the property of the ward learns of any property that was not known to the court at the time of his or her appointment, he or she shall file a report of such property with the court. Upon petition by the guardian, ward, or other interested person, the court, after hearing with appropriate notice, may direct the guardian to take custody and control of such property, without further adjudicatory proceeding under s. 744.331.

History.
S. 1, ch. 74-106; ss. 14, 26, ch. 75-222; s. 62, ch. 89-96; s. 47, ch. 90-271; s. 1096, ch. 97-102.
Editor's Notes.
Created from former s. 744.59.

744.387. Settlement of claims.

(1) When a settlement of any claim by or against the guardian, whether arising as a result of personal injury or otherwise, and whether arising before or after appointment of a guardian, is proposed, but before an action to enforce it is begun, on petition by the guardian of the property stating the facts of the claim, question, or dispute and the proposed settlement, and on any evidence that is introduced, the court may enter an order authorizing the settlement if satisfied that the settlement will be for the best interest of the ward. The order shall relieve the guardian from any further responsibility in connection with the claim or dispute when the settlement has been made in accordance with the order. The order authorizing the settlement may also determine whether an additional bond is required and, if so, shall fix the amount of it.

(2) In the same manner as provided in subsection (1) or as authorized by s. 744.301, the natural guardians or guardian of a minor may settle any claim by or on behalf of a minor that does not exceed $15,000 without bond. A legal guardianship shall be required when the amount of the net settlement to the ward exceeds $15,000.

(3)(a) No settlement after an action has been commenced by or on behalf of a ward shall be effective unless approved by the court having jurisdiction of the action.

(b) In the event of settlement or judgment in favor of the ward or minor, the court may authorize the natural guardians or guardian, or a guardian of the property appointed by a court of competent jurisdiction, to collect the amount of the settlement or judgment and to execute a release or satisfaction. When the amount of net settlement to the ward or judgment exceeds $15,000 and no guardian has been appointed, the court shall require the appointment of a guardian for the property.

(4) In making a settlement under court order as provided in this section, the guardian is authorized to execute any instrument that may be necessary to effect the settlement. When executed, the instrument shall be a complete release of the person making the settlement.

History.
S. 1, ch. 74-106; ss. 14, 26, ch. 75-222; s. 3, ch. 78-342; s. 10, ch. 79-221; s. 63, ch. 89-96; s. 48, ch. 90-271; s. 10, ch. 2002-195.
Editor's Notes.
Created from former s. 744.60.

744.391. Actions by and against guardian or ward.

If an action is brought by the guardian against the ward, or vice versa, or if the interest of the guardian is adverse to that of his or her ward, a guardian ad litem shall be appointed to represent the ward in that particular litigation. In any litigation between the guardian and the ward, a guardian ad litem shall be appointed to represent the ward. If there is a conflict of interest between the guardian and the ward, the guardian ad litem shall petition the court for removal of the guardian. Judgments in favor of the ward shall become the property of the ward without the necessity for any assignment by the guardian or receipt by the ward upon termination of guardianship. The guardian may receive payment and satisfy any judgment in behalf of the ward without joinder by the ward.

History.
S. 1, ch. 74-106; s. 64, ch. 89-96; s. 1097, ch. 97-102.
Editor's Notes.
Created from former s. 744.61.

744.394. Suspension of statutes of limitations in favor of guardian.

If a person entitled to bring an action is declared incapacitated before the expiration of the time limited for the commencement of it and the cause of the action survives, the action may be commenced by the guardian of the property after such expiration and within 1 year from the date of the order appointing the guardian or the time otherwise limited by law, whichever is longer.

History.
S. 1, ch. 74-106; ss. 16, 26, ch. 75-222; s. 65, ch. 89-96; s. 49, ch. 90-271; s. 1098, ch. 97-102.
Editor's Notes.
Created from former s. 744.62.

744.397. Application of income of property of ward.

(1) The court may authorize the guardian of the property to apply the ward's income, first to the ward's care, support, education, and maintenance, and then for the care, support, education, maintenance, cost of final illness, and cost of funeral and burial or cremation of the parent, spouse, or dependents, if any, of the ward, to the extent necessary. If the income is not sufficient for these purposes, the court may authorize the expenditure of part of the principal for such purposes from time to time.

(2) The word "dependents," as used in subsection (1) means, in addition to those persons who are legal dependents of a ward under existing law, the person or persons whom the ward is morally or equitably obligated to aid, assist, maintain, or care for, including, but not limited to, such persons as the indigent spouse of the ward, based upon the showing of an existing need and an ability of the estate of the ward to pay for, provide, or furnish the aid, assistance, maintenance, or care without unreasonably jeopardizing the care, support, and maintenance of the ward.

(3) If the ward is a minor and the ward's parents are able to care for him or her and to support, maintain, and educate him or her, the guardian of the minor shall not so use his or her ward's property unless directed or authorized to do so by the court.

History.
S. 1, ch. 74-106; ss. 16, 26, ch. 75-222; s. 66, ch. 89-96; s. 50, ch. 90-271; s. 1099, ch. 97-102.
Editor's Notes.
Created from former s. 744.64.

744.421. Petition for support of ward's dependents.

Any person dependent on the ward for support may petition for an order directing the guardian of the property to contribute to the support of the dependent person from the property of the ward. The court may enter an order for suitable support and education of the dependent person out of the ward's property that is subject to the guardianship. The grant or denial of an order for support shall not preclude a further petition for increase, decrease, modification, or termination of allowance for support by either the petitioner or the guardian. The order for support shall be valid for payments made pursuant to it, but no valid payments can be made after the termination of the guardianship. The receipt of the petitioner shall be a sufficient release of the guardian for payments made pursuant to the order. If the property of the ward is derived in whole or in part from payments of compensation, adjusted compensation, pension, insurance, or other benefits made directly to the guardian by the United States Department of Veterans Affairs, notice of the petition for support shall be given by the petitioner to the office of the United States Department of Veterans Affairs having jurisdiction over the area in which the court is located and the chief attorney for the Department of Veterans' Affairs in this state at least 15 days before the hearing on the petition. The court may not authorize payments from the ward's property unless the ward has been adjudicated incapacitated to handle such property in accordance with s. 744.331; except in a voluntary guardianship, in which case such petition may be granted only upon the written consent of the ward.

History.
S. 1, ch. 74-106; ss. 16, 26, ch. 75-222; s. 1, ch. 77-174; s. 1, ch. 78-305; s. 80, ch. 81-167; s. 84, ch. 83-55; s. 30, ch. 88-290; s. 67, ch. 89-96; s. 51, ch. 90-271; s. 37, ch. 93-268.
Editor's Notes.
Created from former s. 744.65.

744.441. Powers of guardian upon court approval.

After obtaining approval of the court pursuant to a petition for authorization to act, a plenary guardian of the property, or a limited guardian of the property within the powers granted by the order appointing the guardian or an approved annual or amended guardianship report, may:

(1) Perform, compromise, or refuse performance of a ward's contracts that continue as obligations of the estate, as he or she may determine under the circumstances.

(2) Execute, exercise, or release any powers as trustee, personal representative, custodian for minors, conservator, or donee of any power of appointment or other power that the ward might have lawfully exercised, consummated, or executed if not incapacitated, if the best interest of the ward requires such execution, exercise, or release.

(3) Make ordinary or extraordinary repairs or alterations in buildings or other structures; demolish any improvements; or raze existing, or erect new, party walls or buildings.

(4) Subdivide, develop, or dedicate land to public use; make or obtain the vacation of plats and adjust boundaries; adjust differences in valuation on exchange or partition by giving or receiving consideration; or dedicate easements to public use without consideration.

(5) Enter into a lease as lessor or lessee for any purpose, with or without option to purchase or renew, for a term within, or extending beyond, the period of guardianship.

(6) Enter into a lease or arrangement for exploration and removal of minerals or other natural resources or enter into a pooling or unitization agreement.

(7) Abandon property when, in the opinion of the guardian, it is valueless or is so encumbered or in such condition that it is of no benefit to the estate.

(8) Pay calls, assessments, and other sums chargeable or accruing against, or on account of, securities.

(9) Borrow money, with or without security, to be repaid from the property or otherwise and advance money for the protection of the estate.

(10) Effect a fair and reasonable compromise with any debtor or obligor or extend, renew, or in any manner modify the terms of any obligation owing to the estate.

(11) Prosecute or defend claims or proceedings in any jurisdiction for the protection of the estate and of the guardian in the performance of his or her duties. Before authorizing a guardian to bring an action described in s. 736.0207, the court shall first find that the action appears to be in the ward's best interests during the ward's probable lifetime. There shall be a rebuttable presumption that an action challenging the ward's revocation of all or part of a trust is not in the ward's best interests if the revocation relates solely to a devise. This subsection does not preclude a challenge after the ward's death. If the court denies a request that a guardian be authorized to bring an action described in s. 736.0207, the court shall review the continued need for a guardian and the extent of the need for delegation of the ward's rights.

(12) Sell, mortgage, or lease any real or personal property of the estate, including homestead property, or any interest therein for cash or credit, or for part cash and part credit, and with or without security for unpaid balances.

(13) Continue any unincorporated business or venture in which the ward was engaged.

(14) Purchase the entire fee simple title to real estate in this state in which the guardian has no interest, but the purchase may be made only for a home for the ward, to protect the home of the ward or the ward's interest, or as a home for the ward's dependent family. If the ward is a married person and the home of the ward or of the dependent family of the ward is owned by the ward and spouse as an estate by the entirety and the home is sold pursuant to the authority of subsection (12), the court may authorize the investment of any part or all of the proceeds from the sale toward the purchase of a fee simple title to real estate in this state for a home for the ward or the dependent family of the ward as an estate by the entirety owned by the ward and spouse. If the guardian is authorized to acquire title to real estate for the ward or dependent family of the ward as an estate by the entirety in accordance with the preceding provisions, the conveyance shall be in the name of the ward and spouse and shall be effective to create an estate by the entirety in the ward and spouse.

(15) Exercise any option contained in any policy of insurance payable to, or inuring to the benefit of, the ward.

(16) Pay reasonable funeral, interment, and grave marker expenses for the ward from the ward's estate, up to a maximum of $6,000.

(17) Make gifts of the ward's property to members of the ward's family in estate and income tax planning procedures.

(18) When the ward's will evinces an objective to obtain a United States estate tax charitable deduction by use of a split interest trust (as that term is defined in s. 736.1201), but the maximum charitable deduction otherwise allowable will not be achieved in whole or in part, execute a codicil on the ward's behalf amending said will to obtain the maximum charitable deduction allowable without diminishing the aggregate value of the benefits of any beneficiary under such will.

(19) Create or amend revocable trusts or create irrevocable trusts of property of the ward's estate which may extend beyond the disability or life of the ward in connection with estate, gift, income, or other tax planning or in connection with estate planning. The court shall retain oversight of the assets transferred to a trust, unless otherwise ordered by the court.

(20) Renounce or disclaim any interest by testate or intestate succession or by inter vivos transfer.

(21) Enter into contracts that are appropriate for, and in the best interest of, the ward.

(22) As to a minor ward, pay expenses of the ward's support, health, maintenance, and education, if the ward's parents, or either of them, are alive.

History.
S. 1, ch. 74-106; ss. 22, 26, ch. 75-222; s. 1, ch. 77-174; s. 2, ch. 77-328; s. 281, ch. 79-400; s. 4, ch. 80-203; s. 3, ch. 86-120; s. 2, ch. 87-317; s. 73, ch. 89-96; s. 52, ch. 90-271; s. 1100, ch. 97-102; s. 11, ch. 97-240; s. 5, ch. 2006-77, eff. June 6, 2006; s. 20, ch. 2006-178, eff. July 1, 2006; s. 46, ch. 2006-217, eff. July 1, 2007; s. 12, ch. 2011-183, eff. June 21, 2011.

Editor's Notes.
Created from former ss. 744.501, 745.03(2) and (3), 745.20, 745.23.
Section 14, ch. 2011-183 provides: "Except as otherwise expressly provided in this act, this act shall take effect upon becoming a law and shall apply to all proceedings pending before such date and all cases commenced on or after the effective date."

744.442. Delegation of authority.

(1) A guardian may designate a surrogate guardian to exercise the powers of the guardian if the guardian is unavailable to act. A person designated as a surrogate guardian under this section must be a professional guardian.

(2)(a) A guardian must file a petition with the court requesting permission to designate a surrogate guardian.

(b) If the court approves the designation, the order must specify the name and business address of the surrogate guardian and the duration of appointment, which may not exceed 30 days. The court may extend the appointment for good cause shown. The surrogate guardian may exercise all powers of the guardian unless limited by order of the court. The

surrogate guardian must file with the court an oath swearing or affirming that he or she will faithfully perform the duties delegated. The court may require the surrogate guardian to post a bond.

(3) This section does not limit the responsibility of the guardian to the ward and to the court. The guardian is liable for the acts of the surrogate guardian. The guardian may terminate the authority of the surrogate guardian by filing a written notice of the termination with the court.

(4) The surrogate guardian is subject to the jurisdiction of the court as if appointed to serve as guardian.

History.
S. 21, ch. 2006-178, eff. July 1, 2006.

744.444. Power of guardian without court approval.

Without obtaining court approval, a plenary guardian of the property, or a limited guardian of the property within the powers granted by the order appointing the guardian or an approved annual or amended guardianship report, may:

(1) Retain assets owned by the ward.

(2) Receive assets from fiduciaries or other sources.

(3) Vote stocks or other securities in person or by general or limited proxy or not vote stocks or other securities.

(4) Insure the assets of the estate against damage, loss, and liability and insure himself or herself against liability as to third persons.

(5) Execute and deliver in his or her name as guardian any instrument necessary or proper to carry out and give effect to this section.

(6) Pay taxes and assessments on the ward's property.

(7) Pay valid encumbrances against the ward's property in accordance with their terms, but no prepayment may be made without prior court approval.

(8) Pay reasonable living expenses for the ward, taking into consideration the accustomed standard of living, age, health, and financial condition of the ward. This subsection does not authorize the guardian of a minor to expend funds for the ward's living expenses if one or both of the ward's parents are alive.

(9) Elect to dissent from a will under s. 732.2125(2), seek approval to make an election in accordance with s. 732.401, or assert any other right or choice available to a surviving spouse in the administration of a decedent's estate.

(10) Deposit or invest liquid assets of the estate, including moneys received from the sale of other assets, in federally insured interest-bearing accounts, readily marketable secured loan arrangements, money market mutual funds, or other prudent investments. The guardian may redeem or sell such

deposits or investments to pay the reasonable living expenses of the ward as provided herein.

(11) Pay incidental expenses in the administration of the estate.

(12) Sell or exercise stock subscription or conversion rights and consent, directly or through a committee or other agent, to the reorganization, consolidation, merger, dissolution, or liquidation of a corporation or other business enterprise.

(13) When reasonably necessary, employ persons, including attorneys, auditors, investment advisers, care managers, or agents, even if they are associated with the guardian, to advise or assist the guardian in the performance of his or her duties.

(14) Execute and deliver in his or her name as guardian any instrument that is necessary or proper to carry out the orders of the court.

(15) Hold a security in the name of a nominee or in other form without disclosure of the interest of the ward, but the guardian is liable for any act of the nominee in connection with the security so held.

(16) Pay or reimburse costs incurred and reasonable fees or compensation to persons, including attorneys, employed by the guardian pursuant to subsection (13) from the assets of the guardianship estate, subject to obtaining court approval of the annual accounting.

(17) Provide confidential information about a ward that is related to an investigation arising under part I of chapter 400 to a local or state ombudsman council member conducting such an investigation. Any such ombudsman shall have a duty to maintain the confidentiality of such information.

History.
S. 1, ch. 74-106; ss. 23, 26, ch. 75-222; s. 3, ch. 77-328; s. 282, ch. 79-400; s. 5, ch. 84-31; s. 74, ch. 89-96; s. 53, ch. 90-271; s. 1101, ch. 97-102; s. 8, ch. 2000-155; s. 12, ch. 2003-57; s. 18, ch. 2010-132, eff. Oct. 1, 2010.

744.446. Conflicts of interest; prohibited activities; court approval; breach of fiduciary duty.

(1) It is essential to the proper conduct and management of a guardianship that the guardian be independent and impartial. The fiduciary relationship which exists between the guardian and the ward may not be used for the private gain of the guardian other than the remuneration for fees and expenses provided by law. The guardian may not incur any obligation on behalf of the guardianship which conflicts with the proper discharge of the guardian's duties.

(2) Unless prior approval is obtained by court order, or unless such relationship existed prior to appointment of the guardian and is disclosed to the court in the petition for appointment of guardian, a guardian may not:

(a) Have any interest, financial or otherwise, direct or indirect, in any business transaction or activity with the guardianship;

(b) Acquire an ownership, possessory, security, or other pecuniary interest adverse to the ward;

(c) Be designated as a beneficiary on any life insurance policy, pension, or benefit plan of the ward unless such designation was validly made by the ward prior to adjudication of incapacity of the ward; and

(d) Directly or indirectly purchase, rent, lease, or sell any property or services from or to any business entity of which the guardian or the guardian's spouse or any of the guardian's lineal descendants, or collateral kindred, is an officer, partner, director, shareholder, or proprietor, or has any financial interest.

(3) Any activity prohibited by this section is voidable during the term of the guardianship or by the personal representative of the ward's estate, and the guardian is subject to removal and to imposition of personal liability through a proceeding for surcharge, in addition to any other remedies otherwise available.

(4) In the event of a breach by the guardian of the guardian's fiduciary duty, the court shall take those necessary actions to protect the ward and the ward's assets.

History.
S. 75, ch. 89-96; s. 54, ch. 90-271; s. 1102, ch. 97-102; s. 6, ch. 2002-195.

744.447. Petition for authorization to act.

(1) Application for authorization to perform, or confirmation of, any acts under s. 744.441 or s. 744.446 shall be by petition stating the facts showing the expediency or necessity for the action; a description of any property involved; and the price and terms of a sale, mortgage, or other contract. The application must state whether it conforms to the general terms of the guardianship report and whether the ward has been adjudicated incapacitated to act with respect to the rights to be exercised.

(2) No notice of a petition to authorize a sale of perishable personal property or of property rapidly deteriorating shall be required. Notice of a petition to perform any other acts under s. 744.441 or s. 744.446 shall be given to the ward, to the next of kin, if any, and to those interested persons who have filed requests for notices and copies of pleadings, as provided in the Florida Probate Rules, unless waived by the court. Notice need not be given to a ward who is under 14 years of age or who has been determined to be totally incapacitated.

History.
S. 1, ch. 74-106; ss. 24, 26, ch. 75-222; s. 12, ch. 79-221; s. 76, ch. 89-96; s. 55, ch. 90-271.
Editor's Notes.
Created from former s. 745.06.

744.451. Order.

(1) If a sale or mortgage is authorized, the order shall describe the property, and

(a) If the property is authorized for sale at private sale, the order shall fix the price and the terms of sale.

(b) If the sale is to be public, the order shall state that the sale shall be made to the highest bidder and the court reserves the right to reject all bids.

(2) An order for any other act permitted under s. 744.441 or s. 744.446 shall describe the permitted act and authorize the guardian to perform it.

History.
S. 1, ch. 74-106; ss. 24, 26, ch. 75-222; s. 77, ch. 89-96.
Editor's Notes.
Created from former s. 745.09.

744.454. Guardian forbidden to borrow or purchase; exceptions.

A professional guardian may not purchase property or borrow money from his or her ward. A guardian who is not a professional guardian may do so if:

(1) A court by written order authorizes the sale or loan after a hearing to which interested persons were given notice; or

(2) The property is sold at public sale and the guardian is a spouse, parent, child, brother, or sister of the ward or a cotenant of the ward in the property to be sold.

History.
S. 1, ch. 74-106; ss. 24, 26, ch. 75-222; s. 1, ch. 77-174; s. 78, ch. 89-96; s. 2, ch. 96-184; s. 12, ch. 96-354; s. 1787, ch. 97-102; s. 5, ch. 97-161.
Editor's Notes.
Created from former s. 745.14.

744.457. Conveyance of various property rights by guardians of the property.

(1)(a) All legal or equitable interests in property owned as an estate by the entirety by an incapacitated person for whom a guardian of the property has been appointed may be sold, transferred, conveyed, or mortgaged in accordance with s. 744.447, if the spouse who is not incapacitated joins in the sale, transfer, conveyance, or mortgage of the property. When both spouses are incapacitated, the sale, transfer, conveyance, or mortgage shall be by the guardians only. The sale, transfer, conveyance, or mortgage may be accomplished by one instrument or by separate instruments.

(b) In ordering or approving the sale and conveyance of the real or personal property owned by the ward and the ward's spouse as an estate by the entirety or as joint tenants with right of survivorship, the court may provide that one-half of the net proceeds of the sale shall go to the guardian of the ward and the other one-half to the ward's spouse, or the court may provide for the proceeds of the sale to retain the same character as to survivorship as the original asset.

(c) The guardian of the property shall collect all payments coming due on intangible property, such as notes and mortgages and other securities, and shall retain one-half of all principal and interest payments so collected and shall pay the other one-half of the collections to the spouse who is not incapacitated. If both spouses are incapacitated, the guardian of either shall collect the payments, retain one-half of the principal and interest payments, and pay the other one-half to the guardian of the other spouse.

(d) The spouse of the incapacitated person shall collect all payments of rents on real estate held as an estate by the entirety and, after paying all charges against the property, such as taxes, insurance, maintenance, and repairs, shall retain one-half of the net rents so collected and pay the other one-half to the guardian of the spouse who is incapacitated. If both spouses are incapacitated, the guardian of the property of either may collect the rent, pay the charges, retain one-half of the net rent, and pay the other one-half to the guardian of the other spouse.

(2) In determining the value of life estates or remainder interests, the American Experience Mortality Tables may be used.

(3) Nothing in this section shall prohibit the court in its discretion from appointing a sole guardian to serve as guardian for both spouses.

(4) Any contingent or expectant interest in property, including marital property rights and any right of survivorship incident to joint tenancy or tenancy by the entirety, may be conveyed or released in accordance with s. 744.447.

History.
S. 1, ch. 74-106; ss. 24, 26, ch. 75-222; s. 13, ch. 79-221; s. 3, ch. 87-317; s. 79, ch. 89-96; s. 56, ch. 90-271; s. 1103, ch. 97-102.
Editor's Notes.
Created from former s. 745.15.

744.461. Purchasers and lenders protected.

No person purchasing or leasing from, or taking a mortgage, pledge, or other lien from, a guardian shall be bound to see that the money or other things of value paid to the guardian are actually needed or properly applied. The person is not otherwise bound as to the proprieties or expediencies of the acts of the guardian.

History.
S. 1, ch. 74-106; ss. 24, 26, ch. 75-222; s. 80, ch. 89-96.
Editor's Notes.
Created from former s. 745.21.

744.462. Determination regarding alternatives to guardianship.

Any judicial determination concerning the validity of the ward's durable power of attorney, trust, or trust amendment shall be promptly reported in the guardianship proceeding by the guardian of the property. If the instrument has been judicially determined to be valid or if, after the appointment of a guardian, a petition is filed alleging that there is an alternative to guardianship which will sufficiently address the problems of the ward, the court shall review the continued need for a guardian and the extent of the need for delegation of the ward's rights.

History.
S. 6, ch. 2006-77, eff. June 6, 2006; s. 47, ch. 2006-217, eff. July 1, 2007.

PART VII.
TERMINATION.

744.464.   Restoration to capacity.

(1) Venue. — A suggestion of capacity must be filed with the court in which the guardianship is pending.

(2) Suggestion of capacity.

(a) Any interested person, including the ward, may file a suggestion of capacity. The suggestion of capacity must state that the ward is currently capable of exercising some or all of the rights which were removed.

(b) Upon the filing of the suggestion of capacity, the court shall immediately appoint a physician to examine the ward. The physician must examine the ward and file his or her report with the court within 20 days after the appointment.

(c) The court shall immediately send notice of the filing of the suggestion of capacity to the ward, the guardian, the attorney for the ward, if any, and any other interested persons designated by the court. Formal notice must be served on the guardian. Informal notice may be served on other persons. Notice need not be served on the person who filed the suggestion of capacity.

(d) Any objections to the suggestion of capacity must be filed within 20 days after service of the notice.

(e) If an objection is timely filed, or if the medical examination suggests that full restoration is not appropriate, the court shall set the matter for hearing. If the ward does not have an attorney, the court shall appoint one to represent the ward.

(f) Notice of the hearing and copies of the objections and medical examination reports shall be served upon the ward, the ward's attorney, the guardian, the ward's next of kin, and any other interested persons as directed by the court.

(3) Order of restoration.

(a) If no objections are filed, and the court is satisfied with the medical examination, the court shall enter an order of restoration of capacity, restoring all or some of the rights which were removed from the ward. The order must be issued within 30 days after the medical report is filed.

(b) At the conclusion of a hearing, conducted pursuant to s. 744.1095, the court shall enter an order either denying the suggestion of capacity or restoring all or some of the rights which were removed from the ward.

(c) If only some rights are restored to the ward, the order must state which rights are restored, and

the guardian shall prepare a new guardianship report which addresses only the remaining rights retained by the guardian. The guardian must file a copy of the new report with the court within 60 days after the entry of the order.

History.
SS. 10, 26, ch. 75-222; s. 1, ch. 77-174; s. 81, ch. 89-96; s. 57, ch. 90-271; s. 1104, ch. 97-102; s. 22, ch. 2006-178, eff. July 1, 2006.

744.467.   Resignation of guardian.

A guardian may resign and be relieved of his or her duties after the notice that the court may require and notice to the surety on his or her bond. Before entering an order discharging a guardian of the property, the court shall require the guardian to file a true and correct final report of his or her guardianship and to deliver to the successor guardian all property of the ward, all records concerning the property of the ward or of the guardianship, and all money due to the ward from him or her. A guardian of the person must deliver to the successor guardian copies of all records of medical or personal care, prior to being discharged. Before entering the order, the court shall be satisfied that the interest of the ward will not be placed in jeopardy by the resignation. The acceptance of the resignation shall not exonerate the guardian or the guardian's surety from any liability previously incurred.

History.
S. 1, ch. 74-106; ss. 19, 26, ch. 75-222; s. 1, ch. 77-174; s. 82, ch. 89-96; s. 58, ch. 90-271; s. 1105, ch. 97-102.

Editor's Notes.
Created from former s. 746.01.

744.471.   Appointment of successor.

A successor guardian must be appointed and duly qualified before a guardian shall be relieved of his or her duties and obligations as provided in s. 744.467. A successor guardian shall be appointed if a guardian dies, becomes incapacitated, or is removed. Successor guardians are governed by the laws concerning guardianships.

History.
S. 1, ch. 74-106; s. 83, ch. 89-96; s. 26, ch. 95-401; s. 1106, ch. 97-102.

Editor's Notes.
Created from former s. 746.02.

744.474.   Reasons for removal of guardian.

A guardian may be removed for any of the following reasons, and the removal shall be in addition to any other penalties prescribed by law:

(1) Fraud in obtaining her or his appointment.

(2) Failure to discharge her or his duties.

(3) Abuse of her or his powers.

(4) An incapacity or illness, including substance abuse, which renders the guardian incapable of discharging her or his duties.

(5) Failure to comply with any order of the court.

(6) Failure to return schedules of property sold or accounts of sales of property or to produce and exhibit the ward's assets when so required.

(7) The wasting, embezzlement, or other mismanagement of the ward's property.

(8) Failure to give bond or security for any purpose when required by the court or failure to file with the annual guardianship plan the evidence required by s. 744.351 that the sureties on her or his bond are alive and solvent.

(9) Conviction of a felony.

(10) Appointment of a receiver, trustee in bankruptcy, or liquidator for any corporate guardian.

(11) Development of a conflict of interest between the ward and the guardian.

(12) Having been found guilty of, regardless of adjudication, or entered a plea of nolo contendere or guilty to, any offense prohibited under s. 435.04 or similar statute of another jurisdiction.

(13) A material failure to comply with the guardianship report by the guardian.

(14) A failure to comply with the rules for timely filing the initial and annual guardianship reports.

(15) A failure to fulfill the guardianship education requirements.

(16) The improper management of the ward's assets.

(17) A material change in the ward's financial circumstances such that the guardian is no longer qualified to manage the finances of the ward, or the previous degree of management is no longer required.

(18) After appointment, the guardian becomes a disqualified person as set forth in s. 744.309(3).

(19) Upon a showing by a person who did not receive notice of the petition for adjudication of incapacity, when such notice is required, or who is related to the ward within the relationships specified for nonresident relatives in ss. 744.309(2) and 744.312(2) and who has not previously been rejected by the court as a guardian that the current guardian is not a family member and subsection (20) applies.

(20) Upon a showing that removal of the current guardian is in the best interest of the ward. In determining whether a guardian who is related by blood or marriage to the ward is to be removed, there shall be a rebuttable presumption that the guardian is acting in the best interests of the ward.

History.
S. 1, ch. 74-106; ss. 21, 26, ch. 75-222; s. 84, ch. 89-96; s. 138, ch. 95-418; s. 13, ch. 96-354; s. 1788, ch. 97-102; s. 283, ch. 99-8; s. 2, ch. 99-277; s. 111, ch. 2000-349; s. 32, ch. 2004-267; s. 23, ch. 2006-178, eff. July 1, 2006; s. 54, ch. 2010-114, eff. Aug. 1, 2010.

Editor's Notes.
Created from former s. 746.03.
Section 32, ch. 2004-267, reenacted (12) without change to incorporate amendments to statutory sections referenced therein.
Section 58, ch. 2010-114 provides: "The changes made by this act are intended to be prospective in nature. It is not intended that persons who are employed or licensed on the effective date of this act be rescreened until such time as they are otherwise required to be rescreened pursuant to law, at which time they must meet the requirements for screening as set forth in this act."

744.477. Proceedings for removal of a guardian.

Proceedings for removal of a guardian may be instituted by the court, by any surety or other interested person, or by the ward. Reasonable notice shall be given to the guardian. On the hearing, the court may enter an order that is proper considering the pleadings and the evidence.

History.
S. 1, ch. 74-106; ss. 21, 26, ch. 75-222; s. 85, ch. 89-96; s. 59, ch. 90-271.

Editor's Notes.
Created from former s. 746.04.

744.511. Accounting upon removal.

A removed guardian shall file with the court a true, complete, and final report of his or her guardianship within 20 days after removal and shall serve a copy on the successor guardian and the ward, unless the ward is a minor or has been determined to be totally incapacitated.

History.
S. 1, ch. 74-106; ss. 21, 26, ch. 75-222; s. 86, ch. 89-96; s. 60, ch. 90-271; s. 1107, ch. 97-102; s. 24, ch. 2006-178, eff. July 1, 2006.

Editor's Notes.
Created from former s. 746.05.

744.514. Surrender of property upon removal.

The successor guardian shall demand of the removed guardian or her or his heirs, personal representative, or surety all the property of the ward and copies of all records of the ward. The removed guardian or her or his heirs, personal representative, or surety shall turn over the items to her or his duly qualified successor.

History.
S. 1, ch. 74-106; ss. 21, 26, ch. 75-222; s. 87, ch. 89-96; s. 61, ch. 90-271; s. 1108, ch. 97-102.

Editor's Notes.
Created from former s. 746.06.

744.517. Proceedings for contempt.

If a removed guardian of the property fails to file a true, complete, and final accounting of his or her guardianship; to turn over to his or her successor or to the ward all the property of his or her ward and copies of all records that are in his or her control and that concern the ward; or to pay over to the successor guardian of the property or to the ward all money due the ward by him or her, the court shall issue a show cause order. If cause is shown for the default, the court shall set a reasonable time within which to comply, and, on failure to comply with this or any subsequent order, the removed guardian may be held in contempt. Proceedings for contempt may be instituted by the court, by any interested person, including the ward, or by a successor guardian.

History.
S. 1, ch. 74-106; ss. 21, 26, ch. 75-222; s. 88, ch. 89-96; s. 62, ch. 90-271; s. 1109, ch. 97-102.

Editor's Notes.
Created from former ss. 746.07, 746.08.

744.521. Termination of guardianship.

When a ward becomes sui juris or is restored to capacity, when the guardian has been unable to locate the ward through diligent search, or, for a guardian of the property, when the property subject to the guardianship has been exhausted, the guardian shall file a final report and receive his or her discharge. A guardian of the person is discharged without further proceeding upon filing a certified copy of the ward's death certificate. The court may require proof of the removal of incapacity.

History.
S. 1, ch. 74-106; ss. 21, 26, ch. 75-222; s. 4, ch. 86-120; s. 89, ch. 89-96; s. 63, ch. 90-271; s. 1110, ch. 97-102.
Editor's Notes.
Created from former s. 746.12.

744.524. Termination of guardianship on change of domicile of resident ward.

When the domicile of a resident ward has changed as provided in s. 744.2025, and the foreign court having jurisdiction over the ward at the ward's new domicile has appointed a guardian and that guardian has qualified and posted a bond in an amount required by the foreign court, the guardian in this state may file her or his final report and close the guardianship in this state. The guardian of the property in this state shall cause a notice to be published once a week for 2 consecutive weeks, in a newspaper of general circulation published in the county, that she or he has filed her or his accounting and will apply for discharge on a day certain and that jurisdiction of the ward will be transferred to the state of foreign jurisdiction. If an objection is filed to the termination of the guardianship in this state, the court shall hear the objection and enter an order either sustaining or overruling the objection. Upon the disposition of all objections filed, or if no objection is filed, final settlement shall be made by the Florida guardian. On proof that the remaining property in the guardianship has been received by the foreign guardian, the guardian of the property in this state shall be discharged. The entry of the order terminating the guardianship in this state shall not exonerate the guardian or the guardian's surety from any liability previously incurred.

History.
S. 1, ch. 74-106; ss. 21, 26, ch. 75-222; s. 90, ch. 89-96; s. 64, ch. 90-271; s. 1111, ch. 97-102.
Editor's Notes.
Created from former s. 746.121.

744.527. Final reports and application for discharge; hearing.

(1) When the court terminates the guardianship for any of the reasons set forth in s. 744.521, the guardian shall promptly file his or her final report. If the ward has died, the guardian must file a final report with the court no later than 45 days after he or she has been served with letters of administration or letters of curatorship. If no objections are filed and if it appears that the guardian has made full and complete distribution to the person entitled and has otherwise faithfully discharged his or her duties, the court shall approve the final report. If objections are filed, the court shall conduct a hearing in the same manner as provided for a hearing on objections to annual guardianship reports.

(2) The guardian applying for discharge may retain from the funds in his or her possession a sufficient amount to pay the final costs of administration, including guardian and attorney's fees regardless of the death of the ward, accruing between the filing of his or her final returns and the order of discharge.

History.
S. 1, ch. 74-106; ss. 21, 26, ch. 75-222; s. 91, ch. 89-96; s. 65, ch. 90-271; s. 1112, ch. 97-102; s. 25, ch. 2006-178, eff. July 1, 2006.
Editor's Notes.
Created from former s. 746.13.

744.528. Discharge of guardian named as personal representative.

(1) A guardian authorized to manage property, who is subsequently appointed personal representative, must serve a copy of the guardian's final report and petition for discharge upon the beneficiaries of the ward's estate who will be affected by the report.

(2) All such beneficiaries shall have 30 days to file objections to the final report and petition for discharge.

(3) Any interested person may file a notice of a hearing on any objections filed by the beneficiaries. Notice of the hearing must be served upon the guardian, beneficiaries of the ward's estate, and any other person to whom the court directs service. If a notice of hearing on the objections is not served within 90 days after filing of the objections, the objections are deemed abandoned.

(4) The guardian may not be discharged until:

(a) All objections have been judicially resolved;

(b) The report of the guardian is approved by the court; and

(c) In the case of a guardian of the property, all property has been distributed to the ward's estate or the persons entitled to it.

History.
S. 92, ch. 89-96; s. 66, ch. 90-271; s. 26, ch. 2006-178, eff. July 1, 2006.

744.531. Order of discharge.

If the court is satisfied that the guardian has faithfully discharged her or his duties, has rendered a complete and accurate final report, and, in the case of a guardian of the property, has delivered the property of the ward to the person entitled, and that the interest of the ward is protected, the court shall enter an order of discharge. The discharge shall operate as a release from the duties of the guardianship and as a bar to any action against the guardian or the guardian's surety unless the action is commenced within 3 years after the date of the order.

History.
S. 1, ch. 74-106; ss. 21, 26, ch. 75-222; s. 93, ch. 89-96; s. 67, ch. 90-271; s. 1113, ch. 97-102.

Editor's Notes.
Created from former s. 746.14.

744.534. Disposition of unclaimed funds held by guardian.

(1) In all cases in which it is appropriate for the guardianship to terminate due to the ward's death and in which property in the hands of the guardian cannot be distributed because no estate proceeding has been instituted, the guardian of the property shall be considered an interested person pursuant to s. 733.202 and may, after a reasonable time, institute such a proceeding. In the alternative, the guardian may follow the procedures set forth in subsection (2).

(2)(a) In those cases in which it is appropriate for the guardianship to terminate pursuant to s. 744.521 and in which property in the hands of a guardian cannot be distributed to the ward or the ward's estate solely because the guardian is unable to locate the ward through diligent search, the court shall order the guardian of the property to sell the property of the ward and deposit the proceeds and cash already on hand after retaining those amounts provided for in paragraph (e) with the clerk of the court exercising jurisdiction over the guardianship and receive a receipt. The clerk shall deposit the funds in the registry of the court, to be disposed of as follows:

    1. If the value of the funds is $50 or less, the clerk shall post a notice for 30 days at the courthouse door giving the amount involved, the name of the ward, and other pertinent information that will put interested persons on notice.

    2. If the value of the funds is over $50, the clerk shall publish the notice once a month for 2 consecutive months in a newspaper of general circulation in the county.

    3. After the expiration of 6 months from the posting or first publication, the clerk shall deposit the funds with the Chief Financial Officer after deducting his or her fees and the costs of publication.

(b) Upon receipt of the funds, the Chief Financial Officer shall deposit them to the credit of public guardianship. All interest and all income that may accrue from the money while so deposited shall belong to the fund. The funds so deposited shall constitute and be a permanent appropriation for payments by the Chief Financial Officer in obedience to court orders entered as provided by paragraph (c).

(c) Within 5 years from the date of deposit with the Chief Financial Officer, on written petition to the court that directed the deposit of the funds and informal notice to the Department of Legal Affairs, and after proof of his or her right to them, any person entitled to the funds, before or after payment to the Chief Financial Officer and deposit as provided for in paragraph (a), may obtain a court order directing the payment of the funds to him or her. All funds deposited with the Chief Financial Officer and not claimed within 5 years from the date of deposit shall escheat to the state to be deposited in the Department of Elderly Affairs Administrative Trust Fund to be used solely for the benefit of public guardianship as determined by the Secretary of Elderly Affairs.

(d) Upon depositing the funds with the clerk, the guardian of the property may proceed with the filing of his or her final return and application for discharge under s. 744.527.

(e) The guardian depositing assets with the clerk is permitted to retain from the funds in his or her possession a sufficient amount to pay the final costs of administration, including guardian and attorney's fees accruing between the deposit of the funds with the clerk of the court and the order of discharge. Any surplus funds so retained must be deposited with the clerk prior to discharge of the guardian of the property.

History.
S. 5, ch. 86-120; s. 94, ch. 89-96; s. 68, ch. 90-271; s. 1114, ch. 97-102; s. 7, ch. 2002-195; s. 13, ch. 2003-57; s. 1898, ch. 2003-261.

PART VIII.
VETERANS' GUARDIANSHIP.

744.602. Short title; scope of part.

(1) This part shall be known and may be cited as the "Veterans' Guardianship Law."

(2) The application of this part is limited to veterans and other persons who are entitled to receive benefits from the United States Department of Veterans Affairs. This part is not intended to replace the general law relating to guardianship except insofar as this part is inconsistent with the general law relating to guardianship; in which event, this part and the general law relating to guardianship shall be read together, with any conflict between this part and the general law of guardianship to be resolved by giving effect to this part.

History.
S. 18, ch. 14579, 1929; CGL 1936 Supp. 2146(1); s. 1, ch. 84-62; s. 38, ch. 93-268.

Editor's Notes.
Former s. 293.01.

744.604. Definitions.

As used in this part, the term:

(1) "Adjudication by a court of competent jurisdiction" means a judicial decision or finding that a person is or is not incapacitated as provided in s. 744.331.

(2) "Adjudication by the United States Department of Veterans Affairs" means a determination or finding that a person is competent or incompetent on examination in accordance with the laws and regulations governing the United States Department of Veterans Affairs.

(3) "Secretary" means the Secretary of Veterans Affairs as head of the United States Department of Veterans Affairs or her or his successor.

(4) "Benefits" means arrears of pay, bonus, pension, compensation, insurance, and all other moneys paid or payable by the United States through the United States Department of Veterans Affairs by reason of service in the Armed Forces of the United States.

(5) "Estate" means income on hand and assets acquired in whole or in part with income.

(6) "Guardian" means any person acting as a fiduciary for a ward's person or the ward's estate, or both.

(7) "Income" means moneys received from the United States Department of Veterans Affairs as benefits, and revenue or profit from any property acquired in whole or in part with such moneys.

(8) "Person" means an individual, a partnership, a corporation, or an association.

(9) "United States Department of Veterans Affairs" means the United States Department of Veterans Affairs or its predecessors or successors.

(10) "Ward" means a beneficiary of the United States Department of Veterans Affairs.

History.
S. 1, ch. 14579, 1929; CGL 1936 Supp. 2146(2); s. 1, ch. 73-304; s. 2, ch. 84-62; s. 95, ch. 89-96; s. 39, ch. 93-268; s. 1115, ch. 97-102.
Editor's Notes.
Former s. 293.02.

744.607. Secretary of Veterans Affairs as party in interest.

The Secretary of Veterans Affairs shall be a party in interest in any proceeding for the appointment or removal of a guardian or for the removal of the disability of minority or mental incapacity of a ward, and in any suit or other proceeding affecting in any manner the administration by the guardian of the estate of any present or former ward whose estate includes assets derived in whole or in part from benefits heretofore or hereafter paid by the United States Department of Veterans Affairs. Not less than 15 days prior to hearing in such matter, notice in writing of the time and place thereof shall be given by mail (unless waived in writing) to the office of the United States Department of Veterans Affairs having jurisdiction over the area in which any such suit or any such proceeding is pending.

History.
S. 3, ch. 21795, 1943; s. 3, ch. 84-62; s. 40, ch. 93-268.
Editor's Notes.
Former s. 293.20.

744.609. Procedure for commitment of veteran to United States Department of Veterans Affairs hospital.

The procedure for the placement into a United States Department of Veterans Affairs hospital of a ward hereunder shall be the procedure prescribed in s. 394.4672.

History.
S. 22, ch. 84-62; s. 41, ch. 93-268.

744.613. Appointment of guardian for ward authorized.

(1) Whenever, pursuant to any law of the United States or regulation of the United States Department of Veterans Affairs, the secretary requires, prior to the payment of benefits, that a guardian be appointed for a ward, the appointment may be made in the manner hereinafter provided.

(2) When a petition is filed for the appointment of a guardian of a minor ward, a certificate of the secretary or the secretary's authorized representative setting forth the age of such minor, as shown by the records of the United States Department of Veterans Affairs, and a statement that the appointment of a guardian is a condition precedent to the payment of any moneys due to the minor by the United States Department of Veterans Affairs are prima facie evidence of the necessity for such appointment.

(3) When a petition is filed for the appointment of a guardian of a mentally incompetent ward, a certificate of the secretary or the secretary's authorized representative, setting forth the fact that the person has been found incompetent and has been rated incompetent by the United States Department of Veterans Affairs, on examination in accordance with the laws and regulations governing the United States Department of Veterans Affairs, and that the appointment of a guardian is a condition precedent to the payment of any moneys due to such person by the United States Department of Veterans Affairs, is prima facie evidence of the necessity for such appointment.

History.
SS. 2, 5, 6, ch. 14579, 1929; CGL 1936 Supp. 2146(3), (6), (7); s. 1, ch. 73-304; s. 5, ch. 84-62; s. 42, ch. 93-268; s. 1116, ch. 97-102.
Editor's Notes.
Consolidation of former ss. 293.03, 293.06, 293.07.

744.616. Petition for appointment of guardian.

(1) A petition for the appointment of a guardian may be filed in any court of competent jurisdiction by, or on behalf of, any person who under existing law is entitled to priority of appointment. If no person is so entitled, or if the person so entitled neglects or refuses to file such a petition within 30 days after the mailing of notice by the United States Department of Veterans Affairs to the last known address of such person, indicating the necessity for filing the petition, a petition for such appointment may be filed in any court of competent jurisdiction by, or on behalf of, any responsible person residing in this state.

(2)(a) The petition for appointment shall set forth:

1. The name, age, and place of residence of the ward;

2. The names and places of residence of the nearest relative, if known;

3. The fact that the ward is entitled to receive moneys payable by or through the United States Department of Veterans Affairs;

4. The amount of moneys then due and the amount of probable future payments;

5. The name and address of the person or institution, if any, having actual custody of the ward; and

6. The name, age, relationship, if any, occupation, and address of the proposed guardian.

(b) In the case of a mentally incompetent ward, the petition shall show that the ward has been found incompetent and has been rated incompetent on examination by the United States Department of Veterans Affairs, in accordance with the laws and regulations governing the United States Department of Veterans Affairs.

History.
S. 4, ch. 14579, 1929; CGL 1936 Supp. 2146(5); s. 1, ch. 73-304; s. 6, ch. 84-62; s. 43, ch. 93-268.
Editor's Notes.
Former s. 293.05.

744.617. Notice by court of petition filed for appointment of guardian.

(1) When a petition for the appointment of a guardian has been filed pursuant to s. 744.616, the court shall cause such notice to be given as provided by the general guardianship law. In addition, notice of the petition shall be given to the office of the United States Department of Veterans Affairs having jurisdiction over the area in which the court is located.

(2) A copy of the petition provided for in s. 744.616 shall be mailed by the clerk of the court to the person or persons for whom a guardian is to be appointed, the clerk of court mailing the copy of the petition to the last known address of such person or persons not less than 5 days prior to the date set for the hearing of the petition by the court.

History.
S. 2, ch. 11906, 1927; s. 7, ch. 14579, 1929; CGL 2134; CGL 1936 Supp. 2146(8); s. 7, ch. 84-62; s. 44, ch. 93-268.
Editor's Notes.
Consolidation of former ss. 293.08, 294.03.

744.618. Persons who may be appointed guardian.

(1) Notwithstanding any law with respect to priority of persons entitled to appointment, or nomination in the petition, the court may appoint some other individual or a bank or trust company as guardian if the court determines that the appointment of the other individual or bank or trust company would be in the best interest of the ward.

(2) It is unlawful for a circuit judge to appoint either herself or himself, or a member of her or his family, as guardian for any person entitled to the benefits provided for in 38 U.S.C., as amended, except in a case when the person entitled to such benefits is a member of the family of the circuit judge involved.

History.
S. 4, ch. 11906, 1927; CGL 2136; s. 24, ch. 73-334; s. 6, ch. 84-62; s. 1117, ch. 97-102.
Editor's Notes.
Former s. 294.04.

744.619. Bond of guardian.

When the appointment of a guardian is made, the guardian shall execute and file a bond to be approved by the court in an amount not less than the sum of the amount of moneys then due to the ward and the amount of moneys estimated to become payable during the ensuing year. The bond shall be in the form, and shall be conditioned, as required of guardians appointed under the general guardianship laws of this state. The court has the power to require, from time to time, the guardian to file an additional bond.

History.
S. 8, ch. 14579, 1929; CGL 1936 Supp. 2146(9); s. 7, ch. 84-62.
Editor's Notes.
Former s. 293.09.

744.621. Inventory of ward's property; guardian's failure to file inventory; discharge; forfeiture of commissions.

Every guardian shall, within 30 days after his or her qualification and whenever subsequently required by the circuit judge, file in the circuit court a complete inventory of all the ward's personal property in his or her hands and, also, a schedule of all real estate in the state belonging to his or her ward, describing it and its quality, whether it is improved or not, and, if it is improved, in what manner, and the appraised value of same. The failure on the part of the guardian to conform to the requirements of this section is a ground for the discharge of the guardian, in which case the guardian shall forfeit all commissions.

History.
S. 6, ch. 11906, 1927; CGL 2138; s. 24, ch. 73-334; s. 10, ch. 84-62; s. 1118, ch. 97-102.
Editor's Notes.
Former s. 294.06.

744.622. Guardian empowered to receive moneys due ward from the United States Government.

A guardian appointed under the provisions of s. 744.616 may receive income and benefits payable by the United States through the United States Department of Veterans Affairs and also has the right to receive for the account of the ward any moneys due from the United States Government in the way of arrears of pay, bonus, compensation or insurance, or other sums due by reason of his or her service (or the service of the person through whom the ward claims) in the Armed Forces of the United States and any other moneys due from the United States Government, payable through its agencies or entities, together with the income derived from investments of these moneys.

History.
S. 6, ch. 11906, 1927; CGL 2138; s. 8, ch. 84-62; s. 45, ch. 93-268; s. 1119, ch. 97-102.

744.624. Guardian's application of estate funds for support and maintenance of person other than ward.

A guardian shall not apply any portion of the estate of her or his ward to the support and maintenance of any person other than her or his ward, except upon order of the court after a hearing, notice of which has been given to the proper office of the United States Department of Veterans Affairs as provided in s. 744.625.

History.
S. 13, ch. 14579, 1929; CGL 1936 Supp. 2146(14); s. 1, ch. 73-304; s. 10, ch. 84-62; s. 46, ch. 93-268; s. 1120, ch. 97-102.
Editor's Notes.
Former s. 293.14.

744.625. Petition for support, or support and education, of ward's dependents; payments of apportioned benefits prohibit contempt action against veteran.

(1) Any person who is dependent on a ward for support may petition a court of competent jurisdiction for an order directing the guardian of the ward's estate to contribute from the estate of the ward to the support, or support and education, of the dependent person, when the estate of the ward is derived in whole or in part from payments of compensation, adjusted compensation, pension, insurance, or other benefits made directly to the guardian of the ward by the United States Department of Veterans Affairs. A notice of the application for support, or support and education, shall be given by the applicant to the office of the United States Department of Veterans Affairs having jurisdiction over the area in which the court is located at least 15 days before the hearing on the application.

(2) The grant or denial of an order for support, or support and education, does not preclude a further petition for an increase, decrease, modification, or termination of the allowance for such support, or support and education, by either the petitioner or the guardian.

(3) The order for the support, or support and education, of the petitioner is valid for any payment made pursuant to the order, but no valid payment can be made after the termination of the guardianship. The receipt of the petitioner shall be a sufficient release of the guardian for payments made pursuant to the order.

(4) When a claim for apportionment of benefits filed with the United States Department of Veterans Affairs on behalf of a dependent or dependents of a disabled veteran is approved by the United States Department of Veterans Affairs, subsequent payments of such apportioned benefits by the United States Department of Veterans Affairs prohibit an action for contempt from being instituted against the veteran.

History.
S. 9, ch. 84-62; s. 47, ch. 93-268.

744.626. Exemption of benefits from claims of creditors.

Except as provided by federal law, payments of benefits from the United States Department of Veterans Affairs or the Social Security Administration to or for the benefit of a disabled veteran or the veteran's surviving spouse or dependents are exempt from the claims of creditors and shall not be liable to attachment, levy, or seizure by or under any legal or equitable process whatever, either before or after the receipt of the payments by the guardian or the beneficiary.

History.
S. 9, ch. 84-62; s. 48, ch. 93-268; s. 1121, ch. 97-102.

744.627. Investment of funds of estate by guardian.

Every guardian shall invest the funds of the estate in such manner or in such securities, in which the guardian has no interest, as allowed by chapter 518.

History.
S. 12, ch. 14579, 1929; s. 1, ch. 17473, 1935; CGL 1936 Supp. 2146(13); s. 10, ch. 84-62.
Editor's Notes.
Former s. 293.13.

744.631. Guardian's petition for authority to sell ward's real estate; notice by publication; penalties.

(1) When a guardian of the estate of a minor or an incompetent ward, which guardian has the control or management of any real estate that is the property of such minor or incompetent, deems it necessary or expedient to sell all or part of the real estate, the guardian shall apply, either in term time or in vacation by petition to the judge of the circuit court for the county in which the real estate is situated, for authority to sell all or part of the real estate. If the prayer of the petition appears to the judge to be reasonable and just and financially beneficial to the estate of the ward, the judge may authorize the guardian to sell the real estate described in the petition under such conditions as the interest of the minor or incompetent may, in the opinion of the judge, seem to require.

(2) The authority to sell the real estate described in the petition shall not be granted unless the guardian has given previous notice, published once a week for 4 successive weeks in a newspaper published in the county where the application is made, of his or her intention to make application to the judge for authority to sell such real estate, the guardian setting forth in the notice the time and place and to what judge the application will be made. If the lands lie in more than one county, the application for such authority shall be made in each county in which the lands lie.

(3) The failure on the part of the guardian to comply with the provisions of this section makes the guardian and the guardian's bond agents individually responsible for any loss that may accrue to the estate of the ward involved, and is a ground for the immediate removal of such guardian as to his or her functions, but

does not discharge the guardian as to his or her liability or discharge the liabilities of his or her sureties.

History.
S. 9, ch. 11906, 1927; CGL 2141; s. 24, ch. 73-334; s. 11, ch. 84-62; s. 1122, ch. 97-102.

Editor's Notes.
Former s. 294.10.

744.634. Guardian's accounts, filing with court and certification to United States Department of Veterans Affairs; notice and hearing on accounts; failure to account.

(1) Every guardian who receives on account of his or her ward any moneys from the United States Department of Veterans Affairs shall annually file with the court on the anniversary date of the appointment, in addition to such other accounts as may be required by the court, a full, true, and accurate account under oath, which account is an account of all moneys so received by him or her and of all disbursements from such moneys, and which account shows the balance of the moneys in his or her hands at the date of such filing and shows how the moneys are invested. A certified copy of each of such accounts filed with the court shall be sent by the guardian to the office of the United States Department of Veterans Affairs having jurisdiction over the area in which such court is located. If the requirement of certification is waived in writing by the United States Department of Veterans Affairs, an uncertified copy of each of such accounts shall be sent.

(2) The court, at its discretion or upon the petition of an interested party, shall fix a time and place for the hearing on such account; and notice of the hearing shall be given by the court to the United States Department of Veterans Affairs not less than 15 days prior to the date fixed for the hearing.

(3) The court need not appoint a guardian ad litem to represent the ward at the hearing provided for in subsection (2). If the residence of the next kin of the ward is known, notice by registered mail shall be sent to such relative. Notice also shall be served on the ward; or, if the ward is mentally incapable of understanding the matter at issue, the notice may be served on the person in charge of the institution where the ward is detained, or on the person having charge or custody of the ward.

(4) When a hearing on an account is required by the court or requested in the petition of an interested party as provided in subsection (2), the judge of the court on the day of the hearing as provided for in subsection (2) shall carefully examine the vouchers and audit and state the account between the guardian and ward. Proper evidence shall be required in support of any voucher or item of the account that may appear to the court not to be just and proper, such evidence to be taken by affidavit or by any other legal mode. If any voucher is rejected, the item or items covered by the disapproval of any voucher or vouchers shall be taxed against the guardian personally. After such examina-

tion, the court shall render a decree upon the account, which shall be entered on the record, and the account and vouchers shall be filed. Such partial settlement shall be taken and presumed as correct on final settlement of the guardianship.

(5) If a guardian fails to file any account of the moneys received by him or her from the United States Department of Veterans Affairs on account of his or her ward within 30 days after such account is required by either the court or the United States Department of Veterans Affairs, or fails to furnish the United States Department of Veterans Affairs a copy of his or her accounts as required by subsection (1), such failure shall be a ground for the removal of the guardian.

History.
SS. 7, 8, ch. 11906, 1927; CGL 2139, 2140; ss. 9, 10, ch. 14579, 1929; CGL 1936 Supp. 2146(10), (11); s. 1, ch. 73-304; s. 12, ch. 84-62; s. 49, ch. 93-268; s. 1123, ch. 97-102.

Editor's Notes.
Consolidation of former ss. 293.10, 293.11, 294.08, 294.09.

744.637. Certified copies of public records made available.

When a copy of any public record is required by the United States Department of Veterans Affairs to be used in determining the eligibility of any person to participate in benefits made available by the United States Department of Veterans Affairs, the official charged with the custody of such public record shall, without charge, provide to the applicant for such benefits or any person acting on her or his behalf, or to the authorized representative of the United States Department of Veterans Affairs, a certified copy of such record. For each and every certified copy so furnished by the official, the official shall be paid by the board of county commissioners the fee provided by law for copies.

History.
S. 14, ch. 14579, 1929; CGL 1936 Supp. 2146(15); s. 7, ch. 29749, 1955; s. 1, ch. 73-304; s. 13, ch. 84-62; s. 50, ch. 93-268; s. 1124, ch. 97-102.

Editor's Notes.
Former s. 293.15.

744.638. Clerk of the circuit court; fees; duties.

Upon the filing of the petition for guardianship, granting of same, and entering decree thereon, the clerk of the circuit court is entitled to the service charge as provided by law, which shall include the cost of recording the petition, bond, and decree and the issuing of letters of guardianship. The certificate of the secretary or the secretary's authorized representative provided for in s. 744.613 need not be recorded but must be kept in the file. Upon issuing letters of guardianship or letters appointing a guardian for the estate of a minor or incompetent, the clerk of the circuit court shall send to the regional office of the United States Department of Veterans Affairs having jurisdiction in this state two certified copies of the letters and two certified copies of the bond approved by the court, without charge or expense to the estate involved. The clerk of the circuit court shall also send a certified copy of such letters to the property appraiser and to the tax collector in each county in which the ward owns real property.

History.
S. 10, ch. 11906, 1927; CGL 2142; s. 1, ch. 73-304; s. 24, ch. 73-334; s. 7, ch. 84-62; s. 11, ch. 87-145; s. 51, ch. 93-268; s. 1125, ch. 97-102.

Editor's Notes.
Former s. 294.11.

744.639. Attorney's fee.

The fee for the attorney filing the petition and conducting the proceedings shall be fixed by the court in an amount as small as reasonably possible, not to exceed $250. However, this section is not to be interpreted to exclude a petition for extraordinary attorney's fees, properly filed, and if approved by the United States Department of Veterans Affairs, does not necessitate a hearing before the court for approval, but the court shall enter its order for withdrawal of said attorney's fees from the ward's guardianship account accordingly.

History.
S. 7, ch. 84-62; s. 31, ch. 95-401; s. 16, ch. 97-93.

744.641. Guardian's compensation; bond premiums.

The amount of compensation payable to a guardian shall not exceed 5 percent of the income of the ward during any year and may be taken, by the guardian, on a monthly basis. In the event of extraordinary services rendered by such guardian, the court may, upon petition and after hearing on the petition, authorize additional compensation for the extraordinary services, payable from the estate of the ward. Provided that extraordinary services approved by the United States Department of Veteran's Affairs do not require a court hearing for approval of the fees, but shall require an order authorizing the guardian to withdraw the amount from the guardianship account. No compensation shall be allowed on the corpus of an estate received from a preceding guardian. The guardian may be allowed from the estate of her or his ward reasonable premiums paid by the guardian to any corporate surety upon the guardian's bond.

History.
S. 11, ch. 14579, 1929; CGL 1936 Supp. 2146(12); s. 1, ch. 73-304; s. 14, ch. 84-62; s. 63, ch. 85-62; s. 52, ch. 93-268; s. 32, ch. 95-401; s. 1126, ch. 97-102; s. 85, ch. 99-3.

Editor's Notes.
Former s. 293.12.

744.643. Discharge of guardian of minor or incompetent ward.

When a minor ward, for whom a guardian has been appointed under the provisions of this part or other laws of this state, attains his or her majority and, if such minor ward has been incompetent, is declared compe-

tent by the United States Department of Veterans Affairs and the court, or when an incompetent ward who is not a minor is declared competent by the United States Department of Veterans Affairs and the court, the guardian shall, upon making a satisfactory accounting, be discharged upon a petition filed for that purpose.

History.
S. 16, ch. 14579, 1929; CGL 1936 Supp. 2146(17); s. 1, ch. 73-304; s. 15, ch. 84-62; s. 53, ch. 93-268; s. 1127, ch. 97-102.

Editor's Notes.
Former s. 293.17.

744.646. Final settlement of guardianship; notice required; guardian ad litem fee; papers required by United States Department of Veterans Affairs.

On the final settlement of the guardianship, the notice provided herein for partial settlement must be given and the other proceedings conducted as in the case of partial settlement, except that a guardian ad litem may be appointed to represent the ward, the fee of which guardian ad litem shall in no case exceed $150. However, if the ward has been pronounced competent, is shown to be mentally sound, appears in court, and is 18 years of age, the settlement may be had between the guardian and the ward under the direction of the court without notice to the next of kin, or the appointment of a guardian ad litem. A certified copy of the final settlement so made in every case must be filed with the United States Department of Veterans Affairs by the clerk of the court.

History.
S. 11, ch. 11906, 1927; CGL 2143; s. 1, ch. 73-304; s. 13, ch. 77-121; s. 16, ch. 84-62; s. 54, ch. 93-268.

Editor's Notes.
Former s. 294.12.

744.649. Notice of appointment of general guardian; closing of veteran's guardianship; transfer of responsibilities and penalties to general guardian.

When the appointment of a general guardian has been made in the proper court and such guardian has qualified and taken charge of the other property of the ward, the general guardian shall file notice of such appointment in the court in which the veteran's guardianship is pending and have the veteran's guardianship settled up and closed so that the general guardian may take charge of the moneys referred to and described in ss. 744.613(2) and (3) and 744.622. When the appointment of a general guardian, whether for an incompetent or minor child or another beneficiary entitled to the benefits provided in 38 U.S.C., as amended, has been confirmed by the court having jurisdiction, such general guardian is responsible and is subject to the provisions and penalties contained in 38 U.S.C., as amended, as well as the requirements pertaining to guardians as set forth in this part.

History.
S. 6, ch. 11906, 1927; CGL 2138; s. 17, ch. 84-62.

Editor's Notes.
Former s. 294.07.

744.652. Construction and application of part.

This part shall be construed liberally to secure the beneficial intents and purposes of this part and applies only to beneficiaries of the United States Department of Veterans Affairs. It shall be so interpreted and construed as to effectuate its general purpose of making the welfare of such beneficiaries the primary concern of their guardians and of the court.

History.
SS. 17, 19, ch. 14579, 1929; CGL 1936 Supp. 2146(18); s. 1, ch. 73-304; s. 18, ch. 84-62; s. 55, ch. 93-268.

Editor's Notes.
Former s. 293.18.

744.653. Annual guardianship report.

Guardians appointed under the Veterans' Guardianship Law shall not be required to comply with the provisions of s. 744.367.

History.
S. 6, ch. 91-306.

PART IX.
PUBLIC GUARDIANSHIP.

744.701. Short title.

This act shall be known and may be cited as the "Public Guardianship Act."

History.
S. 1, ch. 86-120; s. 96, ch. 89-96.

744.702. Legislative intent.

The Legislature finds that private guardianship is inadequate where there is no willing and responsible family member or friend, other person, bank, or corporation available to serve as guardian for an incapacitated person, and such person does not have adequate income or wealth for the compensation of a private guardian. The Legislature intends through this act to establish the Statewide Public Guardianship Office, and permit the establishment of offices of public guardian for the purpose of providing guardianship services for incapacitated persons when no private guardian is available. The Legislature further finds that alternatives to guardianship and less intrusive means of assistance should always be explored, including, but not limited to, guardian advocates, before an individual's rights are removed through an adjudication of incapacity. The purpose of this legislation is to provide a public guardian only to those persons whose needs cannot be met through less drastic means of intervention.

History.
S. 1, ch. 86-120; s. 97, ch. 89-96; s. 3, ch. 99-277.

744.7021. Statewide Public Guardianship Office.

There is hereby created the Statewide Public Guardianship Office within the Department of Elderly Affairs.

(1) The Secretary of Elderly Affairs shall appoint the executive director, who shall be the head of the Statewide Public Guardianship Office. The executive director must be a member of The Florida Bar, knowledgeable of guardianship law and of the social services available to meet the needs of incapacitated persons, shall serve on a full-time basis, and shall personally, or through representatives of the office, carry out the purposes and functions of the Statewide Public Guardianship Office in accordance with state and federal law. The executive director shall serve at the pleasure of and report to the secretary.

(2) The executive director shall, within available resources, have oversight responsibilities for all public guardians.

(a) The executive director shall review the current public guardian programs in Florida and other states.

(b) The executive director, in consultation with local guardianship offices, shall develop statewide performance measures and standards.

(c) The executive director shall review the various methods of funding guardianship programs, the kinds of services being provided by such programs, and the demographics of the wards. In addition, the executive director shall review and make recommendations regarding the feasibility of recovering a portion or all of the costs of providing public guardianship services from the assets or income of the wards.

(d) By January 1 of each year, the executive director shall provide a status report and provide further recommendations to the secretary that address the need for public guardianship services and related issues.

(e) The executive director may provide assistance to local governments or entities in pursuing grant opportunities. The executive director shall review and make recommendations in the annual report on the availability and efficacy of seeking Medicaid matching funds. The executive director shall diligently seek ways to use existing programs and services to meet the needs of public wards.

(f) The executive director, in consultation with the Florida Guardianship Foundation, shall develop a guardianship training program curriculum that may be offered to all guardians whether public or private.

(3) The executive director may conduct or contract for demonstration projects authorized by the Department of Elderly Affairs, within funds appropriated or through gifts, grants, or contributions for such purposes, to determine the feasibility or desirability of new concepts of organization, administration,

financing, or service delivery designed to preserve the civil and constitutional rights of persons of marginal or diminished capacity. Any gifts, grants, or contributions for such purposes shall be deposited in the Department of Elderly Affairs Administrative Trust Fund.

(4) The Department of Elderly Affairs has authority to adopt rules pursuant to ss. 120.536(1) and 120.54 to carry out the provisions of this section.

History.
S. 4, ch. 99-277; s. 14, ch. 2003-57; s. 5, ch. 2003-262; s. 140, ch. 2005-2.

744.703. Office of public guardian; appointment, notification.

(1) The executive director of the Statewide Public Guardianship Office, after consultation with the chief judge and other circuit judges within the judicial circuit and with appropriate advocacy groups and individuals and organizations who are knowledgeable about the needs of incapacitated persons, may establish, within a county in the judicial circuit or within the judicial circuit, one or more offices of public guardian and if so established, shall create a list of persons best qualified to serve as the public guardian, who have been investigated pursuant to s. 744.3135. The public guardian must have knowledge of the legal process and knowledge of social services available to meet the needs of incapacitated persons. The public guardian shall maintain a staff or contract with professionally qualified individuals to carry out the guardianship functions, including an attorney who has experience in probate areas and another person who has a master's degree in social work, or a gerontologist, psychologist, registered nurse, or nurse practitioner. A public guardian that is a nonprofit corporate guardian under s. 744.309(5) must receive tax-exempt status from the United States Internal Revenue Service.

(2) The executive director shall appoint or contract with a public guardian from the list of candidates described in subsection (1). A public guardian must meet the qualifications for a guardian as prescribed in s. 744.309(1)(a). Upon appointment of the public guardian, the executive director shall notify the chief judge of the judicial circuit and the Chief Justice of the Supreme Court of Florida, in writing, of the appointment.

(3) If the needs of the county or circuit do not require a full-time public guardian, a part-time public guardian may be appointed at reduced compensation.

(4) A public guardian, whether full-time or part-time, may not hold any position that would create a conflict of interest.

(5) The public guardian is to be appointed for a term of 4 years, after which her or his appointment must be reviewed by the executive director, and may be reappointed for a term of up to 4 years. The executive director may suspend a public guardian with or without the request of the chief judge. If a public guardian is suspended, the executive director shall appoint an acting public guardian as soon as possible to serve until such time as a permanent replacement is selected. A public guardian may be removed from office during the term of office only by the executive director who must consult with the chief judge prior to said removal. A recommendation of removal made by the chief judge must be considered by the executive director.

(6) Public guardians who have been previously appointed by a chief judge prior to the effective date of this act pursuant to this section may continue in their positions until the expiration of their term pursuant to their agreement. However, oversight of all public guardians shall transfer to the Statewide Public Guardianship Office upon the effective date of this act. The executive director of the Statewide Public Guardianship Office shall be responsible for all future appointments of public guardians pursuant to this act.

History.
S. 1, ch. 86-120; s. 98, ch. 89-96; s. 69, ch. 95-211; s. 27, ch. 95-401; s. 16, ch. 96-354; s. 1789, ch. 97-102; s. 5, ch. 99-277; s. 8, ch. 2002-195.

744.704. Powers and duties.

(1) A public guardian may serve as a guardian of a person adjudicated incapacitated under this chapter if there is no family member or friend, other person, bank, or corporation willing and qualified to serve as guardian.

(2) The public guardian shall be vested with all the powers and duties of a guardian under this chapter, except as otherwise provided by law.

(3) The public guardian shall primarily serve incapacitated persons who are of limited financial means, as defined by contract or rule of the Department of Elderly Affairs. The public guardian may serve incapacitated persons of greater financial means to the extent the Department of Elderly Affairs determines to be appropriate.

(4) The public guardian shall be authorized to employ sufficient staff to carry out the duties of his or her office.

(5) The public guardian may delegate to assistants and other members of his or her staff the powers and duties of the office of public guardian, except as otherwise limited by law. The public guardian shall retain ultimate responsibility for the discharge of his or her duties and responsibilities.

(6) The public guardian, when appointed guardian of an incapacitated person, shall seek a family member or friend, other person, bank, or corporation who is qualified and willing to serve as guardian. Upon determining that there is someone qualified and willing to serve as guardian, either the public guardian or the qualified person shall petition the court for appointment of a successor guardian.

(7) A public guardian shall not commit a ward to a mental health treatment facility, as defined in s.

394.455(32), without an involuntary placement proceeding as provided by law.

(8) When a person is appointed successor public guardian, he or she immediately succeeds to all rights, duties, responsibilities, and powers of the preceding public guardian.

(9) When the position of public guardian is vacant, subordinate personnel employed under subsection (4) shall continue to act as if the position of public guardian were filled.

History.
S. 1, ch. 86-120; s. 99, ch. 89-96; s. 45, ch. 96-169; s. 1790, ch. 97-102; s. 86, ch. 99-3; s. 15, ch. 2003-57; s. 71, ch. 2006-227, eff. July 1, 2006.

744.705. Costs of public guardian.

(1) All costs of administration, including filing fees, shall be paid from the budget of the office of public guardian. No costs of administration, including filing fees, shall be recovered from the assets or the income of the ward.

(2) In any proceeding for appointment of a public guardian, or in any proceeding involving the estate of a ward for whom a public guardian has been appointed guardian, the court may waive any court costs or filing fees.

History.
S. 1, ch. 86-120; s. 100, ch. 89-96.

744.706. Preparation of budget.

Each public guardian, whether funded in whole or in part by money raised through local efforts, grants, or any other source or whether funded in whole or in part by the state, shall prepare a budget for the operation of the office of public guardian to be submitted to the Statewide Public Guardianship Office. As appropriate, the Statewide Public Guardianship Office will include such budgetary information in the Department of Elderly Affairs' legislative budget request. The office of public guardian shall be operated within the limitations of the General Appropriations Act and any other funds appropriated by the Legislature to that particular judicial circuit, subject to the provisions of chapter 216. The Department of Elderly Affairs shall make a separate and distinct request for an appropriation for the Statewide Public Guardianship Office. However, this section shall not be construed to preclude the financing of any operations of the office of the public guardian by moneys raised through local effort or through the efforts of the Statewide Public Guardianship Office.

History.
S. 1, ch. 86-120; s. 101, ch. 89-96; s. 6, ch. 99-277.

744.707. Procedures and rules.

The public guardian, subject to the oversight of the Statewide Public Guardianship Office, is authorized to:

(1) Formulate and adopt necessary procedures to assure the efficient conduct of the affairs of the ward and general administration of the office and staff.

(2) Contract for services necessary to discharge the duties of the office.

(3) Accept the services of volunteer persons or organizations and provide reimbursement for proper and necessary expenses.

History.
S. 1, ch. 86-120; s. 102, ch. 89-96; s. 7, ch. 99-277.

744.708. Reports and standards.

(1) The public guardian shall keep and maintain proper financial, case control, and statistical records on all matters in which the public guardian serves as guardian.

(2) No report or disclosure of the ward's personal and medical records shall be made, except as authorized by law.

(3) A public guardian shall file an annual report on the operations of the office of public guardian, in writing, by September 1 for the preceding fiscal year with the Statewide Public Guardianship Office which shall have responsibility for supervision of the operations of the office of public guardian.

(4) Within 6 months of his or her appointment as guardian of a ward, the public guardian shall submit to the clerk of the court for placement in the ward's guardianship file and to the executive director of the Statewide Public Guardianship Office a report on his or her efforts to locate a family member or friend, other person, bank, or corporation to act as guardian of the ward and a report on the ward's potential to be restored to capacity.

(5)(a) Each office of public guardian shall undergo an independent audit by a qualified certified public accountant at least once every 2 years. A copy of the audit report shall be submitted to the Statewide Public Guardianship Office.

(b) In addition to regular monitoring activities, the Statewide Public Guardianship Office shall conduct an investigation into the practices of each office of public guardian related to the managing of each ward's personal affairs and property. If feasible, the investigation shall be conducted in conjunction with the financial audit of each office of public guardian under paragraph (a).

(6) A public guardian shall ensure that each of the guardian's wards is personally visited by the public guardian or by one of the guardian's professional staff at least once each calendar quarter. During this personal visit, the public guardian or the professional staff person shall assess:

(a) The ward's physical appearance and condition.

(b) The appropriateness of the ward's current living situation.

(c) The need for any additional services and the necessity for continuation of existing services, taking into consideration all aspects of social, psychological, educational, direct service, health, and personal care needs.

(7) The ratio for professional staff to wards shall be 1 professional to 40 wards. The Statewide Public Guardianship Office may increase or decrease the ratio after consultation with the local public guardian and the chief judge of the circuit court. The basis for the decision to increase or decrease the prescribed ratio must be included in the annual report to the secretary.

History.
S. 1, ch. 86-120; s. 103, ch. 89-96; s. 17, ch. 96-354; s. 1791, ch. 97-102; s. 8, ch. 99-277; s. 127, ch. 2001-266; s. 27, ch. 2006-178, eff. July 1, 2006; s. 159, ch. 2010-102, eff. May 26, 2010.

744.7081. Access to records by Statewide Public Guardianship Office; confidentiality.

Notwithstanding any other provision of law to the contrary, any medical, financial, or mental health records held by an agency, or the court and its agencies, which are necessary to evaluate the public guardianship system, to assess the need for additional public guardianship, or to develop required reports, shall be provided to the Statewide Public Guardianship Office upon that office's request. Any confidential or exempt information provided to the Statewide Public Guardianship Office shall continue to be held confidential or exempt as otherwise provided by law. All records held by the Statewide Public Guardianship Office relating to the medical, financial, or mental health of vulnerable adults as defined in chapter 415, persons with a developmental disability as defined in chapter 393, or persons with a mental illness as defined in chapter 394, shall be confidential and exempt from s. 119.07(1) and s. 24(a), Art. I of the State Constitution.

History.
S. 1, ch. 99-278; s. 112, ch. 2000-349; s. 1, ch. 2004-361.

744.7082. Direct-support organization; definition; use of property; board of directors; audit; dissolution.

(1) Definition. — As used in this section, the term "direct-support organization" means an organization whose sole purpose is to support the Statewide Public Guardianship Office and is:

(a) A not-for-profit corporation incorporated under chapter 617 and approved by the Department of State;

(b) Organized and operated to conduct programs and activities; to raise funds; to request and receive grants, gifts, and bequests of moneys; to acquire, receive, hold, invest, and administer, in its own name, securities, funds, objects of value, or other property, real or personal; and to make expenditures to or for the direct or indirect benefit of the Statewide Public Guardianship Office; and

(c) Determined by the Statewide Public Guardianship Office to be consistent with the goals of the office, in the best interests of the state, and in accordance with the adopted goals and mission of the Department of Elderly Affairs and the Statewide Public Guardianship Office.

(2) Contract. — The direct-support organization shall operate under a written contract with the Statewide Public Guardianship Office. The written contract must provide for:

(a) Certification by the Statewide Public Guardianship Office that the direct-support organization is complying with the terms of the contract and is doing so consistent with the goals and purposes of the office and in the best interests of the state. This certification must be made annually and reported in the official minutes of a meeting of the direct-support organization.

(b) The reversion of moneys and property held in trust by the direct-support organization:

1. To the Statewide Public Guardianship Office if the direct-support organization is no longer approved to operate for the office;

2. To the Statewide Public Guardianship Office if the direct-support organization ceases to exist;

3. To the Department of Elderly Affairs if the Statewide Public Guardianship Office ceases to exist; or

4. To the state if the Department of Elderly Affairs ceases to exist.

The fiscal year of the direct-support organization shall begin on July 1 of each year and end on June 30 of the following year.

(c) The disclosure of the material provisions of the contract, and the distinction between the Statewide Public Guardianship Office and the direct-support organization, to donors of gifts, contributions, or bequests, including such disclosure on all promotional and fundraising publications.

(3) Board of directors. — The Secretary of Elderly Affairs shall appoint a board of directors for the direct-support organization from a list of nominees submitted by the executive director of the Statewide Public Guardianship Office.

(4) Use of property. — The Department of Elderly Affairs may permit, without charge, appropriate use of fixed property and facilities of the department or the Statewide Public Guardianship Office by the direct-support organization. The department may prescribe any condition with which the direct-support organization must comply in order to use fixed property or facilities of the department or the Statewide Public Guardianship Office.

(5) Moneys. — Any moneys may be held in a separate depository account in the name of the direct-support organization and subject to the provisions of the written contract with the Statewide Public Guardianship Office. Expenditures of the direct-support organization shall be expressly used to support the Statewide Public Guardianship Office. The expenditures of the direct-support organization may not be used for the purpose of lobbying as defined in s. 11.045.

(6) Public records. — Personal identifying information of a donor or prospective donor to the direct-

support organization who desires to remain anonymous is confidential and exempt from s. 119.07(1) and s. 24(a), Art. I of the State Constitution.

(7) Audit. — The direct-support organization shall provide for an annual financial audit in accordance with s. 215.981.

(8) Dissolution. — After July 1, 2004, any not-for-profit corporation incorporated under chapter 617 that is determined by a circuit court to be representing itself as a direct-support organization created under this section, but that does not have a written contract with the Statewide Public Guardianship Office in compliance with this section, is considered to meet the grounds for a judicial dissolution described in s. 617.1430(1)(a). The Statewide Public Guardianship Office shall be the recipient for all assets held by the dissolved corporation which accrued during the period that the dissolved corporation represented itself as a direct-support organization created under this section.

History.
S. 9, ch. 2002-195; s. 14, ch. 2004-260; ss. 1, 2, ch. 2006-179, eff. July 1, 2006; s. 1, ch. 2011-228, eff. Oct. 1, 2011.

744.709.   Surety bond.

Upon taking office, a public guardian shall file a bond with surety as prescribed in s. 45.011 to be approved by the clerk. The bond shall be payable to the Governor and the Governor's successors in office, in the penal sum of not less than $5,000 nor more than $25,000, conditioned on the faithful performance of all duties by the guardian. The amount of the bond shall be fixed by the majority of the judges within the judicial circuit. In form the bond shall be joint and several. The bond shall be purchased from the funds of the local office of public guardian.

History.
S. 1, ch. 86-120; s. 104, ch. 89-96; s. 1128, ch. 97-102; s. 11, ch. 99-277.

744.7101.   Short title.

Sections 744.7101-744.715 may be cited as the "Joining Forces for Public Guardianship Act."

History.
S. 1, ch. 2004-260.

744.711.   Legislative findings and intent.

The Legislature finds that public guardianship programs are necessary to ensure that the rights and best interests of Florida's vulnerable indigent and incapacitated residents are protected. In addition, the Legislature finds that the best solution to this problem is to encourage each county to establish, through the Statewide Public Guardianship Office, a local office of public guardian for the purpose of providing guardianship services to incapacitated persons when a private guardian is not available. Therefore, the Legislature intends to establish the Joining Forces for Public Guardianship matching grant program for the purpose

of assisting counties to establish and fund community-supported public guardianship programs.

History.
S. 2, ch. 2004-260.

744.712.   Joining Forces for Public Guardianship grant program; purpose.

The Joining Forces for Public Guardianship matching grant program shall be established and administered by the Statewide Public Guardianship Office within the Department of Elderly Affairs. The purpose of the program is to provide startup funding to encourage communities to develop and administer locally funded and supported public guardianship programs to address the needs of indigent and incapacitated residents.

(1) The Statewide Public Guardianship Office may distribute the grant funds as follows:

(a) As initial startup funding to encourage counties that have no office of public guardian to establish an office, or as initial startup funding to open an additional office of public guardian within a county whose public guardianship needs require more than one office of public guardian.

(b) As support funding to operational offices of public guardian that demonstrate a necessity for funds to meet the public guardianship needs of a particular geographic area in the state which the office serves.

(c) To assist counties that have an operating public guardianship program but that propose to expand the geographic area or population of persons they serve, or to develop and administer innovative programs to increase access to public guardianship in this state.

Notwithstanding this subsection, the executive director of the office may award emergency grants if he or she determines that the award is in the best interests of public guardianship in this state. Before making an emergency grant, the executive director must obtain the written approval of the Secretary of Elderly Affairs. Subsections (2), (3), and (4) do not apply to the distribution of emergency grant funds.

(2) One or more grants may be awarded within a county. However, a county may not receive an award that equals, or multiple awards that cumulatively equal, more than 20 percent of the total amount of grant funds appropriated during any fiscal year.

(3) If an applicant is eligible and meets the requirements to receive grant funds more than once, the Statewide Public Guardianship Office shall award funds to prior awardees in the following manner:

(a) In the second year that grant funds are awarded, the cumulative sum of the award provided to one or more applicants within the same county may not exceed 75 percent of the total amount of grant funds awarded within that county in year one.

744.713 GUARDIANSHIP 744.715

(b) In the third year that grant funds are awarded, the cumulative sum of the award provided to one or more applicants within the same county may not exceed 60 percent of the total amount of grant funds awarded within that county in year one.

(c) In the fourth year that grant funds are awarded, the cumulative sum of the award provided to one or more applicants within the same county may not exceed 45 percent of the total amount of grant funds awarded within that county in year one.

(d) In the fifth year that grant funds are awarded, the cumulative sum of the award provided to one or more applicants within the same county may not exceed 30 percent of the total amount of grant funds awarded within that county in year one.

(e) In the sixth year that grant funds are awarded, the cumulative sum of the award provided to one or more applicants within the same county may not exceed 15 percent of the total amount of grant funds awarded within that county in year one.

The Statewide Public Guardianship Office may not award grant funds to any applicant within a county that has received grant funds for more than 6 years.

(4) Grant funds shall be used only to provide direct services to indigent wards, except that up to 10 percent of the grant funds may be retained by the awardee for administrative expenses.

(5) Implementation of the program is subject to a specific appropriation by the Legislature in the General Appropriations Act.

History.
S. 3, ch. 2004-260.

744.713. Program administration; duties of the Statewide Public Guardianship Office.

The Statewide Public Guardianship Office shall administer the grant program. The office shall:

(1) Publicize the availability of grant funds to entities that may be eligible for the funds.

(2) Establish an application process for submitting a grant proposal.

(3) Request, receive, and review proposals from applicants seeking grant funds.

(4) Determine the amount of grant funds each awardee may receive and award grant funds to applicants.

(5) Develop a monitoring process to evaluate grant awardees, which may include an annual monitoring visit to each awardee's local office.

(6) Ensure that persons or organizations awarded grant funds meet and adhere to the requirements of this act.

(7) Adopt rules as necessary to administer the grant program and this act.

History.
S. 4, ch. 2004-260.

744.714. Eligibility.

(1) Any person or organization that has not been awarded a grant must meet all of the following conditions to be eligible to receive a grant:

(a) The applicant must meet or directly employ staff that meet the minimum qualifications for a public guardian under this chapter.

(b) The applicant must have already been appointed by, or is pending appointment by, the Statewide Public Guardianship Office to become an office of public guardian in this state.

(2) Any person or organization that has been awarded a grant must meet all of the following conditions to be eligible to receive another grant:

(a) The applicant must meet or directly employ staff that meet the minimum qualifications for a public guardian under this chapter.

(b) The applicant must have been appointed by, or is pending reappointment by, the Statewide Public Guardianship Office to be an office of public guardian in this state.

(c) The applicant must have achieved a satisfactory monitoring score during the applicant's most recent evaluation.

History.
S. 5, ch. 2004-260.

744.715. Grant application requirements; review criteria; awards process.

Grant applications must be submitted to the Statewide Public Guardianship Office for review and approval.

(1) A grant application must contain:

(a) The specific amount of funds being requested.

(b) The proposed annual budget for the office of public guardian for which the applicant is applying on behalf of, including all sources of funding, and a detailed report of proposed expenditures, including administrative costs.

(c) The total number of wards the applicant intends to serve during the grant period.

(d) Evidence that the applicant has:

1. Attempted to procure funds and has exhausted all possible other sources of funding; or

2. Procured funds from local sources, but the total amount of the funds collected or pledged is not sufficient to meet the need for public guardianship in the geographic area that the applicant intends to serve.

(e) An agreement or confirmation from a local funding source, such as a county, municipality, or any other public or private organization, that the local funding source will contribute matching funds to the public guardianship program totaling not less than $1 for every $1 of grant funds awarded.

PROB-479

For purposes of this section, an applicant may provide evidence of agreements or confirmations from multiple local funding sources showing that the local funding sources will pool their contributed matching funds to the public guardianship program for a combined total of not less than $1 for every $1 of grant funds awarded. In-kind contributions, such as materials, commodities, office space, or other types of facilities, personnel services, or other items as determined by rule shall be considered by the office and may be counted as part or all of the local matching funds.

(f) A detailed plan describing how the office of public guardian for which the applicant is applying on behalf of will be funded in future years.

(g) Any other information determined by rule as necessary to assist in evaluating grant applicants.

(2) If the Statewide Public Guardianship Office determines that an applicant meets the requirements for an award of grant funds, the office may award the applicant any amount of grant funds the executive director deems appropriate, if the amount awarded meets the requirements of this act. The office may adopt a rule allocating the maximum allowable amount of grant funds which may be expended on any ward.

(3) A grant awardee must submit a new grant application for each year of additional funding.

(4)(a) In the first year of the Joining Forces for Public Guardianship program's existence, the Statewide Public Guardianship Office shall give priority in awarding grant funds to those entities that:

1. Are operating as appointed offices of public guardians in this state;

2. Meet all of the requirements for being awarded a grant under this act; and

3. Demonstrate a need for grant funds during the current fiscal year due to a loss of local funding formerly raised through court filing fees.

(b) In each fiscal year after the first year that grant funds are distributed, the Statewide Public Guardianship Office may give priority to awarding grant funds to those entities that:

1. Meet all of the requirements of this act for being awarded grant funds; and

2. Submit with their application an agreement or confirmation from a local funding source, such as a county, municipality, or any other public or private organization, that the local funding source will contribute matching funds totaling an amount equal to or exceeding $2 for every $1 of grant funds awarded by the office. An entity may submit with its application agreements or confirmations from multiple local funding sources showing that the local funding sources will pool their contributed matching funds to the public guardianship program for a combined total of not less than $2 for every $1 of grant funds awarded. In-kind contributions allowable under this section shall be evaluated by the Statewide Public Guardianship Office and may be counted as part or all of the local matching funds.

History.
S. 6, ch. 2004-260.

CHAPTER 747.
CONSERVATORSHIP

747.01. Who are absentees under this law.

(1) Any person serving in or with the Armed Forces of the United States, in or with the Red Cross, in or with the Merchant Marine or otherwise, during any period of time when a state of hostilities exists between the United States and any other power and for 1 year thereafter, who has been reported or listed as missing in action, interned in a neutral country, beleaguered, besieged or captured by the enemy, shall be an "absentee" within the meaning of this law; and,

(2) Any resident of this state, or any person owning property herein, who disappears under circumstances indicating that he or she may have died, either naturally, accidentally or at the hand of another, or may have disappeared as the result of mental derangement, amnesia or other mental cause, shall also be an "absentee" within the meaning of this law.

History.
S. 1, ch. 22888, 1945; s. 1, ch. 67-458; s. 1129, ch. 97-102.

747.011. Absentee incompetent for certain purposes.

An "absentee" as defined in s. 747.01 is considered incompetent for the purposes of s. 4, Art. X of the State Constitution.

History.
S. 1, ch. 71-103.

747.02. Jurisdiction.

The circuit court has jurisdiction to appoint a conservator of the estate of an absentee as defined in s. 747.01 upon a showing that:

(1)(a)1. The absentee has an interest in any form of property in this state; or

2. The absentee is a legal resident of this state; or

3. The spouse or next of kin of the absentee is a legal resident of this state; and

(b) The absentee has not provided an adequate power of attorney authorizing another to act in his or her behalf with regard to such property or interest or the term of any such power of attorney has expired; and

(2) A necessity exists for providing care for the property or estate of the absentee or care for or judgments concerning the absentee's spouse and children or, if he or she has no spouse and children, the absentee's mother or father.

History.
S. 2, ch. 22888, 1945; s. 2, ch. 71-103; s. 1130, ch. 97-102.

747.03. Petition.

(1) The jurisdiction of the court shall be invoked by the filing of a petition by any person who would have an interest in the property or estate of the absentee were such absentee deceased or any person who is dependent on said absentee for his or her maintenance or support.

(2) The petition shall be sworn to by the petitioner and shall state:

(a) The names, addresses, and ages of the spouse, children, mother, father, brothers, and sisters, or, if none of these is living, the next of kin, of the absentee;

(b) The name, address, and age of any other person who would have an interest in the property or the estate of the absentee if he or she were deceased;

(c) The exact circumstances which cause the person missing to be an absentee under s. 747.01 including the date he or she was first known to be missing, interned, beleaguered, etc.;

(d) The necessity for establishing a conservatorship;

(e) Whether or not the person alleged to be an absentee has a will and the whereabouts of said will; and

(f) A statement of all property constituting an asset of the alleged absentee's estate or in which he or she has any interest and the approximate value of same.

History.
S. 3, ch. 22888, 1945; s. 5, ch. 71-103; s. 1131, ch. 97-102.

747.031. Notice; hearing.

(1) Notice of the hearing on the petition to appoint a conservator shall be given to all persons named in the petition by registered mail or certified mail with return receipt requested.

(2) The judge shall hear evidence on the question of whether the person alleged to be missing, interned, beleaguered, etc., is an absentee as defined by s. 747.01 and on the question of who is entitled to appointment as conservator. Any person interested in such proceedings may intervene with leave of the court.

(3) The court may in its discretion appoint a guardian ad litem to represent the alleged absentee at the hearing.

History.
S. 6, ch. 71-103.

747.032. Order of appointment.

(1) If, after hearing, the court is satisfied that the person alleged to be an absentee is an absentee as defined in s. 747.01 and that it is necessary that a conservatorship be established, she or he shall appoint a conservator of the estate and property of said absentee to take charge of the absentee's estate and property under the supervision, and subject to the further orders, of the court.

(2) In the appointment of a conservator, the court shall give due consideration to the appointment of one

of the next of kin of the absentee if such next of kin is a fit and proper person and is qualified to act.

History.
S. 7, ch. 71-103; s. 1132, ch. 97-102.

747.033. Oath.

Every conservator, before exercising his or her authority as conservator, shall take oath that he or she will faithfully perform his or her duties as conservator and will render true accounts whenever required according to law, which oath may be administered by any officer authorized to administer oaths under the laws of this state. Such oath shall be filed with the court.

History.
S. 8, ch. 71-103; s. 1133, ch. 97-102.

747.034. Bond.

The court may require the conservator to post a bond as required for a guardian under ss. 744.38 and 744.39. All provisions of chapter 744 which are applicable to bonds are applicable to the bond of the conservator required under this chapter.

History.
S. 9, ch. 71-103.
Editor's Notes.
Sections 744.38 and 744.39, referred to in the first sentence, were repealed by s. 3, ch. 74-106.

747.035. Rights, powers, and duties of conservator.

(1) The conservator shall have all the rights, powers, and duties of a guardian of the property as established in chapter 744 and an absentee and an absentee's dependents shall be entitled to all benefits accruing to a ward or a ward's dependents under said chapter.

(2) The circuit court shall have the same responsibility as to a conservatorship as it has with respect to the guardianship of the property under said chapter.

History.
S. 10, ch. 71-103; s. 32, ch. 73-334; s. 70, ch. 95-211.

747.036. Resignation or removal of conservator.

The provision for resignation and removal of a guardian of the property in chapter 746 shall apply in the circuit court to resignation and removal of a conservator.

History.
S. 11, ch. 71-103.
Editor's Notes.
All sections in chapter 746, referred to in this section, were repealed by s. 3, ch. 74-106.

747.04. Termination of conservatorship.

(1) At any time upon petition signed by the absentee, or on petition of an attorney in fact acting under an adequate power of attorney granted by the absentee, the court shall direct the termination of the conservatorship and the transfer of all property held thereunder to the absentee or to the designated attorney in fact.

(2) Likewise, if at any time subsequent to the appointment of a conservator it shall appear that the absentee has died and an executor or administrator has been appointed for her or his estate, the court shall direct the termination of the conservatorship and the transfer of all property of the deceased absentee held thereunder to such executor or administrator.

(3) When the need for a conservatorship terminates, the conservator shall promptly file her or his final returns and application for discharge with the court. If it appears to the court that the returns are correct and that the conservator has made full and complete transfer of the absentee's assets as directed, the court may approve the returns and discharge the conservator. If objections to the returns are filed, the circuit judge shall conduct a hearing under the same conditions for a hearing on objections to annual returns.

(4) Such discharge shall operate as a release from the duties of the conservatorship and as a bar to any suit against said conservator or her or his surety, unless such suit is commenced within 1 year from the date of discharge.

History.
S. 4, ch. 22888, 1945; s. 12, ch. 71-103; s. 1134, ch. 97-102.

747.051. Summary procedure.

(1) If the wife of any person defined as an absentee in s. 747.01(1), or his next of kin if said absentee has no wife, shall wish to sell or transfer any property of the absentee which has a gross value of less than $5,000, or shall require the consent of the absentee in any matter regarding the absentee's children or in any other matter in which the gross value of the subject matter is less than $5,000, she may apply to the circuit court for an order authorizing said sale, transfer, or consent without opening a full conservatorship proceeding as provided by this chapter. She may make the application without the assistance of an attorney. Said application shall be made by petition on the following form, which form shall be made readily available to the applicant by the clerk of the circuit court:

In the Circuit Court

In re: (Absentee), case number _____.

PETITION FOR SUMMARY RELIEF

Petitioner, (Name), whose residence is (Street & number), (City or town), and (County), Florida, and who is the (Describe relationship to absentee) of the absentee, (Name), states that the absentee has been (Imprisoned or missing in action) since (Date) when (Describe details). Petitioner desires to sell/transfer (Describe property) of the value of (Value) because (Give reasons). The terms of sale/transfer are (Give reasons). Petitioner requires the consent of the absentee for the purpose of _____.

(Petitioner)

State of Florida

County of ⸺

Sworn to (or affirmed) and subscribed before me this ⸺ day of ⸺, (year), by (name of person making statement).

(Signature of Notary Public - State of Florida)

(Print, Type, or Stamp Commissioned Name of Notary Public)

Personally Known ⸺ OR Produced Identification

Type of Identification Produced ⸺

(2) The court shall, without hearing or notice, enter an order on said petition if it deems the relief requested in said petition necessary to protect the best interests of the absentee or her or his dependents.

(3) Such order shall be prima facie evidence of the validity of the proceedings and the authority of the petitioner to make a conveyance or transfer of the property or to give the absentee's consent in any matter prescribed by subsection (1).

History.

S. 3, ch. 71-103; s. 32, ch. 73-334; s. 1135, ch. 97-102; s. 19, ch. 98-246.

747.052. Procedure for order authorizing action by spouse or next of kin.

(1) If the spouse, or the next of kin if there is no spouse, of any person defined as an absentee under s. 747.01(1), shall wish to sell, lease, or mortgage specific property having a gross value of $5,000 or more owned by the absentee or in which the absentee had an interest, or take specific action with respect to the absentee's interest having a gross value of $5,000 or more, he or she may petition the circuit court for an order authorizing the action with respect to such property or interest.

(2) The petition shall be sworn to by the petitioner and shall state:

(a) The names, addresses, and ages of the spouse, children, mother, father, brothers, and sisters, or, if none of these is living, the next of kin, of the absentee;

(b) The name, address, and age of any other person who would have an interest in the property or the estate of the absentee if she or he were deceased;

(c) The exact circumstances which cause the person missing to be an absentee under s. 747.01, including the date she or he was first known to be missing, interned, beleaguered, etc.;

(d) The reasons for the action for which the petition seeks authorization;

(e) Whether or not the person alleged to be an absentee has a will and the whereabouts of said will and contents if known; and

(f) A statement of all property constituting an asset of the alleged absentee's estate or in which she or he has any interest and the approximate value of same.

(3) Notice of the hearing on the petition shall be given to all persons named in the petition by registered mail or certified mail with return receipt requested.

(4) The judge shall hear evidence on the question of whether the person alleged to be missing, interned, beleaguered, etc., is an absentee as defined by s. 747.01 and on the question of whether the action in question should be authorized. Any person interested in such proceedings may intervene with leave of the court.

(5) The court may in its discretion appoint a guardian ad litem to represent the alleged absentee at the hearing.

(6) If, after hearing, the court is satisfied that the person alleged to be an absentee is an absentee as defined in s. 747.01, that the action in question should be authorized, and that there is no necessity for a full conservatorship as provided by s. 747.03, the court shall enter an order appointing the petitioner as conservator for the purposes of the action which is the subject of the petition and authorizing the conservator to take the action requested in the petition. The court shall require the conservator to account for the proceeds of the sale, lease, or other action, but the conservator shall not be required to subject the other property of the absentee to a conservatorship proceeding. The court may retain jurisdiction of the proceeding to make such further orders as it deems proper.

History.

S. 4, ch. 71-103; s. 1136, ch. 97-102.

TITLE XLIV.
CIVIL RIGHTS

CHAPTER 765.
HEALTH CARE ADVANCE DIRECTIVES

PART I.
GENERAL PROVISIONS.

765.101. Definitions.

As used in this chapter:

(1) "Advance directive" means a witnessed written document or oral statement in which instructions are given by a principal or in which the principal's desires are expressed concerning any aspect of the principal's health care, and includes, but is not limited to, the designation of a health care surrogate, a living will, or an anatomical gift made pursuant to part V of this chapter.

(2) "Attending physician" means the primary physician who has responsibility for the treatment and care of the patient.

(3) "Close personal friend" means any person 18 years of age or older who has exhibited special care and concern for the patient, and who presents an affidavit to the health care facility or to the attending or treating physician stating that he or she is a friend of the patient; is willing and able to become involved in the patient's health care; and has maintained such regular contact with the patient so as to be familiar with the patient's activities, health, and religious or moral beliefs.

(4) "End-stage condition" means an irreversible condition that is caused by injury, disease, or illness which has resulted in progressively severe and permanent deterioration, and which, to a reasonable degree of medical probability, treatment of the condition would be ineffective.

(5) "Health care decision" means:

(a) Informed consent, refusal of consent, or withdrawal of consent to any and all health care, including life-prolonging procedures and mental health treatment, unless otherwise stated in the advance directives.

(b) The decision to apply for private, public, government, or veterans' benefits to defray the cost of health care.

(c) The right of access to all records of the principal reasonably necessary for a health care surrogate to make decisions involving health care and to apply for benefits.

(d) The decision to make an anatomical gift pursuant to part V of this chapter.

(6) "Health care facility" means a hospital, nursing home, hospice, home health agency, or health maintenance organization licensed in this state, or any facility subject to part I of chapter 394.

(7) "Health care provider" or "provider" means any person licensed, certified, or otherwise authorized by law to administer health care in the ordinary course of business or practice of a profession.

(8) "Incapacity" or "incompetent" means the patient is physically or mentally unable to communicate a willful and knowing health care decision. For the purposes of making an anatomical gift, the term also includes a patient who is deceased.

(9) "Informed consent" means consent voluntarily given by a person after a sufficient explanation and disclosure of the subject matter involved to enable that person to have a general understanding of the treatment or procedure and the medically acceptable alternatives, including the substantial risks and hazards inherent in the proposed treatment or procedures, and to make a knowing health care decision without coercion or undue influence.

(10) "Life-prolonging procedure" means any medical procedure, treatment, or intervention, including artificially provided sustenance and hydration, which sustains, restores, or supplants a spontaneous vital function. The term does not include the administration of medication or performance of medical procedure, when such medication or procedure is deemed necessary to provide comfort care or to alleviate pain.

(11) "Living will" or "declaration" means:

(a) A witnessed document in writing, voluntarily executed by the principal in accordance with s. 765.302; or

(b) A witnessed oral statement made by the principal expressing the principal's instructions concerning life-prolonging procedures.

(12) "Persistent vegetative state" means a permanent and irreversible condition of unconsciousness in which there is:

(a) The absence of voluntary action or cognitive behavior of any kind.

(b) An inability to communicate or interact purposefully with the environment.

(13) "Physician" means a person licensed pursuant to chapter 458 or chapter 459.

(14) "Principal" means a competent adult executing an advance directive and on whose behalf health care decisions are to be made.

(15) "Proxy" means a competent adult who has not been expressly designated to make health care decisions for a particular incapacitated individual, but who, nevertheless, is authorized pursuant to s. 765.401 to make health care decisions for such individual.

(16) "Surrogate" means any competent adult expressly designated by a principal to make health care decisions on behalf of the principal upon the principal's incapacity.

(17) "Terminal condition" means a condition caused by injury, disease, or illness from which there is no reasonable medical probability of recovery and which, without treatment, can be expected to cause death.

History.
S. 2, ch. 92-199; s. 3, ch. 94-183; s. 46, ch. 96-169; s. 16, ch. 99-331; s. 3, ch. 2001-250; s. 131, ch. 2001-277; s. 104, ch. 2006-1, eff. July 4, 2006; s. 28, ch. 2006-178, eff. July 1, 2006.

Editor's Notes.
For chapter 2003-418, authorizing the Governor to issue a one-time stay to prevent the withholding of nutrition and hydration to a patient under certain circumstances, see the note at s. 765.404.

765.102. Legislative findings and intent.

(1) The Legislature finds that every competent adult has the fundamental right of self-determination regarding decisions pertaining to his or her own health, including the right to choose or refuse medical treatment. This right is subject to certain interests of society, such as the protection of human life and the preservation of ethical standards in the medical profession.

(2) To ensure that such right is not lost or diminished by virtue of later physical or mental incapacity, the Legislature intends that a procedure be established to allow a person to plan for incapacity by executing a document or orally designating another person to direct the course of his or her medical treatment upon his or her incapacity. Such procedure should be less expensive and less restrictive than guardianship and permit a previously incapacitated person to exercise his or her full right to make health care decisions as soon as the capacity to make such decisions has been regained.

(3) The Legislature recognizes that for some the administration of life-prolonging medical procedures may result in only a precarious and burdensome existence. In order to ensure that the rights and intentions of a person may be respected even after he or she is no longer able to participate actively in decisions concerning himself or herself, and to encourage communication among such patient, his or her family, and his or her physician, the Legislature declares that the laws of this state recognize the right of a competent adult to make an advance directive instructing his or her physician to provide, withhold, or withdraw life-prolonging procedures, or to designate another to make the treatment decision for him or her in the event that such person should become incapacitated and unable to personally direct his or her medical care.

(4) The Legislature recognizes the need for all health care professionals to rapidly increase their understanding of end-of-life and palliative care. Therefore, the Legislature encourages the professional regulatory boards to adopt appropriate standards and guidelines regarding end-of-life care and pain management and encourages educational institutions established to train health care professionals and allied health professionals to implement curricula to train such professionals to provide end-of-life care, including pain management and palliative care.

(5) For purposes of this chapter:

(a) Palliative care is the comprehensive management of the physical, psychological, social, spiritual, and existential needs of patients. Palliative care is especially suited to the care of persons who have incurable, progressive illnesses.

(b) Palliative care must include:

1. An opportunity to discuss and plan for end-of-life care.

2. Assurance that physical and mental suffering will be carefully attended to.

3. Assurance that preferences for withholding and withdrawing life-sustaining interventions will be honored.

4. Assurance that the personal goals of the dying person will be addressed.

5. Assurance that the dignity of the dying person will be a priority.

6. Assurance that health care providers will not abandon the dying person.

7. Assurance that the burden to family and others will be addressed.

8. Assurance that advance directives for care will be respected regardless of the location of care.

9. Assurance that organizational mechanisms are in place to evaluate the availability and quality of end-of-life, palliative, and hospice care services, including the evaluation of administrative and regulatory barriers.

10. Assurance that necessary health care services will be provided and that relevant reimbursement policies are available.

11. Assurance that the goals expressed in subparagraphs 1.-10. will be accomplished in a culturally appropriate manner.

(6) The Department of Elderly Affairs, the Agency for Health Care Administration, and the Department of Health shall jointly create a campaign on end-of-life care for purposes of educating the public. This campaign should include culturally sensitive programs to

improve understanding of end-of-life care issues in minority communities.

History.
S. 2, ch. 92-199; s. 1144, ch. 97-102; s. 17, ch. 99-331; s. 7, ch. 2000-295; s. 4, ch. 2001-250; ss. 132, 133, ch. 2001-277.

765.103. Existing advance directives.

Any advance directive made prior to October 1, 1999, shall be given effect as executed, provided such directive was legally effective when written.

History.
S. 2, ch. 92-199; s. 18, ch. 99-331.

765.104. Amendment or revocation.

(1) An advance directive or designation of a surrogate may be amended or revoked at any time by a competent principal:

(a) By means of a signed, dated writing;

(b) By means of the physical cancellation or destruction of the advance directive by the principal or by another in the principal's presence and at the principal's direction;

(c) By means of an oral expression of intent to amend or revoke; or

(d) By means of a subsequently executed advance directive that is materially different from a previously executed advance directive.

(2) Unless otherwise provided in the advance directive or in an order of dissolution or annulment of marriage, the dissolution or annulment of marriage of the principal revokes the designation of the principal's former spouse as a surrogate.

(3) Any such amendment or revocation will be effective when it is communicated to the surrogate, health care provider, or health care facility. No civil or criminal liability shall be imposed upon any person for a failure to act upon an amendment or revocation unless that person has actual knowledge of such amendment or revocation.

(4) Any patient for whom a medical proxy has been recognized under s. 765.401 and for whom any previous legal disability that precluded the patient's ability to consent is removed may amend or revoke the recognition of the medical proxy and any uncompleted decision made by that proxy. The amendment or revocation takes effect when it is communicated to the proxy, the health care provider, or the health care facility in writing or, if communicated orally, in the presence of a third person.

History.
S. 2, ch. 92-199; s. 47, ch. 96-169; s. 19, ch. 99-331; s. 12, ch. 2002-195.

765.105. Review of surrogate or proxy's decision.

The patient's family, the health care facility, or the attending physician, or any other interested person who may reasonably be expected to be directly affected by the surrogate or proxy's decision concerning any health care decision may seek expedited judicial intervention pursuant to rule 5.900 of the Florida Probate Rules, if that person believes:

(1) The surrogate or proxy's decision is not in accord with the patient's known desires or the provisions of this chapter;

(2) The advance directive is ambiguous, or the patient has changed his or her mind after execution of the advance directive;

(3) The surrogate or proxy was improperly designated or appointed, or the designation of the surrogate is no longer effective or has been revoked;

(4) The surrogate or proxy has failed to discharge duties, or incapacity or illness renders the surrogate or proxy incapable of discharging duties;

(5) The surrogate or proxy has abused powers; or

(6) The patient has sufficient capacity to make his or her own health care decisions.

History.
S. 2, ch. 92-199; s. 4, ch. 94-183.

765.106. Preservation of existing rights.

The provisions of this chapter are cumulative to the existing law regarding an individual's right to consent, or refuse to consent, to medical treatment and do not impair any existing rights or responsibilities which a health care provider, a patient, including a minor, competent or incompetent person, or a patient's family may have under the common law, Federal Constitution, State Constitution, or statutes of this state.

History.
S. 2, ch. 92-199; s. 5, ch. 94-183.

765.107. Construction.

(1) This chapter shall not be construed to repeal by implication any provision of s. 766.103, the Florida Medical Consent Law. For all purposes, the Florida Medical Consent Law shall be considered an alternative to provisions of this section.

(2) Procedures provided in this chapter permitting the withholding or withdrawal of life-prolonging procedures do not apply to a person who never had capacity to designate a health care surrogate or execute a living will.

History.
S. 2, ch. 92-199; s. 20, ch. 99-331.

765.108. Effect with respect to insurance.

The making of an advance directive pursuant to the provisions of this chapter shall not affect the sale, procurement, or issuance of any policy of life insurance, nor shall such making of an advance directive be deemed to modify the terms of an existing policy of life insurance. No policy of life insurance will be legally impaired or invalidated by the withholding or withdrawal of life-prolonging procedures from an insured patient in accordance with the provisions of this chapter, nor by any other treatment decision made according to this chapter, notwithstanding any term of the policy to the contrary. A person shall not be required to make an advance directive as a condition for being insured for, or receiving, health care services.

History.

S. 2, ch. 92-199.

765.109. Immunity from liability; weight of proof; presumption.

(1) A health care facility, provider, or other person who acts under the direction of a health care facility or provider is not subject to criminal prosecution or civil liability, and will not be deemed to have engaged in unprofessional conduct, as a result of carrying out a health care decision made in accordance with the provisions of this chapter. The surrogate or proxy who makes a health care decision on a patient's behalf, pursuant to this chapter, is not subject to criminal prosecution or civil liability for such action.

(2) The provisions of this section shall apply unless it is shown by a preponderance of the evidence that the person authorizing or effectuating a health care decision did not, in good faith, comply with the provisions of this chapter.

History.

S. 2, ch. 92-199.

765.110. Health care facilities and providers; discipline.

(1) A health care facility, pursuant to Pub. L. No. 101-508, ss. 4206 and 4751, shall provide to each patient written information concerning the individual's rights concerning advance directives and the health care facility's policies respecting the implementation of such rights, and shall document in the patient's medical records whether or not the individual has executed an advance directive.

(2) A health care provider or health care facility may not require a patient to execute an advance directive or to execute a new advance directive using the facility's or provider's forms. The patient's advance directives shall travel with the patient as part of the patient's medical record.

(3) A health care provider or health care facility shall be subject to professional discipline and revocation of license or certification, and a fine of not more than $1,000 per incident, or both, if the health care provider or health care facility, as a condition of treatment or admission, requires an individual to execute or waive an advance directive.

(4) The Department of Elderly Affairs for hospices and, in consultation with the Department of Elderly Affairs, the Department of Health for health care providers; the Agency for Health Care Administration for hospitals, nursing homes, home health agencies, and health maintenance organizations; and the Department of Children and Family Services for facilities subject to part I of chapter 394 shall adopt rules to implement the provisions of the section.

History.

S. 2, ch. 92-199; s. 6, ch. 94-183; s. 243, ch. 94-218; s. 48, ch. 96-169; s. 284, ch. 99-8; s. 21, ch. 99-331.

765.1103. Pain management and palliative care.

(1) A patient shall be given information concerning pain management and palliative care when he or she discusses with the attending or treating physician, or such physician's designee, the diagnosis, planned course of treatment, alternatives, risks, or prognosis for his or her illness. If the patient is incapacitated, the information shall be given to the patient's health care surrogate or proxy, court-appointed guardian as provided in chapter 744, or attorney in fact under a durable power of attorney as provided in chapter 709. The court-appointed guardian or attorney in fact must have been delegated authority to make health care decisions on behalf of the patient.

(2) Health care providers and practitioners regulated under chapter 458, chapter 459, or chapter 464 must, as appropriate, comply with a request for pain management or palliative care from a patient under their care or, for an incapacitated patient under their care, from a surrogate, proxy, guardian, or other representative permitted to make health care decisions for the incapacitated patient. Facilities regulated under chapter 395, chapter 400, or chapter 429 must comply with the pain management or palliative care measures ordered by the patient's physician.

History.

S. 8, ch. 2000-295; s. 5, ch. 2001-250; s. 134, ch. 2001-277; s. 105, ch. 2006-197, eff. July 1, 2006.

765.1105. Transfer of a patient.

(1) A health care provider or facility that refuses to comply with a patient's advance directive, or the treatment decision of his or her surrogate, shall make reasonable efforts to transfer the patient to another health care provider or facility that will comply with the directive or treatment decision. This chapter does not require a health care provider or facility to commit any act which is contrary to the provider's or facility's moral or ethical beliefs, if the patient:

(a) Is not in an emergency condition; and

(b) Has received written information upon admission informing the patient of the policies of the health care provider or facility regarding such moral or ethical beliefs.

(2) A health care provider or facility that is unwilling to carry out the wishes of the patient or the treatment decision of his or her surrogate because of moral or ethical beliefs must within 7 days either:

(a) Transfer the patient to another health care provider or facility. The health care provider or facility shall pay the costs for transporting the patient to another health care provider or facility; or

(b) If the patient has not been transferred, carry out the wishes of the patient or the patient's surrogate, unless the provisions of s. 765.105 apply.

History.
S. 4, ch. 92-199; s. 11, ch. 94-183; s. 1148, ch. 97-102; s. 30, ch. 99-331.
Editor's Notes.
Former s. 765.308.

765.1115. Falsification, forgery, or willful concealment, cancellation, or destruction of directive or revocation or amendment; penalties.

(1) Any person who willfully conceals, cancels, defaces, obliterates, or damages an advance directive without the principal's consent or who falsifies or forges the revocation or amendment of an advance directive of another, and who thereby causes life-prolonging procedures to be utilized in contravention of the previously expressed intent of the principal, commits a felony of the third degree, punishable as provided in s. 775.082, s. 775.083, or s. 775.084.

(2) Any person who falsifies or forges the advance directive of another or who willfully conceals or withholds personal knowledge of the revocation of an advance directive, with the intent to cause a withholding or withdrawal of life-prolonging procedures contrary to the wishes of the principal, and who thereby because of such act directly causes life-prolonging procedures to be withheld or withdrawn and death to be hastened, commits a felony of the second degree, punishable as provided in s. 775.082, s. 775.083, or s. 775.084.

History.
S. 4, ch. 92-199; s. 31, ch. 99-331.
Editor's Notes.
Former s. 765.310.

765.112. Recognition of advance directive executed in another state.

An advance directive executed in another state in compliance with the law of that state or of this state is validly executed for the purposes of this chapter.

History.
S. 2, ch. 92-199.

765.113. Restrictions on providing consent.

Unless the principal expressly delegates such authority to the surrogate in writing, or a surrogate or proxy has sought and received court approval pursuant to rule 5.900 of the Florida Probate Rules, a surrogate or proxy may not provide consent for:

(1) Abortion, sterilization, electroshock therapy, psychosurgery, experimental treatments that have not been approved by a federally approved institutional review board in accordance with 45 C.F.R. part 46 or 21 C.F.R. part 56, or voluntary admission to a mental health facility.

(2) Withholding or withdrawing life-prolonging procedures from a pregnant patient prior to viability as defined in s. 390.0111(4).

History.
S. 2, ch. 92-199; s. 7, ch. 94-183; s. 87, ch. 99-3.

PART II.
HEALTH CARE SURROGATE.

765.201. Short title.

Sections 765.202-765.205 may be cited as the "Florida Health Care Surrogate Act."

History.
S. 3, ch. 92-199.

765.202. Designation of a health care surrogate.

(1) A written document designating a surrogate to make health care decisions for a principal shall be signed by the principal in the presence of two subscribing adult witnesses. A principal unable to sign the instrument may, in the presence of witnesses, direct that another person sign the principal's name as required herein. An exact copy of the instrument shall be provided to the surrogate.

(2) The person designated as surrogate shall not act as witness to the execution of the document designating the health care surrogate. At least one person who acts as a witness shall be neither the principal's spouse nor blood relative.

(3) A document designating a health care surrogate may also designate an alternate surrogate provided the designation is explicit. The alternate surrogate may assume his or her duties as surrogate for the principal if the original surrogate is unwilling or unable to perform his or her duties. The principal's failure to designate an alternate surrogate shall not invalidate the designation.

(4) If neither the designated surrogate nor the designated alternate surrogate is able or willing to make health care decisions on behalf of the principal and in accordance with the principal's instructions, the health care facility may seek the appointment of a proxy pursuant to part IV.

(5) A principal may designate a separate surrogate to consent to mental health treatment in the event that the principal is determined by a court to be incompetent to consent to mental health treatment and a guardian advocate is appointed as provided under s. 394.4598. However, unless the document designating the health care surrogate expressly states otherwise, the court shall assume that the health care surrogate authorized to make health care decisions under this chapter is also the principal's choice to make decisions regarding mental health treatment.

(6) Unless the document states a time of termination, the designation shall remain in effect until revoked by the principal.

(7) A written designation of a health care surrogate executed pursuant to this section establishes a rebuttable presumption of clear and convincing evidence of the principal's designation of the surrogate.

History.
S. 3, ch. 92-199; s. 8, ch. 94-183; s. 49, ch. 96-169; s. 1797, ch. 97-102.

765.203. Suggested form of designation.

A written designation of a health care surrogate executed pursuant to this chapter may, but need not be, in the following form:

DESIGNATION OF HEALTH CARE SURROGATE

Name: __ (Last) __ (First) __ (Middle Initial) __

In the event that I have been determined to be incapacitated to provide informed consent for medical treatment and surgical and diagnostic procedures, I wish to designate as my surrogate for health care decisions:

Name: _____
Address: _____
Zip Code: _____
Phone: _____

If my surrogate is unwilling or unable to perform his or her duties, I wish to designate as my alternate surrogate:

Name: _____
Address: _____
Zip Code: _____
Phone: _____

I fully understand that this designation will permit my designee to make health care decisions and to provide, withhold, or withdraw consent on my behalf; to apply for public benefits to defray the cost of health care; and to authorize my admission to or transfer from a health care facility.

Additional instructions (optional): _____

_____
_____
_____

I further affirm that this designation is not being made as a condition of treatment or admission to a health care facility. I will notify and send a copy of this document to the following persons other than my surrogate, so they may know who my surrogate is.

Name: _____
Name: _____
_____
_____

Signed: _____
Date: _____
Witnesses: 1. _____
             2. _____

History.
S. 3, ch. 92-199; s. 1145, ch. 97-102; s. 9, ch. 2000-295; s. 1, ch. 2008-223, eff. July 1, 2008.

765.204. Capacity of principal; procedure.

(1) A principal is presumed to be capable of making health care decisions for herself or himself unless she or he is determined to be incapacitated. Incapacity may not be inferred from the person's voluntary or involuntary hospitalization for mental illness or from her or his mental retardation.

(2) If a principal's capacity to make health care decisions for herself or himself or provide informed consent is in question, the attending physician shall evaluate the principal's capacity and, if the physician concludes that the principal lacks capacity, enter that evaluation in the principal's medical record. If the attending physician has a question as to whether the principal lacks capacity, another physician shall also evaluate the principal's capacity, and if the second physician agrees that the principal lacks the capacity to make health care decisions or provide informed consent, the health care facility shall enter both physician's evaluations in the principal's medical record. If the principal has designated a health care surrogate or has delegated authority to make health care decisions to an attorney in fact under a durable power of attorney, the facility shall notify such surrogate or attorney in fact in writing that her or his authority under the instrument has commenced, as provided in chapter 709 or s. 765.203.

(3) The surrogate's authority shall commence upon a determination under subsection (2) that the principal lacks capacity, and such authority shall remain in effect until a determination that the principal has regained such capacity. Upon commencement of the surrogate's authority, a surrogate who is not the principal's spouse shall notify the principal's spouse or adult children of the principal's designation of the surrogate. In the event the attending physician determines that the principal has regained capacity, the authority of the surrogate shall cease, but shall recommence if the principal subsequently loses capacity as determined pursuant to this section.

(4) A determination made pursuant to this section that a principal lacks capacity to make health care decisions shall not be construed as a finding that a principal lacks capacity for any other purpose.

(5) In the event the surrogate is required to consent to withholding or withdrawing life-prolonging procedures, the provisions of part III shall apply.

History.
S. 3, ch. 92-199; s. 1146, ch. 97-102; s. 22, ch. 99-331; s. 10, ch. 2000-295.

765.205. Responsibility of the surrogate.

(1) The surrogate, in accordance with the principal's instructions, unless such authority has been expressly limited by the principal, shall:

(a) Have authority to act for the principal and to make all health care decisions for the principal during the principal's incapacity.

(b) Consult expeditiously with appropriate health care providers to provide informed consent, and make only health care decisions for the principal which he or she believes the principal would have made under the circumstances if the principal were capable of making such decisions. If there is no indication of what the principal would have chosen, the surrogate may consider the patient's best interest in deciding that proposed treatments are to be withheld or that treatments currently in effect are to be withdrawn.

(c) Provide written consent using an appropriate form whenever consent is required, including a physician's order not to resuscitate.

(d) Be provided access to the appropriate medical records of the principal.

(e) Apply for public benefits, such as Medicare and Medicaid, for the principal and have access to information regarding the principal's income and assets and banking and financial records to the extent required to make application. A health care provider or facility may not, however, make such application a condition of continued care if the principal, if capable, would have refused to apply.

(2) The surrogate may authorize the release of information and medical records to appropriate persons to ensure the continuity of the principal's health care and may authorize the admission, discharge, or transfer of the principal to or from a health care facility or other facility or program licensed under chapter 400 or chapter 429.

(3) If, after the appointment of a surrogate, a court appoints a guardian, the surrogate shall continue to make health care decisions for the principal, unless the court has modified or revoked the authority of the surrogate pursuant to s. 744.3115. The surrogate may be directed by the court to report the principal's health care status to the guardian.

History.
S. 3, ch. 92-199; s. 9, ch. 94-183; s. 50, ch. 96-169; s. 23, ch. 99-331; s. 11, ch. 2000-295; s. 6, ch. 2001-250; s. 135, ch. 2001-277; s. 106, ch. 2006-197, eff. July 1, 2006.

PART III.
LIFE-PROLONGING PROCEDURES.

765.301. Short title.

Sections 765.302-765.309 may be cited as the "Life-Prolonging Procedure Act of Florida."

History.
S. 4, ch. 92-199; s. 24, ch. 99-331.

765.302. Procedure for making a living will; notice to physician.

(1) Any competent adult may, at any time, make a living will or written declaration and direct the providing, withholding, or withdrawal of life-prolonging procedures in the event that such person has a terminal condition, has an end-stage condition, or is in a persistent vegetative state. A living will must be signed by the principal in the presence of two subscribing witnesses, one of whom is neither a spouse nor a blood relative of the principal. If the principal is physically unable to sign the living will, one of the witnesses must subscribe the principal's signature in the principal's presence and at the principal's direction.

(2) It is the responsibility of the principal to provide for notification to her or his attending or treating physician that the living will has been made. In the event the principal is physically or mentally incapacitated at the time the principal is admitted to a health care facility, any other person may notify the physician or health care facility of the existence of the living will. An attending or treating physician or health care facility which is so notified shall promptly make the living will or a copy thereof a part of the principal's medical records.

(3) A living will, executed pursuant to this section, establishes a rebuttable presumption of clear and convincing evidence of the principal's wishes.

History.
S. 4, ch. 92-199; s. 1147, ch. 97-102; s. 25, ch. 99-331.

765.303. Suggested form of a living will.

(1) A living will may, BUT NEED NOT, be in the following form:

Living Will

Declaration made this _____ day of _____, (year), I, _____, willfully and voluntarily make known my desire that my dying not be artificially prolonged under the circumstances set forth below, and I do hereby declare that, if at any time I am incapacitated and

(initial) I have a terminal condition

or (initial) I have an end-stage condition

or (initial) I am in a persistent vegetative state

and if my attending or treating physician and another consulting physician have determined that there is no reasonable medical probability of my recovery from such condition, I direct that life-prolonging procedures be withheld or withdrawn when the application of such procedures would serve only to prolong artificially the process of dying, and that I be permitted to die naturally with only the administration of medication or the performance of any medical procedure deemed necessary to provide me with comfort care or to alleviate pain.

It is my intention that this declaration be honored by my family and physician as the final expression of my legal right to refuse medical or surgical treatment and to accept the consequences for such refusal.

In the event that I have been determined to be unable to provide express and informed consent regarding the withholding, withdrawal, or continuation of life-prolonging procedures, I wish to designate, as my surrogate to carry out the provisions of this declaration:

Name: _____

Address: _____

Zip Code: _____
Phone: _____

I understand the full import of this declaration, and I am emotionally and mentally competent to make this declaration.

Additional Instructions (optional):

_____
_____
_____

(Signed)

Witness

Address

Phone

Witness

Address

Phone

(2) The principal's failure to designate a surrogate shall not invalidate the living will.

History.
S. 4, ch. 92-199; s. 35, ch. 99-6; s. 26, ch. 99-331; s. 12, ch. 2000-295.

765.304.   Procedure for living will.

(1) If a person has made a living will expressing his or her desires concerning life-prolonging procedures, but has not designated a surrogate to execute his or her wishes concerning life-prolonging procedures or designated a surrogate under part II, the attending physician may proceed as directed by the principal in the living will. In the event of a dispute or disagreement concerning the attending physician's decision to withhold or withdraw life-prolonging procedures, the attending physician shall not withhold or withdraw life-prolonging procedures pending review under s. 765.105. If a review of a disputed decision is not sought within 7 days following the attending physician's decision to withhold or withdraw life-prolonging procedures, the attending physician may proceed in accordance with the principal's instructions.

(2) Before proceeding in accordance with the principal's living will, it must be determined that:

(a) The principal does not have a reasonable medical probability of recovering capacity so that the right could be exercised directly by the principal.

(b) The principal has a terminal condition, has an end-stage condition, or is in a persistent vegetative state.

(c) Any limitations or conditions expressed orally or in a written declaration have been carefully considered and satisfied.

History.
S. 4, ch. 92-199; s. 10, ch. 94-183; s. 27, ch. 99-331.

765.305.   Procedure in absence of a living will.

(1) In the absence of a living will, the decision to withhold or withdraw life-prolonging procedures from a patient may be made by a health care surrogate designated by the patient pursuant to part II unless the designation limits the surrogate's authority to consent to the withholding or withdrawal of life-prolonging procedures.

(2) Before exercising the incompetent patient's right to forego treatment, the surrogate must be satisfied that:

(a) The patient does not have a reasonable medical probability of recovering capacity so that the right could be exercised by the patient.

(b) The patient has an end-stage condition, the patient is in a persistent vegetative state, or the patient's physical condition is terminal.

History.
S. 4, ch. 92-199; s. 28, ch. 99-331; s. 13, ch. 2000-295.

765.306.   Determination of patient condition.

In determining whether the patient has a terminal condition, has an end-stage condition, or is in a persistent vegetative state or may recover capacity, or whether a medical condition or limitation referred to in an advance directive exists, the patient's attending or treating physician and at least one other consulting physician must separately examine the patient. The findings of each such examination must be documented in the patient's medical record and signed by each examining physician before life-prolonging procedures may be withheld or withdrawn.

History.
S. 4, ch. 92-199; s. 13, ch. 94-183; s. 29, ch. 99-331; s. 14, ch. 2000-295.

765.309.   Mercy killing or euthanasia not authorized; suicide distinguished.

(1) Nothing in this chapter shall be construed to condone, authorize, or approve mercy killing or euthanasia, or to permit any affirmative or deliberate act or omission to end life other than to permit the natural process of dying.

(2) The withholding or withdrawal of life-prolonging procedures from a patient in accordance with any provision of this chapter does not, for any purpose, constitute a suicide.

History.
S. 4, ch. 92-199.

PART IV.
ABSENCE OF ADVANCE DIRECTIVE.

765.401.   The proxy.

(1) If an incapacitated or developmentally disabled patient has not executed an advance directive, or designated a surrogate to execute an advance directive, or the designated or alternate surrogate is no

longer available to make health care decisions, health care decisions may be made for the patient by any of the following individuals, in the following order of priority, if no individual in a prior class is reasonably available, willing, or competent to act:

(a) The judicially appointed guardian of the patient or the guardian advocate of the person having a developmental disability as defined in s. 393.063, who has been authorized to consent to medical treatment, if such guardian has previously been appointed; however, this paragraph shall not be construed to require such appointment before a treatment decision can be made under this subsection;

(b) The patient's spouse;

(c) An adult child of the patient, or if the patient has more than one adult child, a majority of the adult children who are reasonably available for consultation;

(d) A parent of the patient;

(e) The adult sibling of the patient or, if the patient has more than one sibling, a majority of the adult siblings who are reasonably available for consultation;

(f) An adult relative of the patient who has exhibited special care and concern for the patient and who has maintained regular contact with the patient and who is familiar with the patient's activities, health, and religious or moral beliefs; or

(g) A close friend of the patient.

(h) A clinical social worker licensed pursuant to chapter 491, or who is a graduate of a court-approved guardianship program. Such a proxy must be selected by the provider's bioethics committee and must not be employed by the provider. If the provider does not have a bioethics committee, then such a proxy may be chosen through an arrangement with the bioethics committee of another provider. The proxy will be notified that, upon request, the provider shall make available a second physician, not involved in the patient's care to assist the proxy in evaluating treatment. Decisions to withhold or withdraw life-prolonging procedures will be reviewed by the facility's bioethics committee. Documentation of efforts to locate proxies from prior classes must be recorded in the patient record.

(2) Any health care decision made under this part must be based on the proxy's informed consent and on the decision the proxy reasonably believes the patient would have made under the circumstances. If there is no indication of what the patient would have chosen, the proxy may consider the patient's best interest in deciding that proposed treatments are to be withheld or that treatments currently in effect are to be withdrawn.

(3) Before exercising the incapacitated patient's rights to select or decline health care, the proxy must comply with the provisions of ss. 765.205 and 765.305, except that a proxy's decision to withhold or withdraw

life-prolonging procedures must be supported by clear and convincing evidence that the decision would have been the one the patient would have chosen had the patient been competent or, if there is no indication of what the patient would have chosen, that the decision is in the patient's best interest.

(4) Nothing in this section shall be construed to preempt the designation of persons who may consent to the medical care or treatment of minors established pursuant to s. 743.0645.

History.

S. 5, ch. 92-199; s. 12, ch. 94-183; s. 32, ch. 99-331; s. 15, ch. 2000-295; s. 7, ch. 2001-250; s. 136, ch. 2001-277; s. 13, ch. 2002-195; s. 5, ch. 2003-57.

765.404. Persistent vegetative state.

For persons in a persistent vegetative state, as determined by the attending physician in accordance with currently accepted medical standards, who have no advance directive and for whom there is no evidence indicating what the person would have wanted under such conditions, and for whom, after a reasonably diligent inquiry, no family or friends are available or willing to serve as a proxy to make health care decisions for them, life-prolonging procedures may be withheld or withdrawn under the following conditions:

(1) The person has a judicially appointed guardian representing his or her best interest with authority to consent to medical treatment; and

(2) The guardian and the person's attending physician, in consultation with the medical ethics committee of the facility where the patient is located, conclude that the condition is permanent and that there is no reasonable medical probability for recovery and that withholding or withdrawing life-prolonging procedures is in the best interest of the patient. If there is no medical ethics committee at the facility, the facility must have an arrangement with the medical ethics committee of another facility or with a community-based ethics committee approved by the Florida Bio-ethics Network. The ethics committee shall review the case with the guardian, in consultation with the person's attending physician, to determine whether the condition is permanent and there is no reasonable medical probability for recovery. The individual committee members and the facility associated with an ethics committee shall not be held liable in any civil action related to the performance of any duties required in this subsection.

History.

S. 33, ch. 99-331.

Editor's Notes.

One-time stay.— Section 1, ch. 2003-418 provides: "(1) The Governor shall have the authority to issue a one-time stay to prevent the withholding of nutrition and hydration from a patient if, as of October 15, 2003: (a) That patient has no written advance directive; (b) The court has found that patient to be in a persistent vegetative state; (c) That patient has had nutrition and hydration withheld; and (d) A member of that patient's family has challenged the withholding of nutrition and hydration. (2) The Governor's authority to issue the stay expires 15 days after the effective date of this act [October 21, 2003], and the expiration of that authority does not impact the validity or the effect of any stay issued pursuant to this act. The Governor may lift the stay authorized under this act at any time. A person may not be held civilly liable and is not subject to regulatory or disciplinary sanctions for taking any action to comply with a stay issued by the Governor pursuant to this act. (3) Upon the issuance of a stay, the chief judge of the circuit court shall appoint a guardian ad litem for the patient to make recommendations to the Governor and the court."

PART V.
ANATOMICAL GIFTS.

765.510. Legislative declaration.

Because of the rapid medical progress in the fields of tissue and organ preservation, transplantation of tissue, and tissue culture, and because it is in the public interest to aid the medical developments in these fields, the Legislature in enacting this part intends to encourage and aid the development of reconstructive medicine and surgery and the development of medical research by facilitating premortem and postmortem authorizations for donations of tissue and organs. It is the purpose of this part to regulate the gift of a body or parts of a body, the gift to be made after the death of a donor.

History.
S. 1, ch. 74-106; s. 113, ch. 75-220; s. 3, ch. 84-264; s. 60, ch. 2001-226.

Editor's Notes.
Created from former s. 736.21; s. 732.910.

765.511. Definitions.

As used in this part, the term:

(1) "Agency" means the Agency for Health Care Administration.

(2) "Anatomical gift" or "gift" means a donation of all or part of a human body to take effect after the donor's death and to be used for transplantation, therapy, research, or education.

(3) "Bank" or "storage facility" means a facility licensed, accredited, or approved under the laws of any state for storage of human bodies or body parts.

(4) "Death" means the absence of life as determined, in accordance with currently accepted medical standards, by the irreversible cessation of all respiration and circulatory function, or as determined, in accordance with s. 382.009, by the irreversible cessation of the functions of the entire brain, including the brain stem.

(5) "Decedent" means a deceased individual whose body or body parts may be, or are, the source of an anatomical gift.

(6) "Department" means the Department of Highway Safety and Motor Vehicles.

(7) "Disinterested witness" means a witness other than a person listed in s. 765.512(3) or other family member.

(8) "Document of gift" means any of the documents or mechanisms used in making an anatomical gift under s. 765.514.

(9) "Donor" means an individual who makes an anatomical gift of all or part of his or her body.

(10) "Donor registry" means a database that contains records of anatomical gifts and amendments to, or revocations of, such gifts.

(11) "Eye bank" means an entity that is accredited by the Eye Bank Association of America or otherwise regulated under federal or state law to engage in the retrieval, screening, testing, processing, storage, or distribution of human eye tissue.

(12) "Guardian" means a person appointed pursuant to chapter 744. The term does not include a guardian ad litem.

(13) "Hospital" means a hospital licensed, accredited, or approved under the laws of any state and includes a hospital operated by the United States Government or a state, or a subdivision thereof, although not required to be licensed under state laws.

(14) "Identification card" means an official identification card issued by a governmental entity, state agency, or subdivision thereof.

(15) "Organ procurement organization" means an entity that is designated as an organ procurement organization by the Secretary of the United States Department of Health and Human Services and that engages in the retrieval, screening, testing, processing, storage, or distribution of human organs.

(16) "Part of the body" or "body part" means an organ, eye, or tissue of a human being. The term does not include the whole body.

(17) "Physician" or "surgeon" means a physician or surgeon licensed to practice under chapter 458 or chapter 459 or similar laws of any state. "Surgeon" includes dental or oral surgeon.

(18) "Procurement" means any retrieval, recovery, processing, storage, or distribution of human organs or tissues for transplantation, therapy, research, or education.

(19) "Procurement organization" means an organ procurement organization, eye bank, or tissue bank.

(20) "Reasonably available" means able to be contacted by a procurement organization in a timely manner without undue effort, and willing and able to act in a manner consistent with existing medical protocols necessary for the making of an anatomical gift.

(21) "Record" means information that is inscribed on a tangible medium or that is stored in an electronic or other medium and is retrievable in perceivable form.

(22) "Sign" or "signed" means, with the present intent to authenticate or adopt a record, to execute or adopt a tangible symbol, or attach to or logically associate an electronic symbol, sound, or process with the record.

(23) "Tissue bank" means an entity that is accredited by the American Association of Tissue Banks or

otherwise regulated under federal or state law to engage in the retrieval, screening, testing, processing, storage, or distribution of human tissue.

History.
S. 1, ch. 74-106; s. 113, ch. 75-220; s. 973, ch. 97-102; s. 5, ch. 98-68; s. 61, ch. 2001-226; s. 1, ch. 2009-218, eff. July 1, 2009.

Editor's Notes.
Created from former s. 736.22; s. 732.911.

765.512. Persons who may make an anatomical gift.

(1) Any person who may make a will may make an anatomical gift of his or her body.

(a) If the decedent makes an anatomical gift by one of the methods listed in s. 765.514(1), and in the absence of actual notice of contrary indications by the decedent, the document or entry in the donor registry is legally sufficient evidence of the decedent's informed consent to donate an anatomical gift.

(b) An anatomical gift made by a qualified donor and not revoked by the donor, as provided in s. 765.516, is irrevocable after the donor's death. A family member, guardian, representative ad litem, or health care surrogate may not modify, deny, or prevent a donor's wish or intent to make an anatomical gift after the donor's death.

(2) A health care surrogate designated by the decedent pursuant to part II of this chapter may give all or any part of the decedent's body for any purpose specified in s. 765.513 absent actual notice of contrary indications by the decedent.

(3) If the decedent has not made an anatomical gift or designated a health surrogate, a member of one of the classes of persons listed below, in the order of priority listed and in the absence of actual notice of contrary indications by the decedent or actual notice of opposition by a member of a prior class, may give all or any part of the decedent's body for any purpose specified in s. 765.513:

(a) The spouse of the decedent;

(b) An adult son or daughter of the decedent;

(c) Either parent of the decedent;

(d) An adult brother or sister of the decedent;

(e) An adult grandchild of the decedent;

(f) A grandparent of the decedent;

(g) A close personal friend, as defined in s. 765.101;

(h) A guardian of the person of the decedent at the time of his or her death; or

(i) A representative ad litem appointed by a court of competent jurisdiction upon a petition heard ex parte filed by any person, who shall ascertain that no person of higher priority exists who objects to the gift of all or any part of the decedent's body and that no evidence exists of the decedent's having made a communication expressing a desire that his or her body or body parts not be donated upon death.

Those of higher priority who are reasonably available must be contacted and made aware of the proposed gift and a reasonable search must be conducted which shows that there would have been no objection to the gift by the decedent.

(4) A donee may not accept an anatomical gift if the donee has actual notice of contrary indications by the donor or actual notice that an anatomical gift by a member of a class is opposed by a member of a prior class.

(5) The person authorized by subsection (3) may make the anatomical gift after the decedent's death or immediately before the decedent's death.

(6) An anatomical gift authorizes:

(a) Any examination necessary to assure medical acceptability of the gift for the purposes intended.

(b) The decedent's medical provider, family, or a third party to furnish medical records requested concerning the decedent's medical and social history.

(7) Once the anatomical gift has been made, the rights of the donee are paramount to the rights of others, except as provided by s. 765.517.

History.
S. 1, ch. 74-106; s. 45, ch. 75-220; s. 4, ch. 84-264; s. 62, ch. 85-62; s. 5, ch. 95-423; s. 974, ch. 97-102; s. 6, ch. 98-68; s. 12, ch. 99-331; s. 62, ch. 2001-226; s. 2, ch. 2003-46; s. 2, ch. 2008-223, eff. July 1, 2008; s. 2, ch. 2009-218, eff. July 1, 2009.

Editor's Notes.
Section 1, ch. 2003-46, provides: "This act may be cited as the 'Nick Oelrich Gift of Life Act.'"
Created from former s. 736.23; s. 732.912.

765.513. Donees; purposes for which anatomical gifts may be made.

(1) The following persons or entities may become donees of anatomical gifts of bodies or parts of them for the purposes stated:

(a) Any procurement organization or accredited medical or dental school, college, or university for education, research, therapy, or transplantation.

(b) Any individual specified by name for therapy or transplantation needed by him or her.

(2) If multiple purposes are set forth in the document of gift but are not set forth in any priority order, the anatomical gift shall be used first for transplantation or therapy, if suitable. If the gift cannot be used for transplantation or therapy, the gift may be used for research or education.

(3) The Legislature declares that the public policy of this state prohibits restrictions on the possible recipients of an anatomical gift on the basis of race, color, religion, gender, national origin, age, physical disability, health status, marital status, or economic status, and such restrictions are void and unenforceable.

History.
S. 1, ch. 74-106; s. 45, ch. 75-220; s. 1, ch. 94-305; s. 975, ch. 97-102; s. 7, ch. 98-68; s. 63, ch. 2001-226; s. 3, ch. 2009-218, eff. July 1, 2009.

Editor's Notes.
Created from former s. 736.24; s. 732.913.

765.514. Manner of making anatomical gifts.

(1) A person may make an anatomical gift of all or part of his or her body under s. 765.512(1) by:

(a) Signing an organ and tissue donor card.

(b) Registering online with the donor registry.

(c) Signifying an intent to donate on his or her driver's license or identification card issued by the department. Revocation, suspension, expiration, or cancellation of the driver's license or identification card does not invalidate the gift.

(d) Expressing a wish to donate in a living will or other advance directive.

(e) Executing a will that includes a provision indicating that the testator wishes to make an anatomical gift. The gift becomes effective upon the death of the testator without waiting for probate. If the will is not probated or if it is declared invalid for testamentary purposes, the gift is nevertheless valid to the extent that it has been acted upon in good faith.

(f) Expressing a wish to donate in a document other than a will. The document must be signed by the donor in the presence of two witnesses who shall sign the document in the donor's presence. If the donor cannot sign, the document may be signed for him or her at the donor's direction and in his or her presence and the presence of two witnesses who must sign the document in the donor's presence. Delivery of the document of gift during the donor's lifetime is not necessary to make the gift valid. The following form of written document is sufficient for any person to make an anatomical gift for the purposes of this part:

UNIFORM DONOR CARD

The undersigned hereby makes this anatomical gift, if medically acceptable, to take effect on death. The words and marks below indicate my desires:

I give:

(a) _____ any needed organs, tissues, or eyes;

(b) _____ only the following organs, tissues, or eyes

[Specify the organs, tissues, or eyes]

for the purpose of transplantation, therapy, medical research, or education;

(c) _____ my body for anatomical study if needed. Limitations or special wishes, if any:

(If applicable, list specific donee;
this must be arranged in advance with the donee.)

Signed by the donor and the following witnesses in the presence of each other:

_____ (Signature of donor) _____ (Date of birth of donor)

_____ (Date signed) _____ (City and State)

_____ (Witness) _____ (Witness)

_____ (Address) _____ (Address)

(2) The anatomical gift may be made to a donee listed in s. 765.513, and the donee may be specified by name.

(3) Any anatomical gift by a health care surrogate designated by the decedent pursuant to part II of this chapter or a member of a class designated in s. 765.512(3) must be made by a document signed by that person or made by that person's witnessed telephonic discussion, telegraphic message, or other recorded message.

History.
S. 1, ch. 74-106; s. 45, ch. 75-220; s. 1, ch. 83-171; s. 2, ch. 94-305; s. 6, ch. 95-423; s. 976, ch. 97-102; s. 8, ch. 98-68; s. 13, ch. 99-331; s. 64, ch. 2001-226; s. 3, ch. 2008-223, eff. July 1, 2008; s. 4, ch. 2009-218, eff. July 1, 2009.

Editor's Notes.
Created from former s. 736.25; s. 732.914.

765.515. Delivery of donor document.

(1) If an anatomical gift is made pursuant to s. 765.521, the completed donor registration card shall be delivered to the department, and the department must communicate the donor's intent to the donor registry, but delivery is not necessary to the validity of the gift. If the donor withdraws the gift, the records of the department must be updated to reflect such withdrawal, and the department must communicate the withdrawal to the donor registry for the purpose of updating the registry.

(2) If an anatomical gift is made by the donor to a specified donee, the document of gift, other than a will, may be delivered to the donee to expedite the appropriate procedures immediately after death, but delivery is not necessary to the validity of the gift. The document of gift may be deposited in any hospital, bank, storage facility, or registry office that accepts such documents for safekeeping or to facilitate the donation of organs and tissue after death.

(3) At the request of any interested party upon or after the donor's death, the person in possession shall produce the document of gift for examination.

History.
S. 1, ch. 74-106; s. 45, ch. 75-220; s. 2, ch. 83-171; s. 1, ch. 87-372; s. 7, ch. 95-423; s. 33, ch. 96-418; s. 9, ch. 98-68; s. 65, ch. 2001-226; s. 17, ch. 2008-9, eff. July 1, 2008; s. 4, ch. 2008-223, eff. July 1, 2008; s. 5, ch. 2009-218, eff. July 1, 2009.

Editor's Notes.
Created from former s. 736.26; s. 732.915.

765.5155. Donor registry; education program.

(1) The Legislature finds that:

(a) There is a shortage of organ and tissue donors in this state willing to provide the organs and tissue that could save lives or enhance the quality of life for many persons.

(b) There is a need to encourage the various minority populations of this state to donate organs and tissue.

(c) A statewide donor registry having an online donor registration process coupled with an enhanced program of donor education will lead to an increase in the number of organ and tissue donors registered in this state, thus affording more persons who are awaiting organ or tissue transplants the opportunity for a full and productive life.

(2) The agency and the department shall jointly contract for the operation of a donor registry and education program. The contractor shall be procured by competitive solicitation pursuant to chapter 287, notwithstanding any exemption in s. 287.057(3)(f). When awarding the contract, priority shall be given to existing nonprofit groups that are based within the state, have expertise working with procurement organizations, have expertise in conducting statewide organ and tissue donor public education campaigns, and represent the needs of the organ and tissue donation community in the state.

(3) The contractor shall be responsible for:

(a) The development, implementation, and maintenance of an interactive web-based donor registry that, through electronic means, allows for online organ donor registration and the recording of organ and tissue donation records submitted through the driver's license identification program or through other sources.

   1. The registry must be maintained in a manner that allows, through electronic and telephonic methods, immediate access to organ and tissue donation records 24 hours a day, 7 days a week.

   2. Access to the registry must be through coded and secure means to protect the integrity of the data in the registry.

(b) A continuing program to educate and inform medical professionals, law enforcement agencies and officers, other state and local government employees, high school students, minorities, and the public about the laws of this state relating to anatomical gifts and the need for anatomical gifts.

   1. Existing community resources, when available, must be used to support the program and volunteers may assist the program to the maximum extent possible.

   2. The contractor shall coordinate with the head of a state agency or other political subdivision of the state, or his or her designee, to establish convenient times, dates, and locations for educating that entity's employees.

(c) Preparing and submitting an annual written report to the agency by December 31 of each year. The report must include:

   1. The number of donors on the registry and an analysis of the registration rates by location and method of donation;

   2. The characteristics of donors as determined from registry information submitted directly by the donors or by the department;

   3. The annual dollar amount of voluntary contributions received by the contractor;

   4. A description of the educational campaigns and initiatives implemented during the year and an evaluation of their effectiveness in increasing enrollment on the registry; and

   5. An analysis of Florida's registry compared with other states' donor registries.

(4) Costs for the donor registry and education program shall be paid by the agency from the funds deposited into the Health Care Trust Fund pursuant to ss. 320.08047 and 322.08, which are designated for maintaining the donor registry and education program. In addition, the contractor may receive and use voluntary contributions to help support the registry and provide education.

(5) The donor registry established by this section is designated as the "Joshua Abbott Organ and Tissue Registry."

History.
S. 5, ch. 2008-223, eff. July 1, 2008; s. 6, ch. 2009-218, eff. July 1, 2009; s. 40, ch. 2010-151, eff. July 1, 2010.

765.51551. Donor registry; public records exemption.

(1) Information held in the donor registry which identifies a donor is confidential and exempt from s. 119.07(1) and s. 24(a), Art. I of the State Constitution.

(2) Such information may be disclosed to the following:

(a) Procurement organizations that have been certified by the agency for the purpose of ascertaining or effectuating the existence of a gift under s. 765.522.

(b) Persons engaged in bona fide research if the person agrees to:

   1. Submit a research plan to the agency that specifies the exact nature of the information requested and the intended use of the information;

   2. Maintain the confidentiality of the records or information if personal identifying information is made available to the researcher;

   3. Destroy any confidential records or information obtained after the research is concluded; and

   4. Not directly or indirectly contact, for any purpose, any donor or donee.

(3) This section is subject to the Open Government Sunset Review Act in accordance with s. 119.15 and shall stand repealed on October 2, 2013, unless reviewed and saved from repeal through reenactment by the Legislature.

History.
S. 1, ch. 2008-222, eff. July 1, 2008; s. 7, ch. 2009-218, eff. July 1, 2009.

765.516.　Donor amendment or revocation of anatomical gift.

(1) A donor may amend the terms of or revoke an anatomical gift by:

(a) The execution and delivery to the donee of a signed statement witnessed by at least two adults, at least one of whom is a disinterested witness.

(b) An oral statement that is made in the presence of two persons, one of whom is not a family member, and communicated to the donor's family or attorney or to the donee. An oral statement is effective only if the procurement organization, transplant hospital, or physician or technician has actual notice of the oral amendment or revocation before an incision is made to the decedent's body or an invasive procedure to prepare the recipient has begun.

(c) A statement made during a terminal illness or injury addressed to an attending physician, who must communicate the revocation of the gift to the procurement organization.

(d) A signed document found on or about the donor's person.

(e) Removing his or her name from the donor registry.

(f) A later-executed document of gift which amends or revokes a previous anatomical gift or portion of an anatomical gift, either expressly or by inconsistency.

(g) By the destruction or cancellation of the document of gift or the destruction or cancellation of that portion of the document of gift used to make the gift with the intent to revoke the gift.

(2) Any anatomical gift made by a will may also be amended or revoked in the manner provided for the amendment or revocation of wills or as provided in paragraph (1)(a).

History.

S. 1, ch. 74-106; s. 113, ch. 75-220; s. 3, ch. 83-171; s. 8, ch. 95-423; s. 977, ch. 97-102; s. 10, ch. 98-68; s. 66, ch. 2001-226; s. 3, ch. 2003-46; s. 6, ch. 2008-223, eff. July 1, 2008; s. 8, ch. 2009-218, eff. July 1, 2009.

Editor's Notes.

Section 1, ch. 2003-46, provides: "This act may be cited as the 'Nick Oelrich Gift of Life Act.'"

Created from former s. 736.27; s. 732.916.

765.517.　Rights and duties at death.

(1) The donee, pursuant to s. 765.515(2), may accept or reject an anatomical gift. If the donee accepts a gift to be used for research or education purposes, the donee may authorize embalming and the use of the body in funeral services, subject to the terms of the gift. If the gift is of a part of the body, the donee shall cause the part to be removed without unnecessary mutilation upon the death of the donor and before or after embalming. After removal of the body part, custody of the remainder of the body vests in the surviving spouse, next of kin, or other persons under obligation to dispose of the body.

(2) The time of death shall be determined by a physician who attends the donor at the donor's death or, if there is no such physician, the physician who certifies the death. After death, those physicians or the donor's primary care physician may participate in, but may not obstruct, the procedures to preserve the donor's organs or tissues and may not be paid or reimbursed for such participation, nor be associated with or employed by, a procurement organization. These physicians may not participate in the procedures for removing or transplanting a part. However, this subsection does not prevent a physician from serving in a voluntary capacity on the board of directors of a procurement organization or participating on any board, council, commission, or similar body related to the organ and tissue procurement system.

(3) The procurement organizations, or hospital medical professionals under the direction thereof, may perform any and all tests to evaluate the deceased as a potential donor and any invasive procedures on the deceased body in order to preserve the potential donor's organs. These procedures do not include the surgical removal of an organ or penetrating any body cavity, specifically for the purpose of donation, until:

(a) It has been verified that the deceased's consent to donate appears in the donor registry or a properly executed document of gift is located; or

(b) If a properly executed document of gift cannot be located or the deceased's consent is not listed in the donor registry, a person specified in s. 765.512(2) or (3) has been located, has been notified of the death, and has granted legal permission for the donation.

(4) All reasonable additional expenses incurred in the procedures to preserve the donor's organs or tissues shall be reimbursed by the procurement organization.

(5) A person who acts in good faith and without negligence in accord with the terms of this part or under the anatomical gift laws of another state or a foreign country, or attempts to do so, may not be subject to any civil action for damages, may not be subject to any criminal proceeding, and may not be subject to discipline, penalty, or liability in any administrative proceeding.

(6) The provisions of this part are subject to the laws of this state prescribing powers and duties with respect to autopsies.

(7) The person making an anatomical gift and the donor's estate are not liable for any injury or damages that result from the making or use of the gift.

(8) In determining whether an anatomical gift has been made, amended, or revoked under this part, a person may rely upon the representation of an individual listed in s. 765.512, relating to the individual's relationship to the donor or prospective donor, unless the person knows that the representation is untrue.

History.
S. 1, ch. 74-106; s. 45, ch. 75-220; s. 4, ch. 83-171; s. 9, ch. 95-423; s. 978, ch. 97-102; s. 14, ch. 99-331; s. 67, ch. 2001-226; s. 7, ch. 2008-223, eff. July 1, 2008; s. 9, ch. 2009-218, eff. July 1, 2009.
Editor's Notes.
Created from former s. 736.28; s. 732.917.

765.518. Eye banks.

(1) Any state, county, district, or other public hospital may purchase and provide the necessary facilities and equipment to establish and maintain an eye bank for restoration of sight purposes.

(2) The Department of Education may have prepared, printed, and distributed:

(a) A form document of gift for a gift of the eyes.

(b) An eye bank register consisting of the names of persons who have executed documents for the gift of their eyes.

(c) Wallet cards reciting the document of gift.

History.
S. 1, ch. 74-106; s. 45, ch. 75-220; s. 462, ch. 77-147; s. 68, ch. 2001-226.
Editor's Notes.
Created from former s. 736.29; s. 732.918.

765.5185. Corneal removal by medical examiners.

(1) In any case in which a patient is in need of corneal tissue for a transplant, a district medical examiner or an appropriately qualified designee with training in ophthalmologic techniques may, upon request of any eye bank authorized under s. 765.518, provide the cornea of a decedent whenever all of the following conditions are met:

(a) A decedent who may provide a suitable cornea for the transplant is under the jurisdiction of the medical examiner and an autopsy is required in accordance with s. 406.11.

(b) No objection by the next of kin of the decedent is known by the medical examiner.

(c) The removal of the cornea will not interfere with the subsequent course of an investigation or autopsy.

(2) Neither the district medical examiner nor the medical examiner's appropriately qualified designee nor any eye bank authorized under s. 765.518 may be held liable in any civil or criminal action for failure to obtain consent of the next of kin.

History.
S. 1, ch. 77-172; s. 1, ch. 78-191; s. 979, ch. 97-102; s. 69, ch. 2001-226; s. 111, ch. 2002-1.
Editor's Notes.
Former s. 732.9185.

765.519. Enucleation of eyes by licensed funeral directors.

With respect to a gift of an eye as provided for in this part, a licensed funeral director as defined in chapter 497 who has completed a course in eye enucleation and has received a certificate of competence from the Department of Ophthalmology of the University of Florida School of Medicine, the University of South Florida School of Medicine, or the University of Miami School of Medicine may enucleate eyes for gift after proper certification of death by a physician and in compliance with the intent of the gift as defined in this chapter. No properly certified funeral director acting in accordance with the terms of this part shall have any civil or criminal liability for eye enucleation.

History.
S. 1, ch. 74-106; s. 45, ch. 75-220; s. 1, ch. 80-157; s. 70, ch. 2001-226; s. 148, ch. 2004-301.
Editor's Notes.
Created from former s. 736.31; s. 732.919.

765.521. Donations as part of driver license or identification card process.

(1) The agency and the department shall develop and implement a program encouraging and allowing persons to make anatomical gifts as a part of the process of issuing identification cards and issuing and renewing driver licenses. The donor registration card distributed by the department shall include the information required by the uniform donor card under s. 765.514 and such additional information as determined necessary by the department. The department shall also develop and implement a program to identify donors which includes notations on identification cards, driver licenses, and driver records or such other methods as the department develops to clearly indicate the individual's intent to make an anatomical gift. A notation on an individual's driver license or identification card that the individual intends to make an anatomical gift satisfies all requirements for consent to organ or tissue donation. The agency shall provide the necessary supplies and forms from funds appropriated from general revenue or contributions from interested voluntary, nonprofit organizations. The department shall provide the necessary recordkeeping system from funds appropriated from general revenue. The department and the agency shall incur no liability in connection with the performance of any acts authorized herein.

(2) The department, after consultation with and concurrence by the agency, shall adopt rules to implement the provisions of this section according to the provisions of chapter 120.

(3) Funds expended by the agency to carry out the intent of this section may not be taken from funds appropriated for patient care.

History.
S. 1, ch. 75-71; s. 1, ch. 77-16; s. 463, ch. 77-147; s. 1, ch. 77-174; ss. 1, 2, ch. 80-134; s. 5, ch. 83-171; s. 10, ch. 95-423; s. 71, ch. 2001-226; s. 8, ch. 2008-223, eff. July 1, 2008; s. 10, ch. 2009-218, eff. July 1, 2009.
Editor's Notes.
Former s. 732.921.

765.5215. Education program relating to annatomical gifts [Repealed.]

Repealed by s. 10, ch. 2008-223, effective July 1, 2008.

History.
S. 1, ch. 85-247; s. 11, ch. 95-423; s. 65, ch. 99-248; s. s72, ch. 2001-226; s. 112, ch. 2002-1.

765.52155. Florida Organ and Tissue Donor Education and Procurement Trust Fund [Repealed.]
Repealed by s. 18, ch. 2008-9, effective July 1, 2008.
History.
S. 1, ch. 95-316; s. 29, ch. 96-418; s. 73, ch. 2001-226.

765.5216. Organ and tissue education panel [Repealed.]
Repealed by s. 10, ch. 2008-223, effective July 1, 2008.
History.
S. 12, ch. 95-423; s. 11, ch. 98-68; s. 66, ch. 99-248; s. 25, ch. 2000-305; s. 74, ch. 2001-226; s. 113, ch. 2002-1; s. 103, ch. 2003-1.

765.522. Duty of hospital administrators; liability of hospital administrators and procurement organizations.
(1) If, based on accepted medical standards, a hospital patient is a suitable candidate for organ or tissue donation, the hospital administrator or the hospital administrator's designee shall, at or near the time of death, notify the appropriate procurement organization, which shall access the donor registry created by s. 765.5155 or any other donor registry to ascertain the existence of an entry in the registry which has not been revoked or a document of gift executed by the decedent. In the absence of an entry in the donor registry, a document of gift, or other properly executed document, the procurement organization shall request:

    (a) The patient's health care surrogate, as authorized in s. 765.512(2); or

    (b) If the patient does not have a surrogate, or the surrogate is not reasonably available, any of the persons specified in s. 765.512(3), in the order and manner listed,

to consent to the anatomical gift of the decedent's body for any purpose specified in this part. Except as provided in s. 765.512, in the absence of actual notice of opposition, consent need only be obtained from the person or persons in the highest priority class reasonably available.

(2) A document of gift is valid if executed in accordance with this part or the laws of the state or country where it was executed and where the person making the anatomical gift was domiciled, has a place of residence, or was a citizen at the time the document of gift was executed.

(3) The agency shall establish rules and guidelines concerning the education of individuals who may be designated to perform the request and the procedures to be used in making the request. The agency is authorized to adopt rules concerning the documentation of the request, where such request is made.

(4) If a document of gift is valid under this section, the laws of this state govern the interpretation of the document of gift.

(5) A document of gift or amendment of an anatomical gift is presumed to be valid unless it was not validly executed or was revoked.

(6) There shall be no civil or criminal liability against any procurement organization certified under s. 765.542 or against any hospital or hospital administrator or designee who complies with the provisions of this part and agency rules or if, in the exercise of reasonable care, a request for organ donation is inappropriate and the gift is not made according to this part and agency rules.

(7) The hospital administrator or a designee shall, at or near the time of death of a potential donor, directly notify the affiliated organ procurement organization of the potential organ donor. The organ procurement organization must offer any organ from such a donor first to patients on a Florida-based local or state organ sharing transplant list. For the purpose of this subsection, the term "transplant list" includes certain categories of national or regional organ sharing for patients of exceptional need or exceptional match, as approved or mandated by the Organ Procurement and Transplantation Network, or its agent. This notification may not be made to a tissue bank or eye bank in lieu of the organ procurement organization unless the tissue bank or eye bank is also designated as an organ procurement organization.
History.
S. 1, ch. 86-212; s. 2, ch. 87-372; s. 13, ch. 95-423; s. 980, ch. 97-102; s. 12, ch. 98-68; s. 15, ch. 99-331; s. 75, ch. 2001-226; s. 104, ch. 2003-1; s. 9, ch. 2008-223, eff. July 1, 2008; s. 11, ch. 2009-218, eff. July 1, 2009.
Editor's Notes.
Former s. 732.922.

765.53. Organ Transplant Advisory Council; membership; responsibilities.
(1) A statewide technical Organ Transplant Advisory Council is created within the agency, consisting of twelve members who are physicians licensed under chapter 458 or chapter 459, to represent the interests of the public and the clients of the Department of Health or the agency. A person employed by the agency may not be appointed as a member of the council.

(2) The Secretary of Health Care Administration shall appoint all members of the council to serve a term of 2 years.

(3) The Secretary of Health Care Administration shall fill each vacancy on the council for the balance of the unexpired term. Priority consideration must be given to the appointment of an individual whose primary interest, experience, or expertise lies with clients of the Department of Health and the agency. If an appointment is not made within 120 days after a vacancy occurs on the council, the vacancy must be filled by the majority vote of the council.

(4) The members of the council shall elect a chairperson. The term of the chairperson shall be for 2

years, and an individual may not serve as chairperson for more than two consecutive terms.

(5) Members of the council shall receive no compensation, but shall be reimbursed for per diem and travel expenses by the agency in accordance with s. 112.061 while engaged in the performance of their duties.

(6) The responsibilities of the council shall be to recommend to the agency indications for adult and pediatric organ transplants. The council shall also formulate guidelines and standards for organ transplants and for the development of End Stage Organ Disease and Tissue/Organ Transplant programs. The recommendations, guidelines, and standards developed by the council are applicable only to those health programs funded through the agency.

(7) The council shall meet at least annually or upon the call of the chairperson or the Secretary of Health Care Administration.

History.
SS. 1, 2, ch. 86-208; ss. 88, 89, ch. 86-220; s. 3, ch. 87-50; s. 8, ch. 91-49; s. 52, ch. 91-297; s. 5, ch. 91-429; s. 3, ch. 94-305; s. 50, ch. 97-101; s. 1, ch. 99-299; s. 6, ch. 2000-305; s. 33, ch. 2003-1; s. 12, ch. 2009-218, eff. July 1, 2009.

Editor's Notes.
Formerly s. 381.0602: transferred by s. 33, ch. 2003-1, effective July 1, 2003.
Former s. 381.602.

765.541. Certification of procurement organizations; agency responsibilities.

The agency shall:

(1) Establish a program for the certification of organizations, corporations, or other entities engaged in the procurement of organs, tissues, and eyes for transplantation.

(2) Adopt rules that set forth appropriate standards and guidelines for the program in accordance with ss. 765.541-765.546 and part II of chapter 408. These standards and guidelines must be substantially based on the existing laws of the Federal Government and this state and the existing standards and guidelines of the United Network for Organ Sharing (UNOS), the American Association of Tissue Banks (AATB), the South-Eastern Organ Procurement Foundation (SEOPF), the North American Transplant Coordinators Organization (NATCO), and the Eye Bank Association of America (EBAA). In addition, the agency shall, before adopting these standards and guidelines, seek input from all procurement organizations based in this state.

(3) Collect, keep, and make available to the Governor and the Legislature information regarding the numbers and disposition of organs, tissues, and eyes procured by each certified procurement organization.

(4) Monitor procurement organizations for program compliance.

(5) Provide for the administration of the Organ and Tissue Procurement and Transplantation Advisory Board.

History.
SS. 2, 9, ch. 91-271; s. 5, ch. 91-429; s. 5, ch. 94-305; s. 33, ch. 2003-1; s. 201, ch. 2007-230, eff. July 1, 2007; s. 13, ch. 2009-218, eff. July 1, 2009.

Editor's Notes.
Formerly s. 381.6021: transferred by s. 33, ch. 2003-1, effective July 1, 2003.

765.542. Requirements to engage in organ, tissue, or eye procurement.

(1) The requirements of part II of chapter 408 apply to the provision of services that require licensure pursuant to ss. 765.541-765.546 and part II of chapter 408 and to entities licensed or certified by or applying for such licensure or certification from the agency pursuant to ss. 765.541-765.546. A person may not engage in the practice of organ procurement in this state without being designated as an organ procurement organization by the Secretary of the United States Department of Health and Human Services and being appropriately certified by the agency. A physician or organ procurement organization based outside this state is exempt from these certification requirements if:

(a) The organs are procured for an out-of-state patient who is listed on, or referred through, the United Network for Organ Sharing System; and

(b) The organs are procured through an agreement of an organ procurement organization certified by the state.

(2) A person may not engage in tissue procurement in this state unless it is appropriately certified as a tissue bank by the agency.

(3) A person may not engage in the practice of eye procurement in this state without being appropriately certified as an eye bank by the agency. Funeral directors or direct disposers who retrieve eye tissue for an eye bank certified under this subsection are exempt from the certification requirements under this subsection.

(4) A limited certificate may be issued to a tissue bank or eye bank, certifying only those components of procurement which the bank has chosen to perform. The agency may issue a limited certificate if it determines that the tissue bank or eye bank is adequately staffed and equipped to operate in conformity with the rules adopted under this section.

History.
S. 3, ch. 91-271; s. 6, ch. 94-305; s. 33, ch. 2003-1; s. 202, ch. 2007-230, eff. July 1, 2007; s. 14, ch. 2009-218, eff. July 1, 2009.

Editor's Notes.
Formerly s. 381.6022: transferred by s. 33, ch. 2003-1, effective July 1, 2003.

765.543. Organ and Tissue Procurement and Transplantation Advisory Board; creation; duties.

(1) There is hereby created the Organ and Tissue Procurement and Transplantation Advisory Board, which shall consist of 14 members who are appointed by and report directly to the Secretary of Health Care

Administration. The membership must be regionally distributed and must include:

(a) Two representatives who have expertise in vascular organ transplant surgery;

(b) Two representatives who have expertise in vascular organ procurement, preservation, and distribution;

(c) Two representatives who have expertise in musculoskeletal tissue transplant surgery;

(d) Two representatives who have expertise in musculoskeletal tissue procurement, processing, and distribution;

(e) A representative who has expertise in eye and cornea transplant surgery;

(f) A representative who has expertise in eye and cornea procurement, processing, and distribution;

(g) A representative who has expertise in bone marrow procurement, processing, and transplantation;

(h) A representative from the Florida Pediatric Society;

(i) A representative from the Florida Society of Pathologists; and

(j) A representative from the Florida Medical Examiners Commission.

(2) The advisory board members may not be compensated for their services except that they may be reimbursed for their travel expenses as provided by law. Members of the board shall be appointed for 3-year terms of office.

(3) The board shall:

(a) Assist the agency in the development of necessary professional qualifications, including, but not limited to, the education, training, and performance of persons engaged in the various facets of organ and tissue procurement, processing, preservation, and distribution for transplantation;

(b) Assist the agency in monitoring the appropriate and legitimate expenses associated with organ and tissue procurement, processing, and distribution for transplantation and developing methodologies to assure the uniform statewide reporting of data to facilitate the accurate and timely evaluation of the organ and tissue procurement and transplantation system;

(c) Provide assistance to the Florida Medical Examiners Commission in the development of appropriate procedures and protocols to ensure the continued improvement in the approval and release of potential donors by the district medical examiners and associate medical examiners;

(d) Develop with and recommend to the agency the necessary procedures and protocols required to assure that all residents of this state have reasonable access to available organ and tissue transplantation therapy and that residents of this state can be reasonably assured that the statewide procurement transplantation system is able to fulfill their organ

and tissue requirements within the limits of the available supply and according to the severity of their medical condition and need; and

(e) Develop with and recommend to the agency any changes to the laws of this state or administrative rules or procedures to ensure that the statewide organ and tissue procurement and transplantation system is able to function smoothly, effectively, and efficiently, in accordance with the Federal Anatomical Gift Act and in a manner that assures the residents of this state that no person or entity profits from the altruistic voluntary donation of organs or tissues.

History.
SS. 4, 9, ch. 91-271; s. 5, ch. 91-429; s. 7, ch. 94-305; s. 7, ch. 2000-305; s. 33, ch. 2003-1; s. 15, ch. 2009-218, eff. July 1, 2009.

Editor's Notes.
Formerly s. 381.6023: transferred by s. 33, ch. 2003-1, effective July 1, 2003.

765.544. Fees; organ and tissue donor education and procurement.

(1) In accordance with s. 408.805, an applicant or a certificateholder shall pay a fee for each application submitted under this part, part II of chapter 408, and applicable rules. The amount of the fee shall be as follows:

(a) An initial application fee of $1,000 from organ procurement organizations and tissue banks and $500 from eye banks.

(b) Annual fees to be used, in the following order of priority, for the certification program, the advisory board, maintenance of the donor registry, and the organ and tissue donor education program, which may not exceed $35,000 per organization:

1. Each organ procurement organization shall pay the greater of $1,000 or 0.25 percent of its total revenues produced from procurement activity in this state by the certificateholder during its most recently completed fiscal or operational year.

2. Each tissue procurement organization shall pay the greater of $1,000 or 0.25 percent of its total revenues from procurement and processing activity in this state by the certificateholder during its most recently completed fiscal or operational year.

3. Each eye bank shall pay the greater of $500 or 0.25 percent of its total revenues produced from procurement activity in this state by the certificateholder during its most recently completed fiscal or operational year.

(2) The agency shall specify by rule the administrative penalties for the purpose of ensuring adherence to the standards of quality and practice required by this chapter, part II of chapter 408, and applicable rules of the agency for continued certification.

(3)(a) Proceeds from fees, administrative penalties, and surcharges collected pursuant to this section must be deposited into the Health Care Trust Fund.

(b) Moneys deposited in the trust fund pursuant to this section must be used exclusively for the implementation, administration, and operation of the certification program and the advisory board, for maintaining the donor registry, and for organ and tissue donor education.

(4) As used in this section, the term "procurement activity in this state" includes the bringing into this state for processing, storage, distribution, or transplantation of organs or tissues that are initially procured in another state or country.

History.
S. 5, ch. 91-271; s. 8, ch. 94-305; s. 32, ch. 96-418; ss. 3, 4, ch. 98-68; s. 54, ch. 2002-1; s. 33, ch. 2003-1; s. 203, ch. 2007-230, eff. July 1, 2007; s. 19, ch. 2008-9, eff. July 1, 2008; s. 16, ch. 2009-218, eff. July 1, 2009.

Editor's Notes.
Formerly s. 381.6024: transferred by s. 33, ch. 2003-1, effective July 1, 2003.

765.545. Physician supervision of cadaveric organ and tissue procurement coordinators.

Procurement organizations may employ coordinators who are registered nurses, physician's assistants, or other medically trained personnel who meet the relevant standards for procurement organizations adopted by the agency under s. 765.541, to assist in the medical management of organ donors or in the surgical procurement of cadaveric organs, tissues, or eyes for transplantation or research. A coordinator who assists in the medical management of organ donors or in the surgical procurement of cadaveric organs, tissues, or eyes for transplantation or research must do so under the direction and supervision of a physician medical director pursuant to rules and guidelines adopted by the agency. With the exception of organ procurement surgery, this supervision may be indirect supervision. For purposes of this section, the term "indirect supervision" means that the medical director is responsible for the medical actions of the coordinator, that the coordinator is operating under protocols expressly approved by the medical director, and that the medical director or his or her physician designee is always available, in person or by telephone, to provide medical direction, consultation, and advice in cases of organ, tissue, and eye donation and procurement. Although indirect supervision is authorized under this section, direct physician supervision is to be encouraged when appropriate.

History.
S. 6, ch. 91-271; s. 9, ch. 94-305; s. 1035, ch. 95-148; s. 34, ch. 2003-1; s. 17, ch. 2009-218, eff. July 1, 2009.

Editor's Notes.
Formerly s. 381.6025: transferred by s. 34, ch. 2003-1, effective July 1, 2003.

765.546. Procurement of cadaveric organs for transplant by out-of-state physicians.

Any physician currently licensed to practice medicine and surgery in the United States may surgically procure in this state cadaveric organs for transplant if:

(1) The organs are being procured for an out-of-state patient who is listed on, or referred through, the United Network for Organ Sharing System; and

(2) The organs are being procured through the auspices of an organ procurement organization certified in this state.

History.
S. 7, ch. 91-271; s. 33, ch. 2003-1.

Editor's Notes.
Formerly s. 381.6026: transferred by s. 33, ch. 2003-1, effective July 1, 2003.

765.547. Cooperation between medical examiner and procurement organization.

(1) A medical examiner and procurement organization shall cooperate with each other in order to maximize opportunities to recover anatomical gifts for the purpose of transplantation, therapy, research, or education.

(2) The Florida Medical Examiners Commission shall adopt rules establishing cooperative responsibilities between medical examiners and procurement organizations to facilitate and expedite completion of the medical examiner's responsibilities under chapter 406 in a manner that will maximize opportunities to recover anatomical gifts.

(3) This part does not supersede any part of chapter 406 relating to medical examiners and the disposition of dead bodies.

History.
S. 18, ch. 2009-218, eff. July 1, 2009.

Constitution of the State of Florida

ARTICLE X.

Miscellaneous.

4. Homestead; exemptions.

(a) There shall be exempt from forced sale under process of any court, and no judgment, decree or execution shall be a lien thereon, except for the payment of taxes and assessments thereon, obligations contracted for the purchase, improvement or repair thereof, or obligations contracted for house, field or other labor performed on the realty, the following property owned by a natural person:

(1) a homestead, if located outside a municipality, to the extent of one hundred sixty acres of contiguous land and improvements thereon, which shall not be reduced without the owner's consent by reason of subsequent inclusion in a municipality; or if located within a municipality, to the extent of one-half acre of contiguous land, upon which the exemption shall be limited to the residence of the owner or the owner's family;

(2) personal property to the value of one thousand dollars.

(b) These exemptions shall inure to the surviving spouse or heirs of the owner.

(c) The homestead shall not be subject to devise if the owner is survived by spouse or minor child, except the homestead may be devised to the owner's spouse if there be no minor child. The owner of homestead real estate, joined by the spouse if married, may alienate the homestead by mortgage, sale or gift and, if married, may by deed transfer the title to an estate by the entirety with the spouse. If the owner or spouse is incompetent, the method of alienation or encumbrance shall be as provided by law.

History.

Am. H.J.R. 4324, 1972; adopted 1972; Am. H.J.R. 40, 1983; adopted 1984; Am. proposed by Constitution Revision Commission, Revision No. 13, 1998, filed with the Secretary of State May 5, 1998; adopted 1998.

INDEX TO FLORIDIA PROBATE RULES AND STATUTES

DISTRIBUTION —Cont'd
Summary administration, 5.530(d), 735.206.
Taxes, apportionment of, 733.817.
Time for, 733.801(1).
Title of distributee, 733.811.
Unclaimed property.
See UNCLAIMED PROPERTY.

DIVORCE, EFFECT OF.
See DISSOLUTION OF MARRIAGE, EFFECT
OF.

DOMICILE.
Affidavit of, 222.17.
Defined.
Disposition of Unclaimed Property Act, for
purposes of, 717.101(8).
Estate administration, for purposes of,
731.201(13).
Estate tax, for purposes of, 198.015.
Evidence of, 222.17.
Ward.
Change of, 5.670, 744.524.
Generally, 744.201.

DONATION OF BODY OR ORGANS.
See ANATOMICAL GIFTS.

DOWER.
Abolished, 732.111.
Petition for assignment to widow, 5.365.

DURABLE POWER OF ATTORNEY.
See POWER OF ATTORNEY.

E

**EDUCATION REQUIREMENTS FOR
GUARDIAN,** 5.625, 744.1083(3)(b),
744.1083(7), 744.1083(10), 744.1085,
744.3145.

ELECTIVE SHARE.
**Adversary nature of proceeding to determine
amount of share and contribution,** 5.025(a).
Amount of.
Determination of, 5.025(a), 5.360(d).
Generally, 732.2065.
Assets applied to payment of, 732.2075.
Beneficiaries, liability for contributions, 732.2085.
Contribution to satisfy.
Action to enforce, 5.025(a), 732.2145(4).
Beneficiaries, liability of, 732.2085.
Direct recipients, liability of, 732.2085.
Order of, 5.360(b)(5), 732.2145.
Personal representative's duty to collect,
732.2145(2)–(3).

ELECTIVE SHARE —Cont'd
Contribution to satisfy —Cont'd
Relief from duty to enforce, 5.360(e).
Definitions, 732.2025.
**Direct recipients of property included in elective
estate, liability for contributions,** 732.2085.
Effective dates of laws regarding, 732.2155.
Elective estate.
Inventory of, 5.340(g).
Property entering into, 732.2035.
Property excluded from, 732.2045.
Valuation of, 732.2055.
Excluded property, 732.2045.
Extension of time to elect, 5.360(b)(1),
732.2135(2), 732.2135(4).
Interests other than, effect of election on,
732.2105.
**Notice of administration, notice relating to filing
of election to take elective share,** 5.240(b)(5),
733.212(2)(e).
Payors, protection of, 732.2115.
Procedure.
Amount of share.
Determination of, 5.025(a), 5.360(d).
Objection to, 5.360(d)(4).
Contribution.
Determination of, 5.025(a), 5.360(d).
Relief from duty to enforce, 5.360(e).
Entitlement, determination of, 5.360(c).
Extension of time to make election, 5.360(b)(1).
Filing of election, 5.360(a).
Notice.
Election, 5.360(b)(3).
Petition, 5.360(a)(2)(B).
Objections.
Amount of share, to, 5.360(d)(4).
Election, to, 5.360(b)(4).
Order.
Amount of, determining, 5.360(d)(5)–(d)(6).
Contribution to, specifying, 732.2145.
Entitlement to, determining, 5.360(b)(3)(C),
5.360(c).
Filing by attorney-in-fact or guardian,
authorizing, 5.360(a)(2)(C).
Petition.
Approval to make election, 5.360(a)(2)(A).
Determination of amount of, 5.360(d)(1),
5.360(d)(3).
Extension of time to make election,
5.360(b)(1).
Relief of duty to enforce contribution, 5.360(e).
Withdrawal of election, 5.360(b)(2),
732.2135(3).

F

J

JUDGE.
Defined, 5.015(b)(4).
Eligibility as guardian, 744.309(1)(b).

JUDGMENT.
Appeal of.
  See APPEAL.
Motion for rehearing of, 5.020(d).

JURISDICTION.
Acquisition by notice, 731.301(2).
Allegation in petition, 5.020(b).
Conservatorships, 747.02, 747.03(1).
Defect in statement of jurisdictional facts in
    pleadings, 5.020(a).
Estates, settlement of, 717.1242(1).
Foreign personal representative, over, 734.201,
    734.202.
Homestead, proceedings affecting, 222.08–222.10.
In rem proceedings, 731.105.
Objection to, 5.230(e), 5.240(b)(3), 5.240(d),
    733.212(2)–(3), 733.2123.
Removal of personal representative, 733.505.
Retention over guardianships, 744.372.
Standby guardianships, 744.304(5).
Surrogate guardianships, 744.442(4).
Trust proceedings, 736.0201(2), 736.0202,
    736.0203.

K

KILLER NOT ENTITLED TO RECEIVE
    PROPERTY OR BENEFITS, 732.802.

L

LAND TRUST ACT, FLORIDA, 689.071.

LAPSE.
Devise, 732.603.
Disposition by trust, 736.1106.

LAWYERS.
See ATTORNEYS.

LEGISLATIVE INTENT OF GUARDIANSHIP
    ACT, 744.1012.

LENDER OF PROPERTY TO GUARDIAN,
    PROTECTION EXTENDED TO, 744.461.

LETTERS.
Ancillary, 5.470.
Curatorship, 5.122(b).
Guardianship, 744.345.

LETTERS —Cont'd
Probate.
Defined, 731.201(24).
Issuance of, 5.235(b).

LIABILITY.
Claimant, of, 733.812.
Damage to estate property, 733.309, 733.6121.
Distributee, of, 733.812.
Encumbered property, 733.803.
Guardian, of, 744.358, 744.467.
Payee, of, 733.812.
Personal representative, of.
  Breach of fiduciary duty, 733.609.
  Discharge, after, 733.508(2), 733.901(2),
    733.5036(2).
  Environmental laws, violation of, 733.6121.
  Executor de son tort, 733.309.
  Individual, 733.619.
Purchaser of property.
  From distributee, 733.813.
  From guardian, 744.461.
Surety, of, 733.404, 733.405, 733.901(2), 744.357.
Trustee, of.
  See TRUSTEE.

LIEN BY PERSONAL REPRESENTATIVE ON
    PROTECTED HOMESTEAD.
See HOMESTEAD PROPERTY.

LIFE INSURANCE.
See INSURANCE, LIFE.

LIMITATIONS PERIOD.
See STATUTES OF LIMITATIONS.

LIMITED GUARDIAN.
Appointment of, 744.344(1).
Defined, 744.102(9)(a).
Duties of, 744.344(6), 744.345, 744.361,
    744.384(2).

LIVING WILL.
See HEALTH CARE ADVANCE DIRECTIVES.

LOST WILL.
See WILL.

M

MAGISTRATES.
Appointment of, 5.095(a)–(b), 5.697(a)–(b),
    744.369(2).
Bond, 5.095(e).
General, 5.095(a), 5.697(a), 744.369(2).
Hearings before, 5.095(f), 5.697(d).
Oath of, 5.095(a)–(b), 5.697(a)–(b).

Notes

Notes